Initiative and Referendum
Almanac

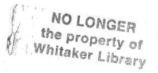

Initiative and Referendum Almanac

M. Dane Waters

Carolina Academic Press
Durham, North Carolina

ISBN 0-89089-969-X
LCCN 2003105098

Carolina Academic Press
700 Kent Street
Durham, NC 27701
Telephone (919) 489-7486
Fax (919) 493-5668
www.cap-press.com

Printed in the United States of America

Thanks to BW whose selfless dedication to the Institute makes our existence possible.

Contents

What Is the Initiative & Referendum Institute?

In 1998, in recognition of the initiative and referendum process' influence on America, the Initiative & Referendum Institute was founded. The Institute, a 501(c)(3) non-profit non-partisan research and educational organization, is dedicated to educating the citizens about how the initiative and referendum process has been utilized and in providing information to the citizens so they understand and know how to utilize the process. No other organization does what we do.

Edwin Meese, III, former U.S. Attorney General under President Ronald Reagan, had this to say about the Institute, "[T]he Initiative & Referendum Institute performs a valuable service to the Nation by providing research and educational programs to protect and expand the democratic process of initiative and referendum by the people in the several states. Having this electoral ability is a critical 'safety valve' for effective citizenship."

The Initiative & Referendum Institute extensively studies the initiative and referendum process and publishes papers and monographs addressing its effect on public policy, citizen participation and its reflection of trends in American thought and culture. We also research and produce a state-by-state guide to the initiative and referendum process that can be used by activists, and we work to educate and update the public on how the process is being utilized across the country. We analyze the relationship between voters and their elected lawmakers and when and why the people turn to initiative and referendum to enact changes in state and local law. The Initiative & Referendum Institute has garnered significant media attention. We have been interviewed or cited by numerous media outlets including, ABC News, Voter News Service, CBS Radio, Pacifica Radio Network, CNN, *The Washington Post, The New York Times, The Chicago Tribune,* Fox News Channel, *The Christian Science Monitor,* The News Hour with Jim Lehrer, *The National Journal, The Wall Street Journal, Governing Magazine, USA Today,* Court TV's "Supreme Court Watch" and "Washington Watch", The Economist, National Public Radio, *Campaigns and Elections Magazine, U.S. News and World Report, Congressional Quarterly,* and dozens of other publications, newspapers and radio stations around the world.

The Institute is uniquely qualified to undertake this mission. Comprising the Institute's Board of Directors, and Advisory Board are some of the world's leading authorities on the initiative and referendum process, including prominent scholars; experienced activists - who know the nuts and bolts of the process and its use; skilled attorneys; and political leaders who have seen first hand the necessity of having a process through which citizens can directly reform their government.

Wayne Pacelle, Senior Vice President of the Humane Society of the United States stated that, "the Initiative & Referendum Institute is the only independent voice for preserving and expanding the right of citizens to make laws directly through the initiative and referendum process. This vital tool of democracy is under siege by special interests, and the Initiative & Referendum Institute is a powerful and persuasive voice for the right of I&R."

For additional information, please visit our two award winning and informative websites at www.iandrinstitute.org and www.ballotwatch.org.

Acknowledgments

The collection and preparation of the data contained in this Almanac could not have occurred without the help of numerous individuals giving their help and support. Individuals like Katrina Haag, Dave Mohel, Bill Piper, Kim Garrett, Dennis Polhill, Karen Connell, Angelo Paparella, Janet Benton, Mark Cullen, Amy Pritchard, Sasha Bruce, Richard Braunstein, Melissa Moses, John Kutinsky, Kurt Gardinier, Dima AbouAlwan, Kristina Wilfore, Jessica Markham, and Blake Conaster. The time and effort they gave to this project was indispensable.

In addition to their support, I must give deep thanks to Dave Schmidt.[1] Dave's countless years of studying the initiative and referendum process and subsequent writings on the subject helped form the basis of all of our work. His book, *Citizen Lawmakers: The Ballot Initiative Revolution* (Temple University Press), is one of the most comprehensive studies to date on the initiative and referendum process. You will notice that we have taken a tremendous amount of information from his book and used it in this Almanac. His groundbreaking efforts not only made this Almanac possible, but the Institute as well.

I must also give the greatest thanks possible to Shirley Starke. Shirley has given hundreds of hours of hard work to the Institute and without her selfless support for the Institute's efforts; this Almanac would not have been possible.

And finally, I must thank Carolina Academic Press. Without their help and support you would no be reading this book today.

---

1. If you would like to contact David Schmidt regarding his research, please write him at 235 Douglass St., San Francisco, California, 94114.

Introduction

For a century, the initiative and referendum process has been **THE** critical tool to check the power of unresponsive and unaccountable government at the national, state and local level. Governor William Janklow of South Dakota—the state that has the distinction of being the first to adopt the statewide initiative and popular referendum process in the United States—had this to say about the process, "it is a tool of true democracy to allow citizens to participate directly in making the laws that affect their lives. People can define and decide the issue themselves if their elected officials aren't doing things to their satisfaction."[1]

However, the initiative and referendum process in the United States has grown in prominence and along with that prominence has come controversy. Questions of how the process has been utilized, the role of money in the process, and whether or not the citizens are competent enough to make informed decisions on complex ballot measures have dominated the debate. Whether these concerns are valid or not is up to the individual observer. However, one thing that is clear is that there exists a tremendous amount of misinformation about the initiative and referendum process.

The purpose of this Almanac is not to persuade people to support the initiative and referendum process, but to discuss the misinformation about it and give the reader a factual and historical base to work from when debating or discussing I&R. Due to the fact that most of the controversy surrounds the initiative process and not the referendum process, more emphasis is given to discussing the initiative.

The data contained within has been collected from numerous sources over several years. In most cases, the information is a compilation of studies, charts, books and articles. A vast amount of the information was derived from the *Book of States,* the **Texas Interim Report on Initiative and Referendum,** *Citizen Lawmakers: The Ballot Initiative Revolution* (Temple University Press) and independent research conducted by the Initiative & Referendum Institute. The data is as accurate as possible given the difficulty in obtaining information from state archives and election officials as well as the fact that state laws change regarding the rules and regulations associated with the initiative and referendum process on a regular basis. Therefore, I encourage you to consult the appropriate state elections officials to confirm the information contained in this Almanac before relying on it exclusively.

This Almanac will be updated every four years and will be a work in progress. We welcome any comments you have about the content and recommendations on how we can make it better.

Though this Almanac may not contain the answer to every question you may have regarding the initiative and referendum process, it is—in our humble opinion—one of the most comprehensive sources of information currently available on this important law making process.

---

1. In a letter to M. Dane Waters, President of the Initiative & Referendum Institute, 1998.

Initiative and Referendum
Almanac

1 The History of the Initiative and Referendum Process in the United States[1]

Setting the Foundation for Initiative and Referendum

Initiative and referendum (I&R) has existed in some form in this country since the 1600s. Citizens of New England placed ordinances and other issues on the agenda for discussion and then a vote utilizing town meetings. These town hall meetings established the precedent which lead to the creation of the legislative referendum process—a process in which the citizens were entrusted with ratifying laws and amendments proposed by their elected officials.

Thomas Jefferson was the first of our founding fathers to propose legislative referendum when he advocated it for the 1775 Virginia state constitution. However, he was attending the Continental Congress and was unable to be present to make certain that this requirement was added to his own state's constitution.[2] His strong support for establishing the process was based on his belief that the people are sovereign and should be the ones to agree to and approve any change to the one document, the constitution, that dictated the laws in which they would have to live by. However, James Madison said it best in Federalist 49 when he stated: "[a]s the people are the only legitimate fountain of power, and it is from them that the constitutional charter, under which the several branches of government hold their power, is derived, it seems strictly consonant to the republican theory to recur to the same original authority ... whenever it may be necessary to enlarge, diminish, or new-model the powers of government."

In 1776, Georgia delegates gathered in Savannah to draft a new constitution. One of the changes that was made was a requirement that the new constitution could only be amended when petitions signed by a majority of voters in each county called for a convention. Though the process was never used and ultimately deleted from the constitution it was the first state to establish a process that recognized the true sovereignty of the people in controlling their constitution.[3]

The first state to hold a statewide legislative referendum for its citizens to ratify its constitution was Massachusetts in 1778. New Hampshire followed in 1792.[4] The next state to require voter approval of a state constitution and any constitutional change was Connecticut in 1818, then Maine in 1819, New York, 1820 and Rhode Island in 1824.[5] The U.S. Congress subsequently made legislative referendum for constitutional changes mandatory for all new states entering the union after 1857.[6] Today, every state has the legislative referendum process.

However, even with advent of legislative referendum, the people began to realize in the late 1800s that they had no direct ability to reign in an out of touch government or government paralyzed by inaction and that something needed to be done to increase their check on representative government.

The Populist and Progressive Era

The 1890s and early 1900s saw the establishment of the Populist and Progressive movements. Both were based on the people's dissatisfaction with government and its inability to deal effectively in addressing the problems of the day. The supporters of both these movements had become especially outraged that moneyed special interest groups controlled government, and that the people had no ability to break this control. They soon began to propose a comprehensive platform of political reforms that included women's suffrage, secret ballots, direct election of U.S. Senators, recall, primary elections, and the initiative process.

The cornerstone of their reform package was the establishment of the initiative process for they knew that without it many of the reforms they wanted—that were being blocked by state legislatures—would not be possible.

Their support for the process was based on a theory of trusting the individual and not as a method of destroying representative government—**but to enhance it.** They believed that our founding fathers at the federal and state levels had done a tremendous job in creating constitutions that established the criteria in which our daily lives should be governed.

---

1. All the statistical data and information contained in this Chapter, unless otherwise noted, was gathered from *Citizen Lawmakers* (Temple University Press) or independently gathered by the Initiative & Referendum Institute and can be verified by visiting the Institute's website at www.iandrinstitute.org.

2. David Schmidt's manuscript of *Citizen Lawmakers*, 1985.

3. Ibid.

4. Ibid.

5. Ibid.

6. Ibid.

However, they knew that these constitutions were based on compromise and were not documents that should be subject to permanent enshrinement. The founding fathers realized this as well and placed in every state constitution and the federal constitution a provision for its revision. The Populists/Progressives took advantage of these methods of amending state constitutions and began the arduous journey of pushing state legislators to add an amendment allowing for the initiative and popular referendum process.

Their efforts soon began to pay off. In 1897, Nebraska became the first state to allow cities to place initiative and referendum in their charters. One year later, the citizens of South Dakota, lead by Father Robert W. Haire, copied initiative and referendum provisions from the 1848 Swiss Constitution and successfully amended them into the South Dakota Constitution. On November 5, 1898, South Dakota became the first state to adopt the statewide initiative and popular referendum process. Utah followed in 1900 and Oregon voters approved their initiative and referendum amendment by an 11-to-1 margin in 1902. Other states soon followed. In 1906 Montana voters approved an initiative and popular referendum amendment proposed by the state legislature. Oklahoma became the first state to provide for the initiative and popular referendum in its original constitution in 1907. Maine and Michigan passed initiative and popular referendum amendments in 1908.

In 1911 California placed initiative and popular referendum in their constitution. Other states were to follow—but even with popular support in many states, the elected class refused the will of the people and did not enact this popular reform. In Texas, for example, the people actually had the opportunity to vote for initiative and popular referendum in 1914, but voted it down because the amendment proposed by the legislature would have required that signatures be gathered from 20% of the registered voters in the state—a number twice as large as what was required in any other state. The proponents for initiative and popular referendum felt it was more important to get a useable process than one that would have maintained the status quo and provided no benefit to the citizenry.

According to David Schmidt, author of *Citizen Lawmakers* (the most comprehensive study on I&R available to date); "In states where I&R activists were unable to gain passage of statewide I&R amendments, they achieved numerous successes at the local level. In 1898, Alfred D. Cridge led a successful drive to incorporate I&R provisions into the city charter of San Francisco; John Randolph Haynes concluded a similar drive in Los Angeles in 1903; Grand Rapids, Michigan followed in 1905; Des Moines, Iowa in 1906; Cedar Rapids, Iowa and Wilmington, Delaware in 1907."[7]

Eventually, between 1898 and 1918, 24 states and numerous cities had adopted initiative or popular referendum—mostly in the West.

The expansion of initiative and popular referendum in the West fit more with the Westerners belief of populism—that the people should rule the elected and not allow the elected to rule the people. Unfortunately in the East and South this was not the case. Those that were in power were opposed to the expansion of initiative and popular referendum because they were concerned that blacks and immigrants would use the process to enact reforms that were not consistent with the beliefs of the ruling class. This was exemplified by a 1911 article in the national I&R movement's newsletter *Equity* in which it was reported that, "many conscientious Southerners oppose direct legislation (I&R) because they fear that this process of government would increase the power of the negro, and therefore increase the danger of negro domination."[8] As to the East Coast states, this racism was exemplified by Massachusetts political leaders who "fear[ed] initiatives [that] could be passed over their objections by Irish-Catholic voting blocs."[9]

By 1915, the push for establishing the initiative process began to wane due to "a developing conviction that German militarism might be a danger to the U.S." which "was generating a crusade for pure, undiluted Americanism—and as usual, patriotism came to be identified with defense of the status quo rather than its alteration."[10] It took 40 years before another state would adopt the initiative process.

A more detailed history of how I&R came about in each state is available in Chapter 4.

---

7. Ibid.
8. Equity, January 1911, pg 19.
9. As quoted from Schmidt's *Citizen Lawmakers* manuscript and footnoted with "Legislative Research Council of Massachusetts, 1975"
10. Chrislock, Carl H., The Progressive Era in Minnesota, 1899–1918, St. Paul: Minnesota Historical Society (1971).

Popular Votes on Adopting the Initiative Process[11]							
State	Year	Passed Failed	Margin	Yes	% Yes	No	% No
South Dakota	1898	Passed	3-2	23,816	59%	16,483	41%
Utah	1900	Passed	5-2	19,219	71%	7,786	29%
Oregon	1902	Passed	11-1	62,024	92%	5,688	8%
Illinois[12]	1902	Passed	5-1	428,469	83%	87,654	17%
Missouri	1904	Failed	2-3	115,741	41%	169,281	59%
Nevada	1905	Passed	5-1	4,393	85%	792	15%
Montana	1906	Passed	5-1	36,374	85%	6,616	15%
Delaware[13]	1906	Passed	6-1	17,405	89%	2,135	11%
Oklahoma	1907	Passed	5-2	180,333	71%	73,059	29%
Missouri	1908	Passed	1-1	177,615	55%	147,290	45%
Maine	1908	Passed	2-1	51,991	69%	23,712	31%
Michigan[14]	1908	Passed	2-1	244,705	65%	130,783	35%
Illinois	1910	Passed	3-1	443,505	63%	127,751	37%
Colorado	1910	Passed	3-1	89,141	76%	28,698	24%
Arkansas	1910	Passed	2-1	91,363	70%	39,680	30%
California	1911	Passed	3-1	138,181	75%	44,850	25%
Arizona	1911	Passed	3-1	12,534	76%	3,920	24%
New Mexico[15]	1911	Passed	5-2	31,724	70%	13,399	30%
Nebraska	1912	Passed	13-1	189,200	93%	15,315	7%
Idaho (I)[16]	1912	Passed	8-3	38,918	72%	15,195	28%
Idaho (PR)	1912	Passed	3-1	43,658	76%	13,490	24%
Nevada[17]	1912	Passed	10-1	9,956	91%	1,027	8%
Ohio	1912	Passed	3-2	312,592	57%	231,312	43%
Washington	1912	Passed	5-2	110,110	71%	43,905	29%
Wyoming[18]	1912	Failed	6-1	20,579	86%	3,446	14%
Mississippi[19]	1912	Failed	2-1	25,153	65%	13,383	35%
Michigan (C)	1913	Passed	5-4	204,796	56%	162,392	44%
Michigan (S)	1913	Passed	3-2	219,057	59%	152,388	41%
Mississippi	1914	Passed	2-1	19,118	69%	8,718	31%
North Dakota	1914	Passed	2-1	43,111	66%	21,815	44%
North Dakota	1914	Passed	5-2	48,783	71%	19,964	29%
Minnesota[20]	1914	Failed	3-1	162,951	77%	47,906	23%
Wisconsin	1914	Failed	2-1	84,934	36%	148,536	64%
Texas	1914	Failed	1-1	62,371	48%	66,785	52%
Maryland	1915	Passed	3-1	33,150	77%	10,022	23%
Minnesota[21]	1916	Failed	4-1	187,713	78%	51,546	22%

11. This information was compiled from research contained in David Schmidt's *Citizen Lawmakers* and from independent research conducted by the Initiative & Referendum Institute.

12. Illinois's 1902 and 1910 votes were advisory—not binding on the legislature. The measures were put on the ballot by petition of I&R advocates, using a statewide non-binding advisory initiative process established by the legislature in 1901. The legislature never followed the people's mandate. A constitutional convention passed a very limited initiative process in 1970, and the voters approved it.

13. Delaware voted on an advisory referendum put on the ballot by the legislature, asking voters whether they wanted the initiative process. Their reply was overwhelmingly "yes", as shown here, but the legislature never followed that mandate. Delaware is also the only state that does not require that the people approve all changes to the state constitution.

14. The initiative procedures put in place in Michigan in 1908 proved so difficult that citizens were unable to put initiatives on the ballot. Reformers got the legislature to approve less restrictive procedures, which were placed on the ballot in 1913 and ratified by the voters. There were two separate initiative amendments on the ballot, one giving voters power to propose and enact initiative statutes (laws), the other giving voters power to propose and enact initiative amendments to the state constitution.

15. New Mexico's new constitution was ratified by the voters in a single vote, not provision by provision and included the popular referendum process but not the initiative process.

16. In Idaho, there were separate amendments for initiative and popular referendum.

17. Nevada's 1905 amendment secured only the popular referendum process. The initiative process was secured by Nevada's 1912 amendment.

18. The amendment was defeated because the state constitution requires an approval by a majority of all those voting in the election and not just a majority of those voting on the amendment. Blank votes count as a no vote against the amendment.

19. Ibid.

20. Ibid.

21. Ibid.

State	Year	Passed Failed	Margin	Yes	% Yes	No	% No
Massachusetts	1918	Passed	1-1	170,646	51%	162,103	49%
North Dakota	1918	Passed	3-2	47,447	59%	32,598	41%
Alaska	1956	Passed	2-1	17,447	68%	8,180	32%
Florida	1968	Passed	1-1	645,233	55%	518,940	45%
Wyoming	1968	Passed	3-1	72,009	75%	24,299	25%
Illinois	1970	Passed	1-1	1,122,425	57%	838,168	43%
Washington, DC	1977	Passed	4-1	27,094	83%	5,627	17%
Minnesota[22]	1980	Failed	1-1	970,407	53%	854,164	47%
Rhode Island[23]	1986	Failed	1-1	129,309	48%	139,294	52%
Mississippi	1992	Passed	3-1	592,536	70%	251,276	30%
Rhode Island	1996	Passed	1-1	165,347	53%	145,808	47%
47 Votes in 32 States and DC		38 Passed 9 Failed	2-1	7,944,583	62%	4,937,179	38%

The Modern Day Movement

In 1959, Alaska was allowed admittance into the Union with initiative and popular referendum in their founding constitution. In 1968, Wyoming voters adopted the process and in 1972 Floridians adopted the statewide initiative process. Mississippians in 1992 restored the initiative process to their constitution, 70 years after the state supreme court had invalidated the election that had established it. Mississippi became the newest and last state to get this valuable tool.

The battle to expand the initiative process is still being waged. But a new front has been opened—the battle to keep the initiative process from being taken away in the states where it exists. However, the factor that causes hesitation among legislators to expand the process is the same reason being used by lawmakers to call for its extinction—how the process has been used.

Initiative Usage

There is little doubt that in recent years the initiative process has become one of the most important mechanisms for altering and influencing public policy at the local, state and even national level. In the last decade alone, utilizing the initiative process, citizens were heard on affirmative action, educational reform, term limits, tax reform, campaign finance reform, drug policy reform and the environment.

The modern day movement to utilize the initiative process can be said to have begun in 1978 in California with the passage of Proposition 13 that cut property taxes from 2.5 percent of market value to just 1 percent. After Proposition 13 passed in California, similar measures were adopted through the initiative process in Michigan and Massachusetts. Within two years, 43 states had implemented some form of property tax limitation or relief and 15 states lowered their income tax rates.

A report from the National Taxpayers Union makes the case that the tax revolt that began with Proposition 13 in the 1970s would never have occurred without the initiative process. The study's author, Pete Sepp, stated: "[w]ith I&R, citizens have created an innovative, effective array of procedural restraints on the growth of state and local government that have even awakened the federal political establishment. Without I&R, citizens almost certainly would be laboring under a more oppressive and unaccountable fiscal regime than they do today…. As initiative and referendum enters its second century of use in the United States, citizens should embrace and nurture this invaluable process. It has transformed the 'Tax Revolt' from a passing fancy to a permanent fixture in American politics."[24]

The citizens, utilizing the initiative process have brought about some of the most fundamental and controversial public policy decisions affecting their daily lives.

---

22. Ibid.
23. An amendment establishing statewide I&R was approved in Rhode Island's 1986 Constitutional Convention; but when placed on the ballot, voters very narrowly defeated it. In 1996 the legislature put a non-binding advisory question on the ballot asking voters if they would like to adopt I&R. Voters said yes, but the legislature did nothing.
24. See "Tax Reform and I&R" by Pete Sepp in Chapter Nine.

Statewide reforms made possible through the use of the initiative process[25]	
Women gained the right to vote *	Ended bi-lingual education
Politicians are elected through direct primaries	Movie theatres and other stores can be open on Sunday
Yellow margarine can be sold	Poll taxes were abolished *
States can't fund abortions *	Parents must be notified prior to the performing of an abortion *
The eight-hour workday was created	Medical marijuana was legalized *
Physician-assisted suicide was legalized	The use of steel traps in hunting was outlawed *
A vote of the people is required before any new tax increases can be adopted *	A super-majority vote of both houses of state legislatures is required before any new tax increase can be adopted *
Ended the use of racial preferences in government hiring and contracting	Bottle taxes to protect the environment were adopted
Term limits on elected officials were adopted *	Campaign finance reform was adopted *
Prohibition was adopted and abolished *	The death penalty was adopted and abolished *

Clearly, reforms have been enacted that represent different ideologies—conservative, liberal, libertarian and populist agendas. This typifies the initiative process—individuals of all different political persuasions use it. Furthermore, because of the diversity of issues that have been placed on the ballot, voters in states with an initiative on the ballot have been more likely to go to the polls than voters in states without an initiative on the ballot. In election after election, no matter what election cycle is analyzed, voter turnout in states with an initiative on the ballot has been usually 3% to 8% higher than in states without an initiative on the ballot. In 1998 voters in the 16 states with an initiative on the ballot went to the polls at a rate of almost 3% greater than voters in the states without an initiative on the ballot.[26] This can be attributed to the fact the people believe that their vote can make a difference when voting on initiatives. They realize that when they vote for an initiative, they get what they voted for. They get term limits, tax limits, and educational or environmental reform. That is the key distinction between voting on an initiative and voting for a candidate. With a candidate there are no guarantees—you can only hope that the candidate delivers on his or her promises.

Since the first statewide initiative appeared on Oregon's ballot in 1904, citizens in the 24 states with the initiative process have placed approximately 2,051 statewide initiatives on the ballot and have only adopted 840 (41%). Even though 24 states have the statewide initiative process, over 60% of all initiative activity has taken place in just six states—Arizona, California, Colorado, North Dakota, Oregon and Washington.[27]

Additionally, it is important to point out that very few initiatives actually make it to the ballot. In California, according to political scientist Dave McCuan, only 26% of all initiatives filed have made it to the ballot and only 8% of those filed actually were adopted by the voters. During the 2000 election cycle, over 350 initiatives were filed in the 24 initiative states and 76 made the ballot—about 22%.[28]

Decades with the lowest number of statewide initiatives on the ballot	Number Proposed	Number Adopted	Passage Rate
1901–1910	56	25	45%
1961–1970	87	37	41%
1951–1960	114	45	39%

The initiative process has been through periods of tremendous use as well as periods in which it was rarely utilized. Initiative usage steadily declined from its peak of 293 from 1911–1920 to its low of 87 in 1961–1970. Many factors contributed to this, but the distraction of two World Wars, the Great Depression and the Korean War are largely responsible.

25. An in-depth overview of the issues marked with an asterisk (*) can be found in Chapter Nine.
26. Based on independent research conducted by the Initiative & Referendum Institute.
27. Ibid.
28. Ibid.

However, in 1978, with the passage of California's Proposition 13, the people began to realize the power of the initiative process once again and its use began to climb. Since 1978, two of the three most prolific decades of initiative use have occurred, 1981–90 (271 initiatives) and 1991–2000 (389 initiatives).[29]

Decades with the highest number of statewide initiatives on the ballot	Number Proposed	Number Adopted	Passage Rate
1991–2000	389	188	48%
1911–1920	293	116	40%
1981–1990	271	115	42%

In 1996, considered by scholars to be the "high water mark" for the use of the initiative process, the citizens placed 93 initiatives on statewide ballots and adopted 44 (47%). In contrast, that year, state legislators in those same 24 states adopted over 14,000 laws and resolutions.[30]

States with the highest number of statewide initiatives on the ballot (1904–2002)	Number Proposed	Number Adopted	Passage Rate
Oregon	325	115	36%
California	279	98	35%
Colorado	183	65	36%
North Dakota	168	76	45%
Arizona	154	64	42%

Since 1996, the number of initiatives actually making the ballot is remaining constant if not falling. In 1998, only 61 statewide initiatives actually made the ballot—the lowest in a decade. In 2000 a total of 76 initiatives found their way to statewide ballots, though more than 1998, it is 17 less than appeared on the 1996 ballot and is consistent with the decade average of 73 initiatives per election cycle. These numbers do not support the accusation that there has been a "drastic" increase in initiative usage over the last decade.

In 2001 there were only four initiatives on statewide ballots. This number is actually two fewer than the number of initiatives that appeared on the 1991 general election ballot. The reason for the low number in odd numbered election years is that the constitutions of only five states allow initiatives in the odd years—Colorado, Maine, Mississippi, Ohio and Washington State.

The 2002 Election Cycle

The 2002 election cycle continues to show that the use of the initiative process is declining—perhaps showing the success that legislatures have had in restricting the public's use of the initiative process. On Election Day 2002, voters cast their ballots on 202 statewide ballot measures in 40 states and approved approximately 60% of them. 53 were placed on the ballot by the people and 149 were placed on the ballot by the state legislatures. Of the measures placed on the ballot by the people, 45% were approved. This number is a little higher than the 100-year average of 41%. In looking at the measures placed on the ballot by the state legislatures, the voters continued the trend of passing those at a higher percentage than citizen measures by adopting almost 66% of them. Arizona and New Mexico hold the top honor of having the most prolific ballot on Election Day—both with 14. The state that had the most issues from the people was Oregon with 7—though a 60% decrease from 2000. Three of the top five most prolific ballots comprised of issues from lawmakers and not the people—New Mexico, Louisiana and Georgia. There was an average of 2.04 initiatives per state and an average of 2.94 legislative referendums per state on the ballot this election (a complete post election report is available in appendix F).

The Future of the Initiative Process in the United States

Whether or not the trend of decreasing numbers of initiatives making the ballot will continue is hard to predict. The history of the initiative process has shown that there are high use periods as well as low use periods. One thing that is for certain—if state lawmakers continue to put more restrictions on the people's ability to utilize the initiative process there

---

29. Ibid.

30. Numbers are approximate due to the fact that a comprehensive list of laws passed by state legislatures is unavailable. The numbers utilized in this section were arrived at utilizing information provided by the National Conference of State Legislatures.

is no doubt that fewer initiatives will be making the ballot. However, there is no doubt that in the upcoming election cycles, there will be numerous initiatives on the ballot that will have a tremendous impact on our daily lives. These initiatives will be derived from the brains of activists of all political persuasions, including those who wish to diminish the size of government and those who wish to increase it. The impact on state governments will be substantial. Whether the impact is positive or negative will be entirely up to the individual observer. If history is any indicator, there is no doubt that the fiscal and social implications will be far-reaching.

But it is hard to predict what will happen with the future of the initiative process itself. The expansion of the process seems to be an uphill battle. Due to the reforms that the citizens have been successful in promoting through the initiative process—reforms that have limited the power of government—legislators in states without I&R have been hostile to advocating it and unfortunately its expansion can only occur by legislators giving it to the people. This in itself is a perfect example of why we need I&R.

2 Comparison of Statewide Initiative Processes[1]

Definitions /Availability

Anything that appears on the ballot other than a candidate for office is called a **ballot measure.** Ballot measures are broken down into two distinct categories—**initiatives and referendums.**

Initiatives are when the citizens, collecting signatures on a petition, place advisory questions, memorials, statutes or constitutional amendments on the ballot for the citizens to adopt or reject. Twenty-four states have the initiative process (see table on next page).

Of the 24 states, 18 have the **constitutional initiative process** which is further broken down into two distinct subcategories—**direct initiative amendments (DA)** and **indirect initiative amendments (IDA). A direct initiative amendment (DA)** is when a constitutional amendment is proposed by the people and is placed directly on the ballot for voter approval or rejection. An **indirect initiative amendment (IDA)** is when a constitutional amendment is proposed by the people but must first be submitted to the state legislature for consideration before the amendment can be placed on the ballot for voter approval or rejection. Sixteen of the 18 states have the **direct initiative amendment** process and two have the **indirect initiative amendment process.**

Twenty-one of the 24 initiative states have the **statutory initiative process** which is further broken down into two distinct subcategories—**direct initiative statutes (DS)** and **indirect initiative statutes (IDS). A direct initiative statute (DS)** is when statutes (laws) or memorials (non-biding laws) proposed by the people are directly placed on the ballot for voter approval or rejection. An **indirect Initiative statute (IDS)** is when statutes (laws) or memorials (non-biding laws) proposed by the people must first be submitted to the state legislature for consideration before they can be placed on the ballot for voter approval or rejection. Fourteen of the 21 states allow **direct initiative statutes (DS)** and nine allow **indirect initiative statutes (IDS).** That adds up to 23—which is greater than the universe of 21 states that allow statutory initiatives. The reason for the difference is that two states—Utah and Washington—allow statutory initiatives through the direct **and** indirect process.

In many of the same states the citizens have the ability to reject laws or amendments proposed by the state legislature. This process is commonly referred to as the **referendum process.** There are two types of referendum in this country—**popular and legislative.**

Popular referendum, which is available in 24 states (see table on next page), is when the people have the power to refer, by collecting signatures on a petition, specific legislation that was enacted by their legislature for the people to either accept or reject. **Legislative referendum,** which is possible in all states, is when the state legislatures, an elected official, state appointed constitutional revision commission or other government agency or department submits propositions (constitutional amendments, statutes, bond issues, etc.) to the people for their approval or rejection. This is either constitutionally required, as in proposing constitutional amendments, or because the legislature, government official or agency voluntarily chooses to submit the proposal to the people (however, not all states allow their state legislature to place statutes on the ballot for voter approval or rejection). Every state requires that constitutional amendments proposed by the legislature be submitted to the citizenry via legislative referendum for approval or rejection. **Legislative referendum** is further broken down into two subcategories. **Legislative amendments (LA)** are constitutional amendments placed on the ballot by the legislature or governmental body. This includes constitutional bond issues and amendments proposed by a constitutional revision commission. **Legislative statues (LS)** are binding and non-binding statues (laws) and statutory bonds placed on the ballot by the legislature or government body.

In the United States, the **initiative process** is used much more frequently than the popular **referendum process** and is considered by many the more important and powerful of the two processes.

Additionally, there is no national initiative or referendum process in the United States. However, the initiative and referendum process is available in thousands of counties, cities and towns across the country and is utilized far more frequently than their statewide counterpart. This will be discussed in greater detail in Chapter 3.

---

1. The information contained in this section was derived primarily from the *Texas Interim Report on the Initiative Process* and from independent research conducted by the Initiative & Referendum Institute.

						Type of initiative process used to propose Constitutional Amendments		Type of initiative process used to propose Statutes (Laws)	
States with Direct (DA) and Indirect (IDA) Initiative Amendments; Direct (DS) and Indirect (IDS) Initiative Statutes and Popular (PR) Referendum[2]									
		Type of process available		Type of Initiative process available					
State	Date adopted	Initiative	Popular Referendum	Constitutional Amendment	Statute	Direct (DA)	Indirect (IDA)	Direct (DS)	Indirect (IDS)
AK	1956	Yes	Yes	No	Yes	No	No	No	Yes
AZ	1911	Yes	Yes	Yes	Yes	Yes	No	Yes	No
AR	1910	Yes	Yes	Yes	Yes	Yes	No	Yes	No
CA[3]	1911/66	Yes	Yes	Yes	Yes	Yes	No	Yes	No
CO	1912	Yes	Yes	Yes	Yes	Yes	No	Yes	No
FL	1972	Yes	No	Yes	No	Yes	No	No	No
ID	1912	Yes	Yes	No	Yes	No	No	Yes	No
IL[4]	1970	Yes	No	Yes	No	Yes	No	No	No
KY	1910	No	Yes	No	No	No	No	No	No
ME	1908	Yes	Yes	No	Yes	No	No	No	Yes
MD	1915	No	Yes	No	No	No	No	No	No
MA	1918	Yes	Yes	Yes	Yes	No	Yes	No	Yes
MI	1908	Yes	Yes	Yes	Yes	Yes	No	No	Yes
MS[5]	1914/92	Yes	No	Yes	No	No	Yes	No	No
MO	1908	Yes	Yes	Yes	Yes	Yes	No	Yes	No
MT[6]	1904/72	Yes	Yes	Yes	Yes	Yes	No	Yes	No
NE	1912	Yes	Yes	Yes	Yes	Yes	No	Yes	No
NV	1905	Yes	Yes	Yes	Yes	Yes	No	No	Yes
NM	1911	No	Yes	No	No	No	No	No	No
ND[7]	1914	Yes	Yes	Yes	Yes	Yes	No	Yes	No
OH	1912	Yes	Yes	Yes	Yes	Yes	No	No	Yes
OK	1907	Yes	Yes	Yes	Yes	Yes	No	Yes	No
OR	1902	Yes	Yes	Yes	Yes	Yes	No	Yes	No
SD[8]	1898/72/88	Yes	Yes	Yes	Yes	Yes	No	Yes	No
UT	1900/17	Yes	Yes	No	Yes	No	No	Yes	Yes
WA	1912	Yes	Yes	No	Yes	No	No	Yes	Yes
WY	1968	Yes	Yes	No	Yes	No	No	No	Yes
Totals		27 states	24 states	24 states	18 states	21 states	16 states	2 states	14 states	9 states

Similarities

Although the initiative process is different in every state, there are certain aspects of the process that are common to all. The five basic steps to any initiative are:

1) Preliminary filing of a proposed initiative with a designated state official;
2) Review of the initiative for compliance with statutory requirements prior to circulation;
3) Circulation of the petition to obtain the required number of signatures;
4) Submission of the petition signatures to the state elections official for verification of the signatures;
5) The placement of the initiative on the ballot and subsequent vote.

---

2. This list does not include the states with legislative referendum (LR). Legislative referendum is when a state legislature places an amendment or statute on the ballot for voter approval or rejection. The legislative referendum process is available in every state.

3. In 1996 California repealed the in-direct initiative process for statutes.

4. In Illinois, the subject matter of proposed constitutional amendments is severely limited to legislative matters. Consequently, initiatives seldom appear on the ballot.

5. Mississippi first adopted the initiative process in 1914 but a State Supreme Court ruling voided the election. The process was "readopted" in 1992.

6. In 1972 Montana adopted a provision that allows for directly initiated constitutional amendments.

7. In North Dakota prior to 1918, constitutional amendments could be initiated only indirectly.

8. In 1972 South Dakota adopted a provision that allows for directly initiated constitutional amendments. In 1988 South Dakota repealed the in-direct Initiative process for statutes.

The Indirect Initiative Process

By Fred Silva[9]

The indirect initiative is a process by which voters can submit a measure to their state legislature for consideration. In general, the legislature has a set period of time to adopt or reject the proposal. If it is adopted by the legislature, the measure becomes law (albeit one subject to referendum). If the measure is rejected or the legislature fails to act within a set period of time, the measure is generally placed on the ballot at the next general election. Currently, the constitutions and provisions of ten states provide for an indirect initiative process: Alaska, Maine, Massachusetts, Michigan, Mississippi, Nevada, Ohio, Utah, Washington, and Wyoming.

This two-step process would in theory seem to lead to a large number of initiatives being proposed since initiative sponsors would only have to collect half of the number of signatures normally required to get their issued addressed by their lawmakers, but in reality that hasn't occurred. This is due to the fact that very rarely do state legislatures actually adopt the initiatives that are placed before them through the indirect process. California and South Dakota, which had *both* the direct and indirect initiative process, repealed the indirect initiative in 1966 and 1988, respectively, for lack of use. The Utah Legislature has never adopted an initiative measure and the Massachusetts legislature, according to the Secretary of State's Office, hasn't adopted an initiative measure in the last decade. The Maine legislature has only adopted two laws placed before them since adopting the indirect initiative process in 1908.[10]

Alaska[11]

Alaska uses a form of the indirect initiative called the legislature's option, and only statutes are eligible. Here, after collecting the proper amount of signatures (10% of those who voted in the preceding election), the petitioners must submit their request prior to the beginning of the legislative session. The legislature is not required to consider the measure, however, and if it does not, the measure goes on the next ballot. If the legislature adopts the measure or a measure that is substantially similar, the initiative does not go on the ballot. Other than Wyoming, Alaska is the only state in which the legislature may vary indirect initiative statutory proposals without creating the possibility of a vote on the amended measure.

Maine[12]

After Massachusetts, Maine is the second largest user of the indirect initiative—but only statutes are allowed. The required number of signatures is 10% of the total votes cast for governor in the last election. The legislature has the entire session in which to act and may decide to place an alternative proposal or recommendation on the ballot. If it chooses to do this, it must construct the ballot so that voters can choose between competing versions (one or more) or reject both. The Legislature can also reject the initiative, in which case it is placed on the ballot. Following enactment, the Legislature can both repeal and amend initiatives.

Massachusetts[13]

Massachusetts is by far the largest user of the indirect initiative. Both constitutional amendments and statutes may be proposed, and signatures that total only 3% of the entire vote cast for Governor are required. The Massachusetts procedure for constitutional amendments is the most indirect of any American initiative procedure, as the proponents have no right to submit their proposal to a vote of the people unless the legislature places the measure on the ballot. The process involves a two-step procedure. In the first step the sponsor must obtain a fairly low number of signatures (3%) to have the legislature consider the proposal. Initiative amendments are acted upon by a joint session of the House and Senate; the Legislature can only amend the initiative by a ? majority vote in a joint session of both houses. If the legislature fails to adopt the proposal, the sponsors must seek additional signatures to get on the ballot. An initiative amendment to the Constitution will not appear on the ballot if, when it comes to a vote in either joint session, less than 25% of the legislators vote in favor of it or if no vote is taken before the legislative term ends. Following enactment, the Legislature can both repeal and amend initiatives. In practice, the indirect initiative process is rarely used for constitutional amendments.

Michigan[14]

Only statutes may be proposed in Michigan's indirect initiative process, and the number of signatures required to qualify is at least 8% of the total votes cast for Governor in the last general election. Once submitted, the legislature has 40 days to act on a petition and may also place an alternative on the ballot. It can approve or reject an initiative, but it can-

9. Fred Silva is a Senior Advisor of Governmental Relations at the Public Policy Institute of California

10. This paragraph was written by M. Dane Waters and is based on research conducted by the Initiative & Referendum Institute. The state by state overviews were written by Fred Silva.

11. Alaska Constitution Article XI; Dubois, Philip L. and Floyd Feeney, Lawmaking by Initiative: Issues, Options and Comparisons. New York: Agathon Press, 1998.

12. Maine Constitution Article IV; ibid.

13. Massachusetts Constitution amendment article XLVIII, Initiative part 5 (statutes), part 4 (cons. Amendment); ibid.

14. Michigan Constitution Article II; ibid.

not amend one. However, it can submit an alternative to an initiative to the ballot. If rejected, the measure can be placed on the next ballot. Following enactment, the Legislature can both repeal and amend initiatives.

Mississippi[15]

Mississippi is the only state in which the indirect initiative process is used for constitutional amendments only. To qualify an amendment for consideration, the number of collected signatures must equal 12% of all votes cast for governor in the last election. These initiatives always appear on the ballot, whether the legislature adopts, rejects, or proposes alternatives to them. If it is amended, both the amended version and the original one are submitted to the ballot. The Legislature is empowered to both repeal and amend these initiatives following enactment. This procedure was adopted in Mississippi in 1992, but has been used only very rarely.

Nevada[16]

Nevada requires that 10% of the total number of voters in the last general election sign a petition in order for it to be considered by the Legislature. After submission, the Legislature has 40 days to act on a petition and may also place an alternative on the ballot. If the measure is rejected by the Legislature or if no action is taken is 40 days, the measure is placed on the ballot. The Legislature can only repeal or amend an approved initiative three years after enactment. Nevada used an indirect procedure for initiative constitutional amendments until 1962. Since then, Nevada has required that initiative constitutional amendments be approved at two separate elections but has allowed the amendments to go directly on the ballot. Because of the two separate elections requirements, the legislature still has an opportunity to deal with any matter proposed before a final ballot. As a result, some see this as really being an "indirect" procedure.

Ohio[17]

Ohio is one of two states (along with Massachusetts) that have a two-step procedure in the indirect initiative process. In the first step the sponsor must obtain a fairly low number of signatures (3% of the total vote cast for governor in the last election) to have the legislature consider the proposal. Only statutes are permitted. If the legislature fails to adopt the proposal (or does not act on it), the sponsors must seek additional signatures to get on the ballot. The Legislature may amend the proposed measure.

Utah[18]

Utah (along with Washington) is one of only two states that allow the initiative sponsor to choose whether they wish to use the direct process or indirect initiative process. In Utah, there is an incentive to use the indirect initiative, since indirect initiatives can go before the legislature with signatures equal to 5% of the last vote, while the direct initiative requires twice that number. If the legislature rejects the indirect initiative, its advantages are lost, however, because sponsors must come up with signatures equal to another 5% of the vote. Only statues can be proposed and signatures that total at least 5% of all votes cast for governor in the last election are required. The proposed law can only be enacted or rejected without change or amendment by the Legislature. Following enactment, the Legislature can both amend and repeal initiatives.

Washington State[19]

Washington (along with Utah) is one of the two states that allow voters to choose between the indirect and direct initiative. The number of signatures required for each type of initiative is the same (8% of the votes cast for governor in the last election); thus, the sponsor chooses the type that seems most advantageous. In practice voters overwhelmingly choose the direct variant. Only statutes can be considered in the indirect process. Following submission to the legislature, the Legislature can approve an amended version of the proposed legislation, in which case both the amended version and the original proposal must be placed on the next state general election ballot. If the Legislature adopts the measure without amending it, it automatically becomes law. After enactment, the Legislature can repeal or amend an initiative by a ⅔ vote of each house during the first two years of enactment, and a majority vote thereafter.

Wyoming[20]

Wyoming, like Alaska, uses the "legislature's option" form of indirect initiative. Initiative sponsors must collect their signatures (15% of those voting in the last election) prior to the beginning of the next legislative session. Only statutes can be proposed using the indirect process. The legislature is not required to consider the measure, however. If it chooses

15. Mississippi Constitution Section 273; ibid.
16. Nevada Constitution Article XIX; ibid.
17. Ohio Constitution Article II; ibid.
18. Utah Code Ann. Sections 2-A-7-201, -208 (Supp. 1994); ibid.
19. Washington Constitution Article II; ibid.
20. Wyoming Constitution Article III, Section 52; ibid.

not to consider the measure, it is placed on the next ballot. If the legislature adopts the measure or a measure that is substantially similar, the initiative does not go on the ballot. As mentioned above, Wyoming and Alaska are the only states in which the legislature may vary indirect initiative statutory proposals without creating the possibility of a vote on the amended measure. After a measure is enacted, the legislature can amend it, and repeal it after two years.

Pre-Circulation Filing Requirements and Review

Prior to circulating a petition, the proposed initiative and a request to circulate must be submitted to the designated public officer such as the Lieutenant Governor, Attorney General or Secretary of State for approval. Nine states require the proposed initiative to be submitted with a certain number of signatures—ranging from five in Montana to 100 in Alaska. Five states require a deposit that is refunded when the completed petition has been filed—Alaska ($100), Mississippi ($500), Ohio ($25), Washington State ($5), and Wyoming ($500).

Depending on the state, the petition may be reviewed for form, language and/or constitutionality. Ten states require the Secretary of State's office or the Attorney General to review initiatives for proper form only. Twelve states **require** some form of pre-circulation/certification review regarding language, content or constitutionality. However, in all but four of these states, the results of the review are advisory only. In Arkansas, the Attorney General has authority to reject a proposal if it utilizes misleading terminology. In Utah, the Attorney General can reject an initiative if it is patently unconstitutional, nonsensical, or if the proposed law could not become law if passed. In Oregon, the Attorney General can stop an initiative from circulating if he believes it violates the single amendment provision for initiatives and in Florida, the State Supreme Court—during its mandatory review—can stop an initiative if it is unconstitutional or violates the state's very strict single subject requirement for initiatives.

Pre-Circulation State Review of Initiative Petitions

State	Assistance Provided
Alaska	Lieutenant Governor reviews for form and legal restrictions on content.
Arizona	Secretary of State reviews for form only.
Arkansas	Attorney General may reject confusing title and summary and instruct petitioners to redesign proposal.
California	Optional assistance from Legislative Council.
Colorado	Mandatory content review by Legislative Council.
Florida	Supreme Court reviews for constitutionality and compliance to single subject after petitioners gather 10% of the signature requirements.
Idaho	Mandatory review of content by Attorney General.
Illinois	None
Maine	Secretary of State reviews for form only.
Massachusetts	Mandatory review of subject by Attorney General
Michigan	Optional public hearing on draft before the Board of State Canvassers.
Mississippi	The state makes advisory recommendations regarding the initiative language. The sponsor may accept or reject any of these recommendations.
Missouri	Attorney General reviews form only.
Montana	Mandatory review of content by Legislative Council. The sponsor may accept or reject any of these recommendations.
Nebraska	The state makes advisory recommendations regarding the initiative language. The sponsor may accept or reject any of these recommendations.
Nevada	Secretary of State reviews for form only.
North Dakota	Secretary of State reviews for form only.
Ohio	Petitioners may revise draft after the indirect initiative legislative hearing.
Oklahoma	Secretary of State reviews for form only.
Oregon	Mandatory review for single subject. The Attorney General can stop an initiative from circulating if he believes it violates the single amendment provision for initiatives.
South Dakota	Legislative Research Council reviews for style and form and makes advisory recommendations regarding the initiative language.
Utah	Attorney General reviews for constitutionality and will reject the measure if it is patently unconstitutional, nonsensical; or if the proposed law could not become a law if passed.
Washington	Mandatory review by Code Reviser. The sponsor may accept or reject any recommendations.
Wyoming	Secretary of State reviews for form only.

Ballot Title/Circulation Title/Summary

At two points in the petition process, an official summary and title must be prepared. A circulation title must be prepared for the signature collection phase, and a ballot title must be prepared for the voter pamphlet (if there is one) and the actual ballot. Typically, the circulation and ballot titles are the same. Procedures for writing the circulation title vary. Some states allow the sponsors to write the title; other states use a committee. Eleven states provide for expedited court challenges to the circulation title.

Every initiative state requires review and approval of the election-day ballot title, caption and summary. Arizona, Arkansas, Florida, Illinois, Ohio and Oklahoma permit proponents to write the ballot title, but it is subject to approval by the Attorney General or Secretary of State. Oklahoma additionally requires that the ballot title be certified by the superintendent of public instruction for readability at the eighth-grade level. Eleven states place responsibility for drafting the ballot title and summary with the Attorney General, Secretary of State or comparable official. Five states assign the task to a special committee or drafting board. Colorado and Oregon allow public comment in drafting the ballot title. Fourteen states make available expedited court review of contested ballot title wording.

Circulation Title and Summary

State	Action	Expedited Review
Alaska	Proponent writes caption and summary, subject to approval by Lt. Governor.	Superior Court
Arizona	Proponent writes caption; no summary.	No
Arkansas	Proponent proposes caption and summary, subject to approval by Attorney General.	Supreme Court
California	Attorney General writes caption and summary.	No
Colorado	Drafting board prepares caption and summary in conduct of public hearings with input from proponent.	Rehearing: Supreme Court
Florida	Proponent writes caption and summary.	No
Idaho	Attorney General writes caption and summary.	Superior Court
Illinois	Proponent writes caption and summary, subject to approval by Board of Elections.	No
Maine	Ballot question written by Secretary of State; no summary.	No
Massachusetts	Proponent writes caption; Secretary of Commonwealth writes summary, approval by Attorney General.	No
Michigan	Proponent writes caption; no summary	No
Mississippi	The Attorney General writes the title and summary.	District Court
Missouri	No caption or summary.	No
Montana	The Attorney General writes the title and summary.	District Court
Nebraska	No caption; proponents writes summary.	No
Nevada	No caption or summary.	No
North Dakota	No caption; summary drafted by Secretary of State, subject to approval by Attorney General.	No
Ohio	Proponents write caption and summary, subject to approval by Attorney General.	No
Oklahoma	No caption, proponent writes summary.	No
Oregon	Attorney General writes caption and summary after receiving public comments.	Supreme Court
South Dakota	No caption or summary.	No
Utah	No caption or summary.	No
Washington	Attorney General writes caption and summary.	Superior Court
Wyoming	No caption; Secretary of State writes summary.	District Court

How an initiative's ballot title is worded can make or break the initiative. In some states, proponents get to recommend a ballot title with final approval being left to the state—but in most states, government officials write the ballot title. Regardless of who writes it, the exact language appearing on the ballot may end up being a subject of a court case. Proponents will sometimes file multiple initiatives very similar in nature but not exact, in the hopes of getting a ballot title that they "like." They will then begin circulating that petition. This is only possible, however, in states in which the ballot title is set before proponents begin gathering signatures. In many states, the ballot title is decided after proponents turn in their signatures and the measure is qualified for the ballot.

Official Ballot Title and Summary

State	Title and Summary Procedures	Is Ballot Title Set Before or After Circulation?	Expedited Review
Alaska	Written by Attorney General; but proponent may negotiate wording with Lt. Governor.	Before	Yes
Arizona	Proponent writes the caption and the Secretary of State drafts the summary, subject to approval by Attorney General.	After	No
Arkansas	Proponent proposes caption and summary, subject to approval by Attorney General.	Before	Yes
California	Attorney General writes caption and summary.	Before	Yes
Colorado	Drafting Board prepares caption and summary in conduct of public hearings, with input from proponents.	Before	Yes
Florida	Proponent writes caption and summary, subject to approval by Secretary of State.	Before	No
Idaho	Attorney General writes caption and summary.	Before	Yes
Illinois	Proponent writes caption and summary, subject to approval by Board of Elections.	Before	No
Maine	Ballot question and summary written by Secretary of State.	Before	No
Massachusetts	Secretary of Commonwealth writes caption and summary, subject to approval by Attorney General.	Before	Yes
Michigan	No caption; Board of State Canvassers writes summary.	After	Yes
Mississippi	The Attorney General writes the title and summary.	Before	Yes
Missouri	No caption, Attorney General writes summary.	Before	Yes
Montana	Attorney General writes ballot title and summary.	Before	Yes
Nebraska	Attorney General writes caption and summary.	After	Yes
Nevada	No caption; Secretary of State writes summary, subject to approval by the Nevada Legislative Commission.	After	No
North Dakota	No caption; summary drafted by Secretary of State, subject to approval by Attorney General.	Before	No
Ohio	Proponent writes caption and summary, subject to approval by Attorney General and Secretary of State.	After	No
Oklahoma	Proponent proposes caption and summary, subject to approval by Attorney General.	After	Yes
Oregon	Attorney General drafts preliminary caption and summary, receives public comments and writes final version.	Before	Yes
South Dakota	Drafted by State Board of Elections.	After	No
Utah	Attorney General writes caption and summary.	After	Yes
Washington	Attorney General writes caption and summary.	Before	Yes
Wyoming	No caption; Secretary of State, with assistance of Attorney General, writes summary.	After	Yes

Subject Limitations

Every state prohibits initiatives from adopting policies that are beyond the permissible boundaries of the legislature. Some states have prohibited initiatives in the subject areas of taxes or appropriations. Nevada, for example, forbids any appropriation by initiative unless the measure also includes a tax sufficient to cover the appropriation. Alaska, Massachusetts, and Wyoming prohibit initiatives from dedicating revenues, making or repealing appropriations, creating courts, and affecting the judicial process. Several states, like Montana and Oregon, distinguish between constitutional amendments, which are permitted and constitutional revisions, which are not. Several states impose a single subject rule for initiatives meaning that all parts of the initiative must be germane.

Initiative Subject Restrictions

State	Restriction
Alaska	Single subject only. No revenue measures, appropriations, acts affecting the judiciary, or any local or special legislation. Also, no laws affecting peace, health or safety.
Arizona	Single subject only; legislative matters only.
Arkansas	Limited to legislative measures.
California	Single subject only.
Colorado	Single subject only.
Florida	Single subject only.
Idaho	No restrictions.
Illinois	Legislative matters only. Can only deal with structural and procedural subjects.
Maine	Any expenditure in excess of appropriations is void 45 days after legislature convenes.
Massachusetts	No measures involving religion, the judiciary, local or special legislation, or specific appropriations.
Michigan	Applicable to statutes that legislature may enact.
Mississippi	No modifications of bill of rights and no modifications of public employees' retirement system or labor-related items. Initiatives rejected by the voters cannot be placed on the ballot for two years after the election.
Missouri	Single subject only; no appropriations without new revenue, and nothing that is prohibited by the constitution.
Montana	Single subject only; no appropriations, and no special or local legislation.
Nebraska	Single subject only. Limited to matters that can be enacted by the legislature. Same subject can't appear on the ballot more than once in three years.
Nevada	No appropriations or expenditures of money, unless the measure includes a sufficient tax not prohibited by Nevada's constitution.
North Dakota	No emergency measures, or appropriations for support and maintenance of state departments and institutions.
Ohio	Single subject only. No measures involving property taxes. Legislative matters only.
Oklahoma	Single subject only. The same subject cannot appear on the ballot more than once every three years. Legislative matters only.
Oregon	Single subject only. Legislative matters only.
South Dakota	Except laws as necessary for the immediate preservation of public peace, health or safety, support of state government and existing public institutions.
Utah	Legislative matters only.
Washington	Single subject only. Limited to legislative matters.
Wyoming	Single Subject. No earmarking, making or repealing appropriations, creating courts, defining jurisdiction of courts or court rules, and no local or special legislation. No measure that is similar to a measure that has been defeated at the ballot within 5 years.

Popular Referendum Limitations

While some states allow voters to undertake a popular referendum on any act of the legislature, others impose restrictions. Twenty-four states grant their citizens the right of popular referendum. The constitutions of fourteen, however, impose some level of restriction on popular referendums when **they concern state appropriations.**

Popular Referendum Limitations

State	Restriction	Comments
Alaska	Yes	Can't repeal appropriations.
Arizona	Yes	Exempts from referendums laws immediately necessary for the support and maintenance of the departments of state government and state institutions.
Arkansas	No	Not Applicable
California	Yes	Exempts from referendum, statutes providing for tax levies or appropriations for current expenses of the state.
Colorado	Yes	Exempts from referendums appropriations for the support and maintenance of the departments of state and state institutions and emergency legislation.
Idaho	No	Not Applicable
Kentucky	Yes	Referendums are only allowed on local tax increases.
Maine	No	Not Applicable
Maryland	No	Not Applicable
Massachusetts	Yes	Exempts from referendums any law that appropriates money for the current or ordinary expenses of the commonwealth or for any of its departments, boards, commissions, or institutions.
Michigan	Yes	The power of referendum does not extend to acts making appropriations for state institutions or to meet deficiencies in state funds.
Missouri	Yes	A referendum may be ordered except as to laws making appropriations for the current expenses of the state government.
Montana	Yes	The people may approve or reject by referendum any act of the legislature except an appropriation of money.
Nebraska	Yes	The referendum may be invoked against any act or part of an act except those making appropriations for the expense of the state government or a state institution existing at the time of such act.
Nevada	No	Not Applicable
New Mexico	Yes	The people reserve the power to disapprove, suspend and annul any law enacted by the legislature, except general appropriation laws.
North Dakota	No	Not Applicable
Ohio	No	Explicitly allows referendums on appropriations.
Oklahoma	No	Not Applicable
Oregon	No	Not Applicable
South Dakota	Yes	Except such laws as may be necessary for the support of the state government and its existing public institutions.
Utah	No	Not Applicable
Washington	Yes	Except such laws as may be necessary for the support of the state government and its existing public institutions.
Wyoming	Yes	The referendum shall not be applied to dedications of revenue or to appropriations.

Limits on the Number and Frequency of Ballot Measures

Six states place restrictions on the number and frequency of ballot measures. In Nebraska, an initiative petition may not be filed that is substantially the same as one that failed on the ballot within the preceding three years. Wyoming has a similar provision, except the time period is five years. Massachusetts's law states that "substantially the same petition cannot have appeared on the ballot at either of the two immediately preceding biennial state elections." Mississippi limits the number of initiative proposals to five: the first five measures meeting the submission requirements will be placed on the ballot. Initiatives rejected by the voters cannot be placed on the ballot for two years after the election.

Limits on the Number and Frequency of Ballot Measures

State	Limitation
Illinois	Limits the number of citizen initiated non-binding advisory questions to no more than three on the same ballot.
Massachusetts	Substantially the same petition cannot have appeared on the ballot at either of the two immediately preceding biennial state elections.
Mississippi	Limits the number of ballot initiatives on the same ballot to five. The first five measures meeting the submission requirements are the ones placed on the ballot. Additionally, an initiative rejected by the voters cannot be placed on another ballot for two years after the election.
Nebraska	Same subject can't appear on the ballot more than once in three years.
Oklahoma	Same subject can't appear on the ballot more than once in three years.
Wyoming	No measure can be put on the ballot that is similar to a measure that has been defeated at the ballot within 5 years.

Petition Circulator Requirements

Up until 1999, several states required petition circulators to be registered voters. The U.S. Supreme Court in **Buckley v. ACLF** ruled that states couldn't require circulators to be registered voters. However, almost all of the states with prior registered voter requirements have now adopted laws requiring that circulators be residents of the state. This new law will most likely be litigated as well. Additionally, several states have limited the amount of money that can be paid to signature gatherers. In Alaska, you can only pay up to $1.00 per signature collected and in North Dakota and Oregon you cannot pay signature gatherers on a per signature basis (a similar ban was struck down in Maine and is being challenged in Oregon).

Circulation Period

Circulation periods range from as brief as 64 days in Massachusetts to an unlimited duration — though there are limits on how long a petition signature is valid. Most states also have deadlines for submitting initiative petitions, so that officials will have time to verify the signatures, publish the initiative, and prepare the ballot. Arkansas, Ohio and Utah have no time limit for signature gathering. Oklahoma at 90 days, California at 150 days, and Massachusetts at 64 days have the shortest circulation periods.

Signature Requirements

Central to the initiative process is gathering the required number of valid signatures. Although the requirements and formulas may differ, all states set the signature threshold at some percentage of the voting public, rather than an absolute number of signatures. Some states require that the number of signatures match a predetermined percentage of the registered voters for the state. Others require a percentage of a previous vote for a designated office to qualify. Signature thresholds vary from a high of 15 percent of qualified voters based on votes cast in the last general election in Wyoming to a low of two percent of the state's resident population in North Dakota. Most states, which have both constitutional and statutory initiatives, require a higher percentage of signatures for constitutional initiatives with Colorado and Nevada being the exceptions. The average number of signatures required for a statute is 7.23% of the votes cast for governor in the last election and 9.17% for a constitutional amendment.

Net Number of Signatures Required for Initiatives

State	Net Signature Requirement for Constitutional Amendments	Estimated NET Number for 2002 Election	Net Signature Requirement for Statutes	Estimated NET Number for 2002 Election
Alaska	Not allowed by state constitution	N/A	10% of votes cast in last general election	28,782
Arizona	15% of votes cast for Governor	152,643	10% of votes cast for Governor	101,762
Arkansas	10% of votes cast for Governor	70,602	8% of votes cast for Governor	54,481
California	8% of votes cast for Governor	670,816	5% of votes cast for Governor	419,094
Colorado	5% of votes cast for SOS	80,571	5% of votes cast for SOS	80,571
Florida	8% of ballots cast in the last Presidential election	488,722	Not allowed by state constitution	N/A
Idaho	Not allowed by state constitution	N/A	6% of registered voters	43,685
Maine	Not allowed by state constitution	N/A	10% of votes cast for Governor	42,101
Massachusetts	3% of votes cast for Governor	57,100	3?% of votes cast for Governor	57,100
Michigan	10% of votes cast for Governor	302,710	8% of votes cast for Governor	242,169
Mississippi	12% of votes cast for Governor	91,673	Not allowed by state constitution	N/A
Missouri	8% of votes cast for Governor	120,571	5% of votes cast for Governor	75,356
Montana	10% of votes cast for Governor	41,019	5% of votes cast for Governor	20,500
Nebraska	10% of registered voters	108,500	7% of registered voters	76,000
Nevada	10% of registered voters	61,366	10% of votes cast in last general election.	61,366
North Dakota	4% of population	25,552	2% of population	12,776
Ohio	10% of votes cast for Governor	334,624	6% of votes cast for Governor	200,774
Oklahoma	15% of votes cast for Governor	185,135	8% of votes cast for Governor	98,739
Oregon	8% of votes cast for Governor	89,048	6% of votes cast for Governor	66,786
South Dakota	10% of votes cast for Governor	26,019	5% of votes cast for Governor	13,010
Utah	Not allowed by state constitution	N/A	Direct statute: 10% of votes cast for Governor Indirect statute: 10% of votes cast for Governor	76,181
Washington	Not allowed by state constitution	N/A	8% of votes cast for Governor	197,588
Wyoming	Not allowed by state constitution	N/A	15% of votes cast in the last general election	33,253
Totals	—————	2,906,671	—————	2,002,074

Signature Collection at Polling Locations

As the initiative process has grown in popularity, states have passed new laws to make the collection of signatures more difficult. One of the primary methods has been to limit when and where signatures could be collected. One of the most popular changes has been to limit signature collection at polling locations. Polling locations are a great place to collect signatures since it is a location where signature gatherers can find a high concentration of registered voters and therefore increase their petition signature validity rates and decrease the total number of signatures necessary to qualify the initiative for the ballot.

Signature Collection at Polling Locations

State	Restriction
Alaska	Circulating petitions within 200 feet of polling places on election day is prohibited.
Arizona	Circulating petitions within 75 feet of polling places on election day is prohibited.
Arkansas	Circulating petitions within 100 feet of polling places on election day is prohibited.
California	Circulating petitions within 100 feet of polling places on election day is prohibited.
Colorado	Circulating petitions within 100 feet of polling places on election day is prohibited.
Florida	Circulating petitions within 50 feet of polling places on election day is prohibited.
Idaho	Circulating petitions within 300 feet of public polling places on election day is prohibited — with 100 feet of private polling places.
Illinois	Circulating petitions within 100 feet of polling places on election day is prohibited.

State	Restriction
Maine	The election warden delegates a spot outside of the voting enclosure and a petitioner can gather signatures but cannot approach a voter until after he or she has voted.
Massachusetts	Circulating petitions within 150 feet of polling places on election day is prohibited.
Michigan	Circulating petitions within 100 feet of polling places on election day is prohibited.
Mississippi	Circulating petitions within 150 feet of polling places on election day is prohibited.
Missouri	Circulating petitions within 25 feet of polling places on election day is prohibited.
Montana	No prohibition.
Nebraska	Circulating petitions within 200 feet of polling places on election day is prohibited.
Nevada	Circulating petitions within 100 feet of polling places on election day is prohibited.
North Dakota	"it is unlawful to obstruct the voting process" — there is no set distance that signature gatherers have to be away from polling locations however an election board has the right to ask them to move back further if they feel there is a problem/obstruction.
Ohio	Circulating petition within 100 feet of polling places on election day is prohibited.
Oklahoma	Circulating petitions within 300 feet of polling places on election day is prohibited.
Oregon	Not applicable — all voting conducted by mail.
South Dakota	Circulating petitions within 100 feet of polling places on election day is prohibited.
Utah	Circulating petitions within 150 feet of polling places on election day is prohibited.
Washington	Circulating petitions within 100 yards of polling places on election day is prohibited.
Wyoming	Circulating petitions within 100 yards of polling places on election day is prohibited.

Geographic Distribution Requirements

Numerous states require some geographic distribution of signatures, often a specified number of signatures from each of a certain number of counties or districts. Distribution requirements can be a deterrent to the use of the initiative process. Over 60% of all initiative activity has taken place in just six states—Arizona, California, Colorado, North Dakota, Oregon and Washington, all without a geographic distribution requirement. States with severe distribution requirements like Idaho, Mississippi, Utah, and Wyoming rarely have initiatives on their ballot. However, Idaho's and Utah's distribution requirement—which were based on a county requirement—were struck down by the courts as unconstitutional. Montana's distribution requirement is currently being challenged in the courts (see chart below for additional information on geographic distribution requirements).

Verification of Petition Signatures

There are three methods to verifying signatures: presumed valid, random sampling, and full certification. Three states use the presumed valid test. This means that the state simply counts the names and assumes that all of the signatures are legitimate. Twelve states require full certification and ten states use the random sampling method.

Signature Verification Process

State	Process
Alaska	Signatures are turned into the Division of Elections who verify each signature until the minimum number needed is met.
Arizona	Signatures are verified by the Secretary of State using a random sampling method.
Arkansas	The Secretary of State will verify signatures up to 10% above the designated number required. However, the Secretary of State will not accept additional signatures if the petition is determined to be sufficient after the initial submission even if the number is one signature over the required number. Nor will the Secretary of State accept additional signatures after the initial submission until a determination of sufficiency is made. If a petition is determined not to contain the requisite number of valid signatures, a sponsor may within 30 days of notification of insufficiency from the Secretary of State do any or all of the following: a) solicit and obtain additional signatures; b) submit proof that the rejected signatures or some of them are good and should be counted; or c) make the petition more definite or certain. The Secretary of State will set designated times to accept the additional signatures from a notified sponsor.

State	Process
California	The signatures are submitted to the county clerks who verify them using a random sampling method and then provide the results to the Secretary of State who will certify the measure for the ballot.
Colorado	The Secretary of State verifies signatures by a random sample procedure. Not less than 5% of the signatures, and in no event fewer than 4,000 signatures, are to be verified. If the sample indicates that the number of valid signatures is 90% or less of the required total, the petition is deemed to have insufficient signatures. If the valid signatures are found to be 110% or more of number required, the petition is deemed sufficient. However, if the number of valid signatures is found to be over 90% but less than 110% of the required number, the law requires that each signature on the petition be verified.
Florida	Proponents must turn their petitions into each county for certification. The county clerks will verify each signature. Florida charges proponents to verify their signatures. For each signature checked, ten cents, or the actual cost of checking a signature, whichever is less, is paid to the supervisor at the time of submitting the petitions, by the political committee sponsoring the initiative petition. However, if a committee is unable to pay the charges without imposing an undue burden on the organization, the organization must submit a written certification of such inability given under oath to the Division of Elections to have the signatures verified at no charge. However, a sponsor of a proposed initiative amendment who uses paid petition circulators may not file an oath of undue burden in lieu of paying the fee required for the verification of signatures gathered. The Division of Elections will then circulate the undue burden oath submitted by the committee to each supervisor of elections in the state.
Idaho	Petitions are turned into the county clerks of the counties in which the petitions are circulated. The county clerks verify every signature.
Maine	Signatures fully verified by the Secretary of State.
Massachusetts	All signatures must be certified by a majority (at least three) of the local registrars or election commissioners in the city or town in which the signatures are collected.
Michigan	Signatures are verified by the Secretary of State using a random sampling method.
Mississippi	County circuit clerks verify every signature.
Missouri	Secretary of State verifies signatures by use of a random sampling.
Montana	County officials check the names of all signers to verify they are registered voters. In addition, they randomly select signatures on each sheet and compare them with the signatures of the electors as they appear in the registration records of the office. If any of the randomly selected signatures do not appear to be genuine, all signatures on that sheet must be compared with the signatures in the registration records of the office.
Nebraska	Petitions are turned into the Secretary of State, who then gives the petitions to the respective counties to verify. Each signature is compared with the voter registration records.
Nevada	The Secretary of State using the random sampling method verifies signatures.
North Dakota	North Dakota does not a have a voter registration process. As a result, there are no registered voters. Proponents, however, must collect the signatures of North Dakota residents. The Secretary of State then conducts a representative random sampling of the signatures contained in the petitions by the use of questionnaires, post cards, telephone calls, personal interviews, or other accepted information gathering techniques to determine the validity of the signatures.
Ohio	The petition and signatures on such petition shall be presumed to be in all respects sufficient, unless, it shall be otherwise proved, and in such event ten (10) additional days shall be allowed for the filing of additional signatures. Each signer must be a qualified elector of the state. Each part-petition must contain signatures of electors of only one county. If a part-petition contains signatures of more than one county, the Secretary of State determines the county from which the majority of signatures came from, and only signatures from that county will be counted.
Oklahoma	Signatures are presumed valid unless challenged.
Oregon	The Secretary of State highlights a random sample and sends them to the appropriate counties for verification.
South Dakota	The Secretary of State verifies each signature until reaching the minimum number of valid signatures needed to qualify the initiative.

State	Process
Utah	Petitions are verified by the county clerks who verify every signature.
Washington	Signatures verified by the Secretary of State using a random sampling method.
Wyoming	The Secretary of State's office verifies every signature to ensure that they are registered voters. They do not, however, match the signatures on the petition to the actual signatures on the voter registration cards.

When Initiatives Can Appear on the Ballot

In most states it is mandatory that a statewide initiative appear on the general election ballot. In some states, an initiative can appear on either a primary or general election ballot. There are exceptions—in Oklahoma for example, the Governor can set any date that he chooses for a vote to take place on an initiative or referendum.

When Initiatives Can Appear on the Ballot

States that Allow Initiatives on General Election Ballots	
Alaska	Missouri
Arizona	Montana
Arkansas	Nebraska
California	Nevada
Colorado	North Dakota
Florida	Ohio
Idaho	Oklahoma
Illinois	Oregon
Maine	South Dakota
Massachusetts	Utah
Michigan	Washington
Mississippi	Wyoming

States that Allow Initiatives on Primary or Special Election Ballots	
Alaska	North Dakota
California	Oklahoma

States that Allow Initiatives on Odd-Year Ballots[21]	
Colorado[22]	Mississippi
Maine	Ohio
Washington	

Publication of Initiatives

A majority of the initiative states distribute a voter pamphlet. Several states also inform the electorate about ballot measures through publication in major newspapers with some states using both methods. States that use the newspaper as their medium for voter information use a variety of styles and format. Some states will publish the entire initiative text in the newspaper; most publish an impartial analysis along with an argument for and against.

The voter pamphlet usually includes the official ballot title, a fiscal impact statement, an "impartial" analysis by public officials and arguments and rebuttals for and against each measure.

Arizona, California, Montana, Nevada, Oregon and Utah specifically mandate that a fiscal impact statement be printed in the pamphlet.

Both Oregon and Montana use a committee system to draft the voter pamphlet analyses. In Oregon, the committee is two proponents and two opponents selected by the Secretary of State. These individuals then select a fifth committee member. Montana establishes a similar committee for each analysis, however the fifth committee member is the Attorney General.

Massachusetts makes full use of legislative hearings to assist in voter information. A summary of the majority and minority reports of the legislative committee that conducted public hearings on the proposal is printed in the pamphlet. Committee members representing both the majority and minority opinions on the issue draft a brief summary of their reasons for supporting or opposing the measure.

The majority of states produce a voter pamphlet essentially at state expense with the exception of Alaska, Arizona, and Oregon. Alaska does not charge to print ballot measure arguments, but it does charge political parties and candidates a

---

21. All the states but Mississippi allow initiatives on the ballot in an even numbered year as well.
22. Only initiatives that raise taxes can appear on the ballot in odd numbered years.

"per page" fee to have information included in the pamphlet. Arizona charges $100 per argument printed in its pamphlet. Oregon charges $500 per argument. This fee may be waived if the submitter collects 2,500 valid signatures in support of the argument.

Voter Guide, Fiscal Impact and Pro/Con Argument Information

State	Does the state publish a voter's Pamphlet?	What's In it?	How is it distributed?	Do they allow for pro and con statements?	Who writes the pro and con statements?	Is there a fiscal impact Statement?	Are there hearings on the initiative?	How many hearings and when and where?
AK	Yes	Title, full text, ballot language, neutral Legislative Affairs Agency summary and pro and con arguments.	Mailed to every registered voter.	Yes	Whoever wants to submit one but can't exceed 500 words.	No	No	N/A
AZ	Yes	Title, full text, form in which it appears on the ballot, a Legislative Council analysis, fiscal impact statement, and pro and con.	Mailed to every registered voter.	Yes	Anyone who agrees to pay $100 but can't exceed 300 words.	Yes	Yes	Hearings in at least three different counties.
AR	No	N/A	N/A	N/A	N/A	No	No	N/A
CA	Yes	Title, summary, full text, fiscal statements and pro and con (and rebuttals to pro and con).	Mailed to every registered voter.	Yes	Proponents — opponents chosen by SOS if more than one.	Yes	Yes	One in the state legislature.
CO	Yes	Title, summary and text, and pro and con.	Mailed to every registered voter.	Yes	The Legislative Council writes the pro and con.	Yes	Yes	At least one
FL	No	N/A	N/A	No	N/A	Yes	No	N/A
ID	Yes	Title, Ballot form, full text, pro and con arguments and rebuttal.	Mailed to every registered voter in the state.	Yes	Selected by the state.	No	No	N/A
ME	Yes	Title, summary, explanatory statement, fiscal statement	Two to every town office and libraries. Also, posted in poster form at voting center. Also, available on request.	No	N/A	No, except for bond issues.	No	N/A
MA	Yes	Title, ballot language, full text and pro and con.	Mailed to every registered voter.	Yes	State legislative committees and proponents	No	Yes	At least one
MI	No	N/A	N/A	No	N/A	No	No	N/A
MS	Yes	Title, summary, full text, fiscal analysis and pro and con.	Newspaper	Yes	Whoever submits one but not to exceed 300 words.	Yes	Yes	At least one in every Congressional district.

State	Does the state publish a voter's Pamphlet?	What's In it?	How is it distributed?	Do they allow for pro and con statements?	Who writes the pro and con statements?	Is there a fiscal impact Statement?	Are there hearings on the initiative?	How many hearings and when and where?
MO	No	N/A	N/A	N/A	N/A	Yes	No	N/A
MT	Yes	Title, text, fiscal statement and pro and con.	Mailed to every registered voter.	Yes	Written by a committee of three chosen by the legislative leadership.	Yes	No	N/A
NE	No	N/A	N/A	No	N/A	No	No	N/A
NV	Yes	Title, text, fiscal statement and pro and con.	Mailed to every registered voter.	No	N/A	Yes	No	N/A
ND	No	N/A	N/A	N/A	N/A	No	No	N/A
OH	Yes	Title, text, fiscal statement and pro and con.	Mailed to every registered voter.	Yes	Groups chosen by the state	Yes	No	N/A
OK	No	N/A	N/A	N/A	N/A	No	No	N/A
OR	Yes	Title, summary, explanatory statement, fiscal statement, etc.	Mailed to every registered voters home.	Yes	Anyone who wants to pay $500	Yes	No	N/A
SD	Yes	Explanation of measure, proponent's and opponent's statement.	Available online and available at any County Auditor's office.	Yes	Proponent writes a statement and the SOS chooses an opponent to write a statement.	No	No	N/A
UT	Yes	Impartial analysis of all ballot issues. Arguments for and against each ballot issue. Complete text of all ballot issues.	In every newspaper in general circulation.	Yes	Proponent writes argument for and state chooses who writes con argument	Yes	No	N/A
WA	Yes	Official ballot title and explanatory statement, statement for and against, fiscal impact statement, and complete text of measure.	Mailed registered to voters and available at county election offices.	Yes	Supporters opponents who apply with the Secretary of State's and office.	Yes	No	N/A
WY	No	N/A	N/A	No	N/A	No	No	N/A

Voter Approval

Once an initiative is on the ballot, the general requirement for passage is a simple majority vote. Exceptions are Nebraska, Massachusetts and Mississippi. These states require a majority, provided the votes cast on the initiative equals a percentage of the total votes cast in the election (35% in Nebraska, 30% in Massachusetts, and 40% in Mississippi.) Wyoming requires "an amount in excess of 50% of those voting in the preceding general election." An initiated constitutional amendment in Nevada must receive a majority vote in two successive general elections. Washington requires a simple majority approval for all measures except those concerning gambling (which requires 60% affirmative vote for passage). Utah has a requirement that any initiative pertaining to the taking of wildlife must pass by a 2/3 vote.

Conflicting Measures

Most states have adopted policies addressing conflicting propositions especially in states that allow the state legislature to place an "alternative" measure on the ballot. Fifteen states have determined that if two or more conflicting initiatives receive voter approval, the one with the most affirmative vote controls.

In Utah, the governor makes the initial decision whether provisions conflict and declares which proposal controls based on the highest number of votes. Voters may challenge this determination within 30 days. In Washington, voters are asked to express two preferences: first, between either measure or neither; second, between one or the other. Maine also forces voters to choose between competing propositions or against both, with a warning that a "yes" vote for both measures will invalidate the ballot. In Massachusetts, the legislature designates prior to the election which initiatives conflict. Voters are then encouraged to choose between one or the other.

Amending Initiative Statutes and Veto Authority

In no state does the governor have the right to veto laws passed by initiative. California is the only initiative state where the legislature may not repeal or amend a statutory initiative. Eleven states allow their legislatures to amend or repeal a statutory initiative statue at any time after its adoption by a simple majority vote of both houses. Nine states impose restrictions on changes to statutory initiatives. Nevada, for example, prohibits legislative amendment or repeal for three years after passage of the statutory initiative. Alaska and Wyoming permit simple majority amendments at any time but prohibit a legislative repeal of the initiative for two years after its passage. Michigan requires a 3/4 vote of the legislature to amend to repeal an initiative (unless otherwise specified by the initiative.) Arkansas imposes a 2/3 legislative vote requirement, and North Dakota requires a 2/3 legislative vote but only in the first seven years after enactment. In states with the constitutional initiative process, any changes proposed by the legislature must be placed on the ballot for a subsequent vote.

Legislative and Executive Power to Change or Repeal Statutory Initiatives

State	Legislative Power
Alaska	Can repeal only after two years but can amend anytime
Arizona	Cannot repeal but can amend an initiative law if the amending legislation furthers the purposes of such measure and at least 3/4 of both houses, by a roll call vote, vote to amend the measure
Arkansas	Can repeal or amend by a 2/3 vote of each house
California	Cannot repeal or amend unless permitted by the initiative
Colorado	Can repeal and amend at anytime
Florida	Florida's initiative process only allows constitutional amendments
Idaho	Can repeal and amend
Maine	Can repeal and amend
Massachusetts	Can repeal and amend
Michigan	Can repeal and amend by a 3/4 vote of each house or as otherwise provided by the initiative
Mississippi	Mississippi's initiative process only allows constitutional amendments
Missouri	Can repeal and amend
Montana	Can repeal and amend
Nebraska	Can repeal and amend
Nevada	Can only repeal or amend after three years of enactment
North Dakota	Can repeal or amend by a 2/3 vote of each house for seven year after passage, majority vote thereafter
Ohio	Can repeal and amend
Oklahoma	Can repeal and amend
Oregon	Can repeal and amend
South Dakota	Can repeal and amend
Utah	Can amend only at subsequent sessions
Washington	Can repeal or amend by a 2/3 vote of each house during the first two years of enactment, majority vote thereafter
Wyoming	Cannot repeal for at least two years after enactment, but may amend at any time

Signature, Geographic Distribution and Single Subject (SS) Requirements for Initiative Petitions

State	Type	SS	Net Signature Requirement for Constitutional Amendments	Net Signature Requirement for Statutes	Geographic Distribution	Deadline for Signature Submission	Circulation Period
AK	IDS	Yes	Not allowed by state constitution	10% of votes cast in last general election.	At least 1 signature in 2/3 of Election Districts	Prior to the convening of the legislature[23]	1 year
AZ	DA/DS	Yes	15% of votes cast for Governor	10% of votes cast for Governor	No geographical distribution	Four months prior to election	20 months
AR	DA/DS	No	10% of votes cast for Governor	8% of votes cast for Governor	5% in 15 of 75 counties	Four months prior to election	Unlimited
CA	DA/DS	Yes	8% of votes cast for Governor	5% of votes cast for Governor	No geographical distribution	To be determined by state each year[24]	150 days
CO	DA/DS	Yes	5% of votes cast for SOS	5% of votes cast for SOS	No geographical distribution	Three months prior to election	6 months
FL	DA	Yes	8% of ballots cast in the last Presidential election	Not allowed by state constitution	8% in 12 of 23 Congressional Districts	90 days prior to election[25]	4 years
ID	DS	No	Not allowed by state constitution	6% of registered voters	6% in 22 of 44 counties[26]	Four months prior to election	18 months
ME	IDS	No	Not allowed by state constitution	10% of votes cast for Governor	No geographical distribution	To be determined by state each year[27]	1 year
MA	IDA/IDS	No	3% of votes cast for Governor	3?% of votes cast for Governor[28]	No more than 25% from a single county	To be determined each year by state[29]	64 days
MI	DA/IDS	No	10% of votes cast for Governor	8% of votes cast for Governor	No geographical distribution	Constitutional amendment[30] Statute[31]	180 days
MS	IDA	No	12% of votes cast for Governor	Not allowed by state constitution	20% from each Congressional District	90 days prior to the convening of the legislature	1 year
MO	DA/DS	Yes	8% of votes cast for Governor	5% of votes cast for Governor	5% in 6 of 9 Congressional Districts	Eight months prior to election	16 months
MT	DA/DS	Yes	10% of votes cast for Governor	5% of votes cast for Governor	Statute: 5% in 34 Legislative Districts; Amendment: 10% in 40 Legislative Districts[32]	Second Friday of the fourth month prior to election	1 year
NE	DA/DS	Yes	10% of registered voters	7% of registered voters	5% in 38 of 93 counties	Four months prior to election	1 year
NV	DA/IDS	No	10% of registered voters	10% of votes cast in last general election.	10% in 13 of 17 counties	Constitutional amendment[33] Statute[34]	CA: 11 months[35] Statute: 10 months[36]
ND	DA/DS	No	4% of population	2% of population	No geographical distribution	90 days prior to election	1 year
OH	DA/IDS	Yes	10% of votes cast for Governor	6% of votes cast for Governor[37]	Statute: 1% in 44 of 88 counties Amendment: 5% in 44 of 88 counties	Constitutional amendment[38] Statute[39]	1 year
OK	DA/DS	Yes	15% of votes cast for Governor	8% of votes cast for Governor	No geographical distribution	Eight months prior to election[40]	90 days
OR	DA/DS	Yes	8% of votes cast for Governor	6% of votes cast for Governor	No geographical distribution	Four months prior to election	Unlimited
SD	DA/DS	No	10% of votes cast for Governor	5% of votes cast for Governor	No geographical distribution	Constitutional amendment[41] Statute[42]	1 year
UT	DS/IDS	No	Not allowed by state constitution	Direct statute: 10% of votes cast for Governor In-direct statute: 10% of votes cast for Governor[43]	10% in 20 of 29 counties	Direct statute[44] In-direct statute[45]	Direct: Unlimited In-direct: Unlimited

State	Type	SS	Net Signature Requirement for Constitutional Amendments	Net Signature Requirement for Statutes	Geographic Distribution	Deadline for Signature Submission	Circulation Period
WA	DS/IDS	No	Not allowed by state constitution	8% of votes cast for Governor	No geographical distribution	Direct: statute[46] In-direct statute[47]	Direct: 6 months In-direct: 10 months
WY	IDS	Yes	Not allowed by state constitution	15% of votes cast in the last general election.	15% of total votes cast in the last election from at least 2/3 of the counties	One day prior to the convening of the legislature[48]	18 months

23. In Alaska, signatures must be submitted prior to the convening of the legislative session in the year in which the initiative is to appear on the ballot. The lieutenant governor shall place the initiative on the election ballot of the first statewide general, special, or primary election that is held after (1) the petition and any supplementary petition signatures have been submitted, (2) a legislative session has convened and adjourned, and (3) a period of 120 days has expired since the adjournment of the legislative session.

24. In California, each year the Secretary of State will set a complete schedule showing the maximum filing deadline and the certification deadline by the counties to the Secretary of State. There is a recommended submission date for "full check" and "random check". These dates are only recommended. Notwithstanding any other provision of law, no initiative shall be placed on a statewide election ballot that qualifies less than 131 days before the date of the election.

25. In Florida, certification must be received by the Secretary of State from the county supervisors stating the number of valid signatures submitted by the initiative proponent no later than 90 days prior to the general election ballot for the initiative to be considered for that ballot. However, there are several additional criteria that must be met prior to the certification of an initiative for the ballot. This includes the requirement that the proposed initiative has been approved for the ballot by the state supreme court. An initiative can only be submitted to the court for review after 10% of the required number of signatures have been collected and certified to the Secretary of State by the county supervisors. The court is under no statutory time frame to render a decision. Therefore, there is no precise date in which the signatures must be submitted in order to insure that you qualify for any specific general election ballot.

26. This distribution requirement was struck down as unconstitutional by the Federal District Court of Idaho in early 2002. The decision was appealed by the state and as of the writing of this Almanac, the appeal had not been decided.

27. In Maine, signatures must be submitted on or before the 50th day after the convening of the Legislature in the first regular session or on or before the 25th day after the convening of the Legislature in the second regular session.

28. In Massachusetts, the initial petition must include 3% of the total votes cast for Governor. If the legislature has not passed an initiated statute by the first Wednesday in May, petitioners must file a supplementary petition with petitions equal in number to one-half of one percent of the total votes cast in the previous gubernatorial election to place the issue on the ballot.

29. In Massachusetts, the initial petition signatures shall be submitted no later than the first Wednesday in December in the year in which the Initiative was submitted. If the legislature has not passed the initiated statute by the first Wednesday in May, petitioners must file a supplementary petition with petitions equal in number to one-half of one percent of the total votes cast in the previous gubernatorial election no sooner than the first Wednesday in June and no later than the first Wednesday in July in for the initiative statute to be placed on the ballot.

30. In Michigan, signatures for constitutional amendments must be submitted not less than 120 days prior to the general election.

31. In Michigan, signatures for statutes must be submitted ten days prior to the start of the legislative session.

32. The legislature placed a constitutional amendment on the November 2002 that was adopted by the voters that increased the state's distribution requirement. The new requirement, which is being challenged in Federal Court requires a percentage of signatures to be gathered in half of the counties.

33. In Nevada, signatures for constitutional amendments must be submitted 90 days prior to the election.

34. In Nevada, signatures for statutes must be submitted 30 days prior to the convening of the legislature.

35. In Nevada, petition language for constitutional amendments can be filed no sooner than September 1 of the year preceding the election and all signatures are due 90 days prior to the election.

36. In Nevada, petition language for statutes can be filed no sooner than January 1st of an even numbered year and signatures must be submitted no later than November 1st of that same even numbered year.

37. In Ohio, the initial petition must include 3% of the total votes cast for Governor. A supplementary petition containing an additional 3% is required in the event the proposed statute is defeated, amended or left idle by the legislature.

38. In Ohio, signatures for amendments must be submitted 90 days prior to the election.

39. In Ohio, signatures for statutes must be submitted 10 days prior to the convening of legislature.

40. In Oklahoma, an initiative must be submitted to the state Supreme Court for review before it can be certified for the ballot by the Secretary of State. Due to the fact that there is no statutory deadline for the court to make this determination, the state recommends that you submit your signatures eight months prior to the election that you desire the measure to be considered for.

41. In South Dakota, signatures for amendments must be submitted at least one year prior to the election.

42. In South Dakota, signatures for statutes must be submitted by the first Tuesday in May in the general election year.

43. In Utah, direct statutes require signatures equal in number to 10% of the votes cast for all candidates for Governor in the next preceding gubernatorial election for the statute to be placed on the ballot. Indirect statutes must contain signatures from 5% of the votes cast for all candidates for Governor in the next preceding gubernatorial election. If the legislature rejects or does not enact the proposed statute, a supplemental petition contacting additional signatures equal in number to 5% of the votes cast for all candidates for Governor in the next preceding gubernatorial election for the statute to be placed on the ballot.

44. In Utah, signatures for direct statutes must be submitted at least four months prior to the election.

45. In Utah, signatures for in-direct statutes must be submitted at least 10 days before the commencement of the annual general legislative session.

46. In Washington, signatures for direct statutes must be submitted four months prior to the election.

47. In Washington, signatures for indirect statutes must be submitted ten days prior to the convening of the regular session of the legislature.

48. In Wyoming, signatures must be submitted prior to the convening of the legislature. The state constitution states that the legislature shall convene at noon on the second Tuesday in January.

3 I&R in American Cities: Basic Patterns

By John G. Matsusaka[1]

Introduction[2]

The bright glare of statewide ballot propositions sometimes makes the local initiative and referendum (I&R) process seem almost invisible. Yet far more Americans have access to I&R in their local government than have access in their state government.[3] The purpose of this article is to try to pull the local I&R process out of the shadows by providing some information on its availability in American cities.

I begin with a detailed discussion of I&R provisions in the 20 largest American cities. After this, basic patterns across all (or substantially all) municipalities in the United States are described using survey data collected by the International City/County Management Association (ICMA). In addition to providing a broad overview of current I&R provisions in cities, I identify some patterns that have not been explicitly noted before, and that seem worthy of further investigation by scholars.[4]

Initiative and Referendum in the Largest Cities

Table 1 (on the next page) reports the initiative and referendum provisions of the 20 largest American cities (according to the 2000 Census). The provisions were identified by consulting city charters, city codes, state constitutions, state codes, city web pages, and by phone and email communications with city clerks.

To define terms, the "initiative" is a process by which citizens can place a new law before the electorate by collecting a given number of signatures from fellow citizens. In effect, the initiative allows voters to pass specific laws without involving their elected representatives. The "referendum" is process whereby an existing law is approved or rejected by vote of the electorate. Most cities use the term "initiative" in the same way, but "referendum" is used in a variety of different ways (see below).

Initiatives can allow voters to propose charter amendments or municipal ordinances. As can be seen, 12 cities allow citizens to initiate both charter amendments and ordinances, 3 allow only charter amendments, and 5 do not provide for either type of initiative. In most cases, the legal authority for ordinance initiatives can be found in the city charter, while amendment initiatives are provided in the state constitution or statutes.

In order to qualify a measure for the ballot, petitioners must collect a predetermined number of signatures. The signature requirement is sometimes stated as an absolute number (such as 50,000 in New York) but more often as a percentage (of registered voters, of votes cast at the previous mayoral election, and so on). In most cases, the petitioner must collect the necessary signatures within a fixed amount of time, typically two or three months.

Once the signatures are collected, the petition is submitted to the city's election official, typically the city clerk, for verification. If an ordinance initiative is determined to have enough signatures, the petition is then submitted to the city council. The council has the option to approve the measure without modification. If the council declines to approve the measure or it is a charter amendment, the proposal goes before the voters and becomes law if it receives a majority of the votes.

Some cities restrict the topics that can be addressed by initiatives. For example, New York limits initiatives to charter amendments that pertain to the "manner of voting" or that abolishes or create offices. San Antonio and Detroit do not allow initiatives to appropriate money or to levy taxes. But in most cases, the petitioners have a free hand. We would expect that in cities with charter initiatives but not ordinance initiatives, petitioners would use the initiative process to write substantive law into the charter.

---

1. John Matsusaka is a Senior Research Fellow of the Initiative & Referendum Institute and a professor at the University of Southern California.

2. I would like to thank Sebia Clark of ICMA for speedy responses to my numerous inquiries, and Natalia Moskvitina for excellent research assistance.

3. Ballpark figures for 1986 are that 41% lived in states with statewide initiatives while 71% lived in cities with the initiative process.

4. Some of this information is drawn from my book, *For the Many or the Few: How the Initiative Process Changes American Government* (currently in manuscript form only), which provides additional historical background, and a detailed analysis of the initiative's effect on government policy. For additional information about local I&R, see David D. Schmidt, *Citizen Lawmakers: The Ballot Initiative Revolution,* Philadelphia, PA: Temple University Press, 1991, and various issues of *Municipal Yearbook,* published by the International City/Council Management Association. Both sources are valuable, but appear to contain some errors.

Table 1. Initiative and Referendum Provisions in the 20 Largest Cities, 2000[5]

City	Initiative				Referendum		Source
	Type available:[6] A=Charter amendment O=Ordinance	Signatures required[7]	Circulation Period[8]	Restricted subjects[9]	Signatures required[10]	Days[11]	
New York	A	50,000	120	Anything but changes in "manner of voting" and offices available	...	...	Charter § 40
Los Angeles	A, O	15%[m]	A=200, O=120	...	10%[m]	30	Charter § 450-455, 460-464; CA Elections Code Div. 9 Ch. 3
Chicago	...	...	...	...	...	...	...
Houston	A, O	A=20,000, O=15%*	...	...	10%[m]	30	Charter VII-b, § 1-3, TX Local Govt. Code 9.004
Philadelphia	...	...	...	...	...	...	...
Phoenix	A, O	15%[m]	6 months	...	10%[m]	30	City Code XV, XVI; AZ Constitution IV Part 1 § 1(8), AZ Stats. 19-141 to 19-143
San Diego	A, O	A=15%, O=10%	A=200, O=180	...	5%	30	Charter § 23; City Code Art. 2 Divs. 10, 11, 28; CA Elections Code Div. 9 Ch. 3
Dallas	A, O	A=20,000, O=10%	O=60	...	...	...	Charter Ch. XVIII § 11-15; TX Local Govt. Code 9.004
San Antonio	A, O	A=20,000, O=10%	...	Appropriations, tax levies, franchises, utility rates, zoning	10%	40	Charter IV § 34-44; TX Local Govt. Code 9.004
Detroit	A, O	A=5%, O=3%[m]	A=1 year, O=6 months	Appropriations	3%m	30	Charter Art. 12; MI Statutes 117.21-117.25

5. The information was collected from city charters, municipal code, state constitutions, state statutes, city web pages, and communications with city clerks. Population according the 2000 census ranks Cities. Asterisks mean that more detailed information is presented below.

6. Type available: Indicates if the initiative can be used to amend the city charter or create municipal ordinances. If blank, then the city does not provide any form of the initiative. When an initiative proposing an ordinance qualifies for the ballot, the city council (or equivalent) has the option to approve the measure without sending it to the voters, except in San Francisco.

7. Signatures required: number of signatures required to qualify a measure for the ballot, expressed either as an absolute number or as a percentage of registered voters (except when noted with a superscript "m," in which case the percentage is in terms of the number of votes cast in the previous mayoral election.) In Houston, the percentage for an ordinance is in terms of the number of votes cast in the preceding Democratic primary for the nomination of mayor and commissioners. In Milwaukee, the percentage is in terms of the number of votes cast in the preceding gubernatorial election. In San Francisco, the signature requirement for a referendum on an ordinance granting a franchise is 3 percent.

8. Circulation period: how much time is allowed to collect signatures. The numbers are given in days, except where noted. When no limit on the circulation period could be found, the entry is left blank.

9. Restricted subjects: proposals that may not appear as initiatives. Also, initiative law is usually interpreted as prohibiting proposals that are "administrative" rather than "legislative" in character.

10. See footnote 7.

11. Days: how much time is allowed to collect signatures. The numbers are given in days beginning with the day the ordinance is approved. In Milwaukee, the signatures must be collected before the ordinance goes into effect.

City	Initiative				Referendum		Source
	Type available: A=Charter amendment O=Ordinance	Signatures required	Circulation Period	Restricted subjects	Signatures required	Days	
San Jose, CA	A, O	A=15%, O=5%	A=200, O=180	...	8%	30	City Charter § 1603; CA Elections Code Div. 9 Ch. 3
Indianapolis	...	...	...	...	...	...	...
San Francisco	A, O	A=10%, O=5%ᵐ	A=200, O=180	...	10%ᵐ*	30	Charter Art. 14; CA Elections Code Div. 9 Ch. 3
Jacksonville	A	5%	...	...	...	...	Charter § 18.05
Columbus	A, O	A=10%, O=5%	...	...	5%	30	Charter § 41-56, OH Constitution XVIII § 9
Austin	A, O	A=20,000, O=10%	...	Appropriations, tax levies	10%	*	Charter Art. IV; TX Local Govt. Code 9.004
Baltimore	A	10,000	...	...	...	...	MD Constitution Art. XI-A
Memphis	...	...	...	...	10%	...	TN Code 6-53-105
Milwaukee	A, O	15%*	60	...	7%*	60	WI Statutes 9.20, 66.0101
Boston	...	...	...	...	...	...	...

Twelve cities also allow referendums. A referendum allows citizens to challenge ordinances and charter amendments that have been approved by the city council. To challenge a measure, a petitioner must collect a given number of signatures within a certain amount of time after the measure has been passed. For example, in San Diego a referendum can be called if petitioners collect the signatures of 5 percent of registered voters within 30 days of a measure being approved. If the signature threshold is met, the council usually has the option to rescind its measure. If the council refuses, the measure is put before the voters and if fewer than half support it, the measure does not go into effect.[12]

Two things are perhaps worth noting about I&R in the largest cities. First, I&R is the rule not the exception. Second, provisions for I&R vary considerably across cities. The observation that a city has the initiative gives only a partial description of its practices.

The ICMA Form of Government Survey

The next step is to look at I&R availability in the thousands of other (smaller) cities in the United States. There is nothing conceptually difficult in calculating the numbers that follow. The hard part is assembling the raw data because there is no central clearinghouse that one can consult to determine the government of any given city. The best starting point appears to be the Form of Government surveys conducted by the International City/County Management Association (ICMA) at five-year intervals beginning in 1981. These surveys include a bit less than half of all cities in the country. The ICMA is a professional organization for administrators of cities, counties, and other local governments. The survey, which contains roughly 40 questions, is distributed to city clerks across the country. As far as I am aware, no attempt is made to verify the accuracy of the responses, and of course, many cities do not respond and are therefore omitted from the survey. Each survey contains about 4,700 cities.

While these surveys contain quite a bit of valuable information, they have their limitations, and the reader should be aware of them. There are two main weaknesses: the numbers are difficult to compare over time, and the information on referendums is difficult to interpret.

---

12. Other processes are sometimes referred to as "referendums." For example, the city council may pass a charter amendment and send it to the voters for approval, sometimes called a "legislative referendum." Or the council may vote to issue debt, and send the proposal to the voters for approval (a "bond referendum").

Table 2 reports the text of the relevant survey questions, and indicates the proportion of responses. Consider first the issue of comparability over time. The initiative question is essentially the same in all four surveys, which is good. However, in 1981 and 1986, the survey gives the respondent the choice of indicating "yes" or "no" to the initiative question while in 1991 and 1996 there is only the option to indicate "yes." The problem is the large number of non-responses in 1981 and 1986. Should these be considered "no" responses, that is, the city does not have the initiative? Or was the question skipped for some other reason? As a practical matter, what I do below is discard the "no response" cities from the analysis in 1981 and 1986 but count "no response" as "no initiative" in 1991 and 1996. This is the most literal way to interpret the question, but there is no guarantee that the city clerks who filled out the surveys took this approach. None of this causes any significant problems when looking at patterns for a given year as long as the precise nature of the questions asked is kept in mind. But it does make comparisons across years tricky. As far as time trends, the only comparable number is the "yes" response, and this is very close to 40 percent in all three samples. The natural conclusion is that there has not been much of a change over time in the availability of the initiative.

Table 2. ICMA Survey Questions Pertaining to Initiative and Referendum, 1981, 1986, 1991, 1996[13]

Questions as they appear in the survey	Responses
1981 Survey (N = 4,761)	
3. Does your municipality have provision for:	
b. Initiative (the process permitting citizens to put proposed charter changes or ordinances on the ballot independent of the action of the legislative body) YES ☐ NO ☐	Yes = 40% No = 38% NR = 22%
c. Referendum (the process whereby council-proposed charter changes or ordinances are placed on the ballot) YES ☐ NO ☐	Yes = 63% No = 20% NR = 17%
1986 Survey (N = 4,630)	
4. Does your municipality have provision for:	
a. Initiative (the process permitting citizens to put proposed charter changes or ordinances on the ballot independent of the action of the legislative body) YES ☐ NO ☐	Yes = 42% No = 42% NR = 16%
b. Referendum (the process whereby council-proposed charter changes or ordinances are placed on the ballot) YES ☐ NO ☐	Yes = 69% No = 20% NR = 11%
1991 Survey (N = 4,967)	
7. Does your municipality have a provision for any of the following? (Check all applicable.)	
1. Initiative. Permits citizens to place charter, ordinance, or home rule changes directly on ballot for approval or disapproval of the voters.	Yes = 37% NR = 63%
2. Referendum. Allows voters to vote on public issues/legislation (i.e. bond issues, charter changes, etc.)	Yes = 67% NR = 33%
4. Petition or Protest Referendum. Allows voters to delay enactment of a local ordinance or bylaw until a referendum is held.	Yes = 24% NR = 76%
1996 Survey (N = 4,552)	
5. Does your municipality have a provision for any of the following? (Check all applicable.)	
a. Initiative. Permits citizens to place charter, ordinance, or home rule changes directly on ballot for approval or disapproval of the voters.	Yes = 39% NR = 61%
b. Binding referendum. Allows voters to determine the outcome on public issues by binding the governing body to act on voters' opinions.	Yes = 28% NR = 72%
c. Non-binding referendum. Allows voters to express an opinion on a specific topic without binding the governing body to act on voters' opinion.	Yes = 26% NR = 74%
e. Petition or Protest Referendum. Allows voters to delay enactment of a local ordinance until a referendum is held.	Yes = 24% NR = 76%

---

13. Note. The questions are taken verbatim from the Form of Government survey questionnaire distributed by the ICMA. N is the number of observations in the full ICMA data set. NR means "no response."

Table 3. Availability of Initiative, 1981, 1986, 1991, 1996[14]

	1981	1986	1991	1996
All cities				
% of cities with initiative	51.0	49.7	36.9	38.5
% of population in a city with initiative	70.4	71.0	61.8	61.2
Cities in initiative states				
% of cities with initiative	75.0	71.4	58.8	57.9
% of population in a city with initiative	90.3	90.3	82.1	77.7
Cities in non-initiative states				
% with initiative	32.2	32.3	21.2	24.0
% of population in a city with initiative	53.1	53.8	44.7	47.3
% of population in a city or state with initiative	73.7	75.6	69.4	71.4

A more severe problem concerns the referendum question. The question asked in 1981 defines the referendum rather broadly and could even be taken to include the initiative. Since we have no idea how the respondents interpreted this question, the responses seem almost worthless. In 1986 and 1991, the survey asked about two kinds of referendums. However, in one case (4.b in 1986 and 7.2 in 1991) the referendum is defined so generally that it could include the initiative or any other type of referendum. "Petition or Protest Referendum" corresponds more closely to a petition referendum as defined for Table 1. However, the question seems to exclude votes on charter amendments. It also says clearly that voters can "delay" a measure but does not explicitly state that they can prevent it from taking effect, which would seem to allow non-binding referendums into this category. In 1996, yet another distinction was introduced between binding and non-binding referendums. Since the respondents were asked about several different kinds of referendums, one definition of which was subsumed in the others, there is also the issue of exactly how they interpreted this. These problems undermine the strength of any interpretation that could be drawn from these questions. As a result, I do not attempt to describe the basic patterns of referendums, and restrict my consideration to initiatives.

Basic Patterns

With the various caveats in mind, I now present some basic patterns. Table 3 reports the percentage cities in which the initiative is available. The percentage ranges from a high of 51.0 percent in 1981 to a low of 36.9 percent in 1991. Remember that the relatively low numbers in 1991 and 1996 are probably artifacts of the way the question was asked. In any event, assuming that the sample is fairly representative, the actual number of American cities with the initiative is somewhere between one-third and one-half.[15]

A second way to view availability of the initiative is in terms of the number of citizens with access to it. It turns out that the initiative is more common in large than small cities, so that the percentage of cities with the initiative is less than the percentage of citizens with the initiative. The percent of the (sample) population that has an initiative available is between 61 to 71 percent.[16] Thus, the numbers suggest that a significant majority of Americans have governments with initiatives.

Table 3 also calculates the availability numbers separately for cities located in initiative states (that is, states that provide the initiative at the state level) and those in non-initiative states. As can be seen, cities are about 40 percent more likely to have the initiative if they are in initiative than non-initiative states.

The numbers in Table 3 allow us to calculate the fraction of the population that has the initiative available at either the state or city level. To do this, we add the number of people residing in initiative states to the number residing in non-

---

14. The data were taken from the ICMA Form of Government Survey, 1981, 1986, 1991, 1996, and Bureau of Census, County and City Data Book, 1983, 1988, and 1993. The number of cities in 1981, 1986, 1991, and 1996 respectively was 3,719, 3,904, and 4,978, and 4,565. The total population of those cities where population could be determined was, respectively, 96.3 million, 92.8 million, 120.9 million, and 110.5 million.93. These difficulties are accentuated by the fact that city clerks often do not even know which I&R provisions are available in their city, something I discovered when trying to collect the information for Table 1.

15. My numbers for 1996 are almost 20 percent less than reported in the Municipal Yearbook, 1998. Municipal Yearbook is a publication of the ICMA and its numbers are based on the Form of Government Survey. The reason for the difference is that in the Municipal Yearbook, a city that did not check any of the boxes in question 5 was deleted from the calculations. I retain these cities in my calculations, and count them as not having the initiative. Since the questionnaire instructs respondents without the initiative not to check the box, it seems strange to delete these observations instead of putting them in the "no initiative category." I believe this problem causes significant overstatement of initiative availability in all the tables reported in the Municipal Yearbook.

16. Population numbers from the Census Bureau's County and City Data Book were linked to the ICMA for these calculations. Some observations were lost if a link could not be established.

Table 4. Percentage of Cities that Provide for the Initiative, by Region[17]

Region	1981	1986	1991	1996
West	82.2 (652)	76.9 (713)	67.6 (792)	62.1 (745)
South	39.6 (1,000)	35.2 (1,102)	27.3 (1,429)	28.8 (1,310)
Midwest	50.0 (1,101)	49.1 (1,178)	36.1 (1,511)	37.0 (1,450)
Northeast	44.4 (904)	46.7 (911)	29.5 (1,246)	36.3 (1,059)

Table 5. Percentage of Cities with the Initiative, by Population of City[18]

| Population | Percentage of Cities with Initiative | | | |
	1981	1986	1991	1996
Less than 5,000	42.0 (1,504)	42.5 (1,720)	24.0 (1,727)	27.6 (1,574)
5,000 to 10,000	45.3 (775)	40.8 (752)	33.4 (1,217)	35.4 (1,133)
10,000 to 25,000	54.8 (766)	54.4 (755)	41.4 (1,123)	44.6 (1,050)
25,000 to 50,000	68.7 (348)	54.4 (755)	41.4 (1,123)	44.6 (1,050)
50,000 to 100,000	79.3 (193)	75.9 (191)	68.0 (25.3)	63.9 (208)
100,000 to 250,000	80.5 (87)	77.6 (76)	67.3 (98)	59.8 (82)
More than 250,000	73.9 (46)	85.4 (41)	77.4 (53)	80.8 (47)

initiative states but in initiative cities, and divide by the total number of people.[19] The percentages are reported in the last row of Table 3. The numbers reveal that almost three-quarters of the population have the initiative available at either the state or local level. This stands in contrast to the conventional view that the initiative is an exotic and unusual instrument in the American political landscape. In fact, it is the norm—only about one quarter of the population does not have the initiative available at some level of government (again, assuming that the sample is representative).

Table 4 reports availability of the initiative by Census region. The initiative is not a stranger to any part of the country, and it is extremely popular in the west.

Table 5 reports availability of the initiative by city size. The striking pattern is the almost uniform increase in initiative availability as city population increases. I chose the size divisions in an ad hoc manner, but the basic pattern is robust to other divisions. Why this should be is something of a mystery, and would seem to be a topic worthy of further investigation. I offer here a speculative explanation: perhaps citizens find it more difficult to monitor and control their representatives as a city grows. As the agency problems associated with weak monitoring become more severe, they find the initiative more useful. This explanation, if correct, suggests that a primary function of the initiative is to allow voters a way to override their representatives when the normal electoral mechanisms lose effectiveness.

Summary

This article reports some basic patterns on initiative availability in American cities in 1981, 1986, 1991, and 1996 based on the ICMA Form of Government Surveys. These surveys cover 4,552 to 4,967 cities, towns, and villages, in which live 90 to 120 million people. This boils down to coverage of about half of the country. Here are the main results.

- Most large cities provide for the initiative, including 15 of the 20 largest.
- One-third to one-half of American cities provide for initiatives.
- Approximately 61 to 71 percent of citizens have the initiative available in their cities.
- Almost 75 percent of citizens have either state or local initiatives available.
- Large cities are more likely to have the initiative than small cities.

17. The main entry in each cell is the percentage of cities in the region that provide for the initiative. In parentheses is the total number of cities in the sample for the region. Regions follow Census classifications. West includes HI, AK, CA, OR, WA, NV, UT, AZ, NM, CO, WY, ID, MT. South includes TX, OK, LA, AR, MS, AL, TN, KY, FL, GA, SC, NC, WV, VA, MD, DE. Midwest includes KS, NE, SD, ND, MO, IA, MN, WI, MI, IL, IN, OH. Northeast includes PA, NJ, NY, CT, RI, MA, VT, NH, ME. Data were taken from the ICMA Form of Government Surveys, 1981, 1986, 1991, 1996.

18. The main entries indicate the percentage of cities with the indicated population in the indicated year that provided for the initiative. In parentheses is the number of cities. The data were taken from the ICMA Form of Government Surveys, 1981, 1986, 1991, 1996, and the Census Bureau's County and City Data Book, 1983, 1988, and 1993.

19. These numbers are biased upward a bit because some people do not live in cities. However, we are undercounting overall initiative access by ignoring county initiatives.

4 State-by-State History and Overview[1]

In this section you will find information on the history of the initiative process in each state. The histories contained within were compiled primarily from David Schmidt's *Citizen Lawmakers: The Ballot Initiative Revolution* (Temple University Press). In some cases the histories have been updated to reflect important initiative activity since the publication of *Citizen Lawmakers.* However, 2002 General Election information is not referenced in these histories since the Almanac was submitted to the publisher prior to the election, but we were able to add at the last minute Appendix F which will give you an overview of the 2002 election.

In addition to the state histories, this section contains the relevant constitutional and statutory provisions associated with using the initiative process in the 24 states with the process. In the 26 states without the initiative process, we have included the relevant constitutional provisions to show the state legislators in those states place legislative referendums on the ballot—primarily constitutional amendments. These have been included so as to allow the reader the ability to compare the lawmaking process in initiative versus non-initiative states.

This section also contains information on what it would take to actually place an initiative on the 2002 ballot in those states with the initiative process. Most of the requirements are the same to place an initiative on the 2004 and future ballots but since this Almanac was submitted to the publisher prior to the election only 2002 information could be included.

Alabama

The movement for direct democracy was not successful in Alabama during the Populist/Progressive era. The only victory recorded by Equity, a publication of the initiative and referendum movement, was a state law giving voters the right of referendum on ordinances in major municipalities, which was invoked by petition of 1,000 voters. It wasn't until the late 1990s that a state elected official advocated the adoption of the initiative process in the state. When Fob James was elected Governor, he strongly advocated the adoption of the initiative process—but to no avail.

Alabama Constitution

The state does not have the statewide initiative process and so therefore the following provisions discuss the procedures used by the state legislature to place constitutional amendments on the ballot.

Article XVIII

Section 284. Manner of proposing amendments; submission of amendments to electors; election on amendments; proclamation of result of election; basis of representation in legislature not to be changed by amendment.

Amendments may be proposed to this Constitution by the legislature in the manner following: The proposed amendments shall be read in the house in which they originate on three several days, and, if upon the third reading three-fifths of all the members elected to that house shall vote in favor thereof, the proposed amendments shall be sent to the other house, in which they shall likewise be read on three several days, and if upon the third reading three-fifths of all the members elected to that house shall vote in favor of the proposed amendments, the legislature shall order an election by the qualified electors of the state upon such proposed amendments, to be held either at the general election next succeeding the session of the legislature at which the amendments are proposed or upon another day appointed by the legislature, not less than three months after the final adjournment of the session of the legislature at which the amendments were proposed. Notice of such election, together with the proposed amendments, shall be given by proclamation of the governor, which shall be published in every county in such manner as the legislature shall direct, for at least eight successive

---

1. All of the histories contained within this chapter were taken from David Schmidt's book *Citizen Lawmakers* (Temple University Press) and have been updated by research from the Initiative & Referendum Institute.

weeks next preceding the day appointed for such election. On the day so appointed an election shall be held for the vote of the qualified electors of the state upon the proposed amendments. If such election be held on the day of the general election, the officers of such general election shall open a poll for the vote of the qualified electors upon the proposed amendments; if it be held on a day other than that of a general election, officers for such election shall be appointed; and the election shall be held in all things in accordance with the law governing general elections. In all elections upon such proposed amendments, the votes cast thereat shall be canvassed, tabulated, and returns thereof be made to the secretary of state, and counted, in the same manner as in elections for representatives to the legislature; and if it shall thereupon appear that a majority of the qualified electors who voted at such election upon the proposed amendments voted in favor of the same, such amendments shall be valid to all intents and purposes as parts of this Constitution. The result of such election shall be made known by proclamation of the governor. Representation in the legislature shall be based upon population, and such basis of representation shall not be changed by constitutional amendments.

Section 285. Election ballots; affirmative vote of majority of electors voting required for passage.

Upon the ballots used at all elections provided for in section 284 of this Constitution the substance or subject matter of each proposed amendment shall be so printed that the nature thereof shall be clearly indicated. Following each proposed amendment on the ballot shall be printed the word "Yes" and immediately under that shall be printed the word "No." The choice of the elector shall be indicated by a cross mark made by him or under his direction, opposite the word expressing his desire, and no amendment shall be adopted unless it receives the affirmative vote of a majority of all the qualified electors who vote at such election.

Section 286. Manner of calling convention for purpose of altering or amending Constitution; repeal of act or resolution calling convention; jurisdiction and power of convention not restricted.

No convention shall hereafter be held for the purpose of altering or amending the Constitution of this state, unless after the legislature by a vote of a majority of all the members elected to each house has passed an act or resolution calling a convention for such purpose the question of convention or no convention shall be first submitted to a vote of all the qualified electors of the state, and approved by a majority of those voting at such election. No act or resolution of the legislature calling a convention for the purpose of altering or amending the Constitution of this state, shall be repealed except upon the vote of a majority of all the members elected to each house at the same session at which such act or resolution was passed; provided, nothing herein contained shall be construed as restricting the jurisdiction and power of the convention, when duly assembled in pursuance of this section, to establish such ordinances and to do and perform such things as to the convention may seem necessary or proper for the purpose of altering, revising, or amending the existing Constitution.

Section 287. Votes by legislature on proposed amendments or bills or resolutions calling conventions; acts or resolutions proposing amendments or calling conventions not to be submitted to governor for approval.

All votes of the legislature upon proposed amendments to this Constitution, and upon bills or resolutions calling a convention for the purpose of altering or amending the Constitution of this state, shall be taken by yeas and nays and entered on the journals. No act or resolution of the legislature passed in accordance with the provisions of this article, proposing amendments to this Constitution, or calling a convention for the purpose of altering or amending the Constitution of this state, shall be submitted for the approval of the governor, but shall be valid without his approval.

Alaska

Alaska became the 20th state to adopt a statewide initiative process when it became a state in 1959. However, the procedure does not include the right to make appropriations or amend the state constitution.

In 1974 voters approved an initiative to relocate the state capitol. Without an appropriation, this decision could be implemented only if the legislature acted. Since the legislature failed to respond, voters passed another initiative in 1978, this time requiring the state government to determine the cost of relocation and stipulating that any bond issue to finance that cost be subject to voter approval. The bond issue went to the voters in 1980, but they rejected it, with the result that Juneau is still the state capital, despite its great distance from the major population center, Anchorage. However, there is a strong likelihood that Alaskans will once again vote on an initiative to move the capitol in 2002.

In 1976 Alaskans passed an initiative to abolish one house of their legislature and create a unicameral lawmaking body like Nebraska's. Unfortunately, a constitutional amendment was needed to accomplish this change, and Alaska's initiative procedure does not allow amendments. Members of the legislature, not wishing to abolish their jobs, predictably ignored the measure. They did pay heed, however, to an initiative sponsored by the Libertarian Party to abolish the state personal income tax. The initiative qualified for the November 1980 ballot but was enacted by the legislature on September 25 of that year, thus making a popular vote unnecessary.

Statewide Initiative Usage

Number of Initiatives	Number Passed	Number Failed	Passage Rate
31	17	14	54%

Statewide Initiatives

Year	Measure Number	Type	Subject Matter	Description	Pass/Fail
1960	N/A I	DS	Administration of Government	To move the state capitol from Juneau to Anchorage.	Failed
1962	N/A	IDS	Administration of Government	To relocate the state Capitol.	Failed
1974	N/A	IDS	Campaign Finance Reform	To require full disclosure of personal finances of candidates and holders of state office.	Passed
1974	N/A	IDS	Administration of Government	Relocating and constructing a new Capitol.	Passed
1976	5	IDS	Animal Rights	Regulate entry into fisheries	Failed
1978	6	IDS	Administration of Government	Cost to relocate state capitol.	Passed
1978	10	IDS	Environmental Reform	Disposal of state lands.	Passed
1978	11	IDS	Environmental Reform	Beverage container deposits.	Failed
1980	N/A	IDS	Administration of Government	Establish the Alaska Stock Ownership Corp.	Failed
1982	5	IDS	Environmental Reform	State ownership of Federal land.	Passed
1982	6	IDS	Abortion	Limit state funding of abortion.	Failed
1982	7	IDS	Animal Rights	Consumption of fish and game.	Failed
1984	N/A	IDS	Business Regulation	Regulate transportation.	Passed
1986	1	M	Nuclear weapons/facilities/waste	Nuclear Weapons Freeze.	Passed
1988	2	IDS	Legal	Civil liability.	Passed
1988	3	IDS	Education Separate	Community College from University.	Failed
1990	N/A	IDS	Gaming	Regulate gambling.	Failed
1990	N/A	IDS	Drug Policy	Reform Penalties for marijuana sale/use.	Passed
1990	N/A	IDS	Utility	Regulation Amendments to Alaska Railroad Act.	Failed
1994	4	IDS	Term Limits	Term limits on Congress 6/12	Passed
1994	N/A	IDS	Administration of Government	Relating to voters right to know the cost of moving the capital.	Passed
1994	N/A	IDS	Administration of Government	Relating to changing the capital to Wasilla.	Failed
1996	3	IDS	Animal Rights	Bans same day airborne hunting of wolf, wolverine, fox or lynx.	Passed
1996	4	IDS	Term Limits	Informed Voter Law.	Passed
1998	5	IDS	Environmental Reform	Would prohibit billboards	Passed
1998	6	IDS	Administration of Government	Would adopt English as official language.	Passed
1998	7	IDS	Term Limits	Self Limit Law.	Passed
1998	8	IDS	Drug Policy Reform	Would allow the medical use of marijuana	Passed
1998	9	IDS	Animal Rights	Would prohibit trapping wolves with snares.	Failed
2000	4	IDS	Taxes	This bill sets the value of property at its assessment on January 1 of the first year the bill is in effect.	Failed
2000	5	IDS	Drug Policy Reform	This bill would shield those 18 years or older from civil and criminal sanctions for the use of marijuana and other hemp products.	Failed

Alaska Constitution

Article XI: Initiative, Referendum, and Recall

Section 1.

The people may propose and enact laws by the initiative, and approve or reject acts of the legislature by the referendum.

Section 2.

An initiative or referendum is proposed by an application containing the bill to be initiated or the act to be referred. The application shall be signed by not less than one hundred qualified voters as sponsors, and shall be filed with the lieutenant governor. If he finds it in proper form he shall so certify. Denial of certification shall be subject to judicial review.

Section 3.

After certification of the application, a petition containing a summary of the subject matter shall be prepared by the lieutenant governor for circulation by the sponsors. If signed by qualified voters, equal in number to ten per cent of those who voted in the preceding general election and resident in at least two-thirds of the house districts of the State, it may be filed with the lieutenant governor.

Section 4.

An initiative petition may be filed at any time. The lieutenant governor shall prepare a ballot title and proposition summarizing the proposed law, and shall place them on the ballot for the first statewide election held more than one hundred-twenty days after adjournment of the legislative session following the filing. If, before the election, substantially the same measure has been enacted, the petition is void.

Section 5.

A referendum petition may be filed only within ninety days after adjournment of the legislative session at which the act was passed. The lieutenant governor shall prepare a ballot title and proposition summarizing the act and shall place them on the ballot for the first statewide election held more than one hundred-eighty days after adjournment of that session.

Section 6.

If a majority of the votes cast on the proposition favor its adoption, the initiated measure is enacted. If a majority of the votes cast on the proposition favor the rejection of an act referred, it is rejected. The lieutenant governor shall certify the election returns. An initiated law becomes effective ninety days after certification, is not subject to veto, and may not be repealed by the legislature within two years of its effective date. It may be amended at any time. An act rejected by referendum is void thirty days after certification. Additional procedures for the initiative and referendum may be prescribed by law.

Section 7.

The initiative shall not be used to dedicate revenues, make or repeal appropriations, create courts, define the jurisdiction of courts or prescribe their rules, or enact local or special legislation. The referendum shall not be applied to dedications of revenue, to appropriations, to local or special legislation, or to laws necessary for the immediate preservation of the public peace, health, or safety.

Section 8.

All elected public officials in the State, except judicial officers, are subject to recall by the voters of the State or political subdivision from which elected. Procedures and grounds for recall shall be prescribed by the legislature.

Alaska Statutes

Chapter 15

Sec. 15.45.010.

The law-making powers assigned to the legislature may be exercised by the people through the initiative. However, an initiative may not be proposed to dedicate revenue, to make or repeal appropriations, to create courts, to define the jurisdiction of courts or prescribe their rules, or to enact local or special legislation.

Sec. 15.45.020.

An initiative is proposed by filing an application with the lieutenant governor. A deposit of $100 must accompany the application. This deposit shall be retained if a petition is not properly filed. If a petition is properly filed, the deposit shall be refunded.

Sec. 15.45.030.

The application shall include (1) the proposed bill to be initiated, (2) a statement that the sponsors are qualified voters who signed the application with the proposed bill attached, (3) the designation of an initiative committee of three sponsors who shall represent all sponsors and subscribers in matters relating to the initiative, and (4) the signatures and addresses of not less than 100 qualified voters.

Sec. 15.45.040.

The proposed bill shall be in the following form:
(1) the bill shall be confined to one subject;
(2) the subject of the bill shall be expressed in the title;
(3) the enacting clause of the bill shall be: "Be it enacted by the People of the State of Alaska;"
(4) the bill may not include subjects restricted by AS 15.45.010.

Sec. 15.45.050.

Notice to the initiative committee on any matter pertaining to the application and petition may be served on any member of the committee in person or by mail addressed to a committee member as indicated on the application.

Sec. 15.45.060.

The qualified voters who subscribe to the application are designated as sponsors. The initiative committee may designate additional sponsors by giving written notice to the lieutenant governor of the names and addresses of those so designated.

Sec. 15.45.070.

The lieutenant governor shall review the application and shall either certify it or notify the initiative committee of the grounds for denial.

Sec. 15.45.080.

The lieutenant governor shall deny certification upon determining in writing that:
(1) the proposed bill to be initiated is not in the required form;
(2) the application is not substantially in the required form; or
(3) there is an insufficient number of qualified sponsors.

Sec. 15.45.090.

If the application is certified, the lieutenant governor shall prescribe the form of and prepare petitions containing (1) a copy of the proposed bill if the number of words included in both the formal and substantive provisions of the bill is 500 or less, (2) an impartial summary of the subject matter of the bill, (3) the warning prescribed in AS 15.45.100, (4) sufficient space for signature and address, (5) sufficient space at the bottom of each page for the information required by AS 15.45.130 (8), and (6) other specifications prescribed by the lieutenant governor to assure proper handling and control. Petitions, for purposes of circulation, shall be prepared by the lieutenant governor in a number reasonably calculated to allow full circulation throughout the state. The lieutenant governor shall number each petition and shall keep a record of the petition delivered to each sponsor. Upon request of the committee, the lieutenant governor shall report the number of persons who voted in the preceding general election.

Sec. 15.45.100.

Each petition shall include a statement of warning that a person who signs a name other than the person's own on the petition, or who knowingly signs more than once for the same proposition at one election, or who signs the petition when knowingly not a qualified voter, is guilty of a class B misdemeanor.

Sec. 15.45.110.

(a) The petitions may be circulated throughout the state only in person.
(b) [Repealed, Sec. 92 ch 82 SLA 2000].

(c) A circulator may not receive payment or agree to receive payment that is greater than $1 a signature, and a person or an organization may not pay or agree to pay an amount that is greater than $1 a signature, for the collection of signatures on a petition.

(d) A person or organization may not knowingly pay, offer to pay, or cause to be paid money or other valuable thing to a person to sign or refrain from signing a petition.

(e) A person or organization that violates (c) or (d) of this section is guilty of a class B misdemeanor.

(f) In this section,

(1) "organization" has the meaning given in AS 11.81.900;

(2) "other valuable thing" has the meaning given in AS 15.56.030 (d);

(3) "person" has the meaning given in AS 11.81.900.

Sec. 15.45.120.

Any qualified voter may subscribe to the petition by signing the voter's name and address. A person who has signed the initiative petition may withdraw the person's name only by giving written notice to the lieutenant governor before the date the petition is filed.

Sec. 15.45.130.

Before being filed, each petition shall be certified by an affidavit by the person who personally circulated the petition. The affidavit must state in substance that (1) the person signing the affidavit meets the residency, age, and citizenship qualifications of AS 15.05.010, (2) the person is the only circulator of that petition, (3) the signatures were made in the circulator's actual presence, (4) to the best of the circulator's knowledge, the signatures are those of the persons whose names they purport to be, (5) the signatures are of persons who were qualified voters on the date of signature, (6) the person has not entered into an agreement with a person or organization in violation of AS 15.45.110 (c), (7) the person has not violated AS 15.45.110 (d) with respect to that petition, and (8) the circulator prominently placed, in the space provided under AS 15.45.090 (5) before circulation of the petition, in bold capital letters, the circulator's name and, if the circulator has received payment or agreed to receive payment for the collection of signatures on the petition, the name of each person or organization that has paid or agreed to pay the circulator for collection of signatures on the petition. In determining the sufficiency of the petition, the lieutenant governor may not count subscriptions on petitions not properly certified.

Sec. 15.45.140.

The sponsors must file the initiative petition within one year from the time the sponsors received notice from the lieutenant governor that the petitions were ready for delivery to them, and the petition must be signed by qualified voters equal in number to 10 percent of those who voted in the preceding general election and resident in at least two-thirds of the house districts of the state. If the petition is not filed within the one-year period provided for in this section, the petition has no force or effect.

Sec. 15.45.150.

Within not more than 60 days of the date the petition was filed, the lieutenant governor shall review the petition and shall notify the initiative committee whether the petition was properly or improperly filed, and at which election the proposition shall be placed on the ballot.

Sec. 15.45.160.

The lieutenant governor shall notify the committee that the petition was improperly filed upon determining that

(1) there is an insufficient number of qualified subscribers; or

(2) the subscribers were not resident in at least two-thirds of the house districts of the state.

Sec. 15.45.170.

Repealed or Renumbered

Sec. 15.45.180.

(a) If the petition is properly filed, the lieutenant governor, with the assistance of the attorney general, shall prepare a ballot title and proposition. The ballot title shall, in not more than six words, indicate the general subject of the proposition. The proposition shall, in not more than 100 words, give a true and impartial summary of the proposed law.

(b) The proposition prepared under (a) of this section shall comply with AS 15.60.005 and shall be worded so that a "Yes" vote on the proposition is a vote to enact the proposed law.

Sec. 15.45.190.

The lieutenant governor shall direct the director to place the ballot title and proposition on the election ballot of the first statewide general, special, or primary election that is held after

(1) the petition has been filed;

(2) a legislative session has convened and adjourned; and

(3) a period of 120 days has expired since the adjournment of the legislative session.

Sec. 15.45.200.

The director shall provide each election board with 10 copies of the proposed law being initiated, and the election board shall display three copies of the proposed law in a conspicuous place in the room where the election is held.

Sec. 15.45.210.

If the lieutenant governor, with the formal concurrence of the attorney general, determines that an act of the legislature that is substantially the same as the proposed law was enacted after the petition had been filed, and before the date of the election, the petition is void and the lieutenant governor shall so notify the committee.

Sec. 15.45.220.

If a majority of the votes cast on the initiative proposition favor its adoption, the proposed law is enacted, and the lieutenant governor shall so certify. The act becomes effective 90 days after certification.

Sec. 15.45.230.

Repealed or Renumbered

Sec. 15.45.240.

Any person aggrieved by a determination made by the lieutenant governor under AS 15.45.010 – 15.45.220 may bring an action in the superior court to have the determination reviewed within 30 days of the date on which notice of the determination was given.

Sec. 15.45.245.

The lieutenant governor may delegate the duties imposed on the lieutenant governor by AS 15.45.010 – 15.45.240 to the director.

Sec. 15.45.250.

The people may approve or reject acts of the legislature by referendum. However, a referendum may not be applied to dedication of revenue, to an appropriation, to local or special legislation, or to laws necessary for the immediate preservation of the public peace, health, or safety.

Sec. 15.45.260.

A referendum is proposed by filing an application with the lieutenant governor. A deposit of $100 must accompany the application. This deposit shall be retained if a petition is not properly filed. If a petition is properly filed, the deposit shall be refunded.

Sec. 15.45.270.

The application shall include

(1) the act to be referred;

(2) a statement that the sponsors are qualified voters who signed the application with the proposed bill attached;

(3) the designation of a referendum committee of three sponsors who shall represent all sponsors and subscribers in matters relating to the referendum; and

(4) the signatures and addresses of not fewer than 100 qualified voters.

Sec. 15.45.280.

Notice to the referendum committee on any matter pertaining to the application and petition may be served on any member of the committee in person or by mail addressed to a committee member as indicated on the application.

Sec. 15.45.290.

The qualified voters who subscribe to the application are designated as sponsors. The referendum committee may designate additional sponsors by giving notice to the lieutenant governor of the names and addresses of those so designated.

Sec. 15.45.300.

Within seven calendar days after the date the application is received, the lieutenant governor shall review the application and shall either certify it or notify the referendum committee of the grounds for denial.

Sec. 15.45.310.

The lieutenant governor shall deny certification upon determining that
(1) the application is not substantially in the required form;
(2) there is an insufficient number of qualified sponsors; or
(3) more than 90 days have expired since the adjournment of the legislative session at which the act being referred was passed.

Sec. 15.45.320.

If the application is certified, the lieutenant governor shall, within seven calendar days after the date of certification, prescribe the form of, and prepare, a petition containing (1) a copy of the act to be referred, if the number of words included in both the formal and substantive provisions of the bill is 500 or less, (2) an impartial summary of the subject matter of the act, (3) the warning prescribed in AS 15.45.330, (4) sufficient space for signatures and addresses, and (5) other specifications prescribed by the lieutenant governor to assure proper handling and control. Petitions, for purposes of circulation, shall be prepared by the lieutenant governor in a number reasonably calculated to allow full circulation throughout the state. The lieutenant governor shall number each petition and shall keep a record of the petitions delivered to each sponsor. Upon request of the referendum committee, the lieutenant governor shall specify the number of persons who voted in the preceding general election.

Sec. 15.45.330.

Each petition shall include a statement of warning that a person who signs a name other than the person's own to the petition, or who knowingly signs more than once for the same proposition at one election, or who signs the petition when knowingly not a qualified voter is guilty of a class B misdemeanor.

Sec. 15.45.340.

The petitions may be circulated throughout the state only in person.

Sec. 15.45.350.

Any qualified voter may subscribe to the petition by signing the voter's name and address. A person who has signed the referendum petition may withdraw the person's name only by giving written notice to the lieutenant governor before the date the petition is filed.

Sec. 15.45.360.

Before being filed, each petition shall be certified by an affidavit by the person who circulated the petition. The affidavit shall state in substance that (1) the person signing the affidavit meets the residency, age, and citizenship qualifications of AS 15.05.010, (2) the person is the only circulator of the petition, (3) the signatures were made in the circulator's actual presence, and (4) to the best of the circulator's knowledge, the signatures are the signatures of persons whose names they purport to be. In determining the sufficiency of the petition, the lieutenant governor may not count subscriptions on petitions not properly certified.

Sec. 15.45.370.

The sponsors may file the petition only within 90 days after the adjournment of the legislative session at which the act was passed and only if signed by qualified voters equal in number to 10 percent of those who voted in the preceding general election and resident in at least two-thirds of the house districts of the state.

Sec. 15.45.380.

Within not more than 60 days of the date the petition was filed, the lieutenant governor shall review the petition and shall notify the committee whether the petition was properly or was improperly filed and at which election the proposition shall be placed on the ballot.

Sec. 15.45.390.

The lieutenant governor shall notify the committee that the petition was improperly filed upon determining that
(1) there is an insufficient number of qualified subscribers;
(2) the subscribers were not resident in at least two-thirds of the house districts of the state; or
(3) the petition was not filed within 90 days after the adjournment of the legislative session at which the act was passed.

Sec. 15.45.400.

Upon receipt of notice that the filing of the petition was improper, the committee may amend and correct the petition by circulating and filing a supplementary petition within 10 days of the date that notice was given if 90 days have not expired after the adjournment of the legislative session at which the act was passed.

Sec. 15.45.410.

(a) The lieutenant governor, with the assistance of the attorney general, shall prepare a ballot title and proposition upon determining that the petition is properly filed. The ballot title shall, in not more than six words, indicate the general subject area of the act. The proposition shall, in not more than 100 words, give a true and impartial summary of the act being referred.
(b) The proposition prepared under (a) of this section shall comply with AS 15.60.005 and shall be worded so that a "Yes" vote on the proposition is a vote to reject the act referred.

Sec. 15.45.420.

The lieutenant governor shall direct the director to place the ballot title and proposition on the election ballot for the first statewide general, special, or primary election held more than 180 days after adjournment of the legislative session at which the act was passed.

Sec. 15.45.430.

The director shall provide each election board with 10 copies of the act being referred, and the election board shall display three copies of the act in a conspicuous place in the room where the election is held.

Sec. 15.45.440.

If a majority of the votes cast on the referendum proposition favor the rejection of the act referred, the act is rejected, and the lieutenant governor shall so certify. The act rejected by referendum is void 30 days after certification.

Sec. 15.45.450.

A referendum submitted to the voters may not be held void because of the insufficiency of the application or petition by which the submission was procured.

Sec. 15.45.460.

Any person aggrieved by any determination made by the lieutenant governor under AS 15.45.250 – 15.45.450 may bring an action in the superior court to have the determination reviewed within 30 days of the date on which notice of the determination was given.

Sec. 15.45.465.

The lieutenant governor may delegate the duties imposed upon the lieutenant governor by AS 15.45.250 – 15.45.460 to the director.

Sec. 15.45.470.

The governor, the lieutenant governor, and members of the state legislature are subject to recall by the voters of the state or the political subdivision from which elected.

Sec. 15.45.480.

The recall of the governor, lieutenant governor, or a member of the state legislature is proposed by filing an application with the director. A deposit of $100 must accompany the application. This deposit shall be retained if a petition is not properly filed. If a petition is properly filed the deposit shall be refunded.

Sec. 15.45.490.

An application may not be filed during the first 120 days of the term of office of any state public official subject to recall.

Sec. 15.45.500.

The application must include
(1) the name and office of the person to be recalled;
(2) the grounds for recall described in particular in not more than 200 words;
(3) a statement that the sponsors are qualified voters who signed the application with the statement of grounds for recall attached;
(4) the designation of a recall committee of three sponsors who shall represent all sponsors and subscribers in matters relating to the recall;
(5) the signatures of at least 100 qualified voters who subscribe to the application as sponsors for purposes of circulation; and
(6) the signatures and addresses of qualified voters equal in number to 10 percent of those who voted in the preceding general election in the state or in the senate or house district of the official sought to be recalled.

Sec. 15.45.510.

The grounds for recall are (1) lack of fitness, (2) incompetence, (3) neglect of duties, or (4) corruption.

Sec. 15.45.520.

Notice on all matters pertaining to the application and petition may be served on any member of the recall committee in person or by mail addressed to a committee member as indicated on the application.

Sec. 15.45.530.

The director, upon request, shall notify the recall committee of the official number of persons who voted in the preceding general election in the state or in the senate or house district of the official to be recalled.

Sec. 15.45.540.

The director shall review the application and shall either certify it or notify the recall committee of the grounds of refusal.

Sec. 15.45.550.

The director shall deny certification upon determining that
(1) the application is not substantially in the required form;
(2) the application was filed during the first 120 days of the term of office of the official subject to recall or within less than 180 days of the termination of the term of office of any official subject to recall;
(3) the person named in the application is not subject to recall; or
(4) there is an insufficient number of qualified subscribers.

Sec. 15.45.560.

Upon certifying the application, the director shall prescribe the form of, and prepare, a petition containing (1) the name and office of the person to be recalled, (2) the statement of the grounds for recall included in the application, (3) the statement of warning required in AS 15.45.570, (4) sufficient space for signatures and addresses, and (5) other specifications prescribed by the director to assure proper handling and control. Petitions, for purposes of circulation, shall be prepared by the director in a number reasonably calculated to allow full circulation throughout the state or throughout the senate or house district of the official sought to be recalled. The director shall number each petition and shall keep a record of the petitions delivered to each sponsor.

Sec. 15.45.570.

Each petition and duplicate copy shall include a statement of warning that a person who signs a name other than the person's own to the petition, or who knowingly signs more than once for the same proposition at one election, or who signs the petition while knowingly not a qualified voter, is guilty of a class B misdemeanor.

Sec. 15.45.580.

The petitions may be circulated only in person throughout the state or senate or house district represented by the official sought to be recalled.

Sec. 15.45.590.

Any qualified voter may subscribe to the petition by signing the voter's name and address. A person who has signed the petition may withdraw the person's name only by giving written notice to the director before the date the petition is filed.

Sec. 15.45.600.

Before being filed, each petition shall be certified by an affidavit by the person who personally circulated the petition. The affidavit shall state in substance that (1) the person signing the affidavit meets the residency, age, and citizenship qualifications of AS 15.05.010, (2) the person is the only circulator of that petition or copy, (3) the signatures were made in the circulator's actual presence, and (4) to the best of the circulator's knowledge, the signatures are those of the persons whose names they purport to be. In determining the sufficiency of the petition, the director may not count subscriptions on petitions not properly certified.

Sec. 15.45.610.

A petition may not be filed within less than 180 days of the termination of the term of office of a state public official subject to recall. The sponsor may file the petition only if signed by qualified voters equal in number to 25 percent of those who voted in the preceding general election in the state or in the senate or house district of the official sought to be recalled.

Sec. 15.45.620.

Within 30 days of the date of filing, the director shall review the petition and shall notify the recall committee and the person subject to recall whether the petition was properly or improperly filed.

Sec. 15.45.630.

The director shall notify the committee that the petition was improperly filed upon determining that
(1) there is an insufficient number of qualified subscribers; or
(2) the petition was filed within less than 180 days of the termination of the term of office of the official subject to recall.

Sec. 15.45.640.

Upon receipt of notice that the filing of the petition was improper, the committee may amend and correct the petition by circulating and filing a supplementary petition within 20 days of the date that notice was given, if filed within less than 180 days of the termination of the term of office of the person subject to recall.

Sec. 15.45.650.

If the director determines the petition is properly filed and if the office is not vacant, the director shall prepare the ballot and shall call a special election to be held on a date not less than 60, nor more than 90, days after the date that notification is given that the petition was properly filed. If a primary or general election is to be held not less than 60, nor more than 90, days after the date that notification is given that the petition was properly filed, the special election shall be held on the date of the primary or general election.

Sec. 15.45.660.

The ballot shall be designed with the question of whether the public official shall be recalled, placed on the ballot in the following manner: "Shall (name of official) be recalled from the office of ......?". Provision shall be made for marking the question "Yes" or "No."

Sec. 15.45.670.

Unless specifically provided otherwise, all provisions regarding the conduct of a general election shall govern the conduct of a special election for the recall of the state public official, including but not limited to, provisions concerning voter qualification; provisions regarding duties, powers, rights and obligations of the director, of other election officials, and of municipalities; provision for notification of the election; provision for the payment of election expenses; provisions regarding employees being allowed time from work to vote; provisions for counting, reviewing, and certification of returns; provision for the determination of votes and of recount contests and court appeal; and provisions for absentee voting.

Sec. 15.45.680.

The director shall provide each election board in the state or in the senate or house district of the person subject to recall with 10 copies of the statement of the grounds for recall included in the application and 10 copies of the statement of not more than 200 words made by the official subject to recall in justification of the official's conduct in office. The person subject to recall may provide the director with the statement within 10 days after the date the director gave notification that the petition was properly filed. The election board shall post three copies of the statements for and against recall in three conspicuous places in the polling place.

Sec. 15.45.690.

If a majority of the votes cast on the question of recall favor the removal of the official, the director shall so certify and the office is vacant on the day after the date of certification.

Sec. 15.45.700.

A vacancy caused by a recall is filled as a vacancy caused by any other means is filled.

Sec. 15.45.710.

A recall submitted to the voters may not be held void because of the insufficiency of the grounds, application, or petition by which the submission was procured.

Sec. 15.45.720.

Any person aggrieved by a determination made by the director under AS 15.45.470 – 15.45.710 may bring an action in the superior court to have the determination reviewed within 30 days of the date on which notice of determination was given.

The Basic Steps to Do an Initiative in Alaska

Statutes — Indirect Initiative Process

Basic Procedures: Proponents must first file an application and leave a deposit with the Lieutenant Governor's office. The deposit is $100 made payable to the State of Alaska; it will be refunded if the petition is properly filed and the measure is certified for the ballot. The application must contain the signatures of 3 prime sponsors with a statement that they are the initiative committee representing all sponsors. Proponents must also file with the application a full copy of the proposed bill, and the signatures of at least 100 qualified voters who will serve as sponsors for circulation purposes. A copy of the proposed bill must be attached to each signature page; and each signature page must contain a statement that the voter signed the application with the proposed bill attached.

After the application is filed, the Lieutenant Governor has the 100 signatures reviewed by the Division of Elections for verification of the required 100 qualified voters. At this time, the Department of Law reviews the application for legal content and advises the Lieutenant Governor. The application would be denied if it is not in proper form or does not include all required elements, there are an insufficient number of qualified voter sponsors, or the bill covers an issue restricted by the constitution. The proposed bill must be confined to one subject and the subject of the bill must be expressed in the title which must contain the enacting clause "Be it enacted by the People of the State of Alaska." The bill can not deal with subjects restricted under the Alaska Constitution; namely, dedicate revenues, make or repeal appropriations, create courts, define jurisdiction of courts, or enact local or special legislation.

When the application is certified, the Lieutenant Governor will notify sponsors of acceptance and include a copy of the Department of Law's formal legal opinion and impartial summary. The prime sponsors have the opportunity to review the impartial summary and title of the bill proposed by the Department of Law. The Division of Elections is responsible for printing 500 petition booklets and the initial distribution of the booklets to the prime sponsors. The prime sponsors distribute petition booklets to each of the other qualified sponsors who will circulate the petition and gather the required signatures.

Proponents file signatures with the Lieutenant Governor who must review them within 60 days from the date the petition was filed. If enough valid signatures have been submitted, the proposition will be placed on the election ballot of the first statewide general, special or primary election that is held after the petition has been filed, a legislative session has convened or adjourned, and a period of 120 has expired since the adjournment of the legislative session.

Date Initiative language can be submitted to the state: Any time.

Signatures are tied to vote of which office: Number of votes cast in the general election prior to when the application was filed.

Next General election: 2002

Number of votes cast in last general election: 287,825 (2000)

Net number of signatures required: 10% of the number of votes cast in the last general election. (28,782)

Distribution Requirement: One signature in 2/3 of state house districts.

Circulation period: Proponents have one year from the day they were notified that petition booklets were available for distribution to gather signatures and submit the petition to the Division of Elections.

Do circulators have to be residents: Yes—additionally, compensation to initiative circulators is limited to $1.00 per signature.

Date when signatures are due for certification: Signatures must be submitted prior to the convening of the legislative session in the year in which the initiative is to appear on the ballot. (Early January for 2002.)

Signature verification process: Signatures are turned into the Division of Elections who verify each signature until the minimum number needed is met.

Single-subject restriction: Yes

Legislative tampering: The legislature can repeal an initiative only after two years of it passing; but the legislature may amend the initiative anytime.

Arizona

Arizona acquired statewide initiative, referendum, and recall rights at the time of statehood in 1912. **Equity** mentions "Hon. A. C. Baker of Phoenix" as a leader of the local direct democracy movement.

The first initiative was for women's suffrage, and it passed by a margin of greater than two to one on November 5, 1912. Two years later, in 1914, a total of 15 initiatives qualified for the Arizona ballot: a record for initiative use in that state.

Organized labor that year was successful in passing four initiatives: one to prohibit blacklisting of union members; a second establishing an "old age and mothers' pension"; a third establishing a state government contract system, printing plant, and banking system, and a fourth requiring that businesses limit employment of non-citizens. Voters passed a fifth initiative barring the governor and legislature from amending or repealing initiatives.

The legislature responded with a constitutional amendment to make it harder to pass initiatives. This amendment however, could take effect only if approved by voters. The Arizona Federation of Labor waged a campaign against the measure, and voters defeated it by a narrow margin in 1916.

Arizona government reforms passed by voter initiative include changes in reapportionment (1918 and 1932), changes in the court system (1960 and 1974), created the voter registration system known as "Motor Voter" (1982), which allows applicants for driver's license renewal to simultaneously register to vote and adopted campaign finance reform in (1986 and 1998). Also in 1988, the voters adopted an initiative that made English the official language and adopted term limits for state legislators in 1992.

Arizonans owe many of their reforms to John Kromko. Kromko, like most Arizonans, is not a native; he was born near Erie, Pennsylvania, in 1940 and moved to Tucson in the mid-1960s. He was active in protests against the Vietnam War, and in the 1970s and 1980s he was elected to the lower house of the state legislature several times. By night, he was a computer-programming instructor; by day, he was Arizona's "Mr. Initiative."

Kromko's first petition was a referendum drive to stop a Tucson city council ordinance banning topless dancing. (He explains with a touch of embarrassment that he was fighting for the principle of free speech.) In 1976 Kromko was among the handful of Arizonans who, in cooperation with the People's Lobby Western Bloc campaign, succeeded in putting on the state ballot an initiative to phase out nuclear power. The initiative lost at the polls, but Kromko's leadership on the issue got him elected to his first term in the legislature.

Once elected, he set his sights on abolishing the sales tax on food, a "regressive" tax that hits the poor hardest. Unsuccessful in the legislature, Kromko launched a statewide initiative petition and got enough signatures to put food tax repeal on the ballot. The legislature, faced with the initiative, acted to repeal the tax.

After the food tax victory, Kromko turned to voter registration reform. Again the legislature was unresponsive, so he launched an initiative petition. He narrowly missed getting enough signatures in 1980, and he failed to win re-election that year. Undaunted, he revived the voter registration campaign and turned to yet another cause: Medicaid funding. Arizona in 1981 was the only state without Medicaid, since the legislature had refused to appropriate money for the state's share of this federal program.

In 1982, with an initiative petition drive under way and headed for success, the legislature got the message and established a Medicaid program. Kromko and his allies on this issue, the state's churches, were satisfied and dropped their petition drive. The voter registration initiative, now under the leadership of Les Miller, a Phoenix attorney, and the state Democratic Party, gained ballot placement and voter approval. In the ensuing four years, this "Motor Voter" initiative increased by over 10 percent the proportion of Arizona's eligible population who were registered to vote.

Kromko, re-elected to the legislature in 1982, took up his petitions again in 1983 to prevent construction of a freeway in Tucson that would have smashed through several residential neighborhoods. The initiative was merely to make freeway plans subject to voter approval, but Tucson officials, seeing the campaign as the death knell for their freeway plans, blocked its placement on the ballot through various legal technicalities. Kromko and neighborhood activists fighting to save their homes refused to admit defeat. They began a new petition drive in 1984, qualified their measure for the ballot, and won voter approval for it in November 1985.

Arizona's moneyed interests poured funds into a campaign to unseat Kromko in 1986. Kromko not only survived but also fought back by supporting a statewide initiative to limit campaign contributions, sponsored by his colleague in the legislature, Democratic State Representative Reid Ewing of Tucson. Voters passed the measure by a two to one margin.

Kromko's initiative exploits have made him the most effective Democratic political figure, besides former governor Bruce Babbitt, in this perennially Republican-dominated state. And Babbitt owes partial credit for one of his biggest successes—enactment of restrictions on the toxic chemical pollution of drinking water—to Kromko. Early in 1986 Kromko helped organize an environmentalist petition drive for an anti-toxic initiative, while Babbitt negotiated with the legislature for passage of a similar bill. When initiative backers had enough signatures to put their measure on the ballot, the legislature bowed to the pressure and passed Babbitt's bill.

Since 1992 several other major initiatives have passed in the state including the banning of cockfighting in 1998 and in 2000 the requirement that all public school instruction be conducted in English. Also in 2000, the voters of Arizona defeated an attempt by the state legislature to require a two-thirds vote of the people before any animal protection initiative could be adopted. This legislative assault on the process was in retaliation to the success of the animal protection movement in the state—however, the voters would have nothing to do with it.

Statewide Initiative Usage

Number of Initiatives	Number Passed	Number Failed	Passage Rate
150	63	87	42%

Statewide Initiatives

Year	Measure Number	Type	Subject Matter	Description	Pass/Fail
1912	N/A	DA	Election Reform	To permit women's suffrage.	Passed
1914	N/A	DS	Business Regulation	Assessment, by owner.	Failed
1914	N/A	DS	Business Regulation	Industrial pursuits.	Passed
1914	N/A	DS	Administration of Government	Create Miami County.	Failed
1914	N/A	DA	Administration of Government	State reclamation services.	Failed
1914	N/A	DA	Bonds	Highway bonds.	Failed
1914	N/A	DS	Environmental Reform	Placing of electric poles	Passed
1914	N/A	DA	Initiative and Referendum	To provide that vote power of the Governor and the power of the legislature to repeal or amend, shall not extend to initiative or Referendum measures approved by a majority of qualified voters.	Passed
1914	N/A	DS	Alien Rights	Non-citizens, employment of.	Passed
1914	N/A	DS	Administration of Government	Expositions appropriations.	Failed
1914	N/A	DS	Welfare	Relative to old age pensions.	Passed
1914	N/A	DS	Civil Rights	Blacklisting prohibited.	Passed
1914	N/A	DS	Taxes	Taxes, delinquent.	Failed
1914	N/A	DS	Death Penalty	Abolishing death penalty.	Failed
1914	N/A	DA	Alcohol Regulation	Providing for statewide prohibition.	Passed
1914	N/A	DA	Alcohol Regulation	Prohibition elections.	Failed
1916	N/A	DA	Labor	Workman's compensation.	Failed
1916	N/A	DS	Environmental Reform	Fish and game regulation.	Passed
1916	N/A	DS	Administration of Government	To hire a state architect.	Failed
1916	N/A	DS	Administration of Government	To establish a department of labor	Failed
1916	N/A	DS	Death Penalty	Abolishing death penalty.	Passed
1916	N/A	DS	Administration of Government	Create laws associated with divorce.	Failed
1916	N/A	DA	Administration of Government	Abolishment of the Senate and establish a unicameral.	Failed
1916	N/A	DA	Alcohol Regulation	To amend the prohibition act.	Passed
1916	N/A	DA	Apportionment/ Redistricting	Legislative redistricting.	Failed
1916	N/A	DA	Administration of Government	Local option.	Failed
1918	N/A	DS	Death Penalty	Reinstating the death penalty.	Passed
1918	N/A	DA	Labor	Workmen's compensation.	Failed
1918	N/A	DS	Health/Medical	Vaccination, minors.	Passed
1918	N/A	DA	Environmental Reform	To authorize the legislature to provide proper laws for the sale of state lands and the lease of the same, and for the protection of bona fide residents and lessee's of said lands.	Passed

Year	Measure Number	Type	Subject Matter	Description	Pass/Fail
1918	N/A	DA	Apportionment/ Redistricting	To give each country in the state equitable representation in the lower house of the legislature based on population; authorizing boards of supervisors to divide counties into legislative districts according to population and permitting each district.	Passed
1918	N/A	DS	Administration of Government	The leasing of state lands	Failed
1918	N/A	DA	Environmental Reform	To limit the sale of agricultural and grazing land.	Passed
1920	N/A	DS	Environmental Reform	Conservation, game and fish.	Failed
1920	N/A	DS	Administration of Government	Civil service.	Failed
1920	N/A	DS	Administration of Government	Establishment of Counties.	Failed
1920	N/A	DS	Environmental Reform	Reclamation.	Failed
1920	N/A	DS	Administration of Government	To establish the State Highway Department.	Failed.
1920	N/A	DA	Education	Publication of teachers salaries	Failed
1922	N/A	DA	Education	Make changes to existing educational statutes.	Failed
1922	N/A	DA	Bonds	Hassayampa — Colorado Highway bonds.	Failed
1924	N/A	DA	Bonds	Hassayampa — Colorado Highway bonds.	Failed
1924	N/A	DS	Gaming	To create board, appointed by Governor, to regulate and license horse racing and pari-mutuel betting within race track enclosure.	Failed
1924	N/A	DS	Administration of Government	Highway commission.	Failed
1924	N/A	DS	Environmental Reform	Colorado River, appropriations.	Failed
1925	N/A	DA	Administration of Government	Tenure of state officers.	Failed
1926	N/A	DS	Taxes	Automobile tax reduction.	Failed
1926	N/A	DS	Administration of Government	Highway Department, finance bill.	Failed
1928	N/A	DS	Administration of Government	To create a Board of Equalization.	Failed
1928	N/A	DS	Administration of Government	To create Commissioner of State Finance.	Failed
1928	N/A	DA	Health/Medical	Medical liberty.	Failed
1928	N/A	DS	Administration of Government	To create a Motor Vehicle Department.	Failed
1930	N/A	DA	Bonds	To authorize issuance and sale of state highway bonds.	Failed
1930	N/A	DA	Taxes	Auto tax exemption.	Failed
1932	N/A	DS	Administration of Government	Industrial Commission, abolishment.	Failed

Year	Measure Number	Type	Subject Matter	Description	Pass/Fail
1932	N/A	DS	Administration of Government	Abolishment of 18 Boards.	Failed
1932	N/A	DA	Apportionment/ Redistricting	Legislature, apportionment.	Passed
1932	N/A	DA	Taxes	County expenditures, limit on.	Failed
1932	N/A	DS	Health/Medical	Chiropractors.	Failed
1932	N/A	DA	Taxes	Gasoline tax distribution.	Failed
1932	N/A	DA	Taxes	State expenditures, limit on.	Failed
1932	N/A	DA	Alcohol Regulation	Repeal of Prohibition.	Passed
1934	N/A	DS	Administration of Government	Legislature, nepotism, rules.	Failed
1934	N/A	DS	Administration of Government	To create a Board of Naturopathic. Examiners	Failed
1938	N/A	DS	Administration of Government	All appointive members of boards and commissions, terms conterminous with Governor.	Failed
1938	N/A	DA	Administration of Government	Legislators not eligible for appointment to public office.	Passed
1938	N/A	DA	Taxes	Tax free homes.	Failed
1940	N/A	DS	Gaming	To permit and authorize the licensing of gambling.	Failed
1940	N/A	DS	Taxes	Relating to motor fuel tax, fixing the tax and the distribution and use thereof.	Failed
1940	N/A	DS	Taxes	Education, state aid; proscribing the state levy for common and high school purposes.	Passed
1940	N/A	DA	Taxes	Tax free homes.	Failed
1940	N/A	DA	Taxes	Uniform auto lien tax.	Passed
1940	N/A	DA	Administration of Government	Establishing irrigation districts.	Passed
1940	N/A	DA	Taxes	Tax limitation.	Failed
1942	N/A	DS	Taxes	Privilege tax, division.	Passed
1944	N/A	D	A Welfare	Annuities for the disabled and blind.	Failed
1946	N/A	DA	Labor	Right to work	Passed
1946	N/A	DS	Taxes	Motor vehicle fuel tax.	Passed
1946	N/A	DA	Labor	Right-to-work.	Passed
1948	N/A	DS	Administration of Government	Highway patrol, merit system.	Passed
1948	N/A	DS	Labor	Limitation to workmen's compensation.	Passed
1948	N/A	DS	Administration of Government	Civil service.	Passed
1948	N/A	DS	Administration of Government	Public employees' retirement.	Passed
1950	N/A	DS	Administration of Government	Merit system for peace officers.	Failed
1950	N/A	DS	Gaming	Legalized gambling.	Failed
1950	N/A	DS	Taxes	Excise tax, increase.	Failed
1950	N/A	DS	Alcohol Regulation	Local option, liquor.	Failed
1950	N/A	DS	Labor	Workmen's compensation — to limit compensation.	Failed
1950	N/A	DS	Welfare	Social security and welfare reform and regulation.	Failed
1950	N/A	DS	Labor	Employment security, extend benefits.	Failed

Year	Measure Number	Type	Subject Matter	Description	Pass/Fail
1950	N/A	DS	Administration of Government	Employment security, agricultural workers.	Failed
1950	N/A	DS	Civil Rights	Segregation in schools.	Failed
1950	N/A	DA	Education	State Board of Education.	Failed
1950	N/A	DA	Administration of Government	Merit system, public employees.	Failed
1950	N/A	DA	Education	Education — maintenance of kindergartens.	Failed
1952	N/A	DS	Labor	Labor organizations — secondary picketing	Passed
1956	N/A	DS	Administration of Government	Pre-marital blood test.	Passed
1958	N/A	DS	Education	Revises laws pertaining to Arizona State University.	Passed
1958	N/A	DS	Administration of Government	Merit system, public employees.	Failed
1960	N/A	DA	Judicial Reform	Revision of state court systems.	Passed
1960	N/A	DS	Taxes	Revenue and taxation; increasing cities' share of sales tax.	Passed
1962	N/A	DA	Business Regulation	Real estate agents may prepare instruments.	Passed
1962	N/A	DS	Taxes	Property taxation reappraisal.	Failed
1964	N/A	DA	Taxes	Inventories exempt from taxation.	Passed
1964	N/A	DA	Term Limits	County officers, 4 year terms.	Passed
1964	N/A	DA	Education	Apportionment of state school funds.	Passed
1964	N/A	DS	Utility Regulation	Railroads; eliminating featherbedding.	Passed
1970	N/A	DS	Gaming	Establishing the Arizona sweepstakes lottery	Failed
1972	N/A	DS	Taxes	Preemption by the state of income and luxury taxation.	Passed
1974	N/A	DA	Judicial Reform	Relating to the Judicial Department.	Passed
1976	200	DS	Nuclear weapons/ facilities/waste	Legislative approval-nuclear facilities.	Failed
1980	106	DA	Taxes	Property tax limitation-2/3 legislature.	Failed
1980	200	DS	Gaming	Provisions for state lottery.	Passed
1982	200	DS	Environmental Reform	Deposit/refund for beverage containers.	Failed
1982	201	DS	Administration of Government	Declare last Sunday in May as Peace Sunday.	Failed
1982	202	DS	Election Reform	Voter registration by driver's license.	Passed
1982	203	DS	Administration of Government	Repeal state control over public lands.	Failed
1984	110	DA	Health/Medical	Health care institutions, regulation	Failed
1984	200	DS	Health/Medical	Regulate cost of health care.	Failed
1986	103	DA	Tort Reform	Personal injury damages, legislative limitations.	Failed
1986	200	DS	Campaign Finance Reform	Limit campaign contributions.	Passed
1988	106	DA	Administration of Government	English as official language.	Passed
1990	103	DA	Education	Classroom Improvement program.	Failed
1990	104	DA	Legal	Victims' bill of rights.	Passed
1990	105	DA	Business Regulation	Vehicle accident compensation law.	Failed
1990	200	DS	Environmental Reform	Arizona state Parks funded by lottery.	Passed

Year	Measure Number	Type	Subject Matter	Description	Pass/Fail
1990	201	DS	Administration of Government	Establish Consumer Insurance Office.	Failed
1990	202	DS	Environmental Reform	Hazardous waste disposal.	Failed
1990	203	DS	Business Regulation	Motor vehicle insurance; rates and damages.	Failed
1992	107	DA	Term Limits	Term limits. State legislature 8/8. Congress 6/12.	Passed
1992	108	DA	Taxes	Public debt, revenue and taxation.	Passed
1992	110	DA	Abortion	Pre-born child protection amendment; abortion.	Failed
1992	200	DS	Animal Rights	Unlawful methods of capturing wildlife.	Failed
1994	103	DA	Tort Reform	A Constitutional Amendment relating to the right to recover damages.	Failed
1994	200	DS	Taxes	Proposing an act by Initiative Petition to increase state taxes on tobacco products.	Passed
1994	201	DS	Animal Rights	Relating to the use of leg hold traps, poison and snares on public lands.	Passed
1996	102	DA	Legal	Requires juveniles ages 15 and older to be tried as an adult for murder, rape and armed robbery.	Passed
1996	200	DS	Drug Policy Reform	Relating to laws on controlled substances and those convicted of personal use or possession of controlled substances.	Passed
1996	201	DS	Gaming	Proposing an act concerning the use of uniform gaming compacts with Indian tribes.	Passed
1996	203	DS	Health/Medical	Allocates lottery revenues for health programs.	Passed
1998	105	DA	Initiative and Referendum	Would prohibit the Governor's veto of initiative and referendum measures. Prohibits legislative repeal of I&R measures and requires 3/4 vote of legislature to amend I&R measures.	Passed
1998	200	DS	Campaign Finance	Would establish a five-member commission to administer alternative campaign financing system and provides for public funding and additional reporting for participating candidates and reduces current contribution limits by 20%.	Passed
1998	201	DS	Animal Rights	Would outlaw cockfighting.	Passed
1998	202	DS	Taxes	Would give Arizona candidates for federal office the option to pledge to support and vote for elimination of the federal income tax and IRS through the passage of a national consumption tax.	Failed
2000	106	DA	Apportionment/Redistricting	Creates a new "citizens' independent redistricting commission" to draw new legislative and congressional district boundaries after each U.S. Census.	Passed

Year	Measure Number	Type	Subject Matter	Description	Pass/Fail
2000	108	DA	Utility Regulation	End rate making by the Corporate Commission of local telephone rates where service is available from two or more competing providers.	Failed
2000	200	DS	Health/Medical	Provide health insurance for uninsured working parents.	Passed
2000	202	DS	Environmental Reform	This initiative would require cities and counties to adopt growth management plans to limit urban sprawl.	Failed
2000	203	DS	Education	Requires that all public school instruction be conducted in English.	Passed
2000	204	DS	Health/Medical	Funds the Healthy Arizona Initiative passed in 1996; increases eligibility of working poor at federal poverty level for health care coverage through AHCCCS.	Passed

Arizona Constitution

Article 4

Section 1. Legislative authority; initiative and referendum

(1) Senate; house of representatives; reservation of power to people. The legislative authority of the state shall be vested in the legislature, consisting of a senate and a house of representatives, but the people reserve the power to propose laws and amendments to the constitution and to enact or reject such laws and amendments at the polls, independently of the legislature; and they also reserve, for use at their own option, the power to approve or reject at the polls any act, or item, section, or part of any act, of the legislature.

(2) Initiative power. The first of these reserved powers is the initiative. Under this power ten per centum of the qualified electors shall have the right to propose any measure, and fifteen per centum shall have the right to propose any amendment to the constitution.

(3) Referendum power; emergency measures; effective date of acts. The second of these reserved powers is the referendum. Under this power the legislature, or five per centum of the qualified electors, may order the submission to the people at the polls of any measure, or item, section, or part of any measure, enacted by the legislature, except laws immediately necessary for the preservation of the public peace, health, or safety, or for the support and maintenance of the departments of the state government and state institutions; but to allow opportunity for referendum petitions, no act passed by the legislature shall be operative for ninety days after the close of the session of the legislature enacting such measure, except such as require earlier operation to preserve the public peace, health, or safety, or to provide appropriations for the support and maintenance of the departments of the state and of state institutions; provided, that no such emergency measure shall be considered passed by the legislature unless it shall state in a separate section why it is necessary that it shall become immediately operative, and shall be approved by the affirmative votes of two-thirds of the members elected to each house of the legislature, taken by roll call of ayes and nays, and also approved by the governor; and should such measure be vetoed by the governor, it shall not become a law unless it shall be approved by the votes of three-fourths of the members elected to each house of the legislature, taken by roll call of ayes and nays.

(4) Initiative and referendum petitions; filing. All petitions submitted under the power of the initiative shall be known as initiative petitions, and shall be filed with the Secretary of State not less than four months preceding the date of the election at which the measures so proposed are to be voted upon. All petitions submitted under the power of the referendum shall be known as referendum petitions, and shall be filed with the Secretary of State not more than ninety days after the final adjournment of the session of the legislature which shall have passed the measure to which the referendum is applied. The filing of a referendum petition against any item, section, or part of any measure shall not prevent the remainder of such measure from becoming operative.

(5) Effective date of initiative and referendum measures. Any measure or amendment to the constitution proposed under the initiative, and any measure to which the referendum is applied, shall be referred to a vote of the qualified electors, and shall become law when approved by a majority of the votes cast thereon and upon proclamation of the governor, and not otherwise.

(6)(A) Veto of initiative or referendum. The veto power of the governor shall not extend to an initiative measure approved by a majority of the votes cast thereon or to a referendum measure decided by a majority of the votes cast thereon.

(6)(B) Legislature's power to repeal initiative or referendum. The legislature shall not have the power to repeal an initiative measure approved by a majority of the votes cast thereon or to repeal a referendum measure decided by a majority of the votes cast thereon.

(6)(C) Legislature's power to amend initiative or referendum. The legislature shall not have the power to amend an initiative measure approved by a majority of the votes cast thereon, or to amend a referendum measure decided by a majority of the votes cast thereon, unless the amending legislation furthers the purposes of such measure and at least three-fourths of the members of each house of the legislature, by a roll call of ayes and nays, vote to amend such measure.

(6)(D) Legislature's power to appropriate or divert funds created by initiative or referendum. The legislature shall not have the power to appropriate or divert funds created or allocated to a specific purpose by an initiative measure approved by a majority of the votes cast thereon, or by a referendum measure decided by a majority of the votes cast thereon, unless the appropriation or diversion of funds furthers the purposes of such measure and at least three-fourths of the members of each house of the legislature, by a roll call of ayes and nays, vote to appropriate or divert such funds.

(7) Number of qualified electors. The whole number of votes cast for all candidates for governor at the general election last preceding the filing of any initiative or referendum petition on a state or county measure shall be the basis on which the number of qualified electors required to sign such petition shall be computed.

(8) Local, city, town or county matters. The powers of the initiative and the referendum are hereby further reserved to the qualified electors of every incorporated city, town, and county as to all local, city, town, or county matters on which such incorporated cities, towns, and counties are or shall be empowered by general laws to legislate. Such incorporated cities, towns, and counties may prescribe the manner of exercising said powers within the restrictions of general laws. Under the power of the initiative fifteen per centum of the qualified electors may propose measures on such local, city, town, or county matters, and ten per centum of the electors may propose the referendum on legislation enacted within and by such city, town, or county. Until provided by general law, said cities and towns may prescribe the basis on which said percentages shall be computed.

(9) Form and contents of initiative and of referendum petitions; verification. Every initiative or referendum petition shall be addressed to the secretary of state in the case of petitions for or on state measures, and to the clerk of the board of supervisors, city clerk, or corresponding officer in the case of petitions for or on county, city, or town measures; and shall contain the declaration of each petitioner, for himself, that he is a qualified elector of the state (and in the case of petitions for or on city, town, or county measures, of the city, town, or county affected), his post office address, the street and number, if any, of his residence, and the date on which he signed such petition. Each sheet containing petitioners' signatures shall be attached to a full and correct copy of the title and text of the measure so proposed to be initiated or referred to the people, and every sheet of every such petition containing signatures shall be verified by the affidavit of the person who circulated said sheet or petition, setting forth that each of the names on said sheet was signed in the presence of the affiant and that in the belief of the affiant each signer was a qualified elector of the state, or in the case of a city, town, or county measure, of the city, town, or county affected by the measure so proposed to be initiated or referred to the people.

(10) Official ballot. When any initiative or referendum petition or any measure referred to the people by the legislature shall be filed, in accordance with this section, with the secretary of state, he shall cause to be printed on the official ballot at the next regular general election the title and number of said measure, together with the words "yes" and "no" in such manner that the electors may express at the polls their approval or disapproval of the measure.

(11) Publication of measures. The text of all measures to be submitted shall be published as proposed amendments to the constitution are published, and in submitting such measures and proposed amendments the secretary of state and all other officers shall be guided by the general law until legislation shall be especially provided therefore.

(12) Conflicting measures or constitutional amendments. If two or more conflicting measures or amendments to the constitution shall be approved by the people at the same election, the measure or amendment receiving the greatest number of affirmative votes shall prevail in all particulars as to which there is conflict.

(13) Canvass of votes; proclamation. It shall be the duty of the secretary of state, in the presence of the governor and the chief justice of the supreme court, to canvass the votes for and against each such measure or proposed amendment to the constitution within thirty days after the election, and upon the completion of the canvass the governor shall forthwith issue a proclamation, giving the whole number of votes cast for and against each measure or proposed amendment, and declaring such measures or amendments as are approved by a majority of those voting thereon to be law.

(14) Reservation of legislative power. This section shall not be construed to deprive the legislature of the right to enact any measure. Except that the legislature shall not have the power to adopt any measure that supersedes, in whole or in part, any initiative measure approved by a majority of the votes cast thereon or any referendum measure decided by a majority of the votes cast thereon unless the superseding measure furthers the purposes of the initiative or referendum

measure and at least three-fourths of the members of each house of the legislature, by a roll call of ayes and nays, vote to supersede such initiative or referendum measure.

(15) Legislature's right to refer measure to the people. Nothing in this section shall be construed to deprive or limit the legislature of the right to order the submission to the people at the polls of any measure, item, section, or part of any measure.

(16) Self-executing. This section of the constitution shall be, in all respects, self-executing.

Section 2. Penalty for violation of initiative and referendum provisions

The legislature shall provide a penalty for any willful violation of any of the provisions of the preceding section.

Article 21

Section 1. Introduction in legislature; initiative petition; election

Any amendment or amendments to this Constitution may be proposed in either House of the Legislature, or by Initiative Petition signed by a number of qualified electors equal to fifteen per centum of the total number of votes for all candidates for Governor at the last preceding general election. Any proposed amendment or amendments which shall be introduced in either House of the Legislature, and which shall be approved by a majority of the members elected to each of the two Houses, shall be entered on the journal of each House, together with the ayes and nays thereon. When any proposed amendment or amendments shall be thus passed by a majority of each House of the Legislature and entered on the respective journals thereof, or when any elector or electors shall file with the Secretary of State any proposed amendment or amendments together with a petition therefor signed by a number of electors equal to fifteen per centum of the total number of votes for all candidates for Governor in the last preceding general election, the Secretary of State shall submit such proposed amendment or amendments to the vote of the people at the next general election (except when the Legislature shall call a special election for the purpose of having said proposed amendment or amendments voted upon, in which case the Secretary of State shall submit such proposed amendment or amendments to the qualified electors at said special election,) and if a majority of the qualified electors voting thereon shall approve and ratify such proposed amendment or amendments in said regular or special election, such amendment or amendments shall become a part of this Constitution. Until a method of publicity is otherwise provided by law, the Secretary of State shall have such proposed amendment or amendments published for a period of at least ninety days previous to the date of said election in at least one newspaper in every county of the State in which a newspaper shall be published, in such manner as may be prescribed by law. If more than one proposed amendment shall be submitted at any election, such proposed amendments shall be submitted in such manner that the electors may vote for or against such proposed amendments separately.

Arizona Statutes

Title 19

19-101. Referendum petition; circulators; violation; classification

A. The following shall be the form for referring to the people by referendum petition a measure or item, section or part of a measure enacted by the legislature, or by the legislative body of an incorporated city, town or county:
Referendum Description
(Insert a description of no more than one hundred words of the principal provisions of the measure sought to be referred.)
Notice: This is only a description of the measure sought to be referred prepared by the sponsor of the measure. It may not include every provision contained in the measure. Before signing, make sure the title and text of the measure are attached. You have the right to read or examine the title and text before signing.

Petition for Referendum
To the secretary of state: (or to the corresponding officer for or on local county, city, or town measures)
We, the undersigned citizens and qualified electors of the state of Arizona, respectfully order that the senate (or house) bill No. ___ (or other local county, city, or town measure) entitled (title of act or ordinance, and if the petition is against less than the whole act or ordinance then set forth here the item, section, or part, of any measure on which the referen-

dum is used), passed by the _____ session of the legislature of the state of Arizona, at the general (or special, as the case may be) session of said legislature, (or by county, city or town legislative body) shall be referred to a vote of the qualified electors of the state, (county, city or town) for their approval or rejection at the next regular general election (or city or town election) and each for himself says:

I have personally signed this petition with my first and last names. I have not signed any other petition for the same measure. I am a qualified elector of the state of Arizona, county of (or city or town and county of, as the case may be) _____.

"Warning: It is a class 1 misdemeanor for any person to knowingly sign an initiative or referendum petition with a name other than his own, except in a circumstance where he signs for a person, in the presence of and at the specific request of such person, who is incapable of signing his own name because of physical infirmity, or to knowingly sign his name more than once for the same measure, or to knowingly sign such petition when he is not a qualified elector."

(Fifteen lines for signatures which shall be numbered)

The validity of signatures on this sheet must be sworn to by the circulator before a notary public on the form appearing on the back of the sheet.

Number _____

B. Each petition sheet shall have printed in capital letters in no less than twelve point bold-faced type in the upper right-hand corner of the face of the petition sheet the following: "_____ paid circulator" "_____ volunteer"

C. A circulator of a referendum petition shall state whether he is a paid circulator or volunteer by checking the appropriate line on the petition form before circulating the petition for signatures.

D. Signatures obtained on referendum petitions in violation of subsection C of this section are void and shall not be counted in determining the legal sufficiency of the petition. The presence of signatures that are invalidated under this subsection on a petition does not invalidate other signatures on the petition that were obtained as prescribed by this section.

19-102. Initiative petition; circulators

A. The form of petition for a law or amendment to the constitution of this state or county legislative measure, or city or town ordinance, or amendment to a city or town charter proposed by the initiative to be submitted directly to the electors, shall be substantially in the form prescribed in section 19-101, except that the title and body of such petition shall read:

Initiative description

(Insert a description of no more than one hundred words of the principal provisions of the proposed measure or constitutional amendment.)

Notice: this is only a description of the proposed measure (or constitutional amendment) prepared by the sponsor of the measure. It may not include every provision contained in the measure. Before signing, make sure the title and text of the measure are attached. You have the right to read or examine the title and text before signing.

Initiative Measure to be Submitted Directly to Electors

We, the undersigned, citizens and qualified electors of the state of Arizona, respectfully demand that the following proposed law (or amendment to the constitution, or other initiative measure), shall be submitted to the qualified electors of the state of Arizona (county, city or town of _____) for their approval or rejection at the next regular general election (or county, city or town election) and each for himself says: (terminate form same as a referendum petition.)

B. Each petition sheet shall have printed in capital letters in no less than twelve point bold-faced type in the upper right-hand corner of the face of the petition sheet the following: "_____ paid circulator" or "_____ volunteer"

C. A circulator of an initiative petition shall state whether he is a paid circulator or volunteer by checking the appropriate line on the petition form before circulating the petition for signatures.

D. Signatures obtained on initiative petitions in violation of subsection C of this section are void and shall not be counted in determining the legal sufficiency of the petition. The presence of signatures that are invalidated under this subsection on a petition does not invalidate other signatures on the petition that were obtained as prescribed by this section.

19-111. Number for petition

A. A person or organization intending to propose a law or constitutional amendment by initiative petition or to file a referendum petition against a measure, item, section or part of a measure shall, before causing the petition to be printed and circulated, file with the secretary of state an application, on a form to be provided by the secretary of state, setting forth his name or, if an organization, its name and the names and titles of its officers, address, his intention to circulate and file a petition, a description of no more than one hundred words of the principal provisions of the proposed law, constitutional amendment or measure and the text of the proposed law, constitutional amendment or measure to be initiated or referred in no less than eight point type, and applying for issuance of an official serial number.

B. On receipt of the application, the secretary of state shall assign an official serial number to the petition, which number shall appear in the lower right-hand corner of each side of each copy thereof, and issue that number to the applicant. Numbers shall be assigned to petitions by the secretary of state in numerical sequence, and a record shall be maintained in his office of each application received and of the numbers assigned and issued to the applicant.

C. The secretary of state shall print in pamphlet form and shall furnish to each applicant, at the time the application is submitted, a copy of the text of this article governing the initiative and referendum and all rules adopted by the secretary of state pursuant to this title. In addition, the secretary of state shall at this time furnish the applicant with a statement of organization form and a notice stating: "This statement must be filed before valid signatures can be collected." The secretary of state shall furnish a sufficient supply of these pamphlets to the county, city and town clerks who shall similarly furnish the pamphlet to each applicant.

D. The eight point type required by subsection A shall not apply to maps, charts or other graphics.

19-112. Signatures and verification; attachment

A. Every qualified elector signing a petition shall do so in the presence of the person who is circulating the petition and who is to execute the affidavit of verification. At the time of signing, the qualified elector shall sign his first and last names in the spaces provided and the elector so signing or the person circulating the petition shall print his first and last names and write, in the appropriate spaces following the signature, the signer's residence address, giving street and number, and if he has no street address, a description of his residence location. The elector so signing or the person circulating the petition shall write, in the appropriate spaces following the elector's address, the date on which the elector signed the petition.

B. The signature sheets shall be attached at all times during circulation to a full and correct copy of the title and text of the measure or constitutional amendment proposed or referred by the petition. The title and text shall be in at least eight point type and shall include both the original and the amended text. The text shall indicate material deleted, if any, by printing the material with a line drawn through the center of the letters of the material and shall indicate material added or new material by printing the letters of the material in capital letters.

C. The person before whom the signatures and addresses were written on the signature sheet shall, on the affidavit form pursuant to this section, subscribe and swear before a notary public that each of the names on the sheet was signed and the name and address were printed in the presence of the elector and the circulator on the date indicated, and that in his belief each signer was a qualified elector of a certain county of the state, or, in the case of a city, town or county measure, of the city, town or county affected by the measure on the date indicated, and that at all times during circulation of the signature sheet a copy of the title and text was attached to the signature sheet. All signatures of petitioners on a signature sheet shall be those of qualified electors who are registered to vote in the same county. However, if signatures from more than one county appear on the same signature sheet, only the valid signatures from the same county which are most numerous on the signature sheet shall be counted. Signature and handwriting comparisons may be made.

D. The affidavit shall be in the following form printed on the reverse side of each signature sheet:

Affidavit of Circulator
State of Arizona)
) ss.:
County of _____)
I, __(print name)__, a person who is qualified to register to vote in the county of _____, in the state of Arizona at all times during my circulation of this petition sheet, and under the penalty of a class 1 misdemeanor, depose and say that each individual signed this sheet of the foregoing petition in my presence on the date indicated, and I believe that each signer's name and residence address or post office address are correctly stated and that each signer is a qualified elector of the state of Arizona (or in the case of a city, town or county measure, of the city, town or county affected by the measure proposed to be initiated or referred to the people) and that at all times during circulation of this signature sheet a copy of the title and text was attached to the signature sheet.

(Signature of affiant) _____

(Residence address, street and number of affiant, or if no street address, a description of residence location)

_____

Subscribed and sworn to before me on _____.

_____

Notary Public

_____, Arizona.

My commission expires on _____.

E. The eight point type required by subsection B shall not apply to maps, charts or other graphics.

19-114. Prohibition on circulating petitions by certain persons

A. No county recorder or justice of the peace and no person other than a person who is qualified to register to vote pursuant to section 16-101 may circulate an initiative or referendum petition and all signatures verified by any such person shall be void and shall not be counted in determining the legal sufficiency of the petition.

B. Signatures obtained on initiative and referendum petitions by a political committee proposing the initiative or referendum or any of its officers, agents, employees or members prior to the filing of the committee's statement of organization are void and shall not be counted in determining the legal sufficiency of the petition.

19-114.01. Prohibition on signing petition for profit; classification

Any person who knowingly gives or receives money or any other thing of value for signing an initiative or referendum petition, excluding payments made to a person for circulating such petition, is guilty of a class 1 misdemeanor.

19-115. Unlawful acts; violations; classification

A. Every qualified elector of the state may sign a referendum or initiative petition upon any measure which he is legally entitled to vote upon.

B. A person knowingly signing any name other than his own to a petition, except in a circumstance where he signs for a person, in the presence of and at the specific request of such person, who is incapable of signing his own name, because of physical infirmity or knowingly signing his name more than once for the same measure, or proposed constitutional amendment, at one election, or who is not at the time of signing a qualified elector of this state, or any officer or person knowingly violating any provision of this chapter, is guilty of a class 1 misdemeanor unless another classification is specifically prescribed in this title.

19-116. Coercion or intimidation with respect to petitions; classification

A person who knowingly coerces any other person by menace or threat, or threatens any other person to the effect that the other person will or may be injured in his business, or discharged from employment, or that he will not be employed, to sign or subscribe, or to refrain from signing or subscribing, his name to an initiative or referendum petition, or, after signing or subscribing his name, to have his name taken there from, is guilty of a class 1 misdemeanor.

19-117. Initiative and referendum petition; changes; applicability

Notwithstanding any other law, any change in the law or procedure adopted by a governing body with respect to circulation or filing of an initiative or referendum petition after an initiative or referendum petition application is filed pursuant to section 19-111 does not apply to the initiative or referendum petition.

19-118. Definition of paid circulator

For the purposes of this title, "paid circulator":

1. Means a natural person who receives monetary or other compensation that is based on the number of signatures obtained on a petition or on the number of petitions circulated that contain signatures.

2. Does not include a paid employee of any political committee organized pursuant to title 16, chapter 6, unless that employee's primary responsibility is circulating petitions to obtain signatures.

19-119. Deceptive mailings; civil penalty

A. In an attempt to influence the outcome of an election held pursuant to this title, an individual or committee shall not deliver or mail any document that falsely purports to be a mailing authorized, approved, required, sent or reviewed by or that falsely simulates a document from the government of this state, a county, city or town or any other political subdivision.

B. An individual or committee that violates this section is liable for a civil penalty equal to twice the total of the cost of the mailing or five hundred dollars, whichever is greater. The attorney general, the county attorney, the city or town attorney or other legal representative of the political subdivision, as appropriate, may assess the civil penalty.

19-121. Signature sheets; petitions; form; procedure for filing

A. Signature sheets filed shall:

1. Be in the form prescribed by law.

2. Have printed in its lower right-hand corner, on each side of such sheet, the official serial number assigned to the petition by the secretary of state.

3. Be attached to a full and correct copy of the title and text of the measure, or amendment to the constitution, proposed or referred by the petition.

4. Be printed in at least eight point type.

5. Be printed in black ink on white or recycled white pages fourteen inches in width by eight and one-half inches in length, with a margin of at least one-half inch at the top and one-fourth inch at the bottom of each page.

B. For purposes of this chapter, a petition is filed when the petition sheets are tendered to the secretary of state, at which time a receipt is immediately issued by the secretary of state based on an estimate made to the secretary of state of the purported number of sheets and signatures filed. After the issuance of the receipt, no additional petition sheets may be accepted for filing.

C. Petitions may be filed with the secretary of state in numbered sections for convenience in handling. Not more than fifteen signatures on one sheet shall be counted.

D. Initiative petitions which have not been filed with the secretary of state as of 5:00 p.m. on the day required by the constitution prior to the ensuing general election after their issuance shall be null and void, but in no event shall the secretary of state accept an initiative petition which was issued for circulation more than twenty-four months prior to the general election at which the measure is to be included on the ballot.

E. For purposes of this article and article 4, the measure to be attached to the petition as enacted by the legislative body of an incorporated city, town or county means the adopted ordinance or resolution or, in the absence of a written ordinance or resolution, that portion of the minutes of the legislative body that reflects the action taken by that body when adopting the measure. In the case of zoning measures the measure shall also include a legal description of the property and any amendments made to the ordinance by the legislative body.

19-121.01. Secretary of state; removal of petition and ineligible signatures; facsimile sheets; random sample

A. Within fifteen days, excluding Saturdays, Sundays and other legal holidays, of the date of filing of an initiative or referendum petition and issuance of the receipt, the secretary of state shall:

1. Remove the following:

(a) Those sheets not attached to a copy of the title and text of the measure.

(b) The copy of the title and text from the remaining petition sheets.

(c) Those sheets not bearing the petition serial number in the lower right-hand corner of each side.

(d) Those sheets containing a circulator's affidavit that is not completed or signed.

(e) Those sheets on which the affidavit of the circulator is not notarized, the notary's signature is missing, the notary's commission has expired or the notary's seal is not affixed.

(f) Those sheets on which the signatures of the circulator or the notary are dated earlier than the dates on which the electors signed the face of the petition sheet.

2. After completing the steps in paragraph 1 of this subsection, review each sheet to determine the county of the majority of the signers and shall:

(a) Place a three or four letter abbreviation designating that county in the upper right-hand corner of the face of the petition.

(b) Remove all signatures of those not in the county of the majority on each sheet by marking an "SS" in red ink in the margin to the right of the signature line.

(c) Cause all signature sheets to be grouped together by county of registration of the majority of those signing and attach them to one or more copies of the title and text of the measure. If the sheets are too bulky for convenient grouping by the secretary of state in one volume by county, they may be bound in two or more volumes with those in each volume attached to a single printed copy of the measure. The remaining detached copies of the title and text of the measure shall be delivered to the applicant.

3. After completing the steps in paragraph 2 of this subsection, remove the following signatures that are not eligible for verification by marking an "SS" in red ink in the margin to the right of the signature line:

(a) If the signature of the qualified elector is missing.

(b) If the residence address or the description of residence location is missing.

(c) If the date on which the petitioner signed is missing.

(d) Signatures in excess of the fifteen signatures permitted per petition.

(e) Signatures withdrawn pursuant to section 1-261.

4. After the removal of petition sheets and signatures, count the number of signatures for verification on the remaining petition sheets and note that number in the upper right-hand corner of the face of each petition sheet immediately above the county designation.

5. Number the remaining petition sheets that were not previously removed and that contain signatures eligible for verification in consecutive order on the front side of each petition sheet in the upper left-hand corner.

6. Count all remaining petition sheets and signatures not previously removed and issue a receipt to the applicant of this total number eligible for verification.

B. If the total number of signatures for verification as determined pursuant to subsection A, paragraph 6 of this section equals or exceeds the constitutional minimum, the secretary of state, during the same fifteen day period provided in subsection A of this section, shall select, at random, five per cent of the total signatures eligible for verification by the county recorders of the counties in which the persons signing the petition claim to be qualified electors. The random sample of signatures to be verified shall be drawn in such a manner that every signature eligible for verification has an equal chance of being included in the sample. The random sample produced shall identify each signature selected by petition page and line number. The signatures selected shall be marked according to the following procedure:

1. Using red ink, mark the selected signature by circling the line number and drawing a line from the base of the circle extending into the left margin.

2. If a signature line selected for the random sample is found to be blank or was removed from the verification process pursuant to subsection A of this section and is marked with an "SS", then the next line down, even if that requires going to the next petition sheet in sequence, on which an eligible signature appears shall be selected as a substitute if that line has not already been selected for the random sample. If the next eligible line is already being used in the random sample, the secretary of state shall proceed back up the page from the signature line originally selected for the random sample to the next previous signature line eligible for verification. If that line is already being used in the random sample, the secretary of state shall continue moving down the page or to the next page from the line originally selected for the random sample and shall select the next eligible signature as its substitute for the random sample. The secretary of state shall use this process of alternately moving forward and backward until a signature eligible for verification and not already included in the random sample can be selected and substituted.

C. After the selection of the random sample and the marking of the signatures selected on the original petition sheets pursuant to subsection B of this section, the secretary of state shall reproduce a facsimile of the front of each signature sheet on which a signature included in the random sample appears. The secretary of state shall clearly identify those signatures marked for verification by color highlighting or other similar method and shall transmit by personal delivery or certified mail to each county recorder a facsimile sheet of each signature sheet on which a signature appears of any individual claiming to be a qualified elector of that county whose signature was selected for verification as part of the random sample.

D. The secretary of state shall retain in custody all signature sheets removed pursuant to this section except as otherwise prescribed in this title.

19-121.02. Certification by county recorder

A. Within ten days, excluding Saturdays, Sundays and other legal holidays, after receiving the facsimile signature sheets from the secretary of state pursuant to section 19-121.01, the county recorder shall determine which signatures of individuals whose names were transmitted shall be disqualified for any of the following reasons:

1. No residence address or description of residence location is provided.

2. No date of signing is provided.

3. The signature is illegible and the signer is otherwise unidentifiable.

4. The address provided is illegible or nonexistent.

5. The individual was not a qualified elector on the date of signing the petition.

6. The individual was a registered voter but was not at least eighteen years of age on the date of signing the petition or affidavit.

7. The signature was disqualified after comparison with the signature on the affidavit of registration.

8. If a petitioner signed more than once, all but one otherwise valid signature shall be disqualified.

9. For the same reasons any signatures or entire petition sheets could have been removed by the secretary of state pursuant to section 19-121.01, subsection A.

B. Within the same time period provided in subsection A of this section, the county recorder shall certify to the secretary of state the following:

1. The name of any individual whose signature was included in the random sample and disqualified by the county recorder together with the petition page and line number of the disqualified signature.

2. The name of any other individual petition signer whose signature was disqualified by the county recorder together with the petition page and line number of the disqualified signature.

3. The total number of signatures selected for the random sample and transmitted to the county recorder for verification and the total number of random sample signatures disqualified as well as the total number of all other individual signatures disqualified.

C. The secretary of state shall prescribe the form of the county recorder's certification.

D. At the time of the certification, the county recorder shall:

1. Return the facsimile signature sheets to the secretary of state.

2. Send notice of the results of the certification by mail to the person or organization that submitted the initiative or referendum petitions and to the secretary of state.

19-121.03. Judicial review of actions by county recorder; venue

A. If the county recorder fails or refuses to comply with the provisions of section 19-121.02, any citizen may apply, within ten calendar days after such failure or refusal, to the superior court for a writ of mandamus. If the court finds that the county recorder has not complied with the provisions of section 19-121.02, the court shall issue an order for the county recorder to comply.

B. Any citizen may challenge in the superior court the certification made by a county recorder pursuant to section 19-121.02 within ten calendar days of the receipt thereof by the secretary of state. The action shall be advanced on the calendar and heard as a trial de novo and decided by the court as soon as possible. Either party may appeal to the supreme court within ten calendar days after judgment.

C. An action commenced under this section shall be brought in the county of such recorder, except that any such action involving more than one recorder shall be brought in Maricopa county.

19-121.04. Disposition of petitions by secretary of state

A. Within forty-eight hours, excluding Saturdays, Sundays and other legal holidays, after receipt of the facsimile signature sheets and the certification of each county recorder, the secretary of state shall determine the total number of valid signatures by subtracting from the total number of eligible signatures determined pursuant to section 19-121.01, subsection A, paragraph 6 in the following order:

1. All signatures on petitions containing a defective circulator's affidavit.

2. All signatures that were found ineligible by the county recorders and that were not subtracted pursuant to paragraph 1 of this subsection.

3. After determining the percentage of all signatures found to be invalid in the random sample, a like percentage from those signatures remaining after the subtractions performed pursuant to paragraphs 1 and 2 of this subsection.

B. If the actual number of signatures after certification pursuant to subsection C of this section on the remaining sheets after any such subtraction equals or exceeds the minimum number required by the constitution or if the number of valid signatures as projected from the random sample pursuant to subsection A of this section is at least one hundred five percent of the minimum number required by the constitution, the secretary of state shall issue the following receipt to the person or organization that submitted them: _____ signature pages bearing _____ signatures for initiative (referendum) petition serial number _____ have been refused for filing in this office because the person circulating them was a county recorder or justice of the peace at the time of circulating the petition or due to defects in the circulator's affidavit. A total of _____ signatures included on the remaining petition sheets were found to be ineligible. Of the total random sample of _____ signatures, a total of _____ signatures were invalidated by the county recorders resulting in a failure rate of _____ percent. The actual number of remaining signatures for such initiative (referendum) petition number _____ are equal to or in excess of the minimum required by the constitution to place a measure on the general election ballot. The number of valid signatures filed with this petition, based on the random sample, appears to be at least one hundred five percent of the minimum required or through examination of each signature has been certified to be greater than the minimum required by the constitution.

The secretary of state shall then forthwith notify the governor that a sufficient number of signatures has been filed and that the initiative or referendum shall be placed on the ballot in the manner provided by law.

C. If the number of valid signatures as projected from the random sample is less than one hundred five but greater than ninety-five per cent of the minimum number required by the constitution, then the secretary of state shall order the examination and verification of each signature filed and shall so notify the county recorders. The county recorder's certification shall be in the form prescribed by the secretary of state.

D. If the number of valid signatures as projected from the random sample is less than ninety-five per cent of the minimum number required by the constitution or if the actual number of signatures on the remaining sheets after any such subtraction from the random sample or after certification fails to equal or exceed the minimum required by the constitution, the secretary of state shall immediately return the original signature sheets, in the form filed by him under section 19-121, to the person or organization that submitted them, together with a certified statement that, for the following reasons, the petition lacks the minimum number of signatures to place it on the general election ballot:

1. Signature sheets bearing secretary of state page numbers _____ and bearing signatures of _____ persons appeared on petitions containing a defective circulator's affidavit.

2. A total of signatures on the remaining petition sheets were found to be ineligible.

3. A total of signatures included in the random sample have been certified by the county recorders as ineligible at the time such petition was signed and a projection from such random sample has indicated that _____ more signatures are ineligible to appear on the petition. A facsimile of the certifications of the county recorders under section 19-121.02 shall accompany the signature sheets returned to the person or organization that submitted them.

19-121.05. Special fund for reimbursement of county recorders

A. The secretary of state shall establish a separate fund from which he shall reimburse a county recorder for actual expenses incurred by the county recorder for performance of his duties under the provisions of section 19-121.02, but not to exceed the rate of fifty cents per signature.

B. A county recorder who claims to be entitled to reimbursement under the provisions of this section shall submit a claim therefor to the secretary of state.

C. The special fund established under the provisions of this section shall be exempt from the provisions of section 35-190 relating to lapsing of appropriations.

19-122. Refusal of secretary of state to file petition or transmit facsimiles of signature sheets or affidavits of circulators; writ of mandamus; venue

A. If the secretary of state refuses to accept and file a petition for the initiative or referendum, or proposal for a constitutional amendment which has been presented within the time prescribed, or if he refuses to transmit the facsimiles of a signature sheet or sheets or affidavits of circulators to the county recorders for certification under section 19-121.01, he shall provide the person who submitted the petition, proposal, signature sheet or affidavit with a written statement of the reason for the refusal. Within ten calendar days after the refusal any citizen may apply to the superior court for a writ of mandamus to compel the secretary of state to file the petition or proposal or transmit the facsimiles, or the citizen may file a complaint with the county attorney or attorney general. The county attorney or attorney general may apply, within ten calendar days after the complaint is made, to the superior court for a writ of mandamus to compel the secretary of state to file the petition or proposal or transmit the facsimiles. The action shall be advanced on the calendar and heard and decided by the court as soon as possible. Either party may appeal to the supreme court within ten calendar days after judgment. If the court finds that the petition is legally sufficient, the secretary of state shall then file it, with a certified copy of the judgment attached as of the date on which it was originally offered for filing in his office.

B. The most current version of the general county register at the time of filing a court action challenging an initiative or referendum petition shall constitute the official record to be used to determine on a prima facie basis by the challenger that the signer of a petition was not registered to vote at the address given on the date of signing the petition. If the address of the signer given on the date of signing the petition is different from that on the most current version of the general county register, the county recorder shall examine the version of the general county register which was current on the date the signer signed the petition to determine the validity of the signature. This subsection does not preclude introducing into evidence a certified copy of the affidavit or registration of any signer dated prior to the signing of the petition if the affidavit is in the possession of the county recorder but has not yet been filed in the general county register.

C. Notwithstanding section 19-121.04, if any petition filed is not legally sufficient, the court may, in an action brought by any citizen, enjoin the secretary or other officers from certifying or printing on the official ballot for the ensuing election the amendment or measure proposed or referred. The action shall be advanced on the calendar and heard and decided by the court as soon as possible. Either party may appeal to the supreme court within ten days after judgment.

D. The superior court in Maricopa county shall have jurisdiction of actions relating to measures and amendments to be submitted to the electors of the state at large. With respect to actions relating to local and special measures, the superior court in the county, or in one of the counties, in which the measures are to be voted upon shall have jurisdiction.

19-123. Publicity pamphlet; printing; distribution; public hearings

A. When the secretary of state is ordered by the legislature, or by petition under the initiative and referendum provisions of the constitution, to submit to the people a measure or proposed amendment to the constitution, the secretary of state shall cause to be printed, at the expense of the state, except as otherwise provided in this article, a publicity pamphlet, which shall contain:

1. A true copy of the title and text of the measure or proposed amendment. Such text shall indicate material deleted, if any, by printing such material with a line drawn through the center of the letters of such material and shall indicate material added or new material by printing the letters of such material in capital letters.

2. The form in which the measure or proposed amendment will appear on the ballot, the official title, the descriptive title prepared by the secretary of state and the number by which it will be designated.

3. The arguments for and against the measure or amendment.

4. For any measure or proposed amendment, a legislative council analysis of the ballot proposal as prescribed by section 19-124.

5. The report of the commission on judicial performance review for any justices of the supreme court, judges of the court of appeals and judges of the superior court who are subject to retention.

6. The summary of a fiscal impact statement prepared by the joint legislative budget committee staff pursuant to subsection D of this section.

B. The secretary of state shall mail one copy of the publicity pamphlet to every household that contains a registered voter. The mailings may be made over a period of days but shall be mailed in order to be delivered to households before the earliest date for receipt by registered voters of any requested early ballots for the general election.

C. Sample ballots for both the primary and general elections shall include a statement that information on how to obtain a publicity pamphlet for the general election ballot propositions is available by calling the secretary of state. The statement shall include a telephone number and mailing address of the secretary of state.

D. On certification of an initiative measure as qualified for the ballot, the secretary of state shall hold or cause to be held at least three public meetings on the ballot measure. Hearings shall be held in at least three different counties and shall be held before the date of the election on the measure. The hearings shall provide an opportunity for proponents, opponents and the general public to provide testimony and request information. Hearings may be scheduled to include more than one qualified ballot measure and shall include a fiscal impact presentation on the measure by the joint legislative budget committee staff. The joint legislative budget committee staff shall prepare a summary of the fiscal impact for each ballot measure, not to exceed three hundred words, for publication in the publicity pamphlet.

19-124. Arguments and analyses on measures; cost; submission at special election

A. The person filing an initiative petition may at the same time file with the secretary of state an argument advocating the measure or constitutional amendment proposed in the petition. Not later than sixty days preceding the regular primary election a person may file with the secretary of state an argument advocating or opposing the measure or constitutional amendment proposed in the petition. Not later than sixty days preceding the regular primary election a person may file with the secretary of state an argument advocating or opposing any measure with respect to which the referendum has been invoked, or any measure or constitutional amendment referred by the legislature. Each argument filed shall contain the original signature of each person sponsoring it. If the argument is sponsored by an organization, it shall be signed by two executive officers thereof or if sponsored by a political committee it shall be signed by the committee's chairman or treasurer. Payment of the deposit required by subsection D or reimbursement of the payor constitutes sponsorship of the argument for purposes of this subsection. The person or persons signing the argument shall identify themselves by giving their residence or post office address and a telephone number, which information shall not appear in the publicity pamphlet. Each argument filed pursuant to this subsection shall not exceed three hundred words in length.

B. Not later than sixty days preceding the regular primary election the legislative council, after providing reasonable opportunity for comments by all legislators, shall prepare and file with the secretary of state an impartial analysis of the provisions of each ballot proposal of a measure or proposed amendment. The analysis shall include a description of the measure and shall be written in clear and concise terms avoiding technical terms wherever possible. The analysis may contain background information, including the effect of the measure on existing law, or any legislative enactment suspended by referendum, if the measure or referendum is approved or rejected.

C. The analyses and arguments shall be included in the publicity pamphlet immediately following the measure or amendment to which they refer. Arguments in the affirmative shall be placed first in order, and first among the affirmative or negative arguments shall be placed the arguments filed by the person filing the initiative petition or the person who introduced the measure or constitutional amendment referred. The remaining affirmative and negative arguments shall be placed in the order in which they were filed with the secretary of state.

D. The person filing an argument shall deposit with the secretary of state, at the time of filing, an amount of money as prescribed by the secretary of state for the purpose of offsetting a portion of the proportionate cost of the paper and printing of the argument. If the person filing an argument requests that the argument appear in connection with more than one proposition, a deposit shall be made for each placement requested. No such deposit or payment shall be required for the analyses prepared and filed by the legislative council. Any proportional balance remaining of the deposit, after paying the cost, shall be returned to the depositor.

E. When a measure is submitted at a special election, and time will not permit full compliance with the provisions of this article, the charter provision or ordinance providing for the special election shall make provision for printing and distribution of the publicity pamphlet.

F. In the case of referendum petitions that are not required to be filed until after the primary election or at a time so close to the primary election that a referendum cannot be certified for the ballot before the deadline for filing ballot arguments pursuant to subsection A, the secretary of state may establish a separate deadline for filing the referendum ballot arguments pursuant to rules adopted by the secretary of state.

19-125. Form of ballot

A. The secretary of state, at the time he transmits to the clerks of the boards of supervisors a certified copy of the name of each candidate for public office, shall transmit to each clerk a certified copy of the official title, the descriptive title and the number of each measure and proposed amendment to the constitution to be voted upon at the ensuing regular general election.

B. Proposed constitutional amendments shall be numbered consecutively beginning with the number one hundred, proposed initiative measures shall be numbered consecutively beginning with the number two hundred, measures submitted under the referendum shall be numbered consecutively beginning with the number three hundred, and county and local issues shall be numbered consecutively beginning with the number four hundred. Numbering shall be consecutive based on the order in which the initiative or referendum petitions are filed with the secretary of state. Proposed constitutional amendments shall be placed by themselves at the head of the ballot column, followed by initiated and referred measures in that order.

C. The officer in charge of elections shall print the official title, the descriptive title and the number of each measure upon the official ballot in the order presented to him by the secretary of state unless otherwise provided by law. The number of the measure shall be in reverse type and at least twelve point type. A proposed constitutional amendment shall be designated "proposed amendment to the constitution by the legislature", or "proposed amendment to the constitution by the initiative", as the case may be. A measure referred by the legislature shall be designated "referred to the people by the legislature", a measure referred by petition shall be designated "referendum ordered by petition of the people" and a measure proposed by initiative petition shall be designated "proposed by initiative petition".

D. There shall be printed on the official ballot immediately below the number of the measure and the official title of each measure a descriptive title containing a summary of the principal provisions of the measure, not to exceed fifty words, which shall be prepared by the secretary of state and approved by the attorney general or the ballot shall comply with subsection E of this section:

A "yes" vote shall have the effect of _____.

A "no" vote shall have the effect of _____.

The blank spaces shall be filled with a brief phrase, approved by the attorney general, stating the essential change in the existing law should the measure receive a majority of votes cast in that particular manner. In the case of a referendum, a "yes" vote shall have the effect of approving the legislative enactment that is being referred. Below the statement of effect of a "yes" vote and effect of a "no" vote there shall be printed the corresponding words "yes" and "no" and a place for the voter to put a mark as defined in section 16-400 indicating his preference.

E. Instead of printing the official and descriptive titles or the full text of each measure or question on the official ballot, the officer in charge of elections may print phrases on the official ballot that contain all of the following:

1. The number of the measure in reverse type and at least twelve point type.

2. The designation of the measure as prescribed by subsection C of this section or as a question, proposition or charter amendment, followed by the words "relating to…" and inserting the subject.

3. Either the statement prescribed by subsection D of this section that describes the effects of a "yes" vote and a "no" vote or, for other measures, the text of the question or proposition.

4. The words "yes" and "no" or "for" and "against", as may be appropriate and a place for the voter to put a mark.

F. For any ballot printed pursuant to subsection E of this section, the instructions on the official ballot shall direct the voter to the full text of the official and descriptive titles and the questions and propositions as printed on the sample ballot and posted in the polling place.

19-126. Counting and canvassing votes; governor's proclamation

A. The votes on measures and proposed constitutional amendments shall be counted, canvassed and returned by the officers of the election boards as votes for candidates are counted, canvassed and returned, and the abstract made by the clerks of the boards of supervisors of the several counties of votes on measures and proposed constitutional amendments shall be returned to the secretary of state on separate abstract sheets in the manner provided by law. The total vote shall then be canvassed and proclamation of the results made in the manner prescribed by the constitution.

B. If two or more conflicting measures or amendments are approved at the same election, the governor shall proclaim which of the measures or amendments received the greatest number of affirmative votes.

19-127. Preservation and publication of approved measures

A. If a measure or proposed constitutional amendment, at the ensuing election, is approved by the people, the preserved copies with the sheets, signatures and affidavits, and a certified copy of the governor's proclamation declaring them to have been approved by the people, shall be bound together in such form that they may be conveniently identified and preserved.

B. The secretary of state shall cause every measure or constitutional amendment submitted under the initiative and approved by the people to be printed with the general laws enacted by the next ensuing session of the legislature, with the date of the governor's proclamation declaring them to have been approved by the people.

19-128. Campaign literature and advertising funding; identification; disclosure; civil penalty; violation; classification; definitions

A. A political committee that makes an expenditure in connection with any literature or advertisement to support or oppose a ballot proposition shall disclose in such literature or advertisement the four largest of its major funding sources. If a political committee has fewer than four major funding sources, the committee shall disclose all major funding sources.

B. For purposes of this section, a major funding source of a political committee is:

1. An industry that is both the largest industry contributor to the committee and whose combined contributions to the committee are five hundred thousand dollars or more, or are fifty thousand dollars or more and constitute twenty-five per cent or more of all contributions, or for political subdivisions with a population of one hundred thousand or more persons, are fifty thousand dollars or more, or are five thousand dollars or more and constitute twenty-five per cent or more of all contributions, or for political subdivisions with a population of less than one hundred thousand persons are ten thousand dollars or more, or are one thousand dollars or more and constitute twenty-five per cent or more of all contributions.

2. A person whose contributions to the committee are fifty thousand dollars or more, or for political subdivisions with a population of one hundred thousand or more persons are ten thousand dollars or more, or for political subdivisions with a population of less than one hundred thousand persons are two thousand dollars or more.

3. Corporations as a group or unions as a group if their combined contributions to the committee are fifty thousand dollars or more, or for political subdivisions with a population of one hundred thousand or more persons are ten thousand dollars or more, or for political subdivisions with a population of less than one hundred thousand persons are two thousand dollars or more.

4. Out-of-state contributions as a group, if their combined contributions to the committee are fifty thousand dollars or more, or for political subdivisions with a population of one hundred thousand or more persons are ten thousand dollars or more, or for political subdivisions with a population of less than one hundred thousand persons are two thousand dollars or more.

5. Contributions by corporations as a group, unions as a group, industries or persons to more than one political committee in support of or opposition to the same ballot proposition if the cumulative total of these contributions in support of or opposition to the ballot proposition would qualify as a major funding source if made to a single political committee.

C. A political committee that receives at least fifteen thousand individual contributions of between five and fifty dollars each may describe these contributions as a group and disclose the group as a major funding source in addition to those funding sources required to be disclosed pursuant to this section.

D. Corporations as a group, unions as a group, industries or persons that make contributions to more than one political committee that supports or opposes the same ballot proposition shall notify each political committee of the cumulative total of these contributions. Cumulative totals must be disclosed by each political committee that received contributions from the same contributor if the cumulative totals qualify as a major funding source to be disclosed pursuant to subsection A.

E. Any disclosure statement required by this section shall be printed clearly and legibly in a conspicuous manner in type at least as large as the majority of the printed text. If the communication is broadcast on radio, the information shall be spoken at the end of the communication. If the communication is broadcast on a telecommunications system, the information shall be both written and spoken at the end of the communication, except that if the disclosure statement is written for at least five seconds of a thirty second advertisement broadcast or ten seconds of a sixty second advertisement broadcast, a spoken disclosure statement is not required. If the communication is broadcast on a telecommunications system, the written disclosure statement shall be printed in letters equal to or larger than four per cent of the vertical picture height.

F. Subsection A does not apply to bumper stickers, pins, buttons, pens and similar small items on which the statements required in subsection A cannot be conveniently printed or to a communication by an organization solely to its members.

G. A committee shall change future literature and advertisements to reflect any change in funding sources that must be disclosed pursuant to subsection A.

H. This section only applies to advertisements the contents of which are more than fifty per cent devoted to one or more ballot propositions or proposed measures on the same subject.

I. Any committee that violates this section is liable in a civil action brought by the attorney general, county attorney or city or town attorney, as appropriate, or by any other person for a civil penalty of three times the total cost of the advertisement, except that a committee is not liable for a violation of subsection D regarding cumulative totals if its donors do not accurately disclose their donations. A donor who does not accurately disclose its contributions is liable for a civil penalty of three times the amount donated.

J. For purposes of this section:

1. "Advertisement" means general public advertising through the print and electronic media, signs, billboards and direct mail.

2. "Industry" means those persons who derive economic benefit from the manufacture, sale or distribution of a like or similar product, commodity or service, including professional services.

3. "Person" means any individual, business, public, private or professional corporation, limited liability corporation, company, partnership, limited partnership, firm, association, society or other organization or group of persons acting in concert.

4. "Population" means the population determined according to the most recent United States decennial census.

19-129. Destroying, suppressing or filing false initiative or referendum petition; classification

A person filing an initiative or referendum petition or measure who, at the time of filing the petition or measure, knows it is falsely made, or who knowingly destroys or suppresses an initiative or referendum petition or measure, or any part thereof, which has been duly filed with the officers of the state, or of any political subdivisions thereof, as provided by this chapter, is guilty of a class 1 misdemeanor.

19-141. Initiative and referendum in counties, cities and towns

A. The provisions of this chapter shall apply to the legislation of cities, towns and counties, except as specifically provided to the contrary in this article. The duties required of the secretary of state as to state legislation shall be performed in connection with such legislation by the city or town clerk, county officer in charge of elections or person performing the duties as such. The duties required of the governor shall be performed by the mayor or the chairman of the board of supervisors, the duties required of the attorney general shall be performed by the city, town or county attorney, and the printing and binding of measures and arguments shall be paid for by the city, town or county in like manner as payment is provided for by the state with respect to state legislation. The provisions of section 19-124 with respect to the legislative council analysis do not apply in connection with initiatives and referenda in cities, towns and counties. The printing shall be done in the same manner as other municipal or county printing is done. Distribution of pamphlets shall be made to every household containing a registered voter in the city or county, so far as possible, by the city or town clerk or by the county officer in charge of elections either by mail or carrier, not less than ten days before the election at which the measures are to be voted upon.

B. Arguments supporting or opposing municipal or county initiative and referendum measures shall be filed with the city or town clerk or the county officer in charge of elections not less than sixty days before the election at which they are to be voted upon.

C. The procedure with respect to municipal and county legislation shall be as nearly as practicable the same as the procedure relating to initiative and referendum provided for the state at large, except the procedure for verifying signatures on initiative or referendum petitions may be established by a city or town by charter or ordinance.

D. References in this section to duties to be performed by city or town officers apply only with respect to municipal legislation, and references to duties to be performed by county officers apply only with respect to county legislation.

E. The duties required of the county recorder with respect to state legislation shall also be performed by the county recorder with respect to municipal or county legislation.

19-142. Referendum petitions against municipal actions; emergency measures; zoning actions

A. The whole number of votes cast at the city or town election at which a mayor or councilmen were chosen last preceding the submission of the application for a referendum petition against an ordinance, franchise or resolution shall be the basis on which the number of electors of the city or town required to file a referendum petition shall be computed. The petition shall be filed with the city or town clerk within thirty days after passage of the ordinance, resolution or franchise.

B. A city or town ordinance, resolution or franchise shall not become operative until thirty days after its passage by the council and approval by the mayor, unless it is passed over the mayor's veto, and then it shall not become operative until thirty days after final approval and until certification by the clerk of the city or town of the minutes of the meeting at which the action was taken, except emergency measures necessary for the immediate preservation of the peace, health or safety of the city or town. An emergency measure shall not become immediately operative unless it states in a separate section the reason why it is necessary that it should become immediately operative, and unless it is approved by the affirmative vote of three-fourths of all the members elected to the city or town council, taken by ayes and noes, and also approved by the mayor.

C. At the time a person or organization intending to file a referendum petition against an ordinance or resolution applies for the issuance of an official number pursuant to section 19-111, the city or town clerk shall provide such person or organization with a full and correct copy of the ordinance or resolution in the form as finally adopted. If the copy of the ordinance or resolution proposed as a referendum is not available to such person or organization at the time of making application for an official number or on the same business day as the application is submitted, the thirty-day period prescribed in subsection A of this section begins on the day that the ordinance or resolution is available from the city or town clerk, and the ordinance or resolution shall not become operative until thirty days after the ordinance or resolution is available.

D. Notwithstanding subsection C of this section, a person or organization may file a referendum petition against the rezoning of a parcel of property on the approval by the city or town council of the ordinance that adopts the rezoning or on the approval of that portion of the minutes of the city or town council that includes the council's approval of the rezoning, whichever occurs first. The thirty day period prescribed in subsection A of this section begins on the day that the rezoning ordinance or approved minutes or portion of the approved minutes are available from the city or town clerk and the ordinance is not operative until thirty days after the ordinance or minutes are available.

19-143. Initiative petition in cities; action of council; amendment of charter

A. The whole number of votes cast at the city or town election at which a mayor or councilman was chosen last preceding the submission of the application for an initiative petition is the basis for computing the number of qualified electors of the city or town required to sign the petition unless the city or town by charter or ordinance provides an alternative basis for computing the number of necessary signatures.

B. If an ordinance, charter or amendment to the charter of a city or town is proposed by initiative petition, it shall be filed with the city or town clerk, who shall submit it to the voters of the city or town at the next ensuing election. The council may enact the ordinance or amendment and refer it to the people or it may enact the ordinance or amendment without referring it to the people, and in that case it is subject to referendum petition as other ordinances. The mayor shall not have power to veto either of such measures.

C. Amendments to a city or town charter may be proposed and submitted to the people by the council, with or without an initiative petition, but they shall be filed with the clerk for submission not less than sixty days before the election at which they are to be voted upon, and no amendment of a charter shall be effective until it is approved by a majority of the votes cast thereon by the people of the city or town to which it applies. The council may by ordinance order special elections to vote on municipal measures.

The Basic Steps to Do an Initiative in Arizona

Statutes and Amendments — Direct Initiative Process

Basic Procedures: As soon as proponents file their application with the full text of the initiative attached and file their Statement of Organization (to adhere to the state's campaign finance regulations), they can begin circulating. Petitions must contain the full text of the initiative, along with a displayed serial number (given to them when they file their initiative). The Secretary of State (SOS) does not review or approve the language; nor does the SOS set a ballot title or summary at this time—they only need the initiative text to be filed with them before circulation can begin.

Date Initiative language can be submitted to state for 2002: Any time after even year general elections. (Anytime after July 6, 2000 for the 2002 general election.)

Signatures are tied to vote of which office: Governor

Next Gubernatorial election: 2002

Votes cast for governor in last election: 1,017,616

Net number of signatures required: For statute—10% of votes cast for governor (101,762). For constitutional amendment—15% (152,643)

Distribution Requirement: None

Circulation period: Two years or less. (Proponents have from July 6, 2000 to July 4, 2002.)

Do circulators have to be residents: Yes

Date when signatures are due for certification: July 4, 2002

Signature verification process: Random Sampling.

Single-subject restriction: Arizona has a single subject requirement.

Legislative tampering: The legislature cannot repeal an initiative—but they can amend an initiative if amending legislation furthers the purposes of such measure and at least three-fourths of the members of each house of the legislature, by a roll call of ayes and nays, vote to amend such measure.

General Comments: When proponents turn in all the petitions, the signatures are verified. If the measure qualifies and is certified for the ballot, then the Secretary of State sets the ballot title and summary. (It generally takes a month to verify the signatures. The SOS sets the ballot title and summary shortly thereafter.) The Secretary of State will take a suggested draft of ballot language from proponents, once all the petitions are turned in. If the proponent's language is objective enough, the SOS may use it—but they are not obligated to. Once the SOS sets the ballot title and summary, they forward it to the Attorney General for final approval. There is no statutory appeals process. If proponents (or opponents) don't like the final ballot language, there is nothing they can do—except bring a lawsuit against the Secretary of State. But unless the Secretary of State is grossly derelict in its duty in writing the ballot language, the Secretary of State will likely win.

The person filing an initiative may at the same time file with the Secretary of State an argument advocating the measure or constitutional amendment proposed in the petition. No later than sixty days preceding the regular primary election a person may file with the secretary of state an argument advocating or opposing the measure or constitutional amendment proposed in the petition.

No later than sixty days preceding the regular primary election the Legislative Council, after providing reasonable opportunity for comments by all legislators, shall prepare and file with the secretary of state an impartial analysis of the provisions of each ballot proposal of a measure or proposed amendment. The analysis shall include a description of the measure and shall be written in clear and concise terms avoiding technical terms wherever possible. The analysis may contain background information, including the effect of the measure on existing law, or any legislative enactment suspended by referendum, if the measure or referendum is approved or rejected.

The analyses and arguments will be included in the voter guides.

After certification, the secretary of state will hold at least three public hearings on the ballot measures. Hearings must be held in at least three different counties and must provide an opportunity for proponents, opponents and the general public to provide testimony and request information.

Arkansas

The Arkansas Populist Party endorsed initiative and referendum in its 1896 state platform, and the Democrats followed suit in 1898. But it was not until a decade later that the Democrat George W. Donaghey won election as governor and, in 1909, successfully shepherded an I&R amendment through the legislature. It won voter ratification on September 5, 1910.

Out-of-state Progressive movement leaders had flocked into Arkansas during the summer to popularize the amendment. George Judson King of Ohio set up a press bureau to provide newspapers with pro-I&R information. William Jennings Bryan and Governor Donaghey made a whistle-stop tour of the state in a specially chartered train. In five days they covered 1,750 miles and gave 55 speeches to between 75,000 and 100,000 people. The presidents of the state Farmers Union and Federation of Labor were on board to urge their members to support I&R. On Election Day, voters approved I&R by a greater than two to one margin.

In 1912, seven initiatives qualified for the ballot, of which three passed: one limiting the legislature's session and members' salaries; a second providing for recall of elected officers; and a third authorizing cities and towns to issue bonds for public works. Opponents of the successful initiatives went to court to overturn them on legal technicalities, and the Arkansas state supreme court encouraged such challenges with a series of decisions that chipped away at Arkansas voters' rights to self-government, beginning with the recall and bond initiative votes. I&R supporters fought back with an initiative to strengthen I&R procedures, only to see it lose with a frustratingly close 48.6 percent of the vote. They tried again by writing I&R provisions into a new constitution proposed by a state constitutional convention in 1917-1918, but that lost also. They tried a third time in 1920 with an initiative that won the popular vote but lost in court on a legal technicality, and the voters rejected a fourth initiative in 1922.

Unexpected salvation for I&R advocates came in 1925, when the state supreme court reversed its decision on the 1920 technicality (Brickhouse v. Hill, 167 Ark. 513 [1925]). Meanwhile, the state Federation of Labor won approval of an initiative prohibiting child labor (1914), and the local bond authority initiative won on a second try in 1918. In 1926 voters approved an initiative to consolidate their state and federal elections, which had been held on different dates.

Like the legislatures of other southern states, voters in Arkansas enacted several regressive measures: a 1928 initiative to ban the teaching of evolution in the schools; a 1930 law to require Bible-reading in the schools; and a 1956 initiative requiring the legislature to use any constitutional means to block school integration. The last won with 56 percent of the vote, thus supporting the segregationist policy of Governor Orval Faubus.

In the same election, however, Arkansans showed a liberal streak by approving, by a nearly three to one margin, an initiative to increase workmen's compensation (a previous initiative had authorized workmen's compensation in 1938). In 1964 they voted by a 56 percent majority to abolish the state's poll tax, which was another liberal move.

Numerous other high profile initiatives were adopted in the state — term limits in 1992 and campaign finance reform in 1996. Also during the 1990s a tax activist by the name of Oscar Stilley attempted numerous tax related initiatives at both the state and local levels. However, many of his initiatives were struck off the ballot by the state supreme court on technicalities.

Statewide Initiative Usage

Number of Initiatives	Number Passed	Number Failed	Passage Rate
113	53	60	47%

Statewide Initiatives

Year	Measure Number	Type	Subject Matter	Description	Pass/Fail
1912	N/A	DS	Education	Free textbooks.	Failed
1912	N/A	DA	Administration of Government	Mileage and per diem, legislature sixty-day session.	Passed
1912	N/A	DA	Election Reform	Recall of elective officers.	Passed
1912	N/A	DA	Administration of Government	Cities and towns can issue bonds.	Passed
1912	N/A	DS	Election Reform	Bipartisan election boards.	Failed
1912	N/A	DS	Alcohol Regulation	Providing for statewide prohibition.	Failed
1914	N/A	DS	Labor	Prohibiting child labor.	Passed
1914	N/A	DA	Administration of Government	Cities and towns issue bonds for improvements.	Passed
1916	N/A	DA	Initiative and Referendum	Initiative and referendum more fully defined.	Failed
1916	N/A	DA	Taxes	Twelve-mill district school tax.	Passed
1916	N/A	DS	Election Reform	New primary laws.	Passed
1918	N/A	DA	Administration of Government	Allow for municipal improvement bonds.	Passed
1920	N/A	DA	Initiative and Referendum	Initiative and referendum better defined.	Passed
1922	N/A	DA	Initiative and Referendum	Initiative and referendum more fully defined.	Failed
1922	N/A	DA	Taxes	To increase school revenues.	Failed
1926	N/A	DS	Election Reform	A measure for consolidation of elections (state and national).	Passed
1926	N/A	DA	Bonds	To allow for municipal improvement bonds.	Passed
1926	N/A	DA	Administration of Government	To prohibit local acts by legislature.	Passed
1928	N/A	DA	Taxes	Tax to aid factories, industries and transportation facilities.	Passed
1928	N/A	DS	Education	Ban the teaching of evolution in schools.	Passed
1930	N/A	DS	Education	To require reading of Bibles in public schools.	Passed
1930	N/A	DA	Unknown	There is no information available at this time. However, the state claims that this initiative appeared on the ballot but state records have been destroyed.	Failed
1930	N/A	DA	Unknown	There is no information available at this time. However, the state claims that this initiative appeared on the ballot but state records have been destroyed.	Failed
1930	N/A	DA	Unknown	There is no information available at this time. However, the state claims that this initiative appeared on the ballot but state records have been destroyed.	Failed
1930	N/A	DA	Unknown	There is no information available at this time. However, the state claims that this initiative appeared on the ballot but state records have been destroyed.	Failed
1930	N/A	DA	Unknown	There is no information available at this time. However, the state claims that this initiative appeared on the ballot but state records have been destroyed.	Failed
1930	N/A	DA	Unknown	There is no information available at this time. However, the state claims that this initiative appeared on the ballot but state records have been destroyed.	Failed

Year	Measure Number	Type	Subject Matter	Description	Pass/Fail
1932	N/A	DS	Administration of Government	To set up a budget system.	Failed
1932	N/A	DS	Taxes	Supplementary act to proposed amendment for a sales tax.	Failed
1932	N/A	DA	Taxes	To reduce state property tax to 1/2 a mill and substituting a sales tax of one per cent.	Failed
1932	N/A	DS	Administration of Government	To give the organization of the minority party (Republican) the power to name its representatives on the election boards and commissions.	Failed
1932	N/A	DA	Education	To require the legislature to appropriate $6 per capita of the school population for the public schools and an additional sum to be arrived at by arithmetical calculation.	Failed
1932	N/A	DA	Taxes	To exempt homesteads (forty acres in the County, a lot fifty by one hundred and fifty in the cities) from all taxes; regardless of value.	Failed
1932	N/A	DA	Administration of Government	To provide for a split session of the legislature and a four-year term for elective state officials who were to be subject to recall.	Failed
1932	N/A	DA	Bonds	Forbidding the issuance of any more highway or bridge bonds with few exceptions until ratified by two-thirds majority of the votes cast on the proposal	Failed
1936	N/A	DA	Apportionment/ Redistricting	To provide for the Board of Apportionment consisting of the Governor, Secretary of state and the Attorney General, to apportion representatives and senators.	Passed
1936	N/A	DA	Taxes	An amendment to provide for an exemption of homesteads from certain state taxes.	Passed
1938	27	DA	Labor	To provide the General Assembly with the power to enact laws providing for workmen's compensation.	Passed
1938	28	DS	Bonds	Highway bond refunding	Failed
1938	29	DA	Taxes	To provide for an industry tax exemption for any new manufacturing or processing establishment or for expansion of existing establishments.	Passed
1938	30	DA	Education	Establishes a State Board of Education	Failed
1938	31	DA	Judicial Reform	The Supreme Court shall make rules regulating the practice of law and the professional conduct of attorneys at law.	Passed
1938	32	DA	Administration of Government	To provide for rules for the filling of vacancies.	Passed
1938	1	DS	Prohibition	Would amend liquor laws	Failed
1940	1	DS	Business Regulation	Payment for employers of compensation for injured employees	Failed

Year	Measure Number	Type	Subject Matter	Description	Pass/Fail
1940	33	DA	Taxes	To provide for a municipal library tax to be authorized in advance by the voters.	Passed
1940	34	DA	Taxes	To provide for the collection of an annual tax on the assessed value of real and personal property from which shall be created a fund to pay retirement salaries and pensions to policemen and firemen.	Passed
1940	35	DA	Administration of Government	Game and Fish Commission.	Failed
1940	36	DA	Welfare	Relative to old age pensions.	Failed
1942	1	DS	Alcohol Regulation	Amend liquor laws, provide for better local option.	Passed
1942	34	DA	Environmental Reform	Game and Fish Commission	Failed
1942	35	DA	Administration of Government	To provide rules and regulations for boards and commissions.	Passed
1944	2	DS	Gaming	Repeals horse and dog racing	Failed
1944	3	DS	Health/Medical	Hollingsworth state hospital system	Failed
1944	34	DA	Taxes	County library tax	Failed
1944	35	DA	Labor	To provide for the right to work.	Passed
1944	36	DA	Environmental Reform	To create the Arkansas state Game and Fish Commission to control, manage, conserve and regulate the birds, fish, game, and wildlife resources of the state.	Passed
1944	37	DA	Civil Rights	To provide that any citizen of Arkansas, while serving in the armed forces of the United States, may vote in any election, without having paid poll tax, if otherwise qualified to vote.	Passed
1944	38	DA	Administration of Government	4 year term for Governor and Lieutenant Governor	Failed
1946	1	DS	Education	School district reorganization	Failed
1946	39	DA	Taxes	To provide for the levy of a tax on real and personal property for the establishment of the County library when approved in advance by qualified electors.	Passed
1948	1	DS	Education	Reorganization of school districts	Passed
1948	2	DS	Alcohol Regulation	Amend liquor laws regarding local option elections.	Failed
1948	3	DS	Election Reform	Provides for direct political party response in holding of all general elections	Passed
1948	4	DS	Labor	Amend workmen's compensation	Passed
1948	41	DA	Taxes	Abolition of state property tax	Failed
1950	1	DS	Animal Rights	General statewide stock law. Unlawful for livestock to run at large	Passed
1950	2	DS	Alcohol Regulation	Statewide prohibition	Failed
1950	41	DA	Education	Public school finance	Failed
1950	44	DA	Administration of Government	4 year term for state and County officers	Failed
1956	1	DS	Labor	To increase Workmen's Compensation.	Passed
1956	2	DS	Education	School pupil assignment law.	Passed

Year	Measure Number	Type	Subject Matter	Description	Pass/Fail
1956	45	DA	Civil Rights	Abolition of poll tax	Failed
1956	46	DA	Judicial Reform	To provide the General Assembly with the authority to set by law the amount and method of payment of salaries and expenses of the Supreme Court, Circuit Courts and Chancery Courts.	Passed
1956	47	DA	Civil Rights	To cause the General Assembly to take appropriate action and pass laws opposing in every Constitutional manner the unconstitutional desegregation decisions of May 17, 1954, and May 3, 1955, of the U.S. Supreme Court.	Passed
1956	48	DA	Apportionment/ Redistricting	An amendment to preserve present apportionment of state senators and existing state senatorial districts.	Passed
1956	49	DA	Gaming	Prohibition of horse and racing betting	Failed
1956	50	DA	Gaming	To provide that horse racing and pari-mutuel wagering thereon shall be lawful in Hot Springs, Garland County, and shall be regulated by the General Assembly.	Passed
1956	51	DA	Banking Reform	Sets maximum interest rates.	Failed
1958	1	DS	Labor	Repeal full crew laws	Failed
1960	1	DS	Labor	Minimum wage and overtime act.	Failed
1962	1	DS	Education	Provide 50% of general revenues for public school fund	Failed
1962	53	DA	Education	Teacher retirement fund	Failed
1962	54	DA E	lection Reform	Permit use of voting machines	Passed
1964	54	DA	Civil Rights	To provide for voter registration system without payment of poll tax.	Passed
1964	55	DA	Gaming	Allow wagering in Garland County	Failed
1964	56	DA	Administration of Government	Establish salaries for County Officials	Failed
1964	57	DA	Education	To provide for the creation of community college districts.	Passed
1966	1	DS	Education	School district reorganization.	Failed
1968	1	DS	Labor	Amend Workmen's Compensation Law	Passed
1970	1	DS	Labor	An Act to repeal the Full Crew Laws.	Failed
1972	1	DS	Labor	An Act to repeal railroad crew laws and to protect present employees.	Passed
1974	57	DA	Banking Reform	Authorize legislature to fix maximum rate of interest.	Failed
1976	59	DA	Labor	Rights of Labor amendment.	Failed
1978	59	DA	Taxes	Food and medicine sales tax exemptions.	Failed
1980	1	DS	Education	Equal education for all children in the state.	Failed
1980	60	DA	Banking Reform	Maximum rate of interest controlled by 2/3 vote of legislature.	Failed
1984	64	DA	Term Limits	Four year terms for state constitutional officers.	Passed
1984	66	DA	Gaming	Authorize gambling in Garland County.	Failed
1984	67	DA	Administration of Government	Sales/use tax for Fish and Game Commission.	Failed

Year	Measure Number	Type	Subject Matter	Description	Pass/Fail
1986	65	DA	Abortion	Limit public funding of abortion.	Failed
1986	66	DA	Administration of Government	Four year terms for elected County officials.	Failed
1986	67	DA	Taxes	Issuance of revenue bonds without election.	Passed
1988	1	DS	Campaign Finance Reform	Conduct and disclosure act — lobbyist, state officials.	Passed
1988	3	DA	Abortion	Prevent abortion funding and restrict abortion.	Passed
1988	4	DA	Taxes	Repeal property tax on household goods.	Failed
1990	1	DS	Campaign Finance Reform	Conduct and disclosure act — candidates and campaigns.	Passed
1992	4	DA	Term Limits	Term limits. State legislature 6/8. Congress 6/12.	Passed
1996	1	DS	Campaign Finance Reform	Establish campaign finance regulations.	Passed
1996	4	DA	Gaming	Would establish a state lottery; permit charitable bingo and raffles, provide for a local vote in Hot Springs concerning casino gambling.	Failed
1996	9	DA	Term Limits	Term limits on state legislature 6/8, Governor, and Congress 6/12.	Passed
2000	1	DS	Health/Medical	Will designate how the tobacco settlement proceeds are dedicated.	Passed
2000	5	DA	Gaming	An amendment to establish a state lottery; to permit charitable bingo games and raffles; to allow Arkansas Casino Corporation to own and operate six casino gambling establishments.	Failed

Arkansas Constitution

Amendment 7.

Initiative and Referendum

The legislative power of the people of this State shall be vested in a General Assembly, which shall consist of the Senate and House of Representatives, but the people reserve to themselves the power to propose legislative measures, laws and amendments to the Constitution, and to enact or reject the same at the polls independent of the General Assembly; and also reserve the power, at their own option, to approve or reject at the polls any entire act or any item of an appropriation bill.

State-wide Petitions

Initiative — The first power reserved by the people is the initiative. Eight percent of the legal voters may propose any law and ten per cent may propose a Constitutional Amendment by initiative petition, and every such petition shall include the full text of the measure so proposed. Initiative petitions for statewide measures shall be filed with the Secretary of State not less than four months before the election at which they are to be voted upon; provided, that at least thirty days before the aforementioned filing, the proposed measure shall have been published once, at the expense of the petitioners, in some paper of general circulation.

Referendum — The second power reserved by the people is the referendum, and any number not less than six per cent of the legal voters may, by petition, order the referendum against any general act, or any item of an appropriation bill, or measure passed by the General Assembly, but the filing of a referendum petition against one or more items, sections or parts of any such act or measure shall not delay the remainder from becoming operative. Such petition shall be filed with the Secretary of State not later than ninety days after the final adjournment of the session at which such act was passed, except when a recess or adjournment shall be taken temporarily for a longer period than ninety days, in which case such petition shall be filed not later than ninety days after such recess or temporary adjournment. Any measure referred to the people by referendum petition shall remain in abeyance until such vote is taken. The total number of votes cast for the office of Governor in the last preceding general election shall be the basis upon which the number of signatures of legal voters upon statewide initiative and referendum petitions shall be computed.

Upon all initiative or referendum petitions provided for in any of the sections of this article, it shall be necessary to file, from at least fifteen of the counties of the State, petitions bearing the signature of not less than one-half of the designated percentage of the electors of such county.

Emergency—If it shall be necessary for the preservation of the public peace, health and safety that a measure shall become effective without delay, such necessity shall be stated in one section, and if upon a yea and nay vote two-thirds of all the members elected to each house, or two-thirds of all the members elected to city or town councils, shall vote upon separate roll call in favor of the measure going into immediate operation, such emergency measure shall become effective without delay. It shall be necessary, however, to state the fact which constitutes such emergency. Provided, however, that an emergency shall not be declared on any franchise or special privilege or act creating any vested right or interest or alienating any property of the State. If a referendum is filed against any emergency measure such measure shall be a law until it is voted upon by the people, and if it is then rejected by a majority of the electors voting thereon, it shall be thereby repealed. The provisions of this subsection shall apply to city or town councils.

Local Petitions

Municipalities and Counties—The initiative and referendum powers of the people are hereby further reserved to the local voters of each municipality and county as to all local, special and municipal legislation of every character in and for their respective municipalities and counties, but no local legislation shall be enacted contrary to the Constitution or any general law of the State, and any general law shall have the effect of repealing any local legislation which is in conflict therewith.

Municipalities may provide for the exercise of the initiative and referendum as to their legal legislation.

General laws shall be enacted providing for the exercise of the initiative and referendum as to counties. Fifteen per cent of the legal voters of any municipality or county may order the referendum, or invoke the initiative upon any local measures. In municipalities the number of signatures required upon any petition shall be computed upon the total vote cast for the office of mayor at the last preceding general election; in counties, upon the office of Circuit Clerk. In municipalities and counties the time for filing an initiative petition shall not be fixed at less than sixty days nor more than ninety days before the election at which it is to be voted upon; for a referendum petition at not less than thirty days nor more than ninety days after the passage of such measure by a municipal council; nor less than ninety days when filed against a local or special measure passed by the General Assembly.

Every extension, enlargement, grant, or conveyance of a franchise or any rights, property, easement, lease, or occupation of or in any road, street, alley or any part thereof in real property or interest in real property owned by municipalities, exceeding in value three hundred dollars, whether the same be by statute, ordinance, resolution, or otherwise, shall be subject to referendum and shall not be subject to emergency legislation.

General Provisions

Definition—The word "measure" as used herein includes any bill, law, resolution, ordinance, charter, constitutional amendment or legislative proposal or enactment of any character.

No Veto—The veto power of the Governor or Mayor shall not extend to measures initiated by or referred to the people.

Amendment and Repeal—No measure approved by a vote of the people shall be amended or repealed by the General Assembly or by any City Council, except upon a yea and nay vote on roll call of two-thirds of all the members elected to each house of the General Assembly, or of the City Council, as the case may be.

Election—All measures initiated by the people, whether for the State, county, city or town, shall be submitted only at the regular elections, either State, congressional or municipal, but referendum petitions may be referred to the people at special elections to be called by the proper official, and such special elections shall be called when fifteen per cent of the legal voters shall petition for such special election, and if the referendum is invoked as to any measure passed by a city or town council, such city or town council may order a special election.

Majority—Any measure submitted to the people as herein provided shall take effect and become a law when approved by a majority of the votes cast upon such measure, and not otherwise, and shall not be required to receive a majority of the electors voting at such elections. Such measures shall be operative on and after the 30th day after the election at which it is approved, unless otherwise specified in the act.

This section shall not be construed to deprive any member of the General Assembly of the right to introduce any measure, but no measure shall be submitted to the people by the General Assembly, except a proposed constitutional amendment or amendments as provided for in this Constitution.

Canvass and Declaration of Result—The result of the vote upon any State measure shall be canvassed and declared by the State Board of Election Commissioners (or legal substitute therefore); upon a municipal or county measure, by the County Election Commissioners (or legal substitute therefore).

Conflicting Measures—If conflicting measures initiated or referred to the people shall be approved by a majority of the votes severally cast for and against the same at the same election, the one receiving the highest number of affirmative votes shall become law.

The Petition

Title—At the time of filing petitions the exact title to be used on the ballot shall by the petitioner be submitted with the petition, and on State-wide measures, shall be submitted to the State Board of Election Commissioners, who shall certify such title to the Secretary of State, to be placed upon the ballot; on county and municipal measures such title shall be submitted to the County Election Board and shall by said board be placed upon the ballot in such county or municipal election.

Limitation—No limitation shall be placed upon the number of constitutional amendments, laws, or other measures which may be proposed and submitted to the people by either initiative or referendum petition as provided in this section. No petition shall be held invalid if it shall contain a greater number of signatures than required herein.

Verification—Only legal votes shall be counted upon petitions. Petitions may be circulated and presented in parts but each part of any petition shall have attached thereto, the affidavit of the persons circulating the same, that all signatures thereon were made in the presence of the affiant, and that to the best of the affiant's knowledge and belief each signature is genuine, and that the person signing is a legal voter, and no other affidavit or verification shall be required to establish the genuineness of such signatures.

Sufficiency—The sufficiency of all State-wide petitions shall be decided in the first instance by the Secretary of State, subject to review by the Supreme Court of the State, which shall have original and exclusive jurisdiction over all such causes. The sufficiency of all local petitions shall be decided in the first instance by the county clerk or the city clerk, as the case may be, subject to review by the Chancery Court.

Court Decisions—If the sufficiency of any petition is challenged such cause shall be a preference cause and shall be tried at once, but the failure of the courts to decide prior to the election as to the sufficiency of any such petition shall not prevent the question from being placed upon the ballot at the election named in such petition, nor militate against the validity of such measure, if it shall have been approved by a vote of the people.

Amendment of Petition—If the Secretary of State, county clerk or city clerk, as the case may be, shall decide any petition to be insufficient, he shall without delay notify the sponsors of such petition, and permit at least thirty days from the date of such notification, in the instance of a State-wide petition, or ten days in the instance of a municipal or county petition, for correction or amendment. In the event of legal proceedings to prevent giving legal effect to any petition upon any grounds, the burden of proof shall be upon the person or persons attacking the validity of the petition.

Unwarranted Restrictions Prohibited—No law shall be passed to prohibit any person or persons from giving or receiving compensation for circulating petitions, nor to prohibit the circulation of petitions, nor in any manner interfering with the freedom of the people in procuring petitions; but laws shall be enacted prohibiting and penalizing perjury, forgery and all other felonies or other fraudulent practices in the securing of signatures or filing of petitions.

Publication—All measures submitted to a vote of the people by petition under the provisions of this section shall be published as is now, or hereafter may be provided by law.

Enacting Clause—The style of all the bills initiated and submitted under the provisions of this section shall be, "Be It Enacted by the People of the State of Arkansas" (municipality, or county as the case may be). In submitting measures to the people, the Secretary of State and all other officials shall be guided by the general election laws or municipal laws, as the case may be, until additional legislation is provided therefor.

Self-Executing—This section shall be self-executing, and all its provisions shall be treated as mandatory, but laws may be enacted to facilitate its operation. No legislation shall be enacted to restrict, hamper or impair the exercise of the rights herein reserved to the people.

Arkansas Statutes

Title 7: Chapter 9

7-9-101. Definitions.

As used in this subchapter, unless the context otherwise requires:

(1) "Act" means any act having general application throughout the state, whether originating in the General Assembly or proposed by the people, and referred acts;

(2) "Amendment" means any proposed amendment to the Arkansas Constitution, whether proposed by the General Assembly or by the people;

(3) "Canvasser" means a person who circulates an initiative or referendum petition or a part or parts of an initiative or referendum petition to obtain the signatures of petitioners thereto;

(4) "Election" means a regular general election at which state and county officers are elected for regular terms;

(5) "Legal voter" means a person who is registered at the time of signing the petition pursuant to Arkansas Constitution, Amendment 51;

(6) "Measure" means either an amendment or an act;

(7) "Petitioner" means a person who signs an initiative or referendum petition ordering a vote upon an amendment or an act having general application throughout the state; and

(8) "Sponsor" means a person or group of persons filing an initiative or referendum petition with the Secretary of State.

7-9-102. Duties of election officers — Penalty for failure to perform.

(a) The duties imposed by this act upon members of the State Board of Election Commissioners and county boards of election commissioners, election officials, and all other officers expressly named in this act are declared to be mandatory. These duties shall be performed in good faith within the time and in the manner provided.

(b)(1) If any member of any board, any election official, or any other officer so charged with the duty shall knowingly and willfully fail or refuse to perform his duty or shall knowingly and willfully commit a fraud in evading the performance of his duty, then he shall be deemed guilty of a misdemeanor.

(2) Upon conviction, he shall be fined any sum not less than one hundred dollars ($100) nor more than one thousand dollars ($1000) and also shall be removed from office.

7-9-103. Signing of petition — Penalty for falsification.

(a) (1) Any person who is a qualified elector of the State of Arkansas may sign an initiative or referendum petition in his own proper handwriting, and not otherwise, to order an initiative or referendum vote upon a proposed measure or referred act.

(2) Any person who is an elector of any municipality of this state may sign any petition for the referendum of any ordinance passed by the council of the municipality.

(b) A person shall be deemed guilty of a Class A misdemeanor if the person:

(1) Signs any name other than his or her own to any petition;

(2) Knowingly signs his or her name more than once to any petition;

(3) Knowingly signs a petition when he or she is not legally entitled to sign it;

(4) Knowingly and falsely misrepresents the purpose and effect of the petition or the measure affected for the purpose of causing anyone to sign a petition;

(5) Acting in the capacity of canvasser, knowingly makes a false statement on a petition verification form; or

(6) Acting in the capacity of a notary, knowingly fails to witness a canvasser's affidavit either by witnessing the signing of the instrument and personally knowing the signer or by being presented with proof of identify of the signer.

7-9-104. Form of initiative petition — Sufficiency of signatures.

(a) The following shall be substantially the form of petition for any ordinance, law, or amendment to the Constitution of the State of Arkansas proposed by initiative:

"INITIATIVE PETITION.
To the Honorable Secretary of State of the State of Arkansas, or County Clerk, or City Clerk
We, the undersigned legal voters of the State of Arkansas, or _____ County, Arkansas, or City of _____ or Incorporated Town of _____, Arkansas (as the case may be) respectfully propose the following amendment to the Constitution of the State, or law, or ordinance (as the case may be), to wit: (Here insert title

and full text of measure proposed.) and by this, our petition, order that the same be submitted to the people of said state, or county, or municipality (as the case may be), to the end that the same may be adopted, enacted, or rejected by the vote of legal voters of said (state, county, or municipality) at the regular general election to be held in said _____ on the _____ day of _____, 19 _____, and each of us for himself says:
I have personally signed this petition; I am a legal voter of the State of Arkansas, and my printed name, date of birth, residence, city or town of residence, and date of signing this petition are correctly written after my signature."

(b) The information provided by the person on the petition may be used as evidence of the validity or invalidity of the signature. However, if a signature of a registered voter on such petition is sufficient to verify the voter's name, then it shall not be adjudged invalid for failure to sign the name or write the residence and city or town of residence exactly as it appears on voter registration records, for failure to print the name in the space provided, for failure to provide the correct date of birth, nor for failure to provide the correct date of signing the petition, all such information being an aid to verification rather than a mandatory requirement to perfect the validity of the signature.
(c) No additional sheets of voter signatures shall be attached to any such petition unless such sheets contain the full language of the petition.

7-9-105. Form of referendum petition — Sufficiency of signatures.

(a) The petition and order of referendum shall be substantially in the following form:

"PETITION FOR REFERENDUM.
To the Honorable Secretary of State of the State of Arkansas, or County Clerk, or City Clerk
We, the undersigned legal voters of the State of Arkansas, or _____ County, Arkansas, or City (or Incorporated Town) of _____, Arkansas (as the case may be) respectfully order by this, our petition, that Act No. _____ of the General Assembly of the State of Arkansas, approved on the _____ day of _____, 19____, entitled 'An Act _____ ' or Ordinance No. _____, passed by the county quorum court, the city (or town) council of the City (or Incorporated Town), or County of _____, Arkansas, on the _____ day of _____, 19____, entitled, 'An Ordinance _____,' be referred to the people of said state, county, or municipality (as the case may be), to the end that the same may be approved or rejected by the vote of the legal voters of the state, or of said county or municipality (as the case may be) at the biennial (or annual, as the case may be, if a city ordinance) regular general election (or at a special election, as the case may be) to be held on the _____ day of _____, 19____ ; and each of us for himself says:
I have personally signed this petition; I am a legal voter of the State of Arkansas, and my printed name, date of birth, residence, city or town of residence, and date of signing this petition are correctly written after my signature."

(b) The information provided by the person on the petition may be used as evidence of the validity or invalidity of the signature. However, if a signature of a registered voter on the petition is sufficient to verify the voter's name, then it shall not be adjudged invalid for failure to sign the name or write the residence and city or town of residence exactly as it appears on voter registration records, for failure to print the name in the space provided, for failure to provide the correct date of birth, nor for failure to provide the correct date of signing the petition, all of that information being an aid to verification rather than a mandatory requirement to perfect the validity of the signature.
(c) No additional sheets of voter signatures shall be attached to any petition unless the sheets contain the full language of the petition.

7-9-106. Required attachments to petitions.

(a) To every petition for the initiative shall be attached a full and correct copy of the title and the measure proposed.
(b) To every petition for the referendum shall be attached a full and correct copy of the measure on which the referendum is ordered.

7-9-107. Approval of ballot titles and popular names of petitions prior to circulation — Publication.

(a) Before any initiative or referendum petition ordering a vote upon any amendment or act shall be circulated for obtaining signatures of petitioners, the sponsors shall submit the original draft to the Attorney General, with a proposed legislative or ballot title and popular name.
(b) The Attorney General shall, within ten (10) days, approve and certify or shall substitute and certify a more suitable and correct ballot title and popular name for each amendment or act. The ballot title so submitted or supplied by the Attorney General shall briefly and concisely state the purpose of the proposed measure.

(c) If, as a result of his review of the ballot title and popular name of a proposed initiated act or a proposed amendment to the Arkansas Constitution, the Attorney General determines that the ballot title, or the nature of the issue, is presented in such manner that the ballot title would be misleading or designed in such manner that a vote "FOR" the issue would be a vote against the matter or viewpoint that the voter believes himself casting a vote for, or, conversely, that a vote "AGAINST" an issue would be a vote for a viewpoint that the voter is against, the Attorney General may reject the entire ballot title, popular name, and petition and state his reasons therefor and instruct the petitioners to redesign the proposed measure and the ballot title and popular name in a manner that would not be misleading.

(d) If the Attorney General refuses to act or if the sponsors feel aggrieved at his acts in such premises, they may, by petition, apply to the Supreme Court for proper relief.

(e)(1)(A) If a sponsor of any proposed statewide initiative elects to submit its popular name and ballot title to the Attorney General for certification prior to September 30 of the year preceding the year in which the initiative would be voted on, then, within ten (10) days of certification by the Attorney General, who shall deliver such certification to the Secretary of State on the day of certification, the Secretary of State shall approve and certify the sufficiency of such popular name and ballot title as certified by the Attorney General and shall cause to be published in a newspaper with statewide circulation the entire proposal with its certified popular name and ballot title and a notice informing the public of such certification and the procedure identified in this section to govern any party who may contest such certification before the Supreme Court.

(B) The procedure shall be as follows:

(i) Any legal action against such certification shall be filed with the Supreme Court within forty-five (45) days of the Secretary of State's publication;

(ii) No such action filed later than forty-five (45) days following publication shall be heard by the Supreme Court; and

(iii) An action timely filed shall be advanced by the Supreme Court as a matter of public interest over all other civil cases except contested election cases and shall be heard and decided expeditiously.

(2) Nothing in this section shall be taken to require any sponsor of a statewide initiative to submit its popular name and ballot title to the Attorney General prior to September 30 of the year preceding the year in which the proposal would be voted on. If the Secretary of State refuses to act as required in this section or if the sponsors feel aggrieved at his acts in such premises, they may, by petition, apply to the Supreme Court for proper relief.

(3) Whenever the sponsor of any initiative or referendum petition has obtained final approval of its ballot title and popular name, the sponsor shall file such petition with the Secretary of State prior to obtaining signatures on the petition.

(f) The cost of the initial publication in a newspaper of the text of a statewide initiative and related information as required in subsection (e) of this section shall be paid by the sponsor of the statewide initiative.

7-9-108. Procedure for circulation of petition.

(a) Each initiative or referendum petition ordering a vote upon a measure having general application throughout the state shall be prepared and circulated in fifteen (15) or more parts, or counterparts, and each shall be an exact copy or counterpart of all other such parts upon which signatures of petitioners are to be solicited. When a sufficient number of parts are signed by a requisite number of qualified electors and are filed and duly certified by the Secretary of State, they shall be treated and considered as one (1) petition.

(b) Each part of any petition shall have attached thereto the affidavit of the person who circulated the petition to the effect that all signatures appearing thereon were made in the presence of the affiant and that to the best of the affiant's knowledge and belief each signature is genuine and that the person so signing is a legal voter.

(c) Preceding every petition, there shall be set out in boldface type, over the signature of the Attorney General, any instructions to canvassers and signers as may appear proper and beneficial informing them of the privileges granted by the Constitution and of the penalties imposed for violations of this act. The instructions on penalties shall be in larger type than the other instructions.

(d) No part of any initiative or referendum petition shall contain signatures of petitioners from more than one (1) county.

7-9-109. Form of verification — Penalty for false statement.

(a) Each petition containing the signatures shall be verified in substantially the following form, by the person who circulated the sheet of the petition by his or her affidavit thereon as a part thereof:

"State of Arkansas)
County of _____)

I, _____, being first duly sworn, state that the foregoing persons signed this sheet of the foregoing petition, and each of them signed his name thereunto in my presence. I believe that each has stated his name, date of birth, residence or town of residence correctly, and that each signer is a legal voter of the State of Arkansas, _____ County, or City or Incorporated Town of _____.

Signature _____

Residence _____

Subscribed and sworn to before me this the _____ day of _____, 19_____.

Signature _____

Clerk, Notary, Judge or J.P.

Residence _____ ”

(b) Forms herein given are not mandatory, and if substantially followed in any petition it shall be sufficient, disregarding clerical and merely technical errors.

(c) A canvasser who knowingly makes a false statement on a petition verification form required by this section shall be deemed guilty of a Class D felony.

7-9-110. Designation of number and popular name.

(a)(1) The Secretary of State shall fix and declare the number by which each amendment to the Arkansas Constitution and each initiated and referred measure shall be designated.

(2) The Attorney General shall fix and declare the popular name by which each amendment to the Arkansas Constitution and each initiated and referred measure shall be designated.

(b) In all legal notices and publications, proceedings, and publicity affecting any such amendment or measure, the amendment or measure shall be designated by both the number and popular name fixed as provided in subsection (a) of this section.

7-9-111. Determination of sufficiency of petition — Corrections.

(a)(1) The Secretary of State shall ascertain and declare the sufficiency or insufficiency of each initiative and referendum petition within thirty (30) days after it is filed.

(2) The Secretary of State may contract with the various county clerks for their assistance in verifying the signatures on petitions. The county clerk shall return the petitions to the Secretary of State within ten (10) days.

(b) In considering the sufficiency of initiative and referendum petitions, if it is made to appear beyond a reasonable doubt that twenty percent (20%) or more of the signatures on any one (1) part thereof are fictitious, forged, or otherwise clouded or that the challenged petitioners were ineligible to sign the petition, which fact was known or could have been ascertained by the exercise of reasonable diligence on the part of the canvasser, then the Secretary of State shall require the sponsors to assume the burden of proving that all other signatures appearing on the part are genuine and that the signers are qualified electors and are in all other respects entitled to sign the petition. If the sponsors refuse or fail to assume and meet the burden, then the Secretary of State shall reject the part and shall not count as petitioners any of the names appearing thereon.

(c) If the petition is found to be sufficient, the Secretary of State shall certify and record the finding and do and perform such other duties relating thereto as are required by law.

(d)(1) If the petition is found to be insufficient, the Secretary of State shall forthwith notify the sponsors in writing, through their designated agent, and shall set forth his reasons for so finding. When the notice is delivered, the sponsors shall have thirty (30) days in which to do any or all of the following:

(A) Solicit and obtain additional signatures;

(B) Submit proof to show that the rejected signatures or some of them are good and should be counted; or

(C) Make the petition more definite and certain.

(2) Any amendments and corrections shall not materially change the purpose and effect of the petition. No change shall be made in the measure, except to correct apparent typographical errors or omissions.

(e)(1) To assist the Secretary of State in ascertaining the sufficiency or insufficiency of each initiative and referendum petition, all county clerks shall furnish at cost to the Secretary of State a single alphabetical list of all registered voters in their respective counties. The list shall be provided at least four (4) months before the election, and an updated list shall be provided at cost by September 1 in the year of the election. The list shall include the date of birth of each registered voter.

(2) The State Board of Election Commissioners, upon the request of the county clerk, may grant a waiver from this provision if the state board determines that the county clerk is unable to provide the list within the time required.

(f) A person filing initiative or referendum petitions with the Secretary of State shall bundle the petitions by county and shall file an affidavit stating the number of petitions and the total number of signatures being filed.

(g) All county initiative and referendum elections shall be held in accordance with the provisions of § 14-14-917.

(h) Municipal referendum petition measures shall be submitted to the electors at a regular general election unless the petition expressly calls for a special election. If the date set by the petition does not allow sufficient time to comply with election procedures, then the city or town council shall fix the date for any special election on the referendum measure. The date of any special election shall not be more than one hundred twenty (120) calendar days after the date of certification of sufficiency by the municipal clerk.

7-9-112. Failure to act on petition — Mandamus — Injunction.

(a) If the Secretary of State shall fail or refuse to examine and file any initiative or referendum petition within the time prescribed in § 7-9-111, any twenty-five (25) qualified electors who feel aggrieved thereby may, within fifteen (15) days thereafter, apply to the Supreme Court for a writ of mandamus to compel the officer to certify the sufficiency of the petition.

(b) If the Supreme Court shall decide that the petition is legally sufficient, it shall order the Secretary of State to file and certify the sufficiency thereof as of the date upon which it was first offered for filing, and a certified copy of the judgment shall be attached to the petition.

(c) On a proper showing that any petition is not sufficient, the Supreme Court may enjoin the Secretary of State from certifying its sufficiency and may also enjoin the various election boards from allowing the ballot title thereof to be printed on the ballots and certifying votes cast on the proposal.

7-9-113. Publication of notice.

(a) The Secretary of State shall be charged with the duty of letting contracts for publishing notices as authorized in this section.

(b)(1) Before the election at which any proposed or referred measure is to be voted upon by the people, notice shall be published in two (2) weekly issues of some newspaper in each county as is provided by law.

(2) Publication of the notice for amendments proposed by the General Assembly shall commence six (6) months, and on all other measures eight (8) weeks, before the election.

(c) At least one (1) notice shall contain the number, the popular name, the ballot title, and a complete text of the measure to be submitted and shall be published in a camera-ready format in a type no smaller than ten point (10 pt.) type.

(d) It shall be the duty of the Secretary of State, in connection with a copy of the proposed amendment, to give notice in the same newspapers that each elector on depositing his ballot at the election shall vote for or against the amendment.

7-9-114. Abstract of proposed measure.

(a) The Attorney General shall prepare a concise abstract of the contents of each statewide initiative and referendum measure proposed under Arkansas Constitution, Amendment 7, and he shall transmit it to the Secretary of State not less than twenty (20) days before the election.

(b) Not fewer than eighteen (18) days before the election, the Secretary of State shall transmit a certified copy of the abstract to the county boards of election commissioners, who shall cause copies to be printed and posted conspicuously at all polling places in the county for the information of the voters.

(c) The cost of printing copies of the abstracts shall be borne by the counties as a regular expense of the election.

7-9-115. Furnishing ballot title and popular name to election commissioners.

Not less than eighteen (18) days before the election, the Secretary of State shall furnish the State Board of Election Commissioners and county boards of election commissioners a certified copy of the ballot title and popular name for each proposed measure and each referred act to be voted upon at the ensuing election.

7-9-116. Captions.

(a) Measures proposed by initiative petition shall be captioned, "PROPOSED BY PETITION OF THE PEOPLE."

(b) Measures referred to a vote by petition shall be captioned, "REFERRED BY ORDER OF THE PEOPLE."

(c) Measures referred to a vote by the General Assembly shall be captioned, "REFERRED TO THE PEOPLE BY THE GENERAL ASSEMBLY."

7-9-117. Ballot form.

(a) It shall be the duty of the county board of election commissioners in each county to cause each title and popular name to be printed upon the official ballot to be used in the election at which the measure is to be voted upon, in the order and manner certified by the Secretary of State.

(b) The title and popular name shall be stated plainly, followed by these words:

FOR PROPOSED INITIATIVE (OR REFERRED) AMENDMENT (OR ACT) NO.

AGAINST PROPOSED INITIATIVE (OR REFERRED) AMENDMENT (OR ACT) NO.

(c) In arranging the ballot titles on the ballot, the county board shall place each measure separate and apart from others.

7-9-118. Failure to place proposal on ballot — Manner of voting.

If any election board shall fail or refuse to submit any proposal after its sufficiency has been duly certified, the qualified electors of the county may vote for or against the measure by writing or stamping on their ballot the proposed ballot title, followed by the word "FOR" or "AGAINST". All votes so cast, if otherwise legal, shall be canvassed, counted, and certified.

7-9-119. Counting, canvass, and return of votes — Proclamation of result — Effective date.

(a) The vote on each measure shall be counted, tabulated, and returned by the proper precinct election officials and the county board of election commissioners in each county at the time and in the manner the vote for candidates for state and county officers is tabulated, canvassed, and returned.

(b) An abstract of all votes cast on any measure shall be certified and delivered by the county board to the Secretary of State within fifteen (15) days after the election is held.

(c) It shall be the duty of the Secretary of State to canvass the returns on each measure not later than ten (10) days thereafter and to certify the result to the Governor and to the State Board of Election Commissioners.

(d)(1)(A) The Governor shall thereupon issue a proclamation showing the total number of votes cast, the number cast for, and the number cast against each measure and shall declare the measure adopted or rejected, as the facts appear.

(B) If the Governor declares any measure adopted, it shall be in full force and effect thirty (30) days after the election unless otherwise provided in the measure.

(2) However, amendments to the Arkansas Constitution shall also be declared adopted or rejected by the Speaker of the House of Representatives, as is provided by the Arkansas Constitution.

7-9-120. Printing of approved measures with general laws — Certification of city ordinances.

(a) The Secretary of State shall cause every measure approved by the people to be printed with the general laws enacted by the next ensuing session of the General Assembly with the date of the Governor's proclamation declaring the same to have been approved by the people.

(b) However, city ordinances approved by the people shall only be certified by the Secretary of State to the city clerk or recorder of the municipality for which the ordinance has been approved, who shall immediately record the same as he is required by law to record other ordinances of the municipality.

7-9-121. Contest of returns and certification.

(a) The right to contest the returns and certification of the votes cast upon any measure is expressly conferred upon any twenty-five (25) qualified electors of the state.

(b) Any contest may be brought in either the Chancery Court of Pulaski County or the Circuit Court of Pulaski County and shall be conducted under any rules and regulations as may be made and promulgated by the Supreme Court. However, the complaint shall be filed within sixty (60) days after the certification of the vote thereon, and the contestants shall not be required to make bond for the costs.

7-9-122. Adoption of conflicting measures.

If two (2) or more conflicting measures shall be approved by a majority of the votes severally cast for and against the measures at the same election, the measure receiving the greatest number of affirmative votes shall become law.

7-9-123. Preservation of records.

All petitions, notices, certificates, or other documentary evidence of procedural steps taken in submitting any measure shall be filed and preserved. Petitions with signatures shall be retained for two (2) years and thereafter destroyed. The measure and the certificates relating thereto shall be recorded in a permanent record and duly attested by the Secretary of State.

7-9-124. Voter registration signature imaging system.

(a) There is hereby established in the office of the Secretary of State a voter registration signature imaging system, and the Secretary of State is authorized to acquire and maintain the necessary equipment and facilities to accommodate the system.

(b) The Department of Information Systems shall cooperate with and assist the Secretary of State in determining the computer equipment and software needed in the office of the Secretary of State for the voter registration signature imaging system.

(c) There is hereby created on the books of the Treasurer of State, the Auditor of State, and the Chief Fiscal Officer of the State a fund to be known as the "Voter Registration Signature Imaging System Fund".

7-9-501. Purpose.

The purpose of this subchapter is to provide for the timely and expeditious review of the legal sufficiency of initiative petitions by the Supreme Court.

7-9-502. Construction.

(a) The General Assembly declares that this subchapter be construed as a measure to facilitate the provisions of Arkansas Constitution, Amendment 7.

(b) The General Assembly declares that this subchapter is not intended to expand the jurisdiction of the Supreme Court under Arkansas Constitution, Amendment 7 but is intended to provide a process to timely review the legal sufficiency of a measure in a manner which avoids voter confusion and frustration which occur when measures are stricken from the ballot on the eve of an election on the measure.

7-9-503. Declaration of sufficiency.

(a)(1) Any Arkansas taxpayer and voter may submit a written petition to the Secretary of State requesting the determination of legal sufficiency of statewide initiative petitions.

(2) The petitioner shall notify the sponsor of the measure of the petition for determination by certified mail on the date that it is submitted to the Secretary of State.

(b) Within thirty (30) days after receipt of the petition for determination, the Secretary of State shall decide and declare, after consultation with the Attorney General, questions on one (1) or both of the following issues:

(1) Whether the popular name and ballot title of the measure are fair and complete; and

(2) Whether the measure, if subsequently approved by the electorate, would violate any state constitutional provision or any federal constitutional, statutory, or regulatory provision or would be invalid for any other reason.

(c) The declaration shall be in writing and shall be mailed to the petitioner and the sponsor of the measure by certified mail on the date that it is issued.

(d) The scope of review authorized by this subchapter shall be strictly limited to the questions referred to in subsection (b) of this section and shall not include questions regarding the sufficiency or validity of signatures on the initiative petitions.

7-9-504. Cure by correction or amendment.

(a) If the Secretary of State declares the initiative petition legally insufficient, the sponsors of such measure may attempt to cure the insufficiency by correction or amendment, as provided in Arkansas Constitution, Amendment 7.

(b) Within fifteen (15) days after a correction or amendment is filed with the Secretary of State, the Secretary of State shall notify the petitioner and sponsor of the measure of this declaration by certified mail on the date that it is issued.

7-9-505. Right of review.

The petitioner, the sponsor of the measure, and any Arkansas taxpayer and voter shall have the immediate right to petition the Supreme Court to review the determination of the Secretary of State regarding the sufficiency of the initiative petition.

7-9-506. Effect on existing petition.

(a)(1) This subchapter shall be applicable to any initiative petition which has received the approval of the Attorney General and has been filed with the Secretary of State, pursuant to § 7-9-107, as of March 25, 1999.

(2) The Secretary of State shall review all initiative petitions approved by the Attorney General within two (2) months after March 25, 1999.

(3) If this review is not completed within the stated period, the initiative petition will be presumed sufficient and subject to immediate review by the Supreme Court.

(b) In addition, this subchapter shall be applicable to all initiative petitions submitted to the Attorney General after March 25, 1999.

Title 14: Chapter 14

14-14-914. Initiative and referendum generally.

(a) County Legislative Powers Reserved. The powers of initiative and referendum are reserved to the electors of each county government pursuant to Arkansas Constitution, Amendment 7.

(b) Restrictions. No county legislative measure shall be enacted contrary to the Arkansas Constitution or any general state law which operates uniformly throughout the state, and any general law of the state shall have the effect of repealing any county ordinance which is in conflict therewith. All ordinances adopted by the county quorum court providing for alternative county organizations and all proposed reorganizations of county government that may be proposed by initiative petition of electors of the county under Arkansas Constitution, Amendment 7 shall be submitted to the electors of the county only at the next following general election. However, such referendum shall be subject to initiative petition.

(c) Petition by Electors. The qualified electors of each county may initiate and amend ordinances and require submission of existing ordinances to a vote of the people by petition if signed by not less than fifteen percent (15%) of the qualified electors voting in the last general election for the office of circuit clerk, or the office of Governor where the electors have abolished the office of circuit clerk.

(d) Suspension of Force. (1) General Ordinance. A referendum petition on a general ordinance, or any part thereof, shall delay the effective date on such part included in the petition until the ordinance is ratified by the electors. However, the filing of a referendum petition against one (1) or more items, sections, or parts of any ordinance shall not delay the remainder from becoming operative.

(2) Emergency Ordinance. A referendum petition on an emergency ordinance shall not suspend the force of the law, but the measure may be law until it is voted upon by the electors.

14-14-915. Initiative and referendum requirements.

(a) Style Requirements of Petitions. A petition for county initiative or referendum filed by the electors shall:

(1) Embrace only a single comprehensive topic and shall be styled and circulated for signatures in the manner prescribed for county ordinances and amendments to ordinances established in this section and § 7-9-101 seq.;

(2) Set out fully in writing the ordinance sought by petitioners; or in the case of an amendment, set out fully in writing the ordinance sought to be amended and the proposed amendment; or in the case of referendum, set out the ordinance, or parts thereof, sought to be repealed; and

(3) Contain a written certification of legal review by an attorney at law duly registered and licensed to practice in the State of Arkansas. This legal review shall be conducted for the purpose of form, proper title, legality, constitutionality, and conflict with existing ordinances. Legal review shall be concluded prior to the circulations of the petition for signatures. No change shall be made in the text of any initiative or referendum petition measure after any or all signatures have been obtained.

(b) Time Requirements for Filing Petitions.

(1) Initiative Petitions. All petitions for initiated county measures shall be filed with the county clerk not less than sixty (60) calendar days nor more than ninety (90) calendar days prior to the date established for the next regular election.

(2) Referendum Petitions. All petitions for referendum on county measures must be filed with the county clerk within sixty (60) calendar days after passage and publication of the measure sought to be repealed.

(3) Certification. All initiative and referendum petitions must be certified sufficient to the county board of election commissioners not less than forty (40) calendar days prior to a regular general election to be included on the ballot. If the adequacy of a petition is determined by the county clerk less than forty (40) days prior to the next regular election, the election on the measure shall be delayed until the following regular election unless a special election is called on a referendum measure as provided by law.

(c) Filing of Petitions. Initiative and referendum petitions ordering the submission of county ordinances or measures to the electors shall be directed to, and filed with, the county clerk.

(d) Sufficiency of Petition. Within ten (10) days after the filing of any petition, the county clerk shall examine and ascertain its sufficiency. Where the petition contains evidence of forgery, perpetuated either by the circulator or with his connivance, or evidence that a person has signed a name other than his own to the petition, the prima facie verity of the circulator's affidavit shall be nullified and disregarded, and the burden of proof shall be upon the sponsors of petitions to establish the genuineness of each signature. If the petition is found sufficient, the clerk shall immediately certify such finding to the county board of election commissioners and the quorum court.

(e) Insufficiency of Petition and Recertification. If the county clerk finds the petition insufficient, the clerk shall, within ten (10) days after the filing thereof, notify the petitioners or their designated agent or attorney of record, in writing, setting forth in detail every reason for the findings of insufficiency. Upon notification of insufficiency of petition, the petitioners shall be afforded ten (10) calendar days, exclusive of the day notice of insufficiency is receipted, in which to solicit and add additional signatures, or to submit proof tending to show that signatures rejected by the county clerk are correct and should be counted. Upon resubmission of a petition which was previously declared insufficient, the county clerk shall, within five (5) calendar days, recertify its sufficiency or insufficiency in the same manner as prescribed in this section and, thereupon, the clerk's jurisdiction as to the sufficiency of the petition shall cease.

(f) Appeal of Sufficiency or Insufficiency Findings. Any taxpayer aggrieved by the action of the clerk in certifying the sufficiency or insufficiency of any initiative or referendum petition, may within fifteen (15) calendar days, but not thereafter, may file a petition in chancery court for a review of the findings.

14-14-916. Judicial jurisdiction over initiative and referendum.

(a) Jurisdiction of Chancery Court. Jurisdiction is vested upon the chancery courts and chancellors in vacation to hear and determine petitions for writs of mandamus, injunctions, and all other actions affecting the submission of any proposed county initiative or referendum petitions. All such proceedings and actions shall be heard summarily in term time or in vacation upon five (5) calendar days' notice in writing and shall have precedence over all other suits and matters before the court or chancellor. When any such action or proceeding is filed, if the court is not in session, it shall be the duty of the chancellor, by order made in vacation, to call a special term of the court to convene, within ten (10) calendar days after notice, to hear and determine the cause.

(b) Limitation of Injunction or Stay of Proceedings. No procedural steps in submitting an initiative or referendum measure shall be enjoined, stayed, or delayed by the order of any court or judge after the petition shall have been declared sufficient, except in chancery on petition to review as provided in this section. During the pendency of any proceeding to review, the findings of the county clerk shall be conclusive and binding and shall not be changed or modified by any temporary order or ruling, and no court or judge shall entertain jurisdiction of any action or proceeding questioning the validity of any such ordinance or measure until after it shall have been adopted by the people.

14-14-917. Initiative and referendum elections.

(a) Time of Election for Initiative and Referendum Measures.

(1) Initiative. Initiative petition measures shall be considered by the electors only at a regular general election at which state and county officers are elected for regular terms.

(2) Referendum. Referendum petition measures may be submitted to the electors during a regular general election and shall be if the adequacy of the petition is determined within the time limitation prescribed in this section. A referendum measure may also be referred to the electors at a special election called for the expressed purpose proposed by petition. However, no referendum petition certified within the time limitations established for initiative measures shall be referred to a special election, but shall be voted upon at the next regular election.

(3) Calling Special Elections. The jurisdiction to establish the necessity for a special election on referendum measures is vested in the electors through the provisions of petition. Where such jurisdiction is not exercised by the electors, the county court of each of the several counties may determine such necessity. However, a quorum court may compel the calling of a special election by a county court through resolution adopted during a regularly scheduled meeting of the quorum court. The resolution may specify a reasonable time limitation in which a county court order calling the special election shall be entered.

(4) Time of Special Election. The county court shall fix the date for the conduct of any special elections on referendum measures. The date shall be not less than thirty (30) calendar days after the date of the order calling the election. However, where the electors exercise their powers to establish the necessity for a special election, the county court shall order an election not more than forty-five (45) calendar days after certification of sufficiency by the county clerk, nor less than thirty (30) calendar days after the date of the order calling the election.

(b) Certification Requirements.

(1) Numeric Designation of Initiative and Referendum Measures. The county clerk shall, upon finding an initiative or referendum petition sufficient and prior to delivery of such certification to a board of election commissioners and quorum court, cause the measure to be entered into the legislative agenda register of the quorum court. This entry shall be in the order of the original filing of petition, and the register entry number shall be the official numeric designation of the proposed measure for election ballot purposes.

(2) Certification of Sufficiency. The certification of sufficiency for initiative and referendum petitions transmitted by the county clerk to the county board of election commissioners and quorum court shall include the ballot title of the proposed measure, the legislative agenda registration number, and a copy of the proposed measure, omitting signatures. The ballot title certified to the board shall be the comprehensive title of the measure proposed by petition, and the delivery of the certification to the chairman or secretary of the board shall be deemed sufficient notice to the members of the board and their successors.

(c) Notice of Election.

(1) Initiative Petitions. The county clerk shall, upon certification of any initiative or referendum petition measure submitted during the time limitations for a regular election, give notice, through publication by a two-time insertion, at not less than a seven-day interval, in a newspaper of general circulation in the county or as provided by law. Publication notice shall state that the measure will be submitted to the electors for adoption or rejection at the next regular election and shall include the full text, the ballot title, and the official numeric designation of the measure.

(2) Referendum Petition. The county clerk shall, upon certifying any referendum petition prior to the time limitations of filing measures established for a regular election, give notice through publication by a one-time insertion in a newspaper of general circulation in the county or as provided by law. Publication notice shall state that the measure will be submitted to the electors for adoption or rejection at the next regular election or a special election when ordered by the county court and shall include the full text, the ballot title, and the official numeric designation of the measure.

(3) Publication of Special Referendum Election Notice. Upon filing of a special election order by the county court, the county clerk shall give notice of the election through publication by a two-time insertion, at not less than a seven-day interval, in a newspaper of general circulation in the county or as provided by law. Publication shall state that the measure will be submitted to the electors for adoption or rejection at a special election and shall include the full text, the date of the election, the ballot title, and official numeric designation of the measure.

(4) Costs. The cost of all publication notices required in this section shall be paid out of the county general fund.

(d) Ballot Specifications for Initiative and Referendum Measures. Upon receipt of any initiative or referendum measure certified as sufficient by a county clerk, it shall be the duty of the members of the county board of election commissioners to take due cognizance and to certify the results of the vote cast thereon. The board shall cause the ballot title to be placed on the ballot to be used in the election, stating plainly and separately the title of the ordinance or measure so initiated or referred to the electors with these words:

FOR PROPOSED INITIATIVE (OR REFERRED) ORDINANCE (OR AMENDMENT) NO . . . .

AGAINST PROPOSED INITIATIVE (OR REFERRED) ORDINANCE (OR AMENDMENT) NO . . . .

so electors may vote upon such ordinance or measure. In arranging the ballot title on the ballot, the commissioners shall place it separate and apart from the ballot titles of the state acts, constitutional amendments, and the like. If the board of election commissioners fails or refuses to submit a proposed initiative or referendum ordinance when it is properly petitioned and certified as sufficient, the qualified electors of the county may vote for or against the ordinance or measure by writing or stamping on their ballots the proposed ballot title, followed by the word "FOR" or "AGAINST," and a majority of the votes so cast shall be sufficient to adopt or reject the proposed ordinance.

(e) Conflicting Measures. Where two (2) or more ordinances or measures shall be submitted by separate petition at any one (1) election, covering the same subject matters and being for the same general purpose, but different in terms, words, and figures, the ordinance or measure receiving the greatest number of affirmative votes shall be declared the law, and all others shall be declared rejected.

(f) Contest of Election. The right to contest the returns and certification of the vote cast upon any proposed initiative or referendum measure is expressly conferred upon any ten (10) qualified electors of the county. The contest shall be brought in the chancery court and shall be conducted under the procedure for contesting the election of county officers, except that the complaint shall be filed within sixty (60) days after the certification of the vote and no bond shall be required of the contestants.

(g) Vote Requirement for Enactment of Ordinance. Any measure submitted to the electors as provided in this section shall take effect and become law when approved by a majority of the votes cast upon the measure, and not otherwise, and shall not be required to receive a majority of the electors voting at the election. The measure so enacted shall be operative on and after the thirtieth day after the election at which it is approved unless otherwise specified in the ordinance or amendment.

14-14-918. Passage of initiative and referendum measures.

(a) Recording of Enactment. Upon passage of any initiative or referendum measure by the electors, the county clerk shall record the enactment in the county ordinance and resolution register in the manner provided by law for all county ordinances and resolutions. The register entry number designation shall thereby become the official reference number designating the enactment.

(b) Quorum Court Authority. No measure approved by a vote of the electors shall be amended or repealed by a quorum court except by affirmative vote of two-thirds (2/3) of the whole number of justices comprising a court. On the passage of an amendment or repealing measure, the yeas and nays shall be called and recorded in the minutes of the meeting.

(c) Preservation of Records. All petitions, certificates, notices, and other evidences of procedural steps taken in submitting any ordinance shall be filed and preserved for a period of three (3) years by the county clerk.

14-14-919. Referendum petitions on county bond issue.

All referendum petitions under Arkansas Constitution, Amendment 7, against any measure, as the term is used and defined in Arkansas Constitution, Amendment 7, pertaining to a county bond issue must be filed with the county clerk within thirty (30) days after the adoption of any such measure.

The Basic Steps to Do an Initiative in Arkansas

Statutes and Amendments — Direct Initiative Process

Basic Procedures: Before proponents can circulate the petition, they must submit the original draft to the Attorney General, with a proposed legislative or ballot title and popular name. The Attorney General has 10 days to approve and certify the ballot title and popular name or substitute and certify a more suitable and correct title and name. If the Attorney General refuses to act, or if the sponsors feel aggrieved at the choice of title and name, they can apply to the Supreme Court for proper relief.

When the proponents have obtained a final approval on the measure's ballot title and popular name, they then must file the petition with the Secretary of State, Elections Division before they can circulate.

The Secretary of State is required to publish the measure in the newspaper, at the proponent's expense at least 30 days before the signatures are filed.

Date Initiative language can be submitted to state for 2002: Any time.

Signatures are tied to vote of which office: Governor

Next Gubernatorial election: 2002

Votes cast for governor in last election: 706,020

Net number of signatures required: For a constitutional amendment it is 10% of the total number of votes cast for Governor in the last gubernatorial election (70,602). For a statute, it is 8% of the total number of votes cast for Governor in the last gubernatorial election. (54,481)

Distribution Requirement: 5% in 15 of 75 counties for amendments and 4% in 15 of 75 counties for statutes.

Circulation period: Unlimited

Do circulators have to be residents: No

Date when signatures are due for certification: July 5, 2002 for 2002 general election ballot.

Signature verification process: The Secretary of State will verify signatures up to 10% above the designated number. However, the Secretary of State will not accept additional signatures if the petition is determined to be sufficient after the initial submission even if the number is one signature over the required number. Nor will the Secretary of State accept additional signatures after the initial submission until a determination of sufficiency is made. If a petition is determined not to contain the requisite number of valid signatures, a sponsor may within 30 days of notification of insufficiency from the Secretary of State do any or all of the following: A) Solicit and obtain additional signatures; B) Submit proof that the rejected signatures or some of them are good and should be counted; C) Make the petition more definite or certain. The Secretary of State will set designated times to accept the additional signatures from a notified sponsor.

Single-subject restriction: No

Legislative tampering: Initiatives can be amended or repealed by a 2/3 vote of each house.

General Comments: Under a new 1999 law, any Arkansas taxpayer and voter may submit a written request to the Secretary of State for a determination of legal sufficiency of a statewide initiative petition. Within 30 days of receipt of this request the Secretary of State shall issue, after consultation with the Attorney General, a declaration stating whether the popular name or ballot title of the measure are fair and complete and whether the measure, if subsequently approved by the electorate, would violate any state constitutional provision or any federal constitutional, statutory or regulatory provision, or would be invalid for any other reason. The petitioner, the sponsor of the measure and any Arkansas taxpayer and voter shall have the immediate right to petition the Arkansas Supreme Court to review the determination of the Secretary of State regarding the sufficiency of the initiative petition.

California

Californians rightly credit Progressive-era Governor Hiram Johnson with leading the successful fight for direct democracy in the Golden State, but few are familiar with the critical groundwork that had been laid by Dr. John Randolph Haynes. A Philadelphian who held doctorates in both medicine and philosophy, Haynes moved west to Los Angeles in 1887, at the age of 34. He established a successful medical practice, counting many prominent Southern Californians among his patients, invested his profits skillfully in real estate, and eventually became a millionaire.

In 1895 Haynes helped found the California Direct Legislation League, dedicated to winning the rights of initiative, referendum, and recall both statewide and in every local jurisdiction. He won election in 1900 to a Los Angeles "board of freeholders" responsible for drafting a new charter for that city. Haynes used this strategic position to make sure that the board included I&R in the new charter, only to see the entire charter thrown out by the courts on a technicality. A new board, without Haynes, was elected in 1902, but he continued to advocate I&R and brought Eltweed Pomeroy of New Jersey, president of the National Direct Legislation League, from the east coast specifically to address the board. After Pomeroy's speech, the board voted to include initiative, referendum, and recall in the new charter. Voters ratified the charter in 1903.

Haynes then concentrated his efforts on winning statewide I&R. The odds against him were daunting. The entire state government had for decades been under the control of the Southern Pacific Railroad. Bribery was the accepted method of doing business in the state capitol. Realizing the hopelessness of dealing with the current officeholders, Haynes and other reformers began a campaign to get rid of them and remake state government from top to bottom. In May 1907 they founded the Lincoln-Roosevelt League of Republican Clubs, and elected several of their candidates to the legislature. Once elected, these legislators worked for a bill to require the nomination of party candidates through primary election rather than the backroom deals of state party conventions. The bill passed, and the League's 1910 gubernatorial candidate, Hiram Johnson, ran in the state's first primary election. Johnson won the primary and the general election and swept dozens of other reformers into the legislature on his political coattails.

Johnson and the new Progressive majority in the legislature made the most sweeping governmental changes ever seen in the history of California. Among these were the introduction of initiative, referendum, and recall at both the state and local levels. Voters ratified these amendments in a special election on October 10, 1911.

Reformers in Los Angeles won voter approval, in December 1911, of a unique local initiative to create a municipally owned, yet editorially independent, newspaper to compete with the anti-labor, anti-reform Los Angeles Times and provide unbiased news and an equal forum for all political views. Each political party was given a column in every weekly edition.

This bold experiment in free speech attracted the state's top newspaper talent and got off to a highly successful start. After less than a year, however, it failed because of the harassment of vendors and an advertiser boycott organized by the Los Angeles reformers' arch-enemy, Harrison Gray Otis, owner of the Times.

The first significant statewide initiative in California abolished the poll tax in 1914, and a construction bond initiative for the University of California also won voter approval that year. Immediately thereafter, anti-initiative forces launched their first counterattack, in the form of a constitutional amendment passed by the legislature to make it more difficult to pass initiative bond proposals. Haynes mobilized his pro-initiative forces and defeated the amendment at the polls in 1915.

Anti-initiative forces tried again in 1920; this time using the initiative process themselves to propose a measure that would have made it virtually impossible to put any tax-related initiatives on future ballots. Haynes mobilized his forces again and defeated the measure at the polls; and he won a third, similar contest in 1922. After this he changed the name of his California Direct Legislation League to "The League to Protect the Initiative," and for the rest of his life kept close watch over the legislature to make sure that it enacted no laws to restrict I&R procedures. Haynes died on October 30, 1937, at the age of 84.

On the ballot in 1934 were four successful constitutional initiatives to revamp the state's law enforcement and criminal justice systems. All four were sponsored by Alameda County District Attorney Earl Warren, who went on to become the state's attorney general in 1938, its governor in 1942, and the Chief Justice of the U.S. Supreme Court in 1953. The principal changes involved procedures for judicial selection and retention, and increasing the woefully inadequate powers and jurisdiction of the office of attorney general. Warren's foresight in revamping the justice system before running for attorney general accounted in no small measure for his effectiveness once elected, which in turn made possible his rise to higher office.

Each decade for the first half of this century, the number of signatures required to put a statewide initiative on the ballot roughly doubled. It was set at 8 percent of the number of votes cast in the previous gubernatorial election. In 1911 this was 30,481 signatures; in 1930, it was 91,529; in 1939, it was 212,117. The rapid change was due to California's explosive population growth and the increasing participation of women as voters. As petition requirements increased, the number of initiatives qualifying for the ballot decreased, particularly in the 1940s, 1950s, and 1960s.

One of the highest stakes initiative campaigns, in terms of campaign spending was the 1956 struggle over changes in the state regulation and taxation of oil and gas production. The initiative was sponsored by one group of oil companies that sought to make their business more profitable, and opposed by another group of oil firms that preferred the existing system. Campaign funds spent by both sides totaled over $5 million. The 1956 initiative lost: California voters, inundated with conflicting claims about a complex measure, took the cautious route and voted "no."

Almost as expensive was the gargantuan 1958 labor-capital conflict over a "Right to Work" (open shop) initiative sponsored by employers. This battle ended in a double defeat for employers: not only did voters decisively reject the initiative, but the opposition campaign mobilized Democrats and union members to vote in droves, resulting in the election of Governor Edmund G. Brown, Sr., the first Democrat to occupy that office in 16 years.

In the 1960s, California liberals soured on the initiative process as a result of two measures passed by voters in 1964. The first repealed the Rumford Fair Housing Act, which the legislature had passed, and Governor Brown had signed, in 1963. The second banned cable television. That measure was sponsored by theater owners who, fearing competition, advertised the initiative as guaranteeing "free television" and eliminating the specter of "pay television." Both 1964 initiatives were later overturned by the courts as unconstitutional.

The California initiative process gave rise to a new breed of campaign professional: the paid petition circulator. With signature requirements doubling nearly every decade, citizen groups were unable to rely solely on volunteer effort. As early as World War I, Joseph Robinson was offering his organizing services to initiative proponents. His firm, which paid its employees a fee for each signature brought in, had a virtual monopoly on the petition business from 1920 to 1948—a period during which, Robinson estimated, his firm was involved in 98 percent of the successful statewide initiative petition drives. Robinson stayed in business into the late 1960s, when he offered his services to Ed and Joyce Koupal, but by then he had competitors.

In 1978 Proposition 13 was adopted. This initiative, which cut property taxes in the state, reinvigorated the initiative process across the country and can be said to have been the catalyst for the modern tax reform movement.

In the last decade, Californians lead the nation in numerous reform efforts including term limits, ending bilingual education, adopting animal protection laws, ending racial preferences, and adopting one of the most comprehensive drug reform measures in the country. This has lead to elected officials across the country vilifying the initiative process and have used the rhetoric "we don't want to be like California" as their rallying cry in opposing the initiative process. They are concerned that the reforms adopted in California would come to their states—even though these are the reforms wanted by the people. However, Californians still overwhelmingly support the initiative process and have no desire for it to be abolished.

Statewide Initiative Usage

Number of Initiatives	Number Passed	Number Failed	Passage Rate
275	96	179	35%

Statewide Initiatives

Year	Measure Number	Type	Subject Matter	Description	Pass/Fail
1912	6	DA	Administration of Government	Relating to the formation of consolidated city and County government, prescribing methods thereof.	Failed
1912	7	DS	Gaming	An act to prohibit bookmaking and pool-selling, and to provide for the appointment of a state racing commission to grant licenses for horse racing.	Failed
1912	8	DA	Taxes	Relating to taxation by counties, cities and counties, cities, towns, districts; prescribing methods and procedures thereof.	Failed
1914	10	DA	Civil Rights	Provides that no poll or head tax shall be levied.	Passed
1914	11	DS	Bonds	To provide for the issuance and sale of state bonds in the sum of $1.8m to create a fund for the completion and construction of buildings at the University of California at Berkeley.	Passed
1914	13	DA	Election Reform	Provides that no elector may vote on question of incurring bonded indebtedness of state or political subdivision thereof, unless he is owner of property taxable for payment of such indebtedness.	Failed
1914	14	DS	Election Reform	To provide for issuance of certificate of identification and ballot to voters who will be absent from home precincts on election day.	Failed
1914	15	DA	Banking Reform	Present section unchanged except, authorizes banks in which public moneys are deposited to furnish, as security, bonds of districts within municipalities, or of a corporation qualified to act as sole surety in value.	Failed
1914	19	DA	Administration of Government	Consolidation of City and County and Limited Annexation of Contiguous Territory.	Passed
1914	2	DA	Alcohol Regulation	To prohibit the manufacture, sale, gift, or transportation of intoxicating liquors.	Failed
1914	20	DS	Gaming	Prohibits the engaging in or furthering in any way prize fights or remunerative boxing exhibitions, training therefore.	Passed
1914	21	DA	Administration of Government	City and County Consolidation and Annexation with Consent of Annexed Territory.	Failed

Year	Measure Number	Type	Subject Matter	Description	Pass/Fail
1914	22	DS	Administration of Government	To provide procedures for certification of land titles and record keeping thereof.	Passed
1914	3	DS	Labor	To establish an eight-hour work day and a forty-eight hour week.	Failed
1914	38	DS	Bonds	To provide for the issuance and sale of state bonds in the sum of $1.25m to create a fund for the acquisition of a site in the city of Los Angeles, for the construction thereon of a state building.	Failed
1914	39	DA	Alcohol Regulation	Suspension of Prohibition Amendment. To suspend the proposed prohibition amendment (if passed) until Feb. 15, 1915 relating to use and transportation of intoxicating liquors.	Passed
1914	45	DS	Labor	To prohibit, except in cases of emergency, the requiring or employing of any person to work more than 6 days or 48 hours a week.	Failed
1914	46	DS	Health/Medical	To create a state board of drugless physicians to regulate the examination and certification of persons to treat all physical or mental ailments of human beings without drugs or medicine.	Failed
1914	47	DA	Alcohol Regulation	Prohibits for 8 years after this election state election on question of prohibiting or permitting transportation of intoxicating liquors.	Failed
1914	9	DS	Business Regulation	To provide for the regulation of investment companies by an auditor of investments appointed by the Governor.	Failed
1916	1	DA	Alcohol Regulation	Prohibits after Jan. 1, 1920, the manufacture, sale or possession of intoxicating liquors except for medicinal, sacramental, scientific and mechanical purposes.	Failed
1916	2	DA	Alcohol Regulation	Defines alcoholic liquor and prohibits its use; neither limits nor repeals state or local prohibition.	Failed
1916	5	DA	Taxes	To declare that all public revenues be raised by taxation of land values, exclusive of its improvements.	Failed
1916	6	DA	Administration of Government	Ineligibility of Office. Declares that no Senator or member of Assembly shall during the term for which he has been elected, hold or accept any office, trust, or employment of this state, except for other elected office.	Passed
1918	1	DS	Alcohol Regulation	To provide for the regulation of liquor use and sales, prohibit drinking saloons, limit the number of municipal licenses for sale of vinous or malt liquors for consumption.	Failed
1918	18	DS	Administration of Government	To create state board of authorization and require each County officer to file financial statements with governing body of County which shall submit same with budget to such state board before making tax levy.	Failed

Year	Measure Number	Type	Subject Matter	Description	Pass/Fail
1918	19	DA	Taxes	To require all public revenue to be raised by taxation of land values irrespective of improvements thereon.	Failed
1918	21	DS	Business Regulation	To regulate the practice of dentistry in the state.	Failed
1918	22	DS	Alcohol Regulation	To make the manufacture, importation or sale of intoxicating liquors a misdemeanor.	Failed
1918	3	DS	Business Regulation	To restrict and regulate rates of interest upon the loan or forbearance of money, goods, and certain other transactions.	Passed
1920	1	DS	Alien Rights	To permit acquisition and transfer of real property by aliens eligible for citizenship, and to permit other aliens to acquire and transfer real property only as prescribed by treaty.	Passed
1920	12	DA	Education	Levies ad valorem tax for state university of one and two-tenths mills to be paid to "State University Fund."	Failed
1920	16	DA	Education	Adds kindergartens to public school system; requires addition to state school fund, and creation of high school fund.	Passed
1920	20	DA	Taxes	Land Value Taxation. To require all public revenues to be raised by taxing land values exclusive of improvements.	Failed
1920	3	DA	Judicial Reform	To increase salaries of Justices of the Supreme Court from $8,000 to $10,000 per year and Justices of District Court from $7,000 to $9,000 per year.	Failed
1920	4	DA	Initiative and Referendum	To increase the number of signatures necessary to file an initiative petition which relates to assessment or collection of taxes.	Failed
1920	5	DS	Business Regulation	To regulate and license the practice of chiropractic.	Failed
1920	6	DA	Health/Medical	Declares that no form of vaccination, inoculation or other medication shall be made a condition for admission or attendance to any public school, college, or university.	Failed
1920	7	DS	Health/Medical	To prohibit vivisection, dissection or torture of any living person or living animal, including experimental physiological and pathological investigation.	Failed
1920	9	DA	Administration of Government	Creates state Highway Finance Board and authorizes the sale of bonds, and relieves counties from payments to state for highway construction.	Passed
1922	1	DA	Veteran Affairs	Permits state aid with money or credit to U.S. Army or Navy veterans who served during war time, in acquiring or developing farms or homes or in land settlement projects.	Passed

Year	Measure Number	Type	Subject Matter	Description	Pass/Fail
1922	10	DA	Utility Regulation	To require all property owned by public utilities to be assessed and taxed in same manner and to same extent as like property held by private corporations and persons.	Failed
1922	11	DA	Utility Regulation	To make all publicly owned utilities regulated by the state Railroad Commission.	Failed
1922	12	DA	Administration of Government	Requires Governor to submit to legislature within first 30 days of each regular session, a budget containing itemized statement of all proposed expenditures and estimated revenues for next biennial period.	Passed
1922	16	DS	Business Regulation	To provide for the regulation and licensing for the practice of chiropractic.	Passed
1922	19	DA	Administration of Government	Water and Power. Creates board appointed by Governor and subject to recall to issue bonds, and develop and distribute water and electric energy.	Failed
1922	20	DS	Health/Medical	Osteopathic Act. To provide for the practice of osteopathic medication.	Passed
1922	28	DS	Health/Medical	To prohibit the vivisection or torture of human beings, animals, or other living creatures, for experimental or pathological investigations, or other purposes.	Failed
1922	29	DA	Taxes	Abolishes present system of taxation, and declares that private property rights attach only to products of labor and not to land.	Failed
1922	30	DA	Administration of Government	Gives Railroad Commission exclusive power to grant franchises for street, interurban and suburban railways, and motor vehicle transportation, and other purposes.	Failed
1924	1	DA	Taxes	Provides for state taxation of highway transportation companies, sets rates and provides that Legislature may change rate with two-thirds vote.	Failed
1924	11	DS	Environmental Reform	To create the Klamath River Fish and Game District and to prohibit the construction or maintenance of any dam or other artificial obstruction in its waters.	Passed
1924	16	DA	Utility Regulation	Creates a Board, to be appointed by the Governor and subject to recall, to develop and distribute water and electric energy, to issue bonds, and for related purposes.	Failed
1924	7	DS	Gaming	To authorize boxing and wrestling contests for prizes and purses, or where admission fee is charged, limiting such boxing contests to 12 rounds.	Passed

Year	Measure Number	Type	Subject Matter	Description	Pass/Fail
1926	17	DA	Education	Permits the study and reading of Bible in public schools.	Failed
1926	18	DA	Utility Regulation	To create a water and power board the members of which are to be appointed by the Governor to develop and distribute water and electricity policies and issue bonds.	Failed
1926	20	DA	Apportionment/ Redistricting	To create a reapportionment commission to act if legislature fails at first session after each census.	Failed
1926	28	DA	Apportionment/ Redistricting	To require legislature to reapportion the state immediately following each federal census.	Passed
1926	4	DS	Taxes	To require every distributor of gasoline, distillate and of motor vehicle fuels, to pay license tax of $.01 per gallon, in addition to $.02 license tax now required by law.	Failed
1926	6	DS	Gaming	To create board, appointed by Governor, to regulate and license horse racing and pari-mutuel betting within race track enclosure.	Failed
1926	8	DA	Administration of Government	Classifies highways within counties and provides funding formulas for construction and maintenance thereof.	Failed
1926	9	DS	Alcohol Regulation	To repeal Wright Act approved by electors on referendum November 7, 1922, which provided for enforcement of the 18th Amendment of the U.S. Constitution (prohibition).	Failed
1928	21	DS	Animal Rights	Prohibiting Certain Acts with Animals. Defines bull-dogging, bull riding, etc., prohibits such acts for sport, exhibitions, or amusement and makes such prohibition inapplicable to farming or dairying.	Failed
1928	5	DS	Gaming	To repeal the initiative act approved by the electors on November 4, 1924, which authorized boxing and wrestling contests for prizes.	Failed
1930	10	DS	Business Regulation	To amend the usury law to require that written agreement for interest rate unnecessary, to provide that the legislature regulate pawnbrokers and "industrial loan companies".	Failed
1930	11	DA	Administration of Government	Creates Fish and Game Commission appointed by Governor to regulate the hunting and conservation of animals, fish and birds.	Failed
1930	14	DS	Election Reform	To change laws regulating registration of voters to require new statewide registration commencing January 1, 1932.	Passed

Year	Measure Number	Type	Subject Matter	Description	Pass/Fail
1930	26	DS	Business Regulation	Prohibits keeping open for business any store, barber show, workshop, factory, or other place of business, or performing or employing labor, on Sunday.	Failed
1930	7	DS	Daylight Savings Time	Provides that annually, at 2 a.m. on last Sunday in April, standard time be advanced one hour and at 2 a.m. on last Sunday in September, retarded one hour.	Failed
1932	1	DS	Alcohol Regulation	Repeals Wright Act that enforced 18th Amendment.	Passed
1932	11	DA	Administration of Government	Grants to City of Huntington Beach tide and submerged lands situated within present boundaries of the city.	Failed
1932	2	DA	Alcohol Regulation	Provides for the sale and use of liquor when the Wright Act is repealed and when lawful under Federal Constitution and laws of California.	Passed
1932	3	DS	Administration of Government	To regulate foreclosure of mortgage as contract, trust deed, instrument, making specific real property security for performance without changing possession.	Failed
1932	5	DS	Gaming	Create California Racing Board, to be appointed by Governor, empowered to regulate and license racing and wagering within race tract enclosure.	Failed
1934	11	DA	Education	To make State Board of Education elective; abolish Superintendent of Public Instruction; and provide for Director of Education.	Failed
1934	13	DA	Alcohol Regulation	Provides for local option for liquor sales and use.	Failed
1934	17	DS	Health/Medical	Creates Naturopathic Association, a public corp.; provides for its organization, government, membership and powers; regulates practice and licensing of naturopathy.	Failed
1934	2	DA	Alcohol Regulation	Prohibits consumption, sale, or disposition for consumption on premises, of intoxicating liquors, except beer, in public saloons or barrooms.	Passed
1934	3	DA	Judicial Reform	Declares Supreme or Appellate Court Justice may declare candidacy to succeed himself, otherwise Governor shall nominate candidate.	Passed
1934	4	DA	Administration of Government	Declares Attorney General, state's Chief law officer, shall see all state laws enforced, directly supervised district attorneys, sheriffs and other enforcement officers designated by law.	Passed

Year	Measure Number	Type	Subject Matter	Description	Pass/Fail
1934	5	DA	Legal	Declares in any criminal case, whether defendant testifies or not, court and counsel may comment on his failures to explain or deny any evidence against him.	Passed
1934	6	DA	Legal	Requires defendant charged with felony be immediately taken before magistrate of court, be delivered copy of complaint and given time to procure counsel.	Passed
1934	7	DA	Administration of Government	Prohibits permanent appointments and promotion in state civil service except on merit, efficiency and fitness ascertained by competitive examination.	Passed
1934	9	DS	Business Regulation	To amend Chiropractic Act creating state Chiropractors Association; and to provide for organization, government, membership powers and duties thereof.	Failed
1936	10	DA	Taxes	Relating to motor vehicle fuel taxes and license fees requiring funds raised there from to be used for highway purposes and vehicle regulation.	Failed
1936	11	DA	Education	To create state Tenure Board to establish tenure procedures for instructors.	Failed
1936	2	DA	Taxes	Repeals 1935 Personal Income Tax Act and provides that no law imposing income tax on individuals is valid unless approved by majority of electors after initiative proceedings.	Failed
1936	3	DA	Alcohol Regulation	Creates Alcoholic Beverage Commission to succeed to liquor regulatory and licensing powers of state Board of Equalization.	Failed
1936	4	DS	Environmental Reform	To prohibit tideland and surface oil drilling and authorizing drilling wells slanted from uplands, and to prohibit pollution of tide, ocean bay or inlet waters.	Failed
1936	7	DA	Administration of Government	Creates County and municipal civil service, to regulate employment and prohibit appointees from political activities.	Failed
1936	9	DA	Alcohol Regulation	Provides for local option for the regulation of alcoholic beverage.	Failed
1938	1	DS	Labor	To establish certain labor practices. Defines lawful picketing, boycotting and display of banners, prohibits seizure of private property.	Failed
1938	2	DS	Animal Rights	To provide for the regulation of pounds. Defines pounds, prescribes duties of pound masters; prohibits sale or surrender of unwanted animals for scientific, medical, experimental, purposes but exempts kennels.	Failed

Year	Measure Number	Type	Subject Matter	Description	Pass/Fail
1938	20	DA	Taxes	To repeal limitation on ad valorem property taxes for state appropriation; to prohibit increasing present assessed valuation of improvements and tangible personal property.	Failed
1938	25	DA	Administration of Government	Provides for state Retirement Life Payments Administrator to administer programs of retirement compensation warrants to qualified electors 50 years of age, not an employer nor employee.	Failed
1938	4	DA	Administration of Government	To create a Highway and Traffic Safety Commission; to abolish existing state Highway Commission and transfer control of California Highway Patrol to new Commission.	Failed
1938	5	IDS	Animal Rights	Prohibits operation in state waters of fishing boats which deliver fish, mollusks or crustaceans, wherever caught, to points beyond state waters.	Passed
1939	1	DA	Administration of Government	To establish system of warrants issued by state to electors 50 years old.	Failed
1939	2	DS	Business Regulation	Provides secretary of Chiropractic Board shall devote full time to duties and increase his salary; increases powers of board; increases educational requirements of applicant.	Failed
1940	5	DS	Daylight Savings Time	Provides for daylight saving time each year from last Sunday in April to the last Sunday in September.	Failed
1942	10	IDS	Business Regulation	Authorizes plans for rehabilitation, readjustment, reorganization, consolidation or merger of building and loan association.	Failed
1942	3	DS	Administration of Government	To create Board of Examiners in basic sciences comprised of 5 members with prescribed qualifications appointed by Governor.	Failed
1942	4	DA	Taxes	Repeal 1935 Personal Income Tax Act and declares no law imposing income tax on persons to be valid until approved by majority of voters after initiative proceedings.	Failed
1944	11	DA	Welfare	To provide $60 monthly to citizens having required residence, who are 60 years old or over, or totally and permanently disabled, including those in military service, or blind.	Failed
1944	12	DA	Labor	Declares right of employment, free from interference because employee does or does not belong to or pay money to a labor organization.	Failed

Year	Measure Number	Type	Subject Matter	Description	Pass/Fail
1944	9	DA	Education	Increase the amount of revenue required to be raised and apportioned by the Legislative for elementary schools. Increases apportionment from 100% to 166 2/3% of amount raised by counties.	Passed
1946	11	DS	Labor	Declares state policy that all persons have the right of equal opportunity to secure employment.	Failed
1946	2	DS	Gaming	To permit greyhound racing and pari-mutual wagering thereon in counties having population over 175,000.	Passed
1946	3	DA	Education	Amends same sections of Constitution and simplifies allocation of school funds in same manner as Proposition No. 13. Establishes minimum salary of $2400 per year for teachers. Increases state support for public schools to $120 per year per student.	Passed
1948	12	DA	Alcohol Regulation	To provide for local control and enforcement of intoxicating liquors.	Failed
1948	13	DA	Apportionment/ Redistricting	To provide for reapportionment of Senate, requires 1949 Legislature to reapportion Senate Districts according to population shown by 1940 census.	Failed
1948	14	DA	Housing	To create state Housing Agency and authorizes state to guarantee obligations of, and furnish operating subsidies to, public housing authorities.	Failed
1948	15	DS	Environmental Reform	Prohibits use of purse nets and round haul nets for fishing in ocean and tide waters of the state south of line extending due west from Point San Simeon in San Luis Obispo County.	Failed
1948	2	DA	Alcohol Regulation	To provide for local control of intoxicating liquors.	Failed
1948	3	DS	Utility Regulation	Empowers Public Utilities Commission to prescribe number of brakemen to be used on railroad trains. Prohibits feather-bed practices in employment of railroad brakemen on trains.	Passed
1948	4	DA	Welfare	Increases maximum aid from $60 to $75 monthly for aged persons, and from $75 to $85 for blind persons and increases income and property exemptions.	Passed
1948	6	DS	Animal Rights	Prohibits use of nets, traps, set lines, or other appliances in commercial fishing in fish and game districts in San Francisco Bay.	Failed
1949	12	DS	Daylight Savings Time	To provide for daylight saving time from the last Sunday in April until the last Sunday in September, annually.	Passed

Year	Measure Number	Type	Subject Matter	Description	Pass/Fail
1949	2	DA	Welfare	To reinstate plan of Old Age Security and Aid to Blind, except next maximum aid payments are retained at present level.	Passed
1950	1	DA	Taxes	To prohibit state and its political subdivision from imposing taxes upon personal property, tangible or intangible.	Failed
1950	10	DA	Housing	To require approval of majority of electors of County or city, voting at an election, as prerequisites for establishment of any low-rent housing project by the state or County, city district.	Passed
1950	6	DA	Gaming	To permit wagering and gambling to licensed establishments.	Failed
1952	10	DA	Administration of Government	Prohibits appropriation or expenditure of public money to California State Chamber of Commerce, local chamber or commerce and County Supervisors Association.	Failed
1952	11	IDS	Welfare	Place old age security program under state administration; terminates County administration, eliminates County share of costs.	Failed
1952	13	IDS	Election Reform	To provide that no person shall be a candidate or nominee of a political party for any office unless he has been registered as affiliated with such party for at least three months prior to filing nominating papers.	Failed
1952	2	DA	Education	Increases required state support for public schools to $180 per year per pupil.	Passed
1954	4	DA	Welfare	To increase monthly aid payments to aged persons who meet eligibility requirements (from $80 to $100).	Failed
1956	4	DS	Environmental Reform	To prohibit waste, defined as production methods which reduce maximum economic quantity of oil or gas ultimately recoverable by good engineering practices.	Failed
1958	16	DA	Taxes	To amend Constitution by providing that school property, religious and other nonprofit organizations be exempted from taxation.	Failed
1958	17	DS	Taxes	Reduces sales and use tax rate from 3% to 2%. Changes income tax rates to new range of 1/2% on incomes over $50,000.	Failed

Year	Measure Number	Type	Subject Matter	Description	Pass/Fail
1958	18	DA	Labor	Prohibits employers and employee organizations from entering into collective bargaining which establish labor organization membership, or payment of dues or charges of any kind thereto, as an entry condition.	Failed
1960	15	DA	Apportionment/ Redistricting	To provide for reapportionment of senate and limiting the number of senatorial districts per County; provides for legislature to reapportion after each Census.	Failed
1962	23	DA	Apportionment/ Redistricting	Establishes and apportions 50 (instead of existing 40) senatorial districts and limits the number of districts which a County could have.	Failed
1962	24	DA	Election Reform	Declares existence, purposes, and objectives of world communist movement; defines communist and subversive organizations and denies them political party status and any tax exemption.	Failed
1964	14	DA	Civil Rights	Prohibits state, subdivision, or agency thereof from denying, limiting, or abridging right of any person to decline to sell, lease, or rent residential real property to any person as he chooses.	Passed
1964	15	DS	Utility Regulation	Declares it contrary to public policy to permit development of subscription television business. Provides no charge shall be made to public for television programs transmitted to home television sets.	Passed
1964	16	DA	Gaming	Provides for statewide lottery with monthly drawings.	Failed
1964	17	DS	Utility Regulation	Declares state policy on manning trains.	Passed
1966	16	DS	Legal	Declares state policy is to prohibit obscene matter and conduct.	Failed
1968	9	DA	Taxes	Provides that total ad valorem tax burden on all property be limited after July 1, 1969 to 1% of market value for property-related services plus 80% of base cost of people-related services.	Failed
1970	8	DA	Education	Requires state provide from sources other than property taxes not less than 50% of costs for public schools, exclusive of capital outlay and federal funds, and 90% of costs for social welfare services.	Failed
1972	14	DA	Taxes	Establishes ad valorem property tax rate limitations for all purposes except payment of designated types of debts and liabilities.	Failed

Year	Measure Number	Type	Subject Matter	Description	Pass/Fail
1972	15	DA	Administration of Government	Requires state Personnel Board, University of California Regents and state University and College Trustees semi-annually to determine prevailing rates in private and public employment.	Failed
1972	16	DA	Administration of Government	Requires state Personnel Board to determine maximum salary for each class of policemen or deputy sheriff in each city and County within state.	Failed
1972	17	DA	Death Penalty	To provide that all state statutes in effect Feb. 17, 1972 requiring, authorizing, imposing, or relating to death penalty are in full force and effect.	Passed
1972	18	DS	Legal	Redefines obscenity, removes "redeeming social importance" defense, etc.	Failed
1972	19	DS	Drug Policy Reform	Proposes a law that no person 18 years or older shall be punished criminally or denied any right or privilege because of his planting, cultivating, harvesting, drying and processing marijuana.	Failed
1972	20	DS	Environmental Reform	Creates Coastal Zone Conservation Commission and 6 regional commissions.	Passed
1972	21	DS	Civil Rights	No public school student shall, because of his race, creed, or color, be assigned to or be required to attend a particular school.	Passed
1972	22	DS	Labor	Sets forth permissible and prohibited labor relation activities of agricultural employers, employees, and labor organizations.	Failed
1972	9	DS	Environmental Reform	Specifies permissible composition and quality of gasoline and other fuel for internal combustion engines.	Failed
1973	1	DA	Taxes	Limits state expenditures; restricts use of defined surplus revenue to tax reductions, refunds or emergencies. Constitutionally eliminates personal income tax for lower income persons.	Failed
1974	17	DS	Environmental Reform	Designates specified portions of the main stem of the Stanislaus River as components of the California Wild and Scenic Rivers System.	Failed
1974	9	DS	Campaign Finance Reform	Requires reports of receipts and expenditures in campaigns for state and local offices and ballot measures. Limits expenditures for state wide candidates.	Passed
1976	13	DS	Gaming	To authorize and regulate greyhound dog racing.	Failed
1976	14	DS	Labor	Agricultural labor relations.	Failed
1976	15	DS	Nuclear weapons/ facilities/waste	Nuclear power plants.	Failed
1978	13	DA	Taxes	Property tax reduction and limitation. Two-thirds vote required for increases.	Passed

Year	Measure Number	Type	Subject Matter	Description	Pass/Fail
1978	5	DS	Health/Medical	Prohibits smoking in specified areas and restaurants must have non-smoking areas.	Failed
1978	6	DS	Civil Rights	School employees can be fired for homosexuality.	Failed
1978	7	DS	Legal	Criminal penalty for murder	Passed
1979	4	DA	Administration of Government	Limit government appropriations.	Passed
1980	10	DS	Health/Medical	Smoking and non-smoking sections in public places.	Failed
1980	10	DA	Housing	Rent control through local ordinance.	Failed
1980	11	DS	Taxes	Taxation. 10% surtax on energy businesses.	Failed
1980	9	DA	Taxes	Taxation: indexing, business inventory exemption.	Failed
1982	11	DS	Environmental Reform	Beverage containers must have refund value of at least five cents.	Failed
1982	12	M	Nuclear weapons/ facilities/waste	Nuclear weapons.	Passed
1982	13	DS	Environmental Reform	Establishes water conservation programs.	Failed
1982	14	DA	Apportionment/ Redistricting	Removes legislature's power over redistricting.	Failed
1982	15	DS	Gun Regulation	Requires registration of concealable firearms.	Failed
1982	5	DS	Taxes	Gift and inheritance taxes.	Passed
1982	6	DS	Taxes	Gift and inheritance taxes.	Passed
1982	7	DS	Taxes	Income tax indexing.	Passed
1982	8	DA	Legal	Criminal Justice.	Passed
1984	24	DS	Administration of Government	Legislature: rules, procedures, powers, funding.	Passed
1984	36	DA	Taxes	Forbids new property tax.	Failed
1984	37	DA	Gaming	Establishes state lottery.	Passed
1984	38	DS	Administration of Government	Voting materials. English only.	Passed
1984	39	DA	Apportionment/ Redistricting	Revising apportionment of members of legislature.	Failed
1984	40	DS	Campaign Finance Reform	Campaign contribution limits.	Failed
1984	41	DS	Welfare	Public aid, medical assistance programs.	Failed
1986	51	DS	Tort Reform	Multiple defendants tort damage liability.	Passed
1986	61	DA	Administration of Government	Compensation of public employees, contractors.	Failed
1986	62	DS	Taxes	Taxation, local governments and districts.	Passed
1986	63	DA	Administration of Government	English as official state language.	Passed
1986	64	DS	Health/Medical	Acquired Immune Deficiency Syndrome (AIDS)	Failed
1986	65	DS	Environmental Reform	Toxic discharge into drinking water.	Passed
1988	100	DS	Business Regulation	Reductions in auto insurance rates, regulation.	Failed

Year	Measure Number	Type	Subject Matter	Description	Pass/Fail
1988	101	DS	Business Regulation	Automobile accident claims, insurance rates.	Failed
1988	102	DS	Health/Medical	Reporting exposure to AIDS virus.	Failed
1988	103	DS	Business Regulation	Insurance rates, regulation, Commission.	Passed
1988	104	DS	Business Regulation	Automobile and other insurance.	Failed
1988	105	DS	Business Regulation	Disclosure to consumers, voters, investors.	Passed
1988	106	DS	Tort Reform	Attorney fee limit for tort claims.	Failed
1988	68	DS	Campaign Finance Reform	Legislative campaigns-spending and contribution limits.	Passed
1988	69	DS	Health/Medical	Acquired Immune Deficiency Syndrome (AIDS)	Failed
1988	73	DS	Campaign Finance Reform	Campaign bundling.	Passed
1988	95	DS	Welfare	Funding for hunger and homelessness programs.	Failed
1988	96	DS	Health/Medical	Communicable disease tests.	Passed
1988	97	DS	Health/Medical	State occupational safety and health plan.	Passed
1988	98	DA	Education	General fund financing — school funding.	Passed
1988	99	DA	Taxes	Cigarette and tobacco tax. Benefit fund.	Passed
1990	115	DA	Legal	Changes criminal law, judicial procedures, expands capital offences.	Passed
1990	116	DS	Bonds	Authorizes bonds for passenger and commuter rail systems.	Passed
1990	117	DS	Animal Rights	Prohibit sport hunting of mountain lions and establishes fund for wildlife protection.	Passed
1990	118	DA	Apportionment/ Redistricting	Changes procedures for redistricting.	Failed
1990	119	DA	Apportionment/ Redistricting	Reapportionment by commission.	Failed
1990	128	DS	Health/Medical	Regulates chemicals in foods and pesticides.	Failed
1990	129	DA	Drug Policy Reform	Creates drug superfund and authorizes bonds for prison construction.	Failed
1990	130	DS	Environmental Reform	Authorizes bonds for forest acquisition and regulates timber harvesting.	Failed
1990	131	DA	Term Limits	Term limits for state officials, changes campaign finance laws, some public funding.	Failed
1990	132	DA	Environmental Reform	Establishes marine protection zone within three miles of coast.	Passed
1990	133	DS	Taxes	Increases sales tax to fund drug enforcement and prevention.	Failed
1990	134	DA	Alcohol Regulation	Alcohol surtax.	Failed
1990	135	DS	Environmental Reform	Pesticide regulation.	Failed
1990	136	DA	Taxes	State and local taxation.	Failed
1990	137	DA	Initiative and Referendum	Initiative and referendum process.	Failed
1990	138	DS	Environmental Reform	Forest acquisition. Timber harvesting. Bond act.	Failed
1990	139	DA	Labor	Prison inmate labor. Tax credit.	Passed

Year	Measure Number	Type	Subject Matter	Description	Pass/Fail
1990	140	DA	Term Limits	Term limits for state officials, limits on legislature's salary and operating costs. 6/8	Passed
1992	161	DS	Physician assisted suicide	Allows a mentally competent adult who is suffering from a terminal illness to request and obtain medication from a physician to end that patient's own life in a humane and dignified manner.	Failed
1992	162	DA	Administration of Government	Public employee retirement systems.	Passed
1992	163	DA	Taxes	End taxation of certain food products.	Passed
1992	164	DS	Term Limits	Term limits on Congress 6/12.	Passed
1992	165	DA	Administration of Government	Lets Governor reduce some expenditures to balance budget.	Failed
1992	166	DS	Health/Medical	Requires employers to provide basic health care coverage.	Failed
1992	167	DS	Taxes	Raises top income tax rates, repeals 1991 sales tax hike, renters' tax credits.	Failed
1993	174	DA	Education	State education vouchers usable for public or private schools.	Failed
1994	184	DS	Legal	Convicted felons with 1 such prior conviction would receive twice the normal sentence for the new offense. Convicted felons with 2 or more such prior convictions would receive a life sentence. Three strikes your out.	Passed
1994	185	DS	Taxes	This measure imposes an additional 4% tax on retail sales of gasoline.	Failed
1994	186	DA	Health/Medical	Establishes health services system with defined medical, prescription drug, long-term, mental health, dental, emergency, other benefits.	Failed
1994	187	DS	Alien Rights	Makes illegal aliens ineligible for public social services, public health care services (unless emergency under federal law), and public school education at elementary, secondary, and post-secondary levels.	Passed
1994	188	DS	Health/Medical	Repeals and preempts local smoking and tobacco regulations. Repeals and replaces existing statewide smoking and tobacco regulations.	Failed
1996	198	DS	Election Reform	Created open blanket primary voting.	Passed
1996	199	DS	Housing	Mobile home rent.	Failed
1996	200	DS	Business Regulation	No-fault motor insurance.	Failed
1996	201	DS	Tort Reform	Attorneys' fees in class action and shareholder suits.	Failed
1996	202	DS	Tort Reform	Limits on attorneys' contingency fees in tort cases.	Failed
1996	207	DS	Tort Reform	Attorneys fees. Right to negotiate. Frivolous lawsuits.	Failed
1996	208	DS	Campaign Finance Reform	Campaign contributions and spending limits. Restricts lobbyist.	Passed
1996	209	DA	Civil Rights	Ending racial preferences.	Passed

Year	Measure Number	Type	Subject Matter	Description	Pass/Fail
1996	210	DS	Labor	Minimum wage increase.	Passed
1996	211	DS	Tort Reform	Attorney — client fee arrangements, securities, fraud, lawsuits.	Failed
1996	212	DS	Campaign Finance Reform	Campaign contributions and spending limits. Repeals gift and honoraria limits. Restricts lobbyist.	Failed
1996	213	DS	Business Regulation	Limitation of recovery to felons. Uninsured motorists. Drunk drivers.	Passed
1996	214	DS	Health/Medical	Regulation of health care business.	Failed
1996	215	DS	Drug Policy Reform	Legalize marijuana for medicinal purposes.	Passed
1996	216	DS	Business Regulation	Consumer protection. Taxes on corporate restructuring.	Failed
1996	217	DS	Taxes	Reinstates expired higher tax rates on top incomes.	Failed
1996	218	DA	Taxes	Establish tax limits	Passed
1998	10	DA	Health/Medical	Would create state commission to provide information and materials and to formulate guidelines for establishment of comprehensive early childhood development and smoking prevention programs.	Passed
1998	223	DA	Education	School districts to spend no more than 5 percent of all funds for administrative costs.	Failed
1998	224	DA	Administration of Government	Regulates state funded design and engineering contracts.	Failed
1998	225	DS	Term Limits	Informed Voter Law.	Passed
1998	226	DS	Campaign Finance Reform	Union member's permission required to use dues for political contributions.	Failed
1998	227	DS	Education	Ending bilingual education.	Passed
1998	4	DS	Animal Rights	Would prohibit trapping mammals classified as fur bearing or non-game with body-gripping traps for recreation or commerce in fur.	Passed
1998	5	DS	Gaming	Would specify terms and conditions of mandatory compact between state and Indian tribes for gambling on tribal land.	Passed
1998	6	DS	Animal Rights	Prohibiting any person from possessing transferring receiving or holding any horse or pony or burro or mule with intent to kill or have it killed.	Passed
1998	7	DS	Environmental Reform	Would authorize State Air Resources Board and delegated air pollution control districts to award $218 million in state tax credits annually until 2011 to encourage air-commissions reduction.	Failed
1998	8	DS	Education	Would create fund for reduction in class sizes. Requires teacher credentialing and testing.	Failed
1998	9	DS	Nuclear weapons/ facilities/waste	Would prohibit assessment of utility tax bond payments or surcharges for payment of costs of nuclear power plants/related assets.	Failed

Year	Measure Number	Type	Subject Matter	Description	Pass/Fail
2000	21	DS	Death Penalty	Increases punishment for gang-related felonies; death penalty for gang-related murder; indeterminate life sentences for home-invasion robbery, carjacking, witness intimidation and drive-by shootings.	Passed
2000	22	DS	Civil Rights	Adds a provision to the Family Code providing that only marriage between a man and a woman is valid or recognized in California.	Passed
2000	23	DS	Election Reform	Provides that in general, special, primary and recall elections, voters may vote for "none of the above" rather than a named candidate.	Failed
2000	25	DS	Campaign Finance Reform	Expands campaign contribution disclosure requirements. Establishes contribution limits. Bans corporate contributions. Limits fundraising to period 12 months before primary election and ninety days after election.	Failed
2000	26	DA	Education	Authorizes school, community college districts, and County education offices that evaluate safety, class size, information technology needs to issue bonds if approved by majority of applicable district or County voters.	Failed
2000	27	DA	Term Limits	Self Limit Law	Failed
2000	28	DS	Taxes	Repeals additional $.50 per pack tax on cigarettes and equivalent increase in state tax on tobacco products previously enacted by Proposition 10 at November 3, 1998, election.	Failed
2000	35	DA	Administration of Government	Overrides constitutional restrictions to allow state, local contracting with private entities for engineering and architectural services in all phases of public works projects.	Passed
2000	36	DS	Drug Policy Reform	Requires drug treatment program and probation for certain non-violent drug possession offenses and similar parole violations not including sale, production or manufacture.	Passed
2000	37	DA	Taxes	Redefines as taxes any compulsory fees enacted by state or local government after July 1, 1999 to monitor, study or mitigate societal or economic effects of activity where such fees impose no regulatory obligation on the payer.	Failed
2000	38	DA	Education	Authorizes annual state payments of at least $4000 per pupil for qualifying private and religious schools as grants for new enrollees.	Failed

Year	Measure Number	Type	Subject Matter	Description	Pass/Fail
2000	39	DA	Education	Authorizes bonds for construction, reconstruction, rehabilitation or replacement of school facilities if approved by 55% vote.	Passed

California Constitution

Article 2

Sec. 8.

(a) The initiative is the power of the electors to propose statutes and amendments to the Constitution and to adopt or reject them.

(b) An initiative measure may be proposed by presenting to the Secretary of State a petition that sets forth the text of the proposed statute or amendment to the Constitution and is certified to have been signed by electors equal in number to 5 percent in the case of a statute, and 8 percent in the case of an amendment to the Constitution, of the votes for all candidates for Governor at the last gubernatorial election.

(c) The Secretary of State shall then submit the measure at the next general election held at least 131 days after it qualifies or at any special statewide election held prior to that general election. The Governor may call a special statewide election for the measure.

(d) An initiative measure embracing more than one subject may not be submitted to the electors or have any effect.

(e) An initiative measure shall not include or exclude any political subdivision of the State from the application or effect of its provisions based upon approval or disapproval of the initiative measure, or based upon the casting of a specified percentage of votes in favor of the measure, by the electors of that political subdivision.

(f) An initiative measure shall not contain alternative or cumulative provisions wherein one or more of those provisions would become law depending upon the casting of a specified percentage of votes for or against the measure.

Sec. 9.

(a) The referendum is the power of the electors to approve or reject statutes or parts of statutes except urgency statutes, statutes calling elections, and statutes providing for tax levies or appropriations for usual current expenses of the State.

(b) A referendum measure may be proposed by presenting to the Secretary of State, within 90 days after the enactment date of the statute, a petition certified to have been signed by electors equal in number to 5 percent of the votes for all candidates for Governor at the last gubernatorial election, asking that the statute or part of it be submitted to the electors. In the case of a statute enacted by a bill passed by the Legislature on or before the date the Legislature adjourns for a joint recess to reconvene in the second calendar year of the biennium of the legislative session, and in the possession of the Governor after that date, the petition may not be presented on or after January 1 next following the enactment date unless a copy of the petition is submitted to the Attorney General pursuant to subdivision (d) of Section 10 of Article II before January 1.

(c) The Secretary of State shall then submit the measure at the next general election held at least 31 days after it qualifies or at a special statewide election held prior to that general election. The Governor may call a special statewide election for the measure.

Sec. 10.

(a) An initiative statute or referendum approved by a majority of votes thereon takes effect the day after the election unless the measure provides otherwise. If a referendum petition is filed against a part of a statute the remainder shall not be delayed from going into effect.

(b) If provisions of 2 or more measures approved at the same election conflict, those of the measure receiving the highest affirmative vote shall prevail.

(c) The Legislature may amend or repeal referendum statutes. It may amend or repeal an initiative statute by another statute that becomes effective only when approved by the electors unless the initiative statute permits amendment or repeal without their approval.

(d) Prior to circulation of an initiative or referendum petition for signatures, a copy shall be submitted to the Attorney General who shall prepare a title and summary of the measure as provided by law.

(e) The Legislature shall provide the manner in which petitions shall be circulated, presented, and certified, and measures submitted to the electors.

Sec. 11.

(a) Initiative and referendum powers may be exercised by the electors of each city or county under procedures that the Legislature shall provide. Except as provided in subdivisions (b) and (c), this section does not affect a city having a charter.

(b) A city or county initiative measure shall not include or exclude any part of the city or county from the application or effect of its provisions based upon approval or disapproval of the initiative measure, or based upon the casting of a specified percentage of votes in favor of the measure, by the electors of the city or county or any part thereof.

(c) A city or county initiative measure shall not contain alternative or cumulative provisions wherein one or more of those provisions would become law depending upon the casting of a specified percentage of votes for or against the measure.

Sec. 12.

No amendment to the Constitution, and no statute proposed to the electors by the Legislature or by initiative, that names any individual to hold any office, or names or identifies any private corporation to perform any function or to have any power or duty, may be submitted to the electors or have any effect.

Sec. 13.

Recall is the power of the electors to remove an elective officer.

Sec. 14.

(a) Recall of a state officer is initiated by delivering to the Secretary of State a petition alleging reason for recall. Sufficiency of reason is not reviewable. Proponents have 160 days to file signed petitions.

(b) A petition to recall a statewide officer must be signed by electors equal in number to 12 percent of the last vote for the office, with signatures from each of 5 counties equal in number to 1 percent of the last vote for the office in the county. Signatures to recall Senators, members of the Assembly, members of the Board of Equalization, and judges of courts of appeal and trial courts must equal in number 20 percent of the last vote for the office.

(c) The Secretary of State shall maintain a continuous count of the signatures certified to that office.

Sec. 15.

(a) An election to determine whether to recall an officer and, if appropriate, to elect a successor shall be called by the Governor and held not less than 60 days nor more than 80 days from the date of certification of sufficient signatures.

(b) A recall election may be conducted within 180 days from the date of certification of sufficient signatures in order that the election may be consolidated with the next regularly scheduled election occurring wholly or partially within the same jurisdiction in which the recall election is held, if the number of voters eligible to vote at that next regularly scheduled election equal at least 50 percent of all the voters eligible to vote at the recall election.

(c) If the majority vote on the question is to recall, the officer is removed and, if there is a candidate, the candidate who receives a plurality is the successor. The officer may not be a candidate, nor shall there be any candidacy for an office filled pursuant to subdivision (d) of Section 16 of Article VI.

Sec. 16.

The Legislature shall provide for circulation, filing, and certification of petitions, nomination of candidates, and the recall election.

Sec. 17.

If recall of the Governor or Secretary of State is initiated, the recall duties of that office shall be performed by the Lieutenant Governor or Controller, respectively.

Sec. 18.

A state officer who is not recalled shall be reimbursed by the State for the officer's recall election expenses legally and personally incurred. Another recall may not be initiated against the officer until six months after the election.

Sec. 19.

The Legislature shall provide for recall of local officers. This section does not affect counties and cities whose charters provide for recall.

Sec. 20.

Terms of elective offices provided for by this Constitution, other than Members of the Legislature, commence on the Monday after January 1 following election. The election shall be held in the last even-numbered year before the term expires.

Article 4: Legislative

Sec. 1.

The legislative power of this State is vested in the California Legislature which consists of the Senate and Assembly, but the people reserve to themselves the powers of initiative and referendum.

California Statutes

9000.

This article applies only to initiative and referendum measures affecting the Constitution or laws of the state.

9001.

The heading of a proposed initiative measure shall be in substantially the following form:

Initiative Measure to Be Submitted Directly to the Voters

The Attorney General of California has prepared the following title and summary of the chief purpose and points of the proposed measure:

(Here set forth the title and summary prepared by the Attorney General. This title and summary must also be printed across the top of each page of the petition whereon signatures are to appear.)

To the Honorable Secretary of State of California

We, the undersigned, registered, qualified voters of California, residents of ____ County (or City and County), hereby propose amendments to the Constitution of California (the ____ Code, relating to ____) and petition the Secretary of State to submit the same to the voters of California for their adoption or rejection at the next succeeding general election or at any special statewide election held prior to that general election or otherwise provided by law. The proposed constitutional (or statutory) amendments (full title and text of the measure) read as follows:

9002.

Prior to the circulation of any initiative or referendum petition for signatures, a draft of the proposed measure shall be submitted to the Attorney General with a written request that a title and summary of the chief purpose and points of the proposed measure be prepared. The title and summary shall not exceed a total of 100 words. The persons presenting the request shall be known as the "proponents." The Attorney General shall preserve the written request until after the next general election.

9003.

In the event that the Attorney General is a proponent of a proposed measure, the title and summary of the chief purpose and points of the proposed measure, including an estimate or opinion on the financial impact of the measure, shall be prepared by the Legislative Counsel, and the other duties of the Attorney General specified in this chapter with respect to the title and summary and an estimate of the financial effect of the measure shall be performed by the Legislative Counsel.

9004.

Upon receipt of a draft of a petition, the Attorney General shall prepare a summary of the chief purposes and points of the proposed measure. The summary shall be prepared in the manner provided for the preparation of ballot titles in Article 5 (commencing with Section 9050), the provisions of which in regard to the preparation, filing, and settlement of titles and summaries are hereby made applicable to the summary. The Attorney General shall provide a copy of the title and summary to the Secretary of State within 15 days after receipt of the final version of a proposed initiative measure, or if a fiscal estimate or opinion is to be included, within 15 days after receipt of the fiscal estimate or opinion prepared by the Department of Finance and the Joint Legislative Budget Committee pursuant to Section 9005.

If during the 15-day period, the proponents of the proposed initiative measure submit amendments, other than technical, nonsubstantive amendments, to the final version of the measure, the Attorney General shall provide a copy of the title and summary to the Secretary of State within 15 days after receipt of the amendments.

The proponents of any initiative measure, at the time of submitting the draft of the measure to the Attorney General, shall pay a fee of two hundred dollars ($200), which shall be placed in a trust fund in the office of the Treasurer and refunded to the proponents if the measure qualifies for the ballot within two years from the date the summary is furnished to the proponents. If the measure does not qualify within that period, the fee shall be immediately paid into the General Fund of the state.

9005.

Notwithstanding Section 9004, the Attorney General, in preparing a title or summary for an initiative measure, shall determine whether the substance thereof if adopted would affect the revenues or expenditures of the state or local government, and if he or she determines that it would, he or she shall include in the title either the estimate of the amount of any increase or decrease in revenues or costs to the state or local government, or an opinion as to whether or not a substantial net change in state or local finances would result if the proposed initiative is adopted.

The estimates as required by this section shall be made jointly by the Department of Finance and the Joint Legislative Budget Committee, who shall deliver them to the Attorney General so that he or she may include them in the titles prepared by him or her.

The estimate shall be delivered to the Attorney General within 25 working days from the date of receipt of the final version of the proposed initiative from the Attorney General, unless in the opinion of both the Department of Finance and the Joint Legislative Budget Committee a reasonable estimate of the net impact of the proposed initiative cannot be prepared within the 25-day period. In the latter case, the Department of Finance and the Joint Legislative Budget Committee shall, within the 25-day period, give the Attorney General their opinion as to whether or not a substantial net change in state or local finances would result if the proposed initiative is adopted.

Any statement of fiscal impact prepared by the Legislative Analyst pursuant to subdivision (b) of Section 12172 of the Government Code may be used by the Department of Finance and the Joint Legislative Budget Committee in the preparation of the fiscal estimate or the opinion.

9006.

If, for any reason, any initiative or referendum measure proposed by petition as provided by this article is not submitted to the voters at the next succeeding statewide election, that failure shall not prevent its submission at a succeeding statewide election.

9007.

Immediately upon the preparation of the summary of an initiative or referendum petition, the Attorney General shall forthwith transmit copies of the text of the measure and summary to the Senate and Assembly. The appropriate committees of each house may hold public hearings on the subject of the measure. However, nothing in this section shall be construed as authority for the Legislature to alter the measure or prevent it from appearing on the ballot.

9008.

Every proposed initiative measure, prior to circulation, shall have placed across the top of the petition in 12-point or larger roman boldface type, all of the following:
(a) The summary prepared by the Attorney General upon each page of the petition on which signatures are to appear.
(b) The summary prepared by the Attorney General upon each section of the petition preceding the text of the measure.
(c) The summary prepared by the Attorney General as required by subdivision (b) shall be preceded by the following statement: "Initiative measure to be submitted directly to the voters."

9009.

A space at least one inch wide shall be left blank across the top of each page of every initiative petition and after the name of each voter who has signed the petition for the use of the county elections official in verifying the petition.

9010.

Across the top of each page of a referendum petition, there shall be printed in 12-point boldface type the following: "Referendum Against an Act Passed by the Legislature."

9011.

Across the top of each page after the first page of every referendum petition or section of a referendum petition, which is prepared and circulated, there shall be printed in 18-point gothic type a short title, in 20 words or less, showing the nature of the petition and the subject to which it relates.

A space at least one inch wide shall be left blank at the top of each page and after each name, for the use of the county elections official, in verifying the petition.

9012.

Officers required by law to receive or file in their offices any initiative or referendum petition shall not receive or file any initiative or referendum petition not in conformity with this article.

9013.

Notwithstanding any other provision of law, no initiative shall be placed on a statewide special election ballot that qualifies less than 131 days before the date of the election.

9014.

Any initiative or referendum petition may be presented in sections, but each section shall contain a full and correct copy of the title and text of the proposed measure. The text of the measure shall be printed in type not smaller than 8 point.

9015.

The Secretary of State shall prepare and provide to any person, upon request, a pamphlet describing the procedures and requirements for preparing and circulating a statewide initiative measure and for filing sections of the petition, and describing the procedure used in determining and verifying the number of qualified voters who have signed the petition.

9020.

The petition sections shall be designed so that each signer shall personally affix all of the following:
(a) His or her signature.
(b) His or her printed name.
(c) His or her residence address, giving street and number, or if no street or number exists, adequate designation of residence so that the location may be readily ascertained.
(d) The name of his or her incorporated city or unincorporated community.
Only a person who is a qualified registered voter at the time of signing the petition is entitled to sign it.
The number of signatures attached to each section shall be at the pleasure of the person soliciting the signatures.

9021.

Any qualified registered voter may circulate an initiative or referendum petition anywhere within the state. Each section of the petition shall bear the name of a county or city and county, and only qualified registered voters of that county or city and county shall sign that section.

Any circulator may sign the section he or she is circulating as provided in Section 106.

9022.

(a) Each section shall have attached thereto the declaration of the person soliciting the signatures setting forth the information required by Section 104 and stating that the circulator is a registered voter of the state.
(b) The circulator shall certify to the content of the declaration as to its truth and correctness, under penalty of perjury under the laws of the State of California, with the signature of his or her name at length, including given name, middle name or initial. The circulator shall state the date and the place of execution on the declaration immediately preceding his or her signature.

No other declaration thereto shall be required.

Petitions so verified shall be prima facie evidence that the signatures thereon are genuine and that the persons signing are qualified voters. Unless and until otherwise proven upon official investigation, it shall be presumed that the petition presented contains the signatures of the requisite number of qualified voters.

9030.

(a) Each section of the petition shall be filed with the elections official of the county or city and county in which it was circulated, but all sections circulated in any county or city and county shall be filed at the same time. Once filed, no petition section shall be amended except by order of a court of competent jurisdiction.

(b) Within eight days after the filing of the petition, excluding Saturdays, Sundays, and holidays, the elections official shall determine the total number of signatures affixed to the petition and shall transmit this information to the Secretary of State. If the total number of signatures filed with all elections officials is less than 100 percent of the number of qualified voters required to find the petition sufficient, the Secretary of State shall so notify the proponents and the elections officials, and no further action shall be taken with regard to the petition.

(c) If the number of signatures filed with all elections officials is 100 percent or more of the number of qualified voters needed to declare the petition sufficient, the Secretary of State shall immediately so notify the elections officials.

(d) Within 30 days after this notification, excluding Saturdays, Sundays, and holidays, the elections official shall determine the number of qualified voters who have signed the petition. If more than 500 names have been signed on sections of the petition filed with an elections official, the elections official shall use a random sampling technique for verification of signatures, as determined by the Secretary of State. The random sample of signatures to be verified shall be drawn in such a manner that every signature filed with the elections official shall be given an equal opportunity to be included in the sample. The random sampling shall include an examination of at least 500 or 3 percent of the signatures, whichever is greater. In determining from the records of registration what number of qualified voters have signed the petition, the elections official may use the duplicate file of affidavits of registered voters or the facsimiles of voters' signatures, provided that the method of preparing and displaying the facsimiles complies with law.

(e) The elections official, upon the completion of the examination, shall immediately attach to the petition, except the signatures thereto appended, a properly dated certificate, showing the result of the examination, and shall immediately transmit the petition and the certificate to the Secretary of State. A copy of this certificate shall be filed in the elections official's office.

(f) If the certificates received from all elections officials by the Secretary of State establish that the number of valid signatures does not equal 95 percent of the number of qualified voters needed to find the petition sufficient, the petition shall be deemed to have failed to qualify, and the Secretary of State shall immediately so notify the proponents and the elections officials.

(g) If the certificates received from all elections officials by the Secretary of State total more than 110 percent of the number of qualified voters needed to find the petition sufficient, the petition shall be deemed to qualify as of the date of receipt by the Secretary of State of certificates showing the petition to have reached the 110 percent, and the Secretary of State shall immediately so notify the proponents and the elections officials.

9031.

(a) If the statistical sampling shows that the number of valid signatures is within 95 to 110 percent of the number of signatures of qualified voters needed to declare the petition sufficient, the Secretary of State shall order the examination and verification of each signature filed, and shall so notify the elections officials.

(b) Within 30 days, excluding Saturdays, Sundays, and holidays, after receipt of the order, the elections official or registrar of voters shall determine from the records of registration what number of qualified voters have signed the petition and if necessary the board of supervisors shall allow the elections official or registrar additional assistance for the purpose of examining the petition and provide for their compensation. In determining from the records of registration what number of qualified voters have signed the petition, the elections official or registrar of voters may use any file or list of registered voters maintained by his or her office, or the facsimiles of voters' signatures, provided that the method of preparing and displaying the facsimiles complies with law.

(c) The elections official or registrar, upon the completion of the examination, shall immediately attach to the petition, except the signatures thereto appended, an amended certificate properly dated, showing the result of the examination and shall immediately transmit the petition, together with the amended certificate, to the Secretary of State. A copy of the amended certificate shall be filed in the elections official's office.

(d) If the amended certificates establish the petition's sufficiency, the petition shall be deemed to be filed as of the date of receipt by the Secretary of State of certificates showing the petition to be signed by the requisite number of voters of the state.

If the amended certificates received from all elections officials by the Secretary of State establish that the petition has still been found insufficient, the Secretary of State shall immediately so notify the proponents and the elections officials.

9032.

The right to file the petition shall be reserved to its proponents, and any section thereof presented for filing by any person or persons other than the proponents of a measure or by persons duly authorized in writing by one or more of the proponents shall be disregarded by the elections official.

9033.

When the Secretary of State has received from one or more elections officials or registrars a petition, certified as herein provided to have been signed by the requisite number of qualified voters, the Secretary of State shall forthwith notify the proponents and immediately transmit to the elections official or registrar of voters of every county or city and county in the state, a certificate showing this fact so that signature verification can be terminated.

A petition shall be deemed to be filed with the Secretary of State upon the date of the receipt by the Secretary of State of a certificate or certificates showing the petition to be signed by the requisite number of voters of the state. Any elections official shall, upon receipt of the copy, file the notification for record in that office.

9034.

Upon the certification of an initiative measure for the ballot, the Secretary of State shall transmit copies of the initiative measure, together with the ballot title as prepared by the Attorney General pursuant to Section 9050, to the Senate and Assembly. Each house shall assign the initiative measure to its appropriate committees. The appropriate committees shall hold joint public hearings on the subject of such measure prior to the date of the election at which the measure is to be voted upon. However, no hearing may be held within 30 days prior to the date of the election.

Nothing in this section shall be construed as authority for the Legislature to alter the initiative measure or prevent it from appearing on the ballot.

9035.

An initiative measure may be proposed by presenting to the Secretary of State a petition that sets forth the text of the proposed statute or amendment to the Constitution and is certified to have been signed by registered voters equal in number to 5 percent in the case of a statute, and 8 percent in the case of an amendment to the Constitution, of the voters for all candidates for Governor at the last gubernatorial election preceding the issuance of the title and summary for the initiative measure by the Attorney General.

9040.

Every constitutional amendment, bond measure, or other legislative measure submitted to the people by the Legislature shall appear on the ballot of the first statewide election occurring at least 131 days after the adoption of the proposal by the Legislature.

9041.

Whenever the Legislature submits any measure to the voters of the state, the author of the measure and no more than two persons appointed by the author may draft an argument for the adoption of the measure, or the author of the measure may appoint no more than three persons to draft the argument. In no case shall more than three persons write the argument. This argument shall not exceed 500 words in length.

If the author of the measure desires separate arguments to be written in its favor by each person appointed, separate arguments may be written, but the combined length of the arguments shall not exceed 500 words.

9042.

If a measure submitted to the voters by the Legislature was not adopted unanimously, one member of each house who voted against it shall be appointed by the presiding officers of the respective houses, at the same time as appointments to draft an argument in its favor are made, to write an argument against the measure. The argument shall not exceed 500 words.

If those members appointed to write an argument against the measure so choose, each may write a separate argument opposing it, but the combined length of the two arguments shall not exceed 500 words.

9043.

Arguments prepared by legislators and their appointees shall be submitted to the Secretary of State no later than a date to be designated by the Secretary of State. The arguments may not be amended or changed after submission.

9044.

If an argument for or an argument against a measure submitted to the voters by the Legislature has not been filed by a Member of the Legislature, any voter may request the Secretary of State's permission to prepare and file an argument for either side, on which no argument has been prepared by a Member of the Legislature. The Secretary of State shall grant permission unless two or more voters request permission to submit arguments on the same side of a measure, in which event the Secretary of State shall designate one of the voters to write the argument. Any argument prepared pursuant to this section shall be submitted to the Secretary of State by a date sufficient to meet ballot printing deadlines.

9050.

The Attorney General shall provide and return to the Secretary of State a ballot title for each measure submitted to the voters of the whole state.

9051.

Any person who is interested in any proposed measure may at any time, prior to 150 days before the election at which the measure is to be voted upon, file a copy of it with the Secretary of State, together with a request that a ballot title be prepared for it. This request shall be accompanied by the address of the person or association of persons proposing the measure. The Secretary of State shall immediately transmit a copy of the measure to the Attorney General. Within 10 days after it is filed, the Attorney General shall provide and return to the Secretary of State a ballot title for the measure. The ballot title may differ from the legislative or other title of the measure and shall express in not exceeding 100 words the purpose of the measure. In providing the ballot title, the Attorney General shall give a true and impartial statement of the purpose of the measure in such language that the ballot title shall neither be an argument, nor be likely to create prejudice, for or against the proposed measure.

9052.

Immediately upon receipt of the ballot title prepared by the Attorney General, the Secretary of State shall mail to all persons who may have requested the preparation of that ballot title, a notice addressed to them at the address accompanying the request, stating that the Attorney General has made and returned the ballot title. The notice shall also contain a copy of the ballot title prepared by the Attorney General.

9053.

Each measure shall be designated on the ballot by the ballot title certified to the Secretary of State by the Attorney General.

9060.

In case either the argument for or the argument against any measure placed on the ballot is not prepared and filed, the Secretary of State shall, by a general press release, request voters to submit arguments.

9061.

The press release shall be mailed at least 120 days prior to the date of the election at which a measure is to be voted upon.

9062.

The press release shall consist of an announcement containing:
(a) A summary of the essential nature or purpose of the measure for or against which no argument has been prepared or filed.
(b) A statement that the affirmative or negative arguments, or both, have not been filed.
(c) An invitation to any voter or group of voters to submit and file with the Secretary of State, within the time limit, arguments for or against the measure as to which affirmative or negative arguments have not been filed.

9063.

The summary of a measure given in the press release shall be the official summary that has been prepared by the Attorney General. The Legislative Counsel Bureau shall prepare the summary on all other measures.

9064.

Any voter or group of voters may, at any time within the time limit, prepare and file with the Secretary of State an argument for or against any measure as to which arguments have not been prepared or filed. This argument shall not exceed 500 words in length.

9065.

A ballot argument shall not be accepted under this article unless accompanied by all of the following:
(a) The name, business or home address, and telephone number of each person submitting the argument.
(b) If the argument is submitted on behalf of an organization, the name, business address, and telephone number of the organization and of at least two of its principal officers.
(c) The name, business or home address, and telephone number of a contact person for each individual or organization submitting the argument.
(d) If the argument is signed by anyone other than the proponent or legislative author, the name and official title of the person or persons authorized by the proponent to sign the argument.
(e) The signed statement required by Section 9600.
(f) No person signing an argument for or against a measure or a rebuttal to an argument for or against a measure may identify himself or herself in reference to that signature as a candidate for any office.

9067.

If more than one argument for or more than one argument against any measure is filed within the time prescribed, the Secretary of State shall select one of the arguments for printing in the ballot pamphlets. In selecting the argument the Secretary of State shall give preference and priority in the order named to the arguments of the following:
(a) In the case of a measure submitted by the Legislature, Members of the Legislature.
(b) In the case of an initiative or referendum measure, the proponent of the petition.
(c) Bona fide associations of citizens.
(d) Individual voters.

9068.

(a) No more than three signatures shall appear with any argument printed in the ballot pamphlet. In case any argument is signed by more than three persons the signatures of the first three shall be printed.
(b) The Secretary of State shall provide, upon request, the name of, and a telephone number for, each signer of a ballot argument printed in the ballot pamphlet.

9069.

When the Secretary of State has received the arguments that will be printed in the ballot pamphlet, the Secretary of State, within five days of receipt thereof, shall send copies of the arguments in favor of the proposition to the authors of the arguments against and copies of the arguments against to the authors of the arguments in favor. The authors may prepare and submit rebuttal arguments not exceeding 250 words, or may authorize in writing any other person or persons to prepare, submit, or sign the rebuttal argument. The rebuttal arguments shall be filed with the Secretary of State no later than a date to be designated by the Secretary of State.

Rebuttal arguments shall be printed in the same manner as the direct arguments. Each rebuttal argument shall immediately follow the direct argument which it seeks to rebut.

9080.

The provisions of Sections 9084 to 9093, inclusive, are a restatement of, and shall be construed in conformity with, Sections 88001 to 88007, inclusive, of the Government Code.

9081.

There shall be a state ballot pamphlet, that the Secretary of State shall prepare.

9082.

The Secretary of State shall cause to be printed as many ballot pamphlets as needed to comply with this code. The ballot pamphlets shall be printed in the Office of State Printing unless the Director of General Services determines that the printing of the pamphlets in the Office of State Printing cannot be done adequately, competently, or satisfactorily, in which case the Secretary of State, subject to the approval of the Director of General Services, shall contract with a private printing concern for the printing of all or a part of the pamphlets.

Copy for preparation of the ballot pamphlets shall be furnished to the Office of State Printing at least 40 days prior to the date for required delivery to the elections officials as provided in Section 9094.

9082.5.

The Secretary of State shall cause to be produced an audiocassette recorded version of the state ballot pamphlet. This recorded cassette version shall be made available in quantities to be determined by the Secretary of State and shall contain an impartial summary, arguments for and against, rebuttal arguments, and other information concerning each measure that the Secretary of State determines will make the cassette recorded version of the state ballot pamphlet easier to understand or more useful to the average voter.

9082.7.

The Secretary of State shall disseminate the complete state ballot pamphlet over the Internet.

9083.

If the ballot contains a question as to the confirmation of a justice of the Supreme Court or a court of appeal, the Secretary of State shall include in the state ballot pamphlet a written explanation of the electoral procedure for justices of the Supreme Court and the courts of appeal. The explanation shall state the following:

"Under the California Constitution, justices of the Supreme Court and the courts of appeal are subject to confirmation by the voters. The public votes "yes" or "no" on whether to retain each justice.

"These judicial offices are nonpartisan.

"Before a person can become an appellate justice, the Governor must submit the candidate's name to the Judicial Nominees Evaluation Commission, which is comprised of public members and lawyers. The commission conducts a thorough review of the candidate's background and qualifications, with community input, and then forwards its evaluation of the candidate to the Governor.

"The Governor then reviews the commission's evaluation and officially nominates the candidate, whose qualifications are subject to public comment before examination and review by the Commission on Judicial Appointments. That commission consists of the Chief Justice of California, the Attorney General of California, and a senior Presiding Justice of the Courts of Appeal. The Commission on Judicial Appointments must then confirm or reject the nomination. Only if confirmed does the nominee become a justice.

"Following confirmation, the justice is sworn into office and is subject to voter approval at the next gubernatorial election, and thereafter at the conclusion of each term. The term prescribed by the California Constitution for justices of the Supreme Court and courts of appeal is 12 years. Justices are confirmed by the Commission on Judicial Appointments only until the next gubernatorial election, at which time they run for retention of the remainder of the term, if any, of their predecessor, which will be either four or eight years."

9084.

The ballot pamphlet shall contain all of the following:
(a) A complete copy of each state measure.
(b) A copy of the specific constitutional or statutory provision, if any, that each state measure would repeal or revise.
(c) A copy of the arguments and rebuttals for and against each state measure.
(d) A copy of the analysis of each state measure.
(e) Tables of contents, indexes, art work, graphics and other materials that the Secretary of State determines will make the ballot pamphlet easier to understand or more useful for the average voter.
(f) A notice, conspicuously printed on the cover of the ballot pamphlet, indicating that additional copies of the ballot pamphlet will be mailed by the county elections official upon request.
(g) A written explanation of the judicial retention procedure as required by Section 9083.

9085.

(a) The ballot pamphlet shall also contain a section, located near the front of the pamphlet, that provides a concise summary of the general meaning and effect of "yes" and "no" votes on each state measure.
(b) The summary statements required by this section shall be prepared by the Legislative Analyst. These statements are not intended to provide comprehensive information on each measure. The Legislative Analyst shall be solely responsible for determining the contents of these statements. The statements shall be available for public examination and amendment pursuant to Section 9092.

9086.

The ballot pamphlet shall contain as to each state measure to be voted upon, the following, in the order set forth in this section:

(a) Upon the top portion of the first page, and not exceeding one-third of the page, shall appear:

(1) Identification of the measure by number and title.

(2) The official summary prepared by the Attorney General.

(3) The total number of votes cast for and against the measure in both the State Senate and Assembly, if the measure was passed by the Legislature.

(b) Beginning at the top of the right page shall appear the analysis prepared by the Legislative Analyst, provided that the analysis fits on a single page. If it does not fit on a single page, the analysis shall begin on the lower portion of the first left page and shall continue on subsequent pages until it is completed.

(c) Arguments for and against the measure shall be placed on the next left and right pages, respectively, following the final page of the analysis of the Legislative Analyst ends. The rebuttals shall be placed immediately below the arguments.

(d) If no argument against the measure has been submitted, the argument for the measure shall appear on the right page facing the analysis.

(e) The complete text of each measure shall appear at the back of the pamphlet. The text of the measure shall contain the provisions of the proposed measure and the existing provisions of law repealed or revised by the measure. The provisions of the proposed measure differing from the existing provisions of law affected shall be distinguished in print, so as to facilitate comparison.

(f) The following statement shall be printed at the bottom of each page where arguments appear: "Arguments printed on this page are the opinions of the authors, and have not been checked for accuracy by any official agency."

9087.

The Legislative Analyst shall prepare an impartial analysis of the measure describing the measure and including a fiscal analysis of the measure showing the amount of any increase or decrease in revenue or cost to state or local government. Any estimate of increased cost to local governments shall be set out in boldface print in the ballot pamphlet. The analysis shall be written in clear and concise terms, so as to be easily understood by the average voter, and shall avoid the use of technical terms wherever possible. The analysis may contain background information, including the effect of the measure on existing law and the effect of enacted legislation which will become effective if the measure is adopted, and shall generally set forth in an impartial manner the information the average voter needs to adequately understand the measure. The Legislative Analyst may contract with professional writers, educational specialists or other persons for assistance in writing an analysis that fulfills the requirements of this section, including the requirement that the analysis be written so that it will be easily understood by the average voter. The Legislative Analyst may also request the assistance of any state department, agency, or official in preparing his or her analysis. Prior to submitting the analysis to the Secretary of State, the Legislative Analyst shall submit the analysis to a committee of five persons, appointed by the Legislative Analyst, for the purpose of reviewing the analysis to confirm its clarity and easy comprehension to the average voter. The committee shall be drawn from the public at large, and one member shall be a specialist in education, one shall be bilingual, and one shall be a professional writer. Members of the committee shall be reimbursed for reasonable and necessary expenses incurred in performing their duties. Within five days of the submission of the analysis to the committee, the committee shall make such recommendations to the Legislative Analyst as it deems appropriate to guarantee that the analysis can be easily understood by the average voter. The Legislative Analyst shall consider the committee's recommendations, and he or she shall incorporate in the analysis those changes recommended by the committee that he or she deems to be appropriate. The Legislative Analyst is solely responsible for determining the content of the analysis required by this section. The title of the measure that appears on the ballot shall be amended to contain a summary of the Legislative Analyst's estimate of the net state and local government financial impact.

9088.

(a) At each statewide election at which state bond measures will be submitted to the voters for their approval or rejection, the ballot pamphlet for that election shall include a discussion, prepared by the Legislative Analyst, of the state's current bonded indebtedness situation.

(b) This discussion shall include information as to the dollar amount of the state's current authorized and outstanding bonded indebtedness, the approximate percentage of the state's General Fund revenues which are required to service this indebtedness, and the expected impact of the issuance of the bonds to be approved at the election on the items specified in this subdivision.

(c) The discussion required by this section shall appear on a separate page in the ballot pamphlet immediately following the rebuttal to the argument against the last ballot measure included in the ballot pamphlet.

9089.

Measures shall be printed in the ballot pamphlet, so far as possible, in the same order, manner and form in which they are designated upon the ballot.

9090.

The ballot pamphlet shall be printed according to the following specifications:
(a) The pages of the pamphlet shall be not smaller than 81/2 x 11 inches in size.
(b) The pamphlet shall be printed in clear readable type, no less than 10-point, except that the text of any measure may be set forth in eight-point type.
(c) The pamphlet shall be printed on a quality and weight of paper which, in the judgment of the Secretary of State, best serves the voters.
(d) The pamphlet shall contain a certificate of correctness by the Secretary of State.

9091.

The Legislative Counsel shall prepare and proofread the texts of all measures and the provisions which are repealed or revised.

9092.

Not less than 20 days before he or she submits the copy for the ballot pamphlet to the State Printer, the Secretary of State shall make the copy available for public examination. Any elector may seek a writ of mandate requiring any copy to be amended or deleted from the ballot pamphlet. A peremptory writ of mandate shall issue only upon clear and convincing proof that the copy in question is false, misleading, or inconsistent with the requirements of this code or Chapter 8 (commencing with Section 88000) of Title 9 of the Government Code, and that issuance of the writ will not substantially interfere with the printing and distribution of the ballot pamphlet as required by law. Venue for a proceeding under this section shall be exclusively in Sacramento County. The Secretary of State shall be named as the respondent and the State Printer and the person or official who authored the copy in question shall be named as real parties in interest. If the proceeding is initiated by the Secretary of State, the State Printer shall be named as the respondent.

9093.

Notwithstanding Section 81012 of the Government Code, the Legislature may without restriction amend this article to add to the ballot pamphlet information regarding candidates or any other information.

9094.

(a) The Secretary of State shall mail ballot pamphlets to voters, in those instances in which the county clerk uses data processing equipment to store the information set forth in the affidavits of registration, before the election at which measures contained in the ballot pamphlet are to be voted on unless a voter has registered fewer than 29 days before the election. The mailing shall commence not less than 40 days before the election and shall be completed no later than 21 days before the election for those voters who registered on or before the 60th day before the election. The Secretary of State shall mail one copy of the ballot pamphlet to each registered voter at the postal address stated on the voter's affidavit of registration, or the Secretary of State may mail only one ballot pamphlet to two or more registered voters having the same surname and the same postal address.
(b) In those instances in which the county clerk does not utilize data processing equipment to store the information set forth in the affidavits of registration, the Secretary of State shall furnish ballot pamphlets to the county clerk not less than 45 days before the election at which measures contained in the ballot pamphlet are to be voted on and the county clerk shall mail ballot pamphlets to voters, on the same dates and in the same manner provided by subdivision (a).
(c) The Secretary of State shall provide for the mailing of ballot pamphlets to voters registering after the 60th day before the election and before the 28th day before the election, by either: (1) mailing in the manner as provided in subdivision (a), or (2) requiring the county clerk to mail ballot pamphlets to those voters registering in the county after the 60th day before the election and before the 28th day before the election pursuant to the provisions of this section. The second mailing of ballot pamphlets shall be completed no later than 10 days before the election. The county clerk shall mail a ballot pamphlet to any person requesting a ballot pamphlet. Three copies, to be supplied by the Secretary of State, shall be kept at every polling place, while an election is in progress, so that they may be freely consulted by the voters.

9095.

Any costs incurred by a county for mailing the ballot pamphlets pursuant to the provisions of subdivisions (b) and (c) of Section 9094 shall be reimbursed to the county by the Secretary of State.

9096.

(a) As soon as copies of the ballot pamphlet are available, the Secretary of State shall immediately mail the following number of copies to the listed persons and places:
(1) Five copies to each county elections official or registrar of voters;
(2) Six copies to each city elections official.
(3) Five copies to each Member of the Legislature.
(4) Five copies to the proponents of each ballot measure.
(b) The Secretary of State shall also mail:
(1) Two copies to each public library and branch thereof.
(2) Twelve copies to each public high school or other public school teaching at least the 11th and 12th grades, and 25 copies to each public institution of higher learning. Upon request, and in the discretion of the Secretary of State, additional copies may be furnished to these persons and institutions.

9100.

In addition to any other method provided by law, ordinances may be enacted by any county pursuant to this article.

9101.

Any proposed ordinance may be submitted to the board of supervisors by filing an initiative petition with the county elections official, signed by not less than the number of voters specified in this article.

Each petition section shall comply with Sections 100 and 9020 and contain a full and correct copy of the notice of intention and accompanying statement including the full text of the proposed ordinance.

9102.

Any proposal to enact, amend, or otherwise revise a county charter by initiative petition may be submitted to the board of supervisors and shall be subject to this article. However, nothing in this article shall be construed to allow a board of supervisors to enact, amend, or otherwise revise a county charter without submitting the proposal to the voters.

9103.

(a) Before circulating any initiative petition in a county, or any petition relating to the annexation of territory by a county, the consolidation of counties, or the dissolution of a county, its proponents shall file with the county elections official a notice of intention to do so. The notice shall include the names and business or residence addresses of at least one but not more than five proponents of the petition, and shall be accompanied by the written text of the initiative and a request that a ballot title and summary be prepared.
(b) Any person filing a notice of intent with the county elections official shall pay a fee to be established by the board of supervisors not to exceed two hundred dollars ($200) to be refunded to the filer if, within one year of the date of filing the notice of intent, the county elections official certifies the sufficiency of the petition.

9104.

The notice of intention shall contain the printed name, signature, and business or residence address of at least one but not more than five proponents, and may include a printed statement, not exceeding 500 words in length, stating the reasons for the proposed petition. The notice shall be in substantially the following form:

Notice of Intention to Circulate Petition

Notice is hereby given by the persons whose names appear hereon of their intention to circulate the petition within the County of ____ for the purpose of ____. A statement of the reasons of the proposed action as contemplated in the petition is as follows: (optional statement).

9105.

(a) The county elections official shall immediately transmit a copy of any proposed measure to the county counsel. Within 15 days after the proposed measure is filed, the county counsel shall provide and return to the county elections official a ballot title and summary for the proposed measure. The ballot title may differ from any other title of the proposed measure and shall express in 500 words or less the purpose of the proposed measure. In providing the ballot title, the county counsel shall give a true and impartial statement of the purpose of the proposed measure in such language that the ballot title shall neither be an argument, nor be likely to create prejudice, for or against the proposed measure.

(b) The county elections official shall furnish a copy of the ballot title and summary to the proponents of the proposed measure. The proponents shall, prior to the circulation of the petition, publish the Notice of Intention, and the ballot title and summary of the proposed measure in a newspaper of general circulation published in that county, and file proof of publication with the county elections official.

(c) The ballot title and summary prepared by the county counsel shall appear upon each section of the petition, above the text of the proposed measure and across the top of each page of the petition on which signatures are to appear, in roman boldface type not smaller than 12 point. The ballot title and summary shall be clearly separated from the text of the measure. The text of the measure shall be printed in type not smaller than 8 point.

The heading of the proposed measure shall be in substantially the following form:

Initiative Measure to be Submitted Directly to the Voters

The county counsel has prepared the following title and summary of the chief purpose and points of the proposed measure:

(Here set forth the title and summary prepared by the county counsel. This title and summary must also be printed across the top of each page of the petition whereon signatures are to appear.)

9106.

The proponent may seek a writ of mandate requiring the ballot title or summary prepared by the county counsel to be amended. The court shall expedite hearing on the writ. A peremptory writ of mandate shall be issued only upon clear and convincing proof that the ballot title or summary is false, misleading, or inconsistent with the requirements of Section 9105.

9107.

The county elections official shall ascertain the number of signatures required to sign the petition by obtaining the number of votes cast within the county for all candidates for Governor at the last gubernatorial election preceding the publication of the notice of intention to circulate the initiative petition.

9108.

The proponents may commence to circulate the petitions among the voters of the county for signatures by any registered voter of the county after publication of the title and summary prepared by the county counsel. Each section of the petition shall bear a copy of the notice of intention, and the title and summary prepared by the county counsel.

9109.

Each petition section shall have attached to it an affidavit to be completed by the circulator. The affidavit shall be substantially in the same form as set forth in Section 104.

9110.

Signatures shall be secured and the petition shall be presented to the county elections official for filing within 180 days from the date of receipt of the title and summary, or after termination of any action for a writ of mandate pursuant to Section 9106 and, if applicable, after receipt of an amended title or summary or both, whichever occurs later.

9111.

(a) During the circulation of the petition or before taking either action described in subdivisions (a) and (b) of Section 9116, or Section 9118, the board of supervisors may refer the proposed initiative measure to any county agency or agencies for a report on any or all of the following:

(1) Its fiscal impact.

(2) Its effect on the internal consistency of the county's general and specific plans, including the housing element, the consistency between planning and zoning, and the limitations on county actions under Section 65008 of the Govern-

ment Code and Chapters 4.2 (commencing with Section 65913) and 4.3 (commencing with Section 65915) of Division 1 of Title 7 of the Government Code.

(3) Its effect on the use of land, the impact on the availability and location of housing, and the ability of the county to meet its regional housing needs.

(4) Its impact on funding for infrastructure of all types, including, but not limited to, transportation, schools, parks, and open space. The report may also discuss whether the measure would be likely to result in increased infrastructure costs or savings, including the costs of infrastructure maintenance, to current residents and businesses.

(5) Its impact on the community's ability to attract and retain business and employment.

(6) Its impact on the uses of vacant parcels of land.

(7) Its impact on agricultural lands, open space, traffic congestion, existing business districts, and developed areas designated for revitalization.

(8) Any other matters the board of supervisors request to be in the report.

(b) The report shall be presented to the board of supervisors within the time prescribed by the board of supervisors, but no later than 30 days after the county elections official certifies to the board of supervisors the sufficiency of the petition.

9112.

On or before April 1 of each odd-numbered year, the county elections official of each county shall file a report with the Secretary of State containing the following information:

(a) The number of county initiative petitions circulated during the preceding two calendar years that did not qualify for the ballot, and the number of these proposed initiatives for which reports were prepared pursuant to Section 9111.

(b) With respect to county initiative measures that qualified for the ballot in the preceding two calendar years, the number that were approved by the voters, and the number of these ballot measures for which reports were prepared pursuant to Section 9111.

(c) With respect to county initiative measures that qualified for the ballot in the preceding two calendar years, the number which were not approved by the voters, and the number of these ballot measures for which reports were prepared pursuant to Section 9111.

9113.

The petition shall be filed by the proponents, or by any person or persons authorized in writing by the proponents. All sections of the petition shall be filed at one time. Any sections of the petition not so filed shall be void for all purposes. Once filed, no petition section shall be amended except by order of a court of competent jurisdiction.

When the petition is filed, the county elections official shall determine the total number of signatures affixed to the petition. If, from this examination, the county elections official determines that the number of signatures, prima facie, equals or is in excess of the minimum number of signatures required, the county elections official shall examine the petition in accordance with Section 9114 or 9115. If, from this examination, the county elections official determines that the number of signatures, prima facie, does not equal or exceed the minimum number of signatures required, no further action shall be taken.

9114.

Except as provided in Section 9115, within 30 days from the date of filing of the petition, excluding Saturdays, Sundays, and holidays, the elections official shall examine the petition, and from the records of registration ascertain whether or not the petition is signed by the requisite number of voters. A certificate showing the results of this examination shall be attached to the petition.

In determining the number of valid signatures, the elections official may use the duplicate file of affidavits maintained, or may check the signatures against facsimiles of voters' signatures, provided that the method of preparing and displaying the facsimiles complies with law.

The elections official shall notify the proponents of the petition as to the sufficiency or insufficiency of the petition.

If the petition is found insufficient, no further action shall be taken. However, the failure to secure sufficient signatures shall not preclude the filing of a new petition on the same subject, at a later date.

If the petition is found sufficient, the elections official shall certify the results of the examination to the board of supervisors at the next regular meeting of the board.

9115.

(a) Within 30 days from the date of filing of the petition, excluding Saturdays, Sundays, and holidays, if, from the examination of petitions pursuant to Section 9114 shows that more than 500 signatures have been signed on the petition, the elections official may use a random sampling technique for verification of signatures. The random sample of signatures to be verified shall be drawn so that every signature filed with the elections official shall be given an equal opportunity to be included in the sample. The random sampling shall include an examination of at least 500, or 3 percent of the signatures, whichever is greater.

(b) If the statistical sampling shows that the number of valid signatures is within 95 to 110 percent of the number of signatures of qualified voters needed to declare the petition sufficient, the elections official shall examine and verify each signature filed.

(c) In determining from the records of registration, what number of valid signatures are signed on the petition, the elections official may use the duplicate file of affidavits maintained, or may check the signatures against facsimiles of voters' signatures, provided that the method of preparing and displaying the facsimiles complies with law.

(d) The elections official shall attach to the petition, a certificate showing the result of this examination, and shall notify the proponents of either the sufficiency or insufficiency of the petition.

(e) If the petition is found insufficient, no action shall be taken on the petition. However, the failure to secure sufficient signatures shall not preclude the filing later of an entirely new petition to the same effect.

(f) If the petition is found to be sufficient, the elections official shall certify the results of the examination to the board of supervisors at the next regular meeting of the board.

9116.

If the initiative petition is signed by voters not less in number than 20 percent of the entire vote cast within the county for all candidates for Governor at the last gubernatorial election preceding the publication of the notice of intention to circulate an initiative petition, and contains a request that the ordinance be submitted immediately to a vote of the people at a special election, the board of supervisors shall do one of the following:

(a) Adopt the ordinance without alteration either at the regular meeting at which the certification of the petition is presented, or within 10 days after it is presented.

(b) Immediately call a special election pursuant to subdivision (a) of Section 1405, at which the ordinance, without alteration, shall be submitted to a vote of the voters of the county.

(c) Order a report pursuant to Section 9111 at the regular meeting at which the certification of the petition is presented. When the report is presented to the board of supervisors, it shall either adopt the ordinance within 10 days or order an election pursuant to subdivision (b).

9118.

If the initiative petition is signed by voters not less in number than 10 percent of the entire vote cast in the county for all candidates for Governor at the last gubernatorial election preceding the publication of the notice of intention to circulate an initiative petition, the board of supervisors shall do one of the following:

(a) Adopt the ordinance without alteration at the regular meeting at which the certification of the petition is presented, or within 10 days after it is presented

(b) Submit the ordinance, without alteration, to the voters pursuant to subdivision (b) of Section 1405, unless the ordinance petitioned for is required to be, or for some reason is, submitted to the voters at a special election pursuant to subdivision (a) of Section 1405.

(c) Order a report pursuant to Section 9111 at the regular meeting at which the certification of the petition is presented. When the report is presented to the board of supervisors, it shall either adopt the ordinance within 10 days or order an election pursuant to subdivision (b).

9119.

Whenever any ordinance is required by this article to be submitted to the voters of a county at any election, the county elections official shall cause the ordinance to be printed. A copy of the ordinance shall be made available to any voter upon request.

9120.

Article 3 (commencing with Section 9160) shall govern the procedures for submitting arguments for county initiatives.

9121.

Any number of proposed ordinances may be voted upon at the same election.

9122.

If a majority of the voters voting on a proposed ordinance vote in its favor, the ordinance shall become a valid and binding ordinance of the county. The ordinance shall be considered as adopted upon the date the vote is declared by the board of supervisors, and shall go into effect 10 days after that date.

9123.

If the provisions of two or more ordinances adopted at the same election conflict, the ordinance receiving the highest number of affirmative votes shall control.

9124.

The enacting clause of an ordinance submitted to the voters of a county shall be substantially in the following form: "The people of the County of ____ ordain as follows:"

9125.

No ordinance proposed by initiative petition and adopted either by the board of supervisors without submission to the voters or adopted by the voters shall be repealed or amended except by a vote of the people, unless provision is otherwise made in the original ordinance. In all other respects, an ordinance proposed by initiative petition and adopted shall have the same force and affect as any ordinance adopted by the board of supervisors.

9126.

This article does not apply to any statewide initiative measure.

9140.

The board of supervisors may submit to the voters, without a petition, an ordinance for the repeal, amendment, or enactment of any ordinance. The ordinance shall be voted upon at any succeeding regular or special election and, if it receives a majority of the votes cast, the ordinance shall be repealed, amended, or enacted accordingly.

9141.

(a) Except an ordinance granting a franchise, the following ordinances shall take effect immediately:
(1) Those calling or otherwise relating to an election.
(2) Those specifically required by law to take immediate effect.
(3) Those fixing the amount of money to be raised by taxation or the rate of taxes to be levied.
(4) Those for the immediate preservation of the public peace, health, or safety. The ordinances referred to in this subdivision shall contain a declaration of the facts constituting the necessity and shall be passed by a four-fifths vote of the board of supervisors.
(b) All other ordinances, including ordinances granting a franchise, shall become effective 30 days from and after the date of final passage.

9142.

(a) Notwithstanding Section 9141, ordinances authorizing the issuance of revenue bonds by a county as part of a joint powers entity pursuant to Section 6547 of the Government Code shall not take effect for 60 days.
(b) When the number of votes cast for all candidates for Governor at the last gubernatorial election within the boundaries of the county described in subdivision (a) exceeds 500,000, the ordinance is subject to referendum upon presentation of a petition bearing signatures of at least 5 percent of the entire vote cast within the boundaries of the county for all candidates for Governor at the last gubernatorial election. When the number of votes cast for all candidates for Governor at the last gubernatorial election within the boundaries of the county is less than 500,000, the ordinance is subject to referendum upon presentation of a petition bearing signatures of at least 10 percent of the entire vote cast within the boundaries of the county for all candidates for Governor at the last gubernatorial election.
(c) For the purpose of submitting the question to the voters pursuant to subdivision (b), the ballot wording shall approximate the following: "Shall the, (county name) as a member of the, (joint powers entity name) authorize the issuance of revenue bonds by the joint powers entity in the amount of $____ pursuant to ordinance number ____, dated ____, the bonds to be used for the following purposes and to be redeemed in the following manner: ____?"

9143.

Notwithstanding Section 9141, that portion of any ordinance that changes supervisorial salaries shall become effective 60 days from the date of its final passage.

9144.

If a petition protesting the adoption of an ordinance is presented to the board of supervisors prior to the effective date of the ordinance, the ordinance shall be suspended and the supervisors shall reconsider the ordinance. The petition shall be signed by voters of the county equal in number to at least 10 percent of the entire vote cast within the county for all candidates for Governor at the last gubernatorial election.

9145.

If the board of supervisors does not entirely repeal the ordinance against which a petition is filed, the board shall submit the ordinance to the voters either at the next regularly scheduled county election occurring not less than 88 days after the date of the order, or at a special election called for that purpose not less than 88 days after the date of the order. The ordinance shall not become effective unless and until a majority of the voters voting on the ordinance vote in favor of it.

9146.

The provisions of this code relating to the form of petitions, the duties of the county elections official, and the manner of holding elections, when an ordinance is proposed by initiative petition, govern the procedure on ordinances against which a protest is filed.

9147.

(a) The heading of a proposed referendum measure shall be in substantially the following form: Referendum Against an Ordinance Passed by the Board of Supervisors.

(b) Each section of the referendum petition shall contain the title and text of the ordinance or the portion of the ordinance which is the subject of the referendum.

9160.

(a) Whenever any county measure qualifies for a place on the ballot, the county elections official shall transmit a copy of the measure to the county auditor and to the county counsel or to the district attorney in any county which has no county counsel.

(b) The county counsel or district attorney shall prepare an impartial analysis of the measure showing the effect of the measure on the existing law and the operation of the measure. The analysis shall be printed preceding the arguments for and against the measure. The analysis shall not exceed 500 words in length. In the event the entire text of the measure is not printed on the ballot, nor in the voter information portion of the sample ballot, there shall be printed immediately below the impartial analysis, in no less than 10-point boldface type, a legend substantially as follows: "The above statement is an impartial analysis of Ordinance or Measure _____. If you desire a copy of the ordinance or measure, please call the elections official's office at (insert telephone number) and a copy will be mailed at no cost to you."

(c) Not later than 88 days prior to an election that includes a county ballot measure, the board of supervisors may direct the county auditor to review the measure and determine whether the substance thereof, if adopted, would affect the revenues or expenditures of the county. He or she shall prepare a fiscal impact statement which estimates the amount of any increase or decrease in revenues or costs to the county if the proposed measure is adopted. The fiscal impact statement is "official matter" within the meaning of Section 13303, and shall be printed preceding the arguments for and against the measure. The fiscal impact statement shall not exceed 500 words in length.

9161.

If there is no other method provided by law, arguments for and against any county measure may be submitted to the qualified voters of the county pursuant to this article. If a method is otherwise provided by law for submitting such arguments as to a particular kind of county measure, that method shall control.

9162.

The board of supervisors or any member or members of the board authorized by the board, or any individual voter who is eligible to vote on the measure, or bona fide association of citizens, or any combination of these voters and associations may file a written argument for or against any county measure. No argument shall exceed 300 words in length. The county elections official shall cause an argument for and an argument against the measure, and the analysis of the measure, to be printed, and shall enclose a copy of both arguments preceded by the analysis with each sample ballot. The printed arguments and the analysis are "official matter" within the meaning of Section 13303.

The following statement shall be printed on the front cover, or if none, on the heading of the first page, of the printed arguments: "Arguments in support of or in opposition to the proposed laws are the opinions of the authors."

Printed arguments submitted to voters in accordance with this section shall be titled either "Argument In Favor Of Measure _____" or "Argument Against Measure _____," accordingly, the blank spaces being filled in only with the letter or number, if any, which designates the measure. At the discretion of the county elections official, the word "Proposition" may be substituted for the word "Measure" in the titles. Words used in the title shall not be counted when determining the length of any argument.

9163.

Based on the time reasonably necessary to prepare and print the arguments, analysis, and sample ballots and to permit the 10-calendar-day public examination as provided in Article 5 (commencing with Section 9190) for the particular election, the county elections official shall fix and determine a reasonable date prior to the election after which no arguments for or against any county measure may be submitted for printing and distribution to the voters as provided in this article. Notice of the date fixed shall be published by the county elections official pursuant to Section 6061 of the Government Code. Arguments may be changed until and including the date fixed by the county elections official.

9164.

A ballot argument shall not be accepted under this article unless accompanied by the printed name and signature or printed names and signatures of the person or persons submitting it, or, if submitted on behalf of an organization, the name of the organization and the printed name and signature of at least one of its principal officers.

No more than five signatures shall appear with any argument submitted under this article. In case any argument is signed by more than five persons, the signatures of the first five shall be printed.

9166.

If more than one argument for or more than one argument against any county measure is submitted to the county elections official within the time prescribed, the county elections official shall select one of the arguments in favor and one of the arguments against the measure for printing and distribution to the voters. In selecting the argument the county elections official shall give preference and priority in the order named to the arguments of the following:
(a) The board of supervisors, or member or members of the board authorized by the board.
(b) The individual voter, or bona fide association of citizens, or combination of voters and associations, who are the bona fide sponsors or proponents of the measure.
(c) Bona fide associations of citizens.
(d) Individual voters who are eligible to vote on the measure.

9167.

When the county elections official has selected the arguments for and against the measure which will be printed and distributed to the voters, the elections official shall send copies of the argument in favor of the measure to the authors of the argument against, and copies of the argument against to the authors of the argument in favor. The authors may prepare and submit rebuttal arguments not exceeding 250 words. The rebuttal arguments must be filed with the county elections official not more than 10 days after the final date for filing direct arguments. Rebuttal arguments shall be printed in the same manner as the direct arguments. Each rebuttal argument shall immediately follow the direct argument which it seeks to rebut and shall be titled "Rebuttal To Argument In Favor Of Measure (or Proposition) _____" or "Rebuttal To Argument Against Measure (or Proposition) _____," the blank spaces being filled in only with the letter or number, if any, which designates the measure. Words used in the title shall not be counted when determining the length of any rebuttal argument.

9168.

(a) Notwithstanding any provision of law to the contrary, this article shall apply to any district bond election called by, and the returns of which are canvassed by, the board of supervisors, or to any district bond election conducted by a district. This article shall also apply to any special election, if the board of supervisors so provides in its proclamation or notice thereof.
(b) At any election subject to this section:
(1) "County measure" shall be deemed to refer to any measure as defined in Section 329. Section 312 shall not apply.

(2) Section 9160, and the reference to the analysis of the measure in Section 9162, shall not apply unless the board of supervisors directs the officer to prepare the analysis.

(c) This article shall not apply to any school district bond election.

9180.

Whenever the county elections official is required to mail official matter, as provided in Sections 9119, 9120, 9160, 9162, and 9167, only one copy of each official matter shall be mailed to a postal address where two or more registered voters have the same surname and the same postal address.

This section shall only apply if the board of supervisors adopts this section.

9190.

Not less than 10 calendar days before the county elections official submits the official election materials referred to in Sections 9119, 9120, 9160, 9162, and 9167 for printing, the county elections official shall make a copy of the materials available for public examination in the county elections official's office. Any person may obtain a copy of the materials from the county elections official for use outside of the county elections official's office. The county elections official may charge a fee to any person obtaining a copy of the material. The fee shall not exceed the actual cost incurred by the county elections official in providing the copy.

During the 10-calendar-day examination period provided by this section, any voter of the jurisdiction in which the election is being held, or the county elections official, himself or herself, may seek a writ of mandate or an injunction requiring any or all of the materials to be amended or deleted. A peremptory writ of mandate or an injunction shall be issued only upon clear and convincing proof that the material in question is false, misleading, or inconsistent with this chapter, and that issuance of the writ or injunction will not substantially interfere with the printing or distribution of official election materials as provided by law. The county elections official shall be named as respondent and the person or official who authored the material in question shall be named as real parties in interest. In the case of the county elections official bringing the mandamus or injunctive action, the board of supervisors of the county shall be named as the respondent and the person or official who authored the material in question shall be named as the real party in interest.

9200.

Ordinances may be enacted by and for any incorporated city pursuant to this article.

9201.

Any proposed ordinance may be submitted to the legislative body of the city by a petition filed with the elections official of the legislative body, in the manner hereinafter prescribed, after being signed by not less than the number of voters specified in this article. The petition may be in separate sections, providing that the petition complies with this article. The first page of each section shall contain the title of the petition and the text of the measure. The petition sections shall be designated in the manner set forth in Section 9020.

9202.

(a) Before circulating an initiative petition in any city, the proponents of the matter shall file with the elections official a notice of intention to do so, which shall be accompanied by the written text of the initiative and may be accompanied by a written statement not in excess of 500 words, setting forth the reasons for the proposed petition. The notice shall be signed by at least one, but not more than three, proponents and shall be in substantially the following form:

Notice of Intent to Circulate Petition

Notice is hereby given by the persons whose names appear hereon of their intention to circulate the petition within the City of _____ for the purpose of _____. A statement of the reasons of the proposed action as contemplated in the petition is as follows:

(b) Any person filing a notice of intent with the elections official shall pay a fee to be established by the legislative body not to exceed two hundred dollars ($200) to be refunded to the filer if, within one year of the date of filing the notice of intent, the elections official certifies the sufficiency of the petition.

9203.

(a) Any person who is interested in any proposed measure shall file a copy of the proposed measure with the elections official with a request that a ballot title and summary be prepared. This request shall be accompanied by the address of the person proposing the measure. The elections official shall immediately transmit a copy of the proposed measure to the city attorney. Within 15 days after the proposed measure is filed, the city attorney shall provide and return to the city elections official a ballot title for and summary of the proposed measure. The ballot title may differ from any other title of the proposed measure and shall express in 500 words or less the purpose of the proposed measure. In providing the ballot title, the city attorney shall give a true and impartial statement of the purpose of the proposed measure in such language that the ballot title shall neither be an argument, nor be likely to create prejudice, for or against the proposed measure.

(b) The elections official shall furnish a copy of the ballot title and summary to the person filing the proposed measure. The person proposing the measure shall, prior to its circulation, place upon each section of the petition, above the text of the proposed measure and across the top of each page of the petition on which signatures are to appear, in roman boldface type not smaller than 12 point, the ballot title prepared by the city attorney. The text of the measure shall be printed in type not smaller than 8 point.

The heading of the proposed measure shall be in substantially the following form:

Initiative Measure to be Submitted Directly to the Voters

The city attorney has prepared the following title and summary of the chief purpose and points of the proposed measure:

(Here set forth the title and summary prepared by the city attorney. This title and summary must also be printed across the top of each page of the petition whereon signatures are to appear.)

9204.

The proponent may seek a writ of mandate requiring the ballot title or summary prepared by the city attorney to be amended. The court shall expedite hearing on the writ. A peremptory writ of mandate shall be issued only upon clear and convincing proof that the ballot title or summary is false, misleading, or inconsistent with the requirements of Section 9203.

9205.

A notice of intention and the title and summary of the proposed measure shall be published or posted or both as follows:

(a) If there is a newspaper of general circulation, as described in Chapter 1 (commencing with Section 6000) of Division 7 of Title 1 of the Government Code, adjudicated as such, the notice, title, and summary shall be published therein at least once.

(b) If the petition is to be circulated in a city in which there is no adjudicated newspaper of general circulation, the notice, title, and summary shall be published at least once, in a newspaper circulated within the city and adjudicated as being of general circulation within the county in which the city is located and the notice, title, and summary shall be posted in three (3) public places within the city, which public places shall be those utilized for the purpose of posting ordinances as required in Section 36933 of the Government Code.

(c) If the petition is to be circulated in a city in which there is no adjudicated newspaper of general circulation, and there is no newspaper of general circulation adjudicated as such within the county, circulated within the city, then the notice, title, and summary shall be posted in the manner described in subdivision (b).

9206.

Within 10 days after the date of publication or posting, or both, of the notice of intention and title and summary, the proponents shall file a copy of the notice and title and summary as published or posted together with an affidavit made by a representative of the newspaper in which the notice was published or, if the notice was posted, by a voter of the city, certifying to the fact of publication or posting.

If the notice and title and summary are both published and posted pursuant to subdivision (b) of Section 9205, the proponents shall file affidavits as required by this section made by a representative of the newspaper in which the notice was published certifying to the fact that the notice was published and by a voter of the city certifying to the fact that the notice was posted.

These affidavits, together with a copy of the notice of intention and title and summary, shall be filed with the elections official of the legislative body of the city in his or her office during normal office hours as posted.

9207.

The proponents may commence to circulate the petitions among the voters of the city for signatures by any registered voter of the city after publication or posting, or both, as required by Section 9205, of the title and summary prepared by the city attorney. Each section of the petition shall bear a copy of the notice of intention and the title and summary prepared by the city attorney.

9208.

Signatures upon petitions and sections of petitions shall be secured, and the petition, together with all sections of the petition, shall be filed within 180 days from the date of receipt of the title and summary, or after termination of any action for a writ of mandate pursuant to Section 9204, and, if applicable, after receipt of an amended title or summary or both, whichever occurs later. Petitions and sections thereof shall be filed in the office of the elections official during normal office hours as posted. If the petitions are not filed within the time permitted by this section, the petitions shall be void for all purposes.

9209.

Each section shall have attached thereto the declaration of the person soliciting the signatures. This declaration shall be substantially in the same form as set forth in Section 9022, except that the declaration shall declare that the circulator is a voter of the city, and shall state the voter's residence address at the time of the execution of the declaration.

9210.

The petition shall be filed by the proponents or by any person or persons authorized in writing by the proponents. All sections of the petition shall be filed at one time. Once filed, no petition section shall be amended except by order of a court of competent jurisdiction.

When the petition is presented for filing, the elections official shall do all of the following:

(a) Ascertain the number of registered voters of the city last reported by the county elections official to the Secretary of State pursuant to Section 2187 effective at the time the notice specified in Section 9202 was published.

(b) Determine the total number of signatures affixed to the petition. If, from this examination, the elections official determines that the number of signatures, prima facie, equals or is in excess of the minimum number of signatures required, he or she shall accept the petition for filing. The petition shall be deemed as filed on that date. Any petition not accepted for filing shall be returned to the proponents.

9211.

After the petition has been filed, as herein provided, the elections official shall examine the petition in the same manner as are county petitions in accordance with Sections 9114 and 9115, except that for the purposes of this section, references to the board of supervisors shall be treated as references to the legislative body of the city.

9212.

(a) During the circulation of the petition, or before taking either action described in subdivisions (a) and (b) of Section 9214, or Section 9215, the legislative body may refer the proposed initiative measure to any city agency or agencies for a report on any or all of the following:

(1) Its fiscal impact.

(2) Its effect on the internal consistency of the city's general and specific plans, including the housing element, the consistency between planning and zoning, and the limitations on city actions under Section 65008 of the Government Code and Chapters 4.2 (commencing with Section 65913) and 4.3 (commencing with Section 65915) of Division 1 of Title 7 of the Government Code.

(3) Its effect on the use of land, the impact on the availability and location of housing, and the ability of the city to meet its regional housing needs.

(4) Its impact on funding for infrastructure of all types, including, but not limited to, transportation, schools, parks, and open space. The report may also discuss whether the measure would be likely to result in increased infrastructure costs or savings, including the costs of infrastructure maintenance, to current residents and businesses.

(5) Its impact on the community's ability to attract and retain business and employment.

(6) Its impact on the uses of vacant parcels of land.

(7) Its impact on agricultural lands, open space, traffic congestion, existing business districts, and developed areas designated for revitalization.

(8) Any other matters the legislative body requests to be in the report.

(b) The report shall be presented to the legislative body within the time prescribed by the legislative body, but no later than 30 days after the elections official certifies to the legislative body the sufficiency of the petition.

9213.

On or before April 1 of each odd-numbered year, the elections official of each legislative body shall file a report with the Secretary of State containing the following information:

(a) The number of municipal initiative petitions circulated during the preceding two calendar years which did not qualify for the ballot, and the number of these proposed initiatives for which reports were prepared pursuant to Section 9212.

(b) With respect to municipal initiative measures that qualified for the ballot in the preceding two calendar years, the number that were approved by the voters, and the number of these ballot measures for which reports were prepared pursuant to Section 9212.

(c) With respect to municipal initiative measures that qualified for the ballot in the preceding two calendar years, the number that were not approved by the voters, and the number of these ballot measures for which reports were prepared pursuant to Section 9212.

9214.

If the initiative petition is signed by not less than 15 percent of the voters of the city according to the last report of registration by the county elections official to the Secretary of State pursuant to Section 2187, effective at the time the notice specified in Section 9202 was published, or, in a city with 1,000 or less registered voters, by 25 percent of the voters or 100 voters of the city, whichever is the lesser number, and contains a request that the ordinance be submitted immediately to a vote of the people at a special election, the legislative body shall do one of the following:

(a) Adopt the ordinance, without alteration, at the regular meeting at which the certification of the petition is presented, or within 10 days after it is presented.

(b) Immediately order a special election, to be held pursuant to subdivision (a) of Section 1405, at which the ordinance, without alteration, shall be submitted to a vote of the voters of the city.

(c) Order a report pursuant to Section 9212 at the regular meeting at which the certification of the petition is presented. When the report is presented to the legislative body, the legislative body shall either adopt the ordinance within 10 days or order an election pursuant to subdivision (b).

9215.

If the initiative petition is signed by not less than 10 percent of the voters of the city, according to the last report of registration by the county elections official to the Secretary of State pursuant to Section 2187, effective at the time the notice specified in Section 9202 was published, or, in a city with 1,000 or less registered voters, by 25 percent of the voters or 100 voters of the city, whichever is the lesser number, the legislative body shall do one of the following:

(a) Adopt the ordinance, without alteration, at the regular meeting at which the certification of the petition is presented, or within 10 days after it is presented.

(b) Submit the ordinance, without alteration, to the voters pursuant to subdivision (b) of Section 1405, unless the ordinance petitioned for is required to be, or for some reason is, submitted to the voters at a special election pursuant to subdivision (a) of Section 1405.

(c) Order a report pursuant to Section 9212 at the regular meeting at which the certification of the petition is presented. When the report is presented to the legislative body, the legislative body shall either adopt the ordinance within 10 days or order an election pursuant to subdivision (b).

9216.

In cities having a mayor, or like officer, with the veto power, when the passage of an ordinance petitioned for by the voters is vetoed, the failure of the legislative body to pass the ordinance over the veto shall be deemed a refusal of the legislative body to pass the ordinance within the meaning of this article.

9217.

If a majority of the voters voting on a proposed ordinance vote in its favor, the ordinance shall become a valid and binding ordinance of the city. The ordinance shall be considered as adopted upon the date that the vote is declared by the legislative body, and shall go into effect 10 days after that date. No ordinance that is either proposed by initiative petition and adopted by the vote of the legislative body of the city without submission to the voters, or adopted by the voters, shall be repealed or amended except by a vote of the people, unless provision is otherwise made in the original ordinance.

9218.

Any number of proposed ordinances may be voted upon at the same election, but the same subject matter shall not be voted upon twice within any 12-month period at a special election under the provisions of this article.

9219.

The persons filing an initiative petition pursuant to this article may file a written argument in favor of the ordinance, and the legislative body may submit an argument against the ordinance. Neither argument shall exceed 300 words in length, and both arguments shall be printed upon the same sheet of paper and mailed to each voter with the sample ballot for the election.

The following statement shall be printed on the front cover, or if none, on the heading of the first page, of the printed arguments: "Arguments in support of or in opposition to the proposed laws are the opinions of the authors."

Printed arguments submitted to voters in accordance with this section shall be titled either "Argument In Favor Of Measure ____" or "Argument Against Measure ____," accordingly, the blank spaces being filled in only with the letter or number, if any, which designates the measure. At the discretion of the elections official, the word "Proposition" may be substituted for the word "Measure" in the titles. Words used in the title shall not be counted when determining the length of any argument.

9220.

(a) If the legislative body submits an argument against the ordinance, it shall immediately send copies of the argument to the persons filing the initiative petition. The persons filing the initiative petition may prepare and submit a rebuttal argument not exceeding 250 words. The legislative body may prepare and submit a rebuttal to the argument in favor of the ordinance not exceeding 250 words. The rebuttal arguments shall be filed with the elections official not more than 10 days after the final date for filing direct arguments. Rebuttal arguments shall be printed in the same manner as the direct arguments. Each rebuttal argument shall immediately follow the direct argument which it seeks to rebut.

(b) Subdivision (a) shall only apply if, not later than the day on which the legislative body calls an election, the legislative body, by a majority vote, approves its application; in which case, subdivision (a) shall apply at the next ensuing municipal election and at each municipal election thereafter, unless later repealed by the legislative body in accord with this subdivision.

9221.

If the provisions of two or more ordinances adopted at the same election conflict, the ordinance receiving the highest number of affirmative votes shall control.

9222.

The legislative body of the city may submit to the voters, without a petition therefore, a proposition for the repeal, amendment, or enactment of any ordinance, to be voted upon at any succeeding regular or special city election, and if the proposition submitted receives a majority of the votes cast on it at the election, the ordinance shall be repealed, amended, or enacted accordingly. A proposition may be submitted, or a special election may be called for the purpose of voting on a proposition, by ordinance or resolution.

9223.

Whenever any ordinance or measure is required by this article to be submitted to the voters of a city at any election, the elections official of the legislative body shall cause the ordinance or measure to be printed. A copy of the ordinance or measure shall be made available to any voter upon request.

9224.

The enacting clause of an ordinance submitted to the voters of a city shall be substantially in the following form: "The people of the City of _____ do ordain as follows:"

9226.

This article does not apply to any statewide initiative measure.

9235.

No ordinance shall become effective until 30 days from and after the date of its final passage, except:
(a) An ordinance calling or otherwise relating to an election.

(b) An ordinance for the immediate preservation of the public peace, health, or safety that contains a declaration of, and the facts constituting, its urgency and is passed by a four-fifths vote of the city council.

(c) Ordinances relating to street improvement proceedings.

(d) Other ordinances governed by particular provisions of state law prescribing the manner of their passage and adoption.

9236.

(a) Notwithstanding Section 9235, ordinances authorizing the issuance of revenue bonds by a city as part of a joint powers entity pursuant to Section 6547 of the Government Code shall not take effect for 60 days.

(b) When the number of votes cast for all candidates for Governor at the last gubernatorial election within the boundaries of the city described in subdivision (a) exceeds 500,000, the ordinance is subject to referendum upon presentation of a petition bearing signatures of at least 5 percent of the entire vote cast within the boundaries of the city for all candidates for Governor at the last gubernatorial election. When the number of votes cast for all candidates for Governor at the last gubernatorial election within the boundaries of the city is less than 500,000, the ordinance is subject to referendum upon presentation of a petition bearing signatures of at least 10 percent of the entire vote cast within the boundaries of the city for all candidates for Governor at the last gubernatorial election.

(c) For the purpose of submitting the question to the voters pursuant to subdivision (b), the ballot wording shall approximate the following: "Shall the, (county name) as a member of the, (joint powers entity name) authorize the issuance of revenue bonds by the joint powers entity in the amount of $____ pursuant to ordinance number ____, dated ____, the bonds to be used for the following purposes and to be redeemed in the following manner: ____?"

9237.

If a petition protesting the adoption of an ordinance and circulated by any qualified registered voter of the city, is submitted to the elections official of the legislative body of the city in his or her office during normal office hours, as posted, within 30 days of the adoption of the ordinance, and is signed by not less than 10 percent of the voters of the city according to the county elections official's last official report of registration to the Secretary of State, or, in a city with 1,000 or less registered voters, is signed by not less than 25 percent of the voters or 100 voters of the city whichever is the lesser, the effective date of the ordinance shall be suspended, and the legislative body shall reconsider the ordinance.

9237.5.

The provisions of this code relating to the form of petitions, the duties of the county elections official, and the manner of holding elections shall govern the petition procedure and submission of the ordinance to the voters.

9238.

(a) Across the top of each page of the referendum petition there shall be printed the following: "Referendum Against an Ordinance Passed by the City Council"

(b) Each section of the referendum petition shall contain (1) the identifying number or title, and (2) the text of the ordinance or the portion of the ordinance that is the subject of the referendum.

The petition sections shall be designed in the same form as specified in Section 9020.

(c) Each section shall have attached thereto the declaration of the person soliciting the signatures. This declaration shall be substantially in the same form as set forth in Section 9022, except that the declaration shall declare that the circulator is a voter of the city and shall state his or her residence address at the time of the execution of the declaration.

9239.

Petitions shall be accepted for filing by the elections official and the determination of the number of signatures thereon shall be made by the elections official in accordance with Section 9210. Petitions shall be filed with the elections official of the legislative body of the city in his or her office during normal office hours, as posted.

9240.

After the petition has been filed as herein provided, the elections official shall examine the petition and certify the results in the same manner, as are county petitions in Sections 9114 and 9115 except that, for the purposes of this section, references to the board of supervisors shall be treated as references to the legislative body of the city.

9241.

If the legislative body does not entirely repeal the ordinance against which the petition is filed, the legislative body shall submit the ordinance to the voters, either at the next regular municipal election occurring not less than 88 days after the order of the legislative body, or at a special election called for the purpose, not less than 88 days after the order of the legislative body. The ordinance shall not become effective until a majority of the voters voting on the ordinance vote in favor of it. If the legislative body repeals the ordinance or submits the ordinance to the voters, and a majority of the voters voting on the ordinance do not vote in favor of it, the ordinance shall not again be enacted by the legislative body for a period of one year after the date of its repeal by the legislative body or disapproval by the voters.

9242.

Signatures upon petitions, and sections thereof, shall be secured, and the petition, together with all sections thereof, shall be filed, within 30 days from the date of the adoption of the ordinance to which it relates. Petitions and sections thereof shall be filed with the elections official of the legislative body of the city in his or her office during normal office hours as posted. Petitions which are not filed within the time permitted by this section shall be void for all purposes.

9243.

Elections pursuant to this article shall be held in accordance with Sections 9217 to 9225, inclusive.

9244.

Whenever the legislative body of a city has voted in favor of the repeal of an ordinance protested against by the voters, as provided in this article, and the mayor, or like officer, has vetoed the repeal, the failure of the legislative body to pass the repeal over the veto shall be deemed a refusal to repeal the ordinance.

9245.

If approval of an ordinance by the mayor or like officer is necessary, the date of approval shall be deemed the date of its final passage by the legislative body within the meaning of this article.

If an ordinance becomes law when the time for approval or veto has expired, and no action has been taken, the date of the expiration of that time shall be deemed the date of its final passage by the legislative body within the meaning of this article.

9246.

Any duty imposed in this chapter upon the legislative body of a city with regard to calling a municipal election, or in connection with an election called pursuant to this chapter, is likewise imposed upon any officer having any duty to perform connected with the election, so far as may be necessary to carry out this chapter.

9247.

Article 1 (commencing with Section 9200) and this article do not apply to cities having a charter adopted under Section 3 of Article XI of the California Constitution, and having in their charters any provision for the direct initiation of ordinances by the voters; nor to proceedings had for the improvement of streets in or rights-of-way owned by cities, the opening or closing of streets, the changing of grades or the doing of other work, the cost of which, or any portion of the cost which is to be borne by special assessments upon real property.

9255.

(a) The following city or city and county charter proposals shall be submitted to the voters at either a special election called for that purpose, at any established municipal election date, or at any established election date pursuant to Section 1000, provided that there are at least 88 days before the election:
(1) A charter proposed by a charter commission, whether elected or appointed by a governing body. A charter commission may also submit a charter pursuant to Section 34455 of the Government Code.
(2) An amendment or repeal of a charter proposed by the governing body of a city or a city and county on its own motion.
(3) An amendment or repeal of a city charter proposed by a petition signed by 15 percent of the registered voters of the city.
(4) An amendment or repeal of a city and county charter proposed by a petition signed by 10 percent of the registered voters of the city and county.
(5) A recodification of the charter proposed by the governing body on its own motion, provided that the recodification does not, in any manner, substantially change the provisions of the charter.
(b) Charter proposals by the governing body and charter proposals by petition of the voters may be submitted at the same election.

(c) The total number of registered voters of the city or city and county shall be determined according to the county elections official's last official report of registration to the Secretary of State.

9256.

The proponents of a measure proposing to amend a charter shall publish or post, or both, a notice of intent to circulate the petition in the same form and manner as prescribed in Sections 9202, 9203, 9204, and 9205. The proponents shall also file an affidavit prescribed in Section 9206 with the clerk of the legislative body of the city, and, with respect to the petition, shall be subject to Section 9207.

9257.

The petition signed by registered voters of the city or city and county proposing an amendment to a charter shall set forth in full the text of the proposed amendment, in no less than 10-point type.

9258.

The petition may be circulated in sections, but each section shall contain a correct copy of the text of the proposed amendment.

9259.

Each signer of the petition shall sign it in the manner prescribed by Section 9020.

9260.

The petition shall be in substantially the following form:

Petition for Submission to Voters of Proposed Amendment to the Charter of the City (or City and County) of _____

To the city council (or other legislative body) of the City (or City and County) of _____:

We, the undersigned, registered and qualified voters of the State of California, residents of the City (or City and County) of _____, pursuant to Section 3 of Article XI of the California Constitution and Chapter 2 (commencing with Section 34450) of Part 1 of Division 2 of Title 4 of the Government Code, present to the city council (or other legislative body) of the city (or city and county) this petition and request that the following proposed amendment to the charter of the city (or city and county) be submitted to the registered and qualified voters of the city (or city and county) for their adoption or rejection at an election on a date to be determined by the city council (or other legislative body).

The proposed charter amendment reads as follows: First. (setting forth the text of the amendment) _____ (etc.)

9261.

Each section shall have attached thereto the affidavit of the person soliciting the signatures. This affidavit shall be substantially in the same form as set forth in Section 9022 and shall comply with Sections 104 and 9209.

9262.

Each petition section shall consist of sheets of white paper, uniform in size, with dimensions no smaller than 81/2 by 11 inches or greater than 81/2 by 14 inches.

9263.

The sheets comprising each petition section shall be fastened together securely and remain so during circulation and filing.

9264.

A voter may withdraw his or her signature from a petition in the manner prescribed in Section 9602.

9265.

The petition shall be filed with the elections official by the proponents, or by any person or persons authorized in writing by the proponents. All sections of the petition shall be filed at one time, and no petition section submitted subsequently shall be accepted by the elections official. The petition shall be filed not more than 200 days after the date on which the notice of intent to circulate was published or posted, or both.

9266.

After the petition has been filed, the elections official shall examine the petition in the same manner as are county petitions in accordance with Sections 9114 and 9115, except that, for the purposes of this section, references in those sections to the board of supervisors shall be treated as references to the legislative body of the city or city and county. The expenses of signature verification shall be provided by the governing body receiving the petition from the elections official.

9267.

Petitions that do not substantially conform to the form requirements of this article shall not be accepted for filing by the elections official.

9268.

The conduct of election and publication requirements shall substantially conform with Part 1 (commencing with Section 10000) and Part 2 (commencing with Section 10100) of Division 10.

9269.

Upon the completion of the canvass of votes, the governing body of a city or city and county shall pass a resolution reciting the fact of the election and such other matters as are enumerated in Section 10264. The elections official of the city or city and county shall then cause the adopted measures to be submitted to the Secretary of State pursuant to Sections 34459 and 34460 of the Government Code.

9280.

Whenever any city measure qualifies for a place on the ballot, the governing body may direct the city elections official to transmit a copy of the measure to the city attorney, unless the organization or salaries of the office of the city attorney are affected. The city attorney shall prepare an impartial analysis of the measure showing the effect of the measure on the existing law and the operation of the measure. If the measure affects the organization or salaries of the office of the city attorney, the governing board may direct the city elections official to prepare the impartial analysis. The analysis shall be printed preceding the arguments for and against the measure. The analysis shall not exceed 500 words in length. In the event the entire text of the measure is not printed on the ballot, nor in the voter information portion of the sample ballot, there shall be printed immediately below the impartial analysis, in no less than 10-point bold type, a legend substantially as follows: "The above statement is an impartial analysis of Ordinance or Measure ____. If you desire a copy of the ordinance or measure, please call the elections official's office at (insert telephone number) and a copy will be mailed at no cost to you."

9281.

If no other method is provided by general law, or, in the case of a chartered city, by the charter or by city ordinance, arguments for and against any city measure may be submitted to the qualified voters of the city pursuant to this article. If a method is otherwise provided by general law, or, in the case of a chartered city, by charter or city ordinance, for submitting arguments as to a particular kind of city measure, that method shall control.

9282.

The legislative body, or any member or members of the legislative body authorized by that body, or any individual voter who is eligible to vote on the measure, or bona fide association of citizens, or any combination of voters and associations, may file a written argument for or against any city measure. No argument shall exceed 300 words in length. The city elections official shall cause an argument for and an argument against the measure to be printed along with the following statement on the front cover, or if none, on the heading of the first page, of the printed arguments: "Arguments in support or opposition of the proposed laws are the opinions of the authors."

The city elections official shall enclose a printed copy of both arguments with each sample ballot; provided, that only those arguments filed pursuant to this section shall be printed and enclosed with the sample ballot. The printed arguments are "official matter" within the meaning of Section 13303.

Printed arguments submitted to voters in accordance with this section shall be titled either "Argument In Favor Of Measure ____" or "Argument Against Measure ____," accordingly, the blank spaces being filled in only with the letter or number, if any, designating the measure. At the discretion of the elections official, the word "Proposition" may be substituted for the word "Measure" in such titles. Words used in the title shall not be counted when determining the length of any argument.

9283.

A ballot argument shall not be accepted under this article unless accompanied by the printed name and signature or printed names and signatures of the person or persons submitting it, or, if submitted on behalf of an organization, the name of the organization and the printed name and signature of at least one of its principal officers.

No more than five signatures shall appear with any argument submitted under this article. In case any argument is signed by more than five persons, the signatures of the first five shall be printed.

9285.

(a) If any person submits an argument against a city measure, and an argument has been filed in favor of the city measure, the elections official shall immediately send copies of that argument to the persons filing the argument in favor of the city measure. The persons filing the argument in favor of the city measure may prepare and submit a rebuttal argument not exceeding 250 words. The elections official shall send copies of the argument in favor of the measure to the persons filing the argument against the city measure, who may prepare and submit a rebuttal to the argument in favor of the city measure not exceeding 250 words. The rebuttal arguments shall be filed with the elections official not more than 10 days after the final date for filing direct arguments. Rebuttal arguments shall be printed in the same manner as the direct arguments. Each rebuttal argument shall immediately follow the direct argument it seeks to rebut.
(b) Subdivision (a) shall only apply if, not later than the day on which the legislative body calls an election, the legislative body, adopts its provisions by majority vote, in which case subdivision (a) shall apply at the next ensuing municipal election and at each municipal election thereafter, unless later repealed by the legislative body in accordance with the procedures of this subdivision.

9286.

Based on the time reasonably necessary to prepare and print the arguments and sample ballots and to permit the 10-calendar-day public examination as provided in Article 6 (commencing with Section 9295) for the particular election, the city elections official shall fix and determine a reasonable date prior to the election after which no arguments for or against any city measure may be submitted for printing and distribution to the voters, as provided in this article. Arguments may be changed or withdrawn by their proponents until and including the date fixed by the city elections official.

9287.

If more than one argument for or more than one argument against any city measure is submitted to the city elections official within the time prescribed, he or she shall select one of the arguments in favor and one of the arguments against the measure for printing and distribution to the voters. In selecting the argument the city elections official shall give preference and priority, in the order named, to the arguments of the following:
(a) The legislative body, or member or members of the legislative body authorized by that body.
(b) The individual voter, or bona fide association of citizens, or combination of voters and associations, who are the bona fide sponsors or proponents of the measure.
(c) Bona fide associations of citizens.
(d) Individual voters who are eligible to vote on the measure.

9290.

Whenever the elections official is required to mail official matter, as provided in Sections 9219, 9220, 9223, 9280, 9281, 9282, and 9285, only one copy of each piece of official matter shall be mailed to a postal address where two or more registered voters have the same surname and the same postal address.

This section shall only apply if the legislative body of the city adopts this section and the election official conducting the election approves of the procedure.

9295.

Not less than 10 calendar days before the elections official submits the official election materials referred to in Sections 9219, 9220, 9223, 9280, 9281, 9282, and 9285 for printing, the elections official shall make a copy of the material available for public examination in the elections official's office. Any person may obtain a copy of the materials from the elections official for use outside of the election official's office. The elections official may charge a fee to any person obtaining a copy of the material. The fee shall not exceed the actual cost incurred by the elections official in providing the copy.

During the 10-calendar-day examination period provided by this section, any voter of the jurisdiction in which the election is being held, or the elections official, himself or herself, may seek a writ of mandate or an injunction requiring any or all of the materials to be amended or deleted. A peremptory writ of mandate or an injunction shall be issued only upon clear and convincing proof that the material in question is false, misleading, or inconsistent with the requirements of this chapter, and that issuance of the writ or injunction will not substantially interfere with the printing or distribution of official election materials as provided by law. The elections official shall be named as respondent, and the person or official who authored the material in question shall be named as real parties in interest. In the case of the elections official bringing the mandamus or injunctive action, the board of supervisors of the county shall be named as the respondent and the person or official who authored the material in question shall be named as the real party in interest.

17200.

(a) Elections officials required by law to receive or file in their offices any initiative or referendum petition shall preserve the petition until eight months after the certification of the results of the election for which the petition qualified or, if the measure, for any reason, is not submitted to the voters, eight months after the final examination of the petition by the elections official.

(b) Thereafter, the petition shall be destroyed as soon as practicable unless it is in evidence in some action or proceeding then pending or unless the elections official has received a written request from the Attorney General, the Secretary of State, the Fair Political Practices Commission, a district attorney, a grand jury, or the governing body of a county, city and county, or district, including a school district, that the petition be preserved for use in a pending or ongoing investigation into election irregularities, the subject of which relates to the petition's qualification or disqualification for placement on the ballot, or in a pending or ongoing investigation into a violation of the Political Reform Act of 1974 (Title 9 (commencing with Section 81000) of the Government Code).

(c) Public access to any such petition shall be restricted in accordance with Section 6253.5 of the Government Code.

(d) This section shall apply to the following petitions:

(1) Statewide initiative and referendum petitions.

(2) County initiative and referendum petitions.

(3) Municipal initiative and referendum petitions.

(4) Municipal city charter amendment petitions.

(5) District initiative and referendum petitions.

18600.

Every person is guilty of a misdemeanor who:

(a) Circulating, as principal or agent, or having charge or control of the circulation of, or obtaining signatures to, any state or local initiative, referendum or recall petition, intentionally misrepresents or intentionally makes any false statement concerning the contents, purport or effect of the petition to any person who signs, or who desires to sign, or who is requested to sign, or who makes inquiries with reference to it, or to whom it is presented for his or her signature.

(b) Willfully and knowingly circulates, publishes, or exhibits any false statement or misrepresentation concerning the contents, purport or effect of any state or local initiative, referendum, or recall petition for the purpose of obtaining any signature to, or persuading or influencing any person to sign, that petition.

(c) Circulating, as principal or agent, or having charge or control of the circulation of, or obtaining signatures to, any state or local initiative, intentionally makes any false statement in response to any inquiry by any voter as to whether he or she is a paid signature gatherer or a volunteer.

18601.

Any person working for the proponent or proponents of an initiative or referendum measure or recall petition who refuses to allow a prospective signer to read the measure or petition is guilty of a misdemeanor.

An arrest or conviction pursuant to this section shall not invalidate or otherwise affect the validity of any signature obtained by the person arrested or convicted.

18602.

Any person working for the proponent or proponents of a statewide initiative or referendum measure who covers or otherwise obscures the summary of the measure prepared by the Attorney General from the view of a prospective signer is guilty of a misdemeanor.

18603.

Every person who offers or gives money or other valuable consideration to another in exchange for his or her signature on a state, county, municipal, or district initiative, referendum, or recall petition is guilty of a misdemeanor.

18610.

Every person who solicits any circulator to affix to any initiative, referendum, or recall petition any false or forged signature, or to cause or permit a false or forged signature to be affixed, is guilty of a misdemeanor.

18611.

Every person is punishable by a fine not exceeding five thousand dollars ($5,000), or by imprisonment in the state prison for 16 months or two or three years or in a county jail not exceeding one year, or by both the fine and imprisonment, who circulates or causes to be circulated any initiative, referendum, or recall petition, knowing it to contain false, forged, or fictitious names.

18612.

Every person is guilty of a misdemeanor who knowingly signs his or her own name more than once to any initiative, referendum, or recall petition, or signs his or her name to that petition knowing himself or herself at the time of signing not to be qualified to sign it.

18613.

Every person who subscribes to any initiative, referendum, or recall petition a fictitious name, or who subscribes thereto the name of another, or who causes another to subscribe such a name to that petition, is guilty of a felony and is punishable by imprisonment in the state prison for two, three, or four years.

18614.

Every person is punishable by a fine not exceeding five thousand dollars ($5,000), or by imprisonment in the state prison for 16 months or two or three years or in a county jail not exceeding one year, or by both the fine and imprisonment, who files in the office of the elections official or other officer designated by law to receive the filing, any initiative, referendum, or recall petition to which is attached, appended or subscribed any signature which the person filing the petition knows to be false or fraudulent or not the genuine signature of the person whose name it purports to be.

18620.

Every person who seeks, solicits, bargains for, or obtains any money, thing of value, or advantage of or from any person, firm, or corporation for the purpose or represented purpose of fraudulently inducing, persuading, or seeking the proponent or proponents of any initiative or referendum measure or recall petition to (a) abandon the measure or petition, (b) fail, neglect, or refuse to file in the office of the elections official or other officer designated by law, within the time required by law, the initiative or referendum measure or recall petition after securing the number of signatures required to qualify the measure or petition, (c) stop the circulation of the initiative or referendum measure or recall petition, or (d) perform any act that will prevent or aid in preventing the initiative or referendum measure or recall petition from qualifying as an initiative or referendum measure, or the recall petition from resulting in a recall election, is punishable by a fine not exceeding five thousand dollars ($5,000), or by imprisonment in the state prison 16 months or two or three years or in a county jail not exceeding one year, or by both the fine and imprisonment.

18621.

Any proponent of an initiative or referendum measure or recall petition who seeks, solicits, bargains for, or obtains any money or thing of value of or from any person, firm, or corporation for the purpose of abandoning the same or stopping the circulation of petitions concerning the same, or failing or neglecting or refusing to file the measure or petition in the office of the elections official or other officer designated by law within the time required by law after obtaining the number of signatures required under the law to qualify the measure or petition, or performing any act that will prevent or aid in preventing the initiative, referendum or recall proposed from qualifying as an initiative or referendum measure, or resulting in a recall election is punishable by a fine not exceeding five thousand dollars ($5,000) or by imprisonment in the state prison for 16 months or two or three years or in a county jail not exceeding one year, or by both the fine and imprisonment.

18622.

Every person who offers to buy or does buy from a circulator any referendum, initiative, or recall petition on which one or more persons have affixed their signatures is guilty of a misdemeanor punishable by imprisonment in the county jail for not more than one year, or by a fine not exceeding one thousand dollars ($1,000), or both. This section is not intended to prohibit compensation of a circulator, for his or her services, by a proponent of the petition or his or her agent.

18630.

Every person who threatens to commit an assault or battery on a person circulating a referendum, initiative, or recall petition or on a relative of a person circulating a referendum, initiative, or recall petition or to inflict damage on the property of the circulator or the relative, with the intent to dissuade the circulator from circulating the petition or in retribution for the circulation, is guilty of a misdemeanor.

18631.

Every person who forcibly or by stealth takes from the possession of a circulator any initiative, referendum, or recall petition on which one or more persons have affixed their signatures is guilty of a misdemeanor.

18640.

Any person working for the proponent or proponents of an initiative or referendum measure or recall petition who solicits signatures to qualify the measure or petition and accepts any payment therefore and who fails to surrender the measure or petition to the proponents thereof for filing is punishable by a fine not exceeding five thousand dollars ($5,000), or by imprisonment in the state prison for 16 months or two or three years or in a county jail not exceeding one year, or by both the fine and imprisonment.

18650.

No one shall knowingly or willfully permit the list of signatures on an initiative, referendum, or recall petition to be used for any purpose other than qualification of the initiative or referendum measure or recall question for the ballot, except as provided in Section 6253.5 of the Government Code. Violation of this section is a misdemeanor.

18660.

Every person is punishable by a fine not exceeding five thousand dollars ($5,000), or by imprisonment in the state prison for 16 months or two or three years or in a county jail not exceeding one year, or by both the fine and imprisonment, who makes any false affidavit concerning any initiative, referendum, or recall petition or the signatures appended thereto.

18661.

Every public official or employee is punishable by a fine not exceeding five thousand dollars ($5,000), or by imprisonment in the state prison for 16 months or two or three years or in a county jail not exceeding one year, or by both the fine and imprisonment, who knowingly makes any false return, certification or affidavit concerning any initiative, referendum, or recall petition or the signatures appended thereto.

18670.

Every person is guilty of a misdemeanor who, either as principal or agent, files in the office of the Secretary of State, county elections official, or in the office of any other officer designated by law to receive the filing, a petition or any section of a petition relating to the Constitution or the laws of this state, authorized by the Constitution or laws of this state regulating the statewide initiative or referendum, with the intention of thereby defeating that initiative or referendum measure that is embraced in the petition. Nothing in this section applies to any person who, in good faith, files a petition embracing an initiative or referendum measure that conflicts with a similar measure already on file.

18671.

Any petition, or any section of a petition, filed by any person other than the proponents of an initiative or referendum measure and with an intention of defeating an expression of the public will is null and void.

18680.

Every person who is entrusted with money or things of value for the purpose of promoting or defeating any initiative, referendum, or recall petition or any measure that has qualified for the ballot is a trustee of the money or things of value. If a person wrongfully appropriates the money or things of value to any use or purpose not in the due and lawful execution of the trust, the person shall be punishable by a fine not exceeding five thousand dollars ($5,000), or by imprisonment in the state prison for 16 months or two or three years or in a county jail not exceeding one year, or by both the fine and imprisonment. The following expenses are within the due and lawful execution of the trust:
(a) Securing signatures to initiative, referendum, or recall petitions.
(b) Circulating initiative, referendum, or recall petitions.
(c) Holding and conducting public meetings.
(d) Printing and circulating prior to an election:
(1) Specimen ballots.
(2) Handbills.
(3) Cards.

(4) Other papers.

(e) Advertising.

(f) Postage.

(g) Expressage.

(h) Telegraphing.

(i) Telephoning.

(j) All salaries and expenses of:

(1) Campaign managers.

(2) Lecturers.

(3) Solicitors.

(4) Agents.

(5) All persons employed in transacting business at headquarters or branch offices, if the business transacted is related to promoting or defeating an initiative, referendum, or recall petition or any measure which has qualified for the ballot.

(k) Maintaining headquarters and branch offices.

(l) Renting of rooms for the transaction of the business of an association.

(m)Attorney's fees and other costs in connection with litigation where the litigation arises directly out of any of the following:

(1) Activities related to promoting or defeating an initiative, referendum, or recall petition or any measure that has qualified for the ballot.

(2) The enactment, by the initiative process, of any ordinance, charter amendment, statute, or constitutional amendment.

(3) An election contest or recount.

(4) A violation of state or local campaign, disclosure, or election laws. The amendment of this section by adding subdivision (m) thereto, made at the 1991-92 Regular Session of the Legislature, does not constitute a change in, but is declaratory of, the existing law.

Expenses for food, clothing, shelter and other personal needs of the trustee are not within the due and lawful execution of the trust.

However, expenses for travel and necessary accommodations for the trustee are within the due and lawful execution of the trust, if the travel and accommodations are related to promoting or defeating an initiative, referendum, or recall petition or any measure that has qualified for the ballot.

The Basic Steps to Do an Initiative Petition in California

Statutes and Amendments — Direct Initiative Process

Basic Procedures: The first step in the process of qualifying an initiative is to write the text of the proposed law. The measure's proponents in many cases may obtain assistance from the Legislative Counsel in drafting the measure. To do so, the proponents must present the idea for the law to the Legislative Counsel, and the request for a draft of the proposed law must be signed by 25 or more electors. The Legislative Counsel will then draft the proposed law if it is determined that there is a reasonable probability the measure will eventually be submitted to the voters. The draft of the proposed measure must then be submitted to the Attorney General, who prepares the title and summary. The Attorney General provides the Secretary of State with a copy of this title and summary within 15 days of the receipt of the final version of the measure. The Attorney General works closely with proponents on this language, but gets the final say.

If the Attorney General determines that the measure requires a fiscal analysis, the Department of Finance and the Joint Legislative Budget Committee are asked to prepare an analysis within 25 working days from the date they receive the final version of the proposed initiative. The fiscal analysis includes either the estimate of the amount of any increase or decrease in revenues or costs to the state or local government, or an opinion as to whether or not a substantial net change in state or local finances would result if the proposed initiative is adopted. If, in the opinion of the Dept. of Finance and the Joint Legislative Budget Committee, a reasonable estimate of the net impact of the proposed initiative cannot be prepared within the 25-day period, the Dept. of Finance and the Budget Committee shall, within the 25-day period, give the Attorney General their opinion as to whether or not a substantial net change in the state or local finances would result if the proposed initiative is adopted. The fiscal analysis is then included in the official summary. (If a fiscal estimate is required, the Attorney General shall prepare the title and summary within 15 days after receipt of the estimate prepared by the Dept. of Finance and the Joint Legislative Budget Committee.)

When the official summary is complete, the Attorney General sends it to the proponents, the Senate, the Assembly, and the Secretary of State. It is at this time that proponents can begin circulating. It generally takes 30-45 days between submitting an initiative and approval for circulation.

The Legislature may conduct public hearings on the proposed initiative, but cannot amend it.

Date Initiative language can be submitted to state for November 2002 ballot: Any time.

Signatures tied to vote of which office: Governor

Next Gubernatorial election: 2002

Votes cast for governor in last election: 8,381,880

Net number of signatures required: 8% of votes cast for Governor for a constitutional amendment (670,816) and 5% for a statute (419,094)

Distribution requirement: None

Circulation period: 150 days

Do circulators have to be residents? No

Date when signatures are due for certification: No petition may be circulated prior to the official summary date. The completed and signed petition must be filed with the county elections official not later than 150 days from the official summary date; no petition may be accepted for filing after that date. Each initiative will be placed on the next statewide general or special election ballot that occurs at least 131 days after the initiative qualifies.

Signature verification process: Random Sampling

Single-subject restriction: Yes

Legislative tampering: The legislature cannot amend or repeal an initiative, unless it is permitted by the initiative.

General Comments: The law specifies the format for the petition. The petition may be circulated by many different people carrying separate, identical parts of the petition called "sections". It is important to follow the prescribed format because the county elections officials will not accept nonconforming petitions for filing. Each section of the petition must contain the full title and text of the measure and each page on which signatures are to appear must contain a copy of the Attorney General's summary in Roman boldface type not smaller than 12-point. The petition must have room for the signature of each petition signer as well as his or her printed name, residence address and community name. Signature spaces must be consecutively numbered commencing with the number 1 for each petition section. A minimum one-inch space shall be left at the top of each page and after each name for use by the county elections official. Pursuant to the Supreme Court's decision in Assembly v. Deukmajian, the petition form must direct signers to include their "residence address" rather than "address as registered" or other address. Non-complying petition forms will be rejected as invalid. Additionally, each section of the petition must contain the name of the county (or city and county) in which it was circulated. Each section shall be circulated among voters of only one county and may be circulated only by registered voters.

Colorado

The effort for I&R in Colorado was started by Dr. Persifor M. Cooke of Denver in the mid-1890s. As secretary and president of the Colorado Direct Legislation League, Cooke and the constitutional lawyer J. Warner Mills of Denver fought for I&R from 1900 until 1910, when Governor John F. Shafroth called a special session of the legislature to consider the issue. The constitutional amendments that were passed provided for initiative, referendum, and recall on both state and local levels.

Coloradans set their state's record for initiative use the first year it was available, in 1912, by putting 22 initiatives and 6 popular referendums on the ballot. Eight of the initiatives passed and challenges to legislatively approved laws were sustained in 5 of the 6 cases. Among these were laws or amendments establishing an eight-hour work day for workers employed in "underground mines, smelters, mills and coke ovens"; giving women workers an eight-hour day; providing pensions for orphans and for widows with children; establishing juvenile courts in major cities and counties; and granting home rule to cities and towns.

Over the years Colorado voters proved sympathetic to the needs of the aged and infirm, approving initiatives providing for the treatment of mental illness in 1916 and 1920, relief for blind adults in 1918, pensions for the aged and for indigent tuberculosis sufferers in 1936, and increased pensions adjusted for inflation in 1956. Colorado voters also remained friendly to organized labor, approving an initiative statute changing the workmen's compensation law to benefit employees in 1936 and defeating an employer-backed "Right to Work" initiative in 1958.

In the early 1970s, Coloradans passed environmentalist-backed initiatives to keep the Winter Olympics from being held in their state (1972) and prohibit underground nuclear explosions except with prior voter approval (1974). Richard Lamm, an obscure state legislator when he sponsored the anti-Olympics initiative, gained sufficient prestige from his leadership of this campaign to later win election as governor.

In 1984 Colorado became the first state to pass an initiative banning the use of state funds for abortion (the second was Arkansas, in 1988). Voters approved the measure by a single percentage point. Less controversial and more popular was the 1984 "Motor Voter" initiative, which set up a system of voter registration at driver's licensing bureaus. This highly successful program increased the number of registered voters in Colorado by 12.4 percent in the 15 months from July 1985 to October 1986.

Hostility to the initiative process by the political establishment manifested itself in the 1976 election with a "No on Everything" campaign that outspent proponents with over 91% of all funds expended. The election was followed by a series of legislative efforts to restrict use of the initiative. Notorious for exceeding the "reasonable regulation" guideline, Federal Courts have struck down more of Colorado initiative restrictions than any other state. Those most famous are *Meyer v. Grant* in 1986 and *Buckley v. ACLF* in 1999—both went all the way to the U.S. Supreme Court.

Colorado is recognized for having spawned the Term Limits movement in 1990. Other states had term limits initiative in 1990 and in previous years. State Senator Terry Considine, frustrated that his peers would not consider his term limits bill, became an activist and drove the term limits law to fruition with a 71% favorable vote. Colorado's initiative was unique in that it also sought to limit members of Congress. Large numbers of states approved term limits for members of Congress in subsequent elections. Colorado passed additional term limits initiatives in 1994, 1996, and 1998.

Coloradans would have preferred that their elected officials exercise self-restraint with taxation. Tax limit initiatives succeeded in making it to the ballot in 1966, 1972, 1976, 1978, 1986, 1988, 1990, and 1992, but failed at the ballot box until 1992. The 1992 effort sponsored by tax activist Doug Bruce and dubbed the Taxpayer Bill of Rights (TABOR), helped to revitalize the lagging taxpayer revolt begun in 1978 when Proposition 13 had been approved in California. Recent use of the initiative peaked in 1992 with 10 initiatives on the ballot. Since 1992, use has been flat with a slight downward trend to 6 in 2000. Average is 8 per 2 year election cycle over the high use decade of the 1990s. Initiatives are blamed for long ballots, yet state issues referred to the ballot by the General Assembly generally equal the number of initiatives. Other issues referred to the ballot by local governments result in several times more referred measures than initiatives.

Statewide Initiative Usage

Number of Initiatives	Number Passed	Number Failed	Passage Rate
178	64	114	35%

Statewide Initiatives

Year	Measure Number	Type	Subject Matter	Description	Pass/Fail
1912	1	DA	Alcohol Regulation	Providing for statewide prohibition.	Failed
1912	10	DS	Election Reform	Amending election laws.	Failed
1912	11	DA	Initiative and Referendum	Providing for the holding of special elections for voting on proposed constitutional amendments and initiated and referred laws.	Failed

Year	Measure Number	Type	Subject Matter	Description	Pass/Fail
1912	12	DA	Legal	Defining contempt of court and providing for trial by jury for contempt in certain cases.	Failed
1912	13	DA	Utility Regulation	Creating a public utilities court with exclusive power to fix and enforce reasonable rates, and for appeal direct to the supreme court from its decision.	Failed
1912	14	DS	Election Reform	Amending election laws, and providing for a "headless ballot".	Passed
1912	15	DA	Education	Providing wider control of the schools by the people.	Failed
1912	16	DA	Judicial Reform	Providing for juvenile courts in cities and counties of 100,000 population.	Passed
1912	17	DS	Welfare	Mothers' compensation act and aid to dependent and neglected children.	Passed
1912	18	DS	Administration of Government	Relating to civil service and amending said law.	Passed
1912	19	DS	Labor	Eight-hour law for work in underground mines, smelters, mills and coke ovens.	Passed
1912	2	DS	Alcohol Regulation	Enforcement of prohibition laws by search and seizure.	Failed
1912	20	DS	Administration of Government	Giving state highway commission control of certain funds.	Failed
1912	3	DS	Labor	Women's eight-hour employment law.	Passed
1912	31	DA	Bonds	Authorizing a bonded indebtedness for public highways.	Failed
1912	32	DS	Administration of Government	Construction of tunnel through James Peak.	Failed
1912	4	DS	Administration of Government	Providing for the regulation of public service corporations.	Failed
1912	5	DS	Administration of Government	Establishing a state fair.	Failed
1912	6	DA	Alien Rights	Providing special funds for the state immigration bureau.	Failed
1912	7	DS	Initiative and Referendum	Reducing costs of publishing constitutional amendments, initiated and referred laws, and publishing arguments for and against.	Failed
1912	8	DA	Administration of Government	Granting home rule to cities and towns.	Passed
1912	9	DA	Election Reform	Providing recall from office.	Passed
1914	N/A	DA	Initiative and Referendum	Giving people right to petition governor to call special elections for submitting measures under the initiative and referendum.	Failed
1914	N/A	DS	Legal	Permitting probation in criminal cases for minors and first offenders.	Failed
1914	N/A	DS	Administration of Government	Providing for codification of laws relating to women and children.	Failed
1914	N/A	DA	Utility Regulation	Designating newspapers as public utilities.	Failed
1914	N/A	DA	Judicial Reform	Providing for a 3/4 jury verdict in civil cases and permitting women to serve on juries if they desire.	Failed

Year	Measure Number	Type	Subject Matter	Description	Pass/Fail
1914	N/A	DA	Alcohol Regulation	Providing for statewide prohibition.	Passed
1914	N/A	DA	Initiative and Referendum	Providing that initiated measures rejected by people cannot again be initiated for six years, and if two conflicting measures be adopted at same election, one receiving largest affirmative vote shall prevail.	Failed
1914	N/A	DS	Taxes	Increasing state road fund by half mill levy for highway construction.	Passed
1916	N/A	DS	Education	Providing for the investment of public school funds in certain securities.	Passed
1916	N/A	DS	Business Regulation	Regulating the running of stock at large.	Failed
1916	N/A	DS	Welfare	Providing for the care and treatment of insane persons.	Passed
1916	N/A	DA	Alcohol Regulation	Declaring beer non-toxicating and providing for its manufacture and sale.	Failed
1916	N/A	DA	Administration of Government	Placing state civil service in the constitution.	Failed
1916	N/A	DS	Taxes	Abolishment of the state tax commission.	Failed
1918	N/A	DS	Welfare	Relief for blind adults.	Passed
1918	N/A	DA	Administration of Government	Placing state civil service in the constitution.	Passed
1918	N/A	DS	Alcohol Regulation	"Bone-dry" prohibition law.	Passed
1920	N/A	DS	Health/Medical	Appropriating $350,000 from the general fund for the establishment o the Psychopathic Hospital and Laboratory.	Passed
1920	N/A	DA	Education	Providing additional one mill levy for state educational institutions.	Passed
1920	N/A	DA	Bonds	Providing for the construction of the Moffat, Monarch and San Juan tunnels, and bond issue therefore.	Failed
1920	N/A	DS	Business Regulation	Relating to the practice of chiropractic, and providing for the regulation and licensing thereof.	Failed
1920	N/A	DS	Administration of Government	Creating the County of Limon.	Failed
1920	N/A	DS	Administration of Government	Creating the County of Flagler.	Failed
1920	N/A	DS	Labor	Fixing hours of employment in city fire departments.	Passed
1922	N/A	DA	Bonds	$1.5m bond issue for construction of public highways.	Passed
1922	N/A	DA	Utility Regulation	Creating a public utilities commission, prescribing its powers and duties, and defining public utilities.	Failed
1922	N/A	DA	Taxes	Giving legislature or people power to exempt certain intangibles from ad valorem taxation, and to impose an income tax in lieu thereof.	Failed
1922	N/A	DS	Business Regulation	Concerning experimental operations on human beings and dumb animals.	Failed
1922	N/A	DS	Apportionment/ Redistricting	Revising apportionment of members of legislature.	Failed

Year	Measure Number	Type	Subject Matter	Description	Pass/Fail
1924	N/A	DA	Administration of Government	Establishing the office of state printer and printing building committee.	Failed
1926	N/A	DA	Administration of Government	Creating a public utilities commission and prescribing its powers and duties.	Failed
1926	N/A	DS	Taxes	Concerning the taxation of petroleum products and registration of motor vehicles, and providing that all such taxes and fees by used exclusively for roads.	Failed
1926	N/A	DS	Business Regulation	Amending law to permit dentists licensed in other states to practice in Colorado without examination.	Failed
1928	N/A	DA	Education	Providing for the election of a board of education, and for the appointment by said board of a commissioner of education to take place of superintendent of public instruction.	Failed
1928	N/A	DA	Bonds	Providing for a $60m bond issue for the construction of highways.	Failed
1930	N/A	DA	Education	Providing for the election of a board of education and for the appointment by said board of a commissioner of education to take place of superintendent of public instruction.	Failed
1932	N/A	DA	Taxes	Limiting taxation of motor fuel and ad valorem taxation of motor vehicles.	Failed
1932	N/A	DS	Apportionment/ Redistricting	Reapportionment of members of legislature.	Passed
1932	N/A	DA	Alcohol Regulation	Repealing statewide prohibition, subject to national repeal.	Passed
1932	N/A	DA	Taxes	Giving legislature power to provide for a limited income tax and a classified personal property tax, to be used for public schools.	Passed
1932	N/A	DA	Taxes	Giving legislature power to provide for a graduated income tax for state purposes, abolishing property tax for state purposes, and giving any excess revenue to the public schools.	Failed
1934	N/A	DA	Taxes	Concerning the taxation of petroleum products and registration of motor vehicles and providing that such taxes and fees be used exclusively for roads.	Passed
1934	N/A	DS	Business Regulation	Imposing license fees on chain stores.	Passed
1934	N/A	DA	Taxes	Limiting tax on motor fuel to $.03 per gallon.	Failed
1934	N/A	DA	Taxes	Giving people sole power to impose or approve imposition of excise taxes through the initiative and referendum.	Failed
1936	N/A	DA	Taxes	Providing for ownership tax on motor vehicles in lieu of ad valorem taxation thereon, and for the distribution thereof.	Passed
1936	N/A	DS	Welfare	Providing for public assistance to indigent tubercular residents.	Passed

Year	Measure Number	Type	Subject Matter	Description	Pass/Fail
1936	N/A	DA	Taxes	Amending "uniformity clause" of constitution principally by limiting rate to taxation for all purposes to 20 mills in cities and towns of first class, and 15 mills in other divisions.	Failed
1936	N/A	DA	Taxes	Amending revenue section of constitution, principally by giving legislature power to provide for an income tax within limitations.	Failed
1936	N/A	DA	Welfare	Providing $45 per month old age pensions and designating certain taxes for the payment thereof.	Passed
1936	N/A	DS	Labor	Amending workmen's compensation act to benefit of employee.	Passed
1938	N/A	DA	Business Regulation	Relating to the practice of the healing arts, and giving practitioners licensed by the state certain rights in tax supported institutions and power to regulate their own professions.	Failed
1938	N/A	DA	Welfare	Repeal of $45 per month old age pension amendment and giving legislature power to provide for pensions.	Failed
1938	N/A	DS	Taxes	Repeal of chain stores tax act.	Failed
1940	N/A	DA	Taxes	Providing for an income tax; requiring the legislature to levy such income tax at not lower than certain specified rates; and providing that the revenues derived there from shall replace property taxes.	Failed
1940	N/A	DA	Environmental Reform	Providing for the conservation of the state's wildlife resources; limiting the use of game and fish revenues for such purposes; and establishing a Game and Fish Commission.	Failed
1940	N/A	DS	Gaming	Establishing a racing commission and legalizing horse and dog racing.	Failed
1940	N/A	DA	Welfare	Providing for a guaranteed old age pension of $30 per month to residents of the state over 65 years who qualify.	Failed
1940	N/A	DA	Taxes	Providing for an ad valorem tax on all intangible property in the state, and allocating the funds derived there from.	Failed
1944	N/A	DA	Alien Rights	Providing that aliens eligible to citizenship may acquire and dispose of real and personal property, and that provision shall be made by law concerning the right of aliens ineligible to citizenship to acquire and dispose of such property.	Failed
1944	N/A	DA	Veteran Affairs	Providing for preference to honorably discharged veterans and their widows in the civil service of the state and its political subdivisions.	Passed
1944	N/A	DS	Welfare	Appropriating $.5m for the then current biennium and $1.5m annually thereafter for old age pensions.	Passed

Year	Measure Number	Type	Subject Matter	Description	Pass/Fail
1948	3	DA	Alcohol Regulation	Political subdivisions may adopt and thereafter modify or repeal local option proposals prohibiting the sale of alcoholic and fermented malt beverages.	Failed
1948	4	DA	Welfare	Providing for a guaranteed minimum $55 per month old age pension and for the allocation and earmarking of certain moneys and excise taxes to pay the same.	Failed
1950	3	DA	Administration of Government	Concerning civil service and providing for additional exemptions there from of governor's staff.	Failed
1952	4	DA	Taxes	Providing for a severance tax on certain petroleum products and natural gas.	Failed
1952	6	DA	Gaming	Legalizing slot machines except where prohibited by local ordinance.	Failed
1952	N/A	DS	Labor	Making it unlawful for any municipality to employ firemen more than 60 hours a week, with certain exceptions.	Failed
1954	8	DA	Administration of Government	Providing for four-year terms of office for certain County officers. (Art. 14, Sec. 8)	Passed
1956	4	DA	Apportionment/Redistricting	Providing for apportionment of members of the general assembly.	Failed
1956	5	DA	Welfare	Revising the old age pension article; establishing a monthly award of $100 to be adjusted to increased living costs; providing for a stabilization fund of $5 million.	Passed
1958	1	DA	Labor	"Right-to-work" amendment; providing that no person shall be denied the freedom to obtain or retain employment because of membership or non-membership in any labor union or labor organization.	Failed
1958	4	DA	Gaming	Legalizing the conduct of games of chance (limited to bingo, lotto, or raffles) by certain organizations which operate without profit to dues paying members.	Passed
1960	3	DA	Environmental Reform	Creates a wildlife management commission and a department of wildlife conservation.	Failed
1960	4	DS	Daylight Savings Time	Providing for and establishing Daylight Saving Time.	Failed
1960	6	DA	Taxes	Authorizing general assembly to vest in counties, cities and towns, the power to impose a retail sales and use tax for local purposes on tangible personal property, except drugs, and food for off-premises consumption.	Failed
1960	7	DA	Administration of Government	Authorizing governor, with consent of Senate, to appoint administrative officers of certain departments, to be excluded from civil service.	Failed

Year	Measure Number	Type	Subject Matter	Description	Pass/Fail
1962	7	DA	Apportionment/ Redistricting	An act providing for the apportionment of the Senate and House of Representatives of the General Assembly.	Passed
1962	8	DA	Apportionment/ Redistricting	Providing for reapportionment of the general assembly.	Failed
1966	3	DA	Administration of Government	Selection, tenure and removal of judges.	Passed
1966	4	DA	Administration of Government	Provide for 35 member senate and 65 member house.	Passed
1966	5	DA	Taxes	Property tax limitation.	Failed
1972	10	DS	Utility Regulation	An Act to protect the consumer of public utility services by defining just and reasonable rates, by creating an Office of Public Consumer Counsel.	Failed
1972	11	DS	Business Regulation	Establishing a system of compulsory insurance and compensation irrespective of fault for victims of motor vehicle accidents, setting forth the basis for recovery.	Failed
1972	12	DA	Taxes	Replacement of property taxes for the financing of schools.	Failed
1972	6	DA	Gaming	An act to amend the Constitution to provide for a privately operated lottery, supervised and regulated by the Department of State and granting an exclusive original ten year license to the United States Sweepstakes Corporation.	Failed
1972	8	DA	Taxes	An Act to Amend Art. 10 and 11 to prohibit the state from levying taxes and appropriating or loaning funds for the purpose of aiding or furthering the 1976 Winter Olympic Games.	Passed
1972	9	DS	Campaign Finance Reform	Require that public officials disclose their private interests and that all lobbyists register and file periodic informational statements.	Passed
1972	7	DA	Taxes	Establishing a maximum limitation of one and one-half percent of the actual value on the annual taxation of property except as permitted by a vote of the qualified electors.	Failed
1974	1	DA	Administration of Government	An act concerning the annexation of property by a County or city and County, and prohibiting the striking off of any territory from a County without first submitting the question to a vote of the qualified electors of the County and city.	Passed
1974	10	DA	Nuclear weapons/ facilities/waste	An act to amend the Constitution to establish procedural steps to be complied with prior to the detonation of nuclear explosive devises including voter approval.	Passed

Year	Measure Number	Type	Subject Matter	Description	Pass/Fail
1974	8	DA	Education	Prohibit the assignment or the transportation of pupils to public educational institutions in order to achieve racial balance of pupils at such institutions.	Passed
1974	9	DA	Apportionment/ Redistricting	Reapportioning of legislative districts by a body to be known as the Colorado Reapportionment Commission which shall consist of electors.	Passed
1976	10	DA	Taxes	An Amendment adding a new Sec. 31 to Art. 10 requiring registered electoral approval of all state and local executive or legislative acts which result in new or increased taxes.	Failed
1976	3	DA	Nuclear weapons/ facilities/waste	An amendment requiring approval by two thirds of each House of the General Assembly prior to any construction or modification of a nuclear power plant or related facility.	Failed
1976	6	DA	Civil Rights	An Act to repeal Sec. 29 of Art. 2 which section provides for equality of rights under the law on account of sex.	Failed
1976	7	DS	Taxes	Exempts food and food products, with certain exceptions, from state sales and use taxes and repeal the food sales tax credit, to require the General Assembly to enact severance taxes and corporate income taxes to offset any revenue lost.	Failed
1976	8	DS	Environmental Reform	Requires a minimum deposit refund value for beverage containers for malt liquor, including beer, and carbonated soft drinks manufactured, distributed, or sold for use in this state.	Failed
1976	9	DS	Utility Regulation	Protects and represents consumers of public utilities services by creating a Department of Public Counselor, and concerning financial disclosures by Public Utilities Commissioners.	Failed
1978	2	DA	Taxes	Limiting annual increases in per capita expenditures by the state and its political subdivisions.	Failed
1982	5	DS	Environmental Reform	Refund on beverage containers.	Failed
1982	6	DA	Nuclear weapons/ facilities/waste	To bring about the cessation of nuclear weapons component production in Colorado.	Failed
1982	7	DS	Business Regulation	Regulate the sale of wine in grocery stores.	Failed
1984	3	DA	Abortion	Ban the state funding of abortion.	Passed
1984	4	DS	Election Reform	To provide for additional voter registration of qualified electors applying for a driver's license.	Passed
1984	5	DA	Gaming	Establish casino gambling in Pueblo.	Failed
1986	4	DA	Taxes	Voter approval for tax increases.	Failed

Year	Measure Number	Type	Subject Matter	Description	Pass/Fail
1988	1	DA	Administration of Government	English as official language.	Passed
1988	6	DA	Taxes	Voter approval: increases in tax revenues.	Failed
1988	7	DA	Abortion	Restore funding for abortions.	Failed
1988	8	DA	Administration of Government	Referral of measures to committees.	Passed
1990	1	DA	Taxes	To require voter approval for certain state and local government revenue increases.	Failed
1990	4	DA	Gaming	Legalizing limited gaming.	Passed
1990	5	DA	Term Limits	Term limits for elected officials. State legislature and Congress. 8/8	Passed
1992	1	DA	Taxes	Voter approval of tax revenue increases.	Passed
1992	10	DS	Animal Rights	Prohibit taking of black bears.	Passed
1992	2	DA	Civil Rights	Repeal local laws passed to ban discrimination based on sexual orientation and prevent similar new laws.	Passed
1992	3	DA	Gaming	Limited gaming; surtax.	Failed
1992	4	DA	Gaming	Limited gaming.	Failed
1992	5	DA	Gaming	Limited gaming.	Failed
1992	6	DS	Education	Act for system of educational standards.	Failed
1992	7	DA	Education	Vouchers for school funding.	Failed
1992	8	DA	Environmental Reform	The Great Outdoors Colorado program.	Passed
1992	9	DA	Gaming	Limited gaming.	Failed
1994	1	DA	Taxes	Would place an additional 50 cents per pack tax on the sale of cigarettes by wholesalers.	Failed
1994	11	DA	Labor	Workers compensation benefits.	Failed
1994	12	DA	Campaign Finance Reform	Placed limitations on elected officials compensation; enacted campaign contribution limitations.	Failed
1994	13	DA	Gaming	To allow slot machines without a local vote in Manitou Springs.	Failed
1994	15	DA	Campaign Finance Reform	Establish campaign contributions limits.	Failed
1994	16	DA	Civil Rights	Would allow the control of the promotion of obscenity by the state and any city, town or County to the full extent permitted by the First Amendment to the United States Constitution.	Failed
1994	17	DA	Term Limits	Term limits on Congress 6/12 and on all localities.	Passed
1994	18	DA	Administration of Government	State medical assistance repayment.	Failed
1996	11	DA	Taxes	Eliminates property tax exemptions of religious and nonprofit organizations.	Failed
1996	12	DA	Term Limits	Informed Voter Law	Passed
1996	13	DA	Initiative and Referendum	Expands initiative and referendum powers.	Failed

Year	Measure Number	Type	Subject Matter	Description	Pass/Fail
1996	14	DA	Animal Rights	Concerns methods of taking wildlife; prohibits use of leg hold traps.	Passed
1996	15	DS	Campaign Finance Reform	Limiting the amount of campaign contributions to candidate committees.	Passed
1996	16	DA	Administration of Government	Concerns management of state's trust lands; expands membership of the State Land Board.	Passed
1996	17	DA	Civil Rights	Grants constitutional status to parents' rights.	Failed
1996	18	DA	Gaming	Allow limited gambling in the city of Trinidad.	Failed
1997	1	DA	Taxes	Funding for transportation	Failed
1998	11	DS	Abortion	Would prohibit partial birth abortion	Failed
1998	12	DS	Abortion	Would require parents be notified prior to a physician performed abortion.	Passed
1998	13	DA	Animal Rights	Would establish uniform livestock regulations.	Failed
1998	14	DS	Animal Rights	Establish regulations for commercial hog farms	Passed
1998	15	DS	Environmental Reform	Would regulate water flow meters.	Failed
1998	16	DA	Education	Would require that payments by the Conservation District be made to the Public School Fund and School Districts.	Failed
1998	17	DA	Education	Would establish Income Tax Credit for education expenses.	Failed
1998	18	DA	Term Limits	Self Limit Law.	Passed
2000	20	DA	Drug Policy Reform	Legalizes marijuana for medical purposes.	Passed
2000	21	DA	Taxes	Amends TABOR — creates tax cuts.	Failed
2000	22	DS	Gun Regulation	An initiative amendment to require background checks for guns purchased at gun shows.	Passed
2000	23	DA	Education	Providing Additional K-12 Funding	Passed
2000	24	DA	Environmental Reform	Citizen Growth Initiative.	Failed
2000	25	DS	Abortion	This measure insures the provision of complete and accurate information to allow a woman to make an informed choice as to whether to give birth or to have an abortion.	Failed
2001	26	DA	Administration of Government	Expends $50 million of 2001 tax refund revenues over a period of three years to fund a high-speed monorail.	Failed

Colorado Constitution

Article V: Section 1. General assembly — initiative and referendum.

(1) The legislative power of the state shall be vested in the general assembly consisting of a senate and house of representatives, both to be elected by the people, but the people reserve to themselves the power to propose laws and amendments to the constitution and to enact or reject the same at the polls independent of the general assembly and also re-

serve power at their own option to approve or reject at the polls any act or item, section, or part of any act of the general assembly.

(2) The first power hereby reserved by the people is the initiative, and signatures by registered electors in an amount equal to at least five percent of the total number of votes cast for all candidates for the office of secretary of state at the previous general election shall be required to propose any measure by petition, and every such petition shall include the full text of the measure so proposed. Initiative petitions for state legislation and amendments to the constitution, in such form as may be prescribed pursuant to law, shall be addressed to and filed with the secretary of state at least three months before the general election at which they are to be voted upon.

(3) The second power hereby reserved is the referendum, and it may be ordered, except as to laws necessary for the immediate preservation of the public peace, health, or safety, and appropriations for the support and maintenance of the departments of state and state institutions, against any act or item, section, or part of any act of the general assembly, either by a petition signed by registered electors in an amount equal to at least five percent of the total number of votes cast for all candidates for the office of the secretary of state at the previous general election or by the general assembly. Referendum petitions, in such form as may be prescribed pursuant to law, shall be addressed to and filed with the secretary of state not more than ninety days after the final adjournment of the session of the general assembly that passed the bill on which the referendum is demanded. The filing of a referendum petition against any item, section, or part of any act shall not delay the remainder of the act from becoming operative.

(4) The veto power of the governor shall not extend to measures initiated by or referred to the people. All elections on measures initiated by or referred to the people of the state shall be held at the biennial regular general election, and all such measures shall become the law or a part of the constitution, when approved by a majority of the votes cast thereon, and not otherwise, and shall take effect from and after the date of the official declaration of the vote thereon by proclamation of the governor, but not later than thirty days after the vote has been canvassed. This section shall not be construed to deprive the general assembly of the power to enact any measure.

(5) The original draft of the text of proposed initiated constitutional amendments and initiated laws shall be submitted to the legislative research and drafting offices of the general assembly for review and comment. No later than two weeks after submission of the original draft, unless withdrawn by the proponents, the legislative research and drafting offices of the general assembly shall render their comments to the proponents of the proposed measure at a meeting open to the public, which shall be held only after full and timely notice to the public. Such meeting shall be held prior to the fixing of a ballot title. Neither the general assembly nor its committees or agencies shall have any power to require the amendment, modification, or other alteration of the text of any such proposed measure or to establish deadlines for the submission of the original draft of the text of any proposed measure.

(5.5) No measure shall be proposed by petition containing more than one subject, which shall be clearly expressed in its title; but if any subject shall be embraced in any measure which shall not be expressed in the title, such measure shall be void only as to so much thereof as shall not be so expressed. If a measure contains more than one subject, such that a ballot title cannot be fixed that clearly expresses a single subject, no title shall be set and the measure shall not be submitted to the people for adoption or rejection at the polls. In such circumstance, however, the measure may be revised and resubmitted for the fixing of a proper title without the necessity of review and comment on the revised measure in accordance with subsection (5) of this section, unless the revisions involve more than the elimination of provisions to achieve a single subject, or unless the official or officials responsible for the fixing of a title determine that the revisions are so substantial that such review and comment is in the public interest. The revision and resubmission of a measure in accordance with this subsection (5.5) shall not operate to alter or extend any filing deadline applicable to the measure.

(6) The petition shall consist of sheets having such general form printed or written at the top thereof as shall be designated or prescribed by the secretary of state; such petition shall be signed by registered electors in their own proper persons only, to which shall be attached the residence address of such person and the date of signing the same. To each of such petitions, which may consist of one or more sheets, shall be attached an affidavit of some registered elector that each signature thereon is the signature of the person whose name it purports to be and that, to the best of the knowledge and belief of the affiant, each of the persons signing said petition was, at the time of signing, a registered elector. Such petition so verified shall be prima facie evidence that the signatures thereon are genuine and true and that the persons signing the same are registered electors.

(7) The secretary of state shall submit all measures initiated by or referred to the people for adoption or rejection at the polls, in compliance with this section. In submitting the same and in all matters pertaining to the form of all petitions, the secretary of state and all other officers shall be guided by the general laws.

(7.3) Before any election at which the voters of the entire state will vote on any initiated or referred constitutional amendment or legislation, the nonpartisan research staff of the general assembly shall cause to be published the text and title of every such measure. Such publication shall be made at least one time in at least one legal publication of general circulation in each county of the state and shall be made at least fifteen days prior to the final date of voter registration for the election. The form and manner of publication shall be as prescribed by law and shall ensure a reasonable opportunity for the voters statewide to become informed about the text and title of each measure.

(7.5) (a) Before any election at which the voters of the entire state will vote on any initiated or referred constitutional amendment or legislation, the nonpartisan research staff of the general assembly shall prepare and make available to the public the following information in the form of a ballot information booklet:

(I) The text and title of each measure to be voted on;

(II) A fair and impartial analysis of each measure, which shall include a summary and the major arguments both for and against the measure, and which may include any other information that would assist understanding the purpose and effect of the measure. Any person may file written comments for consideration by the research staff during the preparation of such analysis.

(b) At least thirty days before the election, the research staff shall cause the ballot information booklet to be distributed to active registered voters statewide.

(c) If any measure to be voted on by the voters of the entire state includes matters arising under section 20 of article X of this constitution, the ballot information booklet shall include the information and the titled notice required by section 20 (3) (b) of article X, and the mailing of such information pursuant to section 20 (3) (b) of article X is not required.

(d) The general assembly shall provide sufficient appropriations for the preparation and distribution of the ballot information booklet pursuant to this subsection (7.5) at no charge to recipients.

(8) The style of all laws adopted by the people through the initiative shall be, "Be it Enacted by the People of the State of Colorado".

(9) The initiative and referendum powers reserved to the people by this section are hereby further reserved to the registered electors of every city, town, and municipality as to all local, special, and municipal legislation of every character in or for their respective municipalities. The manner of exercising said powers shall be prescribed by general laws; except that cities, towns, and municipalities may provide for the manner of exercising the initiative and referendum powers as to their municipal legislation. Not more than ten percent of the registered electors may be required to order the referendum, nor more than fifteen per cent to propose any measure by the initiative in any city, town, or municipality.

(10) This section of the constitution shall be in all respects self-executing; except that the form of the initiative or referendum petition may be prescribed pursuant to law.

Colorado Statutes

1-40-101 — Legislative declaration.

It is not the intention of this article to limit or abridge in any manner the powers reserved to the people in the initiative and referendum, but rather to properly safeguard, protect, and preserve inviolate for them these modern instrumentalities of democratic government.

As used in this article, unless the context otherwise requires:

(1) "Ballot issue" means a non-recall, citizen-initiated petition or legislatively-referred measure which is authorized by the state constitution, including a question as defined in sections 1-41-102 (3) and 1-41-103 (3), enacted in Senate Bill 93-98.

(2) "Ballot title" means the language which is printed on the ballot which is comprised of the submission clause and the title.

(3) (Deleted by amendment, L. 95, p. 430, § 2, effective May 8, 1995.)

(4) "Draft" means the typewritten proposed text of the initiative which, if passed, becomes the actual language of the constitution or statute, together with language concerning placement of the measure in the constitution or statutes.

(5) (Deleted by amendment, L. 95, p. 431, § 2, effective May 8, 1995.)

(6) "Section" means a bound compilation of initiative forms approved by the secretary of state, which shall include pages that contain the warning required by section 1-40-110 (1), the ballot title, and a copy of the proposed measure; succeeding pages that contain the warning, the ballot title, and ruled lines numbered consecutively for registered electors' signatures; and a final page that contains the affidavit required by section 1-40-111 (2). Each section shall be consecutively prenumbered by the petitioner prior to circulation.

(7) (Deleted by amendment, L. 95, p. 431, § 2, effective May 8, 1995.)

(8) "Submission clause" means the language which is attached to the title to form a question which can be answered by "yes" or "no".

(9) (Deleted by amendment, L. 2000, p. 1621, § 3, effective August 2, 2000.)

(10) "Title" means a brief statement that fairly and accurately represents the true intent and meaning of the proposed text of the initiative.

1-40-103 — Applicability of article.

(1) This article shall apply to all state ballot issues that are authorized by the state constitution unless otherwise provided by statute, charter, or ordinance.

(2) The laws pertaining to municipal initiatives, referenda, and referred measures are governed by the provisions of article 11 of title 31, C.R.S.

(3) The laws pertaining to county petitions and referred measures are governed by the provisions of section 30-11-103.5, C.R.S.

(4) The laws pertaining to school district petitions and referred measures are governed by the provisions of section 22-30-104 (4), C.R.S.

1-40-104 — Designated representatives.

At the time of any filing of a draft as provided in this article, the proponents shall designate the names and mailing addresses of two persons who shall represent the proponents in all matters affecting the petition and to whom all notices or information concerning the petition shall be mailed.

1-40-105 — Filing procedure — review and comment — amendments — filing with secretary of state.

(1) The original typewritten draft of every initiative petition for a proposed law or amendment to the state constitution to be enacted by the people, before it is signed by any elector, shall be submitted by the proponents of the petition to the directors of the legislative council and the office of legislative legal services for review and comment. Proponents are encouraged to write such drafts in plain, non-technical language and in a clear and coherent manner using words with common and everyday meaning which are understandable to the average reader. Upon request, any agency in the executive department shall assist in reviewing and preparing comments on the petition. No later than two weeks after the date of submission of the original draft, unless it is withdrawn by the proponents, the directors of the legislative council and the office of legislative legal services, or their designees, shall render their comments to the proponents of the petition concerning the format or contents of the petition at a meeting open to the public. Where appropriate, such comments shall also contain suggested editorial changes to promote compliance with the plain language provisions of this section. Except with the permission of the proponents, the comments shall not be disclosed to any person other than the proponents prior to the public meeting with the proponents of the petition.

(2) After the public meeting but before submission to the secretary of state for title setting, the proponents may amend the petition in response to some or all of the comments of the directors of the legislative council and the office of legislative legal services, or their designees. If any substantial amendment is made to the petition, other than an amendment in direct response to the comments of the directors of the legislative council and the office of legislative legal services, the amended petition shall be resubmitted to the directors for comment in accordance with subsection (1) of this section prior to submittal to the secretary of state as provided in subsection (4) of this section. If the directors have no additional comments concerning the amended petition, they may so notify the proponents in writing, and, in such case, a hearing on the amended petition pursuant to subsection (1) of this section is not required.

(3) To the extent possible, drafts shall be worded with simplicity and clarity and so that the effect of the measure will not be misleading or likely to cause confusion among voters. The draft shall not present the issue to be decided in such manner that a vote for the measure would be a vote against the proposition or viewpoint that the voter believes that he or she is casting a vote for or, conversely, that a vote against the measure would be a vote for a proposition or viewpoint that the voter is against.

(4) After the conference provided in subsections (1) and (2) of this section, a copy of the original typewritten draft submitted to the directors of the legislative council and the office of legislative legal services, a copy of the amended draft with changes highlighted or otherwise indicated, if any amendments were made following the last conference conducted pursuant to subsections (1) and (2) of this section, and an original final draft which gives the final language for printing shall be submitted to the secretary of state without any title, submission clause, or ballot title providing the designation by which the voters shall express their choice for or against the proposed law or constitutional amendment.

1-40-106 — Title board — meetings — titles and submission clause.

(1) For ballot issues, beginning with the first submission of a draft after an election, the secretary of state shall convene a title board consisting of the secretary of state, the attorney general, and the director of the office of legislative legal services or the director's designee. The title board, by majority vote, shall proceed to designate and fix a proper fair title for each proposed law or constitutional amendment, together with a submission clause, at public meetings to be held at 2

p.m. on the first and third Wednesdays of each month in which a draft or a motion for reconsideration has been submitted to the secretary of state. To be considered at such meeting, a draft shall be submitted to the secretary of state no later than 3 p.m. on the twelfth day before the meeting at which the draft is to be considered by the title board. The first meeting of the title board shall be held no sooner than the first Wednesday in December after an election, and the last meeting shall be held no later than the third Wednesday in May in the year in which the measure is to be voted on.

(2) (Deleted by amendment, L. 95, p. 432, § 4, effective May 8, 1995.)

(3) (a) (Deleted by amendment, L. 2000, p. 1620, § 1, effective August 2, 2000.)

(b) In setting a title, the title board shall consider the public confusion that might be caused by misleading titles and shall, whenever practicable, avoid titles for which the general understanding of the effect of a "yes" or "no" vote will be unclear. The title for the proposed law or constitutional amendment, which shall correctly and fairly express the true intent and meaning thereof, together with the ballot title and submission clause, shall be completed within two weeks after the first meeting of the title board. Immediately upon completion, the secretary of state shall deliver the same with the original to the parties presenting it, keeping the copy with a record of the action taken thereon. Ballot titles shall be brief, shall not conflict with those selected for any petition previously filed for the same election, and shall be in the form of a question which may be answered "yes" (to vote in favor of the proposed law or constitutional amendment) or "no" (to vote against the proposed law or constitutional amendment) and which shall unambiguously state the principle of the provision sought to be added, amended, or repealed.

1-40-106.5 — Single-subject requirements for initiated measures and referred constitutional amendments — legislative declaration.

(1) The general assembly hereby finds, determines, and declares that:

(a) Section 1 (5.5) of article V and section 2 (3) of article XIX of the state constitution require that every constitutional amendment or law proposed by initiative and every constitutional amendment proposed by the general assembly be limited to a single subject, which shall be clearly expressed in its title;

(b) Such provisions were referred by the general assembly to the people for their approval at the 1994 general election pursuant to Senate Concurrent Resolution 93-4;

(c) The language of such provisions was drawn from section 21 of article V of the state constitution, which requires that every bill, except general appropriation bills, shall be limited to a single subject, which shall be clearly expressed in its title;

(d) The Colorado supreme court has held that the constitutional single-subject requirement for bills was designed to prevent or inhibit various inappropriate or misleading practices that might otherwise occur, and the intent of the general assembly in referring to the people section 1 (5.5) of article V and section 2 (3) of article XIX was to protect initiated measures and referred constitutional amendments from similar practices;

(e) The practices intended by the general assembly to be inhibited by section 1 (5.5) of article V and section 2 (3) of article XIX are as follows:

(I) To forbid the treatment of incongruous subjects in the same measure, especially the practice of putting together in one measure subjects having no necessary or proper connection, for the purpose of enlisting in support of the measure the advocates of each measure, and thus securing the enactment of measures that could not be carried upon their merits;

(II) To prevent surreptitious measures and apprise the people of the subject of each measure by the title, that is, to prevent surprise and fraud from being practiced upon voters.

(2) It is the intent of the general assembly that section 1 (5.5) of article V and section 2 (3) of article XIX be liberally construed, so as to avert the practices against which they are aimed and, at the same time, to preserve and protect the right of initiative and referendum.

(3) It is further the intent of the general assembly that, in setting titles pursuant to section 1 (5.5) of article V, the initiative title setting review board created in section 1-40-106 should apply judicial decisions construing the constitutional single-subject requirement for bills and should follow the same rules employed by the general assembly in considering titles for bills.

1-40-107 — Rehearing — appeal — fees — signing.

(1) Any person presenting an initiative petition or any registered elector who is not satisfied with a decision of the title board with respect to whether a petition contains more than a single subject pursuant to section 1-40-106.5, or who is not satisfied with the titles and submission clause provided by the title board and who claims that they are unfair or that they do not fairly express the true meaning and intent of the proposed state law or constitutional amendment may file a motion for a rehearing with the secretary of state within seven days after the decision is made or the titles and submission clause are set. The motion for rehearing shall be heard at the next regularly scheduled meeting of the title board; ex-

cept that, if the title board is unable to complete action on all matters scheduled for that day, consideration of any motion for rehearing may be continued to the next available day, and except that, if the titles and submission clause protested were set at the last meeting in May, the motion shall be heard within forty-eight hours after the motion is filed.

(2) If any person presenting an initiative petition for which a motion for a rehearing is filed, any registered elector who filed a motion for a rehearing pursuant to subsection (1) of this section, or any other registered elector who appeared before the title board in support of or in opposition to a motion for rehearing is not satisfied with the ruling of the title board upon the motion, then the secretary of state shall furnish such person, upon request, a certified copy of the petition with the titles and submission clause of the proposed law or constitutional amendment, together with a certified copy of the motion for rehearing and of the ruling thereon. If filed with the clerk of the supreme court within five days thereafter, the matter shall be disposed of promptly, consistent with the rights of the parties, either affirming the action of the title board or reversing it, in which latter case the court shall remand it with instructions, pointing out where the title board is in error.

(3) The secretary of state shall be allowed a fee which shall be determined and collected pursuant to section 24-21-104 (3), C.R.S., for certifying a record of any proceedings before the title board. The clerk of the supreme court shall receive one-half the ordinary docket fee for docketing any such cause, all of which shall be paid by the parties desiring a review of such proceedings.

(4) No petition for any initiative measure shall be circulated nor any signature thereto have any force or effect which has been signed before the titles and submission clause have been fixed and determined as provided in section 1-40-106 and this section.

(5) In the event a motion for rehearing is filed in accordance with this section, the period for filing a petition in accordance with section 1-40-108 shall not begin until a final decision concerning the motion is rendered by the title board or the Colorado supreme court; except that under no circumstances shall the period for filing a petition be extended beyond three months prior to the election at which the petition is to be voted upon.

(6) (Deleted by amendment, L. 2000, p. 1622, § 5, effective August 2, 2000.)

(7) (Deleted by amendment, L. 95, p. 433, § 5, effective May 8, 1995.)

1-40-108 — Petition — time of filing.

(1) No petition for any ballot issue shall be of any effect unless filed with the secretary of state within six months from the date that the titles and submission clause have been fixed and determined pursuant to the provisions of sections 1-40-106 and 1-40-107 and unless filed with the secretary of state within the time required by the state constitution before the election at which it is to be voted upon. A petition for a ballot issue for the election to be held in November of odd-numbered years shall be filed with the secretary of state within the same time before such odd-year election as is required by the state constitution for issues to be voted on at the general election. All filings under this section must be made by 3 p.m. on the day of filing.

(2) (Deleted by amendment, L. 95, p. 433, § 6, effective May 8, 1995.)

1-40-109 — Signatures required.

(1) No petition for any initiated law or amendment to the state constitution shall be of any force or effect, nor shall the proposed law or amendment to the state constitution be submitted to the people of the state of Colorado for adoption or rejection at the polls, as is by law provided for, unless the petition for the submission of the initiated law or amendment to the state constitution is signed by the number of electors required by the state constitution.

(2) (Deleted by amendment, L. 95, p. 433, § 7, effective May 8, 1995.)

(3) Any person who is a registered elector may sign a petition for any ballot issue for which the elector is eligible to vote.

1-40-110 — Warning — ballot title.

(1) At the top of each page of every initiative or referendum petition section shall be printed, in a form as prescribed by the secretary of state, the following:

"WARNING: IT IS AGAINST THE LAW: For anyone to sign any initiative or referendum petition with any name other than his or her own or to knowingly sign his or her name more than once for the same measure or to knowingly sign a petition when not a registered elector who is eligible to vote on the measure.

DO NOT SIGN THIS PETITION UNLESS YOU ARE A REGISTERED ELECTOR AND ELIGIBLE TO VOTE ON THIS MEASURE. TO BE A REGISTERED ELECTOR, YOU MUST BE A CITIZEN OF COLORADO AND REGISTERED TO VOTE.

Before signing this petition, you are encouraged to read the text or the title of the proposed initiative or referred measure."

(2) The ballot title for the measure shall then be printed on each page following the warning.

1-40-111 — Signatures — affidavits.

(1) Any initiative or referendum petition shall be signed only by registered electors who are eligible to vote on the measure. Each registered elector shall sign his or her own signature and shall print his or her name, the address at which he or she resides, including the street number and name, the city and town, the county, and the date of signing. Each registered elector signing a petition shall be encouraged by the circulator of the petition to sign the petition in ink. In the event a registered elector is physically disabled or is illiterate and wishes to sign the petition, the elector shall sign or make his or her mark in the space so provided. Any person, but not a circulator, may assist the disabled or illiterate elector in completing the remaining information required by this subsection (1). The person providing assistance shall sign his or her name and address and shall state that such assistance was given to the disabled or illiterate elector.

(2) To each petition section shall be attached a signed, notarized, and dated affidavit executed by the registered elector who circulated the petition section, which shall include his or her printed name, the address at which he or she resides, including the street name and number, the city or town, the county, and the date he or she signed the affidavit; that he or she has read and understands the laws governing the circulation of petitions; that he or she was a registered elector at the time the section of the petition was circulated and signed by the listed electors; that he or she circulated the section of the petition; that each signature thereon was affixed in the circulator's presence; that each signature thereon is the signature of the person whose name it purports to be; that to the best of the circulator's knowledge and belief each of the persons signing the petition section was, at the time of signing, a registered elector; and that he or she has not paid or will not in the future pay and that he or she believes that no other person has paid or will pay, directly or indirectly, any money or other thing of value to any signer for the purpose of inducing or causing such signer to affix his or her signature to the petition.

The secretary of state shall not accept for filing any section of a petition that does not have attached thereto the notarized affidavit required by this section. Any signature added to a section of a petition after the affidavit has been executed shall be invalid.

1-40-112 — Circulators — requirements.

(1) No section of a petition for any initiative or referendum measure shall be circulated by any person who is not a registered elector and at least eighteen years of age at the time the section is circulated.

(2) (a) All circulators who are not to be paid for circulating petitions concerning ballot issues shall display an identification badge that includes the words "VOLUNTEER CIRCULATOR" in bold-faced type which is clearly legible and the circulator's name.

(b) All circulators who are to be paid for circulating petitions concerning ballot issues shall display an identification badge that includes the words "PAID CIRCULATOR" in bold-faced type which is clearly legible, the circulator's name, and the name and telephone number of the individual employing the circulator.

1-40-113 — Form — representatives of signers.

(1) Each section of a petition shall be printed on a form as prescribed by the secretary of state. No petition shall be printed, published, or otherwise circulated unless the form and the first printer's proof of the petition have been approved by the secretary of state. Each petition section shall designate by name and mailing address two persons who shall represent the signers thereof in all matters affecting the same. The secretary of state shall assure that the petition contains only the matters required by this article and contains no extraneous material. All sections of any petition shall be prenumbered serially, and the circulation of any petition section described by this article other than personally by a circulator is prohibited. Any petition section that fails to conform to the requirements of this article or is circulated in a manner other than that permitted in this article shall be invalid.

(2) Any disassembly of a section of the petition which has the effect of separating the affidavits from the signatures shall render that section of the petition invalid and of no force and effect.

(3) Prior to the time of filing, the persons designated in the petition to represent the signers shall bind the sections of the petition in convenient volumes consisting of one hundred sections of the petition if one hundred or more sections are available or, if less than one hundred sections are available to make a volume, consisting of all sections that are available. Each volume consisting of less than one hundred sections shall be marked on the first page of the volume. However, any volume that contains more or less than one hundred sections, due only to the oversight of the designated representatives of the signers or their staff, shall not result in a finding of insufficiency of signatures therein. Each section of each vol-

ume shall include the affidavits required by section 1-40-111 (2), together with the sheets containing the signatures accompanying the same. These bound volumes shall be filed with the secretary of state.

1-40-114 — Petitions — not election materials — no bilingual language requirement.

The general assembly hereby determines that initiative petitions are not election materials or information covered by the federal "Voting Rights Act of 1965", and therefore are not required to be printed in any language other than English to be circulated in any county in Colorado.

1-40-115 — Ballot — voting — publication.

(1) Measures shall appear upon the official ballot by ballot title only. The measures shall be placed on the ballot in the order in which they were certified to the ballot and as provided in section 1-5-407 (5).

(2) All ballot issues shall be printed on the official ballot in that order, together with their respective letters and numbers prefixed in bold-faced type. Each ballot shall have the following explanation printed one time at the beginning of such ballot issues: "Ballot issues referred by the general assembly or any political subdivision are listed by letter, and ballot issues initiated by the people are listed numerically. A 'yes' vote on any ballot issue is a vote in favor of changing current law or existing circumstances, and a 'no' vote on any ballot issue is a vote against changing current law or existing circumstances." Each ballot title shall appear on the official ballot but once and shall be separated from the other ballot titles next to it by heavy black lines and shall be followed by the words "yes" and "no" with blank spaces to the right and opposite the same as follows:

(HERE SHALL APPEAR THE BALLOT TITLE IN FULL)

YES _____ NO _____

(3) A voter desiring to vote for the measure shall make a cross mark (X) in the blank space to the right and opposite the word "yes"; a voter desiring to vote against the measure shall make a cross mark (X) in the blank space to the right and opposite the word "no"; and the votes marked shall be counted accordingly. Any measure approved by the people of the state shall be printed with the acts of the next general assembly.

1-40-116 — Verification — ballot issues — random sampling.

(1) For ballot issues, each section of a petition to which there is attached an affidavit of the registered elector who circulated the petition that each signature thereon is the signature of the person whose name it purports to be and that to the best of the knowledge and belief of the affiant each of the persons signing the petition was at the time of signing a registered elector shall be prima facie evidence that the signatures are genuine and true, that the petitions were circulated in accordance with the provisions of this article, and that the form of the petition is in accordance with this article.

(2) Upon submission of the petition, the secretary of state shall examine each name and signature on the petition. The petition shall not be available to the public for a period of no more than thirty calendar days for the examination. The secretary shall assure that the information required by sections 1-40-110 and 1-40-111 is complete, that the information on each signature line was written by the person making the signature, and that no signatures have been added to any sections of the petition after the affidavit required by section 1-40-111 (2) has been executed.

(3) No signature shall be counted unless the signer is a registered elector and eligible to vote on the measure. A person shall be deemed a registered elector if the person's name and address appear on the master voting list kept by the secretary of state at the time of signing the section of the petition. In addition, the secretary of state shall not count the signature of any person whose information is not complete or was not completed by the elector or a person qualified to assist the elector. The secretary of state may adopt rules consistent with this subsection (3) for the examination and verification of signatures.

(4) The secretary of state shall verify the signatures on the petition by use of random sampling. The random sample of signatures to be verified shall be drawn so that every signature filed with the secretary of state shall be given an equal opportunity to be included in the sample. The secretary of state is authorized to engage in rule making to establish the appropriate methodology for conducting such random sample. The random sampling shall include an examination of no less than five percent of the signatures, but in no event less than four thousand signatures. If the random sample verification establishes that the number of valid signatures is ninety percent or less of the number of registered eligible electors needed to find the petition sufficient, the petition shall be deemed to be not sufficient. If the random sample verification establishes that the number of valid signatures totals one hundred ten percent or more of the number of required signatures of registered eligible electors, the petition shall be deemed sufficient. If the random sampling shows the number of valid signatures to be more than ninety percent but less than one hundred ten percent of the number of signa-

tures of registered eligible electors needed to declare the petition sufficient, the secretary of state shall order the examination and verification of each signature filed.

1-40-117 — Statement of sufficiency — statewide issues.

(1) After examining the petition, the secretary of state shall issue a statement as to whether a sufficient number of valid signatures appears to have been submitted to certify the petition to the ballot.

(2) If the petition was verified by random sample, the statement shall contain the total number of signatures submitted and whether the number of signatures presumed valid was ninety percent of the required total or less or one hundred ten percent of the required total or more.

(3) (a) If the secretary declares that the petition appears not to have a sufficient number of valid signatures, the statement issued by the secretary shall specify the number of sufficient and insufficient signatures. The secretary shall identify by section number and line number within the section those signatures found to be insufficient and the grounds for the insufficiency. Such information shall be kept on file for public inspection in accordance with section 1-40-118.

(b) In the event the secretary of state issues a statement declaring that a petition, having first been submitted with the required number of signatures, appears not to have a sufficient number of valid signatures, the representatives designated by the proponents pursuant to section 1-40-104 may cure the insufficiency by filing an addendum to the original petition for the purpose of offering such number of additional signatures as will cure the insufficiency. No addendum offered as a cure shall be considered unless the addendum conforms to requirements for petitions outlined in sections 1-40-110, 1-40-111, and 1-40-113, and unless the addendum is filed with the secretary of state within the fifteen-day period after the insufficiency is declared and unless filed with the secretary of state within the time required by the state constitution before the election at which the initiative petition is to be voted on. All filings under this paragraph (b) shall be made by 3 p.m. on the day of filing. Upon submission of a timely filed addendum, the secretary of state shall order the examination and verification of each signature on the addendum. The addendum shall not be available to the public for a period of up to ten calendar days for such examination. After examining the petition, the secretary of state shall, within ten calendar days, issue a statement as to whether the addendum cures the insufficiency found in the original petition.

1-40-118 — Protest.

(1) A protest in writing, under oath, together with three copies thereof, may be filed in the district court for the county in which the petition has been filed by some registered elector, within thirty days after the secretary of state issues a statement as to whether the petition has a sufficient number of valid signatures, which statement shall be issued no later than thirty calendar days after the petition has been filed. If the secretary of state fails to issue a statement within thirty calendar days, the petition shall be deemed sufficient. During the period a petition is being examined by the secretary of state for sufficiency, the petition shall not be available to the public; except that such period shall not exceed thirty calendar days.

(2) If the secretary of state conducted a random sample of the petitions and did not verify each signature, the protest shall specifically allege the defects in the procedure used by the secretary of state in the verification of the petition or the grounds for challenging individual signatures. If the secretary of state verified each name on the petition sections, the protest shall set forth with particularity the grounds of the protest and the signatures protested. No signature may be challenged that is not identified in the protest by section number, line number, name, and reason why the secretary of state is in error. If any party is protesting the finding of the secretary of state regarding the registration of a signer, the protest shall be accompanied by an affidavit of the elector or a copy of the election record of the signer.

(3) (Deleted by amendment, L. 95, p. 436, § 13, effective May 8, 1995.)

(4) The secretary of state shall furnish a requesting protestor with a computer tape or microfiche listing of the names of all registered electors in the state and shall charge a fee which shall be determined and collected pursuant to section 24-21-104 (3), C.R.S., to cover the cost of furnishing the listing.

1-40-119 — Procedure for hearings.

At any hearing held under this article, the party protesting the finding of the secretary of state concerning the sufficiency of signatures shall have the burden of proof. Hearings shall be had as soon as is conveniently possible and shall be concluded within thirty days after the commencement thereof, and the result of such hearings shall be forthwith certified to the designated representatives of the signers and to the protestors of the petition. The hearing shall be subject to the provisions of the Colorado rules of civil procedure. Upon application, the decision of the court shall be reviewed by the Colorado supreme court.

1-40-120 — Filing in federal court.

In case a complaint has been filed with the federal district court on the grounds that a petition is insufficient due to failure to comply with any federal law, rule, or regulation, the petition may be withdrawn by the two persons designated pursuant to section 1-40-104 to represent the signers of the petition and, within fifteen days after the court has issued its order in the matter, may be amended and refiled as an original petition. Nothing in this section shall prohibit the timely filing of a protest to any original petition, including one that has been amended and refiled. No person shall be entitled, pursuant to this section, to amend an amended petition.

1-40-121 — Receiving money to circulate petitions — filing.

(1) The proponents of the petition shall file with the official who receives filings under the "Fair Campaign Practices Act", article 45 of this title, for the election the name, address, and county of voter registration of all circulators who were paid to circulate any section of the petition, the amount paid per signature, and the total amount paid to each circulator. The filing shall be made at the same time the petition is filed with the secretary of state. Any payment made to circulators is an expenditure under article 45 of this title.

(2) The proponents of the petition shall sign and file monthly reports with the secretary of state, due ten days after the last day of each month in which petitions are circulated on behalf of the proponents by paid circulators. Monthly reports shall set forth the following:

(a) The names of the proponents;

(b) The name and the residential and business addresses of each of the paid circulators;

(c) The name of the proposed ballot measure for which petitions are being circulated by paid circulators; and

(d) The amount of money paid and owed to each paid circulator for petition circulation during the month in question.

1-40-122 — Certification of ballot titles.

(1) The secretary of state, at the time the secretary of state certifies to the county clerk and recorder of each county the names of the candidates for state and district offices for general election, shall also certify to them the ballot titles and numbers of each initiated and referred measure filed in the office of the secretary of state to be voted upon at such election.

(2) Repealed.

1-40-123 — Counting of votes — effective date — conflicting provisions.

The votes on all measures submitted to the people shall be counted and properly entered after the votes for candidates for office cast at the same election are counted and shall be counted, canvassed, and returned and the result determined and certified in the manner provided by law concerning other elections. The secretary of state who has certified the election shall, without delay, make and transmit to the governor a certificate of election. The measure shall take effect from and after the date of the official declaration of the vote by proclamation of the governor, but not later than thirty days after the votes have been canvassed, as provided in section 1 of article V of the state constitution. A majority of the votes cast thereon shall adopt any measure submitted, and, in case of adoption of conflicting provisions, the one that receives the greatest number of affirmative votes shall prevail in all particulars as to which there is a conflict.

1-40-124 — Publication.

(1) (a) In accordance with section 1 (7.3) of article V of the state constitution, the director of research of the legislative council of the general assembly shall cause to be published at least one time in every legal newspaper, as defined in sections 24-70-102 and 24-70-103 (1), C.R.S., compactly and without unnecessary spacing, in not less than eight-point standard type, a true copy of:

(I) The title and text of each constitutional amendment, initiated or referred measure, or part of a measure, to be submitted to the people with the number and form in which the ballot title thereof will be printed in the official ballot; and

(II) The text of each referred or initiated question arising under section 20 of article X of the state constitution, as defined in section 1-41-102 (3), to be submitted to the people with the number and form in which such question will be printed in the official ballot.

(b) The charge for publication shall be at the newspaper's then effective current lowest bulk comparable or general rate charged. The director of research shall provide all of the legal newspapers either complete slick proofs or mats of the title and text of the proposed constitutional amendment, initiated or referred measure, or part of a measure, and of the text of a referred or initiated question arising under section 20 of article X of the state constitution, as defined in section 1-41-102 (3), at least one week before the publication date.

(2) (Deleted by amendment, L. 95, p. 437, § 18, effective May 8, 1995.)

1-40-124.5 — Ballot information booklet.

(1) The director of research of the legislative council of the general assembly shall prepare a ballot information booklet for any initiated or referred constitutional amendment or legislation, including a question, as defined in section 1-41-102 (3), in accordance with section 1 (7.5) of article V of the state constitution. If it appears that any measure has a sig-

nificant fiscal impact on the state or any of its political subdivisions, the booklet shall include an estimate of the fiscal impact of such measure, taking into consideration fiscal impact information submitted by the office of state planning and budgeting, the department of local affairs, any proponent, or other interested person. Prior to completion of the booklet, a draft shall be reviewed by the legislative council at a public hearing held after notice. At the hearing, any proponent or other interested person shall be allowed to comment on the accuracy or fairness of the analysis of any ballot issue addressed by the booklet.

(1.5) The executive committee of the legislative council of the general assembly shall be responsible for providing the fiscal information on any ballot issue that must be included in the ballot information booklet pursuant to section 1 (7.5)(c) of article V of the state constitution.

(2) Following completion of the ballot information booklet, the director of research shall arrange for its distribution to every residence of one or more active registered electors in the state. Distribution may be accomplished by such means as the director of research deems appropriate to comply with section 1 (7.5) of article V of the state constitution, including, but not limited to, mailing the ballot information booklet to electors and insertion of the ballot information booklet in newspapers of general circulation in the state. The distribution shall be performed pursuant to a contract or contracts bid and entered into after employing standard competitive bidding practices including, but not limited to, the use of requests for information, requests for proposals, or any other standard vendor selection practices determined to be best suited to selecting an appropriate means of distribution and an appropriate contractor or contractors. The executive director of the department of personnel shall provide such technical advice and assistance regarding bidding procedures as deemed necessary by the director of research.

(3) There is hereby established in the state treasury the ballot information publication and distribution revolving fund. Moneys shall be appropriated to the fund each year by the general assembly in the annual general appropriation act. All interest earned on the investment of moneys in the fund shall be credited to the fund. Moneys in the revolving fund are continuously appropriated to the legislative council of the general assembly to pay the costs of publishing the text and title of each constitutional amendment, initiated or referred measure, or part of a measure, and the text of a referred or initiated question arising under section 20 of article X of the state constitution, as defined in section 1-41-102 (3), in every legal newspaper in the state, as required by section 1-40-124, and the costs of distributing the ballot information booklet, as required by subsection (2) of this section. Any moneys credited to the revolving fund and unexpended at the end of any given fiscal year shall remain in the fund and shall not revert to the general fund.

1-40-125 — Mailing to electors.

(1) The requirements of this section shall apply to any ballot issue involving a local government matter arising under section 20 of article X of the state constitution, as defined in section 1-41-103 (4), for which notice is required to be mailed pursuant to section 20 (3) (b) of article X of the state constitution. A mailing is not required for a ballot issue that does not involve a local government matter arising under section 20 of article X of the state constitution, as defined in section 1-41-103 (4).

(2) Thirty days before a ballot issue election, political subdivisions shall mail at the least cost and as a package where districts with ballot issues overlap, a titled notice or set of notices addressed to "all registered voters" at each address of one or more active registered electors. Except for voter-approved additions, notices shall include only:

(a) The election date, hours, ballot title, text, and local election office address and telephone number;

(b) For proposed district tax or bonded debt increases, the estimated or actual total of district fiscal year spending for the current year and each of the past four years, and the overall percentage and dollar change;

(c) For the first full fiscal year of each proposed political subdivision tax increase, district estimates of the maximum dollar amount of each increase and of district fiscal year spending without the increase;

(d) For proposed district bonded debt, its principal amount and maximum annual and total district repayment cost, and the principal balance of total current district bonded debt and its maximum annual and remaining local district repayment cost;

(e) Two summaries, up to five hundred words each, one for and one against the proposal, of written comments filed with the election officer by thirty days before the election. No summary shall mention names of persons or private groups, nor any endorsements of or resolutions against the proposal. Petition representatives following these rules shall write this summary for their petition. The election officer shall maintain and accurately summarize all other relevant written comments.

(3) The provisions of this section shall not apply to a ballot issue that is subject to the provisions of section 1-40-124.5.

1-40-126 — Explanation of effect of "yes" or "no" vote included in notices provided by mailing or publication.

In any notice to electors provided by the director of research of the legislative council, whether by mailing pursuant to section 1-40-124.5 or publication pursuant to section 1-40-124, there shall be included the following explanation preceding any information about individual ballot issues: "A 'yes' vote on any ballot issue is a vote in favor of changing current law or existing circumstances, and a 'no' vote on any ballot issue is a vote against changing current law or existing circumstances."

1-40-130 — Unlawful acts — penalty.

(1) It is unlawful:

(a) For any person willfully and knowingly to circulate or cause to be circulated or sign or procure to be signed any petition bearing the name, device, or motto of any person, organization, association, league, or political party, or purporting in any way to be endorsed, approved, or submitted by any person, organization, association, league, or political party, without the written consent, approval, and authorization of the person, organization, association, league, or political party;

(b) For any person to sign any name other than his or her own to any petition or knowingly to sign his or her name more than once for the same measure at one election;

(c) For any person to knowingly sign any petition who is not a registered elector at the time of signing the same;

(d) For any person to sign any affidavit as circulator without knowing or reasonably believing the statements made in the affidavit to be true;

(e) For any person to certify that an affidavit attached to a petition was subscribed or sworn to before him or her unless it was so subscribed and sworn to before him or her and unless the person so certifying is duly qualified under the laws of this state to administer an oath;

(f) For any officer or person to do willfully, or with another or others conspire, or agree, or confederate to do, any act which hinders, delays, or in any way interferes with the calling, holding, or conducting of any election permitted under the initiative and referendum powers reserved by the people in section 1 of article V of the state constitution or with the registering of electors therefor;

(g) For any officer to do willfully any act which shall confuse or tend to confuse the issues submitted or proposed to be submitted at any election, or refuse to submit any petition in the form presented for submission at any election;

(h) For any officer or person to violate willfully any provision of this article.

(2) Any person, upon conviction of a violation of any provision of this section, shall be punished by a fine of not more than five hundred dollars, or by imprisonment for not more than one year in the county jail, or by both such fine and imprisonment.

1-40-131 — Tampering with initiative or referendum petition.

Any person who willfully destroys, defaces, mutilates, or suppresses any initiative or referendum petition or who willfully neglects to file or delays the delivery of the initiative or referendum petition or who conceals or removes any initiative or referendum petition from the possession of the person authorized by law to have the custody thereof, or who adds, amends, alters, or in any way changes the information on the petition as provided by the elector, or who aids, counsels, procures, or assists any person in doing any of said acts commits a misdemeanor and, upon conviction thereof, shall be punished as provided in section 1-13-111. The language in this section shall not preclude a circulator from striking a complete line on the petition if the circulator believes the line to be invalid.

1-40-132 — Enforcement.

(1) The secretary of state is charged with the administration and enforcement of the provisions of this article relating to initiated or referred measures and state constitutional amendments. The secretary of state shall have the authority to promulgate rules as may be necessary to administer and enforce any provision of this article that relates to initiated or referred measures and state constitutional amendments. The secretary of state may conduct a hearing, upon a written complaint by a registered elector, on any alleged violation of the provisions relating to the circulation of a petition, which may include but shall not be limited to the preparation or signing of an affidavit by a circulator. If the secretary of state, after the hearing, has reasonable cause to believe that there has been a violation of the provisions of this article relating to initiated or referred measures and state constitutional amendments, he or she shall notify the attorney general, who may institute a criminal prosecution. If a circulator is found to have violated any provision of this article or is otherwise shown to have made false or misleading statements relating to his or her section of the petition, such section of the petition shall be deemed void.

(2) (Deleted by amendment, L. 95, p. 439, § 22, effective May 8, 1995.)

1-40-133 — Retention of petitions.

After a period of three years from the time of submission of the petitions to the secretary of state, if it is determined that the retention of the petitions is no longer necessary, the secretary of state may destroy the petitions.

1-40-134 — Withdrawal of initiative petition.

The designated representatives of the proponents of an initiative petition may withdraw the petition from consideration as a ballot issue by filing a letter with the secretary of state requesting that the petition not be placed on the ballot. The letter shall be signed and acknowledged by both designated representatives before an officer authorized to take acknowledgments and shall be filed no later than thirty-three days prior to the election at which the initiative is to be voted upon.

31-11-104 — Ordinances — initiative — conflicting measures.

(1) Any proposed ordinance may be submitted to the legislative body of any municipality by filing written notice of the proposed ordinance with the clerk and, within one hundred eighty days after approval of the petition pursuant to section 31-11-106 (1), by filing a petition signed by at least five percent of the registered electors of the city or town on the date of such notice. The proposed ordinance may be adopted without alteration by the legislative body within twenty days following the final determination of petition sufficiency. If vetoed by the mayor, the proposed ordinance may be passed over the mayor's veto within ten days after the veto. If the proposed ordinance is not adopted by the legislative body, the legislative body shall forthwith publish the proposed ordinance as other ordinances are published and shall refer the proposed ordinance, in the form petitioned for, to the registered electors of the municipality at a regular or special election held not less than sixty days and not more that one hundred fifty days after the final determination of petition sufficiency, unless otherwise required by the state constitution. The ordinance shall not take effect unless a majority of the registered electors voting on the measure at the election vote in favor of the measure.

(2) Alternative ordinances may be submitted at the same election, and, if two or more conflicting measures are approved by the people, the one that receives the greatest number of affirmative votes shall be adopted in all particulars as to which there is a conflict.

31-11-105 — Ordinances — when effective — referendum.

(1) No ordinance passed by the legislative body of any municipality shall take effect before thirty days after its final passage and publication, except an ordinance calling for a special election or necessary to the immediate preservation of the public peace, health, or safety, and not then unless the ordinance states in a separate section the reasons why it is necessary and unless it receives the affirmative vote of three-fourths of all the members elected to the legislative body taken by ayes and noes.

(2) Within thirty days after final publication of the ordinance, a referendum petition protesting against the effect of the ordinance or any part thereof may be filed with the clerk. The petition must be signed during the thirty-day period by at least five percent of the registered electors of the municipality registered on the date of final publication.

(3) If a referendum petition is filed, the ordinance or part thereof protested against shall not take effect, and, upon a final determination of petition sufficiency, the legislative body shall promptly reconsider the ordinance. If the petition is declared not sufficient by the clerk or found not sufficient in a protest, the ordinance shall forthwith take effect, unless otherwise provided therein.

(4) If, upon reconsideration, the ordinance or part thereof protested is not repealed, the legislative body shall submit the measure to a vote of the registered electors at a regular or special election held not less than sixty days and not more than one hundred fifty days after the final determination of petition sufficiency, unless otherwise required by the state constitution. The ordinance or part thereof shall not take effect unless a majority of the registered electors voting on the measure at the election vote in favor of the measure.

31-11-106 — Form of petition sections.

(1) Each petition section shall be printed in a form consistent with the requirements of this article. No petition section shall be printed or circulated unless the form and the first printer's proof of the petition section have first been approved by the clerk. The clerk shall approve or reject the form and the first printer's proof of the petition no later than five business days following the date on which the clerk received such material. The clerk shall assure that the petition section contains only those elements required by this article and contains no extraneous material. The clerk may reject a petition or a section of a petition on the grounds that the petition or a section of the petition does not propose municipal legislation pursuant to section 1 (9) of article V of the state constitution.

(2) Each petition section shall designate by name and mailing address two persons who shall represent the proponents thereof in all matters affecting the petition and to whom all notices or information concerning the petition shall be mailed.

(3) (a) At the top of each page of every initiative or referendum petition section, the following shall be printed, in a form as prescribed by the clerk:

"WARNING: IT IS AGAINST THE LAW: For anyone to sign any initiative or referendum petition with any name other than his or her own or to knowingly sign his or her name more than once for the same measure or to knowingly sign a petition when not a registered elector who is eligible to vote on the measure.

DO NOT SIGN THIS PETITION UNLESS YOU ARE A REGISTERED ELECTOR AND ELIGIBLE TO VOTE ON THIS MEASURE. TO BE A REGISTERED ELECTOR, YOU MUST BE A CITIZEN OF COLORADO AND REGISTERED TO VOTE.

Do not sign this petition unless you have read or have had read to you the proposed initiative or referred measure or the summary in its entirety and understand its meaning."

(b) A summary of the proposed initiative or ordinance that is the subject of a referendum petition shall be printed following the warning on each page of a petition section. The summary shall be true and impartial and shall not be an argument, or likely to create prejudice, either for or against the measure. The summary shall be prepared by the clerk.

(c) The full text of the proposed initiated measure or ordinance that is the subject of a referendum petition shall be printed following the summary on the first page or pages of the petition section that precede the signature page. Notwithstanding the requirement of paragraph (a) of this subsection (3), if the text of the proposed initiated measure or ordinance requires more than one page of a petition section, the warning and summary need not appear at the top of other than the initial text page.

(d) The signature pages shall consist of the warning and the summary, followed by ruled lines numbered consecutively for registered electors' signatures. If a petition section contains multiple signature pages, all signature lines shall be numbered consecutively, from the first signature page through the last. The signature pages shall follow the page or pages on which the full text of the proposed initiated measure or ordinance that is the subject of the referendum petition is printed.

(e) (I) Following the signature pages of each petition section, there shall be attached a signed, notarized, and dated affidavit executed by the person who circulated the petition section, which shall include the following:

(A) The affiant's printed name, the address at which the affiant resides, including the street name and number, the municipality, the county, and the date the affiant signed the affidavit;

(B) That the affiant has read and understands the laws governing the circulation of petition;

(C) That the affiant was eighteen years of age or older at the time the section of the petition was circulated and signed by the listed electors;

(D) That the affiant circulated the section of the petition;

(E) That each signature thereon was affixed in the affiant's presence;

(F) That each signature thereon is the signature of the person whose name it purports to be;

(G) That, to the best of the affiant's knowledge and belief, each of the persons signing the petition section was, at the time of signing, a registered elector; and

(H) That the affiant has not paid or will not in the future pay and that the affiant believes that no other person has paid or will pay, directly or indirectly, any money or other thing of value to any signer for the purpose of inducing or causing such signer to affix the signer's signature to the petition.

(II) The clerk shall not accept for filing any section of a petition that does not have attached thereto the notarized affidavit required by subparagraph (I) of paragraph (e) of this subsection (3). Any disassembly of a section of the petition that has the effect of separating the affidavit from the signature page or pages shall render that section of the petition invalid and of no force and effect.

(III) Any signature added to a section of a petition after the affidavit has been executed shall be invalid.

(4) All sections of any petition shall be prenumbered serially.

(5) Any petition section that fails to conform to the requirements of this article or that is circulated in a manner other than that permitted by this article shall be invalid.

31-11-107 — Circulators — requirements.

The circulation of any petition section other than personally by a circulator is prohibited. No section of a petition for any initiative or referendum measure shall be circulated by any person who is not at least eighteen years of age at the time the section is circulated.

31-11-108 — Signatures.

Any initiative or referendum petition shall be signed only by registered electors who are eligible to vote on the measure. Each registered elector shall sign his or her own signature and shall print his or her name, the address at which he or she resides, including the street number and name, the city or town, the county, and the date of signing. Each registered elector signing a petition shall be encouraged by the circulator of the petition to sign the petition in ink. In the event a registered elector is physically disabled or is illiterate and wishes to sign the petition, the elector shall sign or make his or her mark in the space so provided. Any person, but not a circulator, may assist the disabled or illiterate elector in completing the remaining information required by this section. The person providing assistance shall sign his or her name and address and shall state that such assistance was given to the disabled or illiterate elector.

31-11-109 — Signature verification — statement of sufficiency.

(1) The clerk shall inspect timely filed initiative or referendum petitions and the attached affidavits, and may do so by examining the information on signature lines for patent defects, by comparing the information on signature lines against a list of registered electors provided by the county, or by other reasonable means.

(2) After examining the petition, the clerk shall issue a statement as to whether a sufficient number of valid signatures have been submitted. A copy of the statement shall be mailed to the persons designated as representing the petition proponents pursuant to section 31-11-106 (2).

(3) The statement of sufficiency or insufficiency shall be issued no later than thirty calendar days after the petition has been filed. If the clerk fails to issue a statement within thirty calendar days, the petition shall be deemed sufficient.

31-11-110 — Protest.

(1) Within forty days after an initiative or referendum petition is filed, a protest in writing under oath may be filed in the office of the clerk by any registered elector who resides in the municipality, setting forth specifically the grounds for such protest. The grounds for protest may include, but shall not be limited to, the failure of any portion of a petition or circulator affidavit to meet the requirements of this article. No signature may be challenged that is not identified in the protest by section and line number. The clerk shall forthwith mail a copy of such protest to the persons designated as representing the petition proponents pursuant to section 31-11-106 (2) and to the protester, together with a notice fixing a time for hearing such protest that is not less than five or more than ten days after such notice is mailed.

(2) The county clerk shall furnish a requesting protester with a list of the registered electors in the municipality and shall charge a fee to cover the cost of furnishing the list.

(3) Every hearing shall be held before the clerk with whom such protest is filed. The clerk shall serve as hearing officer unless some other person is designated by the legislative body as the hearing officer, and the testimony in every such hearing shall be under oath. The hearing officer shall have the power to issue subpoenas and compel the attendance of witnesses. The hearing shall be summary and not subject to delay and shall be concluded within sixty days after the petition is filed. No later than five days after the conclusion of the hearing, the hearing officer shall issue a written determination of whether the petition is sufficient or not sufficient. If the hearing officer determines that a petition is not sufficient, the officer shall identify those portions of the petition that are not sufficient and the reasons therefor. The result of the hearing shall be forthwith certified to the protester and to the persons designated as representing the petition proponents pursuant to section 31-11-106 (2). The determination as to petition sufficiency may be reviewed by the district court for the county in which such municipality or portion thereof is located upon application of the protester, the persons designated as representing the petition proponents pursuant to section 31-11-106 (2), or the municipality, but such review shall be had and determined forthwith.

31-11-111 — Initiatives, referenda, and referred measures — ballot titles.

(1) After an election has been ordered pursuant to section 31-11-104 or 31-11-105, the legislative body of the municipality or its designee shall promptly fix a ballot title for each initiative or referendum.

(2) The legislative body of any municipality may, without receipt of any petition, submit any proposed or adopted ordinance or resolution or any question to a vote of the registered electors of the municipality. The legislative body of the municipality or its designee shall fix a ballot title for the referred measure.

(3) In fixing the ballot title, the legislative body or its designee shall consider the public confusion that might be caused by misleading titles and shall, whenever practicable, avoid titles for which the general understanding of the effect of a "yes" or "no" vote would be unclear. The ballot title shall not conflict with those titles selected for any other measure that will appear on the municipal ballot in the same election. The ballot title shall correctly and fairly express the true intent and meaning of the measure.

(4) Any protest concerning a ballot title shall be conducted as provided by local charter, ordinance, or resolution.

31-11-112 — Petitions — not election materials — no bilingual requirement.

The general assembly hereby determines that initiative and referendum petitions are not election materials or information covered by the federal "Voting Rights Act of 1965", and are therefore not required to be printed in any language other than English in order to be circulated in any municipality in Colorado.

31-11-113 — Receiving money to circulate petitions — filing.

The proponents of the petition shall file with the clerk a report disclosing the amount paid per signature and the total amount paid to each circulator. The filing shall be made at the same time the petition is filed with the clerk. Any payment made to circulators is an expenditure under article 45 of title 1, C.R.S.

31-11-114 — Unlawful acts — penalty.

(1) It is unlawful:

(a) For any person willfully and knowingly to circulate or cause to be circulated or sign or procure to be signed any petition bearing the name, device, or motto of any person, organization, association, league, or political party, or purporting in any way to be endorsed, approved, or submitted by any person, organization, association, league, or political party, without the written consent, approval, and authorization of the person, organization, association, league, or political party;

(b) For any person to sign any name other than his or her own name to any petition or knowingly to sign his or her name more than once for the same measure at one election;

(c) For any person knowingly to sign any petition relating to an initiative or referendum in a municipality who is not a registered elector of that municipality at the time of signing the petition;

(d) For any person to sign any affidavit as circulator without knowing or reasonably believing the statements made in the affidavit to be true;

(e) For any person to certify that an affidavit attached to a petition was subscribed or sworn to before him or her unless it was so subscribed and sworn to before him or her and unless the person so certifying is duly qualified under the laws of this state to administer an oath;

(f) For any officer or person to do willfully, or with another or others conspire, or agree, or confederate to do, any act that hinders, delays, or in any way interferes with the calling, holding, or conducting of any election permitted under the initiative and referendum powers reserved by the people in section 1 of article V of the state constitution or with the registering of electors therefor;

(g) For any officer to do willfully any act that shall confuse or tend to confuse the issues submitted or proposed to be submitted at any election or refuse to submit any petition in the form presented for submission at any election;

(h) For any officer or person to violate willfully any provision of this article.

(2) Any person, upon conviction of a violation of any provision of this section, shall be punished by a fine of not more than five hundred dollars, or by imprisonment for not more than one year in the county jail, or by both such fine and imprisonment.

31-11-115 — Tampering with initiative or referendum petition.

(1) Any person commits a class 2 misdemeanor who:

(a) Willfully destroys, defaces, mutilates, or suppresses any initiative or referendum petition;

(b) Willfully neglects to file or delays the delivery of the initiative or referendum petition;

(c) Conceals or removes any initiative or referendum petition from the possession of the person authorized by law to have custody of the petition;

(d) Adds, amends, alters, or in any way changes the information on the petition as provided by the elector; or

(e) Aids, counsels, procures, or assists any person in doing any of such acts.

(2) Any person convicted of committing such a misdemeanor shall be punished by a fine of not more than one thousand dollars, or by imprisonment in the county jail for not more than one year, or by both such fine and imprisonment.

(3) This section shall not preclude a circulator from striking a complete line on the petition if the circulator believes the line to be invalid.

31-11-116 — Enforcement.

(1) Any person may file with the district attorney an affidavit stating the name of any person who has violated any of the provisions of this article and stating the facts that constitute the alleged offense. Upon the filing of such affidavit, the district attorney shall forthwith investigate, and, if reasonable grounds appear therefor, the district attorney shall prosecute the same.

(2) The attorney general of the state shall have equal power with district attorneys to file information or complaints against any person for violating any provision of this article.

31-11-117 — Retention of petitions.

After a period of three years from the time of submission of the petitions to the clerk, if it is determined that the retention of the petitions is no longer necessary, the clerk may destroy the petitions.

31-11-118 — Powers of clerk and deputy.

(1) Except as otherwise provided in this article, the clerk shall render all interpretations and shall make all initial decisions as to controversies or other matters arising in the operation of this article.

(2) All powers and authority granted to the clerk by this article may be exercised by a deputy clerk in the absence of the clerk or in the event the clerk for any reason is unable to perform the duties of the clerk's office.

The Basic Steps to Do an Initiative in Colorado

Statutes and Amendments — Direct Initiative Process

Basic Procedures: Proponents must submit the original text of the measure to the directors of the Legislative Council Staff and the Office of Legal Services for review and comment. Proponents must designate two people as those representing the proponents in all matters affecting the petition. Drafts are to be submitted in typewritten form and are to be written in plain, non-technical language, using words with common and everyday meaning understandable to the average reader.

Upon receiving the proposed measure, directors set a date for a public hearing no later than two weeks from the date the measure is filed. The director of the Legislative Council Staff provides proper notice of the date, time, and place for the meeting. Measures accepted as a legal filing are a matter of public record and are available for public distribution.

Comments on proposed initiated measures are prepared by the Legislative Council Staff and the Office of Legislative Legal Services for review during the public hearing. The comments typically contain a summary of the proposal followed by a series of questions concerning the wording, intent, and purpose of the proposal. The Legislative Council Staff and Legislative Legal Services directors may request the assistance of state agencies in preparing the comments. Agencies are required to assist when so requested. Proponents receive the comments prior to the meeting, but the comments are not disclosed to the public before the hearing, except with permission of the proponents.

The public hearing conducted by the Legislative Council Staff and Legislative Legal Services is informal in nature. The purpose of the meeting is to give the public notice that a proposal on a given topic is under consideration and to review the purposes and wording with the proponents so that the proposal states what the proponents want it to state. The comments are intended to help proponents clarify their proposal, but proponents are not required to accept the suggestions made in the comments. The meeting is open to the public and, while persons who may oppose a measure are welcome to attend, no testimony or comments are accepted from anyone other than the proponents. The meeting is tape recorded for the public record.

Following the public hearing, proponents may submit the measure to the Secretary of State who chairs the Ballot Title Setting Board. The ballot title, submission clause, and summary are established by a board consisting of the Secretary of State, the Attorney General, and the director of the Office of Legislative Legal Services.

The Ballot Title Setting Board usually completes its work on the ballot title, submission clause, and summary at its first meeting. If the board is unable to complete action on all of its agenda, motions for rehearing may be continued until the board's next meeting.

If a proponent or any registered elector claims that a ballot title, submission clause, or summary is unfair or does not fairly express the meaning of a proposal, that person may request a rehearing by the Ballot Title Setting Board. Such request must be made within seven days after the title and summary are set.

Such rehearing will be held at the next regularly scheduled meeting of the board. If the board is unable to complete action on the request for rehearing, consideration of the request may be continued until the next available day, except that if the request was to be heard on the last meeting date in May, it must be heard within 48 hours after the motion is filed.

An appeal for change in the ballot title, submission clause, and summary may be made to the Colorado Supreme Court, pursuant to Section 1-40-107 (2) and (5), C.R.S.

Once the ballot title, submission clause, and summary are established, petitions may then be circulated throughout the state to obtain the required number of signatures.

Date Initiative language can be submitted to state for November 2002: Can be submitted anytime after the first Wednesday in December of 2000.

Signatures are tied to vote of which office: Secretary of State

Next Secretary of State election: 2002

Votes cast for Secretary of State in last election: 1,611,420 (Note: Although Secretary of States are normally elected every four years, a vacancy was filled in 2000.)

Net number of signatures required: 5% of votes cast for Secretary of State in last election, for both statutes and amendments. (80,571 signatures)

Distribution Requirement: None

Circulation period: 6 months

Do circulators have to be residents: No

Date when signatures are due for certification: The petition must be filed within 6 months from when the final language is set by the Title Board and no later than 3 months before a statewide election. (August 5, 2002 for the November 2002 ballot.)

Signature verification process: The Secretary of State verifies signatures by a random sample procedure. Not less than five percent of the signatures, and in no event fewer than 4,000 signatures, are to be verified. If the sample indicates that the number of valid signatures is 90 percent or less of the required total, the petition is deemed to have insufficient signatures. If the valid signatures are found to be 110 percent or more of number required, the petition is deemed sufficient. However, if the number of valid signatures is found to be over 90 percent but less than 110 percent of the required number, the law requires that each signature on the petition be verified.

Single-subject restriction: Yes

Legislative tampering: The Legislature can repeal and amend an initiative statute passed by the voters.

General Comments: If the Ballot Title Setting Board finds that more than one subject is contained in a proposal, the proponents are permitted to change the measure. If the changes by the proponents involve only the removal of language to achieve a single subject, another review and comment hearing with the Office of Legislative Legal Services and the Legislative Council Staff may not be required. However, if the board finds that revisions are so substantial that another hearing is in the public interest, another review and comment hearing may be required.

If a proposal is revised and resubmitted to the board, a ballot title can be set or the title board can conclude that the proposal still contains more than one subject. In the event of a dispute over the single subject rule, the board can set the title without including reference to the provisions it thought was in violation of the rule. The constitution provides that, if there is any part of a proposal not clearly expressed in the ballot title, that part is to be considered void.

Connecticut

Direct democracy advocates in the Progressive era failed to win initiative and referendum rights at either the state or local levels, except in the city of Bristol. However, citizens in many of the state's small towns still enjoy the right to enact ordinances by popular vote in their town meetings.

Connecticut Constitution

The state does not have the statewide initiative process and so therefore the following provisions discuss the procedures used by the state legislature to place constitutional amendments on the ballot.

Article Third: Sec. 1.

The legislative power of the state shall be vested in two distinct houses or branches; the one to be styled the senate, the other the house of representatives, and both together the general assembly. The style of their laws shall be: Be it enacted by the Senate and House of Representatives in General Assembly convened.

Article Twelfth: Sec. 1.

Amendments to this constitution may be proposed by any member of the senate or house of representatives. An amendment so proposed, approved upon roll call by a yea vote of at least a majority, but by less than three-fourths, of the total membership of each house, shall be published with the laws which may have been passed at the same session and be continued to the regular session of the general assembly elected at the general election to be held on the Tuesday after the first Monday of November in the next even-numbered year. An amendment so proposed, approved upon roll call by a yea vote of at least three-fourths of the total membership of each house, or any amendment which, having been continued from the previous general assembly, is again approved upon roll call by a yea vote of at least a majority of the total membership of each house, shall, by the secretary of the state, be transmitted to the town clerk in each town in the state, whose duty it shall be to present the same to the electors thereof for their consideration at the general election to be held on the Tuesday after the first Monday of November in the next even-numbered year. If it shall appear, in a manner to be provided by law, that a majority of the electors present and voting on such amendment at such election shall have approved such amendment, the same shall be valid, to all intents and purposes, as a part of this constitution. Electors voting by absentee ballot under the provisions of the statutes shall be considered to be present and voting. (Art. Twelfth amended in 1974. See Art. VI of Amendments to the Constitution of the State of Connecticut.)

Article Thirteenth: Sec. 1.

The general assembly may, upon roll call, by a yea vote of at least two-thirds of the total membership of each house, provide for the convening of a constitutional convention to amend or revise the constitution of the state not earlier than ten years from the date of convening any prior convention.

Sec. 2.

The question "Shall there be a Constitutional Convention to amend or revise the Constitution of the State?" shall be submitted to all the electors of the state at the general election held on the Tuesday after the first Monday in November in the even-numbered year next succeeding the expiration of a period of twenty years from the date of convening of the last convention called to revise or amend the constitution of the state, including the Constitutional Convention of 1965, or next succeeding the expiration of a period of twenty years from the date of submission of such a question to all electors of the state, whichever date shall last occur. If a majority of the electors voting on the question shall signify "yes", the general assembly shall provide for such convention as provided in Section 3 of this article.

Sec. 3.

In providing for the convening of a constitutional convention to amend or revise the constitution of the state the general assembly shall, upon roll call, by a yea vote of at least two-thirds of the total membership of each house, prescribe by law the manner of selection of the membership of such convention, the date of convening of such convention, which shall be not later than one year from the date of the roll call vote under Section 1 of this article or one year from the date of the election under Section 2 of this article, as the case may be, and the date for final adjournment of such convention.

Sec. 4.

Proposals of any constitutional convention to amend or revise the constitution of the state shall be submitted to all the electors of the state not later than two months after final adjournment of the convention, either as a whole or in such parts and with such alternatives as the convention may determine. Any proposal of the convention to amend or revise the constitution of the state submitted to such electors in accordance with this section and approved by a majority of such electors voting on the question shall be valid, to all intents and purposes, as a part of this constitution. Such proposals when so approved shall take effect thirty days after the date of the vote thereon unless otherwise provided in the proposal.

Amendments Article VI.

Article Twelfth of the constitution is amended to read as follows: Amendments to this constitution may be proposed by any member of the senate or house of representatives. An amendment so proposed, approved upon roll call by a yea vote of at least a majority, but by less than three-fourths, of the total membership of each house, shall be published with the laws which may have been passed at the same session and be continued to the regular session of the general assembly elected at the next general election to be held on the Tuesday after the first Monday of November in an even-numbered year. An amendment so proposed, approved upon roll call by a yea vote of at least three-fourths of the total membership of each house, or any amendment which, having been continued from the previous general assembly, is again approved upon roll call by a yea vote of at least a majority of the total membership of each house, shall, by the secretary of the state, be transmitted to the town clerk in each town in the state, whose duty it shall be to present the same to the electors thereof for their consideration at the next general election to be held on the Tuesday after the first Monday of November in an even-numbered year. If it shall appear, in a manner to be provided by law, that a majority of the electors present and voting on such amendment at such election shall have approved such amendment, the same shall be valid, to all intents and purposes, as a part of this constitution. Electors voting by absentee ballot under the provisions of the statutes shall be considered to be present and voting.

Delaware

During the Progressive era, the I&R movement publication Equity described Delaware as one of 11 states where "the initiative sentiment is all-powerful."

Delaware's extraordinarily difficult procedure for amending its state constitution stacked the deck against I&R activists from the start. Under the leadership of Wilmington's Francis I. DuPont (of the well-known chemical company family), I&R advocates persuaded the legislature to schedule a statewide advisory referendum on whether I&R should be added to the state constitution. In the 1906 election voters approved the idea by a landslide six to one margin.

Instead of obeying this mandate, the legislature passed a bill giving I&R rights to the city of Wilmington only. Voters there quickly used their new rights to put five initiatives on the city's ballot in early 1907. According to Equity, it was "the first use of Direct Legislation on general questions of public policy in an eastern city, and the first among Negro voters." Meanwhile, the Delaware Referendum League pressed on for statewide I&R. Twelve years later, in 1919, they still did not have the necessary two-thirds majority of both houses of the legislature.

In the 1960s State Representative John P. Ferguson of the town of Churchman's Road sponsored an I&R bill, which he reintroduced in every session. By the mid-1970s, as Speaker of the House, he engineered the amendment's passage by a vote of 33 to 1; it then sailed through the state senate (14 to 3). The state constitution, however, required that a constitutional amendment be approved by two thirds of both houses a second time after the next election. This gave opponents, led by Governor Pierre S. DuPont IV (who did not have the reformist notions of the earlier DuPont), a chance to organize. On March 29, 1979, the house defeated I&R by 22 to 6, ending all hopes for its passage. Ferguson, frustrated by this defeat after so many years of effort, retired.

In 1980 the police and firefighters' unions collected enough signatures to put an initiative on the ballot in Wilmington, only to be told that there was no longer an initiative procedure. The legislature had quietly passed a municipal charter law in 1965 that contained no I&R provision, and this law, state courts ruled, superseded the law that had given I&R to Wilmington in 1907!

Between 1907 and 1987, the people of Delaware voted on only one statewide ballot question, which the legislature put on the ballot in 1984: should the state allow charities to sponsor gambling games to raise money? Voters said "yes" by a 72 percent majority.

Delaware Constitution

The state does not have the statewide initiative process and so therefore the following provisions discuss the procedures used by the state legislature to place constitutional amendments on the ballot.

Article XVI.

§1. Proposal of Constitutional amendments in General Assembly; procedure.

Any amendment or amendments to this Constitution may be proposed in the Senate or House of Representatives; and if the same shall be agreed to by two-thirds of all the members elected to each House, such proposed amendment or amendments shall be entered on their journals, with the yeas and nays taken thereon, and the Secretary of State shall cause such proposed amendment or amendments to be published three months before the next General Election in at least three newspapers in each county in which such newspapers shall be published; and if in the General Assembly next after the said election such proposed amendment or amendments shall upon yea and nay vote be agreed to by two-thirds of all the members elected to each House, the same shall thereupon become part of the Constitution.

§2. Constitutional conventions; procedure; compensation of delegates; quorum; powers and duties; vacancies.

The General Assembly by a two-thirds vote of all the members elected to each House may from time to time provide for the submission to the qualified electors of the State at the general election next thereafter the question, "Shall there be a Convention to revise the Constitution and amend the same?" and upon such submission, if a majority of those voting on said question shall decide in favor of a Convention for such purpose, the General Assembly at its next session shall provide for the election of delegates to such convention at the next general election. Such Convention shall be composed of forty-one delegates, one of whom shall be chosen from each Representative District by the qualified electors thereof, and two of whom shall be chosen from New Castle County, two from Kent County and two from Sussex County by the qualified electors thereof respectively. The delegates so chosen shall convene at the Capital of the State on the first Tuesday in September next after their election. Every delegate shall receive for his services such compensation as shall be provided by law. A majority of the Convention shall constitute a quorum for the transaction of business. The Convention shall have power to appoint such officers, employees and assistants as it may deem necessary, and fix their compensation, and provide for the printing of its documents, journals, debates and proceedings. The Convention shall determine the rules of its proceedings, and be the judge of the elections, returns and qualification of its members. Whenever there shall be a vacancy in the office of delegate from any district or county by reason of failure to elect, ineligibility, death, resignation or otherwise, a writ of election to fill such vacancy shall be issued by the Governor, and such vacancy shall be filled by the qualified electors of such district or county.

§3. Receiving, tallying and counting votes for or against Convention; return of vote; enabling legislation.

The General Assembly shall provide for receiving, tallying and counting the votes for or against a Convention, and for returning to the General Assembly at its next session the state of such vote; and shall also enact all provisions necessary for giving effect to this Article.

§4. Approval of bills or resolutions under this article; exemption from Article III, Section 18.

No bill or resolution passed by the General Assembly under or pursuant to the provisions of this Article, shall require for its validity the approval of the Governor, and the same shall be exempt from the provisions of Section 18 of Article III, of this Constitution.

§5. Separate ballots on question of Convention.

In voting at any general election, upon the question, "shall there be a Convention to revise the Constitution and amend the name?" the ballots shall be separate from those cast for any person voted for at such election, and shall be kept distinct and apart from all other ballots.

Florida

Florida's best-known initiative and referendum backer of the Progressive Era was retired U.S. Senator Wilkinson Call. The closest the Florida legislature came to approving statewide I&R was the state senate's passage, in 1912, of a version so restrictive that it would have made it virtually impossible to put an initiative on the ballot. The senate quickly rescinded even this weak bill.

In the late 1960s, following the transformation of Florida from a southern state to a sunbelt state populated largely by transplanted northerners, the legislature passed an amendment authorizing initiative constitutional amendments only—not initiatives or referendums on statutes. The new provision was successfully employed for the first time in 1976, when Governor Reuben Askew sponsored an initiative requiring public disclosure of campaign contributions. After this measure passed, infuriated state legislators passed bills banning the collection of signatures at polling places and imposing a 10-cent-per-signature "verification fee" to further discourage future initiative proponents.

In 1992 Floridians passed term limits for the state legislature and in 2000 environmentalist won a major victory with the passage of an initiative that established a statewide high-speed monorail system. However, since the adoption of the statewide initiative process, only 16 initiatives have made it on statewide ballots. This is due primarily to the high rate of initiatives that are invalidated because they violate the state's outrageously stringent single subject provision for initiatives. It has become almost impossible to get the proper clearance from the state supreme court necessary to place an initiative on the ballot.

Statewide Initiative Usage

Number of Initiatives	Number Passed	Number Failed	Passage Rate
16	11	5	68%

Statewide Initiatives

Year	Measure Number	Type	Subject Matter	Description	Pass/Fail
1976	1	DA	Campaign Finance Reform	To require full public disclosure by state and County election officials and candidates (sunshine amendment).	Passed
1978	9	DA	Gaming	Establish casino gambling.	Failed
1986	2	DA	Gaming	Allow casino gambling.	Failed
1986	5	DA	Gaming	Establish a state operated lottery.	Passed
1988	10	DA	Tort Reform	Limit damages in civil actions.	Failed
1988	11	DA	Administration of Government	English as official state language.	Passed
1992	10	DA	Taxes	Limit homestead valuations.	Passed
1992	9	DA	Term Limits	Term Limits on state legislature 8/8.	Passed
1994	3	DA	Environmental Reform	Limit marine net fishing	Passed
1994	4	DA	Taxes	Governmental revenue limits.	Passed
1994	8	DA	Gaming	Legalize casinos in limited areas.	Failed
1996	1	DA	Taxes	Requires a 2/3 vote for new constitutionally imposed state taxes or fees.	Passed
1996	4	DA	Taxes	Establishes a fee on Everglades sugar production.	Failed
1996	5	DA	Environmental Reform	Responsibility for paying costs of water pollution abatement in the Everglades.	Passed
1996	6	DA	Environmental Reform	Establishes and Everglade Trust Fund for conservation and protection of natural resources and abatement of water pollution.	Passed
2000	1	DA	Environmental Reform	To reduce traffic and increase travel alternatives, this amendment provides for development of a high speed monorail, fixed guide way or magnetic levitation system linking Florida's five largest urban areas.	Passed

Florida Constitution

Article XI: Section 3. Initiative.

The power to propose the revision or amendment of any portion or portions of this constitution by initiative is reserved to the people, provided that, any such revision or amendment, except for those limiting the power of government to raise revenue, shall embrace but one subject and matter directly connected therewith. It may be invoked by filing with the secretary of state a petition containing a copy of the proposed revision or amendment, signed by a number of electors in each of one half of the congressional districts of the state, and of the state as a whole, equal to eight percent of the votes cast in each of such districts respectively and in the state as a whole in the last preceding election in which presidential electors were chosen.

Florida Statutes

Title IV: Chapter 15: Section 15.21

The Secretary of State shall immediately submit an initiative petition to the Attorney General if the sponsor has:
(1) Registered as a political committee pursuant to s. 106.03;
(2) Submitted the ballot title, substance, and text of the proposed revision or amendment to the Secretary of State pursuant to ss. 100.371 and 101.161; and
(3) Obtained a letter from the Division of Elections confirming that the sponsor has submitted to the appropriate supervisors for verification, and the supervisors have verified forms signed and dated equal to 10 percent of the number of electors statewide and in at least one-fourth of the congressional districts required by s. 3, Art. XI of the State Constitution.

Title IV: Chapter 16: Section 16.061: Initiative Petitions

(1) The Attorney General shall, within 30 days after receipt of a proposed revision or amendment to the State Constitution by initiative petition from the Secretary of State, petition the Supreme Court, requesting an advisory opinion regarding the compliance of the text of the proposed amendment or revision with s. 3, Art. XI of the State Constitution and the compliance of the proposed ballot title and substance with s. 101.161. The petition may enumerate any specific factual issues which the Attorney General believes would require a judicial determination.
(2) A copy of the petition shall be provided to the Secretary of State and the principal officer of the sponsor.

Title IX: Chapter 100: Section 100.371 Initiatives; procedure for placement on ballot.

(1) Constitutional amendments proposed by initiative shall be placed on the ballot for the general election occurring in excess of 90 days from the certification of ballot position by the Secretary of State.
(2) Such certification shall be issued when the Secretary of State has received verification certificates from the supervisors of elections indicating that the requisite number and distribution of valid signatures of electors have been submitted to and verified by the supervisors. Every signature shall be dated when made and shall be valid for a period of 4 years following such date, provided all other requirements of law are complied with.
(3) The sponsor of an initiative amendment shall, prior to obtaining any signatures, register as a political committee pursuant to s. 106.03 and submit the text of the proposed amendment to the Secretary of State, with the form on which the signatures will be affixed, and shall obtain the approval of the Secretary of State of such form. The Secretary of State shall promulgate rules pursuant to s. 120.54 prescribing the style and requirements of such form.
(4) The sponsor shall submit signed and dated forms to the appropriate supervisor of elections for verification as to the number of registered electors whose valid signatures appear thereon. The supervisor shall promptly verify the signatures upon payment of the fee required by s. 99.097. Upon completion of verification, the supervisor shall execute a certificate indicating the total number of signatures checked, the number of signatures verified as valid and as being of registered electors, and the distribution by congressional district. This certificate shall be immediately transmitted to the Secretary of State. The supervisor shall retain the signature forms for at least 1 year following the election in which the issue appeared on the ballot or until the Division of Elections notifies the supervisors of elections that the committee which circulated the petition is no longer seeking to obtain ballot position.
(5) The Secretary of State shall determine from the verification certificates received from supervisors of elections the total number of verified valid signatures and the distribution of such signatures by congressional districts. Upon a determination that the requisite number and distribution of valid signatures have been obtained, the secretary shall issue a certificate of ballot position for that proposed amendment and shall assign a designating number pursuant to s. 101.161. A petition shall be deemed to be filed with the Secretary of State upon the date of the receipt by the secretary of a certificate or certificates from supervisors of elections indicating the petition has been signed by the constitutionally required number of electors.
(6) The Department of State shall have the authority to promulgate rules in accordance with s. 120.54 to carry out the provisions of this section.

Section 101.161: Referenda; ballots

(1) Whenever a constitutional amendment or other public measure is submitted to the vote of the people, the substance of such amendment or other public measure shall be printed in clear and unambiguous language on the ballot after the list of candidates, followed by the word "yes" and also by the word "no," and shall be styled in such a manner that a "yes" vote will indicate approval of the proposal and a "no" vote will indicate rejection. The wording of the substance of the amendment or other public measure and the ballot title to appear on the ballot shall be embodied in the joint resolution, constitutional revision commission proposal, constitutional convention proposal, taxation and budget reform commission proposal, or enabling resolution or ordinance. The substance of the amendment or other public measure shall be an explanatory statement, not exceeding 75 words in length, of the chief purpose of the measure. The ballot title shall consist of a caption, not exceeding 15 words in length, by which the measure is commonly referred to or spoken of.

(2) The substance and ballot title of a constitutional amendment proposed by initiative shall be prepared by the sponsor and approved by the Secretary of State in accordance with rules adopted pursuant to s. 120.54. The Department of State shall give each proposed constitutional amendment a designating number for convenient reference. This number designation shall appear on the ballot. Designating numbers shall be assigned in the order of filing or certification of the amendments. The Department of State shall furnish the designating number, the ballot title, and the substance of each amendment to the supervisor of elections of each county in which such amendment is to be voted on.

Section 104.185: Petitions; knowingly signing more than once; signing another person's name or a fictitious name.

1. A person who knowingly signs a petition or petitions for a candidate, a minor political party, or an issue more than one time commits a misdemeanor of the first degree, punishable as provided in s. 775.082 or s. 775.083.

2. A person who signs another person's name or a fictitious name to any petition to secure ballot position for a candidate, a minor political party, or an issue commits a misdemeanor of the first degree, punishable as provided in s. 775.082 or s. 775.083.

Section 106.19 (3): Violations by candidates, persons connected with campaigns, and political committees.

A political committee sponsoring a constitutional amendment proposed by initiative which submits a petition form gathered by a paid petition circulator which does not provide the name and address of the paid petition circulator on the form is subject to the civil penalties prescribed in s. 106.265, Florida Statutes.

The Basic Steps to Do an Initiative in Florida

Amendments Only — Direct Initiative Process

Basic Procedures: The first step in the process of qualifying an initiative is to register with the Division of Elections as a political committee pursuant to section 106.03 of the Florida Statutes.

Once proponents form and register their committee, they can file their initiative with the Division of Elections. Proponents write their own ballot title (no more than 15 words) and ballot summary (no more than 75 words). Petitions must contain the title, summary, full text and a serial number (given to them when they file the initiative.) The Secretary of State reviews the petition for form only. (This generally takes less than a week — but there is no statutory deadline.) Proponents can begin circulating once the format is approved.

Once proponents gather 10% of the total number of signatures needed from at least 3 congressional districts (48,536 signatures), they turn them into the Local Supervisors of Elections in the various counties. The Supervisors then verify them and submit them to the Secretary of State. (There is no statutory mandated turn-around time) The Secretary of State then certifies them, and sends them to the Attorney General. The Attorney General has 30 days to forward the initiative language to the Florida Supreme Court. The Supreme Court decides if the initiative is legal. The Supreme Court has no time frame — it can take as long as it likes. If the Court approves it, proponents go out and gather the remaining signatures to put it on the ballot. If the Court declares the initiative invalid because it is unconstitutional, violates Florida's strict single subject requirement, or any other reasons, the initiative is dead.

(Proponents may continue to collect signatures while waiting for the Supreme Court to approve or disallow their initiative; but this is not advisable given the Courts history of keeping measures off the ballot.)

Date initiative language can be submitted to state for the November 2002 election: Any time.

Signatures tied to vote of which office: Number of ballots cast in last presidential election.

Next presidential election: 2004

Ballots cast in the last presidential election: 6,109,013

Net number of signatures required: Proponents must gather signatures equal to 8% of the total number of statewide ballots cast in the last presidential election. (488,722 signatures.)

Distribution requirements: Proponents must get 8% of the district-wide vote for President in at least 12 of 23 Congressional Districts.

Circulation period: Four years. (While initiative petitions can stay active for an unlimited amount of time, a voter's signature is no longer valid four years after the date he or she signed the petition. Proponents must obtain the required number of signatures within any four-year period.)

Do circulators have to be residents of the state: No

Date when signatures are due for certification: The deadline for the State to receive the signatures is no later than 5:00 p.m. of the 91st day preceding the General Election (August 6, 2002). However, proponents must turn their petitions into each county for certification. August 6 is the deadline by which the counties must turn the certified petitions into the Secretary of State's office. Thus, proponents must give their signatures to the counties early enough for them to verify them before the August 6 deadline.

Signature verification process: Florida charges proponents to verify their signatures. For each signature checked, ten cents, or the actual cost of checking a signature, whichever is less, is paid to the supervisor at the time of submitting the petitions, by the political committee sponsoring the initiative petition. However, if a committee is unable to pay the charges without imposing an undue burden on the organization, the organization must submit a written certification of such inability given under oath to the Division of Elections to have the signatures verified at no charge. However, a sponsor of a proposed initiative amendment who uses paid petition circulators may not file an oath of undue burden in lieu of paying the fee required for the verification of signatures gathered. The Division of Elections will then circulate the undue burden oath submitted by the committee to each supervisor of elections in the state.

Single subject restriction: Florida has a very strict single subject requirement.

Legislative tampering: Constitutional amendments by initiative become part of the constitution and are thus only alterable by the legislature through regular constitutional procedures, any changes of which must be approved by popular vote.

Georgia

The I&R movement was never a major force in Georgia politics. However, between 1911-1913, the high-water mark of the Progressive era nationwide, the Georgia legislature enacted laws granting initiative, referendum, and recall rights to the residents of four cities, including Atlanta.

Georgia Constitution

The state does not have the statewide initiative process and so therefore the following provisions discuss the procedures used by the state legislature to place constitutional amendments on the ballot.

Article X: Section I. Constitution, How Amended

Paragraph I. Proposals to amend the Constitution; new Constitution.

Amendments to this Constitution or a new Constitution may be proposed by the General Assembly or by a constitutional convention, as provided in this article. Only amendments which are of general an uniform applicability throughout the state shall be proposed, passed, or submitted to the people.

Paragraph II. Proposals by the General Assembly; submission to the people.

A proposal by the General Assembly to amend this Constitution or to provide for a new Constitution shall originate as a resolution in either the Senate or the House of Representatives and, if approved by two-thirds of the members to which each house is entitled in a roll-call vote entered on their respective journals, shall be submitted to the electors of the entire state at the next general election which is held in the even-numbered years. A summary of such proposal shall be prepared by the Attorney General, the Legislative Counsel, and the Secretary of State and shall be published in the official organ of each county and, if deemed advisable by the "Constitutional Amendments Publication Board," in not more than 20 other newspapers in the state designated by such board which meet the qualifications for being selected as the official organ of a county. Said board shall be composed of the Governor, the Lieutenant Governor, and the Speaker of the House of Representatives. Such summary shall be published once each week for three consecutive weeks immediately preceding the day of the general election at which such proposal is to be submitted. The language to be use in submitting a proposed amendment or a new Constitution shall be in such words as the General Assembly may provide in the resolution or, in the absence thereof, in such language as the Governor may prescribe. A copy of the entire proposed amendment or of a new Constitution shall be filed in the office of the judge of the probate court of each county and shall be available for public inspection; and the summary of the proposal shall so indicate. The General Assembly is hereby authorized to provide by law for additional matters relative to the publication and distribution of proposed amendments and summaries not in conflict with the provisions of this Paragraph.

If such proposals is ratified by a majority of the electors qualified to vote for members of the General Assembly voting thereon in such general election, such proposal shall become a part of this Constitution or shall become a new Constitution, as the case may be. Any proposal so approved shall take effect as provided in Paragraph VI of this article. When more than one amendment is submitted at the same time, they shall be so submitted as to enable the electors to vote on each amendment separately, provided that one or more new articles or related changes in one or more articles may be submitted as a single amendment.

Paragraph III. Repeal or amendment of proposal.

Any proposal by the General Assembly to amend this Constitution or for a new Constitution may be amended or repealed by the same General Assembly which adopted such proposal by the affirmative vote of two-thirds of the members to which each house is entitled in a roll-call vote entered on their respective journals, if such action is taken at least two months prior to the date of the election at which such proposal is to be submitted to the people.

Paragraph IV. Constitutional convention; how called.

No convention of the people shall be called by the General Assembly to amend this Constitution or to propose a new Constitution, unless by the concurrence of two-thirds of the members to which each house of the General Assembly is entitled. The representation in said convention shall be based on population as near as practicable. A proposal by the convention to amend this Constitution or for a new Constitution shall be advertised, submitted to, and ratified by the people in the same manner provided for advertisement, submission, and ratification of proposals to amend the Constitution by the General Assembly. The General Assembly is hereby authorized to provide the procedure by which a convention is to be called and under which such convention shall operate and for other matters relative to such constitutional convention.

Paragraph V. Veto not permitted.

The Governor shall not have the right to veto any proposal by the General Assembly or by a convention to amend this Constitution or to provide a new Constitution.

Paragraph VI. Effective date of amendments or of a new Constitution.

Unless the amendment or the new Constitution itself or the resolution proposing the amendment or the new Constitution shall provide otherwise, an amendment to this Constitution or a new Constitution shall become effective on the first day of January following its ratification.

Hawaii

Hawaii's territorial Democratic Party convention of 1907 passed a resolution in favor of I&R, but until the 1950s the territorial government was dominated by Republicans who opposed the initiative process. After the Democrats gained power, however, most of them turned against I&R, and it was not included in the state constitution when Hawaii became a state in 1959. In the state's 1978 constitutional convention, initiative advocates attempted to pass an amendment enacting I&R, but they were narrowly defeated.

Until 1982 the county of Honolulu, on the island of Oahu, allowed initiative charter amendments, but not ordinances. State Senator Mary Jane McMurdo, who routinely sponsored bills in the legislature to get statewide I&R, led a campaign for a Honolulu initiative charter amendment to authorize citizens to pass ordinances by initiative. Voters approved it in November 1982 by a 55 percent margin, despite strong opposition from labor unions. Sen. McMurdo then led a drive for an initiative ordinance to save a block of moderate-income Honolulu apartments that were slated for destruction by high-rise builders. Voters approved this measure in 1984.

In 1986 McMurdo helped place another Honolulu initiative on the ballot, to prevent conversion of Fort DeRussy's 45 acres of mostly open space into a hotel—convention center complex. After a campaign in which pro-development forces spent $200,000, outspending initiative backers by a ratio of 20 to 1, voters turned it down. In 1988, Senator McMurdo and conservationists sponsored an initiative to restrict development at Oahu's Sandy Beach. This time, despite a campaign spending advantage by pro-development forces, voters passed the measure.

On the island of Kauai, voters approved an initiative in 1980 to stop construction of a hotel-condominium complex at Nukoli'i Beach, but the developer sponsored another initiative, which passed in 1984, to authorize completion of the half-built project.

Since 1984 there has been a tremendous amount of interest in trying to get the initiative process in Hawaii. However, the state legislature has remained openly hostile to its adoption.

Hawaii Constitution

The state does not have the statewide initiative process and so therefore the following provisions discuss the procedures used by the state legislature to place constitutional amendments on the ballot.

Article XVII: Revision and Amendment

Section 1. Methods of Proposal

Revisions of or amendments to this constitution may be proposed by constitutional convention or by the legislature. [Ren Const Con 1978 and election Nov 7, 1978]

Section 2. Constitutional Convention

The legislature may submit to the electorate at any general or special election the question, "Shall there be a convention to propose a revision of or amendments to the Constitution?" If any nine-year period shall elapse during which the question shall not have been submitted, the lieutenant governor shall certify the question, to be voted on at the first general election following the expiration of such period.

Election of Delegates

If a majority of the ballots cast upon such a question be in the affirmative, delegates to the convention shall be chosen at the next regular election unless the legislature shall provide for the election of delegates at a special election.

Notwithstanding any provision in this constitution to the contrary, other than Section 3 of Article XVI, any qualified voter of the district concerned shall be eligible to membership in the convention.

The legislature shall provide for the number of delegates to the convention, the areas from which they shall be elected and the manner in which the convention shall convene. The legislature shall also provide for the necessary facilities and equipment for the convention. The convention shall have the same powers and privileges, as nearly as practicable, as provided for the convention of 1978.

Meeting

The constitutional convention shall convene not less than five months prior to the next regularly scheduled general election.

Organization; Procedure

The convention shall determine its own organization and rules of procedure. It shall be the sole judge of the elections, returns and qualifications of its members and, by a two-thirds vote, may suspend or remove any member for cause. The governor shall fill any vacancy by appointment of a qualified voter from the district concerned.

Ratification; Appropriations

The convention shall provide for the time and manner in which the proposed constitutional revision or amendments shall be submitted to a vote of the electorate; provided that each amendment shall be submitted in the form of a question embracing but one subject; and provided further, that each question shall have designated spaces to mark YES or NO on the amendment.

At least thirty days prior to the submission of any proposed revision or amendments, the convention shall make available for public inspection, a full text of the proposed amendments. Every public library, office of the clerk of each county, and the chief election officer shall be provided such texts and shall make them available for public inspection. The full text of any proposed revision or amendments shall also be made available for inspection at every polling place on the day of the election at which such revision or amendments are submitted.

The convention shall, as provided by law, be responsible for a program of voter education concerning each proposed revision or amendment to be submitted to the electorate.

The revision or amendments shall be effective only if approved at a general election by a majority of all the votes tallied upon the question, this majority constituting at least fifty per cent of the total vote cast at the election, or at a special election by a majority of all the votes tallied upon the question, this majority constituting at least thirty per cent of the total number of registered voters.

The provisions of this section shall be self-executing, but the legislature shall make the necessary appropriations and may enact legislation to facilitate their operation. [Am Const Con 1968 and election Nov 5, 1968; ren and am Const Con 1978 and election Nov 7, 1978; am SB 578 (1979) and SB 1703 (1980) and election Nov 4, 1980]

Section 3. Amendments Proposed by Legislature

The legislature may propose amendments to the constitution by adopting the same, in the manner required for legislation, by a two-thirds vote of each house on final reading at any session, after either or both houses shall have given the governor at least ten days' written notice of the final form of the proposed amendment, or, with or without such notice, by a majority vote of each house on final reading at each of two successive sessions.

Upon such adoption, the proposed amendments shall be entered upon the journals, with the ayes and noes, and published once in each of four successive weeks in at least one newspaper of general circulation in each senatorial district wherein such a newspaper is published, within the two months' period immediately preceding the next general election.

At such general election the proposed amendments shall be submitted to the electorate for approval or rejection upon a separate ballot.

The conditions of and requirements for ratification of such proposed amendments shall be the same as provided in section 2 of this article for ratification at a general election.

Section 4. Veto

No proposal for amendment of the constitution adopted in either manner provided by this article shall be subject to veto by the governor.

Section 5. Conflicting Revisions or Amendments

If a revision or amendment proposed by a constitutional convention is in conflict with a revision or amendment proposed by the legislature and both are submitted to the electorate at the same election and both are approved, then the revision or amendment proposed by the convention shall prevail. If conflicting revisions or amendments are proposed by the same body and are submitted to the electorate at the same election and both are approved, then the revision or amendment receiving the highest number of votes shall prevail.

Idaho

In 1911, swept up in the reformist spirit of the times, the Idaho legislature approved an I&R amendment to the state constitution, which was approved by voters the following year. But the amendment was flawed: it did not specify the number of petition signatures required to qualify an initiative for the ballot. This meant that the legislature could set the threshold—and change it at any time. No initiative could qualify for the ballot until the legislature passed a bill to set the signature requirement. The legislature did this in 1915, but Governor Moses Alexander vetoed the bill because he thought the requirement unreasonable. Two decades went by before another such bill was passed.

The first initiative to qualify for the ballot was one to establish the state Fish and Game Commission; the voters approved it in 1938 by a margin of three to one. In 1954, voters passed an anti-pollution measure to ban dredge mining in riverbeds.

In 1974, Idaho voters passed an initiative calling for greater disclosure of campaign contributions and expenditures. In 1978, they approved a property tax cut initiative patterned after California's Proposition 13, but the legislature amended it to benefit businesses rather than homeowners.

In 1982, Idaho voters passed an initiative cutting taxes for homeowners, and in the same year they approved two other measures: one allowing denture technicians to compete with dentists in the sale and fitting of dentures and another supporting the development of nuclear power. This was the only statewide initiative supporting nuclear power that has ever been passed.

In early 1984, anti-initiative forces—primarily timber, mining, and farming interests—persuaded their friends in the legislature to double the number of signatures required to put an initiative on the ballot. The bill was introduced without a hearing, voted on, and sent to the governor's desk within 24 hours. However, initiative supporters reached Governor John Evans first and persuaded him to veto the bill. In 1999, these same forces, along with anti term limits advocates, convinced the state legislature to once again over regulate and restrict the initiative process. This time they were successful. The new law drastically increased the distribution requirement for initiatives that lead to the fact that not a single initiative qualified for the 2000 ballot. However, in litigation sponsored by the Initiative & Referendum Institute, the Federal District Court for Idaho struck down the new regulation as unconstitutional.

Statewide Initiative Usage

Number of Initiatives	Number Passed	Number Failed	Passage Rate
25	13	12	52%

Statewide Initiatives

Year	Measure Number	Type	Subject Matter	Description	Pass/Fail
1938	1	DS	Administration of Government	The Idaho state Fish and Game Commission Act.	Passed
1940	1	DS	Alcohol Regulation	Proposed prohibition districts, prohibiting the possession, purchase, sale and transportation of alcoholic liquors.	Failed
1940	2	DS	Alcohol Regulation	Idaho Sobriety Act proposed to inhibit advertising promotion of sales, limit amount of purchase and to inhibit dispensing of alcoholic liquors in bars and clubs.	Failed
1942	1	DS	Welfare	Provides a minimum of forty dollars monthly and medical, dental, surgical, optical, hospital, nursing care, and artificial limbs, eyes, hearing aids, and other needed appliances to citizens over 65 years of age.	Passed

Year	Measure Number	Type	Subject Matter	Description	Pass/Fail
1946	1	DS	Gaming	The anti gambling act.	Failed
1946	2	DS	Alcohol Regulation	The Local Option Act.	Failed
1946	3	DS	Alcohol Regulation	The Idaho Sobriety Act.	Failed
1954	1	DS	Environmental Reform	The Dredge Mining Initiative Proposal.	Passed
1958	1	DS	Labor	Right to employment regardless of labor organization membership or non-membership.	Failed
1970	1	DS	Administration of Government	Legislative Pay.	Passed
1974	1	DS	Campaign Finance Reform	Establishes campaign finance regulations and disclosure laws.	Passed
1978	1	DS	Taxes	Restrict property valuation or tax changes.	Passed
1982	1	DS	Taxes	Home improvement exemptions: ad valorem tax.	Passed
1982	2	DS	Health/Medical	Practice of Denturitry; licensing board.	Passed
1982	3	DS	Utility Regulation	Use of nuclear power for electricity generation.	Passed
1984	1	DS	Taxes	Sales tax exemption: food for consumption.	Failed
1986	1	DS	Gaming	Establish state lottery and lottery commission.	Passed
1992	1	DS	Taxes	Limit ad valorem property tax rates.	Failed
1994	1	DS	Civil Rights	Act establishing state policies regarding homosexuality.	Failed
1994	2	DS	Term	Limits Term limits on state legislature 8/8 and Congress 6/12.	Passed
1996	1	DS	Taxes	Limit property taxes to one percent of value.	Failed
1996	2	DS	Animal Rights	Prohibit the use of dogs or bait for hunting bear. Limit the bear hunting season.	Failed
1996	3	DS	Nuclear weapons/ facilities/waste	Require legislative and voter approval of agreements for the receipt of additional radioactive waste and nullifying a prior agreement.	Failed
1996	4	DS	Term Limits	Informed Voter Law.	Passed
1998	1	DS	Term Limits	Informed Voter Law.	Passed

Idaho Constitution

Article III: Legislative Department

Section 1. Legislative Power & Enacting Clause & Referendum & Initiative.

The legislative power of the state shall be vested in a senate and house of representatives. The enacting clause of every bill shall be as follows: "Be it enacted by the Legislature of the State of Idaho."

The people reserve to themselves the power to approve or reject at the polls any act or measure passed by the legislature. This power is known as the referendum, and legal voters may, under such conditions and in such manner as may be provided by acts of the legislature, demand a referendum vote on any act or measure passed by the legislature and cause the same to be submitted to a vote of the people for their approval or rejection.

The people reserve to themselves the power to propose laws, and enact the same at the polls independent of the legislature. This power is known as the initiative, and legal voters may, under such conditions and in such manner as may be provided by acts of the legislature, initiate any desired legislation and cause the same to be submitted to the vote of the people at a general election for their approval or rejection.

Idaho Statutes

Title 34: Chapter 18

Initiative and Referendum Elections

34-1801. Statement of Legislative Intent and Legislative Purpose

The legislature of the state of Idaho finds that there have been incidents of fraudulent and misleading practices in soliciting and obtaining signatures on initiative or referendum petitions, or both, that false signatures have been placed upon initiative or referendum petitions, or both, that difficulties have arisen in determining the identity of petition circulators and that substantial danger exists that such unlawful practices will or may continue in the future. In order to prevent and deter such behavior, the legislature determines that it is necessary to provide easy identity to the public of those persons who solicit or obtain signatures on initiative or referendum petitions, or both, and of those persons for whom they are soliciting and obtaining signatures and to inform the public concerning the solicitation and obtaining of such signatures. It is the purpose of the legislature in enacting this act to fulfill the foregoing statement of intent and remedy the foregoing practices.

34-1801A. Petitions

The following shall be substantially the form of petition for any law proposed by the initiative:

WARNING
It is a felony for anyone to sign any initiative or referendum petition with any name other than his own, or to knowingly sign his name more than once for the measure, or to sign such petition when he is not a qualified elector.

INITIATIVE PETITION
To the Honorable ...., Secretary of State of the State of Idaho, "We, the undersigned citizens and qualified electors of the State of Idaho, respectfully demand that the following proposed law, to-wit (setting out full text of measure proposed) shall be submitted to the qualified electors of the State of Idaho, for their approval or rejection at the regular general election, to be held on the .... day of ..., A.D., ...," and each for himself says I have personally signed this petition; I am a qualified elector of the State of Idaho; my residence and post office are correctly written after my name.
(Here follow twenty numbered lines for signatures.)

The petition for referendum on any act passed by the state legislature of the state of Idaho shall be in substantially the same form with appropriate title and changes, setting out in full the text of the act of the legislature to be referred to the people for their approval or rejection.

34-1802. Initiative Petitions — Time for Gathering Signatures — Time for Submission of Signatures to the County Clerk — Time for Filing

(1) Except as provided in section 34-1804, Idaho Code, petitions for an initiative shall be circulated and signatures obtained beginning upon the date that the petitioners receive the official ballot title from the secretary of state and extending eighteen (18) months from that date or April 30 of the year that an election on the initiative will be held, whichever occurs earlier. The last day for circulating petitions and obtaining signatures shall be the last day of April in the year an election on the initiative will be held.

(2) The person or persons or organization or organizations under whose authority the measure is to be initiated shall submit the petitions containing signatures to the county clerk for verification pursuant to the provisions of section 34-1807, Idaho Code. The signatures required shall be submitted to the county clerk not later than the close of business on the first day of May in the year an election on the initiative will be held, or eighteen (18) months from the date the petitioner receives the official ballot title from the secretary of state, whichever is earlier.

(3) The county clerk shall, within sixty (60) calendar days of the deadline for the submission of the signatures, verify the signatures contained in the petitions, but in no event shall the time extend beyond the last day of June in the year an election on the initiative will be held.

(4) Initiative petitions with the requisite number of signatures attached shall be filed with the secretary of state not less than four (4) months before the election at which they are to be voted upon.

34-1803. Referendum Petitions — Time for Filing — When Election Held — Effective Date of Law

Referendum petitions with the requisite number of signatures attached shall be filed with the secretary of state not more than sixty (60) days after the final adjournment of the session of the state legislature which passed on the bill on which the referendum is demanded. All elections on measures referred to the people of the state shall be had at the biennial regular election. Any measure so referred to the people shall take effect and become a law when it is approved by a majority of the votes cast thereon, and not otherwise.

34-1803B. Initiative and Referendum Petitions — Removal of Signatures

(1) The signer of any initiative or referendum petition may remove his or her own name from the petition by crossing out, obliterating or otherwise defacing his or her own signature at any time prior to the time when the petition is presented to the county clerk for signature verification.

(2) The signer of any initiative or referendum petition may have his or her name removed from the petition at any time after presentation of the petition to the county clerk but prior to verification of the signature, by presenting or submitting to the county clerk a signed statement that the signer desires to have his name removed from the petition. The statement shall contain sufficient information to clearly identify the signer. The county clerk shall immediately strike the signer's name from the petition, and adjust the total of certified signatures on the petition accordingly. The statement shall be attached to, and become a part of the initiative or referendum petition.

34-1804. Printing of Petition and Signature Sheets

Before or at the time of beginning to circulate any petition for the referendum to the people on any act passed by the state legislature of the state of Idaho, or for any law proposed by the initiative, the person or persons or organization or organizations under whose authority the measure is to be referred or initiated shall send or deliver to the secretary of state a copy of such petition duly signed by at least twenty (20) qualified electors of the state which shall be filed by said officer in his office, and who shall immediately transmit a copy of the petition to the attorney general for the issuance of the certificate of review as provided in section 34-1809, Idaho Code. All petitions for the initiative and for the referendum and sheets for signatures shall be printed on a good quality of bond or ledger paper in the form and manner as approved by the secretary of state. To every sheet of petitioners' signatures shall be attached a full and correct copy of the measure so proposed by initiative petition; but such petition may be filed by the secretary of state in numbered sections for convenience in handling. Every sheet of petitioners' signatures upon referendum petitions shall be attached to a full and correct copy of the measure on which the referendum is demanded, and may be filed in numbered sections in like manner as initiative petitions. Not more than twenty (20) signatures on one (1) sheet shall be counted. Each signature sheet shall contain signatures of qualified electors from only one (1) county.

34-1805. Sponsors To Print Petition — Number of Signers Required

After the form of the initiative or referendum petition has been approved by the secretary of state as in sections 34-1801A through 34-1822, Idaho Code, provided, the same shall be printed by the person or persons or organization or organizations under whose authority the measure is to be referred or initiated and circulated in the several counties of the state for the signatures of legal voters. Before such petitions shall be entitled to final filing and consideration by the secretary of state there shall be affixed thereto the signatures of legal voters equal in number to not less than six percent (6%) of the qualified electors of the state at the time of the last general election. Provided, that the petition must contain a number of signatures of qualified electors from each of twenty-two (22) counties equal to not less than six percent (6%) of the qualified electors at the time of the last general election in each of those twenty-two (22) counties.

34-1806. Binding of Petition and Signature Sheets — Approved Measures To Be Printed With Session Laws

When any such initiative or referendum petition shall be offered for filing the secretary of state shall detach the sheets containing the signatures and affidavits and cause them all to be attached to one or more printed copies of the measure so proposed by initiative or referendum petitions. The secretary of state shall file and keep such petitions as official public records. The secretary of state shall cause every such measure so approved by the people to be printed with the general laws enacted by the next ensuing session of the state legislature with the date of the governor's proclamation declaring the same to have been approved by the people.

34-1807. Circulation of Petitions — Verification of Petition and Signature Sheet — Comparison of Signatures With Registration Oaths and Records — Certain Petitions and Signatures Void

Any person who circulates any petition for an initiative or referendum shall be a resident of the state of Idaho and at least eighteen (18) years of age. Each and every sheet of every such petition containing signatures shall be verified on the face thereof in substantially the following form, by the person who circulated said sheet of said petition, by his or her affidavit thereon, and as a part thereof:

State of Idaho,
ss.
County of _____
I, _____, being first duly sworn, say: That I am a resident of the State of Idaho and at least eighteen (18) years of age: that every person who signed this sheet of the foregoing petition signed his or her name thereto in my presence: I believe that each has stated his or her name, post-office address and residence correctly, that each signer is a qualified elector of the State of Idaho, and a resident of the county of _____
Signed _____
Post-office address _____
Subscribed and sworn to before me this _____ day of _____
(Notary Seal)   Notary Public _____
Residing at _____

In addition to said affidavit the county clerk shall carefully examine said petitions and shall attach to the signature sheets a certificate to the secretary of state substantially as follows:

State of Idaho
ss.
County of _____
To the honorable _____, Secretary of State for the State of Idaho: I, _____, County Clerk of _____
County, hereby certify that _____ signatures on this petition are those of qualified electors.
Signed _____
County Clerk or Deputy.
(Seal of office)

The county clerk shall deliver the petition or any part thereof to the person from whom he received it with his certificate attached thereto as above provided. The forms herein given are not mandatory and if substantially followed in any petition, it shall be sufficient, disregarding clerical and merely technical error.

Any petition upon which signatures are obtained by a person not a resident of the state of Idaho and at least eighteen (18) years of age, shall be void. The definition of resident in section 34-107, Idaho Code, shall apply to the circulators of initiative and referendum petitions. In addition to (to) being a resident, a petition circulator shall be at least eighteen (18) years of age.

34-1808. Filing of Petition — Mandate — Injunction

If the secretary of state shall refuse to accept and file any petition for the initiative or for the referendum with the requisite number of signatures of qualified electors thereto attached, any citizen may apply, within ten (10) days after such refusal to the district court for a writ of mandamus to compel him to do so. If it shall be decided by the court that such petition is legally sufficient, the secretary of state shall then file it, with a certified copy of the judgment attached thereto, as of the date on which it was originally offered for filing in his office. On a showing that any petition filed is not legally sufficient, the court may enjoin the secretary of state and all other officers from certifying or printing on the official ballot for the ensuing election the ballot title and numbers of such measure. All such suits shall be advanced on the court docket and heard and decided by the court as quickly as possible. Either party may appeal to the Supreme Court within ten (10) days after a decision is rendered. The district court of the fourth judicial district of the state of Idaho in and for Ada County shall have jurisdiction in all cases of measures to be submitted to the qualified electors of the state at large.

34-1809. Review of Initiative and Referendum Measures by Attorney General — Certificate of Review Prerequisite to Assignment of Ballot Title — Ballot Title — Judicial Review

After receiving a copy of the petition from the secretary of state as provided in section 34-1804, Idaho Code, the attorney general may confer with the petitioner and shall, within twenty (20) working days from receipt thereof, review the proposal for matters of substantive import and shall recommend to the petitioner such revision or alteration of the measure as may be deemed necessary and appropriate. The recommendations of the attorney general shall be advisory only and the petitioner may accept or reject them in whole or in part. The attorney general shall issue a certificate of review to the secretary of state certifying that he has reviewed the measure for form and style and that the recommendations thereon, if any, have been communicated to the petitioner, and such certificate shall be issued whether or not the petitioner accepts such recommendations. The certificate of review shall be available for public inspection in the office of the secretary of state. Within fifteen (15) working days after the issuance of the certificate of review, the petitioner, if he desires to proceed with his sponsorship, shall file the measure, as herein provided, with the secretary of state for assignment of a ballot title and the secretary of state shall thereupon submit to the attorney general two (2) copies of the measure filed. Within ten (10) working days after receiving said copies the attorney general shall provide a ballot title therefor and return one of said copies to the secretary of state, together with the ballot title so prepared by him. A copy of the ballot title as prepared by the attorney general shall be furnished by the secretary of state with his approved form of any initiative or referendum petition, as provided herein, to the person or persons or organization or organizations under whose authority the measure is initiated or referred. Said ballot title shall be used and printed on the covers of the petition when in circulation; the short title shall be printed in type not less than twenty (20) points on the covers of all such petitions circulated for signatures. The ballot title shall contain (1) Distinctive short title in not exceeding twenty (20) words by which the measure is commonly referred to or spoken of and which shall be printed in the foot margin of each signature sheet of the petition. (2) A general title expressing in not more than two hundred (200) words the purpose of the measure. The ballot title shall be printed with the numbers of the measure on the official ballot. In making such ballot title the attorney general shall to the best of his ability give a true and impartial statement of the purpose of the measure and in such language that the ballot title shall not be intentionally an argument or likely to create prejudice either for or against the measure. Any person who is dissatisfied with the ballot title or the short title provided by the attorney general for any measure, may appeal from his decision to the Supreme Court by petition, praying for a different title and setting forth the reason why the title prepared by the attorney general is insufficient or unfair. No appeal shall be allowed from the decision of the attorney general on a ballot title unless the same is taken within twenty (20) days after said ballot title is filed in the office of the secretary of state; provided however, that this section shall not prevent any later judicial proceeding to determine the sufficiency of such title, nor shall it prevent any judicial decision upon the sufficiency of such title. A copy of every such ballot title shall be served by the secretary of state upon the person offering or filing such initiative or referendum petition, or appeal. The service of such decision may be by mail or telegraph and shall be made forthwith when it is received from the attorney general by the secretary of state. Said Supreme Court shall thereupon examine said measure, hear argument, and in its decision thereon certify to the secretary of state a ballot title and a short title for the measure in accord with the intent of this section. The secretary of state shall print on the official ballot the title thus certified to him. Any qualified elector of the state of Idaho may, at any time after the attorney general has issued a certificate of review, bring an action in the Supreme Court to determine the constitutionality of any initiative.

34-1810. Printing and Designation of Ballot Titles On Official Ballots

The secretary of state, at the time he furnishes to the county clerks of the several counties certified copies of the names of candidates for state and district offices shall furnish to each of said county clerks a certified copy of the ballot titles and numbers of the several measures to be voted upon at the ensuing general election, and he shall use for each measure the ballot title designated in the manner herein provided. Such ballot title shall not resemble, so far as to probably create confusion, any such title previously filed for any measure to be submitted at that election. The secretary of state shall number the measures consecutively beginning with number (1), in the order in which the measures were finally filed with the secretary. The measures shall be designated on the ballot as a "Proposition One", "Proposition Two," et cetera.

34-1811. Manner of Voting — Procedure When Conflicting Measures Approved

The manner of voting upon measures submitted to the people shall be the same as is now or may be required and provided by law; no measure shall be adopted unless it shall receive an affirmative majority of the aggregate number of votes cast on such measure. If two (2) or more conflicting laws shall be approved by the people at the same election, the law receiving the greatest number of affirmative votes shall be paramount in all particulars as to which there is a conflict, even though such law may not have received the greatest majority of affirmative votes. If two (2) or more conflicting amendments to the constitution shall be approved by the people at the same election, the amendment which receives the greatest number of affirmative votes shall be paramount in all particulars as to which there is a conflict, even though such amendment may not have received the greatest majority of affirmative votes.

34-1812A. Arguments Concerning Initiative and Referendum Measures

Any voter or group of voters may on or before July 20 prepare and file an argument, not to exceed five hundred (500) words, for or against any measure. Such argument shall not be accepted unless accompanied by the name and address or names and addresses of the person or persons submitting it, or, if submitted on behalf of an organization, the name and address of the organization and the names and addresses of at least two (2) of its principal officers.

If more than one (1) argument for or more than one (1) argument against any measure is filed within the time prescribed, the secretary of state shall select one (1) of the arguments for printing in the voters' pamphlets. In selecting the argument the secretary of state shall be required to give priority in the order named to the arguments of the following:
(1) The proponent of the initiative or referendum petition.
(2) Bona fide associations of citizens.
(3) Individual voters.

34-1812B. Submissions of Rebuttal Arguments

When the secretary of state has received the arguments which will be printed in the voters' pamphlet, the secretary of state shall immediately send copies of the arguments in favor of the proposition to the authors of the arguments against and copies of the arguments against to the authors of the arguments in favor. The authors may prepare and submit rebuttal arguments not exceeding two hundred and fifty (250) words. The rebuttal arguments must be filed no later than August 1. Rebuttal arguments shall be printed in the same manner as the direct arguments. Each rebuttal argument shall immediately follow the direct argument which it seeks to rebut.

34-1812C. Voters' Pamphlet

(1) Not later than September 25 before any regular general election at which an initiative or referendum measure is to be submitted to the people, the secretary of state shall cause to be printed a voters' pamphlet which shall contain the following:
(a) A complete copy of the title and text of each measure with the number and form in which the ballot title thereof will be printed on the official ballot;
(b) A copy of the arguments and rebuttals for and against each state measure.
(2) The secretary of state shall mail or distribute a copy of the voters' pamphlet to every household in the state. Sufficient copies of the voters' pamphlet shall also be sent to each county clerk. The county clerk and the secretary of state shall make copies of the voters' pamphlet available upon request.
(3) The voters' pamphlet shall be printed according to the following specifications:
(a) The pages of the pamphlet shall be not smaller than 6 x 9 inches in size;
(b) It shall be printed in clear readable type, no less than 10-point, except that the text of any measure may be set forth in no less than 7-point type;
(c) It shall be printed on a quality and weight of paper which in the judgment of the secretary of state best serves the voters;
(d) If the material described in subsections (a) and (b) of this section is combined in a single publication with constitutional amendments, the entire publication shall be treated as a legal notice.

34-1813. Counting, Canvassing, and Return of Votes

The votes on measures and questions shall be counted, canvassed and returned by the regular boards of judges, clerks and officers, as votes for candidates are counted, canvassed and returned, and the abstract made by the several county auditors of votes on measures shall be returned to the secretary of state on separate abstract sheets in the manner provided for abstract of votes for state and county officers. It shall be the duty of the secretary of state, in the presence of the governor, to proceed within thirty (30) days after the election, and sooner if the returns be all received, to canvass the votes given for each measure, and the governor shall forthwith issue his proclamation, giving the whole number of votes cast in the state for and against such measure and question, and declaring such measures as are approved by a majority of those voted thereon to be in full force and effect as the law of the state of Idaho from the date of said proclamation; provided, that if two (2) or more measures shall be approved at said election which are known to conflict with each other or to contain conflicting provisions he shall also proclaim which is paramount in accordance with the provisions of sections 34-1801 – 34-1822.

34-1814. Who May Sign Petition — Effect of Wrongful Signing — Penalty for Wrongful Signing

Every person who is a qualified elector of the state of Idaho may sign a petition for the referendum or for the initiative for any measure which he is legally entitled to vote upon. Any person signing any name other than his own to any petition, or knowingly signing his name more than once for the same measure at one election, or who is not at the time of signing the same a legal voter of this state, or any officer or person willfully violating any provision of this statute, shall, upon conviction thereof be punished by a fine not exceeding five thousand dollars ($5,000) or by imprisonment in the penitentiary not exceeding two (2) years, or by both such fine and imprisonment, in the discretion of the court before which such conviction shall be had. Any such wrongful signatures are null and void and shall not be counted as a qualified signature. Any person circulating a petition, who knows, or who in the exercise of reasonable care should know, that a signature is forged and who shall thereafter fail to strike through and thereby void such signature, and any person in a position of supervision of such person who suffers or permits a forged signature to remain on a petition shall pay a fine of not less than one thousand dollars ($1,000) for each such signature.

34-1815. False Statements Spoken or Written Concerning Petition Unlawful — Failure to Disclose Material Provisions

It shall be unlawful for any person to willfully or knowingly circulate, publish or exhibit any false statement or representation, whether spoken or written, or to fail to disclose any material provision in a petition, concerning the contents, purport or effect of any petition mentioned in sections 34-1801A through 34-1822, Idaho Code, for the purpose of obtaining any signature to any such petition, or for the purpose of persuading any person to sign any such petition. It shall be unlawful for any person to solicit or obtain any signature on a petition without first showing the signer both the short title and the general title as defined in section 34-1809, Idaho Code, so that the signer has an opportunity to read them before signing the petition.

Any signature obtained without compliance with this section is null and void.

34-1816. Filing Petition With False Signatures Unlawful

It shall be unlawful for any person to file in the office of any officer provided by law to receive such filing any petition mentioned in sections 34-1801 – 34-1822, to which is attached, appended or subscribed any signature which the person so filing such petition knows to be false or fraudulent or not the genuine signature of the person purporting to sign such petition, or whose name is attached, appended or subscribed thereto.

34-1817. Circulating Petition With False, Forged or Fictitious Names Unlawful

It shall be unlawful for any person to circulate or cause to be circulated any petition mentioned in sections 34-1801 – 34-1822, knowing the same to contain false, forged or fictitious names.

34-1818. False Affidavit by Any Person Unlawful

It shall be unlawful for any person to make any false affidavit concerning any petition mentioned in sections 34-1801 – 34-1822, or the signatures appended thereto.

34-1819. False Return, Certification or Affidavit by Public Official Unlawful.

It shall be unlawful for any public official or employee knowingly to make any false return, certification or affidavit concerning any petition mentioned in sections 34-1801 – 34-1822, or the signatures appended thereto.

34-1820. Signing More Than Once or When Not Qualified Unlawful

It shall be unlawful for any person to knowingly sign his own name more than once to any petition mentioned in sections 34-1801 – 34-1822, or to sign his name to any such petition knowing himself at the time of such signing not to be qualified to sign the same.

34-1821. Felonious Acts Enumerated

It shall be a felony for any person to offer, propose or threaten to do any act mentioned in this section of or concerning any petition mentioned in sections 34-1801 – 34-1822, for any pecuniary reward or consideration: (a) To offer, propose, threaten or attempt to sell, hinder or delay any petition or any part thereof or of any signatures thereon mentioned in sections 34-1801 – 34-1822; (b) To offer, propose, or threaten to desist, for a valuable consideration, from beginning, promoting or circulating any petition mentioned in sections 34-1801 – 34-1822, or soliciting signatures to any such petition; (c) To offer, propose, attempt or threaten in any manner or form to use any petition or power of promotion or opposition in any manner or form for extortion, blackmail or secret or private intimidation of any person or business interest.

34-1822. Penalty for Violations

Any person, either as principal or agent, violating any of the provisions of sections 34-1801 – 34-1822 shall be punished upon conviction by imprisonment in the penitentiary or in the county jail not exceeding two (2) years, or by a fine not exceeding $5000.00, or by both, excepting that imprisonment in the penitentiary and punishment by a fine shall be the only penalty for violation of any provision of section 34-1821.

34-1823. Severability

In the event that any part of chapter 18, title 34, Idaho Code, shall for any reason be determined void or unenforceable in any part thereof, the remainder thereof shall remain in full force and effect.

The Basic Steps to Do an Initiative in Idaho

Statutes Only — Direct Initiative Process

Basic Procedures: A copy of the proposed initiative petition shall be filed with the signatures of 20 qualified electors of the state in the Secretary of State's office. The Secretary of State shall immediately transmit a copy of the proposed petition to the Attorney General for a Certificate of Review. The Attorney General may confer with the petitioner and shall, within 20 working days after receipt, review the proposed petition for substantive improvements and shall recommend to the petitioner such revision or alteration of the measure as may be deemed necessary and appropriate. The recommendations of the Attorney General shall be advisory only and the petitioner may accept or reject them in whole or in part.

The Attorney General shall issue a certificate of review to the Secretary of State certifying that he has reviewed the measure for form and style and that the recommendations thereon, if any, have been communicated to the petitioner, and such certificate shall be issued whether or not the petitioner accepts such recommendations.

Any qualified elector of the state of Idaho may, at any time after the certificate of review is issued, bring an action in the Supreme Court to determine the constitutionality of the initiative.

Within 15 working days after the issuance of the Certificate of Review, the petitioner, if he desires to proceed, with his sponsorship, shall inform the Secretary of State, in writing, of his intent. The Attorney General shall provide ballot titles, on the final proposal, within ten (10) working days. Any person who is dissatisfied with ballot titles, may appeal to the Supreme Court within 20 days after said ballot title is filed in the office of the Secretary of State. This shall not prevent later judicial proceedings and decisions on sufficiency of ballot titles. The Secretary of State shall transmit the approved form with the ballot titles to the petitioners with printing instructions. Any voter or group of voters may on or before July 20 prepare and file an argument not to exceed 500 words, for or against any measure. Rebuttal Arguments, not to exceed 250 words may be submitted no later than August 1. Voter Pamphlets will be printed and distributed by the Secretary of State no later than September 25.

Date Initiative language can be submitted to state for 2002: No deadline

Signatures are tied to vote of which office: Number of registered voters at the last general election.

Next general election: 2002

Registered voters at last general election: 728,083

Net number of signatures required: 6% of registered voters at the last general election (43,685)

Distribution Requirement: A minimum of 6% of qualified electors in each of Idaho's 22 counties (this distribution requirement was struck down by the federal courts but the state has appealed that decision).

Circulation period: 18 Months

Do circulators have to be residents: Yes

Date when signatures are filed for certification: The proponents upon receipt of ballot titles and approved form have an 18-month circulation period or until April 30 in an election year whichever occurs earlier.

Signature verification process: Petitions are turned into the county clerks of the counties in which the petitions are circulated. The county clerks verify every signature.

Single-subject restriction: No

Legislative tampering: The legislature can repeal an initiative.

Illinois

The fight for I&R in Illinois began in 1897, when 250 delegates met in Chicago to form the Direct Legislation Union. Encouraged by this organization, the state Democratic Party endorsed I&R, and governor John Peter Altgeld endorsed it in a Labor Day speech in 1899.

The state legislature, seeking to defuse the I&R agitation without giving voters any real lawmaking power, passed a "Public Opinion Law" in 1901 which allowed citizens to petition to put non-binding advisory questions on state or city ballots. It restricted this initiative power further by setting the signature requirement at 10 percent of registered voters for statewide measures, and a nearly impossible 25 percent for local measures.

The initiative advocates reorganized as the Referendum League of Illinois and elected Dr. Maurice F. Doty of Chicago as their leader. The League employed the advisory petition as a means for citizens to demand real I&R lawmaking rights. The first two advisory initiatives on the state ballot called for state and local I&R. Both propositions received 83 percent of the vote—a landslide—on November 4, 1902.

In 1904 the League sponsored a statewide advisory initiative calling for primary elections to replace nominating conventions, which passed by a large majority. The League put more advisory initiatives on the state ballot in the following years: a measure calling for the enactment of a law to restrict corrupt political practices was passed in 1910 by a margin of 422,000 to 122,000, and a measure to shorten the long, complicated election ballots was also approved. However, the legislature did not respond to the people's wishes except to their demand for primary elections.

The League put a measure calling for I&R on the ballot a second time in 1910. Leaders in this campaign included Harold L. Ickes, who later became secretary of the interior under Franklin D. Roosevelt, and suffragist Dr. Anna E. Blount. Illinois voters again demanded I&R, this time by a resounding 78 percent, but the legislature again ignored the people's wishes.

In the four decades following World War II, only one advisory initiative qualified for the state ballot: a measure calling for tax reduction, sponsored by Governor James R. Thompson in 1978. Thompson, running for re-election, was attempting to capitalize on the nationwide popularity of California's tax-cutting Proposition 13, which passed in June of that year. Illinois voters approved the measure and re-elected Thompson, but no tax cuts resulted.

At the local level, the earliest major I&R battle in Illinois began in 1901 between Progressives and the "traction trust," as the price-gouging, politician-bribing streetcar companies were known. In his book Altgeld's America, Ray Ginger gives a detailed account of this convoluted campaign. Between 1902 and 1907, Chicagoans voted on five separate ballot measures calling for city takeover of the streetcar lines. The voters consistently endorsed municipal ownership, but were ultimately forced to settle for a compromise that delayed this goal for 20 years and set up a system of city regulation in the interim.

At the state constitutional convention in 1920, Progressives waged an unsuccessful battle for the passage of a statewide I&R amendment. Since then, little was done to promote the initiative process until the campaigns by the Coalition for Political Honesty in the 1970s and 1980s.

In 1980, the first and only "binding" initiative appeared on Illinois's ballot. The initiative reduced the size of the state legislature from 177 members to 118 members. It passed overwhelmingly.

Due to the fact that the Illinois initiative process is so limited and so difficult, many initiative scholars don't even count it as an initiative state.

Statewide Initiative Usage

Number of Initiatives	Number Passed	Number Failed	Passage Rate
1	1	0	100%

Statewide Initiatives

Year	Measure Number	Type	Subject Matter	Description	Pass/Fail
1980	N/A	DA	Administration of Government	Reduce size of House of Representatives from 177 members to 118 members beginning with elections in 1982.	Passed

Illinois Constitution

Article XI

Section 3. Constitutional Initiative for Legislative Article

Amendments to Article IV of this Constitution may be proposed by a petition signed by a number of electors equal in number to at least eight percent of the total votes cast for candidates for Governor in the preceding gubernatorial election. Amendments shall be limited to structural and procedural subjects contained in Article IV. A petition shall contain the text of the proposed amendment and the date of the general election at which the proposed amendment is to be submitted, shall have been signed by the petitioning electors not more than twenty-four months preceding that general election and shall be filed with the Secretary of State at least six months before that general election. The procedure for determining the validity and sufficiency of a petition shall be provided by law. If the petition is valid and sufficient, the proposed amendment shall be submitted to the electors at that general election and shall become effective if approved by either three-fifths of those voting on the amendment or a majority of those voting in the election.

Article VII

Local Governments

Section 11. Initiative and Referendum

(a) Proposals for actions which are authorized by this Article or by law and which require approval by referendum may be initiated and submitted to the electors by resolution of the governing board of a unit of local government or by petition of electors in the manner provided by law.
(b) Referenda required by this Article shall be held at general elections, except as otherwise provided by law. Questions submitted to referendum shall be adopted if approved by a majority of those voting on the question unless a different requirement is specified in this Article.

Illinois Statutes

Article 28: Chapter 10

Submitting Public Questions

Sec. 28-1.

The initiation and submission of all public questions to be voted upon by the electors of the State or of any political subdivision or district or precinct or combination of precincts shall be subject to the provisions of this Article.

Questions of public policy which have any legal effect shall be submitted to referendum only as authorized by a statute which so provides or by the Constitution. Advisory questions of public policy shall be submitted to referendum pursuant to Section 28-5 or pursuant to a statute which so provides.

The method of initiating the submission of a public question shall be as provided by the statute authorizing such public question, or as provided by the Constitution.

All public questions shall be initiated, submitted and printed on the ballot in the form required by Section 16-7 of this Act, except as may otherwise be specified in the statute authorizing a public question.

Whenever a statute provides for the initiation of a public question by a petition of electors, the provisions of such statute shall govern with respect to the number of signatures required, the qualifications of persons entitled to sign the petition, the contents of the petition, the officer with whom the petition must be filed, and the form of the question to be submitted. If such statute does not specify any of the foregoing petition requirements, the corresponding petition requirements of Section 28-6 shall govern such petition.

Irrespective of the method of initiation, not more than 3 public questions other than (a) back door referenda, (b) referenda to determine whether a disconnection may take place where a city coterminous with a township is proposing to annex territory from an adjacent township or (c) referenda held under the provisions of the Property Tax Extension Limitation Law in the Property Tax Code may be submitted to referendum with respect to a political subdivision at the same election.

If more than 3 propositions are timely initiated or certified for submission at an election with respect to a political subdivision, the first 3 validly initiated, by the filing of a petition or by the adoption of a resolution or ordinance of a political subdivision, as the case may be, shall be printed on the ballot and submitted at that election. However, except as expressly authorized by law not more than one proposition to change the form of government of a municipality pursuant to Article VII of the Constitution may be submitted at an election. If more than one such proposition is timely initiated or certified for submission at an election with respect to a municipality, the first validly initiated shall be the one printed on the ballot and submitted at that election.

No public question shall be submitted to the voters of a political subdivision at any regularly scheduled election at which such voters are not scheduled to cast votes for any candidates for nomination for, election to or retention in public office, except that if, in any existing or proposed political subdivision in which the submission of a public question at a regularly scheduled election is desired, the voters of only a portion of such existing or proposed political subdivision are not scheduled to cast votes for nomination for, election to or retention in public office at such election, but the voters in one or more other portions of such existing or proposed political subdivision are scheduled to cast votes for nomination for, election to or retention in public office at such election, the public question shall be voted upon by all the qualified voters of the entire existing or proposed political subdivision at the election.

Not more than 3 advisory public questions may be submitted to the voters of the entire state at a general election. If more than 3 such advisory propositions are initiated, the first 3 timely and validly initiated shall be the questions printed on the ballot and submitted at that election; provided however, that a question for a proposed amendment to Article IV of the Constitution pursuant to Section 3, Article XIV of the Constitution, or for a question submitted under the Property Tax Cap Referendum Law, shall not be included in the foregoing limitation. (Source: P.A. 88-116; 89-510, eff. 7-11-96.)

Sec. 28-2.

(a) Except as otherwise provided in this Section, petitions for the submission of public questions to referendum must be filed with the appropriate officer or board not less than 78 days prior to a regular election to be eligible for submission on the ballot at such election; and petitions for the submission of a question under Section 18-120 of the Property Tax Code must be filed with the appropriate officer or board not more than 10 months nor less than 6 months prior to the election at which such question is to be submitted to the voters.

(b) However, petitions for the submission of a public question to referendum which proposes the creation or formation of a political subdivision must be filed with the appropriate officer or board not less than 108 days prior to a regular election to be eligible for submission on the ballot at such election.

(c) Resolutions or ordinances of governing boards of political subdivisions which initiate the submission of public questions pursuant to law must be adopted not less than 65 days before a regularly scheduled election to be eligible for submission on the ballot at such election.

(d) A petition, resolution or ordinance initiating the submission of a public question may specify a regular election at which the question is to be submitted, and must so specify if the statute authorizing the public question requires submission at a particular election. However, no petition, resolution or ordinance initiating the submission of a public question, other than a legislative resolution initiating an amendment to the Constitution, may specify such submission at an election more than one year after the date on which it is filed or adopted, as the case may be. A petition, resolution or ordinance initiating a public question which specifies a particular election at which the question is to be submitted shall be so limited, and shall not be valid as to any other election, other than an emergency referendum ordered pursuant to Section 2A-1.4.

(e) If a petition initiating a public question does not specify a regularly scheduled election, the public question shall be submitted to referendum at the next regular election occurring not less than 78 days after the filing of the petition, or not less than 108 days after the filing of a petition for referendum to create a political subdivision.

If a resolution or ordinance initiating a public question does not specify a regularly scheduled election, the public question shall be submitted to referendum at the next regular election occurring not less than 65 days after the adoption of the resolution or ordinance.

(f) In the case of back door referenda, any limitations in another statute authorizing such a referendum which restrict the time in which the initiating petition may be validly filed shall apply to such petition, in addition to the filing deadlines specified in this Section for submission at a particular election. In the case of any back door referendum, the publication of the ordinance or resolution of the political subdivision shall include a notice of (1) the specific number of voters required to sign a petition requesting that a public question be submitted to the voters of the subdivision; (2) the time within which the petition must be filed; and (3) the date of the prospective referendum. The secretary or clerk of the political subdivision shall provide a petition form to any individual requesting one. As used herein, a "back door referendum" is the submission of a public question to the voters of a political subdivision, initiated by a petition of voters or residents of such political subdivision, to determine whether an action by the governing body of such subdivision shall be adopted or rejected.

(g) A petition for the incorporation or formation of a new political subdivision whose officers are to be elected rather than appointed must have attached to it an affidavit attesting that at least 108 days and no more than138 days prior to such election notice of intention to file such petition was published in a newspaper published within the proposed political subdivision, or if none, in a newspaper of general circulation within the territory of the proposed political subdivision in substantially the following form:

NOTICE OF PETITION TO FORM A NEW...

Residents of the territory described below are notified that a petition will or has been filed in the Office of .... requesting a referendum to establish a new ...., to be called the ....

The officers of the new .... will be elected on the same day as the referendum. Candidates for the governing board of the new ... may file nominating petitions with the officer named above until ....

The territory proposed to comprise the new ... is described as follows:
(description of territory included in petition)
(signature) ....

Name and address of person or persons proposing the new political subdivision.

Failure to file such affidavit, or failure to publish the required notice with the correct information contained therein shall render the petition, and any referendum held pursuant to such petition, null and void.

Notwithstanding the foregoing provisions of this subsection (g) or any other provisions of this Code, the publication of notice and affidavit requirements of this subsection (g) shall not apply to any petition filed under Article 7, 7A, 11A, 11B, or 11D of the School Code nor to any referendum held pursuant to any such petition, and neither any petition filed under any of those Articles nor any referendum held pursuant to any such petition shall be rendered null and void because of the failure to file an affidavit or publish a notice with respect to the petition or referendum as required under this subsection (g) for petitions that are not filed under any of those Articles of the School Code.
(Source: P.A. 90-459, eff. 8-17-97.)

Sec. 28-3. Form of petition for public question.

Petitions for the submission of public questions shall consist of sheets of uniform size and each sheet shall contain, above the space for signature, an appropriate heading, giving the information as to the question of public policy to be submitted, and specifying the state at large or the political subdivision or district or precinct or combination of precincts or other territory in which it is to be submitted and, where by law the public question must be submitted at a particular election, the election at which it is to be submitted. In the case of a petition for the submission of a public question described in subsection (b) of Section 28-6, the heading shall also specify the regular election at which the question is to be submitted and include the precincts included in the territory concerning which the public question is to be submitted, as well as a common description of such territory in plain and non-legal language, such description to describe the territory by reference to streets, natural or artificial landmarks, addresses or any other method which would enable a voter signing the petition to be informed of the territory concerning which the question is to be submitted. The heading of each sheet shall be the same. Such petition shall be signed by the registered voters of the political subdivision or district or precinct or combination of precincts in which the question of public policy is to be submitted in their own proper persons only, and opposite the signature of each signer his residence address shall be written or printed, which residence address shall include the street address or rural route number of the signer, as the case may be, as well as the signer's county, and city, village or town, and state; provided that the county or city, village or town, and state of residence of such electors may be printed on the petition forms where all of the such electors signing the petition reside in the same county or city, village or town, and state. Standard abbreviations may be used in writing the residence address, including street number, if any. No signature shall be valid or be counted in considering the validity or sufficiency of such petition unless the requirements of this Section are complied with.

At the bottom of each sheet of such petition shall be added a statement, signed by a registered voter, who has been a registered voter at all times he or she circulated the petition, of the political subdivision or district or precinct or combination of precincts in which the question of public policy is to be submitted, stating the street address or rural route number of the voter, as the case may be, as well as the voter's county, and city, village or town, and state certifying that the signatures on that sheet of the petition were signed in his presence and are genuine, and that to the best of his knowledge and belief the persons so signing were at the time of signing the petition registered voters of the political subdivision or district or precinct or combination of precincts in which the question of public policy is to be submitted and that their respective residences are correctly stated therein. Such statement shall be sworn to before some officer authorized to administer oaths in this State.

Such sheets, before being filed with the proper office or board shall be bound securely and numbered consecutively. The sheets shall not be fastened by pasting them together end to end, so as to form a continuous strip or roll. All petition sheets which are filed with the proper local election officials, election authorities or the State Board of Elections shall be the original sheets which have been signed by the voters and by the circulator, and not photocopies or duplicates of such sheets. A petition, when presented or filed, shall not be withdrawn, altered, or added to, and no signature shall be revoked except by revocation in writing presented or filed with the board or officer with whom the petition is required to be presented or filed, and before the presentment or filing of such petition, except as may otherwise be provided in another statute which authorize the public question. Whoever forges any name of a signer upon any petition shall be deemed guilty of a forgery, and on conviction thereof, shall be punished accordingly.

In addition to the foregoing requirements, a petition proposing an amendment to Article IV of the Constitution pursuant to Section 3 of Article XIV of the Constitution or a petition proposing a question of public policy to be submitted to the voters of the entire State shall be in conformity with the requirements of Section 28-9 of this Article.

If multiple sets of petitions for submission of the same public questions are filed, the State Board of Elections, appropriate election authority or local election official where the petitions are filed shall within 2 business days notify the proponent of his or her multiple petition filings and that proponent has 3 business days after receipt of the notice to notify the State Board of Elections, appropriate election authority or local election official that he or she may cancel prior sets of petitions. If the proponent notifies the State Board of Elections, appropriate election authority or local election official, the last set of petitions filed shall be the only petitions to be considered valid by the State Board of Elections, appropriate election authority or local election official. If the proponent fails to notify the State Board of Elections, appropriate election authority or local election official then only the first set of petitions filed shall be valid and all subsequent petitions shall be void. (Source: P.A. 91-57, eff. 6-30-99.)

Sec. 28-4.

The provisions of Sections 10-8 through 10-10.1 relating to objections to nominating petitions, hearings on objections, and judicial review, shall apply to and govern, insofar as may be practicable, objections to petitions for the submission of questions of public policy required to be filed with local election officials and election authorities, and to petitions for proposed Constitutional amendments and statewide advisory public questions required to be filed with the State Board of Elections, except that objections to petitions for the submission of proposed Constitutional amendments and statewide advisory public questions may be filed within 42 business days after the petition is filed.

The electoral board to hear and pass on objections shall be the electoral board specified in Section 10-9 to have jurisdiction over objections to the nominating petitions of candidates for offices of the political subdivision in which the question of public policy is proposed to be submitted to the electors. The electoral board to hear and pass upon objections to petitions for proposed Constitutional amendments or statewide advisory public questions shall be the State Board of Elections.

Objections to petitions for the submission of public questions which are required by law to be filed with the circuit court shall be presented to and heard by the court with which such petitions are filed. In such cases, unless otherwise provided in the statute authorizing the public question, the court shall (1) set a hearing on the petition, (2) cause notice of such hearing to be published, as soon as possible after the filing of the petition but not later than 14 days after such filing and not less than 5 days before the hearing, in a newspaper of general circulation published in the political subdivision to which the public question relates and if there is no such newspaper, then in one newspaper published in the county and having a general circulation in the political subdivision, (3) conduct such hearing and entertain all objections as may be properly presented on or before such hearing date in the manner as provided in Article 10 for the conduct of proceedings before electoral boards, insofar as practicable, (4) conduct further hearings as necessary to a decision on the objections properly raised, and (5) enter a final order not later than 7 days after the initial hearing.

Where a statute authorizing a public question specifies judicial procedures for the determination of the validity of such petition, or for the determination by the court as to any findings required prior to ordering the proposition submitted to referendum, the procedures specified in that statute shall govern. (Source: P.A. 83-999.)

Sec. 28-5.

Not less than 61 days before a regularly scheduled election, each local election official shall certify the public questions to be submitted to the voters of or within his political subdivision at that election which have been initiated by petitions filed in his office or by action of the governing board of his political subdivision.

Not less than 61 days before a regularly scheduled election, each circuit court clerk shall certify the public questions to be submitted to the voters of a political subdivision at that election which have been ordered to be so submitted by the circuit court pursuant to law. Not less than 30 days before the date set by the circuit court for the conduct of an emergency referendum pursuant to Section 2A-1.4, the circuit court clerk shall certify the public question as herein required.

Local election officials and circuit court clerks shall make their certifications, as required by this Section, to each election authority having jurisdiction over any of the territory of the respective political subdivision in which the public question is to be submitted to referendum.

Not less than 61 days before the next regular election, the county clerk shall certify the public questions to be submitted to the voters of the entire county at that election, which have been initiated by petitions filed in his office or by action of the county board, to the board of election commissioners, if any, in his county.

Not less than 67 days before the general election, the State Board of Elections shall certify any questions proposing an amendment to Article IV of the Constitution pursuant to Section 3, Article XIV of the Constitution and any advisory public questions to be submitted to the voters of the entire State, which have been initiated by petitions received or filed at its office, to the respective county clerks. Not less than 61 days before the general election, the county clerk shall certify such questions to the board of election commissioners, if any, in his county.

The certifications shall include the form of the public question to be placed on the ballot, the date on which the public question was initiated by either the filing of a petition or the adoption of a resolution or ordinance by a governing body, as the case may be, and a certified copy of any court order or political subdivision resolution or ordinance requiring the submission of the public question. Certifications of propositions for annexation to, disconnection from, or formation of political subdivisions or for other purposes shall include a description of the territory in which the proposition is required to be submitted, whenever such territory is not coterminous with an existing political subdivision.

The certification of a public question described in subsection (b) of Section 28-6 shall include the precincts included in the territory concerning which the public question is to be submitted, as well as a common description of such territory, in plain and nonlegal language, and specify the election at which the question is to be submitted. The description of the territory shall be prepared by the local election official as set forth in the resolution or ordinance initiating the public question.

Whenever a local election official, an election authority, or the State Board of Elections is in receipt of an initiating petition, or a certification for the submission of a public question at an election at which the public question may not be placed on the ballot or submitted because of the limitations of Section 28-1, such officer or board shall give notice of such prohibition, by registered mail, as follows:

(a) in the case of a petition, to any person designated on a certificate attached thereto as the proponent or as the proponents' attorney for purposes of notice of objections;

(b) in the case of a certificate from a local election authority, to such local election authority, who shall thereupon give notice as provided in subparagraph (a), or notify the governing board which adopted the initiating resolution or ordinance;

(c) in the case of a certification from a circuit court clerk of a court order, to such court, which shall thereupon give notice as provided in subparagraph (a) and shall modify its order in accordance with the provisions of this Act.

If the petition, resolution or ordinance initiating such prohibited public question did not specify a particular election for its submission, the officer or board responsible for certifying the question to the election authorities shall certify or recertify the question, in the manner required herein, for submission on the ballot at the next regular election no more than one year subsequent to the filing of the initiating petition or the adoption of the initiating resolution or ordinance and at which the public question may be submitted, and the appropriate election authorities shall submit the question at such election, unless the public question is ordered submitted as an emergency referendum pursuant to Section 2A-1.4 or is withdrawn as may be provided by law. (Source: P.A. 86-875.)

Sec. 28-6.

(a) On a written petition signed by 10% of the registered voters of any municipality, township, county or school district it shall be the duty of the proper election officers to submit any question of public policy so petitioned for, to the electors of such political subdivision at any regular election named in the petition at which an election is scheduled to be held throughout such political subdivision under Article 2A. Such petitions shall be filed with the local election official of the political subdivision or election authority, as the case may be. Where such a question is to be submitted to the voters of a municipality which has adopted Article 6, or a township or school district located entirely within the jurisdiction of a municipal board of election commissioners, such petitions shall be filed with the board of election commissioners having jurisdiction over the political subdivision.

(b) In a municipality with more than 1,000,000 inhabitants, when a question of public policy exclusively concerning a contiguous territory included entirely within but not coextensive with the municipality is initiated by resolution or ordinance of the corporate authorities of the municipality, or by a petition which may be signed by registered voters who reside in any part of any precinct all or part of which includes all or part of the territory and who equal in number 10% of the total number of registered voters of the precinct or precincts the registered voters of which are eligible to sign the petition, it shall be the duty of the election authority having jurisdiction over such municipality to submit such question to the electors throughout each precinct all or part of which includes all or part of the territory at the regular election specified in the resolution, ordinance or petition initiating the public question. A petition initiating a public question described in this subsection shall be filed with the election authority having jurisdiction over the municipality. A resolution, ordinance or petition initiating a public question described in this subsection shall specify the election at which the question is to be submitted.

(c) Local questions of public policy authorized by this Section and statewide questions of public policy authorized by Section 28-9 shall be advisory public questions, and no legal effects shall result from the adoption or rejection of such propositions.

(d) This Section does not apply to a petition filed pursuant to Article IX of the Liquor Control Act of 1934. (Source: P.A. 84-1467.)

Sec. 28-7.

In any case in which Article VII or paragraph (a) of Section 5 of the Transition Schedule of the Constitution authorizes any action to be taken by or with respect to any unit of local government, as defined in Section 1 of Article VII of the Constitution, by or subject to approval by referendum, any such public question shall be initiated in accordance with this Section.

Any such public question may be initiated by the governing body of the unit of local government by resolution or by the filing with the clerk or secretary of the governmental unit of a petition signed by a number of qualified electors equal to or greater than 10% of the number of registered voters in the governmental unit, requesting the submission of the proposal for such action to the voters of the governmental unit at a regular election.

If the action to be taken requires a referendum involving 2 or more units of local government, the proposal shall be submitted to the voters of such governmental units by the election authorities with jurisdiction over the territory of the governmental units. Such multi-unit proposals may be initiated by appropriate resolutions by the respective governing bodies or by petitions of the voters of the several governmental units filed with the respective clerks or secretaries.

This Section is intended to provide a method of submission to referendum in all cases of proposals for actions which are authorized by Article VII of the Constitution by or subject to approval by referendum and supersedes any conflicting statutory provisions except those contained in the "County Executive Act".

Referenda provided for in this Section may not be held more than once in any 23-month period on the same proposition, provided that in any municipality a referendum to elect not to be a home rule unit may be held only once within any 47-month period. (Source: P.A. 82-750.)

Sec. 28-8.

If a referendum to be held in accordance with Section 28-7 of this Act involves the question of whether a unit of local government shall become a home rule unit or shall cease to be a home rule unit, the clerk of that unit of local government shall, at least 20 days prior to the referendum, file with the Secretary of State a certified statement indicating when the referendum will be held. Within 30 days after the referendum such clerk shall file with the Secretary of State a certified statement showing the results of the referendum and the resulting status of the unit of local government as a home rule unit or a non-home rule unit. The Secretary of State shall maintain such certified statements in his office as a public record. (Source: P.A. 80-1469.)

Sec. 28-8.1. Proposition publication.

(a) Whenever any proposition required by law to be voted upon before its adoption, other than a constitutional amendment, is submitted to the people, it is the duty of the Secretary of State to prepare a statement setting forth in detail the Section or Sections of the law sought to be amended by the vote, together with statements and suggestions as may be necessary for a proper understanding of the proposition. The statements and suggestions shall be submitted to the Attorney General for his approval.

(b) It shall be the duty of the Secretary of State, after the amendments and suggestions shall have been approved by the Attorney General as provided in subsection (a), to certify to each county clerk, under seal, the statements and suggestions.

(c) It is hereby made the duty of the county clerk to have the statements and suggestions published and posted at the same time, in the same manner and at the same places that the sample ballots and instructions to voters are required by law to be posted. (Source: P.A. 87-1052.)

Sec. 28-9.

Petitions for proposed amendments to Article IV of the Constitution pursuant to Section 3, Article XIV of the Constitution shall be signed by a number of electors equal in number to at least 8% of the total votes cast for candidates for Governor in the preceding gubernatorial election. Such petition shall have been signed by the petitioning electors not more than 24 months preceding the general election at which the proposed amendment is to be submitted and shall be filed with the Secretary of State at least 6 months before that general election.

Upon receipt of a petition for a proposed Constitutional amendment, the Secretary of State shall, as soon as is practicable, but no later than the close of the next business day, deliver such petition to the State Board of Elections.

Petitions for advisory questions of public policy to be submitted to the voters of the entire State shall be signed by at least 10% of the registered voters in the State. Such petition shall have been signed by said petitioners not more than 24 months preceding the date of the general election at which the question is to be submitted and shall be filed with the State Board of Elections at least 6 months before that general election.

The proponents of the proposed Constitutional amendment or statewide advisory public question shall file the original petition in bound election jurisdiction sections. Each section shall be composed of consecutively numbered petition sheets containing only the signatures of registered voters of a single election jurisdiction and, at the top of each petition sheet, the name of the election jurisdiction shall be typed or printed in block letters; provided that, if the name of the election jurisdiction is not so printed, the election jurisdiction of the circulator of that petition sheet shall be controlling with respect to the signatures on that sheet. Any petition sheets not consecutively numbered or which contain duplicate page numbers already used on other sheets, or are photocopies or duplicates of the original sheets, shall not be considered part of the petition for the purpose of the random sampling verification and shall not be counted toward the minimum number of signatures required to qualify the proposed constitutional amendment or statewide advisory public question for the ballot.

Within 7 business days following the last day for filing the original petition, the proponents shall also file copies of the sectioned election jurisdiction petition sheets with each proper election authority and obtain a receipt therefor.

For purposes of this Act, the following terms shall be defined and construed as follows:

1. "Board" means the State Board of Elections.
2. "Election Authority" means a county clerk or city or county board of election commissioners.

3. "Election Jurisdiction" means (a) an entire county, in the case of a county in which no city board of election commissioners is located or which is under the jurisdiction of a county board of election commissioners; (b) the territorial jurisdiction of a city board of election commissioners; and (c) the territory in a county outside of the jurisdiction of a city board of election commissioners. In each instance election jurisdiction shall be determined according to which election authority maintains the permanent registration records of qualified electors.

4. "Proponents" means any person, association, committee, organization or other group, or their designated representatives, who advocate and cause the circulation and filing of petitions for a statewide advisory question of public policy or a proposed constitutional amendment for submission at a general election and who has registered with the Board as provided in this Act.

5. "Opponents" means any person, association, committee, organization or other group, or their designated representatives, who oppose a statewide advisory question of public policy or a proposed constitutional amendment for submission at a general election and who have registered with the Board as provided in this Act. (Source: P.A. 87-1052.)

Sec. 28-10.

Upon receipt of an original petition for a proposed Constitutional amendment or statewide advisory public question, the designated Board staff shall examine the petition sheets in each election jurisdiction section for conformity with the single jurisdiction signature requirement prescribed in Section 28-9. The Board staff shall determine from the name of the election jurisdiction printed at the top of the petition sheet or from the election jurisdiction of the circulator of that petition sheet, as the case may be, whether any signatures on that sheet are not in conformity. If any signatures are determined to be nonconforming, the Board staff shall prepare, for each election jurisdiction section, a list by page and line number of purported nonconforming signatures and shall immediately transmit such lists to the Board Chairman and copies of such lists to the principal proponent of the proposed Constitutional amendment or statewide advisory public question, or the proponent's attorney, whichever is designated on the certificate attached to the petition, as provided in Section 10-8 of this Code.

On the 10th business day following the last day for petition filing, the Board shall conduct a hearing at which the proponents may present arguments and evidence as to the conformity of any purported nonconforming signatures. At the conclusion of the hearing the Board shall make a final determination with respect to each purported nonconforming signature. Any signatures on petition sheets in an election jurisdiction section finally determined to be nonconforming shall not be considered part of the petition for the purpose of the random sample verification and shall not be counted toward the minimum number of signatures required to qualify the proposed Constitutional amendment or statewide advisory public question for the ballot. (Source: P.A. 83-999.)

Sec. 28-11.

The Board shall design a standard and scientific random sampling method for the verification of petition signatures and shall conduct a public test to prove the validity of its sampling method. Notice of the time and place for such test shall be given at least 10 days before the date on which such test is to be conducted and in the manner prescribed for notice of regular Board meetings.

Within 14 business days following the last day for the filing of the original petition as prescribed in Section 28-9, the Board shall apply its proven random sampling method to the petition sheets in each election jurisdiction section for the purpose of selecting and identifying the petition signatures to be included in the sample signature verification for the respective jurisdictions and shall prepare and transmit to each proper election authority a list by page and line number of the signatures from its election jurisdiction selected for verification.

For each election jurisdiction, the sample verification shall include an examination of either (a) 10% of the signatures if 5,010 or more signatures are involved; or (b) 500 signatures if more than 500 but less than 5,010 signatures are involved; or (c) all signatures if 500 or less signatures are involved.

Each election authority with whom jurisdictional copies of petition sheets were filed shall use the proven random sampling method designed and furnished by the Board for the verification of signatures shown on the list supplied by the Board and in accordance with the following criteria for determination of petition signature validity:

1. Determine if the person who signed the petition is a registered voter in that election jurisdiction or was a registered voter therein on the date the petition was signed;

2. Determine if the signature of the person who signed the petition reasonably compares with the signature shown on that person's registration record card.

Within 14 business days following receipt from the Board of the list of signatures for verification, each election authority shall transmit a properly dated certificate to the Board which shall indicate; (a) the page and line number of petition signatures examined, (b) the validity or invalidity of such signatures, and (c) the reasons for invalidity, based on the criteria heretofore prescribed. The Board shall prepare and adopt a standard form of certificate for use by the election authorities which shall be transmitted with the list of signatures for verification.

Upon written request of the election authority that, due to the volume of signatures in the sample for its jurisdiction, additional time is needed to properly perform the signature verification, the Board may grant the election authority additional days to complete the verification and transmit the certificate of results. These certificates of random sample verification results shall be available for public inspection within 24 hours after receipt by the State Board of Elections. (Source: P.A. 83-999.)

Sec. 28-12.

Upon receipt of the certificates of the election authorities showing the results of the sample signature verification, the Board shall:

1. Based on the sample, calculate the ratio of invalid or valid signatures in each election jurisdiction.

2. Apply the ratio of invalid to valid signatures in an election jurisdiction sample to the total number of petition signatures submitted from that election jurisdiction.

3. Compute the degree of multiple signature contamination in each election jurisdiction sample.

4. Adjust for multiple signature contamination and the invalid signatures, project the total number of valid petition signatures submitted from each election jurisdiction.

5. Aggregate the total number of projected valid signatures from each election jurisdiction and project the total number of valid signatures on the petition statewide.

If such statewide projection establishes a total number of valid petition signatures not greater than 95.0% of the minimum number of signatures required to qualify the proposed Constitutional amendment or statewide advisory public question for the ballot, the petition shall be presumed invalid; provided that, prior to the last day for ballot certification to the general election, the Board shall conduct a hearing for the purpose of allowing the proponents to present competent evidence or an additional sample to rebut the presumption of invalidity. At the conclusion of such hearing, the Board shall issue a final order declaring the petition to be valid or invalid and shall, in accordance with its order, certify or not certify the proposition for the ballot.

If such statewide projection establishes a total number of valid petition signatures greater than 95.0% of the minimum number of signatures required to qualify the proposed Constitutional amendment or statewide advisory public question for the ballot, the results of the sample shall be considered inconclusive and, if no specific objections to the petition are filed pursuant to Section 10-8 of this Code, the Board shall issue a final order declaring the petition to be valid and shall certify the proposition for the ballot.

In either event, the Board shall append to its final order the detailed results of the sample from each election jurisdiction which shall include: a) specific page and line numbers of signatures actually verified or determined to be invalid by the respective election authorities, and (b) the calculations and projections performed by the Board for each election jurisdiction. (Source: P.A. 82-750.)

Sec. 28-13.

Each political party and civic organization as well as the registered proponents and opponents of a proposed Constitutional amendment or statewide advisory public question shall be entitled to one watcher in the office of the election authority to observe the conduct of the sample signature verification. However, in those election jurisdictions where a 10% sample is required, the proponents and opponents may appoint no more than 5 assistant watchers in addition to the 1 principal watcher permitted herein.

Within 7 days following the last day for filing of the original petition, the proponents and opponents shall certify in writing to the Board that they publicly support or oppose the proposed Constitutional amendment or statewide advisory public question. The proponents and opponents of such questions shall register the name and address of its group and the name and address of its chairman and designated agent for acceptance of service of notices with the Board. Thereupon, the Board shall prepare a list of the registered proponents and opponents and shall adopt a standard proponents' and opponents' watcher credential form. A copy of such list and sufficient copies of such credentials shall be transmitted with the list for the sample signature verification to the appropriate election authorities. Those election authorities shall issue credentials to the permissible number of watchers for each proponent and opponent group; provided, however, that a prospective watcher shall first present to the election authority a letter of authorization signed by the chairman of the proponent or opponent group he or she represents.

Political party and qualified civic organization watcher credentials shall be substantially in the form and shall be authorized in the manner prescribed in Section 7-34 of this Code.

The rights and limitations of poll watchers as prescribed by Section 7-34 of this Code, insofar as they may be made applicable, shall be applicable to watchers at the conduct of the sample signature verification.

The principal watcher for the proponents and opponents may make signed written objections to the Board relating to procedures observed during the conduct of the sample signature verification which could materially affect the results of the sample. Such written objections shall be presented to the election authority and a copy mailed to the Board and shall be attached to the certificate of sample results transmitted by the election authority to the Board. (Source: P.A. 82-750.)

Indiana

After Ohio voters approved a constitutional amendment establishing I&R in November 1912, the Ohio leaders turned their attention to the state next door. Rev. Herbert S. Bigelow and other leaders spoke throughout the state and helped organize a Citizens' League to work for I&R. Yet a native Indiana reformer gave the situation a gloomy assessment in 1914: "Indiana, politically, is one of the most backward of our States. It must continue to be, under the ironclad restrictions of the present constitution. The state has remained untouched by the progressive movement in the states around it." The only victory for I&R advocates came in 1913, when the legislature approved a Public Utilities Act that included a provision allowing municipal initiatives to mandate municipal purchase and operation of utilities (Public Service Commission Act of 1913, Sect. 8-1-2-99/100 [54-612, 613]).

State Senator John Bushemi of Gary waged a long, lonely battle in the late 1970s and 1980s to pass a statewide I&R amendment, but he received little support from other legislators and constituents.

Indiana Constitution

The state does not have the statewide initiative process and so therefore the following provisions discuss the procedures used by the state legislature to place constitutional amendments on the ballot.

Article 16.

Section 1.

(a) An amendment to this Constitution may be proposed in either branch of the General Assembly. If the amendment is agreed to by a majority of the members elected to each of the two houses, the proposed amendment shall, with the yeas and nays thereon, be entered on their journals, and referred to the General Assembly to be chosen at the next general election.

(b) If, in the General Assembly so next chosen, the proposed amendment is agreed to by a majority of all the members elected to each House, then the General Assembly shall submit the amendment to the electors of the State at the next general election.

(c) If a majority of the electors voting on the amendment ratify the amendment, the amendment becomes a part of this Constitution.

Section 2.

If two or more amendments shall be submitted at the same time, they shall be submitted in such manner that the electors shall vote for or against each of such amendments separately.

Iowa

In 1904, I&R advocates began making headway with an endorsement from the Prohibitionist Party, followed in 1906 by the support of the Socialists and Populists and, in 1910, that of the Democrats. An amendment by Republican State Representative David E. Kulp calling for statewide I&R reached the floor of the lower house of the legislature in 1911, but it was defeated 58 to 42.

In the election campaign of 1912, both the Republican Party and its offspring, the Progressive Party, endorsed I&R. In 1913 the legislature voted overwhelmingly in favor of I&R: approval was nearly unanimous in the senate, and there were only 11 negative votes in the house. But ratification by the voters had to wait because the state constitution specified that any amendments had to be cleared by the legislature twice, in two successive sessions with an election between them. In 1915 the legislature voted against I&R, and the proposed amendment never reached the voters.

Iowa Constitution

The state does not have the statewide initiative process and so therefore the following provisions discuss the procedures used by the state legislature to place constitutional amendments on the ballot.

Article X

Amendments

Sec 1. How proposed — submission.

Any amendment or amendments to this constitution may be proposed in either house of the general assembly; and if the same shall be agreed to by a majority of the members elected to each of the two houses, such proposed amendment shall be entered on their journals, with the yeas and nays taken thereon, and referred to the legislature to be chosen at the next general election, and shall be published, as provided by law, for three months previous to the time of making such choice; and if, in the general assembly so next chosen as aforesaid, such proposed amendment or amendments shall be agreed to, by a majority of all the members elected to each house, then it shall be the duty of the general assembly to submit such proposed amendment or amendments to the people, in such manner, and at such time as the general assembly shall provide; and if the people shall approve and ratify such amendment or amendments, by a majority of the electors qualified to vote for members of the general assembly, voting thereon, such amendment or amendments shall become a part of the constitution of this state.

Sec 2. More than one amendment.

If two or more amendments shall be submitted at the same time, they shall be submitted in such manner that the electors shall vote for or against each of such amendments separately.

Sec 3. Constitutional convention.

At the general election to be held in the year one thousand nine hundred and seventy, and in each tenth year thereafter, and also at such times as the general assembly may, by law, provide, the question, "Shall there be a convention to revise the constitution, and propose amendment or amendments to same?" shall be decided by the electors qualified to vote for members of the general assembly; and in case a majority of the electors so qualified, voting at such election, for and against such proposition, shall decide in favor of a convention for such purpose, the general assembly, at its next session, shall provide by law for the election of delegates to such convention, and for submitting the results of said convention to the people, in such manner and at such time as the general assembly shall provide; and if the people shall approve and ratify such amendment or amendments, by a majority of the electors qualified to vote for members of the general assembly, voting thereon, such amendment or amendments shall become a part of the constitution of this state. If two or more amendments shall be submitted at the same time, they shall be submitted in such a manner that electors may vote for or against each such amendment separately.

Kansas

The movement to establish the initiative process in Kansas was well under way by 1900, when the Democratic and Populist parties in the state endorsed the idea. In 1909, initiative supporters won approval of their amendment in the state's lower house but were defeated in the state senate.

In 1911 Governor W. R. Stubbs called for the enactment of an I&R amendment, and by 1913 all the state's major parties had endorsed it, including Kansas' first state conference of women voters. The nationally known progressive leader William Allen White of Emporia was called Kansas' "foremost champion of Direct Legislation" in a contemporary periodical. Despite all this support, I&R advocates never succeeded in passing a statewide I&R amendment. However, they did push through the legislature a bill establishing I&R in all Kansas cities in 1909, and a statewide recall amendment in 1914.

Kansas Constitution

The state does not have the statewide initiative process and so therefore the following provisions discuss the procedures used by the state legislature to place constitutional amendments on the ballot.

Article 14 — Constitutional Amendment and Revision

§ 1: Proposals by legislature; approval by electors.

Propositions for the amendment of this constitution may be made by concurrent resolution originating in either house of the legislature, and if two-thirds of all the members elected (or appointed) and qualified of each house shall approve such resolution, the secretary of state shall cause such resolution to be published in the manner provided by law. At the next election for representatives or a special election called by con current resolution of the legislature for the purpose of submitting constitutional propositions, such proposition to amend the constitution shall be submitted, both by title and by the amendment as a whole, to the electors for their approval or rejection. The title by which a proposition is submitted shall be specified in the concurrent resolution making the proposition and shall be a brief non-technical statement expressing the intent or purpose of the proposition and the effect of a vote for and a vote against the proposition. If a majority of the electors voting on any such amendment shall vote for the amendment, the same shall become a part of the constitution. When more than one amendment shall be submitted at the same election, such amendments shall be so submitted as to enable the electors to vote on each amendment separately. One amendment of the constitution may revise any entire article, except the article on general provisions, and in revising any article, the article may be renumbered and all o r parts of other articles may be amended, or amended and transferred to the article being revised. Not more than five amendments shall be submitted at the same election.

§ 2: Constitutional conventions; approval by electors.

The legislature, by the affirmative vote of two-thirds of all the members elected to each house, may submit the question "Shall there be a convention to amend or revise t he constitution of the state of Kansas?" or the question "Shall there be a convention limited to revision of article(s) _____ of the constitution of the state of Kansas?" to the electors at the next election for representatives, and the concurrent resolution providing for such question shall specify in such blank appropriate words and figures to identify the article or articles to be considered by the convention. If a majority of all electors voting on the question shall vote in the affirmative, delegates to such convention shall be elected at the next election for representatives thereafter, unless the legislature shall have provided by law for the election of such delegates at a special election. The electors of each representative district as organized at the time of such election of delegates shall elect as many delegates to the convention as there are representatives from such district. Such delegates shall have the same qualifications as provided by the constitution for members of the legislature and members of the legislature and candidates for membership in the legislature shall be eligible for election as delegates to the convention. The delegates so elected shall convene at the state capital on the first Tuesday in May next following such election or at an earlier date if provided by law.

The convention shall have power to choose its own officers, appoint and remove its employees and fix their compensation, determine its rules, judge the qualifications of its members, and carry on the business of the convention in an orderly manner. Each delegate shall receive such compensation as provided by law. A vacancy in the office of any delegate shall be filled as provided by law.

The convention shall have power to amend or revise all or that part of the constitution indicated by the question voted upon to call the convention, subject to ratification by the electors. No proposed constitution, or amendment or revision of an existing constitution, shall be submitted by the convention to the electors unless it has been available to the delegates in final form at least three days on which the convention is in session, prior to final passage, and receives the assent of a majority of all the delegates. The yeas and nays upon final passage of any proposal, and upon any question upon request of one-tenth of the delegates present, shall be entered in the journal of the convention.

Proposals of the convention shall be submitted to the electors at the first general or special statewide election occurring not less than two months after final action thereon by the convention, and shall take effect in accordance with the provisions thereof in such form and with such notice as is directed by the convention upon receiving the approval of a majority of the qualified electors voting thereon.

Kentucky

Populist State Senator J. H. McConnell of Otter Pond, Kentucky, successfully pushed a statewide I&R bill through the state senate in 1900, but the measure failed in the house. Kentucky initiative advocates had to settle for a state law, passed in 1910, establishing the initiative process in most of the state's cities.

By the 1970s this municipal I&R provision (Kentucky Revised Statutes, Ch. 89) applied to all of the state's 27 largest cities except Louisville. In 1980, however, the legislature passed a new municipal government law which abolished the provision.

Kentucky Constitution

The state does not have the statewide initiative process and so therefore the following provisions discuss the procedures used by the state legislature to place constitutional amendments on the ballot.

Section 256. Amendments to Constitution — How proposed and voted upon.

Amendments to this Constitution may be proposed in either House of the General Assembly at a regular session, and if such amendment or amendments shall be agreed to by three-fifths of all the members elected to each House, such proposed amendment or amendments, with the yeas and nays of the members of each House taken thereon, shall be entered in full in their respective journals. Then such proposed amendment or amendments shall be submitted to the voters of the State for their ratification or rejection at the next general election for members of the House of Representatives, the vote to be taken thereon in such manner as the General Assembly may provide, and to be certified by the officers of election to the Secretary of State in such manner as shall be provided by law, which vote shall be compared and certified by the same board authorized by law to compare the polls and give certificates of election to officers for the State at large. If it shall appear that a majority of the votes cast for and against an amendment at said election was for the amendment, then the same shall become a part of the Constitution of this Commonwealth, and shall be so proclaimed by the Governor, and published in such manner as the General Assembly may direct. Said amendments shall not be submitted at an election which occurs less than ninety days from the final passage of such proposed amendment or amendments. Not more than four amendments shall be voted upon at any one time. If two or more amendments shall be submitted at the same time, they shall be submitted in such manner that the electors shall vote for or against each of such amendments separately, but an amendment may relate to a single subject or to related subject matters and may amend or modify as many articles and as many sections of the Constitution as may be necessary and appropriate in order to accomplish the objectives of the amendment. The approval of the Governor shall not be necessary to any bill, order, resolution or vote of the General Assembly, proposing an amendment or amendments to this Constitution.

Section 257. Publication of proposed amendments.

Before an amendment shall be submitted to a vote, the Secretary of State shall cause such proposed amendment, and the time that the same is to be voted upon, to be published at least ninety days before the vote is to be taken thereon in such manner as may be prescribed by law.

Section 258. Constitutional Convention — How proposed, voted upon, and called.

When a majority of all the members elected to each House of the General Assembly shall concur, by a yea and nay vote, to be entered upon their respective journals, in enacting a law to take the sense of the people of the State as to the necessity and expediency of calling a Convention for the purpose of revising or amending this Constitution, and such amendments as may have been made to the same, such law shall be spread upon their respective journals. If the next General Assembly shall, in like manner, concur in such law, it shall provide for having a poll opened in each voting precinct in this state by the officers provided by law for holding general elections at the next ensuing regular election to be held for State officers or members of the House of Representatives, which does not occur within ninety days from the final passage of such law, at which time and places the votes of the qualified voters shall be taken for and against calling the Convention, in the same manner provided by law for taking votes in other State elections. The vote for and against said proposition shall be certified to the Secretary of State by the same officers and in the same manner as in State elections. If it shall appear that a majority voting on the proposition was for calling a Convention, and if the total number of votes cast for the calling of the Convention is equal to one-fourth of the number of qualified voters who voted at the last preceding general election in this State, the Secretary of State shall certify the same to the General Assembly at its next regular session, at which session a law shall be enacted calling a Convention to readopt, revise or amend this Constitution, and such amendments as may have been made thereto.

Louisiana

Progressive reformers, who were never a major force in Louisiana politics, failed to pass a statewide initiative and referendum amendment, but they did succeed in passing laws providing for municipal I&R (1912) and for recall of statewide elected officers (1914).

In the mid-1970s backers of a rent control initiative collected the required 10,000 signatures to put it on the New Orleans ballot, only to be barred by a ruling of the state supreme court that initiative charter amendments must be related to matters in the existing city charter. In April 1981 voters passed an initiative to restrict the city council's power to enact flat-rate taxes on real property and motor vehicles.

The biggest New Orleans initiative battle in recent years, however, was over the city council's power to regulate electric utility rates. The council had this power until 1982, when voters approved the transfer of the authority to the state public service commission. Little more than a year later, a utility company, New Orleans Public Service, Inc. (NOPSI), asked for a huge rate increase to finance the construction of the Grand Gulf nuclear power plant.

Mayor Ernest Morial and Council Members Joseph Giarusso and James Singleton sponsored an initiative in 1983 to return the power to regulate utility rates to the city council. Utility company executives and stockholders raised $800,000 for a campaign to defeat it, an unprecedented amount for a New Orleans election campaign. Backers spent only $35,000 and were narrowly defeated on November 8, 1983: the vote was 78,746 (49.8 percent) in favor and 79,434 against.

The sponsors came back with another initiative a year and a half later. This time the utilities spent $2 million on their "Vote No" advertising blitz, but it did not sway the voters. On May 4, 1985, New Orleans voted by a two to one margin to return control of utility rates to the city.

In 1999, Governor Mike Foster, working with the Initiative & Referendum Institute, supported efforts to add the initiative and referendum process to the state constitution. Though his commitment was strong, the state legislature rebuffed his efforts.

Louisiana Constitution

The state does not have the statewide initiative process and so therefore the following provisions discuss the procedures used by the state legislature to place constitutional amendments on the ballot.

Article XIII

§1. Amendments

(A) Procedure. An amendment to this constitution may be proposed by joint resolution at any regular session of the legislature, but the resolution shall be prefiled, at least ten days before the beginning of the session, in accordance with the rules of the house in which introduced. An amendment to this constitution may be proposed at any extraordinary session of the legislature if it is within the objects of the call of the session and is introduced in the first five calendar days thereof. If two-thirds of the elected members of each house concur in the resolution, pursuant to all of the procedures and formalities required for passage of a bill except submission to the governor, the secretary of state shall have the proposed amendment published once in the official journal of each parish within not less than thirty nor more than sixty days preceding the election at which the proposed amendment is to be submitted to the electors. Each joint resolution shall specify the statewide election at which the proposed amendment shall be submitted. Special elections for submitting proposed amendments may be authorized by law.

(B) Form of Proposal. A proposed amendment shall have a title containing a brief summary of the changes proposed; shall be confined to one object; and shall set forth the entire article, or the sections or other subdivisions thereof, as proposed to be revised or only the article, sections, or other subdivisions proposed to be added. However, the legislature may propose, as one amendment, a revision of an entire article of this constitution which may contain multiple objects or changes. A section or other subdivision may be repealed by reference. When more than one amendment is submitted at the same election, each shall be submitted so as to enable the electors to vote on them separately.

(C) Ratification. If a majority of the electors voting on the proposed amendment approve it, the governor shall proclaim its adoption, and it shall become part of this constitution, effective twenty days after the proclamation, unless the amendment provides otherwise. A proposed amendment directly affecting not more than five parishes or areas within not more than five parishes shall become part of this constitution only when approved by a majority of the electors voting thereon in the state and also a majority of the electors voting thereon in each affected parish. However, a proposed amendment directly affecting not more than five municipalities, and only such municipalities, shall become part of this constitution only when approved by a majority of the electors voting thereon in the state and also a majority of the electors voting thereon in each such municipality.

Maine

In 1908, Maine became the first state east of the Mississippi to adopt a constitutional provision for statewide initiative and referendum. It could not have happened without the work of the state's foremost I&R advocate, Roland T. Patten of Skowhegan.

In the early 1980s, Patten, editor of the Skowhegan Somerset Reporter, was an advocate of municipal ownership of public utilities. "About 1894," he wrote, he "heard something of the idea [of I&R] as made use of in Switzerland" and realized that I&R could be used in the cause of municipal ownership.

A member of the Republican Party, he first pushed for adoption of an I&R resolution at the Republican convention in his county. Failing there, he became a leader of the state's Socialist Party and lobbied all four of the state's major parties—Republican, Democratic, Socialist, and Prohibitionist—to endorse I&R. In 1902 Maine Democrats adopted Patten's I&R resolution verbatim, and in 1903 Democratic State Representative Cyrus W. Davis of Waterville introduced the first statewide I&R bill.

Meanwhile, Patten had founded the Initiative and Referendum League of Maine and had allied with the state Grange and the state Federation of Labor. In 1905 they nearly succeeded: their I&R bill got a tie vote in the state senate. The following year all four parties endorsed I&R, and Davis made it a central issue in his Democratic gubernatorial campaign.

Davis lost to Republican William T. Cobb, who was lukewarm on the issue, but the I&R League succeeded in electing more I&R supporters to the legislature. Despite opposition from banks, timberland owners, and railroads, the legislature passed an initiative bill without a single dissent. However, it was not exactly what the I&R League wanted: it provided for initiative statutes, but not constitutional amendments. The Republicans, who controlled both houses of the legislature, forced the initiative advocates to accept this compromise because they feared that an initiative constitutional amendment might be used to repeal their state's Prohibition amendment.

Governor Cobb signed the I&R amendment on March 20, 1907, but it still had to be ratified by popular vote before taking effect. In the 18 months prior to this vote, most of the state's newspapers published editorials opposing I&R, and Maine's U.S. Senator Hale sent his constituents copies of a vehement speech opposing it by Senator Henry Cabot Lodge of Massachusetts. Nevertheless, voters approved I&R by a margin of more than two to one on September 15, 1908.

The first initiative on the state ballot was a victory for the Progressives: a law mandating the nomination of state and county candidates by popular vote in primary elections, rather than in party conventions. It passed by margin of more than three to one on September 11, 1911.

Only seven initiatives were on the ballot during the first 60 years of the initiative process, and there were none during the 1950s and 1960s. The only successful measure after 1911 was a 1936 statute "to prevent diversions of the general highway fund" (to uses others than highways).

In the 1970s Maine voters, like those in other states, rediscovered their power to make laws by initiative. In 1972 they approved an initiative to change the ballot form to eliminate party columns in order to encourage voters to give each candidate independent consideration.

In the 1970s and 1980s, more than half of Maine's initiatives were about energy and environmental matters. In 1976, voters enacted a beverage container deposit (Bottle Bill) initiative and established a state park at Bigelow Mountain; in 1980 and 1982, they turned down proposed initiatives to ban nuclear power, following massive "Vote No" ad campaigns paid for by the owners of the Maine Yankee nuclear plant. The Maine Nuclear Referendum Committee, sponsors of the nuclear ban initiatives, won only one campaign: a 1985 initiative to require a statewide referendum on any plan to dump low-level radioactive waste.

In 1986, consumer advocates waged a successful battle against the local telephone company to pass an initiative outlawing local measured service, whereby callers are charged by the minute for local calls. The company had set a campaign spending record with its "Vote No" ads, which featured former U.S. senator and 1972 presidential candidate Edmund Muskie.

However, with the passage of term limits in the early 90s, state lawmakers began a crusade against the initiative process by passing numerous changes to the states I&R laws. One law that was passed, prohibiting petition circulators to be paid by signature, was struck down by the Federal Courts as a violation of the First Amendment. The case was sponsored by the Initiative & Referendum Institute. Other new laws designed to regulate and restrict the I&R process are likely which will no doubt lead to additional litigation in the state.

Statewide Initiative Usage

Number of Initiatives	Number Passed	Number Failed	Passage Rate
38	17	21	44%

Statewide Initiatives

Year	Measure Number	Type	Subject Matter	Description	Pass/Fail
1911	N/A	IDS	Election Reform	Nomination of state and County officers by primaries (direct primary law).	Passed
1923	N/A	IDS	Labor	To establish a forty-eight hour week for women and minors.	Failed
1927	N/A	IDS	Election Reform	To repeal the direct primary law.	Failed
1933	N/A	IDS	Utility Regulation	To raise the tax on corporations distributing and supplying electric power.	Failed
1936	N/A	IDS	Administration of Government	To prevent diversions of the general highway fund.	Passed
1947	N/A	IDS	Labor	To regulate collective bargaining Tabb Bill (competing measure).	Failed
1947	N/A	IDS	Administration of Government	Barlow Bill (initiative measure).	Failed
1971	N/A	IDS	Taxes	To repeal the income tax.	Failed
1972	N/A	IDS	Election Reform	To change form of ballot from party column to office type.	Passed
1973	N/A	IDS	Utility Regulation	To create Power Authority of Maine.	Failed
1976	N/A	IDS	Environmental Reform	To establish a public preserve in Bigelow Mountain area.	Passed
1979	N/A	IDS	Environmental Reform	To repeal the forced deposit law (bottle bill)	Failed
1980	N/A	IDS	Gaming	Shall slot machine ban become law?	Passed
1980	N/A	IDS	Nuclear weapons/facilities/waste	Prohibit electric power by nuclear fission.	Failed
1981	N/A	IDS	Utility Regulation	Create Maine Energy Commission.	Failed
1982	N/A	IDS	Nuclear weapons/facilities/waste	End nuclear power for electricity in five years.	Failed
1982	N/A	IDS	Business Regulation	Repeal of milk price controls.	Failed
1982	N/A	IDS	Taxes	Abolish inflation-induce state income tax increases.	Passed
1983	1	IDS	Animal Rights	Repeal hunting season on moose.	Failed
1985	N/A	IDS	Nuclear weapons/facilities/waste	Would require a statewide referendum on any plan to dump low-level radioactive waste in the state.	Passed

Year	Measure Number	Type	Subject Matter	Description	Pass/Fail
1986	N/A	IDS	Civil Rights	Obscenity law.	Failed
1986	N/A	IDS	Utility Regulation	Ban mandatory local phone service; flat rates.	Passed
1987	N/A	IDS	Nuclear weapons/ facilities/waste	No high-waste nuclear plants after July 4, 1988.	Passed
1989	N/A	IDS	Nuclear weapons/ facilities/waste	Stop cruise missile tests.	Passed
1989	N/A	IDS	Campaign Finance Reform	Campaign finance — candidates for Governor.	Failed
1990	N/A	IDS	Business Regulation	Stores open on Sundays/holidays; option to workers.	Passed
1991	N/A	IDS	Administration of Government	Reauthorize widening of the Maine Turnpike.	Passed
1993	1	IDS	Term Limits	Term limits for state legislators 8/8.	Passed
1994	1	IDS	Term Limits	Term limits on Congress 6/12.	Passed
1995	N/A	IDS	Civil Rights	Do you favor the changes in Maine law limiting protected classifications, in future state and local laws to race, color, sex, physical or mental disability, religion, age, national origin, familial status and marital status, and repealing existing laws?	Failed
1996	1	IDS	Term Limits	Informed Voter Law.	Passed
1996	2A	IDS	Environmental Reform	Bans clear cutting.	Failed
1996	3	IDS	Campaign Finance Reform	Campaign finance reform; including voluntary spending limits and public funding.	Passed
1999	1	IDS	Abortion	Bans partial-birth abortions except when such an abortion is necessary to save the life of the mother.	Failed
1999	2	IDS	Drug Policy Reform	Authorizes an eligible patient diagnosed with one or more specified debilitating conditions, including cancer and acquired immune deficiency syndrome, to use marijuana for medical purposes.	Passed
2000	1	IDS	Physician assisted suicide	Allows a mentally competent adult who is suffering from a terminal illness to request and obtain medication from a physician to end that patient's own life in a humane and dignified manner.	Failed
2000	2	IDS	Environmental Reform	Sets limits on timber harvesting on land subject to the Maine Tree Growth Tax Law and requires that a landowner obtain a permit from the Maine Forest Service prior to undertaking harvesting activities that will result in a clear-cut.	Failed
2000	3	IDS	Gaming	This initiated bill authorizes the operation of video lottery terminals at certain existing pari-mutuel facilities.	Failed

Maine Constitution

Article IV

Section 17. Proceedings for people's veto.

1. Petition procedure; petition for people's veto. Upon written petition of electors, the number of which shall not be less than 10% of the total vote for Governor cast in the last gubernatorial election preceding the filing of such petition, and addressed to the Governor and filed in the office of the Secretary of State by the hour of 5:00 p.m., on or before the 90th day after the recess of the Legislature, or if such 90th day is a Saturday, a Sunday, or a legal holiday, by the hour of 5:00 p.m., on the preceding day which is not a Saturday, a Sunday, or a legal holiday, requesting that one or more Acts, bills, resolves or resolutions, or part or parts thereof, passed by the Legislature but not then in effect by reason of the provisions of the preceding section, be referred to the people, such Acts, bills, resolves, or resolutions or part or parts thereof as are specified in such petition shall not take effect until 30 days after the Governor shall have announced by public proclamation that the same have been ratified by a majority of the electors voting thereon at a statewide or general election. CR 1999, c. 1 (amd).

2. Effect of referendum. The effect of any Act, bill, resolve or resolution or part or parts thereof as are specified in such petition shall be suspended upon the filing of such petition. If it is later finally determined, in accordance with any procedure enacted by the Legislature pursuant to the Constitution, that such petition was invalid, such Act, bill, resolve or resolution or part or parts thereof shall then take effect upon the day following such final determination.

3. Referral to electors; proclamation by Governor. As soon as it appears that the effect of any Act, bill, resolve, or resolution or part or parts thereof has been suspended by petition in manner aforesaid, the Governor by public proclamation shall give notice thereof and of the time when such measure is to be voted on by the people, which shall be at the next statewide or general election, whichever comes first, not less than 60 days after such proclamation. If the Governor fails to order such measure to be submitted to the people at the next statewide or general election, the Secretary of State shall, by proclamation, order such measure to be submitted to the people at such an election and such order shall be sufficient to enable the people to vote. CR 1999, c. 1 (amd).

Section 18. Direct initiative of legislation.

1. Petition procedure. The electors may propose to the Legislature for its consideration any bill, resolve or resolution, including bills to amend or repeal emergency legislation but not an amendment of the State Constitution, by written petition addressed to the Legislature or to either branch thereof and filed in the office of the Secretary of State by the hour of 5:00 p.m., on or before the 50th day after the date of convening of the Legislature in first regular session or on or before the 25th day after the date of convening of the Legislature in second regular session. If the 50th or 25th day, whichever applies, is a Saturday, Sunday, or legal holiday, the period runs until the hour of 5:00 p.m., of the next day which is not a Saturday, Sunday, or legal holiday.

2. Referral to electors unless enacted by the Legislature without change; number of signatures necessary on direct initiative petitions; dating signatures on petitions; competing measures. For any measure thus proposed by electors, the number of signatures shall not be less than 10% of the total vote for Governor cast in the last gubernatorial election preceding the filing of such petition. The date each signature was made shall be written next to the signature on the petition, and no signature older than one year from the written date on the petition shall be valid. The measure thus proposed, unless enacted without change by the Legislature at the session at which it is presented, shall be submitted to the electors together with any amended form, substitute, or recommendation of the Legislature, and in such manner that the people can choose between the competing measures or reject both. When there are competing bills and neither receives a majority of the votes given for or against both, the one receiving the most votes shall at the next statewide election to be held not less than 60 days after the first vote thereon be submitted by itself if it receives more than 1/3 of the votes given for and against both. If the measure initiated is enacted by the Legislature without change, it shall not go to a referendum vote unless in pursuance of a demand made in accordance with the preceding section. The Legislature may order a special election on any measure that is subject to a vote of the people.

3. Timing of elections; proclamation by Governor. The Governor shall, by proclamation, order any measure proposed to the Legislature as herein provided, and not enacted by the Legislature without change, referred to the people at an election to be held in November of the year in which the petition is filed. If the Governor fails to order a measure proposed to the Legislature and not enacted without change to be submitted to the people at such an election by proclamation within 10 days after the recess of the Legislature to which the measure was proposed, the Secretary of State shall, by

proclamation, order such measure to be submitted to the people at an election as requested, and such order shall be sufficient to enable the people to vote.

Section 19. Effective date of measures approved by people; veto power limited.

Any measure referred to the people and approved by a majority of the votes given thereon shall, unless a later date is specified in said measure, take effect and become a law in 30 days after the Governor has made public proclamation of the result of the vote on said measure, which the Governor shall do within 10 days after the vote thereon has been canvassed and determined; provided, however, that any such measure which entails expenditure in an amount in excess of available and unappropriated state funds shall remain inoperative until 45 days after the next convening of the Legislature in regular session, unless the measure provides for raising new revenues adequate for its operation. The veto power of the Governor shall not extend to any measure approved by vote of the people, and any measure initiated by the people and passed by the Legislature without change, if vetoed by the Governor and if the veto is sustained by the Legislature shall be referred to the people to be voted on at the next general election. The Legislature may enact measures expressly conditioned upon the people's ratification by a referendum vote.

Section 20. Meaning of words "electors," "people," "recess of Legislature," "statewide election," "measure," "circulator," and "written petition"; written petitions for people's veto; written petitions for direct initiative.

As used in any of the 3 preceding sections or in this section the words "electors" and "people" mean the electors of the State qualified to vote for Governor; "recess of the Legislature" means the adjournment without day of a session of the Legislature; "statewide election" means any election held throughout the State on a particular day; "measure" means an Act, bill, resolve or resolution proposed by the people, or 2 or more such, or part or parts of such, as the case may be; "circulator" means a person who solicits signatures for written petitions, and who must be a resident of this State and whose name must appear on the voting list of the city, town or plantation of the circulator's residence as qualified to vote for Governor; "written petition" means one or more petitions written or printed, or partly written and partly printed, with the original signatures of the petitioners attached, verified as to the authenticity of the signatures by the oath of the circulator that all of the signatures to the petition were made in the presence of the circulator and that to the best of the circulator's knowledge and belief each signature is the signature of the person whose name it purports to be, and accompanied by the certificate of the official authorized by law to maintain the voting list of the city, town or plantation in which the petitioners reside that their names appear on the voting list of the city, town or plantation of the official as qualified to vote for Governor. The oath of the circulator must be sworn to in the presence of a person authorized by law to administer oaths. Written petitions for a people's veto pursuant to Article IV, Part Third, Section 17 must be submitted to the appropriate officials of cities, towns or plantations for determination of whether the petitioners are qualified voters by the hour of 5:00 p.m., on the 5th day before the petition must be filed in the office of the Secretary of State, or, if such 5th day is a Saturday, a Sunday or a legal holiday, by 5:00 p.m., on the next day which is not a Saturday, a Sunday or a legal holiday. Written petitions for a direct initiative pursuant to Article IV, Part Third, Section 18 must be submitted to the appropriate officials of cities, towns or plantations for determination of whether the petitioners are qualified voters by the hour of 5:00 p.m., on the 10th day before the petition must be filed in the office of the Secretary of State, or, if such 10th day is a Saturday, a Sunday or a legal holiday, by 5:00 p.m., on the next day which is not a Saturday, a Sunday or a legal holiday. Such officials must complete the certification of such petitions and must return them to the circulators or their agents within 2 days for a petition for a people's veto and within 5 days for a petition for a direct initiative, Saturdays, Sundays and legal holidays excepted, of the date on which such petitions were submitted to them. The petition shall set forth the full text of the measure requested or proposed. Petition forms shall be furnished or approved by the Secretary of State upon written application signed in the office of the Secretary of State by a resident of this State whose name must appear on the voting list of the city, town or plantation of that resident as qualified to vote for Governor. The full text of a measure submitted to a vote of the people under the provisions of the Constitution need not be printed on the official ballots, but, until otherwise provided by the Legislature, the Secretary of State shall prepare the ballots in such form as to present the question or questions concisely and intelligibly. CR 1995, c. 3 (amd).

Section 21. City council of any city may establish direct initiative and people's veto.

The city council of any city may establish the direct initiative and people's veto for the electors of such city in regard to its municipal affairs, provided that the ordinance establishing and providing the method of exercising such direct initiative and people's veto shall not take effect until ratified by vote of a majority of the electors of said city, voting thereon at a municipal election. Provided, however, that the Legislature may at any time provide a uniform method for the exercise of the initiative and referendum in municipal affairs.

Section 22. Election officers and officials, how governed.

Until the Legislature shall enact further laws not inconsistent with the Constitution for applying the people's veto and direct initiative, the election officers and other officials shall be governed by the provisions of this Constitution and of the general law, supplemented by such reasonable action as may be necessary to render the preceding sections self-executing. The Legislature may enact laws not inconsistent with the Constitution to establish procedures for determination of the validity of written petitions. Such laws shall include provision for judicial review of any determination, to be completed within 100 days from the date of filing of a written petition in the office of the Secretary of State.

Section 23. Municipalities reimbursed annually.

The Legislature shall annually reimburse each municipality from state tax sources for not less than 50% of the property tax revenue loss suffered by that municipality during the previous calendar year because of the statutory property tax exemptions or credits enacted after April 1, 1978. The Legislature shall enact appropriate legislation to carry out the intent of this section.

Maine Statutes

21A Chapter 11 — Elections

§ 901. Petitions

To initiate proceedings for a people's veto referendum or the direct initiative of legislation, provided in the Constitution of Maine, Article IV, Part Third, Sections 17 and 18, a voter shall submit a written application to the Department of the Secretary of State on a form designed by the Secretary of State. The application must contain the names, addresses and signatures of 5 voters, in addition to the applicant, who are designated to receive any notices in proceedings under this chapter. For a direct initiative, the application must contain the full text of the proposed law. The voter submitting the application shall sign the application in the presence of the Secretary of State, the Secretary of State's designee or a notary public. [1993, c. 695, §33 (amd).]

On receipt, the Secretary of State or the Secretary of State's designee shall review the application and determine the form of the petition to be submitted to the voters. The date the approved form of the petition is provided to the voter submitting the application is the date of issuance for the purposes of this chapter. [1993, c. 695, §34 (amd).]

1. Limitation on petitions. An application for a people's veto referendum petition must be filed in the Department of the Secretary of State within 10 business days after Adjournment of the legislative session at which the Act in question was passed. A direct initiative of legislation must meet the filing deadlines specified in the Constitution of Maine, Article IV, Part Third, Section 18.

2. Furnished within 10 days. [1993, c. 352, §1 (rp).]

3. Forms printed by voters. [1993, c. 352, §1 (rp).]

3-A. Review for proper form. The Secretary of State shall review the proposed law for a direct initiative of legislation within 10 business days after receipt of the application and either reject the application or provide a first revised draft of the initiative legislation to the applicant within that time. The Secretary of State may reject the application if the Secretary of State determines that the proposed law:

A. Does not conform to the form prescribed by the Secretary of State; or

B. Does not conform to the essential aspects of the drafting conventions established for the Maine Revised Statutes. The drafting conventions include but are not limited to:

(1) Correct allocation to the statutes and correct integration with existing statutes;

(2) Bill titles and statute section headnotes that objectively reflect the content of the bill, section or sections to which they apply;

(3) Conformity to the statutory numbering system; and

(4) Ensuring that bills enacting statutes do not contain provisions that describe intent or make testimonial statements without creating a legal requirement or duty. [1993, c. 352, §1 (new).]

By consent of the applicant the proposed law may be modified to conform with the requirements of this section. The Secretary of State may request assistance from the Revisor of Statutes in reviewing the proposed law.

The applicant shall submit each subsequent draft of the legislation to the Secretary of State for review following the same process. The Secretary of State shall review each subsequent draft from the applicant and provide a revised draft or written response suggesting how the proposed law may be modified to conform with the requirements of this section within 10 business days. Before the ballot question is drafted by the Secretary of State, written consent to the final language of the proposed law must be given by the applicant.

3-B. Approved petitions printed by voters. A voter must print the petitions in the form approved by the Secretary of State.

4. Ballot question. The ballot question for an initiative or a people's veto referendum must be drafted by the Secretary of State in accordance with section 906 and rules adopted in accordance with the Maine Administrative Procedure Act. The Secretary of State shall provide the ballot question to the applicant for a people's veto referendum within 10 business days after receipt of a properly completed application. The Secretary of State shall provide the ballot question to the applicant for an initiative within 10 business days after the applicant has submitted to the Secretary of State written consent to the final language of the proposed law. The question must be conspicuously displayed on the face of the petition.

5. Summary of proposal. For a direct initiative, the Secretary of State shall request the Revisor of Statutes to recommend a concise summary that objectively describes the content of the proposed law. The Secretary of State shall approve or amend the summary and the summary must be attached to the end of the proposed law.

6. Rejection. If the Secretary of State rejects an application under this section, the Secretary of State shall provide a written statement of the reasons for the decision.

7. Court review. A voter named in the application under this section may appeal any decision made by the Secretary of State under this section using the procedures for court review provided for in section 905, subsections 2 and 3.

§ 902. Verification and certification

The petitions must be signed, verified and certified in the same manner as are nonparty nomination petitions under section 354, subsections 3 and 4 and subsection 7, paragraphs A and C. [1997, c. 581, §5 (new).]

The verification and certification of the petition as required by the Constitution of Maine, Article IV, Part Third, Section 20, must be worded so that a single verification or certification may cover one or more pages fastened together as a single petition.

§ 903. Instructions to be printed on

The Secretary of State shall prepare complete instructions to inform the clerk and the signer or circulator of a petition of the statutory and constitutional requirements. The instructions must specify the conditions which have been held to invalidate either individual signatures or complete petitions. The instructions must be printed in bold type or capital letters on the petition. [1985, c. 161, § 6 (new).]

§ 903-A. Circulation

Petitions issued under this chapter may be circulated by any registered voter.

1. Filing. Filing of petitions in accordance with the deadlines specified in the Constitution of Maine, Article IV, Part Third, Section 18 must be completed within one year of the date of issuance under this chapter.

2. Invalid petition. Petitions not filed in accordance with the deadlines specified in the Constitution of Maine, Article IV, Part Third, Section 18 within one year of the date of issuance under this chapter are invalid for circulation.

§ 904. Violations and Penalties

The commission of any of the following acts is a Class E crime:

1. False statement. A circulator of an initiative or referendum petition who willfully swears that one or more signatures to the petition were made in his presence when those signatures were not made in his presence or that one or more signatures are those of the persons whose names they purport to be when he knows that the signature or signatures are not those of such persons; [1985, c. 161, § 6 (new).]

2. False acknowledgement of oath. A person authorized by law to administer oaths who willfully and falsely acknowledges the oath of a circulator of an initiative or referendum petition when that oath was not made in his presence; [1985, c. 161, § 6 (new).]

3. Unauthorized signature. A person who knowingly signs an initiative or referendum petition with any name other than his own; or [1985, c. 161, § 6 (new).]

4. Duplicate signature. A person who knowingly signs his name more than once on initiative or referendum petitions for the same measure. [1985, c. 161, § 6 (new).]

§ 904-A. Payment per signature; prohibition

A person may not pay a circulator of an initiative or a referendum petition or another person who causes the circulation of an initiative or referendum petition for the collection of signatures if that payment is based on the number of signatures collected. Nothing in this section prohibits a circulator of an initiative or a referendum petition or a person who causes the circulation of an initiative or referendum petition from being paid a salary that is not based on the number of signatures collected. [1997, c. 61, §1 (amd).]

§ 904-B. Payment for signature; prohibition

A circulator of an initiative or a referendum petition or a person who causes the circulation of an initiative or referendum petition may not pay or offer to pay any compensation to a person for the person's signature on the initiative or referendum petition.

§ 905. Review of initiative and referendum petitions

1. Secretary of State. The Secretary of State shall review all petitions filed in the Department of the Secretary of State for a people's veto referendum under the Constitution of Maine, Article IV, Part Third, Section 17, or for a direct initiative under the Constitution of Maine, Article IV, Part Third, Section 18.

The Secretary of State shall determine the validity of the petition and issue a written decision stating the reasons for the decision within 30 days after the final date for filing the petitions in the Department of the Secretary of State under the Constitution of Maine, Article IV, Part Third, Section 17 or 18.

2. Superior Court. Any voter named in the application under section 901, or any person who has validly signed the petitions, if these petitions are determined to be invalid, or any other voter, if these petitions are determined to be valid, may appeal the decision of the Secretary of State by commencing an action in the Superior Court. This action shall be conducted in accordance with the Maine Rules of Civil Procedure, Rule 80C, except as modified by this section. In reviewing the decision of the Secretary of State, the court shall determine whether the description of the subject matter is understandable to a reasonable voter reading the question for the first time and will not mislead a reasonable voter who understands the proposed legislation into voting contrary to his wishes. This action must be commenced within 5 days of the date of the decision of the Secretary of State and shall be tried, without a jury, within 15 days of the date of that decision. Upon timely application, anyone may intervene in this action when the applicant claims an interest relating to the subject matter of the petitions, unless the applicant's interest is adequately represented by existing parties. The court shall issue its written decision containing its findings of fact and stating the reasons for its decision within 30 days of the commencement of the trial or within

3. Supreme Judicial Court. Any aggrieved party may appeal the decision of the Superior Court, on questions of law, by filing a notice of appeal within 3 days of that decision. The appellant must file the required number of copies of the record with the clerk within 3 days after filing notice of appeal. After a notice of appeal is filed, the parties have 10 days to file briefs with the clerk of courts. As soon as the record and briefs have been filed, the court shall immediately consider the case. The standard of review shall be the same as for the Superior Court. The court shall issue its decision within 30 days of the date of the decision of the Superior Court.

§ 906. Form of ballot

The Secretary of State shall prepare the ballots for referendum questions according to the following provisions, subject to the authority contained in section 604-A. [1987, c. 188, § 16]

1. Referendum questions on separate ballot. [1997, c. 581, §6 (rp).]

1-A. Referendum questions on same ballot. Referendum questions may be printed on the same ballot or ballot card used for the election of state candidates or municipal elections, as determined by the Secretary of State in accordance with section 604-A. There must be a place on the ballot for the voter to designate the voter's choice.

2. Bond issues; total interest. Whenever ratification by the electors is essential to the validity of bonds issued on behalf of the State, the ballot must contain the total interest necessary for the retirement of the bonds outstanding and unpaid.

3. Distinctively colored. Referendum ballots must be printed on paper of a distinctive color selected by the Secretary of State, unless the referendum ballot is combined with the same ballot used for the election of state candidates or municipal elections under subsection 1-A.

4. Size. The Secretary of State shall determine the size of the ballots.

5. Contents concealed. [1997, c. 581, §9 (rp).]

6. Wording of ballots for people's veto and direct initiative referenda. Ballots for a statewide vote on a people's veto referendum or a direct initiative must set out the question or questions to be voted on as set forth in this subsection.

A. The Secretary of State shall advise petitioners that the proper suggested format for an initiative question is a separate question for each issue. In determining whether there is more than one issue, each requiring a separate question, considerations include whether:

1. A voter would reasonably have different opinions on the different issues;

2. Having more than one question would help voters to better understand the subject matter; and

3. The questions are severable and can be enacted or rejected separately without negating the intent of the petitioners. [1993, c. 352, §3 (rpr).]

B. The Secretary of State shall write the question in a simple, clear, concise and direct manner that describes the subject matter of the people's veto or direct initiative. [1993, c. 352, §3 (rpr).]

C. The question must be phrased so that an affirmative vote is in favor of the people's veto or direct initiative. [1993, c. 352, §3 (rpr).]

D. If the Legislature adopts a competing measure, the ballot must clearly designate the competing question and legislation as a competing measure and allow voters to indicate whether they support the direct initiative, support the competing measure or reject both. [1993, c. 352, §3 (rpr).]

E. If there is more than one direct initiative referendum on the same general subject, the Secretary of State shall write the questions in a manner that describes the differences between the initiatives. [1993, c. 352, §3 (rpr).]

6-A. Wording of referendum questions enacted by the Legislature. The proper format for a statutory referendum enacted by the Legislature is a separate question for each issue. In determining whether there is more than one issue, each requiring a separate question, considerations include whether:

A. A voter would reasonably have different opinions on the different issues;

B. Having more than one question would help voters to better understand the subject matter; and

C. The Legislature determines the questions are severable and can be enacted or rejected separately without negating the intent of the Legislature.

7. Order of questions on the ballot. The Secretary of State shall arrange questions on the ballot in the following order: carry-over measures from a previous election; people's veto questions; initiated measures; bond issues; constitutional amendments; and other legislatively proposed referenda. Within each group, questions must be arranged in a random order determined by a selection process conducted in public. All ballot questions must be numbered sequentially.

The Basic Steps to Do an Initiative in Maine

Statutes Only — Indirect Initiative Process

Basic procedures: Filing an initiative is a very simple process in Maine. All you need to do is take your initiative language to the Secretary of State—it doesn't have to be in petition format. The Secretary of State then submits the language to the Reviser of Statutes who puts it in the format that is consistent with state law and gives it back to the Secretary of State. The Secretary of State then returns the initiative to the proponent. Once this occurs, the proponent of the initiative will take the language and put it into petition format. Once it is in petition format, it is submitted to the Secretary of State for final approval. This whole process will take approximately six weeks.

Date initiative language can be submitted to the state for the November 2001 or 2002 election: Anytime, but you have only one year from the time the Secretary of State gives the final approval to collect the signatures. Based on this, you shouldn't submit the language until you are ready to go forward.

Signatures tied to vote of which office: Governor

Next Gubernatorial election: 2002

Votes cast for governor in last election: 421,010 (1998)

Net number of signatures required: 10% of votes cast for Governor for a statute (42,101). If proponents have enough signatures, the measure is sent to the Legislature. If the Legislature does not approve the measure, it is placed on the next statewide election.

Distribution requirement: None

Circulation period: One year from date the Secretary of State grants approval.

Do circulators have to be residents and/or registered voters: Yes

Date when signatures are due for certification: January 25, 2001 to be on the November 2001 general election ballot. No later than late January 2002 to be on the November 2002 general election ballot.

Signature verification process: Full certification

Single-subject restriction: Yes (advisory only)

Legislative tampering: By common practice, the legislature can both repeal and amend initiatives.

Maryland

By 1900, reformers had organized a Maryland Direct Legislation League, with A. G. Eichelberger as its president. Ten years later the League claimed "more than 1,000 active, working members." In 1914, the League promoted an I&R bill sponsored by State Senator William J. Odgen of Baltimore, but the legislature amended it to remove the initiative provision. This "referendum only" amendment passed both houses in 1915 and was ratified by the voters. The following year the League pressed the legislature for an initiative amendment. Their bill passed the senate with only six dissenting votes, but was tabled (effectively killed) in the house by a 66 to 27 vote. Never again did an initiative amendment come close to approval. Charles J. Ogle, secretary of the League in 1916, attributed the failure to the committee chairmen, "a very active lobby against" the initiative amendment, and rural legislators' fear of the Baltimore masses.

Since the referendum amendment was ratified in 1915, it has been used 13 times by citizens to force a statewide popular vote on unpopular laws passed by the legislature. In 1970, voters vetoed the legislature's bill regarding a Department of Economic and Community Development, and in 1972 and 1974, they vetoed state aid to nonpublic schools. Until 1988, all subsequent referendum petitions failed because of either insufficient signatures or court decisions barring ballot placement. In 1988, however, the legislature passed a bill banning cheap handguns, and gun control opponents responded with a petition drive that put the measure on the ballot. Despite the record-breaking expenditure by the National Rifle Association of more than $4 million for a "Vote No" campaign, voters approved the law by a 58-percent margin.

Maryland Constitution

The state does not have the statewide initiative process and so therefore the following provisions discuss the procedures used by the state legislature to place constitutional amendments on the ballot. However, the state does allow for the popular referendum process (the ability to refer bills passed by the legislature to the ballot via a petition process). The requirements for undertaking a popular referendum are also included.

Article XIV

Sec. 1.

The General Assembly may propose amendments to this Constitution; provided that each amendment shall be embraced in a separate bill, embodying the Article or Section, as the same will stand when amended and passed by three-fifths of all the members elected to each of the two Houses, by yeas and nays, to be entered on the Journals with the proposed amendment. The requirement in this section that an amendment proposed by the General Assembly shall be embraced in a separate bill shall not be construed or applied to prevent the General Assembly from (1) proposing in one bill a series of amendments to the Constitution of Maryland for the general purpose of removing or correcting constitutional provisions which are obsolete, inaccurate, invalid, unconstitutional, or duplicative; or (2) embodying in a single Constitutional amendment one or more Articles of the Constitution so long as that Constitutional amendment embraces only a single subject. The bill or bills proposing amendment or amendments shall be publicized, either by publishing, by order of the Governor, in at least two newspapers, in each County, where so many may be published, and where not more than one may be published, then in that newspaper, and in three newspapers published in the City of Baltimore, once a week for four weeks, or as otherwise ordered by the Governor in a manner provided by law, immediately preceding the next ensuing general election, at which the proposed amendment or amendments shall be submitted, in a form to be prescribed by the General Assembly, to the qualified voters of the State for adoption or rejection. The votes cast for and against said proposed amendment or amendments, severally, shall be returned to the Governor, in the manner prescribed in other cases, and if it shall appear to the Governor that a majority of the votes cast at said election on said amendment or amendments, severally, were cast in favor thereof, the Governor shall, by his proclamation, declare the said amendment or amendments having received said majority of votes, to have been adopted by the people of Maryland as part of the Constitution thereof, and thenceforth said amendment or amendments shall be part of the said Constitution. If the General Assembly determines that a proposed Constitutional amendment affects only one county or the City of Baltimore, the proposed amendment shall be part of the Constitution if it receives a majority of the votes cast in the State and in the affected county or City of Baltimore, as the case may be. When two or more amendments shall be submitted to the voters of this State at the same election, they shall be so submitted as that each amendment shall be voted on separately (amended by Chapter 476, Acts of 1943, ratified Nov. 7, 1944; Chapter 367, Acts of 1972, ratified Nov. 7, 1972; Chapter 679, Acts of 1977, and Chapter 975, Acts of 1978, ratified Nov. 7, 1978).

Sec. 1A.

A proposed Constitutional amendment which, by provisions that are of limited duration, provides for a period of transition, or a unique schedule under which the terms of the amendment are to become effective, shall set forth those provisions in the amendment as a section or sections of a separate article, to be known as "provisions of limited duration", and state the date upon which or the circumstances under which those provisions shall expire. If the Constitutional amendment is adopted, those provisions of limited duration shall have the same force and effect as any other part of the Constitution, except that they shall remain a part of the Constitution only so long as their terms require. Each new section of the article known as "provisions of limited duration" shall refer to the title and section of the other article of the Constitution of which it, temporarily, is a part (added by Chapter 680, Acts of 1977, ratified Nov. 7, 1978).

Sec. 2.

It shall be the duty of the General Assembly to provide by Law for taking, at the general election to be held in the year nineteen hundred and seventy, and every twenty years thereafter, the sense of the People in regard to calling a Convention for altering this Constitution; and if a majority of voters at such election or elections shall vote for a Convention, the General Assembly, at its next session, shall provide by Law for the assembling of such convention, and for the election of Delegates thereto. Each County, and Legislative District of the City of Baltimore, shall have in such Convention a number of Delegates equal to its representation in both Houses at the time at which the Convention is called. But any Constitution, or change, or amendment of the existing Constitution, which may be adopted by such Convention, shall be submitted to the voters of this State, and shall have no effect unless the same shall have been adopted by a majority of the voters voting thereon (amended by Chapter 99, Acts of 1956, ratified Nov. 6, 1956).

Article XVI

(added by Chapter 673, Acts of 1914, ratified Nov. 2, 1915)

Sec. 1.

(a) The people reserve to themselves power known as The Referendum, by petition to have submitted to the registered voters of the State, to approve or reject at the polls, any Act, or part of any Act of the General Assembly, if approved by the Governor, or, if passed by the General Assembly over the veto of the Governor;
(b) The provisions of this Article shall be self-executing; provided that additional legislation in furtherance thereof and not in conflict therewith may be enacted.

Sec. 2.

No law enacted by the General Assembly shall take effect until the first day of June next after the session at which it may be passed, unless it contains a Section declaring such law an emergency law and necessary for the immediate preservation of the public health or safety and is passed upon a yea and nay vote supported by three-fifths of all the members elected to each of the two Houses of the General Assembly. The effective date of a law other than an emergency law may be extended as provided in Section 3 (b) hereof. If before said first day of June there shall have been filed with the Secretary of the State a petition to refer to a vote of the people any law or part of a law capable of referendum, as in this Article provided, the same shall be referred by the Secretary of State to such vote, and shall not become a law or take effect until thirty days after its approval by a majority of the electors voting thereon at the next ensuing election held throughout the State for Members of the House of Representatives of the United States. An emergency law shall remain in force notwithstanding such petition, but shall stand repealed thirty days after having been rejected by a majority of the qualified electors voting thereon. No measure creating or abolishing any office, or changing the salary, term or duty of any officer, or granting any franchise or special privilege, or creating any vested right or interest, shall be enacted as an emergency law. No law making any appropriation for maintaining the State Government, or for maintaining or aiding any public institution, not exceeding the next previous appropriation for the same purpose, shall be subject to rejection or repeal under this Section. The increase in any such appropriation for maintaining or aiding any public institution shall only take effect as in the case of other laws, and such increase or any part thereof specified in the petition, may be referred to a vote of the people upon petition (amended by Chapter 681, Acts of 1977, ratified Nov. 7, 1978).

Sec. 3.

(a) The referendum petition against an Act or part of an Act passed by the General Assembly, shall be sufficient if signed by three percent of the qualified voters of the State of Maryland, calculated upon the whole number of votes cast for Governor at the last preceding Gubernatorial election, of whom not more than half are residents of Baltimore City, or of any one County. However, any Public Local Law for any one County or the City of Baltimore, shall be referred by the Secretary of State only to the people of the County or City of Baltimore, upon a referendum petition of ten percent of the qualified voters of the County or City of Baltimore, as the case may be, calculated upon the whole number of votes cast respectively for Governor at the last preceding Gubernatorial election.

(b) If more than one-third, but less than the full number of signatures required to complete any referendum petition against any law passed by the General Assembly, be filed with the Secretary of State before the first day of June, the time for the law to take effect and for filing the remainder of signatures to complete the petition shall be extended to the thirtieth day of the same month, with like effect.

If an Act is passed less than 45 days prior to June 1, it may not become effective sooner than 31 days after its passage. To bring this Act to referendum, the first one-third of the required number of signatures to a petition shall be submitted within 30 days after its passage. If the first one-third of the required number of signatures is submitted to the Secretary of State within 30 days after its passage, the time for the Act to take effect and for filing the remainder of the signatures to complete the petition shall be extended for an additional 30 days.

(c) In this Article, "pass" or "passed" means any final action upon any Act or part of an Act by both Houses of the General Assembly; and "enact" or "enacted" means approval of an Act or part of an Act by the Governor.

(d) Signatures on a petition for referendum on an Act or part of an Act may be signed at any time after the Act or part of an Act is passed (amended by Chapter 548, Acts of 1976, ratified Nov. 2, 1976. Sec. 3(a) previously amended by Chapter 6, Acts of 1962, ratified Nov. 6, 1962).

Sec. 4.

A petition may consist of several papers, but each paper shall contain the full text, or an accurate summary approved by the Attorney General, of the Act or part of Act petitioned. There shall be attached to each paper of signatures filed with a petition an affidavit of the person procuring those signatures that the signatures were affixed in his presence and that, based upon the person's best knowledge and belief, every signature on the paper is genuine and bona fide and that the signers are registered voters at the address set opposite or below their names. The General Assembly shall prescribe by law the form of the petition, the manner for verifying its authenticity, and other administrative procedures which facilitate the petition process and which are not in conflict with this Article (amended by Chapter 548, Acts of 1976, ratified Nov. 2, 1976; Chapter 849, Acts of 1982, ratified Nov. 2, 1982).

Sec. 5.

(a) The General Assembly shall provide for furnishing the voters of the State the text of all measures to be voted upon by the people; provided, that until otherwise provided by law the same shall be published in the manner prescribed by Article XIV of the Constitution for the publication of proposed Constitutional Amendments.

(b) All laws referred under the provisions of this Article shall be submitted separately on the ballots to the voters of the people, but if containing more than two hundred words, the full text shall not be printed on the official ballots, but the Secretary of State shall prepare and submit a ballot title of each such measure in such form as to present the purpose of said measure concisely and intelligently. The ballot title may be distinct from the legislative title, but in any case the legislative title shall be sufficient. Upon each of the ballots, following the ballot title or text, as the case may be, of each such measure, there shall be printed the words "For the referred law" and "Against the referred law," as the case may be. The votes cast for and against any such referred law shall be returned to the Governor in the manner prescribed with respect to proposed amendments to the Constitution under Article XIV of this Constitution, and the Governor shall proclaim the result of the election, and, if it shall appear that the majority of the votes cast on any such measure were cast in favor thereof, the Governor shall by his proclamation declare the same having received a majority of the votes to have been adopted by the people of Maryland as a part of the laws of the State, to take effect thirty days after such election, and in like manner and with like effect the Governor shall proclaim the result of the local election as to any Public Local Law which shall have been submitted to the voters of any County or of the City of Baltimore.

Sec. 6.

No law, licensing, regulating, prohibiting, or submitting to local option, the manufacture or sale of malt or spirituous liquors, shall be referred or repealed under the provisions of this Article (amended by Chapter 681, Acts of 1977, ratified Nov. 7, 1978).

Massachusetts

Massachusetts' Populist Party adopted a resolution in 1895 calling for statewide initiative and referendum. In 1900, State Representative Henry Stirling introduced one of the first I&R proposals; Socialist State Representative James Carey introduced another in 1901. In 1905, Mrs. Ella 0. Marshall organized the Massachusetts Referendum League to push for I&R, but results were slow to come.

After a decade of unsuccessful attempts, the Massachusetts Direct Legislation League hired Henry Stirling to organize support for I&R throughout the state. The Progressive and Democratic parties, by now staunch supporters of I&R, used this issue with some success against the Republicans in the electoral campaigns of 1912.

In 1913 the legislature approved a bill establishing a procedure for advisory initiatives to be placed on the ballot by voters in any of the state's senatorial or representative districts; I&R advocates used the procedure in 1914, 1915, and 1916 to get "straw votes" throughout the state showing public support for I&R.

In 1915 Governor David I. Walsh, a Democrat who was the first Irish Catholic elected to statewide office in Massachusetts, formed the Union for a Progressive Constitution to push for a state constitutional convention to consider various reforms, with I&R as a priority. The legislature passed a bill in 1916 authorizing such a convention, if the voters approved it—which they did, in November 1916.

The convention met in 1917 and passed the I&R amendment by a vote of 163 yeas, 125 nays, and 30 delegates not voting. Conservative opposition to I&R, led by former state attorney general Albert E. Pillsbury of Wellesley and railroad counsel Charles F. Choate of Southborough, was strong enough to force numerous compromises in the final version: compromises that even today make the Massachusetts initiative procedure the nation's most cumbersome and complicated. Submitted to the voters for ratification on November 5, 1918, the amendment passed by a narrow margin.

The first initiative to win voter approval was a 1920 measure defining cider and beer as non-intoxicating liquors, and thus exempt from Prohibition. Other successful early initiatives included measures to end the ban on Sunday sports events (1928), repeal the state's Prohibition law (1930), reform candidate nominating procedures (1932), and regulate animal trapping (1930).

On the 1948 ballot was a controversial initiative to legalize contraceptives, which was opposed by the Catholic Church, and three labor relations measures sponsored by employers and bitterly opposed by organized labor: a "Right to Work" initiative, a law regulating strikes, and a third measure regarding the election of union officers. The four initiatives provoked an extraordinarily heavy Democratic turnout, which not only defeated all the initiatives but also swept Republican incumbents out of office.

The Democrats gained a majority in Massachusetts' lower house for the first time in the state's history, tipped the balance of power in the senate, and ousted Republican Governor Robert Bradford. The initiative that got the most favorable vote, though it still lost was on the contraceptive issue: 43 percent of the electorate said "yes."

In 1964, voters passed an initiative statute reducing the powers of the governor's Executive Council. The state's most famous initiative was the tax cutting "Proposition 2 1/2." Dog and cat lovers made successful use of the initiative process in 1983 by proposing a measure to ban research on these animals. The legislature, responding to an initiative petition signed by a record 145,170 voters, passed the initiative in December of that year, thus eliminating the need for it to go on the 1984 ballot. A 1986 initiative mandating cleanup of toxic waste dumps, sponsored by the Massachusetts Public Interest Research Group (MassPIRG), became the most popular initiative in the state's history, garnering 73 percent approval.

In 1994, a term limits initiative was adopted only to have it thrown out several years later by the state supreme court. The court ruled that term limits can only be imposed if the state constitution were amended and since the term limits imposed in 1994 were done statutorily, they were unconstitutional.

In 1998, state voters adopted a campaign finance reform initiative that called for the public funding of campaigns. However, the state legislature, as of April 2002, had still refused to fund the initiative.

Statewide Initiative Usage

Number of Initiatives	Number Passed	Number Failed	Passage Rate
60	31	29	52%

Statewide Initiatives

Year	Measure Number	Type	Subject Matter	Description	Pass/Fail
1920	Question 1	IDS	Alcohol Regulation	Definition of cider, beer, et al. as non-intoxicating liquors.	Passed
1926	Question 2	IDS	Veteran Affairs	Modify veterans' preference law.	Failed
1928	Question 1	IDS	Business Regulation	Authorizing certain Sunday sporting events.	Passed
1930	Question 2	IDS	Alcohol Regulation	Repeal of "Baby Volstead" (Prohibition) Act.	Passed
1930	Question 3	IDS	Animal Rights	Prohibit use of trapping devices	Passed
1932	Question 1	IDS	Business Regulation	Legalizing chiropractic.	Failed
1932	Question 2	IDS	Election Reform	Regulating nominating procedures.	Passed
1938	Question 1	DA	Administration of Government	Biennial legislative session.	Passed
1938	Question 2	IDS	Business Regulation	Free public taxicab stands in cities and towns.	Passed
1942	Question 1	IDS	Abortion	Revision of birth control law.	Failed
1946	Question 1	IDS	Welfare	Relative to old age pensions.	Failed
1946	Question 2	IDS	Labor	Labor relations.	Passed
1948	Question 5	IDS	Labor	Open shop.	Failed
1948	Question 6	IDS	Labor	Election of union officers.	Failed
1948	Question 7	IDS	Labor	Regulation of strikes.	Failed
1950	Question 3	IDS	Welfare	Payments to blind persons who are 63 years of age or older.	Passed
1950	Question 4	IDS	Gaming	Establishing state lottery.	Failed
1950	Question 5	IDS	Business Regulation	Compulsory motor vehicle insurance classifications.	Failed
1958	Question 1	IDS	Administration of Government	Public employee pensions.	Passed
1964	Question 5	IDS	Administration of Government	Reducing powers of Governor's Executive Council.	Passed
1968	Question 4	IDS	Constitutional Convention	Question regarding popular constitutional convention.	Passed
1974	Question 4	DA	Administration of Government	Authorizing use of state highway revenues for mass transportation.	Passed
1974	Question 5	IDS	Campaign Finance Reform	Political contributions and campaign expenditures.	Passed
1976	Question 4	IDS	Utility Regulation	To establish Massachusetts Power Authority.	Failed
1976	Question 5	IDS	Gun Regulation	To prohibit to possession, ownership, or sale of any weapon from which a shot or bullet can be discharged and which has a barrel length of less than 16 inches.	Failed
1976	Question 6	IDS	Environmental Reform	To require every beverage container to have a refund value of $.05 and to ban containers with flip-tops.	Failed
1976	Question 7	IDS	Utility Regulation	To regulate electric utility charges and permit peak load pricing.	Failed
1980	Question 2	IDS	Taxes	Limit local taxes. "Proposition 2 1/2"	Passed
1980	Question 3	IDS	Taxes	Limit taxes; increase state share of education costs.	Failed

Year	Measure Number	Type	Subject Matter	Description	Pass/Fail
1982	Question 3	IDS	Nuclear weapons/ facilities/waste	Restrict radioactive waste disposal; construction.	Passed
1986	Question 3	IDS	Taxes	Limit state revenue tax increases: income surtax.	Passed
1986	Question 4	IDS	Environmental Reform	DEQE to identify/clean hazardous waste sites.	Passed
1986	Question 6	IDS	Election Reform	Mail-in voter registration.	Failed
1988	Question 2	IDS	Labor	Repeal prevailing wage law.	Failed
1988	Question 3	IDS	Animal Rights	Regulate treatment of farm animals.	Failed
1988	Question 4	IDS	Nuclear weapons/ facilities/waste	Ban electric power plants that produce nuclear waste.	Failed
1990	Question 2	IDS	Administration of Government	Limit state use of consultants	Failed
1990	Question 3	IDS	Taxes	Change income tax law; regulate state agency fees.	Failed
1990	Question 4	IDS	Election Reform	Establishment of political parties, nominations.	Passed
1990	Question 5	IDS	Administration of Government	Regulate local aid fund.	Passed
1992	Question 1	IDS	Taxes	Tax on cigarettes and smokeless tobacco.	Passed
1992	Question 2	IDS	Taxes	Public reporting of corporate tax information.	Passed
1992	Question 3	IDS	Environmental Reform	All packaging to be recycled or recyclable.	Failed
1992	Question 4	IDS	Taxes	Tax on oils, hazardous materials.	Failed
1994	Question 1	IDS	Campaign Finance Reform	Regulating spending on ballot question campaigns.	Failed
1994	Question 4	IDS	Term Limits	Term limits on state legislature 8/8 and on Congress 6/12.	Passed
1994	Question 5	IDS	Business Regulation	Opening of retail stores on Sunday morning and certain holidays.	Passed
1994	Question 6	DA	Taxes	Graduated income tax.	Failed
1994	Question 7	IDS	Taxes	Personal income tax changes.	Failed
1994	Question 8	IDS	Administration of Government	State highway fund changes.	Passed
1994	Question 9	DS	Housing	Prohibiting rent control.	Passed
1996	Question 1	IDS	Animal Rights	Prohibits use of leg hold traps and snares. Prohibits use of dogs and bait in hunting bear and bobcats.	Passed
1998	Question 2	IDS	Campaign Finance Reform	Would establish public funding of campaigns.	Passed
1998	Question 3	IDS	Taxes	Would cut state income taxes.	Passed
2000	Question 3	IDS	Animal Rights	This proposed law would prohibit in Massachusetts any dog racing or racing meeting where any form of betting or wagering on the speed or ability of dogs occurs.	Failed
2000	Question 4	IDS	Taxes	This proposed law would repeal the law setting the state personal income tax rate on Part B taxable income.	Passed

Year	Measure Number	Type	Subject Matter	Description	Pass/Fail
2000	Question 5	IDS	Health/Medical	This proposed law would set up a state Health Care Council to review and recommend legislation for a health care system that ensures comprehensive, high quality health care.	Failed
2000	Question 6	IDS	Taxes	This proposed law would allow a state personal income taxpayer a tax credit equal to the amount of tolls the taxpayer paid during the taxable year on all Massachusetts roads.	Failed
2000	Question 7	IDS	Taxes	This proposed law would allow taxpayers who give to charity a state personal income tax deduction for those charitable contributions.	Passed
2000	Question 8	IDS	Drug Policy Reform	This proposed law would create a state Drug Treatment Trust Fund, to be used, subject to appropriations by the state Legislature, solely for the treatment of drug-dependent persons. The Fund would include fines paid under the state's criminal drug laws; money and the proceeds from selling property forfeited because of its use in connection with drug crimes.	Failed

Massachusetts Constitution

Article XLVIII The Initiative.

II. Initiative Petitions.

Section 1. Contents.

An initiative petition shall set forth the full text of the constitutional amendment or law, hereinafter designated as the measure, which is proposed by the petition.

Section 2. Excluded Matters.

No measure that relates to religion, religious practices or religious institutions; or to the appointment, qualification, tenure, removal, recall or compensation of judges; or to the reversal of a judicial decision; or to the powers, creation or abolition of courts; or the operation of which is restricted to a particular town, city or other political division or to particular districts or localities of the commonwealth; or that makes a specific appropriation of money from the treasury of the commonwealth, shall be proposed by an initiative petition; but if a law approved by the people is not repealed, the general court shall raise by taxation or otherwise and shall appropriate such money as may be necessary to carry such law into effect.

Neither the eighteenth amendment of the constitution, as approved and ratified to take effect on the first day of October in the year nineteen hundred and eighteen, nor this provision for its protection, shall be the subject of an initiative amendment.

No proposition inconsistent with any one of the following rights of the individual, as at present declared in the declaration of rights, shall be the subject of an initiative or referendum petition: The right to receive compensation for private property appropriated to public use; the right of access to and protection in courts of justice; the right of trial by jury; protection from unreasonable search, unreasonable bail and the law martial; freedom of the press; freedom of speech; freedom of elections; and the right of peaceable assembly.

No part of the constitution specifically excluding any matter from the operation of the popular initiative and referendum shall be the subject of an initiative petition; nor shall this section be the subject of such a petition. The limitations on the legislative power of the general court in the constitution shall extend to the legislative power of the people as exercised hereunder.

Section 3. Mode of Originating.

Such petition shall first be signed by ten qualified voters of the commonwealth and shall then be submitted to the attorney-general, and if he shall certify that the measure is in proper form for submission to the people, and that it is not, either affirmatively or negatively, substantially the same as any measure which has been qualified for submission or submitted to the people within three years of the succeeding first Wednesday in December and that it contains only subjects not excluded from the popular initiative and which are related or which are mutually dependent, it may then be filed with the secretary of the commonwealth. The secretary of the commonwealth shall provide blanks for the use of subsequent signers, and shall print at the top of each blank a description of the proposed measure as such description will appear on the ballot together with the names and residences of the first ten signers. All initiative petitions, with the first ten signatures attached, shall be filed with the secretary of the commonwealth not earlier than the first Wednesday of the September before the assembling of the general court into which they are to be introduced, and the remainder of the required signatures shall be filed not later than the first Wednesday of the following December.] [Section 3 superseded by section 1 of Amendments, Art. LXXIV.]

Section 4. Transmission to the General Court.

If an initiative petition, signed by the required number of qualified voters, has been filed as aforesaid, the secretary of the commonwealth shall, upon the assembling of the general court, transmit it to the clerk of the house of representatives, and the proposed measure shall then be deemed to be introduced and pending.

III. Legislative Action. General Provisions.

Section 1. Reference to Committee.

If a measure is introduced into the general court by initiative petition, it shall be referred to a committee thereof, and the petitioners and all parties in interest shall be heard, and the measure shall be considered and reported upon to the general court with the committee's recommendations, and the reasons therefor, in writing. Majority and minority reports shall be signed by the members of said committee.

Section 2. Legislative Substitutes.

The general court may, by resolution passed by yea and nay vote, either by the two houses separately, or in the case of a constitutional amendment by a majority of those voting thereon in joint session in each of two years as hereinafter provided, submit to the people a substitute for any measure introduced by initiative petition, such substitute to be designated on the ballot as the legislative substitute for such an initiative measure and to be grouped with it as an alternative therefor.

IV. Legislative Action on Proposed Constitutional Amendments.

Section 1. Definition.

A proposal for amendment to the constitution introduced into the general court by initiative petition shall be designated an initiative amendment, and an amendment introduced by a member of either house shall be designated a legislative substitute or a legislative amendment.

Section 2. Joint Session.

If a proposal for a specific amendment of the constitution is introduced into the general court by initiative petition signed by not less than twenty-five thousand qualified voters, or if in case of a proposal for amendment introduced into the general court by a member of either house, consideration thereof in joint session is called for by vote of either house, such proposal shall, not later than the second Wednesday in June, be laid before a joint session of the two houses, at which the president of the senate shall preside; and if the two houses fail to agree upon a time for holding any joint session hereby required, or fail to continue the same from time to time until final action has been taken upon all amendments pending, the governor shall call such joint session or continuance thereof.] [Section 2 superseded by section 1 of Amendments, Art. LXXXI.]

Section 3. Amendment of Proposed Amendments.

A proposal for an amendment to the constitution introduced by initiative petition shall be voted upon in the form in which it was introduced, unless such amendment is amended by vote of three-fourths of the members voting thereon in joint session, which vote shall be taken by call of the yeas and nays if called for by any member.

Section 4. Legislative Action.

Final legislative action in the joint session upon any amendment shall be taken only by call of the yeas and nays, which shall be entered upon the journals of the two houses; and an unfavorable vote at any stage preceding final action shall be verified by call of the yeas and nays, to be entered in like manner. At such joint session a legislative amendment receiving the affirmative votes of a majority of all the members elected, or an initiative amendment receiving the affirmative votes of not less than one-fourth of all the members elected, shall be referred to the next general court.

Section 5. Submission to the People.

If in the next general court a legislative amendment shall again be agreed to in joint session by a majority of all the members elected, or if an initiative amendment or a legislative substitute shall again receive the affirmative votes of a least one-fourth of all the members elected, such fact shall be certified by the clerk of such joint session to the secretary of the commonwealth, who shall submit the amendment to the people at the next state election. Such amendment shall become part of the constitution if approved, in the case of a legislative amendment, by a majority of the voters voting thereon, or if approved, in the case of an initiative amendment or a legislative substitute, by voters equal in number to at least thirty per cent of the total number of ballots cast at such state election and also by a majority of the voters voting on such amendment.

V. Legislative Action on Proposed Laws.

[Section 1. Legislative Procedure.

If an initiative petition for a law is introduced into the general court, signed by not less than twenty thousand qualified voters, a vote shall be taken by yeas and nays in both houses before the first Wednesday of June upon the enactment of such law in the form in which it stands in such petition. If the general court fails to enact such law before the first Wednesday of June, and if such petition is completed by filing with the secretary of the commonwealth, not earlier than the first Wednesday of the following July nor later than the first Wednesday of the following August, not less than five thousand signatures of qualified voters, in addition to those signing such initiative petition, which signatures must have been obtained after the first Wednesday of June aforesaid, then the secretary of the commonwealth shall submit such proposed law to the people at the next state election. If it shall be approved by voters equal in number to at least thirty per cent of the total number of ballots cast at such state election and also by a majority of the voters voting on such law, it shall become law, and shall take effect in thirty days after such state election or at such time after such election as may be provided in such law.] [Section 1 superseded by section 2 of Amendments, Art. LXXXI.]

[Section 2. Amendment by Petitioners.

If the general court fails to pass a proposed law before the first Wednesday of June, a majority of the first ten signers of the initiative petition therefor shall have the right, subject to certification by the attorney-general filed as hereinafter provided, to amend the measure which is the subject of such petition. An amendment so made shall not invalidate any signature attached to the petition. If the measure so amended, signed by a majority of the first ten signers, is filed with the secretary of the commonwealth before the first Wednesday of the following July, together with a certificate signed by the attorney-general to the effect that the amendment made by such proposers is in his opinion perfecting in its nature and does not materially change the substance of the measure, and if such petition is completed by filing with the secretary of the commonwealth, not earlier than the first Wednesday of the following July nor later than the first Wednesday of the following August, not less than five thousand signatures of qualified voters, in addition to those signing such initiative petition, which signatures must have been obtained after the first Wednesday of June aforesaid, then the secretary of the commonwealth shall submit the measure to the people in its amended form.] [Section 2 superseded by section 3 of Amendments, Art. LXXXI.]

VI. Conflicting and Alternative Measures.

If in any judicial proceeding, provisions of constitutional amendments or of laws approved by the people at the same election are held to be in conflict, then the provisions contained in the measure that received the largest number of affirmative votes at such election shall govern.

A constitutional amendment approved at any election shall govern any law approved at the same election.

The general court, by resolution passed as hereinbefore set forth, may provide for grouping and designating upon the ballot as conflicting measures or as alternative measures, only one of which is to be adopted, any two or more proposed constitutional amendments or laws which have been or may be passed or qualified for submission to the people at any one election: provided, that a proposed constitutional amendment and a proposed law shall not be so grouped, and that the ballot shall afford an opportunity to the voter to vote for each of the measures or for only one of the measures, as may be provided in said resolution, or against each of the measures so grouped as conflicting or as alternative. In case more than one of the measures so grouped shall receive the vote required for its approval as herein provided, only that one for which the largest affirmative vote was cast shall be deemed to be approved.

The Referendum.

I. When Statutes shall take Effect.

No law passed by the general court shall take effect earlier than ninety days after it has become a law, excepting laws declared to be emergency laws and laws which may not be made the subject of a referendum petition, as herein provided.

II. Emergency Measures.

A law declared to be an emergency law shall contain a preamble setting forth the facts constituting the emergency, and shall contain the statement that such law is necessary for the immediate preservation of the public peace, health, safety or convenience. [A separate vote shall be taken on the preamble by call of the yeas and nays, which shall be recorded, and unless the preamble is adopted by two-thirds of the members of each house voting thereon, the law shall not be an emergency law; but] if the governor, at any time before the election at which it is to be submitted to the people on referendum, files with the secretary of the commonwealth a statement declaring that in his opinion the immediate preservation of the public peace, health, safety or convenience requires that such law should take effect forthwith and that it is an emergency law and setting forth the facts constituting the emergency, then such law, if not previously suspended as hereinafter provided, shall take effect without suspension, or if such law has been so suspended such suspension shall thereupon terminate and such law shall thereupon take effect: but no grant of any franchise or amendment thereof, or renewal or extension thereof for more than one year shall be declared to be an emergency law. [See Amendments, Art. LXVII.]

III. Referendum Petitions.

Section 1. Contents.

A referendum petition may ask for a referendum to the people upon any law enacted by the general court which is not herein expressly excluded.

Section 2. Excluded Matters.

No law that relates to religion, religious practices or religious institutions; or to the appointment, qualification, tenure, removal or compensation of judges; or to the powers, creation or abolition of courts; or the operation of which is restricted to a particular town, city or other political division or to particular districts or localities of the commonwealth; or that appropriates money for the current or ordinary expenses of the commonwealth or for any of its departments, boards, commissions or institutions shall be the subject of a referendum petition.

Section 3. Mode of Petitioning for the Suspension of a Law and a Referendum Thereon.

A petition asking for a referendum on a law, and requesting that the operation of such law be suspended, shall first be signed by ten qualified voters and shall then be filed with the secretary of the commonwealth not later than thirty days after the law that is the subject of the petition has become law. [The secretary of the commonwealth shall provide blanks for the use of subsequent signers, and shall print at the top of each blank a description of the proposed law as such description will appear on the ballot together with the names and residences of the first ten signers. If such petition is completed by filing with the secretary of the commonwealth not later than ninety days after the law which is the subject of the petition has become law the signatures of not less than fifteen thousand qualified voters of the commonwealth, then the operation of such law shall be suspended, and the secretary of the commonwealth shall submit such law to the people at the next state election, if thirty days intervene between the date when such petition is filed with the secretary of the commonwealth and the date for holding such state election; if thirty days do not so intervene, then such law shall be submitted to the people at the next following state election, unless in the meantime it shall have been repealed; and if it shall be approved by a majority of the qualified voters voting thereon, such law shall, subject to the provisions of the constitution, take effect in thirty days after such election, or at such time after such election as may be provided in such law;

if not so approved such law shall be null and void; but no such law shall be held to be disapproved if the negative vote is less than thirty per cent of the total number of ballots cast at such state election.] [Section 3 amended by section 2 of Amendments, Art. LXXIV and section 4 of Amendments, Art. LXXXI]

Section 4. Petitions for Referendum on an Emergency Law or a Law the Suspension of Which is Not Asked for.

A referendum petition may ask for the repeal of an emergency law or of a law which takes effect because the referendum petition does not contain a request for suspension, as aforesaid. Such petition shall first be signed by ten qualified voters of the commonwealth, and shall then be filed with the secretary of the commonwealth not later than thirty days after the law which is the subject of the petition has become law. [The secretary of the commonwealth shall provide blanks for the use of subsequent signers, and shall print at the top of each blank a description of the proposed law as such description will appear on the ballot together with the names and residences of the first ten signers. If such petition filed as aforesaid is completed by filing with the secretary of the commonwealth not later than ninety days after the law which is the subject of the petition has become law the signatures of not less than ten thousand qualified voters of the commonwealth protesting against such law and asking for a referendum thereon, then the secretary of the commonwealth shall submit such law to the people at the next state election, if thirty days intervene between the date when such petition is filed with the secretary of the commonwealth and the date for holding such state election. If thirty days do not so intervene, then it shall be submitted to the people at the next following state election, unless in the meantime it shall have been repealed; and if it shall not be approved by a majority of the qualified voters voting thereon, it shall, at the expiration of thirty days after such election, be thereby repealed; but no such law shall be held to be disapproved if the negative vote is less than thirty per cent of the total number of ballots cast at such state election.] [Section 4 superseded by section 3 of Amendments, Art. LXXIV and section 5 of Amendments, Art. LXXXI.]

General Provisions.

I. Identification and Certification of Signatures.

Provision shall be made by law for the proper identification and certification of signatures to the petitions hereinbefore referred to, and for penalties for signing any such petition, or refusing to sign it, for money or other valuable consideration, and for the forgery of signatures thereto. Pending the passage of such legislation all provisions of law relating to the identification and certification of signatures to petitions for the nomination of candidates for state offices or to penalties for the forgery of such signatures shall apply to the signatures to the petitions herein referred to. The general court may provide by law that no co-partnership or corporation shall undertake for hire or reward to circulate petitions, may require individuals who circulate petitions for hire or reward to be licensed, and may make other reasonable regulations to prevent abuses arising from the circulation of petitions for hire or reward.

II. Limitation on Signatures.

Not more than one-fourth of the certified signatures on any petition shall be those of registered voters of any one county.

III. Form of Ballot.

Each proposed amendment to the constitution, and each law submitted to the people, shall be described on the ballots by a description to be determined by the attorney-general, subject to such provision as may be made by law, and the secretary of the commonwealth shall give each question a number and cause such question, except as otherwise authorized herein, to be printed on the ballot in the following form: —

In the case of an amendment to the constitution: Shall an amendment to the constitution (here insert description, and state, in distinctive type, whether approved or disapproved by the general court, and by what vote thereon) be approved?

In the case of a law: Shall a law (here insert description, and state, in distinctive type, whether approved or disapproved by the general court, and by what vote thereon) be approved?

IV. Information for Voters.

The secretary of the commonwealth shall cause to be printed and sent to each registered voter in the commonwealth the full text of every measure to be submitted to the people, together with a copy of the legislative committee's majority and minority reports, if there be such, with the names of the majority and minority members thereon, a statement of the votes of the general court on the measure, and a description of the measure as such description will appear on the ballot; and shall, in such manner as may be provided by law, cause to be prepared and sent to the voters other information and arguments for and against the measure.] [Subheadings III and IV> superseded by section 4 of Amendments, Art. LXXIV.] [Subheading IV superseded by Amendments, Art. CVIII.]

V. The Veto Power of the Governor.

The veto power of the governor shall not extend to measures approved by the people.

VI. The General Court's Power of Repeal.

Subject to the veto power of the governor and to the right of referendum by petition as herein provided, the general court may amend or repeal a law approved by the people.

VII. Amendment Declared to be Self-executing.

This article of amendment to the constitution is self-executing, but legislation not inconsistent with anything herein contained may be enacted to facilitate the operation of its provisions.

Article LXVII.

Article XLVIII of the Amendments to the Constitution is hereby amended by striking out, in that part entitled "II. Emergency Measures", under the heading "The Referendum", the words "A separate vote shall be taken on the preamble by call of the yeas and nays, which shall be recorded, and unless the preamble is adopted by two-thirds of the members of each House voting thereon, the law shall not be an emergency law; but" and substituting the following: — A separate vote, which shall be recorded, shall be taken on the preamble, and unless the preamble is adopted by two-thirds of the members of each House voting thereon, the law shall not be an emergency law. Upon the request of two members of the Senate or of five members of the House of Representatives, the vote on the preamble in such branch shall be taken by call of the yeas and nays.

Article LXXIV. Section 1.

Article XLVIII of the amendments to the constitution is hereby amended by striking out section three, under the heading "THE INITIATIVE. III. Initiative Petitions.", and inserting in place thereof the following: —

Section 3. Mode of Originating.

Such petition shall first be signed by ten qualified voters of the commonwealth and shall be submitted to the attorney-general not later than the first Wednesday of the August before the assembling of the general court into which it is to be introduced, and if he shall certify that the measure and the title thereof are in proper form for submission to the people, and that the measure is not, either affirmatively or negatively, substantially the same as any measure which has been qualified for submission or submitted to the people at either of the two preceding biennial state elections, and that it contains only subjects not excluded from the popular initiative and which are related or which are mutually dependent, it may then be filed with the secretary of the commonwealth. The secretary of the commonwealth shall provide blanks for the use of subsequent signers, and shall print at the top of each blank a fair, concise summary, as determined by the attorney-general, of the proposed measure as such summary will appear on the ballot together with the names and residences of the first ten signers. All initiative petitions, with the first ten signatures attached, shall be filed with the secretary of the commonwealth not earlier than the first Wednesday of the September before the assembling of the general court into which they are to be introduced, and the remainder of the required signatures shall be filed not later than the first Wednesday of the following December.

Section 2.

Section three of that part of said Article XLVIII, under the heading "THE REFERENDUM. III. Referendum Petitions.", is hereby amended by striking out the words "The secretary of the commonwealth shall provide blanks for the use of subsequent signers, and shall print at the top of each blank a description of the proposed law as such description will appear on the ballot together with the names and residences of the first ten signers.", and inserting in place thereof the words "The secretary of the commonwealth shall provide blanks for the use of subsequent signers, and shall print at the top of each blank a fair, concise summary of the proposed law as such summary will appear on the ballot together with the names and residences of the first ten signers."

Section 3.

Section four of that part of said Article XLVIII under the heading "THE REFERENDUM. III. Referendum Petitions.", is hereby amended by striking out the words "The secretary of the commonwealth shall provide blanks for the use of subsequent signers, and shall print at the top of each blank a description of the proposed law as such description will appear on the ballot together with the names and residences of the first ten signers.", and inserting in place thereof the words "The secretary of the commonwealth shall provide blanks for the use of subsequent signers, and shall print at the top of each blank a fair, concise summary of the proposed law as such summary will appear on the ballot together with the names and residences of the first ten signers."

Section 4.

Said Article XLVIII is hereby further amended by striking out, under the heading "GENERAL PROVISIONS", all of sub-heading "III. Form of Ballot." and all of subheading "IV. Information for Voters.", and inserting in place thereof the following: —

III. Form of Ballot.

A fair, concise summary, as determined by the attorney general, subject to such provision as may be made by law, of each proposed amendment to the constitution, and each law submitted to the people, shall be printed on the ballot, and the secretary of the commonwealth shall give each question a number and cause such question, except as otherwise authorized herein, to be printed on the ballot in the following form: —

In the case of an amendment to the constitution: Do you approve of the adoption of an amendment to the constitution summarized below, (here state, in distinctive type, whether approved or disapproved by the general court, and by what vote thereon)?
[Set forth summary here]

In the case of a law: Do you approve of a law summarized below, (here state, in distinctive type, whether approved or disapproved by the general court, and by what vote thereon)?
[Set forth summary here]

IV. Information for Voters.

The secretary of the commonwealth shall cause to be printed and sent to each registered voter in the commonwealth the full text of every measure to be submitted to the people, together with a copy of the legislative committee's majority and minority reports, if there be such, with the names of the majority and minority members thereon, a statement of the votes of the general court on the measure, and a fair, concise summary of the measure as such summary will appear on the ballot; and shall, in such manner as may be provided by law, cause to be prepared and sent to the voters other information and arguments for and against the measure.] [See Amendments, Art. CVIII.]

Article LXXXI. Section 1.

Article XLVIII of the Amendments to the Constitution is hereby amended by striking out section 2, under the heading "THE INITIATIVE. IV. Legislative Action on Proposed Constitutional Amendments.", and inserting in place thereof the following: —

Section 2.

Joint Session. — If a proposal for a specific amendment of the constitution is introduced into the general court by initiative petition signed in the aggregate by not less than such number of voters as will equal three per cent of the entire vote cast for governor at the preceding biennial state election, or if in case of a proposal for amendment introduced into the general court by a member of either house, consideration thereof in joint session is called for by vote of either house, such proposal shall, not later than the second Wednesday in May, be laid before a joint session of the two houses, at which the president of the senate shall preside; and if the two houses fail to agree upon a time for holding any joint session hereby required, or fail to continue the same from time to time until final action has been taken upon all amendments pending, the governor shall call such joint session or continuance thereof.

Section 2.

Section 1 of that part of said Article XLVIII, under the heading "THE INITIATIVE. V. Legislative Action on Proposed Laws.", is hereby amended by striking out said section and inserting in place thereof the following: —

Section 1. Legislative Procedure.

If an initiative petition for a law is introduced into the general court, signed in the aggregate by not less than such number of voters as will equal three per cent of the entire vote cast for governor at the preceding biennial state election, a vote shall be taken by yeas and nays in both houses before the first Wednesday of May upon the enactment of such law in the form in which it stands in such petition. If the general court fails to enact such law before the first Wednesday of May, and if such petition is completed by filing with the secretary of the commonwealth, not earlier than the first Wednesday of the following June nor later than the first Wednesday of the following July, a number of signatures of qualified voters equal in number to not less than one half of one per cent of the entire vote cast for governor at the preceding biennial state election, in addition to those signing such initiative petition, which signatures must have been obtained after the first Wednesday of May aforesaid, then the secretary of the commonwealth shall submit such proposed law to the people at the next state election. If it shall be approved by voters equal in number to at least thirty per cent of the total number of ballots cast at such state election and also by a majority of the voters voting on such law, it shall become law, and shall take effect in thirty days after such state election or at such time after such election as may be provided in such law.

Section 3.

Section 2 of that part of said Article XLVIII, under the heading "THE INITIATIVE. V. Legislative Action on Proposed Laws.", is hereby amended by striking out said section and inserting in place thereof the following:—

Section 2. Amendment by Petitioners.

If the general court fails to pass a proposed law before the first Wednesday of May, a majority of the first ten signers of the initiative petition therefor shall have the right, subject to certification by the attorney-general filed as hereinafter provided, to amend the measure which is the subject of such petition. An amendment so made shall not invalidate any signature attached to the petition. If the measure so amended, signed by a majority of the first ten signers, is filed with the secretary of the commonwealth before the first Wednesday of the following June, together with a certificate signed by the attorney-general to the effect that the amendment made by such proposers is in his opinion perfecting in its nature and does not materially change the substance of the measure, and if such petition is completed by filing with the secretary of the commonwealth, not earlier than the first Wednesday of the following June nor later than the first Wednesday of the following July, a number of signatures of qualified voters equal in number to not less than one half of one per cent of the entire vote cast for governor at the preceding biennial state election in addition to those signing such initiative petition, which signatures must have been obtained after the first Wednesday of May aforesaid, then the secretary of the commonwealth shall submit the measure to the people in its amended form.

Section 4.

Section 3 of that part of said Article XLVIII, under the heading "THE REFERENDUM. III. Referendum Petitions.", is hereby amended by striking out the sentence "If such petition is completed by filing with the secretary of the commonwealth not later than ninety days after the law which is the subject of the petition has become law the signatures of not less than fifteen thousand qualified voters of the commonwealth, then the operation of such law shall be suspended, and the secretary of the commonwealth shall submit such law to the people at the next state election, if thirty days intervene between the date when such petition is filed with the secretary of the commonwealth and the date for holding such state election; if thirty days do not so intervene, then such law shall be submitted to the people at the next following state election, unless in the meantime it shall have been repealed; and if it shall be approved by a majority of the qualified voters voting thereon, such law shall, subject to the provisions of the constitution, take effect in thirty days after such election, or at such time after such election as may be provided in such law; if not so approved such law shall be null and void; but no such law shall be held to be disapproved if the negative vote is less than thirty per cent of the total number of ballots cast at such state election." and inserting in place thereof the following sentence:—If such petition is completed by filing with the secretary of the commonwealth not later than ninety days after the law which is the subject of the petition has become law a number of signatures of qualified voters equal in number to not less than two per cent of the entire vote cast for governor at the preceding biennial state election, then the operation of such law shall be suspended, and the secretary of the commonwealth shall submit such law to the people at the next state election, if sixty days intervene between the date when such petition is filed with the secretary of the commonwealth and the date for holding such state election; if sixty days do not so intervene, then such law shall be submitted to the people at the next following state election, unless in the meantime it shall have been repealed; and if it shall be approved by a majority of the qualified voters voting thereon, such law shall, subject to the provisions of the constitution, take effect in thirty days after such election, or at such time after such election as may be provided in such law; if not so approved such law shall be null and void; but no such law shall be held to be disapproved if the negative vote is less than thirty per cent of the total number of ballots cast at such state election.

Section 5.

Section 4 of that part of said Article XLVIII, under the heading "THE REFERENDUM. III. Referendum Petitions.", is hereby amended by striking out the words "If such petition filed as aforesaid is completed by filing with the secretary of the commonwealth not later than ninety days after the law which is the subject of the petition has become law the signatures of not less than ten thousand qualified voters of the commonwealth protesting against such law and asking for a referendum thereon, then the secretary of the commonwealth shall submit such law to the people at the next state election, if thirty days intervene between the date when such petition is filed with the secretary of the commonwealth and the date for holding such state election. If thirty days do not so intervene, then it shall be submitted to the people at the next following state election, unless in the meantime it shall have been repealed; and if it shall not be approved by a majority of the qualified voters voting thereon, it shall, at the expiration of thirty days after such election, be thereby repealed; but no such law shall be held to be disapproved if the negative vote is less than thirty per cent of the total number of ballots cast at such state election." and inserting in place thereof the following: — If such petition filed as aforesaid is completed by filing with the secretary of the commonwealth not later than ninety days after the law which is the subject of the petition has become law a number of signatures of qualified voters equal in number to not less than one and one half per cent of the entire vote cast for governor at the preceding biennial state election protesting against such law and asking for a referendum thereon, then the secretary of the commonwealth shall submit such law to the people at the next state election, if sixty days intervene between the date when such petition is filed with the secretary of the commonwealth and the date for holding such state election. If sixty days do not so intervene, then it shall be submitted to the people at the next following state election, unless in the meantime it shall have been repealed; and if it shall not be approved by a majority of the qualified voters voting thereon, it shall, at the expiration of thirty days after such election, be thereby repealed; but no such law shall be held to be disapproved if the negative vote is less than thirty per cent of the total number of ballots cast at such state election.

Massachusetts Statutes

Part I. Administration of The Government.

Title VIII. Elections.

Chapter 53: Section 19. Questions of public policy submitted in certain districts upon application.

On an application signed by twelve hundred voters in any senatorial district, or by two hundred voters in any representative district, asking for the submission to the voters in that senatorial or representative district of any question of instructions to the senator or representatives from that district, and stating the substance thereof, the attorney general shall upon request of the state secretary determine whether or not such question is one of public policy, and if such question is determined to be one of public policy, the state secretary and the attorney general shall draft it in such simple, unequivocal and adequate form as shall be deemed best suited for presentation upon the ballot. Upon the fulfillment of the requirements of this and the two following sections the state secretary shall place such question on the official ballot to be used in that senatorial or representative district at the next state election.

Chapter 53: Section 20. Applications; signatures; identification; certification.

The provisions of law relative to the signing of nomination papers of candidates for state office, and to the identification and certification of names thereon and submission to the registrars therefor, shall apply, so far as apt, to applications submitted under section nineteen. Petition forms for such applications submitted under section nineteen shall be made available for use on or before the fifteenth Tuesday preceding the final date for filing as provided in section twenty-one.

Chapter 53: Section 21. Applications; filing; number of questions; resubmission.

Applications shall be filed with the state secretary not later than the first Wednesday of August before the election at which the questions are to be submitted. Not more than three questions under section nineteen shall be placed upon the ballot at one election, and they shall be submitted in the order in which the applications are filed. No question negatived and no question substantially the same shall be submitted again in less than three years.

Chapter 53: Section 22A. Signing initiative and referendum petitions; forms; receipt; filing date.

The provisions of law relative to the signing of nomination papers of candidates for state office, and to the identification and certification of names thereon and submission to the registrars therefor, shall apply, so far as apt, to the signing of initiative and referendum petitions and to the identification and certification of names thereon, and, except as otherwise provided, to the time of their submission to the registrars. Initiative or referendum petition forms shall be made available no later than the fourteenth day after the date such petitions are filed with the state secretary by the first ten signers; provided, however, that in the instance of petitions filed under the provisions of section three or section four of that part of Article XLVIII of the Amendments of the Constitution under the heading "THE REFERENDUM. III. Referendum Petitions.", the petition forms shall be made available no later than the fourteenth day after a summary has been prepared. Registrars shall receipt in writing for each initiative or referendum petition submitted to and received by them, and shall deliver such petitions only on receiving written receipts therefor or other identification acceptable to the registrars. Each initiative and referendum petition shall state the last day and hour for filing such petitions with the registrars and with the state secretary. Certificates showing that each of the ten original signers is a registered voter at the stated address, signed by a majority of the registrars of voters, shall accompany an original initiative or referendum petition. In no case shall any blank forms for such initiative or referendum petitions be larger than eight and one half inches by fourteen inches, nor shall anyone be prohibited from making exact copies of such blanks provided by the secretary of state for the purpose of collecting signatures for such petitions, nor shall any such copies be rejected for certification or submittal to the secretary of state.

The Basic Steps to Do an Initiative in Massachusetts

Statutes and Amendments — Indirect Initiative Process

Basic Procedures: Ten qualified voters may draw up and sign an original petition on which they put forward the full text of the law they want enacted. Each of the ten original signers must obtain certificates of voter registration from the board of registrars or election commission in the city or town where they are registered voters. The certificate of voter registration must be signed by at least three registrars. These certificates and the original petition must be submitted to the Attorney General no later then the first Wednesday of August 2001.

The Attorney General certifies that the measure and the title thereof are in proper form for submission to the people, and that the measure is not, either affirmatively or negatively, substantially the same as any measure which has been qualified for submission or submitted to the people at either of the two preceding biennial state elections, and that it contains only subjects not excluded from the popular initiative. The Constitution excludes from the initiative subjects that relate to religion, judges, the courts, particular localities, specific appropriations, and certain provisions of the state constitution's Declaration of Rights.

Once the Attorney General finds that the petition is acceptable, he prepares a summary and returns the summary and the petition to the petitioners, who must file the petition and summary with the Secretary of State. The initiative can be filed with the Secretary of State sometime after the first Wednesday in September of 2001. The Attorney General almost always reviews the measure and writes the summary by the first Wednesday of September, but is not required by statute to do so. (The Attorney General works closely with proponents on writing the title and summary and proponents can challenge the ultimate language directly in the Massachusetts Supreme Court.)

After the proponents submit the final language to the Secretary of State, the Secretary of State will prepare the initiative petition forms with the summary printed thereon for voters to sign within fourteen days after receiving the papers from the original petitioners.

Date initiative language can be submitted for the November 2002 election: Any time, but not later than the first Wednesday of August 2001. Proponents, however, cannot circulate their petitions until after the first Wednesday in September.

Signatures are tied to vote of which office: Governor

Next Gubernatorial election: 2002

Votes cast for governor in last election: 1,935,277 (1998)

Net number of signatures required: Massachusetts has an in-direct initiative process. In order to be placed before the General Court, the petition (whether a statute or an amendment) must contain certified signatures at least equal to 3% of the total vote cast for all candidates for governor (excluding blanks) at the last state election. This means that until the results of the 2002 state election are certified by the Governor's Council, the initiative petition must be signed by a minimum of 57,100 certified voters. No more than one-quarter of the certified signatures may come from any one county (until the results of the 2002 state election are certified by the Governor's Council, this figure is 14,275).
A) Statutes: If the petition is rejected by the General Court or if the General Court fails to act by the first Wednesday in May of 2002, the proposed ballot measure, in an infrequently used process, may be amended by a majority of the ten original signers. Any amendment proposed pursuant to this infrequently used process must be approved by the Attorney General as perfecting in nature; that is, the amendment does not materially change the substance of the measure. The proponents may force the original or amended petition on the ballot at the next regular state election by submitting a written request to the Secretary of State by the appropriate deadline for additional petition forms and then collecting the

required number of additional certified signatures on these forms. This request should indicate that a majority of the first ten signers wish to obtain additional petition forms. The request need not contain the signatures of all ten signers, and an agent may sign on behalf of a majority of the first ten signers. The signatures of an additional 1/2 of 1% of the vote cast for governor (excluding blanks) at the last state election must be filed with the Secretary of the Commonwealth. This means that, until the Governor's Council certifies the results of the 2002 state election, the additional signature requirement is 9,517 certified signatures. The same provision applies that no more than 1/4 of these signatures may come from one county (until the results of the 2002 state election are certified by the Governor's Council, this is 2,379).

B) Constitutional Amendments: After signatures have been certified and petitions filed, the Secretary transmits the amendment petition to the House clerk for legislative action on the first legislative day of the year.

Initiative amendments are acted upon by joint sessions of the House and Senate sitting together. The amendment must be "laid before" the joint session by the second Wednesday of May. The petition may be amended by a three-fourths affirmative majority vote by the House and Senate. By a majority vote, the Legislature may formulate a proposal of it own, to be grouped on the ballot with the initiative amendment as an alternative choice. The initiative amendment must be placed on the ballot if, in joint sessions held by two successively elected Legislatures, the petition wins the support of at least 25% (50) of the 200 legislators (40 senators and 160 representatives). An initiative amendment to the constitution will not appear on the ballot if, when it comes to a vote in either joint session, less than 25% of the legislators vote in favor of it or no vote is taken before the legislative term ends.

Distribution requirement: No more than one-quarter of the certified signatures may come from any one county (until the results of the 2002 state election are certified by the Governor's Council, this figure is 14,275).

Circulation period: 64 days

Do circulators have to be residents of the state: No

Date when signatures are due for certification: The petitions must be submitted to the Local Registrars of Voters at least 14 days before the first Wednesday in December 2001 for verification, with the exception of Boston, which will be 10 days earlier. (Once signatures are verified by the Local Registrars of Voters, proponents have until the first Wednesday in December to submit them to the Secretary of State.)

Signature verification process: All signatures must be certified by a majority (at least three) of the local registrars or election commissioners in the city or town in which the signatures are collected.

Single Subject Restriction: Massachusetts has no single subject requirement.

Legislative tampering: Legislature can both repeal and amend initiatives. (Massachusetts Constitution Article 48, Gen. Prov. Pt. 6)

General Comments: Even though the state allows the citizens to propose both amendments and statutes through the initiative process, it has been the history of the state that most citizens propose statutory changes versus amendments. This is primarily because when an amendment is submitted to the legislature, they do not have to act and there is no provision to collect additional signatures and place the amendment on the ballot.

In addition, a recent Massachusetts Supreme Judicial Court case has set a strong precedent restricting the circulation and gathering of signatures on ballot question petitions. *Hurst v. State Ballot Law Commission*, 427 Mass. 825 (1998). Specifically, the court ruled that any extraneous markings on the petition sheet would invalidate all of the signatures contained thereon. The court stated that, "...no alterations—additions or deletions—of any sort may be made to the forms provided by the Secretary...." Hurst at 830. The Secretary of State now warns:

"In the past, the Secretary of State has accepted petitions containing various markings. Such markings have included highlighting, underlining, stamped and/or printed return addresses, as well as numbering on each petition. However, in light of the recent court decision the Secretary of State is no longer able to accept the signatures on petitions containing such extraneous markings. This office will therefore reject the signatures contained on any petitions deviating from an 'exact copy' of the blank petition provided by the Secretary."

Thus, DO NOT place a return address (*handwritten, stamped or printed*) on the petitions.

DO NOT use a highlighter or mark any area on the petition, especially the summary.

DO NOT underline any area on the petition.

DO NOT number the petitions.

DO NOT put the name of the signature gatherer on the petition.

Please be aware that any extraneous markings on a petition sheet will result in invalidation of all signatures contained on it.

Michigan

Agitation for initiative and referendum in Michigan started with the formation of the state's Direct Legislation Club in 1895 by George F. Sherman and David Inglis, both Detroit physicians. Inglis was 45 years old, a distinguished professor at the Detroit Medical College. Sherman and Inglis led I&R efforts in Michigan for over a decade without success, despite support from the noted reformer, Detroit mayor, and later Michigan governor Hazen S. Pingree. In 1900 S. D. Williams of Battle Creek cited the legislature's Republican majority as the major obstacle.

The reformers won passage of an I&R amendment at the state constitutional convention of 1907. The voters ratified it in 1908, but the victory turned out to be hollow. The amendment proved so restrictive that citizens were unable to place a single initiative on the ballot.

Michigan I&R advocates resumed lobbying the legislature for a better amendment and gained the support of Governor Chase S. Osborn, a Progressive elected in 1910. The legislature rejected Osborn's attempts, but relented in 1913 during the administration of Governor Ferris, another I&R supporter.

Under the new provisions, it took 39,000 signatures to put a constitutional amendment initiative on the 1914 ballot. The first two initiatives that won voter approval, however, were on the ballot in 1932: a measure to establish a liquor control commission passed overwhelmingly, and an amendment to limit property taxes won 51.1 percent of the vote.

In 1938, voters passed an amendment specifying that gas and vehicle weight tax money must be used for roads and streets; the following year, in an April special election, they approved a system for the nonpartisan election of judges. In 1946, voters enacted an initiative to ensure that part of the state's sales tax revenues were returned to the municipalities; in 1948, they modified the property tax limitation.

The initiative for which Michigan is most famous is the Bottle Bill, approved by a two to one margin in 1976, which put a 10-cent deposit on bottles and cans.

In 1998, the voters rejected a physician assisted suicide initiative and in 2000 defeated a school voucher initiative that was sponsored by Amway founder Dick DeVos.

Statewide Initiative Usage

Number of Initiatives	Number Passed	Number Failed	Passage Rate
60	20	40	33%

Statewide Initiatives

Year	Measure Number	Type	Subject Matter	Description	Pass/Fail
1914	N/A	DA	Business Regulation	Relative to the incorporation, regulation and supervision of beneficiary societies.	Failed
1916	N/A	DA	Business Regulation	Relative to the regulation of beneficiary societies.	Failed
1919	N/A	DA	Alcohol Regulation	Relative to the manufacture of cider, wines, beer, etc.	Failed
1920	N/A	DA	Education	Relative to compulsory attendance at the public schools of all residents of Michigan between the ages of five years and sixteen years.	Failed
1924	N/A	DA	Education	Relative to compulsory attendance in public schools.	Failed
1924	N/A	DA	Taxes	Relative to an income tax.	Failed

Year	Measure Number	Type	Subject Matter	Description	Pass/Fail
1924	N/A	DA	Apportionment/ Redistricting	Relative to division of the state into senatorial and representative districts.	Failed
1930	N/A	DA	Apportionment/ Redistricting	Relative to apportionment of legislative districts.	Failed
1932	N/A	DA	Alcohol Regulation	Relative to establishment of a liquor control commission.	Passed
1932	N/A	DA	Taxes	Relative to limitation of taxes assessed against property.	Passed
1932	N/A	DA	Administration of Government	Relative to term of office and apportionment of senators and representatives in state legislature.	Failed
1932	N/A	DA	Taxes	Relative to exemption from taxation of homesteads, etc.	Failed
1934	N/A	DA	Taxes	Relative to limiting specific taxes upon gasoline and like fuel sold or used to propel motor vehicles, and providing exemptions of certain other taxes for those engaged in manufacturing, etc. gasoline and like fuels.	Failed
1934	N/A	DA	Taxes	Relative to abolishing the uniform rule of taxation and to permit the classification of property for taxation purposes and an income tax for public schools.	Failed
1934	N/A	DA	Taxes	Relative to limiting registration license fees or taxes on all motor vehicles except commercial motor vehicles and motorcycles, and providing for exemptions from certain other taxes.	Failed
1934	N/A	DA	Election Reform	Relative to providing for nonpartisan elections of judges.	Failed
1934	N/A	DA	Administration of Government	Relative to permitting the adoption of home rule government by counties.	Failed
1936	N/A	DA	Taxes	Relative to exempting certain articles of food and prepared meals from the sales tax.	Failed
1936	N/A	DA	Alcohol Regulation	Relative to prohibition after December 31, 1937, certain real property taxes and to provide for an income tax.	Failed
1938	N/A	DA	Administration of Government	Relative to increasing terms of County offices from two- to four-year terms.	Failed
1938	N/A	DA	Judicial Reform	Relative to non-partisan nomination and appointment of supreme court justices for 8 year terms.	Failed
1938	N/A	DA	Taxes	Relative to guaranteeing that gas and weight tax monies be used solely for highways, roads and streets.	Passed
1939	N/A	DA	Election Reform	Relative to nonpartisan election of judges.	Passed
1940	N/A	DA	Administration of Government	Establishing a new system of civil service in state employment.	Passed
1942	N/A	DA	Administration of Government	To permit Wayne County to adopt a charter.	Failed

Year	Measure Number	Type	Subject Matter	Description	Pass/Fail
1946	N/A	DA	Administration of Government	To permit Wayne County to adopt a charter.	Failed
1946	N/A	DA	Administration of Government	Return of portion of sales tax to certain municipalities	Passed
1948	N/A	DA	Taxes	Modify 15 mill limitation.	Passed
1950	N/A	DA	Business Regulation	To permit the sale of oleomargarine.	Passed
1952	N/A	DA	Apportionment/ Redistricting	Establishing senatorial districts and providing decennial reapportionment of representatives by legislatures.	Passed
1952	N/A	DA	Apportionment/ Redistricting	To provide for decennial reapportionment of senate and house of representatives by secretary of state.	Failed
1954	N/A	DA	Gaming	Permit the legislature to authorize charitable lotteries.	Failed
1962	N/A	DA	Constitutional Convention	Relative to calling constitutional convention.	Passed
1972	N/A	DA	Daylight Savings Time	Proposal to change Michigan to Daylight Saving Time.	Passed
1972	N/A	DA	Abortion	Proposal to allow abortion under certain conditions.	Failed
1976	N/A	DA	Administration of Government	Proposal to place a limitation on state spending.	Failed
1976	N/A	DA	Taxes	Proposal to remove the ban on graduated income tax.	Failed
1976	N/A	DA	Environmental Reform	A proposal to ban throw-away bottles and cans.	Passed
1978	B	IDS	Legal	Limit parole-violent criminals; minimum sentence.	Passed
1978	D	DA	Alcohol Regulation	Must be 21 to purchase/posses alcohol.	Passed
1978	E	DA	Taxes	Tax limitation (Headlee Amendment).	Passed
1978	G	DA	Labor	Collective bargaining for Michigan state Troopers.	Passed
1978	H	DA	Education	Exempt property tax from school operations and also would have established a school voucher system.	Failed
1978	J	DA	Taxes	Property and taxes, local mandates, voter approval.	Failed
1980	N/A	DA	Taxes	Taxes for school finance; equal per pupil funding.	Failed
1980	N/A	DA	Taxes	Reduce property taxes; voter approval for new taxes.	Failed
1982	N/A	DA	Administration of Government	Establish elected Public Service Commission.	Failed
1982	N/A	IDS	Business Regulation	Foreclosures: not "due on sale" clauses; security.	Failed
1982	N/A	IDS	Utility Regulation	Hearings on utility rate increases, procedures.	Passed
1982	N/A	M	Nuclear weapons/ facilities/waste	Mutual nuclear weapons freeze with Soviet Union.	Passed
1982	N/A	DA	Administration of Government	Create department of State Police.	Failed
1984	N/A	DA	Taxes	State/local tax rates set to those of 12/31/81.	Failed

Year	Measure Number	Type	Subject Matter	Description	Pass/Fail
1992	B	DA	Term Limits	Term limits on state legislature 6/8 and Congress 6/12.	Passed
1992	N/A	DA	Taxes	Exempt property tax from school funds; increases.	Failed
1992	N/A	IDS	Business Regulation	Amendment of auto insurance laws.	Failed
1996	D	IDS	Animal Rights	Limits the bear hunting season and prohibits the use of bait and dogs to hunt bear.	Failed
1996	E	IDS	Gaming	Permit casino gambling in Detroit.	Passed
1998	B	IDS	Physician assisted suicide	Allows a mentally competent adult who is suffering from a terminal illness to request and obtain medication from a physician to end that patient's own life in a humane and dignified manner.	Failed
2000	1	DA	Education	Create voucher system. Guarantee per-pupil funding in public schools; require testing of teachers in academic subjects.	Failed
2000	2	DA	Administration of Government	Requires supermajority vote of legislature interfere in municipal affairs.	Failed

Michigan Constitution

Article II. Elections

§ 9 Initiative and referendum; limitations; appropriations; petitions.

Sec. 9.

The people reserve to themselves the power to propose laws and to enact and reject laws, called the initiative, and the power to approve or reject laws enacted by the legislature, called the referendum. The power of initiative extends only to laws which the legislature may enact under this constitution. The power of referendum does not extend to acts making appropriations for state institutions or to meet deficiencies in state funds and must be invoked in the manner prescribed by law within 90 days following the final adjournment of the legislative session at which the law was enacted. To invoke the initiative or referendum, petitions signed by a number of registered electors, not less than eight percent for initiative and five percent for referendum of the total vote cast for all candidates for governor at the last preceding general election at which a governor was elected shall be required.

Referendum, approval.

No law as to which the power of referendum properly has been invoked shall be effective thereafter unless approved by a majority of the electors voting thereon at the next general election.

Initiative; duty of legislature, referendum.

Any law proposed by initiative petition shall be either enacted or rejected by the legislature without change or amendment within 40 session days from the time such petition is received by the legislature. If any law proposed by such petition shall be enacted by the legislature it shall be subject to referendum, as hereinafter provided.

Legislative rejection of initiated measure; different measure; submission to people.

If the law so proposed is not enacted by the legislature within the 40 days, the state officer authorized by law shall submit such proposed law to the people for approval or rejection at the next general election. The legislature may reject any measure so proposed by initiative petition and propose a different measure upon the same subject by a yea and nay vote upon separate roll calls, and in such event both measures shall be submitted by such state officer to the electors for approval or rejection at the next general election.

Initiative or referendum law; effective date, veto, amendment and repeal.

Any law submitted to the people by either initiative or referendum petition and approved by a majority of the votes cast thereon at any election shall take effect 10 days after the date of the official declaration of the vote. No law initiated or adopted by the people shall be subject to the veto power of the governor, and no law adopted by the people at the polls under the initiative provisions of this section shall be amended or repealed, except by a vote of the electors unless otherwise provided in the initiative measure or by three-fourths of the members elected to and serving in each house of the legislature. Laws approved by the people under the referendum provision of this section may be amended by the legislature at any subsequent session thereof. If two or more measures approved by the electors at the same election conflict, that receiving the highest affirmative vote shall prevail.

Legislative implementation.

The legislature shall implement the provisions of this section.

Article XII

§ 2 Amendment by petition and vote of electors.

Sec. 2.

Amendments may be proposed to this constitution by petition of the registered electors of this state. Every petition shall include the full text of the proposed amendment, and be signed by registered electors of the state equal in number to at least 10 percent of the total vote cast for all candidates for governor at the last preceding general election at which a governor was elected. Such petitions shall be filed with the person authorized by law to receive the same at least 120 days before the election at which the proposed amendment is to be voted upon. Any such petition shall be in the form, and shall be signed and circulated in such manner, as prescribed by law. The person authorized by law to receive such petition shall upon its receipt determine, as provided by law, the validity and sufficiency of the signatures on the petition, and make an official announcement thereof at least 60 days prior to the election at which the proposed amendment is to be voted upon.

Any amendment proposed by such petition shall be submitted, not less than 120 days after it was filed, to the electors at the next general election. Such proposed amendment, existing provisions of the constitution which would be altered or abrogated thereby, and the question as it shall appear on the ballot shall be published in full as provided by law. Copies of such publication shall be posted in each polling place and furnished to news media as provided by law.

The ballot to be used in such election shall contain a statement of the purpose of the proposed amendment, expressed in not more than 100 words, exclusive of caption. Such statement of purpose and caption shall be prepared by the person authorized by law, and shall consist of a true and impartial statement of the purpose of the amendment in such language as shall create no prejudice for or against the proposed amendment.

If the proposed amendment is approved by a majority of the electors voting on the question, it shall become part of the constitution, and shall abrogate or amend existing provisions of the constitution at the end of 45 days after the date of the election at which it was approved. If two or more amendments approved by the electors at the same election conflict, that amendment receiving the highest affirmative vote shall prevail.

Michigan Statutes

Chapter XXII

168.471 Petitions proposing constitutional amendments; filing.

Petitions under section 2 of article XII of the state constitution of 1963 proposing an amendment to the constitution shall be filed with the secretary of state at least 120 days before the election at which the proposed amendment is to be voted upon. Initiative petitions under section 9 of article II of the state constitution of 1963 shall be filed with the secretary of state at least 160 days before the election at which the proposed law is to be voted upon. Referendum petitions under section 9 of article II of the state constitution of 1963 shall be filed with the secretary of state not more than 90 days following the final adjournment of the legislative session at which the law that is the subject of the referendum was enacted.

168.472 Initiative petitions; filing. [M.S.A. s.1472]

Petitions to initiate legislation shall be filed with the secretary of state not less than 10 days before the beginning of a session of the legislature.

168.472a Presumption as to signature on petition.

It shall be rebuttably presumed that the signature on a petition that proposes an amendment to the constitution or is to initiate legislation, is stale and void if the signature was made more than 180 days before the petition was filed with the office of the secretary of state.

168.473 Referendum petitions; filing. [M.S.A. 6.1473]

Referendum petitions shall be presented to and filed with the secretary of state within 90 days after the final adjournment of the legislature.

168.473b Filing petition after November election.

Signatures on a petition to propose an amendment to the state constitution of 1963 or a petition to initiate legislation collected prior to a November general election at which a governor is elected shall not be filed after the date of that November general election.

168.474 Board of state canvassers; duties; statement of purpose of proposed constitutional amendment. [M.S.A. 6.1474]

Wherever the phrases "the state officer authorized by law" or "the person authorized by law", are used in section 9 of article 2 or section 2 of article 12 of the constitution of this state, such phrases shall mean and have reference to the board of state canvassers and such board shall exercise the duties prescribed in such constitutional provisions. The preparing of a statement of the purpose of any such proposed amendment or question to be designated on the ballots for submission to the electors in not more than 100 words, exclusive of the caption, which said statement shall consist of a true and impartial statement of the purpose of the amendment or question in such language as shall create no prejudice for or against such proposal shall be the duty of the director of elections with the approval of the board of state canvassers.

168.474a Assignment of number designation to appear on ballot for question submitted on statewide basis.

(1) The board of state canvassers shall assign a number designation to appear on the ballot for each question to be submitted on a statewide basis. The designation shall be assigned not less than 60 days before the election. If the question is to appear on a general election ballot the designation shall not be assigned earlier than the primary election preceding that general election.

(2) The number designation under subsection (1) shall consist of 3 or 4 digits. The first 2 digits shall be the last 2 digits of the year of the election. The next digit or, if necessary, 2 digits shall indicate the chronological order in which the question was filed to appear on the ballot. For the purposes of this subsection, a question shall be considered to be filed to appear on the ballot as follows:

(a) A general revision of the constitution under section 3 of article XII of the state constitution of 1963 shall be considered to be the first question filed to appear on the ballot for those elections at which a general revision of the constitution will appear on the ballot.

(b) An amendment to the constitution proposed under section 2 of article XII of the state constitution of 1963, legislation initiated under section 9 of article II of the state constitution of 1963, or a referendum invoked under section 9 of article II of the state constitution of 1963 shall be considered to be filed to appear on the ballot when the petition is filed with the secretary of state.

(c) An amendment to the constitution proposed under section 1 of article XII of the state constitution of 1963 shall be considered to be filed to appear on the ballot when the joint resolution proposing the amendment is filed with the secretary of state.

(d) A referendum under section 34 of article IV of the state constitution of 1963 shall be considered to be filed to appear on the ballot when the legislation is filed with the secretary of state.

168.475 Filing of petition; notification of board of state canvassers; supplemental filings.

(1) Upon the filing of a petition under this chapter, the secretary of state shall immediately notify the board of state canvassers of the filing of the petition. The notification shall be by first-class mail.

(2) After the day on which a petition under this chapter is filed, the secretary of state shall not accept further filings of that petition to supplement the original filing.

168.476 Petitions; canvass by board of state canvassers; use of qualified voter file; hearing upon complaint; investigations; completion date; disposition of challenges; report.

(1) Upon receiving notification of the filing of the petitions, the board of state canvassers shall canvass the petitions to ascertain if the petitions have been signed by the requisite number of qualified and registered electors. The qualified voter file may be used to determine the validity of petition signatures by verifying the registration of signers. If the qualified voter file indicates that, on the date the elector signed the petition, the elector was not registered to vote, there is a rebuttable presumption that the signature is invalid. If the qualified voter file indicates that, on the date the elector signed the petition, the elector was not registered to vote in the city or township designated on the petition, there is a rebuttable presumption that the signature is invalid. The board may cause any doubtful signatures to be checked against the registration records by the clerk of any political subdivision in which the petitions were circulated, to determine the authenticity of the signatures or to verify the registrations. Upon request, the clerk of any political subdivision shall cooperate fully with the board in determining the validity of doubtful signatures by rechecking the signature against registration records in an expeditious and proper manner.

(2) The board of state canvassers may hold hearings upon any complaints filed or for any purpose considered necessary by the board to conduct investigations of the petitions. To conduct a hearing, the board may issue subpoenas and administer oaths. The board may also adjourn from time to time awaiting receipt of returns from investigations that are being made or for other necessary purposes, but shall complete the canvass at least 2 months before the election at which the proposal is to be submitted.

(3) At least 2 business days before the board of state canvassers meets to make a final determination on challenges to and sufficiency of a petition, the bureau of elections shall make public its staff report concerning disposition of challenges filed against the petition. Beginning with the receipt of any document from local election officials pursuant to subsection (1), the board of state canvassers shall make that document available to petitioners and challengers on a daily basis.

168.477 Petitions; official declaration of sufficiency or insufficiency by board of state canvassers; publication of statement of purpose, expense; effectiveness of law that is subject of referendum.

(1) The board of state canvassers shall make an official declaration of the sufficiency or insufficiency of a petition under this chapter at least 2 months before the election at which the proposal is to be submitted. If the board of state canvassers declares that the petition is sufficient, the secretary of state shall send copies of the statement of purpose of the proposal as approved by the board of state canvassers under section 474 to the several daily and weekly newspapers published in this state, with the request that the newspapers give as wide publicity as possible to the proposed amendment or other question. Publication of any matter by any newspaper under this section shall be without expense or cost to the state of Michigan.

(2) For the purposes of the second paragraph of section 9 of article II of the state constitution of 1963, a law that is the subject of the referendum continues to be effective until the referendum is properly invoked, which occurs when the board of state canvassers makes its official declaration of the sufficiency of the referendum petition. The board of state canvassers shall complete the canvass of a referendum petition within 60 days after the petition is filed with the secretary of state, except that 1 15-day extension may be granted by the secretary of state if necessary to complete the canvass.

168.478 Petitions; notice of approval or rejection by board of state canvassers to persons filing. [M.S.A. 6.1478]

At the time of filing any such petition, the person or persons filing the same may request a notice of the approval or rejection of said petitions to be forwarded by said board to such person or persons or any other persons so designated at the time of the filing of such petitions. In any case where such a request is made at the time of filing of the petitions, it shall be the duty of the secretary of state, immediately upon the determination thereof, to transmit by registered or certified mail to said person or persons an official notice of the sufficiency or insufficiency of said petitions.

168.479 Review of determination; mandamus, certiorari or other remedy. [M.S.A. 6.1479]

Any person or persons, feeling themselves aggrieved by any determination made by said board, may have such determination reviewed by mandamus, certiorari, or other appropriate remedy in the supreme court.

168.480 Proposed constitutional amendment or question; certification; copies to voting precincts, posting. [M.S.A. 6.1480]

Whenever a proposed constitutional amendment or other special question is to be submitted to the electors of the state for a popular vote, the secretary of state shall, not less than 49 days before the election, certify the same to the clerk of each county in the state, together with the form in which such amendment or other special questions shall be submitted. The secretary of state shall also furnish the several county clerks in the state 2 copies of the text of each amendment or question and 2 copies of each said statement for each voting precinct in their respective counties. The county clerk shall furnish the said copies of such statement to the several township and city clerks in his county at the time other supplies for the election are furnished; and each such township or city clerk shall, before the opening of the polls on election day, deliver the copies of such text and statement to which each voting precinct in his township or city is entitled to the board of election inspectors of said precinct, who shall post the same in conspicuous places in the room where such election is held.

168.481 Proposed constitutional amendment or question; form. [M.S.A. 6.1481]

Whenever any proposed constitutional amendment or other question is to be submitted to the electors, the board of election commissioners of each county shall cause such proposed constitutional amendment or other special question to be printed in accordance with the form submitted by the secretary of state.

168.482 Petitions; size; form; contents. [M.S.A. 6.1482]

(1) Each petition under this section shall be 8-1/2 inches by 14 inches in size.
(2) If the measure to be submitted proposes a constitutional amendment, initiation of legislation, or referendum of legislation, the heading of each part of the petition shall be prepared in the following form and printed in capital letters in 14-point boldfaced type:
INITIATIVE PETITION
AMENDMENT TO THE CONSTITUTION
OR
INITIATION OF LEGISLATION
OR
REFERENDUM OF LEGISLATION
PROPOSED BY INITIATIVE PETITION
(3) The full text of the amendment so proposed shall follow and be printed in 8-point type. If the proposal would alter or abrogate an existing provision of the constitution, the petition shall so state and the provisions to be altered or abrogated shall be inserted, preceded by the words: "Provisions of existing constitution altered or abrogated by the proposal if adopted."
(4) The following statement shall appear beneath the petition heading: "We, the undersigned qualified and registered electors, residents in the city township (strike one) in the county of ...., state of Michigan, respectively petition for (amendment to constitution) (initiation of legislation) (referendum of legislation) (other appropriate description)."
(5) The following warning shall be printed in 12-point type immediately above the place for signatures, on each part of the petition: WARNING: A person who knowingly signs this petition more than once, signs a name other than his or her own, signs when not a qualified and registered elector, or sets opposite his or her signature on a petition, a date other than the actual date the signature was affixed, is violating the provisions of the Michigan election law.
(6) The remainder of the petition form shall be as provided following the warning to electors signing the petition in section 544c(1). In addition, the petition shall comply with the requirements of section 544c(2).

168.485 Questions submitted to electors; form. [M.S.A. 6.1485]

A question submitted to the electors of this state or the electors of a subdivision of this state shall, to the extent that it will not confuse the electorate, be worded so that a "yes" vote will be a vote in favor of the subject matter of the proposal or issue and a "no" vote will be a vote against the subject matter of the proposal or issue. The question shall be worded so as to apprise the voters of the subject matter of the proposal or issue, but need not be legally precise. The question shall be clearly written using words that have a common everyday meaning to the general public. The language used shall not create prejudice for or against the issue or proposal.

168.486 Certifying and transmitting language of constitutional amendment or legislation initiated by petition. [M.S.A. 6.1486]

If the qualified electors of this state approve a constitutional amendment or legislation initiated by petition, the board of state canvassers shall certify to the secretary of state the language of the amendment or legislation. The secretary of state shall transmit the language of the amendment or legislation to the director of the department of management and budget.

168.487 Reimbursement to county, city, and township for cost of conducting special election. [M.S.A. 6.1487]

(1) If a statewide special election is called to submit a proposed constitutional amendment to the electors of this state, this state shall reimburse each county, city, and township for the cost of conducting the special election as provided in this section. The reimbursement shall not exceed the verified account of actual costs of the special election. This state shall reimburse each county, city, and township under this section notwithstanding that the county, city, or township also holds a local special election in conjunction with the statewide special election.

(2) Payment shall be made upon presentation and approval of a verified account of actual costs to the department of treasury, local government audit division, after the department of treasury and the secretary of state agree as to what constitutes valid costs of conducting an election. Reimbursable costs do not include salaries of permanent local officials, the cost of reusable supplies and equipment, or costs attributable to local special elections held in conjunction with the statewide special election.

(3) The legislature shall appropriate from the general fund of this state an amount necessary to implement this section.

(4) To qualify for reimbursement, a county, city, or township shall submit its verified account of actual costs before the expiration of 90 days after the date of the statewide special election. This state shall pay or disapprove all or a portion of the verified account before the expiration of 90 days after this state receives a verified account of actual costs under this subsection.

(5) If this state disapproves all or a portion of a verified account of actual costs under subsection (4), this state shall send a notice of disapproval along with the reasons for the disapproval to the county, city, or township. Upon request of a county, city, or township whose verified account or portion of a verified account was disapproved under this section, this state shall review the disapproved costs with the county, city, or township.

168.488 Applicability of §§ 168.544c and 168.482(1), (4), (5), and (6).

(1) Section 544c applies to a nominating petition for an office in a political subdivision under a statute that refers to this section, and to the circulation and signing of the petition.

(2) Section 482(1), (4), (5), and (6) apply to a petition to place a question on the ballot before the electorate of a political subdivision under a statute that refers to this section, and to the circulation and signing of the petition.

(3) A person who violates a provision of this act applicable to a petition pursuant to subsection (1) or (2) is subject to the penalties prescribed for that violation in this act.

The Basic Steps to Do an Initiative in Michigan

Statutes and Amendments — Direct Initiative Process (Amendments), Indirect Initiative Process (Statutes)

Basic Procedures: The Michigan Department of State's Bureau of Elections offers its staff for consultations on the designing the petition format of an initiative measure. Upon determining through the consultation process that an initiative of referendum petition is properly formatted, it is submitted to the Board of State Canvassers for approval as to form. While Michigan election law does not require Board approval of an initiative or referendum petition form, such approval greatly reduces the risk that signatures collected on the form will be ruled invalid due to formatting defects. The Board does not review or approve the actual language of the proposed initiative.

When the Secretary of State certifies that enough valid signatures have been collected, the State Director of Elections writes the ballot question and summary. This ballot question and summary is submitted to the Board of Canvassers for review and changes. The Board of Canvassers also holds a public meeting so that proponents, opponents and the general public can comment on the language and ask for changes. Although, the Board of Canvassers relies on the suggestions of proponents, they need not heed them. If proponents are unsatisfied with the final ballot language and think it's unfair, they can take the Board of Canvassers to court to get the ballot language changed.

Date Initiative language can be submitted to state for November 2002: Any time.

Signatures are tied to vote of which office: Governor

Next gubernatorial election: 2002

Votes cast for Governor in Gubernatorial election: 3,027,104

Net number of signatures required: For statutes, 8% of votes cast for Governor (242,169 signatures.) For amendments, 10% of votes cast for Governor (302,710 signatures.) For statutes, if the petition contains a sufficient number of valid signatures the state legislature has 40 session days to adopt or reject the proposal. If the legislature rejects the law, then the measure is placed on the next general election ballot. For amendments, if the petition contains a sufficient number of valid signatures the measure is placed immediately on the next general election ballot.

Distribution Requirement: None.

Circulation period: 180 days. (Michigan law states that proponents must submit signatures that have been gathered within a 180-day period and that the number of valid signatures must be at least equal to the required amount for the initiative to qualify for the ballot. The signatures can be gathered, however, within any 180-day period. Thus, proponents can gather signatures for as long as they want—but they can only submit signatures gathered within the same 180-day period.)

Do circulators have to be residents: Yes

Date when signatures are filed for certification: For amendments, at least 120 days prior to the 2002 general election (Early July) statutes, signatures must be submitted at least 10 days prior to the start of the 2002 legislature (Late May)

Signature verification process: Random sample.

Single-subject restriction: No

Legislative tampering: Legislature can repeal and amend by a ¾ vote of each house or as otherwise provided by the initiative.

Minnesota[2]

Three times in the last century, Minnesotans voted on a measure to establish a statewide process of initiative and referendum and each time a majority favored the process. But that alone was not been enough to enact initiative and referendum in the state.

In 1897 the Minnesota Legislature unintentionally frustrated the initiative process, as well as a great many future proposals to amend the state's constitution, by proposing a supermajority requirement for ratifying amendments to the constitution.

In 1897, the legislators' actual objective was to block passage of a Prohibition amendment, which was bitterly opposed by brewery interests. In 1897 the question of initiative and referendum had not even been seriously discussed. It was still two years before Governor John Lind called for I&R in his message to the legislature, and eight years before the Minnesota suffragist Mrs. Eugenia Farmer helped found the state's I&R League.

The 1897 "Brewer's Amendment," sponsored by state representative (and Hamm Brewing Co. attorney) W. W. Dunn, proposed changing the ratification threshold for state constitutional amendments: instead of requiring ratification by a majority of the popular vote of those voting on each individual amendment, as was then the case (and is now the case in most states), they would require a majority of all votes cast in the election. In effect, under this system those who do not vote on a particular question are counted as voting against it.

Dunn's amendment passed both houses and was placed on the ballot for ratification by the voters in 1898. The amendment could not have passed under its own standard for voter ratification, but it did pass under the old standard. Of those who voted on the question, 68 percent favored it—but less than one-third of those voting in the election voted on this question.

The first Minnesota I&R amendment to get through the legislature was on the ballot in 1914 and was approved by a three to one margin, but lost because the "yes" votes were still less than a majority of all the votes cast in the election. In 1916, the legislature passed an I&R amendment again, and voters supported it by a margin of nearly four to one, but those voting in favor were only 45 percent of all voters at the polls, so it lost again. The Progressives decided the following year that the "supermajority" requirement was an "insurmountable obstacle," and apparently gave up.

---

2. This history is a compilation of work by David Schmidt and Paul Jacob.

Sixty years later, the newly elected liberal State Senator Robert Benedict of Bloomington renewed the fight for a statewide initiative process. By late April 1978 the three leading candidates in that year's gubernatorial election had endorsed L&R. But trouble for the amendment was brewing elsewhere. On April 25, in a special state election in St. Paul, voters approved an initiative to repeal a city ordinance banning discrimination on the basis of "affectionate or sexual preference"—a stunning defeat for gay rights advocates and the entire liberal community. Christian fundamentalists sponsoring the initiative had shrewdly petitioned for a low-turnout special election; such elections tend to favor conservatives, who turn out to vote in greater numbers than liberals.

Republican Al Quie, elected governor in 1978, made I&R the centerpiece of his legislative agenda and by April 1980 had pushed it through the legislature. The state senate approved it 47 to 13; in the house the vote was 86 to 47.

Lobbyists and attorneys for the beverage industry were the first to organize a campaign against voter ratification of the I&R amendment. Just as in 1897, they wanted to prevent Minnesotans from voting on any initiative that might qualify for the ballot, in order to ensure that one specific proposal—in this case, a Bottle Bill—could never pass. The industry lobbyists maintained a low profile and encouraged allies from liberal groups (who were upset about the 1978 gay rights vote in St. Paul) to lead the "Vote No" campaign.

The opposition group was co-chaired by Wayne Popham, a former Republican state senator and vice president of the Minneapolis Chamber of Commerce, and Treva Kahl, who headed the state AFL-CIO's political department. Popham's group made Harriette Burkhalter, president of the state League of Woman Voters, the most visible anti-I&R spokesperson.

On November 4, 1980 the election returns showed 53.2 percent in favor and 46.8 percent against: not enough to win. Of the total that turned out to vote, 12 percent had failed to mark "yes" or "no" on I&R. With these added to the "no" side, the amendment lost.

Former governor Elmer Anderson and Governor Quie had run a lackluster pro-initiative campaign, but a University of Minnesota political scientist, Charles H. Backstrom, identified another reason for the loss: many voters failed to cast ballots on the I&R question because they were not tall enough to see it on their voting machines. This factor alone, Backstrom found, could have changed the outcome of the election.

The long-dead legislators of 1897, combined with voting machines designed for tall people, has thus far defeated the efforts of Minnesotans to get I&R. But after many years of no serious campaign for I&R, efforts are once again underway in the legislature and at the grassroots. Rep. Erik Paulsen has introduced bipartisan legislation in the Minnesota House of Representatives to establish a statewide initiative and referendum process.

Rep. Paulsen's bill has the support of Governor Jesse Ventura and has passed the House twice, in 1999 and again in 2002, but has failed to get a vote on the floor of the state Senate. A new citizens' lobby, Let Minnesota Vote!, sprang up in 2002 to mobilize voters at the grassroots to pressure additional legislators.

It remains to be seen whether the current push for I&R will ultimately succeed, but a recent statewide poll showed 80 percent of Minnesotans favor a statewide initiative and referendum process. That level of public support and the willingness of initiative supporters to continue the battle ultimately bode well for I&R in Minnesota.

Minnesota Constitution

The state does not have the statewide initiative process and so therefore the following provisions discuss the procedures used by the state legislature to place constitutional amendments on the ballot.

Article IX Amendments to the Constitution

Sec. 1. Amendments; Ratification.

A majority of the members elected to each house of the legislature may propose amendments to this constitution. Proposed amendments shall be published with the laws passed at the same session and submitted to the people for their approval or rejection at a general election. If a majority of all the electors voting at the election vote to ratify an amendment, it becomes a part of this constitution. If two or more amendments are submitted at the same time, voters shall vote for or against each separately.

Sec. 2. Constitutional Convention.

Two-thirds of the members elected to each house of the legislature may submit to the electors at the next general election the question of calling a convention to revise this constitution. If a majority of all the electors voting at the election vote for a convention, the legislature at its next session, shall provide by law for calling the convention. The convention shall consist of as many delegates as there are members of the house of representatives. Delegates shall be chosen in the same manner as members of the house of representatives and shall meet within three months after their election. Section 5 of Article IV of the constitution does not apply to election to the convention.

Sec. 3. Submission to People of Constitution Drafted at Convention.

A convention called to revise this constitution shall submit any revision to the people for approval or rejection at the next general election held not less than 90 days after submission of the revision. If three-fifths of all the electors voting on the question vote to ratify the revision, it becomes a new constitution of the state of Minnesota.

Mississippi

Mississippi is the only state that once had a statewide initiative process but lost it: not because the people rejected it, but because the state supreme court in 1922 decided on the basis of a legal technicality to throw the I&R provision out of the state constitution.

Agitation for I&R in Mississippi achieved partial success for the first time in 1912, the peak year for I&R success nationwide. Mississippi voters approved an I&R amendment by a nearly two to one margin, but the measure failed because of the state's requirement that a "supermajority" of all votes cast in the election, rather than a simple majority of votes on the I&R question, ratify it. This was the same requirement that defeated Minnesota's I&R amendment in three elections.

In Mississippi, after the initial defeat, I&R supporters led by State Representatives N. A. Mott of Yazoo City and Frank Burkitt of Okalona succeeded in pushing their proposal through the legislature a second time, and it was on the ballot again in 1914. This time it passed by a margin of more than two to one, though it barely passed the supermajority requirement.

In 1916 voters successfully petitioned to refer a bill passed by the legislature appointing a certain Z. A. Brantley to the office of game and fish commissioner, and then rejected the law by popular vote. Brantley took the case to court, charging that the I&R amendment was not valid. On March 26, 1917 the state supreme court upheld the referendum and the I&R process (State v. Brantley, 113 Miss. 786, 74 South, 662, Ann. Cas. 1917E, 723). An elated Assistant Attorney General Lamar F. Easterling, who defended the I&R process in the case, wrote the following day that the decision "settles the matter finally in this state."

Easterling's assessment proved premature. Five years later, a citizen group backing an initiative to change the salary of the state revenue agent turned in enough petition signatures to qualify the measure for the November 1922 ballot. Stokes V. Robertson, the revenue agent, went to court to keep it off the ballot, again attacking the validity of the I&R amendment.

The state supreme court, reversing its 1917 judgment, held that initiatives or referendums on statutes are one thing, but initiative constitutional amendments are another, and thus the constitutional initiative power should have been approved in 1914 in a separate amendment. And because it was not, the entire I&R provision was held unconstitutional. The court abolished the people's right to self-government by I&R, finding that: "The Constitution is the product of the people in their sovereign capacity. It was intended primarily to secure the rights of the people against the encroachments of the legislative branch of the government" (Power v. Robertson, 130 Miss. 188, 93 So. 769). In effect, the court said that it had to destroy the people's rights to self-government in order to save them. The legislature could have remedied the situation by approving two new amendments, one covering statutory, and the other constitutional, initiatives. But it took no such action.

The issue lay dormant for over half a century, until in 1977 Upton Sisson of Gulfport took up the cause of I&R. Sisson, who served as state representative from 1956 to 1960, was a civil rights attorney who had argued one of the landmark "one man, one vote" reapportionment cases in the U.S. Supreme Court. At age 70 and in failing health, Sisson returned to the legislature to lobby for I&R.

Although unsuccessful, his efforts sparked enough interest in the subject that State Attorney General Bill Allain, running for governor in 1983, pledged to work for passage of an I&R amendment if elected. Allain won, but he was unable to fulfill his pledge.

However, the power of initiative and referendum was eventually restored to the citizens of Mississippi by the passage of Senate Concurrent Resolution No. 616 during the 1992 regular session. Initiative and referendum had been a widely discussed campaign issue in the 1991 fall elections. Its eventual passage in the 1992 regular session of the legislature was widely hailed as a progressive reform of government. It was approved by an astounding 70% of the popular vote in the 1992 fall elections—making Mississippi the last state to adopt the statewide initiative process.

However, the initiative process that was established in the state is one of the most difficult in the country. Since 1992, only two statewide initiatives have made it to the ballot—both to establish term limits—and both were defeated.

Statewide Initiative Usage

Number of Initiatives	Number Passed	Number Failed	Passage Rate
2	0	2	0%

Statewide Initiatives

Year	Measure Number	Type	Subject Matter	Description	Pass/Fail
1995	4	IDA	Term Limits	Term limits on all elected officials in the state.	Failed
1999	9	IDA	Term Limits	Term limits on state legislature 8/8.	Failed

Mississippi Constitution

Article 15

Amendments to the Constitution

Section 273.

(1) Amendments to this Constitution may be proposed by the Legislature or by initiative of the people.

(2) Whenever two-thirds (2/3) of each house of the Legislature, which two-thirds (2/3) shall consist of not less than a majority of the members elected to each house, shall deem any change, alteration or amendment necessary to this Constitution, such proposed amendment, change or alteration shall be read and passed by two-thirds (2/3) vote of each house, as herein provided; public notice shall then be given by the Secretary of State at least thirty (30) days preceding an election, at which the qualified electors shall vote directly for or against such change, alteration or amendment, and if more than one (1) amendment shall be submitted at one (1) time, they shall be submitted in such manner and form that the people may vote for or against each amendment separately; and, notwithstanding the division of the Constitution into sections, the Legislature may provide in its resolution for one or more amendments pertaining and relating to the same subject or subject matter, and may provide for one or more amendments to an article of the Constitution pertaining and relating to the same subject or subject matter, which may be included in and voted on as one (1) amendment; and if it shall appear that a majority of the qualified electors voting directly for or against the same shall have voted for the proposed change, alteration or amendment, then it shall be inserted as a part of the Constitution by proclamation of the Secretary of State certifying that it received the majority vote required by the Constitution; and the resolution may fix the date and direct the calling of elections for the purposes hereof.

(3) The people reserve unto themselves the power to propose and enact constitutional amendments by initiative. An initiative to amend the Constitution may be proposed by a petition signed over a twelve-month period by qualified electors equal in number to at least twelve percent (12%) of the votes for all candidates for Governor in the last gubernatorial election. The signatures of the qualified electors from any congressional district shall not exceed one-fifth (1/5) of the total number of signatures required to qualify an initiative petition for placement upon the ballot. If an initiative petition contains signatures from a single congressional district which exceed one-fifth (1/5) of the total number of required signatures, the excess number of signatures from that congressional district shall not be considered by the Secretary of State in determining whether the petition qualifies for placement on the ballot.

(4) The sponsor of an initiative shall identify in the text of the initiative the amount and source of revenue required to implement the initiative. If the initiative requires a reduction in any source of government revenue, or a reallocation of funding from currently funded programs, the sponsor shall identify in the text of the initiative the program or programs whose funding must be reduced or eliminated to implement the initiative. Compliance with this requirement shall not be a violation of the subject matter requirements of this section of the Constitution.

(5) The initiative process shall not be used:

(a) For the proposal, modification or repeal of any portion of the Bill of Rights of this Constitution;

(b) To amend or repeal any law or any provision of the Constitution relating to the Mississippi Public Employees' Retirement System;

(c) To amend or repeal the constitutional guarantee that the right of any person to work shall not be denied or abridged on account of membership or nonmembership in any labor union or organization; or

(d) To modify the initiative process for proposing amendments to this Constitution.

(6) The Secretary of State shall file with the Clerk of the House and the Secretary of the Senate the complete text of the certified initiative on the first day of the regular session. A constitutional initiative may be adopted by a majority vote of each house of the Legislature. If the initiative is adopted, amended or rejected by the Legislature; or if no action is taken within four (4) months of the date that the initiative is filed with the Legislature, the Secretary of State shall place the initiative on the ballot for the next statewide general election.

The chief legislative budget officer shall prepare a fiscal analysis of each initiative and each legislative alternative. A summary of each fiscal analysis shall appear on the ballot.

(7) If the Legislature amends an initiative, the amended version and the original initiative shall be submitted to the electors. An initiative or legislative alternative must receive a majority of the votes thereon and not less than forty percent (40%) of the total votes cast at the election at which the measure was submitted to be approved. If conflicting initiatives or legislative alternatives are approved at the same election, the initiative or legislative alternative receiving the highest number of affirmative votes shall prevail.

(8) If an initiative measure proposed to the Legislature has been rejected by the Legislature and an alternative measure is passed by the Legislature in lieu thereof, the ballot titles of both such measures shall be so printed on the official ballots that a voter can express separately two (2) preferences: First, by voting for the approval of either measure or against both measures, and, secondly, by voting for one measure or the other measure. If the majority of those voting on the first issue is against both measures, then both measures fail, but in that case the votes on the second issue nevertheless shall be carefully counted and made public. If a majority voting on the first issue is for the approval of either measure, then the measure receiving a majority of the votes on the second issue and also receiving not less than forty percent (40%) of the total votes cast at the election at which the measure was submitted for approval shall be law. Any person who votes for the ratification of either measure on the first issue must vote for one (1) of the measures on the second issue in order for the ballot to be valid. Any person who votes against both measures on the first issue may vote but shall not be required to vote for any of the measures on the second issue in order for the ballot to be valid. Substantially the following form shall be a compliance with this subsection:

Initiative Measure No. __, entitled (here insert the ballot title of the initiative measure).

Alternative Measure No. __ A, entitled (here insert the ballot title of the alternative measure).

VOTE FOR APPROVAL OF EITHER, OR AGAINST BOTH:
FOR APPROVAL OF EITHER Initiative No. __ OR Alternative No. __ A ....()
AGAINST Both Initiative No. __ AND Alternative No. __ A ....()
FOR Initiative Measure No. __ .... ()
FOR Alternative Measure No. __ A ....()

(9) No more than five (5) initiative proposals shall be submitted to the voters on a single ballot, and the first five (5) initiative proposals submitted to the Secretary of State with sufficient petitions shall be the proposals which are submitted to the voters. The sufficiency of petitions shall be decided in the first instance by the Secretary of State, subject to review by the Supreme Court of the state, which shall have original and exclusive jurisdiction over all such cases.

(10) An initiative approved by the electors shall take effect thirty (30) days from the date of the official declaration of the vote by the Secretary of State, unless the measure provides otherwise.

(11) If any amendment to the Constitution proposed by initiative petition is rejected by a majority of the qualified electors voting thereon, no initiative petition proposing the same, or substantially the same, amendment shall be submitted to the electors for at least two (2) years after the date of the election on such amendment.

(12) The Legislature shall provide by law the manner in which initiative petitions shall be circulated, presented and certified.

(13) The Legislature may enact laws to carry out the provisions of this section but shall in no way restrict or impair the provisions of this section or the powers herein reserved to the people.

Mississippi Statutes

Chapter 17

§ 23-17-1. Procedures by which qualified electors may initiate proposed amendments to the constitution

(1) For purposes of this chapter, the following term shall have the meaning ascribed herein: "Measure" means an amendment to the Mississippi Constitution proposed by a petition of qualified electors under Section 273, Mississippi Constitution of 1890.

(2) If any qualified elector of the state desires to initiate a proposed amendment to the Constitution of this state as authorized by subsections (3) through (13) of Section 273 of the Mississippi Constitution of 1890, he shall first file with the Secretary of State a typewritten copy of the proposed initiative measure, accompanied by an affidavit that the sponsor is a qualified elector of this state.

(3) The sponsor of an initiative shall identify in the text of the initiative the amount and source of revenue required to implement the initiative. If the initiative requires a reduction in any source of government revenue, or a reallocation of funding from currently funded programs, the sponsor shall identify in the text of the initiative the program or programs whose funding must be reduced or eliminated to implement the initiative.

(4) The person proposing the measure shall also include all the information required under Section 273, Mississippi Constitution of 1890.

§ 23-17-3. Time for filing petition; length of time petition remains valid.

The petition for a proposed initiative measure must be filed with the Secretary of State not less than ninety (90) days before the first day of the regular session of the Legislature at which it is to be submitted. A petition is valid for a period of twelve (12) months.

§ 23-17-5. Submission of proposed initiative to Attorney General; review; recommendations; certificate of review; filing of proposed initiative and certificate.

Upon receipt of any proposed initiative measure, the Secretary of State shall submit a copy of the proposed measure to the Attorney General and give notice to the person filing the proposed measure of such transmittal. Upon receipt of the measure, the Attorney General may confer with the person filing the proposed measure and shall within ten (10) working days from receipt thereof review the proposal for matters of form and style, and such matters of substantive import as may be agreeable to the person filing the proposed measure, and shall recommend such revision or alteration of the measure as may be deemed necessary and appropriate. The recommendations of the Attorney General shall be advisory only, and the person filing the proposed measure may accept or reject them in whole or in part. The Attorney General shall issue a certificate of review certifying that he has reviewed the measure for form and style and that the recommendations thereon, if any, have been communicated to the person filing the proposed measure, and such certificate shall issue whether or not the person filing the proposed measure accepts such recommendations. Within fifteen (15) working days after notification of submittal of the proposed initiative measure to the Attorney General, the person filing the proposed measure, if he desires to proceed with his sponsorship, shall file the measure together with the certificate of review with the Secretary of State for assignment of a serial number and the Secretary of State shall thereupon submit to the Attorney General a certified copy of the measure filed. Upon submitting the proposal to the Secretary of State for assignment of a serial number the Secretary of State shall refuse to make such assignment unless the proposal is accompanied by a certificate of review.

§ 23-17-7. Assignment of serial number; designation as "Initiative Measure No.."

The Secretary of State shall give a serial number to each initiative measure, and forthwith transmit one (1) copy of the measure proposed bearing its serial number to the Attorney General. Thereafter, a measure shall be known and designated on all petitions, ballots and proceedings as "Initiative Measure No.."

§ 23-17-9. Formulation of ballot title and summary of initiative measure.

Within seven (7) calendar days after the receipt of an initiative measure, the Attorney General shall formulate and transmit to the Secretary of State a concise statement posed as a question and not to exceed twenty (20) words, bearing the serial number of the measure and a summary of the measure, not to exceed seventy-five (75) words, to follow the statement. The statement shall give a true and impartial statement of the purpose of the measure. Neither the statement nor the summary may intentionally be an argument, nor likely to create prejudice, either for or against the measure. Such concise statement shall constitute the ballot title. The ballot title formulated by the Attorney General shall be the ballot title of the measure unless changed on appeal. When practicable, the question posed by the ballot title shall be written in such a way that an affirmative answer to such question and an affirmative vote on the measure would result in a change in then current law, and a negative answer to the question and a negative vote on the measure would result in no change to then current law.

§ 23-17-11. Notice of ballot title and summary to initiator; publication of title and summary.

Upon the filing of the ballot title and summary for an initiative measure in his office, the Secretary of State shall forthwith notify by certified mail return receipt requested, the person proposing the measure and any other individuals who have made written request for such notification of the exact language of the ballot title. The Secretary of State shall publish the title and summary for an initiative measure within ten (10) days after filing such title and summary in a newspaper or newspapers of general circulation throughout the State of Mississippi.

§ 23-17-13. Procedure for appeal of title and summary.

If any person is dissatisfied with the ballot title or summary formulated by the Attorney General, he or she may, within five (5) days from the publications of the ballot title and summary by the office of the Secretary of State, appeal to the circuit court of the First Judicial District of Hinds County by petition setting forth the measure, the title or summary formulated by the Attorney General, and his or her objections to the ballot title or summary and requesting amendment of the title or summary by the court.

A copy of the petition on appeal together with a notice that an appeal has been taken shall be served upon the Secretary of State, upon the Attorney General and upon the person proposing the measure if the appeal is initiated by someone other than that person. Upon the filing of the petition on appeal or at the time to which the hearing may be adjourned by consent of the appellant, the court shall accord first priority to examining the proposed measure, the title or summary prepared by the Attorney General and the objections to that title or summary. The court may hear arguments, and, within ten (10) days, shall render its decision and file with the Secretary of State a certified copy of such ballot title or summary as it determines will meet the requirements of Section 23-17-9. The decision of the court shall be final.

§ 23-17-15. Filing of instrument establishing title and summary of measure; notice to initiator; title and summary to be used in all proceedings.

When the ballot title and summary are finally established, the Secretary of State shall file the instrument establishing it with the proposed measure and transmit a copy thereof by certified mail return receipt requested, to the person proposing the measure and to any other individuals who have made written request for such notification. Thereafter such ballot title shall be the title of the measure in all petitions, ballots and other proceedings in relation thereto. The summary shall appear on all petitions directly following the ballot title.

§ 23-17-17. Initiator of measure to print blank petitions; form of petitions.

(1)   The person proposing an initiative measure shall print blank petitions upon single sheets of paper of good writing quality not less than eight and one-half (8-1/2) inches in width and not less than fourteen (14) inches in length. Each sheet shall have a full, true and correct copy of the proposed measure referred to therein printed on the reverse side of the petition or attached thereto.

(2)   Only a person who is a qualified elector of this state may circulate a petition or obtain signatures on a petition.

§ 23-17-19. Secretary of State to design petitions; form of petitions.

The Secretary of State shall design the form each sheet of which shall contain the following:

"WARNING EVERY PERSON WHO SIGNS THIS PETITION WITH ANY OTHER THAN HIS OR HER TRUE NAME, KNOWINGLY SIGNS MORE THAN ONE OF THESE PETITIONS RELATING TO THE SAME INITIATIVE MEASURE, SIGNS THIS PETITION WHEN HE OR SHE IS NOT A QUALIFIED ELECTOR OR MAKES ANY FALSE STATEMENT ON THIS PETITION MAY BE PUNISHED BY FINE, IMPRISONMENT, OR BOTH.

PETITION FOR INITIATIVE MEASURE

To the Honorable _____, Secretary of State of the State of Mississippi:

We, the undersigned citizens and qualified electors of the State of Mississippi, respectfully direct that this petition and the proposed measure known as Initiative Measure No. _____, entitled (here insert the established ballot title of the measure), a full, true and correct copy of which is printed or attached on the reverse side of this petition, be transmitted to the Legislature of the State of Mississippi at its next ensuing regular session, and we respectfully petition the Legislature to adopt the proposed measure; and each of us for himself or herself says: I have personally signed this petition, I am a qualified elector of the State of Mississippi in the city (or town), county and congressional district written after my name, my residence address is correctly stated and I have knowingly signed this petition only once."

Each sheet shall also provide adequate space for the following information: Petitioner's signature; print name for positive identification; residence address, street and number, if any; city or town; county; precinct; and congressional district.

§ 23-17-21. Certification of petition by the circuit clerk; fee for filing petition.

Before a person may file a petition with the Secretary of State, the petition must be certified by the circuit clerk of each county in which the petition was circulated. The circuit clerk shall certify the signatures of qualified electors of that county and shall state the total number of qualified electors signing the petition in that county. The circuit clerk shall verify the name of each qualified elector signing on each petition. A circuit clerk may not receive any fee, salary or compensation from any private person or private legal entity for the clerk's duties in certifying an initiative petition. When the person proposing any initiative measure has secured upon the petition a number of signatures of qualified electors equal to or exceeding the minimum number required by Section 273(3) of the Mississippi Constitution of 1890 for the proposed measure, and such signatures have been certified by the circuit clerks of the various counties, he may submit the petition to the Secretary of State for filing. The Secretary of State shall collect a fee of Five Hundred Dollars ($500.00) from the person filing the petition to pay part of the administrative and publication costs.

§ 23-17-23. Grounds for refusing to file initiative petition.

The Secretary of State shall refuse to file any initiative petition being submitted upon any of the following grounds:

(a) That the petition is not in the form required by Section 23-17-19;

(b) That the petition clearly bears insufficient signatures;

(c) That one or more signatures appearing on the petition were obtained in violation of Section 23-17-17(2), Section 23-17-57(2) or Section 23-17-57(3);

(d) That the time within which the petition may be filed has expired; or

(e) That the petition is not accompanied by the filing fee provided for in Section 23-17-21.

In case of such refusal, the Secretary of State shall endorse on the petition the word "submitted" and the date, and retain the petition pending appeal.

If none of the grounds for refusal exists, the Secretary of State shall accept and file the petition.

§ 23-17-25. Procedure to compel Secretary of State to file petition.

If the Secretary of State refuses to file an initiative petition when submitted to him for filing, the person submitting it for filing, within ten (10) days after his refusal, may apply to the Supreme Court for an order requiring the Secretary of State to bring the petition before the court and for a writ of mandamus to compel him to file it. The application shall be considered an emergency matter of public concern and shall be heard and determined with all convenient speed. If the Supreme Court decides that the petition is legal in form, apparently contains the requisite number of signatures of qualified electors, was filed within the time prescribed in the Constitution and was accompanied with the proper filing fee, it shall issue its mandate directing the Secretary of State to file the petition in his office as of the date of submission.

§ 23-17-27. Failure to appeal, or loss of appeal of, Secretary's refusal to file petition.

If no appeal is taken from the refusal of the Secretary of State to file a petition within the time prescribed, or if an appeal is taken and the Secretary of State is not required to file the petition by the mandate of the Supreme Court, the Secretary of State shall destroy it.

§ 23-17-29. Filing petition with Legislature; adoption, amendment, or rejection of initiative; placement of initiative on ballot; approval of conflicting initiatives.

The Secretary of State shall file with the Clerk of the House and the Secretary of the Senate on the first day of the regular legislative session the complete text of each initiative for which a petition has been certified and filed with him. A constitutional initiative may be adopted or amended by a majority vote of each house of the Legislature. If the initiative is adopted, amended or rejected by the Legislature; or if no action is taken within four (4) months of the date that the initiative is filed with the Legislature, the Secretary of State shall place the initiative on the ballot for the next statewide general election. If the Legislature amends an initiative, the amended version and the original initiative shall be submitted to the electors. An initiative or legislative alternative must receive a majority of the votes thereon and not less than forty percent (40%) of the total votes cast at the election at which the measure was submitted to be approved. If conflicting initiatives or legislative alternatives are approved at the same election, the initiative or legislative alternative receiving the highest number of affirmative votes shall prevail.

§ 23-17-31. Procedure for rejection of measure and adoption of new measure by Legislature; designation of "Alternative Measure No. A"; fiscal analysis.

(1) Whenever the Legislature rejects a measure submitted to it by initiative petition and adopts an amendment to the measure proposed by initiative petition, then the Secretary of State shall give the measure adopted by the Legislature the same number as that borne by the initiative measure followed by the letter "A." Such measure so designated as "Alternative Measure No. A," together with the ballot title thereof, when ascertained, shall be certified by the Secretary of State to the county election commissioners for printing on the ballots for submission to the voters for their approval or rejection at the next statewide general election.

(2) The chief legislative budget officer shall prepare a fiscal analysis of each initiative and each legislative alternative. A summary of each fiscal analysis shall appear on the ballot.

§ 23-17-33. Ballot title and summary for alternative measures.

For a measure designated by him as "Alternative Measure No. _____ A," the Secretary of State shall obtain from the Attorney General a ballot title in the manner provided by Section 23-17-9. The ballot title therefor shall be different from the ballot title of the measure in lieu of which it is proposed, and shall indicate, as clearly as possible, the essential differences in the measure.

§ 23-17-35. Form of initiative measure as appearing on ballot.

Except in the case of alternative voting on a measure initiated by petition, each measure submitted to the people for approval or rejection shall be so printed on the ballot, under the proper heading, that a voter can, by making one (1) choice, express his approval or rejection of such measure. Substantially the following form shall be a compliance with this section:

INITIATIVE MEASURE NO.   _____
(Here insert the ballot title of the measure.)
YES .... ()
NO ....…................ ()

§ 23-17-37. Voting for initiative when legislative alternative proposed; form of initiative measure and Legislative alternative as appearing on ballot.

If an initiative measure proposed to the Legislature has been rejected by the Legislature and an alternative measure is passed by the Legislature in lieu thereof, the serial numbers and ballot titles of both such measures shall be printed on the official ballots so that a voter can express separately two (2) preferences: First, by voting for the approval of either measure or against both measures, and, secondly, by voting for one measure or the other measure. If the majority of those voting on the first issue is against both measures, then both measures fail, but in that case the votes on the second issue nevertheless shall be carefully counted and made public. If a majority voting on the first issue is for the approval of either measure, then the measure receiving a majority of the votes on the second issue and also receiving not less than forty percent (40%) of the total votes cast at the election at which the measure was submitted for approval shall be law. Any person who votes against both measures on the first issue may vote but shall not be required to vote for any of the measures on the second issue in order for the ballot to be valid. Substantially the following form shall be a compliance with this section:

INITIATED BY PETITION AND ALTERNATIVE BY LEGISLATURE
Initiative Measure No. _____, entitled (here insert the ballot title of the initiative measure).
Alternative Measure No. _____ A, entitled (here insert the ballot title of the alternative measure).

VOTE FOR APPROVAL OF EITHER, OR AGAINST BOTH:
FOR APPROVAL OF EITHER Initiative No. _____OR Alternative No. _____ A .... ()
AGAINST BOTH initiative No. _____ AND Alternative No. _____ A .... ()
AND VOTE FOR ONE:

FOR Initiative Measure No. _____ .... ()
FOR Alternative Measure No. _____ A .... ()

§ 23-17-39. Limit of how many initiative proposals may be submitted to voters on single ballot.

No more than five (5) initiative proposals shall be submitted to the voters on a single ballot, and the first five (5) initiative proposals submitted to the Secretary of State with sufficient petitions shall be the proposals which are submitted to the voters.

The Basic Steps to Do an Initiative in Mississippi

Amendments Only — Indirect Initiative Process

Basic Procedures: Once the sponsor has drafted the proposed initiative language, he or she must file with the Mississippi Secretary of State a typewritten copy of the proposed initiative accompanied by an affidavit affirming that the sponsor is a registered voter in Mississippi. The Secretary of State then submits a copy of the initiative text to the "Revisor of the Statutes," an attorney in the Attorney General's office. Within 10 working days of receipt of the text, the Revisor makes all advisory recommendations to the sponsor regarding the initiative language. The Revisor of the Statutes also issues a Certificate of Review to the sponsor that the initiative has been reviewed. The sponsor may accept or reject any of the recommendations from the Revisor of the Statutes.

Within 15 working days of the of the sponsor's receiving notice that the Secretary of State has submitted the initiative to the Revisor of the Statutes, the sponsor must submit both the initiative measure (including changes, if any) and the Certificate of Review to the Secretary of State. The Secretary of State assigns the initiative a serial number, and then forwards a copy of the initiative text to the Attorney General.

Within seven calendar days of receiving the initiative from the Secretary of State, the Attorney General must draft the ballot title (not to exceed 20 words) and the ballot summary (not to exceed 75 words.) The Attorney General files both the title and summary with the Secretary of State, who then notified the sponsor by certified mail of the exact language in the ballot title and summary. Within ten days of the title and summary being filed, the Secretary of State publishes the title and summary in a newspaper or newspapers of general circulation throughout Mississippi. If the sponsor or another person is dissatisfied with the ballot title or summary, they have five days from the date of publication in the newspaper to file an appeal in the Circuit Court of the First Judicial District of Hinds County, whose decision shall be final.

Once the ballot title and ballot summary have been finalized, the sponsor may begin collecting signatures.

Date Initiative language can be submitted to state for November 2002 or 2003: Any time

Signatures are tied to vote of which office: Governor

Next Gubernatorial election: 2003

Votes cast for governor in last election: 463,938

Net number of signatures required: 12% of the total number of votes cast for governor in the last gubernatorial general election (91,673 signatures.)

Distribution Requirement: 20% from each of the five congressional districts. Thus, at least 19,668 signatures must be gathered from each of the five congressional districts. If less than 19,688 certified signatures are submitted from ANY of the five congressional districts, the entire petition will be invalid.

Circulation period: 1 year

Do circulators have to be residents: Yes

Date when signatures are due for certification: At least 90 days prior to the convening of the legislature to which it will be submitted. A petition filed after the 90th day cannot be submitted to the next legislative session. October 2001 for the 2002 November ballot and October 2002 for the 2003 November ballot.

Signature verification process: County Circuit Clerks verify every signature.

Single-subject restriction: No

Legislative tampering: Constitutional amendments by initiative become part of the constitution and are thus only alterable by the legislature through regular constitutional procedures, any changes of which must be approved by popular vote.

General Comments: The initiative text must include the amount and source of revenue required to implement the initiative. If the initiative requires a reduction in government revenue or a reallocation from currently funded programs, the initiative text must identify the program or programs whose funding must be reduced or eliminated to implement the initiative. The initiative process cannot be used to modify the Bill of Rights, amend any law or constitutional provision relating to the Public Employees Retirement System (PERS), amend or repeal Mississippi's "Right to Work" constitutional provision, or modify the initiative process for proposing amendments to the Mississippi constitution.

Additionally, if the voters reject an initiative proposal, no similar proposal can be submitted to the people for two years after the date of election at which it was rejected.

Missouri

Initiative and referendum became part of Missouri's constitution primarily as the result of a decade of work by three people: St. Louis attorney Silas L. Moser, William Preston Hill, M.D., Ph.D., and Anna Beard, Dr. Hill's assistant.

Moser, as president of the Missouri Direct Legislation League, brought an I&R bill to a vote in the lower house of the state legislature in 1900. A majority of legislators wanted to be recorded as voting in favor of it: which is not to say that it passed, for after the roll call showed a majority in favor, enough legislators switched their votes to make the bill lose by one vote. In 1904 the legislature approved I&R, but Missouri voters rejected it by a 53,000-vote margin.

Refusing to accept defeat, the I&R leaders persuaded the legislature to pass another I&R amendment in 1907. To avoid a repeat of the 1904 disaster, they embarked on a year long voter education campaign. They engaged the Illinois Progressive leader John Z. White to travel through the state making four speeches a week for the entire year before the vote. Dr. Hill prepared a three-piece mailer and sent it to all 60,000 names listed in telephone directories throughout the state. The effort paid off when Missouri's voters backed I&R by a 35,868-vote majority.

Missouri's most notable initiative was probably the 1940 constitutional amendment to establish a nonpartisan system for the nomination, appointment, and retention elections of judges. This was copied by several states and is now known as the "Missouri Plan" for judicial selection.

The first initiative to pass was a 1920 statute requiring that a new state constitution be drawn up. The next was a 1924 measure to provide funding for the maintenance and construction of the state's highways, followed in 1928 by a $75 million bond issue for further construction. Also approved in 1924 was an initiative to allow voters in the city of St. Louis and St. Louis County to consolidate their local governments.

In the 1930s Missouri voters enacted initiatives to allow public employee benefits and to create a Conservation Commission to manage fish, game, and forest resources. In 1980, the voters adopted the "Hancock Amendment" which limited state and local taxes. In 1992 a term limits initiative was adopted and in 1994 campaign finance reform and riverboat gambling initiatives were approved by the voters.

Statewide Initiative Usage

Number of Initiatives	Number Passed	Number Failed	Passage Rate
68	26	42	38%

Statewide Initiatives

Year	Measure Number	Type	Subject Matter	Description	Pass/Fail
1910	N/A	DA	Alcohol Regulation	To provide for prohibition of the manufacture an sale of intoxicating liquors.	Failed
1910	N/A	DA	Education	To provide for the support and maintenance of the state University by direct state levy.	Failed
1912	N/A	DA	Taxes	To provide for raising all revenue by taxes on land, inheritance and franchises for public service utilities; exempting from taxation all personal property and improvements on land.	Failed
1912	N/A	DA	Administration of Government	To provide for abolishing the present state Board of Equalization, and providing for appointment by the Governor, in lieu of such board, of a state tax commission.	Failed
1912	N/A	DA	Education	To provide for levying and collecting, on each hundred dollars assessed valuation, a state tax of ten cents for the support of the public elementary and high schools.	Failed
1914	13	DA	Election Reform	To provide that females shall have the same right to vote at all elections within the state as males.	Failed
1914	14	DA	Bonds	To authorize the state of Missouri to issue fifty million dollars in interest-bearing bonds and sell same and use the proceeds thereof for building and maintaining public highways of this state, and to authorize a tax levy sufficient to pay the fund.	Failed
1914	15	DA	Taxes	To authorize levy and collection of special taxes for road purposes, to issue bonds in any sum for said purposes, upon petition of taxpaying voters.	Failed
1920	N/A	DS	Administration of Government	To provide for new constitution.	Passed
1922	19	DS	Apportionment/ Redistricting	Apportionment of the state into Senatorial Districts.	Failed
1922	18	DS	Labor	To repeal workman's compensation act.	Failed
1924	8	DS	Taxes	To provide for the exemption from taxation of certain property used exclusively for religious worship, and property including endowments or income used exclusively for educational or charitable purposes.	Failed
1924	7	DS	Administration of Government	To authorize the voters of the city of St. Louis and St. Louis County to consolidate the territories and governments thereof into one legal subdivision of the state.	Passed

Year	Measure Number	Type	Subject Matter	Description	Pass/Fail
1924	6	DS	Labor	An act providing a system of compensation for workmen injured in industrial accidents.	Failed
1924	5	DS	Administration of Government	An act to provide funds for the completion and maintenance of the state highway system.	Passed
1926	4	DS	Alcohol Regulation	To repeal the prohibition act.	Failed
1926	3	DS	Labor	To repeal workmen's compensation.	Failed
1928	2	DS	Administration of Government	An act to provide for the creation, maintenance and administration of a police pension system in all cities of this state that now have or may hereafter attain a population of 500,000 inhabitants or over.	Failed
1928	3	DA	Bonds	Providing for an additional bond issue of $75,000,000 for construction of state highways.	Passed
1930	4	DS	Labor	An act to repeal Sec. 25 of the Workmen's Compensation Act relating to employers liability insurance, enacting new sections providing for the establishment of the Missouri Compensation Fund.	Failed
1930	7	DA	Administration of Government	Providing that the sheriff and coroner in the various counties may succeed themselves.	Failed
1930	6	DA	Environmental Reform	Providing for the taking of private lands for public purposes.	Failed
1930	5	DA	Administration of Government	Enabling the voters of St. Louis and St. Louis County to adopt a charter creating a City of Greater St. Louis.	Failed
1932	3	DA	Administration of Government	An amendment providing for an itemized executive budget of estimated revenue and recommended expenditures to be submitted to the General Assembly within 15 days after it convenes.	Passed
1932	2	DA	Administration of Government	An amendment limiting each House of the General Assembly to 75 employees.	Passed
1934	3	DA	Administration of Government	The Constitution of Missouri shall not be construed to not prohibit payments from any public fund or funds, for benefits, upon retirement, disability or death, to persons employed and paid out of any public fund.	Failed
1936	3	DA	Labor	The Constitution of Missouri shall not be construed to nor prohibit payments, from any public fund or funds, for benefits, upon retirement, disability or death, to persons employed and paid out of any public fund.	Passed
1936	4	DA	Administration of Government	An amendment creating Conservation Commission pertaining to fish, game and forestry, and stating its powers, duties and obligations with respect to administration of same.	Passed

Year	Measure Number	Type	Subject Matter	Description	Pass/Fail
1938	9	DA	Administration of Government	Providing sheriffs and coroners may be eligible to succeed themselves in office.	Failed
1938	8	DA	Taxes	Providing plan of assessment, valuation and taxation; appropriating bond money; prohibiting local property tax on motor vehicles; providing state maintained school system.	Failed
1938	7	DA	Apportionment/ Redistricting	Amendment relating to legislative proceedings, apportionment of senators and representatives, their qualifications, election, compensation, tenure and redistricting.	Failed
1938	N/A	DA	Administration of Government	Concerning state highways, fixing motor fuel tax, prescribing powers relating thereto of General Assembly and state Highway Commission.	Failed
1940	7	DA	Taxes	Providing revenue for rural roads and abolishing municipal gasoline taxes.	Failed
1940	4	DA	Initiative and Referendum	Amending Art. IV of Constitution to provide required number of signatures in initiative or referendum petitions be based on vote for Governor.	Failed
1940	5	DA	Environmental Reform	Repealing Wild Life and Forestry Code and all laws and regulations ordained and established by Conservation Commission.	Failed
1940	6	DA	Taxes	Amending Missouri Constitution by addition of Art. 4a fixing motor vehicle license fees at present rate, and providing revenue for road purposes.	Failed
1940	3	DA	Election Reform	Provide for establishment of non-partisan system for nomination appointment and election of judges of certain courts.	Passed
1944	2	DA	Administration of Government	Constitutional amendment to create a unicameral legislature, 50-75 members elected for two years.	Failed
1958	3	DS	Banking Reform	To permit banking institutions, upon prior approval of the Commissioner of Finance, to establish and operate branches within the city, town, County, village, or constitutional charter city in which its principal office is located.	Failed
1974	1	DS	Campaign Finance Reform	Provides for a new campaign financing and election law to replace portions of the present corrupt practices act.	Passed
1976	7	DA	Education	Authorizes enactment of laws providing services for the handicapped, non-religious textbooks, and transportation for all public and non-public elementary and secondary school children.	Failed
1976	1	DS	Utility Regulation	Prohibits charges for electricity based on cost construction in progress upon any existing or new facility or based on cost associated with owning, operating, maintaining, or financing property.	Passed

Year	Measure Number	Type	Subject Matter	Description	Pass/Fail
1976	2	DA	Taxes	Prohibits after Jan. 1, 1978, sales or use tax on food for off premises human consumption or on drugs and devices prescribed for human medical treatment.	Failed
1976	N/A	DA	Taxes	Increase funding for bird, fish, game, forestry and wildlife programs by levying additional sales and use taxes of one-eighth of one percent.	Passed
1978	23	DA	Labor	Right to work.	Failed
1978	5	DA	Taxes	Increase gas tax from 7 to 10 cents.	Failed
1980	5	DA	Taxes	Limit state and local taxes. Hancock Amendment.	Passed
1980	11	DS	Nuclear weapons/ facilities/waste	Nuclear waste.	Failed
1982	N/A	DS	Taxes	One cent sales tax increase.	Passed
1982	N/A	DS	Utility Regulation	Utility Consumers Board.	Failed
1984	7	DA	Gaming	Establish Horse Racing Commission and regulate wagering.	Passed
1984	6	DS	Utility Regulation	Electricity generation cost charges for consumers.	Passed
1988	8	DA	Health/Medical	Trust fund for catastrophic, high-risk illness.	Failed
1988	7	DA	Taxes	Extend use and sales taxes.	Passed
1990	N/A	DS	Environmental Reform	Regulation of streams.	Failed
1992	12	DA	Term Limits	Term limits on Congress 8/12.	Passed
1992	13	DA	Term Limits	Term limits on state legislature 8/8.	Passed
1994	N/A	DA	Environmental Reform	Property protection to require government reimbursement for lost revenue due to the acquisition on lands for park use.	Passed
1994	N/A	DA	Campaign Finance Reform	Establish campaign finance regulations.	Passed
1994	6	DA	Gaming	Allow slot machine gambling on a riverboat.	Passed
1994	7	DA	Taxes	Voter approval of tax increase.	Failed
1996	8	DA	Taxes	Extends, for 10 years, a sales and use tax for soil and water conservation, state parks and historic sites and for payments in lieu of property taxes for park lands.	Passed
1996	9	DA	Term Limits	Informed Voter Law.	Passed
1996	A	DS	Labor	Increases the minimum wage, from $6.25, Jan. 1, 1997, to $6.75, Jan. 1, 1999 and an additional 15 cents per year thereafter.	Failed
1998	9	DA	Gaming	Would overturn a Missouri Supreme Court ruling that games of chance including slot machines may legally be offered only on boats moored in the main channels of the Missouri.	Passed
1998	A	DS	Animal Rights	Would make it a felony to bait or fight animals.	Passed

Year	Measure Number	Type	Subject Matter	Description	Pass/Fail
2000	A	DS	Environmental Reform	Prohibits new billboards from being constructed and restricts existing outdoor advertising along all National Highway System highways in Missouri.	Failed
2000	B	DS	Campaign Finance Reform	Allows candidates that abide by certain requirements (such as campaign spending limits) to receive taxpayer money for their campaigns.	Failed

Missouri Constitution

Article III Initiative and Referendum

Section 49. Reservation of power to enact and reject laws.

The people reserve power to propose and enact or reject laws and amendments to the constitution by the initiative, independent of the general assembly, and also reserve power to approve or reject by referendum any act of the general assembly, except as hereinafter provided.

Section 50. Initiative petitions — signatures required — form and procedure.

Initiative petitions proposing amendments to the constitution shall be signed by eight percent of the legal voters in each of two-thirds of the congressional districts in the state, and petitions proposing laws shall be signed by five percent of such voters. Every such petition shall be filed with the secretary of state not less than six months before the election and shall contain an enacting clause and the full text of the measure. Petitions for constitutional amendments shall not contain more than one amended and revised article of this constitution, or one new article which shall not contain more than one subject and matters properly connected therewith, and the enacting clause thereof shall be "Be it resolved by the people of the state of Missouri that the Constitution be amended:". Petitions for laws shall contain not more than one subject which shall be expressed clearly in the title, and the enacting clause thereof shall be "Be it enacted by the people of the state of Missouri:".

Section 51. Appropriations by initiative — effective date of initiated laws — conflicting laws concurrently adopted.

The initiative shall not be used for the appropriation of money other than of new revenues created and provided for thereby, or for any other purpose prohibited by this constitution. Except as provided in this constitution, any measure proposed shall take effect when approved by a majority of the votes cast thereon. When conflicting measures are approved at the same election the one receiving the largest affirmative vote shall prevail.

Section 52(a). Referendum — exceptions — procedure.

A referendum may be ordered (except as to laws necessary for the immediate preservation of the public peace, health or safety, and laws making appropriations for the current expenses of the state government, for the maintenance of state institutions and for the support of public schools) either by petitions signed by five percent of the legal voters in each of two-thirds of the congressional districts in the state, or by the general assembly, as other bills are enacted. Referendum petitions shall be filed with the secretary of state not more than ninety days after the final adjournment of the session of the general assembly which passed the bill on which the referendum is demanded.

Section 52(b). Veto power — elections — effective date.

The veto power of the governor shall not extend to measures referred to the people. All elections on measures referred to the people shall be had at the general state elections, except when the general assembly shall order a special election. Any measure referred to the people shall take effect when approved by a majority of the votes cast thereon, and not otherwise. This section shall not be construed to deprive any member of the general assembly of the right to introduce any measure.

Section 53. Basis for computation of signatures required.

The total vote for governor at the general election last preceding the filing of any initiative or referendum petition shall be used to determine the number of legal voters necessary to sign the petition. In submitting the same to the people the secretary of state and all other officers shall be governed by general laws.

Article XII Amending the Constitution

Section 2(b) Submission of amendments proposed by general assembly or by the initiative.

All amendments proposed by the general assembly or by the initiative shall be submitted to the electors for their approval or rejection by official ballot title as may be provided by law, on a separate ballot without party designation, at the next general election, or at a special election called by the governor prior thereto, at which he may submit any of the amendments. No such proposed amendment shall contain more than one amended and revised article of this constitution, or one new article which shall not contain more than one subject and matters properly connected therewith. If possible, each proposed amendment shall be published once a week for two consecutive weeks in two newspapers of different political faith in each county, the last publication to be not more than thirty nor less than fifteen days next preceding the election. If there be but one newspaper in any county, publication for four consecutive weeks shall be made. If a majority of the votes cast thereon is in favor of any amendment, the same shall take effect at the end of thirty days after the election. More than one amendment at the same election shall be so submitted as to enable the electors to vote on each amendment separately.

Missouri Statutes

Chapter 116 Initiative and Referendum

116.010. Definitions

As used in this chapter, unless the context otherwise indicates,
(1) "County" means any one of the several counties of this state or the city of St. Louis;
(2) "Election authority" means a county clerk or board of election commissioners, as established by section 115.015, RSMo;
(3) "General election" means the first Tuesday after the first Monday in November in even-numbered years;
(4) "Official ballot title" means the summary statement and fiscal note summary prepared for all statewide ballot measures in accordance with the provisions of this chapter which shall be placed on the ballot and, when applicable, shall be the petition title for initiative or referendum petitions;
(5) "Statewide ballot measure" means a constitutional amendment submitted by initiative petition, the general assembly or a constitutional convention; a statutory measure submitted by initiative or referendum petition; the question of holding a constitutional convention; and a constitution proposed by a constitutional convention;
(6) "Voter" means a person registered to vote in accordance with section 115.151, RSMo.

116.020. Application of Laws

This chapter shall apply to elections on statewide ballot measures. The election procedures contained in chapter 115, RSMo, shall apply to elections on statewide ballot measures, except to the extent that the provisions of chapter 116 directly conflict, in which case chapter 116 shall prevail, and except to the extent that a constitutional convention's provisions under section 3(c) of article XII of the constitution directly conflict, in which case the convention's provisions shall prevail.

116.030. Referendum petition, form — clerical and technical errors to be disregarded, penalties for false signature.

The following shall be substantially the form of each page of referendum petitions on any law passed by the general assembly of the state of Missouri:

County ....
Page No. ....

It is a class A misdemeanor punishable, notwithstanding the provisions of section 560.021, RSMo, to the contrary, for a term of imprisonment not to exceed one year in the county jail or a fine not to exceed ten thousand dollars or both, for anyone to sign any referendum petition with any name other than his or her own, or knowingly to sign his or her name more than once for the same measure for the same election, or to sign a petition when such person knows he or she is not a registered voter.

PETITION FOR REFERENDUM To the Honorable ...., Secretary of State for the state of Missouri:

We, the undersigned, registered voters of the state of Missouri and .... County (or city of St. Louis), respectfully order that the Senate (or House) Bill No..... entitled (title of law), passed by the .... general assembly of the state of Missouri, at the .... regular (or special) session of the .... general assembly, shall be referred to the voters of the state of Missouri, for their approval or rejection, at the general election to be held on the ... day of ...., ..., unless the general assembly shall designate another date, and each for himself or herself says: I have personally signed this petition; I am a registered voter of the state of Missouri and .... County (or city of St. Louis); my registered voting address and the name of the city, town or village in which I live are correctly written after my name.

CIRCULATOR'S AFFIDAVIT STATE OF MISSOURI, COUNTY OF ....

I, ..., being first duly sworn, say (print or type names of signers) REGISTERED VOTING NAME DATE ADDRESS ZIP CONGR. NAME (Signature) SIGNED (Street)(City, CODE DIST. (Printed Town or Village) or Typed)

(Here follow numbered lines for signers) signed this page of the foregoing petition, and each of them signed his or her name thereto in my presence; I believe that each has stated his or her name, registered voting address and city, town or village correctly, and that each signer is a registered voter of the state of Missouri and .... County.
....
Signature of Affiant (Person obtaining signatures)
....
Address of Affiant Subscribed and sworn to before me this ... day of ... A.D ....
....
Signature of Notary   Address of Notary   Notary Public (Seal)
My commission expires ....

If this form is followed substantially and the requirements of section 116.050 are met, it shall be sufficient, disregarding clerical and merely technical errors.

116.040. Initiative petition for law or constitutional amendment, form — clerical and technical errors to be disregarded, penalties for false signature.
The following shall be substantially the form of each page of each petition for any law or amendment to the Constitution of the state of Missouri proposed by the initiative:

County ....
Page No. ....

It is a class A misdemeanor punishable, notwithstanding the provisions of section 560.021, RSMo, to the contrary, for a term of imprisonment not to exceed one year in the county jail or a fine not to exceed ten thousand dollars or both, for anyone to sign any initiative petition with any name other than his or her own, or knowingly to sign his or her name more than once for the same measure for the same election, or to sign a petition when such person knows he or she is not a registered voter.

INITIATIVE PETITION To the Honorable ... Secretary of State for the state of Missouri:

We, the undersigned, registered voters of the state of Missouri and .... County (or city of St. Louis), respectfully order that the following proposed law (or amendment to the constitution) shall be submitted to the voters of the state of Missouri, for their approval or rejection, at the general election to be held on the ... day of ... and each for himself or herself says: I have personally signed this petition; I am a registered voter of the state of Missouri and ... County (or city of St. Louis); my registered voting address and the name of the city, town or village in which I live are correctly written after my name.

CIRCULATOR'S AFFIDAVIT STATE OF MISSOURI, COUNTY OF ....

I, ... being first duly sworn, say (print or type names of signers) REGISTERED VOTING NAME DATE ADDRESS ZIP CONGR. NAME (Signature) Signed (Street)(City, CODE DIST. (Printed Town or Village) or Typed)

(Here follow numbered lines for signers) signed this page of the foregoing petition, and each of them signed his or her name thereto in my presence; I believe that each has stated his or her name, registered voting address and city, town or village correctly, and that each signer is a registered voter of the state of Missouri and .... County.

....
Signature of Affiant (Person obtaining signatures)
....
Address of Affiant Subscribed and sworn to before me this ... day of ... A.D ....
....
Signature of Notary   Address of Notary   Notary Public (Seal)
My commission expires ....

If this form is followed substantially and the requirements of section 116.050 and section 116.080 are met, it shall be sufficient, disregarding clerical and merely technical errors.

116.050. Initiative and referendum petitions, requirements.

Initiative and referendum petitions filed under the provisions of this chapter shall consist of pages of a uniform size. Each page, excluding the text of the measure, shall be no larger than eight and one-half by fourteen inches. Each page of an initiative petition shall be attached to or shall contain a full and correct text of the proposed measure. Each page of a referendum petition shall be attached to or shall contain a full and correct text of the measure on which the referendum is sought.

116.060. Initiative and referendum petitions, who may sign — residents of one county only on a designated page.

Any registered voter of the state of Missouri may sign initiative and referendum petitions. However, each page of an initiative or referendum petition shall contain signatures of voters from only one county. Each petition page filed with the secretary of state shall have the county where the signers are registered designated in the upper right-hand corner of such page. Signatures of voters from counties other than the one designated by the circulator in the upper right-hand corner on a given page shall not be counted as valid.

116.070. Petitioner may sign by mark, procedure.

When any voter wishes to sign an initiative or referendum petition and is unable to sign his name, the circulator shall print the required information on the petition. The voter shall then make his mark, and the circulator shall attest to it by his signature. For purposes of this chapter, all marks made and attested in accordance with this section shall be considered signatures.

116.080. Qualifications of circulator — affidavit, notarization, penalty.

1. Each petition circulator shall be at least eighteen years of age and registered with the secretary of state. Signatures collected by any circulator who has not registered with the secretary of state pursuant to this chapter on or before 5:00 p.m. on the final day for filing petitions with the secretary of state shall not be counted.
2. Each petition circulator shall supply the following information to the secretary of state's office:
(1) Name of petition;
(2) Name of circulator;
(3) Residential address, including street number, city, state and zip code;
(4) Mailing address, if different;
(5) Have you been or do you expect to be paid for soliciting signatures for this petition? [] YES [] NO;
(6) If the answer to subdivision (5) is yes, then identify the payer;
(7) Signature of circulator.
3. The circulator information required in subsection 2 of this section shall be submitted to the secretary of state's office with the following oath and affirmation: I HEREBY SWEAR OR AFFIRM UNDER PENALTY OF PERJURY THAT ALL STATEMENTS MADE BY ME ARE TRUE AND CORRECT.
4. Each petition circulator shall subscribe and swear to the proper affidavit on each petition page such circulator submits before a notary public commissioned in Missouri. When notarizing a circulator's signature, a notary public shall sign his

or her official signature and affix his or her official seal to the affidavit only if the circulator personally appears before the notary and subscribes and swears to the affidavit in his or her presence.

5. Any circulator who falsely swears to a circulator's affidavit knowing it to be false is guilty of a class A misdemeanor punishable, notwithstanding the provisions of section 560.021, RSMo, to the contrary, for a term of imprisonment not to exceed one year in the county jail or a fine not to exceed ten thousand dollars or both.

116.090. Signing petition illegally, penalty.

1. Any person who signs any name other than his own to any petition, or who knowingly signs his or her name more than once for the same measure for the same election, or who knows he or she is not at the time of signing or circulating the same a Missouri registered voter and a resident of this state, shall, upon conviction thereof, be guilty of a class A misdemeanor punishable, notwithstanding the provisions of section 560.021, RSMo, to the contrary, for a term of imprisonment not to exceed one year in the county jail or a fine not to exceed ten thousand dollars or both.

2. Any person who knowingly accepts or offers money or anything of value to another person in exchange for a signature on a petition is guilty of a class A misdemeanor punishable, notwithstanding the provisions of section 560.021, RSMo, to the contrary, for a term of imprisonment not to exceed one year in the county jail or a fine not to exceed ten thousand dollars or both.

116.100. Filing of petition, procedure.

The secretary of state shall not accept any referendum petition submitted later than 5:00 p.m. on the final day for filing referendum petitions. The secretary of state shall not accept any initiative petition submitted later than 5:00 p.m. on the final day for filing initiative petitions. All pages shall be submitted at one time. When an initiative or referendum petition is submitted to the secretary of state, the signature pages shall be in order and numbered sequentially by county, except in counties that include multiple congressional districts, the signatures may be ordered and numbered using an alternate numbering scheme approved in writing by the secretary of state prior to submission of the petition. Any petition that is not submitted in accordance with this section, disregarding clerical and merely technical errors, shall be rejected as insufficient. After verifying the count of signature pages, the secretary of state shall issue a receipt indicating the number of pages presented from each county. When a person submits a petition he or she shall designate to the secretary of state the name and the address of the person to whom any notices shall be sent under sections 116.140 and 116.180.

116.110. Signature may be withdrawn, when, how, effect, penalty.

Any voter who has signed an initiative or referendum petition may withdraw his or her signature from that petition by submitting to the secretary of state, before the petition is filed with the secretary of state, a sworn statement requesting that his or her signature be withdrawn and affirming the name of the petition signed, the name the voter used when signing the petition, the address of the voter and the county of residence. It is a class A misdemeanor punishable, notwithstanding the provisions of section 560.021, RSMo, to the contrary, for a term of imprisonment not to exceed one year in the county jail or a fine not to exceed ten thousand dollars or both, to knowingly file a false withdrawal statement with the secretary of state.

116.120. Secretary of state to determine sufficiency of form and compliance — invalid signatures not counted — signatures may be verified by random sampling, procedure and requirements.

1. When an initiative or referendum petition is submitted to the secretary of state, he or she shall examine the petition to determine whether it complies with the Constitution of Missouri and with this chapter. Signatures on petition pages that have been collected by any person who is not properly registered with the secretary of state as a circulator shall not be counted as valid. Signatures on petition pages that do not have the official ballot title affixed to the page shall not be counted as valid. The secretary of state may verify the signatures on the petition by use of random sampling. The random sample of signatures to be verified shall be drawn in such a manner that every signature properly filed with the secretary of state shall be given an equal opportunity to be included in the sample. The process for establishing the random sample and determining the statistically valid result shall be established by the secretary of state. Such a random sampling shall include an examination of five percent of the signatures.

2. If the random sample verification establishes that the number of valid signatures is less than ninety percent of the number of qualified voters needed to find the petition sufficient in a congressional district, the petition shall be deemed to have failed to qualify in that district. In finding a petition insufficient, the secretary of state does not need to verify all congressional districts on each petition submitted if verification of only one or more districts establishes the petition as insufficient.

3. If the random sample verification establishes that the number of valid signatures total more than one hundred ten percent of the number of qualified voters needed to find the petition sufficient in a congressional district, the petition shall be deemed to qualify in that district.

4. If the random sampling shows the number of valid signatures within a congressional district is within ninety to one hundred ten percent of the number of signatures of qualified voters needed to declare the petition sufficient in that district, the secretary of state shall order the examination and verification of each signature filed.

116.130. Election authorities may be requested to verify signatures either by random sampling or checking signatures, when, how.

1. The secretary of state may send copies of petition pages to election authorities to verify that the persons whose names are listed as signers to the petition are registered voters. Such verification may either be of each signature or by random sampling as provided in section 116.120, as the secretary shall direct. If copies of the petition pages are sent to an election authority for verification, such copies shall be sent pursuant to the following schedule:

(1) Copies of all pages from not less than one petition shall be received in the office of the election authority not later than two weeks after the petition is filed in the office of secretary of state;

(2) Copies of all pages of a total of three petitions shall be received in the office of the election authority not later than three weeks after the petition is filed in the office of secretary of state;

(3) If more than three petitions are filed, all copies of petition pages, including those petitions selected for verification by random sample pursuant to section 116.120, shall be received in the office of the election authority not later than the fourth week after the petition is filed in the office of the secretary of state. Each election authority shall check the signatures against voter registration records in the election authority's jurisdiction, but the election authority shall count as valid only the signatures of persons registered as voters in the county named in the circulator's affidavit. Signatures shall not be counted as valid if they have been struck through or crossed out.

2. If the election authority is requested to verify the petition by random sampling, such verification shall be completed and certified not later than two weeks from the date that the election authority receives the petition from the secretary of state. If the election authority is to verify each signature, such verification must be completed, certified and delivered to the secretary of state by 5:00 p.m. on the last Tuesday in July prior to the election, or in the event of complete verification of signatures after a failed random sample, full verification shall be completed, certified and delivered to the secretary of state by 5:00 p.m. on the last Tuesday in July or by 5:00 p.m. on the Friday of the fifth week after receipt of the signatures by the local election authority, whichever is later.

3. If the election authority or the secretary of state determines that the congressional district number written after the signature of any voter is not the congressional district of which the voter is a resident, the election authority or the secretary of state shall correct the congressional district number on the petition page. Failure of a voter to give the voter's correct congressional district number shall not by itself be grounds for not counting the voter's signature.

4. The election authority shall return the copies of the petition pages to the secretary of state with annotations regarding any invalid or questionable signatures which the election authority has been asked to check by the secretary of state. The election authority shall verify the number of pages received for that county, and also certify the total number of valid signatures of voters from each congressional district which the election authority has been asked to check by the secretary of state.

5. The secretary of state is authorized to adopt rules to ensure uniform, complete, and accurate checking of petition signatures either by actual count or random sampling. No rule or portion of a rule promulgated pursuant to this section shall become effective unless it has been promulgated pursuant to the provisions of section 536.024, RSMo.

6. After a period of three years from the time of submission of the petitions to the secretary of state, the secretary of state, if the secretary determines that retention of such petitions is no longer necessary, may destroy such petitions.

116.140. Secretary of state's authority not to count forged or fraudulent signatures.

Notwithstanding certifications from election authorities under section 116.130, the secretary of state shall have authority not to count signatures on initiative or referendum petitions which are, in his opinion, forged or fraudulent signatures.

116.150. Secretary of state to issue certificate of sufficiency of petition, when — if insufficient, certificate to state reasons.

1. After the secretary of state makes a determination on the sufficiency of the petition and if the secretary of state finds it sufficient, the secretary of state shall issue a certificate setting forth that the petition contains a sufficient number of valid signatures to comply with the Constitution of Missouri and with this chapter.

2. The secretary of state shall issue a certificate only for a petition approved pursuant to section 116.332. If the secretary of state finds the petition insufficient, the secretary of state shall issue a certificate stating the reason for the insufficiency.

3. The secretary of state shall issue a certificate pursuant to this section not later than 5:00 p.m. on the thirteenth Tuesday prior to the general election or two weeks after the date the election authority certifies the results of a petition verification pursuant to subsection 2 of section 116.130, whichever is later.

116.155. Official summaries and fiscal notes may be included in ballot measures, summary to be official ballot title if included.

1. The general assembly may include the official summary statement and a fiscal note summary in any statewide ballot measure that it refers to the voters.

2. The official summary statement approved by the general assembly shall, taken together with the approved fiscal note summary, be the official ballot title and such summary statement shall contain no more than fifty words, excluding articles. The title shall be a true and impartial statement of the purposes of the proposed measure in language neither intentionally argumentative nor likely to create prejudice either for or against the proposed measure.

3. The fiscal note summary approved by the general assembly shall contain no more than fifty words, excluding articles, which shall summarize the fiscal note prepared for the measure in language neither argumentative nor likely to create prejudice for or against the proposed measure.

116.160. Summary statement to be provided by the secretary of state if summary not provided by general assembly — content.

1. If the general assembly adopts a joint resolution proposing a constitutional amendment or a bill without a fiscal note summary, which is to be referred to a vote of the people, after receipt of such resolution or bill the secretary of state shall promptly forward the resolution or bill to the state auditor. If the general assembly adopts a joint resolution proposing a constitutional amendment or a bill without an official summary statement, which is to be referred to a vote of the people, within twenty days after receipt of the resolution or bill, the secretary of state shall prepare and transmit to the attorney general a summary statement of the measure as the proposed summary statement. The secretary of state may seek the advice of the legislator who introduced the constitutional amendment or bill and the speaker of the house or the president pro tem of the legislative chamber that originated the measure. The summary statement may be distinct from the legislative title of the proposed constitutional amendment or bill. The attorney general shall within ten days approve the legal content and form of the proposed statement.

2. The official summary statement shall contain no more than fifty words, excluding articles. The title shall be a true and impartial statement of the purposes of the proposed measure in language neither intentionally argumentative nor likely to create prejudice either for or against the proposed measure.

116.170. Fiscal note and fiscal note summary to be provided by state auditor if not provided by general assembly.

If the general assembly adopts a joint resolution proposing a constitutional amendment or a bill without a fiscal note summary, which is to be referred to a vote of the people, the state auditor shall, within thirty days of delivery to the auditor, prepare and file with the secretary of state a fiscal note and a fiscal note summary for the proposed measure in accordance with the provisions of section 116.175.

116.175. Fiscal impact of proposed measure — fiscal note, fiscal note summary, requirements.

1. Except as provided in section 116.155, upon receipt from the secretary of state's office of any petition sample sheet, joint resolution or bill, the auditor shall assess the fiscal impact of the proposed measure. The state auditor may consult with the state departments, local government entities, the general assembly and others with knowledge pertinent to the cost of the proposal. Proponents or opponents of any proposed measure may submit to the state auditor a proposed statement of fiscal impact estimating the cost of the proposal in a manner consistent with the standards of the governmental accounting standards board and section 23.140, RSMo, provided that all such proposals are received by the state auditor within ten days of his or her receipt of the proposed measure from the secretary of state.

2. Within twenty days of receipt of a petition sample sheet, joint resolution or bill from the secretary of state, the state auditor shall prepare a fiscal note and a fiscal note summary for the proposed measure and forward both to the attorney general.

3. The fiscal note and fiscal note summary shall state the measure's estimated cost or savings, if any, to state or local governmental entities. The fiscal note summary shall contain no more than fifty words, excluding articles, which shall summarize the fiscal note in language neither argumentative nor likely to create prejudice either for or against the proposed measure.

4. The attorney general shall, within ten days of receipt of the fiscal note and the fiscal note summary, approve the legal content and form of the fiscal note summary prepared by the state auditor and shall forward notice of such approval to the state auditor.

116.180. Copies of ballot title, fiscal note and fiscal note summary to designated persons, when — ballot title to be affixed to petition, when.

Within three days after receiving the official summary statement the approved fiscal note summary and the fiscal note relating to any statewide ballot measure, the secretary of state shall certify the official ballot title in separate paragraphs with the fiscal note summary immediately following the summary statement of the measure and shall deliver a copy of the official ballot title and the fiscal note to the speaker of the house or the president pro tem of the legislative chamber that originated the measure or, in the case of initiative or referendum petitions, to the person whose name and address are designated under section 116.332. Persons circulating the petition shall affix the official ballot title to each page of the petition prior to circulation and signatures shall not be counted if the official ballot title is not affixed to the page containing such signatures.

116.185. Identical ballot titles may be changed, how.

Before the ballot is printed, if the title of a ballot issue is identical or substantially identical to the title of another ballot issue that will appear on the same ballot, the election authority shall promptly notify the officer or entity that certifies the election of the identical or substantially identical title, and if such officer or entity submits a new title to the election authority, the election authority may change the title of the ballot issue prior to printing the official ballot.

116.190. Ballot title may be challenged, procedure — who are parties defendant — changes may be made by court — appeal to supreme court, when.

1. Any citizen who wishes to challenge the official ballot title or the fiscal note prepared for a proposed constitutional amendment submitted by the general assembly, by initiative petition, or by constitutional convention, or for a statutory initiative or referendum measure, may bring an action in the circuit court of Cole County. The action must be brought within ten days after the official ballot title is certified by the secretary of state in accordance with the provisions of this chapter.

2. The secretary of state shall be named as a party defendant in any action challenging the official ballot title prepared by the secretary of state. When the action challenges the fiscal note or the fiscal note summary prepared by the auditor, the state auditor shall also be named as a party defendant. The president pro tem of the senate, the speaker of the house and the sponsor of the measure and the secretary of state shall be the named party defendants in any action challenging the official summary statement, fiscal note or fiscal note summary prepared pursuant to section 116.155.

3. The petition shall state the reason or reasons why the official ballot title is insufficient or unfair and shall request a different official ballot title.

4. The action shall be placed at the top of the civil docket. The court shall consider the petition, hear arguments, and in its decision certify the official ballot title to the secretary of state. Any party to the suit may appeal to the supreme court within ten days after a circuit court decision. In making the legal notice to election authorities under section 116.240, the secretary of state shall certify the language which the court certifies to him.

116.195. Costs of court-ordered ballot title change to be paid by the state.

Whenever the reprinting of a statewide ballot measure is necessary as a result of a court-ordered change to the ballot language for such measure, the costs of such reprinting shall be paid by the state.

116.200. Secretary of state's decision as to sufficiency of petition may be reversed, procedure — appeal.

1. After the secretary of state certifies a petition as sufficient or insufficient, any citizen may apply to the circuit court of Cole County to compel him to reverse his decision. The action must be brought within ten days after the certification is made. All such suits shall be advanced on the court docket and heard and decided by the court as quickly as possible.

2. If the court decides the petition is sufficient, the secretary of state shall certify it as sufficient and attach a copy of the judgment. If the court decides the petition is insufficient, the court shall enjoin the secretary of state from certifying the measure and all other officers from printing the measure on the ballot.

3. Within ten days after a decision is rendered, any party may appeal it to the supreme court.

116.210. Numbering of proposed constitutional amendments.

The secretary of state shall number proposed constitutional amendments in the order in which they are passed by the general assembly, or submitted by initiative petition, or adopted by constitutional convention. He shall number the first as "Constitutional Amendment No. 1" and so on consecutively. A new series of numbers shall be started after each general election.

116.220. Labeling of initiative and referendum measures.

The secretary of state shall label statutory initiative and referendum measures alphabetically in the order in which they are submitted by petition or in the order in which they are passed by the general assembly. The secretary of state shall label the first as "Proposition A", and so on consecutively through the letter Z, and then begin labeling as "Proposition AA" and so on. A new series of letters shall be started after each general election. In the event a measure is labeled prior to, but not voted on at, the next succeeding general election, the letter assigned to such measure shall not be reassigned until after such measure has been voted on by the people.

116.230. Sample ballots to be prepared, form.

1. The secretary of state shall prepare sample ballots in the following form.
2. The top of the ballot shall read: "OFFICIAL BALLOT STATE OF MISSOURI"
3. When constitutional amendments are submitted, the first heading shall read: "CONSTITUTIONAL AMENDMENTS" There shall follow the numbers assigned under section 116.210 the official ballot titles prepared under section 116.160 or 116.334, and the fiscal note summaries prepared under section 116.170. Constitutional amendments proposed by the general assembly shall be designated as "Proposed by the general assembly". Constitutional amendments proposed by initiative petition shall be designated "Proposed by initiative petition". Constitutional amendments proposed by constitutional convention shall be designated as "Proposed by constitutional convention".
4. When statutory measures are submitted, the next heading shall read: "STATUTORY MEASURES" There shall follow the letters assigned under section 116.220, the official ballot titles prepared under section 116.160 or 116.334, and the fiscal note summaries prepared under section 116.170. Statutory initiative measures shall be designated "Proposed by initiative petition". Referendum measures shall be designated "Referendum ordered by petition".

116.240. Certification to election authorities of notice to be published — contents.

Not later than the tenth Tuesday prior to an election at which a statewide ballot measure is to be voted on, the secretary of state shall send each election authority a certified copy of the legal notice to be published. The legal notice shall include the date and time of the election and a sample ballot.

116.250. Publication of legal notice.

On receiving a notice under section 116.240, each election authority shall cause the legal notice to be published in accordance with subsection 2 of section 115.127, RSMo.

116.260. Newspapers for publication of text of measures to be designated — measures to be published, how.

The secretary of state shall designate in what newspaper or newspapers in each county the text of statewide ballot measures shall be published. If possible, each shall be published once a week for two consecutive weeks in two newspapers of different political faiths in each county, the last publication to be not more than thirty or less than fifteen days next preceding the election. If there is but one newspaper in any county, publication for four consecutive weeks shall be made, the first publication to be not less than twenty-eight days next preceding the election. If there are two or more newspapers in a county, none of which is of different political faiths from another, the statewide ballot measures shall be published once a week for two consecutive weeks in any two newspapers in the county with the last publication not more than thirty or less than fifteen days next preceding the election.

116.270. Publications fund created — payments from fund for what, how made.

1. There is hereby created a "Publications Fund" which shall be used only to pay printing, publication, and other expenses incurred in submitting statewide ballot measures to the voters.
2. The secretary of state shall certify to the commissioner of administration all valid claims for payment from the publications fund. On receiving the certified claims, the commissioner of administration shall issue warrants on the state treasurer payable to each individual out of the publications fund.

116.280. Paper ballots for statewide measures, form.

In jurisdictions using paper ballots, election authorities shall cause the ballots for statewide ballot measures to be printed on paper not less than four inches wide and ten inches long, and all in the same color and size. Measures may be printed in more than one column.

116.290. Printing of copies of statewide measures — to be posted at polling places — distribution, exception.

1. The secretary of state shall distribute copies of each statewide ballot measure, except proposed constitutions as published in newspapers for legal notice of the election.

2. The secretary of state shall print copies of each proposed constitution in pamphlet form.

3. From copies delivered by the secretary of state, each election authority shall post at least two copies of each notice and pamphlet at each polling place during the time the polls are open.

4. The secretary of state shall print any new language being proposed for adoption or rejection in boldface type.

116.300. Challengers and watchers at polling places, how designated.

Not later than the fourth Tuesday prior to an election on a statewide ballot measure, each chairman of a county campaign committee favoring a measure and each chairman of a county campaign committee opposing a measure shall file with the election authority a list of committee officers and a request to have the right to designate challengers and watchers under section 116.310. If only one committee favoring a particular measure and one committee opposing a particular measure file a list and a request, then each filing chairman shall have the right to designate challengers and watchers under section 116.310. If more than one committee favoring a particular measure or more than one committee opposing a particular measure files a list and request, then the election authority shall determine which chairman has the right to designate challengers and watchers. If the measure was submitted by initiative or referendum petition, the person designated under section 116.100 as the person to receive notice under sections 116.140 and 116.180 shall be entitled to designate the county campaign committee chairmen's names to the proper election authorities by the fourth Tuesday prior to the election on that measure.

116.310. Time limited for designating challengers and watchers for polling places and counting locations — effect of failure to designate by prescribed time.

1. Not later than the Tuesday prior to an election on a statewide ballot measure, each county campaign committee chairman who had the right to designate challengers under section 116.300 shall designate such challengers, who may be present at each polling place during the hours of voting. Each such chairman shall also by the same time designate a challenger for each location at which absentee ballots are counted. The challengers so designated may be present while the ballots are being prepared for counting and being counted.

2. Not later than the Tuesday prior to an election on a statewide ballot measure, each campaign committee chairman who has the right to designate watchers under section 116.300 shall designate a watcher for each place votes are counted.

3. After challengers and watchers have been designated, the provisions contained in sections 115.105, 115.107, 115.109, and 115.111, RSMo, shall apply to them.

4. Failure to designate challengers and watchers by the prescribed times shall cause the county campaign committee to forfeit its right to name such persons for those omitted locations for that election.

116.320. Adoption of measure, vote required — effect of approval of conflicting measures.

1. Each statewide ballot measure receiving a majority of affirmative votes is adopted.

2. If voters approve two or more conflicting statutes at the same election, the statute receiving the largest affirmative vote shall prevail, even if that statute did not receive the greatest majority of affirmative votes.

3. If voters approve two or more conflicting constitutional amendments at the same election, the amendment receiving the largest affirmative vote shall prevail, even if that amendment did not receive the greatest majority of affirmative votes.

116.330. Board of canvassers or governor to issue statement.

1. After an election at which any statewide ballot measure, other than a proposed constitution or constitutional amendment submitted by a constitutional convention, is voted upon, the secretary of state shall convene the board of state canvassers to total the abstracts. Not later than two weeks after receiving all required abstracts, the board shall issue a statement giving the number of votes cast "yes" and "no" on each question. If voters approve two or more measures at one election which are known to conflict with one another, or to contain conflicting provisions, the board shall also state which received the largest affirmative vote.

2. After an election at which a proposed constitution or constitutional amendment adopted by a constitutional convention is submitted, the governor shall proclaim the results in accordance with section 3(c), article XII of the constitution.

116.332. Petitions for constitutional amendments, statutory initiative or referendum, requirements, procedure.

1. Before a constitutional amendment petition, a statutory initiative petition, or a referendum petition may be circulated for signatures, a sample sheet must be submitted to the secretary of state in the form in which it will be circulated. When

a person submits a sample sheet of a petition he or she shall designate to the secretary of state the name and address of the person to whom any notices shall be sent pursuant to sections 116.140 and 116.180. The secretary of state shall refer a copy of the petition sheet to the attorney general for his approval and to the state auditor for purposes of preparing a fiscal note and fiscal note summary. The secretary of state and attorney general must each review the petition for sufficiency as to form and approve or reject the form of the petition, stating the reasons for rejection, if any.

2. Upon receipt of a petition from the office of the secretary of state, the attorney general shall examine the petition as to form. If the petition is rejected as to form, the attorney general shall forward his or her comments to the secretary of state within ten days after receipt of the petition by the attorney general. If the petition is approved as to form, the attorney general shall forward his or her approval as to form to the secretary of state within ten days after receipt of the petition by the attorney general.

3. The secretary of state shall review the comments and statements of the attorney general as to form and make a final decision as to the approval or rejection of the form of the petition. The secretary of state shall send written notice to the person who submitted the petition sheet of the approval within thirty days after submission of the petition sheet. The secretary of state shall send written notice if the petition has been rejected, together with reasons for rejection, within thirty days after submission of the petition sheet.

116.334. Petition approval required, procedure to obtain petition title or summary statement — rejection or approval of petition, procedure — circulation of petition prior to approval, effect.

1. If the petition form is approved, the secretary of state shall within ten days prepare and transmit to the attorney general a summary statement of the measure which shall be a concise statement not exceeding one hundred words. This statement shall be in the form of a question using language neither intentionally argumentative nor likely to create prejudice either for or against the proposed measure. The attorney general shall within ten days approve the legal content and form of the proposed statement.

2. Signatures obtained prior to the date the official ballot title is certified by the secretary of state shall not be counted.

116.340. Publication of approved measures.

When a statewide ballot measure is approved by the voters, the secretary of state shall publish it with the laws enacted by the following session of the general assembly, and the revisor of statutes shall include it in the next edition or supplement of the revised statutes of Missouri. Each of the measures printed above shall include the date of the proclamation or statement of approval under section 116.330.

The Basic Steps to Do an Initiative in Missouri

Statutes and Amendments — Direct Initiative Process

Basic Procedures: After forming their committee, proponents file the full text of their initiative with the Secretary of State (SOS), along with a sample petition form. The Secretary of State reviews the petition for form and also writes a ballot title and summary based on the full text. The SOS will take a suggested title and summary from proponents — but are not obligated to use it. Once the SOS writes the title and summary, it is forwarded to the Attorney General for final approval. After the initiative is filed, the State Auditor writes a fiscal impact statement.

Once the ballot title, summary and fiscal impact statements are written, proponents can begin circulating. The Secretary of State, Attorney General and State Auditor are required to have everything completed within 30 days of when an initiative is filed. There is no statutory procedure for appealing the title, summary or fiscal impact statement. Proponents can, however, sue through normal legal channels.

Date Initiative language can be submitted to state for 2002: Any time.

Signatures are tied to vote of which office: Governor

Next Gubernatorial election: 2004

Votes cast for governor in last election: 2,346,830

Net number of signatures required: For a statute, proponents must collect signatures equal to 5% of votes cast for governor in 6 out of 9 Congressional districts and 8% for constitutional amendments. The actual total number varies, depending on which 6 counties are chosen. A statute initiative circulated in 2000 in the 6 districts with the highest votes cast for governor would require 75,356 signatures. An amendment would require 120,571 in 2000.

Distribution requirement: 5% in 6 out of 9 congressional districts.

Circulation period: 18 months

Do circulators have to be residents of the state: Yes and they must register with the Secretary of State's office.

Date when signatures are due for certification: May 5, 2002

Signature verification process: Secretary of State verifies signatures by use of random sampling.

Single Subject: Missouri has a single subject requirement.

Legislative tampering: The legislature can both repeal and amend initiative statutes.

Montana

Montana's Populist governor Robert B. Smith, elected in 1896, and his successor, Joseph K. Toole, elected in 1900, both called for I&R, but neither made much headway until December 1903, when the reformer F. Augustus Heinze organized and "Anti-Trust Democratic Party" and an "Ant-Trust Republican Party." These groups, combining their efforts with those of the very vocal "seven or eight men" from the state's Direct Legislation League, were able to push an I&R amendment through the legislature. The bill did not include the right to pass state constitutional amendments by initiative.

The I&R amendment won by a six to one margin on the 1906 ballot, receiving a majority of the vote in every single county. Montanans added the right of constitutional initiative to their constitution at the 1972 state constitutional convention, 66 years later.

Montanans first used I&R in 1912, when voters approved four out of four initiatives on the ballot. One required primary elections to nominate state and local candidates; the second established a presidential preference primary; the third called for direct election of U.S. senators; and the fourth limited candidates' campaign expenditures.

The reformers' goal for the 1912 election, which was to "Put the Amalgamated [Copper Company] out of Montana politics," proved to be an elusive one. The legislature and the governors of the World War I era continued to do the company's bidding. Even after the election of Joseph M. Dixon as governor in 1920, which was a victory for the reformers, Amalgamated continued to dominate the legislature. Near the end of his term, Dixon and the reformers turned to the initiative process.

Dixon selected as his key issue the under-taxing of Amalgamated: in 1922 the production of Montana's metal mines was $20 million, but the state got less than seven-hundredths of one percent of that in taxes. To remedy the situation, Dixon drew up Initiative 28, which proposed no taxes on mines with annual production of $100,000 or less, but taxed larger mines at up to 1 percent of the value of their production. The initiative qualified for the ballot in 1924, the same year Dixon was up for re-election. During that campaign, observed K. Ross Toole in his history of Montana, "The people heard little from Dixon himself because he had no medium for expression. The press was controlled [by Amalgamated], and there were no radios." Amalgamated attacked Dixon's policies and Dixon himself, and he lost the election by 15,000 votes. But in their attacks on Dixon they overlooked Initiative 28, and it passed.

A year later, under the new tax, which Amalgamated called "confiscatory and ruinous," the company's net profit for 1925 was nearly three times its net for 1924, and the state of Montana received $300,000. This was 22 times as much as the $13,559 the state took in from its metal mines tax prior to the initiative. Toole considered Initiative 28 the most significant reform won by Montana's Progressive movement.

In 1920, voters approved a 1.5 million property tax for maintenance of the state university, and on the same ballot passed an initiative issuing $5 million in bonds to fund school construction. In 1926, they passed a three-cent-per-gallon gasoline tax to fund road construction, and they approved more highway funding in a 1938 initiative vote.

Numerous other important initiatives have passed in the last decade—term limits and tax reform have been the most controversial with state legislators. These two reforms have led state lawmakers to propose numerous new regulations and restrictions on the initiative process. Additionally, a recent state Supreme Court decision strictly enforcing the state's single amendment provision for initiative amendments has led to a drastic decrease in the number of initiatives appearing on the state's ballot and has in effect shut down the state's constitutional initiative process.

Statewide Initiative Usage

Number of Initiatives	Number Passed	Number Failed	Passage Rate
65	34	31	52%

Statewide Initiatives

Year	Measure Number	Type	Subject Matter	Description	Pass/Fail
1912	I 302-303	DS	Election Reform	Party nominations by direct vote.	Passed
1912	I 304-305	DS	Campaign Finance Reform	Limiting campaign expenses of public candidates.	Passed
1912	I 306-307	DS	Election Reform	Popular referendum for election of Senators.	Passed
1912	I 308-309	DS	Election Reform	Direct presidential preference primary.	Passed
1914	I 7	DS	Labor	Workmen's compensation.	Failed
1914	I 8	DS	Administration of Government	Farm Loan Bill—relating to investment of permanent state funds.	Passed
1914	I 9	DS	Education	Consolidation of state institutions of higher education.	Failed
1916	I 11	DS	Administration of Government	Establishing athletic commission.	Failed
1918	I 12	DS	Business Regulation	An act authorizing and regulating the practice of chiropractors.	Passed
1920	I 18	DS	Taxes	1 1/2 mills levy for maintenance of university.	Passed
1920	I 19	DS	Bonds	$5,000,000 bonds for state educational institutions buildings.	Passed
1920	I 20	DS	Bonds	$20,000,000 bond issue for reclamation of arid lands.	Failed
1922	I 26	DS	Gaming	To create board, appointed by Governor, to regulate and license horse racing and pari-mutuel betting within race track enclosure.	Failed
1924	I 28	DS	Taxes	Metal mines tax.	Passed
1926	I 30	DS	Alcohol Regulation	Relating to repeal of state's intoxicating liquor laws.	Passed
1926	I 31	DS	Taxes	3 cents gasoline tax for good roads.	Passed
1928	I 32	DS	Alcohol Regulation	For adoption and enforcement of the Federal prohibition laws.	Failed
1938	I 41	DS	Administration of Government	State highway treasury anticipation debentures act of 1938.	Passed
1940	I 44	DS	Bonds	Montana state college bonds.	Failed
1944	I 48	DS	Health/Medical	Defining osteopathy—authorizing and regulating practice of osteopathic physicians and surgeons.	Failed

Year	Measure Number	Type	Subject Matter	Description	Pass/Fail
1950	I 54	DS	Administration of Government	Military honorarium.	Passed
1952	I 55	DS	Taxes	Tax on gasoline.	Failed
1968	I 66	DS	Taxes	To reduce taxable valuation of certain personal property including stocks of merchandise.	Failed
1974	CI 1	DA	Administration of Government	Providing for 90 day biennial legislative sessions.	Passed
1976	CI 7	DA	Administration of Government	Providing for a limit on state spending and a phase out of federal funds.	Failed
1976	I 71	DS	Nuclear weapons/ facilities/waste	Requiring legislative approval of any nuclear facility licensed under the Montana Major Facility Sitting Act.	Failed
1976	I 72	DS	Taxes	To provide property tax relief for owner-occupied homesteads.	Passed
1976	I 73	DS	Election Reform	Montana recall and advisory recall act.	Passed
1978	CI 8	DA	Taxes	Property tax assessment and Commission.	Failed
1978	I 79	DS	Legal	Local option: obscenity laws.	Passed
1978	I 80	DS	Nuclear weapons/ facilities/waste	Voter regulation of nuclear facilities.	Passed
1978	I 81	DS	Business Regulation	Table wine retail sales.	Passed
1980	I 84	DS	Nuclear weapons/ facilities/waste	Prohibit disposal of radioactive waste in MT.	Passed
1980	I 85	DS	Campaign Finance Reform	Lobbyist disclosure.	Passed
1980	I 86	DS	Taxes	Tax indexing.	Passed
1980	I 87	DS	Environmental Reform	Montana Litter Control and Recycling Act.	Failed
1982	I 91	DS	Nuclear weapons/ facilities/waste	Opposing placement of MX Missiles in Montana.	Passed
1982	I 92	DS	Gaming	Authorize the expansion of gambling.	Failed
1982	I 94	DS	Alcohol Regulation	Beer and wine quota system.	Failed
1982	I 95	DS	Administration of Government	Invest Coal Tax Trust revenue in Montana economy.	Passed
1984	I 96	DS	Business Regulation	Milk price decontrol.	Failed
1984	I 97	DS	Business Regulation	Allowing practice of Denturitry.	Failed
1986	CI 27	DA	Taxes	Abolish property tax; popular Failed vote for tax change.	
1986	CI 30	DA	Legal	Concerning private liability.	Passed
1986	I 104	DS	Business Regulation	Decontrol of milk prices.	Failed
1986	I 105	DS	Taxes	Limit property taxes to 1986 levels.	Passed
1988	I 110	DS	Health/Medical	Repeal the Montana Seatbelt Use Act.	Failed
1988	I 113	DS	Environmental Reform	Refundable deposits on beverage containers.	Failed
1990	CI 55	DA	Taxes	Repeal existing taxes; charges on business exchange.	Failed
1990	I 115	DS	Taxes	Increase cigarette sales tax.	Failed
1992	CI 63	DA	Taxes	Big Sky Dividend	Failed
1992		CI 64 DA	Term Limits	Term limits on state elected officials 8/8 and Congress 6/12.	Passed
1994	CI 66	DA	Taxes	Requires voter approval of all new or increased taxes.	Failed

Year	Measure Number	Type	Subject Matter	Description	Pass/Fail
1994	CI 67	DA	Taxes	Requires 2/3 vote of the legislature for any new or increased taxes.	Failed
1994	I 118	DS	Campaign Finance Reform	Lower the cap on campaign contributions and other revisions to campaign finance laws.	Passed
1996	I 121	DS	Labor	Increases the minimum wage, from $4.25 to $6.25 by year 2000.	Failed
1996	I 122	DS	Environmental Reform	Increases requirements for treatment of water discharged from mines.	Failed
1996	I 123	DS	Legal	Allows lawsuits for civil damages for unlawful threats or intimidation. Prohibits filing of false liens against property.	Passed
1996	I 125	DS	Campaign Finance Reform	Prohibits contributions from corporations to ballot question committees.	Passed
1996	I 132	DS	Term Limits	Informed Voter Law.	Failed
1998	CI 75	DA	Taxes	Would require voter approval of tax increases.	Passed
1998	I 134	DS	Taxes	Would repeal Montana Retail Motor Fuel Marketing Act.	Passed
1998	I 136	DS	Animal Rights	Would revise outfitter and hunter licensing.	Failed
1998	I 137	DS	Environmental Reform	Would prohibit cyanide process open pit mining.	Passed
2000	I 143	DS	Animal Rights	Prohibit all new alternative livestock ranches, also known as game farms. Existing game farms would be allowed to continue, but would be prohibited from transferring their license to anybody else.	Passed

Montana Constitution

Article III

Section 4. Initiative.

(1) The people may enact laws by initiative on all matters except appropriations of money and local or special laws.

(2) Initiative petitions must contain the full text of the proposed measure, shall be signed by at least five percent of the qualified electors in each of at least one-third of the legislative representative districts and the total number of signers must be at least five percent of the total qualified electors of the state. Petitions shall be filed with the secretary of state at least three months prior to the election at which the measure will be voted upon.

(3) The sufficiency of the initiative petition shall not be questioned after the election is held.

Section 5. Referendum.

(1) The people may approve or reject by referendum any act of the legislature except an appropriation of money. A referendum shall be held either upon order by the legislature or upon petition signed by at least five percent of the qualified electors in each of at least one-third of the legislative representative districts. The total number of signers must be at least five percent of the qualified electors of the state. A referendum petition shall be filed with the secretary of state no later than six months after adjournment of the legislature which passed the act.

(2) An act referred to the people is in effect until suspended by petitions signed by at least 15 percent of the qualified electors in a majority of the legislative representative districts. If so suspended the act shall become operative only after it is approved at an election, the result of which has been determined and declared as provided by law.

Article IV

Section 7. Ballot issues — challenges — elections.

(1) An initiative or referendum that qualifies for the ballot under Article III or Article XIV shall be submitted to the qualified electors as provided in the Article under which the initiative or referendum qualified unless a new election is held pursuant to this section.

(2) A preelection challenge to the procedure by which an initiative or referendum qualified for the ballot or a post election challenge to the manner in which the election was conducted shall be given priority by the courts.

(3) If the election on an initiative or referendum properly qualifying for the ballot is declared invalid because the election was improperly conducted, the secretary of state shall submit the issue to the qualified electors at the next regularly scheduled statewide election unless the legislature orders a special election.

Article XIV

Section 2. Initiative for constitutional convention.

(1) The people may by initiative petition direct the secretary of state to submit to the qualified electors the question of whether there shall be an unlimited convention to revise, alter, or amend this constitution. The petition shall be signed by at least ten percent of the qualified electors of the state. That number shall include at least ten percent of the qualified electors in each of two-fifths of the legislative districts.

(2) The secretary of state shall certify the filing of the petition in his office and cause the question to be submitted at the next general election.

Section 9. Amendment by initiative.

(1) The people may also propose constitutional amendments by initiative. Petitions including the full text of the proposed amendment shall be signed by at least ten percent of the qualified electors of the state. That number shall include at least ten percent of the qualified electors in each of two-fifths of the legislative districts.

(2) The petitions shall be filed with the secretary of state. If the petitions are found to have been signed by the required number of electors, the secretary of state shall cause the amendment to be published as provided by law twice each month for two months previous to the next regular statewide election.

(3) At that election, the proposed amendment shall be submitted to the qualified electors for approval or rejection. If approved by a majority voting thereon, it shall become a part of the constitution effective the first day of July following its approval, unless the amendment provides otherwise.

Section 10. Petition signers.

The number of qualified electors required for the filing of any petition provided for in this Article shall be determined by the number of votes cast for the office of governor in the preceding general election.

Montana Statutes

13-27-104. Time for filing.

Unless a specific time for filing is provided in the constitution, all petitions filed with the secretary of state, certified as provided by law, must be received before 5 p.m. of the third Friday of the fourth month prior to the election at which they are to be voted upon by the people.

13-27-105. Effective date of initiative and referendum issues.

(1) Unless the petition placing an initiative issue on the ballot states otherwise, an initiative issue, other than a constitutional amendment, approved by the people is effective on October 1 following approval. If the issue delegates rulemaking authority, it is effective no sooner than October 1 following approval.

(2) A constitutional amendment proposed by initiative or by the legislature and approved by the people is effective on July 1 following approval unless the amendment provides otherwise.

(3) Unless specifically provided by the legislature in an act referred by it to the people or until suspended by a petition signed by at least 15% of the qualified electors in a majority of the legislative representative districts, an act referred to the people is in effect as provided by law until it is approved or rejected at the election. An act that is rejected is repealed effective the date the result of the canvass is filed by the secretary of state under 13-27-503. An act referred to the people that was in effect at the time of the election and is approved by the people remains in effect. An act that was suspended by a petition and is approved by the people is effective the date the result of the canvass is filed by the secretary of state under 13-27-503. An act referred by the legislature that contains an effective date following the election becomes effective on that date if approved by the people. An act that provides no effective date and whose substantive provisions were delayed by the legislature pending approval at an election and that is approved is effective October 1 following the election.

13-27-106. Violations — penalties.

A person who knowingly makes a false entry upon a petition or affidavit required by this chapter or who knowingly signs a petition to place the same issue on the ballot at the same election more than once is guilty of unsworn falsification or tampering with public records or information, as appropriate, and is punishable as provided in 45-7-203 or 45-7-208, as applicable.

13-27-107 through 13-27-110 reserved.

13-27-111. Definitions. As used in 13-27-112, 13-27-113, and this section, unless otherwise indicated by the context, the following definitions apply:

(1) "Commissioner" means the commissioner of political practices provided for in 13-37-101.

(2) "Paid signature gatherer" means a signature gatherer who is compensated in money for the collection of signatures.

(3) "Person" has the meaning provided in 13-1-101, but does not include a candidate and includes a political committee.

(4) "Signature gatherer" means an individual who collects or intends to collect signatures on a petition for the purpose of an initiative, a referendum, or the calling of a constitutional convention.

13-27-112. Required reports — time and manner of reporting — exceptions — penalty.

(1) Except as provided in this section, a person who employs a paid signature gatherer shall file with the commissioner reports containing those matters required by Title 13, chapter 37, part 2, for a political committee organized to support or oppose a ballot issue or for an independent committee that receives contributions and makes expenditures in connection with a ballot issue, as applicable. If a person who employs a paid signature gatherer is required by Title 13, chapter 37, part 2, to file a report pursuant to those provisions, the person need not file a duplicate report pursuant to this section, but shall report the matter required by subsection (2) as part of that report. As used in this section, "a person who employs a paid signature gatherer" means a political party, political committee, or other person seeking to place a ballot issue before the electors and does not mean an individual who is part of the same signature gathering company, partnership, or other business organization that directly hires, supervises, and pays an individual who is a signature gatherer.

(2) The reports required by subsection (1) must include the amount paid to a paid signature gatherer.

(3) Reports filed pursuant to this section must be filed at the same time, in the same manner, including the certification required by 13-37-231, and upon the same forms as required for reports filed pursuant to Title 13, chapter 37, part 2, except as the rules of the commissioner may otherwise provide.

(4) A person who violates subsection (1) is guilty of a misdemeanor and upon conviction shall be punished as provided by law.

13-27-113. Powers and duties of commissioner.

(1) The commissioner has the same powers and duties regarding the regulation of signature gatherers, as provided in 13-27-112 and this section, as the commissioner has regarding the control of campaign practices as provided in Title 13, chapter 37, including the investigation of alleged violations of 13-27-112 and the issuance of orders of noncompliance for and prosecution of violations of 13-27-112.

(2) The commissioner may adopt rules to implement 13-27-112.

13-27-201. Form of petition generally.

(1) A petition for the initiative, the referendum, or to call a constitutional convention must be substantially in the form provided by this chapter. Clerical or technical errors that do not interfere with the ability to judge the sufficiency of signatures on the petition do not render a petition void.

(2) Petition sheets may not exceed 8 1/2 x 14 inches in size. Separate sheets of a petition may be fastened in sections of not more than 25 sheets. Near the top of each sheet containing signature lines must be printed the title of the statute or constitutional amendment proposed or the measure to be referred or a statement that the petition is for the purpose of calling a constitutional convention. If signature lines are printed on both the front and back of a petition sheet, the information required above must appear on both the front and back of the sheet. The complete text of the measure proposed or referred must be attached to or contained within each signature sheet if sheets are circulated separately. The text of the measure must be in the bill form provided in the most recent issue of the bill drafting manual furnished by the legislative services division. If sheets are circulated in sections, the complete text of the measure must be attached to each section.

13-27-202. Recommendations — approval of form required.

(1) Before submission of a sample sheet to the secretary of state pursuant to subsection (3), the following requirements must be fulfilled:

(a) The text of the proposed measure must be submitted to the legislative services division for review.

(b) The legislative services division staff shall review the text for clarity, consistency, and any other factors that the staff considers when drafting proposed legislation.

(c) Within 14 days after submission of the text, the legislative services division staff shall make to the person submitting the text written recommendations for changes in the text or a statement that no changes are recommended.

(d) The person submitting the text shall consider the recommendations and respond in writing to the legislative services division, accepting, rejecting, or modifying each of the recommended changes. If no changes are recommended, no response is required.

(2) The legislative services division shall furnish a copy of the correspondence provided for in subsection (1) to the secretary of state, who shall make a copy of the correspondence available to any person upon request.

(3) Before a petition may be circulated for signatures, a sample sheet containing the text of the proposed measure must be submitted to the secretary of state in the form in which it will be circulated. The sample petition may not be submitted to the secretary of state more than 1 year prior to the final date for filing the signed petition with the county election administrator. The secretary of state shall refer a copy of the petition sheet to the attorney general for approval. The secretary of state and attorney general shall each review the petition for sufficiency as to form and approve or reject the form of the petition, stating the reasons for rejection, if any. The attorney general shall also review the petition as to its legal sufficiency. If the attorney general determines that the petition is legally deficient, the attorney general shall notify the secretary of state of that fact and provide a copy of the determination to the secretary of state and to the petitioner within the time provided in 13-27-312(8). The petition may not be given final approval by the secretary of state unless the attorney general's determination is overruled pursuant to 13-27-316. As used in this section, "legal sufficiency" means that the petition complies with the statutory prerequisites to submission of the proposed measure to the electors and that the text of the proposed measure complies with constitutional requirements governing submission of ballot measures to the electorate. Review of a petition for legal sufficiency does not include consideration of the merits or application of the measure if adopted by the voters. The secretary of state or the attorney general may not reject the petition solely because the text contains material not submitted to the legislative services division unless the material not submitted to the legislative services division is a substantive change not suggested by the legislative services division.

(4) (a) The secretary of state shall review the comments and statements of the attorney general received pursuant to 13-27-312 and make a final decision as to the approval or rejection of the petition.

(b) The secretary of state shall send written notice to the person who submitted the petition sheet of the approval or rejection of the form of the petition within 28 days after submission of the petition sheet. The secretary of state shall send written notice to the person who submitted the petition sheet of the final approval or rejection of the petition within 5 days of:

(i) the date on which a final court decision is entered under 13-27-316 if a challenge to the attorney general's review of the petition is filed pursuant to that section; or

(ii) the expiration of the time for filing a challenge to the attorney general's review under 13-27-316 if no challenge is filed. If the petition is rejected, the notice must include reasons for rejection.

(5) A petition with technical defects in form may be approved with the condition that those defects will be corrected before the petition is circulated for signatures.

(6) The secretary of state shall upon request provide the person submitting the petition with a sample petition form, including the text of the proposed measure, the statement of purpose, and the statements of implications, all as approved by the secretary of state and the attorney general. The petition may be circulated in the form of the sample prepared by the secretary of state. The petition may be circulated upon approval of the form of the petition by the secretary of state and the attorney general pending a final determination of its legal sufficiency.

13-27-203. Numbering of petitions.

The secretary of state shall serially number all submitted petitions that are approved as to form continuously from year to year. The numbering system shall distinguish the different types of petitions received and include provisions for numbering measures referred to the people by the legislature.

13-27-204. Petition for initiative.

(1) The following is substantially the form for a petition calling for a vote to enact a law by initiative:

PETITION TO PLACE INITIATIVE NO.____ ON THE ELECTION BALLOT

(a) If 5% of the voters in each of 34 legislative representative districts sign this petition and the total number of voters signing this petition is ... this measure will appear on the next general election ballot. If a majority of voters vote for this measure at that election, it will become law.

(b) We, the undersigned Montana voters, propose that the secretary of state place the following measure on the ... 20... general election ballot:

(Title of measure written pursuant to 13-27-312)

(Statement of implication written pursuant to 13-27-312)

(c) Voters are urged to read the complete text of the measure, which appears (on the reverse side of, attached to, etc., as applicable) this sheet. A signature on this petition is only to put the measure on the ballot and does not necessarily mean the signer agrees with the measure.
(d) WARNING: A person who purposefully signs a name other than the person's own to this petition, who signs more than once for the same issue at one election, or who signs when not a legally registered Montana voter is subject to a $500 fine, 6 months in jail, or both.
(e) Each person is required to sign the person's name and address in substantially the same manner as on the person's voter registration card or the signature will not be counted.
(2) Numbered lines must follow the above heading. Each numbered line must contain spaces for the signature, post-office address, legislative representative district number, and printed last name of the signer.

13-27-205. Petition for the referendum.

(1) The following is substantially the form for a petition calling for approval or rejection of an act of the legislature by the referendum:

PETITION TO PLACE REFERENDUM NO.____ ON THE ELECTION BALLOT

(a) If 5% of the voters in each of 34 legislative representative districts sign this petition and the total number of voters signing the petition is ... Senate (House) Bill Number .... will appear on the next general election ballot. If a majority of voters vote for this measure at that election it will become law.
(b) We, the undersigned Montana voters, propose that the secretary of state place the following Senate (House) Bill Number ...., passed by the legislature on ... on the next general election ballot:

(Title of referendum written pursuant to 13-27-312)

(Statement of implication written pursuant to 13-27-312)

(c) Voters are urged to read the complete text of the measure, which appears (on the reverse side of, attached to, etc., as applicable) on this sheet. A signature on this petition is only to put the measure on the ballot and does not necessarily mean the signer agrees with the measure.

(d) WARNING: A person who purposefully signs a name other than his/her own to this petition or who signs more than once for the same issue at one election or signs when not a legally registered Montana voter is subject to a $500 fine, 6 months in jail, or both.

(e) Each person must sign his/her name and address in substantially the same manner as on his/her voter registry card, or the signature will not be counted.

(2) Numbered lines shall follow the above heading. Each numbered line shall contain spaces for the signature, post-office address, legislative representative district number, and printed last name of the signer.

13-27-206. Petition for initiative for constitutional convention.

(1) The following is substantially the form for a petition to direct the secretary of state to submit to the qualified voters the question of whether there will be a constitutional convention:

PETITION TO PLACE INITIATIVE NO._____, CALLING FOR A CONSTITUTIONAL CONVENTION, ON THE ELECTION BALLOT

(a) If 10% of the voters in each of 40 legislative districts sign this petition and the total number of voters signing this petition is ....., the question of whether to have a constitutional convention will appear on the next general election ballot. If a majority of voters vote for the constitutional convention, the legislature shall call for a constitutional convention at its next session.

(b) We, the undersigned Montana voters, propose that the secretary of state place the question of whether to hold a constitutional convention on the ...., 20..., general election ballot:

(Title of the initiative written pursuant to 13-27-312)

(Statement of implication written pursuant to 13-27-312)

(c) A signature on this petition is only to put the call for a constitutional convention on the ballot and does not necessarily mean the signer is in favor of calling a constitutional convention.

(d) WARNING: A person who purposefully signs a name other than the person's own to this petition, who signs more than once for the same issue at one election, or who signs when not a legally registered Montana voter is subject to a $500 fine or 6 months in jail, or both.

(e) Each person is required to sign the person's name and address in substantially the same manner as on the person's voter registration card or the signature will not be counted.

(2) Numbered lines must follow the above heading. Each numbered line must also contain spaces for the signature, post-office address, legislative representative district number, and printed last name of the signer.

13-27-207. Petition for initiative for constitutional amendment.

(1) The following is substantially the form for a petition for an initiative to amend the constitution:

PETITION TO PLACE CONSTITUTIONAL AMENDMENT NO._____ ON THE ELECTION BALLOT

(a) If 10% of the voters in each of 40 legislative districts sign this petition and the total number of voters signing the petition is ....., this constitutional amendment will appear on the next general election ballot. If a majority of voters vote for this amendment at that election, it will become part of the constitution.

(b) We, the undersigned Montana voters, propose that the secretary of state place the following constitutional amendment on the ...., 20..., general election ballot:

(Title of the proposed amendment written pursuant to 13-27-312)

(Statement of implication written pursuant to 13-27-312)

(c) Voters are urged to read the complete text of the measure, which appears (on the reverse side of, attached to, etc., as applicable) this sheet. A signature on this petition is only to put the constitutional amendment on the ballot and does not necessarily mean the signer agrees with the amendment.

(d) WARNING: A person who purposefully signs a name other than the person's own to this petition, who signs more than once for the same issue at one election, or who signs when not a legally registered Montana voter is subject to a $500 fine, 6 months in jail, or both.

(e) Each person is required to sign the person's name and address in substantially the same manner as on the person's voter registration card or the signature will not be counted.

(2) Numbered lines must follow the above heading. Each numbered line must contain spaces for the signature, post-office address, legislative representative district number, and printed last name of the signer.

13-27-208. Petitions to be made available in each county election administrator's office.

When the secretary of state sends written notice of the final approval of a petition as required under 13-27-202(4), the secretary of state shall forward a copy of the petition, along with signature sheets, to the election administrator of each county. The election administrator shall make a copy of each approved petition available for reading and signing in the administrator's office during business hours in an election year until the petitions are submitted under 13-27-301. The secretary of state may charge the person who submitted the petition a fee sufficient to reimburse the secretary of state for the cost of providing copies of the petition and signature sheets to each county election administrator.

13-27-301. Submission of petition sheets — withdrawal of signatures.

(1) Signed sheets or sections of petitions shall be submitted to the official responsible for registration of electors in the county in which the signatures were obtained no sooner than 9 months and no later than 4 weeks before the final date for filing the petition with the secretary of state.

(2) Signatures may be withdrawn from a petition for constitutional amendment, constitutional convention, initiative, or referendum up to the time of final submission of petition sheets as provided in subsection (1). The secretary of state shall prescribe the form to be used by an elector desiring to have his signature withdrawn from a petition.

13-27-302. Certification of signatures.

An affidavit, in substantially the following form, must be attached to each sheet or section submitted to the county official:

I, (name of person who circulated this petition), swear that I circulated or assisted in circulating the petition to which this affidavit is attached, that I believe the signatures on the petition are genuine, are the signatures of the persons whose names they purport to be, and are the signatures of Montana electors who are registered at the address following their signature, and that the signers knew the contents of the petition before signing the petition.

....
(Signature of petition circulator) ....
(Address of petition circulator)
Subscribed and sworn to before me this ... day of ....., 20...

....
Seal (Person authorized to take oaths)

....
(Title or notarial information)

13-27-303. Verification of signatures by county official — allocating voters following reapportionment — duplicate signatures.

(1) Except as required by 13-27-104, within 4 weeks after receiving the sheets or sections of a petition, the county official shall check the names of all signers to verify they are registered electors of the county. In addition, the official shall randomly select signatures on each sheet or section and compare them with the signatures of the electors as they appear in the registration records of the office. If all the randomly selected signatures appear to be genuine, the number of signatures of registered electors on the sheet or section may be certified to the secretary of state without further comparison of signatures. If any of the randomly selected signatures do not appear to be genuine, all signatures on that sheet or section must be compared with the signatures in the registration records of the office.

(2) For the purpose of allocating the signatures of voters among the several legislative representative districts of the state as required to certify a petition for a ballot issue under the provisions of this chapter following the filing of a districting and apportionment plan under 5-1-111 and before the first gubernatorial election following the filing of the plan, the

new districts must be used with the number of signatures needed for each legislative representative district being the total votes cast for governor in the last gubernatorial election divided by the number of legislative representative districts.
(3) Upon discovery of fraudulent signatures or duplicate signatures of an elector on any one issue, the election administrator may submit the name of the elector or the petition circulator, or both, to the county attorney to be investigated under the provisions of 13-27-106 and 13-35-207.

13-27-304. County official to forward verified sheets.

The county official verifying the number of registered electors signing the petition shall forward it to the secretary of state by certified mail with a certificate in substantially the following form attached:

To the Honorable ... Secretary of State of the state of Montana:

I, ..., ... (title) of the County of ...., certify that I have examined the attached (section containing .... sheets) or (.... sheets) of the petition for (referendum, initiative, constitutional convention, or constitutional amendment) No. .... in the manner prescribed by law; and I believe that .... (number) signatures in Legislative Representative District No. .... (repeat for each district included in sheet or section) are valid; and I further certify that the affidavit of the circulator of the (sheet) (section) of the petition is attached and the post-office address and legislative representative district number is completed for each valid signature.

Signed: .... (Date) .... (Signature)
Seal .... (Title)

13-27-305. Retention of copies by county official.

The county official certifying the sheets or sections of a petition shall keep a copy of the sheets or sections certified in the official files of his office. The copies may be destroyed 3 months after the date of the election specified in the petition unless a court action is pending on the sufficiency of the petition.

13-27-306. Challenge to signatures by elector of county.

A registered elector of a county having reason to believe that signatures on a petition that were not among those actually compared with signatures in the registration records of the county are not genuine may file a sworn statement or affirmation of his belief and request for comparison of those signatures he believes are not genuine with the county official certifying the sheet or section of the petition. If any of the challenged signatures are not genuine, the county official must compare all signatures on that sheet or section and issue an amended certificate to the secretary of state, giving the correct number of valid signatures, on or before the deadline, as provided for in 13-27-104, for filing in the office of the secretary of state.

13-27-307. Consideration and tabulation of signatures by secretary of state.

(1) The secretary of state shall consider and tabulate only the signatures on petitions that are certified by the proper county official, and each certificate is prima facie evidence of the facts stated in the certificate. However, the secretary of state may consider and tabulate any signature not certified by the county official that is certified by a notary public of the county in which the signer resides to be the genuine signature of an elector legally qualified to sign the petition.
(2) The official certificate of the notary public for any signature not certified as valid by the county official must be in substantially the following form:
State of Montana)
) ss.
County of ...)

I, ... (name), a duly qualified and acting notary public in and for the above-named county and state, certify that I am personally acquainted with all of the following-named electors whose signatures are affixed to the attached (petition) (copy of a petition) and I know that they are registered electors of the state of Montana and of the county and legislative district written after their names in the petition and that their post-office addresses are correctly stated in the petition .... (Names of electors)

In testimony whereof, I have set my hand and official seal this .... day of ......, 20..(Signature)

Seal .... (Notarial information)

13-27-308. Certification of petition to governor.

When sheets or sections of a petition for referendum, initiative, constitutional convention, or constitutional amendment containing a sufficient number of signatures have been filed with the secretary of state within the time required by the constitution or by law, he shall immediately certify to the governor that the completed petition has been officially filed.

13-27-309. Repealed. Sec. 195, Ch. 575, L. 1981.

13-27-310. Transmittal of issues referred by the legislature and ballot forms to the attorney general.

(1) The secretary of state shall transmit a copy of the form in which a ballot issue proposed by petition will appear on the ballot to the attorney general on the same day the completed petition is certified to the governor.

(2) The secretary of state shall transmit a copy of an act referred to the people or a constitutional amendment proposed by the legislature and a copy of the form in which the issue will appear on the ballot to the attorney general no later than 6 months before the election at which the issue will be voted on by the people.

(3) If the ballot form is not approved by the attorney general pursuant to 13-27-313, the secretary of state shall immediately submit a new ballot form to the attorney general.

13-27-311. Publication of proposed constitutional amendments.

(1) If a proposed constitutional amendment or amendments are submitted to the people, the secretary of state shall have the proposed amendment or amendments published in full twice each month for 2 months previous to the election at which they are to be voted upon by the people, in not less than one newspaper of general circulation in each county.

(2) The secretary of state may arrange for newspaper, radio, or television publication of proposed constitutional amendments in each county. A summary of the amendment as provided by the attorney general, as described in 13-27-312 or 13-27-315, would suffice for the publication required by this section and should be made at least twice each month for 2 months previous to the election.

13-27-312. Review of petition by attorney general — preparation of statements — fiscal note.

(1) Upon receipt of a petition from the office of the secretary of state pursuant to 13-27-202, the attorney general shall examine the petition as to form and legal sufficiency, as provided in 13-27-202, and, if the proposed ballot issue has an effect on the revenues, expenditures, or the fiscal liability of the state, shall order a fiscal note incorporating an estimate of the effect, the substance of which must substantially comply with the provisions of 5-4-205. The budget director, in cooperation with the agency or agencies affected by the petition, is responsible for preparing the fiscal note and shall return it within 6 days unless the attorney general, for good cause shown, extends the time for completing the fiscal note.

(2) If the petition form is approved, the attorney general shall endeavor to seek out parties on both sides of the issue and obtain their advice. The attorney general shall prepare:

(a) a statement, not to exceed 100 words, explaining the purpose of the measure; and

(b) statements, not to exceed 25 words each, explaining the implications of a vote for and a vote against the measure.

(3) The attorney general shall prepare a fiscal statement of no more than 50 words if a fiscal note was prepared for the proposed ballot issue, such statement to be used on the petition and ballot if the measure is placed on the ballot.

(4) The statement of purpose and the statements of implication must express the true and impartial explanation of the proposed ballot issue in plain, easily understood language and may not be arguments or written so as to create prejudice for or against the measure.

(5) The statement of purpose, unless altered by a court under 13-27-316, is the petition title for the measure circulated by the petition and the ballot title if the measure is placed on the ballot.

(6) The statements of implication must be placed beside the diagram provided for marking of the ballot in a manner similar to but not limited to the following example:

FOR extending the right to vote to persons 18 years of age

AGAINST extending the right to vote to persons 18 years of age

(7) If the petition is rejected as to form, the attorney general shall forward the comments to the secretary of state within 21 days after receipt of the petition by the attorney general. If the petition is approved as to form, the attorney general shall forward the statement of purpose, the statements of implication, and the fiscal statement, if applicable, to the secretary of state within 21 days after receipt of the petition by the attorney general.

(8) If the petition is approved as to form, within 30 days of the approval, the attorney general shall forward to the secretary of state the determination regarding legal sufficiency, as provided in 13-27-202.

13-27-313. Review of ballot forms by attorney general.

The attorney general shall examine each ballot form submitted to his office pursuant to 13-27-310 and within 20 days of receipt of the ballot form shall notify the secretary of state of his approval or rejection of the ballot form. If the ballot form is rejected, the attorney general shall approve or reject a new ballot form submitted by the secretary of state pursuant to 13-27-310(3) within 5 days of receiving the new form.

13-27-314. Repealed. Sec. 19, Ch. 400, L. 1979.

13-27-315. Statements by attorney general on issues referred by legislature.

(1) Upon receipt of a copy of a ballot form under 13-27-310(2) for an issue proposed by the legislature, the attorney general shall order a fiscal note as provided in 13-27-312(1) if the issue has an effect on the revenues, expenditures, or the fiscal liability of the state. At the same time the explanatory statement is prepared under subsection (2), the attorney general shall prepare a fiscal statement of no more than 50 words to be forwarded to the secretary of state at the same time as the explanatory statement.

(2) At the same time the attorney general, pursuant to 13-27-313, informs the secretary of state of the approval or rejection of a ballot form for an issue proposed by the legislature, the attorney general shall forward to the secretary of state a statement, not exceeding 100 words, expressing a true and impartial explanation of the purpose of the measure in plain, easily understood language. The statement may not be an argument and may not be written to create a prejudice for or against the issue. The statement prepared under this section is known as the attorney general's explanatory statement.

(3) If statements of the implication of a vote for or against a ballot issue have not been provided by the legislature, the attorney general shall prepare the statements. Requirements for statements of implication for ballot issues referred by the legislature are the same as those provided in 13-27-312 for other ballot issues. Statements of implication prepared by the attorney general must be returned to the secretary of state no later than the time specified for approval of the ballot form.

13-27-316. Court review of attorney general opinion or statements.

(1) If the proponents of a ballot measure believe that the statement of purpose, the statements of implication of a vote, or the fiscal statement formulated by the attorney general pursuant to 13-27-312 do not satisfy the requirements of 13-27-312, or believe that the attorney general was incorrect in determining that the petition was legally deficient, they may, within 10 days of receipt of the notice from the secretary of state or of the attorney general's determination regarding legal sufficiency provided for in 13-27-202, file an action in the district court in and for the county of Lewis and Clark challenging the adequacy of the statement or the attorney general's determination and requesting the court to alter the statement or modify the attorney general's determination.

(2) If the opponents of a ballot measure believe that the statement of purpose, the statements of implication of a vote, or the fiscal statement formulated by the attorney general pursuant to 13-27-312 do not satisfy the requirements of 13-27-312, or believe that the attorney general was incorrect in determining that the petition was legally sufficient, they may, within 10 days of the date of certification to the governor that the completed petition has been officially filed, file an action in the district court in and for the county of Lewis and Clark challenging the adequacy of the statement or the attorney general's conclusion and requesting the court to alter the statement or overrule the attorney general's determination concerning the legal sufficiency of the petition.

(3) (a) Notice must be served upon the secretary of state and upon the attorney general. The action takes precedence over other cases and matters in the district court. The court shall examine the proposed measure and the challenged statement or determination of the attorney general and shall as soon as possible render a decision and certify to the secretary of state a statement which the court determines will meet the requirements of 13-27-312 or an opinion as to the correctness of the attorney general's determination.

(b) A statement certified by the court must be placed on the petition for circulation and on the official ballot.

(4) A copy of the petition in final form must be filed in the office of the secretary of state by the proponents.

(5) Any party may appeal the order of the district court to the Montana supreme court by filing a notice of appeal within 5 days of the date of the order of the district court.

13-27-401. Voter information pamphlet.

(1) The secretary of state shall prepare for printing a voter information pamphlet containing the following information for each ballot issue to be voted on at an election, as applicable:

(a) ballot title, fiscal statement if applicable, and complete text of the issue;

(b) the form in which the issue will appear on the ballot;

(c) arguments advocating approval and rejection of the issue; and

(d) rebuttal arguments.

(2) The pamphlet must also contain a notice advising the recipient where additional copies of the pamphlet may be obtained.

(3) Whenever more than one ballot issue is to be voted on at a single election, the secretary of state may publish a single pamphlet for all of the ballot issues. The secretary of state may arrange the information in the order which seems most appropriate, but the information for all issues in the pamphlet must be presented in the same order.

(4) The secretary of state may prescribe by rule the format and manner of submission of the arguments concerning the ballot issue.

13-27-402. Committees to prepare arguments for and against ballot issues.

(1) The arguments advocating approval or rejection of the ballot issue and rebuttal arguments must be submitted to the secretary of state by committees appointed as provided in this section.

(2) The committee advocating approval of a legislative act referred to the people either by the legislature or by referendum petition or advocating approval of a constitutional amendment referred by the legislature must be composed of:

(a) one senator known to favor the referred measure, appointed by the president of the senate;

(b) one representative known to favor the referred measure, appointed by the speaker of the house of representatives; and

(c) one individual who need not be a member of the legislature, appointed by the first two members.

(3)(a) the committee advocating rejection of an act referred to the people or of a constitutional amendment proposed by the legislature must be composed of:

(i) one senator appointed by the president of the senate;

(ii) one representative appointed by the speaker of the house of representatives; and

(iii) one individual who need not be a member of the legislature, appointed by the first two members.

(b) Whenever possible, the members must be known to have opposed the issue.

(4) The following must be three-member committees and must be appointed by the person submitting the petition to the secretary of state under the provisions of 13-27-202:

(a) the committee advocating approval of a ballot issue proposed by any type of initiative petition; and

(b) the committee advocating rejection of any legislative act referred to the people by referendum petition.

(5) A committee advocating rejection of a ballot issue proposed by any type of initiative petition must be composed of five members. The governor, attorney general, president of the senate, and speaker of the house of representatives shall each appoint one member, and the fifth member must be appointed by the first four members. If possible, members must be known to favor rejection of the issue.

(6) A person may not be required to serve on any committee under this section, and except for legislative appointments made by the president of the senate or by the speaker of the house of representatives, the person making an appointment must have written acceptance of appointment from the appointee. If an appointment is not made by the required time, the committee members that have been appointed may fill the vacancy by unanimous written consent up until the deadline for filing the arguments.

13-27-403. Appointment to committee.

(1) Except as provided in subsection (2), appointments to committees advocating approval or rejection of an act referred to the people, a constitutional amendment proposed by the legislature, or a ballot measure referred to the people by referendum petition or proposed by any type of initiative petition must be made no later than 1 week prior to the deadline for filing arguments on the ballot issue under 13-27-406.

(2) Appointments to committees advocating approval or rejection of a ballot measure referred to the people by referendum petition or proposed by any type of initiative petition must be made no later than 1 week before the deadline for filing arguments on the ballot issue under 13-27-406. All persons responsible for appointing members to the committee shall submit to the secretary of state the names and addresses of the appointees no later than the date set by this subsection. The submission must include the written acceptance of appointment from each appointee required by section 13-27-402(6). If an appointment is not made by the required time, the committee members that have been appointed may fill the vacancy by unanimous written consent up until the deadline for filing the arguments.

(3) Within 5 days after receiving notice under subsection (2), but not later than 5 days after the deadline set for appointment of committee members, the secretary of state shall notify the appointees to a committee appointed pursuant to subsection (1) or (2) by certified mail, with return receipt requested, of the deadlines for submission of the committee's arguments.

13-27-404. Committee chairman.

The appointee of the president of the senate is the chairman of any committee to which that officer makes an appointment. The appointing authority for other committees shall name a chairman at the time the appointments are made.

13-27-405. Committee expenses.

Each committee is entitled to receive funds for the preparation of arguments and expenses of members not to exceed $100 for a three-member committee and $200 for a five-member committee. Itemized claims for actual expenses incurred, approved by a majority of the committee, shall be submitted to the secretary of state for payment from funds appropriated for that purpose.

13-27-406. Limitation on length of argument — time of filing.

An argument advocating approval or rejection of a ballot issue is limited to a single side of a single 7 1/2-inch by 10-inch page and must be filed, in a black-and-white, camera-ready format, with the secretary of state no later than 105 days before the election at which the issue will be voted on by the people. The argument must consist solely of written material prepared by the committee and may not consist of pictures, clippings, or other material. The written material must be prepared in the font and type style required by the secretary of state. With the goal of achieving readability and uniformity, the secretary of state shall prescribe a commonly used font and type style. A majority of the committee responsible for preparation shall approve and sign each argument filed. Separate signed letters of approval of an argument may be filed with the secretary of state by members of a committee if necessary to meet the filing deadline.

13-27-407. Rebuttal arguments.

The secretary of state shall provide copies of the arguments advocating approval or rejection of a ballot issue to the members of the adversary committee no later than 1 day following the filing of both the approval and rejection arguments for the issue. The committees may prepare rebuttal arguments no longer than one-half the size of the arguments under 13-27-406 that must be filed, in a black-and-white, camera-ready format, with the secretary of state no later than 10 days after the deadline for filing the original arguments. The argument must consist solely of written material prepared by the committee and may not consist of pictures, clippings, or other material. The written material must be prepared in the font and type style required by the secretary of state. With the goal of achieving readability and uniformity, the secretary of state shall prescribe a commonly used font and type style. Discussion in the rebuttal argument must be confined to the subject matter raised in the argument being rebutted. The rebuttal argument must be approved and signed by a majority of the committee responsible for its preparation. Separate signed letters of approval may be submitted in the same manner as for the original arguments.

13-27-408. Rejection of improper arguments.

The secretary of state shall reject, with the approval of the attorney general, an argument or other matter held to contain obscene, vulgar, profane, scandalous, libelous, or defamatory matter; any language that in any way incites, counsels, promotes, or advocates hatred, abuse, violence, or hostility toward, or that tends to cast ridicule or shame upon, a group of persons by reason of race, color, religion, or sex; or any matter not allowed to be sent through the mail. Such arguments may not be filed or printed in the voter information pamphlet.

13-27-409. Liability for contents of argument.

Nothing in this chapter relieves an author of any argument from civil or criminal responsibility for statements contained in an argument printed in the voter information pamphlet.

13-27-410. Printing and distribution of voter information pamphlet.

(1) The secretary of state shall arrange with the department of administration by requisition for the printing and delivery of a voter information pamphlet for all ballot issues to be submitted to the people at least 110 days before the election at which they will be submitted. The requisition must include a delivery list providing for shipment of the required number of pamphlets to each county and to the secretary of state.

(2) The secretary of state shall estimate the number of copies necessary to furnish one copy to each voter in each county, except that two or more voters with the same mailing address and the same last name may be counted as one voter. The secretary of state shall provide for an extra supply of the pamphlets in determining the number of voter pamphlets to be ordered in the requisition.

(3) The department of administration shall call for bids and contract with the lowest bidder for the printing and delivery of the voter information pamphlet. The contract must require completion of printing and shipment, as specified on

the delivery list, of the voter information pamphlets by not later than 45 days before the election at which the ballot issues will be voted on by the people.

(4) The county official responsible for voter registration in each county shall mail one copy of the voter information pamphlet to each registered voter in the county who is on the active voter list, except that two or more voters with the same mailing address and the same last name may be counted as one voter. The mailing must take place no later than 2 weeks before the election.

(5) Ten copies of the voter information pamphlet must be available at each precinct for use by any voter wishing to read the explanatory information and complete text before voting on the ballot issues.

The Basic Steps to Do an Initiative in Montana

Statutes and Amendments — Direct Initiative Process

Basic Procedures: Proponents submit the full text of the initiative to the Legislative Services for its review. Within 14 days after receiving the measure, the Legislative Services staff must make recommendations for changes in the text or a statement that no changes are recommended. Proponents must consider the recommendations and respond in writing to Legislative Services accepting, rejecting or modifying each recommended change.

A sample petition, including the complete text of the measure, must submitted to the Secretary of State's office in the form in which it will be circulated. The sample petition may not be submitted to the Secretary of State more than 1 year prior to the final date for filing the signed petition with the county election administrator. The text of the petition submitted to the Secretary of State should be substantially the same as the text submitted to the Legislative Services. If it is substantially different, the proposed ballot issue could be rejected for not having been reviewed by the Legislative Services. The Secretary of State refers a copy of the petition to the Attorney General for his approval. The Secretary of State and Attorney General must each review the petition for sufficiency as to form, approve or reject the form of the petition and state the reasons for rejection, if any.

The Attorney General must forward his or her comments to the Secretary of State within 21 days after receipt of the petition. The Secretary of State will send written notice of the initial approval or rejection of the form to the person who submitted the petition within 28 days after submission. If the petition form is approved, a printed sample copy of the petition to be circulated, containing the title and implication of the vote statements as prepared by the Attorney General, must be filed with the Secretary of State.

The Attorney General will also review all petitions submitted after October 1, 1999 for legal sufficiency. The determination of legal sufficiency shall be forwarded to the Secretary of State within 30 days of the initial form approval. The Secretary of State will notify the sponsor of such a decision.

The Attorney General will also order a fiscal statement if the proposed ballot issue has an effect on the revenues, expenditures or the fiscal liability of the state. The budget director, in cooperation with the agency of agencies affected by the petition, is responsible for preparing the fiscal note. If a fiscal note is prepared for the proposed ballot issue, the Attorney General will prepare a fiscal statement that is to be used on the petition and ballot if the measure is placed on the ballot.

The Attorney General also will write a statement, not to exceed 100 words, explaining the purpose of the measure, and statements, not to exceed 25 words each, explaining the implications for and against the measure.

Date Initiative language can be submitted to state for November 2002: July 21, 2001

Signatures are tied to vote of which office: Governor

Next Gubernatorial election: 2004

Votes cast for governor in last election: 410,192

Net number of signatures required: For a constitutional amendment, 10% of votes cast for governor in last gubernatorial general election (41,019). For a statute initiative, 5% of votes cast for governor (20,500)

Distribution Requirement: For amendments 10% in 40 Legislative Representative Districts and for statutes 5% in 34 Legislative Districts. However, the state adopted a new distribution requirement in 2002 basing the requirement on counties instead of Legislative Districts but the new requirement is currently being challenged in the courts.

Circulation period: 1 year.

Do circulators have to be residents: No.

Date when signatures are due for certification: Signatures are due to the County Election Administrators by June 23, 2002 for the 2002 ballot.

Signature verification process: County officials check the names of all signers to verify they are registered voters. In addition, they randomly select signatures on each sheet and compare them with the signatures of the electors as they appear in the registration records of the office. If any of the randomly selected signatures do not appear to be genuine, all signatures on that sheet must be compared with the signatures in the registration records of the office.

Single-subject restriction: Yes

Legislative tampering: The legislature can both repeal and amend initiatives

General Comments: Once an initiative has qualified to appear on the ballot, committees are formed to write arguments for and against the issue. These arguments appear in an information pamphlet that is distributed before each election to all households with a Montana voter. A three-member committee supporting the issue is appointed by the sponsor who submitted the petition. A five-member committee opposing the issue is appointed by the governor, Attorney General, president of the senate and speaker of the house of representatives. The four appointed persons appoint the fifth member.

Nebraska

Nebraska's legislature in 1897 became the first in the nation to pass a bill allowing initiative and referendum—but only in municipalities, not on the state level. This bill was the Sheldon-Geiser Act, sponsored by state legislator A. E. Sheldon.

Walter Breen of Omaha led early efforts for I&R in Nebraska. Breen, a native of London, emigrated to the United States at age 17 and lived in Lincoln, Nebraska, before settling in Omaha. He became a successful real estate salesman and was among the initial organizers of the Populist Party. By 1897, by the age of 30, he had become secretary of the Omaha Direct Legislation League, as well as a member of the seven-man executive committee of the National Direct Legislation League.

Since Nebraska did not have Prohibition, the Prohibitionists favored I&R, but liquor interests blocked it until 1911. I&R finally made it through the legislature with the support of the orator and presidential candidate William Jennings Bryan, along with H. Mockett, Jr., president of the Nebraska Direct Legislation League, and Professor F. E. Howard of the state university. Bryan, who spoke on behalf of I&R throughout the nation, wrote in a 1909 letter: "I know of nothing that will do more than I&R to restore government to the hands of the people and keep it within their control."

In 1912 Nebraska voters approved I&R by a margin of thirteen to one. It helped that under Nebraska's constitutional amendment ratification procedure, blank ballots were counted as "yes" votes: the opposite of the system that doomed I&R in Minnesota.

Nebraska's most famous initiative was the successful 1934 amendment to create the nation's only unicameral state legislative body. U.S. Sen. George Norris, who is best known for his bill creating the Tennessee Valley Authority, led the unicameral campaign. Another highlight of Nebraska initiative history was the passage, in 1982, of a constitutional amendment prohibiting farm buy-outs by corporations, which was the toughest statewide anti-corporate farm legislation in the nation.

Nebraskans have been infrequent initiative users, placing only 27 such measures on state ballots in 70 years: an average of less than one per election. The first was a 1914 women's suffrage initiative, defeated by a 52.4 percent negative vote of the all-male electorate. Nebraskans in 1930 approved authorization for municipally owned electric utilities to extend their lines. In 1966 they voted by a narrow margin to prohibit property taxes.

As with many initiative states, there has typically been one person who becomes personified as THE tax reformer in the state. Nebraska is no exception. Ed Jacksha is a living legend. He has been involved in almost every tax reduction measure in the state and has championed initiative rights for decades. He was also instrumental, as was State Auditor Kate Witek, Attorney General Don Stenberg, Bob Wright and Omaha Mayor Hal Daub, in getting a term limits initiative for state legislators passed in 2000.

Statewide Initiative Usage

Number of Initiatives	Number Passed	Number Failed	Passage Rate
40	15	25	37%

Statewide Initiatives

Year	Measure Number	Type	Subject Matter	Description	Pass/Fail
1914	N/A	DS	Education	University removal.	Failed
1914	N/A	DA	Election Reform	Woman suffrage, authorizations.	Failed
1916	N/A	DA	Alcohol Regulation	Providing for statewide prohibition.	Passed
1916	N/A	DA	Administration of Government	Creation of Pure Food Department.	Failed
1924	N/A	DA	Election Reform	Direct primary and nonpartisan elections, establishment.	Failed
1930	N/A	DS	Administration of Government	Authorization for cities and villages and public electric and power districts to extend their lines.	Failed
1930	N/A	DS	Utility Regulation	Authorization for cities and towns owning electric light plants to extend their lines.	Passed
1930	N/A	DS	Administration of Government	Prohibition of sale of municipally owned plants except for cash, etc.	Failed
1932	N/A	DS	Administration of Government	Change laws associated with the powers of the state police.	Failed
1934	N/A	DA	Administration of Government	Unicameral legislature, creation.	Passed
1934	N/A	DA	Gaming	Pari-mutual betting, authorization.	Passed
1938	N/A	DA	Gaming	Slot machines, licensing.	Failed
1944	N/A	DS	Taxes	Proposed gasoline tax amendment.	Failed
1944	N/A	DS	Alcohol Regulation	Prohibition of liquor traffic.	Failed
1946	N/A	DA	Labor	Closed shop, abolition.	Passed
1948	N/A	DS	Veteran Affairs	Soldier's bonus.	Failed
1956	N/A	DS	Taxes	Ton mile tax.	Failed
1958	N/A	DA	Gaming	Legalizing bingo.	Passed
1958	N/A	DA	Utility Regulation	Public Power Districts, in lieu of taxes.	Passed
1960	N/A	DA	Administration of Government	Commissioner of Education, election of.	Failed
1964	N/A	DA	Education	Commissioner of Education, election of.	Failed
1966	N/A	DA	Taxes	Property tax, termination of.	Passed
1969	N/A	DA	Taxes	Income tax, prohibit.	Failed
1978	301	DS	Environmental Reform	Five cent deposit on beverage containers.	Failed
1978	302	DS	Administration of Government	Five percent increase limit on political subdivisions.	Failed
1982	300	DA	Administration of Government	NE Family Farm Corporations must own farms.	Passed
1988	402	DS	Environmental Reform	Central Interstate Radioactive Waste Compact.	Failed
1988	403	DA	Gun Regulation	Right to bear arms.	Passed
1990	404	DA	Gaming	Establish state lottery.	Failed
1990	405	DA	Administration of Government	Limits budget appropriations.	Failed

Year	Measure Number	Type	Subject Matter	Description	Pass/Fail
1992	407	DA	Term Limits	Term limits on state elected officials 8 years. Congress 8/12	Passed
1994	408	DA	Term Limits	Term limits on state legislature 8 years and on Congress 6/12.	Passed
1996	409	DA	Term Limits	Term limits on state legislature 8 years and on Congress 6/12.	Passed
1996	410	DA	Initiative and Referendum	Bases number of signatures required on citizen petitions on percentages of votes cast for governor rather than on percentages of the total number of registered voters.	Failed
1996	411	DA	Education	Makes "quality education" a fundamental constitutional right.	Failed
1996	412	DA	Taxes	Limits property taxes.	Failed
1998	413	DA	Taxes	Would slow the growth of state and local government spending and cut taxes.	Failed
1998	414	DS	Utility Regulation	Would require long distance carriers to pass on for the benefit of long distance carriers mandatory reductions in access charges by local exchange carriers.	Failed
2000	415	DA	Term Limits	Term limits on state legislature 8 years.	Passed
2000	416	DS	Civil Rights	Ban on Same Sex Marriage.	Passed

Nebraska Constitution

Article III

CIII-2 First power reserved; initiative.

The first power reserved by the people is the initiative whereby laws may be enacted and constitutional amendments adopted by the people independently of the Legislature. This power may be invoked by petition wherein the proposed measure shall be set forth at length. If the petition be for the enactment of a law, it shall be signed by seven percent of the registered voters of the state, and if the petition be for the amendment of the Constitution, the petition therefore shall be signed by ten percent of such registered voters. In all cases the registered voters signing such petition shall be so distributed as to include five percent of the registered voters of each of two-fifths of the counties of the state, and when thus signed, the petition shall be filed with the Secretary of State who shall submit the measure thus proposed to the electors of the state at the first general election held not less than four months after such petition shall have been filed. The same measure, either in form or in essential substance, shall not be submitted to the people by initiative petition, either affirmatively or negatively, more often than once in three years. If conflicting measures submitted to the people at the same election be approved, the one receiving the highest number of affirmative votes shall thereby become law as to all conflicting provisions. The constitutional limitations as to the scope and subject matter of statutes enacted by the Legislature shall apply to those enacted by the initiative.

CIII-3 Second power reserved; referendum.

The second power reserved is the referendum which may be invoked, by petition, against any act or part of an act of the Legislature, except those making appropriations for the expense of the state government or a state institution existing at the time of the passage of such act. Petitions invoking the referendum shall be signed by not less than five percent of the registered voters of the state, distributed as required for initiative petitions, and filed in the office of the Secretary of State within ninety days after the Legislature at which the act sought to be referred was passed shall have adjourned sine die or for more than ninety days. Such petition shall set out the title of the act against which the referendum is invoked and, in addition thereto, when only a portion of the act is sought to be referred, the number of the section or sections or portion of sections of the act designating such portion. When the referendum is thus invoked, the Secretary of State shall refer the same to the electors for approval or rejection at the first general election to be held not less than thirty days after the filing of such petition. When the referendum is invoked as to any act or part of act, other than emergency acts or those for the immediate preservation of the public peace, health, or safety, by petition signed by not less than ten percent of the registered voters of the state distributed as aforesaid, it shall suspend the taking effect of such act or part of act until the same has been approved by the electors of the state.

CIII-4 Initiative or referendum; signatures required; veto; election returns; constitutional amendments; non-partisan ballot.

The whole number of votes cast for Governor at the general election next preceding the filing of an initiative or referendum petition shall be the basis on which the number of signatures to such petition shall be computed. The veto power of the Governor shall not extend to measures initiated by or referred to the people. A measure initiated shall become a law or part of the Constitution, as the case may be, when a majority of the votes cast thereon, and not less than thirty-five per cent of the total vote cast at the election at which the same was submitted, are cast in favor thereof, and shall take effect upon proclamation by the Governor which shall be made within ten days after the official canvass of such votes. The vote upon initiative and referendum measures shall be returned and canvassed in the manner prescribed for the canvass of votes for president. The method of submitting and adopting amendments to the Constitution provided by this section shall be supplementary to the method prescribed in the article of this Constitution, entitled, "Amendments" and the latter shall in no case be construed to conflict herewith. The provisions with respect to the initiative and referendum shall be self-executing, but legislation may be enacted to facilitate their operation. All propositions submitted in pursuance hereof shall be submitted in a non-partisan manner and without any indication or suggestion on the ballot that they have been approved or endorsed by any political party or organization. Only the title or proper descriptive words of measures shall be printed on the ballot and when two or more measures have the same title they shall be numbered consecutively in the order of filing with the Secretary of State and the number shall be followed by the name of the first petitioner on the corresponding petition.

Nebraska Statutes

Chapter 32: Elections

32-628 Petitions; requirements.

(1) All petitions prepared or filed pursuant to the Election Act or any petition which requires the election commissioner or county clerk to verify signatures by utilizing the voter registration register shall provide a space at least two and one-half inches long for written signatures, a space at least two inches long for printed names, and sufficient space for date of birth and street name and number, city or village, and zip code. Lines on each petition shall not be less than one-fourth inch apart. Petitions may be designed in such a manner that lines for signatures and other information run the length of the page rather than the width. Petitions shall provide for no more than twenty signatures per page.

(2) For the purpose of preventing fraud, deception, and misrepresentation, every sheet of every petition containing signatures shall have upon it, above the signatures, statements printed in boldface type in substantially the following form:

WARNING TO PETITION SIGNERS—VIOLATION OF ANY OF THE FOLLOWING PROVISIONS OF LAW MAY RESULT IN THE FILING OF CRIMINAL CHARGES: Any person who signs any name other than his or her own to any petition or who is not, at the time of signing or circulating the petition, a registered voter and qualified to sign or circulate the petition except as provided for initiative and referendum petitions shall be guilty of a Class I misdemeanor. Any person who falsely swears to a circulator's affidavit on a petition, who accepts money or other things of value for signing a petition, or who offers money or other things of value in exchange for a signature upon any petition shall be guilty of a Class IV felony.

(3) Every sheet of a petition which contains signatures shall have upon it, below the signatures, an affidavit in substantially the following form:

STATE OF NEBRASKA)
) ss.
COUNTY OF ...)
... (name of circulator) being first duly sworn, deposes and says that he or she is the circulator of this petition containing .... signatures, that he or she is a registered voter of the State of Nebraska, that each person whose name appears on the petition personally signed the petition in the presence of the affiant, that the date to the left of each signature is the correct date on which the signature was affixed to the petition and that the date was personally affixed by the person

signing such petition, that the affiant believes that each signer has written his or her name, street and number or voting precinct, and city, village, or post office address correctly, that the affiant believes that each signer was qualified to sign the petition, and that the affiant stated to each signer the object of the petition as printed on the petition before he or she affixed his or her signature to the petition.

....
Circulator

....
Address

Subscribed and sworn to before me, a notary public, this ... day of .... 20.... at ...., Nebraska.

....
Notary Public

(4) Each sheet of a petition shall have upon its face and in plain view of persons who sign the petition a statement in letters not smaller than sixteen-point type in red print on the petition. If the petition is circulated by a paid circulator, the statement shall be as follows: This petition is circulated by a paid circulator. If the petition is circulated by a circulator who is not being paid, the statement shall be as follows: This petition is circulated by a volunteer circulator.

32-1108: Ballot question; contest of election result; petition; service; answer; representation.

The result of any election upon a proposed constitutional amendment or statute submitted or referred to the voters either by the Legislature or by initiative or referendum petition may be contested upon the petition of one or more registered voters directed against the Secretary of State. The petitioning voter or voters shall present a petition to the district court of Lancaster County within forty days after such election. The petition shall set forth the points on which the election will be contested and the facts which will be proved in support of such points and shall ask for leave to produce the proof. The Secretary of State shall be served with a copy of the petition and a notice of the time and place of the presentation of the petition ten days before the petition will be presented. The Secretary of State may, upon the presentation of such petition, file an answer thereto specifying reasons why the election should not be contested. The proponents and opponents of any proposed constitutional amendment or statute shall have the right to engage counsel to represent and act for such parties in all matters involved in and pertaining to the contest.

32-629 Petitions; signers and circulators; qualifications; exception.

Only a registered voter of the State of Nebraska shall qualify as a valid signer or circulator of a petition and may sign or circulate petitions under the Election Act, except that any person who is or will be a registered voter in the State of Nebraska on or before the date on which the petition is required to be filed with the Secretary of State may sign an initiative or referendum petition.

32-630 Petition; signers and circulators; duties; prohibited acts.

(1) Each person who signs a petition shall, at the time of and in addition to signing, personally affix the date, print his or her last name and first name in full, and affix his or her date of birth and address, including the street and number or a designation of a rural route or voting precinct and the city or village or a post office address. A person signing a petition may use his or her initials in place of his or her first name if such person is registered to vote under such initials. No signer shall use ditto marks as a means of personally affixing the date or address to any petition. A wife shall not use her husband's first name when she signs a petition but shall personally affix her first name and her last name by marriage or her surname. Any signature using ditto marks as a means of personally affixing the date or address of any petition or any signature using a spouse's first name instead of his or her own shall be invalid.
(2) Each circulator of a petition shall personally witness the signatures on the petition and shall sign the circulator's affidavit.
(3) No person shall:
(a) Sign any name other than his or her own to any petition;
(b) Knowingly sign his or her name more than once for the same petition effort or measure;
(c) Sign or circulate a petition if he or she is not a registered voter and qualified to sign or circulate the same except as provided in section 32-629;
(d) Falsely swear to any signature upon any such petition;
(e) Accept money or other thing of value for signing any petition; or
(f) Offer money or other thing of value in exchange for a signature upon any petition.

32-631 Petitions; signature verification; procedure.

(1) All petitions that are presented to the election commissioner or county clerk for signature verification shall be retained in the election office and shall be open to public inspection. Upon receipt of the pages of a petition, the election commissioner or county clerk shall issue a written receipt indicating the number of pages of the petition in his or her custody to the person presenting the petition for signature verification. Petitions may be destroyed twenty-two months after the election to which they apply.

(2) The election commissioner or county clerk shall determine the validity and sufficiency of such petition by comparing the names, dates of birth if applicable, and addresses of the signers and circulators with the voter registration records to determine if the signers and circulators were registered voters on the date of signing the petition. If it is determined that a signer has affixed his or her signature more than once to any petition and that only one person is registered by that name, the election commissioner or county clerk shall strike from the pages of the petition all but one such signature. Only one of the duplicate signatures shall be added to the total number of valid signatures. All signatures, dates of birth, and addresses shall be presumed to be valid if the election commissioner or county clerk has found the signers to be registered voters on or before the date on which the petition was signed. This presumption shall not be conclusive and may be rebutted by any credible evidence which the election commissioner or county clerk finds sufficient.

(3) If the election commissioner or county clerk verifies signatures in excess of one hundred ten percent of the number necessary for the issue to be placed on the ballot, the election commissioner or county clerk may cease verifying signatures and certify the number of signatures verified to the person who delivered the petitions for verification.

(4) If the number of signatures verified does not equal or exceed the number necessary to place the issue on the ballot upon completion of the comparison of names and addresses with the voter registration records, the election commissioner or county clerk shall prepare in writing a certification under seal setting forth the name and address of each signer or circulator found not to be a registered voter and the petition page number and line number where the signature is found. If the signature or address is challenged for a reason other than the nonregistration of the signer, the election commissioner or county clerk shall set forth the reasons for the challenge of the signature.

32-632 Petition; removal of name; procedure.

Any person may remove his or her name from a petition by an affidavit signed and sworn to by such person before the election commissioner, the county clerk, or a notary public. The affidavit shall be presented to the Secretary of State, election commissioner, or county clerk prior to or on the day of the petition-filing deadline.

32-1401 Initiative petition; form.

The form of a petition for initiating any law or any amendment to the Constitution of Nebraska shall comply with the requirements of sections 32-628 and 32-1403 and shall be substantially as follows:

Initiative Petition
The object of this petition is to .... (Print a concise statement in large type of the legal effect of the filing of the petition and the object sought to be secured by submitting the measure to the voters).

To the Honorable ...., Secretary of State for the State of Nebraska:

We, the undersigned residents of the State of Nebraska and the county of ...., respectfully demand that the following proposed law (or amendment to the Constitution of Nebraska as the case may be) shall be referred to the registered voters of the state for their approval or rejection at the general election to be held on the .... day of ... 19.., and each for himself or herself says:

I have personally signed this petition on the date opposite my name; I am a registered voter of the State of Nebraska and county of .... and am qualified to sign this petition or I will be so registered and qualified on or before the date on which this petition is required to be filed with the Secretary of State; and my printed name, date of birth, street and number or voting precinct, and city, village, or post office address are correctly written after my signature.

(Here follow numbered lines for signature, printed name, date of birth, date, street and number or voting precinct, and city, village, or post office address.)

32-1402 Referendum petition; form.

The form of a petition for ordering a referendum upon any act or any part of any act passed by the Legislature of the State of Nebraska shall comply with the requirements of sections 32-628 and 32-1403 and shall be substantially as follows:

Referendum Petition

The object of this petition is to .... (Print a concise statement in large type of the legal effect of the filing of the petition and the object sought to be secured by submitting the measure to the voters).

To the Honorable ...., Secretary of State for the State of Nebraska:

We, the undersigned residents of the State of Nebraska and the county of ...., respectfully order that Legislative Bill No. .... entitled .... (title of act and, if the petition is against less than the whole act, then set forth here the part or parts on which the referendum is sought), passed by the .... Legislature of the State of Nebraska at its .... Session, shall be referred to the registered voters of the state for retention or repeal at the general election to be held on the.... day of .... 19.., and each for himself or herself says:

I have personally signed this petition on the date opposite my name; I am a registered voter of the State of Nebraska and county of .... and am qualified to sign this petition or I will be so registered and qualified on or before the date on which this petition is required to be filed with the Secretary of State; and my printed name, date of birth, street and number or voting precinct, and city, village, or post office address are correctly written after my signature.

(Here follow numbered lines for signature, printed name, date, date of birth, street and number or voting precinct, and city, village, or post office address.)

32-1403 Initiative or referendum; petition; title and text required; filing.

A full and correct copy of the title and text of the law or amendment to the Constitution of Nebraska to be proposed by an initiative petition or the measure sought to be referred to the registered voters by a referendum petition shall be printed upon each sheet of the petition which contains signatures. The petition may be filed with the Secretary of State in numbered sections for convenience in handling.

32-1404 Initiative and referendum petitions; signers and circulators; requirements.

Signers and circulators of initiative and referendum petitions shall meet the requirements of sections 32-629 and 32-630. A registered voter who intends to circulate initiative and referendum petitions outside of his or her county of residence shall register with the Secretary of State on forms provided by the Secretary of State prior to circulating initiative and referendum petitions outside of his or her county of residence. The Secretary of State shall make available to the counties a list of registered circulators for each petition drive.

32-1405 Initiative and referendum petitions; sponsors; filing required; Revisor of Statutes; Secretary of State; duties.

(1) Prior to obtaining any signatures on an initiative or referendum petition, a statement of the object of the petition and the text of the measure shall be filed with the Secretary of State together with a sworn statement containing the names and street addresses of every person, corporation, or association sponsoring the petition.

(2) Upon receipt of the filing, the Secretary of State shall transmit the text of the proposed measure to the Revisor of Statutes. The Revisor of Statutes shall review the proposed measure and suggest changes as to form and draftsmanship. The revisor shall complete the review within ten days after receipt from the Secretary of State. The Secretary of State shall provide the results of the review and suggested changes to the sponsor but shall otherwise keep them confidential for five days after receipt by the sponsor. The Secretary of State shall then maintain the opinion as public information and as a part of the official record of the initiative. The suggested changes may be accepted or rejected by the sponsor.

(3) The Secretary of State shall prepare five camera-ready copies of the petition from the information filed by the sponsor and any changes accepted by the sponsor and shall provide the copies to the sponsor within five days after receipt of the review required in subsection (2) of this section. The sponsor shall print the petitions to be circulated from the forms provided.

(4) The changes made to this section by Laws 1995, LB 337 shall apply to initiative and referendum petitions filed on or after September 9, 1995.

32-1405.01 Initiative and referendum measures; informational pamphlet; contents; distribution.

(1) The Secretary of State shall develop and print one informational pamphlet on all initiative and referendum measures to be placed on the ballot. The pamphlet shall include the measure number, the ballot title and text, and the full text of each initiated or referred measure and arguments both for and against each measure.

(2) The Secretary of State shall write the arguments for and against each measure, and each set of arguments shall consist of no more than two hundred fifty words. Information for the arguments may be provided by the sponsors of the measure, opponents to the measure, and other sources.

(3) The Secretary of State shall distribute the pamphlets to election commissioners and county clerks at least six weeks prior to the election. The election commissioners and county clerks shall immediately make the pamphlets available in their offices and in at least three other public locations that will facilitate distribution to the public.

32-1405.02 Initiative and referendum measures; public hearing; notice.

After the Secretary of State certifies the initiative and referendum measures for the ballot under subsection (3) of section 32-1411, the Secretary of State shall hold one public hearing in each congressional district for the purpose of allowing public comment on the measures. Notice of each hearing shall be published once in such newspapers as are necessary to provide for general circulation within the congressional district in which the meeting will be held not less than five days prior to the hearing. The hearings shall be held not more than eight weeks prior to the election.

32-1406 Initiative and referendum petitions; principal circulator; name and address.

The election commissioner or county clerk shall provide the name and address of the principal circulator of an initiative or referendum petition upon request. The principal circulator shall inform the election commissioner or county clerk of the name and address to be provided.

32-1407 Initiative petition; filing deadline; issue placed on ballot; when; referendum petition; filing deadline.

(1) Initiative petitions shall be filed in the office of the Secretary of State at least four months prior to the general election at which the proposal would be submitted to the voters.

(2) When a copy of the form of any initiative petition is filed with the Secretary of State prior to obtaining signatures, the issue presented by such petition shall be placed before the voters at the next general election occurring at least four months after the date that such copy is filed if the signed petitions are found to be valid and sufficient. All signed initiative petitions shall become invalid on the date of the first general election occurring at least four months after the date on which the copy of the form is filed with the Secretary of State.

(3) Petitions invoking a referendum shall be filed in the office of the Secretary of State within ninety days after the Legislature at which the act sought to be referred was passed has adjourned sine die or has adjourned for more than ninety days.

32-1408 Initiative and referendum petitions; Secretary of State; refuse filing; when.

The Secretary of State shall not accept for filing any initiative or referendum petition which interferes with the legislative prerogative contained in the Constitution of Nebraska that the necessary revenue of the state and its governmental subdivisions shall be raised by taxation in the manner as the Legislature may direct.

32-1409 Initiative and referendum petitions; signature verification; procedure; certification; Secretary of State; duties.

(1) Upon the receipt of the petitions, the Secretary of State, with the aid and assistance of the election commissioner or county clerk, shall determine the validity and sufficiency of signatures on the pages of the filed petition. The Secretary of State shall deliver the various pages of the filed petition to the election commissioner or county clerk by hand carrier, by use of law enforcement officials, or by certified mail, return receipt requested. Upon receipt of the pages of the petition, the election commissioner or county clerk shall issue to the Secretary of State a written receipt that the pages of the petition are in the custody of the election commissioner or county clerk. The election commissioner or county clerk shall compare the signature of each person signing upon each of the pages of the petition with the voter registration records to determine if each signer was a registered voter on or before the date on which the petition was required to be filed with the Secretary of State. The election commissioner or county clerk shall also compare the signer's printed name, date of birth, street and number or voting precinct, and city, village, or post office address with the voter registration records to determine whether the signer was a registered voter. The signature, date of birth, and address shall be presumed to be valid only if the election commissioner or county clerk finds the printed name, date of birth, street and number or voting precinct, and city, village, or post office address to match the registration records and that the registration was received on or before the date on which the petition was required to be filed with the Secretary of State. Any signature

which is not accompanied by the information required by section 32-630 shall be invalid. The finding of the election commissioner or county clerk may be rebutted by any credible evidence which the Secretary of State finds sufficient. The express purpose of the comparison of names and addresses with the voter registration records, in addition to helping to determine the validity of such petition, the sufficiency of such petition, and the qualifications of the signer, shall be to prevent fraud, deception, and misrepresentation in the petition process.

(2) Upon completion of the comparison of names and addresses with the voter registration records, the election commissioner or county clerk shall prepare in writing a certification under seal setting forth the name and address of each signer found not to be a registered voter and the petition page number and line number where the name is found, and if the reason for the invalidity of the signature or address is other than the nonregistration of the signer, the election commissioner or county clerk shall set forth the reason for the invalidity of the signature. If the election commissioner or county clerk determines that a signer has affixed his or her signature more than once to any page or pages of the petition and that only one person is registered by that name, the election commissioner or county clerk shall prepare in writing a certification under seal setting forth the name of the duplicate signature and shall count only the earliest dated signature. The election commissioner or county clerk shall deliver all pages of the petition and the certifications to the Secretary of State within forty days after the receipt of such pages from the Secretary of State. The delivery shall be by hand carrier, by use of law enforcement officials, or by certified mail, return receipt requested. The Secretary of State may grant to the election commissioner or county clerk an additional ten days to return all pages of the petition in extraordinary circumstances.

(3) Upon receipt of the pages of the petition, the Secretary of State shall issue a written receipt indicating the number of pages of the petition that are in his or her custody. When all the petitions and certifications have been received by the Secretary of State, he or she shall strike from the pages of the petition all but the earliest dated signature of any duplicate signatures and such stricken signatures shall not be added to the total number of valid signatures. Not more than twenty signatures on one sheet shall be counted. All signatures secured in a manner contrary to sections 32-1401 to 32-1416 shall not be counted. Clerical and technical errors in a petition shall be disregarded if the forms prescribed in sections 32-1401 to 32-1403 are substantially followed. The Secretary of State shall total the valid signatures and determine if constitutional and statutory requirements have been met. The Secretary of State shall immediately serve a copy of such determination by certified or registered mail upon the person filing the initiative or referendum petition. If the petition is found to be valid and sufficient, the Secretary of State shall proceed to place the measure on the general election ballot.

(4) The Secretary of State may adopt and promulgate rules and regulations for the issuance of all necessary forms and procedural instructions to carry out this section.

32-1410 Initiative and referendum petitions; ballot title; statement of effect; Attorney General; duties; appeal.

(1) When an initiative petition is filed with the Secretary of State to propose a measure to the registered voters of the state, the Secretary of State shall transmit a copy of the measure to the Attorney General. Within ten days after receiving the copy, the Attorney General shall provide and return to the Secretary of State a ballot title for such measure. The ballot title shall express the purpose of the measure in not exceeding one hundred words and shall not resemble, so far as to be likely to create confusion, any title previously filed for any measure to be submitted at that election. The Attorney General also shall prepare a statement to be printed in italics immediately preceding the ballot title on the official ballot. Such statement shall in clear and concise language explain the effect of a vote for and against the measure in such language that the statement will not be intentionally an argument or likely to create prejudice, either for or against the measure. The ballot title shall be so worded that those in favor of adopting the measure shall vote for and those opposing the adoption of the measure shall vote against.

(2) When a referendum petition is filed with the Secretary of State to refer a measure to the registered voters of the state, the Secretary of State shall transmit a copy of the measure to the Attorney General. Within ten days after receiving the copy, the Attorney General shall provide and return to the Secretary of State a ballot title for such measure. The ballot title may be distinct from the legislative title of the measure, shall express the purpose of the measure in not exceeding one hundred words, and shall not resemble, so far as to be likely to create confusion, any title previously filed for any measure to be submitted at that election. The Attorney General also shall prepare a statement to be printed in italics immediately preceding the ballot title on the official ballot. Such statement shall in clear and concise language explain the effect of a vote to retain and a vote to repeal the measure in such language that the statement will not be intentionally an argument or likely to create prejudice, either for retention or for repeal of the measure. The ballot title shall be so worded that those in favor of retaining the measure shall vote Retain and those opposing the measure shall vote Repeal.

(3) Any person who is dissatisfied with the ballot title provided by the Attorney General for any measure may appeal from his or her decision to the district court as provided in section 32-1412. The person shall file a petition asking for a different title and setting forth the reasons why the title prepared by the Attorney General is insufficient or unfair. No appeal shall be allowed from the decision of the Attorney General on a ballot title unless the appeal is taken within ten days

after the decision is filed. A copy of every such decision shall be served by the Secretary of State or the clerk of the district court upon the person offering or filing such initiative or referendum petition or appeal. Service of such decision may be by mail or electronic transmission and shall be made forthwith. The district court shall thereupon examine the measure, hear arguments, and in its decision thereon certify to the Secretary of State a ballot title for the measure in accord with the intent of this section by September 1 prior to the statewide general election.

(4) The appeal procedures described in the Administrative Procedure Act shall not apply to this section.

32-1411 Initiative and referendum measures; numbering; placement on ballot.

(1) The Secretary of State shall number the measures proposed by initiative or referendum to be voted upon at the next general election. Beginning with the 1986 general election, the first measure shall be numbered 400 and the succeeding measures shall be numbered consecutively 401, 402, 403, 404, 405, and so on.

(2) When any initiative or referendum petition is regularly and legally filed with the Secretary of State, he or she shall, at the next general election, cause to be printed on an official ballot in a nonpartisan manner the ballot title and number of the measure. The ballot titles shall be printed on the official ballot in a random order as determined by the Secretary of State. The statement prepared by the Attorney General shall be printed in italics immediately preceding the ballot title on the official ballot. Measures proposed by initiative petition shall be designated and distinguished on the ballot by the heading Proposed by Initiative Petition. Measures referred by petition shall be designated Referendum ordered by Petition of the People. All initiative and referendum measures shall be submitted in a nonpartisan manner without any indication or suggestion on the ballot that they have been approved or endorsed by any political party or organization.

(3) At the time the Secretary of State furnishes to the election commissioners or county clerks certified copies of the names of the candidates for state and other offices, the Secretary of State shall furnish to each election commissioner or county clerk a certified copy of the ballot titles and numbers of the measures proposed by initiative or referendum to be voted upon at the next general election. The election commissioner or county clerk shall print such ballot titles and numbers upon the official ballot in the order presented by the Secretary of State and the relative position required by this section.

32-1412 Initiative and referendum measures; refusal of Secretary of State to place on ballot; jurisdiction of district court; parties; appeal.

(1) If the Secretary of State refuses to place on the ballot any measure proposed by an initiative petition presented at least four months preceding the date of the election at which the proposed law or constitutional amendment is to be voted upon or a referendum petition presented within ninety days after the Legislature enacting the law to which the petition applies adjourns sine die or for a period longer than ninety days, any resident may apply, within ten days after such refusal, to the district court of Lancaster County for a writ of mandamus. If it is decided by the court that such petition is legally sufficient, the Secretary of State shall order the issue placed upon the ballot at the next general election.

(2) On a showing that an initiative or referendum petition is not legally sufficient, the court, on the application of any resident, may enjoin the Secretary of State and all other officers from certifying or printing on the official ballot for the next general election the ballot title and number of such measure. If a suit is filed against the Secretary of State seeking to enjoin him or her from placing the measure on the official ballot, the person who is the sponsor of record of the petition shall be a necessary party defendant in such suit.

(3) Such suits shall be advanced on the court docket and heard and decided by the court as quickly as possible. Either party may appeal to the Court of Appeals within ten days after a decision is rendered. The appeal procedures described in the Administrative Procedure Act shall not apply to this section.

(4) The district court of Lancaster County shall have jurisdiction over all litigation arising under sections 32-1401 to 32-1416.

32-1413 Initiative and referendum measures; publication required; rate.

Immediately preceding any general election at which any initiative or referendum measure is to be submitted to the registered voters, the Secretary of State shall cause to be published in all legal newspapers in the state once each week for three consecutive weeks a true copy of the ballot title and text and the number of each measure to be submitted in the form in which the measure will be printed on the official ballot. The publication shall be at a rate charged as provided in section 33-141.

32-1414 Initiative and referendum measures; counting, canvassing, and return of votes; proclamation by Governor.

The votes on initiative and referendum measures shall be counted, canvassed, and returned in the same manner as votes for candidates are counted, canvassed, and returned, and the abstract of votes made by the election commissioners or county clerks shall be returned on abstract sheets in the manner provided by section 32-1034 for abstracts of votes for state and county officers. The board of state canvassers shall canvass the votes upon each initiative or referendum measure in the same manner as is prescribed in the case of presidential electors. The Governor shall, within ten days of the completion of the canvass, issue his or her proclamation giving the whole number of votes cast in the state approving and rejecting each measure and declaring such measures as are approved by the constitutional number or majority of those voting to be in full force and effect as the law of the State of Nebraska from the date of such proclamation. If two or more measures are approved at such election which are known to conflict with each other or to contain conflicting provisions, the Governor shall also proclaim which is paramount in accordance with section 32-1416.

32-1415 Initiative or referendum; approved; preservation and printing.

If an initiative or referendum is approved by the voters at the general election, the copies of the initiative or referendum petition filed with the Secretary of State and a certified copy of the Governor's proclamation declaring the measure approved by the people shall be identified and preserved. The Secretary of State shall cause every measure approved by the people to be printed with the general laws enacted by the next session of the Legislature with the date of the Governor's proclamation declaring the same to have been approved by the people.

32-1416 Conflicting laws; adoption; which law controls.

If two or more conflicting laws are approved by the registered voters at the same election, the law receiving the greatest number of affirmative votes shall be paramount in all particulars as to which there is a conflict even though such law may not have received the greater majority of affirmative votes. If two or more conflicting amendments to the Constitution of Nebraska are approved by the registered voters at the same election, the amendment which receives the greatest number of affirmative votes shall be paramount in all particulars as to which there is conflict even though such amendment may not have received the greater majority of affirmative votes.

32-1417 Constitution of United States; proposed amendment; adoption or rejection; submission to voters for advisory vote.

(1) If a proposed amendment to the Constitution of the United States is duly submitted to the Legislature of the State of Nebraska as provided in Article V of the Constitution of the United States, a petition may be filed with the Secretary of State requesting that such proposed amendment be submitted to a vote of the people for an advisory opinion as to whether the proposed amendment to the Constitution of the United States shall be adopted or rejected. The petition shall set forth at length the proposed amendment and shall be signed by a number of registered voters of the state equal to ten percent of the votes cast at the immediately preceding presidential election. The registered voters signing the petition shall be so distributed as to include two percent of the registered voters of each of three-fifths of the counties of the state. When the petition is filed with the Secretary of State, he or she shall submit the proposed amendment to the registered voters of the state at the first general election held at least four months after such petition has been filed.

(2) The procedure for placing the proposed amendment on the ballot shall be the same as for placing initiated measures on the ballot under the Constitution and laws of Nebraska so far as is applicable. The ballot title on each such question submitted shall be designated as follows:

Advisory Vote on Amendment to Constitution of United States Ordered by Petition of the People.

The question shall be submitted in substantially the following form:

Is it desirable that the Legislature ratify the following proposed amendment to the Constitution of the United States:

(Setting out proposed amendment)

For ratification
Against ratification

(3) The result of the vote cast on a question submitted under this section shall be regarded as advisory to the Legislature of the opinion of the people concerning such proposed amendment to the Constitution of the United States but shall not be binding upon the Legislature or any member thereof or be considered as controlling in any action taken either to ratify or not to ratify such amendment.

The Basic Steps to Do an Initiative in Nebraska

Statutes and Amendments — Direct Initiative Process

Basic Procedures: Once a sponsor has decided to begin an initiative petition effort, the first step is to deliver, to the Secretary of State's office, a copy of the language that they want to see in the statutes or in the constitution and the object clause for the petition. The object clause is a brief statement of what the proposal will accomplish. The sponsor also needs to provide a list of the sponsors of the petition at that time.

From there, the Secretary of State sends the language to the Revisor of Statutes who reviews the submitted language. The Revisor has 10 days to review the language and suggest changes to make the language fit into the constitution or statutes clearly and uniformly. When the suggested changes are returned to the Secretary of State, the sponsors are informed and may accept or reject any suggestions made by the Revisor. The suggested changes are confidential for five days after returned from the Revisor. The sponsor then provides the final language to the Secretary of State and he or she places the language and object clause onto a petition form. The Secretary of State provides 5 camera-ready copies of the form to the sponsor within 5 days. The form must contain a statement in red and 16 pt. type that the petition is circulated by either a paid or volunteer circulator as the case may be.

Once the final form is given to the sponsors the language of the measure may not be changed or amended. However, if a change in the language becomes necessary, sponsors may stop collecting signatures on the petition and begin the process again with revised language.

The procedures for the filing of a referendum petition are very similar to an initiative. Instead of submitting the proposed initiative language, the sponsors submit a copy of the recently passed law along with a statement of the object of the petition. The proposed referendum follows the same path through the Revisor and Secretary of State as an initiative.

Once the sponsors have received the camera-ready copies of the form, they may print or copy the form and begin collecting signatures from registered voters in the state.

Date initiative language can be submitted to the state for the 2002 ballot: Any time.

Signatures are tied to vote of which office: Number of registered voters.

Current signatures total requirements: For statutes 7% of registered voters at the time signatures are submitted and for amendments 10% of the registered voters and for a popular referendum 5%. For a referendum that suspends a law from taking effect, 10% of the registered voters must sign the petition. The exact number needed is hard to calculate, as it depends on the number of registered voters there are in the future—at the time the signatures are submitted. However, as an estimate 76,000 signatures will be needed for a statute and 108,500 for amendment. (These estimates are based on the number of registered voters in November of 2000.)

Distribution Requirement: 5% must be gathered in 38 of 93 counties.

Circulation period: 1 year

Do circulators have to be residents: No

Date when signatures are due for certification: Initiative petition signatures must be submitted to the Secretary of State no later than four months prior to the general election. July 5, 2002 for the 2002 election.

Signature verification process: Petitions are turned into the Secretary of State, who then gives the petitions to the respective counties to verify the signatures. Each signature is compared with the voter registration records.

Single-subject requirement: Nebraska has a strict single-subject requirement.

Legislative tampering: Legislature can repeal and amend initiatives.

General Comments: The legislature can repeal and amend initiative statutes by a simple majority. There is also a statutory restriction on the use of the initiative for issues that interfere with the Legislature's prerogative to raise the necessary revenue for the state and its political subdivisions. In addition, the same measure may not be placed on the ballot more often than once in three years.

When the petition is submitted for verification, the Secretary of State will deliver a copy of the measure to the Attorney General. The Attorney General will write a ballot question or title that summarizes (in 100 words or less) the purpose of the measure. In addition, the Attorney General will provide material that explains the effect of a vote for or against the measure. These items will appear on the ballot.

If anyone believes that the ballot language is not sufficient or fair, they may file in District Court asking for the language to be changed. This must be filed within 10 days after the language is delivered to the Secretary of State.

The final language (either from the Attorney General or the District Court) is sent by the Secretary of State to each local official for placement on the ballot. The language on the ballot will indicate that the voter is to vote either "For" or "Against" an initiative measure and "Repeal" or "Retain" on a referendum.

Prior to the election, there are three informational mechanisms used by the Secretary of State.

The first is the publication of a pamphlet that contains the ballot title and arguments for and against the measure. The pamphlet is available from local election officials and is available at least six weeks prior to the election. Proponents and opponents of the measure may submit suggestions on material to be included in the pamphlet. It should be noted however that the pamphlet is written and produced by the Secretary of State and any submitted material may or may not be used at his or her discretion.

Second, the Secretary of State conducts public hearings on the measures with a public hearing in each congressional district. These hearings occur no more than 8 weeks prior to the general election. Proponents and opponents are encouraged to attend to provide their views on the measure.

The final information source is the publication of the entire text in all legal newspapers in the state once each week for the three weeks prior to the election.

Nevada

In 1905, an amendment giving voters the power of referendum was approved by the Nevada legislature and ratified by the voters by a margin of five to one.

By 1909, initiative supporters included acting governor Denver S. Dickerson and U.S. Senator Francis G. Newlands, architect of the Newlands Reclamation Act of 1901, which set up the federal Bureau of Reclamation and provided for the construction of dams and canals to irrigate the arid lands of the western states. An amendment establishing the initiative process passed the legislature and was approved by Nevada voters in 1912.

The first initiative to pass was a Prohibition statute, approved by a 59 percent majority in 1918. In 1922, a change in the divorce law was initiated by petition, sparking the legislature to place its own alternative on the ballot also. The legislature's version passed, and the initiative lost. In 1936, Nevadans rejected a pension initiative by a margin of nearly three to one, but they changed their minds eight years later and approved by a 53.5 percent margin another initiative to increase the state's old-age benefits. During the 1950s business interests and labor unions clashed in three successive elections over the "Right to Work" issue. Organized labor lost in all three elections.

The battle began in 1952, when voters approved a "Right to Work" measure by a slim 50.7 percent margin. Labor unions fought back with a 1954 initiative to repeal the new law; Nevada voters defeated it by a narrow margin of 51.4 percent. A second union-sponsored repeal initiative on the 1956 ballot was rejected by a 53.9 percent margin. Another union-backed initiative on the same ballot sought to amend the state constitution to prohibit "Right to Work" laws, but was rejected by an even more decisive margin of 57 percent.

In 1958, business interests responded with their own initiative to end the dispute in employers' favor, simply by making it more difficult to put initiatives on the ballot and more difficult to pass them. Approved by a 61.9 percent majority, the new provision required that initiative petitions meet signature quotas in three-quarters of the state's 75 counties. No more could initiative proponents get all the signatures they needed from the heavily populated Las Vegas and Reno areas. Another new requirement specified that initiatives to amend the constitution be approved by voters twice, in two successive elections, before taking effect. Nevada is the only state with such a requirement.

In 1982, an initiative spurred the legislature to pass a similar bill of its own creating a consumer advocate's office to deal with utility matters. Both measures were on the ballot, but sponsors of the initiative liked the legislature's version so much that they campaigned against their own! Not surprisingly, the legislature's measure won the approval of the voters.

In 1998, medical marijuana was legalized via the initiative process as was a ban on same sex marriage in 2000.

Statewide Initiative Usage

Number of Initiatives	Number Passed	Number Failed	Passage Rate
39	25	14	64%

Statewide Initiatives

Year	Measure Number	Type	Subject Matter	Description	Pass/Fail
1918	N/A	IDS	Alcohol Regulation	Providing for statewide prohibition.	Passed
1922	N/A	IDS	Legal	Divorce law	Failed
1934	N/A	IDS	Animal Rights	Bounties on predatory animals.	Passed
1936	N/A	IDS	Welfare	Relative to old age pensions.	Failed
1938	N/A	IDS	Animal Rights	To pay bounties on predatory animals.	Failed
1944	N/A	IDS	Welfare	Relative to old age pensions.	Passed
1952	N/A	IDS	Labor	Right-to-work law.	Passed
1954	N/A	IDS	Labor	To repeal the right-to-work law.	Failed
1956	N/A	DA	Labor	Prohibit "right-to-work laws."	Failed
1956	N/A	IDS	Labor	To repeal the right-to-work law.	Failed
1956	N/A	IDS	Education	Relating to the question of public school financing.	Failed
1958	N/A	DA	Initiative and Referendum	To amend Sec. 3, Art. 19 of the Constitution which would make the requirements to commence and carry through an initiative more strict.	Passed
1960	N/A	DA	Administration of Government	Require the legislature to meet in regular session once each 2 years, in odd-numbered years, instead of once each year.	Passed
1962	N/A	DA	Initiative and Referendum	Make changes to the state's initiative and referendum laws.	Passed
1968	N/A	DA	Gaming	Repeal prohibition on establishing a lottery.	Failed
1978	6	DA	Taxes	Limit property taxes.	Passed
1980	6	DA	Taxes	1978 Measure 6 — Limit property taxes. 2nd vote as required by law	Failed
1980	8	DA	Taxes	Exempt household goods from taxation.	Passed
1980	9	DA	Taxes	Exempt food from taxation.	Passed
1982	12	IDS	Utility Regulation	Protection of public utilities customers.	Failed
1982	8	DA	Taxes	1980 Measure 8 — Exempt household goods from taxation. 2nd vote as required by law.	Passed
1982	9	DA	Taxes	1980 Measure 9 — Exempt food from taxation. 2nd vote as required by law	Failed
1984	12	DA	Taxes	Limit tax increases, all levels of government.	Failed
1988	9	DA	Taxes	Prohibit a state personal income tax.	Passed
1990	6	IDS	Taxes	Net profit tax, franchise fee for corporations.	Failed
1990	9	DA	Taxes	1988 Measure 9 — prohibits a state personal income tax. 2nd vote as required by law.	Passed

Year	Measure Number	Type	Subject Matter	Description	Pass/Fail
1994	10	DA	Campaign Finance Reform	Defines and limits campaign contributions.	Passed
1994	11	DA	Taxes	Require a 2/3 vote in the legislature and a majority vote by referendum for any tax increase.	Passed
1994	8	DA	Term Limits	Term limits on judges and state legislature 12/12.	Passed
1994	9	DA	Term Limits	Term limits on Congress 6/12.	Passed
1996	10	DA	Campaign Finance Reform	Campaign contributions limits. 2nd vote as required by law.	Passed
1996	11	DA	Taxes	Amends constitution to require a 2/3 vote of the legislature to increase taxes. 2nd vote as required by law.	Passed
1996	17	DA	Term Limits	Informed Voter Law.	Passed
1996	9A	DA	Term Limits	Term limits on state legislature 12/12.	Passed
1996	9B	DA	Term Limits	Term limits on judges. (Question 9 was split into two questions, by court order) 2nd vote as required by law.	Failed
1998	17	DA	Term Limits	Informed Voter Law.	Passed
1998	9	DA	Drug Policy Reform	Would let adults on the advice of physicians use marijuana for curing or relieving pain in a number of illnesses such as cancer and AIDS.	Passed
2000	2	DA	Civil Rights	Ban of same sex marriage	Passed
2000	9	DA	Drug Policy Reform	Would let adults on the advice of physicians use marijuana for curing or relieving pain in a number of illnesses such as cancer and AIDS. 2nd vote as required by law.	Passed

Nevada Constitution

Article 19

Section 1. Referendum for approval or disapproval of statute or resolution enacted by legislature.

1. A person who intends to circulate a petition that a statute or resolution or part thereof enacted by the legislature be submitted to a vote of the people, before circulating the petition for signatures, shall file a copy thereof with the secretary of state. He shall file the copy not earlier than August 1 of the year before the year in which the election will be held.

2. Whenever a number of registered voters of this state equal to 10 percent or more of the number of voters who voted at the last preceding general election shall express their wish by filing with the secretary of state, not less than 120 days before the next general election, a petition in the form provided for in section 3 of this article that any statute or resolution or any part thereof enacted by the legislature be submitted to a vote of the people, the officers charged with the duties of announcing and proclaiming elections and of certifying nominations or questions to be voted upon shall submit the question of approval or disapproval of such statute or resolution or any part thereof to a vote of the voters at the next succeeding election at which such question may be voted upon by the registered voters of the entire state. The circulation of the petition shall cease on the day the petition is filed with the secretary of state or such other date as may be prescribed for the verification of the number of signatures affixed to the petition, whichever is earliest.

3. If a majority of the voters voting upon the proposal submitted at such election votes approval of such statute or resolution or any part thereof, such statute or resolution or any part thereof shall stand as the law of the state and shall not be amended, annulled, repealed, set aside, suspended or in any way made inoperative except by the direct vote of the peo-

ple. If a majority of such voters votes disapproval of such statute or resolution or any part thereof, such statute or resolution or any part thereof shall be void and of no effect.

Sec. 2. Initiative petition for enactment or amendment of statute or amendment of constitution.

1. Notwithstanding the provisions of section 1 of article 4 of this constitution, but subject to the limitations of section 6 of this article, the people reserve to themselves the power to propose, by initiative petition, statutes and amendments to statutes and amendments to this constitution, and to enact or reject them at the polls.

2. An initiative petition shall be in the form required by section 3 of this article and shall be proposed by a number of registered voters equal to 10 percent or more of the number of voters who voted at the last preceding general election in not less than 75 percent of the counties in the state, but the total number of registered voters signing the initiative petition shall be equal to 10 percent or more of the voters who voted in the entire state at the last preceding general election.

3. If the initiative petition proposes a statute or an amendment to a statute, the person who intends to circulate it shall file a copy with the secretary of state before beginning circulation and not earlier than January 1 of the year preceding the year in which a regular session of the legislature is held. After its circulation, it shall be filed with the secretary of state not less than 30 days prior to any regular session of the legislature. The circulation of the petition shall cease on the day the petition is filed with the secretary of state or such other date as may be prescribed for the verification of the number of signatures affixed to the petition, whichever is earliest. The secretary of state shall transmit such petition to the legislature as soon as the legislature convenes and organizes. The petition shall take precedence over all other measures except appropriation bills, and the statute or amendment to a statute proposed thereby shall be enacted or rejected by the legislature without change or amendment within 40 days. If the proposed statute or amendment to a statute is enacted by the legislature and approved by the governor in the same manner as other statutes are enacted, such statute or amendment to a statute shall become law, but shall be subject to referendum petition as provided in section 1 of this article. If the statute or amendment to a statute is rejected by the legislature, or if no action is taken thereon within 40 days, the secretary of state shall submit the question of approval or disapproval of such statute or amendment to a statute to a vote of the voters at the next succeeding general election. If a majority of the voters voting on such question at such election votes approval of such statute or amendment to a statute, it shall become law and take effect upon completion of the canvass of votes by the supreme court. An initiative measure so approved by the voters shall not be amended, annulled, repealed, set aside or suspended by the legislature within 3 years from the date it takes effect. If a majority of such voters votes disapproval of such statute or amendment to a statute, no further action shall be taken on such petition. If the legislature rejects such proposed statute or amendment, the governor may recommend to the legislature and the legislature may propose a different measure on the same subject, in which event, after such different measure has been approved by the governor, the question of approval or disapproval of each measure shall be submitted by the secretary of state to a vote of the voters at the next succeeding general election. If the conflicting provisions submitted to the voters are both approved by a majority of the voters voting on such measures, the measure which receives the largest number of affirmative votes shall thereupon become law.

4. If the initiative petition proposes an amendment to the constitution, the person who intends to circulate it shall file a copy with the secretary of state before beginning circulation and not earlier than September 1 of the year before the year in which the election is to be held. After its circulation it shall be filed with the secretary of state not less than 90 days before any regular general election at which the question of approval or disapproval of such amendment may be voted upon by the voters of the entire state. The circulation of the petition shall cease on the day the petition is filed with the secretary of state or such other date as may be prescribed for the verification of the number of signatures affixed to the petition, whichever is earliest. The secretary of state shall cause to be published in a newspaper of general circulation, on three separate occasions, in each county in the state, together with any explanatory matter which shall be placed upon the ballot, the entire text of the proposed amendment. If a majority of the voters voting on such question at such election votes disapproval of such amendment, no further action shall be taken on the petition. If a majority of such voters votes approval of such amendment, the secretary of state shall publish and resubmit the question of approval or disapproval to a vote of the voters at the next succeeding general election in the same manner as such question was originally submitted. If a majority of such voters votes disapproval of such amendment, no further action shall be taken on such petition. If a majority of such voters votes approval of such amendment, it shall become a part of this constitution upon completion of the canvass of votes by the supreme court.

5. If two or more measures which affect the same section of a statute or of the constitution are finally approved pursuant to this section, or an amendment to the constitution is finally so approved and an amendment proposed by the legislature is ratified which affect the same section, by the voters at the same election:

(a) If all can be given effect without contradiction in substance, each shall be given effect.

(b) If one or more contradict in substance the other or others, the measure which received the largest favorable vote, and any other approved measure compatible with it, shall be given effect. If the one or more measures that contradict in substance the other or others receive the same number of favorable votes, none of the measures that contradict another shall be given effect.

6. If, at the same election as the first approval of a constitutional amendment pursuant to this section, another amendment is finally approved pursuant to this section, or an amendment proposed by the legislature is ratified, which affects the same section of the constitution but is compatible with the amendment given first approval, the secretary of state shall publish and resubmit at the next general election the amendment given first approval as a further amendment to the section as amended by the amendment given final approval or ratified. If the amendment finally approved or ratified contradicts in substance the amendment given first approval, the secretary of state shall not submit the amendment given first approval to the voters again.

Sec. 3. Referendum and initiative petitions: Contents and form; signatures; enacting clause; manner of verification of signatures.

1. Each referendum petition and initiative petition shall include the full text of the measure proposed. Each signer shall affix thereto his or her signature, residence address and the name of the county in which he or she is a registered voter. The petition may consist of more than one document, but each document shall have affixed thereto an affidavit made by one of the signers of such document to the effect that all of the signatures are genuine and that each individual who signed such document was at the time of signing a registered voter in the county of his or her residence. The affidavit shall be executed before a person authorized by law to administer oaths in the State of Nevada. The enacting clause of all statutes or amendments proposed by initiative petition shall be: "The People of the State of Nevada do enact as follows:"

2. The legislature may authorize the secretary of state and the other public officers to use generally accepted statistical procedures in conducting a preliminary verification of the number of signatures submitted in connection with a referendum petition or an initiative petition, and for this purpose to require petitions to be filed no more than 65 days earlier than is otherwise required by this article.

Sec. 4. Powers of initiative and referendum of registered voters of counties and municipalities.

The initiative and referendum powers provided for in this article are further reserved to the registered voters of each county and each municipality as to all local, special and municipal legislation of every kind in or for such county or municipality. In counties and municipalities initiative petitions may be instituted by a number of registered voters equal to 15 percent or more of the voters who voted at the last preceding general county or municipal election. Referendum petitions may be instituted by 10 percent or more of such voters.

Sec. 5. Provisions of article self-executing; legislative procedures.

The provisions of this article are self-executing but the legislature may provide by law for procedures to facilitate the operation thereof.

Nevada Statutes

Chapter 293 Circulation and Sufficiency of Certain Petitions

NRS 293.12756 Informational pamphlet concerning petitions; fee.

1. The secretary of state shall prepare an informational pamphlet describing the requirements for filing and circulating petitions. The pamphlet must also contain a sample of a petition to demonstrate an acceptable format for a petition.

2. The pamphlets must be made available to the public and must be distributed to any person who requests a pamphlet upon payment of the applicable fee, if any. The secretary of state may impose a fee for the pamphlet in an amount not to exceed the cost to produce the pamphlet.
(Added to NRS by 1993, 2664)

NRS 293.12757 Qualification to sign petition.

A person may sign a petition required under the election laws of this state on or after the date he is deemed to be registered to vote pursuant to subsection 5 of NRS 293.517 or subsection 5 of NRS 293.5235.
(Added to NRS by 1999, 3546)

NRS 293.12758 Receipt issued by county clerk; requirements for petition.

1. The county clerk shall issue a receipt to any person who submits a petition for the verification of signatures or a petition, declaration of or acceptance of candidacy. The receipt must state:

(a) The number of documents submitted;

(b) The number of pages of each document; and

(c) The number of signatures which the person declares are on the petition.

2. If a petition consists of more than one document, all of the documents must be submitted to the county clerk for verification at the same time.

3. The county clerk shall not accept a petition unless each page of the petition is numbered.

4. Each signature on the petition must be signed in ink. The county clerk shall disregard any signature which is not signed in ink.

5. As used in this section, "document" includes material which is separately compiled and bound together and may consist of one or more sheets of paper.

(Added to NRS by 1993, 2664)

NRS 293.1276 County clerk to forward number of signatures to secretary of state; notice of failure to file required number of signatures; handling of petition.

1. Within 4 days, excluding Saturdays, Sundays and holidays, after the submission of a petition containing signatures which are required to be verified pursuant to NRS 293.128, 293.165, 293.172, 293.200, 295.056, 298.109, 306.035 or 306.110, the county clerk shall determine the total number of signatures affixed to the documents and forward that information to the secretary of state.

2. If the secretary of state finds that the total number of signatures filed with all the county clerks is less than 100 percent of the required number of registered voters, he shall so notify the person who submitted the petition and the county clerks and no further action may be taken in regard to the petition. If the petition is a petition to recall a county, district or municipal officer, the secretary of state shall also notify the officer with whom the petition is to be filed.

3. After the petition is submitted to the county clerk, it must not be handled by any other person except by an employee of the county clerk's office until it is filed with the secretary of state.

NRS 293.1277 Verification of signatures by county clerks.

1. If the secretary of state finds that the total number of signatures submitted to all the county clerks is 100 percent or more of the number of registered voters needed to declare the petition sufficient, he shall immediately so notify the county clerks. Within 9 days, excluding Saturdays, Sundays and holidays, after notification, each of the county clerks shall determine the number of registered voters who have signed the documents submitted in his county.

2. If more than 500 names have been signed on the documents submitted to him, a county clerk shall examine the signatures by sampling them at random for verification. The random sample of signatures to be verified must be drawn in such a manner that every signature which has been submitted to the county clerk is given an equal opportunity to be included in the sample. The sample must include an examination of at least 500 or 5 percent of the signatures, whichever is greater.

3. In determining from the records of registration the number of registered voters who signed the documents, the county clerk may use the signatures contained in the file of applications to register to vote. If the county clerk uses that file, he shall ensure that every application in the file is examined, including any application in his possession which may not yet be entered into his records. The county clerk shall rely only on the appearance of the signature and the address and date included with each signature in making his determination.

4. Except as otherwise provided in subsection 6, upon completing the examination, the county clerk shall immediately attach to the documents a certificate properly dated, showing the result of his examination and transmit the documents with the certificate to the secretary of state. A copy of this certificate must be filed in the clerk's office.

5. A person who submits a petition to the county clerk which is required to be verified pursuant to NRS 293.128, 293.165, 293.172, 293.200, 295.056, 298.109, 306.035 or 306.110 must be allowed to witness the verification of the signatures. A public officer who is the subject of a recall petition must also be allowed to witness the verification of the signatures on the petition.

6. For any petition containing signatures which are required to be verified pursuant to the provisions of NRS 293.165, 293.200, 306.035 or 306.110 for any county, district or municipal office within one county, the county clerk shall not transmit to the secretary of state the documents containing the signatures of the registered voters.

7. The secretary of state may by regulation establish further procedures for carrying out the provisions of this section.

(Added to NRS by 1985, 1090; A 1987, 1361; 1993, 2665; 1995, 2257; 1997, 750; 1999, 2147)

NRS 293.1278 Qualification or disqualification of petition upon receipt of certificates by secretary of state.

1. If the certificates received by the secretary of state from all the county clerks establish that the number of valid signatures is less than 90 percent of the required number of registered voters, the petition shall be deemed to have failed to qualify, and the secretary of state shall immediately so notify the petitioners and the county clerks.

2. If those certificates establish that the petitioners have more than 100 percent of the number of registered voters needed to make the petition sufficient, the petition shall be deemed to qualify as of the date of receipt by the secretary of state of certificates showing the petition to have reached 100 percent, and the secretary of state shall immediately so notify the petitioners and the county clerks.

(Added to NRS by 1985, 1091; A 1993, 2666)

NRS 293.1279 Qualification or disqualification of petition upon verification of signatures.

1. If the statistical sampling shows that the number of valid signatures filed is 90 percent or more but less than 100 percent of the number of signatures of registered voters needed to declare the petition sufficient, the secretary of state shall order the county clerks to examine the signatures for verification. The county clerks shall examine the signatures for verification until they determine that 100 percent of the number of signatures of registered voters needed to declare the petition sufficient are valid.

2. If the statistical sampling shows that the number of valid signatures filed in any county is 90 percent or more but less than 100 percent of the number of signatures of registered voters needed to constitute 10 percent of the number of voters who voted at the last preceding general election in that county, the secretary of state may order the county clerk in that county to examine every signature for verification.

3. Within 12 days, excluding Saturdays, Sundays and holidays, after receipt of such an order, the clerk shall determine from the records of registration what number of registered voters have signed the petition. If necessary, the board of county commissioners shall allow the county clerk additional assistants for examining the signatures and provide for their compensation. In determining from the records of registration what number of registered voters have signed the petition, the clerk may use any file or list of registered voters maintained by his office or facsimiles of voters' signatures. The county clerk may rely on the appearance of the signature and the address and date included with each signature in determining the number of registered voters that signed the petition.

4. Except as otherwise provided in subsection 5, upon completing the examination, the county clerk shall immediately attach to the documents of the petition an amended certificate properly dated, showing the result of the examination and shall immediately forward the documents with the amended certificate to the secretary of state. A copy of the amended certificate must be filed in the county clerk's office.

5. For any petition containing signatures which are required to be verified pursuant to the provisions of NRS 293.165, 293.200, 306.035 or 306.110 for any county, district or municipal office within one county, the county clerk shall not forward to the secretary of state the documents containing the signatures of the registered voters.

6. Except for a petition to recall a county, district or municipal officer, the petition shall be deemed filed with the secretary of state as of the date on which he receives certificates from the county clerks showing the petition to be signed by the requisite number of voters of the state.

7. If the amended certificates received from all county clerks by the secretary of state establish that the petition is still insufficient, he shall immediately so notify the petitioners and the county clerks. If the petition is a petition to recall a county, district or municipal officer, the secretary of state shall also notify the officer with whom the petition is to be filed.

(Added to NRS by 1985, 1091; A 1985, 551; 1987, 1362; 1993, 2666; 1997, 751; 1999, 2148)

NRS 293.12793 Appeal with secretary of state contesting verification of votes; notification of public officer who is subject of petition to recall; consideration and investigation of allegations.

1. If the secretary of state determines that the total number of signatures that the county clerks have certified pursuant to NRS 293.1277 or 293.1279 is less than 100 percent of the number of registered voters needed to make the petition sufficient, the person who submitted the petition may contest the verification of the signatures by filing an appeal with the secretary of state. The appeal must:

(a) Be filed within 5 working days after receipt of notification of the determination of the secretary of state;

(b) Include each reason for the appeal; and

(c) Include a statement of the number of signatures, if any, that the county clerk determined were invalid.

2. The secretary of state shall:

(a) If the petition was circulated pursuant to chapter 306 of NRS, immediately notify the public officer who is the subject of the petition of the appeal by the person who submitted the petition; and

(b) Consider the allegations and conduct an investigation, if necessary.
(Added to NRS by 1993, 2664; A 1997, 752; 1999, 3546)

NRS 293.12795 Action by secretary of state upon review of appeal; judicial review of decision of secretary of state.

1. If an appeal is based upon the results of the verification of signatures on a petition performed pursuant to NRS 293.1277 or 293.1279, the secretary of state shall:
(a) If he finds for the appellant, order the county clerk to recertify the petition, including as verified signatures all contested signatures which the secretary of state determines are valid.
(b) If he does not find for the appellant, notify the appellant and the county clerk that the petition remains insufficient.
2. If the secretary of state is unable to make a decision on the appeal based upon the documents submitted to him, the secretary of state may order the county clerk to reverify the signatures.
3. The decision of the secretary of state is a final decision for the purposes of judicial review. The decision of the secretary of state may only be appealed in the first judicial district court.
(Added to NRS by 1993, 2664)

Chapter 295 — Initiative and Referendum

NRS 295.015 Copy of petition for initiative to be filed with secretary of state before presentation of petition to voters for signatures.

A copy of a petition for initiative must be placed on file in the office of the secretary of state before it may be presented to the registered voters for their signatures.
(Added to NRS by 1963, 1384; A 1981, 12; 1985, 1112)

NRS 295.035 Petition for initiative proposing amendment to constitution: Secretary of state to use same number for identification of petition when submitted at successive elections.

If the initiative petition proposes an amendment to the constitution, in resubmitting the initiative to the voters, the secretary of state shall use the same identifying number or other identification used for the first submission.
(Added to NRS by 1963, 1384; A 1973, 332; 1985, 550)

NRS 295.045 Petition for referendum: Filing; submission to voters at general election.

1. A copy of a petition for referendum must be placed on file in the office of the secretary of state before it may be presented to the registered voters for their signatures.
2. A petition for referendum must be filed with the secretary of state not less than 120 days before the date of the next succeeding general election.
3. The secretary of state shall certify the questions to the county clerks, and they shall publish them in accordance with the provisions of law requiring county clerks to publish questions and proposed constitutional amendments which are to be submitted for popular vote.
4. The title of the statute or resolution must be set out on the ballot, and the question printed upon the ballot for the information of the voters must be as follows: "Shall the statute (setting out its title) be approved?".
5. Where a mechanical voting system is used, the title of the statute must appear on the list of offices and candidates and the statements of measures to be voted on and may be condensed to no more than 25 words.
6. The votes cast upon the question must be counted and canvassed as the votes for state officers are counted and canvassed.
(Added to NRS by 1963, 1383; A 1977, 247; 1979, 268; 1981, 13; 1985, 1112)

NRS 295.055 Petition for initiative or referendum: Regulations specifying format; each document of petition limited to voters of single county; removal of name from petition.

1. The secretary of state shall by regulation specify:
(a)The format for the signatures on a petition for an initiative or referendum and make free specimens of the format available upon request. Each signature must be dated.
(b) The manner of fastening together several sheets circulated by one person to constitute a single document.
2. Each document of the petition must bear the name of a county, and only registered voters of that county may sign the document.
3. A person who signs a petition may remove his name from it by transmitting his request in writing to the county clerk at any time before the petition is filed with the county clerk.
(Added to NRS by 1963, 1385; A 1985, 550; 1987, 1374)

NRS 295.056 Petition for initiative or referendum: Requirements for submission of signatures to county clerk.

1. Before a petition for initiative or referendum is filed with the secretary of state, the petitioners must submit to each county clerk for verification pursuant to NRS 293.1276 to 293.1279, inclusive, the document or documents which were circulated for signature within his county. The clerks shall give the person submitting a document or documents a receipt stating the number of documents and pages and the person's statement of the number of signatures contained therein.

2. If a petition for initiative proposes a statute or an amendment to a statute, the document or documents must be submitted not later than the second Tuesday in November of an even-numbered year.

3. If a petition for initiative proposes an amendment to the constitution, the document or documents must be submitted not later than the third Tuesday in June of an even-numbered year.

4. If the petition is for referendum, the document or documents must be submitted not later than the third Tuesday in May of an even-numbered year.

5. All documents which are submitted to a county clerk for verification must be submitted at the same time.
(Added to NRS by 1983, 923; A 1985, 551, 1113; 1991, 2226; 1993, 2669; 1999, 3560)

NRS 295.061 Challenge to legal sufficiency of petition.

The legal sufficiency of a petition filed pursuant to NRS 295.015 to 295.061, inclusive, may be challenged by filing a complaint in district court not later than 5 days, Saturdays, Sundays and holidays excluded, after the petition is filed with the secretary of state. All affidavits and documents in support of the challenge must be filed with the complaint. The court shall set the matter for hearing not later than 30 days after the complaint is filed and shall give priority to such a complaint over all other matters pending with the court, except for criminal proceedings.
(Added to NRS by 1999, 3560)

County Initiative and Referendum

NRS 295.075 "Board" defined.

As used in NRS 295.075 to 295.125, inclusive, unless the context otherwise requires, "board" means the board of county commissioners.
(Added to NRS by 1967, 380; A 1999, 2120)

NRS 295.085 Registered voters' power of initiative and referendum concerning county ordinances.

The registered voters of a county may:

1. Propose ordinances to the board and, if the board fails to adopt an ordinance so proposed without change in substance, to adopt or reject it at a primary or general election.

2. Require reconsideration by the board of any adopted ordinance and, if the board fails to repeal an ordinance so reconsidered, to approve or reject it at a primary or general election.
(Added to NRS by 1967, 380; A 1993, 1032)

NRS 295.095 Commencement of proceedings: Petitioners' committee; form and requirements of petition; circulator's affidavit; receipt for petition issued by clerk.

1. Any five registered voters of the county may commence initiative or referendum proceedings by filing with the county clerk an affidavit stating they will constitute the petitioners' committee and be responsible for circulating the petition and filing it in proper form, stating their names and addresses and specifying the address to which all notices to the committee are to be sent, and setting out in full the proposed initiative ordinance or citing the ordinance sought to be reconsidered.

2. Initiative petitions must be signed by a number of registered voters of the county equal to 15 percent or more of the number of voters who voted at the last preceding general election in the county.

3. Referendum petitions must be signed by a number of registered voters of the county equal to 10 percent or more of the number of voters who voted at the last preceding general election in the county.

4. A petition must be filed not later than:

(a) One hundred and eighty days after the date that the affidavit required by subsection 1 is filed with the county clerk; or

(b) One hundred days before the election, whichever is earlier.

5. A petition may consist of more than one document, but all documents of a petition must be uniform in size and style, numbered and assembled as one instrument for filing. Each signature must be executed in ink or indelible pencil and

followed by the address of the person signing and the date on which he signed the petition. All signatures on a petition must be obtained within the period specified in paragraph (a) of subsection 4. Each document must contain or have attached thereto throughout its circulation the full text of the ordinance proposed or sought to be reconsidered.

6. Each document of a petition must have attached to it when filed an affidavit executed by the circulator thereof stating:

(a) That he personally circulated the document;

(b) The number of signatures thereon;

(c) That all the signatures were affixed in his presence;

(d) That he believes them to be genuine signatures of the persons whose names they purport to be; and

(e) That each signer had an opportunity before signing to read the full text of the ordinance proposed or sought to be reconsidered.

7. The county clerk shall issue a receipt to any person who submits a petition pursuant to this section. The receipt must set forth the number of:

(a) Documents included in the petition;

(b) Pages in each document; and

(c) Signatures that the person declares are included in the petition.

(Added to NRS by 1967, 380; A 1989, 1182; 1997, 2787)

NRS 295.105 Filing, examination, certification and amendment of petition; court and board to review sufficiency of petition.

1. Within 20 days after the petition is filed, the county clerk shall complete a certificate as to its sufficiency, specifying, if it is insufficient, the particulars wherein it is defective and shall promptly send a copy of the certificate to the petitioners' committee by registered or certified mail.

2. A petition must not be certified insufficient for lack of the required number of valid signatures if, in the absence of other proof of disqualification, any signature on the face thereof does not exactly correspond with the signature appearing on the official register of voters and the identity of the signer can be ascertained from the face of the petition. A petition certified insufficient for lack of the required number of valid signatures may be amended once if the petitioners' committee files a notice of intention to amend it with the county clerk within 2 days after receiving the copy of his certificate and files a supplementary petition upon additional papers within 10 days after receiving the copy of the certificate. A supplementary petition must comply with the requirements of subsections 5 and 6 of NRS 295.095, and within 5 days after it is filed the county clerk shall complete a certificate as to the sufficiency of the petition as amended and promptly send a copy of the certificate to the petitioners' committee by registered or certified mail.

3. If a petition or amended petition is certified sufficient, or if a petition or amended petition is certified insufficient and the petitioners' committee does not elect to amend or request board review under subsection 4 within the time required, the county clerk shall promptly present his certificate to the board and the certificate is a final determination as to the sufficiency of the petition.

4. If a petition has been certified insufficient and the petitioners' committee does not file notice of intention to amend it or if an amended petition has been certified insufficient, the committee may, within 2 days after receiving a copy of the certificate, file a request that it be reviewed by the board. The board shall review the certificate at its next meeting following the filing of the request and approve or disapprove it, and the determination of the board is a final determination as to the sufficiency of the petition.

5. A final determination as to the sufficiency of a petition is subject to court review. A final determination of insufficiency, even if sustained upon court review, does not prejudice the filing of a new petition for the same purpose.

(Added to NRS by 1967, 380; A 1989, 1183)

NRS 295.115 Consideration by board; submission to registered voters; withdrawal of petition.

1. When an initiative or referendum petition has been finally determined sufficient, the board shall promptly consider the proposed initiative ordinance in the manner provided by law for the consideration of ordinances generally or reconsider the referred ordinance by voting its repeal. If the board fails to adopt a proposed initiative ordinance without any change in substance within 60 days or fails to repeal the referred ordinance within 30 days after the date the petition was finally determined sufficient, it shall submit the proposed or referred ordinance to the registered voters of the county.

2. The vote of the county on a proposed or referred ordinance must be held at the next primary or general election. Copies of the proposed or referred ordinance must be made available at the polls.

3. An initiative or referendum petition may be withdrawn at any time before the 30th day preceding the day scheduled for a vote of the county or the deadline for placing questions on the ballot, whichever is earlier, by filing with the county clerk a request for withdrawal signed by at least four members of the petitioners' original committee. Upon the filing of that request, the petition has no further effect and all proceedings thereon must be terminated.

(Added to NRS by 1967, 381; A 1969, 896; 1993, 1032)

NRS 295.121 Appointment of committee to prepare arguments advocating and opposing approval of ballot questions for county; duties of committee; regulations; review of arguments; placement of arguments in sample ballot.

1. In a county whose population is 50,000 or more, for each initiative, referendum or other question to be placed on the ballot by the board or county clerk, including, without limitation, pursuant to NRS 293.482, 295.115 or 295.160, the board shall, in consultation with the county clerk, pursuant to subsection 2, appoint a committee of six persons, three of whom are known to favor approval by the voters of the initiative, referendum or other question and three of whom are known to oppose approval by the voters of the initiative, referendum or other question. A person may serve on more than one committee. Members of the committee serve without compensation. The term of office for each member commences upon appointment and expires upon the publication of the sample ballot containing the initiative, referendum or other question.

2. Before the board appoints a committee pursuant to subsection 1, the county clerk shall:

(a) Recommend to the board persons to be appointed to the committee; and

(b) Consider recommending pursuant to paragraph (a):

(1) Any person who has expressed an interest in serving on the committee; and

(2) A person who is a member of an organization that has expressed an interest in having a member of the organization serve on the committee.

3. If the board of a county whose population is 50,000 or more fails to appoint a committee as required by subsection 1, the county clerk shall appoint the committee.

4. A committee appointed pursuant to this section:

(a) Shall elect a chairman for the committee;

(b) Shall meet and conduct its affairs as necessary to fulfill the requirements of this section;

(c) May seek and consider comments from the general public;

(d) Shall prepare an argument advocating approval by the voters of the initiative, referendum or other question, and prepare a rebuttal to that argument;

(e) Shall prepare an argument opposing approval by the voters of the initiative, referendum or other question, and prepare a rebuttal to that argument; and

(f) Shall submit the arguments and rebuttals prepared pursuant to paragraphs (d) and (e) to the county clerk not later than the date prescribed by the county clerk pursuant to subsection 5.

5. The county clerk of a county whose population is 50,000 or more shall provide, by rule or regulation:

(a) The maximum permissible length of an argument or rebuttal prepared pursuant to this section; and

(b) The date by which an argument or rebuttal prepared pursuant to this section must be submitted by the committee to the county clerk.

6. Upon receipt of an argument or rebuttal prepared pursuant to this section, the county clerk shall reject each statement in the argument or rebuttal that he believes is libelous or factually inaccurate. Not later than 5 days after the county clerk rejects a statement pursuant to this subsection, the committee may appeal that rejection to the district attorney. The district attorney shall review the statement and the reasons for its rejection and may receive evidence, documentary or testimonial, to aid him in his decision. Not later than 3 business days after the appeal by the committee, the district attorney shall issue his decision rejecting or accepting the statement. The decision of the district attorney is a final decision for the purposes of judicial review.

7. The county clerk shall place in the sample ballot provided to the registered voters of the county each argument and rebuttal prepared pursuant to this section, containing all statements that were not rejected pursuant to subsection 6. The county clerk may revise the language submitted by the committee so that it is clear, concise and suitable for incorporation in the sample ballot, but shall not alter the meaning or effect without the consent of the committee.

8. In a county whose population is less than 50,000:

(a) The board may appoint a committee pursuant to subsection 1.

(b) If the board appoints a committee, the county clerk shall provide for rules or regulations pursuant to subsection 5.

(Added to NRS by 1999, 2118)

NRS 295.125 Results of election.

1. If a majority of the registered voters voting on a proposed initiative ordinance vote in its favor, it shall be considered adopted upon certification of the election results and shall be treated in all respects in the same manner as ordinances of the same kind adopted by the council. If conflicting ordinances are approved at the same election, the one receiving the greatest number of affirmative votes shall prevail to the extent of such conflict.

2. If a majority of the registered voters voting on a referred ordinance vote against it, it shall be considered repealed upon certification of the election results.
(Added to NRS by 1967, 382)

County Referendum Concerning Specific Legislative Acts or Resolutions

NRS 295.140 Petition for referendum: Required signatures; filing.

Whenever 10 percent or more of the registered voters of any county of this state, as shown by the number of registered voters who voted at the last preceding general election, express their wish that any act or resolution enacted by the legislature, and pertaining to that county only, be submitted to the vote of the people, they shall file with the county clerk, not less than 4 months before the time set for the next succeeding general election, a petition, which must contain the names and residence addresses of at least 10 percent of the registered voters of that county, demanding that a referendum vote be had by the people of the county at the next primary or general election upon the act or resolution on which the referendum is demanded.
(Added to NRS by 1960, 280; A 1993, 1033)

NRS 295.150 Names of registered voters may be contained in more than one petition; verification of petition.

1. The names of the registered voters petitioning need not be all upon one petition, but may be contained on one or more petitions; but each petition shall be verified by at least one of the voters who has signed such petition.
2. The voter making the verification shall swear, on information and belief, that the persons signing the petition are registered voters of the county and state, and that such signatures are genuine and were executed in his presence.
(Added to NRS by 1960, 280)

NRS 295.160 Submission of question to people; publication.

1. The county clerk shall file the petition upon its receipt by him. At the next primary or general election he shall submit the act or resolution, by appropriate questions on the ballot, for the approval or disapproval of the people of that county.
2. The county clerk shall publish those questions in accordance with the provisions of law requiring county clerks to publish questions and proposed constitutional amendments which are to be submitted for popular vote.
(Added to NRS by 1960, 280; A 1993, 1033)

NRS 295.170 Form of question on ballot; count and canvass of votes.

1. The subject matter of such questions must be stated concisely on the ballot, and the question printed upon the ballot for the information of the voter must be as follows: "Shall the act (setting out the title thereof) be approved?"
2. Where a mechanical voting system is used, the title of the act must appear on the list of offices and candidates and the statements of measures to be voted on and may be condensed by the district attorney to 20 words.
3. The district attorney shall prepare an explanation of each such question, which must be placed on the ballot or the list of offices and candidates and the statements of measures to be voted on, or posted in the polling place.
4. The votes cast upon such question must be counted and canvassed as the votes for county officers are counted and canvassed.
(Added to NRS by 1960, 281; A 1967, 1226; 1977, 248; 1985, 1114)

NRS 295.180 Effect of approval or disapproval of majority of registered voters.

1. When a majority of the registered voters of the county voting upon the question submitted, by their vote, approve the act or resolution, it is the law of the state, and may not be repealed, overruled, annulled, set aside or in any way made inoperative, except by a direct vote of the registered voters of that county.
2. When a majority of the registered voters of that county voting upon the question submitted disapproves, the act or resolution is void.
(Added to NRS by 1960, 281; A 1987, 1374)

Municipal Initiative and Referendum

NRS 295.195 Definitions.

As used in NRS 295.195 to 295.220, inclusive, unless the context otherwise requires:
1. "City" means an incorporated city.
2. "Council" means the governing body of a city.

(Added to NRS by 1967, 377; A 1987, 1719; 1999, 2120)

NRS 295.200 Registered voters' power of initiative and referendum concerning city ordinances.

The registered voters of a city may:

1. Propose ordinances to the council and, if the council fails to adopt an ordinance so proposed without change in substance, adopt or reject it at the next primary or general city election or primary or general election.

2. Require reconsideration by the council of any adopted ordinance and, if the council fails to repeal an ordinance so reconsidered, approve or reject it at the next primary or general city election or primary or general election.

(Added to NRS by 1967, 378; A 1987, 364; 1993, 1033)

NRS 295.205 Commencement of proceedings: Petitioners' committee; form and requirements of petition; circulator's affidavit; receipt for petition issued by clerk.

1. Any five registered voters of the city may commence initiative or referendum proceedings by filing with the city clerk an affidavit:

(a) Stating they will constitute the petitioners' committee and be responsible for circulating the petition and filing it in proper form;

(b) Stating their names and addresses;

(c) Specifying the address to which all notices to the committee are to be sent; and

(d) Setting out in full the proposed initiative ordinance or citing the ordinance sought to be reconsidered.

2. Initiative petitions must be signed by a number of registered voters of the city equal to 15 percent or more of the number of voters who voted at the last preceding city election.

3. Referendum petitions must be signed by a number of registered voters of the city equal to 10 percent or more of the number of voters who voted at the last preceding city election.

4. A petition must be filed not later than:

(a) One hundred and eighty days after the date that the affidavit required by subsection 1 is filed with the city clerk; or

(b) One hundred days before the election,

whichever is earlier.

5. A petition may consist of more than one document, but all documents of a petition must be uniform in size and style, numbered and assembled as one instrument for filing. Each signature must be executed in ink or indelible pencil and followed by the address of the person signing and the date on which he signed the petition. All signatures on a petition must be obtained within the period specified in paragraph (a) of subsection 4. Each document must contain or have attached thereto throughout its circulation the full text of the ordinance proposed or sought to be reconsidered.

6. Each document of a petition must have attached to it when filed an affidavit executed by the circulator thereof stating:

(a) That he personally circulated the document;

(b) The number of signatures thereon;

(c) That all the signatures were affixed in his presence;

(d) That he believes them to be genuine signatures of the persons whose names they purport to be; and

(e) That each signer had an opportunity before signing to read the full text of the ordinance proposed or sought to be reconsidered.

7. The city clerk shall issue a receipt to any person who submits a petition pursuant to this section. The receipt must set forth the number of:

(a) Documents included in the petition;

(b) Pages in each document; and

(c) Signatures that the person declares are included in the petition.

(Added to NRS by 1967, 378; A 1987, 364; 1989, 1184; 1997, 2788)

NRS 295.210 Filing, examination, certification and amendment of petition; council and court to review sufficiency of petition.

1. Within 20 days after the petition is filed, the city clerk shall examine the signatures thereon, complete a certificate as to its sufficiency, specifying, if it is insufficient, the particulars wherein it is defective and shall promptly send a copy of the certificate to the petitioners' committee by registered or certified mail.

2. If more than 500 names are signed on the documents filed with him, the city clerk must examine the signatures by sampling them randomly for verification. The random sample of signatures to be verified must be drawn in such a manner that every signature which has been submitted to the city clerk is given an equal opportunity to be included in the sample. The sample must include an examination of at least 500 signatures or 5 percent of the signatures, whichever is greater.

3. A petition must not be certified insufficient for lack of the required number of valid signatures if, in the absence of other proof of disqualification, any signature on the face thereof does not exactly correspond with the signature appearing on the official register of voters and the identity of the signer can be ascertained from the face of the petition. A petition certified insufficient for lack of the required number of valid signatures may be amended once if the petitioners' committee files a notice of intention to amend it with the city clerk within 2 days after receiving the copy of his certificate and files a supplementary petition upon additional papers within 10 days after receiving the copy of the certificate. A supplementary petition must comply with the requirements of subsections 5 and 6 of NRS 295.205, and within 5 days after it is filed the city clerk shall complete a certificate as to the sufficiency of the petition as amended and promptly send a copy of the certificate to the petitioners' committee by registered or certified mail.

4. If a petition or amended petition is certified sufficient, or if a petition or amended petition is certified insufficient and the petitioners' committee does not elect to amend or request council review under subsection 5 within the time required, the city clerk must promptly present his certificate to the council and the certificate is a final determination as to the sufficiency of the petition.

5. If a petition has been certified insufficient and the petitioners' committee does not file notice of intention to amend it or if an amended petition has been certified insufficient, the committee may, within 2 days after receiving the copy of the certificate, file a request that it be reviewed by the council. The council shall review the certificate at its next meeting following the filing of the request and approve or disapprove it, and the council's determination is a final determination as to the sufficiency of the petition.

6. A final determination as to the sufficiency of a petition is subject to court review. A final determination of insufficiency, even if sustained upon court review, does not prejudice the filing of a new petition for the same purpose.
(Added to NRS by 1967, 378; A 1989, 1184)

NRS 295.215 Consideration by council; submission to registered voters; withdrawal of petition.

1. When an initiative or referendum petition has been finally determined sufficient, the council shall promptly consider the proposed initiative ordinance in the manner provided by law for the consideration of ordinances generally or reconsider the referred ordinance by voting its repeal. If the council fails to adopt a proposed initiative ordinance without any change in substance within 60 days or fails to repeal the referred ordinance within 30 days after the date the petition was finally determined sufficient, it shall submit the proposed or referred ordinance to the registered voters of the city.

2. The vote of the city on a proposed or referred ordinance must be held at the next primary or general city election or primary or general election. Copies of the proposed or referred ordinance must be made available at the polls.

3. An initiative or referendum petition may be withdrawn at any time before the 30th day preceding the day scheduled for a vote of the city or the deadline for placing questions on the ballot, whichever is earlier, by filing with the city clerk a request for withdrawal signed by at least four members of the petitioners' original committee. Upon the filing of that request the petition has no further effect and all proceedings thereon must be terminated.
(Added to NRS by 1967, 379; A 1969, 896; 1987, 364; 1993, 1033)

NRS 295.217 Appointment of committee to prepare arguments advocating and opposing approval of ballot questions for city; duties of committee; regulations; review of arguments; placement of arguments in sample ballot.

1. In a city whose population is 50,000 or more, for each initiative, referendum or other question to be placed on the ballot by the council, including, without limitation, pursuant to NRS 293.482 or 295.215, the council shall, in consultation with the city clerk, pursuant to subsection 2, appoint a committee of six persons, three of whom are known to favor approval by the voters of the initiative, referendum or other question and three of whom are known to oppose approval by the voters of the initiative, referendum or other question. A person may serve on more than one committee. Members of the committee serve without compensation. The term of office for each member commences upon appointment and expires upon the publication of the sample ballot containing the initiative, referendum or other question.

2. Before the council appoints a committee pursuant to subsection 1, the city clerk shall:
(a) Recommend to the council persons to be appointed to the committee; and
(b) Consider recommending pursuant to paragraph (a):
(1) Any person who has expressed an interest in serving on the committee; and
(2) A person who is a member of an organization that has expressed an interest in having a member of the organization serve on the committee.

3. If the council of a city whose population is 50,000 or more fails to appoint a committee as required by subsection 1, the city clerk shall appoint the committee.

4. A committee appointed pursuant to this section:
(a) Shall elect a chairman for the committee;
(b) Shall meet and conduct its affairs as necessary to fulfill the requirements of this section;

(c) May seek and consider comments from the general public;

(d) Shall prepare an argument advocating approval by the voters of the initiative, referendum or other question, and prepare a rebuttal to that argument;

(e) Shall prepare an argument opposing approval by the voters of the initiative, referendum or other question, and prepare a rebuttal to that argument; and

(f) Shall submit the arguments and rebuttals prepared pursuant to paragraphs (d) and (e) to the city clerk not later than the date prescribed by the city clerk pursuant to subsection 5.

5. The city clerk of a city whose population is 50,000 or more shall provide, by rule or regulation:

(a) The maximum permissible length of an argument or rebuttal prepared pursuant to this section; and

(b) The date by which an argument or rebuttal prepared pursuant to this section must be submitted by the committee to the city clerk.

6. Upon receipt of an argument or rebuttal prepared pursuant to this section, the city clerk shall reject each statement in the argument or rebuttal that he believes is libelous or factually inaccurate. Not later than 5 days after the city clerk rejects a statement pursuant to this subsection, the committee may appeal that rejection to the city attorney. The city attorney shall review the statement and the reasons for its rejection and may receive evidence, documentary or testimonial, to aid him in his decision. Not later than 3 business days after the appeal by the committee, the city attorney shall issue his decision rejecting or accepting the statement. The decision of the city attorney is a final decision for the purposes of judicial review.

7. The city clerk shall place in the sample ballot provided to the registered voters of the city each argument and rebuttal prepared pursuant to this section, containing all statements that were not rejected pursuant to subsection 6. The city clerk may revise the language submitted by the committee so that it is clear, concise and suitable for incorporation in the sample ballot, but shall not alter the meaning or effect without the consent of the committee.

8. In a city whose population is less than 50,000:

(a) The council may appoint a committee pursuant to subsection 1.

(b) If the council appoints a committee, the city clerk shall provide for rules or regulations pursuant to subsection 5.

(Added to NRS by 1999, 2119)

NRS 295.220 Results of election.

1. If a majority of the registered voters voting on a proposed initiative ordinance vote in its favor, it shall be considered adopted upon certification of the election results and shall be treated in all respects in the same manner as ordinances of the same kind adopted by the council. If conflicting ordinances are approved at the same election, the one receiving the greatest number of affirmative votes shall prevail to the extent of such conflict.

2. If a majority of the registered voters voting on a referred ordinance vote against it, it shall be considered repealed upon certification of the election results.

(Added to NRS by 1967, 379)

Nevada Administrative Code

295.020 NAC Content of multiple documents; documents consisting of multiple sheets. (NRS 293.124, 293.247)

If a petition for an initiative or referendum consists;

1. of more than one document, each document must contain the full text of the proposed measure and:

Include sequentially numbered spaces for:

The name of each person who signs the petition.

The signature of the person signing.

The street address of the residence where the person signing actually resides, unless a street address has not been assigned. If a street address has not been assigned, the document may contain the mailing address of the person signing.

The name of the county where the person who signs is a registered voter.

The date of the signature.

If the petition is a municipal initiative or referendum proposed pursuant to the provisions of NRS 295.195 to 295.220, inclusive, the name of the city in which the person who signs is registered to vote.

Have attached to it, when filed, an affidavit signed by the person who circulated the document in substantially the following form:

STATE OF NEVADA
COUNTY OF _____

I, _____, (print name), being first duly sworn under penalty of perjury, depose and say: (1) that I reside at (print street, city and state); (2) that I am 18 years of age or older; (3) that I personally circulated this document; (4) that all signatures were affixed in my presence; (5) that I believe them to be genuine signatures; and (6) that I believe each person who signed was at the time of signing a registered voter in the county of his residence.

Subscribed and sworn to or affirmed before me this ____ day of, ____. _____Signature of circulator

_____
Notary public or other person licensed to administer an oath

A document may consist of more than one sheet. If a document consists of more than one sheet:
Each sheet must be numbered sequentially;
All the sheets must be permanently attached together in numerical order; and
The affidavit of the circulator required by NRS 295.095 or 295.205 must appear on the last sheet of the document.
As used in this section, "petition" means a petition described in article 19 of the Nevada constitution or NRS 295.015 or 295.045.
(Added to NAC by Sec'y of State, eff. 7-18-88; A by R217-97, 5-26-98; R013-00, 4-4-2000)

295.040 NAC Disclosure of requirement for participation in constitutional convention. (NRS 293.124)

If passage of an initiative would require this state to participate in a constitutional convention called by the Congress of the United States, that fact must be stated on the first page of each document of the petition for the initiative in at least 12-point type when the petition is presented to registered voters for their signatures.

The Basic Steps to Do an Initiative in Nevada

Amendments and Statutes — Indirect Initiative Process (Statutes), Direct Initiative Process (Amendments)

Basic Procedures: Filing an initiative is a very simple process in Nevada. Prior to circulating a petition for signatures, a copy of the petition must be filed with the Secretary of State. The Secretary of State reviews the petition for acceptable format—but does not review or approve the legality of the language contained on the petition. Proponents are advised to obtain their own legal counsel to review the measure's language and content.

When the measure qualifies for the ballot, the Secretary of State writes the Ballot Summary and Ballot Question; and the Attorney General reviews and comments on both. While writing them, the Secretary of State holds public gathering to obtain input from proponents, opponents and the general public. There is no official process for challenging the Secretary of State's Title and Summary, other then challenging them in court.

Date Initiative language can be submitted to state for November 2002: For amendments, no sooner than early September 2001 for 2002 ballot. For statutes, no sooner than early January 2002 for 2004 ballot.

Signatures are tied to vote of which office: Votes cast in the last general election.

Next general election: 2002

Votes cast in last general election: 613,360

Net number of signatures required: For statutes and amendments, 10% of the total votes cast at the last general election. (61,366 signatures.) If the measure is a statute and enough valid signatures have been gathered, the Secretary of State transmits the petition to the legislature as soon as the legislature convenes. The Legislature has 40 days to enact or reject it. If the proposed statute is enacted by the legislature and approved by the Governor, it shall become law. If rejected, the Secretary of State submits the question of approval or disapproval of the statute to a vote at the next general election. If the measure is an amendment and enough valid signatures have been gathered, the Secretary of State submits the question of approval or disapproval the amendment to a vote at the next general election.

Distribution Requirement: 10% of total number of votes cast in the last general election in at least 13 out of the 17 counties.

Circulation period: 10 months for statutes, 11 months for constitutional amendments.

Do circulators have to be residents: Yes

Date when signatures are due for certification: For amendment, 90 days prior to the election (June 2002 for 2002 ballot). For statutes, 30 days prior to the convening of the legislature. (November 2000 for 2002 ballot, November 2002 for 2004 ballot.)

Signature verification process: Random Sampling

Single-subject restriction: No

Legislative tampering: Legislature can only repeal or amend after three years of enactment.

General Comments: Nevada requires that constitutional amendments adopted by initiative be voted on twice by the people before it can become law.

The Nevada Constitution does not permit the proposal of any statute or statutory amendment which makes an appropriation or otherwise requires the expenditure of money, unless such statute or amendment also imposes a sufficient tax, not prohibited by the constitution, or otherwise constitutionally provides for raising the necessary revenue.

New Hampshire

Initiative and referendum advocates were defeated at New Hampshire's 1902 constitutional convention by an overwhelming 250 to 40 vote of the delegates. George H. Duncan of East Joffrey, secretary of the New Hampshire Direct Legislation League in 1912, led an effort to pass I&R at the next state constitutional convention, but lost again by a vote of 166 to 156. Duncan attributed the defeat to the fact that "officials of the Concord and Montreal Railroad, a subsidiary of the Boston and Maine [Railroad], were using railroad money to defeat us."

New Hampshire Constitution

The state does not have the statewide initiative process and so therefore the following provisions discuss the procedures used by the state legislature to place constitutional amendments on the ballot.

[Art.] 100. [Alternate Methods of Proposing Amendments.]

Amendments to this constitution may be proposed by the general court or by a constitutional convention selected as herein provided.

(a) The senate and house of representatives, voting separately, may propose amendments by a three-fifths vote of the entire membership of each house at any session.

(b) The general court, by an affirmative vote of a majority of all members of both houses voting separately, may at any time submit the question "Shall there be a convention to amend or revise the constitution?" to the qualified voters of the state. If the question of holding a convention is not submitted to the people at some time during any period of ten years, it shall be submitted by the secretary of state at the general election in the tenth year following the last submission. If a majority of the qualified voters voting on the question of holding a convention approves it, delegates shall be chosen at the next regular general election, or at such earlier time as the legislature may provide, in the same manner and proportion as the representatives to the general court are chosen. The delegates so chosen shall convene at such time as the legislature may direct and may recess from time to time and make such rules for the conduct of their convention as they may determine.

(c) The constitutional convention may propose amendments by a three-fifths vote of the entire membership of the convention. Each constitutional amendment proposed by the general court or by a constitutional convention shall be submitted to the voters by written ballot at the next biennial November election and shall become a part of the Constitution only after approval by two-thirds of the qualified voters present and voting on the subject in the towns, wards, and unincorporated places.

New Jersey

It is ironic that New Jersey, the state where the national initiative and referendum movement originated, never adopted provisions for I&R. Certainly it was not for lack of enthusiasm among New Jersey's I&R supporters, including AFL founder Samuel Gompers. At that time the New Jersey branch of the federation, which endorsed I&R, represented 20,000 workers.

In December 1900 the *Direct Legislation Record* published the gloomy prediction of Clarence T. Atkinson that the reform had "no chance of success until the evil of bribery is abolished." By 1907, after 14 years of effort, the New Jersey Direct Legislation League had despaired of passing an amendment to give voters actual lawmaking power and instead sponsored a bill allowing voters to put non-binding, advisory initiatives on the state ballot. That proposal also failed again and again. In 1911 the I&R movement's journal *Equity* explained New Jersey's failure in terms of its being "the Trust State": the nation's biggest businesses were chartered there, and they were the major source of opposition to I&R.

A second attempt to adopt I&R was made at the state's 1947 constitutional convention with the strong support of organized labor, but again without success. Interest revived, however, during the mid-1970s, when the state chapters of Common Cause and the League of Women Voters began supporting I&R.

In 1981 initiative advocates in won state senate approval of an I&R bill by a 30 to 3 vote, but Democratic Party leaders in the assembly kept the bill bottled up in committee. The same thing happened in 1983: the bill received 32 to 4 approval in the senate but no vote at all in the assembly. In 1986, I&R advocates, led by Republican assemblyman (and former state Common Cause director) Richard Zimmer, pushed their bill through the assembly for the first time, but lost in the senate.

New Jersey Constitution

The state does not have the statewide initiative process and so therefore the following provisions discuss the procedures used by the state legislature to place constitutional amendments on the ballot.

Article IX

1. Any specific amendment or amendments to this Constitution may be proposed in the Senate or General Assembly. At least twenty calendar days prior to the first vote thereon in the house in which such amendment or amendments are first introduced, the same shall be printed and placed on the desks of the members of each house. Thereafter and prior to such vote a public hearing shall be held thereon. If the proposed amendment or amendments or any of them shall be agreed to by three-fifths of all the members of each of the respective houses, the same shall be submitted to the people. If the same or any of them shall be agreed to by less then three-fifths but nevertheless by a majority of all the members of each of the respective houses, such proposed amendment or amendments shall be referred to the Legislature in the next legislative year; and if in that year the same or any of them shall be agreed to by a majority of all the members of each of the respective houses, then such amendment or amendments shall be submitted to the people.
2. The proposed amendment or amendments shall be entered on the journal of each house with the yeas and nays of the members voting thereon.
3. The Legislature shall cause the proposed amendment or amendments to be published at least once in one or more newspapers of each county, if any be published therein, not less than three months prior to submission to the people.
4. The proposed amendment or amendments shall then be submitted to the people at the next general election in the manner and form provided by the Legislature.
5. If more than one amendment be submitted, they shall be submitted in such manner and form that the people may vote for or against each amendment separately and distinctly.

6. If the proposed amendment or amendments or any of them shall be approved by a majority of the legally qualified voters of the State voting thereon, the same shall become part of the Constitution on the thirtieth day after the election, unless otherwise provided in the amendment or amendments.

7. If at the election a proposed amendment shall not be approved, neither such proposed amendment nor one to effect the same or substantially the same change in the Constitution shall be submitted to the people before the third general election thereafter.

New Mexico

In 1910 statehood was just around the corner, and New Mexico voters elected delegates to a convention that drew up a constitution for the proposed new state.

Of the 100 delegates, initiative and referendum supporters included 23 Democrats, 19 Democrat-Populist "Fusionists," and at least a dozen independent Republicans: a majority of at least 54 percent. The *Albuquerque Journal* noted, however, that "every one of the candidates whom the Journal attacked as bosses, railroad attorneys, and corporation lawyers have [sic] been elected to the Constitutional Convention."

The Republican Party, which dominated the convention with 58 delegates, set up procedures so that its leaders—the anti-I&R "Old Guard"—ran the meeting. The independent Republicans were enticed to drop their push for I&R by a promise of support for their pet proposal, a constitutional provision mandating popular election of state supreme court justices and corporation commissioners. Once this was done, the Democrats and Fusionists knew that the Republican leaders could prevent I&R from even coming up for a vote. Rather than lose on both initiative and referendum, the Democrats and Fusionists decided to drop initiative and push for a referendum provision alone.

The referendum provision passed by a vote of 65 to 25 in October 1910. A month later the convention approved the entire constitution, which was then sent to the voters for ratification. It passed, although there was much public dissatisfaction with the lack of an initiative provision.

George Judson King, a leader of the national I&R movement who visited New Mexico while the convention was in progress, described the situation as typical: "It is the same story here as in every state, people for it, corporations against it, politicians trying to straddle the issue and save their scalps."

Between 1912 and 1988 only two referred measures qualified for the ballot (in 1950 and 1964). Both were sponsored by citizen groups seeking to overrule laws governing state nominating conventions. In both cases the majority of voters cast their ballots to uphold the enactments of the legislature.

New Mexico Constitution

The state does not have the statewide initiative process and so therefore the following provisions discuss the procedures used by the state legislature to place constitutional amendments on the ballot. However, New Mexico does have the popular referendum process. The provisions of this process are included as well.

Article IV

Sec. 1. [Vesting of legislative power; location of sessions; referendum on legislation.]

The legislative power shall be vested in a senate and house of representatives which shall be designated the legislature of the state of New Mexico, and shall hold its sessions at the seat of government.

The people reserve the power to disapprove, suspend and annul any law enacted by the legislature, except general appropriation laws; laws providing for the preservation of the public peace, health or safety; for the payment of the public debt or interest thereon, or the creation or funding of the same, except as in this constitution otherwise provided; for the maintenance of the public schools or state institutions, and local or special laws. Petitions disapproving any law other than those above excepted, enacted at the last preceding session of the legislature, shall be filed with the secretary of state not less than four months prior to the next general election. Such petitions shall be signed by not less than ten per centum of the qualified electors of each of three-fourths of the counties and in the aggregate by not less than ten per centum of the qualified electors of the state, as shown by the total number of votes cast at the last preceding general election. The question of the approval or rejection of such law shall be submitted by the secretary of state to the electorate at the next general election; and if a majority of the legal votes cast thereon, and not less than forty per centum of the total number of legal votes cast at such general election, be cast for the rejection of such law, it shall be annulled and thereby repealed with the same effect as if the legislature had then repealed it, and such repeal shall revive any law repealed by the act so annulled; otherwise, it shall remain in force unless subsequently repealed by the legislature. If such petition or petitions be signed by not less than twenty-five per centum of the qualified electors under each of the foregoing conditions, and be filed with the secretary of state within ninety days after the adjournment of the session of the legislature at which such law was enacted, the operation thereof shall be thereupon suspended and the question of its approval or rejection shall be likewise submitted to a vote at the next ensuing general election. If a majority of the votes cast thereon and not less than forty per centum of the total number of votes cast at such general election be cast for its rejection, it shall be thereby annulled; otherwise, it shall go into effect upon publication of the certificate of the secretary of state declaring the result of the vote thereon. It shall be a felony for any person to sign any such petition with any name other than his own, or to sign his name more than once for the same measure, or to sign such petition when he is not a qualified elector in the county specified in such petition; provided, that nothing herein shall be construed to prohibit the writing thereon of the name of any person who cannot write, and who signs the same with his mark. The legislature shall enact laws necessary for the effective exercise of the power hereby reserved.

Article XIX

Sec. 1. [Proposing and ratifying amendments.]

An amendment or amendments to this constitution may be proposed in either house of the legislature at a regular session; and if a majority of all members elected to each of the two houses voting separately votes in favor thereof, the proposed amendment or amendments shall be entered on their respective journals with the yeas and nays thereon. An amendment or amendments may also be proposed by an independent commission established by law for that purpose, and the amendment or amendments shall be submitted to the legislature for its review in accordance with the provisions of this section. The secretary of state shall cause any such amendment or amendments to be published in at least one newspaper in every county of the state, where a newspaper is published once each week, for four consecutive weeks, in English and Spanish when newspapers in both of said languages are published in such counties, the last publication to be not more than two weeks prior to the election at which time said amendment or amendments shall be submitted to the electors of the state for their approval or rejection; and shall further provide notice of the content and purpose of legislatively approved constitutional amendments in both English and Spanish to inform electors about the amendments in the time and manner provided by law. The secretary of state shall also make reasonable efforts to provide notice of the content and purpose of legislatively approved constitutional amendments in indigenous languages and to minority language groups to inform electors about the amendments. Amendments approved by the legislature shall be voted upon at the next regular election held after the adjournment of that legislature or at a special election to be held not less than six months after the adjournment of that legislature, at such time and in such manner as the legislature may by law provide. An amendment that is ratified by a majority of the electors voting on the amendment shall become part of this constitution. If two or more amendments are initiated by the legislature, they shall be so submitted as to enable the electors to vote on each of them separately. Amendments initiated by an independent commission created by law for that purpose may be submitted to the legislature separately or as a single ballot question, and any such commission-initiated amendments that are not substantially altered by the legislature may be submitted to the electors in the separate or single ballot question form recommended by the commission. No amendment shall restrict the rights created by Sections One and Three of Article VII hereof, on elective franchise, and Sections Eight and Ten of Article XII hereof, on education, unless it be proposed by vote of three-fourths of the members elected to each house and be ratified by a vote of the people of this state in an election at which at least three-fourths of the electors voting on the amendment vote in favor of that amendment. (As amended November 7, 1911 and November 5, 1996.)

Sec. 2. [Constitutional conventions.]

Whenever the legislature, by a two-thirds vote of the members elected to each house, deems it necessary to call a convention to revise or amend this constitution, they shall submit the question of calling such convention to the electors at the next general election, and if a majority of all the electors voting on such questions at said election in the state votes in favor of calling a convention, the legislature shall, at the next session, provide by law for calling the same. Such convention shall consist of at least as many delegates as there are members of the house of representatives. Revisions or amendments proposed by a constitutional convention shall be submitted to the voters of the state at an election held on a date set by the convention. The revisions or amendments proposed by the convention may be submitted in whole or in part, or with alternatives, as determined by the convention. If a majority vote favors a proposal or alternative, it is adopted and becomes effective thirty days after the certification of the election returns unless otherwise provided by the convention. (As amended November 7, 1911 and November 5, 1996.)

Sec. 3. [Initiative restricted.]

If this constitution be in any way so amended as to allow laws to be enacted by direct vote of the electors the laws which may be so enacted shall be only such as might be enacted by the legislature under the provisions of this constitution. (As amended November 7, 1911.)

Sec. 4. [Amendment of compact with United States.]

When the United States shall consent thereto, the legislature, by a majority vote of the members in each house, may submit to the people the question of amending any provision of Article XXI of this constitution on compact with the United States to the extent allowed by the act of congress permitting the same, and if a majority of the qualified electors who vote upon any such amendment shall vote in favor thereof the said article shall be thereby amended accordingly.

New York

In 1911 the I&R movement organ *Equity* explained the failure to win initiative and referendum rights in New York: "No Direct Legislationist has expected New York State to come into the fold until about the last. The 'interests' are so strong, so thoroly intrenched [sic], and have so much at stake in that state, that it is expected that their strongest fight against real popular control of public affairs will be made there."

In 1907 the attorney and "prominent club woman" Mrs. Harriet M. Johnston-Wood of New York City had helped organize the state Direct Legislation League. Hamilton Holt was elected President of the group. The League proved ineffective. In July 1909 *Equity* reported: "The introduction of I&R in the New York legislature seems to have been taken as a joke. It was referred to committee, and we find no other allusion to it."

In 1914 *Equity* told its readers that Tammany Hall's recent electoral defeat should help I&R, but later reported that despite the decline of New York City's machine, "the legislature in Albany was still sufficiently in the control of reactionary leaders not to take any definite action in favor of I&R."

By mid-1917, Buffalo's referendum provision was the only example of direct legislation in the state. Over the years the legislature proved willing to allow limited I&R in local jurisdictions, but never at the statewide level. The most important such I&R provision is the section of the New York City charter that allows voters to propose a charter amendment by petition of 50,000 registered voters, about 2 percent of the city's voters.

It was last successfully used in 1966 when police officers petitioned for—and voters approved—an amendment giving the police more control over the Civilian Review Board that had been set up to investigate citizens' complaints about the police. New Yorkers petitioned in the late 1960s for an anti-Vietnam War initiative and, in 1985, for an initiative to prohibit harboring ships with nuclear weapons, but state courts ruled against ballot placement on the ground that these were not proper subjects to go into the city charter.

In 1999, Governor George Pataki in his first "State of the State" address called for the establishment of the initiative and referendum process, however, the state legislature wasn't interested in supporting establishing the process. In 2002, Pataki once again called for the legislature to pass a constitutional amendment establishing the initiative and referendum process. The proposal was strongly supported by the state's Independence Party, Conservative Party and Republican Party. In April, the New York Senate passed the initiative amendment with only three dissenting votes. However, as of the writing of this history, the State Assembly had not acted on the Governor's proposal.

New York Constitution

The state does not have the statewide initiative process and so therefore the following provisions discuss the procedures used by the state legislature to place constitutional amendments on the ballot.

Article XIX

Section 1.

Any amendment or amendments to this constitution may be proposed in the senate and assembly whereupon such amendment or amendments shall be referred to the attorney-general whose duty it shall be within twenty days thereafter to render an opinion in writing to the senate and assembly as to the effect of such amendment or amendments upon other provisions of the constitution. Upon receiving such opinion, if the amendment or amendments as proposed or as amended shall be agreed to by a majority of the members elected to each of the two houses, such proposed amendment or amendments shall be entered on their journals, and the ayes and noes taken thereon, and referred to the next regular legislative session convening after the succeeding general election of members of the assembly, and shall be published for three months previous to the time of making such choice; and if in such legislative session, such proposed amendment or amendments shall be agreed to by a majority of all the members elected to each house, then it shall be the duty of the legislature to submit each proposed amendment or amendments to the people for approval in such manner and at such times as the legislature shall prescribe; and if the people shall approve and ratify such amendment or amendments by a majority of the electors voting thereon, such amendment or amendments shall become a part of the constitution on the first day of January next after such approval. Neither the failure of the attorney general to render an opinion concerning such a proposed amendment nor his failure to do so timely shall affect the validity of such proposed amendment or legislative action thereon.

Sec. 2.

At the general election to be held in the year nineteen hundred fifty-seven, and every twentieth year thereafter, and also at such times as the legislature may by law provide, the question "Shall there be a convention to revise the constitution and amend the same?" shall be submitted to and decided by the electors of the state; and in case a majority of the electors voting thereon shall decide in favor of a convention for such purpose, the electors of every senate district of the state, as then organized, shall elect three delegates at the next ensuing general election, and the electors of the state voting at the same election shall elect fifteen delegates-at-large. The delegates so elected shall convene at the capitol on the first Tuesday of April next ensuing after their election, and shall continue their session until the business of such convention shall have been completed. Every delegate shall receive for his services the same compensation as shall then be annually payable to the members of the assembly and be reimbursed for actual traveling expenses, while the convention is in session, to the extent that a member of the assembly would then be entitled thereto in the case of a session of the legislature. A majority of the convention shall constitute a quorum for the transaction of business, and no amendment to the constitution shall be submitted for approval to the electors as hereinafter provided, unless by the assent of a majority of all the delegates elected to the convention, the ayes and noes being entered on the journal to be kept. The convention shall have the power to appoint such officers, employees and assistants as it may deem necessary, and fix their compensation and to provide for the printing of documents, journal, proceedings and other expenses of said convention. The convention shall determine the rules of its own proceedings, choose its own officers, and be the judge of the election, returns and qualifications of its members. In case of a vacancy, by death, resignation or other cause, of any district delegate elected to the convention, such vacancy shall be filled by a vote of the remaining delegates representing the district in which such vacancy occurs. If such vacancy occurs in the office of a delegate-at-large, such vacancy shall be filled by a vote of the remaining delegates-at-large. Any proposed constitution or constitutional amendment which shall have been adopted by such convention, shall be submitted to a vote of the electors of the state at the time and in the manner provided by such convention, at an election which shall be held not less than six weeks after the adjournment of such convention. Upon the approval of such constitution or constitutional amendments, in the manner provided in the last preceding section, such constitution or constitutional amendment, shall go into effect on the first day of January next after such approval.

Sec. 3.

Any amendment proposed by a constitutional convention relating to the same subject as an amendment proposed by the legislature, coincidently submitted to the people for approval shall, if approved, be deemed to supersede the amendment so proposed by the legislature.

North Carolina

Though unsuccessful at the state level, initiative and referendum backers managed by 1917 to persuade the legislature to grant local I&R powers to the citizens of nine North Carolina cities.

In 1977 voters in Charlotte passed an initiative sponsored by civil rights activists to change the system of at-large city council elections (which had previously guaranteed domination of the council by white businessmen) to one of district representation. In Wilmington, voters put an initiative on the ballot for the first time in a special election held on June 29,1982. By a margin of nearly two to one, they approved an ordinance to change the zoning laws to prohibit construction of a planned coal storage facility.

North Carolina Constitution

The state does not have the statewide initiative process and so therefore the following provisions discuss the procedures used by the state legislature to place constitutional amendments on the ballot.

Article XIII

Sec. 1. Convention of the People.

No Convention of the People of this State shall ever be called unless by the concurrence of two-thirds of all the members of each house of the General Assembly, and unless the proposition "Convention or No Convention" is first submitted to the qualified voters of the State at the time and in the manner prescribed by the General Assembly. If a majority of the votes cast upon the proposition are in favor of a Convention, it shall assemble on the day prescribed by the General Assembly. The General Assembly shall, in the act submitting the convention proposition, propose limitations upon the authority of the Convention; and if a majority of the votes cast upon the proposition are in favor of a Convention, those limitations shall become binding upon the Convention. Delegates to the Convention shall be elected by the qualified voters at the time and in the manner prescribed in the act of submission. The Convention shall consist of a number of delegates equal to the membership of the House of Representatives of the General Assembly that submits the convention proposition and the delegates shall be apportioned as is the House of Representatives. A Convention shall adopt no ordinance not necessary to the purpose for which the Convention has been called.

Sec. 2. Power to revise or amend Constitution reserved to people.

The people of this State reserve the power to amend this Constitution and to adopt a new or revised Constitution. This power may be exercised by either of the methods set out hereinafter in this Article, but in no other way.

Sec. 3. Revision or amendment by Convention of the People.

A Convention of the People of this State may be called pursuant to Section 1 of this Article to propose a new or revised Constitution or to propose amendments to this Constitution. Every new or revised Constitution and every constitutional amendment adopted by a Convention shall be submitted to the qualified voters of the State at the time and in the manner prescribed by the Convention. If a majority of the votes cast thereon are in favor of ratification of the new or revised Constitution or the constitutional amendment or amendments, it or they shall become effective January first next after ratification by the qualified voters unless a different effective date is prescribed by the Convention.

Sec. 4. Revision or amendment by legislative initiation.

A proposal of a new or revised Constitution or an amendment or amendments to this Constitution may be initiated by the General Assembly, but only if three-fifths of all the members of each house shall adopt an act submitting the proposal to the qualified voters of the State for their ratification or rejection. The proposal shall be submitted at the time and in the manner prescribed by the General Assembly. If a majority of the votes cast thereon are in favor of the proposed new or revised Constitution or constitutional amendment or amendments, it or they shall become effective January first next after ratification by the voters unless a different effective date is prescribed in the act submitting the proposal or proposals to the qualified voters.

North Dakota

The father of the North Dakota initiative process was L. A. Ueland of Edgeley, a state legislator who served on the executive committee of the National Direct Legislation League from its founding in 1896. If Ueland was the father of the process, however, Katherine King of McKenzie was the mother. Mrs. King, married to Royal V. King, in 1902 organized a state chapter of the League. Mrs. King's League won passage of Ueland's I&R bill through both houses of the legislature in 1907, despite opposition from Prohibitionists who feared the possibility of an initiative to repeal the state's anti-liquor amendment.

The 1907 I&R amendment needed to be approved by the legislature twice, in two successive sessions with an election in between. In 1909 the legislature reversed itself and killed the I&R amendment. Mrs. King and Ueland pressed on nonetheless, and won the necessary legislative approvals in 1911 and 1913. The I&R amendment finally went to the voters for ratification in 1914 and passed.

The watershed event in North Dakota's century of statehood was the agrarian revolt of 1915-1916, which spawned the Non-Partisan League, one of the most successful state-level reform organizations in the nation's history. In that revolt, which was dramatized in the 1979 movie Northern Lights, farmers united against an unresponsive state government controlled by banks, railroads, and big grain dealers.

The League put seven constitutional amendment initiatives on the 1918 ballot. All seven passed by similar majorities of about 58 percent. Taken together, they brought about a revolutionary change in state government by:

• Reducing the number of signatures required for initiative petitions
• Forbidding the legislature to exempt any bills from referendum petitions
• Abolishing the requirement that proposed constitutional amendments be approved in two successive legislatures (in favor of a single approval)
• Authorizing the legislature to classify personal property for purposes of tax exemptions
• Authorizing the legislature to impose an acreage tax on land to insure crops against hail damage
• Authorizing the state to issue up to $10 million in bonds rather than the existing $200,000 limit, allowing mortgages on state industries
• Authorizing the state, counties, and cities to engage in business activities, thus clearing the way for bills that set up the state-owned bank, mill, and grain elevator, which continue to operate to the present day. Considered "socialistic" enterprises by critics, they provided a model for President Franklin D. Roosevelt's Tennessee Valley Authority.

Bankers and grain dealers sponsored an initiative backlash against the state-owned industries in 1920, gaining voter approval of measures requiring public audits of such industries, banning real estate loans by the state bank, and limiting state bank deposits to the assets of the state, rather than including local governments' assets. But North Dakotans in 1921 defeated four initiatives to further restrict the operations of state-owned industries, including one that would have abolished the state bank outright. In 1922 voters again confirmed their support for the state bank by approving an initiative doubling the state's bonded indebtedness limit so that the bank could make more farm loans.

A state record of 18 initiatives qualified for the ballot in 1932. Among the measures passed by voters were initiatives reducing property taxes, prohibiting crop mortgages, banning corporations from farming, reducing salaries of judges and state and local elected and appointed officials, reducing officials' travel expenses, and abolishing the requirement of published, public notice regarding auction of land to pay delinquent taxes.

In 1938, North Dakotans passed an initiative providing for pensions for senior citizens, and in 1940, they approved measures earmarking sales tax revenues for schools and welfare and increasing funding for financially distressed schools. In 1944, the voters initiated over $12 million worth of bonds to match federal funds for highway construction, and in 1948, they voted to ban parking meters. Notable initiatives passed in the 1950s include a conflict-of-interest measure prohibiting legislators from doing over $10,000 worth of business annually with the state or local governments (1954), and an initiative that set up a $1 million college student loan fund from state bank profits (1955). In 1962 voters struck a blow for ballot-box freedom by passing an initiative abolishing the requirement that they publicly state their party affiliation when they vote.

In 1963 Robert P. McCarney, a Bismarck auto dealer, sponsored three referendum petitions to block tax increase bills which just been approved by the legislature. Although the state's voters upheld each of the bills, McCarney was not about to give up. Years earlier, as chauffeur to Non-Partisan League Governor (and later U.S. Senator) William ("Wild Bill") Langer, McCarney had learned the value of tenacity in politics. Over the next 17 years, he sponsored 10 successful petition drives for initiatives or referendums on tax issues. In 1978 his initiative to lower the North Dakota income tax on individuals, but raise it for corporations, won—the capstone of his activist career. It is still said in state government circles that North Dakota's tax structure is more a product of McCarney than of the legislature.

In 1980, before he was elected to Congress, Byron Dorgan sponsored an initiative to more than double the tax on oil production (from 5 percent to 11.5 percent). Despite strong opposition from oil companies, it passed with 56 percent of the vote.

The other most hotly contested initiative of the state's history was a 1978 measure to establish a state agency to regulate health care costs. Sponsored by state Insurance Commissioner Byron Knudsen, it provoked intense opposition from hospitals' and doctors' organizations, which raised $175,000 for their effort to oppose it—a huge amount by North Dakota standards. Voters rejected the initiative by a three to one margin. Since 1978, numerous other issues have been voted on through the initiative process—term limits and environmental regulation—to name a few. However, even though North Dakota ranks as one of the top five most prolific initiative states since 1904, not a single statewide initiative has qualified for the ballot since 1998.

Statewide Initiative Usage

Number of Initiatives	Number Passed	Number Failed	Passage Rate
166	75	91	45%

Statewide Initiatives

Year	Measure Number	Type	Subject Matter	Description	Pass/Fail
1918	N/A	IDA	Administration of Government	Authorizing the state, counties, and cities to engage in business activities.	Passed
1918	N/A	IDA	Administration of Government	Authorizing the state to bond up to $10 million instead of $200,000 and providing for mortgages on state industries.	Passed
1918	N/A	IDA	Taxes	Authorizing the Legislature to impose an acreage tax on land to insure crops against hail damage.	Passed
1918	N/A	IDA	Taxes	Authorizing the Legislature to classify personal property for purposes of exemptions.	Passed
1918	N/A	IDA	Initiative and Referendum	Amending provision for initiative and referendum by changing required signatures to 10,000 for initiating a statutory measure; to 7,000 for referring legislation actions; and providing that initiated measures would go directly to a vote of the people.	Passed
1918	N/A	IDA	Initiative and Referendum	Providing for submission of constitutional amendments to people by simple majority vote of one legislative session, and providing for initiated constitutional amendments with 20,000 signatures.	Passed
1918	N/A	IDA	Administration of Government	Forbidding the Legislature to grant a franchise or special interest as an emergency measure.	Passed
1920	N/A	DS	Administration of Government	Requiring an examination of state industrial institutions twice yearly by a state Board of Auditors consisting of the Attorney General, state Auditor, and the Secretary of state.	Passed
1920	N/A	DS	Education	Restoring certain powers regarding teacher certification to the Superintendent of Public Instruction.	Passed
1920	N/A	DS	Administration of Government	Permitting legal publication in other than official newspapers.	Passed

Year	Measure Number	Type	Subject Matter	Description	Pass/Fail
1920	N/A	DS	Banking Reform	Requiring the deposit of only state funds in the Bank of North Dakota instead of the funds of all public bodies.	Passed
1920	N/A	DS	Civil Rights	Prohibiting the display of red and black flags or signs bearing anti-government inscriptions; prohibiting the carrying in parade or the display of any flag other than the national flag or the flag or a friendly nation.	Passed
1920	N/A	DS	Business Regulation	Permitting baseball on Sunday.	Passed
1920	N/A	DS	Health/Medical	Legalizing the sale of cigarettes but prohibiting sale to minors.	Failed
1920	N/A	DS	Administration of Government	Creating a state Athletic Commission to regulate boxing and deduction of 10% of the boxing gate receipts for the state highway fund.	Failed
1920	N/A	DS	Banking Reform	Prohibiting real estate loans by the Bank of North Dakota.	Passed
1920	N/A	DS	Business Regulation	Permitting the operation of motion picture theaters on Sunday.	Failed
1921	N/A	DS	Election Reform	Changing the form of ballot for national and partisan elections.	Failed
1921	N/A	DS	Banking Reform	Abolishing the Bank of North Dakota and providing a liquidation procedure.	Failed
1921	N/A	DS	Administration of Government	Establishing a rural credit system to take over the farm loans from the Bank of North Dakota.	Failed
1921	N/A	DS	Banking Reform	Providing for public depositories to disqualify the Bank of North Dakota from receiving public funds.	Failed
1921	N/A	DS	Election Reform	Providing for the nonpartisan election of state and County officials.	Failed
1921	N/A	DS	Business Regulation	Reorganizing the Industrial Commission by removing the state officials and providing for the appointment of a 3-man commission by the Governor with confirmation by the state Senate.	Failed
1922	N/A	DS	Administration of Government	Creating the office of state Supervisor of grades, weights and measures and authorizing the office to set standards of quality on grain and conditions for marketing grain.	Passed
1922	N/A	DS	Education	Repealing minimum training and salary standards for teachers.	Passed
1922	N/A	DS	Bonds	Raising the limits of bonded indebtedness from $10 million to $20 million to enable the farm loan department of the Bank of North Dakota to make more loans.	Passed
1924	N/A	DS	Taxes	Reducing the amount of property taxes to be levied and spent in 1925-1927 biennium to not more than 75% of what was collected in 1923.	Failed

Year	Measure Number	Type	Subject Matter	Description	Pass/Fail
1924	N/A	DS	Election Reform	Changing the election of precinct committeemen from the regular June primary to the March presidential primary.	Failed
1924	N/A	DS	Labor	Giving priority to a labor lien running to a farmer and his family for their work between April 1 and December 1.	Failed
1926	N/A	DS	Taxes	Increasing the state gasoline tax from one to two cents per gallon for state highway purposes and providing for refunds when gas is used for non-highway purposes.	Passed
1928	N/A	DA	Alcohol Regulation	Repealing the clause of the constitution providing for prohibition.	Failed
1928	N/A	DS	Bonds	Authorizing a $25 million bond issue for the state to indemnify depositors who lost money in bank closings between January 1, 1910 and May 15, 1928.	Failed
1930	N/A	DA	Administration of Government	Lengthening the terms of state and County officials from two to four years.	Failed
1930	N/A	DS	Business Regulation	Permitting the operation of motion picture theaters on Sunday after 1:30 p.m.	Failed
1930	N/A	DS	Taxes	Increasing the state gasoline tax from two to four cents, with three cents to go to state highway fund and one cent to the County highway funds.	Failed
1932	N/A	DS	Administration of Government	Prohibiting crop mortgages.	Passed
1932	N/A	DA	Alcohol Regulation	Repeal prohibition.	Passed
1932	N/A	DS	Administration of Government	Abolishing the office of District Tax Supervisor created in 1919.	Passed
1932	N/A	DS	Administration of Government	Reducing salaries of elected and appointed state officials by 20%.	Passed
1932	N/A	DS	Judicial Reform	Reducing salaries of Supreme Court Judges from $5,500 to $5,000.	Passed
1932	N/A	DS	Judicial Reform	Reducing salaries of District Judges from $4,000 to $3,500 per year.	Passed
1932	N/A	DS	Administration of Government	Repealing requirement to publish public notice of sale of real estate for delinquent taxes.	Passed
1932	N/A	DS	Administration of Government	Reducing fees paid to newspapers for publication of legal notices.	Passed
1932	N/A	DS	Administration of Government	Providing a 3-year partial moratorium on debts.	Failed
1932	N/A	DA	Administration of Government	Removing the state capital from Bismarck to Jamestown.	Failed
1932	N/A	DS	Administration of Government	Reducing salaries of County officials and basing them on County population.	Passed
1932	N/A	DS	Election Reform	Extending the use of the absentee ballot to include any qualified elector who expected to be absent from his precinct and those restricted by physical disability.	Failed
1932	N/A	DS	Taxes	Reducing the taxable assessed valuation of property from 75% to 50%.	Passed

Year	Measure Number	Type	Subject Matter	Description	Pass/Fail
1932	N/A	DS	Business Regulation	Prohibiting farming by corporation.	Passed
1932	N/A	DS	Administration of Government	Reducing travel expenses for County officials.	Passed
1932	N/A	DS	Administration of Government	Reducing travel expenses for state officials.	Passed
1932	N/A	DS	Administration of Government	Providing 5-year partial moratorium on debts, public or private, except on those able to pay.	Failed
1932	N/A	DS	Administration of Government	Repealing the prohibition against crop mortgages.	Failed
1933	N/A	DS	Alcohol Regulation	Permitting the manufacture and sale of beer in North Dakota.	Passed
1933	N/A	DS	Business Regulation	Permitting operation of motion picture theaters on Sunday after 2 p.m.	Failed
1934	N/A	DS	Education	Setting the maximum amount of levy of school taxes but permitting additional levy if limitations wouldn't permit the raising of a least $70 per pupil.	Failed
1934	N/A	DS	Alcohol Regulation	Legalizing the sale of liquor by any individual or business.	Failed
1934	N/A	DS	Alcohol Regulation	Legalizing and regulating the sale of intoxicating liquor in drug stores, hotels, restaurants an clubs; creating the office of Liquor Control Commissioner, and giving portion of taxes to school districts.	Failed
1934	N/A	DS	Alcohol Regulation	Repealing all state prohibition laws.	Failed
1934	N/A	DS	Business Regulation	Permitting operation of motion picture theaters on Sunday after 2 p.m.	Passed
1936	N/A	DS	Election Reform	Abolishing the use of absent voters' ballots.	Failed
1936	N/A	DS	Campaign Finance Reform	Making it unlawful to expend federal funds in the state for political purposes.	Failed
1936	N/A	DS	Alcohol Regulation	Legalizing the sale of liquor and allocating the tax and license revenue for apportionment to counties to reduce real estate taxes.	Passed
1938	N/A	DS	Banking Reform	Reducing the legal rate of interest to 3% on indebtedness instead of 4% on borrowing and 7% on contracts.	Failed
1938	N/A	DA	Education	Creating a state Board of Higher Education to replace the Board of Administration as administrator of institutions of higher learning.	Passed
1938	N/A	DA	Administration of Government	Clarifying which public funds are to be deposited in the state treasury for appropriation and which moneys are to be kept in trust.	Passed
1938	N/A	DA	Administration of Government	Prohibiting members of the Legislature from accepting state employment during their terms of office.	Passed
1938	N/A	DS	Alcohol Regulation	Repealing liquor control act of November 1936.	Failed

Year	Measure Number	Type	Subject Matter	Description	Pass/Fail
1938	N/A	DS	Welfare	Providing a minimum pension under state old age assistance of $40 per month unless more than one member of a family received aid in which case it would be $30 per month.	Passed
1938	N/A	DS	Administration of Government	Requiring approval of County Treasurer, Judge and Register of Deeds for transactions in County securities by County Commissioners.	Failed
1938	N/A	DS	Administration of Government	Creating a state civil service for state employees.	Failed
1938	N/A	DS	Administration of Government	Providing for a commission consisting of the Governor, Lieutenant Governor and Attorney General to appoint city and village officials.	Failed
1938	N/A	DS	Administration of Government	Abolishing the state Regulatory Department; creating the state laboratories Department to be governed by board of the Governor, Attorney General and Treasurer.	Passed
1938	N/A	DA	Election Reform	Providing for the election of the Tax Commissioner in 1940 for a 4-year term on the no-party ballot.	Passed
1939	N/A	DS	Welfare	Diverting state gasoline and vehicle tax from highway construction to state old age assistance fund for two years.	Failed
1939	N/A	DS	Alcohol Regulation	Providing for the sale of liquor through municipal liquor stores in towns of 150 or more having a regular police department.	Failed
1939	N/A	DS	Taxes	Imposing a gross income tax of 2% on businesses, professions, and occupations, with some exceptions, for the various funds of the state and counties.	Failed
1940	N/A	DS	Taxes	Proposing three classes of property for tax purposes: 100% valuation for property assessed by state Board of Equalization; 75% on business inventories: 50% on household goods.	Failed
1940	N/A	DS	Taxes	Permitting abatement of past, present and future taxes based on excessive valuation.	Failed
1940	N/A	DA	Taxes	Permitting enactment of graduated land tax on farms in excess of $15,000 valuation.	Failed
1940	N/A	DA	Administration of Government	Changing name of state Board of Railroad Commissioners to Public Service Commission.	Passed
1940	N/A	DA	Taxes	Dedicating highway user taxes to defray cost of construction and maintenance of highways.	Passed
1940	N/A	DA	Taxes	Providing for a graduated land tax with a homestead exception of $5,000 for legal owner-resident farmers.	Failed
1940	N/A	DS	Education	Earmarking sales tax revenue for schools and welfare.	Passed

Year	Measure Number	Type	Subject Matter	Description	Pass/Fail
1940	N/A	DS	Administration of Government	Establishing a state Board of Finance and Administration to handle all trust funds.	Failed
1940	N/A	DS	Education	Earmarking sales tax revenues specifically 7/12ths for the school equalization fund and 5/12ths for the state welfare fund.	Passed
1940	N/A	DS	Education	Increasing the funds for financially distressed schools.	Passed
1940	N/A	DS	Education	Reducing the state per pupil payment to schools regardless of need and increasing the emergency funds for schools in distress.	Failed
1942	N/A	DS	Alcohol Regulation	Prohibiting the sale of alcoholic beverages in restaurants.	Failed
1942	N/A	DS	Taxes	Providing for three classes of property for tax purposes.	Failed
1944	N/A	DS	Taxes	Repealing state income tax.	Failed
1944	N/A	DS	Bonds	Authorizing issuance of $12,360,000 in bonds for state highway construction and maintenance.	Passed
1944	N/A	DS	Alcohol Regulation	Prohibiting the sale of alcoholic beverages where commodities other than tobacco and soft drinks are sold.	Failed
1946	N/A	DS	Taxes	Reverting back to refunding procedure for taxes paid on gasoline used for non-highway purposes.	Passed
1948	N/A	DS	Education	Prohibiting the wearing of religious dress by public school teachers.	Passed
1948	N/A	DS	Administration of Government	Legalizing parking meters in political subdivisions.	Failed
1948	N/A	DS	Administration of Government	Prohibiting parking meters in state political subdivisions.	Passed
1948	N/A	DS	Alcohol Regulation	Repealing the law that prohibits sale of alcoholic beverages where commodities other than tobacco and soft drinks are sold.	Failed
1950	N/A	DA	Taxes	Permitting the enactment of a graduated land tax.	Failed
1950	N/A	DS	Alcohol Regulation	Permitting municipal and County option on sale of liquor.	Failed
1950	N/A	DS	Taxes	Increasing personal exemption on state income tax and establishing the basis for computing tax on joint returns.	Failed
1952	N/A	DS	Taxes	Exempting food and drugs from state sales tax.	Passed
1952	N/A	DS	Alcohol Regulation	Setting hours of operation of liquor establishments between 8 a.m. and 10:30pm.	Failed
1952	N/A	DS	Banking Reform	Requiring clearance of all checks by banks without fee for cashing checks.	Failed
1954	N/A	DA	Taxes	Permitting the enactment of a graduated land tax.	Failed
1954	N/A	DS	Taxes	Exempting food from the sales tax.	Failed

Year	Measure Number	Type	Subject Matter	Description	Pass/Fail
1954	N/A	DS	Alcohol Regulation	Setting hours of liquor establishments between 8 a.m. and 11 p.m.	Failed
1954	N/A	DS	Taxes	Providing for an additional one cent non-refundable motor vehicle fuel tax for secondary highways.	Failed
1954	N/A	DS	Campaign Finance Reform	Prohibiting members of the Legislature from doing over $10,000 worth of business annually with the state or its political subdivisions.	Passed
1954	N/A	DS	Taxes	Diverting sales tax collected on automobiles from school and welfare funds to highway construction.	Failed
1955	N/A	DS	Education	Providing for state loan fund for college students with $1 million from profits of the Bank of North Dakota.	Passed
1956	N/A	DA	Term Limits	Removing 2-term limitation on office of County treasurer.	Passed
1958	N/A	DS	Education	Providing $450,000 to move the school for the blind from Pembina County to a location near Grand Forks.	Passed
1958	N/A	DA	Administration of Government	Permitting changing the name of the North Dakota Agriculture College to the North Dakota State University of Agriculture and Applied Sciences.	Failed
1958	N/A	DS	Education	Requiring the reorganization of school districts not operating high schools and providing for their annexation to districts operating high schools.	Failed
1960	N/A	DA	Administration of Government	Changing the name of the North Dakota Agriculture College to the North Dakota State University of Agriculture and Applied Sciences.	Passed
1962	N/A	DA	Bonds	Allowing the state to bond itself to make loans to companies desiring to establish power generating facilities.	Passed
1962	N/A	DS	Election Reform	Providing for a secret primary election ballot instead of requiring voters to only declare party preference at the polls.	Passed
1962	N/A	DA	Administration of Government	Changing terms of office for the most County officials from two to four years.	Passed
1964	N/A	DA	Taxes	Exempt personal property from taxation.	Failed
1964	N/A	DS	Utility Regulation	Repealing statute requiring certain number of crew members on freight trains and self-propelled equipment.	Passed
1964	N/A	DS	Utility Regulation	Requiring daily mixed passenger-freight trains by railroads.	Failed
1964	N/A	DS	Alcohol Regulation	Permitting sale of alcoholic beverages in eating establishments under certain circumstances.	Passed
1964	N/A	DA	Administration of Government	Changing two-year terms to four-year terms for most state officials and the County superintendent of schools.	Passed
1964	N/A	DS	Utility Regulation	Requiring 5-man crew on trains over one-half mile long and switching in municipalities.	Failed

Year	Measure Number	Type	Subject Matter	Description	Pass/Fail
1965	N/A	DS	Taxes	Exempting personal property from taxation.	Failed
1965	N/A	DS	Taxes	Increasing sales tax from 2 1/4% to 3%.	Failed
1966	N/A	DS	Education	Requiring publication of school board proceedings in newspaper.	Passed
1968	N/A	DA	Gaming	Authorizing certain kinds of betting.	Failed
1970	N/A	DS	Administration of Government	Repealing the law relating to the Combined Law Enforcement Council.	Failed
1972	N/A	DS	Abortion	To allow physicians to terminate pregnancy if certain per-conditions are present.	Failed
1973	N/A	DA	Apportionment/ Redistricting	Requiring that the state be divided into individual Senate Districts and House sub-districts by an appointed nine-member commission.	Failed
1974	N/A	DS	Business Regulation	Authorizes small family-owned corporations to engage in farming.	Failed
1974	N/A	DS	Labor	Authorizes new programs to increase employment opportunities.	Failed
1976	N/A	DS	Taxes	Motor vehicle excise tax rates.	Passed
1976	N/A	DS	Administration of Government	Limit General Fund expenditures.	Failed
1978	N/A	DS	Health/Medical	State control of health care costs, insurance.	Failed
1978	N/A	DS	Administration of Government	Funds to Fish and Game Department.	Passed
1978	N/A	DS	Taxes	Income tax rates: individual, corporate.	Passed
1978	N/A	DS	Administration of Government	State sharing of General Fund revenues.	Passed
1980	N/A	DS	Bonds	Tax-exempt bonds for low-income mortgages.	Passed
1980	N/A	DS	Taxes	6.5% oil extraction tax, use of revenues.	Passed
1982	N/A	M	Nuclear weapons/ facilities/waste	Limits development/production of nuclear weapons.	Passed
1982	N/A	DS	Gaming	Place limits on charitable gambling.	Failed
1984	N/A	DA	Gun Regulation	Right to bear arms as a state right.	Passed
1984	N/A	DS	Education	Three junior colleges to local school board control.	Failed
1986	N/A	DS	Labor	Sunday grocery employees — from six to three.	Failed
1986	N/A	DS	Gaming	Establish a state lottery.	Failed
1986	N/A	DS	Business Regulation	More businesses allowed open for retail on Sundays.	Failed
1988	N/A	DA	Gaming	Legislative assembly to establish state lottery.	Failed
1988	N/A	DS	Veteran Affairs	Restore Veterans' Postwar Trust Fund, 1987 balance.	Passed
1990	N/A	DA	Gaming	Electronic video gaming, proceeds.	Failed
1990	N/A	DS	Taxes	Sales, use, motor vehicle taxes for education.	Failed
1990	N/A	DS	Business Regulation	Insurance agents can rebate their commission.	Failed
1990	N/A	DS	Gaming	Regulates private games of chance: video gaming.	Failed
1990	N/A	DA	Gaming	Games of chance: proceeds, Roland Township.	Failed

Year	Measure Number	Type	Subject Matter	Description	Pass/Fail
1992	Measure 5	DS	Term Limits	Term limits on Congress 12/12.	Passed
1992	N/A	DS	Taxes	Water development, sales and use tax.	Failed
1992	N/A	DS	Legal	Prohibit stopping/searching vehicles at random.	Failed
1992	N/A	DS	Environmental Reform	Environmental protection fund, fees on waste.	Failed
1994	N/A	DS	Administration of Government	Provides that cities vote every four years whether to publish the minutes of their meetings.	Passed
1994	N/A	DS	Health/Medical	Provides for the repeal of North Dakota's mandatory seat belt law.	Failed
1996	Measure 4	DA	Veteran Affairs	Makes the veteran's postwar trust fund a permanent fund.	Passed
1996	Measure 5	DA	Term Limits	Informed Voter Law and term limits on state legislature 8/8.	Failed
1996	Measure 6	DA	Term Limits	Direct application for constitutional convention to consider a term limits amendment.	Failed
1998	Measure 2	DA	Election Reform	Would set up a process for the election of Sheriffs	Passed

North Dakota Constitution

Article III

Section 1.

While the legislative power of this state shall be vested in a legislative assembly consisting of a senate and a house of representatives, the people reserve the power to propose and enact laws by the initiative, including the call for a constitutional convention; to approve or reject legislative Acts, or parts thereof, by the referendum; to propose and adopt constitutional amendments by the initiative; and to recall certain elected officials. This article is self-executing and all of its provisions are mandatory. Laws may be enacted to facilitate and safeguard, but not to hamper, restrict, or impair these powers.

Section 2.

A petition to initiate or to refer a measure shall be presented to the secretary of state for approval as to form. A request for approval shall be presented over the names and signatures of twenty-five or more electors as sponsors, one of whom shall be designated as chairman of the sponsoring committee. The secretary of state shall approve the petition for circulation if it is in proper form and contains the names and addresses of the sponsors and the full text of the measure.

Section 3.

The petition shall be circulated only by electors. They shall swear thereon that the electors who have signed the petition did so in their presence. Each elector signing a petition shall also write in the date of signing and his post-office address. No law shall be enacted limiting the number of copies of a petition. The copies shall become part of the original petition when filed.

Section 4.

The petition may be submitted to the secretary of state if signed by electors equal in number to two percent of the resident population of the state at the last federal decennial census.

Section 5.

An initiative petition shall be submitted not less than ninety days before the statewide election at which the measure is to be voted upon. A referendum petition may be submitted only within ninety days after the filing of the measure with the secretary of state. The submission of a petition shall suspend the operation of any measure enacted by the legislative assembly except emergency measures and appropriation measures for the support and maintenance of state departments and institutions. The submission of a petition against one or more items or parts of any measure shall not prevent the remainder from going into effect. A referred measure may be voted upon at a statewide election or at a special election called by the governor.

Section 6.

The secretary of state shall pass upon each petition, and if he finds it insufficient, he shall notify the "committee for the petitioners" and allow twenty days for correction or amendment. All decisions of the secretary of state in regard to any such petition shall be subject to review by the supreme court. But if the sufficiency of such petition is being reviewed at the time the ballot is prepared, the secretary of state shall place the measure on the ballot and no subsequent decision shall invalidate such measure if it is at such election approved by a majority of the votes cast thereon. If proceedings are brought against any petition upon any ground, the burden of proof shall be upon the party attacking it.

Section 7.

All decisions of the secretary of state in the petition process are subject to review by the supreme court in the exercise of original jurisdiction. If his decision is being reviewed at the time the ballot is prepared, he shall place the measure on the ballot and no court action shall invalidate the measure if it is approved at the election by a majority of the votes cast thereon.

Section 8.

If a majority of votes cast upon an initiated or a referred measure are affirmative, it shall be deemed enacted. An initiated or referred measure which is approved shall become law thirty days after the election, and a referred measure which is rejected shall be void immediately. If conflicting measures are approved, the one receiving the highest number of affirmative votes shall be law. A measure approved by the electors may not be repealed or amended by the legislative assembly for seven years from its effective date, except by a two-thirds vote of the members elected to each house.

Section 9.

A constitutional amendment may be proposed by initiative petition. If signed by electors equal in number to four percent of the resident population of the state at the last federal decennial census, the petition may be submitted to the secretary of state. All other provisions relating to initiative measures apply hereto.

Section 10.

Any elected official of the state, of any county or of any legislative or county commissioner district shall be subject to recall by petition of electors equal in number to twenty-five percent of those who voted at the preceding general election for the office of governor in the state, county, or district in which the official is to be recalled. The petition shall be filed with the official with whom a petition for nomination to the office in question is filed, who shall call a special election if he finds the petition valid and sufficient. No elector may remove his name from a recall petition. The name of the official to be recalled shall be placed on the ballot unless he resigns within ten days after the filing of the petition. Other candidates for the office may be nominated in a manner provided by law. When the election results have been officially declared, the candidate receiving the highest number of votes shall be deemed elected for the remainder of the term. No official shall be subject twice to recall during the term for which he was elected.

North Dakota Statutes

16.1-01-09. Initiative, referendum, or recall petitions — Signature — Form — Circulation.

a. A request of the secretary of state for approval of a petition to initiate or refer a measure may be presented over the signatures of the sponsoring committee on individual signature forms that have been notarized. The secretary of state shall prepare a signature form that includes provisions for identification of the measure; the printed name, signature, and address of the committee member; and notarization of the signature.

b. Upon receipt of a petition to initiate or refer a measure, the secretary of state shall draft a short and concise statement that fairly represents the measure. The statement must be submitted to the attorney general for approval or disapproval. An approved statement must be affixed to the petition before it is circulated for signatures, must be called the "ballot title", and must be placed immediately before the full text of the measure.

c. The secretary of state and the attorney general shall complete their review of a petition in not less than five, nor more than seven, business days, excluding Saturdays.

2. No person may sign any initiative, referendum, or recall petition circulated pursuant to article III of the Constitution of North Dakota unless the person is a qualified elector. No person may sign any petition more than once, and each signer shall add the signer's post-office address including the signer's residential address or post-office box number and the date of signing. Every qualified elector signing a petition shall do so in the presence of the person circulating the petition. A referendum or initiative petition must be in substantially the following form:

REFERENDUM [INITIATIVE] PETITION TO THE SECRETARY OF STATE, STATE OF NORTH DAKOTA

We, the undersigned, being qualified electors request [House (Senate) Bill _____ passed by the _____ Legislative Assembly] [the following initiated law] be placed on the ballot as provided by law.

SPONSORING COMMITTEE
The following are the names and addresses of the qualified electors of the state of North Dakota who, as the sponsoring committee for the petitioners, represent and act for the petitioners in accordance with law:

BALLOT TITLE
(To be drafted by the secretary of state, approved by the attorney general, and attached to the petition before circulation.)

FULL TEXT OF THE MEASURE

IF MATERIAL IS UNDERSCORED, IT IS NEW MATERIAL WHICH IS BEING ADDED. IF MATERIAL IS OVER-STRUCK BY DASHES, THE MATERIAL IS BEING DELETED. IF NO MATERIAL IS UNDERSCORED OR OVER-STRUCK, THE MEASURE CONTAINS ALL NEW MATERIAL WHICH IS BEING ADDED.

[The full text of the measure must be inserted here.]

INSTRUCTIONS TO PETITION SIGNERS
You are being asked to sign a petition. You must be a qualified elector. This means you are eighteen years old, you have lived in North Dakota thirty days, and you are a United States citizen. All signers must add their entire post-office address, including post-office box number, and the date of signing. Every qualified elector signing a petition must do so in the presence of the person circulating the petition.

QUALIFIED ELECTORS
[Insert signature lines here]

The number of signature lines on each page of a printed petition may vary if necessary to accommodate other required textual matter. In this section for referral petitions "full text of the measure" means the bill as passed by the legislative assembly excluding the session and sponsor identification. In this section for initiative petitions "full text of the measure" means an enacting clause which must be: "BE IT ENACTED BY THE PEOPLE OF THE STATE OF NORTH DAKOTA" and the body of the bill. If the measure amends the law, all new statutory material must be underscored and all statutory material to be deleted must be overstruck by dashes. When repealing portions of the law, the measure must contain a repealer clause and, in brackets, the text of the law being repealed.

3. Each copy of any petition provided for in this section, before being filed, must have attached an affidavit executed by the circulator in substantially the following form:

State of North Dakota)
) ss.
County of (county where signed)

I, _____, being sworn, say that I am a qualified elector; that I (circulator) reside at _____; (address) that each signature contained on the attached petition was executed in my presence; and that to the best of my knowledge and belief each person whose signature appears on the attached petition is a qualified elector; and that each signature contained on the attached petition is the genuine signature of the person whose name it purports to be.

_____
(signature of circulator)

Subscribed and sworn to before me on _____, _____, at _____, North Dakota.
(city)

(Notary Seal) _____
(signature of notary)
My commission expires_____

4. A petition for recall must include, before the signature lines for the qualified electors as provided in subsection 2, the name of the person being recalled, the office from which that person is being recalled, and a list of the names and post-office addresses including the residential addresses or post-office box numbers of not less than five qualified electors of the state, political subdivision, or district in which the official is to be recalled who are sponsoring the recall.

5. No petition shall be circulated under the authority of article III of the Constitution of North Dakota by a person who is less than eighteen years of age, nor shall the affidavit called for by subsection 3 be executed by a person who is less than eighteen years of age at the time of signing. All petitions circulated under the authority of the constitution and of this section must be circulated in their entirety. A petition may not include a statement of intent or similar explanatory information.

6. When signed petitions are delivered to the secretary of state, the chairperson of the sponsoring committee shall submit to the secretary of state an affidavit stating that to the best of that person's knowledge, the petitions contain at least the required number of signatures.

7. An initiative or referendum petition may be submitted to the secretary of state until midnight of the day designated as the deadline for submitting the petition.

16.1-01-10. Secretary of state to pass upon sufficiency of petitions — Method — Time limit.

The secretary of state shall have a reasonable period, not to exceed thirty-five days, in which to pass upon the sufficiency of any petition mentioned in section 16.1-01-09. The secretary of state shall conduct a representative random sampling of the signatures contained in the petitions by the use of questionnaires, postcards, telephone calls, personal interviews, or other accepted information gathering techniques, or any combinations thereof, to determine the validity of the signatures. Signatures determined by the secretary of state to be invalid may not be counted and all violations of law discovered by the secretary of state must be reported to the attorney general for prosecution.

16.1-01-11. Certain questions not to be voted upon for three months.

Whenever at any election a bond issue or mill levy question has failed to receive the required number of votes for approval by the electors, the matter may not again be submitted to a vote until a period of at least three months has expired, and in no event may more than two elections on the same general matter be held within twelve consecutive calendar months.

16.1-01-12. Election offenses — Penalty.

It is unlawful for a person to:
1. Fraudulently alter another person's ballot or substitute one ballot for another or to otherwise defraud a voter of that voter's vote.
2. Obstruct a qualified elector on the way to a polling place.
3. Vote or offer to vote more than once in any election.
4. Knowingly vote in the wrong election precinct or district.
5. Disobey the lawful command of an election officer as defined in chapter 16.1-05.
6. Knowingly exclude a qualified elector from voting or knowingly allow an unqualified person to vote.
7. Knowingly vote when not qualified to do so.
8. Sign an initiative, referendum, recall, or any other election petition when not qualified to do so.

9. Sign a name other than that person's own name to an initiative, referendum, recall, or any other election petition.

10. Circulate an initiative, referendum, recall, or any other election petition not in its entirety or circulate such a petition when unqualified to do so.

11. Pay or offer to pay any person, or receive payment or agree to receive payment, on a basis related to the number of signatures obtained for circulating an initiative, referendum, or recall petition. This subsection does not prohibit the payment of salary and expenses for circulation of the petition on a basis not related to the number of signatures obtained, as long as the circulators file their intent to remunerate prior to submitting the petitions and fully disclose all expenditures and revenues upon submission of the petitions to the secretary of state.

12. Willfully fail to perform any duty of an election officer after having accepted the responsibility of being an election officer by taking the oath as prescribed in this title.

13. Willfully violate any rule adopted by the secretary of state pursuant to this title.

14. Willfully make any false canvass of votes, or make, sign, publish, or deliver any false return of an election, knowing the same to be false, or willfully deface, destroy, or conceal any statement or certificate entrusted to the person's care.

15. Destroy ballots, ballot boxes, election lists, or other election supplies except as provided by law.

A violation of subsections 1 through 14 is a class A misdemeanor. Any signature obtained in violation of subsection 11 is void and may not be counted. A violation of subsection 15 occurring after an election but before the final canvass, or during an election, is a class C felony, and in other cases is a class A misdemeanor.

Every act which by this chapter is made criminal when committed with reference to the election of a candidate is equally criminal when committed with reference to the determination of a question submitted to qualified electors to be decided by votes cast at an election.

The Basic Steps to Do an Initiative in North Dakota

Statutes and Amendments — Direct Initiative Process

Basic Procedures: Proponents must file their petition with the Secretary of State for approval before they can circulate. The request for approval must be presented over the names and signatures of twenty-five or more electors as sponsors, one of whom must be designated as chairman of the sponsoring committee. The Secretary of State will approve the petition for circulation if it is in proper form and contains the names and addresses of the sponsors and the full text of the measure.

Additionally, upon receipt of the petition, the Secretary of State will draft a short and concise statement which must fairly represent the measure. The statement must be submitted to the Attorney General for approval or disapproval. An approved statement must be affixed to the petition before it is circulated for signatures, must me called the "ballot title", and must be placed immediately before the full text of the measure.

The Secretary of State and the Attorney General must complete their review of the petition in not less than five, nor more than seven, business days.

Date Initiative language can be submitted to state for 2001 or 2002: Any time. Initiatives are placed on the next election ballot after signatures are certified, which could be the general election ballot, a primary ballot, or even a special election. (Exception: Sometimes when the legislature calls a special election for a referred ballot measure they ban the placement of any initiatives on that special election ballot, in which case the initiative will be on the next ballot.)

Signatures are tied to vote of which office: Resident population at the last federal decennial census [Next federal census—2010. Resident Population in last federal census—1990: 638,800. North Dakota's new census population will be certified sometime before the end of 2001.]

Net number of signatures required: For statutes, 2% of the population. (12,776) and for amendments, 4% of the population. (25,552) (These numbers will change after the 2000 census is certified sometime in 2001.)

Distribution Requirement: None.

Circulation period: 1 year.

Do circulators have to be residents: Yes.

Date when signatures are due for certification: 90 days before the election. (March 13, 2002 for the June 11th Primary Election. August 7, 2002 for the November 5, 2002 General Election.)

Signature verification process: North Dakota does not a have a voter registration process. As a result, there are no registered voters. Proponents, however, must collect the signatures of North Dakota residents. The Secretary of State then conducts a representative random sampling of the signatures contained in the petitions by the use of questionnaires, post cards, telephone calls, personal interviews, or other accepted information gathering techniques to determine the validity of the signatures.

Single-subject restriction: No.

Legislative tampering: Legislature can repeal or amend by a 2/3 vote of each house for seven year after passage, majority vote thereafter.

Ohio

When the founding convention of the National Direct Legislation League met in St. Louis in 1896, it elected 56 vice presidents, four of whom were from Ohio. None of the other 36 states which were represented provided so many.

The leader who guided Ohio initiative and referendum forces to victory was the Reverend Herbert S. Bigelow of Cincinnati's Vine Street Congregational Church. Church members who disapproved of his political work quit in droves; his salary diminished to the point that he and his wife had to take in boarders to make ends meet. When he invited the I&R advocate and Prohibitionist R. S. Thompson to speak to the congregation, the church's trustees locked the doors. Later, the trustees filed formal charges of heresy against Bigelow before a church court, but he was never tried. Eventually, Bigelow's supporters won control of the board of trustees and helped him make Vine Street a nerve center of the state's Progressive movement.

When the Ohio state senate approved an I&R amendment in 1906, Bigelow sensed that success was near and took a leave of absence from the church, with his congregation's consent, to work full time for I&R, "for a time, perhaps two or three years." In 1908, despite opposition from Governor Grosvenor, "the well-known machine representative," (as *Equity* called him), the I&R bill passed both houses, but was killed by legislators voting secretly in a conference committee. I&R backers charged that "the Republican bosses and their tools in the state senate" were responsible.

The Progressives finally got their I&R amendment, not through the legislature, but in a state constitutional convention, along with some 41 other amendments, which were submitted for voter approval in a special election held 3 September 1912. A contemporary account of the campaign called it "the most bitter and momentous struggle known in the state for a generation. Every ruse and trick known to Big Business politicians was employed to frighten the people of Ohio from adopting the I&R. The whole corporate power of the state backed by Wall Street money and influence was thrown into the fight. The Catholic Church stood against the people's power measures and issued printed instructions to their members, at the Sunday services, on how to vote."

The fight for the I&R amendment and for other vitally important amendments was led by Reverend Bigelow, ably assisted by Mayor Brand Whitlock of Toledo and Mayor Baker of Cleveland. The I&R amendment passed with 57.5 percent of the vote.

The first initiatives to win voter approval were a Prohibition measure and a law, which later was ruled unconstitutional, to allow voters to veto the legislature's ratification of a federal constitutional amendment (1918).

Voters in 1933 approved aid to the aged and, in 1936, overwhelmingly passed an initiative banning taxes on food. In 1949 they dealt a serious blow to political machines in the state, abolishing the voting-booth system of electing an entire party slate of candidates with the flick of a single lever. Henceforth, voters decided the merits of each candidate independently.

During the next 39 years, voters rejected all but one initiative put before them. The exception was a 1977 vote to repeal a law, approved only months previously by the legislature, that allowed people to register to vote at the polls on election day rather than requiring them to register beforehand.

In 1992, a term limits initiative was approved by the voters overwhelmingly and in 1994 an initiative prohibiting "the current wholesale tax on soft drinks" was approved. It was the last statewide initiative to be adopted by the citizens.

Statewide Initiative Usage

Number of Initiatives	Number Passed	Number Failed	Passage Rate
65	16	49	25%

Statewide Initiatives

Year	Measure Number	Type	Subject Matter	Description	Pass/Fail
1913	Issue No. 1	DA	Administration of Government	Reduce the size of the legislature.	Failed
1914	Issue No. 1	DA	Alcohol Regulation	Home rule on subject of intoxicating liquors.	Passed
1914	Issue No. 2	DA	Taxes	Limitation of tax rate and for classification of property for purpose of taxation.	Failed
1914	Issue No. 3	DA	Election Reform	To extend suffrage to women.	Failed
1914	Issue No. 4	DA	Alcohol Regulation	Prohibition of the sale and manufacture for sale, and importation for sale of intoxicating liquor as a beverage.	Failed
1915	Issue No. 1	DA	Alcohol Regulation	Prohibition of the sale and manufacture for sale of intoxicating liquor as a beverage.	Failed
1915	Issue No. 2	DA	Administration of Government	To fix the terms of all County officers at four years to provide for their election quadrennially, and applying the amendment to incumbents.	Failed
1915	Issue No. 3	DA	Initiative and Referendum	To limit elections on twice defeated constitutional proposals and to prevent the abuse of the initiative and referendum.	Failed
1917	Issue No. 1	DA	Alcohol Regulation	Prohibition of the sale and manufacture for sale of intoxicating liquors.	Failed
1918	Issue No. 1	DA	Initiative and Referendum	Referendum provision, reserving to the people the power to approve or reject an action of the General Assembly ratifying any proposed amendment to the Constitution of the United States.	Passed
1918	Issue No. 2	DA	Alcohol Regulation	Prohibition of the sale and manufacture for sale of intoxicating liquors as a beverage.	Passed
1918	Issue No. 3	DA	Taxes	The General Assembly shall classify property for taxation purposes.	Passed
1919	Issue No. 1	DA	Alcohol Regulation	Defining the phrase "Intoxicating Liquor".	Failed
1919	Issue No. 2	DA	Alcohol Regulation	To repeal statewide prohibition.	Failed
1922	Issue No. 1	DA	Taxes	To provide for 2.75 percent beverage tax.	Failed
1922	Issue No. 2	DA	Administration of Government	To provide for debt limitation for counties, school districts, townships, municipal corporations, or other political subdivisions.	Failed
1922	Issue No. 3	DA	Taxes	To provide a limitation on tax rates of 15 mills, but additional levies may be authorized by vote. State tax rate limited to 1 mil.	Failed
1923	Issue No. 1	IDS	Welfare	Relative to old age pensions.	Failed
1926	Issue No. 1	DA	Election Reform	To eliminate the compulsory primary.	Failed

Year	Measure Number	Type	Subject Matter	Description	Pass/Fail
1927	Issue No. 1	IDS	Administration of Government	To provide for a State board of Chiropractic Examiners.	Failed
1928	Issue No. 1	DA	Judicial Reform	To equalize the compensation of judges.	Failed
1933	Issue No. 1	IDS	Welfare	Relative to old age pensions.	Passed
1933	Issue No. 1	DA	Taxes	To provide a ten mill tax limitation on real estate.	Passed
1933	Issue No. 2	DA	Administration of Government	Relative to County and township organizations and government, and granting counties home rule government.	Passed
1934	N/A	DA	Taxes	Prohibiting the taxation as property of motor vehicles.	Failed
1934	N/A	DA	Taxes	Requiring motor vehicle fuel excise taxes to be measured by a sum for each gallon or other like unit.	Failed
1936	Issue No. 1	DA	Taxes	Prohibiting the levy or collection of an excise tax on the sale or purchase of food for human consumption off the premises where sold.	Passed
1938	Issue No. 1	DA	Judicial Reform	To provide for the original appointment of judges of the Supreme Court and Courts of appeals.	Failed
1939	Issue No. 1	DA	Welfare	Relative to old age pensions.	Failed
1939	Issue No. 2	DA	Initiative and Referendum	Requirements necessary to qualify initiative petitions.	Failed
1947	Issue No. 4	DA	Taxes	Relative to the prohibition of the expenditure of money from motor vehicle license taxes and gasoline taxes for other than highway and related purposes.	Passed
1949	Issue No. 1	IDS	Business Regulation	To permit the manufacture and sale of colored oleomargarine.	Passed
1949	Issue No. 2	DA	Election Reform	Providing that electors of the state of Ohio may vote for candidates only by separately indicating their vote for each candidate.	Passed
1955	Issue No. 1	IDS	Labor	To increase unemployment compensation.	Failed
1958	Issue No. 2	DA	Labor	To forbid labor contracts which established union membership as a condition for continuing employment (called "right-to-work").	Failed
1962	Issue No. 1	DA	Business Regulation	To limit the power of the State to forbid the sale of certain goods and services on Sunday.	Failed
1965	Issue No. 1	IDS	Education	To amend the school foundation program and to increase taxes to support it.	Failed
1972	Issue No. 1	DA	Taxes	Conditions for and prohibitions upon the levy of a tax on income except a municipal income tax, or increasing the rates thereof, without the approval of a majority of the voting electors.	Failed
1975	Issue No. 2	DA	Taxes	To create and preserve jobs by the authorization of tax incentives to industrial plants.	Failed
1975	Issue No. 3	DA	Bonds	To authorize the issuance of bonds and notes in an amount not to exceed $1,750,000,000 to be paid from and additional levy of 9/10 of 1 cent per gallon gasoline tax.	Failed

Year	Measure Number	Type	Subject Matter	Description	Pass/Fail
1975	Issue No. 4	DA	Health/Medical	Relative to the authority of the state, municipal corporation and counties to provide assistance with respect to housing and nursing, extended care and other health facilities.	Failed
1975	Issue No. 5	DA	Bonds	To authorize the issuance of bonds and notes in the amount not to exceed $2,750,000,000 with the principal and interest to be paid by an additional levy of 7/10 of 1% sales and use tax.	Failed
1976	Issue No. 4	DA	Utility Regulation	Limiting the rates which may be charged to residential consumers for fixed amounts of gas and electricity.	Failed
1976	Issue No. 5	DA	Utility Regulation	Providing for representation of residential utility regulatory actions affecting their interests.	Failed
1976	Issue No. 6	DA	Nuclear weapons/ facilities/waste	Relative to establishing procedures for legislative hearings and approval of safety features of nuclear power plants and related facilities.	Failed
1976	Issue No. 7	DA	Initiative and Referendum	Relative to simplifying the procedures for initiative and referendum.	Failed
1977	Issue No. 1	DA	Election Reform	Entitlement to vote if registered for thirty days.	Passed
1977	Issue No. 2	DA	Animal Rights	Ban trapping devices causing prolonged suffering.	Failed
1979	Issue No. 1	IDS	Environmental Reform	Mandatory deposits on bottles; prohibit pull-tabs.	Failed
1980	N/A	IDS	Taxes	To restructure state taxes on personal income.	Failed
1981	Issue No. 1	DA	Labor	Workers compensation insurance; private companies.	Failed
1981	Issue No. 2	DA	Apportionment/ Redistricting	General Assembly and Congressional redistricting.	Failed
1982	Issue No. 3	DA	Administration of Government	Election of members of Public Utilities Commission.	Failed
1983	Issue No. 1	DA	Alcohol Regulation	Minimum age, beer consumption: twenty-one.	Failed
1983	Issue No. 2	DA	Taxes	3/5 majority of General Assembly to raise taxes.	Failed
1983	Issue No. 3	DA	Taxes	Repeal all taxes passed since 1982.	Failed
1987	Issue No. 3	DA	Judicial Reform	Abolish election of Supreme, Appeals Court judges.	Failed
1990	Issue No. 3	DA	Gaming	Casino resort hotel in Lorain as pilot project.	Failed
1992	Issue No. 2	DA	Term Limits	Term limits on Congress 8/12.	Passed
1992	Issue No. 3	DA	Term Limits	Term limits on Governor.	Passed
1992	Issue No. 4	DA	Term Limits	Term limits on state legislature 8/8.	Passed
1992	Issue No. 5	IDS	Business Regulation	Businesses to provide warnings for toxic substances.	Failed
1994	Issue No. 4	DA	Taxes	Prohibiting the current wholesale tax on soft drinks and other carbonated, non-alcoholic beverages.	Passed
1996	Issue No. 1	DA	Gaming	Authorize moored river boat casino gambling.	Failed

Year	Measure Number	Type	Subject Matter	Description	Pass/Fail
1998	Issue No. 1	IDS	Animal Rights	Would ban the hunting of mourning doves.	Failed

Ohio Constitution

Article II

§ 2.01 In whom power vested

The legislative power of the state shall be vested in a general assembly consisting of a senate and house of representatives but the people reserve to themselves the power to propose to the general assembly laws and amendments to the constitution, and to adopt or reject the same at the polls on a referendum vote as hereinafter provided. They also reserve the power to adopt or reject any law, section of any law or any item in any law appropriating money passed by the general assembly, except as hereinafter provided; and independent of the general assembly to propose amendments to the constitution and to adopt or reject the same at the polls. The limitations expressed in the constitution, on the power of the general assembly to enact laws, shall be deemed limitations on the power of the people to enact laws.

§ 2.01a The initiative

The first aforestated power reserved by the people is designated the initiative, and the signatures of ten per centum of the electors shall be required upon a petition to propose an amendment to the constitution. When a petition signed by the aforesaid required number of electors, shall have been filed with the secretary of state, and verified as herein provided, proposing an amendment to the constitution, the full text of which shall have been set forth in such petition, the secretary of state shall submit for the approval or rejection of the electors, the proposed amendment, in the manner hereinafter provided, at the next succeeding regular or general election in any year occurring subsequent to ninety days after the filing of such petition. The initiative petitions, above described, shall have printed across the top thereof: Amendment to the Constitution Proposed by Initiative Petition to be Submitted Directly to the Electors."

§ 2.01b Initiative, continued

When at any time, not less than ten days prior to the commencement of any session of the general assembly, there shall have been filed with the secretary of state a petition signed by three per centum of the electors and verified as herein provided, proposing a law, the full text of which shall have been set forth in such petition, the secretary of state shall transmit the same to the general assembly as soon as it convenes. If said proposed law shall be passed by the general assembly, either as petitioned for or in an amended form, it shall be subject to the referendum. If it shall not be passed, or if it shall be passed in an amended form, or if no action shall be taken thereon within four months from the time it is received by the general assembly, it shall be submitted by the secretary of state to the electors for their approval or rejection at the next regular or general election, if such submission shall be demanded by supplementary petition verified as herein provided and signed by not less than three per centum of the electors in addition to those signing the original petition, which supplementary petition must be signed and filed with the secretary of state within ninety days after the proposed law shall have been rejected by the general assembly or after the expiration of such term of four months, if no action has been taken thereon, or after the law as passed by the general assembly shall have been filed by the governor in the office of the secretary of state. The proposed law shall be submitted in the form demanded by such supplementary petition, which form shall be either as first petitioned for or with any amendment or amendments which may have been incorporated therein by either branch or by both branches, of the general assembly. If a proposed law so submitted is approved by a majority of the electors voting thereon, it shall be the law and shall go into effect as herein provided in lieu of any amended form of said law which may have been passed by the general assembly, and such amended law passed by the general assembly shall not go into effect until and unless the law proposed by supplementary petition shall have been rejected by the electors. All such initiative petitions, last above described, shall have printed across the top thereof, in case of proposed laws: "Law Proposed by Initiative Petition First to be Submitted to the General Assembly." Ballots shall be so printed as to permit an affirmative or negative vote upon each measure submitted to the electors. Any proposed law or amendment to the constitution submitted to the electors as provided in section 1a and section 1b, if approved by a majority of the electors voting thereon, shall take effect thirty days after the election at which it was approved and shall be published by the secretary of state. If conflicting proposed laws or conflicting proposed amendments to the constitution shall be approved at the same election by a majority of the total number of votes cast for and against the same, the one receiving the highest number of affirmative votes shall be the law, or in the case of amendments to the constitution shall be the amendment to the constitution. No law proposed by initiative petition and approved by the electors shall be subject to the veto of the governor.

§ 2.01c The referendum

The second aforestated power reserved by the people is designated the referendum, and the signatures of six per centum of the electors shall be required upon a petition to order the submission to the electors of the state for their approval or rejection, of any law, section of any law or any item in any law appropriating money passed by the general assembly. No law passed by the general assembly shall go into effect until ninety days after it shall have been filed by the governor in the office of the secretary of state, except as herein provided. When a petition, signed by six per centum of the electors of the state and verified as herein provided, shall have been filed with the secretary of state within ninety days after any law shall have been filed by the governor in the office of the secretary of state, ordering that such law, section of such law or any item in such law appropriating money be submitted to the electors of the state for their approval or rejection, the secretary of state shall submit to the electors of the state for their approval or rejection such law, section or item, in the manner herein provided, at the next succeeding regular or general election in any year occurring subsequent to sixty days after the filing of such petition, and no such law, section or item shall go into effect until and unless approved by a majority of those voting upon the same. If, however, a referendum petition is filed against any such section or item, the remainder of the law shall not thereby be prevented or delayed from going into effect.

§ 2.01d Emergency laws; not subject to referendum

Laws providing for tax levies, appropriations for the current expenses of the state government and state institutions, and emergency laws necessary for the immediate preservation of the public peace, health or safety, shall go into immediate effect. Such emergency laws upon a yea and nay vote must receive the vote of two-thirds of all the members elected to each branch of the general assembly, and the reasons for such necessity shall be set forth in one section of the law, which section shall be passed only upon a yea and nay vote, upon a separate roll call thereon. The laws mentioned in this section shall not be subject to the referendum.

§ 2.01e Powers; limitation of use

The powers defined herein as the "initiative" and "referendum" shall not be used to pass a law authorizing any classification of property for the purpose of levying different rates of taxation thereon or of authorizing the levy of any single tax on land or land values or land sites at a higher rate or by a different rule than is or may be applied to improvements thereon or to personal property

§ 2.01f Power of municipalities

The initiative and referendum powers are hereby reserved to the people of each municipality on all questions which such municipalities may now or hereafter be authorized by law to control by legislative action; such powers shall be exercised in the manner now or hereafter provided by law.

§ 2.01g Petition requirements and preparation

Any initiative, supplementary, or referendum petition may be presented in separate parts but each part shall contain a full and correct copy of the title, and text of the law, section or item thereof sought to be referred, or the proposed law or proposed amendment to the constitution. Each signer of any initiative, supplementary, or referendum petition must be an elector of the state and shall place on such petition after his name the date of signing and his place of residence. A signer residing outside of a municipality shall state the county and the rural route number, post office address, or township of his residence. A resident of a municipality shall state the street and number, if any, of his residence and the name of the municipality or the post office address. The names of all signers to such petitions shall be written in ink, each signer for himself. To each part of such petition shall be attached the statement of the circulator, as may be required by law, that he witnessed the affixing of every signature. The petition and signatures upon such petitions shall be presumed to be in all respects sufficient, unless not later than forty days before the election, it shall be otherwise proved and in such event ten additional days shall be allowed for the filing of additional signatures to such petition. No law or amendment to the constitution submitted to the electors by initiative and supplementary petition and receiving an affirmative majority of the votes cast thereon, shall be held unconstitutional or void on account of the insufficiency of the petitions by which such submission of the same was procured; nor shall the rejection of any law submitted by referendum petition be held invalid for such insufficiency. Upon all initiative, supplementary, and referendum petitions provided for in any of the sections of this article, it shall be necessary to file from each of one-half of the counties of the state, petitions bearing the signatures of not less than one-half of the designated percentage of the electors of such county. A true copy of all laws or proposed laws or proposed amendments to the constitution, together with an argument or explanation, or both, for, and also an argument or explanation, or both, against the same, shall be prepared. The person or persons who prepare the argument or explanation, or both, against any law, section, or item, submitted to the electors by referendum petition, may be named in such petition and the persons who prepare the argument or explanation, or both, for any proposed law or proposed amendment to the constitution may be named in the petition proposing the same. The person or persons who prepare the argument or explanation, or both, for the law, section, or item, submitted to the electors by referendum petition, or against any proposed law submitted by supplementary petition, shall be named by the general assembly, if in session, and if not in session then by the governor. The law, or proposed law, or proposed amendment to the constitution, together with the arguments and explanations, not exceeding a total of three hundred words for each, and also the arguments and explanations, not exceeding a total of three hundred words against each, shall be published once a week for three consecutive weeks preceding the election, in at least one newspaper of general circulation in each county of the state, where a newspaper is published. The secretary of state shall cause to be placed upon the ballots, the ballot language for any such law, or proposed law, or proposed amendment to the constitution, to be submitted. The ballot language shall be prescribed by the Ohio ballot board in the same manner, and subject to the same terms and conditions, as apply to issues submitted by the general assembly pursuant to Section 1 of Article XVI of this constitution. The ballot language shall be so prescribed and the secretary of state shall cause the ballots so to be printed as to permit an affirmative or negative vote upon each law, section of law, or item in a law appropriating money, or proposed law, or proposed amendment to the constitution. The style of all laws submitted by initiative and supplementary petition shall be: "Be it Enacted by the People of the State of Ohio," and of all constitutional amendments: "Be it Resolved by the People of the State of Ohio." The basis upon which the required number of petitioners in any case shall be determined shall be the total number of votes cast for the office of governor at the last preceding election therefor. The foregoing provisions of this section shall be self-executing, except as herein otherwise provided. Laws may be passed to facilitate their operation, but in no way limiting or restricting either such provisions or the powers herein reserved.

Ohio Statutes

Chapter 3519

§ 3519.01 Certification of initiative or referendum proposal by attorney general and secretary of state.

(A) Whoever seeks to propose a law or constitutional amendment by initiative petition shall, by a written petition signed by one hundred qualified electors, submit the proposed law or constitutional amendment and a summary of it to the attorney general for examination. If in the opinion of the attorney general the summary is a fair and truthful statement of the proposed law or constitutional amendment, he shall so certify. A verified copy of the proposed law or constitutional amendment, together with the summary and the attorney general's certification, shall then be filed with the secretary of state.

(B)(1) Whoever seeks to file a referendum petition against any law, section, or item in any law shall, by a written petition signed by one hundred qualified electors, submit the measure to be referred and a summary of it to the secretary of state and, on the same day or within one business day before or after that day, submit a copy of the petition, measure, and summary to the attorney general.

(2) Not later than ten business days after receiving the petition, measure, and summary, the secretary of state shall do both of the following:

(a) Have the validity of the signatures on the petition verified;

(b) After comparing the text of the measure to be referred with the copy of the enrolled bill on file in his office containing the law, section, or item of law, determine whether the text is correct and, if it is, so certify.

(3) Not later than ten business days after receiving a copy of the petition, measure, and summary, the attorney general shall examine the summary and, if in his opinion the summary is a fair and truthful statement of the measure to be referred, so certify.

§ 3519.02 Committee for petitioners.

The petitioners shall designate in any initiative, referendum, or supplementary petition and on each of the several parts of such petition a committee of not less than three nor more than five of their number who shall represent them in all matters relating to such petitions. Notice of all matters or proceedings pertaining to such petitions may be served on said committee, or any of them, either personally or by registered mail, or by leaving such notice at the usual place of residence of each of them.

§ 3519.03 Committee to prepare arguments.

The committee named in an initiative petition may prepare the argument or explanation, or both, in favor of the measure proposed and the committee named in a referendum petition may prepare the argument or explanation, or both, against any law, section, or item of law. The persons who prepare the argument or explanation, or both, in opposition to the initiated proposal, or the argument or explanation, or both, in favor of the measure to be referred shall be named by the general assembly, if in session, and if not in session, then by the governor. Such argument or explanation, or both, shall not exceed three hundred words, and shall be filed with the secretary of state at least seventy-five days prior to the date of the election at which the measure is to be voted upon.

§ 3519.04 Estimate of proposed annual expenditures and annual yield of proposed taxes.

Upon receipt of the verified copy of a proposed state law or constitutional amendment proposing the levy of any tax or involving a matter which will necessitate the expenditure of any funds of the state or any political subdivision thereof, the secretary of state shall request of the tax commissioner an estimate of any annual expenditure of public funds proposed and the annual yield of any proposed taxes. The tax commissioner on receipt of such request shall prepare the estimate and file it in the office of the secretary of state. The secretary of state shall distribute copies of such estimate with the pamphlets prescribed in section 3519.19 of the Revised Code.

§ 3519.05 Form of petition.

If the measure to be submitted proposes a constitutional amendment, the heading of each part of the petition shall be prepared in the following form, and printed in capital letters in type of the approximate size set forth:

"INITIATIVE PETITION Number ....
Issued to ....
(Name of solicitor)
Date of issuance ....
Amendment to the Constitution Proposed by Initiative Petition To be submitted directly to the electors."

"Amendment" printed in fourteen-point boldface type shall precede the title, which shall be briefly expressed and printed in eight-point type. The summary shall then be set forth printed in ten-point type, and then shall follow the certification of the attorney general, under proper date, which shall also be printed in ten-point type. The petition shall then set forth the names and addresses of the committee of not less than three nor more than five to represent the petitioners in all matters relating to the petition or its circulation.

Immediately above the heading of the place for signatures on each part of the petition the following notice shall be printed in boldface type:

"NOTICE: Whoever knowingly signs this petition more than once, signs a name other than his own, or signs when not a qualified voter, is liable to prosecution.

In consideration of his services in soliciting signatures to this petition the solicitor has received or expects to receive ....
from ....
(Whose address is) ...."

Before any elector signs the part-petition, the solicitor shall completely fill in the above blanks if the solicitor has received or will receive any consideration and if the solicitor has not received and will not receive any consideration he shall insert "nothing."

The heading of the place for signatures shall be substantially as follows:

"(Sign with ink or indelible pencil. Your name, residence, and date of signing must be given.)

Rural Route or Post Office/County Township/Month—Day—Year/Signature
(Voters who do not live in a municipal corporation should fill in the information called for by headings printed above.)
(Voters who reside in municipal corporations should fill in the information called for by headings printed below.)

Rural Route or Post Office/County Township/Ward-Precinct/Month—Day—Year /Signature

The text of the proposed amendment shall be printed in full, immediately following the place for signatures, and shall ·be prefaced by "Be it resolved by the people of the State of Ohio." Immediately following the text of the proposed amendment must appear the following form:

"..., declares under penalty of election falsification that he is the circulator of the foregoing petition paper containing the signatures of .... electors, that the signatures appended hereto were made and appended in his presence on the date set opposite each respective name, and are the signatures of the persons whose names they purport to be, and that the electors signing this petition did so with knowledge of the contents of same.

(Signed) .... (Solicitor)
(Address) ....…...

THE PENALTY FOR ELECTION FALSIFICATION IS IMPRISONMENT FOR NOT MORE THAN SIX MONTHS, OR A FINE OF NOT MORE THAN ONE THOUSAND DOLLARS, OR BOTH.

If the measure proposes a law, the heading of each part of the petition shall be prepared as follows:

INITIATIVE PETITION Number ....
Issued to …...
(Name of solicitor)
Date of issuance ....…………………........
Law proposed by initiative petition first to be submitted to the General Assembly."

In all other respects the form shall be as provided for the submission of a constitutional amendment, except that the text of the proposed law shall be prefaced by "Be it enacted by the people of the state of Ohio."
The form for a supplementary initiative petition shall be the same as that provided for an initiative petition, with the exception that "supplementary" shall precede "initiative" in the title thereof.
The general provisions set forth in this section relative to the form and order of an initiative petition shall be, so far as practical, applicable to a referendum petition, the heading of which shall be as follows:

"REFERENDUM PETITION Number ....
Issued to …..
(Name of solicitor)
Date of issuance ....…………………........
To be submitted to the electors for their approval or rejection"

The title, which follows the heading, shall contain a brief legislative history of the law, section, or item of law to be referred. The text of the law so referred shall be followed by the certification of the secretary of state, in accordance with division (B)(2)(b) of section 3519.01 of the Revised Code, that it has been compared with the copy of the enrolled bill, on file in his office, containing such law, section, or item of law, and found to be correct.

§ 3519.06 Verification of petition.

No initiative or referendum part-petition is properly verified if it appears on the face thereof, or is made to appear by satisfactory evidence:
(A) That the statement required by section 3519.05 of the Revised Code is not properly filled out;
(B) That the statement is not properly signed;
(C) That the statement is altered by erasure, interlineations, or otherwise;
(D) That the statement is false in any respect;
(E) That any one person has affixed more than one signature thereto.

§§<BD+ 3519.07, 3519.08, 3519.09 Repealed.

§ 3519.10 Signer must be qualified elector; information to be given; each petition to contain signatures of electors of only one county.

Each signer of any initiative or referendum petition must be a qualified elector of the state. He shall place on such petition after his name the date of signing and the location of his voting residence, including the street and number in which such voting residence is located, if in a municipal corporation, and the rural route or other post-office address and township in which such voting residence is located, if outside a municipal corporation. Each signer may also print his name so as to clearly identify his signature. Each part-petition which is filed shall contain signatures of electors of only one county. Petitions containing signatures of electors of more than one county shall not thereby be declared invalid. In case petitions containing signatures of electors of more than one county are filed, the secretary of state shall determine the county from which the majority of signatures came, and only signatures from such county shall be counted. Signatures from any other county shall be invalid.

§ 3519.11 Repealed.

§§<BD+ 3519.12, 3519.13 Repealed.

§ 3519.14 Petition may not be filed with insufficient signatures.

The secretary of state shall not accept for filing any initiative or referendum petition which does not purport to contain at least the minimum number of signatures required for the submission of the amendment, proposed law, or law to be submitted under the initiative or referendum power.

§ 3519.15 Part-petitions sent to boards of elections; procedure by boards.

Whenever any initiative or referendum petition has been filed with the secretary of state, he shall forthwith separate the part-petitions by counties and transmit such part-petitions to the boards of elections in the respective counties. The several boards shall proceed at once to ascertain whether each part-petition is properly verified, and whether the names on each part-petition are on the registration lists of such county, or whether the persons whose names appear on each part-petition are eligible to vote in such county, and to determine any repetition or duplication of signatures, the number of illegal signatures, and the omission of any necessary details required by law. The boards shall make note opposite such signatures and submit a report to the secretary of state indicating the sufficiency or insufficiency of such signatures and indicating whether or not each part-petition is properly verified, eliminating, for the purpose of such report, all signatures on any part-petition that are not properly verified. In determining the sufficiency of such a petition, only the signatures of those persons shall be counted who are electors at the time the boards examine the petition.

§ 3519.16 Protest against board's findings; establishing of sufficiency or insufficiency of signatures; supplementary petition.

If the circulator of any part-petition, the committee interested therein, or any elector files with the board of elections a protest against the board's findings made pursuant to section 3519.15 of the Revised Code, then the board shall proceed to establish the sufficiency or insufficiency of the signatures and of the verification thereof in an action before the court of common pleas in the county. Such action must be brought within three days after the protest has been filed, and the case shall be heard forthwith by a judge of such court whose decision shall be certified to the board. The signatures which are adjudged sufficient or the part-petitions which are adjudged properly verified shall be included with the others by the board, and those found insufficient and all those part-petitions which are adjudged not properly verified shall not be included. The properly verified part-petitions, together with the report of the board, shall be returned to the secretary of state not less than fifty days before the election, provided that in the case of an initiated law to be presented to the general assembly the boards shall promptly check and return the petitions together with their report. The secretary of state shall notify the chairman of the committee in charge of the circulation as to the sufficiency or insufficiency of the petition and the extent of the insufficiency. If the petition is found insufficient because of an insufficient number of valid signatures, such committee shall be allowed ten additional days after such notification by the secretary of state for the filing of additional signatures to such petition. The part-petitions of the supplementary petition which appear to the secretary of state to be properly verified, upon receipt thereof by the secretary of state, shall forthwith be forwarded to the boards of the several counties together with the part-petitions of the original petition which have been properly verified, and shall be immediately examined and passed upon as to the validity and sufficiency of the signatures thereon by each of such boards and returned within five days to the secretary of state with the boards' report. No signature on a supplementary part-petition which is the same as a signature on an original part-petition shall be counted. The number of signatures in both the original and supplementary petitions, properly verified, shall be used by the secretary of state in determining the total number of signatures to the petition which he shall record and announce. If they are sufficient, then such amendment, proposed law, or law shall be placed on the ballot as required by law. If the petition is found insufficient, the secretary of state shall notify the committee in charge of the circulation of the petition.

§ 3519.17 Repealed.

§ 3519.18 Power of boards of elections.

In the performance of the duties required of the boards of elections, the boards may subpoena witnesses, compel the production of books, records, and other evidence, administer oaths, and take evidence.

§§<BD+ 3519.19, 3519.20 Repealed.

§ 3519.21 Ballot title of propositions or issues.

The order in which all propositions, issues, or questions, including proposed laws and constitutional amendments, shall appear on the ballot and the ballot title of all such propositions, issues, or questions shall be determined by the secretary of state in case of propositions to be voted upon in a district larger than a county, and by the board of elections in a county in the case of a proposition to be voted upon in a county or a political subdivision thereof. In preparing such a ballot title the secretary of state or the board shall give a true and impartial statement of the measures in such language that the ballot title shall not be likely to create prejudice for or against the measure. The person or committee promoting such measure may submit to the secretary of state or the board a suggested ballot title, which shall be given full consideration by the secretary of state or board in determining the ballot title.

Except as otherwise provided by law, all propositions, issues, or questions submitted to the electors and receiving an affirmative vote of a majority of the votes cast thereon are approved.

§ 3519.22 Election unaffected by insufficiency; number of petitioners needed.

No measure submitted to the electors and receiving an affirmative majority of the votes cast on the measure shall be held ineffective or void on account of the insufficiency of the petitions by which such submission was procured.

The basis upon which the required number of petitioners in any case is determined shall be the total number of votes cast for the office of governor, in the case of state, county, or municipal referendum, at the most recent election therefor.

The Basic Steps to Do an Initiative in Ohio

Statutes and Amendments — Indirect Initiative Process (Statutes), Direct Initiative Process (Amendments)

Basic procedures: Filing an initiative is a very simple process in Ohio. First, the proponent of the measure must designate a committee of not less than three (3) nor more than five (5) persons to represent them in all matters relating to the petition. Second, the written petition signed by 100 electors must be submitted to the Attorney General with the full text and summary of the proposed statute. The Attorney General certifies if, in her opinion, the summary is a fair and truthful statement of the proposed statute. A verified copy of the statute, together with the summary and Attorney General's certification must then be filed with the Secretary of State. Petitioners draw up the petition. It may be made up of part-petitions, but all separate petitions shall be filed at one time as one instrument. Each part-petition must have a copy of the full text of the proposed statute. The heading must be as specified in Art. II, Sec. 1b and R.C. 3519.05.

Date initiative language can be submitted to the state for the November 2001 or 2002 election: No Deadline

Signatures tied to vote of which office: Governor

Next Gubernatorial election: 2002

Votes cast for governor in last election: 3,346,238 (1998)

Net number of signatures required: For constitutional amendments, the total number of signatures must equal at least ten percent (10%) of the total vote cast for the office of governor at the last gubernatorial election (334,624 signatures). For statutes, the total number of signatures on the petition must equal at least three percent (3%) of the total vote cast for the office of governor at the last gubernatorial election (100,387). The Secretary of State may not accept for filing any initiative petition that does not purport to contain at least the minimum number of signatures required. If the General Assembly adopts the law then no additional signatures are needed. If the General Assembly fails to enact the proposed statute, passes it in amended form, or takes no action within four (4) months from the time it was received by the General Assembly, supplemental petitions may be circulated by the petitioners demanding that the proposal be submitted to the electors at the next general election. The supplemental petition must contain signatures of electors equal to three percent (3%) of the most recent vote for governor (another 100,387). Such petition must be signed and filed with the Secretary of State within ninety (90) days after the General Assembly fails to enact the proposed statute, passes it in amended form, or takes no action within four (4) months from the time it was received by the General Assembly. The petition may present the proposed law as worded on the original petition or with any amendments incorporated by the General Assembly.

Distribution requirement: The signatures for both amendments and statutes must be obtained from at least 44 of the 88 counties of the state. For statutes: From each of these 44 counties, there must be signatures equal to at least one and five-tenths percent (1.5%) of the total vote cast for the office of governor in that county at the last gubernatorial election. For amendments: From each of these 44 counties, there must be signatures equal to at least five percent (5%) of the total vote cast for the office of governor in that county at the last gubernatorial election.

Circulation period: unlimited

Do circulators have to be residents: No

Date when signatures are due for certification: For Statutes: The petition must be filed with the Secretary of State not less than ten (10) days prior to commencement of any session of the General Assembly. Legislative sessions begin on the first Monday in January. Filing must be accompanied by a twenty-five dollar ($25.00) filing fee. The Secretary of State transmits the proposal to the General Assembly as soon as it convenes. For Amendments: The petition must be filed with the Secretary of State not later than ninety (90) days prior to the General Election at which the amendment is to be submitted. (Early August of each year.)

Signature verification process: The petition and signatures on such petition shall be presumed to be in all respects sufficient, unless, it shall be otherwise proved, and in such event ten (10) additional days shall be allowed for the filing of additional signatures. Each signer must be a qualified elector of the state. Each part-petition must contain signatures of electors of only one county. If a part-petition contains signatures of more than one county, the Secretary of State determines the county from which the majority of signatures came from, and only signatures from that county will be counted.

Single-subject restriction: Yes

Legislative Tampering: The legislature can both repeal and amend initiatives.

General comments: The committee named on the petition may prepare an argument and/or explanation in favor of the amendment. The argument and/or explanation in opposition to the amendment is prepared by persons named by the General Assembly, if in session, or if not in session, by the Governor. The arguments and/or explanations may not exceed 300 words and must be filed with the Secretary of State not later than seventy-five (75) days before the election.

Oklahoma

Oklahoma's earliest advocate of initiative and referendum was Theodore L. Sturgis of Perry, who founded the territory's Direct Legislation League in 1899, eight years prior to statehood. The I&R movement soon picked up a formidable champion: Robert Latham Owen, who became the state's U.S. senator. Through the efforts of Sturgis' growing League, 102 of the 112 delegates elected in 1906 to Oklahoma's founding constitutional convention were committed in writing to supporting I&R. In early 1907 the convention voted 80 to 5 to include I&R in the constitution. Oklahoma's I&R provision, however, contained a quirk that was to cause initiative proponents endless headaches: it required that for any ballot measure to pass, it must be approved not just by a majority of the ballots cast on the proposition, but by a majority of all ballots cast in the election. The state's first successful initiative, which was on the ballot in a June 11, 1910 special election, proposed two questions in one: (1) Shall a permanent state capitol be established, and (2) if "yes" on the first, shall the capitol be at (a) Guthrie, (b) Oklahoma City, or (c) Shawnee? It passed, and voters chose Oklahoma City by a wide margin, but the state supreme court overruled their decision owing to the ballot's deviation from the single-question, "yes or no" norm. Nevertheless, Oklahoma City ultimately became the permanent state capital.

In the August 1910 primary, Oklahomans passed an initiative requiring a literacy test as a qualification for voting, which included a "grandfather clause" that made it apply solely to blacks. The U.S. Supreme Court (223 U.S. 347) struck down the measure as unconstitutional. Yet the election had been unfair for another reason as well: racist state officials, instead of printing "yes" and "no" on ballots, printed in small type: "For the amendment." Anyone wishing to vote against it was supposed to scratch out those words with a pencil. If they left their ballot as it was, it was counted as a vote in favor. In some precincts voters were not even provided with pencils. Casting further doubt on the accuracy of the 1910 vote count was a "literacy test" measure placed on the ballot by the legislature in the 1916 primary, six years later: voters rejected it by a 59 percent margin.

On the 1910 ballot, voters rejected an initiative to allow liquor sales in cities, which had been prohibited in Oklahoma's original constitution. It was the first of several Prohibition-repeal initiatives. The Oklahoma humorist Will Rogers would later say, "Oklahomans vote dry as long as they can stagger to the polls." Indeed, liquor was so plentiful that voters in 1914 passed an initiative to make "drunkenness and excessive use of intoxicating liquors" cause for the impeachment of elected officials.

In 1912, a majority of the voters favored one initiative to require the direct election (by the people, instead of by state legislators) of U.S. senators, and another to move the state capital to Guthrie. The first was superseded by passage of the Seventeenth Amendment to the U.S. Constitution, ratified the following year, while the second failed to win a majority of all ballots cast in the election.

The worst victim of the supermajority requirement was the 1914 gubernatorial candidate Charles West, who sponsored four initiatives: one to reduce the number of appellate courts, a second to reduce the property tax by 29 percent, a third to tax oil and gas production, and a fourth to abolish the state senate, thereby creating a unicameral legislature. All four garnered majorities of ballots cast on each proposition, but not majorities of the total cast in the election, and therefore failed.

In 1916 this unfair requirement brought down two more initiatives, to the chagrin of their Socialist sponsors. Ironically, the measures were designed to ensure the fairness of elections. One would have altered voting registration procedures; the other would have created a state election board composed of three members, one appointed by each of the state's three major political parties (the Socialists were the third-largest party at that time). In the 1920s, corruption in state government prompted an initiative to establish a procedure to convene the legislature promptly to investigate allegations of corruption; it passed by a nearly three to one margin but was thrown out by the state supreme court, which ruled that it was not the proper subject of a constitutional amendment. When the court threw out a 1926 initiative that would have established a procedure for contesting property tax levies, however, its sponsors persisted: they rewrote their initiative in conformity to the court's requirements, and voters passed it the second time in 1928 by a margin of nearly five to one.

The Great Depression hit Oklahoma hard, and Oklahomans turned to the initiative process to propose economic reforms. Among these were a 1935 initiative establishing a state welfare program and appropriating $2.5 million for it (passed by a 65 percent margin); a 1936 initiative increasing the automobile tag and sales taxes to provide assistance to needy elderly and disabled persons and children (approved by a 60 percent margin); and a 1936 constitutional amendment authorizing the latter initiative statute (passed by a 62 percent margin).

In the 1940s Oklahomans passed initiatives that provided retirement pensions for teachers (1942), allowed local property tax increases to aid schools (1946), and allowed the legislature to raise additional school funds (1946).

The only initiative to gain approval in the 1950s was a 1956 reapportionment measure; despite a four to three margin in favor, it failed to get a majority of those voting in the election. In the 1960s two more initiatives failed for the same reason: a 1962 reapportionment proposal and a 1964 measure changing the property tax limits. In 1974 the state constitution was finally amended so that an initiative would win if a majority of those voting on the individual initiative approved it.

However, in 2001, the state legislature placed a constitutional amendment on the ballot that would have required twice the number of signatures for initiatives pertaining to wildlife. This action was taken to stop animal protection advocates attempts to ban cockfighting in the state, however the voters defeated it.

Statewide Initiative Usage

Number of Initiatives	Number Passed	Number Failed	Passage Rate
83	38	45	47%

Statewide Initiatives

Year	Measure Number	Type	Subject Matter	Description	Pass/Fail
1908	5	DS	Administration of Government	The authorization of the sale of school and other public lands at auction giving the lessee the right of acceptance of the land at the highest bid, limiting the sales to 160 acres of land to the individual.	Failed
1910	15	DS	Administration of Government	A proposition to permanently locate State Capitol.	Passed
1910	16	DA	Business Regulation	Regulation of railroad, transportation or transmission companies.	Failed
1910	17	DA	Election Reform	No person shall be registered as an elector in this State, be allowed to vote in any election held herein, unless he be able to read and write any section of the Constitution of the State.	Passed
1910	22	DA	Alcohol Regulation	Provide for the licensed sale of intoxicating liquors in incorporated cities, towns, and villages after an election to determine whether said municipality shall license the sale of liquors to be consumed.	Failed
1910	6	DS	Administration of Government	The selection by a majority vote of New Jerusalem District compound of not less than six sections of land compactly located within 50 miles of the center of the State.	Failed
1910	8	DA	Election Reform	To authorize women to vote under the same circumstances and conditions as men may now do under the laws of this State.	Failed
1912	38	DA	Administration of Government	Qualifications and duties of members of the Board of Agriculture and the manner of selecting same.	Passed
1912	40	DA	Administration of Government	To move the State Capitol to a location at Guthrie.	Failed
1912	41	DS	Election Reform	That the United State Senators should be selected by direct vote of the people.	Passed
1914	68	DS	Taxes	To re-enact the direct and redirect system of taxation contained in Chap. 240, Session Laws 1913.	Passed
1914	71	DA	Judicial Reform	Reducing the number of final appellate Courts in the State from two to one, styled "The Supreme Court", to comprise nine associate justices and one chief justice; fixing their terms.	Passed
1914	73	DA	Alcohol Regulation	To make drunkenness and excessive use of intoxicating liquors cause for impeachment or removal from office.	Passed

Year	Measure Number	Type	Subject Matter	Description	Pass/Fail
1914	74	DA	Taxes	Reduces the maximum levy of State taxes, assessed on ad valorem basis, from 3.5 mills (.003 1/2) to 2.5 mills (.002 1/2) and prohibiting the Legislature from making appropriations in excess thereof.	Passed
1914	75	DA	Taxes	Levying and collecting a mine production tax, not exceeding two percent upon the gross value of such productions, upon natural gas, petroleum and other crude oils.	Passed
1914	77	DA	Administration of Government	To amend the Constitution as to reduce the Legislature to one body of 80 members styled and create a unicameral.	Passed
1916	78	DA	Education	Abolishing all existing election boards and providing for State Election Board.	Passed
1916	80	DA	Initiative and Referendum	To prevent Legislature from passing any law concerning registration of electors providing the initiative as the only method to enact such law and providing for registration in cities and towns.	Passed
1920	109	DA	Taxes	Providing for levying upon all property within the State not exempt from taxation an annual tax of not less than 16 mills and not more than 10 mills for maintenance	Failed
1920	99	DA	Taxes	Levying upon the pro-party of the general public service corporations of the State, those operating in more than one County, an annual tax for maintaining common schools.	Failed
1922	116	DA	Veteran Affairs	To make provision for paying a bonus to each soldier, sailor, marine and nurse inducted into the army or navy of the US during the war with Germany.	Passed
1923	119	DA	Administration of Government	To provide a method for promptly convening the Legislature for investigating the conduct of State officials.	Passed
1926	138	DS	Taxes	To provide a method for ascertaining the average ad valorem rate effective for each year, same to be the basis for gross production tax rates for the succeeding year.	Failed
1926	139	DS	Bonds	That all bonds hereafter authorized in the State, whether voted funding, or refunding shall become due and payable in equal annual installments as near as practicable.	Failed
1926	141	DS	Taxes	Provides authority and procedure for testing any tax levy and striking the illegal portion, if any, before same is spread of record.	Passed
1928	152	DS	Taxes	An act provides a method of contesting alleged illegal ad valorem tax levies; requiring copies of all appropriations and levies to be filed with the County clerk and State Auditor.	Passed
1931	167	DS	Taxes	An act repealing existent State Income Tax laws and money and credits tax law.	Failed

Year	Measure Number	Type	Subject Matter	Description	Pass/Fail
1931	169	DA	Business Regulation	Forbidding the ownership of lands by corporations outside of cities and towns, except such as may be necessary for use under their charters or licenses.	Failed
1931	172	DS	Education	Creating a State Board of Education of nine members, each appointed by Governor and confirmed by Senate and to receive for service $10 per day and expenses.	Failed
1931	173	DA	Administration of Government	Creating a budget officer appointed by the Governor, confirmed by the Senate and removable at pleasure of Governor.	Failed
1932	168	DA	Taxes	Limiting ad valorem rate upon personal property to not exceed 23 mills, upon real property to not exceed 15 mills, and appropriating same to subdivisions of government.	Failed
1932	170	DS	Business Regulation	An Act making unlawful the planting of cotton, wheat or other soil exhausting plants in excess of 30% of area of each separately owned tract of land in cultivation previous year.	Failed
1932	171	DS	Administration of Government	Creating new Commission, making Governor member; authorizing construction of reservoirs and farm-to-market roads.	Failed
1932	175	DS	Taxes	An Act for reduction of ad valorem taxes by levying taxes on incomes of individuals, associations and trusts; and excise taxes on incomes of corporations and banks.	Failed
1935	201	DA	Taxes	A proposed amendment to the Constitution providing that all homesteads within said state may be exempted from ad valorem taxation by the Legislature.	Passed
1935	214	DA	Welfare	Relative to old age pensions.	Passed
1935	220	DS	Administration of Government	Appropriating from State Treasury to State Board of Public welfare, $1.5 million and $1 million respectively for fiscal years ending June 30, 1936, and June 30, 1937, to be allocated to counties.	Passed
1936	222	DA	Alcohol Regulation	A Constitutional amendment repealing prohibition provisions; authorizing manufacture, sale and transportation of alcohol and alcoholic beverages in Oklahoma.	Failed
1936	225	DA	Welfare	Authorizing legislation providing for relief and care of needy aged persons who are unable to provide for themselves.	Failed
1936	226	DS	Welfare	An Act providing assistance to needy persons aged 65 or over, needy blind persons, needy crippled children, and needy persons aged fifteen or younger.	Passed
1936	230	DS	Environmental Reform	An Act designating the OK Conservation Commission as a State agency to co-operate with Federal Government in designated projects.	Failed

Year	Measure Number	Type	Subject Matter	Description	Pass/Fail
1938	205	DA	Administration of Government	Proposed constitutional amendment empowering bodies politic, including rural utility districts, organized there under, to assume revenue indebtedness.	Failed
1940	215	DA	Taxes	Authorizing the levy of a graduated tax on land; levying for State Old Age Security, until otherwise provided, an additional tax upon land owned by any person in excess of 640 acres.	Passed
1940	241	DS	Administration of Government	Abolishing alternate members of State Board of Medical Examiners; prohibiting one school of medical practice from having majority membership on said Board.	Passed
1940	253	DS	Taxes	Providing for allocation, apportionment, distribution and use of moneys received by State of OK through levy.	Passed
1940	281	DA	Administration of Government	Qualifications for office.	Passed
1940	289	DA	Alcohol Regulation	A Constitutional amendment authorizing and regulating importation, manufacture, transportation and sale of whiskey and other alcoholic beverages.	Failed
1942	306	DA	Education	Authorizing the Legislature to enact laws to provide for the retirement of meritorious service teachers and other employees in the public schools, colleges and universities in this state.	Passed
1946	314	DA	Taxes	The annual ad valorem tax rate for school purposes may be increased in any school district, but not to exceed 15 mills on the dollar valuation upon all property therein.	Passed
1946	315	DA	Taxes	The Legislature shall raise and appropriate funds for annual support of common schools.	Passed
1949	325	DA	Administration of Government	Creating a four member highway commission of not exceeding two members from any political party nor one from any congressional district members to be appointed by Governor.	Failed
1950	326	DA	Taxes	Prohibits the diversion of any highway users' revenue, including gasoline taxes, registration fees and operators' licenses, in excess of the cost of collection and administration.	Failed
1952	349	DS	Taxes	Increase the tax rate from 2% to 3% upon the gross proceeds of sales to consumers or users.	Failed
1956	357	DS	Apportionment/ Redistricting	An Act to divide the state into 6 new congressional districts with populations according to the 1950 federal decennial census as follows.	Passed
1956	377	DA	Administration of Government	Creating the County offices of County Attorney, County Clerk, Sheriff, County Treasurer, County Surveyor, County Assessor and County Superintendent of Schools.	Failed

Year	Measure Number	Type	Subject Matter	Description	Pass/Fail
1957	376	DA	Alcohol Regulation	Authorize County option and the holding of special elections in and by counties at County expense not more often than every two years, to prohibit or permit beverages containing more than 1/2 of 1% of alcohol by volume.	Failed
1960	396	DA	Administration of Government	Creating a constitutional State Highway Commission to develop and plan a state-wide road program.	Failed
1960	397	DA	Apportionment/ Redistricting	Providing for legislative apportionment by a commission composed of the Attorney General, State Treasurer and Secretary of State.	Failed
1960	398	DS	Administration of Government	Providing for each County to determine whether it shall transfer the construction and maintenance of County roads to State Highway Commission.	Failed
1962	408	DA	Apportionment/ Redistricting	Providing method for enforcement of the present constitutional formula apportioning members of the House of Representatives and Senate, vesting this duty in the Attorney General, Secretary of State and State Treasurer.	Passed
1964	409	DA	Labor	Providing that no person shall be denied the freedom to obtain or retain employment because of membership or non-membership in any labor union or labor organization.	Failed
1964	421	DA	Education	Abolishing authorization for emergency levy for school districts, and authorizing a local support levy for benefit of schools of a school district of not to exceed 15 mills.	Passed
1964	422	DS	Education	Relating to the payment of State Aid to school districts; increasing allowance in minimum program of school districts for certain items of expenditures fixing basis for calculation for teachers' salaries.	Failed
1964	423	DS	Education	Shall a bill relating to school districts; providing for disorganization of school districts not maintaining 12 years of accredited instruction and annexation of territory.	Failed
1964	424	DS	Education	Relating to County superintendents of schools; providing County superintendents shall conduct joint programs for school districts when requested to do so, and prescribing manner of payment of cost thereof.	Failed
1968	441	DA	Judicial Reform	Creating a judicial department; vesting judicial power; providing for the establishment, organization and jurisdiction of the court; the nomination, selection and compensation.	Failed
1971	478	DS	Business Regulation	Making it unlawful to sell certain enumerated merchandise on the consecutive days of Saturday and Sunday at the same location.	Failed

Year	Measure Number	Type	Subject Matter	Description	Pass/Fail
1972	480	DA	Alcohol Regulation	Permitting the sale of intoxicating alcoholic beverages by individual drink for on premise consumption.	Failed
1976	515	DA	Alcohol Regulation	Sale of alcoholic beverages, licensees, terms.	Failed
1978	524	DS	Administration of Government	License/registration through mail; Tax Commission.	Passed
1979	539	DS	Taxes	Deduct individual Federal Income tax from state income.	Failed
1982	553	DS	Gaming	Creation of Oklahoma Horse Racing Commission.	Passed
1982	556	DS	Apportionment/ Redistricting	Creation of new Congressional districts.	Failed
1984	563	DA	Alcohol Regulation	Renaming Alcoholic Beverage Commission; taxation.	Passed
1989	620	DA	Administration of Government	Legislative Session: dates and times.	Passed
1990	627	DA	Administration of Government	Create five-member Ethics Commission.	Passed
1990	632	DA	Term Limits	State legislative term limits. Twelve years limit.	Passed
1991	639	DS	Education	Repeal minimum standards for school accreditation.	Failed
1992	640	DA	Taxes	Revenue bills approval by voters or 3/4 Legislature and Governor.	Passed
1994	658	DA	Gaming	Would create a state lottery.	Failed
1994	662	DA	Term Limits	Term limits on Congress 6/12.	Passed
1996	669	DA	Taxes	Would limit property taxes.	Failed
1998	672	DA	Gaming	To establish casino gambling.	Failed

Oklahoma Constitution

Article V

Section V-2. Designation and definition of reserved powers — Determination of percentages.

The first power reserved by the people is the initiative, and eight per centum of the legal voters shall have the right to propose any legislative measure, and fifteen per centum of the legal voters shall have the right to propose amendments to the Constitution by petition, and every such petition shall include the full text of the measure so proposed. The second power is the referendum, and it may be ordered (except as to laws necessary for the immediate preservation of the public peace, health, or safety), either by petition signed by five per centum of the legal voters or by the Legislature as other bills are enacted. The ratio and per centum of legal voters hereinbefore stated shall be based upon the total number of votes cast at the last general election for the State office receiving the highest number of votes at such election.

Section V-3. Petitions — Veto power — Elections — Time of taking effect — Style of bills — Duty of legislature.

Referendum petitions shall be filed with the Secretary of State not more than ninety (90) days after the final adjournment of the session of the Legislature which passed the bill on which the referendum is demanded. The veto power of the Governor shall not extend to measures voted on by the people. All elections on measures referred to the people of the state shall be had at the next election held throughout the state, except when the Legislature or the Governor shall order a special election for the express purpose of making such reference. Any measure referred to the people by the initiative or referendum shall take effect and be in force when it shall have been approved by a majority of the votes cast thereon and not otherwise. The style of all bills shall be: "Be it Enacted By the People of the State of Oklahoma."

Petitions and orders for the initiative and for the referendum shall be filed with the Secretary of State and addressed to the Governor of the state, who shall submit the same to the people. The Legislature shall make suitable provisions for carrying into effect the provisions of this article.

Section V-4. Referendum against part of act.

The referendum may be demanded by the people against one or more items, sections, or parts of any act of the Legislature in the same manner in which such power may be exercised against a complete act. The filing of a referendum petition against one or more items, sections, or parts of an act shall not delay the remainder of such act from becoming operative.

Section V-5. Reservation of powers to voters of counties and districts — Manner of exercising.

The powers of the initiative and referendum reserved to the people by this Constitution for the State at large, are hereby further reserved to the legal voters of every county and district therein, as to all local legislation, or action, in the administration of county and district government in and for their respective counties and districts. The manner of exercising said powers shall be prescribed by general laws, except that Boards of County Commissioners may provide for the time of exercising the initiative and referendum powers as to local legislation in their respective counties and districts.

The requisite number of petitioners for the invocation of the initiative and referendum in counties and districts shall bear twice, or double, the ratio to the whole number of legal voters in such county or district, as herein provided therefor in the State at large.

Section V-5a. Township organization or government — Abolition and restoration.

Each county in the State of Oklahoma may by a majority of the legal voters of such county voting upon the proposition, abolish township organization or government. The Board of County Commissioners of such county, upon a petition signed by sixteen per centum of the total number of votes cast at the last general election for the county office receiving the highest number of votes, praying that the question of abolishing township organization or government be submitted to a vote of the county, shall within thirty days after the regular meeting of such board next convening after the filing of such petition, call a special election for such purpose, or the board may in their discretion submit such question at the next general election held after the filing of such petition. If such question shall be carried, township organization or government shall cease in such county, and all the duties theretofore performed by the township officers shall be cast upon and be performed by such county officers having like duties to perform in relation to the county at large as such township officers performed in relation to the township at large. At any general election after the abolition of township organization or government the question of returning to township government may be submitted as provided for the submission of the question of abolishing such government, and if a majority of the votes cast upon such question be in favor of township government the same shall thereupon be established, and the Board of County Commissioners shall appoint the full quota of township officers, who shall hold their offices and perform the duties thereof until their successors shall have been elected at the next general election and until they have been qualified. Except as otherwise specifically provided by this section, the law relating to carrying into effect the initiative and referendum provisions of the Constitution shall govern.

Section V-6. Subsequent proposal of rejected measure.

Any measure rejected by the people, through the powers of the initiative and referendum, cannot be again proposed by the initiative within three years thereafter by less than twenty-five per centum of the legal voters.

Section V-7. Powers of Legislature not affected.

The reservation of the powers of the initiative and referendum in this article shall not deprive the Legislature of the right to repeal any law, propose or pass any measure, which may be consistent with the Constitution of the State and the Constitution of the United States.

Article XXIV

Section XXIV-3. Right of amendment by initiative petition not impaired.

This article shall not impair the right of the people to amend this Constitution by a vote upon an initiative petition therefor.

Oklahoma Statutes

§34-1.

The referendum petition shall be substantially as follows:

PETITION FOR REFERENDUM

To the Honorable _____, Governor of Oklahoma (or To the Honorable _____, Mayor, Chairman of County Commissioners, or other chief executive officer, as the case may be, of the city, county or other municipal corporation of _____):

We, the undersigned legal voters of the State of Oklahoma (or district of _____, county of _____, or city of _____, as the case may be), respectfully order that Senate (or House) Bill No. _____ (or ordinance No. _____), entitled (title of Act, and if the petition is against less than the whole Act, then set forth here the part or parts on which the referendum is sought), passed by the _____ Legislature of the State of Oklahoma, at the regular (or special) session of said legislature, shall be referred to the people of the State (district of _____, county of _____, or city of _____, as the case may be) for their approval or rejection at the regular (or special) election to be held on the _____ day of _____, 19__, and each for himself says:

I have personally signed this petition; I am a legal voter of the State of Oklahoma (and district of _____, county of _____, or city of _____, as the case may be); my residence or post office are correctly written after my name. Referendum petitions shall be filed with the Secretary of State not more than ninety days after the final adjournment of the session of the legislature which passed the bill on which the referendum is demanded. (For county, city or other municipality the length of time shall be thirty days.) The question we herewith submit to our fellow voters is:

Shall the following bill of the legislature (or ordinance or resolution—local legislation) be approved? (Insert here an exact copy of the title and text of the measure.) Name and Address of Proponents (not to exceed three) Name _____ Residence _____ Post Office _____ If in city, street and number.

(Here follow twenty numbered lines for signatures.)

§34-2.

The form of initiative petition shall be substantially as follows:

INITIATIVE PETITION

To the Honorable _____, Governor of Oklahoma (or To the Honorable _____, Mayor, Chairman of County Commissioners, or other chief executive officers, as the case may be, for the city, county or other municipality):

We, the undersigned legal voters of the State of Oklahoma (and of the district of _____, county of _____, or city of _____, as the case may be), respectfully order that the following proposed law (or amendment to the constitution, ordinance, or amendment to the city charter, as the case may be) shall be submitted to the legal voters of the State of Oklahoma (or of the district of _____, county of _____, or city of _____, as the case may be) for their approval or rejection at the regular general election (or regular or special city election), to be held on the _____ day of _____, 19__, and each for himself says:

I have personally signed this petition; I am a legal voter of the State of Oklahoma (and of the district of _____, county of _____, city of _____, as the case may be); my residence or post office are correctly written after my name. The time for filing this petition expires ninety days from (insert date when petition is to be opened for signatures). (This for State initiative. For county, city, or other municipality the length of time shall be ninety days.) The question we herewith submit to our fellow voters is:

Shall the following bill (or proposed amendment to the Constitution or resolution) be approved? (Insert here an exact copy of the title and text of the measure.) Name and Address of Proponents (not to exceed three) Name _____ Residence _____ Post Office_____ If in the city, street and number.

(Here follow twenty numbered lines for signatures.)

§34-3.

Each initiative petition and each referendum petition shall be duplicated for the securing of signatures, and each sheet for signatures shall be attached to a copy of the petition. Each copy of the petition and sheets for signatures is hereinafter termed a pamphlet. On the outer page of each pamphlet shall be printed the word "Warning", and underneath this in ten-point type the words, "It is a felony for anyone to sign an initiative or referendum petition with any name other than his own, or knowingly to sign his name more than once for the measure, or to sign such petition when he is not a legal voter". A simple statement of the gist of the proposition shall be printed on the top margin of each signature sheet. Not more than twenty (20) signatures on one sheet on lines provided for the signatures shall be counted. Any signature sheet not in substantial compliance with this act shall be disqualified by the Secretary of State.

§34-3.1.

It shall be unlawful for any person other than a qualified elector of the State of Oklahoma to circulate any initiative or referendum petition to amend, add to, delete, strike or otherwise change in any way the Constitution or laws of the State of Oklahoma, or of any subdivision of the State of Oklahoma. Every person convicted of a violation of this section shall be punished by a fine of not to exceed One Thousand Dollars ($1,000.00), or by imprisonment in the county jail for not to exceed one (1) year, or by both said fine and imprisonment.

§34-4.

When any such initiative or referendum petition shall be offered for filing, the Secretary of State, in the presence of the person offering the same for filing, shall detach the sheets containing the signatures and affidavits and cause them all to be attached to one or more printed copies of the measure so proposed by initiative or referendum petition. All petitions for the initiative and referendum and sheets for signatures shall be printed on pages eight and one-half (8 1/2) inches in width by fourteen (14) inches in length, with a margin of one and three-fourths (1 3/4) inches at the top for binding; if the aforesaid sheets shall be too bulky for convenient binding in one volume, they may be bound in two or more volumes, those in each volume to be attached to a single printed copy of such measure; the detached copies of such measures shall be delivered to the person offering the same for filing. Each of the volumes and each signature sheet therein shall be numbered consecutively, and a cover sheet shall be attached, showing the purported number of signature sheets, the series of numbers assigned to the signature sheets and the total number of signatures counted per volume. The Secretary of State shall render a signed receipt to the person offering the petition for filing, which receipt shall include a report, volume by volume, showing the number of signature sheets in each volume, the series of numbers assigned to the signature sheets in each volume, and the number of purported signatures in each volume. Duplicate copies of the cover sheets, with necessary corrections, may be used as receipts. If the volume of signatures is sufficiently large, the Secretary of State shall seal the petitions in such manner that they cannot be opened unless the seal is broken, and if requested by those filing said petition, they shall not be opened before 9:00 a.m. on the day following the date said petitions are filed and said procedure shall continue until such time as the Secretary shall be able to receipt the petitions so filed; but additional signature sheets shall not be accepted after 5:00 p.m. on ninetieth day. The Secretary of State shall not provide any copies of signature sheets to anyone until the sheets have been bound as provided in this section. Provided, that whenever reference is made in this act to the Secretary of State, such reference shall include the Secretary of State or any officer constitutionally designated to perform the duties herein prescribed.

§34-5.

A. If any measure shall, at the ensuing election, be approved by the people, then the copies so preserved, with the sheets of signatures and affidavits, and a certified copy of the Governor's proclamation declaring the same to have been approved by the people, shall be bound together in such form that they may be conveniently identified. The material required to be bound together shall be preserved by the Secretary of State for two (2) years after the measure was filed with the Secretary of State or, if objections or protests are filed on a measure, for two (2) years after the final decision of the Supreme Court on any objections or protests filed. Thereafter, the Secretary of State may dispose of the material in cooperation with the Archives and Records Commission.

B. The Secretary of State may dispose of materials from measures which were filed prior to this act in cooperation with the Archives and Records Commission. C. The Secretary of State shall cause every such measure so approved by the people to be printed with the general laws enacted by the next ensuing session of the Legislature with the date of the Governor's proclamation declaring the same to have been approved by the people.

§34-6.

Each sheet of every such petition containing signatures shall be verified on the back thereof, in substantially the following form, by the person who circulated said sheet of said petition, by his or her affidavit thereon and as a part thereof.

State of Oklahoma,)
) ss.
County of _____)

I, _____, being first duly sworn, say: That I am a qualified elector of the State of Oklahoma and that (Here shall be legibly written or typewritten the names of the signers of the sheet), signed this sheet of the foregoing petition, and each of them signed his name thereto in my presence; I believe that each has stated his name, post office address, and residence correctly, and that each signer is a legal voter of the State of Oklahoma and county of _____ or of the city of _____ (as the case may be).

_____
(Signature and post office address of affiant.)

Subscribed and sworn to before me this _____ day of _____ A.D. 19__. (Signature and title of the officer before whom oath is made, and his post office address.)

§34-6.1.

A. The Secretary of State shall make or cause to be made a physical count of the number of signatures on the petitions. In making such count, the Secretary of State shall not include in such physical count:
1. All signatures on any sheet of any petition which is not verified by the person who circulated the sheet of the petition as provided in Section 6 of this title;
2. All signatures of nonresidents;
3. All signatures on a sheet that is not attached to a copy of the petition;
4. All multiple signatures on any printed signature line;
5. All signatures not on a printed signature line;
6. Those signatures by a person who signs with any name other than his own or signs more than once; and
7. All signatures on any sheet on which a notary has failed to sign, the seal of the notary is absent, the commission of the notary has expired or the expiration date is not on the signature sheet.
B. The Secretary of State shall notify the Attorney General of any and all violations of this title of which he has knowledge.

§34-7.

Each order for a direct ballot by the voters that is filed with the Secretary of State by initiative petition, referendum petition, and by the Legislature shall be numbered consecutively, each in a series by itself, beginning with one, to be continued year after year, without duplication of numbers.

§34-8.

A. When a citizen or citizens desire to circulate a petition initiating a proposition of any nature, whether to become a statute law or an amendment to the Constitution, or for the purpose of invoking a referendum upon legislative enactments, such citizen or citizens shall, when such petition is prepared, and before the same is circulated or signed by electors, file a true and exact copy of same in the office of the Secretary of State and, within ninety (90) days after such filing of an initiative petition, the signed copies thereof shall be filed with the Secretary of State, but the signed copies of a referendum petition shall be filed with the Secretary of State within ninety (90) days after the adjournment of the Legislature enacting the measure on which the referendum is invoked. The electors shall sign their legally-registered name, their address or post office box, and the name of the county in which they reside. Any petition not filed in accordance with this provision shall not be considered. The proponents of a referendum or an initiative petition, any time before the final submission of signatures, may withdraw the referendum or initiative petition upon written notification to the Secretary of State.

B. The proponents of a referendum or an initiative petition may terminate the circulation period any time during the ninety-day circulation period by certifying to the Secretary of State that:

1. All signed petitions have already been filed with the Secretary of State;

2. No more petitions are in circulation; and

3. The proponents will not circulate any more petitions. If the Secretary of State receives such a certification from the proponents, the Secretary of State shall begin the counting process.

C. When the signed copies of a petition are timely filed, the Secretary of State shall certify to the Supreme Court of the state:

1. The total number of signatures counted pursuant to procedures set forth in this title; and

2. The total number of votes cast for the state office receiving the highest number of votes cast at the last general election. The Supreme Court shall make the determination of the numerical sufficiency or insufficiency of the signatures counted by the Secretary of State. Upon order of the Supreme Court it shall be the duty of the Secretary of State to forthwith cause to be published, in at least one newspaper of general circulation in the state, a notice of such filing and the apparent sufficiency or insufficiency thereof and notice that any citizen or citizens of the state may file a protest to the petition or an objection to the count made by the Secretary of State, by a written notice to the Supreme Court of the state and to the proponent or proponents filing the petition, said protest to be filed within ten (10) days after publication. A copy of the protest or objection to the count shall be filed with the Secretary of State. In case of the filing of an objection to the count, notice shall also be given to the Secretary of State and the party filing a protest, if one was filed.

D. The Secretary of State shall deliver the bound volumes of signatures to the Supreme Court.

E. Upon the filing of an objection to the count, the Supreme Court shall resolve the objection with dispatch. The Supreme Court shall adopt rules to govern proceedings to apply to the challenge of a measure on the grounds that the proponents failed to gather sufficient signatures.

F. Upon the filing of a protest to the petition, the Supreme Court of the state shall then fix a day, not less than ten (10) days thereafter, at which time it will hear testimony and arguments for and against the sufficiency of such petition.

G. A protest filed by anyone hereunder may, if abandoned by the party filing same, be revived within five (5) days by any other citizen. After such hearing the Supreme Court of the state shall decide whether such petition be in form as required by the statutes. If the Court be at the time adjourned, the Chief Justice shall immediately convene the same for such hearing. No objection to the sufficiency shall be considered unless the same shall have been made and filed as herein provided.

H. If in the opinion of the Supreme Court, any objection to the count or protest to the petition is frivolous, the Court may impose appropriate sanctions, including an award of costs and attorneys fees to either party as the court deems equitable.

I. Whenever reference is made in this act to the Supreme Court of the state, such reference shall include the members of the Supreme Court of the state or any officer constitutionally designated to perform the duties herein prescribed.

§34-9.

A. When a referendum is ordered by petition of the people against any measure passed by the Legislature or when any measure is proposed by initiative petition, whether as an amendment to the Constitution or as a statute, it shall be the duty of the parties submitting the measure to prepare and file one copy of the measure with the Secretary of State and one copy with the Attorney General.

B. The parties submitting the measure shall also submit a suggested ballot title which shall be filed on a separate sheet of paper and shall not be deemed part of the petition. The suggested ballot title:

1. Shall not exceed two hundred (200) words;

2. Shall explain in basic words, which can be easily found in dictionaries of general usage, the effect of the proposition;

3. Shall be written on the eighth-grade reading comprehension level;

4. Shall not contain any words which have a special meaning for a particular profession or trade not commonly known to the citizens of this state;

5. Shall not reflect partiality in its composition or contain any argument for or against the measure;

6. Shall contain language which clearly states that a "yes" vote is a vote in favor of the proposition and a "no" vote is a vote against the proposition; and

7. Shall not contain language whereby a "yes" vote is, in fact, a vote against the proposition and a "no" vote is, in fact, a vote in favor of the proposition.

C. When a measure is proposed as a constitutional amendment by the Legislature or when the Legislature proposes a statute conditioned upon approval by the people:

1. After final passage of a measure, the Secretary of State shall submit the proposed ballot title to the Attorney General for review as to legal correctness. Within five (5) business days, the Attorney General shall, in writing, notify the Secre-

tary of State, the President Pro Tempore of the Senate and the Speaker of the House of Representatives whether or not the proposed ballot title complies with applicable laws. The Attorney General shall state with specificity any and all defects found and, if necessary, within ten (10) business days of determining that the proposed ballot title is defective, prepare and file a ballot title which complies with the law;

2. After receipt of the measure and the official ballot title, as certified by the Attorney General, the Secretary of State shall within five (5) days transmit to the Secretary of the State Election Board an attested copy of the measure, including the official ballot title.

D. The following procedure shall apply to ballot titles of referendums ordered by a petition of the people or any measure proposed by an initiative petition:

1. After the filing and binding of the petition pamphlets, the Secretary of State shall submit the proposed ballot title to the Attorney General for review as to legal correctness. Within five (5) business days after the filing of the measure and ballot title, the Attorney General shall, in writing, notify the Secretary of State whether or not the proposed ballot title complies with applicable laws. The Attorney General shall state with specificity any and all defects found and, if necessary, within ten (10) business days of determining that the proposed ballot title is defective, prepare and file a ballot title which complies with the law; and

2. Within ten (10) business days after completion of the review by the Attorney General, the Secretary of State shall, if no appeal is filed, transmit to the Secretary of the State Election Board an attested copy of the measure, including the official ballot title, and a certification that the requirements of this section have been met. If an appeal is taken from such ballot title within the time specified in Section 10 of this title, then the Secretary of State shall certify to the Secretary of the State Election Board the ballot title which is finally approved by the Supreme Court.

§34-10.

A. Any person who is dissatisfied with the wording of a ballot title may, within ten (10) days after the same is filed by the Attorney General with the Secretary of State as provided for in Section 9 of this title, appeal to the Supreme Court by petition in which shall be offered a substitute ballot title for the one from which the appeal is taken. Upon the hearing of such appeal, the court may correct or amend the ballot title before the court, or accept the substitute suggested, or may draft a new one which will conform to the provisions of Section 9 of this title.

B. No such appeal shall be allowed as to the ballot title of constitutional and legislative enactments proposed by the Legislature.

§34-11.

Notice of the appeal provided for in the preceding section shall be served upon the Attorney General and upon the party who filed such ballot title, or on any of such parties, at least five (5) days before such appeal is heard by the court. The Attorney General shall, and any citizen interested may, defend the ballot title from which the appeal is taken. Other procedure upon such appeals shall be the same as is prescribed for appeals from petitions filed as set forth in Section 8 of this title.

§34-12.

When the ballot title has been decided upon, the Secretary of State shall, in writing, notify the Governor, who forthwith shall issue a proclamation setting forth the substance of the measure and the date on which the vote will be held.

§34-17.

It shall be the duty of the Secretary of State, not less than five (5) days before any election held throughout the state at which any proposed law, part of an act, or amendment to the constitution is to be submitted to the people of the state for their approval or rejection, to cause to be published once in two different newspapers of general statewide circulation and in a newspaper of general circulation in each county, a copy of all ballots on initiated and referred questions, measures, and constitutional amendments, and an explanation of how to vote for or against propositions. The Secretary of State shall designate the newspapers in which the publication shall be made. The publication shall be paid for at the legal rate for other publications, out of any funds of the state appropriated therefor.

§34-18.

In the event any official of this state shall fail or neglect to prepare or have published the argument and other matter as provided by law, or to perform any other duty required in connection therewith, any elector may petition the district court, without cost to him, where any such officer has his official residence, for a writ of mandamus to require such officer to perform such duty, and the district courts of this state are hereby given jurisdiction to issue writs of mandamus and require performance of such duty as provided by law.

§34-19.

The failure to prepare and have published the argument and other matter as provided by law shall not invalidate the election held on any initiative or referendum or Constitutional amendment proposed by the Legislature, and no election on any such measure shall be declared or held invalid on the grounds that such publication was not so prepared or published.

§34-21.

Where there are competing measures and neither receives a majority of the votes cast for and against the one receiving the greatest number of votes shall, if it has received more than one-third (1/3) of the votes cast for and against both bills, be submitted by itself at the next general election. If two or more conflicting laws shall be approved by the people at the same election, the law receiving the greatest number of affirmative votes shall be paramount in all particulars as to which there is a conflict, even though such law may not have received the greatest majority of affirmative votes. If two or more conflicting amendments to the constitution shall be approved by the people at the same election, the amendment which receives the greatest number of affirmative votes shall be paramount in all particulars as to which there is a conflict even though such amendment may not have received the greatest majority of affirmative votes.

§34-22.

Whenever any measure or proposition is submitted to a vote by the initiative or referendum, it shall be the duty of the precinct election board of the precinct to make and transmit to the county election board the returns thereof in the same manner that they make their returns in the case of an election of public officers, transmitting to such county election board a certificate of the total number of electors voting in such elections; and the county election board shall keep a record showing such total number of votes cast in each of such precincts as shown by such returns. Should the proposition be one covering the state at large, or any district therein, or be of such other nature as to require it the county election board shall certify the result of such election to the State Election Board in the same manner as it certifies the result of election for public officers, and such county election board shall transmit to the State Election Board a certificate showing the total number of votes cast at any such election. It shall be the duty of the State Election Board to keep a record of all such election returns made to it under the provisions of this section.

§34-23.

Every person who is a qualified elector of the State of Oklahoma may sign a petition for the referendum or for the initiative for any measure upon which he is legally entitled to vote. Any person signing any name other than his own to any petition, or knowingly signing his name more than once for the same measure at one election, or who is not at the time of signing the same a legal voter of this state, or whoever falsely makes or willfully destroys a petition or any part thereof, or who signs or files any certificate or petition knowing the same or any part thereof to be falsely made, or suppresses any certificate or petition or any part thereof which has been duly filed or who shall violate any provision of this statute, or who shall aid or abet any other person in doing any of said acts; and any person violating any provision of this chapter, shall upon conviction thereof be guilty of a felony and shall be punished by a fine of not exceeding Five Hundred Dollars ($500.00) or by imprisonment in the State Penitentiary not exceeding two (2) years, or by both such fine and imprisonment in the discretion of the court before which such conviction shall be had.

§34-24.

The procedure herein prescribed is not mandatory, but if substantially followed will be sufficient. If the end aimed at can be attained and procedure shall be sustained, clerical and mere technical errors shall be disregarded.

§34-25.

Whenever any measure shall be initiated by the people in the manner provided by law, or whenever the referendum shall be demanded against any measure passed by the Legislature, same shall be submitted to the people for their approval or rejection at the next regular election; provided, the Governor shall have power, in his discretion, to call a special election to vote upon such questions, or to designate the mandatory primary election as a special election for such purpose.

§34-27.

The Secretary of State may prepare and distribute information to the public on the initiative and referendum process. The information shall include, but not be limited to relevant statutes and constitutional provisions related to the initiative and referendum process. The information should also outline the initiative and referendum process in a chronological order.

The Basic Steps to Do an Initiative in Oklahoma

Statutes and Amendments — Direct Initiative Process

Basic procedures to file with the state: Filing an initiative is a very simple process in Oklahoma. All you need to do is take your initiative petition—in final camera-ready artwork form—to the Secretary of State. Once you have filed—that day in fact—you can begin to collect signatures. The Secretary of State writes the ballot title after the signatures are submitted.

Date initiative language can be submitted to the state for the November 2002 election: Anytime

Signatures tied to vote of which office: Total votes cast for the office receiving the most votes in the last General Election. (Which was the President in 2000.)

Next General election: 2002

Votes cast for President in last election: 1,234,237 (2000)

Net number of signatures required: 15% of votes cast for Governor for a constitutional amendment (185,135) and 8% of votes cast for Governor for a statute (98,739).

Distribution requirement: None.

Circulation period: 90 days

Do circulators have to be residents: Yes (They have to be qualified electors.)

Date when signatures are due for certification: The Secretary of State recommends that you submit your signatures eight months prior to the election that you desire the measure to be considered for. This is primarily because the state has a provision that the ballot title set by the Secretary of State can be challenged. If a ballot title is challenged, the state supreme court reviews the challenge. There is no statutory requirement for the state to rule on this challenge. There have been instances when the court has taken over a year to make a ruling. The latest they can be submitted is 60 days before the election, which can be either a Primary or a General election.

Signature verification process: Presumed valid unless challenged

Single-subject restriction: Yes

Legislative tampering: The legislature can both repeal and amend initiatives, according to a court ruling.

General comments: Please note that the legislature or the Governor can order an initiative to appear on a special election ballot. The legislature did this in 1998 with the last initiative to appear on the state's ballot, which legalized gaming—it was defeated.

Oregon

Oregon holds the records for the most statewide initiatives (there were 318 between 1904 and 2000), the highest average initiative use (6.6 per general election), and the most statewide initiatives on the ballot in a single year—27 in 1912.

Historians identify one man as the driving force behind I&R: William Simon U'Ren known as early as 1898 as "Referendum U'Ren" for his single-minded devotion to the cause. U'Ren was born on 10 January 1859 in Lancaster, Wisconsin, the son of a blacksmith who, with his wife, had emigrated from Cornwall in England. Young U'Ren accompanied his family westward to Nebraska, then to Colorado, learning the blacksmith's trade from his father. In 1885, at age 26, he earned a law degree in Denver, and then moved to Iowa, Hawaii, and California before settling in Milwaukee, Oregon, in 1889. By this time he had been a miner, a newspaper editor, and a Republican Party worker, in addition to practicing law.

In 1892 he was forced to give up his law practice as a result of an asthma attack and, having no family in the area, was nursed back to health by the Lewellings, a local family of fruit growers. The Lewellings were also reformers, "good government being to us what religion is to most people," wrote the lady of the house. Albert Lewelling brought U'Ren a copy of James W. Sullivan's book, Direct Legislation, and U'Ren, at age 33, found his life's work. As he later told an interviewer: "Blacksmithing was my trade and it has always given color to my view of things. I wanted to fix the evils in the conditions of life. I couldn't. There were no tools. We had tools to do almost anything with in the blacksmith shop; wonderful tools. So in other trades, arts and professions ... in everything but government. In government, the common trade of all men and the basis of social life, men worked still with old tools, with old laws, with institutions and charters which hindered progress more than they helped it. Men suffered from this. There were enough lawyers: many of our ablest men were lawyers. Why didn't some of them invent legislative implements to help people govern themselves: Why had we no tool makers for democracy?"

U'Ren, with the financial support of the Lewellings, took it upon himself to forge the tools of democracy: initiative, referendum, and recall. He brought together representatives of the state Farmer's Alliance and labor unions to form the Oregon Direct Legislation League, of which he was named secretary.

In 1894 U'Ren was elected chairman of the state's Populist Party convention, and won approval of an I&R platform plank. That same year the League published a pamphlet explaining I&R and distributed it throughout the state: 50,000 copies in English and 15,000 in German.

In 1896 U'Ren won a seat in the state's lower house and in 1897 worked the legislature—without success—to gain approval for I&R. Warned that he might go to purgatory for his wheeling and dealing, U'Ren replied thunderously: "I'd go to hell for the people of Oregon!"

Following the 1897 defeat, U'Ren reorganized the League to broaden the base of I&R support. In addition to farmers and labor unionists, the new 17-member executive committee included bankers, the president of the state bar association (such attorneys' associations were notorious during the Progressive era for opposing I&R), and Portland Oregonian editor Harvey W. Scott.

U'Ren ran for the state senate in 1898 and lost, but nevertheless won passage of his I&R amendment the following year. Under Oregon's constitution, amendments had to be approved by two successive sessions of the legislature. In 1901 I&R passed with a single dissenting vote, and a year later voters ratified it by an eleven to one margin.

U'Ren joined other reformers in sponsoring dozens of initiatives during the next two decades. In 1906, he was among the sponsors of an initiative to ban free railroad passes, which the railroads routinely handed out as gifts to politicians and which he himself had once received. In 1908, he proposed initiatives to make Oregon the first state with popular election of U.S. senators and to reform election laws. Both passed by overwhelming margins. In 1910, Oregonians passed an initiative to establish the first presidential primary election system in the nation. The margin was small (43,353 to 41,624), but two dozen other states copied it within six years.

The closeness of the 1910 vote showed that the voters were not quite as ready for reform as was U'Ren, and they rejected his 1912 initiative proposing a unicameral legislature by a greater than two to one margin.

Other early initiatives that bear the mark of U'Ren were a 1906 constitutional amendment extending I&R powers to local jurisdictions, approved by three to one, and a 1908 amendment that gave voters power to recall elected officials.

And these were just the beginning, for U'Ren associated himself with many more initiative efforts before his death, at age 90, in Portland on March 5, 1949. In Oregon, I&R had worked just as its early advocates said it would: this one reform opened the door to all the others.

As a Progressive reformer and practitioner of initiative and referendum campaigns, U'Ren had no equal in any state. Lest he get all the credit for establishing I&R in Oregon, however, another man must be mentioned as the state's number two I&R advocate: Max Burgholzer of Buxton (near Eugene), Oregon, who some contemporaries claimed deserved equal credit.

Oregon is one of two states (the other is Arizona) where women gained the right to vote by an initiative. But it lost on the first try in 1906, and lost again by an even bigger margin in 1908. In 1910 suffragists tried a different approach: an initiative giving only female taxpayers the right to vote, a compromise that was rejected by about the same margin as the 1908 suffrage amendment. Finally, in 1912, suffragists led by Abigail Scott Duniway won their long struggle: their measure passed by a margin of 61,265 in favor to 57,104 against.

Leading the fight against women's suffrage were the liquor and saloon interests, which (rightly, in this instance) feared women would vote for Prohibition. In 1914, the first year Oregon women voted, a Prohibition initiative passed by a wide margin. Women also provided the slim 157-vote victory margin (out of over 200,000 votes cast) for a 1914 initiative constitutional amendment abolishing the death penalty in Oregon. In 1912 a similar initiative had failed, 41,951 to 64,578.

Labor unions won approval of a 1912 initiative establishing an eight-hour day for workers on public works projects, and two other measures prohibiting private employers from hiring convicts from state or local jails.

Some of the most innovative Oregon initiatives of the early days were those that failed to pass. One was a 1914 full-employment initiative sponsored by the Socialist Party. The proposal would have set up a job creation fund derived from an inheritance tax on estates worth more than $50,000 (a huge fortune in those days); the state labor commissioner would then have had the duty to employ any citizen demanding work in a "Department of Industry and Public Works." The measure failed 57,859 to 126,201.

In 1930, another unique proposal—a state constitutional amendment to ban cigarettes—was put on the ballot by citizen petition. By a three to one margin, Oregonians rejected the idea. They did, however, approve an initiative amendment that year establishing a procedure to set up independent, locally owned "People's Utility Districts" to market water and power. In 1938, Oregonians approved the "Townsend Plan" old-age pension initiative. The idea was the brainchild of Dr. Francis E. Townsend of Long Beach, California, who proposed making monthly payments to senior citizens if they promised to spend their entire allotment each month and thus stimulate the economy. Also on the ballot that year was an initiative to clean up the Willamette River, which was heavily polluted by pulp and paper mills and sewage. The measure had been passed by the legislature in 1937 but vetoed by Governor Charles Martin. Voters passed the initiative by a wide margin.

In the late 1940s a University of Oregon at Eugene student, Clay Myers, a leader of the campus Young Republicans, began a movement for reapportionment of the state's legislative and congressional districts, whose boundaries had not been redrawn for over 50 years. Rebuffed by the legislature, Myers sponsored an initiative constitutional amendment specifying that if the legislature failed to reapportion the state during its first six-month session after the census data were released every ten years, the secretary of state would reapportion it. Voters approved the initiative by a nearly two to one margin in 1952. Myers went on to reapportion the state himself during his 1967-1977 term as secretary of state.

In the 1960s, Oregonians put only seven initiatives on the state ballot in five elections, far below their average. In 1960, scenery-conscious citizens sponsored an initiative to limit billboards through the state, but the electorate rejected it by a nearly two to one margin. In the 1970s, however, leading the national trend, initiative use rebounded, with 17 qualifying for the ballot. Among those approved was a "denturism" initiative (1978) that broke dentists' monopoly by allowing denture technicians to sell and fit dentures at a lower cost. Ron Wyden, a young lobbyist for senior citizens, championed this initiative. Dentists opposed the measure with a saturation advertising campaign that voters found so obnoxious that they approved the initiative by a seven to two margin. Voter interest ran so high that the number of ballots cast on the "denturism" question was only a tenth of a percent less than the number cast for gubernatorial candidates. For Wyden, the initiative was a starting point for his successful 1980 campaign to win election to Congress.

None of this could have occurred had it not been for the work of William Simon U'Ren. U'Ren is perhaps the only person to be honored by a monument commemorating his initiative work. The monument can be found in front of the Clackamas County Courthouse, on Main Street in Oregon City. The bronze plaque reads; "In honor of William Simon U'Ren, author of Oregon's constitutional provisions for initiative, referendum, and recall, giving the people control of law making and lawmakers and known in his lifetime as father of Oregon's enlightened system of government."

In the 1990s saw the rise of an initiative proponent by the name of Bill Sizemore. Sizemore became known as Mr. Initiative. He drew the ire of the progressives (liberals) because all of the initiatives he sponsored (literally dozens) were all aimed at them—tax cuts, paycheck protection, labor reform and term limits. His success rate at the ballot box wasn't stellar, but his impact on the initiative scene is indisputable.

Unfortunately, his success has also led to a backlash against the initiative process. His opponents, primarily labor unions, have sponsored initiatives themselves to try and make the initiative process more difficult—with limited success. However, they were successful in getting the state legislature to place on the ballot a constitutional amendment that would have drastically increased the number of signatures required for a constitutional amendment. It was defeated handily. But undeterred by this defeat, the labor unions were eventually successful in placing an initiative on the 2002 ballot that would ban paying signature gatherers by the signature. It was adopted by the voters but a court challenge was being planned.

Statewide Initiative Usage

Number of Initiatives	Number Passed	Number Failed	Passage Rate
318	112	206	35%

Statewide Initiatives

Year	Measure Number	Type	Subject Matter	Description	Pass/Fail
1904	2	DS	Election Reform	Direct primary nominating convention law.	Passed
1904	3	DS	Alcohol Regulation	Local option liquor law.	Passed
1906	10	DS	Taxes	Gross earning tax on sleeping, refrigerator and oil car companies.	Passed
1906	11	DS	Taxes	Gross earning tax on express, telephone and telegraph companies.	Passed
1906	2	DA	Election Reform	Equal suffrage amendment.	Failed
1906	3	DS	Alcohol Regulation	Amendment to local option liquor law.	Failed
1906	4	DS	Administration of Government	Law to abolish tolls on the Mt. Hood and Barlow road and providing for its ownership by the state.	Failed
1906	5	DA	Election Reform	Requiring referendum on any act calling a constitutional convention.	Passed
1906	6	DA	Administration of Government	Giving cities sole powers to amend their charters.	Passed
1906	7	DA	Business Regulation	Authorizing state printers compensation to be regulated by law at any time.	Passed
1906	8	DA	Initiative and Referendum	Initiative and referendum to apply to all local, special and municipal laws.	Passed
1906	9	DS	Utility Regulation	Prohibition of free passes on railroads.	Passed
1908	11	DA	Alcohol Regulation	Giving cities control of liquor selling, poolrooms, theaters, etc, subject to local option law.	Failed
1908	12	DA	Taxes	Modified form of single tax amendment.	Failed
1908	13	DA	Election Reform	Recall power on public officials.	Passed
1908	14	DS	Election Reform	Instructing legislature to vote for people's choice for U.S. Senator.	Passed
1908	16	DS	Campaign Finance Reform	Corrupt practices act governing elections.	Passed
1908	17	DS	Animal Rights	Fishery law proposed by gillnet operators.	Passed
1908	18	DA	Legal	Requiring indictment to be by grand jury.	Passed
1908	19	DS	Administration of Government	Creating Hood River County.	Passed
1908	9	DA	Election Reform	Equal suffrage.	Failed
1910	1	DA	Election Reform	Permitting female taxpayers to vote.	Failed
1910	10	DS	Education	To establish a state normal school at Monmouth.	Passed
1910	11	DS	Administration of Government	Creating Otis County from parts of Harney, Malheur and Grant.	Failed
1910	12	DS	Administration of Government	Annexing part of Clackamas County to Multnomah.	Failed
1910	13	DS	Administration of Government	Creating Williams County from parts of Lane and Douglas.	Failed
1910	14	DA	Civil Rights	Permitting people of each County to regulate taxation for County purposes and abolishing poll taxes.	Passed
1910	15	DA	Alcohol Regulation	Giving cities and towns exclusive power to regulate liquor traffic within their limits.	Passed
1910	16	DS	Labor	For protection of laborers in hazardous employment, fixing employers' liability, etc.	Passed

Year	Measure Number	Type	Subject Matter	Description	Pass/Fail
1910	17	DS	Administration of Government	Creating Orchard County from part of Umatilla.	Failed
1910	18	DS	Administration of Government	Creating Clark County from part of Grant.	Failed
1910	19	DS	Education	To establish state normal school at Weston.	Failed
1910	20	DS	Administration of Government	To annex part of Washington County to Multnomah County.	Failed
1910	21	DS	Education	To establish a state normal school at Ashland.	Failed
1910	22	DA	Alcohol Regulation	Prohibiting liquor traffic.	Failed
1910	23	DS	Alcohol Regulation	Prohibiting the sale of liquors and regulating shipments of same, and providing for search for liquor.	Failed
1910	24	DS	Business Regulation	Creating board to draft employers' liability law for submission to legislature.	Failed
1910	25	DS	Animal Rights	Prohibiting taking of fish in Rogue River except with hook and line.	Passed
1910	26	DS	Administration of Government	Creating Deschutes County out of part of Crook.	Failed
1910	27	DS	Administration of Government	Bill for general law under which new counties may be created or boundaries changed.	Failed
1910	28	DA	Administration of Government	Permitting counties to vote bonds for permanent road improvement.	Passed
1910	29	DS	Election Reform	Permitting voters in direct primaries to express choice for president and vice president, to select delegates to national convention and nominate candidates for presidential electors.	Passed
1910	30	DS	Administration of Government	Creating board of people's inspectors of government, providing for reports of board in Official State Gazette to be mailed to all registered voters bi-monthly.	Failed
1910	31	DA	Administration of Government	Extending initiative and referendum, making term of members of legislature 6 years, increasing salaries, requiring proportional representation in legislature.	Failed
1910	32	DA	Judicial Reform	Permitting 3/4 verdict in civil cases.	Passed
1910	9	DS	Administration of Government	Creating Nesmith County from parts of Lane and Douglas.	Failed
1912	1	DA	Election Reform	To permit women's suffrage.	Passed
1912	10	DS	Taxes	Mileage tax for university and agricultural college.	Failed
1912	11	DA	Initiative and Referendum	Majority rule on initiated laws.	Failed
1912	12	DS	Administration of Government	County bond and real construction act — Grange bill.	Failed
1912	14	DS	Administration of Government	Changing date state printer bill becomes effective.	Failed
1912	15	DS	Administration of Government	Creating office of hotel inspector.	Failed
1912	16	DS	Labor	Eight-hour day on public works.	Passed
1912	17	DS	Environmental Reform	Blue sky law.	Failed
1912	18	DS	Labor	Prohibiting private employment of convicts.	Passed

Year	Measure Number	Type	Subject Matter	Description	Pass/Fail
1912	19	DS	Labor	Relating to employment of County and city prisoners.	Passed
1912	20	DS	Administration of Government	State road bond act.	Failed
1912	21	DA	Administration of Government	Limiting state road indebtedness.	Passed
1912	22	DS	Administration of Government	County bonding act.	Failed
1912	23	DA	Administration of Government	Limiting County road indebtedness.	Passed
1912	24	DS	Administration of Government	Providing method for consolidating cities and creating new counties.	Failed
1912	25	DA	Taxes	Income tax amendment.	Failed
1912	26	DS	Taxes	Tax exemption on household effects.	Passed
1912	27	DS	Taxes	Tax exemption on moneys and credits.	Failed
1912	28	DS	Taxes	Revising inheritance tax laws.	Failed
1912	29	DS	Administration of Government	Freight rates act.	Passed
1912	30	DA	Administration of Government	County road bonding act.	Failed
1912	31	DA	Administration of Government	Abolishing senate and establish a unicameral.	Failed
1912	32	DA	Taxes	Statewide single tax with graduated tax provision.	Failed
1912	33	DS	Death Penalty	Abolishing capital punishment.	Failed
1912	34	DS	Labor	Prohibiting boycotting.	Failed
1912	35	DS	Civil Rights	Giving mayor authority to control street speaking. Prohibits use of public streets, parks and grounds in cities over 5,000 without a permit.	Failed
1912	9	DS	Administration of Government	Creating Cascade County.	Failed
1914	11	DA	Labor	Universal constitutional eight-hour day amendment.	Failed
1914	12	DS	Labor	Eight-hour day and room-ventilation law for female workers.	Failed
1914	13	DS	Election Reform	Nonpartisan judiciary bill prohibiting party nominations for judicial officers.	Failed
1914	14	DA	Taxes	$1,500 tax exemption amendment.	Failed
1914	15	DA	Environmental Reform	Public docks and water frontage amendment.	Failed
1914	16	DS	Administration of Government	Municipal wharves and docks bill.	Failed
1914	17	DA	Alcohol Regulation	Providing for statewide prohibition.	Passed
1914	18	DA	Death Penalty	Abolishing death penalty.	Passed
1914	19	DA	Taxes	Specific personal graduated extra-tax amendment of Art. 10.	Failed
1914	20	DS	Administration of Government	Consolidating corporation and insurance departments.	Failed
1914	21	DS	Health/Medical	Dentistry bill.	Failed
1914	22	DA	Administration of Government	County officers term amendment.	Failed
1914	23	DS	Administration of Government	A tax code commission bill.	Failed

Year	Measure Number	Type	Subject Matter	Description	Pass/Fail
1914	24	DS	Administration of Government	Abolishing desert land board and reorganizing certain state offices.	Failed
1914	25	DA	Election Reform	Proportional representation amendment.	Failed
1914	26	DA	Administration of Government	State senate constitutional amendment.	Failed
1914	27	DA	Administration of Government	Department of industry and public works amendment.	Failed
1914	28	DS	Election Reform	Primary delegate election bill.	Failed
1914	29	DA	Taxes	Equal assessment and taxation $300 exemption.	Failed
1916	10	DA	Taxes	Rural credits amendment.	Passed
1916	11	DA	Taxes	Statewide tax and indebtedness limitation amendment.	Passed
1916	4	DA	Taxes	Full rental value land tax and homemakers' loan fund amendment.	Failed
1916	5	DA	Education	Establish Pendleton normal school and ratifying location for certain state institutions.	Failed
1916	6	DA	Health/Medical	Anti-compulsory vaccination bill.	Failed
1916	7	DA	Business Regulation	Bill repealing and abolishing the Sunday closing law.	Passed
1916	8	DA	Alcohol Regulation	Permitting manufacture and regulating sale 4% malt liquors.	Failed
1916	9	DA	Alcohol Regulation	Prohibition amendment forbidding importation of intoxicating liquors for beverage purposes.	Passed
1918	5	DS	Taxes	Delinquent tax notice bill.	Passed
1918	6	DS	Administration of Government	Fixing compensation for publication of legal notice.	Passed
1920	10	DA	Administration of Government	Divided legislative session.	Failed
1920	11	DS	Administration of Government	State market commission.	Failed
1920	4	DA	Taxes	Single tax.	Failed
1920	5	DA	Administration of Government	Fixing term of certain County officers.	Passed
1920	7	DA	Health/Medical	Anti-compulsory vaccinations.	Failed
1920	8	DA	Banking Reform	Fixing legal rate of interest in Oregon.	Failed
1920	9	DS	Environmental Reform	Roosevelt bird refuge.	Failed
1920	N/A	DS	Administration of Government	Port of Portland dock commission consolidation.	Failed
1922	3	DA	Taxes	Single tax amendment.	Failed
1922	4	DA	Taxes	1925 exposition tax amendment.	Failed
1922	5	DA	Taxes	Income tax amendment.	Failed
1922	6	DS	Education	Compulsory education bill.	Passed
1924	4	DS	Business Regulation	Oleomargarine condensed milk bill.	Failed
1924	5	DS	Health/Medical	Naturopath bill.	Failed
1924	6	DA	Labor	Workmen's compulsory compensation law for hazardous occupations.	Failed
1924	7	DS	Taxes	Income tax repeal.	Passed
1926	15	DS	Taxes	Income tax bill with property tax offset.	Failed
1926	16	DS	Business Regulation	Bus and truck operating license bill.	Failed
1926	17	DS	Animal Rights	Fish wheel, trap, seine, and gillnet bill.	Passed

Year	Measure Number	Type	Subject Matter	Description	Pass/Fail
1926	18	DS	Taxes	Income tax bill.	Failed
1926	19	DS	Utility Regulation	Oregon water and power board development measures.	Failed
1928	1	DS	Taxes	Five cent gasoline tax bill.	Failed
1928	2	DS	Taxes	Bill for reduction of motor vehicle license fees.	Failed
1928	3	DS	Taxes	Income tax bill.	Failed
1928	5	DS	Environmental Reform	Deschutes River water and fish bill.	Failed
1928	6	DS	Environmental Reform	Rogue River water and fish bill.	Failed
1928	7	DS	Environmental Reform	Umpqua River water and fish bill.	Failed
1928	8	DS	Environmental Reform	McKenzie River water and fish bill.	Failed
1928	N/A	DA	Initiative and Referendum	Limiting power of legislature over laws approved by the people.	Failed
1930	10	DA	Health/Medical	Anti-cigarette constitutional amendment.	Failed
1930	11	DA	Animal Rights	Rogue River fishing constitutional amendment.	Failed
1930	12	DA	Administration of Government	Lieutenant governor constitutional amendment.	Failed
1930	13	DA	Utility Regulation	Water and power utility districts.	Passed
1932	10	DA	Taxes	Tax and debt control.	Failed
1932	11	DS	Taxes	Tax supervising and conservation bill.	Failed
1932	12	DS	Taxes	Personal income tax law amendment.	Failed
1932	13	DA	Utility Regulation	State water power and hydroelectric.	Passed
1932	7	DS	Alcohol Regulation	Bill to repeal state prohibition law of Oregon.	Passed
1932	8	DS	Business Regulation	The freight truck and bus bill.	Failed
1932	9	DS	Education	Bill moving university, normal and law schools, establishing junior colleges.	Failed
1933	8	DA	Alcohol Regulation	Repeal of prohibition constitutional amendment.	Passed
1934	2	DA	Taxes	Limitations of taxes on taxable property.	Failed
1934	3	DA	Health/Medical	Healing arts.	Failed
1936	2	DA	Business Regulation	Amendment forbidding prevention or regulation of certain advertising if truthful.	Failed
1936	3	DA	Taxes	Tax limitation for school districts having 100,000 population.	Failed
1936	4	DS	Administration of Government	Noncompulsory military training bill.	Failed
1936	5	DA	Taxes	Amendment limiting and reducing permissible taxes on tangible property.	Failed
1936	6	DS	Administration of Government	State power bill.	Failed
1936	7	DA	Administration of Government	State hydroelectric temporary administrative board.	Failed
1936	8	DS	Banking Reform	State bank bill.	Failed
1938	10	DS	Environmental Reform	Water purification and prevention of pollution bill.	Passed
1938	11	DS	Alcohol Regulation	Bill regulating sale of alcoholic liquor for beverage purposes.	Failed

Year	Measure Number	Type	Subject Matter	Description	Pass/Fail
1938	7	DS	Administration of Government	Townsend Plan bill.	Passed
1938	8	DS	Taxes	Citizens' retirement annuity bill; levying transactions tax to provide fund.	Failed
1938	9	DS	Labor	Bill regulating picketing and boycotting by labor groups and organizations.	Passed
1938	N/A	DA	Gaming	Constitutional amendment legalizing certain lotteries and other forms of gambling.	Failed
1940	7	DS	Alcohol Regulation	Bill repealing present liquor law; authorizing private sale, license, taxing.	Failed
1940	8	DA	Gaming	Amendment legalizing certain gambling and gambling device and certain lotteries.	Failed
1940	9	DS	Business Regulation	Bill to repeal the Oregon milk control law.	Failed
1942	7	DS	Education	Bill distributing surplus funds to school districts reducing taxes therein.	Passed
1944	8	DA	Education	Increasing state fund for public school support.	Failed
1944	9	DA	Taxes	Providing monthly annuities from a gross income tax.	Failed
1946	8	DS	Welfare	Relative to old age pensions.	Failed
1946	9	DS	Taxes	To create basic school support fund by annual tax levy.	Passed
1946	N/A	DA	Education	Schools, state aid.	Failed
1948	10	DS	Animal Rights	Prohibiting salmon fishing in Columbia river with fixed appliances.	Passed
1948	5	DA	Election Reform	Fixing qualifications of voters in school elections.	Passed
1948	6	DS	Welfare	Relative to old age pensions.	Passed
1948	7	DS	Taxes	Increasing personal income tax exemptions.	Passed
1948	8	DS	Alcohol Regulation	Oregon liquor dispensing licensing act.	Failed
1948	9	DA	Veteran Affairs	World War II veterans' bonus.	Failed
1950	7	DA	Veteran Affairs	World War II veterans' compensation fund.	Passed
1950	8	DA	Apportionment/ Redistricting	Legislative representation reapportionment.	Failed
1950	9	DS	Alcohol Regulation	Making sale of promotively advertised alcoholic beverage unlawful.	Failed
1952	13	DS	Daylight Savings Time	Standard time initiative.	Passed
1952	14	DA	Gaming	Pari-mutuel betting prohibition.	Failed
1952	15	DA	Alcohol Regulation	Liquor by the drink sales.	Passed
1952	16	DA	Taxes	Motor carrier tax decrease.	Failed
1952	17	DS	Business Regulation	Milk control bill.	Failed
1952	18	DA	Apportionment/ Redistricting	Legislative reapportionment.	Passed
1954	6	DS	Daylight Savings Time	Establishing Daylight Saving Time.	Failed
1954	7	DS	Animal Rights	Prohibiting certain fishing in coastal streams.	Failed
1954	8	DS	Business Regulation	Repealing milk control law.	Passed
1956	7	DS	Animal Rights	Prohibiting certain fishing in control streams.	Passed
1958	13	DS	Administration of Government	Persons eligible to serve in legislature.	Passed

Year	Measure Number	Type	Subject Matter	Description	Pass/Fail
1960	15	DS	Environmental Reform	Billboard control.	Failed
1962	8	DA	Apportionment/ Redistricting	Legislative apportionment.	Failed
1962	9	DS	Education	To repeal school district reorganization law.	Failed
1964	3	DS	Labor	Amending State workmen's compensation law.	Failed
1964	4	DS	Animal Rights	Prohibiting commercial fishing salmon, steelhead.	Failed
1968	6	DA	Bonds	Bond issue to acquire ocean beaches.	Failed
1968	7	DA	Taxes	Constitutional amendment changing property tax limitation.	Failed
1970	10	DA	Taxes	New property bases for schools.	Failed
1970	11	DA	Environmental Reform	Restricts governmental powers over rural property.	Failed
1970	9	DS	Environmental Reform	Scenic waterways bill.	Passed
1972	7	DA	Administration of Government	Repeals Governor's Retirement Act.	Passed
1972	8	DA	Administration of Government	Changes succession to Office of Governor.	Passed
1972	9	DA	Education	Prohibits property tax for school operations.	Failed
1974	15	DS	Business Regulation	To prohibit the purchase or sale of steelhead.	Passed
1976	10	DS	Environmental Reform	Repeals land use planning coordination statutes.	Failed
1976	11	DS	Health/Medical	Prohibit adding fluoridation to water systems.	Failed
1976	12	DS	Administration of Government	Repeals intergovernmental cooperation, planning district statutes.	Failed
1976	9	DS	Nuclear weapons/ facilities/waste	Regulates nuclear power plant construction approval.	Failed
1978	10	DA	Environmental Reform	Land use planning, zoning amendment.	Failed
1978	4	DS	Utility Regulation	Shorten formation procedures: utility districts.	Failed
1978	5	DS	Business Regulation	Practice of denture technology.	Passed
1978	6	DA	Taxes	Limitations on ad valorem property taxes	Passed
1978	7	DA	Abortion	Prohibits state spending or programs for abortions.	Failed
1978	8	DS	Death Penalty	Death penalty for murder, specific conditions.	Passed
1978	9	DS	Utility Regulation	Limit public utility rate base	Passed
1980	5	DS	Animal Rights	Forbid use, sale of snare leg hold traps.	Failed
1980	6	DA	Taxes	Property tax limit: 85% districts' 1977 revenue.	Failed
1980	7	DS	Nuclear weapons/ facilities/waste	Nuclear plant licensing: voter approval, disposal.	Passed
1982	3	DA	Taxes	Property tax limit: 85% districts' 1979 revenue.	Failed
1982	4	DS	Business Regulation	Permit retail self-service dispensing of fuel.	Failed
1982	5	DS	Nuclear weapons/ facilities/waste	Mutual freeze on nuclear weapons development.	Passed

Year	Measure Number	Type	Subject Matter	Description	Pass/Fail
1982	6	DS	Environmental Reform	End State's land use planning powers; localities.	Failed
1984	2	DA	Taxes	Property tax limit.	Failed
1984	3	DS	Utility Regulation	Establish a citizens' utility board.	Passed
1984	4	DA	Gaming	State lottery; profits for economic development.	Passed
1984	5	DS	Gaming	Statutory provisions for State operated lottery.	Passed
1984	6	DA	Death Penalty	Death penalty exempt: guarantees against cruelty.	Passed
1984	7	DS	Legal	Death/mandatory imprisonment: aggravated murder.	Passed
1984	8	DS	Legal	Criminal laws: police powers, evidence, sentences.	Failed
1984	9	DS	Nuclear weapons/ facilities/waste	Naturally occurring radioactive isotopes: disposal.	Passed
1986	10	DS	Legal	Criminal laws: victims, evidence, sentences, parole.	Passed
1986	11	DS	Taxes	Property tax relief program; sales tax limitation.	Failed
1986	12	DS	Taxes	State income tax changes, property tax relief.	Failed
1986	13	DA	Election Reform	Twenty day pre-election voter registration cutoff.	Passed
1986	14	DS	Nuclear weapons/ facilities/waste	Nuclear Power: permanent waste site licensed.	Failed
1986	15	DS	Nuclear weapons/ facilities/waste	"Radioactive waste" defined; energy facility payments.	Failed
1986	16	DS	Nuclear weapons/ facilities/waste	Nuclear weapons funded by tax credits. Civil penalty.	Failed
1986	5	DS	Drug Policy Reform	Legalize marijuana for personal use.	Failed
1986	6	DA	Abortion	Prohibits state funding of abortions.	Failed
1986	7	DA	Taxes	Sales tax. Funds schools, reduces property taxes.	Failed
1986	8	DS	Utility Regulation	Mandatory local measured telephone service.	Passed
1986	9	DA	Taxes	Limit property tax rate, assessed value increases.	Failed
1988	4	DS	Legal	Full sentences, no parole; probation, repeat felonies.	Passed
1988	5	DS	Taxes	Sin taxes to finance Intercollegiate Athletic Fund.	Failed
1988	6	DS	Environmental Reform	Indoor Clean Air Law revisions — ban public smoking.	Failed
1988	7	DS	Environmental Reform	Oregon Scenic Waterway System.	Passed
1988	8	DS	Civil Rights	Revoke ban on sexual orientation discrimination.	Passed
1990	10	DS	Abortion	Parental notice before minor's abortion.	Failed
1990	11	DA	Education	Choice of public schools; tax credit, private schools.	Failed
1990	4	DS	Nuclear weapons/ facilities/waste	Prohibit Trojan operation until standards met.	Failed
1990	5	DA	Taxes	Property tax limit; schools, government operations.	Passed

Year	Measure Number	Type	Subject Matter	Description	Pass/Fail
1990	6	DS	Environmental Reform	Product packaging: recycling, hard ship waivers.	Failed
1990	7	DS	Welfare	Work in lieu of welfare benefits pilot program.	Passed
1990	8	DA	Abortion	Prohibit abortion.	Failed
1990	9	DS	Health/Medical	Requires use of safety belts.	Passed
1992	3	DA	Term Limits	Term limits on state legislature 6/8 and Congress 6/12.	Passed
1992	4	DS	Business Regulation	Ban triple truck-trailers on Oregon highways.	Failed
1992	5	DS	Nuclear weapons/ facilities/waste	Close Trojan: waste, cost, and earth quake orders.	Failed
1992	6	DS	Nuclear weapons/ facilities/waste	Bans Trojan operation unless conditions met.	Failed
1992	7	DA	Taxes	Raises limit on property tax; renters' tax relief.	Failed
1992	8	DS	Animal Rights	Lower Columbia fish harvest.	Failed
1992	9	DA	Civil Rights	Government to discourage homosexual "behaviors."	Failed
1994	10	DA	Initiative and Referendum	Legislature cannot reduce voter approved sentences without 2/3 vote	Passed
1994	11	DS	Legal	Mandatory sentences for listed felonies; covers persons 15 and up	Passed
1994	12	DS	Labor	Repeals prevailing rate wage requirement for workers on public works.	Failed
1994	13	DA	Civil Rights	Governments cannot approve, create classifications based on homosexuality.	Failed
1994	14	DA	Environmental Reform	Amends chemical process mining laws — adds requirements, prohibitions, standards, fees.	Failed
1994	15	DA	Education	State must maintain funding for schools, community colleges.	Failed
1994	16	DS	Physician assisted suicide	Allows a mentally competent adult who is suffering from a terminal illness to request and obtain medication from a physician to end that patient's own life in a humane and dignified manner.	Passed
1994	17	DA	Legal	Requires state prison inmates to work fulltime.	Passed
1994	18	DS	Animal Rights	Bans hunting bears with bait. Hunting bears, cougars with dogs.	Passed
1994	19	DA	Civil Rights	No free speech protection for obscenity, child pornography.	Failed
1994	20	DA	Taxes	"Equal Tax" on trade replaces current taxes.	Failed
1994	5	DA	Taxes	Bars new or increased taxes without voter approval.	Failed
1994	6	DA	Campaign Finance Reform	Candidates may use only contributions from district residents.	Passed
1994	7	DA	Civil Rights	Guarantees Equal protection and lists prohibited grounds of discrimination.	Failed
1994	8	DA	Labor	Public employees must pay part of salary for pension	Passed

Year	Measure Number	Type	Subject Matter	Description	Pass/Fail
1994	9	DS	Campaign Finance Reform	Sets contribution and spending limits and adopts other campaign finance law changes.	Passed
1996	33	DA	Initiative and Referendum	Prohibits the legislature from amending or repealing, for five years, statutes approved by the voters.	Failed
1996	34	DS	Environmental Reform	Gives Fish & Wildlife Commission exclusive authority to manage wildlife; repeals 1994 initiative that prohibited the use of dogs or bait to hunt bear or cougar.	Failed
1996	35	DS	Health/Medical	Restricts bases on which health care providers may receive payment.	Failed
1996	36	DS	Labor	Increases minimum wage to $6.50 over three years.	Passed
1996	37	DS	Environmental Reform	Broadens types of beverage containers that require deposits and refunds.	Failed
1996	38	DS	Environmental Reform	Prohibits livestock in or near polluted waters or on adjacent lands.	Failed
1996	39	DA	Health/Medical	Prohibits government and private entities from discriminating among health care provider categories.	Failed
1996	40	DA	Legal	Victims' rights.	Passed
1996	41	DA	Labor	Makes complete information regarding employer costs of public employees available to the public.	Failed
1996	42	DA	Education	Requires annual testing of public school students, grades 4-12.	Failed
1996	43	DS	Labor	Reinstates collective bargaining law for public safety employees.	Failed
1996	44	DS	Taxes	Increases cigarette and tobacco product taxes; changes tax revenue distribution.	Passed
1996	45	DA	Labor	Raises public employees' retirement age to qualify for benefits; reduces benefits.	Failed
1996	46	DA	Taxes	Counts non-voters as "no" votes on tax measures.	Failed
1996	47	DA	Taxes	Reduces and limits property taxes; limits revenue available for schools and other local services funded by property taxes; allows lost revenue to be replaced only with state income tax.	Passed
1996	48	DA	Term Limits	Informed Voter Law.	Failed
1998	58	DS	Administration of Government	Would require issuing copy of original birth certificates to adoptee.	Passed
1998	59	DA	Campaign Finance Reform	Would prohibit using public resources to collect money for political purposes.	Failed
1998	60	DS	Election Reform	Would require vote by mail in biennial primary and general elections.	Passed
1998	62	DA	Campaign Finance Reform	Would require campaign finance disclosures and regulates signature gathering.	Passed
1998	63	DA	Election Reform	Would establish super-majority voting requirements and require same super-majority for passage.	Passed

Year	Measure Number	Type	Subject Matter	Description	Pass/Fail
1998	64	DS	Environmental Reform	Would prohibit many present timber harvest practices and imposes more restrictive regulations.	Failed
1998	65	DA	Administration of Government	Would create process for requiring legislature to review administrative rules.	Failed
1998	66	DA	Environmental Reform	Would dedicate some lottery funding to parks and beaches habitat and watershed protection.	Passed
1998	67	DS	Drug Policy Reform	Would allow medical use of marijuana within limits and establishes permit system.	Passed
2000	1	DA	Education	Accountability and equity in school funding.	Passed
2000	2	DA	Administration of Government	Creates process for requiring legislature to review administrative rules	Failed
2000	3	DA	Drug Policy Reform	Limits asset forfeitures and restricts use of proceeds.	Passed
2000	4	DS	Health/Medical	An initiative statute to use tobacco settlement money for low-income health care.	Failed
2000	5	DS	Gun Regulation	An initiative statute to require background checks at gun shows.	Passed
2000	6	DS	Campaign Finance Reform	Provides public funding to candidates who limit spending.	Failed
2000	7	DA	Environmental Reform	Requires payment to landowner if government regulation reduces property value.	Passed
2000	8	DA	Administration of Government	Limits state appropriations to percentage of state's prior personal income.	Failed
2000	9	DS	Civil Rights	Prohibits public school instruction encouraging, promoting, sanctioning homosexual and/or bisexual behaviors.	Failed
2000	91	DA	Taxes	This measure makes all federal income tax paid by personal and corporate income taxpayers a deduction on the taxpayer's Oregon income tax returns.	Failed
2000	92	DA	Campaign Finance Reform	Prohibits payroll deductions for political purposes without specific written authorization	Failed
2000	93	DA	Taxes	Requires Voter Approval Of Most New And Increased Taxes, Fees.	Failed
2000	94	DS	Legal	Repeals Mandatory Minimum Sentences For Certain Felonies, Requires Re-sentencing	Failed
2000	95	DA	Education	Job performance must determine public school teacher pay.	Failed
2000	96	DA	Initiative and Referendum	Prohibits increasing expense, difficulty of initiative process except through initiative.	Failed
2000	97	DS	Animal Rights	Restricts use of certain animal traps, poisons and commerce in fur.	Failed

Year	Measure Number	Type	Subject Matter	Description	Pass/Fail
2000	98	DA	Campaign Finance Reform	Prohibits using public resources for political purposes. Limits payroll deductions.	Failed
2000	99	DA	Health/Medical	Creates commission ensuring quality home care services for elderly and disabled.	Passed

Oregon Constitution

Article IV

Section 1. Legislative power; initiative and referendum.

(1) The legislative power of the state, except for the initiative and referendum powers reserved to the people, is vested in a Legislative Assembly, consisting of a Senate and a House of Representatives.

(2)(a) The people reserve to themselves the initiative power, which is to propose laws and amendments to the Constitution and enact or reject them at an election independently of the Legislative Assembly.

(b) An initiative law may be proposed only by a petition signed by a number of qualified voters equal to six percent of the total number of votes cast for all candidates for Governor at the election at which a Governor was elected for a term of four years next preceding the filing of the petition.

(c) An initiative amendment to the Constitution may be proposed only by a petition signed by a number of qualified voters equal to eight percent of the total number of votes cast for all candidates for Governor at the election at which a Governor was elected for a term of four years next preceding the filing of the petition.

(d) An initiative petition shall include the full text of the proposed law or amendment to the Constitution. A proposed law or amendment to the Constitution shall embrace one subject only and matters properly connected therewith.

(e) An initiative petition shall be filed not less than four months before the election at which the proposed law or amendment to the Constitution is to be voted upon.

(3)(a) The people reserve to themselves the referendum power, which is to approve or reject at an election any Act, or part thereof, of the Legislative Assembly that does not become effective earlier than 90 days after the end of the session at which the Act is passed.

(b) A referendum on an Act or part thereof may be ordered by a petition signed by a number of qualified voters equal to four percent of the total number of votes cast for all candidates for Governor at the election at which a Governor was elected for a term of four years next preceding the filing of the petition. A referendum petition shall be filed not more than 90 days after the end of the session at which the Act is passed.

(c) A referendum on an Act may be ordered by the Legislative Assembly by law. Notwithstanding section 15b, Article V of this Constitution, bills ordering a referendum and bills on which a referendum is ordered are not subject to veto by the Governor.

(4)(a) Petitions or orders for the initiative or referendum shall be filed with the Secretary of State. The Legislative Assembly shall provide by law for the manner in which the Secretary of State shall determine whether a petition contains the required number of signatures of qualified voters. The Secretary of State shall complete the verification process within the 30-day period after the last day on which the petition may be filed as provided in paragraph (e) of subsection (2) or paragraph (b) of subsection (3) of this section.

(b) Initiative and referendum measures shall be submitted to the people as provided in this section and by law not inconsistent therewith.

(c) All elections on initiative and referendum measures shall be held at the regular general elections, unless otherwise ordered by the Legislative Assembly.

(d) Notwithstanding section 1, Article XVII of this Constitution, an initiative or referendum measure becomes effective 30 days after the day on which it is enacted or approved by a majority of the votes cast thereon. A referendum ordered by petition on a part of an Act does not delay the remainder of the Act from becoming effective.

(5) The initiative and referendum powers reserved to the people by subsections (2) and (3) of this section are further reserved to the qualified voters of each municipality and district as to all local, special and municipal legislation of every character in or for their municipality or district. The manner of exercising those powers shall be provided by general laws, but cities may provide the manner of exercising those powers as to their municipal legislation. In a city, not more than 15 percent of the qualified voters may be required to propose legislation by the initiative, and not more than 10 percent of the qualified voters may be required to order a referendum on legislation.

(6) Making Signature Gatherers Be Registered Oregon Voters. A person gathering signatures on an initiative or referendum petition shall be registered to vote in this state in the manner provided by law.

Oregon Statutes

250.015 Form of petition; numbering of signature sheets.

The Secretary of State by rule shall:
(1) Design the form of the prospective petition, and the initiative and the referendum petition, including the signature sheets, to be used in any initiative or referendum in this state.
(2) Designate the quality of paper to be used for signature sheets in order to assure the legibility of the signatures.
(3) Prescribe by rule a system for numbering the signature sheets to be used in any initiative or referendum in this state.
[1979 c.190 s.141; 1979 c.345 s.1; 1981 c.909 s.1; 1989 c.68 s.5]

250.020

[Amended by 1957 c.608 s.121; 1961 c.121 s.4; 1979 c.190 s.232; 1979 c.519 s.17; renumbered 254.085]

250.025 Qualifications for signers of petition; removal of signatures.

(1) Any elector may sign an initiative or referendum petition for any measure on which the elector is entitled to vote.
(2) After an initiative or referendum petition is submitted for signature verification, no elector who signed the petition may remove the signature of the elector from the petition. [Formerly 254.160; 1985 c.808 s.24]

250.029 Withdrawal of initiative or referendum petition; form.

The chief petitioners of an initiative or referendum petition may withdraw the petition at any time prior to the submission of the petition for signature verification. The Secretary of State by rule shall design a form for use in filing a withdrawal of any initiative or referendum petition. The withdrawal form must be signed by all of the chief petitioners and filed with the filing officer. [1995 c.607 s.25]

250.030

[Amended by 1957 c.608 s.122; 1961 c.121 s.5; 1979 c.190 s.233; 1979 c.317 s.8a; 1979 c.519 s.18a; renumbered 254.095]

250.031 Rules for conduct of election under section 11, Article XI of Oregon Constitution.

The Secretary of State shall adopt administrative rules for the conduct of elections under section 11, Article XI of the Oregon Constitution, that include but are not limited to provisions that:
(1) Set forth the requirements for an election to which section 11 (8), Article XI of the Oregon Constitution, is applicable that are consistent with the voter registration requirements of ORS chapter 247 and with the federal National Voter Registration Act of 1993 (P.L. 103-31);
(2) Provide directions to election officers for calculating whether the required number of registered voters eligible to vote voted in the election; and
(3) Interpret the words "cast a ballot" in section 11 (8), Article XI of the Oregon Constitution, as meaning that a ballot was lawfully cast, whether or not the vote of that ballot may lawfully be counted for reasons other than the eligibility of the voter to vote. [1997 c.541 s.310]

250.035 Form of ballot titles for state and local measures.

(1) The ballot title of any measure, other than a state measure, to be initiated or referred shall consist of:
(a) A caption of not more than 10 words which reasonably identifies the subject of the measure;
(b) A question of not more than 20 words which plainly phrases the chief purpose of the measure so that an affirmative response to the question corresponds to an affirmative vote on the measure; and
(c) A concise and impartial statement of not more than 175 words summarizing the measure and its major effect.
(2) The ballot title of any state measure to be initiated or referred shall consist of:
(a) A caption of not more than 15 words that reasonably identifies the subject matter of the state measure. The caption of an initiative or referendum amendment to the constitution shall begin with the phrase, "Amends Constitution," which shall not be counted for purposes of the 15-word caption limit;
(b) A simple and understandable statement of not more than 25 words that describes the result if the state measure is approved. The statement required by this paragraph shall include either the phrase, "I vote" or "vote yes," or a substantially similar phrase, which may be placed at any point within the statement;

(c) A simple and understandable statement of not more than 25 words that describes the result if the state measure is rejected. The statement required by this paragraph shall not describe existing statutory or constitutional provisions in a way that would lead an average elector to believe incorrectly that one of those provisions would be repealed by approval of the state measure, if approval would not have that result. Any thing or action described both in the statement required by paragraph (b) of this subsection and in the statement required by this paragraph shall be described using the same terms in both statements, to the extent practical. Any different terms must be terms that an average elector would understand to refer to the same thing or action. The statement shall include either the phrase, "I vote" or "vote no," or a substantially similar phrase, which may be placed at any point within the statement; and

(d) A concise and impartial statement of not more than 125 words summarizing the state measure and its major effect.

(3) The statements required by subsection (2)(b) and (c) of this section shall be written so that, to the extent practical, the language of the two statements is parallel.

(4) The statement required by subsection (2)(b) of this section shall be written so that an affirmative response to the statement corresponds to an affirmative vote on the state measure.

(5) The statement required by subsection (2)(c) of this section shall be written so that an affirmative response to the statement corresponds to a negative vote on the state measure.

(6) To avoid confusion, a ballot title shall not resemble any title previously filed for a measure to be submitted at that election.

(7) In the statements required by subsection (2)(b), (c) and (d) of this section, reasonable discretion shall be allowed in the use of articles and conjunctions, but the statements shall not omit articles and conjunctions that are necessary to avoid confusion to or misunderstanding by an average elector. [1979 c.190 s.143; 1979 c.675 s.1; 1985 c.405 s.1; 1987 c.556 s.1; 1987 c.875 s.1; 1995 c.534 s.1; 1997 c.541 s.312; 1999 c.793 s.1]

Note: Section 3, chapter 793, Oregon Laws 1999, provides:

Sec. 3.

(1) The amendments to ORS 250.035 by section 1 of this 1999 Act do not apply to any ballot title prepared for:

(a) Any initiative petition that, if filed with the Secretary of State with the required number of signatures of qualified electors, will be submitted to the people at the general election held on the first Tuesday after the first Monday in November 2000; or

(b) Any state measure to be referred that is to be voted upon at an election held prior to or on the first Tuesday after the first Monday in November 2000.

(2) The amendments to ORS 250.035 by section 1 of this 1999 Act apply to ballot titles prepared for:

(a) Any initiative petition that, if filed with the Secretary of State with the required number of signatures of qualified electors, will be submitted to the people at a general election occurring after the first Tuesday after the first Monday in November 2000, regardless of when the prospective petition for the initiative petition is filed; or

(b) Any state measure to be referred that is to be voted upon at an election held after the first Tuesday after the first Monday in November 2000.

(3) The amendments to ORS 250.045 by section 2 of this 1999 Act apply to petitions to initiate or refer a state measure for which a prospective petition is filed on or after the effective date of this 1999 Act [October 23, 1999]. [1999 c.793 s.3]

250.036 Form of ballot title for measure subject to section 11 (8), Article XI of Oregon Constitution; exception.

(1) Notwithstanding any other provision of law, all ballot titles subject to section 11 (8), Article XI of the Oregon Constitution, shall include the following statement as the first statement of the ballot title summary: This measure may be passed only at an election with at least a 50 percent voter turnout.

(2) As used in this section, "at least a 50 percent voter turnout" means a voter turnout that meets the requirements of section 11 (8), Article XI of the Oregon Constitution.

(3) The statement required by this section shall not be counted in determining the word count requirements of ORS 250.035.

(4) Subsection (1) of this section shall not apply to the ballot title of a measure submitted to voters in a general election in an even-numbered year. [1997 c.541 s.311]

250.037 Form of ballot title for measure requesting approval of certain bonds; elections by mail.

(1) The ballot title of any measure requesting elector approval of bonds, the principal and interest on which will be payable from taxes imposed on property or property ownership that are not subject to the limitations of sections 11 and 11b, Article XI of the Oregon Constitution, shall contain, in addition to the matters required by ORS 250.035, the following statement immediately after the ballot title question and appearing with it, in this manner:

Question: (herein the question is stated) If the bonds are approved, they will be payable from taxes on property or property ownership that are not subject to the limits of sections 11 and 11b, Article XI of the Oregon Constitution.

(2) The words of the statement required by subsection (1) of this section shall not be counted for purposes of ORS 250.035.

(3) The ballot title statement for any measure requesting elector approval of bonds, the principal and interest on which is to be payable from taxes imposed on property or property ownership that are not subject to the limitations of sections 11 and 11b, Article XI of the Oregon Constitution, shall contain, in addition to the other requirements of ORS 250.035 and this section, a reasonably detailed, simple and understandable description of the use of proceeds.

(4) If the election for a measure to which this section applies is to be conducted by mail, the front of the outer envelope in which the ballot title is mailed shall state, clearly and boldly printed in red, "CONTAINS VOTE ON PROPOSED TAX INCREASE." [1991 c.902 s.119; 1997 c.541 s.313]

250.038 Form of ballot title for measure authorizing imposition of local option taxes or establishing permanent rate limitation; elections by mail.

In addition to meeting other applicable requirements of this chapter:

(1) The ballot title for a measure authorizing the imposition of local option taxes shall contain the statement required by ORS 280.070 (4)(a) and the information required by ORS 280.070 (5);

(2) The ballot title for a measure authorizing the establishment of a permanent rate limitation shall contain the information required by ORS 280.070 (6); and

(3) If the election on a measure authorizing the imposition of local option taxes or the establishment of a permanent rate limitation is to be conducted by mail, the front of the outer envelope in which the ballot title is mailed shall state, clearly and boldly printed in red, "CONTAINS VOTE ON PROPOSED TAX INCREASE." [1999 c.632 s.25]

250.039

[Formerly ORS 250.055; repealed by 1995 c.534 s.19]

250.040

[Repealed by 1957 c.608 s.231]

250.041 Applicability of ORS 250.005 to 250.037 to counties and cities.

ORS 250.005 to 250.037 apply to the exercise of initiative or referendum powers:

(1) Regarding a county measure, regardless of anything to the contrary in the county charter or ordinance.

(2) Regarding a city measure, regardless of anything to the contrary in the city charter or ordinance. [1983 c.514 s.11]

250.043 Acceptance of initiative or referendum petition without original signatures.

(1) Notwithstanding ORS 250.105, 250.215, 250.315 and 255.175, an initiative or referendum petition for which original signatures are otherwise required may be accepted by the appropriate filing officer for signature verification with photographic copies of one or more signature sheets if:

(a) The signature sheets containing the original signatures were stolen or destroyed by fire, a natural disaster or other act of God; and

(b) The photographic copy of each original signature sheet contains the number of the original signature sheets prescribed by the Secretary of State under ORS 250.015.

(2) As used in this section:

(a) "Act of God" means an unanticipated grave natural disaster or other natural phenomenon of an exceptional, inevitable and irresistible character, the effects of which could not have been prevented or avoided by the exercise of due care or foresight.

(b) "Filing officer" means the Secretary of State in the case of an initiative or referendum petition relating to a state measure, the county clerk in the case of an initiative or referendum petition relating to a county measure, the city elections officer in the case of an initiative or referendum petition relating to a city measure and the elections officer as defined in ORS 255.005 in the case of an initiative or referendum petition relating to a district measure. [1989 c.68 s.13]

250.044 Actions challenging constitutionality of state measure to be filed in Marion County Circuit Court.

(1) An action that challenges the constitutionality of a measure initiated by the people or referred to the people for a vote must be commenced in the Circuit Court for Marion County if:

(a) The action is filed by a plaintiff asserting a claim for relief that challenges the constitutionality of a state statute or an amendment to the Oregon Constitution initiated by the people or referred to the people under section 1 (1) to (4), Article IV of the Oregon Constitution;

(b) The action is commenced on or after the date that the Secretary of State certifies that the challenged measure has been adopted by the electors and within 180 days after the effective date of the measure; and

(c) The action may not be commenced in the Oregon Tax Court.

(2) An action under subsection (1) of this section must be within the jurisdiction of circuit courts and must present a justiciable controversy. The plaintiff in an action subject to the requirements of this section must serve a copy of the complaint on the Attorney General.

(3) If an action subject to the requirements of this section is filed in a court other than the Circuit Court for Marion County, the other court, on its own motion or the motion of any party to the action, shall dismiss the action or transfer the action to the Circuit Court for Marion County.

(4) This section does not apply to any civil or criminal proceeding in which the constitutionality of a state statute or provision of the Oregon Constitution is challenged in a responsive pleading.

(5) If a judgment in an action subject to the requirements of this section holds that a challenged measure is invalid in whole or in part, a party to the action may appeal the judgment only by filing a notice of appeal directly with the Supreme Court within the time and in the manner specified in ORS chapter 19 for civil appeals to the Court of Appeals. Any party filing a notice of appeal under this subsection must note in the notice of appeal that the case is subject to this subsection.

(6) If a judgment in an action subject to the requirements of this section holds that a challenged measure is valid, a party to the action may appeal the judgment by filing a notice of appeal in the Court of Appeals within the time and in the manner specified in ORS chapter 19 for civil appeals. Notwithstanding ORS 19.405 (1), the party may move the Court of Appeals to certify the appeal to the Supreme Court, and the Court of Appeals acting in its sole discretion may so certify the appeal. If the Court of Appeals certifies the appeal to the Supreme Court, the Supreme Court shall accept or deny acceptance of the certification as provided in ORS 19.405 (2). [1997 c.794 s.2]

250.045 Submitting prospective petition; form of petition; statement regarding payment of petition circulators; signature sheet requirements.

(1) Before circulating a petition to initiate or refer a state measure under section 1, Article IV, Oregon Constitution, the petitioner shall file with the Secretary of State a prospective petition. The prospective petition for a state measure to be initiated shall contain a statement of sponsorship signed by at least 25 electors. The signatures in the statement of sponsorship must be accompanied by a certificate of the county clerk of each county in which the electors who signed the statement reside, stating the number of signatures believed to be genuine. The Secretary of State shall date and time stamp the prospective petition and specify the form on which the petition shall be printed for circulation. The secretary shall approve or disapprove the form of any petition signature sheet within five business days after the signature sheet is submitted for review by the secretary. The secretary shall retain the prospective petition.

(2) The chief petitioner may amend the proposed initiated measure filed with the Secretary of State without filing another prospective petition, if:

(a) The Attorney General certifies to the Secretary of State that the proposed amendment will not substantially change the substance of the measure; and

(b) The deadline for submitting written comments on the draft title has not passed.

(3) The cover of an initiative or referendum petition shall designate the name and residence address of not more than three persons as chief petitioners and shall contain instructions for persons obtaining signatures of electors on the petition. The instructions shall be adopted by the Secretary of State by rule. The cover of a referendum petition shall contain the title described in ORS 250.065 (1). If a petition seeking a different ballot title is not filed with the Supreme Court by the deadline for filing a petition under ORS 250.085, the cover of an initiative petition shall contain the ballot title described in ORS 250.067 (2). However, if the Supreme Court has reviewed the ballot title, the cover of the initiative petition shall contain the title certified by the court.

(4) The chief petitioners shall include with the prospective petition a statement declaring whether one or more persons will be paid money or other valuable consideration for obtaining signatures of electors on the initiative or referendum petition. After the prospective petition is filed, the chief petitioners shall notify the filing officer not later than the 10th day after any of the chief petitioners first has knowledge or should have had knowledge that:

(a) Any person is being paid for obtaining signatures, when the statement included with the prospective petition declared that no such person would be paid.

(b) No person is being paid for obtaining signatures, when the statement included with the prospective petition declared that one or more such persons would be paid.

(5)(a) Each sheet of signatures on an initiative petition shall contain the caption of the ballot title. Each sheet of signatures on a referendum petition shall contain the subject expressed in the title of the Act to be referred.

(b) Each sheet of signatures on an initiative or referendum petition shall:

(A) Contain only the signatures of electors of one county; and

(B) If one or more persons will be paid for obtaining signatures of electors on the petition, contain a notice stating: "Some Circulators For This Petition Are Being Paid." The notice shall be in boldfaced type and shall be prominently displayed on the sheet.

(c) The Secretary of State by rule shall adopt a method of designation to distinguish signature sheets of referendum petitions containing the same subject reference and being circulated during the same period.

(6) The reverse side of the cover of an initiative or referendum petition shall be used for obtaining signatures on an initiative or referendum petition.

(7) Not more than 20 signatures on the signature sheet of the initiative or referendum petition shall be counted. The circulator shall certify on each signature sheet of the initiative or referendum petition that the individuals signed the sheet in the presence of the circulator and that the circulator believes each individual is an elector.

(8) The person obtaining signatures on the petition shall carry at least one full and correct copy of the measure to be initiated or referred and shall allow any person to review a copy upon request of the person. [1979 c.190 s.144; 1979 c.345 s.2; 1981 c.909 s.2; 1983 c.514 s.8; 1983 c.756 s.9; 1985 c.447 s.1; 1985 c.808 s.25; 1987 c.519 s.1; 1989 c.959 s.3; 1992 c.1 s.1; 1995 c.607 s.26; 1997 c.846 s.1; 1999 c.262 s.2; 1999 c.318 s.27; 1999 c.793 s.2]

Note: See note under 250.035.

250.050

[Repealed by 1957 c.608 s.231]

250.055

[1979 c.675 s.3; 1981 c.145 s.1; renumbered 250.039]

250.060

[Repealed by 1957 c.608 s.231]

250.065 Preparation of ballot title for certain state measures.

(1) When a prospective petition for a state measure to be referred is filed with the Secretary of State, the secretary shall authorize the circulation of the petition using the final measure summary of the measure in lieu of the ballot title. After the referendum petition has been filed containing the required number of verified signatures, the Secretary of State immediately shall send two copies of the prospective petition to the Attorney General.

(2) When an approved prospective petition for a state measure to be initiated is filed with the Secretary of State, the secretary immediately shall send two copies of it to the Attorney General.

(3) Not later than the fifth business day after receiving the copies of the prospective petition for a state measure to be initiated, the Attorney General shall provide a draft ballot title for the state measure to be initiated and return one copy of the prospective petition and the ballot title to the Secretary of State.

(4) Not later than the 10th business day after receiving the copies of the prospective petition for a state measure to be referred, the Attorney General shall provide a draft ballot title for the state measure to be referred and return one copy of the prospective petition and the draft ballot title to the Secretary of State. [Formerly 254.055; 1985 c.447 s.2]

250.067 Notice of draft ballot title; written comments; certification of title.

(1) The Secretary of State, upon receiving a draft ballot title from the Attorney General under ORS 250.065 or 250.075, shall provide reasonable statewide notice of having received the draft ballot title and of the public's right to submit written comments as provided in this section. Written comments concerning a draft ballot title shall be submitted to the Secretary of State not later than the 10th business day after the Secretary of State receives the draft title from the Attorney General. The Secretary of State immediately shall send a copy of all written comments to the Attorney General and shall maintain a record of written comments received.

(2) The Attorney General shall consider any written comments submitted under subsection (1) of this section and shall certify to the Secretary of State either the draft ballot title or a revised ballot title not later than the fifth business day after receiving the comments from the Secretary of State. If no written comments are submitted to the Secretary of State, the Attorney General shall certify the draft ballot title not later than the 15th business day after the Secretary of State receives the draft title from the Attorney General. The Secretary of State shall furnish the chief petitioner with a copy of the ballot title.

(3) Unless the Supreme Court certifies a different ballot title, the ballot title provided by the Attorney General under subsection (2) of this section shall be the title printed in the voters' pamphlet and on the ballot.

(4) If a petition for review of a ballot title is filed with the Supreme Court as provided in ORS 250.085, the Secretary of State shall file with the Supreme Court a copy of the written comments received as part of the record on review of the ballot title.

(5) The Secretary of State by rule shall specify the means for providing reasonable statewide notice for submitting comments on a draft ballot title. [1985 c.447 s.5; 1989 c.503 s.5]

250.070

[Amended by 1957 c.608 s.123; 1961 c.121 s.6; 1979 c.190 s.234; renumbered 254.107]

250.075 Legislature may prepare ballot titles for certain measures.

(1) When the Legislative Assembly refers a measure to the people, a ballot title for the measure may be prepared by the assembly. The ballot title shall be filed with the Secretary of State when the measure is filed with the Secretary of State.

(2) If the title is not prepared under subsection (1) of this section, when the measure is filed with the Secretary of State, the secretary shall send two copies of the referred measure to the Attorney General. Not later than the 30th day after the Legislative Assembly adjourns, the Attorney General shall provide a draft ballot title for the measure. The Attorney General shall send a copy of the draft ballot title to each member of the Legislative Assembly, and file with the Secretary of State a copy of the referred measure and the draft ballot title and a certificate of mailing of the draft ballot title to each member. [Formerly 254.073; 1985 c.447 s.3; 1995 c.607 s.27]

250.080

[Amended by 1979 c.190 s.242; renumbered 254.185]

250.085 Procedure for elector dissatisfied with title of state measure.

(1) Any elector dissatisfied with a ballot title prepared by the Legislative Assembly for a measure referred to the people by the assembly and filed with the Secretary of State may petition the Supreme Court seeking a different title. The petition shall state the reasons that the title filed with the Secretary of State does not substantially comply with the requirements of ORS 250.035.

(2) Any elector dissatisfied with a ballot title for an initiated or referred measure certified by the Attorney General and who timely submitted written comments on the draft ballot title may petition the Supreme Court seeking a different title. The petition shall state the reasons that the title filed with the Secretary of State does not substantially comply with the requirements of ORS 250.035.

(3) The petition shall name the Attorney General as the respondent and must be filed:

(a) Not later than the 10th business day after the Attorney General certifies a ballot title to the Secretary of State; or

(b) If the title is provided by the Legislative Assembly under ORS 250.075, not later than the 10th business day after the Legislative Assembly files the ballot title with the Secretary of State.

(4) An elector filing a petition under this section shall notify the Secretary of State in writing that the petition has been filed. The notice shall be given not later than 5 p.m. on the next business day following the day the petition is filed.

(5) The court shall review the title for substantial compliance with the requirements of ORS 250.035, and shall certify a title meeting this standard to the Secretary of State.

(6) When reviewing a title prepared by the Attorney General, the court shall not consider arguments concerning the ballot title not presented in writing to the Secretary of State unless the court determines that the argument concerns language added to or removed from the draft title after expiration of the comment period provided in ORS 250.067.

(7) The review by the Supreme Court shall be conducted expeditiously to insure the orderly and timely circulation of the petition or conduct of the election at which the measure is to be submitted to the electors. [Formerly 254.077; 1983 c.514 s.9; 1985 c.447 s.6; 1987 c.519 s.2; 1989 c.503 s.6; 1993 c.493 s.96; 1995 c.534 s.2]

250.090

[Amended by 1957 c.608 s.124; 1979 c.190 s.243; renumbered 254.195]

250.095 State measures affecting a county or district.

A law enacted by the Legislative Assembly relating only to a county or district may be referred by the Legislative Assembly or by petition to the people of the county or district. The percentage of signatures required under section 1, Article

IV, Oregon Constitution, for a referendum petition filed under this section shall be based on the vote for Governor within the county or district. [1979 c.190 s.148]

250.100

[Repealed by 1957 c.608 s.231]

250.105 Filing officer; filing requirements; signature verification.

(1) An initiative or referendum petition relating to a state measure shall be filed with the Secretary of State for the purpose of verifying whether the petition contains the required number of signatures of electors. The filed petition shall contain only original signatures. Each petition shall be verified in the order in which the petitions are filed with the secretary.

(2) An initiative or referendum petition relating to a state measure shall not be accepted for filing if it contains less than 100 percent of the required number of signatures.

(3) If an initiative or referendum petition is submitted not less than 165 days before the election at which the proposed measure is to be voted upon and if the Secretary of State determines that insufficient signatures have been submitted but the deadline for filing the petition has not passed, the petitioners may submit additional signatures.

(4) The Secretary of State by rule shall designate a statistical sampling technique to verify whether a petition contains the required number of signatures of electors. A petition shall not be rejected for the reason that it contains less than the required number of signatures unless two separate sampling processes both establish that the petition lacks the required number of signatures. The second sampling must contain a larger number of signatures than the first sampling. If two samplings are required under this subsection, the total number of signatures verified on the petition shall be not less than five percent of the total number of signatures on the petition.

(5) For purposes of estimating the number of duplicate signatures contained in a petition, the Secretary of State shall apply at least an eight percent duplication rate in the first sampling of signatures on all petitions. If a second sampling of signatures is required under subsection (4) of this section, the secretary shall calculate an estimated signature duplication rate for each petition for which a second sampling is required. For purposes of calculating an estimated signature duplication rate for each petition for which a second sampling is required, the county clerks shall report to the secretary the number of electors determined to have signed a specific petition more than once.

(6) When verifying signatures for a state initiative or referendum petition, the county clerk shall identify on an elector's voter registration record or other database that the elector signed the specific initiative or referendum petition.

(7) The Secretary of State may employ professional assistance to determine the sampling technique to be designated under subsection (4) of this section. [1979 c.190 s.149; 1985 c.447 s.7; 1989 c.68 s.6; 1999 c.1021 s.1]

250.110

[Amended by 1953 c.632 s.6; 1957 c.608 s.126; 1961 c.170 s.2; subsection (7) enacted as 1967 c.26 s.4; 1977 c.508 s.6; 1979 c.190 s.237; renumbered 254.135]

250.115 Numbering of state measures.

(1) The Secretary of State shall number the measures to be voted on in the state at large consecutively, beginning with number one, and not repeating any number in any subsequent election until the number of measures reaches 99. When the number of measures reaches 99, the numbering sequence shall recommence with the number 1 at the next election at which a state measure is voted on. The measures shall be assigned numbers in the order in which the measures are filed with the secretary.

(2) The Secretary of State shall number state measures not referred to under subsection (1) of this section consecutively, beginning with the number after the last number assigned under subsection (1) of this section, in the order in which the measures are filed with the secretary. [1979 c.190 s.150; 1993 c.493 s.14]

250.120

[Amended by 1953 c.632 s.6; repealed by 1957 c.608 s.231]

250.121

[1957 c.608 s.130; 1961 c.68 s.2; 1979 c.190 s.244; renumbered 254.205]

250.125 Estimate of financial impact of state measures.

(1) When a state measure involves expenditure of public money by the state, reduction of expenditure of public money by the state, reduction of state revenues or raising of funds by the state by imposing any tax or incurring any indebted-

ness, the Secretary of State, the State Treasurer, the Director of the Oregon Department of Administrative Services and the Director of the Department of Revenue shall estimate the amount of direct expenditure, direct reduction of expenditure, direct reduction in state revenues, direct tax revenue or indebtedness and interest which will be required to meet the provisions of the measure if it is enacted. The estimate shall state the recurring annual amount involved or, if the measure does not involve a recurring annual amount, the total amount.

(2) The officials named in subsection (1) of this section shall also estimate the aggregate amount of direct expenditure, direct reduction of expenditure, direct reduction in revenues, direct tax revenue or indebtedness and interest which will be required by any city, county or district to meet the provisions of the measure.

(3) The estimates shall be printed in the voters' pamphlet and on the ballot unless the measure involves only state agency expenses not exceeding $100,000 per year.

(4) If the officials named in subsection (1) of this section determine that the measure, if it is enacted, will have no financial effect except as described in subsection (3) of this section, the words "no financial effect on state or local government expenditures or revenues" shall be printed in the voters' pamphlet and on the ballot.

(5) The Legislative Administration Committee shall provide any administrative staff assistance required by the officials named in subsection (1) of this section to facilitate the work of the officials under this section or ORS 250.127. [Formerly 254.180; 1987 c.724 s.6; 1991 c.971 s.1; 1993 c.493 s.15; 1999 c.844 s.1]

250.127 Preparation and filing of estimates of financial impact of state measure.

(1) Not later than the 99th day before a special election held on the date of a biennial primary election or any general election at which any state measure is to be submitted to the people, the officials named in ORS 250.125 shall prepare and file with the Secretary of State, estimates as described in ORS 250.125. The officials named in ORS 250.125 may begin preparation of the estimates described in ORS 250.125 on the date that a petition is accepted for verification of signatures under ORS 250.105 or the date that a measure referred by the Legislative Assembly is filed with the Secretary of State, whichever is applicable.

(2) Not sooner than the 98th nor later than the 95th day before the election, the Secretary of State shall hold a hearing in Salem upon reasonable statewide notice to receive suggested changes to the estimates or other information. At the hearing any person may submit suggested changes or other information orally or in writing. Written suggestions or other information also may be submitted at any time before the hearing.

(3) The officials named in ORS 250.125 shall consider suggestions and any other information submitted under subsection (2) of this section, and may file revised estimates with the Secretary of State not later than the 90th day before the election.

(4) Except as provided in subsection (5) of this section, the original estimates and any revised estimates shall be approved by at least three of the officials named in ORS 250.125. If an official does not concur, the estimates shall show only that the official dissents. The Secretary of State shall certify final estimates not later than the 90th day before the election at which the measure is to be voted upon. All estimates prepared under ORS 250.125 and this section shall be made available to the public.

(5) If two or more of the officials named in ORS 250.125 do not approve the estimates, the Secretary of State alone shall prepare, file and certify the estimates not later than the 88th day before the election at which the measure is to be voted upon with the data upon which it is based.

(6) The support or opposition of any official named in ORS 250.125 to the original or revised estimates shall be indicated in the minutes of any meeting of the officials. Meetings of the officials shall be open to the public. Designees of the officials named in ORS 250.125 may attend any meetings of the officials in the place of the officials, but the designees may not vote to approve or oppose any estimates.

(7) A failure to prepare, file or certify estimates under ORS 250.125, this section or ORS 250.131 shall not prevent the inclusion of the measure in the voters' pamphlet or placement of the measure on the ballot.

(8) If the estimates are not delivered to the county clerk by the 61st day before the election, the county clerk may proceed with the printing of ballots. The county clerk shall not be required to reprint ballots to include the estimates or to provide supplemental information that includes the estimates. [1991 c.971 s.3; 1993 c.493 s.16; 1995 c.712 s.33; 1999 c.318 s.19]

250.130

[Repealed by 1957 c.608 s.231]

250.131 Court review of procedures under which estimates of financial impact of state measure were prepared.

(1) Any person alleging that an estimate required under ORS 250.125 was prepared, filed or certified in violation of the procedures specified in ORS 250.125 or 250.127 may petition the Supreme Court seeking that the required procedures be followed and stating the reasons the estimate filed with the court does not satisfy the required procedures. No petition shall be allowed concerning the amount of the estimate or regarding whether an estimate should be prepared.

(2) If the petition is filed not later than the 85th day before the election at which the measure is to be voted upon, the court shall review the procedures under which the estimate was prepared, filed and certified, hear arguments and determine whether the procedures required under ORS 250.125 and 250.127 were satisfied. The review by the Supreme Court shall be conducted expeditiously to insure the orderly and timely conduct of the election at which the measure is to be submitted to the electors.

(3) If the court determines that the procedures described in ORS 250.125 and 250.127 were not satisfied, the court shall order the preparation of a second estimate, to be prepared, filed and certified as provided in ORS 250.125 and 250.127 except that:

(a) The officials named in ORS 250.125 shall prepare and file with the Secretary of State an estimate not later than two days following the decision of the court;

(b) A hearing shall be held within two days after the estimate is filed; and

(c) An estimate shall be certified not later than seven days after the decision of the court. The procedures under which the second estimate is filed and certified may not be appealed. [1991 c.971 s.4]

250.135 Retention of petition materials.

The Secretary of State shall retain the signature sheets of a filed initiative or referendum petition with a copy of the state measure. If the measure is approved by the people, the signature sheets and copy of the measure shall be bound with a certified copy of the Governor's proclamation declaring the measure approved. A copy of the measure and the Governor's proclamation shall be preserved as a permanent public record. The signature sheets shall be preserved for six years. [1979 c.190 s.152]

250.140

[Amended by 1957 c.608 s.127; repealed by 1979 c.190 s.431]

250.145

[1953 c.58 s.1; 1955 c.52 s.1; 1969 c.104 s.1; repealed by 1979 c.190 s.431]

250.150

[Amended by 1957 c.608 s.128; 1961 c.74 s.2; 1967 c.340 s.2; 1979 c.190 s.245; renumbered 254.215]

250.155 Application of subchapter.

(1) ORS 250.165 to 250.235 carry out the provisions of section 10, Article VI, Oregon Constitution, and shall apply to the exercise of initiative or referendum powers regarding a county measure, unless the county charter or ordinance provides otherwise.

(2) ORS 250.165 to 250.235 applies to the exercise of initiative or referendum powers regarding a county measure in a county that has not adopted a charter under section 10, Article VI, Oregon Constitution. [1979 c.190 s.153]

250.160

[Repealed by 1957 c.608 s.231]

250.161

[1957 c.608 s.131; 1979 c.190 s.240; renumbered 254.165]

250.165 Submitting prospective petition; form of petition; statement regarding payment of petition circulators; signature sheet requirements; annual statement.

(1) Before circulating a petition to initiate or refer a county measure, the petitioner shall file with the county clerk a prospective petition. The county clerk immediately shall date and time stamp the prospective petition, and specify the form on which the petition shall be printed for circulation. The clerk shall retain the prospective petition.

(2) The cover of an initiative or referendum petition shall designate the name and residence address of not more than three persons as chief petitioners and shall contain instructions for persons obtaining signatures of electors on the petition. The instructions shall be adopted by the Secretary of State by rule. The cover of a referendum petition shall contain the title described in ORS 250.175 (1). If the circuit court has not reviewed the ballot title under ORS 250.195, the cover of an initiative petition shall contain the ballot title described in ORS 250.175 (3). If the circuit court has reviewed the ballot title, the cover of the initiative petition shall contain the title certified by the court.

(3) The chief petitioners shall include with the prospective petition a statement declaring whether one or more persons will be paid money or other valuable consideration for obtaining signatures of electors on the initiative or referendum

petition. After the prospective petition is filed, the chief petitioners shall notify the filing officer not later than the 10th day after any of the chief petitioners first has knowledge or should have had knowledge that:

(a) Any person is being paid for obtaining signatures, when the statement included with the prospective petition declared that no such person would be paid.

(b) No person is being paid for obtaining signatures, when the statement included with the prospective petition declared that one or more such persons would be paid.

(4)(a) Each sheet of signatures on an initiative petition shall contain the caption of the ballot title. Each sheet of signatures on a referendum petition shall contain the number of the ordinance or resolution to be referred, if any, and the date it was adopted by the county governing body.

(b) Each sheet of signatures on an initiative or referendum petition shall:

(A) If one or more persons will be paid for obtaining signatures of electors on the petition, contain a notice stating: "Some Circulators For This Petition Are Being Paid"; and

(B) If the person obtaining the signatures on the initiative or referendum petition is being paid, contain a notice stating that the person obtaining the signatures is being paid. The notice shall be in boldfaced type and shall be prominently displayed on the sheet.

(5) The reverse side of the cover of an initiative or referendum petition shall be used for obtaining signatures on an initiative or referendum petition.

(6) Not more than 20 signatures on the signature sheet of the initiative or referendum petition shall be counted. The circulator shall certify on each signature sheet that the individuals signed the sheet in the presence of the circulator and that the circulator believes each individual is an elector registered in the county.

(7) If the gathering of signatures exceeds the period of one year from the time the petition is approved for circulation, any of the chief petitioners, on or before the anniversary of approval of the petition for circulation:

(a) Shall file annually, with the county clerk, a statement that the initiative petition is still active; and

(b) May submit to the county clerk for verification any signatures gathered on the petition in the preceding year.

(8) Not later than 30 days before the date that the chief petitioners must file a statement and submit signatures under subsection (7) of this section, the county clerk shall notify the chief petitioners in writing of the requirements of subsection (7) of this section. The notice shall be sent by certified mail, return receipt requested.

(9) A county clerk shall not accept for filing any petition which has not met the provisions of subsection (7) of this section.

(10) The person obtaining signatures on the petition shall carry at least one full and correct copy of the measure to be initiated or referred and shall allow any person to review a copy upon request of the person. [1979 c.190 s.154; 1981 c.909 s.3; 1983 c.756 s.10; 1991 c.106 s.1; 1992 c.1 s.2; 1995 c.607 s.28; 1997 c.846 s.2; 1999 c.318 s.28]

250.168 One subject determination; notice; appeal.

(1) Not later than the fifth business day after receiving a prospective petition for an initiative measure, the county clerk shall determine in writing whether the initiative measure meets the requirements of section 1 (2)(d), Article IV of the Oregon Constitution.

(2) If the county clerk determines that the initiative measure meets the requirements of section 1 (2)(d), Article IV of the Oregon Constitution, the clerk shall proceed as required in ORS 250.175. The clerk shall include in the publication required under ORS 250.175 (5) a statement that the initiative measure has been determined to meet the requirements of section 1 (2)(d), Article IV of the Oregon Constitution.

(3) If the county clerk determines that the initiative measure does not meet the requirements of section 1 (2)(d), Article IV of the Oregon Constitution, the clerk shall immediately notify the petitioner, in writing by certified mail, return receipt requested, of the determination.

(4) Any elector dissatisfied with a determination of the county clerk under subsection (1) of this section may petition the circuit court of the judicial district in which the county is located seeking to overturn the determination of the clerk. If the elector is dissatisfied with a determination that the initiative measure meets the requirements of section 1 (2)(d), Article IV of the Oregon Constitution, the petition must be filed not later than the seventh business day after the ballot title is filed with the clerk. If the elector is dissatisfied with a determination that the initiative measure does not meet the requirements of section 1 (2)(d), Article IV of the Oregon Constitution, the petition must be filed not later than the seventh business day after the written determination is made by the clerk.

(5) The review by the circuit court shall be the first and final review, and shall be conducted expeditiously to insure the orderly and timely circulation of the petition. [1991 c.719 s.34]

250.170

[Repealed by 1957 c.608 s.231]

250.175 Preparation of ballot title for certain county measures; notice.

(1) When a prospective petition for a county measure to be referred is filed with the county clerk, the clerk shall authorize the circulation of the petition containing the title of the measure as enacted by the county governing body or, if there is no title, the title supplied by the petitioner filing the prospective petition. The county clerk immediately shall send two copies of the prospective petition to the district attorney.

(2) Not later than the sixth business day after a prospective petition for a county measure to be initiated is filed with the county clerk, the clerk shall send two copies of it to the district attorney if the measure to be initiated has been determined to be in compliance with section 1 (2)(d), Article IV of the Oregon Constitution, as provided in ORS 250.168.

(3) Not later than the fifth business day after receiving the copies of the prospective petition, and notwithstanding ORS 203.145 (3), the district attorney shall prepare a ballot title for the county measure to be initiated or referred and return one copy of the prospective petition and the ballot title to the county clerk. Unless the circuit court certifies a different title, this ballot title shall be the title printed on the ballot.

(4) A copy of the ballot title shall be furnished to the chief petitioner.

(5) The county clerk, upon receiving a ballot title for a county measure to be referred or initiated from the district attorney or the county governing body, shall publish in the next available edition of a newspaper of general circulation in the county a notice of receipt of the ballot title including notice that an elector may file a petition for review of the ballot title not later than the date referred to in ORS 250.195. [1979 c.190 s.155; 1983 c.567 s.12; 1985 c.808 s.26; 1987 c.707 s.8; 1991 c.719 s.21]

250.180

[Repealed by 1957 c.608 s.231]

250.185 County governing body may prepare ballot titles for certain measures.

(1) When the county governing body refers a measure to the people, a ballot title for the measure may be prepared by the body. The measure and the ballot title prepared under this subsection shall be filed at the same time with the county clerk.

(2) If the title is not prepared under subsection (1) of this section, when the measure is filed with the county clerk, the clerk shall send two copies to the district attorney. Not later than the fifth business day after receiving the copies the district attorney shall provide a ballot title for the measure and send a copy of it to the county governing body and the county clerk. [1979 c.190 s.156; 1983 c.15 s.3; 1985 c.808 s.27]

250.190

[Amended by 1957 c.608 s.132; repealed by 1979 c.190 s.431]

250.195 Procedure for elector dissatisfied with title of county measure.

(1) Any elector dissatisfied with a ballot title filed with the county clerk by the district attorney or the county governing body, may petition the circuit court of the judicial district in which the county is located seeking a different title and stating the reasons the title filed with the court is insufficient, not concise or unfair. The petition shall name as respondent either the district attorney or county governing body, depending on who prepared the ballot title, and must be filed not later than the seventh business day after the title is filed with the county clerk. The court shall review the title and measure to be initiated or referred, hear arguments, if any, and certify to the county clerk a title for the measure which meets the requirements of ORS 250.035.

(2) An elector filing a petition under this section shall notify the county clerk in writing that the petition has been filed. The notice shall be given not later than 5 p.m. on the next business day following the day the petition is filed.

(3) The review by the circuit court shall be the first and final review, and shall be conducted expeditiously to insure the orderly and timely circulation of the petition or conduct of the election at which the measure is to be submitted to the electors. [1979 c.190 s.157; 1983 c.514 s.9a; 1987 c.707 s.9; 1989 c.503 s.7; 1993 c.493 s.97; 1995 c.534 s.3]

250.200

[Amended by 1957 c.608 s.133; 1961 c.89 s.1; repealed by 1979 c.190 s.431]

250.205 Filing and signature requirements for nonhome rule counties.

(1) This section applies to a county that has not adopted a charter under section 10, Article VI, Oregon Constitution.

(2) A referendum petition must be filed not later than the 90th day after the adoption of a nonemergency county measure.

(3) A petition to refer a county measure must contain at least the number of signatures of electors residing in the county that is equal to four percent of the total number of votes cast in the county for all candidates for Governor at the election at which a Governor is elected for a four-year term next preceding the filing of the petition for verification of signatures. [1979 c.190 s.158; 1995 c.607 s.29]

(4) A petition to initiate a county measure must contain at least the number of signatures of electors residing in the county equal to six percent of the total number of votes cast in the county for all candidates for Governor at the election at which a Governor is elected for a four-year term next preceding the filing of the petition for verification of signatures. [1979 c.190 s.158; 1995 c.607 s.29]

250.210

[Amended by 1957 c.608 s.134; 1979 c.519 s.19; repealed by 1979 c.190 s.431]

250.215 Filing officer for county measure; filing requirements; signature verification.

(1) An initiative or referendum petition relating to a county measure shall be filed with the county clerk for signature verification. The filed petition shall contain only original signatures.

(2) An initiative or referendum petition relating to a county measure shall not be accepted for filing if it contains less than 100 percent of the required number of signatures.

(3) For any petition requiring a number of signatures exceeding 4,500, the Secretary of State by rule shall designate a statistical sampling technique to verify whether a petition contains the required number of signatures of electors. A petition may not be rejected for the reason that it contains less than the required number of signatures unless two separate sampling processes both establish that the petition lacks the required number of signatures. The second sampling must contain a larger number of signatures than the first sampling.

(4) The Secretary of State may employ professional assistance to determine the sampling technique referred to in subsection (3) of this section. [1979 c.190 s.159; 1989 c.68 s.7; 1991 c.580 s.2]

250.220

[Amended by 1957 c.608 s.135; 1961 c.89 s.2; repealed by 1979 c.190 s.431]

250.221 Date of election.

If an initiative or referendum petition contains the required number of verified signatures, the election on the county measure shall be held on the next available election date in ORS 203.085 that is not sooner than the 90th day after the measure was filed with the county clerk. [1981 c.909 s.4]

250.225

[1963 c.345 ss.5,6; 1979 c.190 s.269; 1979 c.519 s.29a; renumbered 254.475]

250.226

[1979 c.190 s.160; repealed by 1987 c.724 s.7]

250.230

[Amended by 1957 c.608 s.136; 1979 c.190 s.227; 1979 c.317 s.9; renumbered 254.035]

250.235 Retention of petition materials.

The county clerk shall retain the signature sheets of a filed initiative or referendum petition with a copy of the county measure. If the measure is approved by the electors, a copy of the measure shall be preserved as a permanent public record, and the signature sheets shall be preserved for six years. [1979 c.190 s.161]

250.255 Application of subchapter.

ORS 250.265 to 250.346 applies to the exercise of initiative or referendum powers regarding a city measure under section 1, Article IV, Oregon Constitution, unless the city charter or ordinance provides otherwise. [1979 c.190 s.162]

250.265 Submitting prospective petition; form of petition; statement regarding payment of petition circulators; signature sheet requirements; annual statement.

(1) Before circulating a petition to initiate or refer a city measure, the petitioner shall file with the city elections officer a prospective petition. The officer immediately shall date and time stamp the prospective petition, and specify the form on which the petition shall be printed for circulation. The officer shall retain the prospective petition.

(2) The cover of an initiative or referendum petition shall designate the name and residence address of not more than three persons as chief petitioners and shall contain instructions for persons obtaining signatures of electors on the petition. The instructions shall be adopted by the Secretary of State by rule. The cover of a referendum petition shall contain the title described in ORS 250.275 (1). If the circuit court has not reviewed the ballot title under ORS 250.296, the cover of an initiative petition shall contain the ballot title described in ORS 250.275 (3). If the circuit court has reviewed the ballot title, the cover of the initiative petition shall contain the title certified by the court.

(3) The chief petitioners shall include with the prospective petition a statement declaring whether one or more persons will be paid money or other valuable consideration for obtaining signatures of electors on the initiative or referendum petition. After the prospective petition is filed, the chief petitioners shall notify the filing officer not later than the 10th day after any of the chief petitioners first has knowledge or should have had knowledge that:

(a) Any person is being paid for obtaining signatures, when the statement included with the prospective petition declared that no such person would be paid.

(b) No person is being paid for obtaining signatures, when the statement included with the prospective petition declared that one or more such persons would be paid.

(4)(a) Each sheet of signatures on an initiative petition shall contain the caption of the ballot title. Each sheet of signatures on a referendum petition shall contain the number of the ordinance or resolution to be referred, if any, and the date it was adopted by the city governing body.

(b) Each sheet of signatures on an initiative or referendum petition shall:

(A) If one or more persons will be paid for obtaining signatures of electors on the petition, contain a notice stating: "Some Circulators For This Petition Are Being Paid"; and

(B) If the person obtaining the signatures on the initiative or referendum petition is being paid, contain a notice stating that the person obtaining the signatures is being paid. The notice shall be in boldfaced type and shall be prominently displayed on the sheet.

(5) The reverse side of the cover of an initiative or referendum petition shall be used for obtaining signatures on an initiative or referendum petition.

(6) Not more than 20 signatures on the signature sheet of the initiative or referendum petition shall be counted. The circulator shall certify on each signature sheet that the individuals signed the sheet in the presence of the circulator and that the circulator believes each individual is an elector registered in the city.

(7) If the gathering of signatures exceeds the period of one year from the time the petition is approved for circulation, any of the chief petitioners, on or before the anniversary of approval of the petition for circulation:

(a) Shall file annually, with the city elections officer, a statement that the initiative petition is still active; and

(b) May submit to the city elections officer for verification any signatures gathered on the petition in the preceding year.

(8) Not later than 30 days before the date that the chief petitioners must file a statement and submit signatures under subsection (7) of this section, the city elections officer shall notify the chief petitioners in writing of the requirements of subsection (7) of this section. The notice shall be sent by certified mail, return receipt requested.

(9) A city elections officer shall not accept for filing any petition which has not met the provisions of subsection (7) of this section.

(10) The person obtaining signatures on the petition shall carry at least one full and correct copy of the measure to be initiated or referred and shall allow any person to review a copy upon request of the person. [1979 c.190 s.163; 1981 c.909 s.6; 1983 c.756 s.11; 1991 c.106 s.2; 1992 c.1 s.3; 1995 c.607 s.30; 1997 c.846 s.3; 1999 c.318 s.29]

250.270 One subject determination; notice; appeal.

(1) Not later than the fifth business day after receiving a prospective petition for an initiative measure, the city elections officer shall determine in writing whether the initiative measure meets the requirements of section 1 (2)(d), Article IV of the Oregon Constitution.

(2) If the city elections officer determines that the initiative measure meets the requirements of section 1 (2)(d), Article IV of the Oregon Constitution, the city elections officer shall proceed as required in ORS 250.275. The city elections officer shall include in the publication required under ORS 250.275 (5) a statement that the initiative measure has been determined to meet the requirements of section 1 (2)(d), Article IV of the Oregon Constitution.

(3) If the city elections officer determines that the initiative measure does not meet the requirements of section 1 (2)(d), Article IV of the Oregon Constitution, the city elections officer shall immediately notify the petitioner, in writing by certified mail, return receipt requested, of the determination.

(4) Any elector dissatisfied with a determination of the city elections officer under subsection (1) of this section may petition the circuit court of the judicial district in which the city is located seeking to overturn the determination of the city elections officer. If the elector is dissatisfied with a determination that the initiative measure meets the requirements of section 1 (2)(d), Article IV of the Oregon Constitution, the petition must be filed not later than the seventh business

day after the ballot title is filed with the city elections officer. If the elector is dissatisfied with a determination that the initiative measure does not meet the requirements of section 1 (2)(d), Article IV of the Oregon Constitution, the petition must be filed not later than the seventh business day after the written determination is made by the city elections officer.

(5) The review by the circuit court shall be the first and final review, and shall be conducted expeditiously to insure the orderly and timely circulation of the petition. [1991 c.719 s.36]

250.275 Preparation of ballot title for certain city measures; notice.

(1) When a prospective petition for a city measure to be referred is filed with the city elections officer, the officer shall authorize the circulation of the petition containing the title of the measure as enacted by the city governing body or, if there is no title, the title supplied by the petitioner filing the prospective petition. The city elections officer immediately shall send two copies of the prospective petition to the city attorney.

(2) Not later than the sixth business day after a prospective petition for a city measure to be initiated is filed with the city elections officer, the officer shall send two copies of it to the city attorney if the measure to be initiated has been determined to be in compliance with section 1 (2)(d), Article IV of the Oregon Constitution, as provided in ORS 250.270.

(3) Not later than the fifth business day after receiving the copies of the prospective petition, the city attorney shall provide a ballot title for the city measure to be initiated or referred and return one copy of the prospective petition and the ballot title to the city elections officer. Unless the circuit court certifies a different title, this ballot title shall be the title printed on the ballot.

(4) A copy of the ballot title shall be furnished to the chief petitioner.

(5) The city elections officer, upon receiving a ballot title for a city measure to be referred or initiated from the city attorney or city governing body, shall publish in the next available edition of a newspaper of general distribution in the city a notice of receipt of the ballot title including notice that an elector may file a petition for review of the ballot title not later than the date referred to in ORS 250.296. [1979 c.190 s.164; 1985 c.808 s.28; 1987 c.707 s.9a; 1991 c.719 s.22]

250.285 City governing body may prepare ballot titles for certain measures.

(1) When the city governing body refers a measure to the people, a ballot title for the measure may be prepared by the body. The ballot title shall be filed with the city elections officer.

(2) If the title is not prepared under subsection (1) of this section, when the measure is filed with the city elections officer, the officer shall send two copies to the city attorney. Not later than the fifth business day after receiving the copies the city attorney shall provide a ballot title for the measure, and send a copy of it to the city governing body and the city elections officer. [1979 c.190 s.165; 1985 c.808 s.29]

250.290

[Amended by 1965 s.s. c.1 s.1; repealed by 1971 c.767 s.1]

250.295

[1971 c.767 s.2; 1979 c.190 s.395; renumbered 188.130]

250.296 Procedure for elector dissatisfied with title of city measure.

(1) Any elector dissatisfied with a ballot title filed with the city elections officer by the city attorney or the city governing body, may petition the circuit court of the judicial district in which the city is located seeking a different title and stating the reasons the title filed with the court is insufficient, not concise or unfair. The petition shall name as respondent the city attorney or city governing body, depending on who prepared the ballot title, and must be filed not later than the seventh business day after the title is filed with the city elections officer. The court shall review the title and measure to be initiated or referred, hear arguments, if any, and certify to the city elections officer a title for the measure which meets the requirements of ORS 250.035.

(2) An elector filing a petition under this section shall notify the city elections officer in writing that the petition has been filed. The notice shall be given not later than 5 p.m. on the next business day following the day the petition is filed.

(3) The review by the circuit court shall be the first and final review, and shall be conducted expeditiously to insure the orderly and timely circulation of the petition or conduct of the election at which the measure is to be submitted to the electors. [1979 c.190 s.166; 1983 c.514 s.9b; 1987 c.707 s.10; 1989 c.503 s.8; 1993 c.493 s.98; 1995 c.534 s.4]

250.300

[Amended by 1979 c.190 s.396; renumbered 188.310]

250.305 Signature requirements.

(1) A petition to refer a city measure must be signed by not less than 10 percent of the electors registered in the city at the time the prospective petition is filed. The petition must be filed with the city elections officer not later than the 30th day after adoption of the city legislation sought to be referred.

(2) A petition to initiate a city measure must be signed by not less than 15 percent of the electors registered in the city at the time the prospective petition is filed. [1979 c.190 s.167; 1983 c.350 s.67; 1989 c.251 s.1]

250.310

[Amended by 1955 c.726 s.1; 1957 c.608 s.137; 1959 c.317 s.3; 1961 c.114 s.11; repealed by 1979 c.190 s.431]

250.315 Filing officer; filing requirements; signature verification.

(1) An initiative or referendum petition relating to a city measure shall be filed with the city elections officer for signature verification. The filed petition shall contain only original signatures.

(2) An initiative or referendum petition relating to a city measure shall not be accepted for filing if it contains less than 100 percent of the required number of signatures.

(3) For any petition requiring a number of signatures exceeding 4,500, the Secretary of State by rule shall designate a statistical sampling technique to verify whether a petition contains the required number of signatures of electors. A petition may not be rejected for the reason that it contains less than the required number of signatures unless two separate sampling processes both establish that the petition lacks the required number of signatures. The second sampling must contain a larger number of signatures than the first sampling.

(4) The Secretary of State may employ professional assistance to determine the sampling technique referred to in subsection (3) of this section. [1979 c.190 s.168; 1989 c.68 s.8; 1991 c.580 s.3]

250.320

[Repealed by 1957 c.608 s.231]

250.325 Procedure following filing of initiative petition.

(1) If an initiative petition contains the required number of verified signatures, the city elections officer shall file the initiated measure with the city governing body at its next meeting.

(2) The governing body, not later than the 30th day after the measure is filed with it, may adopt or reject the measure unless the measure is required to be submitted to city electors under the city charter or state law. If the measure is not adopted, or the measure is required to be submitted to city electors under the city charter or state law, it shall be submitted to city electors on the next available election date in ORS 221.230 held not sooner than the 90th day after the measure was filed with the city governing body.

(3) The governing body may refer a competing measure to city electors at the same election at which the initiated measure is submitted. If the governing body refers a competing measure to city electors, it must prepare the measure not later than the 30th day after the initiated measure is filed with it. The mayor shall not have the power to veto an initiated measure or a competing measure. [1979 c.190 s.169; 1979 c.316 s.14a; 1981 c.909 s.7; 1987 c.471 s.1]

250.330

[Amended by 1957 c.608 s.138; 1979 c.190 s.252; 1979 c.749 s.3; renumbered 254.295]

250.335

[1979 c.190 s.170; repealed by 1987 c.724 s.7]

250.340

[Amended by 1957 c.608 s.139; 1979 c.190 s.255; renumbered 254.325]

250.345

[1967 c.609 s.1; repealed by 1977 c.301 s.15]

250.346 Retention of petition materials.

The city elections officer shall retain the signature sheets of a filed initiative or referendum petition with a copy of the city measure. If the measure is approved by the electors, a copy of the measure shall be preserved as a permanent public record, and the signature sheets shall be preserved for six years. [1979 c.190 s.171]

250.350

[Amended by 1957 c.608 s.140; 1977 c.508 s.7; 1977 c.644 s.4a; 1979 c.190 s.264; renumbered 254.415]

250.355 Date of election.

If a referendum petition contains the required number of verified signatures, the election on the city measure shall be held on the next available election date in ORS 221.230 that is not sooner than the 90th day after the referendum measure was filed with the city elections officer. [1989 c.503 s.35]

The Basic Steps to Do an Initiative in Oregon

Statutes and Amendments — Direct Initiative Process

Basic Procedures: When the proponent files the initiative and application with the Secretary of State, the Secretary of State immediately sends a copy to the Attorney General. The Attorney General has 5 days to write the ballot title and summary. The Attorney General then sends the title and summary to the Secretary of State. The Secretary of State sends copies of the full text, title and summary to the Legislature, proponents and other interested parties (like journalists and activists who are on the Secretary of State's e-mail list.)

There is then a 15 day comment period during which the public can review and debate the ballot title, summary and full text. (There are no official public hearings.) It is during this 15-day comment period that proponents can challenge the wording of the title or summary in the Oregon Supreme Court. The Court, however, does not have a set time frame for dealing with any disputes. If the proponent agrees with the ballot title, then the proponent will put the petition in the correct format with the ballot title and begin collecting signatures after the 15 days.

It is normally the practice to file several measures with the Secretary of State with slightly different wording so you can get different ballot titles to chose from before circulating.

Date initiative language can be submitted to state for the November 2002 ballot: Any time after July 7, 2000 for the 2002 ballot.

Signatures are tied to vote of which office: Governor

Next Gubernatorial election: 2002

Votes cast for governor in last election: 1,113,098

Net number of signatures required: 8% of votes cast for Governor for a constitutional amendment (89,048) and 6% for a statute (66,786)

Distribution requirement: None

Circulation Period: About two years. (Maximum circulation period is from July 7, 2000 to July 5, 2002.

Do circulators have to be residents: No.

Date when signatures are due for certification: July 5, 2002

Signature verification process: Petitions are turned into the Secretary of State's office. The Secretary of State highlights a random sample and sends them to the appropriate counties for verification.

Single-subject restriction: Oregon has a very strict single subject requirement.

Legislative tampering: Legislature can repeal and amend initiative statutes by simple majority.

General Comment: On November 5, 2002 the voters adopted a constitutional amendment — which will go into affect on December 5, 2002 — that states, "it shall be unlawful to pay or receive money or other thing of value based on the number of signatures obtained on an initiative or referendum petition. Nothing herein prohibits payment for signature gathering which is not based, either directly or indirectly, on the number of signatures obtained."

Pennsylvania

Among the earliest initiative and referendum advocates in Pennsylvania was Charles Fremont Thylor, M.D., of Philadelphia. Dr. Taylor, one of the movement's most successful publicists, edited and published its periodical *Equity* (originally *Equity Series)* for over a decade. Thylor collaborated with Prof. Frank Parsons of Boston in publishing several of Parson's reformist works. Parsons' *The City for the People,* a guide to the reform of city government, included a 132-page chapter on initiative, referendum, and recall, which they later published separately.

Although Thylor's publications had a nationwide impact, efforts for I&R foundered in his own state. Under the leadership of Finley Acker of Philadelphia and Clarence Van Dyke Tiers of Pittsburgh, the Pennsylvania Direct Legislation League waged an unsuccessful, 20-year battle against "the rule of the corporation machine" headed by Republican boss Boies Penrose. In July 1909 State Rep. Hyatt M. Cribbs wrote that the state house of representatives "is so overwhelmingly machine that I have little hope of ever getting my [I&R] bill out of committee."

The biggest victory for I&R advocates came in 1914, when they succeeded in persuading the legislature to pass a law allowing I&R in third-class cities—a category that included most of the major cities of the state except the two biggest, Philadelphia and Pittsburgh.

Few initiative campaigns in Pennsylvania have attracted much attention outside the local jurisdictions in which they have taken place. One exception was the May 1983 vote in Bucks County (an elite rural area just north of Philadelphia) to block construction of a massive pump that would have drawn water from the Delaware River. The project drew opposition from environmentalists and voters, who passed the anti-pump initiative by a 56 percent margin. The Philadelphia Electric Company, which wanted the water to cool a nuclear plant, fought a five-year legal battle to build the pump anyway, and won a state ruling in its favor in 1988.

Pennsylvania Constitution

The state does not have the statewide initiative process and so therefore the following provisions discuss the procedures used by the state legislature to place constitutional amendments on the ballot.

Article XI Amendments

Section 1. Proposal of Amendments by the General Assembly and Their Adoption

Amendments to this Constitution may be proposed in the Senate or House of Representatives; and if the same shall be agreed to by a majority of the members elected to each House, such proposed amendment or amendments shall be entered on their journals with the yeas and nays taken thereon, and the Secretary of the Commonwealth shall causes the same to be published three months before the next general election, in at least two newspapers in every county in which such newspapers shall be published; and if, in the General Assembly next afterwards chosen, such proposed amendment or amendments shall be agreed to by a majority of the members elected to each House, the Secretary of the Commonwealth shall cause the same again to be published in the manner aforesaid; and such proposed amendment or amendments shall be submitted to the qualified electors of the State in such manner, and at such time at least three months after being so agreed to by the two Houses, as the General Assembly shall prescribe; and, if such amendment or amendments shall be approved by a majority of those voting thereon, such amendment or amendments shall become a part of the Constitution; but no amendment or amendments shall be submitted oftener than once in five years. When two or more amendments shall be submitted they shall be voted upon separately.

(a) In the event a major emergency threatens or is about to threaten the Commonwealth and if the safety or welfare of the Commonwealth required prompt amendment of this Constitution, such amendments to this Constitution may be proposed in the Senate or House of Representatives at any regular or special session of the General Assembly, and if agreed to by at least two-thirds of the members elected to each House, a proposed amendment shall be entered on the journal of each House with the yeas and nays taken thereon and the official in charge of statewide elections shall promptly publish such proposed amendment in at least two newspapers in every county in which such newspapers are published. Such amendment shall then be submitted to the qualified electors of the Commonwealth in such manner, and at such time, at least one month after being agreed to by both Houses as the General assembly prescribes.

(b) If an emergency amendment is approved by a majority of the qualified electors voting thereon, it shall become part of this constitution. When two or more emergency amendments are submitted they shall be voted on separately.

Rhode Island

By 1917, Rhode Island was one of only four states in the Union where the state legislature had completely blocked initiative and referendum for both the state and local governments. Like Pennsylvania, Rhode Island was controlled from the Civil War to the Great Depression by a Republican Party machine allied with the state's big industrialists, in this case textile mill owners.

Foremost among its I&R advocates was Lucius F. C. Garvin, a state legislator who was elected governor in 1902. Garvin called for passage of an I&R bill in his 1903 message to the legislature and continued pushing for I&R after his term was over. Lewis A. Waterman, Democratic candidate for governor in 1910, also called for I&R, but to no avail.

In the 1980s, agitation for I&R resumed under the leadership of Marilyn Hines, director of the state chapter of Common Cause. The group won approval of a statewide initiative amendment in a state constitutional convention in 1986, but voters, probably not comprehending its meaning due to a lack of publicity on the issue, rejected it by a narrow margin.

The next big opportunity came in 1996 when the citizens voted on a statewide advisory question asking them if they wanted the initiative process. Voters said yes by a 53% to 47% margin. However, as would be expected, the state legislature ignored the people's wishes once again.

Rhode Island Constitution

The state does not have the statewide initiative process and so therefore the following provisions discuss the procedures used by the state legislature to place constitutional amendments on the ballot.

Article VI

Section 1. Constitution supreme law of the state.

This Constitution shall be the supreme law of the state, and any law inconsistent therewith shall be void. The general assembly shall pass all laws necessary to carry this Constitution into effect.

Article XIV

Section 1. Procedure for proposing and approving amendments.

The general assembly may propose amendments to the constitution of the state by a roll call vote of a majority of the members elected to each house. Any amendment thus proposed shall be published in such manner as the general assembly shall direct, and submitted to the electors at the next general election as provided in the resolution of approval; and, if then approved by a majority of the electors voting thereon, it shall become a part of the constitution.

Section 2. Constitutional conventions.

The general assembly, by a vote of a majority of the members elected to each house, may at any general election submit the question, "Shall there be a convention to amend or revise the constitution?" to the qualified electors of the state. If the question be not submitted to the people at some time during any period of ten years, the secretary of state shall submit it at the next general election following said period. Prior to a vote by the qualified electors on the holding of a convention, the general assembly, or the governor if the general assembly fails to act, shall provide for a bi-partisan preparatory commission to assembly information on constitutional questions for the electors. If a majority of the electors voting at such election on said question shall vote to hold a convention, the general assembly at its next session shall provide by law for the election of delegates to such convention. The number of delegates shall be equal to the number of members of the house of representatives and shall be apportioned in the same manner as the members of the house of representatives. No revision or amendment of this constitution agreed upon by such convention shall take effect until the same has been submitted to the electors and approved by a majority of those voting thereon.

South Carolina

The only victory for South Carolina initiative and referendum advocates in the Progressive era was the enactment of a state law allowing I&R at the municipal level in 1910.

However, in 1999 there was a major court case that limited the referendum authority of the state legislature. In *Joytime Distributors v. State of South Carolina,* the South Carolina Supreme Court ruled that the state legislature did not have the authority to place statutes on the ballot for a general vote of the people.

South Carolina Constitution

The state does not have the statewide initiative process and so therefore the following provisions discuss the procedures used by the state legislature to place constitutional amendments on the ballot.

Article XVI

Section 1. Amendments.

Any amendment or amendments to this Constitution may be proposed in the Senate or House of Representatives. However, for the general election in 1990, revision of an entire article or the addition of a new article may be proposed as a single amendment with only one question being required to be submitted to the electors. The amendment may delete, revise, and transpose provisions from other articles of the Constitution provided the provisions are germane to the subject matter of the article being revised or being proposed. If it is agreed to by two-thirds of the members elected to each House, the amendment or amendments must be entered on the Journals respectively, with the yeas and nays taken on it and must be submitted to the qualified electors of the State at the next general election for Representatives. If a majority of the electors qualified to vote for members of the General Assembly voting on the question vote in favor of the amendment or amendments and a majority of each branch of the next General Assembly, after the election and before another, ratify the amendment or amendments, by yeas and nays, they become part of the Constitution. The amendment or amendments must be read three times, on three several days, in each House. (1976 (59) 2215; 1977 (60) 23; 1979 Act No. 5; 1985 Act No. 6, eff February 26, 1985; 1989 Act No. 11, Section 1, eff February 8, 1989.)

Section 2. Two or more amendments.

If two or more amendments shall be submitted at the same time, they shall be submitted in such manner that the electors shall vote for or against each of such amendments separately.

Section 3. Constitutional convention.

Whenever two-thirds of the members elected to each branch of the General Assembly shall think it necessary to call a Convention to revise, amend or change this Constitution, they shall recommend to the electors to vote for or against a Convention at the next election for Representatives; and if a majority of all the electors voting at said election shall have voted for a Convention, the General Assembly shall, at its next session, provide by law for calling the same; and such Convention shall consist of a number of members equal to that of the most numerous branch of the General Assembly.

South Dakota

South Dakota, the first state to adopt initiative and referendum on a statewide level, did so in 1898. The *Direct Legislation Record* for December of that year gave credit for this achievement to the organizing efforts of Walter E. Kidd of Brown County. Kidd, born in Michigan in 1849, spent "half his mature years" in farming and the other half in "newspaper work" as publisher of the *Dakota Ruralist,* whose front-page motto was "Socialism in Our Time." Kidd claimed that it was the "only daily paper in the country advocating socialism." He had served as chair of the Populist Party State Central Committee, and as state representative from his district.

South Dakota was also the only state in which the I&R idea originated on home soil. According to an article by a Mr. Doane Robinson, originally published in the St. Paul Pioneer Press and reprinted in the October 1910 *Equity Series,* I&R "originated in the fertile mind of Rev. Robert W. Haire, a Catholic clergyman of Aberdeen.... With him the plan was pure invention, for he had not heard of the Swiss I&R when in 1885 he proposed a people's legislation embodying the features of the present constitutional provision. Father Haire was active in the Knights of Labor and he exploited his scheme widely through the literature of that organization."

Later the Farmers' Alliance took it up. The populists, too, stood for the measure, and when they secured control of the legislature in 1897 they submitted an amendment to adopt I&R. Hon. H. L. Loucks, widely known as the father of populism, was earnestly in favor of the amendment. At the general election that fall [1898] it was adopted by a vote of 23,816 to 16,483.

South Dakotans in 1912 passed a primary election initiative known as the "Richards primary election law," and they passed another statute on the same subject, by the same author, in 1918.

South Dakota voters approved no other statewide initiatives for the next 60 years. The citizens saw a revival of initiative use in 1978-1988, when 16 initiatives qualified for ballot placement, a tally equal to the total number of initiatives on the ballot during the previous 55 years. In the last decade, South Dakotans have approved initiatives regarding term limits, tax reform and gaming. The renewed use of the initiative process can be tied to Governor William Janklow. Janklow was a strong supporter of the initiative process and advocated its use.

Statewide Initiative Usage

Number of Initiatives	Number Passed	Number Failed	Passage Rate
48	17	31	35%

Statewide Initiatives

Year	Measure Number	Type	Subject Matter	Description	Pass/Fail
1908	N/A	IDS	Alcohol Regulation	An act for licensing, restricting and regulating of the business of manufacture and sale of intoxicating liquors.	Failed
1912	N/A	IDS	Election Reform	Richards primary election law.	Passed
1914	N/A	IDS	Election Reform	Coffey primary election law for making party nominations for members of Congress, State, County, and Judicial officers, delegates to National and State conventions.	Failed
1914	N/A	IDS	Alcohol Regulation	To provide for licensing, restricting, and regulating sale of liquor and for the sale of liquor at local option.	Failed
1916	N/A	IDS	Administration of Government	Create State Banking Board.	Failed
1916	N/A	IDS	Election Reform	Richard primary election law — for regulation of political party transactions.	Failed
1916	N/A	IDS	Banking Reform	Create Department of Banking and Finance.	Failed
1918	N/A	IDS	Election Reform	Richards primary election law.	Passed
1920	N/A	IDS	Election Reform	Primary election law.	Failed
1922	N/A	IDS	Education	Moving state university from Vermillion to Sioux Falls.	Failed
1922	N/A	IDS	Administration of Government	Abolish state constabulary.	Failed
1922	N/A	IDS	Utility Regulation	Build and operate state hydroelectric power plants and transmission systems.	Failed

Year	Measure Number	Type	Subject Matter	Description	Pass/Fail
1922	N/A	IDS	Banking Reform	Establish state owned banks.	Failed
1922	N/A	IDS	Business Regulation	Against Sunday performance.	Failed
1948	N/A	IDS	Alcohol Regulation	To prohibit the sale of liquor where food is sold.	Failed
1950	N/A	IDS	Alcohol Regulation	Prohibit sale of liquor where food is sold.	Failed
1970	1	IDS	Health/Medical	To require fluoridation.	Failed
1970	2	IDS	Taxes	Income tax.	Failed
1972	1	IDS	Animal Rights	Prohibit mourning dove hunting	Passed
1978	1	IDS	Utility Regulation	Lifeline utility rate reform.	Failed
1978	2	IDS	Business Regulation	Repeal of Dairy Marketing Act.	Passed
1978	3	IDS	Legal	New regulation of Obscenity Statute.	Failed
1980	2	IDS	Nuclear weapons/ facilities/waste	Uranium, nuclear waste, plants: voter approval.	Failed
1980	B	DA	Taxes	Relating to real property taxes.	Failed
1980	C	DA	Initiative and Referendum	Legislature cannot change initiative-enacted laws.	Failed
1982	A	DA	Administration of Government	Single member senate districts in legislature.	Passed
1984	1	IDS	Nuclear weapons/ facilities/waste	Voter approval: nuclear waste disposal, compacts.	Passed
1984	2	IDS	Education	School begins day after Labor Day.	Passed
1984	3	M	Nuclear weapons/ facilities/waste	SD mandates a verifiable nuclear freeze.	Failed
1986	1	IDS	Administration of Government	Memorial Day observed last Monday in May.	Passed
1988	1	IDS	Taxes	Additional tax on surface mining.	Failed
1988	2	IDS	Environmental Reform	Surface mining reclamation.	Failed
1988	3	IDS	Animal Rights	Ban on corporate hog farms.	Passed
1988	B	DA	Gaming	Permit gambling in city of Deadwood.	Passed
1988	C	DA	Taxes	Add section limiting property taxes.	Failed
1990	1	DS	Utility Regulation	Legislative approval: large scale waste facilities.	Passed
1990	2	DS	Environmental Reform	Permits for large scale gold/silver mining.	Failed
1992	2	DS	Environmental Reform	Regulation, reclamation: gold/silver mining.	Passed
1992	3	DS	Taxes	Various tax reductions, redistribution.	Failed
1992	4	DS	Gaming	Repeal the video lottery.	Failed
1992	A	DA	Term Limits	Term limits on state legislature 8/8 and on Congress 12/12.	Passed
1994	1	DS	Taxes	Property tax reform.	Failed
1996	1	DS	Term Limits	Informed Voter Law.	Passed
1998	A	DA	Taxes	Would prohibit property taxes for school funding.	Failed
1998	E	DA	Administration of Government	Would address issues relating to corporate farming.	Passed
2000	1	DS	Gaming	Initiated measure to change the maximum bet limit in Deadwood.	Passed
2000	C	DA	Taxes	No tax may be levied on any inheritance, and the Legislature may not enact any law imposing such a tax.	Passed
2000	D	DA	Gaming	Constitutional amendment prohibiting video lottery.	Failed

South Dakota Constitution

Article III

§ 1. Legislative power — Initiative and referendum.

The legislative power of the state shall be vested in a Legislature which shall consist of a senate and house of representatives. However, the people expressly reserve to themselves the right to propose measures, which shall be submitted to a vote of the electors of the state, and also the right to require that any laws which the Legislature may have enacted shall be submitted to a vote of the electors of the state before going into effect, except such laws as may be necessary for the immediate preservation of the public peace, health, or safety, support of the state government and its existing public institutions. Not more than five percent of the qualified electors of the state shall be required to invoke either the initiative or the referendum. This section shall not be construed so as to deprive the Legislature or any member thereof of the right to propose any measure. The veto power of the Executive shall not be exercised as to measures referred to a vote of the people. This section shall apply to municipalities. The enacting clause of all laws approved by vote of the electors of the state shall be: "Be it enacted by the people of South Dakota." The Legislature shall make suitable provisions for carrying into effect the provisions of this section.

South Dakota Statutes

Chapter 1

2-1-1.   Initiative petitions — Number of signatures required.

All measures proposed by initiative shall be presented by petition. The petition shall be signed by not less than five percent of the qualified electors of the state.

2-1-2.   Filing and transmittal of initiative petitions — Submission to voters at general election.

The petition shall be filed in the Office of the Secretary of State by the first Tuesday in May of a general election year for submission to the electors at the next general election.

2-1-2.1. Filing of initiated constitutional amendment — Submission to voters.

A petition of the voters proposing an amendment to the Constitution shall be filed in the Office of the Secretary of State at least one year before the next general election and, if timely filed, shall be submitted to the voters at the next general election in the same manner as other questions and measures are submitted under the provisions of chapter 12-13.

2-1-2.2. Withdrawal of initiated constitutional amendment.

A petition of the voters proposing an amendment to the Constitution may be withdrawn within the meaning of S.D. Const., Art. XXIII, § 3 not later than one hundred twenty days prior to the next general election, if not less than two-thirds of the named sponsors file with the secretary of state, in writing, their request for withdrawal of the question from the ballot. The secretary of state shall attach to the petitions on file the request for withdrawal and shall take no other action thereon.

2-1-3.   Referendum — Laws subject to petition — Form.

Any law which the Legislature may have enacted, except one which may be necessary for the immediate preservation of the public peace, health, or safety, or support of the state government and its existing public institutions, shall, upon the filing of a petition as hereinafter provided, be submitted to a vote of the electors of the state at the next general election. Such petition shall be signed by not less than five percent of the qualified electors of the state. The form of the petition shall be prescribed by the State Board of Elections.

2-1-4.   Time for filing of referendum petition.

The petition shall be filed in the Office of the Secretary of State within ninety days after the adjournment of the Legislature which passed such law.

2-1-5.   Total vote used to determine number of signers required in petitions.

The total number of votes cast for Governor at the last preceding gubernatorial election, shall for the purposes of this chapter, be the basis for determining the number of petitioners required.

2-1-6.   Persons qualified to sign petitions — False or unqualified signing as misdemeanor.

Every person who is a qualified voter may sign a petition to propose a measure or submit a law. Whoever signs a petition for initiation or referendum of legislation, when he is not a qualified voter of the state, or signs a name other than his own, is guilty of a Class 1 misdemeanor.

2-1-6.1.   Filing of petition required prior to circulation.

Repealed by SL 1989, ch 23, § 3.

2-1-6.2.   Filing petition prior to circulation — Collection and filing of signatures — Time limit — Affidavits.

The full text of any initiative petition, referred law petition, or initiated constitutional amendment petition, the date of the general election at which the initiated law or initiated constitutional amendment is to be submitted, and the names and addresses of the petition sponsors shall be filed with the secretary of state prior to circulation for signatures. The signer's post office box number may be given in lieu of a street address if the signer lives within a municipality of the second or third class. The form of the petitions shall be prescribed by the State Board of Elections. For any initiated constitutional amendment petition, no signatures may be obtained more than twenty-four months preceding the general election that was designated at the time of filing of the full text. For any initiative petition, no signatures may be obtained more than eighteen months preceding the general election that was designated at the time of filing of the full text. An initiative petition and an initiated constitutional amendment petition shall be filed with the secretary of state by the date set forth in § 2-1-2 or 2-1-2.1, as applicable. All sections of any petition filed under this chapter shall be filed with the secretary of state simultaneously together with a sworn affidavit on forms promulgated by the State Board of Elections, signed by two-thirds of the sponsors stating that the documents filed constitute the entire petition and to the best of their knowledge contain a sufficient number of signatures.

2-1-6.3.   Applicability of 2000 amendments to § 2-1-6.2.

The 2000 amendments to § 2-1-6.2 do not apply to any initiative petition or initiated constitutional amendment petition filed with the secretary of state, prior to circulation for signatures, before July 1, 2000.

2-1-7.   Petitions to describe initiated and referred measures — Personal signature required.

Every petition proposing a measure must contain the substance of the law desired and must be signed in person by the petitioners, and every petition to submit a law to a vote of the electors must be signed in person by the petitioners and must describe the law desired to be submitted, by setting forth its title, together with the date of its passage and approval.

2-1-8.   Ditto marks to show residence of signers or date of signing.

Repealed by SL 1990, ch 104, § 1.

2-1-9.   Separate papers constituting single petition.

A single petition may be made up of one or more papers, each having the requisite heading and verification.

2-1-10.   Affidavit of persons circulating initiative and referendum petitions — Witness.

Each person who circulates and secures signatures to a petition to initiate or submit to the electors any law pursuant to S.D. Const., Art. III, § 1, shall sign a verification of circulator before filing the petition with the officer in whose office it is by law required to be filed. The State Board of Elections shall prescribe the form for the verification of circulator. The verification of circulator shall be witnessed by a notary public commissioned in South Dakota or other officer authorized to administer oaths pursuant to §18-3-1.

2-1-11.   Petitions liberally construed.

The petitions herein provided for shall be liberally construed, so that the real intention of the petitioners may not be defeated by a mere technicality.

2-1-12.   Effective date of measures approved by voters.

The constitutional amendments and initiated and referred measures that have been approved by a majority of all votes cast become effective the day after the completion of the official canvass by the State Canvassing Board.

2-1-13.   Circulators of petitions — Qualifications — Compensation prohibited — Expenses.

Repealed by SL 1989, ch 23, § 5.

2-1-14.   Signatures secured contrary to chapter not to be counted.

All signatures secured in a manner contrary to the provisions of this chapter may not be counted.

Chapter 20

9-20-1.   Percentage of voters required to propose ordinance or resolution.

The right to propose ordinances and resolutions for the government of any municipality shall rest with any five percent of the voters thereof, such percentage to be based upon the whole number of voters of said municipality as determined by the "precinct registration lists" or the "district registration lists" prepared by the county auditor from the master registration list in conformity to law as of the time of the filing of the petition mentioned in § 9-20-2.

9-20-2.   Petition proposing ordinance or resolution — Contents.

A petition to propose an ordinance or resolution shall be filed with the finance officer, containing in proper form the proposed ordinance or resolution. It shall be signed by the required number of the resident registered voters of the municipality. The signer or circulator shall add the signer's residence address, county of voter registration, and date of signing. The signer's post office box number may be given in lieu of a street address if the signer lives within a municipality of the second or third class. No signature on a petition is valid if signed more than six months prior to the filing of the petitions.

9-20-3.   Ordinance may not be initiated to nullify bond purposes.

The right to initiate an ordinance shall not be applicable to ordinances proposed to nullify the purpose for which bonds have been sold by a municipality pursuant to statutory authority.

9-20-4.   Presentation of initiative petition to governing body — Enactment and submission to voters.

When a petition to initiate is filed with the auditor or clerk, he shall present it to the governing body at its first ensuing regular or special meeting. The governing body shall enact the proposed ordinance or resolution and shall submit it to a vote of the voters in the manner prescribed for a referendum.

9-20-5.   Majority vote at election required for initiated ordinance or resolution — Effective date.

No initiated ordinance or resolution shall become operative unless approved by a majority of the votes cast for and against the same. If so approved, it shall take effect upon the completion of the canvass of the election returns relating thereto.

9-20-5.1.   Year's waiting period required before amendment or repeal.

No initiated ordinance or resolution may be amended or repealed by the governing body of a municipality until at least one year has passed from its effective date.

9-20-6.   Time for filing referendum petition.

The required number of voters residing in any municipality may file within twenty days after the publication of any ordinance or resolution subject to referendum a petition with the auditor or clerk, requiring the submission of any such ordinance or resolution to a vote of the voters of the municipality for its rejection or approval. If filed on the twentieth day after publication, such petitions shall be filed no later than normal closing hours of the city hall or city auditor's office on said twentieth day.

9-20-7.   Description in referendum petition of matter covered.

If the matter intended to be covered by the referendum petition is the whole of any ordinance or resolution, the petition shall contain the title of such ordinance or the subject of such resolution, and the date of its passage, but if only a portion of such ordinance or resolution is intended to be covered by the petition, such portion shall be set out at length.

9-20-8. Number of signers required for referendum petition — Data concerning signers.

The referendum petition shall be signed by at least five percent of the legal voters residing in the municipality. The percentage shall be based on the whole number of voters of the municipality as determined by the precinct registration lists or the district registration lists prepared by the county auditor from the master registration list in conformity to law as of the time of the filing of the petition. The signer or circulator shall add the signer's residence address, county of voter registration, and date of signing. The signer's post office box number may be given in lieu of a street address if the signer lives within a municipality of the second or third class.

9-20-9 Requirements for persons circulating petition — Board of Elections to promulgate rules — Scope of rules.

Any person circulating an initiative or referendum petition shall verify that each person signing the petition is a resident and qualified voter of the municipality. The State Board of Elections shall promulgate rules pursuant to chapter 1-26 prescribing the format for an initiative and referendum petition and its verification.

9-20-10. Liberal construction of referendum petition.

Such petition may be made up and signed and shall be liberally construed as provided by the statute governing an initiated law.

9-20-11. Date of election on referendum petition — No action taken pending election.

The governing body shall, upon the presentation of a petition pursuant to § 9-20-6, submit the question to the electors at the next annual municipal election or the next general election, whichever is earlier. Pending the election, the governing body may take no action with respect to the subject matter of the petition that would alter or preempt the effect of the proposed petition. However, the governing body may expedite the date of the election by ordering, within ten days of receiving the petition, a special election to be held on a Tuesday not less than thirty days from the date of the order of the governing body.

9-20-11.1. Submission of question prohibited after first Tuesday in August of general election year.

No municipality may submit a question to the electors at the next general election pursuant to § 9-20-11 after the first Tuesday in August of the year of the general election.

9-20-11.2. Date to certify ballot language to county auditor.

If a municipality submits a question to the electors at the next general election pursuant to § 9-20-11, the municipality shall certify the ballot language to the county auditor by the third Tuesday in August of the year of the general election.

9-20-11.3. Additional election costs paid by municipality.

If a municipality submits a question to the electors at the next general election pursuant to § 9-20-11, the municipality shall pay the additional election cost related to the municipal question. The cost shall be agreed upon by the county auditor and the municipal finance officer.

9-20-12. Publication of referred ordinance or resolution — Notice of election.

The auditor or clerk shall cause the entire referred ordinance or resolution to be published once a week for two successive weeks immediately preceding the election. Such publication shall include a notice that on the day of election therein stated such ordinance or resolution will be submitted to the voters or, if only a portion thereof is covered by the petition, then notice as to what portion will be submitted.

9-20-13. Ballots used in referendum election — Form and contents.

The auditor or clerk shall have ballots printed for the vote upon such referred ordinance or resolution and cause the same to be distributed as other official ballots are distributed. Such ballots shall conform as near as may be to the law governing the submission of questions by the Legislature, except that the statement required to be printed on the ballots shall be prepared by the city attorney, or if there be no city attorney, by an attorney at law employed by the governing body for that purpose. All questions to be voted upon at the same election may be submitted upon the same ballot.

9-20-14. General municipal election law applicable to referendum elections.

The elections provided for in this chapter shall be governed by the provisions of chapter 9-13 except as to the form of the ballots otherwise specifically provided.

9-20-15. Majority vote required for approval of referred measure — Effective date.

No referred ordinance or resolution so submitted shall become operative unless approved by a majority of the votes cast for and against the same. If so approved, it shall take effect upon completion of the canvass of the election returns relating thereto.

9-20-16. Preservation of referendum petitions — Open to public inspection.

The auditor or clerk shall preserve all petitions invoking the referendum filed in his office for a period of at least two years, during which time such petitions shall be open to public inspection upon reasonable request.

9-20-17. Waiting period for new action after referendum election.

No referred ordinance or resolution may be again voted upon by the government of any municipality within one year from the date of the election thereon.

9-20-18. Legislative finding — Actions of municipal governing boards subject to referendum.

The Legislature finds that in making past grants of decision-making authority to municipal governing authorities, its intent was to grant that authority to the governing bodies of municipalities and that such actions, unless otherwise excluded from the referendum and initiative process by other state law, are subject to the initiative and referendum process. Therefore, the contrary holding in Baker v. Jackson, 372 NW 2d 142 (SD, July 31, 1985) is hereby abrogated.

9-20-19. Legislative decision of governing body subject to referendum — Administrative decision not subject to referendum.

Any legislative decision of a governing body is subject to the referendum process. A legislative decision is one that enacts a permanent law or lays down a rule of conduct or course of policy for the guidance of citizens or their officers. Any matter of a permanent or general character is a legislative decision. No administrative decision of a governing body is subject to the referendum process, unless specifically authorized by this code. An administrative decision is one that merely puts into execution a plan already adopted by the governing body itself or by the Legislature. Supervision of a program is an administrative decision. Hiring, disciplining, and setting the salaries of employees are administrative decisions.

The Basic Steps to Do an Initiative in South Dakota

Statutes and Amendments — Direct Initiative Process

Basic Procedures: The sponsors of any initiated measure or constitutional amendment must submit that text to the director of the Legislative Research Council who will within 15 days provide written comments on the measure to the sponsors and the secretary of state. The comments must be received by the Secretary of State prior to filing the measure's full text.

The full text of any petition to be circulated to put a question on the general election ballot complete with names and addresses of the petition sponsors must be filed with the Secretary of State prior to circulation for signatures. No signatures obtained before that filing date will be counted.

All sections of any completed ballot question petition shall be filed simultaneously together with a sworn affidavit prescribed by the State Board of Elections signed by two-thirds of the sponsors.

Date Initiative language can be submitted to state for November 2002: Any time.

Signatures are tied to vote of which office: Governor

Next gubernatorial election: 2002

Votes cast for governor in last election: 260,187

Net number of signatures required: For statutes, 5% of the total vote for governor in the last gubernatorial election (13,010). For amendments, 10%. (26,019)

Distribution Requirement: None.

Circulation period: 1 year.

Do circulators have to be residents: No.

Date when signatures are due for certification: For Statutes, May 7, 2002. For Amendment, November 5, 2001.

Signature verification process: Each signature is verified until reaching the minimum number of valid signatures needed to qualify an issue for the ballot.

Single-subject restriction: No.

Legislative tampering: Legislature can both repeal and amend statute initiatives.

General Comments: The secretary of state, at least twelve weeks prior to the general election, will deliver to each county auditor in this state four certified copies of each initiated measure together with the statement, title and attorney general's explanation to be published preceding the text of the proposed amendment. In the publication of initiated measures and on official ballots upon which the initiated measures are submitted, initiated measures must be preceded by a statement in the form prescribed by the state board of elections. Not later than the fourth Tuesday in July, the Attorney General will prepare and deliver to the Secretary of State the explanatory statement required by § 12-13-1 of the purpose and legal effect of proposed or initiated amendments to the Constitution and of initiated measures and referred laws. This explanatory statement shall not exceed two hundred words. The explanatory statement shall be followed by a recitation of the effect of a 'Yes' or 'No' vote and shall be in the form prescribed by the state board of elections. The explanatory statement shall immediately follow the title on the printed ballots.

Tennessee

The Progressives and labor unions never won enactment of statewide initiative and referendum rights, and had to settle for a 1913 law granting such rights to residents of a few municipalities.

Tennessee Constitution

The state does not have the statewide initiative process and so therefore the following provisions discuss the procedures used by the state legislature to place constitutional amendments on the ballot.

ARTICLE XI.

Miscellaneous Provisions

Section 3.

Any amendment or amendments to this Constitution may be proposed in the Senate or House of Representatives, and if the same shall be agreed to by a majority of all the members elected to each of the two houses, such proposed amendment or amendments shall be entered on their journals with the yeas and nays thereon, and referred to the General Assembly then next to be chosen; and shall be published six months previous to the time of making such choice; and if in the General Assembly then next chosen as aforesaid, such proposed amendment or amendments shall be agreed to by two-thirds of all the members elected to each house, then it shall be the duty of the General Assembly to submit such proposed amendment or amendments to the people at the next general election in which a governor is to be chosen. And if the people shall approve and ratify such amendment or amendments by a majority of all the citizens of the state voting for governor, voting in their favor, such amendment or amendments shall become a part of this Constitution. When any amendment or amendments to the Constitution shall be proposed in pursuance of the foregoing provisions the same shall at each of said sessions be read three times on three several days in each house. The Legislature shall have the right by law to submit to the people, at any general election, the question of calling a convention to alter, reform, or abolish this Constitution, or to alter, reform or abolish any specified part or parts of it; and when, upon such submission, a majority of all the voters voting upon the proposal submitted shall approve the proposal to call a convention, the delegates to such convention shall be chosen at the next general election and the convention shall assemble for the consideration of such proposals as shall have received a favorable vote in said election, in such mode and manner as shall be prescribed. No change in, or amendment to, this Constitution proposed by such convention shall become effective, unless within the limitations of the call of the convention, and unless approved and ratified by a majority of the qualified voters voting separately on such change or amendment at an election to be held in such manner and on such date as may be fixed by the convention. No such convention shall be held oftener than once in six years.

Texas

The founders of the Texas initiative and referendum movement were two ministers: Rev. A. B. Francisco of Milano and Rev. B. F. Foster of Galveston. Also important in Texas I&R leadership before 1900 was Judge Thomas B. King of Stephenville, county judge of Erath County.

The movement was slow to catch on in Texas. By 1912 Congressman (later U.S. Senator) Morris Shepard had declared himself in favor of I&R; in 1913 the legislature passed a bill allowing I&R as an option for home rule cities and a state constitutional amendment providing for statewide I&R.

The latter amendment would have required more petition signatures to put an initiative on the ballot than were needed in any other state: 20 percent of the number of ballots cast in the previous election. When the amendment was put on the ballot for voter approval in 1914, voters rejected it, to the delight of I&R advocates, who believed that they could get the legislature to pass a better version. They were unable to do so.

After a hiatus of more than half a century, Texans' interest in getting statewide I&R was revived when Californians approved their electrifying Proposition 13 tax cut initiative in 1978. Leading the movement was Republican State Senator Walter Mengden of Houston, who had pushed unsuccessfully for I&R at the state's 1974 constitutional convention and in the legislature until his retirement in 1982. Within a month of the California vote, Governor Dolph Briscoe and gubernatorial candidate William Clements had announced their support for statewide I&R.

Clements reiterated his commitment once elected, telling the legislature on 25 May 1979: "I have made it absolutely clear to everyone that if I do not get I&R passed, I will call a special session." But Clements failed to keep his promise. Leading the opposition was the Houston lobbyist James K. Nance, whose law firm represented such major corporate clients as Union Carbide, DuPont, Houston Power and Light, Pennzoil, and United Texas Gas Transmission.

In 1980 the state's Republicans put an I&R measure on their May 2 statewide primary election ballot, and party members endorsed it by a seven to one margin. Initiative advocates lost a strong ally when Senator Mengden retired, however, and the effort for statewide I&R seemed to be running out of steam. Nevertheless, Texas Republicans put the I&R question on their primary ballot again on May 6, 1982, and party voters favored it by a five to one margin.

However, when George W. Bush was elected Governor in 1994, he allowed the state's Republican Party to remove the pro I&R plank from the Party's platform and replace it with an anti I&R platform. This change effectively ended any chances of I&R being adopted in the state for the foreseeable future. Nonetheless, state I&R activist Mike Ford—founder of the group Initiatives for Texas—has pledged to continue the fight. His group has been instrumental in educating the citizens of Texas about the importance of the I&R process.

Texas Constitution

The state does not have the statewide initiative process and so therefore the following provisions discuss the procedures used by the state legislature to place constitutional amendments on the ballot.

Article 17 — Mode of Amending the Constitution of This State

Section 1 — Proposed Amendments; Publication; Submission to Voters; Adoption

(a)The Legislature, at any regular session, or at any special session when the matter is included within the purposes for which the session is convened, may propose amendments revising the Constitution, to be voted upon by the qualified voters for statewide offices and propositions, as defined in the Constitution and statutes of this State. The date of the elections shall be specified by the Legislature. The proposal for submission must be approved by a vote of two-thirds of all the members elected to each House, entered by yeas and nays on the journals.

(b) A brief explanatory statement of the nature of a proposed amendment, together with the date of the election and the wording of the proposition as it is to appear on the ballot, shall be published twice in each newspaper in the State which meets requirements set by the Legislature for the publication of official notices of offices and departments of the state government. The explanatory statement shall be prepared by the Secretary of State and shall be approved by the Attorney General. The Secretary of State shall send a full and complete copy of the proposed amendment or amendments to each county clerk who shall post the same in a public place in the courthouse at least 30 days prior to the election on said amendment. The first notice shall be published not more than 60 days nor less than 50 days before the date of the election, and the second notice shall be published on the same day in the succeeding week. The Legislature shall fix the standards for the rate of charge for the publication, which may not be higher than the newspaper's published national rate for advertising per column inch.

(c) The election shall be held in accordance with procedures prescribed by the Legislature, and the returning officer in each county shall make returns to the Secretary of State of the number of legal votes cast at the election for and against each amendment. If it appears from the returns that a majority of the votes cast have been cast in favor of an amendment, it shall become a part of this Constitution, and proclamation thereof shall be made by the Governor.

Utah

Utah was the second state to win statewide initiative and referendum, passing its amendment through the legislature in 1899 and ratifying it by popular vote in 1900. The man most responsible for this early victory was State Representative Sherman S. Smith of Ogden, the legislature's "lone Populist." But another I&R advocate, Henry W. Lawrence of Salt Lake City, wondered whether the legislature would pass reasonable implementing legislation: "The great trouble now will be to get the Legislature to adopt legislation to ... make it [I&R] effective, as our Legislature will be Republican and no doubt generally opposed to the principle."

Lawrence's concern was on target. Sixteen years later, I&R advocates were still waiting for the legislature to pass an implementing law. Finally, in 1916, they organized the Popular Government League of Utah to lobby for such a law. Its officers were Parley P. Christensen, president; Dr. Grace Stratton-Airey, vice president; and Parker B. Cady, secretary-treasurer.

The legislature reluctantly passed an implementing bill, but it was worthless: among other restrictions, it specified that anyone signing a petition to put an initiative on the ballot had to sign "in the office and in the presence of an officer competent to administer oaths." The reformers were outraged. The law effectively prohibited initiative sponsors from circulating petitions. After World War II, the restrictions finally were eased, but it was still not easy to put an initiative on the ballot.

In 1960, Utah voters approved a statewide initiative for the first time. It established a merit system procedure for hiring and employing county deputy sheriffs, thus ending the corrupting patronage system.

Over the years, the animal protection movement was very active in Utah—putting fear in the hearts of hunters. Out of fear of how the animal protection groups would use the initiative process, pro-hunting groups began a crusade against the initiative process. In 2000 they were successful in convincing the state legislature to drastically curb the initiative process by increasing the distribution requirements for initiatives and also requiring that animal protection initiatives must pass by a two-thirds vote of the people.

Statewide Initiative Usage

Number of Initiatives	Number Passed	Number Failed	Passage Rate
18	4	14	22%

Statewide Initiatives

Year	Measure Number	Type	Subject Matter	Description	Pass/Fail
1952	A	DS	Welfare	To repeal the welfare "Lien Law."	Failed
1958	A	DS	Gaming	To permit pari-mutuel wagering at horse racing meets and create a state racing commission.	Failed

Year	Measure Number	Type	Subject Matter	Description	Pass/Fail
1960	A	DS	Administration of Government	To establish merit systems and merit system commissions in the counties of the State of Utah for the qualification, employment and tenure of Deputy Sheriffs.	Passed
1968	A	DS	Alcohol Regulation	Liquor initiative.	Failed
1976	A	DS	Health/Medical	To provide for freedom from compulsory fluoridation and medication.	Passed
1976	B	DS	Election Reform	To provide for a recall and advisory recall procedure.	Failed
1976	C	DS	Administration of Government	To provide for a budgetary procedures act ceiling.	Failed
1980	A	DS	Taxes	Elimination of sales tax on food.	Failed
1980	B	DS	Taxes	Tax limitation act.	Failed
1984	A	DS	Legal	Cable television decency act.	Failed
1988	A	DS	Taxes	Tax and spending limitations.	Failed
1988	B	DS	Taxes	Tax reductions.	Failed
1988	C	DS	Taxes	Income tax credit for private education.	Failed
1990	A	DS	Taxes	Removal of state, local sales tax from food.	Failed
1992	A	DS	Gaming	State-regulated horse races; pari-mutual wagering.	Failed
1994	A	IDS	Term Limits	Term limits on state legislature 8 years and on Congress 8/12.	Failed
2000	A	DS	Administration of Government	Declaring English to be the official language for the conduct of government business.	Passed
2000	B	DS	Drug Policy Reform	Relating to forfeiture of assets and property; establishing uniform procedures for the forfeiture of property; forbidding forfeiture against innocent owners.	Passed

Utah Constitution

Article VI

Section 1 Power vested in Senate, House, and People

(1) The Legislative power of the State shall be vested in:

(a) a Senate and House of Representatives which shall be designated the Legislature of the State of Utah; and

(b) the people of the State of Utah as provided in Subsection (2)

(2)(a)(i) The legal voters of the State of Utah, in the numbers, under the conditions, in the manner, and within the time provided by statute, may:

(A) initiate any desired legislation and cause it to be submitted to the people for adoption upon a majority vote of those voting on the legislation, as provided by statute; or

(B) require any law passed by the Legislature, except those laws passed by a two-thirds vote of the members elected to each house of the Legislature, to be submitted to the voters of the State, as provided by statute, before the law may take effect.

(ii) Notwithstanding Subsection (2)(a)(i)(A), legislation initiated to allow, limit, or prohibit the taking of wildlife or the season for or method of taking wildlife shall be adopted upon approval of two-thirds of those voting.

(b) The legal voters of any county, city, or town, in the numbers, under the conditions, in the manner, and within the time provided by statute, may:

(i) initiate any desired legislation and cause it to be submitted to the people of the county, city, or town for adoption upon a majority vote of those voting on the legislation, as provided by statute; or

(ii) require any law or ordinance passed by the law making body of the county, city, or town to be submitted to the voters thereof, as provided by statute, before the law or ordinance may take effect.

Utah Statutes

20A-7-103. Constitutional amendments and other questions — Procedures for submission to popular vote.

(1) The procedures contained in this section govern when:

(a) the Legislature submits a proposed constitutional amendment or other question to the voters; and

(b) an act of the Legislature is referred to the voters by referendum petition.

(2) The lieutenant governor shall, not later than 60 days before the regular general election, publish the full text of the amendment, question, or statute in at least one newspaper in every county of the state where a newspaper is published.

(3) The legislative general counsel shall:

(a) designate the amendment or question by number and order of presentation on the ballot;

(b) draft and designate a ballot title that summarizes the subject matter of the amendment or question; and

(c) deliver them to the lieutenant governor.

(4) The lieutenant governor shall certify the number and ballot title of each amendment or question to the county clerk of each county no later than the second Friday after the primary election.

(5) The county clerk of each county shall:

(a) ensure that both the number and title of the amendment, question, or referendum is printed on the sample ballots and official ballots; and

(b) publish them as provided by law.

20A-7-201. Statewide initiatives — Signature requirements — Submission to the Legislature or to a vote of the people.

(a) A person seeking to have an initiative submitted to the Legislature for approval or rejection shall obtain:

(i) legal signatures equal to 5% of the cumulative total of all votes cast for all candidates for governor at the last regular general election at which a governor was elected; and

(ii) from each of at least 20 counties, legal signatures equal to 5% of the total of all votes cast in that county for all candidates for governor at the last regular general election at which a governor was elected.

(b) If, at any time not less than ten days before the beginning of an annual general session of the Legislature, the lieutenant governor declares sufficient any initiative petition that is signed by enough voters to meet the requirements of this Subsection (1), the lieutenant governor shall deliver a copy of the petition and the cover sheet required by Subsection (1)(c) to the president of the Senate, the speaker of the House, and the director of the Office of Legislative Research and General Counsel.

(c) In delivering a copy of the petition, the lieutenant governor shall include a cover sheet that contains:

(d) the cumulative total of all votes cast for all candidates for governor at the last regular general election at which a governor was elected;

(ii) the total of all votes cast in each county for all candidates for governor at the last regular general election at which a governor was elected;

(iii) the total number of certified signatures received for the submitted initiative; and

(iv) the total number of certified signatures received from each county for the submitted initiative.

(2)(a) A person seeking to have an initiative submitted to a vote of the people for approval or rejection shall obtain:

(i) legal signatures equal to 10% of the cumulative total of all votes cast for all candidates for governor at the last regular general election at which a governor was elected; and

(ii) from each of at least 20 counties, legal signatures equal to 10% of the total of all votes cast in that county for all candidates for governor at the last regular general election at which a governor was elected.

(b) If, at any time not less than four months before any regular general election, the lieutenant governor declares sufficient any initiative petition that is signed by enough legal voters to meet the requirements of this subsection, the lieutenant governor shall submit the proposed law to a vote of the people at the next regular general election.

(3) The lieutenant governor shall provide the following information from the official canvass of the last regular general election at which a governor was elected to any interested person:

(a)the cumulative total of all votes cast for all candidates for governor; and

(b) for each county, the total of all votes cast in that county for all candidates for governor.

20A-7-202. Statewide initiative process — Application procedures — Time to gather signatures — Grounds for rejection.

(1) Persons wishing to circulate an initiative petition shall file an application with the lieutenant governor.

(2) The application shall contain:

(a) the name and residence address of at least five sponsors of the initiative petition;

(b) a statement indicating that each of the sponsors:

(i) is a resident of Utah; and

(ii) has voted in a regular general election in Utah within the last three years;

(c) the signature of each of the sponsors, attested to by a notary public; and

(d) a copy of the proposed law.

(3) The application and its contents are public when filed with the lieutenant governor.

(4)(a) The sponsors shall qualify the petition for the regular general election ballot no later than the second regular general election after the application is filed.

(b) If the sponsors fail to qualify the petition for that ballot, the sponsors must:

(i) submit a new application;

(ii) obtain new signature sheets; and

(iii) collect signatures again.

(5) The lieutenant governor shall reject the application and not issue circulation sheets if:

(a) the law proposed by the initiative is patently unconstitutional;

(b) the law proposed by the initiative is nonsensical; or

(c) the proposed law could not become law if passed.

20A-7-203. Form of initiative petition and signature sheets.

(1)(a) Each proposed initiative petition shall be printed in substantially the following form:

"INITIATIVE PETITION To the Honorable ____, Lieutenant Governor:

We, the undersigned citizens of Utah, respectfully demand that the following proposed law be submitted to the legal voters/Legislature of Utah for their/its approval or rejection at the regular general election/session to be held/ beginning on _____ (month\day\year);

Each signer says: I have personally signed this petition; I am registered to vote in Utah or intend to become registered to vote in Utah before the certification of the petition names by the county clerk; and My residence and post office address are written correctly after my name."

(b) The sponsors of an initiative shall attach a copy of the proposed law to each initiative petition.

(2) Each signature sheet shall:

(a) be printed on sheets of paper 8-1/2 inches long and 11 inches wide;

(b) be ruled with a horizontal line 3/4 inch from the top, with the space above that line blank for the purpose of binding;

(c) contain the title of the initiative printed below the horizontal line;

(d) contain the word "Warning" printed or typed at the top of each signature sheet under the title of the initiative;

(e) contain, to the right of the word "Warning," the following statement printed or typed in not less than eight-point, single leaded type: "It is a class A misdemeanor for anyone to sign any initiative petition with any other name than his own, or knowingly to sign his name more than once for the same measure, or to sign an initiative petition when he knows he is not a registered voter and knows that he does not intend to become registered to vote before the certification of the petition names by the county clerk.";

(f) contain horizontally ruled lines, 3/8 inch apart under the "Warning" statement required by this section; and

(g) be vertically divided into columns as follows:

(i) the first column shall appear at the extreme left of the sheet, be 5/8 inch wide, be headed with "For Office Use Only," and be subdivided with a light vertical line down the middle with the left subdivision entitled "Registered" and the right subdivision left untitled;

(ii) the next column shall be three inches wide, headed "Registered Voter's Printed Name (must be legible to be counted)";

(iii) the next column shall be three inches wide, headed "Signature of Registered Voter"; and

(iv) the final column shall be 4-3/8 inches wide, headed "Street Address, City, Zip Code".

(3) The final page of each initiative packet shall contain the following printed or typed statement:

"Verification

State of Utah, County of _____

I, _____, of _____, hereby state that: I am a resident of Utah and am at least 18 years old; All the names that appear in this packet were signed by persons who professed to be the persons whose names appear in it, and each of them signed his name on it in my presence; I believe that each has printed and signed his name and written his post office address and residence correctly, and that each signer is registered to vote in Utah or intends to become registered to vote before the certification of the petition names by the county clerk.

_____
(Name) (Residence Address) (Date)"

(4) The forms prescribed in this section are not mandatory, and, if substantially followed, the initiative petitions are sufficient, notwithstanding clerical and merely technical errors.

20A-7-204. Circulation requirements — Lieutenant governor to provide sponsors with materials.

(1) In order to obtain the necessary number of signatures required by this part, the sponsors shall circulate initiative packets that meet the form requirements of this part.
(2) The lieutenant governor shall furnish to the sponsors:
(a) a copy of the initiative petition; and
(b) one signature sheet.
(3) The sponsors of the petition shall:
(a) arrange and pay for the printing of all additional copies of the petition and signature sheets; and
(b) ensure that the copies of the petition and signature sheets meet the form requirements of this section.
(4)(a) The sponsors may prepare the initiative for circulation by creating multiple initiative packets.
(b) The sponsors shall create those packets by binding a copy of the initiative petition, a copy of the proposed law, and no more than 50 signature sheets together at the top in such a way that the packets may be conveniently opened for signing.
(c) The sponsors need not attach a uniform number of signature sheets to each initiative packet.
(5)(a) After the sponsors have prepared sufficient initiative packets, they shall return them to the lieutenant governor.
(b) The lieutenant governor shall:
(i) number each of the initiative packets and return them to the sponsors within five working days; and
(ii) keep a record of the numbers assigned to each packet.
20A-7-205. Obtaining signatures — Verification — Removal of signature.
(1) Any Utah voter may sign an initiative petition if the voter is a legal voter.
(2) The sponsors shall ensure that the person in whose presence each signature sheet was signed:
(a) is at least 18 years old and meets the residency requirements of Section 20A-2-105; and
(b) verifies each signature sheet by completing the verification printed on the last page of each initiative packet.
(3)(a)(i) Any voter who has signed an initiative petition may have his signature removed from the petition by submitting a notarized statement to that effect to the county clerk.
(ii) In order for the signature to be removed, the statement must be received by the county clerk before he delivers the petition to the lieutenant governor.
(b) Upon receipt of the statement, the county clerk shall remove the signature of the person submitting the statement from the initiative petition.
(c) No one may remove signatures from an initiative petition after the petition is submitted to the lieutenant governor.

20A-7-205.5. Monthly reports.

(1) When petitions are being circulated by paid circulators, the sponsors of the initiative shall file a report with the lieutenant governor on the last Tuesday in April and on the Tuesday before the regular general election.
(2) The report shall contain:
(a) the names of the sponsors; and
(b) the name of the proposed measure for which petitions are being circulated by paid circulators.

20A-7-206. Submitting the initiative petition — Certification of signatures by the county clerks — Transfer to lieutenant governor.

(1) In order to qualify an initiative petition for placement on the regular general election ballot, the sponsors shall deliver each signed and verified initiative packet to the county clerk of the county in which the packet was circulated by the June 1 before the regular general election.
(2) No later than June 15 before the regular general election, the county clerk shall:

(a) check the names of all persons completing the verification for the initiative packet to determine whether or not those persons are residents of Utah and are at least 18 years old; and

(b) submit the name of each of those persons who is not a Utah resident or who is not at least 18 years old to the attorney general and county attorney.

(3) No later than July 1 before the regular general election, the county clerk shall:

(a) check all the names of the signers against the official registers to determine whether or not the signer is a registered voter;

(b) certify on the petition whether or not each name is that of a registered voter; and

(c) deliver all of the packets to the lieutenant governor.

(4) In order to qualify an initiative petition for submission to the Legislature, the sponsors shall deliver each signed and verified initiative packet to the county clerk of the county in which the packet was circulated by the November 15 before the annual general session of the Legislature.

(5) No later than December 1 before the annual general session of the Legislature, the county clerk shall:

(a) check the names of all persons completing the verification for the initiative packet to determine whether or not those persons are Utah residents and are at least 18 years old; and

(b) submit the name of each of those persons who is not a Utah resident or who is not at least 18 years old to the attorney general and county attorney.

(6) No later than December 15 before the annual general session of the Legislature, the county clerk shall:

(a) check all the names of the signers against the official registers to determine whether or not the signer is a registered voter;

(b) certify on the petition whether or not each name is that of a registered voter; and

(c) deliver all of the packets to the lieutenant governor.

(7) Initiative packets are public once they are delivered to the county clerks.

(8) The sponsor or their representatives may not retrieve initiative packets from the county clerks once they have submitted them.

20A-7-206.5. Financial disclosure — Paid circulators.

(1) When the proponents of a proposed initiative have paid persons to circulate the petition, the proponents shall, at the time the last initiative packet is filed with the county clerk, file a form with the lieutenant governor detailing the amount of money paid per signature.

(2) The lieutenant governor shall develop a form to disclose the information required by this section.

20A-7-207. Evaluation by the lieutenant governor.

(1) When each initiative packet is received from a county clerk, the lieutenant governor shall check off from his record the number of each initiative packet filed.

(2)(a) After all of the initiative packets have been received by the lieutenant governor, the lieutenant governor shall:

(i) count the number of the names certified by the county clerks that appear on each verified signature sheet; and

(ii) declare the petition to be sufficient or insufficient by July 6 before the regular general election.

(b) If the total number of certified names from each verified signature sheet equals or exceeds the number of names required by Section 20A-7-201, the lieutenant governor shall mark upon the front of the petition the word "sufficient."

(c) If the total number of certified names from each verified signature sheet does not equal or exceed the number of names required by Section 20A-7-201, the lieutenant governor shall mark upon the front of the petition the word "insufficient."

(d) The lieutenant governor shall immediately notify any one of the sponsors of his finding.

(3)(a) Once a petition is declared insufficient, the sponsors may not submit additional signatures to qualify the petition for the pending regular general election.

(b) The petition sponsors may submit additional signatures to qualify the petition for the regular general election following the pending regular general election if:

(i) the petition is declared insufficient; and

(ii) the pending general election is the first regular general election after the application was filed.

(4)(a) If the lieutenant governor refuses to accept and file any initiative petition that a sponsor believes is legally sufficient, any voter may, by July 20, apply to the supreme court for an extraordinary writ to compel the lieutenant governor to do so.

(b) The supreme court shall:

(i) determine whether or not the initiative petition is legally sufficient; and

(ii) certify its findings to the lieutenant governor by July 30.

(c) If the supreme court certifies that the initiative petition is legally sufficient, the lieutenant governor shall file it, with a verified copy of the judgment attached to it, as of the date on which it was originally offered for filing in his office.

(d) If the supreme court determines that any petition filed is not legally sufficient, the supreme court may enjoin the lieutenant governor and all other officers from certifying or printing the ballot title and numbers of that measure on the official ballot for the next election.

20A-7-208. Disposition of initiative petitions by the Legislature.

(1)(a) Except as provided in Subsection (1)(b), when the lieutenant governor delivers an initiative petition to the Legislature, the law proposed by that initiative petition shall be either enacted or rejected without change or amendment by the Legislature.

(b) The speaker of the House and the president of the Senate may direct legislative staff to:

(i) make technical corrections authorized by Section 36-12-12; and

(ii) prepare a legislative review note and a legislative fiscal note on the law proposed by the initiative petition.

(c) If any law proposed by an initiative petition is enacted by the Legislature, it is subject to referendum the same as other laws.

(2) If any law proposed by a petition is not enacted by the Legislature, that proposed law shall be submitted to a vote of the people at the next regular general election if:

(a) sufficient additional signatures to the petition are first obtained to bring the total number of signatures up to the number required by Subsection 20A-7-201(2); and

(b) those additional signatures are verified, certified by the county clerks, and declared sufficient by the lieutenant governor as provided in this part.

20A-7-209. Ballot title — Duties of lieutenant governor and Office of Legislative Research and General Counsel.

(1) By July 6 before the regular general election, the lieutenant governor shall deliver a copy of all of the proposed laws that have qualified for the ballot to the Office of Legislative Research and General Counsel.

(2)(a) The Office of Legislative Research and General Counsel shall:

(i) prepare a ballot title for each initiative; and

(ii) return each petition and ballot title to the lieutenant governor by July 20.

(b)The ballot title may be distinct from the title of the proposed law attached to the initiative petition, and shall express, in not more than 100 words, the purpose of the measure.

(c)The ballot title and the number of the measure as determined by the Office of Legislative Research and General Counsel shall be printed on the official ballot.

(d) In preparing ballot titles, the Office of Legislative Research and General Counsel shall, to the best of its ability, give a true and impartial statement of the purpose of the measure.

(e) The ballot title may not intentionally be an argument, or likely to create prejudice, for or against the measure.

(3) By July 21, the lieutenant governor shall mail a copy of the ballot title to any sponsor of the petition.

(4)(a) If the ballot title furnished by the Office of Legislative Research and General Counsel is unsatisfactory or does not comply with the requirements of this section, at least three of the sponsors of the petition may, by July 30, appeal the wording of the ballot title prepared by the Office of Legislative Research and General Counsel to the Supreme Court.

(b) The Supreme Court shall:

(i) examine the ballot title;

(ii) hear arguments; and

(iii) by August 10, certify to the lieutenant governor a ballot title for the measure that fulfills the intent of this section.

(c) By September 1, the lieutenant governor shall certify the title verified to him by the supreme court to the county clerks to be printed on the official ballot.

20A-7-210. Form of ballot — Manner of voting.

(1) The county clerks shall ensure that the number and ballot title verified to them by the lieutenant governor are printed upon the official ballot with, immediately to the right of them, the words "For" and "Against," each word followed by a square in which the elector may indicate his vote.

(2) Electors desiring to vote in favor of enacting the law proposed by the initiative petition shall mark the square following the word "For," and those desiring to vote against enacting the law proposed by the initiative petition shall mark the square following the word "Against."

20A-7-211. Return and canvass — Conflicting measures — Law effective on proclamation.

(1) The votes on the law proposed by the initiative petition shall be counted, canvassed, and delivered as provided in Title 20A, Chapter 4, Part 3, Canvassing Returns.

(2) After the state board of canvassers completes its canvass, the lieutenant governor shall certify to the governor the vote for and against the law proposed by the initiative petition.

(3)(a) The governor shall immediately issue a proclamation that:

(i) gives the total number of votes cast in the state for and against each law proposed by an initiative petition; and

(ii) declares those laws proposed by an initiative petition that were approved by majority vote to be in full force and effect as the law of the state of Utah.

(b) When the governor believes that two proposed laws, or that parts of two proposed laws approved by the people at the same election are entirely in conflict, he shall proclaim that measure to be law that has received the greatest number of affirmative votes, regardless of the difference in the majorities which those measures have received.

(c)(i) Within ten days after the governor's proclamation, any qualified voter who signed the initiative petition proposing the law that is declared by the governor to be superseded by another measure approved at the same election may apply to the Supreme Court to review the governor's decision.

(ii) The court shall:

(A) immediately consider the matter and decide whether or not the proposed laws are in conflict; and

(B) within ten days after the matter is submitted to it for decision, certify its decision to the governor.

(4) Within 30 days after his previous proclamation, the governor shall:

(a) proclaim all those measures approved by the people as law that the Supreme Court has determined are not in conflict; and

(b) of all those measures approved by the people as law that the Supreme Court has determined to be in conflict, proclaim as law the one that received the greatest number of affirmative votes, regardless of difference in majorities.

20A-7-212. Effective date.

(1) A proposed law submitted to the Legislature by initiative petition and enacted by them takes effect 60 days after the final adjournment of the session of the Legislature that passed it, unless a different effective date is included in the proposed law and the proposed law passes the Legislature by a two-thirds vote of the members elected to each house of the Legislature.

(2)(a) Any proposed law submitted to the people by initiative petition that is approved by the voters at any election does not take effect until at least five days after the date of the official proclamation of the vote by the governor.

(b) Any act or law submitted to the people by initiative that is approved by the voters at any election takes effect on the date specified in the initiative petition.

(c) If the initiative petition does not specify an effective date, a law approved by the voters at any election takes effect five days after the date of the official proclamation of the vote by the governor.

(3)(a)The governor may not veto a law adopted by the people.

(b) The Legislature may amend any laws approved by the people at any legislative session after the law has taken effect.

20A-7-213. Misconduct of electors and officers — Penalty.

(1) It is unlawful for any person to:

(a) sign any name other than his own to any initiative petition;

(b) knowingly sign his name more than once for the same measure at one election;

(c) sign an initiative knowing he is not a legal voter; or

(d) knowingly and willfully violate any provision of this part.

(2) It is unlawful for any person to sign the verification for an initiative packet knowing that:

(a) he does not meet the residency requirements of Section 20A-2-105;

(b) he has not witnessed the signatures of those persons whose names appear in the initiative packet; or

(c) one or more persons whose signatures appear in the initiative packet is either:

(i) not registered to vote in Utah; or

(ii) does not intend to become registered to vote in Utah.

(3) Any person violating this section is guilty of a class A misdemeanor.

(4) The attorney general or the county attorney shall prosecute any violation of this section.

20A-7-301. Referendum — Signature requirements — Submission to voters.

(1)(a) A person seeking to have a law passed by the Legislature submitted to a vote of the people shall obtain:
(i) legal signatures equal to 10% of the cumulative total of all votes cast for all candidates for governor at the last regular general election at which a governor was elected; and
(ii) from each of at least 15 counties, legal signatures equal to 10% of the total of all votes cast in that county for all candidates for governor at the last regular general election at which a governor was elected.
(b) When the lieutenant governor declares a referendum petition sufficient under this part, the governor shall issue an executive order that:
(i) directs that the referendum be submitted to the voters at the next regular general election; or
(ii) calls a special election according to the requirements of Section 20A-1-203 and directs that the referendum be submitted to the voters at that special election.
(2) When a referendum petition has been declared sufficient, the law that is the subject of the petition does not take effect unless and until it is approved by a vote of the people at a regular general election or a statewide special election.
(3) The lieutenant governor shall provide to any interested person from the official canvass of the last regular general election at which a governor was elected:
(a) the cumulative total of all votes cast for all candidates for governor; and
(b) for each county, the total of all votes cast in that county for all candidates for governor.

20A-7-302. Referendum process — Application procedures.

(1) Persons wishing to circulate a referendum petition shall file an application with the lieutenant governor within five calendar days after the end of the legislative session at which the law passed.
(2) The application shall contain:
(a) the name and residence address of at least five sponsors of the referendum petition;
(b) a certification indicating that each of the sponsors:
(i) is a voter; and
(ii) has voted in a regular general election in Utah within the last three years;
(c) the signature of each of the sponsors, attested to by a notary public; and
(d) a copy of the law.

20A-7-303. Form of referendum petition and signature sheets.

(1)(a) Each proposed referendum petition shall be printed in substantially the following form:

"REFERENDUM PETITION To the Honorable _____, Lieutenant Governor:
We, the undersigned citizens of Utah, respectfully order that Senate (or House) Bill No. _____, entitled (title of act, and, if the petition is against less than the whole act, set forth here the part or parts on which the referendum is sought), passed by the _____ Session of the Legislature of the state of Utah, be referred to the people of Utah for their approval or rejection at a regular general election or a statewide special election; Each signer says: I have personally signed this petition; I am registered to vote in Utah or intend to become registered to vote in Utah before the certification of the petition names by the county clerk; and My residence and post office address are written correctly after my name."

(b) The sponsors of a referendum shall attach a copy of the law that is the subject of the referendum to each referendum petition.
(2) Each signature sheet shall:
(a) be printed on sheets of paper 8-1/2 inches long and 11 inches wide;
(b) be ruled with a horizontal line 3/4 inch from the top, with the space above that line blank for the purpose of binding;
(c) contain the title of the referendum printed below the horizontal line;
(d) contain the word "Warning" printed or typed at the top of each signature sheet under the title of the referendum;
(e) contain, to the right of the word "Warning," the following statement printed or typed in not less than eight-point, single leaded type: "It is a class A misdemeanor for anyone to sign any referendum petition with any other name than his own, or knowingly to sign his name more than once for the same measure, or to sign a referendum petition when he knows he is not a registered voter and knows that he does not intend to become registered to vote before the certification of the petition names by the county clerk.";

(f) contain horizontally ruled lines, 3/8 inch apart under the "Warning" statement required by this section; and
(g) be vertically divided into columns as follows:
(i) the first column shall appear at the extreme left of the sheet, be 5/8 inch wide, be headed with "For Office Use Only," and be subdivided with a light vertical line down the middle;
(ii) the next column shall be three inches wide, headed "Registered Voter's Printed Name (must be legible to be counted)";
(iii) the next column shall be three inches wide, headed "Signature of Registered Voter"; and
(iv) the final column shall be 4-3/8 inches wide, headed "Street Address, City, Zip Code".
(3) The final page of each referendum packet shall contain the following printed or typed statement:

"Verification State of Utah, County of _____
I, _____, of _____, hereby state that: I am a Utah resident and am at least 18 years old; All the names that appear in this packet were signed by persons who professed to be the persons whose names appear in it, and each of them signed his name on it in my presence; I believe that each has printed and signed his name and written his post office address and residence correctly, and that each signer is registered to vote in Utah or intends to become registered to vote before the certification of the petition names by the county clerk.
_____(Name) (Residence Address) (Date)"

(4) The forms prescribed in this section are not mandatory, and, if substantially followed, the referendum petitions are sufficient, notwithstanding clerical and merely technical errors.

20A-7-304. Circulation requirements — Lieutenant governor to provide sponsors with materials.

(1) In order to obtain the necessary number of signatures required by this part, the sponsors shall circulate referendum packets that meet the form requirements of this part.
(2) The lieutenant governor shall furnish to the sponsors:
(a) a copy of the referendum petition; and
(b) a signature sheet.
(3) The sponsors of the petition shall:
(a) arrange and pay for the printing of all additional copies of the petition and signature sheets; and
(b) ensure that the copies of the petition and signature sheets meet the form requirements of this section.
(4)(a) The sponsors may prepare the referendum for circulation by creating multiple referendum packets.
(b) The sponsors shall create those packets by binding a copy of the referendum petition, a copy of the law that is the subject of the referendum, and no more than 50 signature sheets together at the top in such a way that the packets may be conveniently opened for signing.
(c) The sponsors need not attach a uniform number of signature sheets to each referendum packet.
(5)(a) After the sponsors have prepared sufficient referendum packets, they shall return them to the lieutenant governor.
(b) The lieutenant governor shall:
(i) number each of the referendum packets and return them to the sponsors within five working days; and
(ii) keep a record of the numbers assigned to each packet.

20A-7-305. Obtaining signatures — Verification — Removal of signature.

(1) Any Utah voter may sign a referendum petition if the voter is a legal voter.
(2) The sponsors shall ensure that the person in whose presence each signature sheet was signed:
(a) is at least 18 years old and meets the residency requirements of Section 20A-2-105; and
(b) verifies each signature sheet by completing the verification printed on the last page of each signature sheet.
(3)(a)(i) Any voter who has signed a referendum petition may have his signature removed from the petition by submitting a notarized statement to that effect to the county clerk.
(ii) In order for the signature to be removed, the statement must be received by the county clerk before he delivers the petition to the lieutenant governor.
(b) Upon receipt of the statement, the county clerk shall remove the signature of the person submitting the statement from the referendum petition.
(c) No one may remove signatures from a referendum petition after the petition is submitted to the lieutenant governor.

20A-7-306. Submitting the referendum petition — Certification of signatures by the county clerks — Transfer to lieutenant governor.

(1) No later than 40 days after the end of the legislative session at which the law passed, the sponsors shall deliver each signed and verified referendum packet to the county clerk of the county in which the packet was circulated.

(2) No later than 55 days after the end of the legislative session at which the law passed, the county clerk shall:

(a) check the names of all persons completing the verification on the back of each signature sheet to determine whether or not those persons are Utah residents and are at least 18 years old; and

(b) submit the name of each of those persons who is not a Utah resident or who is not at least 18 years old to the attorney general and county attorney.

(3) No later than 55 days after the end of the legislative session at which the law passed, the county clerk shall:

(a) check all the names of the signers against the official registers to determine whether or not the signer is a voter;

(b) certify on the referendum petition whether or not each name is that of a voter; and

(c) deliver all of the referendum packets to the lieutenant governor.

20A-7-307. Evaluation by the lieutenant governor.

(1) When each referendum packet is received from a county clerk, the lieutenant governor shall check off from his record the number of each referendum packet filed.

(2)(a) After all of the referendum packets have been received by the lieutenant governor, the lieutenant governor shall:

(i) count the number of the names certified by the county clerks that appear on each verified signature sheet; and

(ii) declare the petition to be sufficient or insufficient no later than 60 days after the end of the legislative session at which the law passed.

(b) If the total number of certified names from each verified signature sheet equals or exceeds the number of names required by Section 20A-7-301, the lieutenant governor shall mark upon the front of the petition the word "sufficient."

(c) If the total number of certified names from each verified signature sheet does not equal or exceed the number of names required by Section 20A-7-301, the lieutenant governor shall mark upon the front of the petition the word "insufficient."

(d) The lieutenant governor shall immediately notify any one of the sponsors of his finding.

(3)(a) If the lieutenant governor refuses to accept and file any referendum petition, any voter may apply to the supreme court for an extraordinary writ to compel him to do so within ten days after the refusal.

(b) If the supreme court determines that the referendum petition is legally sufficient, the lieutenant governor shall file it, with a verified copy of the judgment attached to it, as of the date on which it was originally offered for filing in his office.

(c) If the supreme court determines that any petition filed is not legally sufficient, the supreme court may enjoin the lieutenant governor and all other officers from certifying or printing the ballot title and numbers of that measure on the official ballot for the next election.

20A-7-308. Ballot title — Duties of lieutenant governor and Office of Legislative Research and General Counsel.

(1) Whenever a referendum petition is declared sufficient for submission to a vote of the people, the lieutenant governor shall deliver a copy of the petition and the proposed law to the Office of Legislative Research and General Counsel.

(2)(a)The Office of Legislative Research and General Counsel shall:

(i) prepare a ballot title for the referendum; and

(ii) return the petition and the ballot title to the lieutenant governor within 15 days after its receipt.

(b) The ballot title may be distinct from the title of the law that is the subject of the petition, and shall express, in not more than 100 words, the purpose of the measure.

(c) The ballot title and the number of the measure as determined by the Office of Legislative Research and General Counsel shall be printed on the official ballot.

(d) In preparing ballot titles, the Office of Legislative Research and General Counsel shall, to the best of its ability, give a true and impartial statement of the purpose of the measure.

(e) The ballot title may not intentionally be an argument, or likely to create prejudice, for or against the measure.

(3) Immediately after the Office of Legislative Research and General Counsel files a copy of the ballot title with the lieutenant governor, the lieutenant governor shall mail a copy of the ballot title to any of the sponsors of the petition.

(4)(a) If the ballot title furnished by the Office of Legislative Research and General Counsel is unsatisfactory or does not comply with the requirements of this section, at least three of the sponsors of the petition may, within 15 days of the date the lieutenant governor mails the ballot title, appeal the wording of the ballot title prepared by the Office of Legislative Research and General Counsel to the supreme court.

(b) The supreme court shall:

(i) examine the ballot title;

(ii) hear arguments; and

(iii) within five days of its decision, certify to the lieutenant governor a ballot title for the measure that fulfills the intent of this section.

(c) The lieutenant governor shall certify the title verified to him by the supreme court to the county clerks to be printed on the official ballot.

20A-7-309. Form of ballot — Manner of voting.

(1) The county clerks shall ensure that the number and ballot title verified to them by the lieutenant governor are printed upon the official ballot with, immediately to the right of them, the words "For" and "Against," each word followed by a square in which the elector may indicate his vote.

(2) Voters desiring to vote in favor of enacting the law proposed by the referendum petition shall mark the square following the word "For," and those desiring to vote against enacting the law proposed by the referendum petition shall mark the square following the word "Against."

20A-7-310. Return and canvass — Conflicting measures — Law effective on proclamation.

(1) The votes on the law proposed by the referendum petition shall be counted, canvassed, and delivered as provided in Title 20A, Chapter 4, Part 3, Canvassing Returns.

(2) After the state board of canvassers completes its canvass, the lieutenant governor shall certify to the governor the vote for and against the law proposed by the referendum petition.

(3)(a) The governor shall immediately issue a proclamation that:

(i) gives the total number of votes cast in the state for and against each law proposed by a referendum petition; and

(ii) declares those laws proposed by a referendum petition that were approved by majority vote to be in full force and effect as the law of Utah.

(b) When the governor believes that two proposed laws, or that parts of two proposed laws approved by the people at the same election are entirely in conflict, he shall proclaim that measure to be law that has received the greatest number of affirmative votes, regardless of the difference in the majorities which those measures have received.

(4)(a) Within ten days after the governor's proclamation, any qualified voter who signed the referendum petition proposing the law that is declared by the governor to be superseded by another measure approved at the same election may apply to the Supreme Court to review the governor's decision.

(b) The Supreme Court shall:

(i) immediately consider the matter and decide whether or not the proposed laws are in conflict; and

(ii) within ten days after the matter is submitted to it for decision, certify its decision to the governor.

(5) Within 30 days after his previous proclamation, the governor shall:

(a) proclaim all those measures approved by the people as law that the Supreme Court has determined are not in conflict; and

(b) of all those measures approved by the people as law that the Supreme Court has determined to be in conflict, proclaim as law the one that received the greatest number of affirmative votes, regardless of difference in majorities.

20A-7-311. Effective date.

(1)(a) Any proposed law submitted to the people by referendum petition that is approved by the voters at any election does not take effect until at least five days after the date of the official proclamation of the vote by the governor.

(b) Any act or law submitted to the people by referendum that is approved by the voters at any election takes effect on the date specified in the referendum petition.

(c) If the referendum petition does not specify an effective date, a law approved by the voters at any election takes effect five days after the date of the official proclamation of the vote by the governor.

(2)(a) The governor may not veto a law adopted by the people.

(b) The Legislature may amend any laws approved by the people at any legislative session after the law has taken effect.

20A-7-312. Misconduct of electors and officers — Penalty.

(1) It is unlawful for any person to:

(a) sign any name other than his own to any referendum petition;

(b) knowingly sign his name more than once for the same measure at one election;

(c) sign a referendum knowing he is not a legal voter; or

(d) knowingly and willfully violate any provision of this part.

(2) It is unlawful for any person to sign the verification for a referendum packet knowing that:

(a) he does not meet the residency requirements of Section 20A-2-105;

(b) he has not witnessed the signatures of those persons whose names appear in the referendum packet; or

(c) one or more persons whose signatures appear in the referendum packet is either:

(i) not registered to vote in Utah; or

(ii) does not intend to become registered to vote in Utah.

(3) Any person violating this section is guilty of a class A misdemeanor.

(4) The attorney general or the county clerk shall prosecute any violation of this section.

20A-7-401. Limitation — Budgets.

(1) The legal voters of any county, city, or town may not initiate budgets or changes in budgets.

(2) The legal voters of any county, city, or town may not require any budget adopted by the local legislative body to be submitted to the voters.

20A-7-402. Local voter information pamphlet — Contents — Limitations — Preparation — Statement on front cover.

(1) The county or municipality that is the subject of an initiative or referenda shall prepare a local voter information pamphlet that meets the requirements of this part.

(2)(a) The arguments for and against initiatives and referenda shall conform to the requirements of this section.

(b) Persons wishing to prepare arguments for and against initiatives and referenda shall file a request with the local legislative body at least 45 days before the election at which the proposed measure is to be voted upon.

(c) If more than one person or group requests the opportunity to prepare arguments for or against any measure, the governing body shall make the final designation according to the following criteria:

(i) sponsors have priority in making the argument for a measure; and

(ii) members of the local legislative body have priority over others.

(d) The arguments in favor of the measure shall be prepared by the sponsors, whether of the local legislative body or of a voter or voter group, but not more than five names shall appear as sponsors.

(e) The arguments against the measure shall be prepared by opponents from among the local legislative body, if any, or from among voters requesting permission of the local legislative body to prepare these arguments.

(f) The arguments may not exceed 500 words in length.

(g) The arguments supporting and opposing any county or municipal measure shall be filed with the local clerk not less than 30 days before the election at which they are to be voted upon.

(3)(a) In preparing the local voter information pamphlet, the local legislative body shall:

(i) ensure that the arguments are printed on the same sheet of paper upon which the proposed measure is also printed;

(ii) ensure that the following statement is printed on the front cover or the heading of the first page of the printed arguments: "The arguments for or against the proposed measure(s) are the opinions of the authors.";

(iii) pay for the printing and binding of the local voter information pamphlet; and

(iv) ensure that the local clerk distributes the pamphlets either by mail or carrier not less than eight days before the election at which the measures are to be voted upon.

(b)(i) If the proposed measure exceeds 500 words in length, the local legislative body may direct the local clerk to summarize the measure in 500 words or less.

(ii) The summary shall state where a complete copy of the measure is available for public review.

20A-7-501. Initiatives.

(1)(a) Except as provided in Subsection (b), a person seeking to have an initiative submitted to a local legislative body or to a vote of the people for approval or rejection shall obtain legal signatures equal to:

(i) 10% of all the votes cast in the county, city, or town for all candidates for governor at the last election at which a governor was elected if the total number of votes exceeds 25,000;

(ii) 12-1/2% of all the votes cast in the county, city, or town for all candidates for governor at the last election at which a governor was elected if the total number of votes does not exceed 25,000 but is more than 10,000;

(iii) 15% of all the votes cast in the county, city, or town for all candidates for governor at the last election at which a governor was elected if the total number of votes does not exceed 10,000 but is more than 2,500;

(iv) 20% of all the votes cast in the county, city, or town for all candidates for governor at the last election at which a governor was elected if the total number of votes does not exceed 2,500 but is more than 500;

(v) 25% of all the votes cast in the county, city, or town for all candidates for governor at the last election at which a governor was elected if the total number of votes does not exceed 500 but is more than 250; and

(vi) 30% of all the votes cast in the county, city, or town for all candidates for governor at the last election at which a governor was elected if the total number of votes does not exceed 250.

(b) In addition to the signature requirements of Subsection (a), a person seeking to have an initiative submitted to a local legislative body or to a vote of the people for approval or rejection in a county, city, or town where the local legislative body is elected from council districts shall obtain, from each of a majority of council districts, legal signatures equal to the percentages established in Subsection (a).

(2) If the total number of certified names from each verified signature sheet equals or exceeds the number of names required by this section, the clerk or recorder shall deliver the proposed law to the local legislative body at its next meeting.

(3)(a) The local legislative body shall either adopt or reject the proposed law without change or amendment within 30 days of receipt of the proposed law.

(b) The local legislative body may:

(i) adopt the proposed law and refer it to the people;

(ii) adopt the proposed law without referring it to the people; or

(iii) reject the proposed law.

(c) If the local legislative body adopts the proposed law but does not refer it to the people, it is subject to referendum as with other local laws.

(d)(i) If a county legislative body rejects a proposed county ordinance or amendment, or takes no action on it, the county clerk shall submit it to the voters of the county at the next regular general election.

(ii) If a local legislative body rejects a proposed municipal ordinance or amendment, or takes no action on it, the municipal recorder or clerk shall submit it to the voters of the municipality at the next municipal general election.

(e)(i) If the local legislative body rejects the proposed ordinance or amendment, or takes no action on it, the local legislative body may adopt a competing local law.

(ii) The local legislative body shall prepare and adopt the competing local law within the 30 days allowed for its action on the measure proposed by initiative petition.

(iii) If the local legislative body adopts a competing local law, the clerk or recorder shall submit it to the voters of the county or municipality at the same election at which the initiative proposal is submitted.

(f) If conflicting local laws are submitted to the people at the same election and two or more of the conflicting measures are approved by the people, then the measure that receives the greatest number of affirmative votes shall control all conflicts.

20A-7-502. Local initiative process — Application procedures.

(1) Persons wishing to circulate an initiative petition shall file an application with the local clerk.

(2) The application shall contain:

(a) the name and residence address of at least five sponsors of the initiative petition;

(b) a statement indicating that each of the sponsors:

(i) is a registered voter; and

(ii)(A) if the initiative seeks to enact a county ordinance, has voted in a regular general election in Utah within the last three years; or

(B) if the initiative seeks to enact a municipal ordinance, has voted in a regular municipal election in Utah:

(I) except as provided in Subsection (2)(b)(ii)(B)(II), within the last three years; or

(II) within the last five years, if the sponsor's failure to vote within the last three years is due to the sponsor's residing in a municipal district that participates in a municipal election every four years;

(c) the signature of each of the sponsors, attested to by a notary public; and

(d) a copy of the proposed law.

20A-7-503. Form of initiative petitions and signature sheets.

(1)(a) Each proposed initiative petition shall be printed in substantially the following form:

"INITIATIVE PETITION To the Honorable ____, County Clerk/City Recorder/Town Clerk:

We, the undersigned citizens of Utah, respectfully demand that the following proposed law be submitted to: the legislative body for its approval or rejection at its next meeting; and the legal voters of the county/city/town, if the legislative body rejects the proposed law or takes no action on it.

Each signer says: I have personally signed this petition; I am registered to vote in Utah or intend to become registered to vote in Utah before the certification of the petition names by the county clerk; and My residence and post office address are written correctly after my name."

(b) The sponsors of an initiative shall attach a copy of the proposed law to each initiative petition.

(2) Each signature sheet shall:

(a) be printed on sheets of paper 8-1/2 inches long and 11 inches wide;

(b) be ruled with a horizontal line 3/4 inch from the top, with the space above that line blank for the purpose of binding;

(c) contain the title of the initiative printed below the horizontal line;
(d) contain the word "Warning" printed or typed at the top of each signature sheet under the title of the initiative;
(e) contain, to the right of the word "Warning," the following statement printed or typed in not less than eight-point, single leaded type: "It is a class A misdemeanor for anyone to sign any initiative petition with any other name than his own, or knowingly to sign his name more than once for the same measure, or to sign an initiative petition when he knows he is not a registered voter and knows that he does not intend to become registered to vote before the certification of the petition names by the county clerk.";
(f) contain horizontally ruled lines, 3/8 inch apart under the "Warning" statement required by this section;
(g) be vertically divided into columns as follows:
(i) the first column shall appear at the extreme left of the sheet, be 5/8 inch wide, be headed with "For Office Use Only", and be subdivided with a light vertical line down the middle with the left subdivision entitled "Registered" and the right subdivision left untitled;
(ii) the next column shall be three inches wide, headed "Registered Voter's Printed Name (must be legible to be counted)";
(iii) the next column shall be three inches wide, headed "Signature of Registered Voter"; and
(iv) the final column shall be 4-3/8 inches wide, headed "Street Address, City, Zip Code"; and
(h) contain the following statement, printed or typed upon the back of each sheet:

"Verification
State of Utah, County of _____
I, _____, of _____, hereby state that: I am a resident of Utah and am at least 18 years old; All the names that appear on this sheet were signed by persons who professed to be the persons whose names appear in it, and each of them signed his name on it in my presence; I believe that each has printed and signed his name and written his post office address and residence correctly, and that each signer is registered to vote in Utah or intends to become registered to vote before the certification of the petition names by the county clerk. _____"
(3) The forms prescribed in this section are not mandatory, and, if substantially followed, the initiative petitions are sufficient, notwithstanding clerical and merely technical errors.

20A-7-504. Circulation requirements — Local clerk to provide sponsors with materials.

(1) In order to obtain the necessary number of signatures required by this part, the sponsors shall circulate initiative packets that meet the form requirements of this part.
(2) The local clerk shall furnish to the sponsors:
(a) one copy of the initiative petition; and
(b) one signature sheet.
(3) The sponsors of the petition shall:
(a) arrange and pay for the printing of all additional copies of the petition and signature sheets; and
(b) ensure that the copies of the petition and signature sheets meet the form requirements of this section.
(4)(a) The sponsors may prepare the initiative for circulation by creating multiple initiative packets.
(b) The sponsors shall create those packets by binding a copy of the initiative petition, a copy of the proposed law, and no more than 50 signature sheets together at the top in such a way that the packets may be conveniently opened for signing.
(c) The sponsors need not attach a uniform number of signature sheets to each initiative packet.
(5)(a) After the sponsors have prepared sufficient initiative packets, they shall return them to the local clerk.
(b) The local clerk shall:
(i) number each of the initiative packets and return them to the sponsors within five working days; and
(ii) keep a record of the numbers assigned to each packet.

20A-7-505. Obtaining signatures — Verification — Removal of signature.

(1) Any Utah voter may sign a local initiative petition if the voter is a legal voter and resides in the local jurisdiction.
(2) The sponsors shall ensure that the person in whose presence each signature sheet was signed:
(a) is at least 18 years old and meets the residency requirements of Section 20A-2-105; and
(b) verifies each signature sheet by completing the verification printed on the back of each signature sheet.
(3)(a)(i) Any voter who has signed an initiative petition may have his signature removed from the petition by submitting a notarized statement to that effect to the local clerk.
(ii) In order for the signature to be removed, the statement must be received by the local clerk before he delivers the petition to the county clerk to be certified.
(b) Upon receipt of the statement, the local clerk shall remove the signature of the person submitting the statement from the initiative petition.

(c) No one may remove signatures from an initiative petition after the petition is submitted to the county clerk to be certified.

20A-7-506. Submitting the initiative petition — Certification of signatures by the county clerks — Transfer to local clerk.

(1) No later than 120 days before any regular general election, for county initiatives, or municipal general election, for municipal initiatives, the sponsors shall deliver each signed and verified initiative packet to the county clerk of the county in which the packet was circulated.

(2) No later than 90 days before any general election, the county clerk shall:

(a) check the names of all persons completing the verification on the back of each signature sheet to determine whether or not those persons are residents of Utah and are at least 18 years old; and

(b) submit the name of each of those persons who is not a Utah resident or who is not at least 18 years old to the attorney general and county attorney.

(3) No later than 60 days before any general election, the county clerk shall:

(a) check all the names of the signers against the official registers to determine whether or not the signer is a voter;

(b) certify on the petition whether or not each name is that of a voter; and

(c) deliver all of the packets to the local clerk.

20A-7-507. Evaluation by the local clerk.

(1) When each initiative packet is received from a county clerk, the local clerk shall check off from his record the number of each initiative packet filed.

(2)(a) After all of the initiative packets have been received by the local clerk, the local clerk shall count the number of the names certified by the county clerk that appear on each verified signature sheet.

(b) If the total number of certified names from each verified signature sheet equals or exceeds the number of names required by Section 20A-7-501, the local clerk shall mark upon the front of the petition the word "sufficient."

(c) If the total number of certified names from each verified signature sheet does not equal or exceed the number of names required by Section 20A-7-501, the local clerk shall mark upon the front of the petition the word "insufficient."

(d) The local clerk shall immediately notify any one of the sponsors of his finding.

(3) If the local clerk finds the total number of certified signatures from each verified signature sheet to be insufficient, any sponsor may file a written demand with the local clerk for a recount of the signatures appearing on the initiative petition in the presence of any sponsor.

(4)(a) If the local clerk refuses to accept and file any initiative petition, any voter may apply to the supreme court for an extraordinary writ to compel him to do so within ten days after the refusal.

(b) If the supreme court determines that the initiative petition is legally sufficient, the local clerk shall file it, with a verified copy of the judgment attached to it, as of the date on which it was originally offered for filing in his office.

(c) If the supreme court determines that any petition filed is not legally sufficient, the supreme court may enjoin the local clerk and all other officers from certifying or printing the ballot title and numbers of that measure on the official ballot for the next election.

20A-7-508. Ballot title — Duties of local clerk and local attorney.

(1) Whenever an initiative petition is declared sufficient for submission to a vote of the people, the local clerk shall deliver a copy of the petition and the proposed law to the local attorney.

(2)(a) The local attorney shall:

(i) prepare a ballot title for the initiative; and

(ii) return the petition and the ballot title to the local clerk within 15 days after its receipt.

(b) The ballot title may be distinct from the title of the proposed law attached to the initiative petition, and shall express, in not exceeding 100 words, the purpose of the measure.

(c) The ballot title and the number of the measure as determined by the local attorney shall be printed on the official ballot.

(d) In preparing ballot titles, the local attorney shall, to the best of his ability, give a true and impartial statement of the purpose of the measure.

(e) The ballot title may not intentionally be an argument, or likely to create prejudice, for or against the measure.

(3) Immediately after the local attorney files a copy of the ballot title with the local clerk, the local clerk shall serve a copy of the ballot title by mail upon any of the sponsors of the petition.

(4)(a) If the ballot title furnished by the local attorney is unsatisfactory or does not comply with the requirements of this section, at least three of the sponsors of the petition may, by motion, appeal the decision of the local attorney to the Supreme Court.

(b) The Supreme Court shall examine the measures and hear arguments, and, in its decision, shall certify to the local clerk a ballot title for the measure that fulfills the intent of this section.

(c) The local clerk shall print the title verified to him by the Supreme Court on the official ballot.

20A-7-509. Form of ballot — Manner of voting.

(1) The local clerk shall ensure that the number and ballot title are printed upon the official ballot with, immediately to the right of them, the words "For" and "Against," each word followed by a square in which the elector may indicate his vote.

(2) Electors desiring to vote in favor of enacting the law proposed by the initiative petition shall mark the square following the word "For," and those desiring to vote against enacting the law proposed by the initiative petition shall mark the square following the word "Against."

20A-7-510. Return and canvass — Conflicting measures — Law effective on proclamation.

(1) The votes on the law proposed by the initiative petition shall be counted, canvassed, and delivered as provided in Title 20A, Chapter 4, Part 3, Canvassing Returns.

(2) After the local board of canvassers completes its canvass, the local clerk shall certify to the local legislative body the vote for and against the law proposed by the initiative petition.

(3)(a) The local legislative body shall immediately issue a proclamation that:

(i) gives the total number of votes cast in the local jurisdiction for and against each law proposed by an initiative petition; and

(ii) declares those laws proposed by an initiative petition that were approved by majority vote to be in full force and effect as the law of the local jurisdiction.

(b) When the local legislative body determines that two proposed laws, or that parts of two proposed laws approved by the people at the same election are entirely in conflict, they shall proclaim that measure to be law that has received the greatest number of affirmative votes, regardless of the difference in the majorities which those measures have received.

(c)(i) Within ten days after the local legislative body's proclamation, any qualified voter who signed the initiative petition proposing the law that is declared by the local legislative body to be superseded by another measure approved at the same election may apply to the supreme court to review the decision.

(ii) The court shall:

(A) immediately consider the matter and decide whether or not the proposed laws are in conflict; and

(B) within ten days after the matter is submitted to it for decision, certify its decision to the local legislative body.

(4) Within 30 days after its previous proclamation, the local legislative body shall:

(a) proclaim all those measures approved by the people as law that the supreme court has determined are not in conflict; and

(b) of all those measures approved by the people as law that the supreme court has determined to be in conflict, proclaim as law the one that received the greatest number of affirmative votes, regardless of difference in majorities.

20A-7-511. Effective date.

(1)(a) Any proposed law submitted to the people by initiative petition that is approved by the voters at any election takes effect on the date specified in the initiative petition.

(b) If the initiative petition does not specify an effective date, a law approved by the voters at any election takes effect five days after the date of the official proclamation of the vote by the county legislative body.

(2) The local legislative body may amend any laws approved by the people at any meeting after the law has taken effect.

20A-7-512. Misconduct of electors and officers — Penalty.

(1) It is unlawful for any person to:

(a) sign any name other than his own to any initiative petition;

(b) knowingly sign his name more than once for the same measure at one election;

(c) sign an initiative knowing he is not a legal voter;

(d) knowingly and willfully violate any provision of this part.

(2) Any person violating this part is guilty of a class A misdemeanor.

20A-7-601. Referenda — General signature requirements — Signature requirements for land use laws — Time requirements.

(1) Except as provided in Subsection (2), a person seeking to have a law passed by the local legislative body submitted to a vote of the people shall obtain legal signatures equal to:

(a) 10% of all the votes cast in the county, city, or town for all candidates for governor at the last election at which a governor was elected if the total number of votes exceeds 25,000;

(b) 12-1/2% of all the votes cast in the county, city, or town for all candidates for governor at the last election at which a governor was elected if the total number of votes does not exceed 25,000 but is more than 10,000;

(c) 15% of all the votes cast in the county, city, or town for all candidates for governor at the last election at which a governor was elected if the total number of votes does not exceed 10,000 but is more than 2,500;

(d) 20% of all the votes cast in the county, city, or town for all candidates for governor at the last election at which a governor was elected if the total number of votes does not exceed 2,500 but is more than 500;

(e) 25% of all the votes cast in the county, city, or town for all candidates for governor at the last election at which a governor was elected if the total number of votes does not exceed 500 but is more than 250; and

(f) 30% of all the votes cast in the county, city, or town for all candidates for governor at the last election at which a governor was elected if the total number of votes does not exceed 250.

(2)(a) As used in this Subsection (2), "land use law" includes a land use development code, an annexation ordinance, and comprehensive zoning ordinances.

(b) A person seeking to have a land use law passed by the local legislative body submitted to a vote of the people shall obtain legal signatures equal to:

(i) in counties and first and second class cities, 20% of all votes cast in the county or city for all candidates for governor at the last election at which a governor was elected; and

(ii) in third class cities and towns, 35% of all the votes cast in the city or town for all candidates for governor at the last election at which a governor was elected.

(3)(a) Sponsors of any referendum petition challenging, under Subsection (1) or (2), any local law passed by a local legislative body shall file the petition within 35 days after the passage of the local law.

(b) The local law remains in effect until repealed by the voters via referendum.

(4) If the referendum passes, the local law that was challenged by the referendum is repealed as of the date of the election.

20A-7-602. Local referendum process — Application procedures.

(1) Persons wishing to circulate a referendum petition shall file an application with the local clerk.

(2) The application shall contain:

(a) the name and residence address of at least five sponsors of the referendum petition;

(b) a certification indicating that each of the sponsors:

(i) is a resident of Utah; and

(ii)(A) if the referendum challenges a county ordinance, has voted in a regular general election in Utah within the last three years; or

(B) if the referendum challenges a municipal ordinance, has voted in a regular municipal election in Utah within the last three years;

(c) the signature of each of the sponsors, attested to by a notary public; and

(d) one copy of the law.

20A-7-603. Form of referendum petition and signature sheets.

(1)(a) Each proposed referendum petition shall be printed in substantially the following form:

"REFERENDUM PETITION To the Honorable ____, County Clerk/City Recorder/Town Clerk:

We, the undersigned citizens of Utah, respectfully order that Ordinance No. ____, entitled (title of ordinance, and, if the petition is against less than the whole ordinance, set forth here the part or parts on which the referendum is sought), passed by the ____ be referred to the voters for their approval or rejection at the regular/municipal general election to be held on _____(month\day\year);

Each signer says: I have personally signed this petition; I am registered to vote in Utah or intend to become registered to vote in Utah before the certification of the petition names by the county clerk; and

My residence and post office address are written correctly after my name."

(b) The sponsors of a referendum shall attach a copy of the law that is the subject of the referendum to each referendum petition.

(2) Each signature sheet shall:

(a) be printed on sheets of paper 8-1/2 inches long and 11 inches wide;

(b) be ruled with a horizontal line 3/4 inch from the top, with the space above that line blank for the purpose of binding;

(c) contain the title of the referendum printed below the horizontal line;

(d) contain the word "Warning" printed or typed at the top of each signature sheet under the title of the referendum;

(e) contain, to the right of the word "Warning," the following statement printed or typed in not less than eight-point, single leaded type: "It is a class A misdemeanor for anyone to sign any referendum petition with any other name than his own, or knowingly to sign his name more than once for the same measure, or to sign a referendum petition when he knows he is not a registered voter and knows that he does not intend to become registered to vote before the certification of the petition names by the county clerk.";

(f) contain horizontally ruled lines, 3/8 inch apart under the "Warning" statement required by this section;

(g) be vertically divided into columns as follows:

(i) the first column shall appear at the extreme left of the sheet, be 5/8 inch wide, be headed with "For Office Use Only," and be subdivided with a light vertical line down the middle;

(ii) the next column shall be three inches wide, headed "Registered Voter's Printed Name (must be legible to be counted)";

(iii) the next column shall be three inches wide, headed "Signature of Registered Voter"; and

(iv) the final column shall be 4-3/8 inches wide, headed "Street Address, City, Zip Code"; and

(h) contain the following statement, printed or typed upon the back of each sheet:

"Verification

State of Utah, County of _____

I, _____, of _____, hereby state that: I am a resident of Utah and am at least 18 years old; All the names that appear on this sheet were signed by persons who professed to be the persons whose names appear in it, and each of them signed his name on it in my presence;

I believe that each has printed and signed his name and written his post office address and residence correctly, and that each signer is registered to vote in Utah or intends to become registered to vote before the certification of the petition names by the county clerk."

(3) The forms prescribed in this section are not mandatory, and, if substantially followed, the referendum petitions are sufficient, notwithstanding clerical and merely technical errors.

20A-7-604. Circulation requirements — Local clerk to provide sponsors with materials.

(1) In order to obtain the necessary number of signatures required by this part, the sponsors shall circulate referendum packets that meet the form requirements of this part.

(2) The local clerk shall furnish to the sponsors:

(a) five copies of the referendum petition; and

(b) five signature sheets.

(3) The sponsors of the petition shall:

(a) arrange and pay for the printing of all additional copies of the petition and signature sheets; and

(b) ensure that the copies of the petition and signature sheets meet the form requirements of this section.

(4)(a) The sponsors may prepare the referendum for circulation by creating multiple referendum packets.

(b) The sponsors shall create those packets by binding a copy of the referendum petition, a copy of the law that is the subject of the referendum, and no more than 50 signature sheets together at the top in such a way that the packets may be conveniently opened for signing.

(c) The sponsors need not attach a uniform number of signature sheets to each referendum packet.

(5)(a) After the sponsors have prepared sufficient referendum packets, they shall return them to the local clerk.

(b) The local clerk shall:

(i) number each of the referendum packets and return them to the sponsors within five working days; and

(ii) keep a record of the numbers assigned to each packet.

20A-7-605. Obtaining signatures — Verification — Removal of signature.

(1) Any Utah voter may sign a local referendum petition if the voter is a legal voter and resides in the local jurisdiction.

(2) The sponsors shall ensure that the person in whose presence each signature sheet was signed:

(a) is at least 18 years old and meets the residency requirements of Section 20A-2-105; and

(b) verifies each signature sheet by completing the verification printed on the back of each signature sheet.

(3)(a) Any voter who has signed a referendum petition may have his signature removed from the petition by submitting a notarized statement to that effect to the local clerk.

(b) Except as provided in Subsection (3)(c), upon receipt of the statement, the local clerk shall remove the signature of the person submitting the statement from the referendum petition.

(c) A local clerk may not remove signatures from a referendum petition after the petition has been submitted to the county clerk to be certified.

20A-7-606. Submitting the referendum petition — Certification of signatures by the county clerks — Transfer to local clerk.

(1) No later than 120 days before any regular general election for county referenda, or municipal general election for local referenda, the sponsors shall deliver each signed and verified referendum packet to the county clerk of the county in which the packet was circulated.

(2) No later than 90 days before any general election, the county clerk shall:

(a) check the names of all persons completing the verification on the back of each signature sheet to determine whether or not those persons are Utah residents and are at least 18 years old; and

(b) submit the name of each of those persons who is not a Utah resident or who is not at least 18 years old to the attorney general and county attorney.

(3) No later than 60 days before any general election, the county clerk shall:

(a) check all the names of the signers against the official registers to determine whether or not the signer is a voter;

(b) certify on the referendum petition whether or not each name is that of a voter; and

(c) deliver all of the referendum packets to the local clerk.

20A-7-607. Evaluation by the local clerk.

(1) When each referendum packet is received from a county clerk, the local clerk shall check off from his record the number of each referendum packet filed.

(2)(a) After all of the referendum packets have been received by the local clerk, the local clerk shall count the number of the names certified by the county clerks that appear on each verified signature sheet.

(b) If the total number of certified names from each verified signature sheet equals or exceeds the number of names required by Section 20A-7-601, the local clerk shall mark upon the front of the petition the word "sufficient."

(c) If the total number of certified names from each verified signature sheet does not equal or exceed the number of names required by Section 20A-7-601, the local clerk shall mark upon the front of the petition the word "insufficient."

(d) The local clerk shall immediately notify any one of the sponsors of his finding.

(3) If the local clerk finds the total number of certified signatures from each verified signature sheet to be insufficient, any sponsor may file a written demand with the local clerk for a recount of the signatures appearing on the referendum petition in the presence of any sponsor.

(4)(a) If the local clerk refuses to accept and file any referendum petition, any voter may apply to the Supreme Court for an extraordinary writ to compel him to do so within ten days after the refusal.

(b) If the Supreme Court determines that the referendum petition is legally sufficient, the local clerk shall file it, with a verified copy of the judgment attached to it, as of the date on which it was originally offered for filing in his office.

(c) If the Supreme Court determines that any petition filed is not legally sufficient, the Supreme Court may enjoin the local clerk and all other officers from certifying or printing the ballot title and numbers of that measure on the official ballot for the next election.

20A-7-608. Ballot title — Duties of local clerk and local attorney.

(1) Whenever a referendum petition is declared sufficient for submission to a vote of the people, the local clerk shall deliver a copy of the petition and the proposed law to the local attorney.

(2)(a) The local attorney shall:

(i) prepare a ballot title for the referendum; and

(ii) return the petition and the ballot title to the local clerk within 15 days after its receipt.

(b) The ballot title may be distinct from the title of the law that is the subject of the petition, and shall express, in not exceeding 100 words, the purpose of the measure.

(c) The ballot title and the number of the measure as determined by the local attorney shall be printed on the official ballot.

(d) In preparing ballot titles, the local attorney shall, to the best of his ability, give a true and impartial statement of the purpose of the measure.

(e) The ballot title may not intentionally be an argument, or likely to create prejudice, for or against the measure.

(3) Immediately after the local attorney files a copy of the ballot title with the local clerk, the local clerk shall serve a copy of the ballot title by mail upon any of the sponsors of the petition.

(4)(a) If the ballot title furnished by the local attorney is unsatisfactory or does not comply with the requirements of this section, at least three of the sponsors of the petition may, by motion, appeal the decision of the local attorney to the Supreme Court.

(b) The Supreme Court shall examine the measures and hear arguments, and, in its decision, shall certify to the local clerk a ballot title for the measure that fulfills the intent of this section.

(c) The local clerk shall print the title verified to him by the Supreme Court on the official ballot.

20A-7-609. Form of ballot — Manner of voting.

(1) The local clerk shall ensure that the number and ballot title are printed upon the official ballot with, immediately to the right of them, the words "For" and "Against," each word followed by a square in which the elector may indicate his vote.

(2)(a) Unless the county legislative body calls a special election, the county clerk shall ensure that referenda that have qualified for the ballot appear on the next regular general election ballot.

(b) Unless the municipal legislative body calls a special election, the municipal recorder or clerk shall ensure that referenda that have qualified for the ballot appear on the next regular municipal election ballot.

(3) Voters desiring to vote in favor of enacting the law proposed by the referendum petition shall mark the square following the word "For," and those desiring to vote against enacting the law proposed by the referendum petition shall mark the square following the word "Against."

20A-7-610. Return and canvass — Conflicting measures — Law effective on proclamation.

(1) The votes on the law proposed by the referendum petition shall be counted, canvassed, and delivered as provided in Title 20A, Chapter 4, Part 3, Canvassing Returns.

(2) After the local board of canvassers completes its canvass, the local clerk shall certify to the local legislative body the vote for and against the law proposed by the referendum petition.

(3)(a) The local legislative body shall immediately issue a proclamation that:

(i) gives the total number of votes cast in the local jurisdiction for and against each law proposed by a referendum petition; and

(ii) declares those laws proposed by a referendum petition that were approved by majority vote to be in full force and effect as the law of the local jurisdiction.

(b) When the local legislative body determines that two proposed laws, or that parts of two proposed laws approved by the people at the same election are entirely in conflict, they shall proclaim that measure to be law that has received the greatest number of affirmative votes, regardless of the difference in the majorities which those measures have received.

(4)(a) Within ten days after the local legislative body's proclamation, any qualified voter who signed the referendum petition proposing the law that is declared by the local legislative body to be superseded by another measure approved at the same election may apply to the supreme court to review the decision.

(b) The supreme court shall:

(i) immediately consider the matter and decide whether or not the proposed laws are in conflict; and

(ii) within ten days after the matter is submitted to it for decision, certify its decision to the local legislative body.

(5) Within 30 days after its previous proclamation, the local legislative body shall:

(a) proclaim all those measures approved by the people as law that the supreme court has determined are not in conflict; and

(b) of all those measures approved by the people as law that the supreme court has determined to be in conflict, proclaim as law the one that received the greatest number of affirmative votes, regardless of difference in majorities.

20A-7-611. Effective date.

Any proposed law submitted to the people by referendum petition that is rejected by the voters at any election is repealed as of the date of the election.

20A-7-612. Misconduct of electors and officers — Penalty.

(1) It is unlawful for any person to:

(a) sign any name other than his own to any referendum petition;

(b) knowingly sign his name more than once for the same measure at one election;

(c) sign a referendum knowing he is not a legal voter;

(d) knowingly and willfully violate any provision of this part.

(2) Any person violating this part is guilty of a class A misdemeanor.

20A-7-701. Voter information pamphlet to be prepared.

(1) The lieutenant governor shall cause to be printed a voter information pamphlet designed to inform the voters of the state of the content, effect, operation, fiscal impact, and the supporting and opposing arguments of any measure submitted to the voters by the Legislature or by initiative or referendum petition.

(2) The pamphlet shall also include a separate section prepared, analyzed, and submitted by the Judicial Council describing the judicial selection and retention process.

(3) The lieutenant governor shall cause to be printed as many voter information pamphlets as needed to comply with the provisions of this chapter.

20A-7-702. Voter information pamphlet — Form — Contents — Distribution.

(1) The lieutenant governor shall ensure that all information submitted for publication in the voter information pamphlet is:

(a) printed and bound in a single pamphlet;

(b) printed in clear readable type, no less than ten-point, except that the text of any measure may be set forth in eight-point type; and

(c) printed on a quality and weight of paper that best serves the voters.

(2) The voter information pamphlet shall contain the following items in this order:

(a) a cover title page;

(b) an introduction to the pamphlet by the lieutenant governor;

(c) a table of contents;

(d) a list of all candidates for constitutional offices;

(e) a list of candidates for each legislative district;

(f) a 100-word statement of qualifications for each candidate for the office of governor, lieutenant governor, attorney general, state auditor, or state treasurer, if submitted by the candidate to the lieutenant governor's office before July 15 at 5 p.m.;

(g) information pertaining to all measures to be submitted to the voters, beginning a new page for each measure and containing, in the following order for each measure:

(i) a copy of the number and ballot title of the measure;

(ii) the final vote cast by the Legislature on the measure if it is a measure submitted by the Legislature or by referendum;

(iii) the impartial analysis of the measure prepared by the Office of Legislative Research and General Counsel;

(iv) the arguments in favor of the measure, the rebuttal to the arguments in favor of the measure, the arguments against the measure, and the rebuttal to the arguments against the measure, with the name and title of the authors at the end of each argument or rebuttal;

(v) for each constitutional amendment, a complete copy of the text of the constitutional amendment, with all new language underlined, and all deleted language placed within brackets; and

(vi) for each initiative qualified for the ballot, a copy of the measure as certified by the lieutenant governor;

(h) a description provided by the Judicial Council of the selection and retention process for judges of courts of record, including, in the following order:

(i) a description of the judicial selection process;

(ii) a description of the judicial performance evaluation process;

(iii) a description of the judicial retention election process;

(iv) a list of the criteria and minimum standards of judicial performance evaluation;

(v) the names of the judges standing for retention election; and

(vi) for each judge:

(A) the counties in which the judge is subject to retention election;

(B) a short biography of professional qualifications and a recent photograph;

(C) for each standard of performance, a statement identifying whether or not the judge met the standard and, if not, the manner in which the judge failed to meet the standard;

(D) a statement identifying the cumulative number of public orders issued by the Utah Supreme Court under Utah Constitution Article VIII, Section 13 during the judge's current term and the immediately preceding term, and a statement of the basis for each order that the judge has received; and

(E) a statement identifying whether or not the judge was certified by the Judicial Council;

(vii)(A) except as provided in Subsection (2)(h)(vii)(B), for each judge, in graphic format, the favorable response rating for each attorney, jury, and other survey question used by the Judicial Council for certification of judges, displayed in 1% increments and identifying the minimum standards of performance for each question;

(B) notwithstanding Subsection (2)(h)(vii)(A), if the sample size for the survey for a particular judge is too small to provide statistically reliable information in 1% increments, the survey results for that judge shall be reported as being above or below 70% and a statement by the surveyor explaining why the survey is statistically unreliable shall also be included;

(i) an explanation of ballot marking procedures prepared by the Office of Legislative Research and General Counsel, indicating the ballot marking procedure used by each county and explaining how to mark the ballot for each procedure;

(j) voter registration information;

(k) a list of all county clerks' offices and phone numbers;

(l) an index of subjects in alphabetical order; and

(m)on the back cover page, a printed copy of the following statement signed by the lieutenant governor:

"I, _____ (print name), Lieutenant Governor of Utah, certify that the measures contained in this pamphlet will be submitted to the voters of Utah at the election to be held throughout the state on ____ (date of election), and that this pamphlet is complete and correct according to law. SEAL

Witness my hand and the Great Seal of the State, at Salt Lake City, Utah this ____ day of ____ (month), ____ (year)

(signed) _____ Lieutenant Governor"

(1) The lieutenant governor shall:

(a) ensure that one copy of the voter information pamphlet is placed in one issue of every newspaper of general circulation in the state not more than 40 nor less than 15 days before the day fixed by law for the election;

(b) ensure that a sufficient number of printed voter information pamphlets are available for distribution as required by this section;

(c) provide voter information pamphlets to each county clerk for free distribution upon request and for placement at polling places; and

(d) ensure that the distribution of the voter information pamphlets is completed 15 days before the election.

20A-7-703. Impartial analysis of measure — Determination of fiscal effects.

(1) The director of the Office of Legislative Research and General Counsel, after the approval of the legislative general counsel as to legal sufficiency, shall:

(a) prepare an impartial analysis of each measure submitted to the voters by the Legislature or by initiative or referendum petition; and

(b) submit the impartial analysis to the lieutenant governor no later than August 20 of the year in which the measure will appear on the ballot.

(2) The director shall ensure that the impartial analysis:

(a) is not more than 1,000 words long;

(b) is prepared in clear and concise language that will easily be understood by the average voter;

(c) avoids the use of technical terms as much as possible;

(d) shows the effect of the measure on existing law;

(e) identifies any potential conflicts with the United States or Utah Constitutions raised by the measure;

(f) fairly describes the operation of the measure;

(g) identifies the measure's fiscal effects for the first full year of implementation and the first year when the last provisions to be implemented are fully effective; and

(h) identifies the amount of any increase or decrease in revenue or cost to state or local government.

(3) The director shall analyze the measure as it is proposed to be adopted without considering any implementing legislation, unless the implementing legislation has been enacted and will become effective upon the adoption of the measure by the voters.

(4)(a) In determining the fiscal effects of a measure, the director shall confer with the legislative fiscal analyst.

(b) The director shall consider any measure that requires implementing legislation in order to take effect to have no financial effect, unless implementing legislation has been enacted that will become effective upon adoption of the measure by the voters.

(5) If the director requests the assistance of any state department, agency, or official in preparing his analysis, that department, agency, or official shall assist the director.

20A-7-704. Initiative measures — Arguments for and against — Voters' requests for argument — Ballot arguments.

(1)(a)(i)(A) By August 20 of the regular general election year, the sponsors of any initiative petition that has been declared sufficient by the lieutenant governor may deliver to the lieutenant governor an argument for the adoption of the measure.

(B) If two or more sponsors wish to submit arguments for the measure, the lieutenant governor shall designate one of them to submit the argument for his side of the measure.

(ii)(A) Any member of the Legislature may request permission to submit an argument against the adoption of the measure.

(B) If two or more legislators wish to submit an argument against the measure, the presiding officers of the Senate and House of Representatives shall jointly designate one of them to submit the argument to the lieutenant governor.

(b) The sponsors and the legislators submitting arguments shall ensure that each argument:

(i) does not exceed 500 words in length; and

(ii) is delivered by August 20.

(2)(a)(i) If an argument for or against a measure to be submitted to the voters by initiative petition has not been filed within the time required by Subsection (1), any voter may request the lieutenant governor for permission to prepare an argument for the side on which no argument has been prepared.

(ii) If two or more voters request permission to submit arguments on the same side of a measure, the lieutenant governor shall designate one of the voters to write the argument.

(b) Any argument prepared under this subsection shall be submitted to the lieutenant governor by August 30.

(3) The lieutenant governor may not accept a ballot argument submitted under this section unless it is accompanied by:

(a) the name and address of the person submitting it, if it is submitted by an individual voter; or

(b) the name and address of the organization and the names and addresses of at least two of its principal officers, if it is submitted on behalf of an organization.

(4)(a) Except as provided in Subsection (4)(c), the authors may not amend or change the arguments after they are submitted to the lieutenant governor.

(b) Except as provided in Subsection (4)(c), the lieutenant governor may not alter the arguments in any way.

(c) The lieutenant governor and the authors of an argument may jointly modify an argument after it is submitted if:

(i) they jointly agree that changes to the argument must be made to correct spelling or grammatical errors; and

(ii) the argument has not yet been submitted for typesetting.

20A-7-705. Measures to be submitted to voters and referendum measures — Preparation of argument of adoption.

(1)(a) Whenever the Legislature submits any measure to the voters or whenever an act of the Legislature is referred to the voters by referendum petition, the presiding officer of the house of origin of the measure shall appoint the sponsor of the measure or act and one member of either house who voted with the majority to pass the act or submit the measure to draft an argument for the adoption of the measure.

(b)(i) The argument may not exceed 500 words in length.

(ii) If the sponsor of the measure or act desires separate arguments to be written in favor by each person appointed, separate arguments may be written but the combined length of the two arguments may not exceed 500 words.

(2)(a) If a measure or act submitted to the voters by the Legislature or by referendum petition was not adopted unanimously by the Legislature, the presiding officer of each house shall, at the same time as appointments to an argument in its favor are made, appoint one member who voted against the measure or act from their house to write an argument against the measure or act.

(b)(i) The argument may not exceed 500 words.

(ii) If those members appointed to write an argument against the measure or act desire separate arguments to be written in opposition to the measure or act by each person appointed, separate arguments may be written, but the combined length of the two arguments may not exceed 500 words.

(3)(a) The legislators appointed by the presiding officer of the Senate or House of Representatives to submit arguments shall submit them to the lieutenant governor not later than June 1.

(b) Except as provided in Subsection (3)(d), the authors may not amend or change the arguments after they are submitted to the lieutenant governor.

(c) Except as provided in Subsection (3)(d), the lieutenant governor may not alter the arguments in any way.

(d) The lieutenant governor and the authors of an argument may jointly modify an argument after it is submitted if:

(i) they jointly agree that changes to the argument must be made to correct spelling or grammatical errors; and

(ii) the argument has not yet been submitted for typesetting.

(4)(a) If an argument for or an argument against a measure submitted to the voters by the Legislature or by referendum petition has not been filed by a member of the Legislature within the time required by this section, any voter may request the presiding officer of the house in which the measure originated for permission to prepare and file an argument for the side on which no argument has been prepared by a member of the Legislature.

(b)(i) The presiding officer of the house of origin shall grant permission unless two or more voters request permission to submit arguments on the same side of a measure.

(ii) If two or more voters request permission to submit arguments on the same side of a measure, the presiding officer shall designate one of the voters to write the argument.

(c) Any argument prepared under this subsection shall be submitted to the lieutenant governor not later than June 15.

(d) The lieutenant governor may not accept a ballot argument submitted under this section unless it is accompanied by:

(i) the name and address of the person submitting it, if it is submitted by an individual voter; or

(ii) the name and address of the organization and the names and addresses of at least two of its principal officers, if it is submitted on behalf of an organization.

(e) Except as provided in Subsection (4)(g), the authors may not amend or change the arguments after they are submitted to the lieutenant governor.

(f) Except as provided in Subsection (4)(g), the lieutenant governor may not alter the arguments in any way.

(g) The lieutenant governor and the authors of an argument may jointly modify an argument after it is submitted if:

(i) they jointly agree that changes to the argument must be made to correct spelling or grammatical errors; and

(ii) the argument has not yet been submitted for typesetting.

20A-7-706. Copies of arguments to be sent to opposing authors — Rebuttal arguments.

(1) When the lieutenant governor has received the arguments for and against a measure to be submitted to the voters, the lieutenant governor shall immediately send copies of the arguments in favor of the measure to the authors of the arguments against and copies of the arguments against to the authors of the arguments in favor.

(2) The authors may prepare and submit rebuttal arguments not exceeding 250 words.

(3)(a) The rebuttal arguments must be filed with the lieutenant governor not later than June 30.

(b) Except as provided in Subsection (3)(d), the authors may not amend or change the rebuttal arguments after they are submitted to the lieutenant governor.

(c) Except as provided in Subsection (3)(d), the lieutenant governor may not alter the arguments in any way.

(d) The lieutenant governor and the authors of a rebuttal argument may jointly modify a rebuttal argument after it is submitted if:

(i) they jointly agree that changes to the rebuttal argument must be made to correct spelling or grammatical errors; and

(ii) the rebuttal argument has not yet been submitted for typesetting.

(4) The lieutenant governor shall ensure that:

(a) rebuttal arguments are printed in the same manner as the direct arguments; and

(b) each rebuttal argument follows immediately after the direct argument which it seeks to rebut.

The Basic Steps to Do an Initiative in Utah

Statutes Only — Direct and Indirect Initiative Process

Basic procedures: Persons wishing to circulate a statewide initiative petition must file an application and a copy of the proposed law with the Lieutenant Governor. The application requires five sponsors who are registered voters and have voted in regular general election in Utah in the last three years. The Lieutenant Governor then forwards it to the Attorney General who reviews it (which usually takes about 5 business days.) After the Attorney General reviews it, he sends it back to the Lieutenant Governor who notifies the proponents that they can begin circulating.

The Lieutenant Governor can reject an initiative petition application if the law proposed by the initiative is patently unconstitutional; the proposed law is nonsensical; or if the proposed law could not become a law if passed.

As soon as the signatures are verified and the Lieutenant Governor qualifies it for the ballot, the Lieutenant Governor transmits a copy of the petition to the Office of Legislative Research and General Counsel, which will prepare the ballot title within 15 days after its receipt. At least three of the sponsors may appeal the decision to the Supreme Court. The Supreme Court will examine the measures and hear arguments, and, in its decision, certify to the lieutenant governor a ballot title.

Within 15 days after the lieutenant governor declares an initiative petition sufficient, the sponsors of the petition may deliver to the lieutenant governor an argument for the adoption of the measure. Any member of the legislature may request permission to submit an argument against the adoption of the measure. Each argument must not exceed 600 words and be delivered within the 15-day period. These arguments go in the state voter guide, along with the initiative text and a fiscal impact statement.

Date initiative language can be submitted to the state for 2002 election: any time

Signatures are tied to vote of which office: Governor

Next Gubernatorial election: 2004

Votes Cast for Governor in last election: 761,810

Net number of signatures required: For direct initiatives statutes, proponents must gather signatures equal to 10% of the total votes cast in the last gubernatorial election (76,181 signatures), plus they must get 10% of the vote cast in at least 20 of the 29 counties. For indirect initiatives statutes, proponents must get 5% of the total votes cast in last gubernatorial election and 5% in at least 20 of 29 counties for the initiative to be submitted to the legislature. If the legislature votes it down, proponents can then go out and get the remaining 5% to qualify it for the ballot. Utah has no provision for constitutional amendment initiatives.

Distribution requirement: For direct initiatives, proponents must gather 10% of the vote cast in at least 20 of the 29 counties. For indirect initiatives, proponents must gather 5% in at least 20 of 29 counties.

Circulation period: Unlimited

Do circulators have to be residents: Yes

Date when signatures are filed for certification: June 1, 2002 for direct initiatives. November 15, 2001 for in-direct initiatives.

Signature verification process: Petitions are verified by the county clerks, who will verify every signature.

Single-subject restriction: Utah has no single subject restrictions.

Legislative tampering: Initiatives that are approved by the voters treated as regular statutes and may be amended or repealed by the Legislature at any legislative session after the act or law has taken effect.

Vermont

Winston Allen Flint, writing in *The Progressive Movement in Vermont,* noted that "no serious attempt was ever made in Vermont" to get a statewide initiative process: "There is little evidence to show that it was given any important recognition in Vermont by party platforms, legislators, press, or public opinion."

In 1981 and 1982, however, Vermonters used their local initiative process in over 200 town meetings to vote on a resolution calling for U.S.-Soviet nuclear arms freeze. More than 160 towns backed the freeze, which therefore had much the same effect as a statewide initiative.

Vermont Constitution

The state does not have the statewide initiative process and so therefore the following provisions discuss the procedures used by the state legislature to place constitutional amendments on the ballot.

Amendment of the Constitution

Section 72. Amending constitution

At the biennial session of the General Assembly of this State which convenes in A.D. 1975, and at the biennial session convening every fourth year thereafter, the Senate by a vote of two-thirds of its members, may propose amendments to this Constitution, with the concurrence of a majority of the members of the House of Representatives with the amendment as proposed by the Senate. A proposed amendment so adopted by the Senate and concurred in by the House of

Representatives shall be referred to the next biennial session of the General Assembly; and if at that last session a majority of the members of the Senate and a majority of the House of Representatives concur in the proposed amendment, it shall be the duty of the General Assembly to submit the proposal directly to the voters of the state. Any proposed amendment submitted to the voters of the state in accordance with this section which is approved by a majority of the voters voting thereon shall become part of the Constitution of this State.

Prior to the submission of a proposed amendment to a vote in accordance with this section, public notice of the proposed amendment shall be given by proclamation of the Governor.

The General Assembly shall provide for the manner of voting on amendments proposed under this section, and shall enact legislation to carry the provisions of this section into effect.

Virginia

While the Populist call for "more democracy" was gaining strength throughout most of the nation, Virginia's ruling Democratic Party was giving its citizens less democracy. In May 1901, voters elected 100 delegates to a state constitutional convention, 89 of them Democrats. The new constitution they approved included a poll tax and a literacy test, both designed to prevent poor whites and blacks from voting. The delegates did not even submit the new constitution to the voters for ratification, having it take effect instead "by [their own] proclamation." In this context, it is surprising not that Virginia's Progressives failed to amend their state constitution to include I&R, but that they even tried.

The Progressives' hopes for a statewide I&R amendment ran highest in 1914, when state Attorney General John Garland Pollard was elected president of the newly formed Progressive Democratic League, which included I&R on its reform agenda. That same year the House of Delegates approved an I&R amendment by a lopsided 64 to 24 vote, but the measure died in the senate.

The next serious discussion of a statewide I&R amendment came 50 years later, in 1969, when Norfolk State Senator (and unsuccessful 1977 gubernatorial candidate) Henry Howell and Fairfax delegate Vincent Callahan proposed it again without success.

In 1980, three northern Virginians—Gwendolyn F. Cody, James W. Roncaglione, and Harley M. Williams—organized Virginians for Initiative and Referendum. In 1981, both houses passed a bill adding I&R provisions to the city charter of Hampton, which were approved by voters of that city by a greater than three to one margin. Cody won election to the House of Delegates; I&R endorser Charles Robb became governor. But Cody was unable to get the statewide I&R bill out of committee, and Robb did nothing to support it. Prospects dimmed further with the death of Williams in 1986.

Virginia Constitution

The state does not have the statewide initiative process and so therefore the following provisions discuss the procedures used by the state legislature to place constitutional amendments on the ballot.

Article XII

Section 1. Amendments.

Any amendment or amendments to this Constitution may be proposed in the Senate or House of Delegates, and if the same shall be agreed to by a majority of the members elected to each of the two houses, such proposed amendment or amendments shall be entered on their journals, the name of each member and how he voted to be recorded, and referred to the General Assembly at its first regular session held after the next general election of members of the House of Delegates. If at such regular session or any subsequent special session of that General Assembly the proposed amendment or amendments shall be agreed to by a majority of all the members elected to each house, then it shall be the duty of the General Assembly to submit such proposed amendment or amendments to the voters qualified to vote in elections by the people, in such manner as it shall prescribe and not sooner than ninety days after final passage by the General Assembly. If a majority of those voting vote in favor of any amendment, it shall become part of the Constitution on the date prescribed by the General Assembly in submitting the amendment to the voters.

Section 2. Constitutional convention.

The General Assembly may, by a vote of two-thirds of the members elected to each house, call a convention to propose a general revision of, or specific amendments to, this Constitution, as the General Assembly in its call may stipulate.

The General Assembly shall provide by law for the election of delegates to such a convention, and shall also provide for the submission, in such manner as it shall prescribe and not sooner than ninety days after final adjournment of the convention, of the proposals of the convention to the voters qualified to vote in elections by the people. If a majority of those voting vote in favor of any proposal, it shall become effective on the date prescribed by the General Assembly in providing for the submission of the convention proposals to the voters.

Washington

In 1897 State Representative L. E. Reeder of Ollalla introduced a constitutional amendment for initiative and referendum that passed the lower house by a 63 to 12 vote, but it failed in the state senate. Influential in that partial victory was House Speaker Charles E. Cline of Olympia, who became secretary of the state's Direct Legislation League.

Another state legislator, George F. Cotterill of Seattle, had become president of the League by 1900. By this time, however, Cline was no longer House Speaker, and the I&R movement stagnated.

In 1907 the state's organized labor and farm groups cooperated with the Direct Legislation League in deluging the legislature with petitions calling for statewide I&R. Soon after, the I&R bill introduced by State Rep. Glenn N. Ranck of Vancouver passed the lower house 66 to 26, but the state senate defeated it 25 to 15. An I&R supporter noted that "just two forces" opposed I&R: "special privileged corporation interests and the organized liquor traffic," the latter because it feared voters would enact a Prohibition initiative.

The state Federation of Labor, whose president was Charles Case, and the state Grange, whose "master" (i.e., president) was C. B. Kegley, formed a Joint Legislative Committee that finally got the I&R amendment through both houses of the legislature in 1911. However, the version passed by the legislature did not allow voters to initiate state constitutional amendments, because certain state senators, with the active support of Governor Hay, insisted that an amendment receive at least 60 percent of all votes cast in a general election in order to pass. The pro-I&R committee refused to accept this compromise, and over 70 years later, there is still no provision for initiatives to amend the state constitution in Washington. Voters ratified the legislature's I&R bill by a five to two margin in 1912, and in the same election, George Cotterill was elected mayor of Seattle.

The farmer-labor Joint Legislative Committee put the voters' newly established lawmaking powers to use immediately. They circulated petitions to put seven initiatives on the 1914 ballot, of which five qualified, though only one was approved by voters: a measure to abolish private employment agencies. The intent behind this law was to stop the well-documented exploitation of unemployed workers, particularly lumberjacks, by such agencies.

A statewide Prohibition initiative also passed in 1914, just as the liquor interests had feared. The following year anti-initiative forces in the legislature—which was "dominated by the whiskey, lumber, and fish interests," according to Grange Master Kegley—struck back by passing a bill (deceptively titled "An Act to Facilitate the Operation of the Initiative and Referendum") that would have made it virtually impossible to get an initiative on the ballot.

Progressive forces used the power of referendum to stop the bill from going into effect. They quickly circulated petitions to block it until voters could reject it in the November 1916 election (which they did, by a three to one margin).

The legislature soon found a way to obstruct the referendum provision: by attaching an "emergency clause" to a bill, they could cause it to take effect immediately and thus make it invulnerable to referendum petitions. Eventually, in 1929, the state supreme court ruled that the legislature could not add an "emergency clause" to a bill in the absence of a real emergency (*State ex. rel. Satterthwaite v. Hinkle,* 152 Wash. 221 [1929]).

Property tax limitation initiatives were on the ballot five times between 1924 and 1938. The proposals, which sought to limit the tax levy on real and personal property to 40 mills, were passed by voters in 1932, 1934, 1936, and 1938, before the legislature acted to make the tax limit permanent by putting it into the state constitution, a move that was approved by voters in 1940.

Washington voters twice approved redistricting initiatives, once in 1930 and again in 1956. The latter initiative was sponsored by the state League of Women Voters. Another successful election reform passed by voter initiative was permanent voter registration, enacted in 1932.

In the years of the Great Depression, economic concerns frequently became the subject of Washington state initiatives. Voters passed an initiative authorizing creation of public utility districts in 1930, a measure that helped make possible the state's current system of locally controlled, publicly owned electric utilities.

Perhaps the most innovative initiative of the 1930s was the 1936 "Production for Use" proposal. "Production for Use" was conceived by Upton Sinclair, the Socialist author of *The Jungle,* who became a Democrat in 1934 in order to run for California's governorship. This economic recovery plan called for the government to acquire idle production facilities such as factories, hire the unemployed to work in them, and promote sales of the goods through cooperatives. After Sinclair lost in California, his Washington admirers decided to give the concept a second chance by putting it on the ballot there in 1936. The Washington Commonwealth Federation, which sponsored the initiative, was split by internal dissension that year, and little was accomplished to promote the measure's passage. It lost by a nearly four to one margin.

Washington voters turned generous in 1948, when they approved initiatives granting a bonus to veterans and increasing Social Security benefits. In 1954 they rejected by a three to one margin an initiative to restrict advertising for alcoholic beverages on television: a unique proposal that, like "Production for Use" in 1936, never appeared on any other ballot in the nation.

One of the most important postwar reforms accomplished by voter initiative was the establishment of the state's civil service system, which was approved by the electorate in 1958 for county sheriff employees and in 1960 for state employees. Prior to this, the "patronage" or "spoils system" had filled bureaucracies with incompetent party hacks.

In 1968, the Washington State Medical Association sponsored an initiative requiring drivers stopped by police for driving under the influence of liquor to submit to breath tests. Voters approved it by a two to one margin. That same year they approved a measure putting a lid on interest rates paid by retail credit customers.

In 1970, environmentalists launched a petition drive for an initiative to restrict shoreline development, more than a year before California ecology groups launched their drive for a similar initiative. The Washington state petition qualified for the ballot and prompted the legislature to propose an alternative bill, which was on the 1972 ballot along with the initiative measure. The legislature's bill received more votes, and therefore it took effect instead of the initiative. In 1988, however, when the choice was between an environmentalist-backed toxic waste tax and cleanup initiative and the legislature's version, voters chose the initiative.

In 2000 along came a new initiative advocate, Tim Eyman. Like Bill Sizemore in Oregon and Doug Bruce in Colorado, his passion was tax reduction. He placed several initiatives on the ballot in 2000 and 2001 that passed overwhelmingly. However, the state supreme court struck them down as violating the state's stringent single subject rule for initiatives.

Statewide Initiative Usage

Number of Initiatives	Number Passed	Number Failed	Passage Rate
136	68	68	50%

Statewide Initiatives

Year	Measure Number	Type	Subject Matter	Description	Pass/Fail
1914	I-10	DS	Legal	Convict Labor Road Measure.	Failed
1914	I-13	DS	Labor	Eight hour workday	Failed
1914	I-3	DS	Alcohol Regulation	Providing for statewide prohibition.	Passed
1914	I-6	DS	Daylight Savings Time	Blue Sky Law.	Failed
1914	I-7	DS	Administration of Government	Abolishing Bureau of Inspection.	Failed
1914	I-8	DS	Administration of Government	Abolish Employment Offices.	Passed
1914	I-9	DS	Legal	First Aid to Injured.	Failed
1916	I-18	IDS	Alcohol Regulation	Brewer's Hotel Bill.	Failed
1916	I-24	DS	Alcohol Regulation	Brewer's Bill.	Failed
1922	I-40	DS	Civil Rights	Repealing Chapter 174, Laws of 1921, relating to the Poll Tax.	Passed
1922	I-46	DS	Education	"30-10" School Plan.	Failed
1924	I-49	DS	Education	Compulsory school attendance.	Failed
1924	I-50	DS	Taxes	Limitation of Taxation.	Failed
1924	I-52	DS	Utility Regulation	Electric Power Measure.	Failed

Year	Measure Number	Type	Subject Matter	Description	Pass/Fail
1930	I-1	IDS	Administration of Government	District Power Measure.	Passed
1930	I-57	DS	Apportionment/ Redistricting	Redistricting State for Legislative Purpose.	Passed
1932	I-58	DS	Election Reform	Permanent voter registration.	Passed
1932	I-61	DS	Alcohol Regulation	Relating to intoxicating liquors.	Passed
1932	I-62	DS	Administration of Government	Creating Department of Game.	Passed
1932	I-64	DS	Taxes	Limits Tax levy on Real and Personal Property to 40 Mills.	Passed
1932	I-69	DS	Taxes	Income Tax Measure.	Passed
1934	I-77	DS	Animal Rights	Fish Traps and Fishing Regulations.	Passed
1934	I-94	DS	Taxes	40-Mill Tax Limit.	Passed
1936	I-101	DS	Administration of Government	Civil Service.	Failed
1936	I-114	DS	Taxes	40-Mill Tax Limit.	Passed
1936	I-115	DS	Welfare	Relative to old age pensions.	Failed
1936	I-119	DS	Business Regulation	Production for Use.	Failed
1938	I-126	DS	Election Reform	Non-Partisan School Election.	Passed
1938	I-129	DS	Taxes	40-Mill Tax Limit.	Passed
1938	I-130	DS	Labor	Regulation of Labor Disputes.	Failed
1940	I-139	DS	Bonds	P.U.D. Bonds.	Failed
1940	I-141	DS	Welfare	Relative to old age pensions.	Passed
1944	I-157	DS	Welfare	Relative to old age assistance laws.	Failed
1944	I-158	DS	Welfare	Liberalization of Old Age Assistance Laws by the Townsend Clubs of Washington.	Failed
1946	I-166	DS	Utility Regulation	Relating to Public Utility Districts; requiring approval of voters as prerequisite to acquisition of any operating electrical utility properties.	Failed
1948	I 13	IDS	Alcohol Regulation	Restricting sales of Beer and Wine to State Liquor Stores.	Failed
1948	I-169	DS	Veteran Affairs	Providing Bonus to Veterans of World War. [State Supreme Court ruled measure unconstitutional Feb. 4, 1949. A similar measure was passed into law by the 1949 Legislature.]	Passed
1948	I-171	DS	Alcohol Regulation	Providing liquor by the drink with certain restrictions.	Passed
1948	I-172	DS	Administration of Government	Relating to Liberalization of Social Security Laws.	Passed
1950	I-176	DS	Welfare	Increasing to $65 monthly the minimum grant for certain categories of public assistance, otherwise extending the social security program, and making appropriation.	Failed
1950	I-178	DS	Health/Medical	Modifying the Citizens' Security Act of 1948 and transferring the public assistance medical program to the State Department of Health.	Passed
1952	I-180	DS	Business Regulation	Authorizing the manufacture, sale and use of colored oleomargarine.	Passed
1952	I-181	DS	Daylight Savings Time	Prescribing the Observance of Standard Time.	Passed

Year	Measure Number	Type	Subject Matter	Description	Pass/Fail
1952	I-184	DS	Welfare	Relative to old age pensions.	Failed
1954	I-188	DS	Business Regulation	Raising standards for chiropractic examinations.	Failed
1954	I-192	DS	Environmental Reform	Regulation of Commercial Salmon Fishing.	Failed
1954	I-193	DS	Daylight Savings Time	Statewide Daylight Saving Time.	Failed
1954	I-194	DS	Alcohol Regulation	Restricting television alcoholic beverage advertising.	
1956	I-198	DS	Labor	Affecting Employer-Employee Relations.	Failed
1956	I-199	DS	Apportionment/ Redistricting	Legislative Reapportionment and Redistricting. [In 1957 the Legislature extensively amended this act by passing Chapter 289, Laws of 1947 by two-thirds approval of both branches of the Legislature.]	
1958	I-202	DS	Labor	Restricting Labor Agreements.	Failed
1958	I-23	IDS	Administration of Government	Civil service for sheriff's employees.	Passed
1960	I-205	DS	Alcohol Regulation	Authorizing tavern spirituous liquor licenses.	Failed
1960	I-207	DS	Administration of Government	Civil Service for State Employees.	Passed
1960	I-208	DS	Housing	Authorizing Joint Tenancies in Property.	Passed
1960	I-210	DS	Daylight Savings Time	Statewide Daylight Saving Time.	Passed
1960	I-25	IDS	Administration of Government	Dam construction and water diversion measure.	Passed
1962	I-211	DS	Apportionment/ Redistricting	State Legislature Reapportionment and Redistricting.	Failed
1964	I-215	DS	Environmental Reform	Marine Recreation Land Act.	Passed
1966	I-226	DS	Administration of Government	Cities Sharing Sales — Use Taxes.	Failed
1966	I-229	DS	Business Regulation	Repealing Sunday Activities Blue Law.	Passed
1966	I-233	DS	Utility Regulation	Repealing Freight Train Crew Law.	Passed
1968	I-242	DS	Legal	Drivers' Implied consent — Intoxication Tests.	Passed
1968	I-245	DS	Banking Reform	Reducing maximum retain service charges.	Passed
1968	I-32	IDS	Environmental Reform	Local processing of State timber.	Failed
1970	I-251	DS	Taxes	State Taxation — To Regulate Imposition.	Failed
1970	I-256	DS	Environmental Reform	Prohibiting certain nonrefundable beverage receptacles.	Failed
1972	I-258	DS	Gaming	Certain Cities — Greyhound Racing Franchises.	Failed
1972	I-261	DS	Alcohol Regulation	Liquor sales by licensed retailers.	Failed
1972	I-276	DS	Campaign Finance Reform	Establishes disclosure laws and other campaign finance regulations.	Passed
1972	I-40	IDS	Environmental Reform	Litter Control Act.	Passed

Year	Measure Number	Type	Subject Matter	Description	Pass/Fail
1972	I-43	IDS	Environmental Reform	Regulating Shoreline Use and Development.	Passed
1972	I-44	IDS	Taxes	Statutory Tax Limitation — 20 Mills.	Passed
1973	I-282	DS	Administration of Government	Shall state elected officials' salary increases be limited to 5.5% over 1965 levels, and judges' the same over 1972 levels?	Passed
1975	I-314	DS	Taxes	Shall corporations pay a 12% excise tax measured by income so that special school levies may be reduced or eliminated.	Failed
1975	I-316	DS	Death Penalty	Shall the death penalty be mandatory in the case of aggravated murder in the first degree?	Passed
1976	I-322	DS	Health/Medical	Shall fluoridation of public water supplies be made unlawful and violation subject to criminal penalties.	Failed
1976	I-325	DS	Nuclear weapons/ facilities/waste	Shall future nuclear power facilities which do not meet certain conditions and receive two-thirds approval by the legislature be prohibited.	Failed
1977	I-335	DS	Legal	Regulation of pornography.	Passed
1977	I-345	DS	Taxes	State, local sales and use taxes: food exemptions.	Passed
1977	I-348	DS	Taxes	Repeal of variable fuel tax.	Failed
1977	I-59	IDS	Administration of Government	Limit appropriations of public water: agriculture.	Passed
1978	I-350	DS	Education	Assignment of students to schools — prohibitions.	Passed
1979	I-61	IDS	Environmental Reform	Five cent refund on beverage containers.	Failed
1979	I-62	IDS	Taxes	State tax revenue limitation.	Passed
1980	I-383	DS	Nuclear weapons/ facilities/waste	Bans on radioactive wastes generated out of State.	Passed
1981	I-394	DS	Bonds	Voter approval: bonds for public energy projects.	Passed
1981	I-402	DS	Taxes	Abolition of state inheritance and gift tax.	Passed
1982	I-412	DS	Business Regulation	Maximum interest rate on retail sales.	Failed
1982	I-414	DS	Environmental Reform	Five cent refund on beverage containers.	Failed
1982	I-435	DS	Taxes	Sales, other business taxes replaced by franchise tax.	Failed
1984	I-456	M	Business Regulation	Petition Congress to de-commercialize steelhead.	Passed
1984	I-464	DS	Taxes	Trade-in values; sales tax computation.	Passed
1984	I-471	DS	Abortion	No public funding of abortions.	Failed
1986	I-90	IDS	Taxes	Sales/use tax for conservation, recreation programs.	Failed
1987	I-92	IDS	Welfare	Charges to Medicare patients; reasonable charges.	Failed

Year	Measure Number	Type	Subject Matter	Description	Pass/Fail
1988	I-518	DS	Labor	Minimum wage increases: include agricultural sector.	Passed
1989	I-102	IDS	Taxes	$360K new taxes for family services, K-12 education.	Failed
1990	I-547	DS	Environmental Reform	Growth and environmental protection goals, fees.	Failed
1991	I-119	IDS	Physician assisted suicide	Allows a mentally competent adult who is suffering from a terminal illness to request and obtain medication from a physician to end that patient's own life in a humane and dignified manner.	Failed
1991	I-120	IDS	Abortion	Revise abortion laws — a woman's right to choose.	Passed
1991	I-553	DS	Term Limits	Term limits on state and federal officers. 6/12	Failed
1991	I-559	DS	Taxes	Adjust property value for tax purposes.	Failed
1992	I-134	IDS	Campaign Finance Reform	Limit campaign contributions, funding, campaigns.	Passed
1992	I-573	DS	Term Limits	Term limits on state legislature 6/8, Governor, and Congress 6/12.	Passed
1993	I-593	DS	Legal	This measure imposes a "three strikes your out" rule for major criminal convictions.	Passed
1993	I-601	DS	Taxes	Limits state expenditures and provides for a popular vote on new taxes.	Passed
1993	I-602	DS	Taxes	This measure would limit state taxes and expenditures to a set formula, as well as repeal certain revenue measures.	Failed
1994	I-607	DS	Business Regulation	Shall persons other than dentists be licensed to make and sell dentures to the public, as regulated by a new state board of denture technology?	Passed
1995	I-640	DS	Environmental Reform	Regulation of state fishing	Failed
1995	I-651	DS	Gaming	Should gambling be allowed on Native American lands?	Failed
1996	I-173	DS	Education	Scholarship vouchers.	Failed
1996	I-177	DS	Education	Provides for publicly-funded charter schools	Failed
1996	I-655	DS	Animal Rights	Prohibits baiting of bear; prohibits hunting bear, cougar, bobcat or lynx with dogs.	Passed
1996	I-670	DS	Term Limits	Informed Voter Law.	Failed
1996	I-671	DS	Gaming	Allows limited electronic gaming on Indian lands	Failed
1997	I-673	DS	Health/Medical	Shall health insurance plans be regulated as to provision of services by designated health care providers, managed care provisions, and disclosure of certain plan information?	Failed

Year	Measure Number	Type	Subject Matter	Description	Pass/Fail
1997	I-676	DS	Gun Regulation	Shall the transfer of handguns without trigger-locking devices be prohibited and persons possessing or acquiring a hand gun be required to obtain a handgun safety license?	Failed
1997	I-677	DS,	Civil Rights	Shall discrimination based on sexual orientation be prohibited in employment, employment agency, and union membership practices, without requiring employee partner benefits or preferential treatment?	Failed
1997	I-678	DS	Business Regulation	Shall dental hygienist who obtain a special license endorsement be permitted to perform designated dental hygiene services without the supervision of a licensed dentist?	Failed
1997	I-685	DS	Drug Policy Reform	Shall penalties for drug possession and drug-related violent crime be revised, medical use of Schedule I controlled substances be permitted, and a drug prevention commission established?	Failed
1998	I-200	IDS	Civil Rights	Would prohibit state and local government entities from discriminating against or granting preferential treatment to any individual or group based on race and sex and color and ethnicity or national origin.	Passed
1998	I-688	DS	Labor	Would increase the minimum wage for workers eighteen years and older.	Passed
1998	I-692	DS	Drug Policy Reform	Would permit the medical use of marijuana by patients with certain terminal or debilitating conditions.	Passed
1998	I-694	DS	Abortion	Would make it a felony to kill a fetus in the "process of birth" except when such procedure is the only way to prevent death of the mother.	Failed
1999	I-695	DS	Taxes	This measure would establish license tab fees at $30 per year for motor vehicles. No new taxes without vote of people.	Passed
1999	I-696	DS	Environmental Reform	Prohibit certain commercial net, troll, and trawl fishing in fresh and marine waters, except tribal treaty fisheries.	Failed
2000	I-713	DS	Animal Rights	This measure would make it a gross misdemeanor to capture an animal with a steel-jawed leg hold trap, neck snare, or other body-gripping trap.	Passed
2000	I-722	DS	Taxes	This measure would declare null and void tax and fee increases adopted without voter approval by state and local governments between July 2, 1999, and December 31, 1999.	Passed
2000	I-728	DS	Education	This measure would direct that certain existing state revenue, including all unobligated lottery revenue, be placed in a student achievement fund and in the education construction fund.	Passed

Year	Measure Number	Type	Subject Matter	Description	Pass/Fail
2000	I-729	DS	Education	This measure would authorize school districts and public universities to sponsor charter public schools.	Failed
2000	I-732	DS	Education	This measure would provide annual cost-of-living salary adjustments to school district employees.	Passed
2000	I-745	DS	Taxes	This measure would require that 90% of state and local transportation funds, including local transit taxes bus excluding ferry and transit fares, be spent on road construction, improvement, and maintenance. Road and lane construction and maintenance would be the top transportation priority.	Failed
2001	I-747	DS	Taxes	This measure would establish new "limit factors" for taxing districts in setting their property tax levies each year.	Passed
2001	I-773	DS	Taxes	This measure would impose an additional sales tax on cigarettes and a surtax on wholesaled tobacco products.	Passed
2001	I-775	DS	Health/Medical	Creates a "home care quality authority" to establish qualifications, standards, accountability, training, referral and employment relations for publicly funded individual providers of in-home care services.	Passed

Washington State Constitution

Article II

Legislative Department

Section 1 Legislative Powers, Where Vested.

The legislative authority of the state of Washington shall be vested in the legislature, consisting of a senate and house of representatives, which shall be called the legislature of the state of Washington, but the people reserve to themselves the power to propose bills, laws, and to enact or reject the same at the polls, independent of the legislature, and also reserve power, at their own option, to approve or reject at the polls any act, item, section, or part of any bill, act, or law passed by the legislature.

a. Initiative: The first power reserved by the people is the initiative. Every such petition shall include the full text of the measure so proposed. In the case of initiatives to the legislature and initiatives to the people, the number of valid signatures of legal voters required shall be equal to eight percent of the votes cast for the office of governor at the last gubernatorial election preceding the initial filing of the text of the initiative measure with the secretary of state.

Initiative petitions shall be filed with the secretary of state not less than four months before the election at which they are to be voted upon, or not less than ten days before any regular session of the legislature. If filed at least four months before the election at which they are to be voted upon, he shall submit the same to the vote of the people at the said election. If such petitions are filed not less than ten days before any regular session of the legislature, he shall certify the results within forty days of the filing. If certification is not complete by the date that the legislature convenes, he shall provisionally certify the measure pending final certification of the measure. Such initiative measures, whether certified or provisionally certified, shall take precedence over all other measures in the legislature except appropriation bills and shall be either enacted or rejected without change or amendment by the legislature before the end of such regular session. If any such initiative measures shall be enacted by the legislature it shall be subject to the referendum petition, or it may be enacted and referred by the legislature to the people for approval or rejection at the next regular election. If it is rejected or if no action is taken upon it by the legislature before the end of such regular session, the secretary of state shall submit it to the people for approval or rejection at the next ensuing regular general election. The legislature may reject any measure so proposed by initiative petition and propose a different one dealing with the same subject, and in such event both measures shall be submitted by the secretary of state to the people for approval or rejection at the next ensuing regular general election. When conflicting measures are submitted to the people the ballots shall be so printed that a voter can express separately by making one cross (X) for each, two preferences, first, as between either measure and neither, and secondly, as between one and the other. If the majority of those voting on the first issue is for neither, both fail, but in that case the votes on the second issue shall nevertheless be carefully counted and made public. If a majority voting on the first issue is for either, then the measure receiving a majority of the votes on the second issue shall be law.

b. Referendum. The second power reserved by the people is the referendum, and it may be ordered on any act, bill, law, or any part thereof passed by the legislature, except such laws as may be necessary for the immediate preservation of the public peace, health or safety, support of the state government and its existing public institutions, either by petition signed by the required percentage of the legal voters, or by the legislature as other bills are enacted: Provided, That the legislature may not order a referendum on any initiative measure enacted by the legislature under the foregoing subsection (a). The number of valid signatures of registered voters required on a petition for referendum of an act of the legislature or any part thereof, shall be equal to or exceeding four percent of the votes cast for the office of governor at the last gubernatorial election preceding the filing of the text of the referendum measure with the secretary of state.

c. No act, law, or bill subject to referendum shall take effect until ninety days after the adjournment of the session at which it was enacted. No act, law, or bill approved by a majority of the electors voting thereon shall be amended or repealed by the legislature within a period of two years following such enactment: Provided, That any such act, law, or bill may be amended within two years after such enactment at any regular or special session of the legislature by a vote of two-thirds of all the members elected to each house with full compliance with section 12, Article III, of the Washington Constitution, and no amendatory law adopted in accordance with this provision shall be subject to referendum. But such enactment may be amended or repealed at any general regular or special election by direct vote of the people thereon.

d. The filing of a referendum petition against one or more items, sections, or parts of any act, law, or bill shall not delay the remainder of the measure from becoming operative. Referendum petitions against measures passed by the legislature shall be filed with the secretary of state not later than ninety days after the final adjournment of the session of the legislature which passed the measure on which the referendum is demanded. The veto power of the governor shall not extend to measures initiated by or referred to the people. All elections on measures referred to the people of the state shall be had at the next succeeding regular general election following the filing of the measure with the secretary of state, except when the legislature shall order a special election. Any measure initiated by the people or referred to the people as herein provided shall take effect and become the law if it is approved by a majority of the votes cast thereon: Provided, That the vote cast upon such question or measure shall equal one-third of the total votes cast at such election and not otherwise. Such measure shall be in operation on and after the thirtieth day after the election at which it is approved. The style of all bills proposed by initiative petition shall be: "Be it enacted by the people of the State of Washington." This section shall not be construed to deprive any member of the legislature of the right to introduce any measure. All such petitions shall be filed with the secretary of state, who shall be guided by the general laws in submitting the same to the people until additional legislation shall especially provide therefor. This section is self-executing, but legislation may be enacted especially to facilitate its operation.

The legislature shall provide methods of publicity of all laws or parts of laws, and amendments to the Constitution referred to the people with arguments for and against the laws and amendments so referred. The secretary of state shall send one copy of the publication to each individual place of residence in the state and shall make such additional distribution as he shall determine necessary to reasonably assure that each voter will have an opportunity to study the measures prior to election. [AMENDMENT 72, 1981 Substitute Senate Joint Resolution No. 133, p 1796. Approved November 3, 1981.]

Washington State Statutes

RCW 29.79.010 Filing proposed measures with secretary of state.

If any legal voter of the state, either individually or on behalf of an organization, desires to petition the legislature to enact a proposed measure, or submit a proposed initiative measure to the people, or order that a referendum of all or part of any act, bill, or law, passed by the legislature be submitted to the people, he or she shall file with the secretary of state a typewritten copy of the measure proposed, or the act or part of such act on which a referendum is desired, accompanied by an affidavit that the proposer is a legal voter and a filing fee prescribed under RCW 43.07.120, as now or hereafter amended.

RCW 29.79.015 Review of initiative measures by code reviser's office — Certificate of review required for assignment of serial number.

Upon receipt of any petition proposing an initiative to the people or an initiative to the legislature, and prior to giving a serial number thereto, the secretary of state shall submit a copy thereof to the office of the code reviser and give notice to the petitioner of such transmittal. Upon receipt of the measure, the assistant code reviser to whom it has been assigned may confer with the petitioner and shall within seven working days from receipt thereof review the proposal for matters of form and style, and such matters of substantive import as may be agreeable to the petitioner, and shall recommend to the petitioner such revision or alteration of the measure as may be deemed necessary and appropriate. The recommendations of the reviser's office shall be advisory only, and the petitioner may accept or reject them in whole or in part. The code reviser shall issue a certificate of review certifying that he has reviewed the measure for form and style and that the recommendations thereon, if any, have been communicated to the petitioner, and such certificate shall issue whether or not the petitioner accepts such recommendations. Within fifteen working days after notification of submittal of the petition to the reviser's office, the petitioner, if he desires to proceed with his sponsorship, shall file the measure together with the certificate of review with the secretary of state for assignment of serial number and the secretary of state shall thereupon submit to the reviser's office a certified copy of the measure filed. Upon submitting the proposal to the secretary of state for assignment of a serial number the secretary of state shall refuse to make such assignment unless the proposal is accompanied by a certificate of review.

RCW 29.79.020 Time for filing various types.

Initiative measures proposed to be submitted to the people must be filed with the secretary of state within ten months prior to the election at which they are to be submitted, and the petitions therefor must be filed with the secretary of state not less than four months before the next general state-wide election.

Initiative measures proposed to be submitted to the legislature must be filed with the secretary of state within ten months prior to the next regular session of the legislature at which they are to be submitted and the petitions therefor must be filed with the secretary of state not less than ten days before such regular session of the legislature.

A petition ordering that any act or part thereof passed by the legislature be referred to the people must be filed with the secretary of state within ninety days after the final adjournment of the legislative session at which the act was passed. It may be submitted at the next general state-wide election or at a special election ordered by the legislature.

A proposed initiative or referendum measure may be filed no earlier than the opening of the secretary of state's office for business pursuant to RCW 42.04.060 on the first day filings are permitted, and any initiative or referendum petition must be filed not later than the close of business on the last business day in the specified period for submission of signatures. If a filing deadline falls on a Saturday, the office of the secretary of state shall be open on that Saturday for the transaction of business under this section from 8:00 a.m. to 5:00 p.m. on that Saturday.

RCW 29.79.030 Numbering — Transmittal to attorney general.

The secretary of state shall give a serial number to each initiative or referendum measure, using a separate series for initiatives to the legislature, initiatives to the people, and referendum measures, and forthwith transmit one copy of the measure proposed bearing its serial number to the attorney general. Thereafter a measure shall be known and designated on all petitions, ballots, and proceedings as "Initiative Measure No. ...." or "Referendum Measure No. ....".

RCW 29.79.035 Ballot title — Formulation, ballot display.

(1) The ballot title for an initiative to the people, an initiative to the legislature, a referendum bill, or a referendum measure consists of: (a) A statement of the subject of the measure; (b) a concise description of the measure; and (c) a question in the form prescribed in this section for the ballot measure in question. The statement of the subject of a measure must be sufficiently broad to reflect the subject of the measure, sufficiently precise to give notice of the measure's subject matter, and not exceed ten words. The concise description must contain no more than thirty words, be a true and impartial description of the measure's essential contents, clearly identify the proposition to be voted on, and not, to the extent reasonably possible, create prejudice either for or against the measure.
(2) For an initiative to the people, or for an initiative to the legislature for which the legislature has not proposed an alternative, the ballot title must be displayed on the ballot substantially as follows:

"Initiative Measure No. ... concerns (statement of subject). This measure would (concise description). Should this measure be enacted into law?"
Yes ....
No ....

STATE-BY-STATE HISTORY AND OVERVIEW: WASHINGTON

(3) For an initiative to the legislature for which the legislature has proposed an alternative, the ballot title must be displayed on the ballot substantially as follows:

Initiative Measure Nos. ... and ... B concern (statement of subject).
Initiative Measure No. ... would (concise description).

As an alternative, the legislature has proposed Initiative Measure No. ... B, which would (concise description).
1.   Should either of these measures be enacted into law?
Yes ....
No ....
2.   Regardless of whether you voted yes or no above, if one of these measures is enacted, which one should it be?
Measure No ....
Or
Measure No ....

(4) For a referendum bill submitted to the people by the legislature, the ballot issue must be displayed on the ballot substantially as follows:

The legislature has passed .... Bill No. ... concerning (statement of subject). This bill would (concise description). Should this bill be:
Approved ....
Rejected ....

(5) For a referendum measure by state voters on a bill the legislature has passed, the ballot issue must be displayed on the ballot substantially as follows:

The legislature passed ... Bill No. ... concerning (statement of subject) and voters have filed a sufficient referendum petition on this bill. This bill would (concise description). Should this bill be:
Approved ....
Rejected ....

(6) The legislature may specify the statement of subject or concise description, or both, in a referendum bill that it refers to the people. The legislature may specify the concise description for an alternative it submits for an initiative to the legislature. If the legislature fails to specify these matters, the attorney general shall prepare the material that was not specified. The statement of subject and concise description as so provided must be included as part of the ballot title unless changed on appeal.

The attorney general shall specify the statement of subject and concise description for an initiative to the people, an initiative to the legislature, and a referendum measure. The statement of subject and concise description as so provided must be included as part of the ballot title unless changed on appeal.

RCW 29.79.040 Ballot title and summary — Formulation by attorney general.

Within five days after the receipt of an initiative or referendum the attorney general shall formulate the ballot title, or portion of the ballot title that the legislature has not provided, required by RCW 29.79.035 and a summary of the measure, not to exceed seventy-five words, and transmit the serial number for the measure, complete ballot title, and summary to the secretary of state. Saturdays, Sundays, and legal holidays are not counted in calculating the time limits in this section.

RCW 29.79.050 Ballot title and summary — Notice.

Upon the filing of the ballot title and summary for a state initiative or referendum measure in the office of secretary of state, the secretary of state shall notify by telephone and by mail, and, if requested, by other electronic means, the person proposing the measure, the prime sponsor of a referendum bill or alternative to an initiative to the legislature, the chief clerk of the house of representatives, the secretary of the senate, and any other individuals who have made written request for such notification of the exact language of the ballot title and summary.

RCW 29.79.060 Ballot title and summary — Appeal to superior court.

Any persons, including the attorney general or either or both houses of the legislature, dissatisfied with the ballot title or summary for a state initiative or referendum may, within five days from the filing of the ballot title in the office of the secretary of state appeal to the superior court of Thurston county by petition setting forth the measure, the ballot title or summary, and their objections to the ballot title or summary and requesting amendment of the ballot title or summary by the court. Saturdays, Sundays, and legal holidays are not counted in calculating the time limits contained in this section.

A copy of the petition on appeal together with a notice that an appeal has been taken shall be served upon the secretary of state, upon the attorney general, and upon the person proposing the measure if the appeal is initiated by someone other than that person. Upon the filing of the petition on appeal or at the time to which the hearing may be adjourned by consent of the appellant, the court shall accord first priority to examining the proposed measure, the ballot title or summary, and the objections to that ballot title or summary, may hear arguments, and shall, within five days, render its decision and file with the secretary of state a certified copy of such ballot title or summary as it determines will meet the requirements of RCW 29.79.040. The decision of the superior court shall be final. Such appeal shall be heard without costs to either party.

RCW 29.79.070 Ballot title and summary — Mailed to proponents and other persons — Appearance on petitions.

When the ballot title and summary are finally established, the secretary of state shall file the instrument establishing it with the proposed measure and transmit a copy thereof by mail to the person proposing the measure, the chief clerk of the house of representatives, the secretary of the senate, and to any other individuals who have made written request for such notification. Thereafter such ballot title shall be the title of the measure in all petitions, ballots, and other proceedings in relation thereto. The summary shall appear on all petitions directly following the ballot title.

RCW 29.79.075 Fiscal impact statements.

The office of financial management, in consultation with the secretary of state, the attorney general, and any other appropriate state or local agency, shall prepare a fiscal impact statement for each of the following state ballot measures: (1) An initiative to the people that is certified to the ballot; (2) an initiative to the legislature that will appear on the ballot; (3) an alternative measure appearing on the ballot that the legislature proposes to an initiative to the legislature; (4) a referendum bill referred to voters by the legislature; and (5) a referendum measure appearing on the ballot. Fiscal impact statements must be written in clear and concise language and avoid legal and technical terms when possible, and may include easily understood graphics.

A fiscal impact statement must describe any projected increase or decrease in revenues, costs, expenditures, or indebtedness that the state or local governments will experience if the ballot measure were approved by state voters. Where appropriate, a fiscal impact statement may include both estimated dollar amounts and a description placing the estimated dollar amounts into context. A fiscal impact statement must include both a summary of not to exceed one hundred words and a more detailed statement that includes the assumptions that were made to develop the fiscal impacts.

Fiscal impact statements must be available online from the secretary of state's web site and included in the state voters' pamphlet.

RCW 29.79.080 Petitions — Paper — Size — Contents.

The person proposing the measure shall print blank petitions upon single sheets of paper of good writing quality (including but not limited to newsprint) not less than eleven inches in width and not less than fourteen inches in length. Each petition at the time of circulating, signing, and filing with the secretary of state shall consist of not more than one sheet with numbered lines for not more than twenty signatures, with the prescribed warning and title, shall be in the form required by RCW 29.79.090, 29.79.100, or 29.79.110, as now or hereafter amended, and shall have a full, true, and correct copy of the proposed measure referred to therein printed on the reverse side of the petition.

RCW 29.79.090 Petitions to legislature — Form.

Petitions for proposing measures for submission to the legislature at its next regular session, shall be substantially in the following form:

WARNING

Every person who signs this petition with any other than his or her true name, knowingly signs more than one of these petitions, signs this petition when he or she is not a legal voter, or makes any false statement on this petition may be punished by fine or imprisonment or both.

INITIATIVE PETITION FOR SUBMISSION TO THE LEGISLATURE

To the Honorable . . . . . ., Secretary of State of the State of Washington:

We, the undersigned citizens and legal voters of the State of Washington, respectfully direct that this petition and the proposed measure known as Initiative Measure No. . . . . and entitled (here set forth the established ballot title of the measure), a full, true, and correct copy of which is printed on the reverse side of this petition, be transmitted to the legislature of the State of Washington at its next ensuing regular session, and we respectfully petition the legislature to enact said proposed measure into law; and each of us for himself or herself says: I have personally signed this petition; I am a legal voter of the State of Washington in the city (or town) and county written after my name, my residence address is correctly stated, and I have knowingly signed this petition only once.

Petitioners Signature / Print name for positive identification / Residence address, street and number if any / City or Town / County
(Here follow 20 numbered lines divided into columns for each category above)

RCW 29.79.100 Petitions to people — Form.

Petitions for proposing measures for submission to the people for their approval or rejection at the next ensuing general election, shall be substantially in the following form:

WARNING
Every person who signs this petition with any other than his or her true name, knowingly signs more than one of these petitions, signs this petition when he or she is not a legal voter, or makes any false statement on this petition may be punished by fine or imprisonment or both.

INITIATIVE PETITION FOR SUBMISSION TO THE PEOPLE
To the Honorable . . . . . ., Secretary of State of the State of Washington:

We, the undersigned citizens and legal voters of the State of Washington, respectfully direct that the proposed measure known as Initiative Measure No. . . . ., entitled (here insert the established ballot title of the measure), a full, true and correct copy of which is printed on the reverse side of this petition, be submitted to the legal voters of the State of Washington for their approval or rejection at the general election to be held on the . . . . . day of November, 19. . .; and each of us for himself or herself says: I have personally signed this petition; I am a legal voter of the State of Washington, in the city (or town) and county written after my name, my residence address is correctly stated, and I have knowingly signed this petition only once.

Petitioners Signature / Print name for positive identification / Residence address, street and number if any / City or Town / County
(Here follow 20 numbered lines divided into columns for each category above)

RCW 29.79.110 Referendum petitions — Form.

Petitions ordering that acts or parts of acts passed by the legislature be referred to the people at the next ensuing general election, or special election ordered by the legislature, shall be substantially in the following form:

WARNING
Every person who signs this petition with any other than his or her true name, knowingly signs more than one of these petitions, signs this petition when he or she is not a legal voter, or makes any false statement on this petition may be punished by fine or imprisonment or both.

PETITION FOR REFERENDUM

To the Honorable . . . . . ., Secretary of State of the State of Washington:

We, the undersigned citizens and legal voters of the State of Washington, respectfully order and direct that Referendum Measure No. ....., filed to revoke a (or part or parts of a) bill that (concise statement required by RCW 29.79.055) and that was passed by the ...... legislature of the State of Washington at the last regular (special) session of said legislature, shall be referred to the people of the state for their approval or rejection at the regular (special) election to be held on the .... day of November, 19...; and each of us for himself or herself says: I have personally signed this petition; I am a legal voter of the State of Washington, in the city (or town) and county written after my name, my residence address is correctly stated, and I have knowingly signed this petition only once.

Petitioners Signature / Print name for positive identification / Residence address, street and number if any / City or Town / County
(Here follow 20 numbered lines divided into columns for each category above)

RCW 29.79.115 Warning statement — Further requirements.

The word "warning" and the warning statement regarding signing petitions that must appear on petitions as prescribed by RCW 29.79.090, 29.79.100, and 29.79.110 shall be printed on each petition sheet such that they occupy not less than four square inches of the front of the petition sheet.

RCW 29.79.120 Petitions — Signatures — Number necessary.

When the person proposing any initiative measure has secured upon such initiative petition a number of signatures of legal voters equal to or exceeding eight percent of the votes cast for the office of governor at the last regular gubernatorial election prior to the submission of the signatures for verification, or when the person or organization demanding any referendum of an act of the legislature or any part thereof has secured upon any such referendum petition a number of signatures of legal voters equal to or exceeding four percent of the votes cast for the office of governor at the last regular gubernatorial election prior to the submission of the signatures for verification, he or they may submit the petition to the secretary of state for filing.

RCW 29.79.140 Petitions — Time for filing.

The time for submitting initiative or referendum petitions to the secretary of state for filing is as follows:
(1) A referendum petition ordering and directing that the whole or some part or parts of an act passed by the legislature be referred to the people for their approval or rejection at the next ensuing general election or a special election ordered by the legislature, must be submitted not more than ninety days after the final adjournment of the session of the legislature which passed the act;
(2) An initiative petition proposing a measure to be submitted to the people for their approval or rejection at the next ensuing general election, must be submitted not less than four months before the date of such election;
(3) An initiative petition proposing a measure to be submitted to the legislature at its next ensuing regular session must be submitted not less than ten days before the commencement of the session.

The Basic Steps to Do an Initiative in Washington

Statutes Only — Direct and Indirect Initiative Process

Basic procedures: The sponsor must file a printed or typewritten copy of the complete text of the proposed initiative or referendum with the Secretary of State. The sponsor must include an affidavit of sponsorship and a five-dollar ($5.00) filing fee. Each measure, when filed with the Secretary of State, must be accompanied by a sworn affidavit that the sponsor is a legal voter of the state. (Affidavits are available from the state.) The sponsor of an initiative should contact and file with the Public Disclosure Commission in conjunction with the preliminary filing of the initiative language.

There are two types of initiatives: 1) **Initiatives to the People:** Initiatives to the people, if certified to have sufficient signatures, are submitted for a vote of the people at the next state general election and 2) **Initiatives to the Legislature:** Initiatives to the Legislature, if certified, are submitted to the Legislature at its regular session each January. Once submitted, the Legislature must take one of the following three actions: a) the Legislature can adopt the initiative as proposed, in which case it becomes law without a vote of the people; b) the Legislature can reject or refuse to act on the proposed initiative, in which case the initiative must be placed on the ballot at the next state general election; or c) the Legislature can approve an amended version of the proposed initiative, in which case both the amended version and the original proposal must be placed on the next state general election ballot.

Date initiative language can be submitted to state for the 2001 or 2002 election: *Initiatives to the people* must be filed within 10 months prior to the next state general election, and the petitions (signatures) must be filed not less than 4 months before such general election. *Initiatives to the Legislature* must be filed within 10 months prior to the next regular session of the Legislature, and the petitions (signatures) must be filed not less than 10 days before such regular session of the Legislature.

Signatures are tied to vote of which office: Governor

Next Gubernatorial election: 2004

Votes cast for governor in last election: 2,469,852 (2000)

Net number of signatures required: 8% of votes cast for Governor in last gubernatorial election for both direct and indirect initiatives. (197,588).

Distribution requirement: None.

Circulation period: For initiatives to the people—6 months and for initiatives to the Legislature it is 10 months.

Do circulators have to be residents: No

Date when signatures are due for certification: Petitions supporting an initiative to the people must be filed with the Secretary of State no later than four (4) months before the date of the state general election (first week of July 2001 and 2002) and petitions supporting an **initiative to the Legislature** must be filed with the Secretary of State no later than 10 days before a regular session of the Legislature convenes (Early January 2001 for 2001 general election and early January 2002 for 2002 general election.) Petitions must be filed not later than the close of business (5:00 p.m.) on the last business day in the specified period for submission of signatures. If a filing deadline falls on a Saturday, the office of the Secretary of State will be open on that Saturday for the transaction of business from 8:00 am to 5:00 p.m.

Signature verification process: Random sampling

Single-subject restriction: Yes

Legislative tampering: The legislature can repeal or amend an initiative by a ⅔ vote of each house during the first 2 years of enactment, majority vote thereafter.

General comments: Following is a more detailed outline of what occurs once the initiative language is filed:
1) A copy of the text of a proposed initiative is sent to the office of the Code Reviser by the Secretary of State immediately after filing. The Code Reviser must, within seven (7) **working** days, perform the following:
a) Review the draft for technical errors and style;
b) Advise the sponsor of any potential conflicts between the proposal and existing statutes; and
c) Return the proposal with a "certificate of review" to the sponsor with any recommended changes. All changes made by the Code Reviser are advisory and are subject to approval by the sponsor.
2) The sponsor has 15 **working** days after the submittal of the initiative to the Code Reviser to file the final draft of the measure, accompanied by the Code Reviser's certificate of review, with the Secretary of State. If the sponsor has made changes in the final draft as prepared by the Code Reviser, those changes should be initialed by the sponsor prior to filing that draft with the Secretary of State. At this point, the Secretary of State will assign a serial number to the proposal and forward the initiative measure to the office of the Attorney General for formulation of the ballot title and summary. Referendum measures are **not** reviewed by the Code Reviser; they are immediately assigned a serial number and transmitted to the Attorney General.
3) Upon receipt of a proposed ballot measure, the Attorney General has seven (7) **calendar** days to formulate and return a ballot title and a summary to the Secretary of State. The **ballot title** for initiatives must be no more than 20 words, phrased as a question, and impartial and non-argumentative in nature; the **ballot summary** must be no more than 75 words and impartial and non-argumentative in nature. Immediately after receiving the ballot title and summary, the Secretary of State must notify the sponsor by telephone and by mail of the wording of the ballot title. Any person dissatis-

fied with either the ballot title or summary prepared by the Attorney General may seek judicial review of those statements by petitioning the Thurston County Superior Court in Olympia. Such action must be taken within five (5) days of the filing of those statements with the Secretary of State and the court is required to expeditiously review the statements and render a decision within five (5) days. The decision of the court is final. After filing the proposal and obtaining an official serial number and a ballot title and summary, the sponsor of an initiative or referendum measure may print signature petition sheets (sheets are printed at the sponsor's own expense). The Secretary of State may reject any petition that does not meet statutory requirements. The statute requires:

a) Petitions must be printed on sheets of good quality paper. (Petitions printed on newsprint will be accepted by the Secretary of State, assuming other statutory requirements are met.)

b) The petition sheets must measure not less than 11 inches in width and not less than 14 inches in length.

c) In addition, the following must be printed on the **front** of each petition sheet:

i) The official ballot title and summary as prepared by the Attorney General;

ii) The serial number assigned by the Secretary of State;

iii) The heading specified by RCW 29.79.090, 29.79.100 or 29.79.110;

iv) Not more than 20 numbered lines, each with space for a voter's signature, his/her printed name and his/her legal voting address; and

v) The following warning, which must occupy not less than four (4) square inches: "Every person who signs this petition with any other than his or her true name, knowingly signs more than one of these petitions, signs this petition when he or she is not a legal voter or makes any false statement on this petition may be punished by fine or imprisonment or both."

vi) The **full text** of the measure must also appear on the petition. To verify the signatures on any petition, the Secretary of State must be able to ascertain that the signer, at the time of signing the petition, had the opportunity to read the complete text of the measure.

West Virginia

A state senator (Campbell) introduced an initiative and referendum bill in 1907, and a state delegate (Williams) introduced one in 1908. Both were defeated. In 1915, Governor Hatfield called for I&R in his annual message to the legislature, but his words went unheeded. The biggest obstacle to I&R in the Progressive era was probably the corporate-backed Republican Party's domination of West Virginia politics, which lasted from 1896 to 1932. Still, the state's I&R advocates were not without success, for a 1917 chart in the I&R movement organ *Equity* indicated that the legislature had passed "special acts" granting I&R rights to residents of some (unidentified) local jurisdictions.

West Virginia Constitution

The state does not have the statewide initiative process and so therefore the following provisions discuss the procedures used by the state legislature to place constitutional amendments on the ballot.

Article XIV

CON 14-1. Amendments.

No convention shall be called, having the authority to alter the constitution of the state, unless it be in pursuance of law, passed by the affirmative vote of a majority of the members elected to each house of the Legislature and providing that polls shall be opened throughout the state, on the same day therein specified, which shall not be less than three months after the passage of such law, for the purpose of taking the sense of the voters on the question of calling a convention. And such convention shall not be held unless a majority of the votes cast at such polls be in favor of calling the same; nor shall the members be elected to such convention, until, at least, one month after the result of the vote shall be duly ascertained, declared and published. And all acts and ordinances of the said convention shall be submitted to the voters of the State for ratification or rejection, and shall have no validity whatever until they are ratified.

CON 14-2. How amendments are made.

Any amendment to the constitution of the state may be proposed in either house of the Legislature at any regular or extra-ordinary session thereof; and if the same, being read on three several days in each house, be agreed to on its third reading, by two thirds of the members elected thereto, the proposed amendment, with the yeas and nays thereon, shall be entered on the journals, and it shall be the duty of the Legislature to provide by law for submitting the same to the voters of the state for rat-ification or rejection, at a special election, or at the next general election thereafter, and cause the same to be published, at least three months before such election in some newspaper in every county in which a newspaper is printed. If a majority of the qualified voters, voting on the question at the polls held pursuant to such law, ratify the proposed amendment, it shall be in force from the time of such ratification, as part of the constitution of the state. If two or more amendments be submitted at the same time, the vote on the ratification or rejection shall be taken on each separately, but an amendment may relate to a single subject or to related subject matters and may amend or modify as many articles and as many sections of the consti-tution as may be necessary and appropriate in order to accomplish the objectives of the amendment. Whenever one or more amendments are submitted at a special election, no other question, issue or matter shall be voted upon at such special elec-tion, and the cost of such special election throughout the state shall be paid out of the state treasury.

Wisconsin

The name Wisconsin is practically synonymous with Progressivism, yet this state has never had a statewide initiative and referendum process. Indeed, it is one of only three states where voters turned down their opportunity to get it (Texas and Rhode Island are the others). The circumstances were as follows.

In 1907 Lieutenant Governor W. D. Connor and State Senator W. D. Brazeau took up the cause and secured approval in the state senate by a 19 to 5 vote, but lost in the lower house. The Progressive reformers had been in power since 1900 and had enacted a host of reforms, but I&R was apparently not a priority.

Any state constitutional amendment needed to pass both houses by a three-fifths majority in two successive sessions of the legislature, with an election in between. Only then, after two years or more, could it be put on the ballot for rati-fication by the voters. The I&R amendment finally passed both houses in the 1911-1912 legislature with the support of Governor Francis E. McGovern, U.S. Senator Robert M. La Follette and his Progressive Republican followers, and the state's Socialists. It passed again in the 1913-1914 legislature, and was placed on the November 1914 ballot.

After 13 years in power, the Progressives had become overconfident. In the 1913 legislature, they passed a series of big tax increases to finance an ambitious public works program, as well as giving final approval to a constitutional amend-ment raising their salaries. This amendment went on the November 1914 ballot along with the I&R amendment and eight others, including one to allow recall of all state elected officers except judges.

After paying the higher taxes in 1914, the voters had had their fill of the liberal reformers and all their works. The amendments on the 1914 ballot offered an easy target for the voters' wrath. Leading candidates of both major parties damned all the amendments, without informing voters that the initiative, referendum, and recall amendments offered just the mechanism they needed to block legislation they deplored. The state Democratic convention that year disap-proved I&R in its platform, and Republican gubernatorial candidate Emmanuel L. Phillipp also urged voters to reject I&R.

On Election Day, all 10 amendments were defeated overwhelmingly. The voters discriminated hardly at all between them: the least popular amendments won 26 percent approval; the most popular, 38 percent. The I&R amendment and the recall amendment were approved by 36 percent of the voters. Because they decided to vote "no" on everything, Wis-consin voters in 1914 denied themselves the right to vote on issues of their choice.

Wisconsin Constitution

The state does not have the statewide initiative process and so therefore the following provisions discuss the procedures used by the state legislature to place constitutional amendments on the ballot.

Article XII, §1 Constitutional Amendments.

Any amendment or amendments to this constitution may be proposed in either house of the legislature, and if the same shall be agreed to by a majority of the members elected to each of the two houses, such proposed amendment or amendments shall be entered on their journals, with the yeas and nays taken thereon, and referred to the legislature to be chosen at the next general election, and shall be published for three months previous to the time of holding such election; and if, in the legislature so next chosen, such proposed amendment or amendments shall be agreed to by a majority of all the members elected to each house, then it shall be the duty of the legislature to submit such proposed amendment or amendments to the people in such manner and at such time as the legislature shall prescribe; and if the people shall approve and ratify such amendment or amendments by a majority of the electors voting thereon, such amendment or amendments shall become part of the constitution; provided, that if more than one amendment be submitted, they shall be submitted in such manner that the people may vote for or against such amendments separately.

Article XII, §1 — ANNOT.

It is within the discretion of the legislature to submit several distinct propositions to the electorate as one constitutional amendment if they relate to the same subject matter and are designed to accomplish one general purpose. Milwaukee Alliance v. Elections Board, 106 Wis. 2d 593, 317 N.W.2d 420 (1982).

Article XII, §1 — ANNOT.

The several propositions contained in the amendment to sec. 7, art. VIII, are dependent upon or connected with each other and are all related to the single subject of authorizing limited state debt. Under such circumstances the several propositions were properly submitted to the people as a single amendment. 58 Atty. Gen. 194.

Article XII, §1 — ANNOT.

1971 Enrolled Joint Resolution 26 includes 2 propositions that may be submitted to the electors as one amendment to the Wisconsin Constitution. 63 Atty. Gen. 28.

Article XII, §1 — ANNOT.

The taking of yea and nay votes and the entry on the journals of the senate and assembly can be complied with by recording the total aye vote together with a listing of the names of those legislators who voted no, were absent or not voting or were paired on the question. Art. V, sec. 10; Art. VIII, sec. 8; Art. XII, sec. 1 discussed. 63 Atty. Gen. 346.

Article XII, §1 — ANNOT.

The legislature must resubmit a proposed amendment to the people where previous referendum was voided by court order, notwithstanding an appeal there from. 65 Atty. Gen. 42.

Article XII, §2 Constitutional conventions.

If at any time a majority of the senate and assembly shall deem it necessary to call a convention to revise or change this constitution, they shall recommend to the electors to vote for or against a convention at the next election for members of the legislature. And if it shall appear that a majority of the electors voting thereon have voted for a convention, the legislature shall, at its next session, provide for calling such convention.

Wisconsin Statutes

9.20

Direct legislation.

(1) A number of electors equal to at least 15% of the votes cast for governor at the last general election in their city or village may sign and file a petition with the city or village clerk requesting that an attached proposed ordinance or resolution, without alteration, either be adopted by the common council or village board or be referred to a vote of the electors. The individual filing the petition on behalf of the electors shall designate in writing an individual to be notified of any insufficiency or improper form under sub. (3).
(2) The preparation and form of the direct legislation petition shall be governed by s. 8.40.
(2m) After the petition has been offered for filing, no name may be erased or removed. No signature may be considered valid or counted unless the date is less than 60 days before the date offered for filing.
(3) Within 15 days after the petition is filed, the clerk shall determine by careful examination whether the petition is sufficient and whether the proposed ordinance or resolution is in proper form. The clerk shall state his or her findings in a signed and dated certificate attached to the petition. If the petition is found to be insufficient or the proposed ordinance

or resolution is not in proper form, the certificate shall give the particulars, stating the insufficiency or improper form. The petition may be amended to correct any insufficiency or the proposed ordinance or resolution may be put in proper form within 10 days following the affixing of the original certificate and notification of the individual designated under sub. (1). When the original or amended petition is found to be sufficient and the original or amended ordinance or resolution is in proper form, the clerk shall so state on the attached certificate and forward it to the common council or village board immediately.

(4) The common council or village board shall, without alteration, either pass the ordinance or resolution within 30 days following the date of the clerk's final certificate, or submit it to the electors at the next spring or general election, if the election is more than 6 weeks after the date of the council's or board's action on the petition or the expiration of the 30-day period, whichever first occurs. If there are 6 weeks or less before the election, the ordinance or resolution shall be voted on at the next election thereafter. The council or board by a three-fourths vote of the members-elect may order a special election for the purpose of voting on the ordinance or resolution at any time prior to the next election, but not more than one special election for direct legislation may be ordered in any 6-month period.

(5) The clerk shall cause notice of the ordinance or resolution that is being submitted to a vote to be given as provided in s. 10.06 (3) (f).

(6) The ordinance or resolution need not be printed in its entirety on the ballot, but a concise statement of its nature shall be printed together with a question permitting the elector to indicate approval or disapproval of its adoption.

(7) If a majority vote in favor of adoption, the proposed ordinance or resolution shall take effect upon publication under sub. (5). Publication shall be made within 10 days after the election.

(8) City ordinances or resolutions adopted under this section shall not be subject to the veto power of the mayor and city or village ordinances or resolutions adopted under this section shall not be repealed or amended within 2 years of adoption except by a vote of the electors. The common council or village board may submit a proposition to repeal or amend the ordinance or resolution at any election.

9.20 — ANNOT.

This section implements legislative powers reserved by the people. Subject to certain conditions, a common council has no authority to make an initial judgment of the constitutionality or validity of proposed direct legislation. *State ex rel. Althouse v. Madison,* 79 Wis. 2d 97, 255 N.W.2d 449.

9.20 — ANNOT.

A proposal that is administrative, rather than legislative in character, is not the proper subject of initiative proceedings. *State ex rel. Becker v. Common Council,* 101 Wis. 2d 680, 305 N.W.2d 178 (Ct. App. 1981).

9.20 — ANNOT.

A city clerk has a mandatory duty to forward to the common council a sufficient petition and ordinance in proper form. *State ex rel. North v. Goetz,* 116 Wis. 2d 239, 342 N.W.2d 747 (Ct. App. 1983).

9.20 — ANNOT.

The power of initiative does not extend to legislative decisions that have already been made by the legislative body. *Schaefer v. Potosi Village Board,* 177 Wis. 2d 287, 501 N.W.2d 901 (Ct. App. 1993).

9.20 — ANNOT.

If statutes establish procedures for the accomplishment of legislation in a certain area, an initiative may not effect legislation that would modify the statutory directives that would bind a municipality if it were legislating in the same area. Section 62.23 establishes such procedures for zoning; zoning may not be legislated or modified by initiative. An ordinance constituting a pervasive regulation of, or prohibition on, the use of land is zoning. *Heitman v. City of Mauston,* 226 Wis. 2d 542, 595 N.W.2d 450 (Ct. App. 1999).

Wyoming

Wyoming's initiative and referendum pioneer was State Rep. L. C. Tidball of Sheridan. In the early 1890s Tidball was one of the first state legislators in the nation—possibly the very first—to introduce a bill to amend a state constitution to provide for statewide I&R.

The Wyoming legislature waited 19 years before finally taking favorable action on an I&R bill in 1912, after all the surrounding states had already put I&R into their constitutions. It was favored by a six to one margin of the voters who cast ballots on its ratification. It still failed to take effect, however, because Wyoming constitutional amendments required ratification by a "supermajority" of all the voters casting ballots in the election, which made blank ballots count as "no" votes. By this standard, the I&R amendment narrowly failed.

Finally, in 1968, Wyoming's legislature passed an I&R amendment, and it won voter ratification. But the procedures, specified by the legislature, included the most difficult petition requirement for initiatives of any state law in the nation: 15 percent of the number of ballots cast in the preceding gubernatorial election. And it did not allow voters to propose or vote on initiative constitutional amendments at all.

Though several attempts were made, only one initiative qualified for the ballot in 20 years: a proposed law, titled "Instream Flows," that would allow the state's fish and game department to claim water rights on behalf of fish and wildlife, so that future development—and particularly energy projects like a proposed water-guzzling coal slurry pipeline—would not drain essential water sources. The backers' first petition drive, in 1981, fell 1,000 names short, and they were forced to start again. By early 1986 they had finally qualified their measure for the November 1986 ballot. The legislature enacted it in March 1986, making a citizen vote on the measure unnecessary.

In 1992, the first statewide initiative qualified for the ballot. It was an initiative to ban triple trailers from state highways—it passed overwhelmingly. That same year, two other initiatives qualified for the ballot—a term limits measure and an initiative that would regulate railroads and hazardous materials. They both passed. Since 1992, only three other initiatives have made the ballot. The reason for the low number is that the initiative process in Wyoming ranks as one of the most difficult in the country. Attempts by pro-initiative legislators in 2002 to try and lessen the restrictions on the initiative process went nowhere.

Statewide Initiative Usage

Number of Initiatives	Number Passed	Number Failed	Passage Rate
6	3	3	50%

Statewide Initiatives

Year	Measure Number	Type	Subject Matter	Description	Pass/Fail
1992	1	DS	Business Regulation	Ban triple trailers from State highways.	Passed
1992	2	DS	Term Limits	Term limits on state and federal officials.	Passed
1992	3	DS	Utility Regulation	Railroads: emergencies, toxins, hazardous materials.	Passed
1994	2	DS	Gaming	Local option gambling.	Failed
1994	3	DS	Administration of Government	Investment of state funds	Failed
1996	1	DS	Term Limits	Informed Voter Law.	Failed

Wyoming Constitution

97-3-052. Initiative and referendum.

(a) The people may propose and enact laws by the initiative, and approve or reject acts of the legislature by the referendum.

(b) An initiative or referendum is proposed by an application containing the bill to be initiated or the act to be referred. The application shall be signed by not less than one hundred (100) qualified voters as sponsors, and shall be filed with the secretary of state. If he finds it in proper form he shall so certify. Denial of certification shall be subject to judicial review.

(c) After certification of the application, a petition containing a summary of the subject matter shall be prepared by the secretary of state for circulation by the sponsors. If signed by qualified voters, equal in number to fifteen per cent (15%)

of those who voted in the preceding general election and resident in at least two-thirds (2/3) of the counties of the state, it may be filed with the secretary of state.

(d) An initiative petition may be filed at any time except that one may not be filed for a measure substantially the same as that defeated by an initiative election within the preceding (5) years. The secretary of state shall prepare a ballot title and proposition summarizing the proposed law, and shall place them on the ballot for the first statewide election held more than one hundred twenty (120) days after adjournment of the legislative session following the filing. If, before the election, substantially the same measure has been enacted, the petition is void.

(e) A referendum petition may be filed only within ninety (90) days after adjournment of the legislative session at which the act was passed, except that a referendum petition respecting any act previously passed by the legislature may be filed within six months after the power of referendum is adopted. The secretary of state shall prepare a ballot title and proposition summarizing the act and shall place them on the ballot for the first statewide election held more than one hundred eighty (180) days after adjournment of that session.

(f) If votes in an amount in excess of fifty percent (50%) of those voting in the general election are cast in favor of adoption of an initiated measure, the measure is enacted. If votes in an amount in excess of fifty percent (50%) of those voted in the general election are cast in favor of rejection of an act referred, it is rejected. The secretary of state shall certify the election returns. An initiated law becomes effective ninety (90) days after certification, is not subject to veto, and may not be repealed by the legislature within two (2) years of its effective date. It may be amended at any time. An act rejected by referendum is void thirty (30) days after certification. Additional procedures for the initiative and referendum may be prescribed by law.

(g) The initiative shall not be used to dedicate revenues, make or repeal appropriations, create courts, define the jurisdiction of courts or prescribe their rules, enact local or special legislation, or enact that prohibited by the constitution for enactment by the legislature. The referendum shall not be applied to dedications of revenue, to appropriations, to local or special legislation, or to laws necessary for the immediate preservation of the public peace, health, or safety.

Wyoming Statute

Title 22 Chapter 24 Initiative and Referendum

Article 1 In General

22-24-101. Right of initiative; limitations.

The people may propose and enact laws by the initiative. However, the initiative shall not be used to dedicate revenues, make or repeal appropriations, create courts, define the jurisdiction of courts or prescribe their rules, enact local or special legislation, enact that prohibited by the constitution for enactment by the legislature, or enact that substantially the same as that defeated by an initiative election within five (5) years preceding the time of filing of the petition.

22-24-102. Right of referendum; limitations.

The people may approve or reject acts of the legislature by the referendum. However, the referendum shall not be applied to dedications of revenue, to appropriations, to local or special legislation, or to laws necessary for the immediate preservation of the public peace, health or safety.

22-24-103. Application; filing and fee.

An initiative or a referendum shall be proposed by filing an application with the secretary of state. A fee of five hundred dollars ($500.00) shall accompany the application. This fee shall be deposited in the general fund.

22-24-104. Application; contents.

(a) The application shall include:
(i) The proposed bill to be initiated or the act to be referred;
(ii) Repealed By Laws 1998, ch. 100, § 5.
(iii) The designation of a committee of three (3) sponsors who shall represent all sponsors and subscribers in matters relating to the initiative or to the referendum;
(iv) In a referendum, the signatures and addresses of not less than one hundred (100) qualified registered voters; and
(v) Repealed By Laws 1998, ch. 100, § 5.
(vi) A statement that the committee of sponsors are qualified registered voters who signed the application with the proposed bill or the proposed act attached.

22-24-105. Requirements as to proposed bill.

(a) In an initiative, the proposed bill shall be confined to one (1) subject, the entire subject of the bill shall be expressed in the title, the enacting clause shall be: "Be it enacted by the people of the state of Wyoming:" and the bill shall not include subjects restricted by W.S. 22-24-101.

(b) In an initiative, concurrently with the filing of the application, the proposed bill shall be submitted by the committee of sponsors to the secretary of state for review and comment. Upon request of the secretary of state, the legislative service office or any agency in the executive department shall render assistance in reviewing and preparing comments on the proposed bill. No later than fourteen (14) calendar days after the date of submission, at a conference scheduled by the secretary of state, the secretary shall render to the committee of sponsors comments on any problems encountered concerning the format or contents of the proposed bill. The comments shall not be disclosed prior to the conference with the committee of sponsors but, at such time as the application is certified, the comments shall become a public record. After the conference but before the certification the sponsors may amend the proposed bill in response to some or all of the comments of the secretary of state and resubmit the proposed bill in accordance with this subsection, or they may disregard the comments entirely. The committee of sponsors shall notify the secretary of state within five (5) calendar days after the conference whether the proposed bill will be amended. If the proposed bill is to be amended it shall be resubmitted for review and comment in accordance with this subsection. If the proposed bill will not be amended it shall be submitted by the committee of sponsors together with the comments to the secretary of state.

(c)If in the opinion of the secretary of state the proposed bill will have a fiscal impact on the state, the comments prepared pursuant to subsection (b) of this section shall contain an estimate and explanation of the fiscal impact. The explanation shall include a statement that it is an estimate of fiscal impact to the state only and does not include an estimate of any impact upon political subdivisions. The estimate and explanation shall be disclosed to the committee of sponsors at the conference held pursuant to subsection (b) of this section and may be revised if in the opinion of the secretary of state the committee demonstrates the estimate or explanation is inaccurate. If the final estimated fiscal impact by the secretary of state and the final estimated fiscal impact by the committee of sponsors differ by more than twenty-five thousand dollars ($25,000.00), the secretary of state's comments under this section and the ballot proposition shall contain an estimated range of fiscal impact reflecting both estimates.

(d) The committee of sponsors shall notify the secretary of state within five (5) calendar days after the conference whether the proposed bill will be amended. If the proposed bill is to be amended it shall be resubmitted for review and comment in accordance with this subsection.

(e) If the proposed bill will not be amended the committee of sponsors shall submit the names, signatures, addresses and the date of signing of one hundred (100) qualified registered voters to act as sponsors supporting the application in its final form to the secretary of state.

22-24-106. Notice to committee.

Notice to the committee on any matter pertaining to the application and petition shall be served on any member of the committee in person or by mail addressed to a committee member at the address indicated on the application.

22-24-107. Sponsors.

(a)The qualified registered voters who subscribe to the application are designated as sponsors. The committee may designate additional qualified individuals to act as circulators of the petitions by giving written notice to the secretary of state verifying under oath the names, qualifications and addresses of those so designated. An individual shall not be qualified to act as a circulator unless he is a citizen of the United States, a bona fide resident of Wyoming and is at least eighteen (18) years of age. For purposes of this section "resident" means a person who has maintained a residence in Wyoming, as defined by W.S. 22-1-102, for a period of at least ninety (90) days prior to circulating a petition.

(b)The committee of sponsors shall file receipt and expenditure reports as required by W.S. 22-25-106.

22-24-108. Review by secretary of state.

Within seven (7) calendar days after receiving the proposed bill, and the comments received under W.S. 22-24-105 and estimated state fiscal impact, the secretary of state shall review the application and shall either certify it or notify the committee in writing of the grounds for denial.

22-24-109. Grounds for denying certification of initiative or referendum application.

(a)The secretary of state shall deny certification of an initiative application if he determines that:

(i)The proposed bill to be initiated is not in the required form;

(ii) The application is not in the required form;

(iii)There is an insufficient number of qualified registered voters as sponsors; or

(iv)The proposed bill was not submitted for review and comment in accordance with W.S. 22-24-105.

(b)The secretary of state shall deny certification of a referendum application if he determines that:

(i) There is an insufficient number of qualified registered voters as sponsors;

(ii) The application is not substantially in the required form; or

(iii) More than ninety (90) days have expired since the adjournment of the legislative session at which the act being referred was passed.

22-24-110. Petitions; generally.

(a) If the application is certified, the secretary of state shall prescribe the form of and prepare petitions containing:

(i) A copy of the proposed bill or of the act to be referred;

(ii) An impartial summary of the subject matter of the bill;

(iii) The warning required by W.S. 22-24-111;

(iv) Sufficient space for signatures and addresses;

(v)If the circulator is being paid to solicit signatures, each signature page circulated by that circulator shall contain, in sixteen (16) point or larger red boldface type, the following statement: "This circulator is being paid to solicit signatures for this ballot proposition." The statement shall be prominently displayed and made visible to the petition signer by the circulator; and

(vi) Other specifications necessary to assure proper handling and control.

(b)Petitions, for purposes of circulation, shall be prepared by the secretary of state at the sponsor's expense in a number reasonably calculated to allow full circulation throughout the state. A paid circulator shall solicit signatures on a petition only if each signature page circulated by that circulator contains the statement required under paragraph (a)(v) of this section.

(c)The secretary of state shall number each petition and shall keep a record of the petition delivered to each sponsor.

(d)Upon request of the committee, the secretary of state shall report the number of persons who voted in the preceding general election.

(e)The secretary of state, on any printed material circulated by the secretary of state describing the proposition, shall include notice whether any paid circulator was used to gather signatures as required by paragraph (a)(v) of this section.

22-24-111. Petitions; statement of warning.

Each petition shall include a statement of warning that a person who signs a name other than his own on the petition, or who knowingly signs his name more than once for the same proposition at one (1) election, or who signs the petition knowing that he is not a qualified registered voter, upon conviction, is punishable by a fine of not more than one thousand dollars ($1,000.00) or by imprisonment for not more than one (1) year or both.

22-24-112. Petitions; circulation; contests.

(a)The petitions shall be circulated throughout the state only by a sponsor or an individual designated in accordance with W.S. 22-24-107 as a circulator and only in person.

(b)Any person may contest the qualifications of an individual designated as a circulator by filing a petition in the justice of the peace court or county [circuit] court within the county where the circulator was soliciting signatures or in the district court within ten (10) days of the solicitation activity. The court shall hear and decide any such action within five (5) days from the date the petition is filed. Among the criteria the court may use in determining the qualifications of the circulator are the following:

(i) Term and location of dwelling of the circulator and family;

(ii) Term and location of employment;

(iii)Term and location of vehicle registration;

(iv)Length of driver's license registration;

(v)Time of property ownership or lease rental;

(vi)Any other residency qualifications either provided by law or deemed reasonable by the court to render a judicious determination.

(c) Any party prevailing in any action filed pursuant to subsection (b) of this section may be awarded costs and reasonable attorney's fees by the court. The court shall notify the secretary of state of its findings as to the qualifications of a circulator within five (5) days of the determination.

22-24-113. Petitions; subscribing to and withdrawing name.

Any qualified registered voter may subscribe to the petition by signing his name and listing his address. A person who has signed the petition may withdraw his name only by giving written notice to the secretary of state before the time that the petition is filed.

22-24-114. Petitions; verification.

(a)Before a petition is filed, it shall be verified by the sponsor or other individual who personally circulated it. The verification shall be in affidavit form and shall state in substance that:

(i)The person signing the affidavit is a sponsor or an individual designated and qualified in accordance with W.S. 22-24-107 and is the only circulator of that petition;

(ii)The signatures on the petition were made in his presence; and

(iii)To the best of his knowledge, such signatures are those of the persons whose names they purport to be. In determining the sufficiency of the petition, the secretary of state shall not:

(A)Count signatures on petitions not properly verified;

(B) Count signatures on a petition circulated by an individual who has been determined not to be a qualified circulator pursuant to W.S. 22-24-112 or by the secretary of state in accordance with rules of his office.

22-24-115. Petitions; filing by sponsors.

(a) Petitions may be filed with the secretary of state if signed by a sufficient number of qualified registered voters as required by the Wyoming constitution. The sponsor of a petition for referendum may file the petition only within ninety (90) days after the adjournment of the legislative session at which the act was passed.

(b) Petitions for an initiative shall be submitted to the secretary of state for verification within the eighteen (18) month period following the date the first set of petition forms are provided to the sponsors. Any petition not submitted within the eighteen (18) month period is void for all purposes.

(c) The eighteen (18) month period set forth in subsection (b) of this section shall commence on the effective date of this act as to all petitions for an initiative that are outstanding on the effective date.

22-24-116. Petitions; review by secretary of state.

(a) Within not more than sixty (60) days of the date the petition is filed, the secretary of state shall review it and shall notify the committee whether the petition was properly or improperly filed. The petition shall be determined to be improperly filed if:

(i) There is an insufficient total number of signatures of qualified registered voters;

(ii) There is an insufficient number of signatures of qualified registered voters in at least two-thirds (2/3) of the counties of the state; or

(iii)The petition is for referendum and was not filed within ninety (90) days after the adjournment of the legislative session at which the act was passed.

22-24-117. Ballot proposition; preparation and contents.

(a) If the petition is properly filed, the secretary of state, with the assistance of the attorney general, shall prepare a ballot proposition. The ballot proposition shall give a true and impartial summary of the proposed law or of the referred act, including the estimated fiscal impact or range of estimated fiscal impact on the state and explanation of the impact prepared in accordance with W.S. 22-24-105(c), and shall make provision for approval and for disapproval thereof.

(b) When any proposal relating to the investment of the permanent funds of the state of Wyoming is placed on the ballot, the secretary of state shall include in the ballot statement an estimate from the state treasurer of the estimated loss or gain in revenue from the proposal. If the final estimated loss or gain by the state treasurer and the final estimated loss or gain by the committee of sponsors of the ballot proposition differ by more than twenty-five thousand dollars ($25,000.00), the ballot statement shall contain the range of estimated loss or gain reflecting both estimates.

22-24-118. Ballot proposition; procedure for placing on ballot; publication requirements.

(a) Except as required under subsection (b) of this section, the same procedure for placing constitutional amendment questions on the ballot shall be used to place the initiative or referendum ballot proposition on the ballot.

(b) The ballot proposition for an initiative or referendum shall be published by the secretary of state in a newspaper of general circulation in the state in the newspaper edition immediately preceding the general election. Publication under this subsection shall contain the entire text of the initiative or referendum.

22-24-119. Ballot proposition; when placed on ballot.

(a) The ballot proposition for an initiative shall be placed on the election ballot of the first statewide general election that is held after:

(i) The petition is filed;

(ii)A legislative session has convened and adjourned; and

(iii)A period of one hundred twenty (120) days has expired since the adjournment of the legislative session. If the attorney general determines that an act of the legislature enacted after the petition is filed is substantially the same as the proposed law, the petition shall be void and the ballot proposition shall not be placed on the election ballot, and the secretary of the state shall so notify the committee.

(b) The ballot proposition for a referendum shall be placed on the election ballot of the first statewide general election held more than one hundred eighty (180) days after adjournment of the legislative session at which the act was passed.

22-24-120. Repealed By Laws 1998, ch. 100, § 5.

22-24-121. Insufficiency of application or petition.

An initiative or a referendum submitted to the voters shall not be void because of the insufficiency of the application or petition by which the submission was procured.

22-24-122. Action for review of determination.

Any person aggrieved by any determination made under this article, by the secretary of state or by the attorney general, may bring an action in the district court of Laramie county to have the determination reviewed by filing application within thirty (30) days of the date on which notice of the determination was given.

22-24-123. Penalties.

(a) Any person who signs a name other than his own on a petition for initiative or on a petition for referendum, or who knowingly signs his name more than once for the same proposition at one (1) election, or who signs such petition knowing that he is not a qualified registered voter, upon conviction shall be fined not more than one thousand dollars ($1,000.00) or imprisoned for not more than one (1) year, or both.

(b) Any sponsor or circulator who knowingly and willfully makes a false verification of the qualifications of a circulator pursuant to W.S. 22-24-107(a) or knowingly and willfully makes a false verification under W.S. 22-24-114, shall be guilty of false swearing and subject to the penalties provided by W.S. 22-26-101.

22-24-124. Repealed By Laws 1998, ch. 100, § 5.

22-24-125. Petitions; payment for signatures; misrepresentation of petition; prohibition; penalty.

(a) A circulator of an initiative or a referendum petition or a person who causes the circulation of an initiative or a referendum petition may not receive payment for the collection of signatures if that payment is based upon the number of signatures collected. Nothing in this section prohibits a circulator of an initiative or a referendum petition or a person who causes the circulation of an initiative or a referendum petition from being paid a salary that is not based upon the number of signatures collected.

(b) A circulator of an initiative or a referendum petition or a person who causes the circulation of an initiative or a referendum petition may not pay or offer to pay any compensation to another person for that person's signature on the initiative or referendum petition.

(c) A circulator of an initiative or a referendum petition or a person who causes the circulation of an initiative or a referendum petition shall not collect another person's signature on the petition by knowingly making a false statement with respect to or otherwise misrepresenting the proposed law or referred act contained within the initiative or referendum petition. A violation of this subsection is subject to the penalty imposed under W.S.

Article 2 Paid Advertising in Any Communication Medium or Printed Literature to Support, Oppose or Influence Legislation

22-24-201. Paid advertising; penalty.

(a) Any group of persons who are associated for the purpose of raising, collecting or spending money for paid advertising in any communication media or for printed literature to support, oppose or otherwise influence legislation by the legislature of the state of Wyoming, which is or was the subject of a statewide initiative or referendum within the past four (4) years, shall:

(i) File a statement of formation listing the names and addresses of its chairman and treasurer with the secretary of state within ten (10) days after formation and prior to the publication, dissemination or broadcast of any paid advertising from the group;

(ii) File with the secretary of state a statement of receipts and expenditures setting forth the full and complete record of receipts including cash, goods or services and actual and promised expenditures, on a form prescribed by the secretary of state, on the last Friday in December of each calendar year. In addition to the annual report, while the legislature is in session, there shall be filed an interim monthly statement for each month or portion thereof that the legislature is in session, within ten (10) days of the first day of the month for the previous month;

(iii) If the total receipts and expenditures reported under paragraph (a)(ii) of this section lists any contribution in excess of one thousand dollars ($1,000.00) from any source or sources other than an individual, the report shall include a full and complete disclosure of the funding source or sources of any nonindividual contributor which funded the advertising.

(b) Any group formed under this section shall file a termination report within thirty (30) days after it ceases the regulated activity but cessation of activity shall not relieve the group of the reporting requirement for that filing period.

(c) No group subject to this section shall pay for advertising in any communication media or printed literature without full disclosure of the name of the group.

(d) Nothing in this section shall require an individual or individuals who pay for advertising or literature to support, oppose or otherwise influence legislation to file under this section, provided the name of the individual or individuals is fully disclosed in the advertising or literature.

(e) As used in this section:

(i) "Communication media" means advertising on television, radio, in print media, on billboards and other electronic media;

(ii) "Printed literature" means any printed material but shall not include any member association printed communication not intended for public dissemination, bumper stickers, pens, pencils, buttons, rulers, nail files, balloons and yard signs.

(f) Any person who willfully and knowingly violates any of the provisions of this section is guilty of a misdemeanor punishable as provided by W.S. 22-26-112.

The Basic Steps to Do an Initiative in Wyoming

Statutes Only — Indirect Initiative Process

Basic Procedures: The application must be filed with the Secretary of State. A fee of $500 must accompany the application. After the application is filed, the Secretary of State will hold a conference with the sponsors to discuss problems with the format or contents, fiscal impact to the state, and the initiative amendment process. The sponsor may then amend the initiative language. If the proposed bill will not be amended the committee of sponsors shall submit the names, signatures, addresses and the date of signing of one hundred (100) qualified electors to act as sponsors supporting the application in its final form to the Secretary of State. If the application meets all constitutional and statutory requirements, the SOS will certify the application as filed. If the application is denied, the Secretary of State will notify the committee in writing of the grounds for denial. Denial of certification is subject to judicial review if any aggrieved person files an application within 30 days of the notification.

Date Initiative language can be submitted to state for the November 2002 election: Anytime.

Signatures are tied to vote of which office: Number of votes cast in last general election.

Next general election: 2002

Number of votes cast in last general election (2000): 221,685

Net number of signatures required: 15% of all votes cast in the last general election (33,253)

Distribution Requirement: 15% of votes cast in at least 2/3 of the counties.

Circulation period: 18 Months

Do circulators have to be residents: Yes

Date when signatures are due for certification: One day prior to the convening of the legislature. (Early January, 2002)

Signature verification process: Wyoming has a statewide voter registration process. The Secretary of State's office verifies every signature to ensure that they are registered voters. They do not match the signatures on the petition to the actual signatures on the voter registration cards.

Single-subject restriction: Yes

Legislative tampering: The legislature can repeal or amend an initiative by a majority vote at any time.

5 Common Questions Regarding the Initiative Process

As was discussed in Chapter One, the increasing use of the initiative process has lead to numerous questions about its use. This section will address some of the common questions and concerns that have been raised about the initiative process.

Does the Initiative Process Run Contrary to a Republican Form of Government?[1]

A recurring theme in discussions of the initiative and referendum ("I&R") process has been whether, and to what extent, I&R violates that portion of Article IV, section 4 of the U.S. Constitution providing that the United States shall guarantee every state a "republican form of government—the Guarantee Clause."[2] In short, it doesn't.

In 1912, the U.S. Supreme Court refused to invalidate Oregon's I&R system on the grounds that whether a state had a republican form of government was a political question for Congress, and therefore non-justiciable.[3] The Court made clear that it was the sole responsibility of Congress to decide what constitutes a republican form of government. Congress's actions over the years have shown that they do not believe that the initiative process is inconsistent with republican government as evidenced by the fact that they allowed Oklahoma and Alaska into the Union with the initiative process as part of their constitutions. This seems to settle the issue at the federal level.

At the state level, when courts have reached the issue they have almost uniformly decided that I&R is consistent with republican government.[4] Some courts, in fact, have held that I&R is a fundamental part of republican government.[5]

Don't Hundreds of Initiatives Appear on the Ballot Every Election Cycle?

Contrary to popular belief, the initiative process has not been used that frequently. Literally hundreds of initiatives are filed each year but a very small percentage actually make it to the ballot—around 21%.[6] Approximately 2,051 statewide initiatives have been voted on since 1904 and 840 have been adopted—a passage rate of only 41%.

The average number of initiatives on statewide ballots each election cycle since 1904 is 42. The average number of initiatives on the ballot each election cycle between 1981–1990 is 54 and between 1991–2000 the number is 73. Therefore, since only 24 states have the statewide initiative process, since 1904 an average of 1.75 initiatives have appeared on each state's ballot each election cycle. Between 1981–1990 that number is 2.25 and between 1991–2000 the number is 3.04. We define an election cycle as an election that occurs every two years in even numbered years.

Additionally, the use of the initiative process has been centered in just a few states. A little over 60% of all initiative activity has taken place in just six states, Oregon, California, Colorado, North Dakota, Arizona and Washington State.

---

1. This essay was taken from a presentation prepared by Rob Natelson of the University of Montana School of Law. The presentation was made at the Initiative & Referendum Institute's 1999 National I&R conference in Washington, DC.

2. U.S. Const., Art. IV, Section 4 states: The United States shall guarantee to every State in this Union a Republican Form of Government, and shall protect each of them against invasion; and on Application of the Legislature, or of the Executive (when the Legislature cannot be convened) against domestic Violence.

3. *Pacific States Tel. & Tel. Co. v. Oregon*, 223 U.S. 118 (1912).

4. *State ex rel. Billingston v. Sinclair*, 28 Wash. 2d 575, 183 P.2d 813 (1947); *Bernzen v. City of Boulder*, 186 Colo. 81, 525 P.2d 416 (1974); *McKee v. City of Louisville*, 200 Colo. 525, 616 P.2d 969 (1980); *Margolis v. District Court*, 638 P.2d 297 (Colo. 1981); *Cagle v. Qualified Electors of Winston Co.*, 470 So.2d 1208 (Ala. 1985); *Westerberg v. Andrus*, 114 Idaho 401, 757 P.2d 664 (1988); *State of Oregon v. Montez*, 309 Or. 564, 789 P.2d 1352 (1989); *State of Washington v. Davis*, 133 Wash.2d 187, 943 P.2d 283 (1997); *Amador Valley Joint Union High Sch. Dist. v. State Bd. of Equalization*, 22 Cal.3d 208, 237, 149 Cal. Rptr. 239, 583 P.2d 1281 (1978) (two thirds vote to raise local taxes).

5. The Colorado courts take this position. See, e.g., *Bernzen v. Boulder*, 186 Colo. 81, 525 P.2d 416 (1974) (viewing recall, as well as initiative and referendum, as fundamental rights of a republican form of government which the people have reserved unto themselves); see also *Margolis v. District Court*, 638 P.2d 297 (Colo. 1981); *McKee v. City of Louisville*, 200 Colo. 525, 616 P.2d 969 (1980).

6. See Chapter One—Initiative usage.

It is important to point out that the primary reason that the people believe that there are so many initiatives on the ballot is because they have to vote on hundreds of ballot measures each election cycle and they wrongfully assume that they were placed there by the citizens. In fact, a very large percentage of ballot measures that are voted on each election cycle are placed there by the government—and not the people. For example, in Colorado in 2000, at least 297 governments placed 537 legislative referendum before the voters—representing 98.7% of all ballot measures in the 2000 election. In contrast, the citizens placed only seven initiatives on the ballot representing just 1.3% of all ballot measure activity.[7]

Are Voters Competent Enough to Vote on Complex Issues? [8]

Research suggests that voters are capable of responding reasonably well to the information demands associated with the choices they make on numerous ballot measures. The research illustrates that voters find multiple sources of information that can allow them to make choices that reflect their preferences, despite having little or no knowledge of the technical details of the measure they are evaluating.

Research shows that voters find cues about how their interests might be affected by a proposed initiative or referendum. One of the most useful of these cues is knowing who favors or opposes a measure. Responsiveness to these and other cues suggest that voters reason about their ballot decisions in an informed manner, at least in a minimalist sense. Other cues include knowledge of how the proposal might affect them personally, how it might affect their local area, their group, their party, or the state economy.

Using a 1999 public opinion poll conducted in Washington state, and others from California, researchers found that most voters say they rely upon the voter's pamphlets, and most cite it is a "very important" source of information. Other research suggests that the single most important item in these pamphlets are the pro and con arguments, specifically, the elite endorsements of these arguments. Newspapers and TV (news) rank next in reported importance.

Researchers also assessed how low educated voters might be handicapped by a lack of information, and how they compare with other voters. It was found that with nearly all information sources, the less educated are least likely to use the source. Low education does not appear to prevent a citizen from finding information, nor does it force them to rely on commercial advertising. Low educated voters are not more likely than the well educated to report they rely upon paid media (TV, radio, or newspaper ads, or campaign mailings). The average low educated voter reports using at least 3 different information sources, compared to 4.2 for the well educated. These results suggest that the vast majority of participating voters are unlikely to be "manipulated" by duplicitous, commercial campaign information. The research also found that some voters do abstain when information demands are too great.

In short, voters make informed decisions when voting on ballot measures and when they are in doubt they simply either abstain or vote no.

What Impact Does Money Have in the Initiative Process?

In recent years, economic interest groups with vast financial resources have used the initiative process with increasing frequency. Such groups often spend millions of dollars to promote their political causes, taking their cases directly to voters. These expensive, high profile campaigns have lead many observers to conclude that by spending vast sums, narrow, wealthy economic interest groups are now able to use the initiative process to pass laws at the expense of broader citizen interests. But can this point be proven? In short, no.

There is no doubt that individuals, industry sectors and special interest groups with large sums of money are using the initiative process to seek reforms they want—but this isn't new. In the early days of the initiative process, businesses with an interest in selling alcohol and other spirits to the masses used the initiative process to try and overturn prohibition laws—but they were rarely successful. In the 1920s and 30s, the chiropractic industry used the initiative process, with varying degrees of success, to get states to allow them to practice. In the 1980s and 90s, denturists (the people who make dentures, etc) used the initiative process to try and get state laws changed so that they, in addition to dentists, could

7. Polhill, *Murder the Messenger*, an op-ed for the Independence Institute, 2001

8. This essay was taken from a presentation prepared by Todd Donovan of Western Washington University and Shaun Bowler, UC Riverside. The presentation was made at the Initiative & Referendum Institute's 1999 National I&R conference in Washington, DC.

be licensed to make and sell dentures to the public. They felt that dentists had a monopoly and so they tried to stop it—but they were only moderately successful. Since 1912, gambling and lottery interests have used the initiative process to expand their industry. However, after spending tens of millions of dollars over a 90-year period, the industry has only been successful in passing less than 25% of the initiatives they attempted. This is why the industry has chosen not to pursue initiatives to expand their interests. They realize that money alone will not pass an initiative.

In the last decade alone, numerous wealthy individuals have tried to enact reform through the initiative process only to lose after spending millions of dollars. George Soros, Gene Sperling and Peter Lewis spent millions of dollars in 2000 to try and get a drug policy reform initiative passed in Massachusetts only to be defeated. Dick DeVos (the founder of Amway), along with several other wealthy individuals spent almost $30 million dollars in the 2000 election cycle to try and get school choice initiatives adopted—they too were left empty handed on election night. In yet another example, millionaire Ron Unz, the successful architect of the California and Arizona initiatives to require that schools teach in English only (with some exceptions), saw his campaign finance reform initiative handily defeated in California in 2000—after spending a substantial amount of his own money. Numerous more examples can be given, but in short, just because you have money doesn't mean you can buy a law at the ballot box. But let's look passed the anecdotal examples and look at the academic research that has been conducted in this area.

Professor Liz Gerber of the University of California, San Diego and arguably one of the most well respected academics in the study of the initiative process, wrote a book on the role and influence of money in the initiative process. For the book, *The Populist Paradox* (Princeton University Press, 1999), she analyzed surveys of interest group activities and motivations, as well as campaign finance records from 168 different direct legislation campaigns in eight states. Her research found that "…economic interest groups are severely limited in their ability to pass new laws by initiative. Simply put, money is necessary but not sufficient for success at the ballot box. By contrast, research found that citizen groups with broad-based support could much more effectively use direct legislation to pass new laws. When they are able to mobilize sufficient financial resources to get out their message, citizen groups are much more successful at the ballot box, even when economic interest groups greatly outspend them."

Additional research by political scientists Todd Donovan, Shaun Bowler, David McCuan, and Ken Fernandez found that while 40% of ALL initiatives on the Californian ballot from 1986–1996 passed, only 14% of initiatives pushed by special interests passed. They concluded, "[o]ur data reveals that these are indeed the hardest initiatives to market in California, and that money spent by proponents in this arena is largely wasted." This research complements political scientist Anne Campbell's research on special interest-backed initiatives in Colorado from 1966 to 1994. Her research found that during those 28 years, only ONE initiative pushed by special interests was successful at the ballot box.

This is not to say, however, that wealthy economic interest groups have no influence on initiatives appearing on the ballot. They have been very successful in blocking initiatives they do not like. Not because they are buying a "no" vote, but because voters are 1) predisposed to vote against any new law—regardless of if it is proposed by the people or the state legislature and 2) are more likely to vote no and maintain the status quo when confronted with a new law that they are uncertain about. This is supported by the fact that only 41% of all the statewide initiatives to appear on the ballot have been approved by the citizens.

Regardless of the fact that research shows that money can't buy a new law at the ballot box, there have been numerous attempts at regulating the amount of money spent on ballot measure campaigns. In most cases, the proposed laws have attempted to limit the amount of money corporations could spend in either support or opposition of ballot measures. However, state and federal courts, including the U.S. Supreme Court in 1977, have consistently ruled that states cannot limit the amount of money in ballot measure campaigns. Their basic logic has been that you can't corrupt a piece of paper (the ballot measure) and therefore there is no need in limiting the amount of money spent on these campaigns. This is where they apply a different standard in those cases pertaining to contributions to candidate campaigns—the courts have upheld contribution limits to candidates because of the possibility of corruption. In short, any attempt to regulate the amount of money in ballot measure campaigns would be viewed as unconstitutional given the current case law.

There is no doubt that there will continue to be large sums of money associated with initiative campaigns. But it is important to understand why. The main reason is the growing regulation of the initiative process by state legislators. They have been swayed by the rhetoric that money has corrupted the initiative process—even though there is no academic research to support this viewpoint. Their new regulations are the cause for the growing amount of money in initiative campaigns. More regulation just means that initiative proponents will just spend more money to overcome these hurdles. The loser in this scenario is the average citizen. They do not have the resources to overcome these hurdles and therefore are locked out of the process. If legislators are concerned about wealthy individuals and special interest being the only ones using the process, then they should make the process more accessible to those individuals without access to large sums of money.

Does the Initiative Process Impact Voter Turnout?

Two recent scholarly studies find the presence of initiatives on the ballot has a positive effect on turnout rates in the United States.

Examining initiatives (and popular referenda) on state ballots between 1972 and 1996, University of Washington political scientist Mark Smith found that states with "salient" initiatives and popular referendums measured by the percent of front-page newspaper coverage devoted to ballot issues on the day following an election tend to have higher turnout in midterm elections (by roughly 3%) than non-initiative states, but not in presidential years. Smith's study, "The Contingent Effects of Ballot Initiatives and Candidate Races on Turnout," was published in the American Journal of Political Science in 2001.

Similarly, using pooled time series data for the 50 states over a twenty-six year period (1970–1996), political scientists Caroline Tolbert (Kent State), John Grummel (Kent State), and Daniel Smith (University of Denver) found that states with more initiatives measured by the actual number of initiatives appearing on statewide ballots have higher voter turnout in both presidential (roughly 4%) and midterm elections (roughly 8%) than states without the process. Their 2001 study, "The Effects of Ballot Initiatives on Voter Turnout in the United States," was published in American Politics Research.

Both studies demonstrate that higher turnout in initiative states is most pronounced in midterm elections or non-competitive presidential elections, when ballot initiatives do not compete with presidential candidates for media attention.

What Are the Fiscal Implications of the Initiative Process?

When the budgetary numbers were compared for states that allow voter initiatives (from 1960 to 1990) and states that do not, several clear patterns emerged:[9]

Initiatives led to significantly lower spending and taxes. Per capita spending, for example, was about $83 per capita lower in a typical initiative state than a typical non-initiative state, which translates into $332 less expenditure (and hence taxes and fees) for a family of four. Compared to the average level of state and local spending, $2300 per capita, initiatives caused a reduction of 4 percent.

Initiatives led states to decentralize spending decisions. Local spending was 10 percent higher in initiative states than non-initiative states, while state spending was 12 percent lower. Thus, voters used initiatives to force spending decisions to be made closer to home.

Initiatives led states to adopt a less redistributional revenue system. In initiative states, broad-based taxes (primarily on property, income, and sales) were 8 percent lower than in non-initiative states, while fees for services (such as college tuition) were 7 percent higher. Initiative states charged users for services they received instead passing the costs on to other taxpayers.

The period from 1960 to 1990 covers the high point of the big government era and the rise of the taxpayer rebellion. The evidence analyzed provides the first broad statistical overview of the consequences of voter initiatives for tax and spending policies. Taken together, the findings show that voter initiatives are not the most important factor determining state fiscal policies, but they do make a difference. Voters have used the initiative to cut back the size of their state governments and put a break on redistribution.

---

9. This summary was prepared by John G. Matsusaka, a Senior Research Fellow and Board Member of the Initiative & Referendum Institute and author of numerous articles regarding the fiscal impact of initiatives.

6 The Courts and the Initiative Process

By Kenneth P. Miller[1]

A great irony of initiative lawmaking is that *judges* have become the system's most important players. The citizen's initiative process was designed to establish "pure democracy." Instead, it is controlled and often thwarted by undemocratic and countermajoritarian courts.

A prominent example of the conflict between initiative voters and the courts comes from the term limits movement. Between 1990 and 1994, voters in over 20 states used the initiative process to impose term limits on Members of Congress and state elected officials. This blitz was a powerful, coast-to-coast exercise of direct democracy. In 1995, however, the U.S. Supreme Court dealt the movement a decisive setback. In *U.S. Term Limits, Inc. v. Thornton*[2] the court overturned the will of millions of voters by declaring Congressional term limits unconstitutional. Several state courts meanwhile struck down term limits on state officials.[3]

The term limits saga demonstrates that citizen lawmakers can bypass legislatures and other institutions of representative government to enact "the will of the people," but they cannot bypass the courts. Courts are the one institutional check on the people's initiative power.

Judicial invalidation of voter-approved initiatives is remarkable, but it is not rare. Courts have struck down (in whole or in part) many landmark measures, including initiatives to regulate campaign finance, establish a "blanket" primary system, restrict the rights of illegal immigrants, and impose tough criminal penalties, just to name a few. Indeed, a recent study of four high-use initiative states over the past four decades confirms that voter-approved initiatives are challenged in court *more often than not*—and courts invalidate roughly half of all challenged initiatives in part or in their entirety.[4] Clearly, courts exercise a powerful institutional check on the initiative process.

Why are so many initiatives invalidated?

There are at least three important reasons why so many initiatives have trouble in the courts: (1) the subject matter of many initiatives; (2) the polarized process of initiative lawmaking; and (3) the growing hostility of some courts toward the initiative process.

First, the *subject matter* of many initiatives invites legal challenge. Initiatives often tackle issues involving constitutional rights and other norms—the very things American courts seek to protect. A survey of voter-approved initiatives indicates that some (e.g., those related to environmental protection, taxation, and economic regulation) address areas where courts generally defer to policymakers. Such initiatives are rarely challenged on substantive grounds, and rarely invalidated. However, a larger percentage of initiatives touch on areas courts closely guard, such as the rights of criminal defendants or racial or other protected minorities, political rights (e.g., campaign contributions or expenditures), and the institutions of representative government. These types of initiatives are challenged and invalidated at high rates.[5]

Second, the *process* of initiative lawmaking encourages litigation. Kelly Clark, a former Oregon state legislator and supporter of the initiative process, observes: "As a legislator over a decade ago, I was constantly amazed at how any piece of legislation with 'sharp edges'—that is to say legislation that really rocked the status quo—ran into a quick death in the legislative process. What would come out would be some 'moderate' version of the previously radical or conservative leg-

---

1. Kenneth P. Miller is a practicing attorney and a Visiting Assistant Professor of Politics at the University of San Francisco where he teaches courses in constitutional law, American politics, and public policy. He is a graduate of Pomona College (1985) and Harvard Law School (1988) and will receive a doctorate in political science from the University of California at Berkeley in 2002. He has recently published articles in law reviews and edited volumes regarding interaction between courts and the initiative process.

2. 514 U.S. 779 (1995).

3. See, e.g., Gerberding. v. Munro, 134 Wash. 2d 188 (1998); Lehman v. Bradbury, 333 Ore. 231 (2002).

4. Kenneth P. Miller, "Judging Initiatives: A Unique Role for Courts," unpublished paper presented at the 2000 Annual Meeting of the Western Political Science Association, San Jose, CA, March 2000.

5. Id.

islation. The initiative process offers no such softening. It offers extremes of both the Left and the Right. It is supposed to do that."[6]

While this may be so, one effect of a polarized process is that it increases the likelihood of litigation. If an initiative's opponents have no opportunities to "soften" the proposal, their only remaining options are to defeat the measure at the polls or try to kill it in court.

Third, evidence suggests that judges in a number of states have grown increasingly hostile toward the initiative process. Over a decade ago, former California Supreme Court Justice Stanley Mosk wrote: "The initiative process is out of control in California."[7] Increasing numbers of judges in other states have expressed similar sentiments. How is judicial hostility toward the initiative process manifested? One way is through strict enforcement of technical rules for initiative lawmaking, such as the rule that an initiative may contain only one subject. As UCLA Law Professor Daniel H. Lowenstein has argued, "single subject" rules are "infinitely malleable" — if a court chooses to strictly enforce such a rule, it can strike down almost any ballot measure.[8] In 1998, the Oregon State Supreme Court issued a landmark decision in *Armatta v. Kitzhaber*[9], which established a strict new interpretation of the state constitution's rule that each amendment to the constitution requires a separate vote. This landmark Oregon case, and other tough "one amendment" or "single subject" decisions in states such as Florida, Montana, Colorado, Washington, and California, have created new opportunities for those challenging initiatives in court.

How much deference should courts give to initiatives and the initiative process?

Although the U.S. Supreme Court has held that judges should apply the same level of review to ballot initiatives as they do to any other law,[10] a lively debate continues over how courts should treat initiatives. Some believe courts should defer more to initiatives than to "ordinary legislation" because initiatives more closely reflect the "pure" will of the people.[11] Others, such as the late Professor Julian Eule, have argued just the opposite, namely that courts should give less deference to initiatives than to ordinary legislation, because unlike a legislature, the initiative process lacks checks and balances; since courts are the only institutional check in the process, judges need to be extra-vigilant in reviewing initiatives.[12]

Over the past century, with some exceptions, courts have given both the initiative process and individual initiatives a large measure of deference. Importantly, courts have expressly rejected invitations to declare the initiative process itself in violation of Art. IV, Section 4 of the U.S. Constitution, which guarantees each state a "Republican Form of Government."[13] And in other decisions, courts have declared their strong desire to uphold individual ballot measures. For example the California Supreme Court, upheld the state's landmark Proposition 13 tax-cutting initiative against a multi-pronged legal challenge, arguing: "It is our solemn duty to jealously guard the initiative power, it being one of the most precious rights of our democratic process."

Recent signs of judicial hostility in Oregon and elsewhere, however, suggest that a growing number of judges are adopting a less deferential approach.

Potential for voter backlash against the courts

Aggressive invalidation of initiatives creates risks for courts. If judges continue to strike down voter-approved initiatives at high rates, there is a good possibility that initiative activists will seek revenge. The filing of initiatives across the country designed to alter and change the way the judiciary operates, as well as the undertaking of recall campaigns for judges who strike down initiatives, has emphasized this point. These efforts will further politicize the judiciary and many people believe threaten its independence. The courts are a powerful check on initiative lawmaking, but also a vulnerable one.

---

6. Kelly Clark, "Who Owns the Constitution?: Term Limits, Measure 7, and the Oregon Supreme Court" (2002).
7. Legislature v. Eu, 54 Cal. 3d 492, 536 (1990), Mosk, J., dissenting.
8. Daniel H. Lowenstein, "California Initiatives and the Single Subject Rule", 30 UCLA Law Rev. 936, 967 (1983).
9. 327 Ore. 250 (1998).
10. See, Citizens for Rent Control, Coalition for Fair Housing v. City of Berkeley, 454 U.S. 290, 295 (1981).
11. See, e.g., former Supreme Court Justice Hugo Black's comments in oral argument, Reitman v. Mulkey, 387 U.S. 369 (1967) in 64 Landmark Briefs of the Supreme Court of the United States: Constitutional Law 668 (Phillip B. Kurland and Gerhard Caspar, eds., 1975).
12. Julian N. Eule, "Judicial Review of Direct Democracy," 99 Yale L.J. 1503 (1990).
13. Pacific States Telephone and Telegraph Co. v. Oregon, 223 U.S. 118 (1912). In this case, the U.S. Supreme Court held that a "Guarantee Clause" challenge to the initiative process is a non-justiciable political question. See also, Hartig v. City of Seattle, 53 Wash. 432 (1909), and Kadderly v. City of Portland, 74 P. 710 (Ore 1903), rejecting Guarantee Clause challenges.

Listing of major initiative and referendum court decisions [14]

Amalgamated Transit Union Local 587 v. State of Washington (99-2-27054-1 SEA) (2000) Superior Court of the State of Washington in and for the County of King

This case struck down initiative I-695, which had been adopted by the voters, as violating the state's single subject requirement for initiatives. The ruling was appealed to the Washington State Supreme Court, which affirmed the lower court's decision.

Armatta v. Kitzhaber, S44955 (1998)

The Oregon Supreme Court invalidated a criminal justice initiative on the grounds that it involved multiple changes to the constitution that should have been considered separately by voters.

Bates v. Director of the Office of Campaign and Political Finance, SJC-08677 (2002)

In this Massachusetts case, the Supreme Judicial Court for the County of Suffolk ruled that the state legislature must provide funding to implement the Clean Elections Law, which was passed by popular initiative. It is the first case in which a state high court has ordered a legislature to fund a ballot measure.

Bernbeck v. Moore, 96-3503 (1997) United States Court of Appeals for the Eighth Circuit, No. 96-3503

On October 9, 1997 the 8th U.S. Court of Appeals struck down a Nebraska law that required petitioners to be registered voters in Nebraska for at least 30 days before circulating an initiative petition. The court ruled the voter registration requirement violated the First Amendment.

Bernzen v. Boulder, 186 Colo. 81, 525 P.2d 416 (1974)

In this case, the court ruled that recall, as well as initiative and referendum, were fundamental rights of a republican form of government that the people have reserved unto themselves.

Bilofsky v. Deukmajian, 124 Cal.App.3d 825 (1981) Civ. No. 60462. Court of Appeals of California, Second Appellate District, Division Four. October 21, 1981.

The court upheld as constitutional a California statute that prevents the use of names gathered on initiative petitions. The statute prohibits the proponent and circulator from communicating by mail with signers by obtaining their names and addresses from the petition, whether or not the communication relates to the subject of the initiative petition.

Boyette v. Galvin (No. 98-CV-10377-GAO) (2000)

On March 3, 1998, The Becket Fund filed a lawsuit on behalf of a group of Massachusetts's citizens challenging provisions of the Massachusetts constitution that forbid citizens from using the initiative process for issues pertaining to private school funding. In September 1998, a federal judge signed an order permitting a petition to be circulated for signatures while the court challenge was pending. In 1999, more than 78,000 signatures were certified, easily surpassing the minimum requirement. But in order for the petition to come before the legislature, and henceforth the voters, the Attorney General must certify that it is proper for the legislators to take it up. In a letter of September 1, 1999, he declared that one of the very constitutional provisions being challenged prohibits him from doing so. The Federal Court upheld the state's constitutional prohibition on prohibiting initiatives that pertain to religion and by extension private school funding.

---

14. A copy of these decisions are available in the legal section on the Initiative & Referendum Institute's website at www.iandrinstitute.org.

U. S. Supreme Court
Buckley v. American Constitutional Law (97-930), 120 F.3d 1092 (1999)

The question before the court in Buckley was whether the State of Colorado may constitutionally regulate the process of circulating initiative petitions by requiring that: (1) petition circulators who verify the signatures of petition signers must be registered electors; (2) petition circulators must wear identification badges; and (3) proponents of an initiative must file reports disclosing the amounts paid to circulators and the identity of petition circulators. The U.S. Supreme Court ruled on January 12, 1999 striking down Colorado's regulation and restrictions on their initiative process as "undue hindrances to political conversations and the exchange of ideas," according to Justice Ruth Bader Ginsburg who wrote for the court.

U.S. Supreme Court
Buckley v. Valeo, 424 U.S. 1 (1976)

Landmark First Amendment protection case pertaining to campaign spending. The ruling helped establish the fact that spending on ballot measure campaigns cannot be limited.

California Trial Lawyers Assn. v. Eu, 200 Cal.App.3d 351 (1988) No. C003936. Court of Appeals of California, Third Appellate District. April 15, 1988.

This case was the first successful pre-ballot challenge to a California initiative under the single subject rule. The court prohibited the Secretary of State from qualifying or placing on the ballot a lengthy measure embracing several subjects.

Campbell, Hamilton, Initiative & Referendum Institute, et al v. Buckley, 98-1329 (1998) United States Court of Appeals, Tenth Circuit, No. 98-1329 Appeal from the United States District Court for the District of Colorado (D.C. No. 98-K-1022)

This case was filed in 1998 and challenged Colorado's constitutional, statutory, and administrative procedures for review of initiative measures before they are placed on the ballot. The lower court ruled against the complaint.

Canvasser Services v. Employment Department, 997-TAX-00099; CA A100171 (1999) Filed: October 13, 1999, in the Court of Appeals of the State of Oregon

In this Oregon case, the courts ruled that signature gatherers cannot be independent contractors and must be paid as employees.

Chandler v. City of Arvada, CO, Federal District Court for the State of Colorado, 00-N-0342 (2001)

This case struck down as unconstitutional a local ordinance requiring petition circulators to be residents of the city.

Chemical Specialties Manufacturers Assn., Inc. v. Deukmejian, 227 Cal.App.3d 663 (1991) No. A048489. First Dist., Div. Three. Feb. 8, 1991.

The California Appellate Court found Proposition 105, which required disclosure in a wide variety of areas (campaigns, hospitals, South African contracts, etc.), to violate the single subject rule of the state constitution.

U.S. Supreme Court
Citizens Against Rent Control v. Berkeley, 454 U.S. 290 (1981) Appeal from the Supreme Court of California, No. 80-737. Argued October 14, 1981, decided December 14, 1981

The U.S. Supreme Court held that a California city's ordinance to impose a limit on contributions to committees formed to support or oppose ballot measures violated the First Amendment. The Court based its decision on the right of individuals to bear and obtain information. In doing so, it equated free political spending with free speech.

Citizens for Jobs & Energy v. Fair Political Practices Commission, 16 Cal.3d 671 (1976) [S.F. No. 23391. Supreme Court of California. April 7, 1976.]

The California Supreme Court declared that the Political Reform Act couldn't limit expenditures by ballot measure committees.

Dale v. Keisling (98C-18552; CA A105873) (2000) FILED: May 24, 2000 IN THE COURT OF APPEALS OF THE STATE OF ORE-GON

The Oregon Court of Appeals ruled that "a constitutional initiative or referral is invalid (and none of its provisions take effect, regardless of the vote), unless the court determines that voters would necessarily have approved every single element of the measure, if those elements were stated separately."

Finn v. McCuen, 303 Ark. 418, 798 S.W. 2d 34 (1990)

Since the title of a lottery measure was misleading, the court ruled that the measure should not be allowed on the ballot.

U.S. Supreme Court
First National Bank of Boston v. Bellotti, 435 U.S. 765 (1978) APPEAL FROM THE SUPREME JUDICIAL COURT OF MASSA-CHUSETTS, No. 76-1172. Argued November 9, 1977, decided April 26, 1978

The Supreme Court has supported the notion that one-sided spending is not a crucial factor in ballot issue elections. In this case, the U.S. Supreme Court invalidated a Massachusetts statute prohibiting business corporations from making contributions or expenditures "... for the purpose of ... influencing or affecting the vote on any question submitted to the voters, other than one materially affecting any of the property, business or assets of the corporation."

Hardie v. Eu, 18 Cal.3d 371 (1976) S.F. No. 23450. Supreme Court of California. November 29, 1976.

The California Supreme Court found unconstitutional the Political Reform Act's cap on expenditures for qualifying ballot measures since it violated First Amendment rights.

Hartig v. City of Seattle, 53 Wash. 432, 102 P. 408 (1909)

In 1909, the Washington Supreme Court considered whether I&R violated the Guarantee Clause of the Federal Constitution. The Washington court did not think the question of representative government was relevant at all to the question of whether a form of government was republican. They stated: "[I]t can scarcely be contended that this plan is inconsistent with a republican form of government, the central idea of which is a government by the people. Whether the expression of the will of the people is made directly by their own acts or through representatives chosen by them is not material. The important consideration is a full expression."

H-CHH Associates v. Citizens for Representative Government, 193 Cal.App.3d 1193 (1987) No. B019051. Court of Appeals of California, Second Appellate District, Division One. July 28, 1987.

The California Appellate Court ruled that an indoor shopping mall cannot ban petition gatherers but can impose reasonable rules on circulators.

Initiative & Referendum Institute, Idaho Coalition United for Bears, et al v. Cenarussa, D.C. No. 00-0668-S-BLW (2001)

The U.S District Court struck down Idaho state laws that required signatures from 6% of each of Idaho's 22 counties, prohibited the payment of circulators on a per-signature basis, and prohibited circulators from willfully making a false statement to obtain signatures, but upheld the law that requires circulators to be residents of the state.

Initiative & Referendum Institute v. Costco (California State District Court BC 18052) (1998)

This case was filed in 1998 and sought to require Costco stores to adhere to existing California law and establish standard and reasonable time, place and manner restrictions for petitioners. The case was decided in favor of Costco.

Initiative & Referendum Institute v. Ralph's (California State District Court BC 187162) (1998)

This case was filed in 1998 and sought to require Ralph's stores to adhere to existing California law and establish standard and reasonable time, place and manner restrictions for petitioners. The case was decided in favor of Ralph's.

Initiative & Referendum Institute et al v. Alvin Jaeger, 99-3434 (2001) Appeal from the Federal District Court for the State of North Dakota, Initiative & Referendum Institute et al v. State of North Dakota, A1-98-70 (1998)

This case sought to overturn North Dakota's prohibition on paying circulators on a per-signature basis and the requirement that circulators be eligible North Dakota voters. The District Court upheld the state laws. The case was appealed to the U.S. Court of Appeals for the 8th Circuit, which affirmed the lower court's ruling.

Initiative & Referendum Institute et al v. Secretary of State of Maine (Federal District Court for the State of Maine, Civil No. 98-104-B-C, 1999)

The Federal judge upheld the state's residency and voter registration requirements for petition circulators but ruled that the state's law on banning a petitioner's pay on a per signature bases was unconstitutional.

Initiative & Referendum Institute et al v. State of Utah (2-00-cv-837) (2000) United States District Court for the District of Utah, Central Division

This case asked the court to review, declare unconstitutional and enjoin enforcement of Proposition 5, the 1998 legislatively sponsored amendment to the Utah Constitution. The amendment requires any citizen ballot initiative involving wildlife to pass with a two-thirds supermajority vote of the Utah electorate. The Court ruled the law was constitutional. An appeal is pending.

Initiative & Referendum Institute v. United States Postal Service, 1:00CV01246 (2000) In the United States District Court for the District of Columbia

The suit seeks to overturn the USPS regulation prohibiting citizens from collecting petition signatures on initiative petitions on postal property. The new postal regulation severely limits the ability of citizens around the country to place issues before their fellow voters.

Insurance Industry Initiative Campaign Com. v. Eu, 203 Cal.App.3d 961 (1988) No. C004348. Court of Appeals of California, Third Appellate District. August 12, 1988.

The court ruled that an initiative measure can be prevented from being circulated if it violates the single subject rule.

In re Pfahler, 150 Cal. 71, 88 P. 270 (1906)

In this case, the California Supreme Court upheld a local initiative law against a Guarantee Clause challenge while implying that similar measures on the state level would be constitutional as well. The court stated: "In saying this, we do not wish to be understood as intimating that the people of a state may not reserve the supervisory control as to general state legislation afforded by the initiative and referendum, without violating this provision of the federal constitution."

Jordon v. City of Seattle (Washington Supreme Court No. 68805-2) (2001)

In this case, citizens submitted a petition with the requisite number of signatures to the Seattle City Council on a proposed ordinance regarding the funding of neighborhood branch library facilities. The Seattle City Council amended the initiative in such a way as to nullify it and adopted the amended version. The City refused to place the initiative on the ballot, and the case is now on appeal to the Washington State Supreme Court. The issue is the right of referendum over local ordinances.

Joytime Distributors v. State of South Carolina (1999) In the Supreme Court of the State of South Carolina, Opinion No. 25007 Heard October 12, 1999 — Filed October 14, 1999

In this case, the South Carolina Supreme Court ruled that the state legislature did not have the authority to place statutes on the ballot for a general vote of the people.

Kadderly v. City of Portland, 44 Or. 118, 74 P. 710 (1903)

In this case, the Oregon Supreme Court sustained initiative and referendum against a Guarantee Clause attack. The courts states, "The initiative and referendum amendment does not abolish or destroy the republican form of government, or substitute another in its place. The representative character of the government still remains. The people have simply reserved to themselves a larger share of legislative power, but they have not overthrown the republican form of the government, or substituted another in its place."

Kean, Initiative & Referendum Institute, et al v. Clark, 56 F. Supp. 2d 719 (S. District of Miss. 1999)

In this Mississippi case, the Federal District Court concluded that although a voter registration requirement for petition circulators would be unconstitutional, a residency requirement was permissible. They also ruled that changes to the state's initiative laws couldn't be applied retroactively.

Lehman v. Bradbury, SC S48771 (2002)

The Oregon State Supreme Court struck down term limits on state elected officials as being unconstitutional. The Court ruled that the constitutional amendment, passed in 1992, violated the state's requirement that initiative amendments could not affect more than one section of the state constitution.

LIMIT v. Maleng, 874 F. Supp. 1138 (W.D. Wash., 1994)

In this Washington State case, the Federal District Court found that the state's prohibition against paying circulators on a per-signature basis was an unconstitutional infringement on freedom of political speech.

Marijuana Policy Project et al v. DC Board of Elections and Ethics et al, Civil Action No. 01-2595 (2002)

In this precedent setting case, the U.S. District Court for the District of Columbia overturned the Barr Amendment (so named because it was sponsored by Congressman Bob Barr), which prohibited the District of Columbia from expending any monies to decrease the penalties for use or distribution of a Schedule I controlled substance. The amendment would have prohibited validation of the election results of a medical marijuana initiative. The court found the Barr Amendment unconstitutional as applied to ballot initiatives and stated that Congress had overstepped its bounds and had improperly infringed upon the First Amendment Rights of the initiative proponents.

McIntire v. Bradbury, A0006-06252 (2000) In the circuit court of the State of Oregon, in and for the County of Multnomah

The plaintiffs in this Oregon case alleged that state election officials had violated their constitutional rights by declaring certain voters to be "inactive," thereby making them ineligible to sign initiative petitions. They requested a temporary injunction against this declaration, but it was denied.

U.S. Supreme Court
McIntyre v. Ohio Elections Commission, 115 U.S. 1511 (1995) Certiorari to the Supreme Court of Ohio, No. 93-986. Argued October 12, 1994, decided April 19, 1995

The U.S. Supreme Court upheld as constitutional an Ohio statute which prohibits the distribution of campaign literature that does not contain the name and address of the person or campaign official issuing the literature.

U.S. Supreme Court
Meyer v. Grant, 486 U.S. 414 (1988) Appeal from the United States Court of Appeals for the Tenth Circuit, No. 87-920. Argued April 25, 1988, decided June 6, 1988

The states of Colorado, Idaho and Nebraska each passed laws prohibiting the payment of petition circulators. The United States Supreme Court overturned these laws in this 1988 decision. Such a law, the Court ruled unanimously, restricts freedom of expression guaranteed by the First Amendment and that it restricts access to the most effective fundamental and perhaps economical avenue of political discourse, direct one-on-one communication.

Michigan Chamber of Commerce v. Austin, 832 F. 2d 947 (1987)

The federal appellate court ruled that Michigan's provisions limiting corporate contributions to ballot measure campaigns violated the right of association and free speech guarantees of the First Amendment. Another portion of the Michigan statute, prohibiting corporations from making independent expenditures on behalf of political candidates from general treasury funds, was upheld by the U.S. Supreme Court in Austin v. Michigan State Chamber of Commerce, U.S., ll0 S. Ct. 1391 (1990)

Michigan United Conservation Coalition v. Secretary of State, No. 119274 (2001)

In this case the Michigan State Supreme Court ruled that a concealed weapons law could not be referred because it included a clause for financial appropriations, which are not subject to referral. The dissent argued that the legislature had included the appropriations clause only to prevent the law from being referred.

Missourians to Protect Initiative Process v. Blunt, 799 S.W. 824 (1990)

The Missouri Supreme Court ruled an initiative off the ballot because it violated the single subject rule.

Montana Chamber of Commerce v. Argenbright, U.S. 9th 98-36256 (2000) U.S. 9th Circuit of Appeals 98-36256, Opinion issued September 26, 2000

The court of appeals affirmed judgments of the district court. The court held that the First Amendment does not permit restricting corporate expenditures as a means of expression on public issues presented through a state's ballot initiative process.

U.S. Supreme Court
Pacific States Telephone & Telegraph Co. v. State of Oregon, 223 U.S. 118 (1912)

This U.S. Supreme Court case addressed whether Oregon's initiative and referendum system violated the Guarantee Clause of the U.S. Constitution. The Court sidestepped the issue by holding that whether a state has a republican form of government is a political question and therefore non-justiciable, The court concluded that any such determination should be made by Congress, which seemed to settle the issue at the federal level.

Planning and Conservation League, Inc., et al, v. Daniel A. Lungren 38 Cal. App. 4th 497, (1995) No. C016761, Court of Appeal of California, Third Appellate District, September 22, 1995

This case invalidated a legislative attempt to regulate the fashion in which initiatives could qualify for the ballot.

U.S. Supreme Court
Pruneyard Shopping Center v. Robins, 447 U.S. 74 (1980) Appeal from the Supreme Court of California, No. 79-289 Argued March 18, 1980, decided June 9, 1980.

The U.S. Supreme Court ruled that state constitutional provisions that permit political activity at a privately owned shopping center do not violate federal constitutional private property rights of the owner.

Roberts v. Priest, 00-485 (2000) Original Action Petition, Arkansas Supreme Court

The Arkansas Supreme Court prohibited the Secretary of State from placing an initiative on the ballot because the language of the proposal was misleading. The Court said that the wording must be specific and the effects clear before a proposal can be submitted to the voters.

San Francisco Forty-Niners v. Nishioka, 75 Cal.App.4th 637 (1999) No. A083687. First Dist., Div. One. Oct 6, 1999. Superior Court of the City and County of San Francisco, No. 995661

In this case the San Francisco superior court issued a writ of mandate prohibiting respondent San Francisco Director of Elections from qualifying an initiative measure for the ballot. The writ was issued on the grounds that the circulating initiative petition contained false statements intended to mislead voters and induce them to sign the petition.

Senate of the State of California v. Bill Jones, SO83194 (1999) Filed 12/13/99, in the Supreme Court of California

This 1999 decision struck an initiative off the California primary ballot because it violated the state's single subject provision for initiatives.

Stanson v. Mott, 17 Cal.3d 206 (1976) L.A. No. 30567. Supreme Court of California. June 22, 1976.

The California Supreme Court ruled that the use of public funds for election campaigning to promote or oppose a ballot measure is illegal.

State ex rel. Nelson v. Jordan, 104 Ariz. 193 (1969)

The Arizona Supreme Court ruled that when two initiatives conflict, it is the duty of the court to harmonize both.

Stenberg v. Moore, 258 Neb. 199 (1999) Filed November 19, 1999. No. S-98-983.

The Nebraska Supreme Court dealt with the constitutionality of a Nebraskan statute that required that the information a voter puts on an initiative petition (signature, address, etc.) be an exact match of what is in the voter registration records in order for the signature to be counted as a valid signature. The Nebraska Supreme Court ruled that this law was facially unconstitutional.

Stranahan v. Meyer (CC 9110-06504; CA A88372; SC S45547) (2000) In the Supreme Court of the State of Oregon Argued and submitted November 5, 1999. Filed: September 14, 2000

In this case the Oregon State Supreme Court reversed one of its earlier decisions and ruled that the collection of signatures is banned on all private property.

Taxpayers to Limit Campaign Spending v. Fair Political Practices Commission, 51 Cal.3d 744 (1990) No. S012016. Supreme Court of California. Nov 1, 1990.

The California Supreme Court finds that when two initiatives covering the same topic appears on the same ballot, the one initiative receiving the most votes supersedes the other measure in all respects, even though some of the provisions of the one initiative with fewer voters do not conflict with the provisions of the other measure receiving the higher number of votes.

Telford v. Thurston County Board of Commissioners, No. 23559-5-11 (1999)

In November 1996, Paul Telford filed a lawsuit against the Thurston Board of County Commissioners, the Washington State Association of Counties (WSAC), and the Washington State Association of County Officials (WACO) to prevent their use of public funds in political campaigns. The trial court filed a memorandum opinion and an order granting partial summary judgment in favor of Telford, ruling that WSAC and WACO are "quasi-public agencies" subject to RCW 42.17 and therefore cannot use their funds to oppose ballot measures.

Thomas J. Walsh et al v. Secretary to the Commonwealth, SCJ-07986 (1999) Dates: May 7, 1999. — July 16, 1999. Civil action commenced in the Supreme Judicial Court for the county of Suffolk on January 6, 1999

This litigation pertained to the validity of a petition and petition signatures if the petition had been altered in any way. The court ruled that signatures on petitions could be invalidated just because a coffee stain appeared on the petition.

Waremart v. Progressive Campaigns, Inc., 67029-3 (1999) Filed December 16, 1999 in the Supreme Court of the State of Washington

The State Supreme Court ruled that grocery stores do not have to allow initiative petitioning on their property.

WIN v. Warheit, 98-35412 (2000) U.S. 9th Circuit Court of Appeals, No. 98-35412; D.C. No. CV-97-05427-RJB Appeal from the United States District Court for the Western District of Washington Argued and Submitted February 16, 2000 — Seattle, Washington Filed May 25, 2000

The court struck down as unconstitutional the Washington State requirement that requires disclosure of the names, addresses and salaries of people hired to gather signatures for ballot initiatives.

7 Legislative Attempts to Regulate the Initiative and Referendum Process

The Initiative process has been used throughout its history as a tool for the people to utilize to reign in government when it has become too powerful and when government refuses to deal with the issues supported by the people. Since the end result of most initiatives, especially those that reign in government, has been to limit the government's power, elected officials have taken offense. *Congress Daily* on April 14, 2000 said it best when they said:

"[t]hese are difficult times for advocates of ballot initiatives. First, the U.S. Postal Service ruled that initiative supporters had to stop gathering signatures at post offices. Then, the Supreme Judicial Court in Massachusetts ruled that state law justified the rejection of signatures because of stray pen marks in the margins. Later, a Washington State court ruled that a grocery chain could bar petition circulators from its property. And now, a bevy of states have begun pursuing further procedural restrictions on initiatives."

Legislative attempts to "reform" the process aren't new. Legislators since the first use of the process have been trying to restrict its use for they see it — rightfully so — as a means reserved to the people to limit their power. But as William Jennings Bryon said in 1920:

"[W]e have the initiative and referendum in Nebraska; do not disturb them. If defects are discovered, correct them and perfect the machinery ... make it possible for the people to have what they want ... we are the world's teacher in democracy; the world looks to us for an example. We cannot ask others to trust the people unless we are ourselves willing to trust them."

California is a perfect example. Since the voters first adopted the initiative process in 1912, the state legislature has consistently tried to make it more difficult. When California first adopted the process, the citizens had an unlimited amount of time to collect signatures. Then, as the population of the state ballooned — which meant that the signatures had to collect more signatures on petitions — the state legislature was busy shortening the circulation period. It went from unlimited to four years and then to the current requirement of 180 days to collect over 750,000 signatures. One could legitimately question the rationale of drastically decreasing the circulation period during a period of high population growth.

Modern day attempts to reform the process is even more prevalent. From 1998 to 2002, nine states — Arizona, Idaho, Mississippi, Missouri, Montana, Oklahoma, Utah and Wyoming — have tightened procedural restrictions on initiatives.

In November 2000, Nebraska voters rejected a law placed on the ballot by the state legislature that would require initiatives to pass twice before becoming law. Legislators in Alaska, Arizona and Washington are debating whether to impose new geographic distribution requirements for petition circulators, while California and Florida legislators are mulling whether to change the majorities required to pass initiatives. And on May 16th, 2000 Oregon voters went to the polls and defeated an increase in the number of signatures required to place a constitutional amendment on the ballot — an amendment placed on the ballot by the state legislature.

Despite the fact that the citizens adopted the initiative process to ensure citizen government, most of the states where the citizens provided that they retain initiative rights have seen the legislature enact legislation that restricts rather than facilitates the use of these powers by the people. The legislatures' regulation of the initiative and referendum have often violated the citizenry's First Amendment rights as articulated by the U.S. Supreme Court in *Meyer v. Grant,* 486 U.S. 414 (1986). It can be argued that not a single example of truly facilitating legislation has ever been enacted by any state legislature. Furthermore, the restrictions imposed on the citizenry are typically not imposed on other individuals seeking to use a state's electoral processes to invoke changes in state government, whether it be through lobbying, legislating, or running for political office.

States do have a compelling interest in ensuring that all elections, including those on the initiative and referendum, are conducted in a non-fraudulent manner. However, if the state legislatures wish to regulate lawmaking by the people they should impose the same restrictions on their own powers. Lobbyists, for example, who seek to have the legislature enact new laws or propose amendments to the state constitution typically have no voter registration or residency requirements imposed on them — but signature collectors for initiatives do. The purported purpose behind legislatively imposed limitations on the citizenry in the initiative and/or referendum process should be viewed skeptically in the absence of evidence of unique voter fraud during these processes.

A variety of legislative enactments in various states demonstrate how the legislatures have reacted to the use of the initiative process. Many argue that their response appears based on self-interest rather than an interest in protecting a system of government where the citizens are an independent branch of government. A review of the various legislatures' responses, many argue, reveal that control of a distinct branch of government, the people, by legislative action is not about fraud but about raw political power. Let's look at some examples:

States have banned paying petition circulators on a 'per signature' basis.

Several states have prohibited sponsors of initiative petitions from paying or compensating persons who circulate or obtain signatures on petitions according to the number of signatures collected or petitions circulated. These laws were enacted despite the absence of any showing that the initiative process needed correction.

A) Florida

In Florida, the citizenry may propose constitutional amendments in a manner controlled by the legislature. In both 1990 and 1991, when the statewide campaigns for term limits on the legislature were moving forward, the legislature introduced bills that would have changed the process for collecting signatures for initiative petitions.

First, in 1990, Senate Bill 870 required that each signature on a petition be witnessed and the sponsor certify that no per signature fee was paid. Second, the 1991 bill required initiative sponsors to certify that they had not paid a per signature fee for the collection of signatures. These two attempts by the legislature to make the collection of initiative signatures more difficult were vetoed.

Both Governor Martinez and Chiles concluded that this proposed legislation would "so stringently limit access to certification of a citizen initiative that it must be viewed as an effort to quash or severely limit the ability of the people to revise their constitution, in contradiction to the spirit expressed by this reservation of power." Interestingly, these bills were introduced while term limit petitions were circulating. In 1992, term limits were enacted on Florida's state legislature.

In 1998, the Florida legislature attempted to require sponsors of initiatives who intend to use paid petition circulators to file an affidavit with Florida's election division. This was being done despite the U.S. Supreme Court's statement in *Meyer v. Grant* that it was not prepared to assume that a professional circulators whose qualifications for similar future assignments may well depend on a reputation for competence and integrity; is any more likely to accept false signatures than a volunteer who is motivated entirely by an interest in having the proposition placed on the ballot.

B) Mississippi

Florida is not alone. The Mississippi legislature in 1998 overrode the Governor's veto to enact legislation making it unlawful for persons who pay other persons to circulate initiative petitions or who collect signatures on a petition to base that pay on the number of signatures collected or petitions circulated. This law required the State to refuse to accept any initiative petitions, even if only one signature on the entire petition was obtained in violation of the "per signature" ban. This legislation coincided with a term limits initiative for the state legislature. Mississippi's Constitution directed the legislature not to restrict or impair the people's reserved power to propose constitutional amendments. This law was ultimately struck down by the Federal District Court as a violation of the First Amendments protection on free speech.

C) Washington State

Like Mississippi, the Washington legislature, in 1993, one year after term limits were approved by the voters via the initiative, enacted a statute making it a "gross misdemeanor" to pay or compensate circulators according to the number of signatures collected. The legislature asserted that this form of compensation "encourages the introduction of fraud in the signature gathering process . . . Such payments also threaten the integrity of the initiative and referendum process by providing an incentive for misrepresenting the nature or effect of a ballot measure in securing petition signatures for the measure."

This restriction was struck down because the State failed to produce proof of fraud or an actual threat to the "citizens' confidence in government" resulting from circulators being compensated based on the number of signatures they procured.

D) North Dakota, Maine, and Wyoming

Three other states enacted measures similar to those previously discussed. Wyoming and Maine enacted legislation prohibiting the payment of initiative petition circulators based on the number of signatures they collect. Maine's legislature passed its statute in 1994, one-year after the voters through the initiative passed term limits. Wyoming's legislature imposed its restriction on the people in 1996, at a time when there was an initiative campaign underway that would inform voters on the ballot whether candidates for the state and federal legislatures supported a term limits amendment to the United States Constitution.

North Dakota enacted legislation in 1988 that also precluded paying initiative and referendum petition circulators based on the number of signatures collected. This was a legislative response to the criminal convictions of five paid circulators for petition fraud in a 1986 initiative involving the lottery. Thus, this one time experience with petition fraud, fraud that was detected and powerfully prosecuted, was used to permanently deprive the people of an effective method for exercising their constitutional right to the initiative and referendum.

Both the Maine and North Dakota statutes were challenged in Federal Court. The U.S. District Court of Maine ruled, citing *Meyer v. Grant,* that the circulation of an initiative or referendum petition "involves the type of interactive communication concerning change that is appropriately described as core political speech" and citing *Buckley v. ACLF,* that a state may not, consistent with the First Amendment, severely burden such speech unless the regulation at issue is "narrowly tailored to serve a compelling state interest." The Court ruled that although the regulation didn't have the effect of halting all initiative and referendum activity in Maine (and that the proponents probably could have put their initiative on the ballot if they had worked harder and spent more), that the Statute nevertheless severely burdened the plaintiffs' attempt to mount their drive. However, the North Dakota Federal District Court ruled that the law was constitutional. It will be up to the U.S. Supreme Court to sort this issue out.

"Notice" requirement of circulators who are being paid.

Although not prohibiting the payment of petition circulators, some states have sought to limit the initiative by requiring some form of "notice" or disclosure either on the initiative petition itself or in a statement to be filed with an official informing potential signers and the appropriate officials whether and how much such circulators are or will be paid. These states include Idaho, Colorado, Arizona, Ohio, Oregon, and California.

A) Oregon

Oregon's statutes provide that the chief petitioners of a measure must include a statement with their prospective petition indicating whether persons will be paid money or "other valuable consideration" for collecting signatures on the petition. In 1992, the same year that term limits were enacted on legislators via the initiative, the legislature proposed an amendment to that section that would also require that each sheet of the petition indicate whether circulators were paid. The "notice" would state "Some Circulators For This Petition Are Being Paid." This bill was passed over the Governor's veto.

B) Arizona

Arizona requires each petition sheet to have a space for indicating whether a circulator is a paid circulator or is a volunteer. This provision was added by the legislature in 1991 just before the people through the initiative process adopted term limits in 1992. Arizona invalidates those signatures obtained by a circulator who does not indicate whether he or she is paid or is a volunteer.

C) California

In the same year that legislative term limits were approved by the voters via the initiative in California, the legislature added its "notice" provision to California's Elections Code in 1990 as Section 41.5.57 This section provided that:

"Notwithstanding any other provision of law, any state or local initiative petition required to be signed by voters shall contain in 12-point type, prior to that portion of the petition for voters' signatures, printed names, and residence addresses, the following language: **NOTICE TO THE PUBLIC THIS PETITION MAY BE CIRCULATED BY A PAID SIGNATURE GATHERER OR A VOLUNTEER. YOU HAVE THE RIGHT TO ASK.** (Emphasis added)."

Only initiative petitions require such a notice.

D) Idaho

The Idaho legislature revised in 1997 its state's statutory provisions governing the initiative and referendum. The legislature imposed new restrictions making it more difficult for the citizens to successfully qualify an initiative or referendum petition for the ballot.

Included in these revisions was a specific statement that "Any person who circulates any petition for an initiative or referendum shall be a qualified elector of the state of Idaho." Section 34-1807 further states, "Any petition upon which signatures are obtained by a person not a qualified elector of the state of Idaho shall be void." Thus, like Mississippi, Idaho not only punishes the circulator, but it also punishes the signers of these petitions, even when the signatures are valid.

Idaho also now requires that initiative and referendum petitions circulated by paid circulators have printed in bold red type the statement:

THIS INITIATIVE (OR REFERENDUM as the case may be) PETITION IS BEING CIRCULATED BY A PAID SIGNATURE GATHERER. THE SIGNATURE GATHERER IS EMPLOYED BY OR HAS CONTRACTED WITH (insert name), THE MAIN OFFICE OR HEADQUARTERS OF WHICH IS LOCATED AT (city and state).

If the person is a volunteer, however, the petition must have printed in bold red type:

"THIS INITIATIVE (OR REFERENDUM as the case may be) PETITION IS BEING CIRCULATED BY AN UNPAID VOLUNTEER."

No "Notice" requirements must be placed on legislative nominating petitions indicating to signers of such petitions that the circulator is being paid, is a volunteer, or even is an employee of a state legislator.

E) Colorado

In 1993, the Colorado legislature amended its entire statutory article governing initiatives and referendums. It added a subsection that not only required "notice" whether a petition circulator was paid, but also required the circulator to wear a badge while circulating. This badge was to have printed on it in bold-faced type "VOLUNTEER CIRCULATOR" or "PAID CIRCULATOR." Moreover, if the circulator was paid, the name and telephone number of the person who hired them was also to be printed on the badge. This "badge" was purportedly necessary to help "prevent fraud by enabling the public to identify individuals who make false or fraudulent statements while circulating."

The U.S. Supreme Court upheld the trial court's ruling striking down this requirement as unconstitutional. While agreeing that the state has a "compelling interest" in maintaining the integrity of its initiative process, the Court held that this provision was not narrowly tailored to serve the state's interest.

Residency requirements for petition circulators.

In addition to the above restrictions, most of the states that provide for the initiative and referendum now require that petition circulators be residents of the state in which they circulate. Prior to adopting legislation requiring circulators to be residents of the states, many of these states had a requirement that circulators be registered voters of the state. The U.S. Supreme Court ruled in 1999 in *Buckley v. ACLF* that the registered voter requirement was unconstitutional because it violated the citizens First Amendment rights.

In 1999 the Arizona legislature passed new legislation that required that all petition circulators must be qualified to be registered to vote (i.e. a resident of the state, etc.)

Additionally in 1999, the Idaho and Utah legislatures passed new laws requiring all petition circulators be residents of the state and in that same year, the Missouri legislature not only passed legislation requiring that all petition circulators be residents of the state, but also required that all signature-gatherers register with the state and provided that all signatures gathered by unregistered circulators be declared invalid.

A residency requirement for petition circulators, as did the registered voter requirement, diminishes the number of persons available to promote a political message through the initiative petition. However, the residency requirement has yet to reach the U.S. Supreme Court. Certainly, such restrictions make it less likely that sponsors of initiatives will collect signatures necessary to place the initiative on the ballot.

Yet, some of the states that now require circulators to be residents did so because the legislatures claimed they were dealing with problems associated with paid circulators. However, the same requirements have not been placed on nominating petitions and the courts have consistently found that fraud, though existing, is not prevalent enough to warrant such action by the legislatures.

A) Nebraska

Nebraska's unicameral limited initiative petition circulators to Nebraskans. The legislative debates surrounding the voter registration requirements acknowledged that such a requirement was enacted to address problems associated with paid circulators. The legislature sought to do indirectly that which the U.S. Supreme Court ruled a state could not do, prohibit the use of paid professional circulators. However, this law was struck down by the 1999 *Buckley v. ACLF* decision.

B) Colorado

Although Colorado's Constitution was amended to require that circulators of petitions be "registered electors," the U.S. Supreme Court ruled that this law "unconstitutionally infringed on free expression." Without deciding whether a state's interest in preserving the integrity of its initiative process required that all circulators be residents of the state, the court found that Colorado's voter registration requirement was not narrowly tailored to satisfy a compelling state interest.

C) Mississippi

Article 15. §273(12) of Mississippi's Constitution states that the legislature "shall provide by law the manner in which initiative petitions shall be circulated, presented and certified." Subsection 13 continues by stating that while the legislature may enact laws so as to allow the people to exercise this initiative power, the legislature "shall in no way restrict or impair the provisions of this section or the powers herein reserved to the people."

The legislature enacted legislation implementing the initiative process in 1993. However, along with the restriction that prohibited circulators from being paid "per signature," the legislature overrode the Governor's veto in 1996 and required circulators to be qualified electors of Mississippi. This law was struck down.

Despite this recent ruling striking down the requirement that petition circulators had to be "qualified electors," the legislature in 1998 proposed an amendment to its Constitution that would require circulators to be "residents" and additionally made the change retroactive in the hopes of striking a term limits measure off the November 1999 ballot. This proposed amendment was challenged in Federal Court and the court ruled that the retroactive aspect of the law was unconstitutional but let stand the residency requirement for circulators.

Mississippi's legislature has fervently sought to impose restrictions on the people's initiative right, despite the fact that its constitution specifically prohibits it from enacting legislation that restricts or impairs the people's power to the initiative. These limitations have been successful—only two initiatives have ever appeared on Mississippi's ballot.

Different voting schemes are used for legislation versus initiatives.

In addition to placing additional qualifications on persons seeking to use the initiative process, several states have also imposed unique voting schemes on initiatives; thereby making it more difficult for the people to successfully enact their proposals.

In Mississippi, constitutional amendments proposed by the legislature become part of the constitution "if it shall appear that a majority of the qualified electors voting directly for or against the same shall have voted for the proposed change, alteration or amendment". However, for constitutional amendments proposed by the people through the initiative, the initiative or legislative alternative "must receive a majority of the votes thereon and not less than forty percent (40%) of the total votes cast at the election at which the measure was submitted to be approved."

Wyoming allows passage of an initiative only when "an amount in excess of fifty percent (50%) of those voting in the general election" cast a vote in favor of the proposed measure, not just a majority of those voting on the proposed measure. Thus, if voters choose not to vote on a measure, their non-vote is counted against it.

Massachusetts provides that legislative constitutional amendments, "if approved by a majority of the voters voting thereon," become part of the constitution. On the other hand, amendments proposed through the initiative or legislative substitutes become part of the constitution if approved "by voters equal in number to at least thirty percent of the total number of ballots cast at such state election and also by a majority of the voters voting on such amendment."

Utah amended their constitution in 1998 to require a two-thirds vote of the people in order to adopt by initiative a state law allowing, limiting, or prohibiting the taking of wildlife or the season for or method of taking wildlife.

Changes to the circulation period for initiatives.

In 1998, the Missouri legislature changed the deadline for submitting initiative petitions from four months prior to the election to six months prior—effectively decreasing the circulation period by two months.

Changes to distribution requirements for initiatives.

In 1998, the Wyoming legislature changed the distribution requirement for initiatives. The change required initiative proponents to not only gather signatures equal to 15% of the number of voters in the last general election, but to gather signatures equal to 15% of the number of voters in the last general election in 2/3 of Wyoming counties—making petitioners collect an impossible number of signatures in very sparsely populated areas. In 2000, the Utah legislature drastically increased the state's distribution requirement and in 2001 the Montana legislature placed on the ballot a constitutional amendment doubling the distribution requirement for initiative petitions which was subsequently adopted by the voters. The Utah legislation was ultimately overturned by the State Supreme Court and the Montana change is currently being litigated. In 1999 the Idaho legislature drastically increased the distribution requirement for initiatives only to have the law overturned by the Federal District Court of Idaho as being an unconstitutional restriction on the process. These rulings will no doubt lead to litigation in other states to strike down other cumbersome distribution requirements.

Similar restrictions are not imposed on lobbyists or other campaign workers.

Throughout this section, it has been noted that legislators enacted restrictions for the apparent purpose of "maintaining the integrity of the initiative process." Despite this asserted interest, however, the legislatures in the initiative states have failed to impose the same or similar restrictions on lobbyists hired to influence legislation and/or executive policy or individuals hired to work on a candidate's campaign for political office, including the circulation of a candidate's nominating petitions.

This disparate treatment can be seen in Mississippi's Lobbying Reform Act of 1994. While the Act defines "lobbying" as including "(i) Influencing or attempting to influence legislative or executive action through oral or written communication;" the legislature has imposed no restrictions on who may come into the state seeking to influence the course of legislative and executive policymaking. Yet, it requires those utilizing the initiative to be residents of the state.

Similarly, despite having residency requirements for circulators of initiative and referendum petitions, Wyoming fails to impose similar restrictions on lobbyists. Furthermore, while Wyoming requires petitions for candidates who are nominated by petition as independent candidates to include a circulator's verification, no statements indicate that the nomination petitions must be circulated by "qualified registered voters." Nor does Wyoming prohibit paying these circulators based on the number of signatures they collect.

In Colorado, while circulators of petitions for candidacy and recall must be eligible electors in the political subdivision where they are circulating petitions and they must affiliated with the political party of the candidate for at least two (2) months prior to filing the petition, no provisions exist regarding paying such circulators and having such payment information printed on nomination petitions as there exist for initiative petition circulators. Nor does it make provisions for such circulators to wear identification badges or to file monthly disclosure requirements for paid nominating petition circulators. Similarly, Colorado imposes no residency or voter registration requirements for lobbyists nor does it require lobbyists to wear identification badges.

Oddly, at the time the Colorado Legislature deemed it necessary to enact restrictions on those seeking to use the initiative process, it did not also impose the same limitations on lobbyists who are, like sponsors of initiatives, seeking to influence Colorado's elected officials.

Maine does not impose the same restrictions regarding residency and voter registration on lobbyists as it does on initiative and referendum petition circulators. Nor does it impose the initiative restrictions on circulators of nominating petitions.

In Idaho, lobbyists are not required to wear display tags at the time of lobbying. More importantly, while the legislature requires persons seeking to evoke change through the initiative and referendum to be residents of the state, persons seeking to accomplish the same thing via lobbying are not required to be residents or registered voters of Idaho.

Sampling of major initiative legislation

1998 Legislation
• Mississippi: Passed legislation requiring that only a person who is a resident of the state may circulate an initiative petition or obtain signatures on an initiative petition.
• Missouri: Changed the deadline for submitting initiative petitions from four months prior to the election to six months prior—effectively decreasing the circulation period by two months.
• Utah: Amended constitution to require a two-thirds vote of the people in order to adopt by initiative any state law allowing, limiting, or prohibiting the taking of wildlife or the season for or method of taking wildlife.
• Wyoming: Required initiative proponents to not only gather signatures equal to 15% of the number of voters in the last general election, but to gather signatures equal to 15% of the number of voters in the last general election in 2/3 of Wyoming counties—making petitioners have to collect an impossible number of signatures in very sparsely populated areas.

1999 Legislation

• Arkansas: Legislation requires the reporting of state funds in excess of $100 used to support or oppose a ballot measure.

• Arkansas: Gives the Arkansas Supreme Court original jurisdiction to determine the sufficiency of initiative and referendum petitions and proposed constitutional amendments.

• Arizona: Required that all petition circulators must be qualified to be registered to vote (i.e. a resident of the state, etc.)

• Idaho: Required that all petition circulators be a resident of the state.

• Missouri: Required that all petition circulators must be residents of the state. Also required that all signature-gatherers register with the state and provided that all signatures gathered by unregistered circulators be declared invalid.

• Montana: Required that employers of paid signature gatherers file financial disclosure reports.

• Montana: Gave Attorney General the authority to deny certification of an improper ballot measure.

• Nebraska: Passed legislation providing that in order for a constitutional amendment to become law it must be approved twice by the voters in separate elections. Also requires that initiative petitions be filed with the Secretary of State eight months prior to an election, rather than the existing requirement of four months. (Defeated by voters on November 7, 2000.)

• Oregon: Passed legislation increasing the number of signatures needed to get a constitutional amendment on the ballot from eight to twelve percent. (Defeated by voters on May 16th, 2000.)

• Oregon: Passed legislation extending the time period for the Secretary of State to verify signatures on petitions from 15 to 30 days. (Adopted by voters on May 16th, 2000.)

• South Dakota: Provided a procedure for opponents of an initiative to contest the validity of signatures.

• Utah: Required that political issues committees for initiatives and employers of paid signature gatherers file financial disclosure reports.

• Utah: Required that circulators must be a resident of the state.

2000 Legislation

• Alaska: Prohibits initiatives that permit, regulate or prohibit the taking or transportation of wildlife, or prescribes seasons or methods for the taking of wildlife. (Defeated by voters on November 7, 2000.)

• Alaska: Passed legislation limiting the amount you can pay a signature gatherer to no more than $1.00 per signature.

• Arizona: Requires a supermajority vote of the people for all future wildlife and hunting initiatives. (Defeated by voters on November 7, 2000.)

• Arizona: Allows a person to withdraw their signature from a petition.

• Minnesota: Senate Committee kills legislation passed by the House in 1999 allowing the citizens to vote on the establishment of initiative and referendum at the state level.

• South Dakota: Changes South Dakota's circulation period for collecting signatures by not allowing collection time to roll over to future ballots. For example, South Dakota's current circulation period is one year. It use to be that if you started collecting signatures in January and the deadline to make the upcoming ballot was May and you didn't have enough signatures by then, you could keep petitioning until your one year time limit was up—and the measure would go on the next available ballot. Now you still have one year, but no matter when you start you only have until the deadline for the closest election ballot to gather signatures.

• Wyoming: Requires petition circulators be registered voters and citizens of the state.

2001 Legislation

• Montana: Passed legislation that was adopted by the voters in November 2002 that would change the state's distribution requirement. The amendments would require signatures to be gathered from 50% of the counties. This is the exact same distribution requirement that was struck down by the Federal Court in Idaho.

• Oklahoma: Passed legislation that was defeated by the voters in November 2002 that would establish a higher signature requirement for initiatives that pertain to animal issues.

Conclusion

Many, if not most, of the restrictions discussed above were enacted or proposed during the recent wave of term limit, tax limitation and campaign finance initiatives enacted by the citizens. However, legislatures have always vigilantly inhibited the people's right to the initiative and referendum. Restrictions imposed on the people's use of these powers have typically been direct responses by the legislature to the people's use of these powers.

These are just a few examples of how the legislatures have acted to limit the people's right to initiate laws and/or amendments. The true motivations of lawmakers in passing these regulations must be scrutinized. Reforms should be considered. But the reforms being passed by these legislators are only increasing the cost of undertaking an initiative and doing nothing to address the legitimate concerns about the process that need to be considered. If lawmakers truly want to address the concerns raised about the process they should consider increasing circulation periods so the need for paying signature gatherers is diminished, establishing a requirement that public hearings on initiatives be held before the election so voters can be better informed, establishing more comprehensive financial disclosure requirements so the citizens know who is behind certain measures, establish a procedure where the state can help initiative proponents draft initiative language so the citizens can take advantage of their "expertise", and by creating the indirect initiative process so legislators have the opportunity to adopt and/or amend initiatives before they are voted on by the people.

8 Polling

The People's Support of I&R

By Alan Lindsey[1]

In 1999–2000, Portrait of America (POA) conducted a series of statewide telephone polls that asked voters if the initiative and referendum (I&R) process was good public policy. POA also conducted a national survey for the Initiative & Referendum Institute (IRI) in the spring of 2001 that asked voters nationally how they felt about the initiative and referendum process. In every case, POA found a majority of voters favor I&R. In fact, only four states had support under 55% (see chart below).

In every state, I&R supporters outnumbered opponents by at least 30% and in 17 states supporters outnumbered opponents by more than 50%. In five states the spread was 60% or more.

In the 24 states where the I&R process already exists, support is significantly higher than in the 26 states that do not have a statewide initiative process. On average, support was 8% higher in states that have I&R. Additionally, POA looked at the opposition to the initiative process and found it was five points lower among people who lived in initiative states than in non-initiative states.

One of the most interesting findings was the correlation between the level of support for I&R and the number of initiatives that appeared on the ballot. States that used the process more frequently in the four years before the survey have higher levels of support for I&R than states where the process was used less frequently. This finding would seem to be at odds with pundits who say voters are overwhelmed by a large number of issues on the ballot and hence dislike the initiative process.

Among states where voters used the initiative process 15 to 29 times, supporters outnumbered opponents by an average of 61%. In states where the process was used three to nine times, the average difference fell to 54% and where two or fewer initiatives were on the ballot the average difference was only 47%.

Where 15 to 29 issues made the ballot support averaged 72%. Where three to nine issues made the ballot support averaged 68%. Where less than two issues made the ballot support averaged only 61%.

The trend is also seen in opposition to I&R. In states with the most citizen-sponsored measures on the ballot (15–29) opposition was only 12%. The group in the middle (3–9 measures) averaged 14% opposition and the group at the bottom (0–2 measures) averaged 16% opposition.

The polling data suggests that greater use of I&R fosters support for the process. POA looked at the results from several perspectives and considered the mean averages cited above as well as the median averages. POA also evaluated the minimum and maximum values in each category. By every measure, support is significantly higher among I&R states. The 1999–2001 surveys conclusively demonstrate that the experience of voting on initiatives and referendum actually increases support for the process.

Portrait of America 1999–2000 Statewide Polling[2]

"In many states, citizens can place initiatives on the ballot by collecting petition signatures. If a majority of voters approve the initiative on Election Day, it becomes law. Is this a good idea?"

State	Percent Yes	Percent No	Percent Differential
Alabama	57	18	39
Alaska	70	14	56

---

1. Portrait of America (POA) is a non-profit polling firm. POA President Alan Lindsay has been featured in the national media and is well known for seeking public opinion on many timely and controversial topics of national interest. For more information contact Alan at alan@portraitofamerica.com or at (919) 280-4342.

2. Surveys were conducted telephonically with a 1,000 sampling. Margin of error is +/- 3%.

State	Percent Yes	Percent No	Percent Differential
Arizona	71	12	59
Arkansas	67	12	55
California	74	11	63
Colorado	71	12	59
Connecticut	63	16	47
Delaware	56	21	35
Florida	62	18	44
Georgia	61	18	43
Hawaii	62	20	42
Idaho	67	16	51
Illinois	57	18	39
Indiana	59	17	42
Iowa	51	19	32
Kansas	61	16	45
Kentucky	61	16	45
Louisiana	52	22	30
Maine	N/A	N/A	N/A
Maryland	66	15	51
Massachusetts	68	14	54
Michigan	65	16	49
Minnesota	61	16	45
Mississippi	58	18	40
Missouri	61	14	47
Montana	69	15	54
Nebraska	65	13	52
Nevada	74	12	62
New Hampshire	61	16	45
New Jersey	66	17	49
New Mexico	60	19	41
New York	54	20	34
North Carolina	52	21	31
North Dakota	66	12	54
Ohio	66	18	48
Oklahoma	60	17	43
Oregon	69	13	56
Pennsylvania	63	23	40
Rhode Island	57	22	35
South Carolina	58	19	39
South Dakota	75	09	66
Tennessee	55	19	36
Texas	63	16	47
Utah	71	11	60
Vermont	58	21	37
Virginia	57	20	37
Washington	75	10	65
Washington DC	59	16	43
West Virginia	60	17	43
Wisconsin	55	19	36
Wyoming	68	14	54

Initiative & Referendum Institute National Survey[3]
Conducted by Portrait of America on 04/29/01–5/01/01

In 24 states, citizens can propose laws by petitioning. This is called a "citizen's initiative." Do you favor such a process in your state?

	Total	Gender		Age					Race		
		Men	Women	18–29	30–39	40–49	50–64	65+	White	Black	Other
Yes	67.8%	67.9%	67.7%	73.7%	69.9%	65.7%	65.9%	61.9%	70.0%	56.8%	65.2%
No	13.2%	15.2%	11.4%	12.0%	11.5%	13.5%	16.4%	12.8%	12.4%	20.9%	11.5%
Not sure	18.6%	16.5%	20.7%	13.5%	18.3%	20.7%	17.7%	25.0%	17.2%	22.3%	23.3%
Declined to answer	.3%	.4%	.2%	.9%	.4%	.0%	.0%	.3%	.4%	.0%	.0%

Should there be a similar process where citizens can place laws on the ballot nationwide?

	Total	Gender		Age					Race		
		Men	Women	18–29	30–39	40–49	50–64	65+	White	Black	Other
Yes	56.7%	56.3%	57.1%	64.2%	58.0%	57.9%	55.9%	44.3%	56.4%	62.9%	53.7%
No	20.9%	25.2%	17.0%	19.4%	18.4%	23.1%	22.5%	21.7%	22.2%	19.5%	15.3%
Not sure	21.7%	18.1%	25.0%	15.0%	22.3%	19.0%	21.6%	33.7%	20.9%	17.6%	29.1%
Declined to answer	.6%	.4%	.8%	1.4%	1.4%	.0%	.0%	.3%	.5%	.0%	1.8%

All other things being equal, which do you think is more likely to produce laws that are in the public interest; When the law is adopted by the legislature, or when the voters adopt the law.

	Total	Gender		Age					Race		
		Men	Women	18–29	30–39	40–49	50–64	65+	White	Black	Other
By the legislature	20.4%	25.1%	16.0%	19.2%	19.0%	16.6%	21.2%	27.3%	22.3%	13.4%	16.1%
By the voters	65.5%	61.3%	69.3%	69.4%	62.4%	72.3%	65.4%	55.7%	64.0%	77.2%	64.2%
Not sure	13.6%	13.0%	14.1%	9.9%	17.9%	11.1%	13.2%	16.9%	13.3%	9.4%	18.7%
Declined to answer	.5%	.5%	.5%	1.5%	.7%	.0%	.2%	.0%	.5%	.0%	1.1%

President Bush has proposed a 1.6 trillion dollar tax cut. The US Senate passed a smaller tax cut. Should we let the voters choose between them in a national referendum?

	Total	Gender		Age					Race		
		Men	Women	18–29	30–39	40–49	50–64	65+	White	Black	Other
Yes	55.0%	52.0%	57.7%	63.2%	56.0%	56.8%	51.1%	44.5%	54.1%	58.7%	56.3%
No	31.9%	39.1%	25.2%	25.5%	34.1%	29.2%	36.7%	35.4%	33.5%	25.3%	28.4%
Not sure	12.6%	8.7%	16.2%	10.5%	9.2%	14.0%	11.2%	19.9%	11.9%	14.4%	15.3%
Declined to answer	.6%	.2%	.9%	.8%	.7%	.0%	.9%	.3%	.5%	1.6%	.0%

Should the legislature impose additional regulations on citizen petitions?

	Total	Gender		Age					Race		
		Men	Women	18–29	30–39	40–49	50–64	65+	White	Black	Other
Yes	22.1%	23.4%	21.0%	29.9%	22.8%	20.3%	18.3%	17.2%	22.0%	18.9%	25.7%
No	50.3%	53.8%	47.0%	45.1%	46.4%	53.3%	54.0%	54.1%	50.8%	51.3%	46.7%
Not sure	27.0%	22.4%	31.3%	24.5%	29.9%	26.1%	26.8%	28.5%	26.8%	28.2%	27.6%
Declined to answer	.5%	.4%	.7%	.4%	.9%	.3%	.9%	.3%	.5%	1.6%	.0%

Should there be a national referendum before sending troops into a foreign conflict, where the United States has not been attacked?

	Total	Gender		Age					Race		
		Men	Women	18–29	30–39	40–49	50–64	65+	White	Black	Other
Should be national referendum	41.4%	38.0%	44.5%	56.7%	39.7%	35.3%	30.8%	41.9%	38.2%	56.2%	46.5%
Should not be national referendum	45.5%	52.4%	39.1%	32.2%	43.9%	53.8%	55.3%	44.2%	48.8%	36.4%	34.7%
Not sure	12.5%	9.4%	15.3%	10.7%	15.0%	10.6%	13.0%	13.4%	12.4%	5.8%	17.9%
Declined to answer	.7%	.2%	1.1%	.4%	1.4%	.3%	.9%	.5%	.5%	1.6%	.9%

---

3. Survey was conducted telephonically with a 1,000 sampling. Margin of error is +/- 3%.

If an organization supported a measure that would improve the way government works which group would be more receptive to the idea, the legislature, or the voters?

	Total	Gender		Age					Race		
		Men	Women	18–29	30–39	40–49	50–64	65+	White	Black	Other
Legislature	13.5%	14.0%	13.0%	16.0%	11.9%	11.7%	13.1%	14.3%	12.5%	20.9%	12.5%
Voters	59.6%	63.5%	56.0%	60.4%	49.8%	64.9%	61.2%	62.1%	59.4%	56.9%	63.0%
Equally likely	17.7%	14.9%	20.3%	15.8%	24.7%	14.5%	16.8%	16.8%	18.3%	9.8%	20.6%
Not sure	8.8%	7.5%	10.1%	7.7%	12.9%	8.9%	7.6%	6.8%	9.5%	10.8%	3.9%
Declined to answer	.4%	.1%	.6%	.0%	.7%	.0%	1.3%	.0%	.3%	1.6%	.0%

If an organization supported a measure that would harm your state, which group would be more receptive to arguments against the measure: the legislature, or the voters?

	Total	Gender		Age					Race		
		Men	Women	18–29	30–39	40–49	50–64	65+	White	Black	Other
Legislature	20.6%	23.8%	17.6%	30.2%	17.9%	15.3%	16.0%	22.1%	20.6%	19.0%	21.7%
Voters	61.5%	59.5%	63.3%	55.0%	59.2%	68.4%	66.8%	58.6%	61.7%	65.2%	57.5%
Equally likely	12.6%	12.1%	13.1%	10.6%	16.0%	11.8%	12.3%	13.0%	13.0%	8.3%	14.4%
Not sure	4.8%	4.3%	5.3%	4.2%	6.6%	4.1%	4.0%	5.3%	4.5%	4.3%	6.5%
Declined to answer	.5%	.4%	.7%	.0%	.4%	.5%	.9%	1.0%	.2%	3.2%	.0%

Generally speaking, when legislators propose regulations on petitioning, are they generally trying to protect the public, or are they trying to preserve their own power?

	Total	Gender		Age					Race		
		Men	Women	18–29	30–39	40–49	50–64	65+	White	Black	Other
Protect the public	16.4%	17.6%	15.3%	18.8%	15.8%	12.5%	17.3%	17.5%	17.7%	13.0%	12.5%
Preserve their power	66.9%	68.7%	65.3%	67.2%	64.0%	72.3%	66.0%	64.6%	66.4%	75.0%	63.1%
Not sure	16.2%	13.5%	18.6%	13.6%	19.8%	14.6%	15.8%	17.6%	15.5%	10.4%	24.5%
Declined to answer	.5%	.2%	.8%	.4%	.4%	.5%	.9%	.3%	.4%	1.6%	.0%

As the polls above indicate, the citizen's support for the initiative process is strong and since its inception the citizens have desired to preserve it. Numerous polls and surveys prove this point—all of which can be found at www.iandrinstitute.org. Additional information regarding these polls can be found at www.portraitofamerica.com.

9 A Sampling of Issues Brought Forth through the Initiative and Referendum Process[1]

Throughout the history of the initiative and referendum process, the citizens have used I&R to address some of the most controversial issues of their day and age; abortion, animal rights, campaign finance reform, death penalty, drug policy reform, education reform, environmental reform, gaming, gay rights, gun control, poll taxes, physician assisted suicide, prohibition, taxes, term limits, and women's suffrage—to name a few.

Contrary to popular belief, the initiative and referendum process has not been controlled by any one ideological group. In fact, the process has been used almost equally by people of all political persuasions. Following is a listing of the different types of issues that have been addressed utilizing the I&R process and how they rank:

Category[2]	Number of Statewide Initiatives	Rank by Use (highest to lowest)
Taxes	363	1
Administration of Government	317	2
Education Reform	120	3
Alcohol Regulation	114	4
Environmental Reform	108	5
Business Regulation	94	6
Labor Reform	92	7
Gaming	90	8
Election Reform	80	9
Term Limits	62	10
Health/Medical	61	11
Animal Rights/Protection	53	12
Utility Regulation	50	13
Campaign Finance Reform	47	14
Welfare	45	15
Apportionment/Redistricting	39	16/17
Nuclear Weapons/Facilities/Waste	39	16/17
Legal	36	18
Civil Rights	34	19
Initiative and Referendum	31	20
Bonds	30	21
Drug Policy Reform	23	22
Abortion	20	23
Judicial Reform	18	24
Banking Regulation	16	25
Daylight Savings Time	11	26
Death Penalty	10	27/28
Veteran Affairs	10	27/28
Tort Reform	9	29
Gun Regulation	7	30
Housing	6	31
Unknown	6	32
Alien Rights	5	33
Physician Assisted Suicide	5	34

1. The Initiative & Referendum Institute takes no position on any ballot measure or subject matter addressed by a specific ballot measure, nor does it take a position on the essays contained within. They are being provided for educational purposes only as a way to help students of the initiative and referendum process gain a better understanding of the complex and controversial issues that have been addressed using the initiative and referendum process.

2. We have attempted to place each initiative into the broadest category possible. Many initiatives could easily be categorized in multiple categories. However, for simplicity, we have chosen to place each initiative into one specific category.

The following essays will hopefully provide you with a greater understanding of how the initiative process has been used to address some of the more controversial issues.

The Animal Protection Movement and I&R

By Wayne Pacelle[3]

The formation of the first animal protection organization, the American Society for the Prevention of Cruelty to Animals in 1866, preceded by more than three decades the earliest adoptions of the initiative and referendum process in western states.

Throughout the first 40 years when the initiative process was available in many states, animal protection groups did not use the process frequently, focusing primarily on local concerns and direct care of horses, dogs, and cats. Few groups focused on state policy, and fewer still on national policy. Nonetheless, there were several initiatives dealing with vivisection, rodeo, and trapping in the 1920s and 1930s, with voters rejecting most of the measures.

Between 1940 and 1990, animal advocates qualified just a handful of animal protection initiatives, and only one of them passed—a 1972 measure in South Dakota to ban dove hunting. Voters reversed the dove hunting ban just eight years later. Maine voters rejected a ban on moose hunting in 1983, for instance, and Ohio and Oregon voters rejected anti-trapping initiatives in 1978 and 1980, respectively. This 50-year period marked a period of hegemonic control over policies related to the use of animals by agricultural, hunting, and other industries.

Since 1990, there has been a proliferation of animal protection initiatives, largely spearheaded by the organizing efforts of The Humane Society of the United States and The Fund for Animals. These groups approached the initiatives in a highly professional manner, carefully identifying issues in demographically favorable states, organizing volunteer petitioners, conducting public attitude surveys, raising money, and persuading voters primarily by airing emotionally compelling advertising showing direct harm to animals.

After the California Fish and Game Commission voted to institute a mountain lion hunting season in 1988, animal advocates sued the state to delay the onset of the hunting. Concomitantly, they launched and qualified an initiative—with volunteers amassing in excess of 600,000 signatures—to ban any trophy hunting of lions. In June 1990, voters approved the measure, and its passage sparked renewed interest in the initiative process by animal advocates, whose prior experiences had left them skeptical about the usefulness of the process for their issues.

Between November 1992 and November 2000, animal advocates squared off against hunters and other animal use industries in 33 statewide ballot campaigns, marking a huge surge in the use of the process on animal issues. Twenty-two of the measures were initiatives pushed by animal protection advocates, two measures were initiatives by animal use industries, and nine were pro-hunting referenda placed on ballots by state legislators.

While two measures related to cockfighting, one dealt with greyhound racing, and one with the slaughter of horses for human consumption, most of the initiatives and referenda related to the taking of wildlife. Animal protection advocates had very limited successes in appealing to state legislatures and to executive agencies on hunting and trapping issues. Hunters have dominated state wildlife commissions, and the agencies have viewed themselves primarily as service agencies for this user group. In state legislatures, many wildlife protection bills were assigned to fish and wildlife committees, whose members were by and large elected officials from rural areas with little sympathy for animal protection values.

Animal advocates had long despised the use of steel-jawed leghold traps, which they regarded as inhumane and indiscriminate. Animal advocates worked to place anti-trapping initiatives on seven ballots during the last decade, prevailing in five battles. Six other initiatives dealt with hound hunting and baiting of predators, and animal advocates prevailed in four races. One measure related to the shooting of captive animals, in so-called canned hunts, and two measures related to the airborne hunting of wolves in Alaska—voters approved all three of these measures.

In short, the hunting initiatives did not seek to ban all hunting, but to combat certain hunting and trapping practices viewed as particularly cruel and unsportsmanlike. Voters backed a very high percentage of these measures, sending shock waves through the hunting community and causing state fish and wildlife agencies to reassess their relationships with animal protection advocates.

After the initiative success of the early 1990s, hunting groups and their legislative allies struck back. In California, hunting groups convinced the legislature to place a measure on the ballot to overturn the initiative to ban the trophy hunting of mountain lions. But voters rejected that effort by a wide margin. In the same year, in Oregon, hunting groups qualified an initiative to repeal the 1994 measure that banned hounding and baiting. As in California, voters soundly drubbed the repeal effort, retaining the hunting restrictions.

---

3. Wayne Pacelle is senior vice president for communications and government affairs for The Humane Society of the United States.

Taking the message from the public that it was reluctant to repeal initiatives it had previously approved, hunting groups worked in state legislatures to place measures on the ballot to raise the passage standard or to eliminate the possibility of placing wildlife protection measures on the ballot.

In 1998, the Utah Legislature referred a measure to the ballot to require a two-thirds majority to pass any measure to restrict the taking of wildlife—making the process unusable for animal protectionists. Thanks to a 15 to 1 campaign spending disparity favoring hunters, voters approved the measure. In 2000, however, Arizona voters rejected an identical initiative by 63 percent "no" vote, even though hunters outspent animal groups by a five to one margin. In Alaska, voters rejected a measure to bar any future initiative dealing with wildlife protection by nearly a two to one margin.

For 2002, animal use industries have developed a new strategy to thwart animal protection initiatives. In Oklahoma, legislators sympathetic to hunters, farmers, and cockfighters have placed a legislative referendum on the ballot to double the number of signatures needed to place any animal welfare measure on the ballot.

Hunting groups have had success in one area: constitutional amendments that seek to enshrine hunting rights. Legislatures have referred these measures to ballots in Alabama in 1996, Minnesota in 1998, and in North Dakota and Virginia in 2000, and voters have approved them by very wide margins. Michigan legislators referred a measure to the ballot in 1996 to give the state Natural Resources Commission "exclusive authority" over wildlife management decisions, and voters approved it. Animal protection groups have provided little resistance to the measures, arguing that the measures have little practical effect and amount to little more than a political statement in state constitutions.

In sum, animal protection groups have used the initiative process as a safety valve, resorting to its use when legislators fail to enact popular reforms. The issue of cockfighting provides the clearest example. In Arizona and Missouri, rural legislators bottled up anti-cockfighting legislation for decades, until voters settled the issue through direct voting in lopsided campaigns. Oklahoma voters are expected to vote on an anti-cockfighting initiative in 2002.

Animal protection groups have relied more on volunteer petition gatherers than any other social movement. Not possessing major financial resources, the groups have rank-and-file activists who believe passionately in the cause, and they have been the shock troops that help to qualify these measures.

When animal use industries dominate the legislative process, one can expect that animal advocates will resort to the initiative process. Because the animal use groups are politically powerful in more traditional venues, lawmakers can be counted on to develop strategies to restrict the initiative process by raising qualification and passage standards.

Animal Protection Initiatives and Referendum

Year	State	Issue	Measure Number	Pass/Fail	Yes %	No %
1930	MA	Prohibit use of trapping devices	Question 3	Passed	69%	31%
1972	SD	Prohibit mourning dove hunting	Measure 1	Passed	67%	33%
1977	OH	Prohibit use of trapping devices	Measure 2	Failed	37%	63%
1980	OR	Prohibit use, sale of snares, leg hold traps	Measure 5	Failed	37%	63%
1980	SD	Repeal of mourning dove hunting ban	Measure 1	Failed	42%	58%
1983	ME	Repeal moose hunting season	Measure 1	Failed	39%	61%
1990	CA	Prohibit sport hunting of mountain lions	Proposition 117	Passed	52%	48%
1992	AZ	Ban steel jawed traps and other body gripping traps	Proposition 200	Failed	38%	62%
1992	CO	Prohibit spring, bait, and hound hunting of black bears	Amendment 10	Passed	70%	30%
1994	AZ	Prohibit steel jawed traps	Proposition 201	Passed	58%	42%
1994	OR	Ban bear baiting and hound hunting of mountain lions	Measure 18	Passed	52%	48%
1996	AL	Constitutional recognition of hunting	Amendment 1	Passed	81%	19%
1996	AK	Ban same day airborne hunting of wolves and foxes	Measure 3	Passed	58%	42%
1996	CA	Allow the trophy hunting of mountain lions	Proposition 197	Failed	42%	58%
1996	CO	Ban leg hold traps and other body gripping traps	Amendment 14	Passed	52%	48%
1996	ID	Ban spring, bait, and hound hunting of black bears	Proposition 2	Failed	40%	60%
1996	MA	Restrict steel traps and other body-gripping traps, ban hound hunting of bears and bobcats	Question 1	Passed	64%	36%
1996	MI	Ban baiting and hounding of black bears	Proposal D	Failed	40%	60%
1996	MI	Management of wildlife populations	Proposal G	Passed	69%	31%
1996	OR	Repeal ban on bear baiting and hound hunting of bears and cougars	Measure 34	Failed	42%	58%

Year	State	Issue	Measure Number	Pass/Fail	Yes %	No %
1996	WA	Ban bear baiting and hound hunting of bears, cougars, bobcats and lynx	Initiative 655	Passed	63%	37%
1998	AK	Ban wolf snare trapping	Proposition 9	Failed	36%	64%
1998	AZ	Prohibit cockfighting	Proposition 201	Passed	68%	32%
1998	CA	Ban the use of cruel and indiscriminate traps and poisons	Proposition 4	Passed	57%	43%
1998	CA	Prohibit slaughter of horses and sale of horse meat for human consumption	Proposition 6	Passed	59%	41%
1998	CO	Uniform regulations of livestock	Amendment 13	Failed	39%	61%
1998	CO	Regulation of commercial hog facilities	Amendment 14	Passed	62%	38%
1998	MN	Constitutional recognition of hunting	Amendment 2	Passed	77%	23%
1998	MO	Prohibit cockfighting	Proposition A	Passed	63%	37%
1998	OH	Restore the ban on mourning dove hunting	Issue 1	Failed	40%	60%
1998	UT	Require 2/3 majority for wildlife ballot issues	Proposition 5	Passed	56%	44%
2000	AK	Ban wildlife issues from ballot	Measure 1	Failed	36%	64%
2000	AK	Ban land-and-shoot wolf hunting	Measure 6	Passed	53%	47%
2000	AZ	Require 2/3 majority for wildlife ballot issues	Proposition 102	Failed	38%	62%
2000	MA	Ban greyhound racing	Question 3	Failed	49%	51%
2000	MT	Prohibit new game farm licenses	Initiative 143	Passed	52%	48%
2000	ND	Constitutional recognition of hunting	Question 1	Passed	77%	23%
2000	OR	Restrict steel traps and certain poisons	Measure 97	Failed	41%	59%
2000	VA	Constitutional recognition of hunting	Question 2	Passed	60%	40%
2000	WA	Restrict steel traps and certain poisons	Initiative 713	Passed	55%	45%

Drug Policy Reform Initiatives and Referenda

By Scott Ehlers[4]

Over the past three decades, two different types of organizations have attempted to use the initiative and referendum process to bring about drug policy reform in the United States: (1) grassroots organizations, primarily made up of volunteer activists, and (2) professional campaigns funded by three major funders, directed by paid campaign professionals, whose sole mission is to coordinate drug policy reform initiatives.

"Grassroots" Drug Policy Reform Initiative Campaigns

The first two drug policy reform initiatives to qualify for state ballots were grassroots efforts. In 1972, activists in California gathered the required signatures to qualify an initiative for the ballot that would have decriminalized adult possession and cultivation of marijuana for personal use. The California Marijuana Initiative, Proposition 19, only garnered 34 percent of the vote, but it is credited with creating the impetus for California's 1975 marijuana decriminalization law.

In 1986, activists in Oregon placed an initiative on the ballot that would have legalized the private possession and cultivation of marijuana for personal use. Amid much anti-drug sentiment in the country at the time, Measure 5 was defeated with 26 percent support.

It would be another ten years before another drug policy reform initiative would be on a state ballot. In 1996, medical marijuana activists in California began the arduous task of gathering the required signatures to place a medical marijuana initiative on the ballot. When it became clear that the grassroots activists would not be able to gather the required signatures with their limited resources, three major funders stepped in to pay for the remaining signatures, and a professional campaign consultant, Bill Zimmerman, was hired to run the campaign.

"Professional" Drug Policy Reform Initiatives and Referenda Campaigns

Since the 1996 passage of the California medical marijuana initiative, Proposition 215, the vast majority of statewide drug policy reform initiatives and referenda(I&R) have been organized by three organizations supported by three pri-

---

4. Scott is the Director of Research at the Campaign for New Drug Policies.

mary benefactors.[5] As opposed to the largely volunteer efforts of the grassroots organizations, these organizations are directed by paid campaign professionals with paid staff. The three "professional" drug policy reform organizations are the Campaign for New Drug Policies (CNDP), its affiliated medical marijuana project, Americans for Medical Rights (AMR), and in Arizona, The People Have Spoken. The three primary financial backers of these organizations are: George Soros, financier; Peter Lewis, CEO of Progressive Insurance; and John Sperling, CEO of the Apollo Group.

The "professional" drug policy reform I&R campaigns begin each election cycle by deciding which states they should work in for the next general election. Initiative states are chosen using a number of factors, including: a state's national political prominence; relative impact of, and need for a policy reform; geographical location; cost; signature-gathering requirements (deadlines; geographical requirements; number of signatures, etc.); and the level of pre-election voter support. Polling and focus groups are used to measure voter opinions, and initiatives are drafted, in part, on these results. The final text of the initiatives are drafted to maximize the policy impact of the reform while retaining enough public opinion support to be victorious at the polls.

Since 1996, the "professional" drug policy reform I&R campaigns have won 15 of 17 initiatives and referenda they have sponsored. These campaigns fall into three major categories: (1) legalization of the medical use of marijuana; (2) requiring drug treatment instead of incarceration for non-violent drug possession offenders; and (3) the reform of civil asset forfeiture laws. Also, in 1998 Oregonians voted to keep their state's policy of marijuana decriminalization by rejecting a law passed by the legislature through a referendum which would have re-criminalized marijuana. In 1998, Arizona voters also rejected attempts to alter a 1996 drug policy reform initiative through two different referenda.

Medical Marijuana

Under federal law, marijuana is classified as a Schedule 1 drug, which means that the government considers it a drug that has no acceptable medical use and is highly addictive. Other Schedule 1 drugs include heroin and LSD, and along with marijuana, these drugs are completely prohibited for medical or non-medical use.

Despite its prohibited status, many patients have found marijuana to be beneficial in treating: nausea associated with cancer chemotherapy or HIV/AIDS treatment; spasticity associated with multiple sclerosis; eye pressure associated with glaucoma; as well as relieving the pain and suffering associated with a number of other diseases and chronic pain. Because of marijuana's prohibited (and politically unpopular) status, medical research has been effectively stifled by the federal government, thus making legal access to the drug impossible except for the eight patients who legally receive marijuana from the federal government today.

In 1996, Californians for Medical Rights (now Americans for Medical Rights) helped pass Proposition 215, the first statewide ballot initiative that effectively legalized the possession, use, and cultivation of marijuana for medical use. Patients and/or caregivers are exempt from the state's marijuana possession and cultivation laws if the patient has a written recommendation from his/her doctor to use medical marijuana, and the patient or caregiver possesses a quantity of the plant that is consistent with medical use.

In 1998, Americans for Medical Rights (AMR) organized medical marijuana initiatives in a number of other states, including: Alaska, Washington State, Oregon, and Nevada. All of these initiatives differed from California's Proposition 215 in that they established confidential medical marijuana patient registries in state health departments. Patients (and their caregivers) with a valid doctor's recommendation to use medical marijuana are given identification cards to verify that they are medical marijuana patients who can legally possess or grow small quantities of marijuana.

In 1999, Maine voters approved an AMR medical marijuana initiative, and in 2000, voters in Colorado and Nevada (once again) approved similar measures. (In Nevada, constitutional amendments must be approved by the voters twice, so the medical marijuana initiative had to be voted on in 1998 and 2000.)

Drug Treatment Instead of Incarceration

The first ballot initiative to require that non-violent drug possession offenders be placed in treatment rather than being incarcerated was Arizona's Proposition 200, which was sponsored by Arizonans for Drug Policy Reform (now The People Have Spoken) and which passed in 1996. Treatment services are paid for with a new alcohol tax. Proposition 200 also allows doctors to prescribe Schedule 1 drugs (such as marijuana), if at least two doctors feel that the medication is appropriate for the patient and they have scientific documentation that supports their decision.

---

5. Since 1996, there have been two other statewide "grassroots" drug policy reform initiatives that were not organized by the Campaign for New Drug Policies, Americans for Medical Rights, or The People Have Spoken, nor paid for by George Soros, Peter Lewis, and John Sperling. In 1998, AIDS activists in Washington, DC placed a medical marijuana initiative on the ballot. Initiative 59 passed with 69 percent support, but it had not been approved by Congress as of this publication. In 2000, activists in Alaska placed an initiative on the ballot that would have legalized and regulated the sale of marijuana in a manner similar to alcohol. Ballot Measure 5 garnered 41 percent support.

The organizers of Proposition 200 attempted to take the initiative to Washington State in 1997. As was the case with the Arizona initiative, this new measure, Initiative 685, required treatment instead of incarceration for first and second time drug possession offenders and allowed doctors to prescribe Schedule 1 drugs to seriously ill patients under certain circumstances. Initiative 685 only garnered 40 percent of the vote, because, according to press reports following the election, "talk of hard drugs scared initiative voters."

In 2000, the Campaign for New Drug Policies placed initiatives on the ballot in California and Massachusetts that would have required that first and second time drug possession offenders receive probation and drug treatment in lieu of incarceration. The Massachusetts initiative also went one step further: low-level drug dealers who could prove in court that they were dealing to support their drug addiction could receive treatment at the discretion of the judge. Drug treatment would have been paid for, in part, from money and property forfeited from convicted drug dealers.

Despite opposition by Governor Gray Davis, U.S. Senator Diane Feinstein, 57 of 58 county sheriffs, and most of the state's major editorial boards, California's Proposition 36 passed with 61 percent support. It is arguably one of the most far-reaching criminal justice reform laws passed in decades, and according to the state Legislative Analysts' Office, is expected to result in 36,000 drug possession offenders receiving drug treatment instead of being incarcerated, at an estimated savings of over $1 billion over five years.

The Massachusetts initiative, Question 8, failed with 48 percent of the vote.

Civil Asset Forfeiture Reform

Civil asset forfeiture is based on the premise that property that is involved in the commission of a crime is "guilty" and can be seized and "forfeited" by the government. The property owner doesn't have to be proven guilty of a crime to have his/her property forfeited. The owner does not have many of the due process protections given to defendants in criminal cases because the property—not the owner—is on trial, and forfeiture proceedings are held in civil court. Additionally, in most states and at the federal level, the proceeds of forfeited property are given to the law enforcement agency that seized the property, which many critics see as a conflict of interest. The vast majority of civil asset forfeiture cases are drug-related.

In 2000, the Campaign for New Drug Policies placed civil asset forfeiture reform initiatives on the ballot in Utah and Oregon. Both initiatives essentially require that a person be convicted of a crime before their property can be forfeited, in addition to providing for a number of other due process protections for property owners. Oregon's Measure 3 passed with 67 percent of the vote. Utah's initiative B passed with 69 percent support. In Oregon, drug-related forfeiture proceeds are now used for drug treatment, and in Utah they are used for public schools.

Post-Election Results

Since the passage of these various drug policy reform initiatives, polling indicates that public support for these reforms has increased and a number of state legislatures have taken up similar reform measures. Some recent state legislative drug policy reforms include: medical marijuana in Hawaii in 2000 (S.B. 862); civil asset forfeiture reform (S.B. 36) and the decriminalization of the personal possession of marijuana (A.B. 453) in Nevada in 2001; and a variety of drug-related sentencing, welfare and civil asset forfeiture reforms in New Mexico in 2002.

"Grassroots" Drug Policy Reform Initiative Campaigns

Year	State	Ballot Number	Statutory or Constitutional; Initiative	Type of Initiative	Vote	Pass/Fail
1972	CA	Proposition 19	Statutory Initiative	Marijuana Decriminalization	34%-Yes 66%-No	Fail
1986	OR	Measure 5	Statutory Initiative	Marijuana Legalization	26 %-Yes 74%-No	Fail
1998	DC	Initiative 59	Statutory Initiative	Medical Marijuana	69%-Yes 31%-No	Passed
2000	AK	Measure 5	Statutory Initiative	Marijuana Legalization	41%-Yes 59%-No	Fail

"Professional" Drug Policy Reform Initiative and Referendum Campaigns

Year	State	Ballot Number	Statutory or Constitutional; Initiative or Referendum	Type of Initiative	Vote	Pass/Fail
1996	CA	Proposition 215	Statutory Initiative	Medical Marijuana	56%-Yes 44%-No	Passed
1996	AZ	Proposition 200	Statutory Initiative	Drug Treatment; Medical Marijuana	65%-Yes 35%-No	Passed
1997	WA	Initiative 685	Statutory Initiative	Drug Treatment; Medical Marijuana	40%-Yes 60%-No	Failed
1998	AK	Measure 8	Statutory Initiative	Medical Marijuana	58%-Yes 42%-No	Passed
1998	AZ	Proposition 300	Statutory Referendum	Medical Marijuana; Other	43%-Yes 57%-No	Reform Passed by Voter Rejection of Law
1998	AZ	Proposition 301	Statutory Referendum	Drug Treatment; Other	48%-Yes 52%-No	Reform Passed by Voter Rejection of Law
1998	NV	Question 9	Constitutional Initiative	Medical Marijuana	59%-Yes 41%-No	Passed
1998	OR	Measure 57	Statutory Referendum	Marijuana Decriminalization	34%-Yes 66%-No	Reform Passed by Voter Rejection of Law
1998	OR	Measure 67	Statutory Initiative	Medical Marijuana	55%-Yes 45%-No	Passed
1998	WA	Initiative 692	Statutory Initiative	Medical Marijuana	59%-Yes 41%-No	Passed
1999	ME	Question 2	Statutory Initiative	Medical Marijuana	61%-Yes 39%-No	Passed
2000	CA	Proposition 36	Statutory Initiative	Drug Treatment	61%-Yes 39%-No	Passed
2000	CO	Amendment 20	Constitutional Initiative	Medical Marijuana	54%-Yes 46%-No	Passed
2000	MA	Question 8	Statutory Initiative	Drug Treatment; Civil Asset Forfeiture Reform	48%-Yes 52%-No	Failed
2000	NV	Question 9	Constitutional Initiative	Medical Marijuana	65%-Yes 35%-No	Passed
2000	OR	Measure 3	Constitutional Initiative	Civil Asset Forfeiture Reform	67%-Yes 33%-No	Passed
2000	UT	Initiative B	Statutory Initiative	Civil Asset Forfeiture Reform	69%-Yes 31%-No	Passed

Statewide Education Initiatives and Referendum

By Earl Bender and Katrien H. Bartelds[6]

Like many countries, the United States has two education systems that run in parallel with one another. Public education in the U.S. is the government-run and supported school system. Private schools are not run by government—they are supported and paid for by a wide variety of other entities, including religious institutions and profit making businesses.

Across the history of initiatives and referenda (I&R), public education ballot measures have focused first on the question of how to pay for public education. Other issue clusters that have been the subject of public education ballot measures include the appropriate role of public education in the United States, curriculum and school policies, and regulation of school employees. Lastly, because schools impact nearly everyone, many of the ballot measures dealt with social controversies and their affect on public schools.

---

6. Earl Bender is President of Avenel Associates, Inc. a political consulting firm that has specialized in ballot measure campaigns for two decades. He is also a founder of the Ballot Initiative Strategy Center (BISC) which is a resource to progressive organizations and individuals working on ballot measure campaigns. Katrien H. Bartelds an American Studies graduate from the University of Groningen in the Netherlands is a research associate at Avenel.

Paying for Public Education.

From public education's 18th century beginnings up until the 1970s or even later, public schools have primarily been funded by property taxes levied and collected at local levels. However, counties, towns or cities have not always had sufficient resources to meet the needs of growing school systems. Statewide public education ballot measures have frequently been used to provide additional monies for underfunded local schools. School bonds—ballot measures in which citizens approve public borrowing and vote to impose additional property taxes upon themselves for the length of time necessary to repay the principal and interest—are the most common tool used to help fund education.[7] U.S. voters are generally skeptical about new or higher taxes. For this reason, bond ballot measures are most often used to pay for capital improvements—so-called "bricks and mortar" physical projects that allow voters to see exactly what new school buildings or facilities they are buying with their taxes. These bond measures have been used to fund everything from expansion of state higher education systems to construction of local school buildings across the state.

School bond ballot measures tend to pass when economic times are prosperous and when specific projects to be financed are listed. When either element is missing, the fortunes of these measures are quite uncertain. As the population ages and fewer voters feel directly connected to their local schools, school-funding measures face greater voter resistance.

The increasing costs of public education also produced an opposing response. The tax revolt that began in the late 1970s impacted education by reducing tax revenues available to states and localities through property tax limitations. California's Proposition 13 touched off this wildfire in 1978. Arguing that schools were too costly and that tax money was being wasted, anti-tax groups and public school opponents encouraged voters to reduce their tax burdens. Many of these measures passed, particularly during uncertain and difficult economic times.

Tax levy changes were also designed to accomplish other public school funding goals. For example, to fund state supreme court-mandated fairer redistribution of finances across the states wealthier and poorer school districts, Ohio's legislature referred new property tax levies to the ballot, which failed.

Recognizing that their historic reliance upon local property taxes no longer provided adequate funding for public education, public education proponents began considering alternative ways to fund public education. Ballot measures guaranteeing funding levels are one response to declining state support for public education. California led this trend by passing Proposition 98 in 1988. This initiated amendment embedded a requirement into the state constitution that education funding must be at least 40% of the state budget—that is, it set a floor for spending on education. This inspired supporters of public education in many other states to propose numerous measures designed to mandate funding formulas that would maintain or increase public school funding. Most of these measures failed. Yet, in 2000 Colorado voters approved a constitutional amendment requiring the state to increase K-12 public education funding at least 1% per year.

Opposing Public Education.

Another source of public education ballot measures has been a sustained assault on public education emanating from conservative social forces. The long-dominant public philosophy in the United States strongly supports public education as an institution that supports democracy and helps effectively create good citizens. In recent decades, a vital minority believes that government has no appropriate role in education and seeks to completely privatize education. These opponents of public education have innovatively used direct democracy to in their efforts to reduce or dismantle the public schools.

Foremost have been the attempts to defund public education by reducing or eliminating its funding mechanisms through tax reductions or rollbacks. Other proposals to defund public education via initiative and referenda include voucher and charter schools initiatives. School voucher proposals are the most controversial proposals, dividing proponents and opponents of public education. Voucher supporters want government to pay for their children to attend private schools. Public education supporters claim this takes money away from already under funded public schools.

Some public school opponents find fault with educators themselves. They have supported numerous ballot measures controlling conditions of employment or union activity, including attempts to limit or eliminate union political participation. Topics as varied as requiring union members to sign-up annually for membership or political participation and reducing or otherwise restricting school employee pensions have been proposed and sometimes passed.

Determining School Policy.

Another set of ballot measures has sought to prescribe education policy. With mixed success, the innovative west coast states have pioneered attempts to change school operations in various ways, including lowering class size, promoting or eliminating bilingual teaching, and setting teachers salaries or COLAs (cost of living adjustment wage increases). To date,

---

7. Notably, local school bonds and tax levies rather than statewide issues, are the most prevalent use of direct democracy in the United States.

efforts to use initiatives to translate social agendas into curriculum requirements have not qualified for ballot. Circulated curriculum issues have included what to teach about gay relationships and abstinence only programs.

Schools as a Social Prism.

Social conflicts in the United States have a way of intersecting with the public schools. This includes social battles fought out through the I&R process. Immigration issues have had public education components such as prohibitions on teaching English as a second language and California's Proposition 187, which included provisions compelling school-teachers and nurses to report illegal aliens.

Conclusion.

Public education I&R efforts have primarily focused on paying for schools. Methods of school operation, including curriculum issues, and the socialization of citizens in a democracy are increasingly the subject of statewide pubic education ballot measures. These trends will continue into the foreseeable future. One interesting developing trend in the battle over public education financing is earmarking taxes to pay for public education. With revenue sources declining and the pressures to reduce property taxes constantly increasing, some public education supporters are considering initiated measures to dedicate sales taxes, lottery revenues and other sources specifically to help pay for public schools.

Major Education Related Initiatives

Year	State	Measure Number	Description	Pass/Fail
1912	Arkansas	N/A	Free textbooks.	Failed
1920	Arizona	N/A	Publication of teachers salaries	Failed
1920	California	16	Adds kindergartens to public school system.	Passed
1920	Michigan	N/A	Compulsory school attendance.	Failed
1922	Oregon	6	Compulsory school attendance.	Passed
1924	Washington	I-49	Compulsory school attendance.	Failed
1924	Michigan	N/A	Compulsory school attendance.	Failed
1926	California	17	Permits the study and reading of Bible in public schools.	Failed
1928	Arkansas	N/A	Anti-evolution law.	Passed
1930	Arkansas	N/A	To require reading of Bibles in public schools.	Passed
1948	North Dakota	N/A	Prohibiting the wearing of religious dress by public school teachers.	Passed
1962	Arkansas	1	Provide 50% of general revenues for public school fund.	Failed
1972	Oregon	9	Prohibits property tax for school operations.	Failed
1974	Colorado	N/A	Prohibit the assignment or the transportation of pupils to public educational institutions in order to achieve racial balance of pupils at such institutions.	Passed
1978	Washington	I-350	Prohibits assignment of students to schools.	Passed
1978	Michigan	H	Exempt property tax from school operations and also would have established a school voucher system.	Failed
1980	Arkansas	1	Equal education for all children in the state.	Failed
1988	California	98	Establishes minimum level of funding for education	Passed
1990	Oregon	11	Choice of public schools; tax credit, private schools.	Failed
1992	Colorado	N/A	Vouchers for school funding.	Failed
1993	California	174	State education vouchers usable for public or private schools.	Failed
1996	Washington	I-173	Scholarship vouchers.	Failed
1996	Nebraska	411	Makes "quality education" a fundamental constitutional right.	Failed
1996	Oregon	42	Requires annual testing of public school students, grades 4–12.	Failed
1996	Washington	I-177	Provides for publicly-funded charter schools	Failed
1998	California	223	School districts to spend no more than 5 percent of all funds for administrative costs.	Failed
1998	California	227	Requires that all public school instruction be conducted in English.	Passed

Year	State	Measure Number	Description	Pass/Fail
1998	California	8	Would create fund for reduction in class sizes. Requires teacher credentialing and testing.	Failed
1998	Colorado	17	Would establish Income Tax Credit for education expenses.	Failed
2000	California	26	Authorizes bonds for construction, reconstruction, rehabilitation or replacement of school facilities if approved by 50% vote.	Failed
2000	Arizona	203	Requires that all public school instruction be conducted in English.	Passed
2000	California	38	Authorizes annual state payments of at least $4000 per pupil for qualifying private and religious schools for new enrollees.	Failed
2000	Oregon	95	Job performance must determine public school teacher pay.	Failed
2000	Michigan	1	Create voucher system. Guarantee per-pupil funding in public schools; require testing of teachers in academic subjects.	Failed
2000	Washington	I-728	Would direct that certain existing state revenue, including all unobligated lottery revenue, be placed in a student achievement fund and in the education construction fund.	Passed
2000	Washington	I-729	This measure would authorize school districts and public universities to sponsor charter public schools.	Failed
2000	California	39	Authorizes bonds for construction, reconstruction, rehabilitation or replacement of school facilities if approved by 55% vote.	Passed
2000	Colorado	23	Providing additional K–12 funding	Passed
2000	Washington	I-732	This measure would provide annual cost-of-living salary adjustments to school district employees.	Passed

Statewide Death Penalty Initiatives and Referendum

By Earl Bender And Katrien H. Bartelds[8]

The United States continues to actively use the death penalty, while capital punishment is largely disappearing throughout the world. As with many controversial issues, states view and practice the death penalty differently—currently 38 states have capital punishment, while 12 states and the District of Columbia have abolished it. There is constant tension between those who support this punishment and those who want to eliminate it.

The controversy surrounding the appropriateness of capital punishment has been brought before voters for their specific consideration in statewide plebiscites less than twenty times since 1912.[9] Citizen legislation concerning the death penalty can be divided into three periods: the Progressive Era, Developing Conscience, and Tinkering with the Machinery of Death. As the debate about the death penalty in America has evolved, each of these eras has its own characteristics and controversies.

Progressive Era 1912–1920.

As with the powers of the initiative and referendum themselves, the death penalty was one issue fermenting in the rich stew of Progressive Era social change sweeping America. It is no wonder that these new tools of direct democracy became one way in which policy battles over capital punishment were waged. Arizona and Oregon, two states that embraced the Initiative and Referenda (I&R) process early, repetitively contested their approach to capital punishment through ballot measures.

---

8. Earl Bender is President of Avenel Associates, Inc. a political consulting firm that has specialized in ballot measure campaigns for two decades. He is also a founder of the Ballot Initiative Strategy Center (BISC) which is a resource to progressive organizations and individuals working on ballot measure campaigns. Katrien H. Bartelds an American Studies graduate from the University of Groningen in the Netherlands is a research associate at Avenel.

9. Voters have also occasionally voted upon capital punishment as part of their omnibus consideration of new state constitutions. For example, Michigan voters enshrined a prohibition against capital punishment when they adopted their current state constitution.

Upon joining the union in 1912, Arizona incorporated initiative and referendum into its state constitution. Two years later the death penalty became one of the earliest issues fought out at the ballot box. A 1914 initiative to repeal the death penalty failed. Undaunted, Arizona abolitionists initiated another measure in 1916, and this time state voters passed repeal. The rubber match was fought out in the very next general election with the 1918 electorate reinstating the death penalty and ending Arizona's plebiscites on capital punishment.

Progressive Era Oregon was every bit the ballot measure hotbed the state is today. Four times in one decade Oregonians voted on the death penalty. In 1912 an initiative to repeal capital punishment failed. Like Arizona, populist proponents of abolition brought the measure back two years later and passed the repeal. In short order, Oregon's legislature jumped into the fray referring restoration of the death penalty to the ballot in 1918. It failed. Here too, second efforts succeeded when a 1920 referendum restoring the death penalty passed.

Restoration by voters in both Arizona and Oregon closed out the Progressive Era I&R contests over the death penalty. While votes were held in just two states, it was the vigorousness of the contests and the seesaw nature of the battles for the peoples' hearts and minds that characterized the debate and votes about the death penalty during the Progressive Era. At era's end, supporters of the death penalty had prevailed, temporarily settling the balance in favor of capital punishment.

Developing Conscience 1958–1970.

As the I&R process fell into disuse nationally, the focus on death penalty ballot measures waned. Nonetheless, the national conscience about capital punishment was changing profoundly as support for the death penalty steadily eroded after World War II. With the rejection of Jim Crow and the emergence of the Civil Rights movement, the death penalty again became controversial as some citizens began to see it as a vestige of an arbitrary, discriminatory and unfair process. State by state experience during this era showed that opinion about the death penalty was anything but settled.

In the late 1950s, as efforts to end the death penalty gathered steam, citizens again began employing the tools of direct democracy to contest capital punishment policy. Predictably, Oregon led the way as its 1958 legislature referred a measure ending the death penalty to the voters—this failed. Six years later, sensing the conscience of the state had changed; the legislature again referred abolition of the death penalty to the voters in 1964. This time it passed, temporarily deciding the issue in this state.

Colorado, with this era's sole citizen initiated statute, was next to let voters choose. In 1966, they rejected an initiative seeking to repeal the death penalty.

Two years later Massachusetts's voters considered an advisory referendum to the legislature encouraging them to keep the death penalty. It passed.

This era's last direct vote on capital punishment occurred in 1970, as Illinois voters were ratifying their newly revised state constitution. In a separate question, the voters were asked to vote to repeal the death penalty. This vote failed, keeping capital punishment in the new constitution.

During this period of Developing Conscience, no state voted to eliminate capital punishment. Nonetheless, opinion about support for the death penalty had weakened. Despite the relatively spare use of ballot measures during these decades, capital punishment issues reached the ballot in several states. While these ballot measures did not themselves change policy, they contributed to a critical tide of citizen support that helped spur the Supreme Court to act and set the stage for our current era.

"Tinkering with the Machinery of Death" 1972–Present.

This title quotes Justice Brennan's evocative characterization, which aptly describes both the Supreme Court's death penalty decisions and the changing political attitudes about the death penalty. This era's ballot measures have responded to anticipated changing requirements that the Supreme Court has placed on states wishing to retain the death penalty.

In 1972, the Supreme Court declared Georgia's—and by extension every other state's death penalty—unconstitutional in *Furman v. Georgia*. One effect of this case was to eliminate the death penalty in the United States for four years. The *Furman* decision also suggested how states could re-draft constitutional death penalty statutes. The Supreme Court approved Georgia's revised death penalty law in the 1976 *Gregg v. Georgia* case. State legislatures and citizen death penalty supporters dueled with abolitionists throughout this period. They have all used ballot measures to either eliminate or preserve the death penalty in accordance with continually developing Supreme Court standards.

Modern era initiatives began with the passage of a 1972 California initiative restoring the state's death penalty. Like all death penalty laws then on the books, the *Furman* decision rendered this citizen initiated statute unconstitutional. Next, Washington voters hoping to reinstate capital punishment, approved a 1975 initiative to require a mandatory death penalty.

Tinkering further, another stream of ballot measures sought to expand the death penalty by specifying more conditions under which states can impose capital charges. As often happens, innovative Oregon went first passing a 1978 initiative that restored and expanded that state's death penalty. Ohio voters passed a 1984 amendment (placed on the ballot by the state legislature) streamlining legal appeals to make it easier to execute death row inmates. While citizens have tried initiating expansion measures in other states, these efforts often fail to gather sufficient signatures to qualify for the ballot.

Initiated and referred measures have been used to anticipate and perhaps preempt the Supreme Court. Oregon (1984) and Florida (1998) voters have both passed measures designed to exempt their capital punishment statutes from any eventual declaration by the Supreme Court that the death penalty is a "cruel and unusual punishment". The Oregon measure was citizen initiated. Florida's Constitutional Revision Commission, concerned that the U.S. Supreme Court might eventually declare the state's use of the electric chair cruel and unusual punishment, referred a similar exemption to Florida voters who passed it.

In the dynamic opinion environment surrounding the death penalty, capital punishment opponents are manifesting the latest wave of citizen legislative activity. They are again collecting signatures in states like Missouri and Oregon for measures to repeal each state's death penalty. These new abolitionist organizing efforts have not yet achieved the critical mass that was evident during the earlier "Developing Conscience" period.

Since 1972, several influences have surrounded the policy debate regarding the death penalty, including the ballot measures presented to citizens in several states. Foremost, citizens as well as other policy-makers respond to changing Supreme Court requirements for death penalty statutes that are not arbitrary. During an era where citizens fear crime, some politicians have made support for the death penalty emblematic of a tough approach to crime. Citizen legislation reflects this trend too, expanding the death penalty to make more crimes death eligible. Finally, opinion about the death penalty within the United States continues to change. The Supreme Court reveals this in its changing approach to capital punishment. The same dynamism is apparent in how citizens use direct democracy to further—and lead—the debate about this complex moral issue. As innovative as citizens are in using the tools of direct democracy, we can expect the shape of any eventual consensus on capital punishment to reveal itself early through the I&R process.

Initiatives Pertaining to the Death Penalty

Year	State	Measure Number	Description	Pass/Fail
1912	Oregon	33	Abolishing capital punishment.	Failed
1914	Arizona	N/A	Abolishing death penalty.	Failed
1914	Oregon	18	Abolishing death penalty.	Passed
1916	Arizona	N/A	Abolishing death penalty.	Passed
1918	Arizona	N/A	Reinstating the death penalty.	Passed
1966	Colorado	N/A	Abolishing death penalty.	Failed
1972	California	17	All state statutes in effect Feb. 17, 1972 requiring, authorizing, imposing, or relating to death penalty are in full force and effect.	Passed
1974	Colorado	N/A	Shall the death penalty be imposed upon persons convicted of Class 1 felonies where certain mitigating circumstances are not present and certain aggravating circumstances are present?	Passed
1975	Washington	I-316	Shall the death penalty be mandatory in the case of aggravated murder in the first degree?	Passed
1978	Oregon	8	Death penalty for murder, specific conditions.	Passed
1984	Oregon	6	Death penalty exempt — guarantees against cruelty.	Passed
2000	California	21	Increases punishment for gang-related felonies; death penalty for gang-related murder.	Passed

A Brief History of Abortion Related Initiatives and Referendum

By Amy L. Pritchard[10]

Since the early 1970s, there have been two dozen measures on statewide ballots dealing in some way with abortions. The initiative and referendum process has been used by both advocates for safe and legal abortion (pro-choice advocates) and opponents of abortion (pro-life advocates).

---

10. Amy Pritchard is a board member of the Ballot Initiative Strategy Center (BISC) and a partner in the political consulting firm of Mammen Pritchard. She has been involved in numerous initiative and referendum campaigns.

The first two of these ballot measures preceded the landmark 1973 Supreme Court decision in *Roe v. Wade* (Roe) which legalized abortions in the United States. In the fall of 1972, and just less than three months before the *Roe v. Wade* decision, North Dakota and Michigan voted on initiatives put on the ballot by pro-choice advocates to loosen abortion laws. By majorities of 77% in North Dakota and 61% in Michigan, they were defeated.

After Roe, pro-life advocates tried to chip away at this decision mostly by targeting state funding of abortions. Between 1973 and the 1989 there were 11 statewide votes dealing with abortion. Each of these dealt with state funding of abortions—8 were attempts to restrict state funding and 3 were attempts to restore funding that had been cut off by the states.

In 1989, pro-life advocates were handed a big legal victory with the *Webster v. Reproductive Health Services* decision. In Webster, the Supreme Court said states could limit abortions in several ways. Since the Webster decision, there have been 11 statewide votes on abortion related ballot measures. These have been on a variety of subjects; and all but one was put on the ballot by pro-life advocates.

In 1990, there were two measures on the ballot in Oregon. One was an attempt to require parental notification before an abortion could be obtained by a minor. The other measure was an attempt to ban all abortions except those that would save the life of the mother, or in cases of rape and incest. Both were defeated.

In 1991, pro-choice advocates in Washington State put forth an initiative to codify *Roe v. Wade* in the state. They needed to collect 150,000 signatures to put the measure before the Legislature. They collected over 242,000 signatures, the most ever gathered for an initiative in the state's history at that time. In 1992, Maryland held a similar referendum to codify *Roe v. Wade*. Both of these measures were successful, but they were the last measures to be promoted by Pro-choice advocates.

There have been six statewide measures since the 1992 elections advanced by pro-life advocates: four in Colorado and one each in Maine and Washington. Three were on the so called "partial birth abortion procedure", two on parental consent and one on waiting periods. All but one (the parental consent measure in Colorado) were defeated.

What is happening now? As of March 31, 2002, there were three abortion related measures that have been filed or qualified for circulation for the 2002 election cycle, but it does not appear that any of these will make it to the November ballot.

The impact and significance of these statewide ballot measures should be viewed in the context of legislative, judicial and executive action at the state and federal levels. Victories and losses in the legislatures and courts have had a profound impact of the type, timing, and substance of abortion related measures. Ballot measures have served as a forth branch of government—each branch being used to promote, protect, and defend as well as create, change, and overturn a variety of laws that relate to abortion.

Initiatives and Referendum Pertaining to Abortion

Year	State	Proponent	Description	Yes %	No %	Pass/Fail
1972	MI	Pro-Choice	Make abortion legal	39%	61%	Failed
1972	ND	Pro-Choice	Make abortion legal	23%	77%	Failed
1978	OR	Pro-Life	Restrict Funding	48%	52%	Failed
1982	AK	Pro-Life	Restrict Funding	41%	59%	Failed
1984	CO	Pro-Choice	Restore Funding	50.39%	49.61%	Passed
1984	WA	Pro-Life	Restrict Funding	47%	53%	Failed
1986	AR	Pro-Life	Restrict Funding	49.96%	50.04%	Failed
1986	MA	Pro-Life	Restrict Funding	42%	58%	Failed
1986	OR	Pro-Life	Restrict Funding	45%	55%	Failed
1986	RI	Pro-Life	Restrict Funding	N/A	N/A	Failed
1988	AR	Pro-Life	Restrict Funding	52%	48%	Passed
1988	CO	Pro-Choice	Restore Funding	40%	60%	Failed
1988	MI	Pro-Choice	Restore Funding	57%	43%	Failed
1990	OR	Pro-Life	Make abortions illegal with exceptions	32%	68%	Failed
1990	OR	Pro-Life	Parental Notice	48%	52%	Failed
1991	WA	Pro-Choice	Codify Roe v. Wade	50.1%	49.9%	Passed
1992	AZ	Pro-Life	Limit abortions	31%	69%	Failed
1992	MD	Pro-Choice	Codify Roe v Wade	62%	38%	Passed
1996	CO	Pro-Life	Parental Notice	42%	58%	Failed
1998	CO	Pro-Life	Partial Birth Abortion	48%	52%	Failed
1998	CO	Pro-Life	Parental Notice	55%	45%	Passed
1998	WA	Pro-Life	Partial Birth Abortion	43%	57%	Failed
1999	ME	Pro-Life	Partial Birth Abortion	45%	55%	Failed
2000	CO	Pro-Life	Waiting Period	40%	60%	Failed

By state: Twelve states have held statewide votes on abortion. Colorado has held the most with 6 ('84, '88, '96, '98, '98, '00), followed by Oregon with 4 ('78, '86, '90, '90), Washington State with 3 ('84, '91, '98), Arkansas with 2 ('86, '88) and Michigan with 2 ('72, '88). North Dakota ('72), Alaska ('82), Massachusetts ('86), Rhode Island ('86), Arizona ('92), Maryland ('92), and Maine ('99) have each had one statewide ballot measure related to abortion.

• Only 5 of the 24 were passed by a majority of voters. Of these, 3 were pro-choice victories and 2 were pro-life victories.
• Pro-choice advocates were proponents in 7 or 29% of the 24. Of these, 3 passed (43%) and 4 failed (67%).
• Pro-life advocates were proponents in 17 or 71% of the 24. Of these, 2 passed (12%) and 15 failed (88%).
• Pro-choice advocates were victorious in 18 elections or 75% of the total "wins".
• Pro-life advocates were victorious in 6 elections or 25% of the total "wins".

A Brief History of Gay Rights Related Initiatives and Referendum

By Amy L. Pritchard[11]

Gay rights leaders point to the Stonewall riots as the beginning of the modern gay rights movement but what kicked off the anti-gay political movement was the 1977 campaign lead by Anti-gay Crusader Anita Bryant in Dade County (Miami) Florida. Since that time the initiative and referendum process has been used as a political tool by advocates on both sides of the issue—though far more frequently by anti-gay religious conservatives. The vast majority of these ballot measures have been held at a county and municipal level—but there have been significant statewide initiatives and referenda as well.

Since 1977 there have been 16 statewide ballot measures dealing with gay rights. The first major initiative to directly deal with the gay and lesbian community was California's 1978 Briggs Amendment. The Briggs Amendment was an attempt to make it illegal for gays and lesbians to be public school teachers as well as prohibiting anyone from saying anything that could be perceived as supporting a gay lifestyle. This highly controversial measure was defeated by 58% of the voters. It would be ten more years before there was another statewide gay rights ballot measure.

The vast majority of local measures and statewide measures have been efforts to repeal or stop laws which protect gays and lesbians from discrimination. The gay and lesbian community has been struggling to gain protected status under federal law. Currently there are no laws at the federal level which protect gays and lesbians from discrimination in the areas of employment, credit, public accommodation or housing. Most Americans wrongly assume that is illegal to fire someone because of their sexual orientation. While there has been movement to pass a federal law—gay rights advocates have worked at the state level to pass non-discrimination laws. These laws—few of which have actually passed state legislatures—have been the target of several statewide ballot measures.

In 1988, the Oregon Citizens Alliance (O.C.A.) headed by Lon Mabon qualified the first Oregon anti-gay statewide initiative. The 1988 measure was the first in the country to specifically target laws governing discrimination. This measure successfully revoked a ban on sexual orientation discrimination. Buoyed by success of this ballot measure, Mabon went onto to sponsor seven more anti-gay statewide initiatives—three of which qualified for ballots between 1988 and 2000—as well as dozens of county and municipal anti-gay ordinances.

In November 1992, Colorado voters passed Amendment 2, which sought to repeal several local non-discrimination ordinances and to prevent any from being passed in the state. The Amendment passed with 53% of the vote but a district court stopped it from going into effect due to lawsuits that claimed Amendment 2 was unconstitutional. Despite this, a national tourism boycott was called for against the state, causing between 35 and 120 million dollars in lost revenue—depending on whose figures are to be used.

Amendment 2 was appealed to the U.S. Supreme court in *Romer v. Evans*. The court ruled in May of 1996 that Amendment 2 was unconstitutional because it did discriminate against an identifiable class of people, and violated their rights to due process and equal protection under the law. In between the Colorado vote and the *Romer* decision, three other states—Idaho, Oregon, and Maine—voted on anti-gay initiatives that attempted to prevent sexual orientation from receiving protected classifications in civil rights laws. Each of these measures failed.

In 1997, gay-rights advocates in Washington State placed an initiative on the ballot which would have added sexual orientation to the state civil rights laws which bars discrimination on the basis of age, race, gender, and religion. This was the first pro-active gay rights measure in the country. The measure was defeated by 60% of voters who also turned out to overwhelmingly defeat a gun control measure.

Maine, a state that has held three votes on gay rights—and the only state to vote on both anti-gay and pro-gay ballot measures—has a mixed history on the issue. In 1995, Maine voters defeated an attempt to mimic Colorado's Amend-

---

11. Amy Pritchard is a board member of the Ballot Initiative Strategy Center (BISC) and a partner in the political consulting firm of Mammen Pritchard. She has been involved in numerous initiative and referendum campaigns.

ment 2 by repealing local gay rights ordinances and preventing any new civil rights laws from being passed. After "winning" this vote, gay rights advocates managed to get a law passed by the legislature adding sexual orientation to the protected class list in the civil rights code. This law was the target of a successful popular referendum or "citizen's veto" to repeal the vote. A special election was held in February of 1998, in the middle of an ice storm, and 51% of the voters agreed to repeal the law. Believing that they lost in 1998 due to low turnout in a special election, gay rights advocates supported a legislative referral in 2000 to put this issue to the voters again as a pro-active vote. Maine voters, by a narrow margin of 50.5% voted to defeat this attempt to pass a gay rights bill.

In the mid 1990s, anti-gay advocates changed their course and turned their offensive to gay marriage—due in large part to a much touted 1993 Hawaii State Supreme Court case that said that three gay couples who had filed suit over being denied a marriage license were victims of discrimination because of their sexual orientation. While this case was eventually overturned at the Circuit Court level, several states, in anticipation of legal gay marriages in Hawaii, attempted to pass or successfully passed laws limiting marriage to a man and a women. In 1998 both Alaska and Hawaii held statewide votes on this issue—both ballot measures had been placed on the ballot by the state legislatures. The Alaska measure was a constitutional ban on gay marriages—which was passed by 68% of the voters. The Hawaii measure said that the legislature could reserve marriage to opposite sex couples—which also passed with just over 70% of the vote.

Gay marriage was the topic of three more statewide votes in 2000. California, Nebraska, and Nevada voters all adopted gay marriage bans. The California measure was on the primary ballot which some thought was meant to increase conservative participation in the Republican primary. The Nebraska and Nevada measures were on the November ballot and were passed by 70% of the voters in each state.

Two measures have targeted homosexuality and pubic schools—the first, the 1978 California Briggs Amendment and the 2000 O.C.A. sponsored initiative in Oregon. Both measures failed.

In 2001, anti-gay activists in Maryland collected signatures to force a newly passed gay rights bill to a statewide referendum vote. It was assumed that this referendum would be on the November 2002 ballot until legal representatives of gay rights advocates found evidence of signature fraud and the anti-gay proponents withdrew their petitions.

But what is on the horizon. As of the writing of this essay, Oregon has an anti-gay measure in circulation, similar to the unsuccessful 2000 measure that attempted to prohibit public schools from promoting or sanctioning homosexual behaviors. It is unclear if this measure will qualify. In 2002 we know that there will be at least one statewide anti-gay initiative, a Nevada initiative that bans same sex marriage. Additionally, in Massachusetts, there is a ban on gay marriage initiative being circulated. However, this initiative will not likely be on the ballot before 2004.

Like other issues that have appeared on the ballot, it can be misleading to look at the initiatives and referendum in a vacuum. Many other events, including state and local legislation as well as court cases can and have had important impacts on the type and timing of each of these ballot measure. Further, there have been dozens of county and municipal measures that are not enumerated here due to lack of space.

Statewide Initiatives and Referendum Pertaining to Gay Rights

Election	Year	State	Proponent Description	Yes %	No %	Pass/Fail
1978	CA	Anti-gay	Ban gay teachers	41.56%	58.44%	Failed
1988	OR	Anti-gay	Revoke ban on sexual orientation discrimination.	52.75%	47.25%	Passed
1992	CO	Anti-gay	Repeal local laws passed to ban discrimination based on sexual orientation and prevent similar new laws	53.41%	46.59%	Passed
1992	OR	Anti-gay	Government to discourage homosexual "behaviors"	43.53%	56.47%	Failed
1994	ID	Anti-gay	Act establishing state policies regarding homosexuality.	49.62%	50.38%	Failed
1994	OR	Anti-gay	Governments cannot approve, create classifications based on, homosexuality.	48.45%	51.55%	Failed
1995	ME	Anti-gay	Limiting protected classes to exclude sexual orientation	46.68%	53.32%	Failed
1997	WA	Pro-gay	Add sexual orientation to the civil rights laws.	40.34%	59.66%	Failed
1998	ME	Anti-gay	Repeal law passed to ban discrimination based on sexual orientation	51.29%	48.71%	Passed
1998	AK	Anti-gay	Anti-gay marriage	68.11%	31.89%	Passed
1998	HI	Anti-gay	Anti-gay marriage	70.78%	29.22%	Passed
2000	CA	Anti-gay	Anti-gay marriage	61.38%	38.62%	Passed
2000	ME	Pro-gay	Make discrimination unlawful based on sexual orientation	49.45%	50.55%	Failed
2000	NE	Anti-gay	Anti-gay marriage	70.36%	29.64%	Passed

Election	Year	State	Proponent Description	Yes %	No %	Pass/Fail
2000	NV	Anti-gay	Anti-gay marriage	69.62%	30.38%	Passed
2000	OR	Anti-gay	Prohibits public school instruction encouraging, promoting, sanctioning homosexual, bisexual behaviors	47.11%	52.89%	Failed

By state: Seven states have held votes on statewide gay rights ballot measures. Oregon leads with four measures ('88, '92, '94, '00). Maine follows with three ('95, '98, '00). California held two ('78, '00) and Colorado ('92), Idaho ('94), Hawaii ('98), Alaska ('98), Nebraska ('00), and Nevada ('00) have each held one. Several other states have had county or municipal ballot measures on gay rights including Florida, Michigan, and Texas.

• 14 were anti-gay and 2 were pro-gay.
• 8 of the 16 (50%) were passed by a majority of voters. All of these were anti-gay initiatives.
• Pro-gay advocates lost both measures where they were proponents (Washington '97 and Maine '00).
• Anti-gay advocates were victorious in 8 or 57% of the 14 measures where they were proponents.
• Anti-gay advocates won 66% or 10 of the 16 measures that were on statewide ballots.

A Brief History of I&R and the Tax Revolt

By Pete Sepp[12]

From the Boston Tea Party to the Whiskey Rebellion to the repeal of Lincoln's "War Tax," American history is replete with tax rebellions brought on by political and economic factors peculiar to those times. But the *Tax Revolt*—the ongoing political movement for limited government—could not have sustained itself without institutional mechanisms, chief among them the initiative and referendum (I&R) process.

Political observers trace the catalyst behind the rise of I&R to the progressive and populist movements of the late 19th and early 20th centuries. And from its beginning, I&R attracted tax reform advocates of all ideological persuasions who were concerned that the elected establishment was unresponsive to their cause.

In the 1880s Oregon activist William S. U'Ren became convinced of I&R's utility in enacting philosopher Henry George's "Single Tax" on land speculation and unearned income, a proposal that likely appealed more to the political left at that time, "I forgot, for [a] time, all about Henry George and the Single Tax. The one important thing was to restore the lawmaking power where it belonged—in the hands of the people. Once give us that, we could get anything we wanted—Single Tax, anything."

Although more recent I&R efforts have centered upon the fiscally conservative notions of tax reduction and limitation, analysts on both ends of the ideological spectrum acknowledge I&R's profound impact on the modern Tax Revolt. According to James Ring Adams, "[t]his experiment in direct democracy made little difference in fiscal affairs at first, but the means were at hand. In the Great Depression, Midwestern voters used the ballot to cut their property tax rates. In the course of the economic catastrophe, voters in some twenty states adopted one form or another of constitutional tax limits. But it remained for our day to discover the full potential of the initiative."

Populist political commentator Pat McGuigan went so far as to suggest that the Tax Revolt owes its continued existence to I&R, "[T]he reality is that the most frequent subject of significant ballot propositions since 1978 has been one or another aspect of taxing and spending. No other "issue cluster"—not utilities, not the environment, not even the nuclear freeze—has faced such popular scrutiny more often. Win or lose, the tax … movement has, in most states, been deciding the bounds of political debate on tax and fiscal policy."

Although the historical connection between I&R and tax policy spans more than a century, many Americans mark the modern starting point of this phenomenon with California's Proposition 13, a property tax limitation measure adopted in 1978. The measure cut property taxes from 2.5 percent of market value and capped the actual rate at just 1 percent. Additionally, it requires a 2/3 "supermajority" (as opposed to a simple majority) of the state legislature to increase other state taxes.

But Proposition 13's success was part of a coast-to-coast tax limitation movement. In 1980, Question 2 (also known as "Proposition 2-1/2") was adopted at the polls in Massachusetts. This law restricts local property taxes to no more than 2-1/2 percent of a home's full and fair cash value, and stipulates 2/3 voter approval for any increase in the rate. Missourians enacted the so-called "Hancock Amendment" that year as well, a measure that limits total state tax and spend-

---

12. Peter J. Sepp is Vice President for Communications with the 335,000-member National Taxpayers Union (NTU), a non-profit, non-partisan citizen organization that works for lower taxes, less wasteful spending, taxpayer rights, and accountable government. Since its founding in 1969, NTU and its members have participated in virtually every major tax-related ballot issue campaign. For further information, call (703) 683-5700 or visit www.ntu.org.

ing growth and subjects most local tax and fee increases to 2/3 voter consent in the affected jurisdiction. Over the next decade, tax rollbacks or lids met with varying degrees of success in states as diverse as Michigan, Montana, Nebraska, Oregon, and Washington.

These efforts, which often tended to focus on property taxes, later encouraged public officials to look elsewhere for tax and expenditure increases. Citizen activists, in turn, responded by incorporating some of the more successful elements of earlier initiatives into broader based constraints that relied somewhat more heavily on processes (voter approval and legislative supermajorities) than outcomes (mathematical growth formulas or percentage limits).

Two measures typified this "second wave" of the tax revolt. In March of 1992, Oklahomans passed State Question 640, a measure that subjects all state-level tax increases to a ¾ legislative "supermajority" vote or a majority vote of the people for approval. Colorado's Amendment 1, adopted in November 1992, limits the growth of state spending and revenues to the rate of inflation and population. Excess revenues the government wishes to retain, or any new tax increases, require majority voter consent. Subsequently, activists in many states and localities—including Arizona, Florida, Montana, Nevada, and Washington—employed similar safeguards against higher taxes in their own proposals.

Even as the technical provisions of these ballot measures have evolved in several directions over the past 25 years, the political challenges surrounding them remain virtually unchanged. Supporters of the limits are typically outfunded by opponents (chiefly public employee unions), at ratios as high as 15 to 1. It is therefore no surprise that even tax limits that are tremendously popular today—such as those in California and Colorado—fell short of adoption in their first appearances on statewide ballots.

Another constant has been the vocal opposition of most government officials and many media outlets. Californians passed Proposition 13 amidst warnings that "drastic staff cutbacks" were in store for local governments. Instead, government's share of Californians' personal income simply grew more slowly after Proposition 13, leading one San Jose newspaper that editorialized against the measure to later write that "Armageddon is not exactly upon us."

In Colorado, Sheriffs predicted lawless streets if Amendment 1 took effect on local governments, and one investment banker warned it would increase the chances for the Pope's assassination during a planned visit to Denver. The limit passed, and according to Governor Bill Owens, "has proved its worth" in helping the economy grow without catastrophic cuts in government services.

Numerous statistics and studies now attest to the importance of I&R to tax issues.

Prior to 1978, only 4 voter approval/supermajority tax safeguards could be found in state constitutions, all of which were proposed by legislatures. Since 1978, 10 such laws have been added to the books, only 3 of which were proposed by legislatures.

The 7 citizen-initiated measures adopted since 1978 are by far the most sweeping—3 require legislative supermajorities of 2/3 or 3/4, or voter approval for higher taxes. The typical legislatively proposed constraint has a supermajority requirement of 3/5 or 2/3, and only 1 has ever mandated voter approval for even some types of tax hikes.

In a 1994 study of statutory and Constitutional Tax and Expenditure Limitations (TELS), Dean Stansel found that the 5-year growth rate of per-capita state spending in TEL states fell from 0.8 percentage points above the national average to 2.9 percentage points below the average after enactment. However, the "swing" in states with **voter initiated and referred** TELs was much stronger: from 6.5 points above the national average to 2.2 points *below* average over the periods studied.

More recently, the Cato Institute determined that all other factors being constant, state and local expenditures per capita will decrease by approximately $16 every year a citizen-initiated TEL is in effect. Yet, in those states operating under TELs enacted by state legislatures, per-capita expenditures will actually *increase* by $24. Personal income growth has likewise tended to benefit from limits imposed through I&R.

Aside from direct economic effects, statewide I&R has had other impacts on fiscal policy. The notion of a "supermajority" as a *political* constraint exists in the original U.S. Constitution, but the states' modern successful application of this concept to taxes has encouraged members of congress to propose similar legislation on the federal level. Meanwhile, the drive to limit city and county taxes has intensified. California's Proposition 62 (1986) and Proposition 218 (1996), created majority and supermajority voter approval requirements for certain classes of local levies.

In addition, I&R can be a powerful deterrent to other moves to inflate government. Oregon voters have rejected nine separate attempts to permit the state to levy a sales tax. Because of the state's I&R provisions, the legislature effectively must submit such a sweeping proposal to the voters, or risk a citizen-mounted referendum or initiative drive. And, in 1990, Nevadans amended their state constitution through I&R to ban the imposition of a personal income tax, a proposal that had been frequently debated in the legislature.

As initiative and referendum enters its second century of existence in the United States, an increasingly significant factor in its future use will be the courts. In November 1998, for example, Montana citizens adopted CI-75, an initiated constitutional amendment to mandate voter approval for most state tax increases (temporary emergency taxes could be adopted by a ⅔ vote of both Houses of the legislature). Montana's Supreme Court ruled the measure unconstitutional, contending in part that CI-75 violated the so-called "single amendment" rule requiring initiatives to address just one part of the state's constitution.

Later that same year, Washington State citizens passed Initiative 695, which reduced motor vehicle taxes as well as subjected future state or local tax increases to voter approval. Shortly afterwards a state court struck down the voter consent provision of I-695 because it supposedly violated the states "single subject" rule for initiatives.

Despite these developments, the evidence is clear that I&R has transformed the "Tax Revolt" from a passing fancy to a permanent fixture in American politics. In 2001 and 2002, activists in states like Oregon and Washington, as well as individual communities like San Diego, CA, continue to pursue tax limits through I&R. This process has given at least some Americans a choice between meaningless elections and outright revolution, ironically providing the very kind of political stability that critics say I&R seeks to upset.

Significant Statewide Tax Related Initiatives

Year	State	Measure Number	Description	Yes %	No %	Pass/Fail
1978	CA	13	Property tax reduction and limitation. Two-thirds vote required for increases.	65%	35%	Passed
1978	MI	E	Establish tax limitations. Headlee Amendment	53%	47%	Passed
1980	MA	2	Limit local taxes. "Proposition 2½?"	60%	40%	Passed
1980	MO	N/A	Limit state and local taxes. Hancock Amendment	55%	45%	Passed
1990	OR	5	Property tax limit; schools, government operations.	52%	48%	Passed
1992	AZ	108	Public debt, revenue and taxation.	78%	22%	Passed
1992	CO	1	Voter approval of tax revenue increases.	54%	46%	Passed
1992	OK	640	Revenue bills approval by voters or 3/4 Legislature and Governor.	54%	46%	Passed
1993	WA	601	Limits state expenditures and provides for a popular vote on new taxes.	51%	49%	Passed
1996	CA	218	Establish tax limits	57%	43%	Passed
1996	FL	1	Requires a 2/3 vote for new constitutionally imposed state taxes or fees.	69%	31%	Passed
1996	NV	11	Amends constitution to require a 2/3 vote of the legislature to increase taxes.	71%	29%	Passed
1999	WA	695	This measure would establish license tab fees at $30 per year for motor vehicles. No new taxes without vote of people.	58%	42%	Passed
2001	WA	747	This measure would establish new "limit factors" for taxing districts in setting their property tax levies each year.	59%	41%	Passed

State Supermajority/Voter Approval For New Taxes[13]

State	Vote Requirement (Each House)	Description/History
AR	3/4 elected	Required only for taxes levied since 1934.
AZ	2/3 elected	Constitutional requirement adopted in 1992. (Citizen Initiative.)
CA	2/3 elected	Constitutional requirement adopted in 1978. (Citizen Initiative.)
CO	2/3 elected (Temporary emergency taxes only; otherwise voter approval required.)	Constitutional requirement adopted in 1992. (Citizen Initiative.)
DE	3/5 elected	Constitutional requirement adopted in 1980.
FL	3/5 elected	Applies only to changes in corporate income tax, adopted in 1971.
FL	2/3 of voters voting in election	Applies only to taxes proposed by constitutional amendment. (Citizen Initiative, 1996.)
LA	2/3 elected	Adopted by legislature.
MS	2/3 elected	Adopted by legislature.
MO	2/3 elected (Emergency taxes only.)	Voter approval required for taxes that exceed $50 million or 1% of state revenues, whichever is less. (Legislative referendum adopted in 1996.)

13. Source: National Taxpayers Union staff research.

State	Vote Requirement (Each House)	Description/History
NV	2/3 elected or voter approval	Constitutional requirement adopted in 1996. (Citizen Initiative.)
OK	3/4 elected or voter approval	Constitutional requirement adopted in 1992. (Citizen Initiative.)
OR	3/5 elected	Constitutional requirement adopted in 1996. (Legislative referendum)
SD	2/3 elected	Required to enact new tax or increase existing tax rate or base. Adopted in 1978, amended to apply to new taxes in 1996. (Citizen Initiative 1978, Legislative referendum 1996.)
WA	2/3 or voter approval	Tax increases that raise revenue under the expenditure limit require 2/3 vote. Revenue over the limit requires voter approval. (Citizen Initiative, 1993.)

Campaign Finance Reform and the I&R Process

By Galen Nelson[14]

The emergence of giant corporations in the last years of the nineteenth century sparked calls to reduce the influence of wealthy donors and big companies on election campaigns. Railroad, oil and banking firms created huge fortunes for their principle stockholders and directors who contributed great amounts of money to help sympathetic candidates win public office. To counter this development, progressive politicians demanded regulations to prevent them from corrupting government officials. This lead to the first federal campaign finance legislation, the Tillman Act in 1907. This landmark legislation prohibited corporations and national banks from contributing to campaigns for federal office, a prohibition that still stands.

Three years later, Congress enacted additional legislation on campaign financing, the Federal Corrupt Act. However, the law fell short of the reformers expectations and was repealed a year later. Additional attempts were made after 1910 to regulate campaign finance, but none of them proved successful.

The postwar development of television escalated the cost of campaigning for public office. In 1956, before most Americans owned television sets, total campaign spending was about $155 million, of which $ 8.9 million went to radio and television advertising. By the 1968 election, campaign spending had nearly doubled to $300 million, while spending on media ads had grown almost six-fold to $58.9 million. Many incumbents and candidates worried that public office was becoming an exclusive territory of the wealthy. Congress responded to these concerns with the Federal Election Campaign Act (FECA) of 1971, which limited candidates' contributions to their own campaigns. Despite this effort, however, the law failed to halt the growth of campaign spending, which reached $425 million in 1972. President Nixon, for example, spent twice as much in his re-election campaign that year as he did in 1968.

The modern day campaign finance reform movement began in 1974, following the Watergate scandal, when Congress passed campaign finance legislation that strictly limited the amount of money that politicians could raise and spend on political campaigns. Though the law's contribution limits were eventually upheld, the Supreme Court struck down campaign spending limits as a violation of the First Amendment's free speech clause in a now famous 1976 decision Buckley v. Valeo.

Later, a 1978 ruling by the Federal Election Commission opened a loophole in federal campaign finance regulations allowing large, unregulated contributions known as "soft money" to flow to the political parties. Campaign spending spiraled upward at both the national and state level during the seventies, eighties, and nineties. In recent years, soft money contributions jumped 1,400 percent, from $33.8 million in 1992 to nearly $500 million in 2000. The corrosive by-products of large contributions in American democracy are well-documented and widely recognized:

• The public believes that special interests have a disproportionate influence over the creation of public policy, thus discouraging voter participation in the political process and sewing cynicism about government.
• Due to the staggering costs of political campaigns, fewer challengers are running for office giving voters fewer choices while weakening democracy.
• State and federal candidates are forced in many instances to spend an inordinate amount of their time raising money instead of talking to regular voters about issues that concern them.

Since reform efforts at the federal level were met with resistance prior to the recent passage of the Shays/Meehan, Mc-Cain/Feingold legislation, reformers focused their efforts in the states. Still, reformers were caught between the constitutional constraints under the Supreme Court's *Buckley* decision that overturned campaign spending limits, and state leg-

---

14. Galen Nelson is the Executive Director of Ballotfunding.org and is an expert on campaign finance reform.

islatures' resistance to reform. Laws that provided public financing for elections passed via ballot initiative allowed reformers to overcome both barriers. Tailor-made to circumvent the power of entrenched legislatures, the ballot initiative process became campaign finance reformers' best friend as they sought to achieve four goals at the state level:

• Increase electoral competition and voter choice.
• Enable candidates to spend more time connecting with voters and less time raising money.
• Grant access to candidates who would normally not be able to mount credible campaigns due to financial reasons.
• Reduce the influence of special interest money in American politics.

In 1993 and 1994, Maine campaign finance reform and civic organizations plotted a strategy to pass an initiative that would provide public financing to candidates who agreed to strict spending limits and who gathered a prescribed number of small qualifying contributions from voters in their district. The qualifying contributions guarantee that candidates enjoy a reasonable amount of support in their district. Public financing of elections enables qualified candidates without access to special interest money to mount credible campaigns. In addition, lower contribution limits on those not participating in the public financing system were proposed to significantly reduce the influence of private special interest money.

The reform community in Maine began to lay the groundwork for their initiative campaign by educating voters about the problem "big money" creates in Maine's political process. A strong, diverse coalition comprised of labor, civic, and environmental organizations was formed to reach as many voters as possible and to finalize the ballot petition. In one day, Election Day 1995, volunteers gathered over 65,000 signatures to qualify the measure for the ballot. The coalition conducted polling to sharpen their message and campaign staff and consultants produced television and radio ads to deploy in the final weeks before the November, 1996 election.

Their hard work and grassroots organizing paid off. Maine voters approved the initiative by a 56% to 44% margin.

Reform advocates exported nearly identical versions of the successful Maine model to other states. The groundwork had been laid for years in Massachusetts and campaign finance reformers set their sights on the November 1998 ballot. Reform groups in Arizona also qualified a clean elections measure in 1998. Both measures passed.

By the time the campaign finance reform community launched similar efforts via initiative in Oregon and Missouri during the 2000 election cycle, special interest groups including the Chamber of Commerce, and traditional political insiders recognized the threat clean elections posed to their power. Whereas the initiative campaigns in Maine and Massachusetts saw little organized resistance, opponents of reform in Missouri and Oregon fed voters a steady stream of disinformation about the proposals and those who backed them, and eventually, negative campaign ads focusing on the costs of clean elections in an effort to undermine support for reform. Their efforts paid off as voters rejected both ballot measures overwhelmingly.

The ballot initiative process still offers hope for advocates of campaign finance reform at the state level. State legislators are loath to cede power and resistant to change the way in which political campaigns are conducted since they benefit from the status quo where campaign war chests and political patronage render incumbents nearly invincible. The judicial branch has, for the time being, limited the extent to which the influence of "big money" in politics can be checked. In three states, Maine, Massachusetts, and Arizona, the initiative process enabled well-organized citizen groups to make significant changes to their state's campaign finance system. Now it looks as though reformers will use the initiative process in other states to fight for reform, despite the losses in Missouri and Oregon.

Perhaps most important, these successful ballot campaigns at the state level created a groundswell of support for reform at the national level. It is not insignificant that, years before Enron, Maine's two Republican Senators backed the McCain-Feingold legislation. Though the Enron scandal created an atmosphere in Washington ripe for reform, state level ballot measure organizers can take some credit for the recently passed federal campaign finance reform legislation.

Campaign Finance Reform Initiatives

Year	State	Measure Number	Description	Pass/Fail
1908	Oregon	16	Corrupt practices act governing elections.	Passed
1912	Montana	I 304-305	Limiting campaign expenses of public candidates.	Passed
1936	North Dakota	N/A	Making it unlawful to expend federal funds in the state for political purposes.	Failed
1972	Washington	I-276	Establishes disclosure laws and other campaign finance regulations.	Passed

Year	State	Measure Number	Description	Pass/Fail
1974	California	9	Requires reports of receipts and expenditures in campaigns for state and local offices and ballot measures. Limits expenditures for state wide candidates.	Passed
1974	Idaho	1	Establishes campaign finance regulations and disclosure laws.	Passed
1974	Massachusetts	5	Political contributions and campaign expenditures.	Passed
1974	Missouri	N/A	Provides for a new campaign financing and election law to replace portions of the present corrupt practices act.	Passed
1976	Florida	1	To require full public disclosure by state and county election officials and candidates (sunshine amendment).	Passed
1984	California	40	Campaign contribution limits.	Failed
1986	Arizona	200	Campaign contribution limits.	Passed
1988	California	68	Campaign contribution limits.	Passed
1988	California	73	Campaign bundling.	Passed
1989	Maine	N/A	Campaign finance — candidates for Governor.	Failed
1990	Arkansas	1	Conduct and disclosure act — candidates and campaigns.	Passed
1992	Washington	I-134	Limit campaign contributions, funding, campaigns.	Passed
1994	Colorado	12	Placed limitations on elected officials compensation; enacted campaign contribution limitations and placed restrictions on the use of campaign funds.	Failed
1994	Colorado	15	Campaign contribution limits.	Failed
1994	Oregon	6	Candidates may use only contributions from district residents.	Passed
1994	Oregon	9	Sets contribution and spending limits and adopts other campaign finance law changes.	Passed
1994	Massachusetts	1	Regulating spending on ballot question campaigns.	Failed
1994	Montana	118	Lower the cap on campaign contributions and other revisions to campaign finance laws.	Passed
1994	Missouri	N/A	Establish campaign finance regulations.	Passed
1994	Nevada	10	Defines and limits campaign contributions.	Passed
1996	Arkansas	1	Establish campaign finance regulations.	Passed
1996	California	208	Campaign contributions and spending limits.	Passed
1996	California	212	Campaign contributions and spending limits. Repeals gift and honoraria limits.	Failed
1996	Colorado	15	Statutory amendments concerning campaign finance.	Passed
1996	Maine	3	Campaign finance reform; including voluntary spending limits and public funding.	Passed
1996	Montana	125	Prohibits contributions from corporations to ballot question committees.	Passed
1996	Nevada	10	Campaign contributions limits. 2nd vote as required by law.	Passed
1998	California	226	Union member's permission required to use dues for political contributions.	Failed
1998	Arizona	200	Would establish a five-member commission to administer alternative campaign financing system and provides for public funding and additional reporting for participating candidates and reduces current contribution limits 20%.	Passed
1998	Massachusetts	2	Would establish public funding of campaigns.	Passed
1998	Oregon	59	Would prohibit using public resources to collect money for political purposes.	Failed
1998	Oregon	62	Would require campaign finance disclosures and regulates signature gathering.	Passed
2000	California	25	Expands campaign contribution disclosure requirements. Establishes contribution limits. Bans corporate contributions. Limits fundraising to period 12 months before primary election and ninety days after election.	Failed
2000	Oregon	98	Prohibits using public resources for political purposes. Limits payroll deductions.	Failed
2000	Oregon	92	Prohibits payroll deductions for political purposes without specific written authorization	Failed

Year	State	Measure Number	Description	Pass/Fail
2000	Missouri	B	Allows candidates that abide by certain requirements (such as campaign spending limits) to receive taxpayer money for their campaigns.	Failed
2000	Oregon	6	Provides public funding to candidates who limit spending.	Failed

The Impact of the Initiative Process on Abolishing Poll Taxes

By Kim Garrett[15]

The 15th Amendment to the United States Constitution was ratified in 1870 and reads, "1. The right of citizens of the United States to vote shall not be denied or abridged by the United States or by any state on account of race, color, or previous condition of servitude. 2. The Congress shall have power to enforce this article by appropriate legislation." The intent of the amendment was clear, to broaden the right to vote to all adult males, regardless of race. However, not everyone agreed with its intent.

After the amendment passed, those opposed to the intent of the amendment began working to make sure that it would have little to no effect at the state level. One way people this was accomplished was through a poll tax. Between 1889 and 1910 the largest number of poll taxes were implemented. The poll tax was a tax collected on people, rather than on property. Thus, those in favor of suppressing blacks were successful in halting, or at least offsetting their vote because most blacks and lower-class whites could not afford to pay the tax.

One way the payment of poll taxes affected the black vote was because poll taxes usually had to be paid about six months before the actual election, and in cash. The problem during this time is that most people (especially the poor) lived off of credit, so they rarely, if ever, saw cash and therefore were unable to pay the poll tax and could not vote.

Some people, especially Southerners, argued that poll taxes did not discourage blacks from voting, but studies have shown a different result. According to J. Morgan Kousser, a professor at the California Institute of Technology, "Overall turnout in presidential elections in the 1880s in Georgia, the only southern state with a poll tax in force at the time, was less than two-thirds as high as in the rest of the South. Estimated black turnout in Georgia was less than half of that in Florida, a state with the same percentage of African-Americans, in the same elections. No one has suggested any variable or combination of variables other than the poll tax that can account for these stark differences." Thus, not only did poll taxes keep people from voting, they were the main cause for black disenfranchisement in the south.

Oddly, the tax began to gain popularity as a democratic advance to replace restraining property qualifications, and ended up disenfranchising most poverty-stricken citizens, especially blacks. One reason the poll tax was so successful for so long was that it helped to fund schools. Since no one wanted to take funding away from the schools, few poll taxes were questioned. Still, some states felt a poll tax was unfair and decided to do something about it.

In Oregon, the poll tax was assessed on every white male from the age of twenty-one to fifty, with the exception of firemen who were members of a company for at least one year preceding the assessment of the tax. Understanding that this was unfair, citizens pushed for a change in the law. On November 8, 1910, Oregon passed a statewide initiative, "Permitting People of Each County to Regulate Taxation of County Purposes and Abolishing Poll Taxes." The passage of this initiative marked the first time in history that an initiative was used to abolish poll taxes in any state.

The issue of poll taxes could not have advanced as much as it did without the help of the initiative process. In fact, four states were able to overcome this issue, (before abolishing poll taxes became a national amendment to the U.S. Constitution in 1964), because of the use of the initiative—Arkansas (three different initiatives each relating to poll taxes), California, Oregon, and Washington. In California, this was the first major statewide Initiative; it passed on November 3, 1914.

By the time the 24th Amendment was ratified in 1964, only five states retained poll taxes. Still, getting Congress to pass the 24th Amendment was not an easy task. According to the American Memory Library of Congress: "On three separate occasions, the House of Representatives passed legislation prohibiting collection of poll taxes in national elections, only to be outmaneuvered by filibusters in the Senate. In 1949, Senator Spessard L. Holland of Florida initiated efforts to abolish the poll tax by constitutional amendments. The Senate finally approved the measure in 1962 by a vote of 77 to 16. The amendment was submitted to the states for ratification on September 14, 1962."

Poll taxes vanished altogether in the late 1960s due to the ratification of the 24th Amendment and the Voting Rights Act of 1965. However, many argue that if it had not been for the early successes of abolishing the poll tax through the initiative process, Congress would have never considered the issue.

---

15. Kim Garrett is a research assistant for the Initiative & Referendum Institute and a student at the University of Denver.

Initiatives Pertaining to the Abolishment of the Poll Tax

State	Year	Description	Yes Votes	No Votes	Pass/Fail
Oregon	1910	Permitting people of each county to regulate taxation for county purposes and abolishing poll taxes.	44,171	42,127	Passed
California	1914	Provides that no poll or head tax shall be levied.	405,375	374,487	Passed
Washington	1922	Repealing the Poll Tax.	193,356	63,494	Passed
Arkansas	1944	To provide that any citizen of Arkansas, while serving in the armed forces of the United States, may vote in any election, without having paid poll tax.	151,564	38,964	Passed
Arkansas	1956	To abolish the poll tax	161,403	210,237	Failed
Arkansas	1964	To provide for voter registration system without payment of poll taxes.	277,087	218,681	Passed

The Role of I&R in Aiding the Women's Suffrage Movement

By Dennis Polhill and Kim Garrett[16]

One of the first instances of the discussion of women's suffrage was in 1776 when Abigail Adams wrote to her husband, John Adams, asking him to include women in the Declaration of Independences' wording. John writes back with humor, stating that he understands Abigail's views but to Abigail's dismay, the document states, "all men are created equal." Upset with this wording, Abigail confides in many colleagues that this lack of including women in the Declaration might be something that needed to be taken directly to the people. However, it wasn't until the mid 1800s that women's suffrage became a dominant issue again.

Wyoming was the pioneer equal suffrage state when its first legislative council, after its organization as a territory in 1869, passed a bill providing that women should have the same rights as men to vote and hold office. When Wyoming was granted statehood in 1890, equal suffrage was part of its constitution—before any other state had given women the right to vote. Utah followed in 1896. From 1906 to 1920, thirteen states voted on women suffrage ballot measures, both initiatives and legislative referendum; Oregon (1906 by initiative/failed), Oregon (1908 by initiative/failed), Oklahoma and Oregon (1910 by initiative/failed), California (1911 by legislative referendum/passed), Arizona and Oregon (1912 by initiative/passed), Kansas (1912 by legislative referendum/passed), Nevada and Montana (1913 by legislative referendum/passed), Ohio, Nebraska, Missouri (1914 by initiative/failed), New York (1917 by legislative referendum/passed), Michigan, South Dakota and Oklahoma (1918 by legislative referendum/passed).[17]

In both Arizona and Oregon the battle for equal suffrage was long and strong. For nearly fifteen years Arizona women worked without success to get their territorial legislature to confer full suffrage upon them. Nor were they successful in their efforts to get a woman suffrage clause included in the constitution when Arizona was granted statehood. A bill creating a women's suffrage amendment to the constitution was introduced in the first legislature of the new state but lost by one vote in the Senate—although it passed in the House. The women then turned to the people, and in less than two months time succeeded in collecting the signatures necessary to place an initiative on the ballot granting women suffrage. The measure went to the voters in 1912 and won by 7,240 votes.

In Oregon, equal suffrage initiatives lost in 1906 and 1908. In 1910 suffragists tried a different approach: an initiative giving only female taxpayers the right to vote, a compromise that was rejected at the ballot box by a three to one margin. Finally, in 1912, suffragists led by Abigail Scott Duniway won their long struggle. An initiative they placed on the ballot for women's suffrage passed—61,265 in favor to 57,104 against.

One of the reasons the battle for equal suffrage was so difficult was the link between the women's suffrage movement and the prohibition movement. The Women's Crusade of 1873 and the organization of the Women's Christian Temperance Union in 1874 (WCTU), which pioneered the movement for equal suffrage, strongly advocated prohibition. The Ohio WCTU, for example, circulated a speech by Anna Howard Shaw entitled *"Influence versus Power,"* which defined women's suffrage as an important weapon in the fight for prohibition. Brewers and distillers, believing that all suffragists favored prohibition, opposed women's suffrage vehemently and in 1911 created the National Association Opposed to

---

16. Dennis Polhill is the Chairman of the Initiative & Referendum Institute. Kim Garrett is a research assistant for the Institute and a student at the University of Denver.

17. McDonagh, Eileen L. and H. Douglas Price (1984). "Woman Suffrage in the Progressive Era: Patterns of Opposition and Support in Referenda Voting, 1910–1920," in *The American Political Science Review* 79 (3).

Woman Suffrage (NAOWS). NAOWS was instrumental in delaying Congress from passing a women's suffrage amendment.[18]

In 1912 Theodore Roosevelt's Progressive Party adopted a women's suffrage plank—a major breakthrough. In the summer of 1913, suffragists presented U.S. Senators with 200,000 signatures in support of a constitutional amendment establishing women's suffrage—but they refused to act. They also began to speak out through hunger strikes, picketing the White House, and other forms of civil disobedience.

On March 2, 1914, U.S. Senator John Shafroth of Colorado introduced a constitutional amendment that would grant all states I&R to achieve suffrage. The "Shafroth Amendment" would have advanced both I&R and the women's suffrage issue by empowering the people to decide within their own state. Although the amendment failed in Congress, it helped the initiative and referendum process gain public credibility as a method of dealing with these types of issues.

In 1914 and 1915, both houses of Congress again rejected women's suffrage amendments. Finally, in 1918, President Woodrow Wilson changed his position and gave his support to a women's suffrage amendment. His support helped get the amendment through the House, but not the Senate. Then in 1919, President Wilson once again urged passage of a women's suffrage amendment and fifteen days after the House passed the amendment, the Senate passed it as well. The 19th Amendment became part of the U.S. Constitution in 1920—just 14 months after Congress sent it to the states for ratification.

Carrie Chapman Catt summarized the women's suffrage effort when she said, "[t]o get the word 'male' in effect out of the Constitution cost the women of the country fifty-two years of pauseless campaign… During that time they were forced to conduct fifty-six [initiative] referenda campaigns to male voters; 480 campaigns to get legislatures to submit suffrage amendments to voters; 47 campaigns to get state constitutional conventions to write woman suffrage into state constitutions; 277 campaigns to get state party conventions to include woman suffrage planks in party platforms, 30 campaigns to get presidential party conventions to adopt women's suffrage planks into party platforms, and 19 campaigns with 19 successive Congresses."

As Catt points out, the relationship between women's suffrage and I&R is not trivial. When momentum began to lag, I&R appeared on the horizon to instill the suffragists with new hope, inspiration, and energy. However, even though most of the women's suffrage initiatives were defeated at the ballot box, their presence raised the awareness of the issue and helped lead the way to the 19th Amendment.

Women's Suffrage Initiatives (I) and Legislative Referendum (LR)

State	Year	Description	Type	Pass/Fail
OR	1906	To extend suffrage to women.	I	Failed
OR	1908	To extend suffrage to women.	I	Failed
OK	1910	To authorize women to vote under the same circumstances/conditions as men.	I	Failed
OR	1910	To extend suffrage to female taxpayers.	I	Failed
CA	1911	To extend suffrage to women.	LR	Passed
AZ	1912	To extend suffrage to women.	I	Passed
KS	1912	To extend suffrage to women.	LR	Passed
OR	1912	To extend suffrage to women.	I	Passed
MT	1913	To extend suffrage to women.	LR	Passed
NV	1913	To extend suffrage to women.	LR	Passed
OH	1914	To extend suffrage to women.	I	Failed
NE	1914	To extend suffrage to women.	I	Failed
MO	1914	To provide that females shall have the same right to vote at all elections within the state as males.	I	Failed
NY	1917	To extend suffrage to women.	LR	Passed
MI	1918	To extend suffrage to women.	LR	Passed
OK	1918	To extend suffrage to women.	LR	Passed
SD	1918	To extend suffrage to women.	LR	Passed

18. McDonagh, Eileen L. and H. Douglas Price (1984). "Woman Suffrage in the Progressive Era: Patterns of Opposition and Support in Referenda Voting, 1910–1920," in The American Political Science Review 79 (3), and Schmidt, David D. (1989). *Citizen Lawmakers: The Ballot Initiative Revolution*. Philadelphia, PA: Temple University Press; Connors, Arthur (1917). *"Direct Legislation in 1916,"* in The American Political Science Review 11 (1).

Term Limits and the I&R Process
By Paul Jacob[19]

Proponents and opponents of term limits have debated just how the issue leapt onto the political scene in the 1990s. Proponents trace the root causes to increased careerism and sky-high reelection rates, as well as a renewed public interest in domestic governance after the end of the Cold War. Opponents see the issue crystallizing from a combination of slow economic growth in the late 80s and early 90s and congressional scandals like the House Bank fiasco.

Yet, as much as political observers might disagree about the causes of the public's desire for term limitation, no one can rationally quibble over the political delivery vehicle for term limits. Without the citizen initiative process, there would be no term limits movement.

Term limits on state legislators were enacted in 21 states—all initiative states, except for Louisiana, which not surprisingly has the weakest term limits law on the books. (Of these 21 states, 17 states have those limits in effect currently. Massachusetts and Washington State courts ruled that limits could not be passed through the citizen initiative procedures specific to each state. Two other states are seeking to place a restoration of term limits on the 2002 general election ballot—Oregon, after a court invalidated the term limits initiative some 10 years after passage, and Idaho, the only state where legislators have repealed a statutory term limits law.)

In 1990, California, Colorado and Oklahoma passed initiatives term-limiting their state legislatures. Colorado's measure also placed limits on that state's congressional delegation. While all three measures passed, the initiatives in Colorado (71 percent in favor) and Oklahoma (67 percent in favor) passed handily.

In California, however, then Speaker of the Assembly Willie Brown organized a campaign to defeat Proposition 140—in part by tying it to Proposition 131, which combined a softer term limits proposal with public financing of political campaigns. Brown raised over $5 million to run television and radio ads, far exceeding the meager media budget of Prop. 140's proponents. Still, the term limits initiative eked out a victory, 52 to 48 percent. That victory in the face of such well-funded opposition convinced many political observers across the country that term limits were largely unstoppable, once voters where given an opportunity to decide at the ballot box.

Yet, just a year later, term limits were defeated at the ballot box in Washington State. An initiative to limit terms of statewide officials, state legislators and the state's congressional delegation met strong opposition from public employees unions and a number of major corporations. The measure was different than previous term limits initiatives in that it applied the limits retroactively, meaning that then Speaker of the House Tom Foley would have to leave office after his next term.

Toward the end of the campaign, Speaker Foley returned to actively campaign against Initiative 553, which failed 46 to 54 percent. Foley's involvement in opposing term limits—both at the ballot box and in legal proceedings—would later lead to his historic defeat in 1994, making him the first Speaker of the House to be defeated since the Civil War.

Yet, the loss of the Washington State initiative did little to stem the term limits tide. Instead, the movement reorganized and launched initiatives in 14 states in 1992—the most states to ever vote on a single issue in American history. All 14 states had measures placing limits on congressional tenure and many included limits on state legislators or statewide officials. All the measures won, including a turnaround victory in Washington State.

In 1993, Maine voters passed a measure limiting their state legislature and New York City voters limited their mayor and city council. The initiative in New York City, the nation's media center, brought term limits to the forefront of national political debate.

Nine more states voted on term limits in 1994. Eight states passed initiatives, while a Utah measure was beaten badly. The Utah Legislature headed off the citizen initiative by passing their own statutory term limits measure, which allowed longer service. The citizen initiative was attacked for exempting current officeholders and for an additional provision to provide for runoff elections in cases where no candidate garnered a clear majority. This latter provision was widely seen as serving the interest of the term limits initiative's chief backer, Merrill Cook, who had twice lost narrowly in three-way races in which no candidate received a majority of the vote.

Congressional Action

The success of term limits initiatives in the states—and in large population centers such as New York, Los Angeles, Dallas, Cincinnati, Houston, and even Washington, D.C.—provided the momentum necessary to put term limits on the congressional agenda. No small feat, indeed, considering the natural opposition of long-serving congressmen.

19. Paul Jacob is the president of Citizens in Charge, a grassroots lobby for citizen initiative rights, and the Senior Fellow of U.S. Term Limits, the nation's leading term limits organization.

Democrats had controlled Congress for four decades. With numerous Republican challengers campaigning on the term limits issue, Newt Gingrich and the minority Republicans embracing term limits as the anchor of their *Contract With America*—following their polling, which suggested that dozens of seats could turn on the issue. In November of 1994, Republicans ended the long reign of Democrats in the U.S. House.

Though Republicans had won their majority in no small part on support for term limits, the vote in the House the following session was marked by all manner of phony measures advanced by outspoken opponents of the issue. Furthermore, the House GOP leadership refused to "whip" votes on the issue that anchored the Republican's *Contract* just six months earlier. A constitutional amendment for term limits gained a slight majority of House members, but fell well short of the constitutionally mandated two-thirds. Term limits supporters and Republican congressional leaders became determined enemies.

Much of the pressure for congressional action was driven by the fact that 23 states (in 1995, New Hampshire Legislature passed a statute to limit their congressional delegation) had placed a binding limit on their members in Congress. Over 40 percent of the U.S. House and 45 percent of the U.S. Senate faced term limits, regardless of whether Congress took action on a universal amendment for term limits. Yet, when the U.S. Supreme Court invalidated these state-imposed limits in *U.S. Term Limits v. Thornton,* this leverage on Congress was lost.

In November of 1995, Mississippi voters defeated a term limits initiative that limited every elected and appointed official in the state, 46 to 54 percent. The initiative found strong opposition from local officials and suffered when proponents could not state whether volunteer officials on library or public hospital boards were covered by the measure. Yet, the defeat did little to dampen public support for the concept of term limits.

Informed Voter Laws

To restore pressure on Congress to propose an amendment to the Constitution, the term limits movement launched a new round of statewide citizen initiatives in 1996. These new measures were premised on the successful initiative strategy employed by progressives in the early 1900s to achieve direct election of U.S. Senators.

Before the 17th Amendment, U.S. Senators were elected by state legislatures, not voters. But progressives passed measures in numerous states requiring candidates for the state legislature to pledge they would support the voters' choice for U.S. Senator, determined in non-binding voter plebiscite. In some cases, this information about legislative candidates was listed directly on ballots so voters could know in casting their vote whether that legislator would give them *de facto* direct election of their U.S. Senators. State legislators pledging to abide by the voters choice for Senator consistently defeated those who refused to pledge and many states began sending Senators to Congress thus effectively elected by the voters.

Using this historical precedent, term limit proponents placed initiatives on 14 state ballots in 1996. These measures instructed congressmen to do everything within their power to propose a constitutional amendment for term limits and listed specific actions that a congressman must take in order to pass the amendment. If a congressman failed to take these actions a notation would be placed next to the name of that congressman on the ballot in the next election. Voters thus could create a system whereby they could gain information on whether their federal representatives were following their instructions to pass term limits. Supporters called these initiatives "Informed Voter Laws," while opponents dubbed them "Scarlet Letter Laws."

These measures were much more complex than previous initiatives that directly limited elected officials and, not surprisingly, were less successful. Still, nine of the 14 states passed the propositions. Congressmen were furious with this tactic that threatened their reelections, but congressional leadership had promised to bring term limits up in the subsequent congressional session. When the issue was brought to the House floor, support for the serious amendment proposals in these nine states fell just one vote short of the required two-thirds majority. This initial result bolstered confidence that these laws might, if spread to enough states, enable voters to overcome the natural resistance of officeholders to term limitation. But lawsuits challenging these newly minted measures were successful in overturning them. Ultimately, term limits reached the U.S. Supreme Court a second time as they upheld the unconstitutionality of this approach in Cook v. Gralike.

Nevertheless, term limits supporters merely regrouped and struck back with a new approach, wherein initiatives played a far smaller role. The new strategy sought to use public support, particularly in open seat races, to convince candidates to voluntarily limit their terms in office as a condition of their election. The main tactic became issue education advertising informing people of the stated intentions of declared candidates to abide by self-imposed term limits.

In 1998, "Term Limits Pledge" or "Self-Limit" initiatives gained a place on three state ballots: Alaska, Colorado and Idaho. These initiatives made the commitment of candidates to limit their terms an official document and allowed a ballot notation that would inform voters if a candidate made a voluntary term limits pledge. The initiatives passed in all three states, but by fairly narrow margins.

Many supporters of term limits were themselves skeptical that candidates elected on such a pledge could be counted on to abide by their commitment once elected and empowered with the advantages of incumbency. Though most who pledged did indeed keep their commitment, a few broke their word and were able to gain reelection.

Term Limits Today

Though candidates continue to make term limits pledges, the term limits movement has been more focused on defending and expanding term limits at the state and local level. In 1999, Mississippi again defeated a term limits initiative, but Nebraska passed limits for their legislature in 2000.

Numerous efforts by legislators and powerful lobbies to roll back term limits laws have failed. The most notable being a 2002 California proposition funded by various politician-controlled PACs, major corporations, unions and the state's Democratic Party. While Proposition 45's proponents outspent opponents better than 10 to 1, the measure was soundly defeated, 42 to 58 percent.

In 2002, the Idaho Legislature became the only one in the nation to repeal term limits, which as a statute did not require voter approval. However, petitions are now being circulated to send the legislature's repeal back to the voters in a popular referendum. Idaho voters have passed four term limits initiatives since 1994 and seem likely to overturn the legislature's repeal and thus restore the term limits law. Yet, the Speaker of Idaho's House told the *New York Times* he would lead an effort to again overturn the voters if necessary. The battle continues.

After more than a decade of initiative activity by voters, term limits are the law for 37 governors, 17 state legislatures, numerous statewide officials, and thousands of local officials, including seven of the largest 10 cities in the nation. Moreover, voters in Oregon, Idaho and a number of populous cities and counties throughout the country are working to place new term limits initiatives before voters.

Even in Congress, term limits remain in effect for committee chairmen in the House forcing a number of powerful chairman to give back their gavels and step down from their lofty perches. The term limits that have swept the nation at the state and local level, almost exclusively through citizen initiative, may ultimately lead to limits at the congressional level as they begin to change the political culture from the bottom up.

Statewide Term Limits Initiatives

Year	State	Measure Number	Description	Pass/Fail
1990	California	131	Term limits for state officials, changes campaign finance laws, some public funding.	Failed
1990	California	140	Term limits for state officials, limits on legislature's salary and operating costs. 6/8	Passed
1990	Colorado	5	Term limits for elected officials. State legislature and Congress. 8/8	Passed
1990	Oklahoma	632	State legislative term limits. Twelve years limit.	Passed
1991	Washington	I-553	Term limits on state and federal officers. 6/12	Failed
1992	Nebraska	407	Term limits on state elected officials 8 years and on Congress 8/12	Passed
1992	Oregon	3	Term limits on state legislature 6/8 and on Congress 6/12.	Passed
1992	South Dakota	A	Term limits on state legislature 8/8 and on Congress 12/12.	Passed
1992	Washington	I-573	Term limits on state legislature 6/8, Governor, and Congress 6/12.	Passed
1992	Wyoming	2	Term limits on state and federal officials.	Passed
1992	Arizona	107	Term limits on state legislature 8/8. Congress 6/12.	Passed
1992	Arkansas	4	Term limits on state legislature 6/8. Congress 6/12.	Passed
1992	California	164	Term limits on Congress 6/12.	Passed
1992	Florida	9	Term Limits on state legislature 8/8.	Passed
1992	Michigan	B	Term limits on state legislature 6/8 and Congress 6/12.	Passed
1992	Missouri	13	Term limits on state legislature 8/8.	Passed
1992	Missouri	12	Term limits on Congress 8/12.	Passed
1992	Montana	CI 64	Term limits on state elected officials 8/8 and Congress 6/12.	Passed
1992	North Dakota	5	Term limits on Congress 12/12.	Passed
1992	Ohio	2	Term limits on Congress 8/12.	Passed
1992	Ohio	3	Term limits on Governor.	Passed
1992	Ohio	4	Term limits on state legislature 8/8.	Passed
1993	Maine	1	Term limits for state legislators 8/8.	Passed
1994	Colorado	17	Term limits on Congress 6/12 and on all localities.	Passed
1994	Alaska	4	Term limits on Congress 6/12	Passed

Year	State	Measure Number	Description	Pass/Fail
1994	Maine	1	Term limits on Congress 6/12.	Passed
1994	Utah	A	Term limits on state legislature 8 years and on Congress 8/12.	Failed
1994	Massachusetts	4	Term limits on state legislature 8/8 and on Congress 6/12.	Passed
1994	Idaho	2	Term limits on state legislature 8/8 and Congress 6/12.	Passed
1994	Oklahoma	662	Term limits on Congress 6/12.	Passed
1994	Nebraska	408	Term limits on state legislature 8 years and on Congress 6/12.	Passed
1994	Nevada	8	Term limits on judges and state legislature 12/12.	Passed
1994	Nevada	9	Term limits on Congress 6/12.	Passed
1995	Mississippi	4	Term limits on all elected officials in the state.	Failed
1996	Alaska	4	Informed Voter Law.	Passed
1996	Arkansas	9	Term limits on state legislature 6/8, Governor, and Congress 6/12.	Passed
1996	Idaho	4	Informed Voter Law.	Passed
1996	Maine	1	Informed Voter Law.	Passed
1996	Missouri	9	Informed Voter Law.	Passed
1996	Washington	I-670	Informed Voter Law.	Failed
1996	Colorado	12	Term limits on Congress 6/12 and all localities.	Passed
1996	Montana	I 132	Informed Voter Law.	Failed
1996	Nebraska	409	Term limits on state legislature 8 years and on Congress 6/12.	Passed
1996	Nevada	17	Informed Voter Law.	Passed
1996	Nevada	9 A	Term limits on state legislature 12/12.	Passed
1996	Nevada	9B	Term limits on judges. (Question 9 was split into two questions, by court order) 2nd vote as required by law.	Failed
1996	North Dakota	5	Informed Voter Law and term limits on state legislature 8/8.	Failed
1996	North Dakota	6	Direct application for constitutional convention to consider a term limits amendment.	Failed
1996	Oregon	48	Informed Voter Law.	Failed
1996	South Dakota	1	Informed Voter Law.	Passed
1996	Wyoming[20]	20 1	Informed Voter Law.	Failed
1998	California	225	Informed Voter Law.	Passed
1998	Alaska	7	Self Limit Law.	Passed
1998	Colorado	18	Self Limit Law.	Passed
1998	Idaho	1	Self Limit Law.	Passed
1998	Nevada	17	Informed Voter Law.	Passed
1999	Mississippi	9	Term limits on state legislature 8/8.	Failed
2000	California	27	Self Limit Law	Failed
2000	Nebraska	415	Term limits on state legislature 8 years.	Passed
2002	California	45	Would allow term limited state legislators to serve more time if they could collect a specified number of signatures on a petition.	Failed

Gun Control and the I&R Process
By Joe Sudbay[21]

Gun control has been one of the most contentious issues in American politics. The National Rifle Association (NRA) has long dominated the legislative process on the gun issue through lobbying, grassroots and financial resources. This legislative monopoly has forced gun control advocates to turn to the initiative process for reform.

Early gun control efforts were successful in the wake of the assassinations of Robert Kennedy and Martin Luther King in 1968 when Congress enacted the Gun Control Act. The centerpiece of the legislation was the establishment of categories of prohibited persons who could neither purchase nor possess firearms. However, in 1986, Congress acted to weaken provisions of the Gun Control Act. It was not until 1993 that gun control advocates got another victory. That year Con-

20. Wyoming law requires initiatives & referendums to get 50%+1 of everyone who votes in the election. Those who choose not to cast a ballot for or against an initiative are considered a NO vote. Under this requirement both measures lost by only several hundred votes.

21. Joe Sudbay is Public Policy Director of the Violence Policy Center.

gress passed the Brady Law, requiring background checks on firearm sales. However, the lack of ongoing success at the Federal level, forced gun control advocates to turn to the states for reform.

Gun control at the state level

The gun lobby hold on the state legislative process was just as strong as it was at the Federal level forcing gun control activists to look at the initiative process as the only way to counter this legislative monopoly.

In 1976, Massachusetts's voters cast their vote on a statewide initiative that called for an outright ban on handguns, with the state buying back all privately held guns. The initiative lost by more than a 2 to 1 margin.

Following the shootings of John Lennon and President Reagan, gun control supporters launched in initiative in California for the November 1982 ballot. The initiative, know as Proposition 15, would have limited the number of guns in circulation, required state registration of all handguns and forced automatic jail terms for those convicted of carrying unregistered handguns on the street. Opponents of Proposition 15 outspent their rivals by a four-to-one margin and defeated the initiative.

No other gun control ballot measure was considered until 1990 when the Florida legislature placed a constitutional amendment on the ballot that established a three-day waiting period on handgun sales by retailers. Despite opposition from the gun lobby, the amendment passed by an overwhelming majority—84% to16%.

Then in 1997, gun control activists in Washington State, frustrated by legislative inaction, filed an initiative (I-676) calling for comprehensive gun control legislation. The proponents of I-676 were outspent by opponents (primarily the NRA) and the initiative was defeated. The proposal was a long and complicated initiative that allowed the opponents to focus on several sections that could be exploited. This defeat helped gun control advocates realize that the way to victory was to undertake straightforward and uncomplicated gun control initiatives—like background checks.

In 1998, Florida's Constitutional Revision Commission, which meets every twenty years to consider changes to the state's constitution, placed a constitutional amendment on the ballot to allow counties to enact waiting periods and background checks on all firearm sales. The amendment was designed to close the gun show loophole. Gun shows are venues where both licensed sellers and private individuals sell firearms. At the shows, licensed sellers are required to conduct background checks, while in most states, including Florida, private sellers are under no similar obligation—hence the loophole. On Election Day, Floridians once again showed strong support for gun control by passing the amendment by a wide margin—72% to 28%.

That same year, the Missouri legislature began consideration of a law that would allow citizens to carry concealed handguns in public. Governor Carnahan, who had vowed to veto the measure, suggested that if the backers wanted the law they should put it on the ballot for a public vote. At the close of the 1998 legislative session, lawmakers passed the bill and placed it on the ballot. However they didn't place it on the upcoming 1998 general election, but on a special election ballot scheduled for April 6, 1999. Supporters on the bill spent $4.2 million on their campaign compared to $850,000 by the opposition. Opponents of the bill employed a similar strategy used by the NRA in Washington State in 1997. They identified several controversial sections of the bill and focused on them with a consistent message. The measure was defeated by a 52% to 48% margin giving gun control advocates a big victory.

Then on April 20, 1999, the Columbine High School massacre occurred. This prompted the U.S. Congress and a number of state legislatures to consider legislation to close the gun show loophole. A friend of the shooters had purchased the guns used in the shooting at a local gun show. But the congressional effort, as well as many of the state efforts, failed. This caused gun control activists in Colorado and Oregon to push initiatives for the 2000 ballot that would require background checks at gun shows. Both initiatives were passed by wide margins.

Conclusion

The initiative and referendum process has been used by both pro-gun and gun control activists seeking reform—with varied success. However, the Florida referendum on gun shows provided the best example of a state measure giving impetus to national legislation. The Saturday after the measure passed, November 7, 1998, in his weekly radio address, President Clinton took note of the Florida results and ordered a report on the gun show issue. The President stated, "[o]n Tuesday, the people of Florida voted overwhelmingly to put a stop to these tainted transactions and make it harder for criminals to buy firearms. Under the new Florida law, communities now can take action to require background checks for the public sale of all guns. I believe this should be the law of the land: no background check, no gun, no exceptions. Therefore, I am directing Secretary Rubin and Attorney General Reno to report back to me in 60 days with a plan to close the loophole in the law and prohibit any gun sale without a background check. We didn't fight as we hard as we did to pass the Brady Law only to let a handful of unscrupulous gun dealers disrespect the law, undermine our progress, put the safety of our families at risk."

Major Gun Control Initiatives

Year	State	Measure Number	Description	Pass/Fail
1976	Massachusetts	5	To prohibit to possession, ownership, or sale of any weapon from which a shot or bullet can be discharged and which has a barrel length of less than 16 inches.	Failed
1982	California	15	Requires registration of concealable firearms.	Failed
1984	North Dakota	N/A	Right to bear arms as a state right.	Passed
1988	Nebraska	403	Right to bear arms.	Passed
1997	Washington	I-676	Shall the transfer of handguns without trigger-locking devices be prohibited and persons possessing or acquiring a handgun be required to obtain a handgun safety license?	Failed
2000	Oregon	5	An initiative statute to require background checks at gun shows.	Passed
2000	Colorado	22	An initiative amendment to require background checks for guns purchased at gun shows.	Passed

Alcohol and the Initiative and Referendum Process

By M. Dane Waters[22]

According to the historian David E. Williams, one could argue that the American temperance (prohibition) movement is the oldest movement in U.S. history. Organized efforts to limit the use of alcoholic beverages began in the United States during the 1820s. A by product of the religious revivalism sweeping the nation, prohibition soon became part of the whole social reform movement that preceded the Civil War. The earliest reformers called for moderation, not total abstinence, but as the movement gained strength it demanded a complete prohibition of all beer, wine and liquor.

Two major temperance organizations emerged in the decade after the Civil War. The National Prohibition Party (NPP) was founded in 1869 and the Women's Christian Temperance Union (WCTU) in 1874. As was discussed in the earlier essay on the women's suffrage movement, the issue of women's suffrage became intertwined with the push for temperance.

The first state or territorial prohibition law on record was enacted in 1843 by the Territorial Legislature of Oregon (which was repealed in 1848 and re-enacted in 1914 by a citizen initiative). The 1880s, however, proved crucial for the prohibition movement. The decade began with dry Americans confident that they could achieve their goals through the legislative referendum process (in short, having state legislators place prohibition amendments on the ballot). A successful constitutional amendment on prohibition in Kansas in 1880 led the prohibition movement to embark on amendment campaigns elsewhere, "[l]et a prohibition law not be a party but a people's measure," said Ellen Foster, one of the most prominent women in the nineteenth century WCTU.

The establishment in Ohio in 1893 of the Anti-Saloon League (ASL) pushed the nation further on the road to prohibition. A major part of the ASL's success was the nature of its organization: a loose confederation of evangelical churches that crossed denominational boundaries. Each of these churches had an ASL chapter. To join a chapter, individuals had to sign an anti-saloon pledge and make a personal vow of abstinence. ASL members were instrumental in pushing state legislators to put prohibition amendments on the ballot.

Most of the prohibition legislation was achieved through the legislative referendum process. Starting with Kansas in 1880, at least twenty states prohibited the sale, distribution and possession of liquor over a thirty-nine year period using the legislative referendum process. In addition, prohibition initiatives were adopted in seven more states; Arizona, Colorado, Nebraska, Nevada, Ohio, Oregon and Washington, making the total number of dry states in the Union thirty-seven. This activity in the states was the impetus for the passage of the 18th Amendment in 1919 that prohibited the manufacture, sale, or transportation of intoxicating liquors.

However, what makes prohibition particularly interesting to students of the initiative process is that when public opinion turned against prohibition in the late 1920s and early 1930s, voters in six states (Arizona, Colorado, Massachusetts, Montana, North Dakota and Oregon) passed initiatives to legalize liquor. This lead to the adoption in 1933 of the 21st Amendment that repealed the 19th Amendment. As a result, the initiative and referendum process was instrumental not only in the adoption of prohibition but the repeal of prohibition as well.

---

22. Dane is President of the Initiative & Referendum Institute and an internationally recognized expert on the initiative and referendum process.

The first states to attempt the repeal of prohibition using initiatives were Michigan and Ohio in 1919 but they were defeated. The first state to actually repeal its prohibition statute was New York in 1923. Legally, repealing prohibition meant little; the 18th Amendment still outlawed the sale or possession of liquor. As a practical matter, however, the repeal placed the main burden of enforcing prohibition on about two hundred and fifty federal agents instead of twenty-five thousand state and local officers.

Repeal advocates had urged that the repeal question should be resolved by conventions in the states, which is one of two methods prescribed in the Constitution for ratifying amendments. The reason why is that repeal advocates were convinced that the legislatures would not respond to repeal petitions. "To 'wets', [to lobby the legislatures] was out of the question, as state legislatures were notorious 'dry', being dominated by rural, fundamental interests, passionate in their defense of prohibition." The repeal process in Oregon seems to support this argument. In both 1925 and 1931 the Oregon legislature refused to pass bills that would have sent to the voters a call to reconsider statewide prohibition. "Wet" interests finally used the initiative process to put the question on the ballot in 1932, which was passed by the voters. A year later, constitutional conventions were held in thirty-eight states to discuss the proposed 21st Amendment (which role was to repeal Prohibition in the United States). Later that year, the Amendment was successfully ratified by thirty-seven of these conventions ending the prohibition movement.

However, even with the repeal of prohibition, the regulation of alcohol has been a constant fixture on ballots across the country. From initiatives dealing with the manner in which alcohol can be sold to establishing the legal drinking age, the citizens have continued to use the initiative process as a tool to deal with this controversial subject.

Major Prohibition and Alcohol Related Initiatives

Year	State	Measure Number	Description	Pass/Fail
1908	South Dakota	N/A	An act for licensing, restricting and regulating of the business of manufacture and sale of intoxicating liquors.	Failed
1910	Oregon	23	Prohibiting the sale of liquors and regulating shipments of same, and providing for search for liquor.	Failed
1910	Oregon	15	Giving cities and towns exclusive power to regulate liquor traffic within their limits.	Passed
1910	Oregon	22	Prohibiting liquor traffic.	Failed
1910	Oklahoma	22 cities,	Provide for the licensed sale of intoxicating liquors in incorporated towns, and villages after an election to determine whether said municipality shall license the sale of liquors to be consumed.	Failed
1910	Missouri	N/A	To provide for prohibition of the manufacture an sale of intoxicating liquors.	Failed
1912	Arkansas	N/A	Providing for statewide prohibition.	Failed
1912	Colorado	1	Providing for statewide prohibition.	Failed
1912	Colorado	2	Enforcement of prohibition laws by search and seizure.	Failed
1914	Oregon	17	Providing for statewide prohibition.	Passed
1914	Arizona	N/A	Providing for statewide prohibition.	Passed
1914	Arizona	N/A	Prohibition elections.	Failed
1914	South Dakota	N/A	To provide for licensing, restricting, and regulating sale of liquor and for the sale of liquor at local option.	Failed
1914	Washington	3	Providing for statewide prohibition.	Passed
1914	Ohio	1	Home rule on subject of intoxicating liquors.	Passed
1914	Ohio	4	Prohibition of the sale and manufacture for sale, and importation for sale of intoxicating liquor as a beverage.	Failed
1914	Oklahoma	73	To make drunkenness and excessive use of intoxicating liquors cause for impeachment or removal from office.	Passed
1914	California	39	Suspension of Prohibition Amendment. To suspend the proposed prohibition amendment (if passed) until Feb. 15, 1915 relating to use and transportation of intoxicating liquors.	Passed
1914	California	47	Prohibits for 8 years after this election state election on question of prohibiting or permitting transportation of intoxicating liquors.	Failed
1914	California	2	To prohibit the manufacture, sale, gift, or transportation of intoxicating liquors.	Failed
1914	Colorado	N/A	Providing for statewide prohibition.	Passed

Year	State	Measure Number	Description	Pass/Fail
1915	Ohio	1	Prohibition of the sale and manufacture for sale of intoxicating liquor as a beverage.	Failed
1916	California	1	Prohibits after Jan. 1, 1920, the manufacture, sale or possession of intoxicating liquors except for medicinal, sacramental, scientific and mechanical purposes.	Failed
1916	California	2	Defines alcoholic liquor and prohibits its use; neither limits nor repeals state or local prohibition.	Failed
1916	Oregon	8	Permitting manufacture and regulating sale 4% malt liquors.	Failed
1916	Oregon	9	Prohibition amendment forbidding importation of intoxicating liquors for beverage purposes.	Passed
1916	Colorado	N/A	Declaring beer non-toxicating and providing for its manufacture and sale.	Failed
1916	Nebraska	N/A	Providing for statewide prohibition.	Passed
1917	Ohio	1	Prohibition of the sale and manufacture for sale of intoxicating liquors.	Failed
1918	Nevada	N/A	Providing for statewide prohibition.	Passed
1918	Ohio	2	Prohibition of the sale and manufacture for sale of intoxicating liquors as a beverage.	Passed
1918	California	1	To provide for the regulation of liquor use and sales, prohibit drinking saloons, limit the number of municipal licenses for sale of vinous or malt liquors for consumption.	Failed
1918	California	22	To make the manufacture, importation or sale of intoxicating liquors a misdemeanor.	Failed
1918	Colorado	N/A	"Bone-dry" prohibition law.	Passed
1919	Ohio	1	Defining the phrase "Intoxicating Liquor".	Failed
1919	Ohio	2	To repeal statewide prohibition.	Failed
1919	Michigan	N/A	Relative to the manufacture of cider, wines, beer, etc.	Failed
1920	Massachusetts	1	Definition of cider, beer, et al. as non-intoxicating liquors.	Passed
1926	California	9	To repeal Wright Act approved by electors on referendum November 7, 1922, which provided for enforcement of the 18th Amendment of the U.S. Constitution.	Failed
1926	Missouri	N/A	To repeal the prohibition act.	Failed
1926	Montana	30	Relating to repeal of state's intoxicating liquor laws.	Passed
1928	North Dakota	N/A	Repealing the clause of the constitution providing for prohibition.	Failed
1928	Montana	32	For adoption and enforcement of the Federal prohibition laws.	Failed
1930	Massachusetts	2	Repeal of "Baby Volstead" (Prohibition) Act.	Passed
1932	California	1	Repeals Wright Act that enforced 18th Amendment.	Passed
1932	Oregon	7	Bill to repeal state prohibition law of Oregon.	Passed
1932	Washington	61	Relating to intoxicating liquors.	Passed
1932	North Dakota	N/A	Repeal prohibition.	Passed
1932	Colorado	N/A	Repealing statewide prohibition, subject to national repeal.	Passed
1932	California	2	Provides for the sale and use of liquor when the Wright Act is repealed and when lawful under Federal Constitution and laws of California.	Passed
1932	Arizona	N/A	Repeal of Prohibition.	Passed
1932	Michigan	N/A	Relative to establishment of a liquor control commission.	Passed
1933	Oregon	8	Repeal of prohibition constitutional amendment.	Passed
1933	North Dakota	N/A	Permitting the manufacture and sale of beer in North Dakota.	Passed
1934	California	2	Prohibits consumption, sale, or disposition for consumption on premises, of intoxicating liquors, except beer, in public saloons or barrooms.	Passed
1934	California	13	Provides for local option for liquor sales and use.	Failed
1934	North Dakota	N/A	Legalizing and regulating the sale of intoxicating liquor in drug stores, hotels, restaurants an clubs; creating the office of Liquor Control Commissioner, and giving portion of taxes to school districts.	Failed
1934	North Dakota	N/A	Legalizing the sale of liquor by any individual or business.	Failed
1934	North Dakota	N/A	Repealing all state prohibition laws.	Failed
1936	California	9	Provides for local option for the regulation of alcoholic beverage.	Failed
1936	Michigan	N/A	Relative to prohibition after December 31, 1937, certain real property taxes and to provide for an income tax.	Failed

Year	State	Measure Number	Description	Pass/Fail
1936	North Dakota	N/A	Legalizing the sale of liquor and allocating the tax and license revenue for apportionment to counties to reduce real estate taxes.	Passed
1936	Oklahoma	222	A Constitutional amendment repealing prohibition provisions; authorizing manufacture, sale and transportation of alcohol and alcoholic beverages in Oklahoma.	Failed
1938	Oregon	11	Bill regulating sale of alcoholic liquor for beverage purposes.	Failed
1938	North Dakota	N/A	Repealing liquor control act of November 1936.	Failed
1939	North Dakota	N/A	Providing for the sale of liquor through municipal liquor stores in towns of 150 or more having a regular police department.	Failed
1940	Oregon	7	Bill repealing present liquor law; authorizing private sale, license, taxing.	Failed
1940	Idaho	1	Proposed prohibition districts, prohibiting the possession, purchase, sale and transportation of alcoholic liquors.	Failed
1940	Idaho	2	Idaho Sobriety Act proposed to inhibit advertising promotion of sales, limit amount of purchase and to inhibit dispensing of alcoholic liquors in bars and clubs.	Failed
1940	Oklahoma	289	A Constitutional amendment authorizing and regulating importation, manufacture, transportation and sale of whiskey and other alcoholic beverages.	Failed
1942	Arkansas	1	Amend liquor laws, provide for better local option.	Passed
1942	North Dakota	N/A	Prohibiting the sale of alcoholic beverages in restaurants.	Failed
1944	North Dakota	N/A	Prohibiting the sale of alcoholic beverages where commodities other than tobacco and soft drinks are sold.	Failed
1944	Nebraska	N/A	Prohibition of liquor traffic.	Failed
1948	Oregon	8	Oregon liquor dispensing licensing act.	Failed
1948	South Dakota	N/A	To prohibit the sale of liquor where food is sold.	Failed
1948	Washington	171	Providing liquor by the drink with certain restrictions.	Passed
1948	North Dakota	N/A	Repealing the law that prohibits sale of alcoholic beverages where commodities other than tobacco and soft drinks are sold.	Failed
1948	Washington	13	Restricting sales of Beer and Wine to State Liquor Stores.	Failed
1948	California	12	To provide for local control and enforcement of intoxicating liquors.	Failed
1948	California	2	To provide for local control of intoxicating liquors.	Failed
1948	Colorado	3	Political subdivisions may adopt and thereafter modify or repeal local option proposals prohibiting the sale of alcoholic and fermented malt beverages.	Failed
1950	Arkansas	2	Statewide prohibition	Failed
1950	Oregon	9	Making sale of promotively advertised alcoholic beverage unlawful.	Failed
1950	South Dakota	N/A	Prohibit sale of liquor where food is sold.	Failed
1950	North Dakota	N/A	Permitting municipal and County option on sale of liquor.	Failed
1952	Oregon	15	Liquor by the drink sales.	Passed
1952	North Dakota	N/A	Setting hours of operation of liquor establishments between 8 a.m. and 10:30pm.	Failed
1954	Washington	I-194	Restricting television alcoholic beverage advertising.	Failed
1954	North Dakota	N/A	Setting hours of liquor establishments between 8 a.m. and 11 p.m.	Failed
1957	Oklahoma	376	Authorize County option and the holding of special elections in and by counties at County expense not more often than every two years, to prohibit or permit beverages containing more than 1/2 of 1% of alcohol by volume.	Failed
1960	Washington	205	Authorizing tavern spirituous liquor licenses.	Failed
1964	North Dakota	N/A	Permitting sale of alcoholic beverages in eating establishments under certain circumstances.	Passed
1972	Oklahoma	480	Permitting the sale of intoxicating alcoholic beverages by individual drink for on premise consumption.	Failed
1972	Washington	261	Liquor sales by licensed retailers.	Failed
1976	Oklahoma	515	Sale of alcoholic beverages, licensees, terms.	Failed
1978	Michigan	D	Must be 21 to purchase/posses alcohol.	Passed
1982	Montana	I 94	Beer and wine quota system.	Failed
1983	Ohio	1	Minimum age, beer consumption: twenty-one.	Failed

Major Environmental Ballot Initiatives and Referendum

By Derek Cressman[23]

Environmentalists have actively used the initiative and referendum process over the past 30 years. Sometimes environmentalists have won important victories, most recently in the realm of environmental bond measures to preserve open spaces. However, when a particular industry is impacted by regulations to protect the environment, that industry often raises significant sums to oppose ballot questions and often defeats them. Nonetheless, environmentalists have wound up winning larger policy debates even while losing on particular ballot questions, by successfully using those initiatives to place issues on the public agenda.

Sprawl/Open Space

Environmental bond questions to provide funding for open space acquisition and land preservation have proven very popular with voters. In 1998, environmentalists won 172 local ballot measures dealing with development, preservation of open space, and habitat protection. This was an impressive 72% victory rate of the 240 measures of this type that were on the ballot that year. A total of $7.5 billion was approved to protect parks, open space, farmland, watersheds and ecosystems. Statewide bond questions passed in Florida and New York in 1996, New Jersey, Oregon, Michigan and Maine in 1998, Rhode Island and California in 2000, Maine in 2001, and California in March of 2002. More comprehensive statewide sprawl control measures that go beyond land acquisition and improvement and regulate new developments have had a more difficult time, with efforts in Arizona and Colorado failing in 2000.

Toxics

After concerns over toxic chemicals were highlighted by Love Canal and other dumpsites, Massachusetts's voters approved a 1986 initiative sponsored by the Massachusetts Campaign to Clean Up Hazardous Waste (since renamed Toxics Action Center). This law instructed the state to identify and clean up hazardous waste sites.

Also in 1986, California voters enacted the landmark Proposition 65, the Safe Drinking Water and Toxic Enforcement Act. It passed by a two to one margin and required businesses to disclose the presences of toxic chemicals to consumers and employees. A similar measure in Ohio failed in 1992.

In 1988, voters in Washington State established the state's Superfund program by ballot initiative 97. In a classic case of industry attempting to undermine the measure, the state's oil and chemical industry worked with the legislature to place a competing initiative 97B, on the ballot. Voters overwhelmingly approved the citizen initiative after a major grassroots campaign led by every major citizen organization in the state including Washington Environmental Council, WashPIRG, League of Women Voters, and others. The campaign was helped by remnants of the federal Fairness Doctrine that allowed proponents to run a small number of no on 97B ads.

In 1990, a proposal to ban cancer-causing pesticides from use in California was placed on the ballot along with a host of other environmental protections that would have protected old growth forests, banned offshore oil drilling, phased out ozone depleting CFC's, and protected beaches from sewage pollution in an omnibus initiative called Big Green.

Big Green was defeated after opponents spent $16 million to proponents $4 million.

Energy

Environmentalists waged a series of ballot battles against nuclear power, often losing but successfully raising the issue to the public debate. In 1976, the nuclear industry successfully defeated initiatives in Arizona, California, Colorado, Montana, Ohio, Oregon, and Washington that would have required legislative approval of nuclear power facilities. But in 1978, Montana passed an initiative requiring voter approval of nuclear facilities, and Oregon passed an initiative to prevent utilities from saddling ratepayers with investments in nuclear power that didn't pay off. Oregon followed that in 1980 by passing a voter approval initiative for new facilities. Also in 1980, Massachusetts passed restrictions on radioactive waste disposal and Montana passed a ballot question to prohibit disposal of nuclear waste in Montana, while South Dakota defeated a voter approval measure. Although losing many of these battles, environmentalists began winning the war as no new nuclear plants began construction after 1978.

Environmentalists began raising their goals from regulation of new plants to shutting existing plants down. Maine defeated an outright ban on nuclear fission for power generation in 1980 and again in 1982 defeated a measure that would

---

23. Derek Cressman works with the Public Interest Research Groups (PIRGs), a coalition of state-based organizations that work on consumer protection, public health, environmental preservation, and good government. Cressman has worked on nine ballot initiative campaigns in California, Colorado, and Massachusetts.

have phased out nuclear power over five years. In 1986, Washington voters approved a non-binding referendum telling the legislature to oppose the Hanford site for consideration of a national nuclear waste repository and asking for voter approval should Hanford ever is considered. And in 1987 Maine voters passed a ban on new high-waste nuclear power plants. Massachusetts's utilities defeated an initiative to shut down the state's two nuclear plants in 1988, but a few years later closed down one of them anyhow.

The most recent phase of nuclear ballot questions dealt with who would pay for the costs of nuclear plants that environmentalists had never wanted and that had proven to be economic boondoggles. As deregulation of the utility market was approved at the state level, environmentalists including many State Public Interest Research Groups took to the ballot to try to prevent utilities from dumping their "stranded" costs of bad nuclear investments on consumers. A 1998 MA ballot question to rollback deregulation was defeated, as was a 2000 effort in California after a $40 million campaign by the utilities. However, Oregon voters repealed a deregulation deal that would have left Oregon consumers stuck with a $304 million tab in lost profits caused by the closing of the flawed Trojan Nuclear power plant.

Environmentalists have recently begun using the ballot to promote alternatives to nuclear power and fossil fuels. In November 2001, San Francisco voters approved a sweeping local initiative to implement solar power and more efforts like this are underway.

Recycling

The modern recycling ethic got much of its start from state bottle bills—laws that placed a small deposit such as 5 cents on beer and soda cans to encourage consumers to return them for recycling and reclaim their deposit. These laws reduced roadside litter, but also got citizens in the habit of saving some waste for recycling. This ethic has since transformed into successful curbside recycling programs across the country, and a greatly increase sensitivity to reduction of waste and favoring of reusables over disposables. Washington state voters approved a litter control act in 1972, although it was never implemented by the legislature. Michigan voters approved a bottle bill in 1976. Environmentalists then suffered a series of defeats on the ballot as beer manufacturers and grocers waged concerted campaigns to stop bottle bills. Initiatives were defeated in Massachusetts in 1976, Nebraska and Alaska in 1978, Washington and Ohio in 1979, Montana in 1980, Washington, Colorado, California, and Arizona in 1982, and Montana in 1988. Environmentalists did manage to get bottle bills passed through legislatures, and in MASSPIRG successfully defended a bottle bill on the Massachusetts ballot by defeating an industry referendum to repeal law passed by the legislature.

As more recycled materials became available through bottle bills and other programs, environmentalists again looked to the ballot to require packagers to use recycled materials and were again rebuffed by strong industry opposition. In 1990, Oregon voters defeated a measure to require recycled content or reduced packaging after a $2.5 million campaign against it. In 1992, Massachusetts defeated a similar proposal after opponents spent $6 million against it. This continues to be a challenge for environmentalists.

Natural Resource Preservation

Environmentalists have also tried to use the initiative process to preserve wilderness and ecosystems. In 1972, California voters approved a ballot question to create the Coastal Zone Conservation Commission and in Florida voters created a state Fish and Wildlife Conservation Commission in 1998. But more sweeping efforts to protect forests have not fared well. In 1990, California voters rejected an initiative to protect old growth forests. Maine voters in 1996 rejected both a measure backed by environmentalists and compromise measure backed by the logging industry. The industry-backed plan was again rejected in 1997, but an environmentalist backed initiative in 2000 to require permits for clear cutting also failed. Oregon environmentalists also failed to pass an initiative to restrict logging in 1998.

In 1998 Alaska voters re-affirmed and strengthened a ban on billboards backed by the Alaska Center for the Environment. It won by 72 percent, but in 2000 a Missouri ballot campaign to ban construction of new billboards was defeated.

Clean water

At the beginnings of the modern environmental movement, Oregon voters passed an initiative to protect scenic waterways in 1970. An effort to protect the Stanislaus River from damming in California failed in 1974, but ten years later an environmental initiative to protect drinking water from toxic discharges passed. In 1988, Oregon again passed an initiative to create the Oregon Scenic Water Way system to protect important sections of rivers, but in 1994 an environmental initiative in Oregon called Stop Toxic Open Pit Mines that would have mitigated mine runoff was defeated. Montana voters also defeated a mine runoff law in 1996, but in 1998 they approved a similar initiative to ban cyanide leach mining. Significantly, this initiative was run under a Montana reform law (passed through a MontPIRG sponsored ballot question in 1996) that prohibited corporate contributions to ballot question campaigns. This prevented mining corporations from overwhelming environmentalists as they had in the 1996 campaign. Many environmentalists feel that reforms such as this are needed for environmental questions to receive a fair hearing at the ballot box. A 1992 study by Americans for the Environment found that 32 environmental ballot questions drew $18 million in opposition from more than 2,000 corporations.

Factory Farms

South Dakota passed a ban on corporate hog farms in 1988 and in 1998 went even further to ban all corporate ownership of farms. Also in 1998, Colorado environmentalists won restrictions on corporate hog farms, which can be a major source of water pollution.

Transportation

In 1990, and again in 1992 and subsequent years, California voters approved ballot measures to provide funding for the Passenger Rail and Clean Air act aimed at increasing light rail use in California. In 2000, Florida voters approved a plan for a high-speed monorail. Project such as these can reduce traffic and associated air pollution.

Leveraging the Initiative Process

Environmentalists have also won victories through preparing to use the initiative process but seeing legislatures enact environmental laws in response to the threat of a tougher ballot question. The Massachusetts legislature passed a Toxics Use Reduction law in 1989 with the support of the Associated Industries of Massachusetts because AIM was worried that MASSPIRG would take the issue to the ballot. A story in the *Chemistry and Industry* report noted that industry supported the compromise because "Looming in the background was the prospect of an even more onerous ballot initiative should a statute not be enacted." Similarly, the legislature passed a Pesticide Use Reduction act in 1998 After MASSPIRG made preparations to go to the ballot once again.

Major Environmental Ballot Initiatives[24]

State	Type	Measure Number	Description	Year	Pass/Fail
Oregon	DS	17	Blue sky law.	1912	Failed
Arizona	DS	N/A	Placing of electric poles	1914	Passed
Oregon	DA	15	Public docks and water frontage amendment.	1914	Failed
Arizona	DS	N/A	Fish and game regulation.	1916	Passed
Arizona	DA	N/A	To authorize the legislature to provide proper laws for the sale of state lands.	1918	Passed
Arizona	DA	N/A	To limit the sale of agricultural and grazing land.	1918	Passed
Arizona	DS	N/A	Conservation, game and fish.	1920	Failed
Arizona	DS	N/A	Reclamation.	1920	Failed
Oregon	DS	9	Roosevelt bird refuge.	1920	Failed
Arizona	DS	N/A	Colorado River, appropriations.	1924	Failed
California	DS	11	To create the Klamath River Fish and Game District.	1924	Passed
Oregon	DS	5	Deschutes River water and fish bill.	1928	Failed
Oregon	DS	6	Rogue River water and fish bill.	1928	Failed
Oregon	DS	7	Umpqua River water and fish bill.	1928	Failed
Oregon	DS	8	McKenzie River water and fish bill.	1928	Failed
Missouri	DA	N/A	Providing for the taking of private lands for public purposes.	1930	Failed
Oklahoma	DS	230	An Act designating the OK Conservation Commission as a State agency to co-operate with Federal Government in designated projects.	1936	Failed

24. The Institute uses different categories for some of the ballot measures discussed in this chapter. For example, some of the measures that are discussed in this chapter as environmental measures are listed in our database as "Nuclear Freeze", "Animal Protection" and "Transportation". Therefore, some of the ballot measures discussed in this chapter will not appear on this list but can be found in the appendix.

State	Type	Measure Number	Description	Year	Pass/Fail
California	DS	4	To prohibit tideland and surface oil drilling and authorizing drilling wells slanted from uplands, and to prohibit pollution of tide, ocean bay or inlet waters.	1936	Failed
Oregon	DS	10	Water purification and prevention of pollution bill.	1938	Passed
Colorado	DA	N/A	Providing for the conservation of the state's wildlife resources; limiting the use of game and fish revenues for such purposes; and establishing a Game and Fish Commission.	1940	Failed
Missouri	DA	N/A	Repealing Wild Life and Forestry Code and all laws and regulations ordained and established by Conservation Commission.	1940	Failed
Arkansas	DA	34	Game and Fish Commission	1942	Failed
Arkansas	DA	36	To create the Arkansas state Game and Fish Commission to control, manage, conserve and regulate the birds, fish, game, and wildlife resources of the state.	1944	Passed
California	DS	15	Prohibits use of purse nets and round haul nets for fishing in ocean and tide waters of the state south of line extending due west from Point San Simeon in San Luis Obispo County.	1948	Failed
Washington	DS	I-192	Regulation of Commercial Salmon Fishing.	1954	Failed
Idaho	DS	1	The Dredge Mining Initiative Proposal.	1954	Passed
California	DS 4		To prohibit waste, defined as production methods which reduce maximum economic quantity of oil or gas ultimately recoverable by good engineering practices.	1956	Failed
Oregon	DS	15	Billboard control.	1960	Failed
Colorado	DA	3	Creates a wildlife management commission and a department of wildlife conservation.	1960	Failed
Washington	DS	I-215	Marine Recreation Land Act.	1964	Passed
Washington	IDS	I-32	Local processing of State timber.	1968	Failed
Oregon	DA	11	Restricts governmental powers over rural property.	1970	Failed
Oregon	DS	9	Scenic waterways bill.	1970	Passed
Washington	DS	I-256	Prohibiting certain nonrefundable beverage receptacles.	1970	Failed
Washington	IDS	I-40	Litter Control Act.	1972	Passed
Washington	IDS	I-43	Regulating Shoreline Use and Development.	1972	Passed
California	DS	9	Specifies permissible composition and quality of gasoline and other fuel for internal combustion engines.	1972	Failed
California	DS	20	Creates Coastal Zone Conservation Commission and 6 regional commissions.	1972	Passed
California	DS	17	Designates specified portions of the main stem of the Stanislaus River as components of the California Wild and Scenic Rivers System.	1974	Failed
Oregon	DS	10	Repeals land use planning coordination statutes.	1976	Failed
Colorado	DS	8	Requires a minimum deposit refund value for beverage containers for malt liquor, including beer, and carbonated soft drinks manufactured, distributed, or sold for use in this state.	1976	Failed
Maine	IDS	N/A	To establish a public preserve in Bigelow Mountain area.	1976	Passed
Massachusetts	IDS	Question 6	To require every beverage container to have a refund value of $.05 and to ban containers with flip-tops.	1976	Failed
Michigan	DA	N/A	A proposal to ban throw-away bottles and cans.	1976	Passed
Oregon	DA	10	Land use planning, zoning amendment.	1978	Failed
Alaska	IDS	4	Disposal of state lands.	1978	Passed
Alaska	ID	S 5	Beverage container deposits.	1978	Failed
Nebraska	DS	301	Five cent deposit on beverage containers.	1978	Failed
Washington	ID	S I-61	Five cent refund on beverage containers.	1979	Failed
Ohio	IDS	Issue No. 1	Mandatory deposits on bottles; prohibit pull-tabs.	1979	Failed
Montana	DS	I 87	Montana Litter Control and Recycling Act.	1980	Failed

State	Type	Measure Number	Description	Year	Pass/Fail
Washington	DS	I-414	Five cent refund on beverage containers.	1982	Failed
Oregon	DS	6	End State's land use planning powers; localities.	1982	Failed
Alaska	IDS	5	State ownership of Federal land.	1982	Passed
Arizona	DS	200	Deposit/refund for beverage containers.	1982	Failed
California	DS	11	Beverage containers must have refund value of at least five cents.	1982	Failed
California	DS	13	Establishes water conservation programs.	1982	Failed
Colorado	DS	5	Refund on beverage containers.	1982	Failed
California	DS	65	Toxic discharge into drinking water.	1986	Passed
Massachusetts	IDS	Question 4	DEQE to identify/clean hazardous waste sites.	1986	Passed
Oregon	DS	6	Indoor Clean Air Law revisions — ban public smoking.	1988	Failed
Oregon	DS	7	Oregon Scenic Waterway System.	1988	Passed
South Dakota	IDS	2	Surface mining reclamation.	1988	Failed
Montana	DS	I-113	Refundable deposits on beverage containers.	1988	Failed
Washington	ID	S I-97	Would establish a superfund for environmental cleanup	1988	Passed
Nebraska	DS	402	Central Interstate Radioactive Waste Compact.	1988	Failed
Oregon	DS	6	Product packaging: recycling, hardship waivers.	1990	Failed
South Dakota	DS	2	Permits for large scale gold/silver mining.	1990	Failed
Washington	DS	I-547	Growth and environmental protection goals, fees.	1990	Failed
Arizona	DS	200	Arizona state Parks funded by lottery.	1990	Passed
Arizona	DS	202	Hazardous waste disposal.	1990	Failed
California	DA	132	Establishes marine protection zone within three miles of coast.	1990	Passed
California	DS	130	Authorizes bonds for forest acquisition and regulates timber harvesting.	1990	Failed
California	DS	135	Pesticide regulation.	1990	Failed
California	DS	138	Forest acquisition. Timber harvesting. Bond act.	1990	Failed
Missouri	DS	N/A	Regulation of streams.	1990	Failed
Ohio	IDS	5	Businesses would be required to provide warnings for toxic substances.	1992	Failed
South Dakota	DS	2	Regulation, reclamation: gold/silver mining. 1992 Passed Colorado DA 8 The Great Outdoors Colorado program.	1992	Passed
Massachusetts	IDS	Question 3	All packaging to be recycled or recyclable.	1992	Failed
North Dakota	DS	N/A	Environmental protection fund, fees on waste.	1992	Failed
Florida	DA	3	Limit marine net fishing	1994	Passed
Oregon	DA	14	Amends chemical process mining laws — adds requirements, prohibitions, standards, fees.	1994	Failed
Missouri	DA	N/A	Property protection to require government reimbursement for lost revenue due to the acquisition on lands for park use.	1994	Passed
Washington	DS	I-640	Regulation of state fishing	1995	Failed
Florida	DA	5	Responsibility for paying costs of water pollution abatement in the Everglades.	1996	Passed
Florida	DA	6	Establishes and Everglade Trust Fund for conservation and protection of natural resources and abatement of water pollution.	1996	Passed
Maine	IDS	2A	Bans clear cutting.	1996	Failed
Montana	DS I	122	Increases requirements for treatment of water discharged from mines.	1996	Failed
Oregon	DS	34	Gives Fish & Wildlife Commission exclusive authority to manage wildlife; repeals 1994 initiative that prohibited the use of dogs or bait to hunt bear or cougar.	1996	Failed
Oregon	DS	37	Broadens types of beverage containers that require deposits and refunds.	1996	Failed
Oregon	DS	38	Prohibits livestock in or near polluted waters or on adjacent lands.	1996	Failed
Alaska	IDS	5	Would prohibit billboards	1998	Passed
California	DS	7	Would authorize State Air Resources Board and delegated air pollution control districts to award $218 million in state tax credits annually until 2011 to encourage air-commissions reduction.	1998	Failed

State	Type	Measure Number	Description	Year	Pass/Fail
Colorado	DS	15	Would regulate water flow meters.	1998	Failed
Montana	DS I	137	Would prohibit cyanide process open pit mining.	1998	Passed
Oregon	DS	64	Would prohibit many present timber harvest practices and imposes more restrictive regulations.	1998	Failed
Oregon	DA	66	Would dedicate some lottery funding to parks and beaches habitat and watershed protection.	1998	Passed
Washington	DS	I-696	Prohibit certain commercial net, troll, and trawl fishing in fresh and marine waters, except tribal treaty fisheries.	1999	Failed
Maine	IDS	2	Sets limits on timber harvesting on land subject to the Maine Tree Growth Tax Law and requires that a landowner obtain a permit from the Maine Forest Service prior to undertaking harvesting activities that will result in a clear-cut.	2000	Failed
Arizona	DS	202	This initiative would require cities and counties to adopt growth management plans to limit urban sprawl.	2000	Failed
Florida	DA	1	To reduce traffic and increase travel alternatives, this amendment provides for development of a high speed monorail, fixed guide way or magnetic levitation system linking Florida's five largest urban areas.	2000	Passed
Oregon	DA	7	Requires payment to landowner if government regulation reduces property value.	2000	Passed
Missouri	DS	A	Prohibits new billboards from being constructed and restricts existing outdoor advertising along all National Highway System highways in Missouri.	2000	Failed
Colorado	DA	24	Citizen Growth Initiative.	2000	Failed

Nuclear and Energy Related Initiatives

State	Type	Measure Number	Description	Year	Pass/Fail
Colorado	DA	10	An act to amend the Constitution to establish procedural steps to be complied with prior to the detonation of nuclear explosive devises including voter approval.	1974	Passed
Oregon	DS	9	Regulates nuclear power plant construction approval.	1976	Failed
Washington	DS	I-325	Shall future nuclear power facilities which do not meet certain conditions and receive two-thirds approval by the legislature be prohibited.	1976	Failed
Arizona	DS	200	Legislative approval-nuclear facilities.	1976	Failed
Ohio	DA	Issue No. 6	Relative to establishing procedures for legislative hearings and approval of safety features of nuclear power plants and related facilities.	1976	Failed
Colorado	DA	3	An amendment requiring approval by two thirds of each House of the General Assembly prior to any construction or modification of a nuclear power plant or related facility.	1976	Failed
Montana	DS	I 71	Requiring legislative approval of any nuclear facility licensed under the Montana Major Facility Sitting Act.	1976	Failed
California	DS	15	Nuclear power plants.	1976	Failed
Montana	DS	I 80	Voter regulation of nuclear facilities.	1978	Passed
Washington	DS	I-383	Bans on radioactive wastes generated out of State.	1980	Passed
Oregon	DS	7	Nuclear plant licensing: voter approval, disposal.	1980	Passed
South Dakota	IDS	2	Uranium, nuclear waste, plants: voter approval.	1980	Failed
Maine	IDS	N/A	Prohibit electric power by nuclear fission.	1980	Failed
Missouri	DS	N/A	Nuclear waste.	1980	Failed
Montana	DS	I 84	Prohibit disposal of radioactive waste in MT.	1980	Passed
Oregon	DS	5	Mutual freeze on nuclear weapons development.	1982	Passed

State	Type	Measure Number	Description	Year	Pass/Fail
California	M	12	Nuclear weapons.	1982	Passed
Colorado	M	6	To bring about the cessation of nuclear weapons component production in Colorado.	1982	Failed
Maine	IDS	N/A	End nuclear power for electricity in five years.	1982	Failed
Massachusetts	IDS	Question 3	Restrict radioactive waste disposal; construction.	1982	Passed
Michigan	M	N/A	Mutual nuclear weapons freeze with Soviet Union.	1982	Passed
Montana	DS	I 91	Opposing placement of MX Missiles in Montana.	1982	Passed
North Dakota	M	N/A	Limits development/production of nuclear weapons.	1982	Passed
South Dakota	M	3	SD mandates a verifiable nuclear freeze.	1984	Failed
Oregon	DS	9	Naturally occurring radioactive isotopes: disposal.	1984	Passed
South Dakota	IDS	1	Voter approval: nuclear waste disposal, compacts.	1984	Passed
Oregon	DS	14	Nuclear Power: permanent waste site licensed.	1986	Failed
Oregon	DS	15	"Radioactive waste" defined; energy facility payments.	1986	Failed
Oregon	DS	16	Nuclear weapons funded by tax credits. Civil penalty.	1986	Failed
Alaska	M	1	Nuclear Weapons Freeze.	1986	Passed
Maine	IDS	N/A	No high-waste nuclear plants after July 4, 1988.	1987	Passed
Massachusetts	IDS	Question 4	Ban electric power plants that produce nuclear waste.	1988	Failed
Maine	M	N/A	Stop cruise missile tests.	1989	Passed
Oregon	DS	4	Prohibit Trojan operation until standards met.	1990	Failed
Oregon	DS	5	Close Trojan: waste, cost, and earthquake orders.	1992	Failed
Oregon	DS	6	Bans Trojan operation unless conditions met.	1992	Failed
Idaho	DS	3	Require legislative and voter approval of agreements for the receipt of additional radioactive waste and nullifying a prior agreement.	1996	Failed
California	DS	9	Would prohibit assessment of utility tax bond payments or surcharges for payment of costs of nuclear power plants/related assets.	1998	Failed

10 The Issue of a National Initiative Process

By Dennis Polhill [1]

National referendums are a regular event among the world's democracies. With four national elections per year Switzerland has held approximately half of the 800 national referendums in world history.

One application of national referendums has been in exercising the "self determination" of a people. A referendum unified fragmented Italian states into a nation. Norway separated from Sweden in 1905 via national referendum. Only "five major democracies have never had a national referendum: India, Israel, Japan, the Netherlands, and the United States." [2] In recent years Israel and the Netherlands have seriously contemplated the idea of a national referendum to advance intractable issues.

The demise of the Soviet Union was a byproduct of the largest national referendum in world history; the Soviet Union's first and last referendum. To advance his reforms Mikhail Gorbachev sought popular support by proposing the March 17, 1991 All-Union referendum. The All-Union Referendum would reaffirm the Union Treaty of 1922 that created the Soviet Union. The referendum opened a floodgate. The 15 Republics did not conform. Some redrafted the language; several added questions to the ballot; others declared their independence and still others boycotted the event. Although the All-Union Referendum passed overwhelmingly, periphery events turned out to be more relevant than the specific outcome. The Soviet Republics had discovered a way to articulate their frustration with central control and busily went about acting as independent states.

But Has the National Referendum Process Been Abused?

The prospect of manipulation of a national referendum is real. Gorbachev directed the military to manage the election in Republics that boycotted the All-Union Referendum with the result that voter turn out approximated the local ethnic Russian population.

Hitler used national referendums to withdraw Germany from the League of Nations in 1933 and to consolidate his powers in 1934. The ability of the Nazi propaganda machine to insure the desired result is well known. This problem with referred measures was well expressed when Benito Mussolini said, "Give me the right to nominate and you can vote for whomever you please." The control of the language and what questions appear on ballots is not a minor detail. A recent example is the election held in April 2002 in Pakistan. President Musharraf clearly manipulated the wording of the referendum in order to ensure he was reelected to another five year term as President of Pakistan.

So What about National I&R in the United States?

If I&R has been a means for dealing with the conflicts at the state level, why not resolve similar national conflicts with national I&R? Lincoln is said to have proposed a national vote to reconcile slavery. There have been 3 major efforts in the U.S. for national I&R: the Progressive movement (prior to 1920), the anti-war movement (during both World Wars I and II), and the environmental movement (during the 1970s). [3]

An early advocate for national I&R was U.S. Senator and former Colorado Governor John Shafroth. The Shafroth Amendment [4] was proposed as an amendment to the U.S. Constitution in 1914. It would have given the people of every state I&R for determining women's suffrage. When 8% of voters signed a petition, the issue would be determined by a majority vote at the next state election. Mounting pressure eventually forced Congress to deal with the issue. Had it become law, the Shafroth Amendment might very well have expedited resolution of women's suffrage. Perhaps more importantly, it would have set a precedent as a means of addressing other difficult national issues.

When the U.S. entered World War I, isolationists and pacifists called for a national referendum, arguing that only the people should decide whether to go to war. Advocates proposed an Amendment to the U.S. Constitution (also called the

---

1. Dennis currently serves as Chairman of the Initiative & Referendum Institute and is a Senior Fellow at the Independence Institute in Golden, Colorado.
2. "Referendums around the World," by David Butler amd Austin Ranney, AEI Press, 1994, p. 258.
3. "Direct Democracy," by Thomas E. Cronin, Harvard University Press, 1988, p. 164.
4. "Equal Suffrage to Equal Rights," by Christine A. Lunardini, New York University Press, 1986, Appendix I.

Peace Referendum) that would have required a nationwide popular vote to go to war, unless the U.S. was attacked or invaded. A similar movement emerged during World War II but was never approved by Congress.

After World War II, the use of the statewide initiative process declined and was largely forgotten by many activists until it was rediscovered in the 1970s by the environmental movement. Coincident with rediscovery of state I&R, was a renewed interest in national I&R. Senator Abourezk (D-SD) introduced the National Voter Initiative Amendment in 1977. The NVIA would have taken an issue to nationwide vote, when 3% of voters in at least 10 states signed a petition. A majority of voters nationwide would decide the issue. The difference between the Shafroth and the Abourezk approaches merit elaboration. Shafroth empowered the people of the states, acknowledging that the Federal government is a collection of state governments. Abourezk did not account for the division of powers between Federal and State governments itemized in the U.S. Constitution or provide a means of addressing state issues. Shafroth did not provide a means for directly resolving national concerns. A well-designed system of national I&R should do both: work within the bounds of the constitution and provide a means for addressing issues reserved to the respective Federal and State levels.

National I&R Proposals

There have been two distinct approaches to obtaining a national I&R process in the United States. One is working through the states and the other is by getting Congress to pass an amendment establishing the initiative process.

In the states, several organizations, like USPIRG, have worked hard to generate support for a national I&R process. In addition to the "PIRGs", another organization, "Philadelphia Two" has been working to establish a national initiative process. Former U.S. Senator Mike Gravel heads the group. Though their approach is somewhat controversial (basically to set up an "electoral trust" that is not accountable to the government), they are working hard to build support for a national initiative process.

At the Congressional level, between 1895 and 1943, 108 proposals[5] to amend the U.S. Constitution by adding national I&R were submitted. Seven would have created a general I&R, that would have allowed for consideration of any issue. The others created I&R for specific issues only or that had issue-specific prohibitions. For example, Abourezk would not permit the declaring of war, calling up troops, or amending the constitution and would permit statutory modifications by Congress with a two-thirds majority or simple majority after two years. Implementation of national I&R is more complicated in the U.S. than in other nations due to the unique Constitutional division of responsibilities between the Federal and State governments. In most countries, governments are centralized to either a greater or lesser extent. Other variations of national I&R that have been proposed in the U.S. include:

• The first proposal for national I&R was in 1895 by Populist Party U.S. Senator William Peffer from Kansas. It provided for a national vote on an issue when 20% of voters nationwide or 20% of state legislatures requested it.
• In 1907 U.S. Representative Elmer Lincoln Fulton from Oklahoma suggested that 8% of the voters in each of 15 states could put either a constitutional amendment or statute proposal to a national vote or that 5% of the voters in each of 15 states or their state legislatures could challenge a statute passed by Congress.
• In 1911 Senator Bristow from Kansas proposed that the Initiative be used to reign in the court. Any law held unconstitutional by the Supreme Court would go to a vote of the people. This was the first proposal for using I&R as the method by which to reconcile conflicts between the equal branches of the Federal government.
• Socialist Party U.S. Representative Victor Berger of Wisconsin introduced the most radical proposal ever. It would have abolished the Presidency, the Senate and the Supreme Court. Five percent of the voters in three-fourths of the state could propose a law or challenge a law passed by Congress.
• U.S. Senator Bob La Follette from Wisconsin in 1916 proposed a non-binding national advisory referendum that would be held when 1% of the voters in 25 states petitioned.
• The National approach would require some percentage (usually in the range of 3%) of voters nationwide to sign a petition. Because elections are managed by the states and there are no national voter rolls or other election systems, leaving states out of the process would require changes in election management.
• Nullification advocates in the 1980s and 1990s suggested that Federal statutes should go to a nationwide vote when 10% of the voters in 1/3 of the states sign a petition challenging it. Nullification proposals were in reaction to "unfunded mandates" and directives imposed upon the states by Congress. A nullification mechanism would effectively be a national application of the referendum petition or challenge petition.

---

5. "Congress and the People," by Donald R. Wolfensberger, Woodrow Wilson Press, 2000, page 72.

The "States Approach" to National I&R

The question of national I&R in the U.S. is not whether it will be. Rather, the question is when it will be and what form it will have. When the Confederate States wrote their constitution, they substantially replicated the constitution they had lived under for over 70 years. Perhaps the most substantial variation cured a significant structural flaw in the U.S. Constitution: how Amendments are proposed for ratification. Recognizing that a constitution is the delegation of consent to govern and, therefore, a limitation on government, and acknowledging Congress' inherent conflict of interest, the authority of Congress to draft proposed amendments was revoked. A proposed amendment would go to ratification when 25% of the states passed resolutions supporting the same proposal. This, in fact, is what the Founders had intended with Article V; but their intent was subsequently subverted by Congress.

The "States Approach" may be the best form for national I&R. The "States Approach" would permit a number of states (25%) to agree either by state initiative petition and vote or by state legislature resolution, that a question should be addressed nationally. When a number of states concur, the Federal statute (simple majority) or constitution (3/4 majority) is changed. Obviously, over-reaching Federal statutes could be stricken by the same means.

The "States Approach" acknowledges the respective constitutional roles of the State and Federal governments. It provides a means for addressing both state and national issues. It can cure both actions of omission and acts of commission by Congress and by individual state legislatures. It utilizes the existing election management systems of the states. It answers the problem of Congressional conflict of interest. It can deal with both Federal statutory or constitutional problems. It acknowledges the sovereignty of the people at every level. It might be a viable means for resolving conflicts between the equal branches of the Federal government or deadlocked Federal legislation. The fear of majoritarian abuse of I&R is reduced. National issues are resolved gradually via ongoing public debate and incremental approval by the states. A critical part of the Constitution is restored to the functionality intended by the Founders.

The "States Approach" also offers a practical means of implementation and can be achieved gradually by increasing the number of states with I&R until critical mass is reached. Critical mass is when the numbers of states with I&R is sufficient to press the issue of nationally.

Summary

National I&R in the U.S. would offer a mechanism to address national issues that partisan politics or Congressional inherent conflict of interest prohibits a solution. Several attempts have been made in Congress and in the states—but to no avail. However, as citizens enlarge their participation in their government, it appears inevitable that the U.S. will find a way to exercise this fundamental right in the near future.

Appendix

Section A: Timeline

Year	Event
1775	In his proposed 1775 Virginia state constitution, Thomas Jefferson includes a requirement that the constitution must be approved by the voters in a statewide referendum before it can take effect. Unfortunately, because he was hundred of miles from Virginia at the time attending the Continental Congress, delegates to the Virginia Convention did not receive the proposal until after the convention was already over.
1776	Georgia delegates gather in Savannah to draft their state's constitution. The constitution includes a provision that would allow amendments whenever a majority of voters in each county signed petitions calling for a convention, but the provision is never invoked.
1778	Massachusetts becomes the first state to hold a statewide legislative referendum to adopt its constitution. The voters reject it by a five-to-one margin, forcing the legislature to rewrite its proposal.
1792	New Hampshire becomes the second state to hold a statewide legislative referendum to adopt its constitution.
1830	Voters in Virginia demand the power to veto amendments to their state constitution and are given it.
1834	Alabama, Connecticut, Georgia, Maine, Mississippi, New York, North Carolina, and Rhode Island adopt provisions preventing their state constitutions from being amended without the approval of the voters.
1848	The 1848 Swiss Constitution includes provisions for initiative and popular referendum.
1857	Congress requires that voters must approve all state constitutions proposed after 1857.
1885	Father Robert Haire, a priest and labor activist from Aberdeen, South Dakota, and Benjamin Urner, a newspaper publisher from New Jersey become the first Americans to propose giving the people statewide initiative and popular referendum power.
1897	Nebraska becomes the first state to allow its cities to use initiative and popular referendum.
1897	South Dakota becomes the first state to adopt statewide initiative and popular referendum.
1900	Utah becomes the second state to adopt statewide initiative and popular referendum.
1901	The Illinois legislature creates a statewide non-binding advisory initiative process.
1902	Oregon becomes the third state to adopt statewide initiative and popular referendum. In Illinois, using a statewide non-binding advisory initiative process, citizens place an advisory question on the ballot asking whether or not Illinois should adopt a real initiative and referendum process — voters say yes, but the legislature ignores them.
1904	Oregon is the first state to place a statewide initiative on the ballot. In Missouri, voters defeat a measure that would have established statewide initiative and popular referendum.
1905	Nevada adopts statewide popular referendum only.
1906	Montana adopts statewide initiative and popular referendum. Delaware voters approve an advisory referendum put on the ballot by the state legislature, asking whether they want the initiative process — but the legislature ignores the mandate.
1907	Oklahoma becomes the first state to provide for statewide initiative and popular referendum in its original constitution.
1908	Michigan and Maine adopt statewide initiative and popular referendum. Unfortunately, Michigan's initiative procedures are so difficult that, under them, citizens are unable to place a single initiative on the ballot. Missouri adopts statewide initiative and popular referendum.
1910	Arkansas and Colorado adopt statewide initiative and popular referendum. Kentucky adopts statewide popular referendum. Illinois voters again approve a citizen-initiated non-binding advisory question in support of statewide initiative and popular referendum — and the legislature again ignores them.
1911	Arizona and California adopt statewide initiative and popular referendum. New Mexico adopts only statewide popular referendum.

Year	Event
1912	Idaho, Nebraska, Ohio and Washington adopt statewide initiative and popular referendum. Nevada adopts a statewide initiative process, complementing its statewide popular referendum process adopted in 1905. A majority of Wyoming voters voting on a constitutional amendment to adopt statewide initiative and popular referendum approve the amendment; but
	Wyoming's constitution requires that all amendments also receive a majority vote of all voters voting in the election, regardless of whether or not they vote on the actual amendment itself — so the measure fails. A majority of Mississippi voters voting on a constitutional amendment to adopt statewide initiative and popular referendum also approve the amendment; but, like Wyoming, a constitutional requirement that all amendments also receive a majority vote of all voters voting in the election, defeats the measure.
1913	Michigan initiative and popular referendum supporters lobby the legislature to pass amendments simplifying its statewide initiative and popular referendum process, a process so difficult that it is unusable. The legislature passes the amendments and voters approve them.
1914	Mississippi and North Dakota adopt statewide initiative and popular referendum. Wisconsin and Texas voters defeat measures creating a statewide initiative and popular referendum process. A majority of Minnesota voters voting on a constitutional amendment to adopt statewide initiative and popular referendum approve the amendment; but Minnesota's constitution requires that all amendments also receive a majority vote of all voters voting in the election, regardless of whether or not they vote on the actual amendment itself — so the measure fails.
1915	Maryland adopts the popular referendum process.
1916	A majority of Minnesota voters voting on a constitutional amendment to adopt statewide initiative and popular referendum again approve the amendment; but the Minnesota constitution's requirement that all amendments also receive a majority vote of all voters voting in the election, regardless of whether or not they vote on the actual amendment itself — again dooms the measure.
1918	Massachusetts adopts statewide initiative and popular referendum. North Dakotans vote and approve a more lenient initiative process. The amendment passed by the North Dakota legislature and adopted by the voters in 1914 had such strict procedures that no initiatives qualified for the ballot in the following election, so initiative proponents put an initiative on the 1918 ballot to ease the procedures.
1922	Mississippi Supreme Court overturns Mississippi's initiative and popular referendum process.
1956	Alaska adopts statewide initiative and popular referendum as part of its new constitution.
1968	Wyoming adopts statewide initiative and popular referendum.
1970	Illinois adopts a very limited initiative process.
1972	Florida adopts statewide initiative.
1977	*Hardie v. Eu* is decided by the California Supreme Court that finds unconstitutional the Political Reform Act's cap on expenditures for qualifying ballot measures since it violates the First Amendment of the U.S. Constitution. The District of Columbia adopts initiative and popular referendum. The U.S. Supreme Court rules in *First National Bank of Boston v. Bellotti* that state laws prohibiting or limiting corporate contributions or spending in initiative campaigns violates the First and Fourteenth Amendments of the U.S. Constitution.
1980	For the third time, a majority of Minnesota voters voting on a constitutional amendment to adopt statewide initiative and popular referendum approve the measure; but for the third time the Minnesota constitution's requirement that all amendments also receive a majority vote of all voters voting in the election, regardless of whether or not they vote on the actual amendment itself dooms the measure. The U.S. Supreme Court rules in *Pruneyard Shopping Center v. Robins* that state constitutional provisions that permit political activity at a privately-owned shopping center does not violate federal constitutional private property rights of owner.
1981	The U.S. Supreme Court rules in Citizens Against Rent Control v. Berkeley that a California city's ordinance to impose a limit on contributions to committees formed to support or oppose ballot measures violates the First Amendment.
1986	Rhode Island voters defeat a measure establishing statewide initiative and popular referendum.
1988	The U.S. Supreme Court rules in *Meyer v. Grant* that states cannot prohibit paid signature gathering, saying that initiative petitions are protected political speech.
1992	Mississippi adopts statewide initiative for the second time.
1996	Rhode Island voters approve a non-binding advisory question put on the ballot by the legislature asking if they would like to have a statewide initiative and popular referendum process — but the legislature ignores them.

Year	Event
1998	The Initiative & Referendum Institute is formed to study and defend the I&R process on the 100 year anniversary of the adoption of statewide initiative and popular referendum process in the United States.
1999	The Minnesota House of Representatives approves a constitutional amendment that would establish the initiative and popular referendum process; the Senate voted against it. The U.S. Supreme Court declares in *Buckley v. American Constitutional Law Foundation* that, among other things, states cannot require that petition circulators be registered voters.
2000	The Initiative & Referendum Institute files suit against the U.S. Postal Service's prohibition on collecting signatures on postal property. The voters of Oregon reject the state legislatures attempt to increase the number of signatures for initiatives.
2001	The Oklahoma legislature passes legislation requiring that animal protection initiatives must gather more signatures than any other type of initiatives. The Montana legislature passed legislation that would increase the distribution requirement for initiative petitions.
2002	The Federal District Court for Idaho invalidates Idaho's draconian distribution requirement for initiative petitions. The Minnesota House of Representatives pass an I&R amendment. The New York Senate passes an I&R amendment.

Section B: Statements Regarding the Initiative and Referendum Process

Since the founding of our nation, the issue of citizen participation in the lawmaking process has been hotly debated. Following is a variety of statements from prominent individuals regarding their views on citizen lawmaking and the initiative and referendum process.

"We are cleaning house and in order to clean house the one thing we need is a good broom. Initiative and referendum are good brooms?"
President Woodrow Wilson[1]

"I believe in the Initiative and Referendum, which should be used not to destroy representative government, but to correct it whenever it becomes misrepresentative."
President Teddy Roosevelt[2]

"I know of no safe repository of the ultimate power of society but the people…"
Thomas Jefferson[3]

"As the people are the only legitimate fountain of power, and it is from them that the constitutional charter, under which the several branches of government hold their power, is derived, it seems strictly consonant to the republican theory to recur to the same original authority … whenever it may be necessary to enlarge, diminish, or new-model the powers of government."
James Madison[4]

"I most strongly urge, that the first step in our design to preserve and perpetuate popular government shall be the adoption of the Initiative, Referendum, and Recall."
Hiram Johnson, Governor of the State of California[5]

"Twenty years ago, citizens of California were being taxed out of their homes by an out-of-control property tax system. While elected officials did little but talk about the problem, the voters acted. Using the initiative process they passed Proposition 13, a citizen's law which cut and capped the property tax."
Joel Fox, Past President of the Howard Jarvis Taxpayers Association[6]

"Initiative and Referendum is the citizen activist's 'ace in the hole.'"
Ralph Nader[7]

"One big difference between initiatives and elected representatives is that initiatives do not change their minds once you vote them in."
Grover Norquist, President of Americans for Tax Reform[8]

---

1. Quoted in Equity Magazine, January 13, page 18
2. "Characted of Democracy" speech to the 1912 Ohio constitutional convention.
3. In a letter to James Madison, December 20, 1787. Reprinted in Richard Hofstadter, ed., Great Issues in American History (New York: Vintage Books, 1958), p. 115
4. Federalist 49.
5. January 4, 1911 Inaugural speech as Governor.
6. In a letter to M. Dane Waters, President of the Initiative & Referendum Institute, 1998.
7. Endorsement from back cover of David Schmidt's book Citizen Lawmakers (Temple University Press).
8. In a letter to M. Dane Waters, President of the Inititative & Referendum Institute, 1998.

"At the very heart of the democratic process is our Constitutionally given right to change, through representation or by Constitutional amendment, the laws which govern us. In states across the country, the initiative and referendum process has become a necessary key to unlocking this democratic process in such a way that true democratic decision-making occurs."
Hal Daub, Mayor of Omaha, Nebraska[9]

"The initiative and referendum process is an important means to bypass legislatures who refuse to vote on crucial issues. Initiative and Referendum reminds us the citizens of our republic are the rulers and elected officials are the servants."
Kirk Fordice, Governor of the State of Mississippi[10]

"Having this electoral ability [the initiative and referendum process] is a critical 'safety valve' for effective citizenship."
Edwin Meese, III, former U.S. Attorney General under Ronald Reagan[11]

"I was born in North Dakota. We had I&R. I thought everyone did. I think everyone should? It is very difficult to get good new ideas to be considered by Legislative bodies. New ideas have to be taken to the people. That's why we need the initiative process."
Dick Armey, Majority Leader, U.S. House of Representatives

"In an era when politicians have rigged the system to guarantee 95 percent reelection rates and are increasingly disdainful of the will of the people, the need for initiative and referendum has never been greater. I&R strikes fear in the hearts of bureaucrats and politicians alike, because it implies self-government, hence reducing their importance."
Ed Crane, President of the Cato Institute[12]

"The PIRGs have been a leading practitioner of the citizens initiative process to pass environmental, consumer protection, and good government measures. We will continue to use the process and will work to promote and defend the process itself."
Gene Karpinski, Executive Director of U.S.PIRG[13]

"America's political systems have served us well, but are hopelessly archaic for dealing with the complex issues of the future. Because the establishment is incapable of implementing (or even perceiving) the needed reforms, I&R is the people's tool for change."
Dennis Polhill, Chairman of the Initiative & Referendum Institute[14]

"Without initiatives and referendums, elites would barely bother at all to take note of public opinion on issues they disdained—from supermajority requirements to raise taxes to term limits. They serve as a reminder that the experts' sometimes have to pay attention to good old common sense."
John Fund of *The Wall Street Journal*[15]

"The citizen initiative process is today the political life-blood of the people. Without initiative and referendum the politicians can ignore the people and monopolize power. Some may prefer all decision-making to take place in the backrooms of the Capitol, but I say let we the people vote on the issues that impact our lives. That's what freedom is all about."
Paul Jacob, Senior Fellow of U.S. Term Limits[16]

"For 15 I taught my classes that the Initiative and Referendum wouldn't work. I can prove it now—but the trouble is they do!"
President Woodrow Wilson[17]

---

9. Ibid., 1999.
10. Ibid.
11. Ibid.
12. Ibid., 2000.
13. Ibid.
14. Ibid., 1998.
15. Ibid.
16. Ibid.
17. Quoted in Equity Magazine, January 1913, page 18.

"…the will of the majority should always prevail."
Thomas Jefferson[18]

"Men by their makeup are naturally divided into two camps: those who fear and distrust the people and wish to draw all powers from them into the hands of higher classes; and those who identify themselves with the people, have confidence in them, cherish and consider them the safest and most honest, if always the wisest repository of the public interest. These two camps exist in every country, and wherever men are free to think, speak, and write, they will identify themselves."
Thomas Jefferson

"The world is spattered with unrest: rebel forces, civil disobedience, war, civil war, tyranny, and genocide. Any place average citizens have no voice or are losing ground in the fight to control their own lives is one place too many. If we believe in liberty, if we believe in the dignity of the human spirit, if we believe in justice for all, then Citizen Lawmaking is as essential to the future as it was to the past. This process is terribly important to the well being of this country. It must accompany us into the new century. By reviewing and honing the process, and most importantly by understanding and using these tools of democracy, we can preserve and even expand every citizen's right to have a voice in the government."
William J. Janklow, Governor of the State of South Dakota[19]

"The right of citizens to propose changes in government must be protected. Our country was founded with the revolutionary idea that people could govern themselves. As governments grow larger and career politicians flourish, the preservation of the Founding Father's legacy of self-government must be guarded and enhanced. I believe many of the problems we face as a nation could be resolved with more direct input from America citizens."
Kirk Fordice, Governor of the State of Mississippi[20]

"There is nothing more sacred to a free people than the right to govern themselves and take matters into their own hands when their elected officials have failed them. When the very government which the people have created to secure their liberty and domestic tranquility imposes restraints on their freedom, the people have a duty to try to break the shackles themselves. I, along with many of you assembled here this weekend, have responded to that high calling and have utilized the initiative or referendum processes when representative government becomes despotic either by negligence or design? In defense of liberty and in opposition to tyranny, I pray that we continue to empower the American people to mold and shape their own future and the long-term prosperity and pursuit of happiness for generations to come."
Ward Connerly, Chairman of the American Civil Rights Coalition[21]

"Those states that have the initiative and referendum process have tended to have less scandals and more honest state government than those states without that process."
Paul Weyrich, President of the Free Congress Foundation[22]

"The initiative and referendum process is a wonderful tool for citizens. It embodies a fundamental right of self-government that is at the very core of democracy. Every community, state and the federal government should provide for some form of direct democracy."
Doug Phelps, Chairman of U.S.PIRG[23]

"I&R is a critical tool for taxpayers in the fight against unaccountable government and it has been the single most important factor behind the rise of constitutional limits on state and local taxes. I&R enables citizens to make a real difference in how they are governed and thus can reverse the twin problems of rising cynicism and declining participation."
John Berthoud, President of the National Taxpayers Union[24]

---

18. In a letter to James Madison, December 20, 1787. Reprinted in Richard Hofstadter, ed., Great Issues in American History (New York: Vintage Books, 1958), p. 115.
19. Ibid.
20. Ibid.
21. Ibid.
22. Ibid.
23. Ibid
24. Ibid.

"The further the departure from direct and constant control by the citizens, the less has the government the ingredient of republicanism."
Thomas Jefferson[25]

"George Bush and I Congratulate you on your efforts to attain, for the people of New Jersey, the right to initiative and referendum. We urge you to keep up your fight and we endorse your efforts."
President Ronald Reagan[26]

"This initiative and referendum proposal is a cornerstone of our effort to ensure that the voices of all the people of New York are heard. This fundamental reform will empower all New Yorkers by enabling them to become an integral part of the lawmaking process and giving them the power to propose and approve new laws. By reforming the democratic process, we renew our allegiance to the sacred principle that all power ultimately rests in the hands of the people."
George Pataki, Governor of the State of New York[27]

"[W] have the initiative and referendum in Nebraska; do not disturb them. If defects are discovered, correct them and perfect the machinery … make it possible for the people to have what they want … we are the world's teacher in democracy; … the world looks to us for an example. We cannot ask others to trust the people unless we ourselves are willing to trust them."
William Jennings Bryan[28]

---

25. In a letter to James Taylor, 1816.
26. In a telegram to Sam Perelli of the United Taxpayers of New Jersey, October 23, 1980.
27. In a March 12, 2002 press release announcing his support for an initiative and referendum constitutional amendment.
28. In his address to the Nebraska Constitutional Conventional in 1920.

Section C: Model I&R Legislation

Section 1: The legislative power of the people of this State shall be vested in a General Assembly, which shall consist of the Senate and House of Representatives, but the people reserve to themselves the power to propose legislative measures, laws and amendments to the Constitution, and to enact or reject the same at the polls independent of the General Assembly; and also reserve the power, at their own option, to approve or reject at the polls any entire act or any item passed by the General Assembly.

Section 2: The first power reserved by the people is the initiative. Eight percent of the citizens who cast a vote for Governor in the last statewide election may propose a constitutional amendment by initiative petition and five percent of the citizens who cast a vote for Governor in the last statewide election may propose any law. Every such petition shall include the full text of the measure so proposed. Initiative petitions for statewide measures shall be filed with the Secretary of State not less than four months before the election at which they are to be voted upon.

Section 3: The second power reserved by the people is the popular referendum. Five percent of the citizens who cast a vote for Governor in the last statewide election may, by petition, place on the ballot any general act, bill or measures passed by the General Assembly. Such petition shall be filed with the Secretary of State not later than 120 days after the final adjournment of the session at which such act was passed. Any act, bill or measure referred to the people by popular referendum petition shall not be effective until the popular referendum is voted on by the people.

Section 4: No initiative approved by a vote of the people shall be amended or repealed by the General Assembly. The veto power of the Governor shall not extend to initiatives or popular referendum voted on by the people.

Section 5: All initiatives and popular referendum shall be submitted only at regular statewide elections.

Section 6: Any initiative or popular referendum submitted to the people as herein provided shall take effect and become law when approved by a majority of the votes cast upon such measure, and not otherwise, and shall not be required to receive a majority of the electors voting at such elections. Such measures shall be operative on and after the 30th day after the election at which it was approved, unless otherwise specified in the act.

Section 7: Nothing in these sections shall be construed to deprive any member of the General Assembly of the right to carry out his or her constitutional duties.

Section 8: If conflicting initiatives shall be approved by a majority of the votes severally cast for and against the same at the same election, the one receiving the highest number of affirmative votes shall become law.

Section 9: No limitation shall be placed upon the number of constitutional amendments, laws or other measures which may be proposed and submitted to the people by either initiative or popular referendum as provided in this act.

Section 10: Only the signatures of registered voters shall be counted upon petitions. All signatures upon petitions shall be deemed valid unless challenged. The sufficiency of all statewide petitions shall be decided in the first instance by the Secretary of State, subject to review by the Supreme Court of the State, which shall have original and exclusive jurisdiction over all such causes. If the sufficiency of any petition is challenged, such cause shall be a preference cause and shall be tried at once, but the failure of the courts to decide prior to the election as to the sufficiency of any such petition shall not prevent the question from being placed upon the ballot at the election named in such petition, nor militate against the validity of such measure, if it shall have been approved by a vote of the people.

Section 11: If the Secretary of State shall decide any petition to be insufficient, he shall without delay notify the sponsors of such petition, and permit at least thirty days from the date of such notification for the sponsors to submit additional signatures so as to make the petition sufficient.

Section 12: No law shall be passed to prohibit any person or persons from giving or receiving compensation for circulating petitions, nor to prohibit the circulation of petitions, nor in any manner interfering with the freedom of the people in procuring petitions; but laws shall be enacted prohibiting and penalizing perjury, forgery and all other felonies or other fraudulent practices in the securing of signatures or filing petitions.

Section 13: The style of all laws initiated by and submitted under the provisions of this act shall be, "Be It Enacted by the People of the State of (insert state name)". In submitting initiatives to the people, the Secretary of State shall be guided by the general election laws of the state until additional legislation is provided therefor.

Section 14: This act shall be self executing, and all its provisions shall be treated as mandatory, but laws may be enacted to facilitate its operation. No legislation shall be enacted to restrict, hamper or impair the exercise of the rights herein reserved to the people.

Section D: Initiative Usage by Decade

Decade	Number of Statewide Initiatives	Number Adopted	Number Defeated	Percentage Passed
1901–1910	56	25	31	45%
1911–1920	293	116	177	40%
1921–1930	172	40	132	23%
1931–1940	269	106	163	40%
1941–1950	145	58	87	41%
1951–1960	114	45	69	39%
1961–1970	87	37	50	41%
1971–1980	201	85	116	43%
1981–1990	271	115	156	44%
1991–2000	389	189	200	48%
Totals	1,997	816	1181	41%

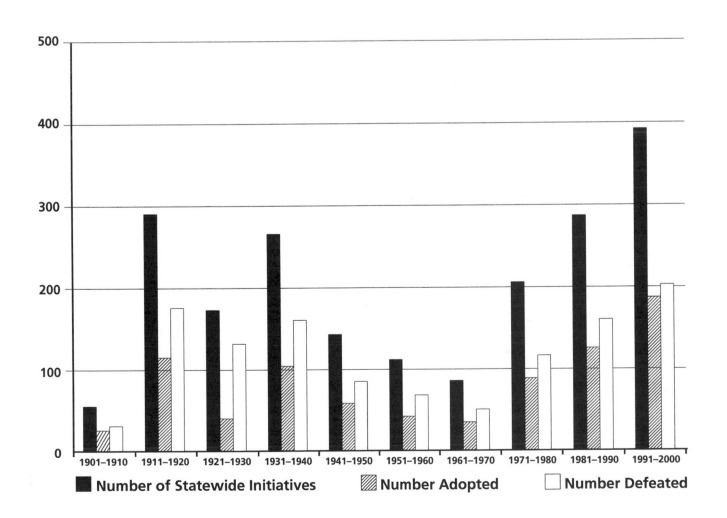

Section E: Listing of Statewide Initiatives Since 1904[1]

Year	State	Type	Measure Number	Subject Matter	Description	Pass/Fail
1904	Oregon	DS	2	Election Reform	Direct primary nominating convention law.	Passed
1904	Oregon	DS	3	Alcohol Regulation	Local option liquor law.	Passed
1906	Oregon	DS	10	Taxes	Gross earning tax on sleeping, refrigerator and oil car companies.	Passed
1906	Oregon	DS	11	Taxes	Gross earning tax on express, telephone and telegraph companies.	Passed
1906	Oregon	DA	2	Election Reform	Equal suffrage amendment.	Failed
1906	Oregon	DS	3	Alcohol Regulation	Amendment to local option liquor law.	Failed
1906	Oregon	DS	4	Administration of Government	Law to abolish tolls on the Mt. Hood and Barlow road and providing for its ownership by the state.	Failed
1906	Oregon	DA	5	Election Reform	Requiring referendum on any act calling a constitutional convention.	Passed
1906	Oregon	DA	6	Administration of Government	Giving cities sole powers to amend their charters.	Passed
1906	Oregon	DA	7	Business Regulation	Authorizing state printers compensation to be regulated by law at any time.	Passed
1906	Oregon	DA	8	Initiative and Referendum	Initiative and referendum to apply to all local, special and municipal laws.	Passed
1906	Oregon	DS	9	Utility Regulation	Prohibition of free passes on railroads.	Passed
1908	Oklahoma	DS	5	Administration of Government	The authorization of the sale of school and other public lands at auction giving the lessee the right of acceptance of the land at the highest bid, limiting the sales to 160 acres of land to the individual.	Failed
1908	Oregon	DA	11	Alcohol Regulation	Giving cities control of liquor selling, poolrooms, theaters, etc, subject to local option law.	Failed
1908	Oregon	DA	12	Taxes	Modified form of single tax amendment.	Failed
1908	Oregon	DA	13	Election Reform	Recall power on public officials.	Passed
1908	Oregon	DS	14	Election Reform	Instructing legislature to vote for people's choice for U.S. Senator.	Passed
1908	Oregon	DS	16	Campaign Finance Reform	Corrupt practices act governing elections.	Passed
1908	Oregon	DS	17	Animal Rights	Fishery law proposed by gillnet operators.	Passed
1908	Oregon	DA	18	Legal	Requiring indictment to be by grand jury.	Passed
1908	Oregon	DS	19	Administration of Government	Creating Hood River County.	Passed
1908	Oregon	DA	9	Election Reform	Equal suffrage.	Failed
1908	South Dakota	IDS	N/A	Alcohol Regulation	An act for licensing, restricting and regulating of the business of manufacture and sale of intoxicating liquors.	Failed
1910	Missouri	DA	N/A	Alcohol Regulation	To provide for prohibition of the manufacture an sale of intoxicating liquors.	Failed
1910	Missouri	DA	N/A	Education	To provide for the support and maintenance of the state University by direct state levy.	Failed
1910	Oklahoma	DS	15	Administration of Government	A proposition to permanently locate State Capitol.	Passed
1910	Oklahoma	DA	16	Business Regulation	Regulation of railroad, transportation or transmission companies.	Failed
1910	Oklahoma	DA	17	Election Reform	No person shall be registered as an elector in this State, be allowed to vote in any election held herein, unless he be able to read and write any section of the Constitution of the State.	Passed

---

1. This list would not have been possible without the help of the University of South Dakota and specifically Rich Braunstein and Mark Cullen.

Year	State	Type	Measure Number	Subject Matter	Description	Pass/Fail
1910	Oklahoma	DA	22	Alcohol Regulation	Provide for the licensed sale of intoxicating liquors in incorporated cities, towns, and villages after an election to determine whether said municipality shall license the sale of liquors to be consumed.	Failed
1910	Oklahoma	DS	6	Administration of Government	The selection by a majority vote of New Jerusalem District compound of not less than six sections of land compactly located within 50 miles of the center of the State.	Failed
1910	Oklahoma	DA	8	Election Reform	To authorize women to vote under the same circumstances and conditions as men may now do under the laws of this State.	Failed
1910	Oregon	DA	1	Election Reform	Permitting female taxpayers to vote.	Failed
1910	Oregon	DS	10	Education	To establish a state normal school at Monmouth.	Passed
1910	Oregon	DS	11	Administration of Government	Creating Otis County from parts of Harney, Malheur and Grant.	Failed
1910	Oregon	DS	12	Administration of Government	Annexing part of Clackamas County to Multnomah.	Failed
1910	Oregon	DS	13	Administration of Government	Creating Williams County from parts of Lane and Douglas.	Failed
1910	Oregon	DA	14	Civil Rights	Permitting people of each County to regulate taxation for County purposes and abolishing poll taxes.	Passed
1910	Oregon	DA	15	Alcohol Regulation	Giving cities and towns exclusive power to regulate liquor traffic with in their limits.	Passed
1910	Oregon	DS	16	Labor	For protection of laborers in hazardous employment, fixing employers' liability, etc.	Passed
1910	Oregon	DS	17	Administration of Government	Creating Orchard County from part of Umatilla.	Failed
1910	Oregon	DS	18	Administration of Government	Creating Clark County from part of Grant.	Failed
1910	Oregon	DS	19	Education	To establish state normal school at Weston.	Failed
1910	Oregon	DS	20	Administration of Government	To annex part of Washington County to Multnomah County.	Failed
1910	Oregon	DS	21	Education	To establish a state normal school at Ashland.	Failed
1910	Oregon	DA	22	Alcohol Regulation	Prohibiting liquor traffic.	Failed
1910	Oregon	DS	23	Alcohol Regulation	Prohibiting the sale of liquors and regulating shipments of same, and providing for search for liquor.	Failed
1910	Oregon	DS	24	Business Regulation	Creating board to draft employers' liability law for submission to legislature.	Failed
1910	Oregon	DS	25	Animal Rights	Prohibiting taking of fish in Rogue River except with hook and line.	Passed
1910	Oregon	DS	26	Administration of Government	Creating Deschutes County out of part of Crook.	Failed
1910	Oregon	DS	27	Administration of Government	Bill for general law under which new counties may be created or boundaries changed.	Failed
1910	Oregon	DA	28	Administration of Government	Permitting counties to vote bonds for permanent road improvement.	Passed
1910	Oregon	DS	29	Election Reform	Permitting voters in direct primaries to express choice for president and vice president, to select delegates to national convention and nominate candidates for presidential electors.	Passed
1910	Oregon	DS	30	Administration of Government	Creating board of people's inspectors of government, providing for reports of board in Official State Gazette to be mailed to all registered voters bi-monthly.	Failed
1910	Oregon	DA	31	Administration of Government	Extending initiative and referendum, making term of members of legislature 6 years, increasing salaries, requiring proportional representation in legislature.	Failed

Year	State	Type	Measure Number	Subject Matter	Description	Pass/Fail
1910	Oregon	DA	32	Judicial Reform	Permitting 3/4 verdict in civil cases.	Passed
1910	Oregon	DS	9	Administration of Government	Creating Nesmith County from parts of Lane and Douglas.	Failed
1911	Maine	IDS	N/A	Election Reform	Nomination of state and County officers by primaries (direct primary law).	Passed
1912	Arizona	DA	N/A	Election Reform	To permit women's suffrage.	Passed
1912	Arkansas	DS	N/A	Election Reform	Bipartisan election boards.	Failed
1912	Arkansas	DS	N/A	Alcohol Regulation	Providing for statewide prohibition.	Failed
1912	Arkansas	DS	N/A	Education	Free textbooks.	Failed
1912	Arkansas	DA	N/A	Administration of Government	Cities and towns can issue bonds.	Passed
1912	Arkansas	DA	N/A	Election Reform	Recall of elective officers.	Passed
1912	Arkansas	DA	N/A	Administration of Government	Mileage and per diem, legislature sixty-day session.	Passed
1912	California	DA	6	Administration of Government	Relating to the formation of consolidated city and County government, prescribing methods thereof.	Failed
1912	California	DS	7	Gaming	An act to prohibit bookmaking and pool-selling, and to provide for the appointment of a state racing commission to grant licenses for horse racing.	Failed
1912	California	DA	8	Taxes	Relating to taxation by counties, cities and counties, cities, towns, districts; prescribing methods and procedures thereof.	Failed
1912	Colorado	DA	1	Alcohol Regulation	Providing for statewide prohibition.	Failed
1912	Colorado	DS	10	Election Reform	Amending election laws.	Failed
1912	Colorado	DA	11	Initiative and Referendum	Providing for the holding of special elections for voting on proposed constitutional amendments and initiated and referred laws.	Failed
1912	Colorado	DA	12	Legal	Defining contempt of court and providing for trial by jury for contempt in certain cases.	Failed
1912	Colorado	DA	13	Utility Regulation	Creating a public utilities court with exclusive power to fix and enforce reasonable rates, and for appeal direct to the supreme court from its decision.	Failed
1912	Colorado	DS	14	Election Reform	Amending election laws, and providing for a "headless ballot".	Passed
1912	Colorado	DA	15	Education	Providing wider control of the schools by the people.	Failed
1912	Colorado	DA	16	Judicial Reform	Providing for juvenile courts in cities and counties of 100,000 population.	Passed
1912	Colorado	DS	17	Welfare	Mothers' compensation act and aid to dependent and neglected children.	Passed
1912	Colorado	DS	18	Administration of Government	Relating to civil service and amending said law.	Passed
1912	Colorado	DS	19	Labor	Eight-hour law for work in underground mines, smelters, mills and coke ovens.	Passed
1912	Colorado	DS	2	Alcohol Regulation	Enforcement of prohibition laws by search and seizure.	Failed
1912	Colorado	DS	20	Administration of Government	Giving state highway commission control of certain funds.	Failed
1912	Colorado	DS	3	Labor	Women's eight-hour employment law.	Passed
1912	Colorado	DA	31	Bonds	Authorizing a bonded indebtedness for public highways.	Failed
1912	Colorado	DS	32	Administration of Government	Construction of tunnel through James Peak.	Failed
1912	Colorado	DS	4	Administration of Government	Providing for the regulation of public service corporations.	Failed
1912	Colorado	DS	5	Administration of Government	Establishing a state fair.	Failed

Year	State	Type	Measure Number	Subject Matter	Description	Pass/Fail
1912	Colorado	DA	6	Alien Rights	Providing special funds for the state immigration bureau.	Failed
1912	Colorado	DS	7	Initiative and Referendum	Reducing costs of publishing constitutional amendments, initiated and referred laws, and publishing arguments for and against.	Failed
1912	Colorado	DA	8	Administration of Government	Granting home rule to cities and towns.	Passed
1912	Colorado	DA	9	Election Reform	Providing recall from office.	Passed
1912	Missouri	DA	N/A	Taxes	To provide for raising all revenue by taxes on land, inheritance and franchises for public service utilities; exempting from taxation all personal property and improvements on land.	Failed
1912	Missouri	DA	N/A	Education	To provide for levying and collecting, on each hundred dollars assessed valuation, a state tax of ten cents for the support of the public elementary and high schools.	Failed
1912	Missouri	DA	N/A	Administration of Government	To provide for abolishing the present state Board of Equalization, and providing for appointment by the Governor, in lieu of such board, of a state tax commission.	Failed
1912	Montana	DS	I 302-303	Election Reform	Party nominations by direct vote.	Passed
1912	Montana	DS	I 304-305	Campaign Finance Reform	Limiting campaign expenses of public candidates.	Passed
1912	Montana	DS	I 306-307	Election Reform	Popular referendum for election of Senators.	Passed
1912	Montana	DS	I 308-309	Election Reform	Direct presidential preference primary.	Passed
1912	Oklahoma	DA	38	Administration of Government	Qualifications and duties of members of the Board of Agriculture and the manner of selecting same.	Passed
1912	Oklahoma	DA	40	Administration of Government	To move the State Capitol to a location at Guthrie.	Failed
1912	Oklahoma	DS	41	Election Reform	That the United State Senators should be selected by direct vote of the people.	Passed
1912	Oregon	DA	1	Election Reform	To permit women's suffrage.	Passed
1912	Oregon	DS	10	Taxes	Mileage tax for university and agricultural college.	Failed
1912	Oregon	DA	11	Initiative and Referendum	Majority rule on initiated laws.	Failed
1912	Oregon	DS	12	Administration of Government	County bond and real construction act — Grange bill.	Failed
1912	Oregon	DS	14	Administration of Government	Changing date state printer bill becomes effective.	Failed
1912	Oregon	DS	15	Administration of Government	Creating office of hotel inspector.	Failed
1912	Oregon	DS	16	Labor	Eight-hour day on public works.	Passed
1912	Oregon	DS	17	Environmental Reform	Blue sky law.	Failed
1912	Oregon	DS	18	Labor	Prohibiting private employment of convicts.	Passed
1912	Oregon	DS	19	Labor	Relating to employment of County and city prisoners.	Passed
1912	Oregon	DS	20	Administration of Government	State road bond act.	Failed
1912	Oregon	DA	21	Administration of Government	Limiting state road indebtedness.	Passed
1912	Oregon	DS	22	Administration of Government	County bonding act.	Failed
1912	Oregon	DA	23	Administration of Government	Limiting County road indebtedness.	Passed
1912	Oregon	DS	24	Administration of Government	Providing method for consolidating cities and creating new counties.	Failed
1912	Oregon	DA	25	Taxes	Income tax amendment.	Failed
1912	Oregon	DS	26	Taxes	Tax exemption on household effects.	Passed
1912	Oregon	DS	27	Taxes	Tax exemption on moneys and credits.	Failed
1912	Oregon	DS	28	Taxes	Revising inheritance tax laws.	Failed
1912	Oregon	DS	29	Administration of Government	Freight rates act.	Passed

Year	State	Type	Measure Number	Subject Matter	Description	Pass/Fail
1912	Oregon	DA	30	Administration of Government	County road bonding act.	Failed
1912	Oregon	DA	31	Administration of Government	Abolishing senate and establish a unicameral.	Failed
1912	Oregon	DA	32	Taxes	Statewide single tax with graduated tax provision.	Failed
1912	Oregon	DS	33	Death Penalty	Abolishing capital punishment.	Failed
1912	Oregon	DS	34	Labor	Prohibiting boycotting.	Failed
1912	Oregon	DS	35	Civil Rights	Giving mayor authority to control street speaking. Prohibits use of public streets, parks and grounds in cities over 5,000 without a permit.	Failed
1912	Oregon	DS	9	Administration of Government	Creating Cascade County.	Failed
1912	South Dakota	IDS	N/A	Election Reform	Richards primary election law.	Passed
1913	Ohio	DA	Issue No. 1	Administration of Government	Reduce the size of the legislature.	Failed
1914	Arizona	DA	N/A	Initiative and Referendum	To provide that vote power of the Governor and the power of the legislature to repeal or amend, shall not extend to Initiative or Referendum measures approved by a majority of qualified voters.	Passed
1914	Arizona	DA	N/A	Administration of Government	State reclamation services.	Failed
1914	Arizona	DS	N/A	Taxes	Taxes, delinquent.	Failed
1914	Arizona	DS	N/A	Welfare	Relative to old age pensions.	Passed
1914	Arizona	DA	N/A	Bonds	Highway bonds.	Failed
1914	Arizona	DS	N/A	Business Regulation	Industrial pursuits.	Passed
1914	Arizona	DS	N/A	Death Penalty	Abolishing death penalty.	Failed
1914	Arizona	DS	N/A	Civil Rights	Blacklisting prohibited.	Passed
1914	Arizona	DS	N/A	Administration of Government	Create Miami County.	Failed
1914	Arizona	DS	N/A	Administration of Government	Expositions appropriations.	Failed
1914	Arizona	DS	N/A	Alien Rights	Non-citizens, employment of.	Passed
1914	Arizona	DS	N/A	Business Regulation	Assessment, by owner.	Failed
1914	Arizona	DS	N/A	Environmental Reform	Placing of electric poles	Passed
1914	Arizona	DA	N/A	Alcohol Regulation	Providing for statewide prohibition.	Passed
1914	Arizona	DA	N/A	Alcohol Regulation	Prohibition elections.	Failed
1914	Arkansas	DA	N/A	Administration of Government	Cities and towns issue bonds for improvements.	Passed
1914	Arkansas	DS	N/A	Labor	Prohibiting child labor.	Passed
1914	California	DA	10	Civil Rights	Provides that no poll or head tax shall be levied.	Passed
1914	California	DS	11	Bonds	To provide for the issuance and sale of state bonds in the sum of $1.8m to create a fund for the completion and construction of buildings at the University of California at Berkeley.	Passed
1914	California	DA	13	Election Reform	Provides that no elector may vote on question of incurring bonded indebtedness of state or political subdivision thereof, unless he is owner of property taxable for payment of such indebtedness.	Failed
1914	California	DS	14	Election Reform	To provide for issuance of certificate of identification and ballot to voters who will be absent from home precincts on election day.	Failed
1914	California	DA	15	Banking Reform	Present section unchanged except, authorizes banks in which public moneys are deposited to furnish, as security, bonds of districts within municipalities, or of a corporation qualified to act as sole surety in value.	Failed
1914	California	DA	19	Administration of Government	Consolidation of City and County and Limited Annexation of Contiguous Territory.	Passed
1914	California	DA	2	Alcohol Regulation	To prohibit the manufacture, sale, gift, or transportation of intoxicating liquors.	Failed

Year	State	Type	Measure Number	Subject Matter	Description	Pass/Fail
1914	California	DS	20	Gaming	Prohibits the engaging in or furthering in any way prize fights or remunerative boxing exhibitions, training therefore.	Passed
1914	California	DA	21	Administration of Government	City and County Consolidation and Annexation with Consent of Annexed Territory.	Failed
1914	California	DS	22	Administration of Government	To provide procedures for certification of land titles and record keeping thereof.	Passed
1914	California	DS	3	Labor	To establish an eight-hour work day and a forty-eight hour week.	Failed
1914	California	DS	38	Bonds	To provide for the issuance and sale of state bonds in the sum of $1.25m to create a fund for the acquisition of a site in the city of Los Angeles, for the construction thereon of a state building.	Failed
1914	California	DA	39	Alcohol Regulation	Suspension of Prohibition Amendment. To suspend the proposed prohibition amendment (if passed) until Feb. 15, 1915 relating to use and transportation of intoxicating liquors.	Passed
1914	California	DS	45	Labor	To prohibit, except in cases of emergency, the requiring or employing of any person to work more than 6 days or 48 hours a week.	Failed
1914	California	DS	46	Health/Medical	To create a state board of drugless physicians to regulate the examination and certification of persons to treat all physical or mental ailments of human beings without drugs or medicine.	Failed
1914	California	DA	47	Alcohol Regulation	Prohibits for 8 years after this election state election on question of prohibiting or permitting transportation of intoxicating liquors.	Failed
1914	California	DS	9	Business Regulation	To provide for the regulation of investment companies by an auditor of investments appointed by the Governor.	Failed
1914	Colorado	DA	N/A	Initiative and Referendum	Providing that initiated measures rejected by people cannot again be initiated for six years, and if two conflicting measures be adopted at same election, one receiving largest affirmative vote shall prevail.	Failed
1914	Colorado	DS	N/A	Legal	Permitting probation in criminal cases for minors and first offenders.	Failed
1914	Colorado	DA	N/A	Alcohol Regulation	Providing for statewide prohibition.	Passed
1914	Colorado	DS	N/A	Administration of Government	Providing for codification of laws relating to women and children.	Failed
1914	Colorado	DA	N/A	Judicial Reform	Providing for a 3/4 jury verdict in civil cases and permitting women to serve on juries if they desire.	Failed
1914	Colorado	DS	N/A	Taxes	Increasing state road fund by half mill levy for highway construction.	Passed
1914	Colorado	DA	N/A	Initiative and Referendum	Giving people right to petition governor to call special elections for submitting measures under the initiative and referendum.	Failed
1914	Colorado	DA	N/A	Utility Regulation	Designating newspapers as public utilities.	Failed
1914	Michigan	DA	N/A	Business Regulation	Relative to the incorporation, regulation and supervision of beneficiary societies.	Failed
1914	Missouri	DA	N/A	Taxes	To authorize levy and collection of special taxes for road purposes, to issue bonds in any sum for said purposes, upon petition of taxpaying voters.	Failed
1914	Missouri	DA	N/A	Election Reform	To provide that females shall have the same right to vote at all elections within the state as males.	Failed

Year	State	Type	Measure Number	Subject Matter	Description	Pass/Fail
1914	Missouri	DA	N/A	Bonds	To authorize the state of Missouri to issue fifty million dollars in interest-bearing bonds and sell same and use the proceeds thereof for building and maintaining public highways of this state, and to authorize a tax levy sufficient to pay the fund.	Failed
1914	Montana	DS	I 7	Labor	Workmen's compensation.	Failed
1914	Montana	DS	I 8	Administration of Government	Farm Loan Bill — relating to investment of permanent state funds.	Passed
1914	Montana	DS	I 9	Education	Consolidation of state institutions of higher education.	Failed
1914	Nebraska	DS	N/A	Education	University removal.	Failed
1914	Nebraska	DA	N/A	Election Reform	Woman suffrage, authorizations.	Failed
1914	Ohio	DA	Issue No. 1	Alcohol Regulation	Home rule on subject of intoxicating liquors.	Passed
1914	Ohio	DA	Issue No. 2	Taxes	Limitation of tax rate and for classification of property for purpose of taxation.	Failed
1914	Ohio	DA	Issue No. 3	Election Reform	To extend suffrage to women.	Failed
1914	Ohio	DA	Issue No. 4	Alcohol Regulation	Prohibition of the sale and manufacture for sale, and importation for sale of intoxicating liquor as a beverage.	Failed
1914	Oklahoma	DS	68	Taxes	To re-enact the direct and redirect system of taxation contained in Chap. 240, Session Laws 1913	Passed
1914	Oklahoma	DA	71	Judicial Reform	Reducing the number of final appellate Courts in the State from two to one, styled "The Supreme Court", to comprise nine associate justices and one chief justice; fixing their terms.	Passed
1914	Oklahoma	DA	73	Alcohol Regulation	To make drunkenness and excessive use of intoxicating liquors cause for impeachment or removal from office.	Passed
1914	Oklahoma	DA	74	Taxes	Reduces the maximum levy of State taxes, assessed on ad valorem basis, from 3.5 mills (.003 1/2) to 2.5 mills (.002 1/2) and prohibiting the Legislature from making appropriations in excess thereof.	Passed
1914	Oklahoma	DA	75	Taxes	Levying and collecting a mine production tax, not exceeding two percent upon the gross value of such productions, upon natural gas, petroleum and other crude oils.	Passed
1914	Oklahoma	DA	77	Administration of Government	To amend the Constitution as to reduce the Legislature to one body of 80 members styled and create a unicameral.	Passed
1914	Oregon	DA	11	Labor	Universal constitutional eight-hour day amendment.	Failed
1914	Oregon	DS	12	Labor	Eight-hour day and room-ventilation law for female workers.	Failed
1914	Oregon	DS	13	Election Reform	Nonpartisan judiciary bill prohibiting party nominations for judicial officers.	Failed
1914	Oregon	DA	14	Taxes	$1,500 tax exemption amendment.	Failed
1914	Oregon	DA	15	Environmental Reform	Public docks and water frontage amendment.	Failed
1914	Oregon	DS	16	Administration of Government	Municipal wharves and docks bill.	Failed
1914	Oregon	DA	17	Alcohol Regulation	Providing for statewide prohibition.	Passed
1914	Oregon	DA	18	Death Penalty	Abolishing death penalty.	Passed
1914	Oregon	DA	19	Taxes	Specific personal graduated extra-tax amendment of Art. 10.	Failed
1914	Oregon	DS	20	Administration of Government	Consolidating corporation and insurance departments.	Failed
1914	Oregon	DS	21	Health/Medical	Dentistry bill.	Failed

Year	State	Type	Measure Number	Subject Matter	Description	Pass/Fail
1914	Oregon	DA	22	Administration of Government	County officers term amendment.	Failed
1914	Oregon	DS	23	Administration of Government	A tax code commission bill.	Failed
1914	Oregon	DS	24	Administration of Government	Abolishing desert land board and reorganizing certain state offices.	Failed
1914	Oregon	DA	25	Election Reform	Proportional representation amendment.	Failed
1914	Oregon	DA	26	Administration of Government	State senate constitutional amendment.	Failed
1914	Oregon	DA	27	Administration of Government	Department of industry and public works amendment.	Failed
1914	Oregon	DS	28	Election Reform	Primary delegate election bill.	Failed
1914	Oregon	DA	29	Taxes	Equal assessment and taxation $300 exemption.	Failed
1914	South Dakota	IDS	N/A	Election Reform	Coffey primary election law for making party nominations for members of Congress, State, County, and Judicial officers, delegates to National and State conventions.	Failed
1914	South Dakota	IDS	N/A	Alcohol Regulation	To provide for licensing, restricting, and regulating sale of liquor and for the sale of liquor at local option.	Failed
1914	Washington	DS	I-10	Legal	Convict Labor Road Measure.	Failed
1914	Washington	DS	I-13	Labor	Eight hour workday	Failed
1914	Washington	DS	I-3	Alcohol Regulation	Providing for statewide prohibition.	Passed
1914	Washington	DS	I-6	Daylight Savings Time	Blue Sky Law.	Failed
1914	Washington	DS	I-7	Administration of Government	Abolishing Bureau of Inspection.	Failed
1914	Washington	DS	I-8	Administration of Government	Abolish Employment Offices.	Passed
1914	Washington	DS	I-9	Legal	First Aid to Injured.	Failed
1915	Ohio	DA	Issue No. 1	Alcohol Regulation	Prohibition of the sale and manufacture for sale of intoxicating liquor as a beverage.	Failed
1915	Ohio	DA	Issue No. 2	Administration of Government	To fix the terms of all County officers at four years to provide for their election quadrennially, and applying the amendment to incumbents.	Failed
1915	Ohio	DA	Issue No. 3	Initiative and Referendum	To limit elections on twice defeated constitutional proposals and to prevent the abuse of the initiative and referendum.	Failed
1916	Arizona	DA	N/A	Alcohol Regulation	To amend the prohibition act.	Passed
1916	Arizona	DS	N/A	Death Penalty	Abolishing death penalty.	Passed
1916	Arizona	DS	N/A	Administration of Government	To establish a department of labor	Failed
1916	Arizona	DS	N/A	Administration of Government	To hire a state architect.	Failed
1916	Arizona	DS	N/A	Environmental Reform	Fish and game regulation.	Passed
1916	Arizona	DS	N/A	Administration of Government	Create laws associated with divorce.	Failed
1916	Arizona	DA	N/A	Apportionment/Redistricting	Legislative redistricting.	Failed
1916	Arizona	DA	N/A	Administration of Government	Local option.	Failed
1916	Arizona	DA	N/A	Labor	Workman's compensation.	Failed
1916	Arizona	DA	N/A	Administration of Government	Abolishment of the Senate and establish a unicameral.	Failed
1916	Arkansas	DA	N/A	Taxes	Twelve-mill district school tax.	Passed
1916	Arkansas	DA	N/A	Initiative and Referendum	Initiative and referendum more fully defined.	Failed
1916	Arkansas	DS	N/A	Election Reform	New primary laws.	Passed
1916	California	DA	1	Alcohol Regulation	Prohibits after Jan. 1, 1920, the manufacture, sale or possession of intoxicating liquors except for medicinal, sacramental, scientific and mechanical purposes.	Failed
1916	California	DA	2	Alcohol Regulation	Defines alcoholic liquor and prohibits its use; neither limits nor repeals state or local prohibition.	Failed

Year	State	Type	Measure Number	Subject Matter	Description	Pass/Fail
1916	California	DA	5	Taxes	To declare that all public revenues be raised by taxation of land values, exclusive of its improvements.	Failed
1916	California	DA	6	Administration of Government	Ineligibility of Office. Declares that no Senator or member of Assembly shall during the term for which he has been elected, hold or accept any office, trust, or employment of this state, except for other elected office.	Passed
1916	Colorado	DA	N/A	Alcohol Regulation	Declaring beer non-toxicating and providing for its manufacture and sale.	Failed
1916	Colorado	DS	N/A	Business Regulation	Regulating the running of stock at large.	Failed
1916	Colorado	DS	N/A	Taxes	Abolishment of the state tax commission.	Failed
1916	Colorado	DA	N/A	Administration of Government	Placing state civil service in the constitution.	Failed
1916	Colorado	DS	N/A	Welfare	Providing for the care and treatment of insane persons.	Passed
1916	Colorado	DS	N/A	Education	Providing for the investment of public school funds in certain securities.	Passed
1916	Michigan	DA	N/A	Business Regulation	Relative to the regulation of beneficiary societies.	Failed
1916	Montana	DS	I 11	Administration of Government	Establishing athletic commission.	Failed
1916	Nebraska	DA	N/A	Alcohol Regulation	Providing for statewide prohibition.	Passed
1916	Nebraska	DA	N/A	Administration of Government	Creation of Pure Food Department.	Failed
1916	Oklahoma	DA	78	Education	Abolishing all existing election boards and providing for State Election Board.	Passed
1916	Oklahoma	DA	80	Initiative and Referendum	To prevent Legislature from passing any law concerning registration of electors providing the initiative as the only method to enact such law and providing for registration in cities and towns.	Passed
1916	Oregon	DA	10	Taxes	Rural credits amendment.	Passed
1916	Oregon	DA	11	Taxes	Statewide tax and indebtedness limitation amendment.	Passed
1916	Oregon	DA	4	Taxes	Full rental value land tax and homemakers' loan fund amendment.	Failed
1916	Oregon	DA	5	Education	Establish Pendleton normal school and ratifying location for certain state institutions.	Failed
1916	Oregon	DA	6	Health/Medical	Anti-compulsory vaccination bill.	Failed
1916	Oregon	DA	7	Business Regulation	Bill repealing and abolishing the Sunday closing law.	Passed
1916	Oregon	DA	8	Alcohol Regulation	Permitting manufacture and regulating sale 4% malt liquors.	Failed
1916	Oregon	DA	9	Alcohol Regulation	Prohibition amendment forbidding importation of intoxicating liquors for beverage purposes.	Passed
1916	South Dakota	IDS	N/A	Administration of Government	Create State Banking Board.	Failed
1916	South Dakota	IDS	N/A	Banking Reform	Create Department of Banking and Finance.	Failed
1916	South Dakota	IDS	N/A	Election Reform	Richard primary election law — for regulation of political party transactions.	Failed
1916	Washington	IDS	I-18	Alcohol Regulation	Brewer's Hotel Bill.	Failed
1916	Washington	DS	I-24	Alcohol Regulation	Brewer's Bill.	Failed
1917	Ohio	DA	Issue No. 1	Alcohol Regulation	Prohibition of the sale and manufacture for sale of intoxicating liquors.	Failed
1918	Arizona	DA	N/A	Environmental Reform	To limit the sale of agricultural and grazing land.	Passed
1918	Arizona	DA	N/A	Environmental Reform	To authorize the legislature to provide proper laws for the sale of state lands and the lease of same, and for the protection of bona fide residents and lessee's of said lands.	Passed

Year	State	Type	Measure Number	Subject Matter	Description	Pass/Fail
1918	Arizona	DA	N/A	Apportionment/Redistricting	To give each country in the state equitable representation in the lower house of the legislature based on population; authorizing boards of supervisors to divide counties into legislative districts according to population and permitting each district.	Passed
1918	Arizona	DA	N/A	Labor	Workmen's compensation.	Failed
1918	Arizona	DS	N/A	Administration of Government	The leasing of state lands	Failed
1918	Arizona	DS	N/A	Death Penalty	Reinstating the death penalty.	Passed
1918	Arizona	DS	N/A	Health/Medical	Vaccination, minors.	Passed
1918	Arkansas	DA	N/A	Administration of Government	Allow for municipal improvement bonds.	Passed
1918	California	DS	1	Alcohol Regulation	To provide for the regulation of liquor use and sales, prohibit drinking saloons, limit the number of municipal licenses for sale of vinous or malt liquors for consumption.	Failed
1918	California	DS	18	Administration of Government	To create state board of authorization and require each County officer to file financial statements with governing body of County which shall submit same with budget to such state board before making tax levy.	Failed
1918	California	DA	19	Taxes	To require all public revenue to be raised by taxation of land values irrespective of improvements thereon.	Failed
1918	California	DS	21	Business Regulation	To regulate the practice of dentistry in the state.	Failed
1918	California	DS	22	Alcohol Regulation	To make the manufacture, importation or sale of intoxicating liquors a misdemeanor.	Failed
1918	California	DS	3	Business Regulation	To restrict and regulate rates of interest upon the loan or forbearance of money, goods, and certain other transactions.	Passed
1918	Colorado	DS	N/A	Alcohol Regulation	"Bone-dry" prohibition law.	Passed
1918	Colorado	DA	N/A	Administration of Government	Placing state civil service in the constitution.	Passed
1918	Colorado	DS	N/A	Welfare	Relief for blind adults.	Passed
1918	Montana	DS	I 12	Business Regulation	An act authorizing and regulating the practice of chiropractors.	Passed
1918	Nevada	IDS	N/A	Alcohol Regulation	Providing for statewide prohibition.	Passed
1918	North Dakota	IDA	N/A	Administration of Government	Forbidding the Legislature to grant a franchise or special interest as an emergency measure.	Passed
1918	North Dakota	IDA	N/A	Administration of Government engage in business activities.	Authorizing the state, counties, and cities to	Passed
1918	North Dakota	IDA	N/A	Taxes	Authorizing the Legislature to impose an acreage tax on land to insure crops against hail damage.	Passed
1918	North Dakota	IDA	N/A	Administration of Government	Authorizing the state to bond up to $10 million instead of $200,000 and providing for mortgages on state industries.	Passed
1918	North Dakota	IDA	N/A	Initiative and Referendum	Amending provision for initiative and referendum by changing required signatures to 10,000 for initiating a statutory measure; to 7,000 for referring legislation actions; and providing that initiated measures would go directly to a vote of the people.	Passed
1918	North Dakota	IDA	N/A	Initiative and Referendum	Providing for submission of constitutional amendments to people by simple majority vote of one legislative session, and providing for initiated constitutional amendments with 20,000 signatures.	Passed
1918	North Dakota	IDA	N/A	Taxes	Authorizing the Legislature to classify personal property for purposes of exemptions.	Passed

Year	State	Type	Measure Number	Subject Matter	Description	Pass/Fail
1918	Ohio	DA	Issue No. 1	Initiative and Referendum	Referendum provision, reserving to the people the power to approve or reject an action of the General Assembly ratifying any proposed amendment to the Constitution of the United States.	Passed
1918	Ohio	DA	Issue No. 2	Alcohol Regulation	Prohibition of the sale and manufacture for sale of intoxicating liquors as a beverage.	Passed
1918	Ohio	DA	Issue No. 3	Taxes	The General Assembly shall classify property for taxation purposes.	Passed
1918	Oregon	DS	5	Taxes	Delinquent tax notice bill.	Passed
1918	Oregon	DS	6	Administration of Government	Fixing compensation for publication of legal notice.	Passed
1918	South Dakota	IDS	N/A	Election Reform	Richards primary election law.	Passed
1919	Michigan	DA	N/A	Alcohol Regulation	Relative to the manufacture of cider, wines, beer, etc.	Failed
1919	Ohio	DA	Issue No. 1	Alcohol Regulation	Defining the phrase "Intoxicating Liquor".	Failed
1919	Ohio	DA	Issue No. 2	Alcohol Regulation	To repeal statewide prohibition.	Failed
1920	Arizona	DA	N/A	Education	Publication of teachers salaries	Failed
1920	Arizona	DS	N/A	Administration of Government	Establishment of Counties.	Failed
1920	Arizona	DS	N/A	Administration of Government	To establish the State Highway Department.	Failed
1920	Arizona	DS	N/A	Environmental Reform	Reclamation.	Failed
1920	Arizona	DS	N/A	Administration of Government	Civil service.	Failed
1920	Arizona	DS	N/A	Environmental Reform	Conservation, game and fish.	Failed
1920	Arkansas	DA	N/A	Initiative and Referendum	Initiative and referendum better defined.	Passed
1920	California	DS	1	Alien Rights	To permit acquisition and transfer of real property by aliens eligible for citizenship, and to permit other aliens to acquire and transfer real property only as prescribed by treaty.	Passed
1920	California	DA	12	Education	Levies ad valorem tax for state university of one and two-tenths mills to be paid to "State University Fund."	Failed
1920	California	DA	16	Education	Adds kindergartens to public school system; requires addition to state school fund, and creation of high school fund.	Passed
1920	California	DA	20	Taxes	Land Value Taxation. To require all public revenues to be raised by taxing land values exclusive of improvements.	Failed
1920	California	DA	3	Judicial Reform	To increase salaries of Justices of the Supreme Court from $8,000 to $10,000 per year and Justices of District Court from $7,000 to $9,000 per year.	Failed
1920	California	DA	4	Initiative and Referendum	To increase the number of signatures necessary to file an initiative petition which relates to assessment or collection of taxes.	Failed
1920	California	DS	5	Business Regulation	To regulate and license the practice of chiropractic.	Failed
1920	California	DA	6	Health/Medical	Declares that no form of vaccination, inoculation or other medication shall be made a condition for admission or attendance to any public school, college, or university.	Failed
1920	California	DS	7	Health/Medical	To prohibit vivisection, dissection or torture of any living person or living animal, including experimental physiological and pathological investigation.	Failed
1920	California	DA	9	Administration of Government	Creates state Highway Finance Board and authorizes the sale of bonds, and relieves counties from payments to state for highway construction.	Passed
1920	Colorado	DA	N/A	Education	Providing additional one mill levy for state educational institutions.	Passed

Year	State	Type	Measure Number	Subject Matter	Description	Pass/Fail
1920	Colorado	DA	N/A	Bonds	Providing for the construction of the Moffat, Monarch and San Juan tunnels, and bond issue therefore.	Failed
1920	Colorado	DS	N/A	Business Regulation	Relating to the practice of chiropractic, and providing for the regulation and licensing thereof.	Failed
1920	Colorado	DS	N/A	Administration of Government	Creating the County of Limon.	Failed
1920	Colorado	DS	N/A	Administration of Government	Creating the County of Flagler.	Failed
1920	Colorado	DS	N/A	Health/Medical	Appropriating $350,000 from the general fund for the establishment of the Psychopathic Hospital and Laboratory.	Passed
1920	Colorado	DS	N/A	Labor	Fixing hours of employment in city fire departments.	Passed
1920	Massachusetts	IDS	Question 1	Alcohol Regulation	Definition of cider, beer, et al. as non-intoxicating liquors.	Passed
1920	Michigan	DA	N/A	Education	Relative to compulsory attendance at the public schools of all residents of Michigan between the ages of five years and sixteen years.	Failed
1920	Missouri	DS	N/A	Administration of Government	To provide for new constitution.	Passed
1920	Montana	DS	I 18	Taxes	1 1/2 mills levy for maintenance of university.	Passed
1920	Montana	DS	I 19	Bonds	$5,000,000 bonds for state educational institutions buildings.	Passed
1920	Montana	DS	I 20	Bonds	$20,000,000 bond issue for reclamation of arid lands.	Failed
1920	North Dakota	DS	N/A	Education	Restoring certain powers regarding teacher certification to the Superintendent of Public Instruction.	Passed
1920	North Dakota	DS	N/A	Administration of Government	Creating a state Athletic Commission to regulate boxing and deduction of 10% of the boxing gate receipts for the state highway fund.	Failed
1920	North Dakota	DS	N/A	Health/Medical	Legalizing the sale of cigarettes but prohibiting sale to minors.	Failed
1920	North Dakota	DS	N/A	Business Regulation	Permitting baseball on Sunday.	Passed
1920	North Dakota	DS	N/A	Business Regulation	Permitting the operation of motion picture theaters on Sunday.	Failed
1920	North Dakota	DS	N/A	Civil Rights	Prohibiting the display of red and black flags or signs bearing anti-government inscriptions; prohibiting the carrying in parade or the display of any flag other than the national flag or the flag or a friendly nation.	Passed
1920	North Dakota	DS	N/A	Administration of Government	Requiring an examination of state industrial institutions twice yearly by a state Board of Auditors consisting of the Attorney General, state Auditor, and the Secretary of state.	Passed
1920	North Dakota	DS	N/A	Banking Reform	Requiring the deposit of only state funds in the Bank of North Dakota instead of the funds of all public bodies.	Passed
1920	North Dakota	DS	N/A	Administration of Government	Permitting legal publication in other than official newspapers.	Passed
1920	North Dakota	DS	N/A	Banking Reform	Prohibiting real estate loans by the Bank of North Dakota.	Passed
1920	Oklahoma	DA	109	Taxes	Providing for levying upon all property within the State not exempt from taxation an annual tax of not less than 16 mills and not more than 10 mills for maintenance	Failed
1920	Oklahoma	DA	99	Taxes	Levying upon the pro-party of the general public service corporations of the State, those operating in more than one County, an annual tax for maintaining common schools.	Failed

Year	State	Type	Measure Number	Subject Matter	Description	Pass/Fail
1920	Oregon	DA	10	Administration of Government	Divided legislative session.	Failed
1920	Oregon	DS	11	Administration of Government	State market commission.	Failed
1920	Oregon	DA	4	Taxes	Single tax.	Failed
1920	Oregon	DA	5	Administration of Government	Fixing term of certain County officers.	Passed
1920	Oregon	DA	7	Health/Medical	Anti-compulsory vaccinations.	Failed
1920	Oregon	DA	8	Banking Reform	Fixing legal rate of interest in Oregon.	Failed
1920	Oregon	DS	9	Environmental Reform	Roosevelt bird refuge.	Failed
1920	Oregon	DS	N/A	Administration of Government	Port of Portland dock commission consolidation.	Failed
1920	South Dakota	IDS	N/A	Election Reform	Primary election law.	Failed
1921	North Dakota	DS	N/A	Administration of Government	Establishing a rural credit system to take over the farm loans from the Bank of North Dakota.	Failed
1921	North Dakota	DS	N/A	Banking Reform	Abolishing the Bank of North Dakota and providing a liquidation procedure.	Failed
1921	North Dakota	DS	N/A	Banking Reform	Providing for public depositories to disqualify the Bank of North Dakota from receiving public funds.	Failed
1921	North Dakota	DS	N/A	Election Reform	Providing for the nonpartisan election of state and County officials.	Failed
1921	North Dakota	DS	N/A	Election Reform	Changing the form of ballot for national and partisan elections.	Failed
1921	North Dakota	DS	N/A	Business Regulation	Reorganizing the Industrial Commission by removing the state officials and providing for the appointment of a 3-man commission by the Governor with confirmation by the state Senate.	Failed
1922	Arizona	DA	N/A	Bonds	Hassayampa — Colorado Highway bonds.	Failed
1922	Arizona	DA	N/A	Education	Make changes to existing educational statutes.	Failed
1922	Arkansas	DA	N/A	Taxes	To increase school revenues.	Failed
1922	Arkansas	DA	N/A	Initiative and Referendum	Initiative and referendum more fully defined.	Failed
1922	California	DA	1	Veteran Affairs	Permits state aid with money or credit to U.S. Army or Navy veterans who served during war time, in acquiring or developing farms or homes or in land settlement projects.	Passed
1922	California	DA	10	Utility Regulation	To require all property owned by public utilities to be assessed and taxed in same manner and to same extent as like property held by private corporations and persons.	Failed
1922	California	DA	11	Utility Regulation	To make all publicly owned utilities regulated by the state Railroad Commission.	Failed
1922	California	DA	12	Administration of Government	Requires Governor to submit to legislature within first 30 days of each regular session, a budget containing itemized statement of all proposed expenditures and estimated revenues for next biennial period.	Passed
1922	California	DS	16	Business Regulation	To provide for the regulation and licensing for the practice of chiropractic.	Passed
1922	California	DA	19	Administration of Government	Water and Power. Creates board appointed by Governor and subject to recall to issue bonds, and develop and distribute water and electric energy.	Failed
1922	California	DS	20	Health/Medical	Osteopathic Act. To provide for the practice of osteopathic medication.	Passed
1922	California	DS	28	Health/Medical	To prohibit the vivisection or torture of human beings, animals, or other living creatures, for experimental or pathological investigations, or other purposes.	Failed

Year	State	Type	Measure Number	Subject Matter	Description	Pass/Fail
1922	California	DA	29	Taxes	Abolishes present system of taxation, and declares that private property rights attach only to products of labor and not to land.	Failed
1922	California	DA	30	Administration of Government	Gives Railroad Commission exclusive power to grant franchises for street, interurban and suburban railways, and motor vehicle transportation, and other purposes.	Failed
1922	Colorado	DA	N/A	Taxes	Giving legislature or people power to exempt certain intangibles from ad valorem taxation, and to impose an income tax in lieu thereof.	Failed
1922	Colorado	DA	N/A	Utility Regulation	Creating a public utilities commission, prescribing its powers and duties, and defining public utilities.	Failed
1922	Colorado	DS	N/A	Apportionment/Redistricting	Revising apportionment of members of legislature.	Failed
1922	Colorado	DA	N/A	Bonds	$1.5m bond issue for construction of public highways.	Passed
1922	Colorado	DS	N/A	Business Regulation	Concerning experimental operations on human beings and dumb animals.	Failed
1922	Missouri	DS	N/A	Apportionment/Redistricting	Apportionment of the state into Senatorial Districts.	Failed
1922	Missouri	DS	N/A	Labor	To repeal workman's compensation act.	Failed
1922	Montana	DS	I 26	Gaming	To create board, appointed by Governor, to regulate and license horse racing and pari-mutuel betting within race track enclosure.	Failed
1922	Nevada	IDS	N/A	Legal	Divorce law	Failed
1922	North Dakota	DS	N/A	Education	Repealing minimum training and salary standards for teachers.	Passed
1922	North Dakota	DS	N/A	Bonds	Raising the limits of bonded indebtedness from $10 million to $20 million to enable the farm loan department of the Bank of North Dakota to make more loans.	Passed
1922	North Dakota	DS	N/A	Administration of Government	Creating the office of state Supervisor of grades, weights and measures and authorizing the office to set standards of quality on grain and conditions for marketing grain.	Passed
1922	Ohio	DA	Issue No. 1	Taxes	To provide for 2.75 percent beverage tax.	Failed
1922	Ohio	DA	Issue No. 2	Administration of Government	To provide for debt limitation for counties, school districts, townships, municipal corporations, or other political subdivisions.	Failed
1922	Ohio	DA	Issue No. 3	Taxes	To provide a limitation on tax rates of 15 mills, but additional levies may be authorized by vote. State tax rate limited to 1 mil.	Failed
1922	Oklahoma	DA	116	Veteran Affairs	To make provision for paying a bonus to each soldier, sailor, marine and nurse inducted into the army or navy of the US during the war with Germany.	Passed
1922	Oregon	DA	3	Taxes	Single tax amendment.	Failed
1922	Oregon	DA	4	Taxes	1925 exposition tax amendment.	Failed
1922	Oregon	DA	5	Taxes	Income tax amendment.	Failed
1922	Oregon	DS	6	Education	Compulsory education bill.	Passed
1922	South Dakota	IDS	N/A	Utility Regulation	Build and operate state hydroelectric power plants and transmission systems.	Failed
1922	South Dakota	IDS	N/A	Business Regulation	Against Sunday performance.	Failed
1922	South Dakota	IDS	N/A	Banking Reform	Establish state owned banks.	Failed
1922	South Dakota	IDS	N/A	Education	Moving state university from Vermillion to Sioux Falls.	Failed
1922	South Dakota	IDS	N/A	Administration of Government	Abolish state constabulary.	Failed

Year	State	Type	Measure Number	Subject Matter	Description	Pass/Fail
1922	Washington	DS	I-40	Civil Rights	Repealing Chapter 174, Laws of 1921, relating to the Poll Tax.	Passed
1922	Washington	DS	I-46	Education	"30-10" School Plan.	Failed
1923	Maine	IDS	N/A	Labor	To establish a forty-eight hour week for women and minors.	Failed
1923	Ohio	IDS	Issue No. 1	Welfare	Relative to old age pensions.	Failed
1923	Oklahoma	DA	119	Administration of Government	To provide a method for promptly convening the Legislature for investigating the conduct of State officials.	Passed
1924	Arizona	DS	N/A	Environmental Reform	Colorado River, appropriations.	Failed
1924	Arizona	DS	N/A	Administration of Government	Highway commission.	Failed
1924	Arizona	DS	N/A	Gaming	To create board, appointed by Governor, to regulate and license horse racing and pari-mutuel betting within race track enclosure.	Failed
1924	Arizona	DA	N/A	Bonds	Hassayampa — Colorado Highway bonds.	Failed
1924	California	DA	1	Taxes	Provides for state taxation of highway transportation companies, sets rates and provides that Legislature may change rate with two-thirds vote.	Failed
1924	California	DS	11	Environmental Reform	To create the Klamath River Fish and Game District and to prohibit the construction or maintenance of any dam or other artificial obstruction in its waters.	Passed
1924	California	DA	16	Utility Regulation	Creates a Board, to be appointed by the Governor and subject to recall, to develop and distribute water and electric energy, to issue bonds, and for related purposes.	Failed
1924	California	DS	7	Gaming	To authorize boxing and wrestling contests for prizes and purses, or where admission fee is charged, limiting such boxing contests to 12 rounds.	Passed
1924	Colorado	DA	N/A	Administration of Government	Establishing the office of state printer and printing building committee.	Failed
1924	Michigan	DA	N/A	Education	Relative to compulsory attendance in public schools.	Failed
1924	Michigan	DA	N/A	Apportionment/Redistricting	Relative to division of the state into senatorial and representative districts.	Failed
1924	Michigan	DA	N/A	Taxes	Relative to an income tax.	Failed
1924	Missouri	DS	N/A	Taxes	To provide for the exemption from taxation of certain property used exclusively for religious worship, and property including endowments or income used exclusively for educational or charitable purposes.	Failed
1924	Missouri	DS	N/A	Administration of Government	To authorize the voters of the city of St. Louis and St. Louis County to consolidate the territories and governments thereof into one legal subdivision of the state.	Passed
1924	Missouri	DS	N/A	Labor	An act providing a system of compensation for workmen injured in industrial accidents.	Failed
1924	Missouri	DS	N/A	Administration of Government	An act to provide funds for the completion and maintenance of the state highway system.	Passed
1924	Montana	DS	I 28	Taxes	Metal mines tax.	Passed
1924	Nebraska	DA	N/A	Election Reform	Direct primary and nonpartisan elections, establishment.	Failed
1924	North Dakota	DS	N/A	Election Reform	Changing the election of precinct committeemen from the regular June primary to the March presidential primary.	Failed
1924	North Dakota	DS	N/A	Labor	Giving priority to a labor lien running to a farmer and his family for their work between April 1 and December 1.	Failed

Year	State	Type	Measure Number	Subject Matter	Description	Pass/Fail
1924	North Dakota	DS	N/A	Taxes	Reducing the amount of property taxes to be levied and spent in 1925–1927 biennium to not more than 75% of what was collected in 1923.	Failed
1924	Oregon	DS	4	Business Regulation	Oleomargarine condensed milk bill.	Failed
1924	Oregon	DS	5	Health/Medical	Naturopath bill.	Failed
1924	Oregon	DA	6	Labor	Workmen's compulsory compensation law for hazardous occupations.	Failed
1924	Oregon	DS	7	Taxes	Income tax repeal.	Passed
1924	Washington	DS	I-49	Education	Compulsory school attendance.	Failed
1924	Washington	DS	I-50	Taxes	Limitation of Taxation.	Failed
1924	Washington	DS	I-52	Utility Regulation	Electric Power Measure.	Failed
1925	Arizona	DA	N/A	Administration of Government	Tenure of state officers.	Failed
1926	Arizona	DS	N/A	Administration of Government	Highway Department, finance bill.	Failed
1926	Arizona	DS	N/A	Taxes	Automobile tax reduction.	Failed
1926	Arkansas	DA	N/A	Bonds	To allow for municipal improvement bonds.	Passed
1926	Arkansas	DA	N/A	Administration of Government	To prohibit local acts by legislature.	Passed
1926	Arkansas	DS	N/A	Election Reform	A measure for consolidation of elections (state and national).	Passed
1926	California	DA	17	Education	Permits the study and reading of Bible in public schools.	Failed
1926	California	DA	18	Utility Regulation	To create a water and power board the members of which are to be appointed by the Governor to develop and distribute water and electricity policies and issue bonds.	Failed
1926	California	DA	20	Apportionment/Redistricting	To create a reapportionment commission to act if legislature fails at first session after each census.	Failed
1926	California	DA	28	Apportionment/Redistricting	To require legislature to reapportion the state immediately following each federal census.	Passed
1926	California	DS	4	Taxes	To require every distributor of gasoline, distillate and of motor vehicle fuels, to pay license tax of $.01 per gallon, in addition to $.02 license tax now required by law.	Failed
1926	California	DS	6	Gaming	To create board, appointed by Governor, to regulate and license horse racing and pari-mutuel betting within race track enclosure.	Failed
1926	California	DA	8	Administration of Government	Classifies highways within counties and provides funding formulas for construction and maintenance thereof.	Failed
1926	California	DS	9	Alcohol Regulation	To repeal Wright Act approved by electors on referendum November 7, 1922, which provided for enforcement of the 18th Amendment of the U.S. Constitution (prohibition).	Failed
1926	Colorado	DS	N/A	Business Regulation	Amending law to permit dentists licensed in other states to practice in Colorado without examination.	Failed
1926	Colorado	DA	N/A	Administration of Government	Creating a public utilities commission and prescribing its powers and duties.	Failed
1926	Colorado	DS	N/A	Taxes	Concerning the taxation of petroleum products and registration of motor vehicles, and providing that all such taxes and fees by used exclusively for roads.	Failed
1926	Massachusetts	IDS	Question 2	Veteran Affairs	Modify veterans' preference law.	Failed
1926	Missouri	DS	N/A	Alcohol Regulation	To repeal the prohibition act.	Failed
1926	Missouri	DS	N/A	Labor	To repeal workmen's compensation.	Failed
1926	Montana	DS	I 30	Alcohol Regulation	Relating to repeal of state's intoxicating liquor laws.	Passed

Year	State	Type	Measure Number	Subject Matter	Description	Pass/Fail
1926	Montana	DS	I 31	Taxes	3 cents gasoline tax for good roads.	Passed
1926	North Dakota	DS	N/A	Taxes	Increasing the state gasoline tax from one to two cents per gallon for state highway purposes and providing for refunds when gas is used for non-highway purposes.	Passed
1926	Ohio	DA	Issue No. 1	Election Reform	To eliminate the compulsory primary.	Failed
1926	Oklahoma	DS	138	Taxes	To provide a method for ascertaining the average ad valorem rate effective for each year, same to be the basis for gross production tax rates for the succeeding year.	Failed
1926	Oklahoma	DS	139	Bonds	That all bonds hereafter authorized in the State, whether voted funding, or refunding shall become due and payable in equal annual installments as near as practicable.	Failed
1926	Oklahoma	DS	141	Taxes	Provides authority and procedure for testing any tax levy and striking the illegal portion, if any, before same is spread of record.	Passed
1926	Oregon	DS	15	Taxes	Income tax bill with property tax offset.	Failed
1926	Oregon	DS	16	Business Regulation	Bus and truck operating license bill.	Failed
1926	Oregon	DS	17	Animal Rights	Fish wheel, trap, seine, and gillnet bill.	Passed
1926	Oregon	DS	18	Taxes	Income tax bill.	Failed
1926	Oregon	DS	19	Utility Regulation	Oregon water and power board development measures.	Failed
1927	Maine	IDS	N/A	Election Reform	To repeal the direct primary law.	Failed
1927	Ohio	IDS	Issue No. 1	Administration of Government	To provide for a State board of Chiropractic Examiners.	Failed
1928	Arizona	DS	N/A	Administration of Government	To create a Board of Equalization.	Failed
1928	Arizona	DA	N/A	Health/Medical	Medical liberty.	Failed
1928	Arizona	DS	N/A	Administration of Government	To create a Motor Vehicle Department.	Failed
1928	Arizona	DS	N/A	Administration of Government	To create Commissioner of State Finance.	Failed
1928	Arkansas	DS	N/A	Education	Ban the teaching of evolution in schools.	Passed
1928	Arkansas	DA	N/A	Taxes	Tax to aid factories, industries and transportation facilities.	Passed
1928	California	DS	21	Animal Rights	Prohibiting Certain Acts with Animals. Defines bull-dogging, bull riding, etc., prohibits such acts for sport, exhibitions, or amusement and makes such prohibition inapplicable to farming or dairying.	Failed
1928	California	DS	5	Gaming	To repeal the initiative act approved by the electors on November 4, 1924, which authorized boxing and wrestling contests for prizes.	Failed
1928	Colorado	DA	N/A	Education	Providing for the election of a board of education, and for the appointment by said board of a commissioner of education to take place of superintendent of public instruction.	Failed
1928	Colorado	DA	N/A	Bonds	Providing for a $60m bond issue for the construction of highways.	Failed
1928	Massachusetts	IDS	Question 1	Business Regulation	Authorizing certain Sunday sporting events.	Passed
1928	Missouri	DA	N/A	Bonds	Providing for an additional bond issue of $75,000,000 for construction of state highways.	Passed
1928	Missouri	DS	N/A	Administration of Government	An act to provide for the creation, maintenance and administration of a police pension system in all cities of this state that now have or may hereafter attain a population of 500,000 inhabitants or over.	Failed
1928	Montana	DS	I 32	Alcohol Regulation	For adoption and enforcement of the Federal prohibition laws.	Failed

Year	State	Type	Measure Number	Subject Matter	Description	Pass/Fail
1928	North Dakota	DS	N/A	Bonds	Authorizing a $25 million bond issue for the state to indemnify depositors who lost money in bank closings between January 1, 1910 and May 15, 1928.	Failed
1928	North Dakota	DA	N/A	Alcohol Regulation	Repealing the clause of the constitution providing for prohibition.	Failed
1928	Ohio	DA	Issue No. 1	Judicial Reform	To equalize the compensation of judges.	Failed
1928	Oklahoma	DS	152	Taxes	An act provides a method of contesting alleged illegal ad valorem tax levies; requiring copies of all appropriations and levies to be filed with the County clerk and State Auditor.	Passed
1928	Oregon	DS	1	Taxes	Five cent gasoline tax bill.	Failed
1928	Oregon	DS	2	Taxes	Bill for reduction of motor vehicle license fees.	Failed
1928	Oregon	DS	3	Taxes	Income tax bill.	Failed
1928	Oregon	DS	5	Environmental Reform	Deschutes River water and fish bill.	Failed
1928	Oregon	DS	6	Environmental Reform	Rogue River water and fish bill.	Failed
1928	Oregon	DS	7	Environmental Reform	Umpqua River water and fish bill.	Failed
1928	Oregon	DS	8	Environmental Reform	McKenzie River water and fish bill.	Failed
1928	Oregon	DA	N/A	Initiative and Referendum	Limiting power of legislature over laws approved by the people.	Failed
1930	Arizona	DA	N/A	Bonds	To authorize issuance and sale of state highway bonds.	Failed
1930	Arizona	DA	N/A	Taxes	Auto tax exemption.	Failed
1930	Arkansas	DA	N/A	Unknown	There is no information available at this time. However, the state claims that this initiative appeared on the ballot but state records have been destroyed.	Failed
1930	Arkansas	DA	N/A	Unknown	There is no information available at this time. However, the state claims that this initiative appeared on the ballot but state records have been destroyed.	Failed
1930	Arkansas	DA	N/A	Unknown	There is no information available at this time. However, the state claims that this initiative appeared on the ballot but state records have been destroyed.	Failed
1930	Arkansas	DA	N/A	Unknown	There is no information available at this time. However, the state claims that this initiative appeared on the ballot but state records have been destroyed.	Failed
1930	Arkansas	DS	N/A	Education	To require reading of Bibles in public schools.	Passed
1930	Arkansas	DA	N/A	Unknown	There is no information available at this time. However, the state claims that this initiative appeared on the ballot but state records have been destroyed.	Failed
1930	Arkansas	DA	N/A	Unknown	There is no information available at this time. However, the state claims that this initiative appeared on the ballot but state records have been destroyed.	Failed
1930	California	DS	10	Business Regulation	To amend the usury law to require that written agreement for interest rate unnecessary, to provide that the legislature regulate pawnbrokers and "industrial loan companies".	Failed
1930	California	DA	11	Administration of Government	Creates Fish and Game Commission appointed by Governor to regulate the hunting and conservation of animals, fish and birds.	Failed
1930	California	DS	14	Election Reform	To change laws regulating registration of voters to require new statewide registration commencing January 1, 1932.	Passed
1930	California	DS	26	Business Regulation	Prohibits keeping open for business any store, barber show, workshop, factory, or other place of business, or performing or employing labor, on Sunday.	Failed

Year	State	Type	Measure Number	Subject Matter	Description	Pass/Fail
1930	California	DS	7	Daylight Savings Time	Provides that annually, at 2 a.m. on last Sunday in April, standard time be advanced one hour and at 2 a.m. on last Sunday in September, retarded one hour.	Failed
1930	Colorado	DA	N/A	Education	Providing for the election of a board of education and for the appointment by said board of a commissioner of education to take place of superintendent of public instruction.	Failed
1930	Massachusetts	IDS	Question 2	Alcohol Regulation	Repeal of "Baby Volstead" (Prohibition) Act.	Passed
1930	Massachusetts	IDS	Question 3	Animal Rights	Prohibit use of trapping devices	Passed
1930	Michigan	DA	N/A	Apportionment/Redistricting	Relative to apportionment of legislative districts.	Failed
1930	Missouri	DA	N/A	Administration of Government	Enabling the voters of St. Louis and St. Louis County to adopt a charter creating a City of Greater St. Louis.	Failed
1930	Missouri	DS	N/A	Labor	An act to repeal Sec. 25 of the Workmen's Compensation Act relating to employers liability insurance, enacting new sections providing for the establishment of the Missouri Compensation Fund.	Failed
1930	Missouri	DA	N/A	Administration of Government	Providing that the sheriff and coroner in the variouscounties may succeed themselves.	Failed
1930	Missouri	DA	N/A	Environmental Reform	Providing for the taking of private lands for public purposes.	Failed
1930	Nebraska	DS	N/A	Administration of Government	Prohibition of sale of municipally owned plants except for cash, etc.	Failed
1930	Nebraska	DS	N/A	Utility Regulation	Authorization for cities and towns owning electric light plants to extend their lines.	Passed
1930	Nebraska	DS	N/A	Administration of Government	Authorization for cities and villages and public electric and power districts to extend their lines.	Failed
1930	North Dakota	DA	N/A	Administration of Government	Lengthening the terms of state and County officials from two to four years.	Failed
1930	North Dakota	DS	N/A	Taxes	Increasing the state gasoline tax from two to four cents, with three cents to go to state highway fund and one cent to the County highway funds.	Failed
1930	North Dakota	DS	N/A	Business Regulation	Permitting the operation of motion picture theaters on Sunday after 1:30 p.m.	Failed
1930	Oregon	DA	10	Health/Medical	Anti-cigarette constitutional amendment.	Failed
1930	Oregon	DA	11	Animal Rights	Rogue River fishing constitutional amendment.	Failed
1930	Oregon	DA	12	Administration of Government	Lieutenant governor constitutional amendment.	Failed
1930	Oregon	DA	13	Utility Regulation	Water and power utility districts.	Passed
1930	Washington	IDS	I-1	Administration of Government	District Power Measure.	Passed
1930	Washington	DS	I-57	Apportionment/Redistricting	Redistricting State for Legislative Purpose.	Passed
1931	Oklahoma	DS	167	Taxes	An act repealing existent State Income Tax laws and money and credits tax law.	Failed
1931	Oklahoma	DA	169	Business Regulation	Forbidding the ownership of lands by corporations outside of cities and towns, except such as may be necessary for use under their charters or licenses.	Failed
1931	Oklahoma	DS	172	Education	Creating a State Board of Education of nine members, each appointed by Governor and confirmed by Senate and to receive for service $10 per day and expenses.	Failed
1931	Oklahoma	DA	173	Administration of Government	Creating a budget officer appointed by the Governor, confirmed by the Senate and removable at pleasure of Governor.	Failed
1932	Arizona	DA	N/A	Alcohol Regulation	Repeal of Prohibition.	Passed
1932	Arizona	DA	N/A	Taxes	County expenditures, limit on.	Failed
1932	Arizona	DA	N/A	Apportionment/Redistricting	Legislature, apportionment.	Passed
1932	Arizona	DS	N/A	Health/Medical	Chiropractors.	Failed

Year	State	Type	Measure Number	Subject Matter	Description	Pass/Fail
1932	Arizona	DS	N/A	Administration of Government	Abolishment of 18 Boards.	Failed
1932	Arizona	DA	N/A	Taxes	State expenditures, limit on.	Failed
1932	Arizona	DA	N/A	Taxes	Gasoline tax distribution.	Failed
1932	Arizona	DS	N/A	Administration of Government	Industrial Commission, abolishment.	Failed
1932	Arkansas	DA	N/A	Administration of Government	To provide for a split session of the legislature and a four-year term for elective state officials who were to be subject to recall.	Failed
1932	Arkansas	DS	N/A	Taxes	Supplementary act to proposed amendment for a sales tax.	Failed
1932	Arkansas	DS	N/A	Administration of Government	To set up a budget system.	Failed
1932	Arkansas	DA	N/A	Taxes	To exempt homesteads (forty acres in the County, a lot fifty by one hundred and fifty in the cities) from all taxes; regardless of value.	Failed
1932	Arkansas	DA	N/A	Education	To require the legislature to appropriate $6 per capita of the school population for the public schools and an additional sum to be arrived at by arithmetical calculation.	Failed
1932	Arkansas	DS	N/A	Administration of Government	To give the organization of the minority party (Republican) the power to name its representatives on the election boards and commissions.	Failed
1932	Arkansas	DA	N/A	Taxes	To reduce state property tax to 1/2 a mill and substituting a sales tax of one per cent.	Failed
1932	Arkansas	DA	N/A	Bonds	Forbidding the issuance of any more highway or bridge bonds with few exceptions until ratified by two-thirds majority of the votes cast on the proposal.	Failed
1932	California	DS	1	Alcohol Regulation	Repeals Wright Act that enforced 18th Amendment.	Passed
1932	California	DA	11	Administration of Government	Grants to City of Huntington Beach tide and submerged lands situated within present boundaries of the city.	Failed
1932	California	DA	2	Alcohol Regulation	Provides for the sale and use of liquor when the Wright Act is repealed and when lawful under Federal Constitution and laws of California.	Passed
1932	California	DS	3	Administration of Government	To regulate foreclosure of mortgage as contract, trust deed, instrument, making specific real property security for performance without changing possession.	Failed
1932	California	DS	5	Gaming	Create California Racing Board, to be appointed by Governor, empowered to regulate and license racing and wagering within race tract enclosure.	Failed
1932	Colorado	DA	N/A	Alcohol Regulation	Repealing statewide prohibition, subject to national repeal.	Passed
1932	Colorado	DA	N/A	Taxes	Giving legislature power to provide for a graduated income tax for state purposes, abolishing property tax for state purposes, and giving any excess revenue to the public schools.	Failed
1932	Colorado	DA	N/A	Taxes	Giving legislature power to provide for a limited income tax and a classified personal property tax, to be used for public schools.	Failed
1932	Colorado	DA	N/A	Taxes	Limiting taxation of motor fuel and ad valorem taxation of motor vehicles.	Failed
1932	Colorado	DS	N/A	Apportionment/Redistricting	Reapportionment of members of legislature .	Passed
1932	Massachusetts	IDS	Question 1	Business Regulation	Legalizing chiropractic.	Failed
1932	Massachusetts	IDS	Question 2	Election Reform	Regulating nominating procedures.	Passed
1932	Michigan	DA	N/A	Taxes	Relative to limitation of taxes assessed against property.	Passed

Year	State	Type	Measure Number	Subject Matter	Description	Pass/Fail
1932	Michigan	DA	N/A	Alcohol Regulation	Relative to establishment of a liquor control commission.	Passed
1932	Michigan	DA	N/A	Taxes	Relative to exemption from taxation of homesteads, etc.	Failed
1932	Michigan	DA	N/A	Administration of Government	Relative to term of office and apportionment of senators and representatives in state legislature.	Failed
1932	Missouri	DA	N/A	Administration of Government	An amendment limiting each House of the General Assembly to 75 employees.	Passed
1932	Missouri	DA	N/A	Administration of Government	An amendment providing for an itemized executive budget of estimated revenue and recommended expenditures to be submitted to the General Assembly within 15 days after it convenes.	Passed
1932	Nebraska	DS	N/A	Administration of Government	Change laws associated with the powers of the state police.	Failed
1932	North Dakota	DS	N/A	Administration of Government	Reducing salaries of elected and appointed state officials by 20%.	Passed
1932	North Dakota	DS	N/A	Administration of Government	Reducing fees paid to newspapers for publication of legal notices.	Passed
1932	North Dakota	DS	N/A	Administration of Government	Repealing requirement to publish public notice of sale of real estate for delinquent taxes.	Passed
1932	North Dakota	DS	N/A	Judicial Reform	Reducing salaries of Supreme Court Judges from $5,500 to $5,000.	Passed
1932	North Dakota	DS	N/A	Administration of Government	Repealing the prohibition against crop mortgages.	Failed
1932	North Dakota	DS	N/A	Administration of Government	Reducing travel expenses for County officials.	Passed
1932	North Dakota	DS	N/A	Judicial Reform	Reducing salaries of District Judges from $4,000 to $3,500 per year.	Passed
1932	North Dakota	DS	N/A	Business Regulation	Prohibiting farming by corporation.	Passed
1932	North Dakota	DS	N/A	Election Reform	Extending the use of the absentee ballot to include any qualified elector who expected to be absent from his precinct and those restricted by physical disability.	Failed
1932	North Dakota	DS	N/A	Administration of Government	Abolishing the office of District Tax Supervisor created in 1919.	Passed
1932	North Dakota	DS	N/A	Taxes	Reducing the taxable assessed valuation of property from 75% to 50%.	Passed
1932	North Dakota	DS	N/A	Administration of Government	Reducing travel expenses for state officials.	Passed
1932	North Dakota	DS	N/A	Administration of Government	Providing 5-year partial moratorium on debts, public or private, except on those able to pay.	Failed
1932	North Dakota	DA	N/A	Administration of Government	Removing the state capital from Bismarck to Jamestown.	Failed
1932	North Dakota	DA	N/A	Alcohol Regulation	Repeal prohibition.	Passed
1932	North Dakota	DS	N/A	Administration of Government	Reducing salaries of County officials and basing them on County population.	Passed
1932	North Dakota	DS	N/A	Administration of Government	Providing a 3-year partial moratorium on debts.	Failed
1932	North Dakota	DS	N/A	Administration of Government	Prohibiting crop mortgages.	Passed
1932	Oklahoma	DA	168	Taxes	Limiting ad valorem rate upon personal property to not exceed 23 mills, upon real property to not exceed 15 mills, and appropriating same to subdivisions of government.	Failed
1932	Oklahoma	DS	170	Business Regulation	An Act making unlawful the planting of cotton, wheat or other soil exhausting plants in excess of 30% of area of each separately owned tract of land in cultivation previous year.	Failed
1932	Oklahoma	DS	171	Administration of Government	Creating new Commission, making Governor member; authorizing construction of reservoirs and farm-to-market roads.	Failed

Year	State	Type	Measure Number	Subject Matter	Description	Pass/Fail
1932	Oklahoma	DS	175	Taxes	An Act for reduction of ad valorem taxes by levying taxes on incomes of individuals, associations and trusts; and excise taxes on incomes of corporations and banks.	Failed
1932	Oregon	DA	10	Taxes	Tax and debt control.	Failed
1932	Oregon	DS	11	Taxes	Tax supervising and conservation bill.	Failed
1932	Oregon	DS	12	Taxes	Personal income tax law amendment.	Failed
1932	Oregon	DA	13	Utility Regulation	State water power and hydroelectric.	Passed
1932	Oregon	DS	7	Alcohol Regulation	Bill to repeal state prohibition law of Oregon.	Passed
1932	Oregon	DS	8	Business Regulation	The freight truck and bus bill.	Failed
1932	Oregon	DS	9	Education	Bill moving university, normal and law schools, establishing junior colleges.	Failed
1932	Washington	DS	I-58	Election Reform	Permanent voter registration.	Passed
1932	Washington	DS	I-61	Alcohol Regulation	Relating to intoxicating liquors.	Passed
1932	Washington	DS	I-62	Administration of Government	Creating Department of Game.	Passed
1932	Washington	DS	I-64	Taxes	Limits Tax levy on Real and Personal Property to 40 Mills.	Passed
1932	Washington	DS	I-69	Taxes	Income Tax Measure.	Passed
1933	Maine	IDS	N/A	Utility Regulation	To raise the tax on corporations distributing and supplying electric power.	Failed
1933	North Dakota	DS	N/A	Business Regulation	Permitting operation of motion picture theaters on Sunday after 2 p.m.	Failed
1933	North Dakota	DS	N/A	Alcohol Regulation	Permitting the manufacture and sale of beer in North Dakota.	Passed
1933	Ohio	DA	Issue No. 1	Taxes	To provide a ten mill tax limitation on real estate.	Passed
1933	Ohio	IDS	Issue No. 1	Welfare	Relative to old age pensions.	Passed
1933	Ohio	DA	Issue No. 2	Administration of Government	Relative to County and township organizations and government, and granting counties home rule government.	Passed
1933	Oregon	DA	8	Alcohol Regulation	Repeal of prohibition constitutional amendment.	Passed
1934	Arizona	DS	N/A	Administration of Government	Legislature, nepotism, rules.	Failed
1934	Arizona	DS	N/A	Administration of Government	To create a Board of Naturopathic Examiners.	Failed
1934	California	DA	11	Education	To make State Board of Education elective; abolish Superintendent of Public Instruction; and provide for Director of Education.	Failed
1934	California	DA	13	Alcohol Regulation	Provides for local option for liquor sales and use.	Failed
1934	California	DS	17	Health/Medical	Creates Naturopathic Association, a public corp.; provides for its organization, government, membership and powers; regulates practice and licensing of naturopathy.	Failed
1934	California	DA	2	Alcohol Regulation	Prohibits consumption, sale, or disposition for consumption on premises, of intoxicating liquors, except beer, in public saloons or barrooms.	Passed
1934	California	DA	3	Judicial Reform	Declares Supreme or Appellate Court Justice may declare candidacy to succeed himself, otherwise Governor shall nominate candidate.	Passed
1934	California	DA	4	Administration of Government	Declares Attorney General, state's Chief law officer, shall see all state laws enforced, directly supervised district attorneys, sheriffs and other enforcement officers designated by law.	Passed
1934	California	DA	5	Legal	Declares in any criminal case, whether defendant testifies or not, court and counsel may comment on his failures to explain or deny any evidence against him.	Passed

Year	State	Type	Measure Number	Subject Matter	Description	Pass/Fail
1934	California	DA	6	Legal	Requires defendant charged with felony be immediately taken before magistrate of court, be delivered copy of complaint and given time to procure counsel.	Passed
1934	California	DA	7	Administration of Government	Prohibits permanent appointments and promotion in state civil service except on merit, efficiency and fitness ascertained by competitive examination.	Passed
1934	California	DS	9	Business Regulation	To amend Chiropractic Act creating state Chiropractors Association; and to provide for organization, government, membership powers and duties thereof.	Failed
1934	Colorado	DS	N/A	Business Regulation	Imposing license fees on chain stores.	Passed
1934	Colorado	DA	N/A	Taxes	Limiting tax on motor fuel to $.03 per gallon.	Failed
1934	Colorado	DA	N/A	Taxes	Giving people sole power to impose or approve imposition of excise taxes through the initiative and referendum.	Failed
1934	Colorado	DA	N/A	Taxes	Concerning the taxation of petroleum products and registration of motor vehicles and providing that such taxes and fees be used exclusively for roads.	Passed
1934	Michigan	DA	N/A	Taxes	Relative to limiting specific taxes upon gasoline and like fuel sold or used to propel motor vehicles, and providing exemptions of certain other taxes for those engaged in manufacturing, etc. gasoline and like fuels.	Failed
1934	Michigan	DA	N/A	Election Reform	Relative to providing for nonpartisan elections of judges.	Failed
1934	Michigan	DA	N/A	Administration of Government	Relative to permitting the adoption of home rule government by counties.	Failed
1934	Michigan	DA	N/A	Taxes	Relative to abolishing the uniform rule of taxation and to permit the classification of property for taxation purposes and an income tax for public schools.	Failed
1934	Michigan	DA	N/A	Taxes	Relative to limiting registration license fees or taxes on all motor vehicles except commercial motor vehicles and motorcycles, and providing for exemptions from certain other taxes.	Failed
1934	Missouri	DA	N/A	Administration of Government	The Constitution of Missouri shall not be construed to not prohibit payments from any public fund or funds, for benefits, upon retirement, disability or death, to persons employed and paid out of any public fund.	Failed
1934	Nebraska	DA	N/A	Gaming	Pari-mutual betting, authorization.	Passed
1934	Nebraska	DA	N/A	Administration of Government	Unicameral legislature, creation.	Passed
1934	Nevada	IDS	N/A	Animal Rights	Bounties on predatory animals.	Passed
1934	North Dakota	DS	N/A	Business Regulation	Permitting operation of motion picture theaters on Sunday after 2 p.m.	Passed
1934	North Dakota	DS	N/A	Alcohol Regulation	Legalizing and regulating the sale of intoxicating liquor in drug stores, hotels, restaurants an clubs; creating the office of Liquor Control Commissioner, and giving portion of taxes to school districts.	Failed
1934	North Dakota	DS	N/A	Alcohol Regulation	Legalizing the sale of liquor by any individual or business.	Failed
1934	North Dakota	DS	N/A	Alcohol Regulation	Repealing all state prohibition laws.	Failed
1934	North Dakota	DS	N/A	Education	Setting the maximum amount of levy of school taxes but permitting additional levy if limitations wouldn't permit the raising of a least $70 per pupil.	Failed

Year	State	Type	Measure Number	Subject Matter	Description	Pass/Fail
1934	Ohio	DA	N/A	Taxes	Prohibiting the taxation as property of motor vehicles.	Failed
1934	Ohio	DA	N/A	Taxes	Requiring motor vehicle fuel excise taxes to be measured by a sum for each gallon or other like unit.	Failed
1934	Oregon	DA	2	Taxes	Limitations of taxes on taxable property.	Failed
1934	Oregon	DA	3	Health/Medical	Healing arts.	Failed
1934	Washington	DS	I-77	Animal Rights	Fish Traps and Fishing Regulations.	Passed
1934	Washington	DS	I-94	Taxes	40-Mill Tax Limit.	Passed
1935	Oklahoma	DA	201	Taxes	A proposed amendment to the Constitution providing that all homesteads within said state may be exempted from ad valorem taxation by the Legislature.	Passed
1935	Oklahoma	DA	214	Welfare	Relative to old age pensions.	Passed
1935	Oklahoma	DS	220	Administration of Government	Appropriating from State Treasury to State Board of Public welfare, $1.5 million and $1 million respectively for fiscal years ending June 30, 1936, and June 30, 1937, to be allocated to counties.	Passed
1936	Arkansas	DA	N/A	Apportionment/Redistricting	To provide for the Board of Apportionment consisting of the Governor, Secretary of state and the Attorney General, to apportion representatives and senators.	Passed
1936	Arkansas	DA	N/A	Taxes	An amendment to provide for an exemption of homesteads from certain state taxes.	Passed
1936	California	DA	10	Taxes	Relating to motor vehicle fuel taxes and license fees requiring funds raised there from to be used for highway purposes and vehicle regulation.	Failed
1936	California	DA	11	Education	To create state Tenure Board to establish tenure procedures for instructors.	Failed
1936	California	DA	2	Taxes	Repeals 1935 Personal Income Tax Act and provides that no law imposing income tax on individuals is valid unless approved by majority of electors after initiative proceedings.	Failed
1936	California	DA	3	Alcohol Regulation	Creates Alcoholic Beverage Commission to succeed to liquor regulatory and licensing powers of state Board of Equalization.	Failed
1936	California	DS	4	Environmental Reform	To prohibit tideland and surface oil drilling and authorizing drilling wells slanted from uplands, and to prohibit pollution of tide, ocean bay or inlet waters.	Failed
1936	California	DA	7	Administration of Government	Creates County and municipal civil service, to regulate employment and prohibit appointees from political activities.	Failed
1936	California	DA	9	Alcohol Regulation	Provides for local option for the regulation of alcoholic beverage.	Failed
1936	Colorado	DA	N/A	Taxes	Amending revenue section of constitution, principally by giving legislature power to provide for an income tax within limitations.	Failed
1936	Colorado	DA	N/A	Welfare	Providing $45 per month old age pensions and designating certain taxes for the payment thereof.	Passed
1936	Colorado	DA	N/A	Taxes	Amending "uniformity clause" of constitution principally by limiting rate to taxation for all purposes to 20 mills in cities and towns of first class, and 15 mills in other divisions.	Failed
1936	Colorado	DS	N/A	Welfare	Providing for public assistance to indigent tubercular residents.	Passed
1936	Colorado	DS	N/A	Labor	Amending workmen's compensation act to benefit of employee.	Passed

Year	State	Type	Measure Number	Subject Matter	Description	Pass/Fail
1936	Colorado	DA	N/A	Taxes	Providing for ownership tax on motor vehicles in lieu of ad valorem taxation thereon, and for the distribution thereof.	Passed
1936	Maine	IDS	N/A	Administration of Government	To prevent diversions of the general highway fund.	Passed
1936	Michigan	DA	N/A	Alcohol Regulation	Relative to prohibition after December 31, 1937, certain real property taxes and to provide for an income tax.	Failed
1936	Michigan	DA	N/A	Taxes	Relative to exempting certain articles of food and prepared meals from the sales tax.	Failed
1936	Missouri	DA	N/A	Labor	The Constitution of Missouri shall not be construed to nor prohibit payments, from any public fund or funds, for benefits, upon retirement, disability or death, to persons employed and paid out of any public fund.	Passed
1936	Missouri	DA	N/A	Administration of Government	An amendment creating Conservation Commission pertaining to fish, game and forestry, and stating its powers, duties and obligations with respect to administration of same.	Passed
1936	Nevada	IDS	N/A	Welfare	Relative to old age pensions.	Failed
1936	North Dakota	DS	N/A	Campaign Finance Reform	Making it unlawful to expend federal funds in the state for political purposes.	Failed
1936	North Dakota	DS	N/A	Election Reform	Abolishing the use of absent voters' ballots.	Failed
1936	North Dakota	DS	N/A	Alcohol Regulation	Legalizing the sale of liquor and allocating the tax and license revenue for apportionment to counties to reduce real estate taxes.	Passed
1936	Ohio	DA	Issue No. 1	Taxes	Prohibiting the levy or collection of an excise tax on the sale or purchase of food for human consumption off the premises where sold.	Passed
1936	Oklahoma	DA	222	Alcohol Regulation	A Constitutional amendment repealing prohibition provisions; authorizing manufacture, sale and transportation of alcohol and alcoholic beverages in Oklahoma.	Failed
1936	Oklahoma	DA	225	Welfare	Authorizing legislation providing for relief and care of needy aged persons who are unable to provide for themselves.	Failed
1936	Oklahoma	DS	226	Welfare	An Act providing assistance to needy persons aged 65 or over, needy blind persons, needy crippled children, and needy persons aged fifteen or younger.	Passed
1936	Oklahoma	DS	230	Environmental Reform	An Act designating the OK Conservation Commission as a State agency to co-operate with Federal Government in designated projects.	Failed
1936	Oregon	DA	2	Business Regulation	Amendment forbidding prevention or regulation of certain advertising if truthful.	Failed
1936	Oregon	DA	3	Taxes	Tax limitation for school districts having 100,000 population.	Failed
1936	Oregon	DS	4	Administration of Government	Noncompulsory military training bill.	Failed
1936	Oregon	DA	5	Taxes	Amendment limiting and reducing permissible taxes on tangible property.	Failed
1936	Oregon	DS	6	Administration of Government	State power bill.	Failed
1936	Oregon	DA	7	Administration of Government	State hydroelectric temporary administrative board.	Failed
1936	Oregon	DS	8	Banking Reform	State bank bill.	Failed
1936	Washington	DS	I-101	Administration of Government	Civil Service.	Failed
1936	Washington	DS	I-114	Taxes	40-Mill Tax Limit.	Passed
1936	Washington	DS	I-115	Welfare	Relative to old age pensions.	Failed
1936	Washington	DS	I-119	Business Regulation	Production for Use.	Failed

Year	State	Type	Measure Number	Subject Matter	Description	Pass/Fail
1938	Arizona	DA	N/A	Taxes	Tax free homes.	Failed
1938	Arizona	DA	N/A	Administration of Government	Legislators not eligible for appointment to public office.	Passed
1938	Arizona	DS	N/A	Administration of Government	All appointive members of boards and commissions, terms conterminous with Governor.	Failed
1938	Arkansas	DA	27	Labor	To provide the General Assembly with the power to enact laws providing for workmen's compensation.	Passed
1938	Arkansas	DS	28	Bonds	Highway bond refunding.	Failed
1938	Arkansas	DA	29	Taxes	To provide for an industry tax exemption for any new manufacturing or processing establishment or for expansion of existing establishments.	Passed
1938	Arkansas	DA	30	Education	Establishes a State Board of Education.	Failed
1938	Arkansas	DA	31	Judicial Reform	The Supreme Court shall make rules regulating the practice of law and the professional conduct of attorneys at law.	Passed
1938	Arkansas	DA	32	Administration of Government	To provide for rules for the filling of vacancies.	Passed
1938	Arkansas	DS	1	Prohibition	Would amend liquor laws	Failed
1938	California	DS	1	Labor	To establish certain labor practices. Defines lawful picketing, boycotting and display of banners, prohibits seizure of private property.	Failed
1938	California	DS	2	Animal Rights	To provide for the regulation of pounds. Defines pounds, prescribes duties of pound masters; prohibits sale or surrender of unwanted animals for scientific, medical, experimental, purposes but exempts kennels.	Failed
1938	California	DA	20	Taxes	To repeal limitation on ad valorem property taxes for state appropriation; to prohibit increasing present assessed valuation of improvements and tangible personal property.	Failed
1938	California	DA	25	Administration of Government	Provides for state Retirement Life Payments Administrator to administer programs of retirement compensation warrants to qualified electors 50 years of age, not an employer nor employee.	Failed
1938	California	DA	4	Administration of Government	To create a Highway and Traffic Safety Commission; to abolish existing state Highway Commission and transfer control of California Highway Patrol to new Commission.	Failed
1938	California	IDS	5	Animal Rights	Prohibits operation in state waters of fishing boats which deliver fish, mollusks or crustaceans, wherever caught, to points beyond state waters.	Passed
1938	Colorado	DA	N/A	Welfare	Repeal of $45 per month old age pension amendment and giving legislature power to provide for pensions.	Failed
1938	Colorado	DA	N/A	Business Regulation	Relating to the practice of the healing arts, and giving practitioners licensed by the state certain rights in tax supported institutions and power to regulate their own professions.	Failed
1938	Colorado	DS	N/A	Taxes	Repeal of chain stores tax act.	Failed
1938	Idaho	DS	1	Administration of Government	The Idaho state Fish and Game Commission Act.	Passed
1938	Massachusetts	DA	Question 1	Administration of Government	Biennial legislative session.	Passed
1938	Massachusetts	IDS	Question 2	Business Regulation	Free public taxicab stands in cities and towns.	Passed
1938	Michigan	DA	N/A	Administration of Government	Relative to increasing terms of County offices from two- to four-year terms.	Failed
1938	Michigan	DA	N/A	Judicial Reform	Relative to non-partisan nomination and appointment of supreme court justices for 8 year terms.	Failed

Year	State	Type	Measure Number	Subject Matter	Description	Pass/Fail
1938	Michigan	DA	N/A	Taxes	Relative to guaranteeing that gas and weight tax monies be used solely for highways, roads and streets.	Passed
1938	Missouri	DA	N/A	Administration of Government	Concerning state highways, fixing motor fuel tax, prescribing powers relating thereto of General Assembly and state Highway Commission.	Failed
1938	Missouri	DA	N/A	Apportionment/Redistricting	Amendment relating to legislative proceedings, apportionment of senators and representatives, their qualifications, election, compensation, tenure and redistricting.	Failed
1938	Missouri	DA	N/A	Administration of Government	Providing sheriffs and coroners may be eligible to succeed themselves in office.	Failed
1938	Missouri	DA	N/A	Taxes	Providing plan of assessment, valuation and taxation; appropriating bond money; prohibiting local property tax on motor vehicles; providing state maintained school system.	Failed
1938	Montana	DS	I 41	Administration of Government	State highway treasury anticipation debentures act of 1938.	Passed
1938	Nebraska	DA	N/A	Gaming	Slot machines, licensing.	Failed
1938	Nevada	IDS	N/A	Animal Rights	To pay bounties on predatory animals.	Failed
1938	North Dakota	DS	N/A	Administration of Government	Requiring approval of County Treasurer, Judge and Register of Deeds for transactions in County securities by County Commissioners.	Failed
1938	North Dakota	DA	N/A	Administration of Government	Clarifying which public funds are to be deposited in the state treasury for appropriation and which moneys are to be kept in trust.	Passed
1938	North Dakota	DA	N/A	Election Reform	Providing for the election of the Tax Commissioner in 1940 for a 4-year term on the no-party ballot.	Passed
1938	North Dakota	DA	N/A	Administration of Government	Prohibiting members of the Legislature from accepting state employment during their terms of office.	Passed
1938	North Dakota	DS	N/A	Welfare	Providing a minimum pension under state old age assistance of $40 per month unless more than one member of a family received aid in which case it would be $30 per month.	Passed
1938	North Dakota	DS	N/A	Banking Reform	Reducing the legal rate of interest to 3% on indebtedness instead of 4% on borrowing and 7% on contracts.	Failed
1938	North Dakota	DS	N/A	Alcohol Regulation	Repealing liquor control act of November 1936.	Failed
1938	North Dakota	DS	N/A	Administration of Government	Creating a state civil service for state employees.	Failed
1938	North Dakota	DS	N/A	Administration of Government	Providing for a commission consisting of the Governor, Lieutenant Governor and Attorney General to appoint city and village officials.	Failed
1938	North Dakota	DS	N/A	Administration of Government	Abolishing the state Regulatory Department; creating the state laboratories Department to be governed by board of the Governor, Attorney General and Treasurer.	Passed
1938	North Dakota	DA	N/A	Education	Creating a state Board of Higher Education to replace the Board of Administration as administrator of institutions of higher learning.	Passed
1938	Ohio	DA	Issue No. 1	Judicial Reform	To provide for the original appointment of judges of the Supreme Court and Courts of appeals.	Failed
1938	Oklahoma	DA	205	Administration of Government	Proposed constitutional amendment empowering bodies politic, including rural utility districts, organized there under, to assume revenue indebtedness.	Failed
1938	Oregon	DS	10	Environmental Reform	Water purification and prevention of pollution bill.	Passed

Year	State	Type	Measure Number	Subject Matter	Description	Pass/Fail
1938	Oregon	DS	11	Alcohol Regulation	Bill regulating sale of alcoholic liquor for beverage purposes.	Failed
1938	Oregon	DS	7	Administration of Government	Townsend Plan bill.	Passed
1938	Oregon	DS	8	Taxes	Citizens' retirement annuity bill; levying transactions tax toprovide fund.	Failed
1938	Oregon	DS	9	Labor	Bill regulating picketing and boycotting by labor groups and organizations.	Passed
1938	Oregon	DA	N/A	Gaming	Constitutional amendment legalizing certain lotteries and other forms of gambling.	Failed
1938	Washington	DS	I-126	Election Reform	Non-Partisan School Election.	Passed
1938	Washington	DS	I-129	Taxes	40-Mill Tax Limit.	Passed
1938	Washington	DS	I-130	Labor	Regulation of Labor Disputes.	Failed
1939	California	DA	1	Administration of Government	To establish system of warrants issued by state to electors 50 years old.	Failed
1939	California	DS	2	Business Regulation	Provides secretary of Chiropractic Board shall devote full time to duties and increase his salary; increases powers of board; increases educational requirements of applicant.	Failed
1939	Michigan	DA	N/A	Election Reform	Relative to nonpartisan election of judges.	Passed
1939	North Dakota	DS	N/A	Taxes	Imposing a gross income tax of 2% on businesses, professions, and occupations, with some exceptions, for the various funds of the state and counties.	Failed
1939	North Dakota	DS	N/A	Welfare	Diverting state gasoline and vehicle tax from highway construction to state old age assistance fund for two years.	Failed
1939	North Dakota	DS	N/A	Alcohol Regulation	Providing for the sale of liquor through municipal liquor stores in towns of 150 or more having a regular police department.	Failed
1939	Ohio	DA	Issue No. 1	Welfare	Relative to old age pensions.	Failed
1939	Ohio	DA	Issue No. 2	Initiative and Referendum	Requirements necessary to qualify initiative petitions.	Failed
1940	Arizona	DS	N/A	Taxes	Education, state aid; proscribing the state levy for common and high school purposes.	Passed
1940	Arizona	DA	N/A	Taxes	Tax free homes.	Failed
1940	Arizona	DA	N/A	Taxes	Uniform auto lien tax.	Passed
1940	Arizona	DS	N/A	Gaming	To permit and authorize the licensing of gambling.	Failed
1940	Arizona	DA	N/A	Taxes	Tax limitation.	Failed
1940	Arizona	DA	N/A	Administration of Government	Establishing irrigation districts.	Passed
1940	Arizona	DS	N/A	Taxes	Relating to motor fuel tax, fixing the tax and the distribution and use thereof.	Failed
1940	Arkansas	DS	1	Business Regulation	Payment for employers of compensation for injured employees	Failed
1940	Arkansas	DA	33	Taxes	To provide for a municipal library tax to be authorized in advance by the voters.	Passed
1940	Arkansas	DA	34	Taxes	To provide for the collection of an annual tax on the assessed value of real and personal property from which shall be created a fund to pay retirement salaries and pensions to policemen and firemen.	Passed
1940	Arkansas	DA	35	Administration of Government	Game and Fish Commission.	Failed
1940	Arkansas	DA	36	Welfare	Relative to old age pensions.	Failed
1940	California	DS	5	Daylight Savings Time	Provides for daylight saving time each year from last Sunday in April to the last Sunday in September.	Failed

Year	State	Type	Measure Number	Subject Matter	Description	Pass/Fail
1940	Colorado	DS	N/A	Gaming	Establishing a racing commission and legalizing horse and dog racing.	Failed
1940	Colorado	DA	N/A	Taxes	Providing for an ad valorem tax on all intangible property in the state, and allocating the funds derived there from.	Failed
1940	Colorado	DA	N/A	Environmental Reform	Providing for the conservation of the state's wildlife resources; limiting the use of game and fish revenues for such purposes; and establishing a Game and Fish Commission.	Failed
1940	Colorado	DA	N/A	Taxes	Providing for an income tax; requiring the legislature to levy such income tax at not lower than certain specified rates; and providing that the revenues derived there from shall replace property taxes.	Failed
1940	Colorado	DA	N/A	Welfare	Providing for a guaranteed old age pension of $30 per month to residents of the state over 65 years who qualify.	Failed
1940	Idaho	DS	1	Alcohol Regulation	Proposed prohibition districts, prohibiting the possession, purchase, sale and transportation of alcoholic liquors.	Failed
1940	Idaho	DS	2	Alcohol Regulation	Idaho Sobriety Act proposed to inhibit advertising promotion of sales, limit amount of purchase and to inhibit dispensing of alcoholic liquors in bars and clubs.	Failed
1940	Michigan	DA	N/A	Administration of Government	Establishing a new system of civil service in state employment.	Passed
1940	Missouri	DA	N/A	Election Reform	Provide for establishment of non-partisan system for nomination appointment and election of judges of certain courts.	Passed
1940	Missouri	DA	N/A	Taxes	Providing revenue for rural roads and abolishing municipal gasoline taxes.	Failed
1940	Missouri	DA	N/A	Taxes	Amending Missouri Constitution by addition of Art. 4a fixing motor vehicle license fees at present rate, and providing revenue for road purposes.	Failed
1940	Missouri	DA	N/A	Environmental Reform	Repealing Wild Life and Forestry Code and all laws and regulations ordained and established by Conservation Commission.	Failed
1940	Missouri	DA	N/A	Initiative and Referendum	Amending Art. IV of Constitution to provide required number of signatures in initiative or referendum petitions be based on vote for Governor.	Failed
1940	Montana	DS	I 44	Bonds	Montana state college bonds.	Failed
1940	North Dakota	DS	N/A	Administration of Government	Establishing a state Board of Finance and Administration to handle all trust funds.	Failed
1940	North Dakota	DS	N/A	Taxes	Permitting abatement of past, present and future taxes based on excessive valuation.	Failed
1940	North Dakota	DA	N/A	Taxes	Dedicating highway user taxes to defray cost of construction and maintenance of highways.	Passed
1940	North Dakota	DS	N/A	Taxes	Proposing three classes of property for tax purposes: 100% valuation for property assessed by state Board of Equalization; 75% on business inventories: 50% on household goods.	Failed
1940	North Dakota	DA	N/A	Administration of Government	Changing name of state Board of Railroad Commissioners to Public Service Commission.	Passed
1940	North Dakota	DS	N/A	Education	Earmarking sales tax revenue for schools and welfare.	Passed
1940	North Dakota	DA	N/A	Taxes	Providing for a graduated land tax with a homestead exception of $5,000 for legal owner-resident farmers.	Failed

Year	State	Type	Measure Number	Subject Matter	Description	Pass/Fail
1940	North Dakota	DA	N/A	Taxes	Permitting enactment of graduated land tax on farms in excess of $15,000 valuation.	Failed
1940	North Dakota	DS	N/A	Education	Reducing the state per pupil payment to schools regardless of need and increasing the emergency funds for schools in distress.	Failed
1940	North Dakota	DS	N/A	Education	Earmarking sales tax revenues specifically 7/12ths for the school equalization fund and 5/12ths for the state welfare fund.	Passed
1940	North Dakota	DS	N/A	Education	Increasing the funds for financially distressed schools.	Passed
1940	Oklahoma	DA	215	Taxes	Authorizing the levy of a graduated tax on land; levying for State Old Age Security, until otherwise provided, an additional tax upon land owned by any person in excess of 640 acres.	Passed
1940	Oklahoma	DS	241	Administration of Government	Abolishing alternate members of State Board of Medical Examiners; prohibiting one school of medical practice from having majority membership on said Board.	Passed
1940	Oklahoma	DS	253	Taxes	Providing for allocation, apportionment, distribution and use of moneys received by State of OK through levy.	Passed
1940	Oklahoma	DA	281	Administration of Government	Qualifications for office.	Passed
1940	Oklahoma	DA	289	Alcohol Regulation	A Constitutional amendment authorizing and regulating importation, manufacture, transportation and sale of whiskey and other alcoholic beverages.	Failed
1940	Oregon	DS	7	Alcohol Regulation	Bill repealing present liquor law; authorizing private sale, license, taxing.	Failed
1940	Oregon	DA	8	Gaming	Amendment legalizing certain gambling and gambling device and certain lotteries.	Failed
1940	Oregon	DS	9	Business Regulation	Bill to repeal the Oregon milk control law.	Failed
1940	Washington	DS	I-139	Bonds	P.U.D. Bonds.	Failed
1940	Washington	DS	I-141	Welfare	Relative to old age pensions.	Passed
1942	Arizona	DS	N/A	Taxes	Privilege tax, division.	Passed
1942	Arkansas	DS	1	Alcohol Regulation	Amend liquor laws, provide for better local option.	Passed
1942	Arkansas	DA	34	Environmental Reform	Game and Fish Commission	Failed
1942	Arkansas	DA	35	Administration of Government	To provide rules and regulations for boards and commissions.	Passed
1942	California	IDS	10	Business Regulation	Authorizes plans for rehabilitation, readjustment, reorganization, consolidation or merger of building and loan association.	Failed
1942	California	DS	3	Administration of Government	To create Board of Examiners in basic sciences comprised of 5 members with prescribed qualifications appointed by Governor.	Failed
1942	California	DA	4	Taxes	Repeal 1935 Personal Income Tax Act and declares no law imposing income tax on persons to be valid until approved by majority of voters after initiative proceedings.	Failed
1942	Idaho	DS	1	Welfare	Provides a minimum of forty dollars monthly and medical, dental, surgical, optical, hospital, nursing care, and artificial limbs, eyes, hearing aids, and other needed appliances to citizens over 65 years of age.	Passed
1942	Massachusetts	IDS	Question 1	Abortion	Revision of birth control law.	Failed
1942	Michigan	DA	N/A	Administration of Government	To permit Wayne County to adopt a charter.	Failed

Year	State	Type	Measure Number	Subject Matter	Description	Pass/Fail
1942	North Dakota	DS	N/A	Taxes	Providing for three classes of property for tax purposes.	Failed
1942	North Dakota	DS	N/A	Alcohol Regulation	Prohibiting the sale of alcoholic beverages in restaurants.	Failed
1942	Oklahoma	DA	306	Education	Authorizing the Legislature to enact laws to provide for the retirement of meritorious service teachers and other employees in the public schools, colleges and universities in this state.	Passed
1942	Oregon	DS	7	Education	Bill distributing surplus funds to school districts reducing taxes therein.	Passed
1944	Arizona	DA	N/A	Welfare	Annuities for the disabled and blind.	Failed
1944	Arkansas	DS	2	Gaming	Repeals horse and dog racing	Failed
1944	Arkansas	DS	3	Health/Medical	Hollingsworth state hospital system	Failed
1944	Arkansas	DA	34	Taxes	County library tax	Failed
1944	Arkansas	DA	35	Labor	To provide for the right to work.	Passed
1944	Arkansas	DA	36	Environmental Reform	To create the Arkansas state Game and Fish Commission to control, manage, conserve and regulate the birds, fish, game, and wildlife resources of the state.	Passed
1944	Arkansas	DA	37	Civil Rights	To provide that any citizen of Arkansas, while serving in the armed forces of the United States, may vote in any election, without having paid poll tax, if otherwise qualified to vote.	Passed
1944	Arkansas	DA	38	Administration of Government	4 year term for Governor and Lieutenant Governor.	Failed
1944	California	DA	11	Welfare	To provide $60 monthly to citizens having required residence, who are 60 years old or over, or totally and permanently disabled, including those in military service, or blind.	Failed
1944	California	DA	12	Labor	Declares right of employment, free from interference because employee does or does not belong to or pay money to a labor organization.	Failed
1944	California	DA	9	Education	Increase the amount of revenue required to be raised and apportioned by the Legislative for elementary schools. Increases apportionment from 100% to 166 2/3% of amount raised by counties.	Passed
1944	Colorado	DA	N/A	Veteran Affairs	Providing for preference to honorably discharged veterans and their widows in the civil service of the state and its political subdivisions.	Passed
1944	Colorado	DA	N/A	Alien Rights	Providing that aliens eligible to citizenship may acquire and dispose of real and personal property, and that provision shall be made by law concerning the right of aliens ineligible to citizenship to acquire and dispose of such property.	Failed
1944	Colorado	DS	N/A	Welfare	Appropriating $.5m for the then current biennium and $1.5m annually thereafter for old age pensions.	Passed
1944	Missouri	DA	N/A	Administration of Government	Constitutional amendment to create a unicameral legislature, 50–75 members elected for two years.	Failed
1944	Montana	DS	I 48	Health/Medical	Defining osteopathy — authorizing and regulating practice of osteopathic physicians and surgeons.	Failed
1944	Nebraska	DS	N/A	Taxes	Proposed gasoline tax amendment.	Failed
1944	Nebraska	DS	N/A	Alcohol Regulation	Prohibition of liquor traffic.	Failed
1944	Nevada	IDS	N/A	Welfare	Relative to old age pensions.	Passed
1944	North Dakota	DS	N/A	Bonds	Authorizing issuance of $12,360,000 in bonds for state highway construction and maintenance.	Passed
1944	North Dakota	DS	N/A	Alcohol Regulation	Prohibiting the sale of alcoholic beverages where commodities other than tobacco and soft drinks are sold.	Failed

Year	State	Type	Measure Number	Subject Matter	Description	Pass/Fail
1944	North Dakota	DS	N/A	Taxes	Repealing state income tax.	Failed
1944	Oregon	DA	8	Education	Increasing state fund for public school support.	Failed
1944	Oregon	DA	9	Taxes	Providing monthly annuities from a gross income tax.	Failed
1944	Washington	DS	I-157	Welfare	Relative to old age assistance laws.	Failed
1944	Washington	DS	I-158	Welfare	Liberalization of Old Age Assistance Laws by the Townsend Clubs of Washington.	Failed
1946	Arizona	DS	N/A	Taxes	Motor vehicle fuel tax.	Passed
1946	Arizona	DA	N/A	Labor	Right to work	Passed
1946	Arizona	DA	N/A	Labor	Right-to-work.	Passed
1946	Arkansas	DS	1	Education	School district reorganization	Failed
1946	Arkansas	DA	39	Taxes	To provide for the levy of a tax on real and personal property for the establishment of the County library when approved in advance by qualified electors.	Passed
1946	California	DS	11	Labor	Declares state policy that all persons have the right of equal opportunity to secure employment.	Failed
1946	California	DS	2	Gaming	To permit greyhound racing and pari-mutuel wagering thereon in counties having population over 175,000.	Passed
1946	California	DA	3	Education	Amends same sections of Constitution and simplifies allocation of school funds in same manner as Proposition No. 13. Establishes minimum salary of $2400 per year for teachers. Increases state support for public schools to $120 per year per student.	Passed
1946	Idaho	DS	1	Gaming	The anti gambling act.	Failed
1946	Idaho	DS	2	Alcohol Regulation	The Local Option Act.	Failed
1946	Idaho	DS	3	Alcohol Regulation	The Idaho Sobriety Act.	Failed
1946	Massachusetts	IDS	Question 1	Welfare	Relative to old age pensions.	Failed
1946	Massachusetts	IDS	Question 2	Labor	Labor relations.	Passed
1946	Michigan	DA	N/A	Administration of Government	To permit Wayne County to adopt a charter.	Failed
1946	Michigan	DA	N/A	Administration of Government	Return of portion of sales tax to certain municipalities	Passed
1946	Nebraska	DA	N/A	Labor	Closed shop, abolition.	Passed
1946	North Dakota	DS	N/A	Taxes	Reverting back to refunding procedure for taxes paid on gasoline used for non-highway purposes.	Passed
1946	Oklahoma	DA	314	Taxes	The annual ad valorem tax rate for school purposes may be increased in any school district, but not to exceed 15 mills on the dollar valuation upon all property therein.	Passed
1946	Oklahoma	DA	315	Taxes	The Legislature shall raise and appropriate funds for annual support of common schools.	Passed
1946	Oregon	DS	8	Welfare	Relative to old age pensions.	Failed
1946	Oregon	DS	9	Taxes	To create basic school support fund by annual tax levy.	Passed
1946	Oregon	DA	N/A	Education	Schools, state aid.	Failed
1946	Washington	DS	I-166	Utility Regulation	Relating to Public Utility Districts; requiring approval of voters as prerequisite to acquisition of any operating electrical utility properties.	Failed
1947	Maine	IDS	N/A	Administration of Government	Barlow Bill (initiative measure).	Failed
1947	Maine	IDS	N/A	Labor	To regulate collective bargaining Tabb Bill (competing measure).	Failed
1947	Ohio	DA	Issue No. 4	Taxes	Relative to the prohibition of the expenditure of money from motor vehicle license taxes and gasoline taxes for other than highway and related purposes.	Passed

Year	State	Measure Type	Number	Subject Matter	Description	Pass/Fail
1948	Arizona	DS	N/A	Administration of Government	Highway patrol, merit system.	Passed
1948	Arizona	DS	N/A	Administration of Government	Civil service.	Passed
1948	Arizona	DS	N/A	Administration of Government	Public employees' retirement.	Passed
1948	Arizona	DS	N/A	Labor	Limitation to workmen's compensation.	Passed
1948	Arkansas	DS	1	Education	Reorganization of school districts.	Passed
1948	Arkansas	DS	2	Alcohol Regulation	Amend liquor laws regarding local option elections.	Failed
1948	Arkansas	DS	3	Election Reform	Provides for direct political party response in holding of all general elections.	Passed
1948	Arkansas	DS	4	Labor	Amend workmen's compensation.	Passed
1948	Arkansas	DA	41	Taxes	Abolition of state property tax.	Failed
1948	California	DA	12	Alcohol Regulation	To provide for local control and enforcement of intoxicating liquors.	Failed
1948	California	DA	13	Apportionment/Redistricting	To provide for reapportionment of Senate, requires 1949 Legislature to reapportion Senate Districts according to population shown by 1940 census.	Failed
1948	California	DA	14	Housing	To create state Housing Agency and authorizes state to guarantee obligations of, and furnish operating subsidies to, public housing authorities.	Failed
1948	California	DS	15	Environmental Reform	Prohibits use of purse nets and round haul nets for fishing in ocean and tide waters of the state south of line extending due west from Point San Simeon in San Luis Obispo County.	Failed
1948	California	DA	2	Alcohol Regulation	To provide for local control of intoxicating liquors.	Failed
1948	California	DS	3	Utility Regulation	Empowers Public Utilities Commission to prescribe number of brakemen to be used on railroad trains. Prohibits feather-bed practices in employment of railroad brakemen on trains.	Passed
1948	California	DA	4	Welfare	Increases maximum aid from $60 to $75 monthly for aged persons, and from $75 to $85 for blind persons and increases income and property exemptions	Passed
1948	California	DS	6	Animal Rights	Prohibits use of nets, traps, set lines, or other appliances in commercial fishing in fish and game districts in San Francisco Bay.	Failed
1948	Colorado	DA	3	Alcohol Regulation	Political subdivisions may adopt and thereafter modify or repeal local option proposals prohibiting the sale of alcoholic and fermented malt beverages.	Failed
1948	Colorado	DA	4	Welfare	Providing for a guaranteed minimum $55 per month old age pension and for the allocation and earmarking of certain moneys and excise taxes to pay the same.	Failed
1948	Massachusetts	IDS	Question 5	Labor	Open shop.	Failed
1948	Massachusetts	IDS	Question 6	Labor	Election of union officers.	Failed
1948	Massachusetts	IDS	Question 7	Labor	Regulation of strikes.	Failed
1948	Michigan	DA	N/A	Taxes	Modify 15 mill limitation.	Passed
1948	Nebraska	DS	N/A	Veteran Affairs	Soldier's bonus.	Failed
1948	North Dakota	DS	N/A	Alcohol Regulation	Repealing the law that prohibits sale of alcoholic beverages where commodities other than tobacco and soft drinks are sold.	Failed
1948	North Dakota	DS	N/A	Education	Prohibiting the wearing of religious dress by public school teachers.	Passed
1948	North Dakota	DS	N/A	Administration of Government	Legalizing parking meters in political subdivisions.	Failed
1948	North Dakota	DS	N/A	Administration of Government	Prohibiting parking meters in state political subdivisions.	Passed

Year	State	Type	Measure Number	Subject Matter	Description	Pass/Fail
1948	Oregon	DS	10	Animal Rights	Prohibiting salmon fishing in Columbia river with fixed appliances.	Passed
1948	Oregon	DA	5	Election Reform	Fixing qualifications of voters in school elections.	Passed
1948	Oregon	DS	6	Welfare	Relative to old age pensions.	Passed
1948	Oregon	DS	7	Taxes	Increasing personal income tax exemptions.	Passed
1948	Oregon	DS	8	Alcohol Regulation	Oregon liquor dispensing licensing act.	Failed
1948	Oregon	DA	9	Veteran Affairs	World War II veterans' bonus.	Failed
1948	South Dakota	IDS	N/A	Alcohol Regulation	To prohibit the sale of liquor where food is sold.	Failed
1948	Washington	IDS	I-13	Alcohol Regulation	Restricting sales of Beer and Wine to State Liquor Stores.	Failed
1948	Washington	DS	I-169	Veteran Affairs	Providing Bonus to Veterans of World War [State Supreme Court ruled measure unconstitutional Feb. 4, 1949. A similar measure was passed into law by the 1949 Legislature.].	Passed
1948	Washington	DS	I-171	Alcohol Regulation	Providing liquor by the drink with certain restrictions.	Passed
1948	Washington	DS	I-172	Administration of Government	Relating to Liberalization of Social Security Laws.	Passed
1949	California	DS	12	Daylight Savings Time	To provide for daylight saving time from the last Sunday in April until the last Sunday in September, annually.	Passed
1949	California	DA	2	Welfare	To reinstate plan of Old Age Security and Aid to Blind, except next maximum aid payments are retained at present level.	Passed
1949	Ohio	IDS	Issue No. 1	Business Regulation	To permit the manufacture and sale of colored oleomargarine.	Passed
1949	Ohio	DA	Issue No. 2	Election Reform	Providing that electors of the state of Ohio may vote for candidates only by separately indicating their vote for each candidate.	Passed
1949	Oklahoma	DA	325	Administration of Government	Creating a four member highway commission of not exceeding two members from any political party nor one from any congressional district members to be appointed by Governor.	Failed
1950	Arizona	DA	N/A	Education	State Board of Education.	Failed
1950	Arizona	DA	N/A	Administration of Government	Merit system, public employees.	Failed
1950	Arizona	DS	N/A	Civil Rights	Segregation in schools.	Failed
1950	Arizona	DS	N/A	Administration of Government	Employment security, agricultural workers.	Failed
1950	Arizona	DS	N/A	Labor	Employment security, extend benefits.	Failed
1950	Arizona	DS	N/A	Alcohol Regulation	Local option, liquor.	Failed
1950	Arizona	DA	N/A	Education	Education — maintenance of kindergartens.	Failed
1950	Arizona	DS	N/A	Administration of Government	Merit system for peace officers.	Failed
1950	Arizona	DS	N/A	Taxes	Excise tax, increase.	Failed
1950	Arizona	DS	N/A	Gaming	Legalized gambling.	Failed
1950	Arizona	DS	N/A	Labor	Workmen's compensation — to limit compensation.	Failed
1950	Arizona	DS	N/A	Welfare	Social security and welfare reform and regulation.	Failed
1950	Arkansas	DS	1	Animal Rights	General statewide stock law. Unlawful for livestock to run at large	Passed
1950	Arkansas	DS	2	Alcohol Regulation	Statewide prohibition	Failed
1950	Arkansas	DA	41	Education	Public school finance	Failed
1950	Arkansas	DA	44	Administration of Government	4 year term for state and County officers	Failed
1950	California	DA	1	Taxes	To prohibit state and its political subdivision from imposing taxes upon personal property, tangible or intangible.	Failed

Year	State	Type	Measure Number	Subject Matter	Description	Pass/Fail
1950	California	DA	10	Housing	To require approval of majority of electors of County or city, voting at an election, as prerequisites for establishment of any low-rent housing project by the state or County, city district.	Passed
1950	California	DA	6	Gaming	To permit wagering and gambling to licensed establishments.	Failed
1950	Colorado	DA	3	Administration of Government	Concerning civil service and providing for additional exemptions there from of governor's staff.	Failed
1950	Massachusetts	IDS	Question 3	Welfare	Payments to blind persons who are 63 years of age or older.	Passed
1950	Massachusetts	IDS	Question 4	Gaming	Establishing state lottery.	Failed
1950	Massachusetts	IDS	Question 5	Business Regulation	Compulsory motor vehicle insurance classifications.	Failed
1950	Michigan	DA	N/A	Business Regulation	To permit the sale of oleomargarine.	Passed
1950	Montana	DS	I 54	Administration of Government	Military honorarium.	Passed
1950	North Dakota	DA	N/A	Taxes	Permitting the enactment of a graduated land tax.	Failed
1950	North Dakota	DS	N/A	Taxes	Increasing personal exemption on state income tax and establishing the basis for computing tax on joint returns.	Failed
1950	North Dakota	DS	N/A	Alcohol Regulation	Permitting municipal and County option on sale of liquor.	Failed
1950	Oklahoma	DA	326	Taxes	Prohibits the diversion of any highway users' revenue, including gasoline taxes, registration fees and operators' licenses, in excess of the cost of collection and administration.	Failed
1950	Oregon	DA	7	Veteran Affairs	World War II veterans' compensation fund.	Passed
1950	Oregon	DA	8	Apportionment/Redistricting	Legislative representation reapportionment.	Failed
1950	Oregon	DS	9	Alcohol Regulation	Making sale of promotively advertised alcoholic beverage unlawful.	Failed
1950	South Dakota	IDS	N/A	Alcohol Regulation	Prohibit sale of liquor where food is sold.	Failed
1950	Washington	DS	I-176	Welfare	Increasing to $65 monthly the minimum grant for certain categories of public assistance, otherwise extending the social security program, and making appropriation.	Failed
1950	Washington	DS	I-178	Health/Medical	Modifying the Citizens' Security Act of 1948 and transferring the public assistance medical program to the State Department of Health.	Passed
1952	Arizona	DS	N/A	Labor	Labor organizations — secondary picketing.	Passed
1952	California	DA	10	Administration of Government	Prohibits appropriation or expenditure of public money to California State Chamber of Commerce, local chamber or commerce and County Supervisors Association.	Failed
1952	California	IDS	11	Welfare	Place old age security program under state administration; terminates County administration, eliminates County share of costs.	Failed
1952	California	IDS	13	Election Reform	To provide that no person shall be a candidate or nominee of a political party for any office unless he has been registered as affiliated with such party for at least three months prior to filing nominating papers.	Failed
1952	California	DA	2	Education	Increases required state support for public schools to $180 per year per pupil.	Passed
1952	Colorado	DA	4	Taxes	Providing for a severance tax on certain petroleum products and natural gas.	Failed
1952	Colorado	DA	6	Gaming	Legalizing slot machines except where prohibited by local ordinance.	Failed

Year	State	Type	Measure Number	Subject Matter	Description	Pass/Fail
1952	Colorado	DS	N/A	Labor	Making it unlawful for any municipality to employ firemen more than 60 hours a week, with certain exceptions.	Failed
1952	Michigan	DA	N/A	Apportionment/Redistricting	Establishing senatorial districts and providing decennial reapportionment of representatives by legislatures.	Passed
1952	Michigan	DA	N/A	Apportionment/Redistricting	To provide for decennial reapportionment of senate and house of representatives by secretary of state.	Failed
1952	Montana	DS	I 55	Taxes	Tax on gasoline.	Failed
1952	Nevada	IDS	N/A	Labor	Right-to-work law.	Passed
1952	North Dakota	DS	N/A	Alcohol Regulation	Setting hours of operation of liquor establishments between 8 a.m. and 10:30pm.	Failed
1952	North Dakota	DS	N/A	Banking Reform	Requiring clearance of all checks by banks without fee for cashing checks.	Failed
1952	North Dakota	DS	N/A	Taxes	Exempting food and drugs from state sales tax.	Passed
1952	Oklahoma	DS	349	Taxes	Increase the tax rate from 2% to 3% upon the gross proceeds of sales to consumers or users.	Failed
1952	Oregon	DS	13	Daylight Savings Time	Standard time initiative.	Passed
1952	Oregon	DA	14	Gaming	Pari-mutual betting prohibition.	Failed
1952	Oregon	DA	15	Alcohol Regulation	Liquor by the drink sales.	Passed
1952	Oregon	DA	16	Taxes	Motor carrier tax decrease.	Failed
1952	Oregon	DS	17	Business Regulation	Milk control bill.	Failed
1952	Oregon	DA	18	Apportionment/Redistricting	Legislative reapportionment.	Passed
1952	Utah	DS	A	Welfare	To repeal the welfare "Lien Law."	Failed
1952	Washington	DS	I-180	Business Regulation	Authorizing the manufacture, sale and use of colored oleomargarine.	Passed
1952	Washington	DS	I-181	Daylight Savings Time	Prescribing the Observance of Standard Time.	Passed
1952	Washington	DS	I-184	Welfare	Relative to old age pensions.	Failed
1954	California	DA	4	Welfare	To increase monthly aid payments to aged persons who meet eligibility requirements (from $80 to $100).	Failed
1954	Colorado	DA	8	Administration of Government	Providing for four-year terms of office for certain County officers. (Art. 14, Sec. 8)	Passed
1954	Idaho	DS	1	Environmental Reform	The Dredge Mining Initiative Proposal.	Passed
1954	Michigan	DA	N/A	Gaming	Permit the legislature to authorize charitable lotteries.	Failed
1954	Nevada	IDS	N/A	Labor	To repeal the right-to-work law.	Failed
1954	North Dakota	DS	N/A	Taxes	Providing for an additional one cent non-refundable motor vehicle fuel tax for secondary highways.	Failed
1954	North Dakota	DS	N/A	Alcohol Regulation	Setting hours of liquor establishments between 8 a.m. and 11 p.m.	Failed
1954	North Dakota	DS	N/A	Taxes	Exempting food from the sales tax.	Failed
1954	North Dakota	DA	N/A	Taxes	Permitting the enactment of a graduated land tax.	Failed
1954	North Dakota	DS	N/A	Taxes	Diverting sales tax collected on automobiles from school and welfare funds to highway construction.	Failed
1954	North Dakota	DS	N/A	Campaign Finance Reform	Prohibiting members of the Legislature from doing over $10,000 worth of business annually with the state or its political subdivisions.	Passed
1954	Oregon	DS	6	Daylight Savings Time	Establishing Daylight Saving Time.	Failed
1954	Oregon	DS	7	Animal Rights	Prohibiting certain fishing in coastal streams.	Failed

Year	State	Type	Measure Number	Subject Matter	Description	Pass/Fail
1954	Oregon	DS	8	Business Regulation	Repealing milk control law.	Passed
1954	Washington	DS	I-188	Business Regulation	Raising standards for chiropractic examinations.	Failed
1954	Washington	DS	I-192	Environmental Reform	Regulation of Commercial Salmon Fishing.	Failed
1954	Washington	DS	I-193	Daylight Savings Time	Statewide Daylight Saving Time.	Failed
1954	Washington	DS	I-194	Alcohol Regulation	Restricting television alcoholic beverage advertising.	Failed
1955	North Dakota	DS	N/A	Education	Providing for state loan fund for college students with $1 million from profits of the Bank of North Dakota.	Passed
1955	Ohio	IDS	Issue No. 1	Labor	To increase unemployment compensation.	Failed
1956	Arizona	DS	N/A	Administration of Government	Pre-marital blood test.	Passed
1956	Arkansas	DS	1	Labor	To increase Workmen's Compensation.	Passed
1956	Arkansas	DS	2	Education	School pupil assignment law.	Passed
1956	Arkansas	DA	45	Civil Rights	Abolition of poll tax	Failed
1956	Arkansas	DA	46	Judicial Reform	To provide the General Assembly with the authority to set by law the amount and method of payment of salaries and expenses of the Supreme Court, Circuit Courts and Chancery Courts.	Passed
1956	Arkansas	DA	47	Civil Rights	To cause the General Assembly to take appropriate action and pass laws opposing in every Constitutional manner the unconstitutional desegregation decisions of May 17, 1954, and May 3, 1955, of the U.S. Supreme Court.	Passed
1956	Arkansas	DA	48	Apportionment/Redistricting	An amendment to preserve present apportionment of state senators and existing state senatorial districts.	Passed
1956	Arkansas	DA	49	Gaming	Prohibition of horse and racing betting.	Failed
1956	Arkansas	DA	50	Gaming	To provide that horse racing and pari-mutuel wagering there on shall be lawful in Hot Springs, Garland County, and shall be regulated by the General Assembly.	Passed
1956	Arkansas	DA	51	Banking Reform	Sets maximum interest rates.	Failed
1956	California	DS	4	Environmental Reform	To prohibit waste, defined as production methods which reduce maximum economic quantity of oil or gas ultimately recoverable by good engineering practices.	Failed
1956	Colorado	DA	4	Apportionment/Redistricting	Providing for apportionment of members of the general assembly.	Failed
1956	Colorado	DA	5	Welfare	Revising the old age pension article; establishing a monthly award of $100 to be adjusted to increased living costs; providing for a stabilization fund of $5 million.	Passed
1956	Nebraska	DS	N/A	Taxes	Ton mile tax.	Failed
1956	Nevada	DA	N/A	Labor	Prohibit "right-to-work laws."	Failed
1956	Nevada	IDS	N/A	Education	Relating to the question of public school financing.	Failed
1956	Nevada	IDS	N/A	Labor	To repeal the right-to-work law.	Failed
1956	North Dakota	DA	N/A	Term Limits	Removing 2-term limitation on office of County treasurer.	Passed
1956	Oklahoma	DS	357	Apportionment/Redistricting	An Act to divide the state into 6 new congressional districts with populations according to the 1950 federal decennial census as follows.	Passed
1956	Oklahoma	DA	377	Administration of Government	Creating the County offices of County Attorney, County Clerk, Sheriff, County Treasurer, County Surveyor, County Assessor and County Superintendent of Schools.	Failed

Year	State	Type	Measure Number	Subject Matter	Description	Pass/Fail
1956	Oregon	DS	7	Animal Rights	Prohibiting certain fishing in control streams.	Passed
1956	Washington	DS	I-198	Labor	Affecting Employer-Employee Relations.	Failed
1956	Washington	DS	I-199	Apportionment/Redistricting	Legislative Reapportionment and Redistricting. [In 1957 the Legislature extensively amended this act by passing Chapter 289, Laws of 1947 by two-thirds approval of both branches of the Legislature.]	Passed
1957	Oklahoma	DA	376	Alcohol Regulation	Authorize County option and the holding of special elections in and by counties at County expense not more often than every two years, to prohibit or permit beverages containing more than 1/2 of 1% of alcohol by volume.	Failed
1958	Arizona	DS	N/A	Administration of Government	Merit system, public employees.	Failed
1958	Arizona	DS	N/A	Education	Revises laws pertaining to Arizona State University.	Passed
1958	Arkansas	DS	1	Labor	Repeal full crew laws.	Failed
1958	California	DA	16	Taxes	To amend Constitution by providing that school property, religious and other nonprofit organizations be exempted from taxation.	Failed
1958	California	DS	17	Taxes	Reduces sales and use tax rate from 3% to 2%. Changes income tax rates to new range of 1/2% on incomes over $50,000.	Failed
1958	California	DA	18	Labor	Prohibits employers and employee organizations from entering into collective bargaining which establish labor organization membership, or payment of dues or charges of any kind thereto, as an entry condition.	Failed
1958	Colorado	DA	1	Labor	"Right-to-work" amendment; providing that no person shall be denied the freedom to obtain or retain employment because of membership or non-membership in any labor union or labor organization.	Failed
1958	Colorado	DA	4	Gaming	Legalizing the conduct of games of chance (limited to bingo, lotto, or raffles) by certain organizations which operate without profit to dues paying members.	Passed
1958	Idaho	DS	1	Labor	Right to employment regardless of labor organization membership or non-membership.	Failed
1958	Massachusetts	IDS	Question 1	Administration of Government	Public employee pensions.	Passed
1958	Missouri	DS	N/A	Banking Reform	To permit banking institutions, upon prior approval of the Commissioner of Finance, to establish and operate branches within the city, town, County, village, or constitutional charter city in which its principal office is located.	Failed
1958	Nebraska	DA	N/A	Utility Regulation	Public Power Districts, in lieu of taxes.	Passed
1958	Nebraska	DA	N/A	Gaming	Legalizing bingo.	Passed
1958	Nevada	DA	N/A	Initiative and Referendum	To amend Sec. 3, Art. 19 of the Constitution which would make the requirements to commence and carry through an initiative more strict.	Passed
1958	North Dakota	DS	N/A	Education	Requiring the reorganization of school districts not operating high schools and providing for their annexation to districts operating high schools.	Failed
1958	North Dakota	DS	N/A	Education	Providing $450,000 to move the school for the blind from Pembina County to a location near Grand Forks.	Passed
1958	North Dakota	DA	N/A	Administration of Government	Permitting changing the name of the North Dakota Agriculture College to the North Dakota State University of Agriculture and Applied Sciences.	Failed

Year	State	Type	Measure Number	Subject Matter	Description	Pass/Fail
1958	Ohio	DA	Issue No. 2	Labor	To forbid labor contracts which established union membership as a condition for continuing employment (called "right-to-work").	Failed
1958	Oregon	DS	13	Administration of Government	Persons eligible to serve in legislature.	Passed
1958	Utah	DS	A	Gaming	To permit pari-mutuel wagering at horse racing meets and create a state racing commission.	Failed
1958	Washington	DS	I-202	Labor	Restricting Labor Agreements.	Failed
1958	Washington	IDS	I-23	Administration of Government	Civil service for sheriff's employees.	Passed
1960	Alaska	IDS	N/A	Administration of Government	To move the state capitol from Juneau to Anchorage.	Failed
1960	Arizona	DS	N/A	Taxes	Revenue and taxation; increasing cities' share of sales tax.	Passed
1960	Arizona	DA	N/A	Judicial Reform	Revision of state court systems.	Passed
1960	Arkansas	DS	1	Labor	Minimum wage and overtime act.	Failed
1960	California	DA	15	Apportionment/Redistricting	To provide for reapportionment of senate and limiting the number of senatorial districts per County; provides for legislature to reapportion after each Census.	Failed
1960	Colorado	DA	3	Environmental Reform	Creates a wildlife management commission and a department of wildlife conservation.	Failed
1960	Colorado	DS	4	Daylight Savings Time	Providing for and establishing Daylight Saving Time.	Failed
1960	Colorado	DA	6	Taxes	Authorizing general assembly to vest in counties, cities and towns, the power to impose a retail sales and use tax for local purposes on tangible personal property, except drugs, and food for off-premises consumption.	Failed
1960	Colorado	DA	7	Administration of Government	Authorizing governor, with consent of Senate, to appoint administrative officers of certain departments, to be excluded from civil service.	Failed
1960	Nebraska	DA	N/A	Administration of Government	Commissioner of Education, election of.	Failed
1960	Nevada	DA	N/A	Administration of Government	Require the legislature to meet in regular session once each 2 years, in odd-numbered years, instead of once each year.	Passed
1960	North Dakota	DA	N/A	Administration of Government	Changing the name of the North Dakota Agriculture College to the North Dakota State University of Agriculture and Applied Sciences.	Passed
1960	Oklahoma	DA	396	Administration of Government	Creating a constitutional State Highway Commission to develop and plan a state-wide road program.	Failed
1960	Oklahoma	DA	397	Apportionment/Redistricting	Providing for legislative apportionment by a commission composed of the Attorney General, State Treasurer and Secretary of State.	Failed
1960	Oklahoma	DS	398	Administration of Government	Providing for each County to determine whether it shall transfer the construction and maintenance of County roads to Sate Highway Commission.	Failed
1960	Oregon	DS	15	Environmental Reform	Billboard control.	Failed
1960	Utah	DS	A	Administration of Government	To establish merit systems and merit system commissions in the counties of the State of Utah for the qualification, employment and tenure of Deputy Sheriffs.	Passed
1960	Washington	DS	I-205	Alcohol Regulation	Authorizing tavern spirituous liquor licenses.	Failed
1960	Washington	DS	I-207	Administration of Government	Civil Service for State Employees.	Passed
1960	Washington	DS	I-208	Housing	Authorizing Joint Tenancies in Property.	Passed
1960	Washington	DS	I-210	Daylight Savings Time	Statewide Daylight Saving Time.	Passed
1960	Washington	IDS	I-25	Administration of Government	Dam construction and water diversion measure.	Passed
1962	Alaska	IDS	N/A	Administration of Government	To relocate the state Capitol.	Failed

Year	State	Type	Measure Number	Subject Matter	Description	Pass/Fail
1962	Arizona	DS	N/A	Taxes	Property taxation reappraisal.	Failed
1962	Arizona	DA	N/A	Business Regulation	Real estate agents may prepare instruments.	Passed
1962	Arkansas	DS	1	Education	Provide 50% of general revenues for public school fund.	Failed
1962	Arkansas	DA	53	Education	Teacher retirement fund.	Failed
1962	Arkansas	DA	54	Election Reform	Permit use of voting machines.	Passed
1962	California	DA	23	Apportionment/Redistricting	Establishes and apportions 50 (instead of existing 40) senatorial districts and limits the number of districts which a County could have.	Failed
1962	California	DA	24	Election Reform	Declares existence, purposes, and objectives of world communist movement; defines communist and subversive organizations and denies them political party status and any tax exemption.	Failed
1962	Colorado	DA	7	Apportionment/Redistricting	An act providing for the apportionment of the Senate and House of Representatives of the General Assembly.	Passed
1962	Colorado	DA	8	Apportionment/Redistricting	Providing for reapportionment of the general assembly.	Failed
1962	Michigan	DA	N/A	Constitutional Convention	Relative to calling constitutional convention.	Passed
1962	Nevada	DA	N/A	Initiative and Referendum	Make changes to the state's initiative and referendum laws.	Passed
1962	North Dakota	DS	N/A	Election Reform	Providing for a secret primary election ballot instead of requiring voters to only declare party preference at the polls.	Passed
1962	North Dakota	DA	N/A	Administration of Government	Changing terms of office for the most County officials from two to four years.	Passed
1962	North Dakota	DA	N/A	Bonds	Allowing the state to bond itself to make loans to companies desiring to establish power generating facilities.	Passed
1962	Ohio	DA	Issue No. 1	Business Regulation	To limit the power of the State to forbid the sale of certain goods and services on Sunday.	Failed
1962	Oklahoma	DA	408	Apportionment/Redistricting	Providing method for enforcement of the present constitutional formula apportioning members of the House of Representatives and Senate, vesting this duty in the Attorney General, Secretary of State and State Treasurer.	Passed
1962	Oregon	DA	8	Apportionment/Redistricting	Legislative apportionment.	Failed
1962	Oregon	DS	9	Education	To repeal school district reorganization law.	Failed
1962	Washington	DS	I-211	Apportionment/Redistricting	State Legislature Reapportionment and Redistricting.	Failed
1964	Arizona	DS	N/A	Utility Regulation	Railroads; eliminating featherbedding.	Passed
1964	Arizona	DA	N/A	Education	Apportionment of state school funds.	Passed
1964	Arizona	DA	N/A	Term Limits	County officers, 4 year terms.	Passed
1964	Arizona	DA	N/A	Taxes	Inventories exempt from taxation.	Passed
1964	Arkansas	DA	54	Civil Rights	To provide for voter registration system without payment of poll tax.	Passed
1964	Arkansas	DA	55	Gaming	Allow wagering in Garland County	Failed
1964	Arkansas	DA	56	Administration of Government	Establish salaries for County Officials	Failed
1964	Arkansas	DA	57	Education	To provide for the creation of community college districts.	Passed
1964	California	DA	14	Civil Rights	Prohibits state, subdivision, or agency thereof from denying, limiting, or abridging right of any person to decline to sell, lease, or rent residential real property to any person as he chooses.	Passed

Year	State	Type	Measure Number	Subject Matter	Description	Pass/Fail
1964	California	DS	15	Utility Regulation	Declares it contrary to public policy to permit development of subscription television business. Provides no charge shall be made to public for television programs transmitted to home television sets.	Passed
1964	California	DA	16	Gaming	Provides for statewide lottery with monthly drawings.	Failed
1964	California	DS	17	Utility Regulation	Declares state policy on manning trains.	Passed
1964	Massachusetts	IDS	Question 5	Administration of Government	Reducing powers of Governor's Executive Council.	Passed
1964	Nebraska	DA	N/A	Education	Commissioner of Education, election of.	Failed
1964	North Dakota	DS	N/A	Utility Regulation	Requiring daily mixed passenger-freight trains by railroads.	Failed
1964	North Dakota	DS	N/A	Utility Regulation	Requiring 5-man crew on trains over one-half mile long and switching in municipalities.	Failed
1964	North Dakota	DS	N/A	Utility Regulation	Repealing statute requiring certain number of crew members on freight trains and self-propelled equipment.	Passed
1964	North Dakota	DS	N/A	Alcohol Regulation	Permitting sale of alcoholic beverages in eating establishments under certain circumstances.	Passed
1964	North Dakota	DA	N/A	Taxes	Exempt personal property from taxation.	Failed
1964	North Dakota	DA	N/A	Administration of Government	Changing two-year terms to four-year terms for most state officials and the County superintendent of schools.	Passed
1964	Oklahoma	DA	409	Labor	Providing that no person shall be denied the freedom to obtain or retain employment because of membership or non-membership in any labor union or labor organization.	Failed
1964	Oklahoma	DA	421	Education	Abolishing authorization for emergency levy for school districts, and authorizing a local support levy for benefit of schools of a school district of not to exceed 15 mills.	Passed
1964	Oklahoma	DS	422	Education	Relating to the payment of State Aid to school districts; increasing allowance in minimum program of school districts for certain items of expenditures fixing basis for calculation for teachers' salaries.	Failed
1964	Oklahoma	DS	423	Education	Shall a bill relating to school districts; providing for disorganization of school districts not maintaining 12 years of accredited instruction and annexation of territory.	Failed
1964	Oklahoma	DS	424	Education	Relating to County superintendents of schools; providing County superintendents shall conduct joint programs for school districts when requested to do so, and prescribing manner of payment of cost thereof.	Failed
1964	Oregon	DS	3	Labor	Amending State workmen's compensation law.	Failed
1964	Oregon	DS	4	Animal Rights	Prohibiting commercial fishing salmon, steelhead.	Failed
1964	Washington	DS	I-215	Environmental Reform	Marine Recreation Land Act.	Passed
1965	North Dakota	DS	N/A	Taxes	Increasing sales tax from 2 1/4% to 3%.	Failed
1965	North Dakota	DS	N/A	Taxes	Exempting personal property from taxation.	Failed
1965	Ohio	IDS	Issue No. 1	Education	To amend the school foundation program and to increase taxes to support it.	Failed
1966	Arkansas	DS	1	Education	School district reorganization.	Failed
1966	California	DS	16	Legal	Declares state policy is to prohibit obscene matter and conduct.	Failed

Year	State	Type	Measure Number	Subject Matter	Description	Pass/Fail
1966	Colorado	DA	3	Administration of Government	Selection, tenure and removal of justics.	Passed
1966	Colorado	DA	4	Administration of Government	Provide for 35 member senate and 65 member house.	Passed
1966	Colorado	DA	5	Taxes	Establish property tax limitations.	Failed
1966	Nebraska	DA	N/A	Taxes	Property tax, termination of.	Passed
1966	North Dakota	DS	N/A	Education	Requiring publication of school board proceedings in newspaper.	Passed
1966	Washington	DS	I-226	Administration of Government	Cities Sharing Sales — Use Taxes.	Failed
1966	Washington	DS	I-229	Business Regulation	Repealing Sunday Activities Blue Law.	Passed
1966	Washington	DS	I-233	Utility Regulation	Repealing Freight Train Crew Law.	Passed
1968	Arkansas	DS	1	Labor	Amend Workmen's Compensation Law	Passed
1968	California	DA	9	Taxes	Provides that total ad valorem tax burden on all property be limited after July 1, 1969 to 1% of market value for property-related services plus 80% of base cost of people-related services.	Failed
1968	Massachusetts	IDS	Question 4	Constitutional Convention	Question regarding popular constitutional convention.	Passed
1968	Montana	DS	I 66	Taxes	To reduce taxable valuation of certain personal property including stocks of merchandise.	Failed
1968	Nevada	DA	N/A	Gaming	Repeal prohibition on establishing a lottery.	Failed
1968	North Dakota	DA	N/A	Gaming	Authorizing certain kinds of betting.	Failed
1968	Oklahoma	DA	441	Judicial Reform	Creating a judicial department; vesting judicial power; providing for the establishment, organization and jurisdiction of the court; the nomination, selection and compensation.	Failed
1968	Oregon	DA	6	Bonds	Bond issue to acquire ocean beaches.	Failed
1968	Oregon	DA	7	Taxes	Constitutional amendment changing property tax limitation.	Failed
1968	Utah	DS	A	Alcohol Regulation	Liquor initiative.	Failed
1968	Washington	DS	I-242	Legal	Drivers' Implied consent — Intoxication Tests.	Passed
1968	Washington	DS	I-245	Banking Reform	Reducing maximum retain service charges.	Passed
1968	Washington	IDS	I-32	Environmental Reform	Local processing of State timber.	Failed
1969	Nebraska	DA	N/A	Taxes	Income tax, prohibit.	Failed
1970	Arizona	DS	N/A	Gaming	Establishing the Arizona sweepstakes lottery.	Failed
1970	Arkansas	DS	1	Labor	An Act to repeal the Full Crew Laws.	Failed
1970	California	DA	8	Education	Requires state provide from sources other than property taxes not less than 50% of costs for public schools, exclusive of capital outlay and federal funds, and 90% of costs for social welfare services.	Failed
1970	Idaho	DS	1	Administration of Government	Legislative Pay.	Passed
1970	North Dakota	DS	N/A	Administration of Government	Repealing the law relating to the Combined Law Enforcement Council.	Failed
1970	Oregon	DA	10	Taxes	New property bases for schools.	Failed
1970	Oregon	DA	11	Environmental Reform	Restricts governmental powers over rural property.	Failed
1970	Oregon	DS	9	Environmental Reform	Scenic waterways bill.	Passed
1970	South Dakota	IDS	1	Health/Medical	To require fluoridation.	Failed
1970	South Dakota	IDS	2	Taxes	Income tax.	Failed
1970	Washington	DS	I-251	Taxes	State Taxation — To Regulate Imposition.	Failed
1970	Washington	DS	I-256	Environmental Reform	Prohibiting certain nonrefundable beverage receptacles.	Failed
1971	Maine	IDS	N/A	Taxes	To repeal the income tax.	Failed

Year	State	Type	Measure Number	Subject Matter	Description	Pass/Fail
1971	Oklahoma	DS	478	Business Regulation	Making it unlawful to sell certain enumerated merchandise on the consecutive days of Saturday and Sunday at the same location.	Failed
1972	Arizona	DS	N/A	Taxes	Preemption by the state of income and luxury taxation.	Passed
1972	Arkansas	DS	1	Labor	An Act to repeal railroad crew laws and to protect present employees.	Passed
1972	California	DA	14	Taxes	Establishes ad valorem property tax rate limitations for all purposes except payment of designated types of debts and liabilities.	Failed
1972	California	DA	15	Administration of Government	Requires state Personnel Board, University of California Regents and state University and College Trustees semi-annually to determine prevailing rates in private and public employment.	Failed
1972	California	DA	16	Administration of Government	Requires state Personnel Board to determine maximum salary for each class of policemen or deputy sheriff in each city and County within state.	Failed
1972	California	DA	17	Death Penalty	To provide that all state statutes in effect Feb. 17, 1972 requiring, authorizing, imposing, or relating to death penalty are in full force and effect.	Passed
1972	California	DS	18	Legal	Redefines obscenity, removes "redeeming social importance" defense, etc.	Failed
1972	California	DS	19	Drug Policy Reform	Proposes a law that no person 18 years or older shall be punished criminally or denied any right or privilege because of his planting, cultivating, harvesting, drying and processing marijuana.	Failed
1972	California	DS	20	Environmental Reform	Creates Coastal Zone Conservation Commission and 6 regional commissions.	Passed
1972	California	DS	21	Civil Rights	No public school student shall, because of his race, creed, or color, be assigned to or be required to attend a particular school.	Passed
1972	California	DS	22	Labor	Sets forth permissible and prohibited labor relation activities of agricultural employers, employees, and labor organizations.	Failed
1972	California	DS	9	Environmental Reform	Specifies permissible composition and quality of gasoline and other fuel for internal combustion engines.	Failed
1972	Colorado	DS	10	Utility Regulation	An Act to protect the consumer of public utility services by defining just and reasonable rates, by creating an Office of Public Consumer Counsel.	Failed
1972	Colorado	DS	11	Business Regulation	Establishing a system of compulsory insurance and compensation irrespective of fault for victims of motor vehicle accidents, setting forth the basis for recovery.	Failed
1972	Colorado	DA	12	Taxes	Replacement of property taxes for school financing.	Failed
1972	Colorado	DA	6	Gaming	An act to amend the Constitution to provide for a privately operated lottery, supervised and regulated by the Department of State and granting an exclusive original ten year license to the United States Sweepstakes Corporation.	Failed
1972	Colorado	DA	8	Taxes	An Act to Amend Art. 10 and 11 to prohibit the state from levying taxes and appropriating or loaning funds for the purpose of aiding or furthering the 1976 Winter Olympic Games.	Passed
1972	Colorado	DS	9	Campaign Finance Reform	Require that public officials disclose their private interests and that all lobbyists register and file periodic informational statements.	Passed

Year	State	Type	Measure Number	Subject Matter	Description	Pass/Fail
1972	Colorado	DA	N/A	Taxes	Establishing a maximum limitation of one and one-half percent of the actual value on the annual taxation of property except as permitted by a vote of the qualified electors.	Failed
1972	Maine	IDS	N/A	Election Reform	To change form of ballot from party column to office type.	Passed
1972	Michigan	DA	N/A	Daylight Savings Time	Proposal to change Michigan to Daylight Saving Time.	Passed
1972	Michigan	DA	N/A	Abortion	Proposal to allow abortion under certain conditions.	Failed
1972	North Dakota	DS	N/A	Abortion	To allow physicians to terminate pregnancy if certain per-conditions are present.	Failed
1972	Ohio	DA	Issue No. 1	Taxes	Conditions for and prohibitions upon the levy of a tax on income except a municipal income tax, or increasing the rates thereof, without the approval of a majority of the voting electors.	Failed
1972	Oklahoma	DA	480	Alcohol Regulation	Permitting the sale of intoxicating alcoholic beverages by individual drink for on premise consumption.	Failed
1972	Oregon	DA	7	Administration of Government	Repeals Governor's Retirement Act.	Passed
1972	Oregon	DA	8	Administration of Government	Changes succession to Office of Governor.	Passed
1972	Oregon	DA	9	Education	Prohibits property tax for school operations.	Failed
1972	South Dakota	IDS	1	Animal Rights	Prohibit mourning dove hunting	Passed
1972	Washington	DS	I-258	Gaming	Certain Cities — Greyhound Racing Franchises.	Failed
1972	Washington	DS	I-261	Alcohol Regulation	Liquor sales by licensed retailers.	Failed
1972	Washington	DS	I-276	Campaign Finance Reform	Establishes disclosure laws and other campaign finance regulations.	Passed
1972	Washington	IDS	I-40	Environmental Reform	Litter Control Act.	Passed
1972	Washington	IDS	I-43	Environmental Reform	Regulating Shoreline Use and Development.	Passed
1972	Washington	IDS	I-44	Taxes	Statutory Tax Limitation — 20 Mills.	Passed
1973	California	DA	1	Taxes	Limits state expenditures; restricts use of defined surplus revenue to tax reductions, refunds or emergencies. Constitutionally eliminates personal income tax for lower income persons.	Failed
1973	Maine	IDS	N/A	Utility Regulation	To create Power Authority of Maine.	Failed
1973	North Dakota	DA	N/A	Apportionment/Redistricting	Requiring that the state be divided into individual Senate Districts and House sub-districts by an appointed nine-member commission.	Failed
1973	Washington	DS	I-282	Administration of Government	Shall state elected officials' salary increases be limited to 5.5% over 1965 levels, and judges' the same over 1972 levels?	Passed
1974	Alaska	IDS	N/A	Campaign Finance Reform	To require full disclosure of personal finances of candidates and holders of state office.	Passed
1974	Alaska	IDS	N/A	Administration of Government	Relocating and constructing a new Capitol.	Passed
1974	Arizona	DA	N/A	Judicial Reform	Relating to the Judicial Department.	Passed
1974	Arkansas	DA	57	Banking Reform	Authorize legislature to fix maximum rate of interest.	Failed
1974	California	DS	17	Environmental Reform	Designates specified portions of the main stem of the Stanislaus River as components of the CaliforniaWild and Scenic Rivers System.	Failed
1974	California	DS	9	Campaign Finance Reform	Requires reports of receipts and expenditures in campaigns for state and local offices and ballot measures. Limits expenditures for state wide candidates.	Passed

Year	State	Type	Measure Number	Subject Matter	Description	Pass/Fail
1974	Colorado	DA	1	Administration of Government	An act concerning the annexation of property by a County or city and County, and prohibiting the striking off of any territory from a County without first submitting the question to a vote of the qualified electors of the County and city.	Passed
1974	Colorado	DA	10	Nuclear weapons/facilities/waste	An act to amend the Constitution to establish procedural steps to be complied with prior to the detonation of nuclear explosive devises including voter approval.	Passed
1974	Colorado	DA	8	Education	Prohibit the assignment or the transportation of pupils to public educational institutions in order to achieve racial balance of pupils at such institutions.	Passed
1974	Colorado	DA	9	Apportionment/Redistricting	Reapportioning of legislative districts by a body to be known as the Colorado Reapportionment Commission which shall consist of electors.	Passed
1974	Idaho	DS	1	Campaign Finance Reform	Establishes campaign finance regulations and disclosure laws.	Passed
1974	Massachusetts	DA	Question 4	Administration of Government	Authorizing use of state highway revenues for mass transportation.	Passed
1974	Massachusetts	IDS	Question 5	Campaign Finance Reform	Political contributions and campaign expenditures.	Passed
1974	Missouri	DS	N/A	Campaign Finance Reform	Provides for a new campaign financing and election law to replace portions of the present corrupt practices act.	Passed
1974	Montana	DA	CI 1	Administration of Government	Providing for 90 day biennial legislative sessions.	Passed
1974	North Dakota	DS	N/A	Business Regulation	Authorizes small family-owned corporations to engage in farming.	Failed
1974	North Dakota	DS	N/A	Labor	Authorizes new programs to increase employment opportunities.	Failed
1974	Oregon	DS	15	Business Regulation	To prohibit the purchase or sale of steelhead.	Passed
1975	Ohio	DA	Issue No. 2	Taxes	To create and preserve jobs by the authorization of tax incentives to industrial plants.	Failed
1975	Ohio	DA	Issue No. 3	Bonds	To authorize the issuance of bonds and notes in an amount not to exceed $1,750,000,000 to be paid from and additional levy of 9/10 of 1 cent per gallon gasoline tax.	Failed
1975	Ohio	DA	Issue No. 4	Health/Medical	Relative to the authority of the state, municipal corporation and counties to provide assistance with respect to housing and nursing, extended care and other health facilities.	Failed
1975	Ohio	DA	Issue No. 5	Bonds	To authorize the issuance of bonds and notes in the amount not to exceed $2,750,000,000 with the principal and interest to be paid by an additional levy of 7/10 of 1% sales and use tax.	Failed
1975	Washington	DS	I-314	Taxes	Shall corporations pay a 12% excise tax measured by income so that special school levies may be reduced or eliminated.	Failed
1975	Washington	DS	I-316	Death Penalty	Shall the death penalty be mandatory in the case of aggravated murder in the first degree?	Passed
1976	Alaska	IDS	5	Animal Rights	Regulate entry into fisheries	Failed
1976	Arizona	DS	200	Nuclear weapons/facilities/waste	Legislative approval-nuclear facilities.	Failed
1976	Arkansas	DA	59	Labor	Rights of Labor amendment.	Failed
1976	California	DS	13	Gaming	To authorize and regulate greyhound dog racing.	Failed
1976	California	DS	14	Labor	Agricultural labor relations.	Failed
1976	California	DS	15	Nuclear weapons/facilities/waste	Nuclear power plants.	Failed

Year	State	Type	Measure Number	Subject Matter	Description	Pass/Fail
1976	Colorado	DA	10	Taxes	An Amendment adding a new Sec. 31 to Art. 10 requiring registered electoral approval of all state and local executive or legislative acts which result in new or increased taxes.	Failed
1976	Colorado	DA	3	Nuclear weapons/facilities/waste	An amendment requiring approval by two thirds of each House of the General Assembly prior to any construction or modification of a nuclear power plant or related facility.	Failed
1976	Colorado	DA	6	Civil Rights	An Act to repeal Sec. 29 of Art. 2 which section provides for equality of rights under the law on account of sex.	Failed
1976	Colorado	DS	7	Taxes	Exempts food and food products, with certain exceptions, from state sales and use taxes and repeal the food sales tax credit, to require the General Assembly to enact severance taxes and corporate income taxes to offset any revenue lost.	Failed
1976	Colorado	DS	8	Environmental Reform	Requires a minimum deposit refund value for beverage containers for malt liquor, including beer, and carbonated soft drinks manufactured, distributed, or sold for use in this state.	Failed
1976	Colorado	DS	9	Utility Regulation	Protects and represents consumers of public utilities services by creating a Department of Public Counselor, and concerning financial disclosures by Public Utilities Commissioners.	Failed
1976	Florida	DA	1	Campaign Finance Reform	To require full public disclosure by state and County election officials and candidates (sunshine amendment).	Passed
1976	Maine	IDS	N/A	Environmental Reform	To establish a public preserve in Bigelow Mountain area.	Passed
1976	Massachusetts	IDS	Question 4	Utility Regulation	To establish Massachusetts Power Authority.	Failed
1976	Massachusetts	IDS	Question 5	Gun Regulation	To prohibit to possession, ownership, or sale of any weapon from which a shot or bullet can be discharged and which has a barrel length of less than 16 inches.	Failed
1976	Massachusetts	IDS	Question 6	Environmental Reform	To require every beverage container to have a refund value of $.05 and to ban containers with flip-tops.	Failed
1976	Massachusetts	IDS	Question 7	Utility Regulation	To regulate electric utility charges and permit peak load pricing.	Failed
1976	Michigan	DA	N/A	Taxes	Proposal to remove the ban on graduated income tax.	Failed
1976	Michigan	DA	N/A	Environmental Reform	A proposal to ban throw-away bottles and cans.	Passed
1976	Michigan	DA	N/A	Administration of Government	Proposal to place a limitation on state spending.	Failed
1976	Missouri	DA	N/A	Education	Authorizes enactment of laws providing services for the handicapped, non-religious textbooks, and transportation for all public and non-public elementary and secondary school children.	Failed
1976	Missouri	DA	N/A	Taxes	Increase funding for bird, fish, game, forestry and wildlife programs by levying additional sales and use taxes of one-eighth of one percent.	Passed
1976	Missouri	DA	N/A	Taxes	Prohibits after Jan. 1, 1978, sales or use tax on food for off premises human consumption or on drugs and devices prescribed for human medical treatment.	Failed
1976	Missouri	DS	N/A	Utility Regulation	Prohibits charges for electricity based on cost construction in progress upon any existing or new facility or based on cost associated with owning, operating, maintaining, or financing property.	Passed

Year	State	Type	Measure Number	Subject Matter	Description	Pass/Fail
1976	Montana	DA	CI 7	Administration of Government	Providing for a limit on state spending and a phase out of federal funds.	Failed
1976	Montana	DS	I 71	Nuclear weapons/facilities/waste	Requiring legislative approval of any nuclear facility licensed under the Montana Major Facility Sitting Act.	Failed
1976	Montana	DS	I 72	Taxes	To provide property tax relief for owner-occupied homesteads.	Passed
1976	Montana	DS	I 73	Election Reform	Montana recall and advisory recall act.	Passed
1976	North Dakota	DS	N/A	Taxes	Motor vehicle excise tax rates.	Passed
1976	North Dakota	DS	N/A	Administration of Government	Limit General Fund expenditures.	Failed
1976	Ohio	DA	Issue No. 4	Utility Regulation	Limiting the rates which may be charged to residential consumers for fixed amounts of gas and electricity.	Failed
1976	Ohio	DA	Issue No. 5	Utility Regulation	Providing for representation of residential utility regulatory actions affecting their interests.	Failed
1976	Ohio	DA	Issue No. 6	Nuclear weapons/facilities/waste	Relative to establishing procedures for legislative hearings and approval of safety features of nuclear power plants and related facilities.	Failed
1976	Ohio	DA	Issue No. 7	Initiative and Referendum	Relative to simplifying the procedures for initiative and referendum.	Failed
1976	Oklahoma	DA	515	Alcohol Regulation	Sale of alcoholic beverages, licensees, terms.	Failed
1976	Oregon	DS	10	Environmental Reform	Repeals land use planning coordination statutes.	Failed
1976	Oregon	DS	11	Health/Medical	Prohibit adding fluoridation to water systems.	Failed
1976	Oregon	DS	12	Administration of Government	Repeals intergovernmental cooperation, planning district statutes.	Failed
1976	Oregon	DS	9	Nuclear weapons/facilities/waste	Regulates nuclear power plant construction approval.	Failed
1976	Utah	DS	A	Health/Medical	To provide for freedom from compulsory fluoridation and medication.	Passed
1976	Utah	DS	B	Election Reform	To provide for a recall and advisory recall procedure.	Failed
1976	Utah	DS	C	Administration of Government	To provide for a budgetary procedures act ceiling.	Failed
1976	Washington	DS	I-322	Health/Medical	Shall fluoridation of public water supplies be made unlawful and violation subject to criminal penalties.	Failed
1976	Washington	DS	I-325	Nuclear weapons/facilities/waste	Shall future nuclear power facilities which do not meet certain conditions and receive two-thirds approval by the legislature be prohibited.	Failed
1977	Ohio	DA	Issue No. 1	Election Reform	Entitlement to vote if registered for thirty days.	Passed
1977	Ohio	DA	Issue No. 2	Animal Rights	Ban trapping devices causing prolonged suffering.	Failed
1977	Washington	DS	I-335	Legal	Regulation of pornography.	Passed
1977	Washington	DS	I-345	Taxes	State, local sales and use taxes: food exemptions.	Passed
1977	Washington	DS	I-348	Taxes	Repeal of variable fuel tax.	Failed
1977	Washington	IDS	I-59	Administration of Government	Limit appropriations of public water: agriculture.	Passed
1978	Alaska	IDS	3	Administration of Government	Relocate state capitol.	Passed
1978	Alaska	IDS	4	Environmental Reform	Disposal of state lands.	Passed
1978	Alaska	IDS	5	Environmental Reform	Beverage container deposits.	Failed
1978	Arkansas	DA	59	Taxes	Food and medicine sales tax exemptions.	Failed
1978	California	DA	13	Taxes	Property tax reduction and limitation. Two-thirds vote required for increases.	Passed
1978	California	DS	5	Health/Medical	Prohibits smoking in specified areas and restaurants must have non-smoking areas.	Failed
1978	California	DS	6	Civil Rights	School employees can be fired for homosexuality.	Failed
1978	California	DS	7	Legal	Criminal penalty for murder.	Passed

Year	State	Type	Measure Number	Subject Matter	Description	Pass/Fail
1978	Colorado	DA	2	Taxes	Limiting annual increases in per capita expenditures by the state and its political subdivisions.	Failed
1978	Florida	DA	9	Gaming	Establish casino gambling.	Failed
1978	Idaho	DS	1	Taxes	Restrict property valuation or tax changes.	Passed
1978	Michigan	IDS	B	Legal	Limit parole-violent criminals; minimum sentence.	Passed
1978	Michigan	DA	D	Alcohol Regulation	Must be 21 to purchase/posses alcohol.	Passed
1978	Michigan	DA	E	Taxes	Tax limitation (Headlee Amendment).	Passed
1978	Michigan	DA	G	Labor	Collective bargaining for Michigan state Troopers.	Passed
1978	Michigan	DA	H	Education	Exempt property tax from school operations and also would have established a school voucher system.	Failed
1978	Michigan	DA	J	Taxes	Property and taxes, local mandates, voter approval.	Failed
1978	Missouri	DA	N/A	Labor	Right to work.	Failed
1978	Missouri	DA	N/A	Taxes	Increase gas tax from 7 to 10 cents.	Failed
1978	Montana	DA	CI 8	Taxes	Property tax assessment and Commission.	Failed
1978	Montana	DS	I 79	Legal	Local option: obscenity laws.	Passed
1978	Montana	DS	I 80	Nuclear weapons/facilities/waste	Voter regulation of nuclear facilities.	Passed
1978	Montana	DS	I 81	Business Regulation	Table wine retail sales.	Passed
1978	Nebraska	DS	301	Environmental Reform	Five cent deposit on beverage containers.	Failed
1978	Nebraska	DS	302	Administration of Government	Five percent increase limit on political subdivisions.	Failed
1978	Nevada	DA	6	Taxes	Limit property taxes.	Passed
1978	North Dakota	DS	N/A	Health/Medical	State control of health care costs, insurance.	Failed
1978	North Dakota	DS	N/A	Administration of Government	State sharing of General Fund revenues.	Passed
1978	North Dakota	DS	N/A	Taxes	Income tax rates: individual, corporate.	Passed
1978	North Dakota	DS	N/A	Administration of Government	Funds to Fish and Game Department.	Passed
1978	Oklahoma	DS	524	Administration of Government	License/registration through mail; Tax Commission.	Passed
1978	Oregon	DA	10	Environmental Reform	Land use planning, zoning amendment.	Failed
1978	Oregon	DS	4	Utility Regulation	Shorten formation procedures: utility districts.	Failed
1978	Oregon	DS	5	Business Regulation	Practice of denture technology.	Passed
1978	Oregon	DA	6	Taxes	Limitations on ad valorem property taxes	Passed
1978	Oregon	DA	7	Abortion	Prohibits state spending or programs for abortions.	Failed
1978	Oregon	DS	8	Death Penalty	Death penalty for murder, specific conditions.	Passed
1978	Oregon	DS	9	Utility Regulation	Limit public utility rate base	Passed
1978	South Dakota	IDS	1	Utility Regulation	Lifeline utility rate reform.	Failed
1978	South Dakota	IDS	2	Business Regulation	Repeal of Dairy Marketing Act.	Passed
1978	South Dakota	IDS	3	Legal	New regulation of Obscenity Statute.	Failed
1978	Washington	DS	I-350	Education	Assignment of students to schools — prohibitions.	Passed
1979	California	DA	4	Administration of Government	Limit government appropriations.	Passed
1979	Maine	IDS	N/A	Environmental Reform	To repeal the forced deposit law (bottle bill).	Failed
1979	Ohio	IDS	Issue No. 1	Environmental Reform	Mandatory deposits on bottles; prohibit pull-tabs.	Failed
1979	Oklahoma	DS	539	Taxes	Deduct individual Federal Income tax from state income.	Failed
1979	Washington	IDS	I-61	Environmental Reform	Five cent refund on beverage containers.	Failed
1979	Washington	IDS	I-62	Taxes	State tax revenue limitation.	Passed
1980	Alaska	IDS	N/A	Administration of Government	Establish the Alaska Stock Ownership Corp.	Failed
1980	Arizona	DA	106	Taxes	Property tax limitation — 2/3 legislature.	Failed
1980	Arizona	DS	200	Gaming	Provisions for state lottery.	Passed
1980	Arkansas	DS	1	Education	Equal education for all children in the state.	Failed

Year	State	Type	Measure Number	Subject Matter	Description	Pass/Fail
1980	Arkansas	DA	60	Banking Reform	Maximum rate of interest controlled by 2/3 vote of legislature.	Failed
1980	California	DS	10	Health/Medical	Smoking and non-smoking sections in public places.	Failed
1980	California	DA	10	Housing	Rent control through local ordinance.	Failed
1980	California	DS	11	Taxes	Taxation. 10% surtax on energy businesses.	Failed
1980	California	DA	9	Taxes	Taxation: indexing, business inventory exemption.	Failed
1980	Illinois	DA	N/A	Administration of Government	Reduce size of House of Representatives from 177 members to 118 members beginning with elections in 1982.	Passed
1980	Maine	IDS	N/A	Nuclear weapons/facilities/waste	Prohibit electric power by nuclear fission.	Failed
1980	Massachusetts	IDS	Question 2	Taxes	Limit local taxes. "Proposition 2 1/2"	Passed
1980	Massachusetts	IDS	Question 3	Taxes	Limit taxes; increase state share of education costs.	Failed
1980	Michigan	DA	N/A	Taxes	Taxes for school finance; equal per pupil funding.	Failed
1980	Michigan	DA	N/A	Taxes	Reduce property taxes; voter approval for new taxes.	Failed
1980	Missouri	DA	N/A	Taxes	Limit state and local taxes. Hancock Amendment.	Passed
1980	Missouri	DS	N/A	Nuclear weapons/facilities/waste	Nuclear waste.	Failed
1980	Montana	DS	I 84	Nuclear weapons/facilities/waste	Prohibit disposal of radioactive waste in MT.	Passed
1980	Montana	DS	I 85	Campaign Finance Reform	Lobbyist disclosure.	Passed
1980	Montana	DS	I 86	Taxes	Tax indexing.	Passed
1980	Montana	DS	I 87	Environmental Reform	Montana Litter Control and Recycling Act.	Failed
1980	Nevada	DA	6	Taxes	1978 Measure 6 — Limit property taxes. 2nd vote as required by law	Failed
1980	Nevada	DA	8	Taxes	Exempt household goods from taxation.	Passed
1980	Nevada	DA	9	Taxes	Exempt food from taxation.	Passed
1980	North Dakota	DS	N/A	Bonds	Tax-exempt bonds for low-income mortgages.	Passed
1980	North Dakota	DS	N/A	Taxes	6.5% oil extraction tax, use of revenues.	Passed
1980	Ohio	IDS	N/A	Taxes	To restructure state taxes on personal income.	Failed
1980	Oregon	DS	5	Animal Rights	Forbid use, sale of snare leg hold traps.	Failed
1980	Oregon	DA	6	Taxes	Property tax limit: 85% districts' 1977 revenue.	Failed
1980	Oregon	DS	7	Nuclear weapons/facilities/waste	Nuclear plant licensing: voter approval, disposal.	Passed
1980	South Dakota	IDS	2	Nuclear weapons/facilities/waste	Uranium, nuclear waste, plants: voter approval.	Failed
1980	South Dakota	DA	B	Taxes	Relating to real property taxes.	Passed
1980	South Dakota	DA	C	Initiative and Referendum	Legislature cannot change initiative-enacted laws.	Failed
1980	Utah	DS	A	Taxes	Elimination of sales tax on food.	Failed
1980	Utah	DS	B	Taxes	Tax limitation act.	Failed
1980	Washington	DS	I-383	Nuclear weapons/facilities/waste	Bans on radioactive wastes generated out of State.	Passed
1981	Maine	IDS	N/A	Utility Regulation	Create Maine Energy Commission.	Failed
1981	Ohio	DA	Issue No. 1	Labor	Workers compensation insurance; private companies.	Failed
1981	Ohio	DA	Issue No. 2	Apportionment/Redistricting	General Assembly and Congressional redistricting.	Failed
1981	Washington	DS	I-394	Bonds	Voter approval: bonds for public energy projects.	Passed
1981	Washington	DS	I-402	Taxes	Abolition of state inheritance and gift tax.	Passed
1982	Alaska	IDS	5	Environmental Reform	State ownership of Federal land.	Passed
1982	Alaska	IDS	6	Abortion	Limit state funding of abortion.	Failed
1982	Alaska	IDS	7	Animal Rights	Consumption of fish and game.	Failed
1982	Arizona	DS	200	Environmental Reform	Deposit/refund for beverage containers.	Failed
1982	Arizona	DS	201	Administration of Government	Declare last Sunday in May as Peace Sunday.	Failed
1982	Arizona	DS	202	Election Reform	Voter registration by driver's license.	Passed
1982	Arizona	DS	203	Administration of Government	Repeal state control over public lands.	Failed

Year	State	Type	Measure Number	Subject Matter	Description	Pass/Fail
1982	California	DS	11	Environmental Reform	Beverage containers must have refund value of at least five cents.	Failed
1982	California	M	12	Nuclear weapons/facilities/waste	Nuclear weapons.	Passed
1982	California	DS	13	Environmental Reform	Establishes water conservation programs.	Failed
1982	California	DA	14	Apportionment/Redistricting	Removes legislature's power over redistricting.	Failed
1982	California	DS	15	Gun Regulation	Requires registration of concealable firearms.	Failed
1982	California	DS	5	Taxes	Gift and inheritance taxes.	Passed
1982	California	DS	6	Taxes	Gift and inheritance taxes.	Passed
1982	California	DS	7	Taxes	Income tax indexing.	Passed
1982	California	DA	8	Legal	Criminal Justice.	Passed
1982	Colorado	DS	5	Environmental Reform	Refund on beverage containers.	Failed
1982	Colorado	DA	6	Nuclear weapons/facilities/waste	To bring about the cessation of nuclear weapons component production in Colorado.	Failed
1982	Colorado	DS	7	Business Regulation	Regulate the sale of wine in grocery stores.	Failed
1982	Idaho	DS	1	Taxes	Home improvement exemptions: ad valorem tax.	Passed
1982	Idaho	DS	2	Health/Medical	Practice of Denturitry; licensing board.	Passed
1982	Idaho	DS	3	Utility Regulation	Use of nuclear power for electricity generation.	Passed
1982	Maine	IDS	N/A	Taxes	Abolish inflation-induce state income tax increases.	Passed
1982	Maine	IDS	N/A	Business Regulation	Repeal of milk price controls.	Failed
1982	Maine	IDS	N/A	Nuclear weapons/facilities/waste	End nuclear power for electricity in five years.	Failed
1982	Massachusetts	IDS	Question 3	Nuclear weapons/facilities/waste	Restrict radioactive waste disposal; construction.	Passed
1982	Michigan	IDS	N/A	Business Regulation	Foreclosures: not "due on sale" clauses; security.	Failed
1982	Michigan	IDS	N/A	Utility Regulation	Hearings on utility rate increases, procedures.	Passed
1982	Michigan	DA	N/A	Administration of Government	Establish elected Public Service Commission.	Failed
1982	Michigan	DA	N/A	Administration of Government	Create department of State Police.	Failed
1982	Michigan	M	N/A	Nuclear weapons/facilities/waste	Mutual nuclear weapons freeze with Soviet Union.	Passed
1982	Missouri	DS	N/A	Taxes	One cent sales tax increase.	Passed
1982	Missouri	DS	N/A	Utility Regulation	Utility Consumers Board.	Failed
1982	Montana	DS	I 91	Nuclear weapons/facilities/waste	Opposing placement of MX Missiles in Montana.	Passed
1982	Montana	DS	I 92	Gaming	Authorize the expansion of gambling.	Failed
1982	Montana	DS	I 94	Alcohol Regulation	Beer and wine quota system.	Failed
1982	Montana	DS	I 95	Administration of Government	Invest Coal Tax Trust revenue in Montana economy.	Passed
1982	Nebraska	DA	300	Administration of Government	NE Family Farm Corporations must own farms.	Passed
1982	Nevada	IDS	12	Utility Regulation	Protection of public utilities customers.	Failed
1982	Nevada	DA	8	Taxes	1980 Measure 8 — Exempt household goods from taxation. 2nd vote as required by law.	Passed
1982	Nevada	DA	9	Taxes	1980 Measure 9 — Exempt food from taxation. 2nd vote as required by law	Failed
1982	North Dakota	DS	N/A	Gaming	Place limits on charitable gambling.	Failed
1982	North Dakota	M	N/A	Nuclear weapons/facilities/waste	Limits development/production of nuclear weapons.	Passed
1982	Ohio	DA	Issue No. 3	Administration of Government	Election of members of Public Utilities Commission.	Failed
1982	Oklahoma	DS	553	Gaming	Creation of Oklahoma Horse Racing Commission.	Passed
1982	Oklahoma	DS	556	Apportionment/Redistricting	Creation of new Congressional districts.	Failed
1982	Oregon	DA	3	Taxes	Property tax limit: 85% districts' 1979 revenue.	Failed
1982	Oregon	DS	4	Business Regulation	Permit retail self-service dispensing of fuel.	Failed
1982	Oregon	DS	5	Nuclear weapons/facilities/waste	Mutual freeze on nuclear weapons development.	Passed
1982	Oregon	DS	6	Environmental Reform	End State's land use planning powers; localities.	Failed
1982	South Dakota	DA	Constitutional Amendment A	Administration of Government	Single member senate districts in legislature.	Passed

Year	State	Type	Measure Number	Subject Matter	Description	Pass/Fail
1982	Washington	DS	I-412	Business Regulation	Maximum interest rate on retail sales.	Failed
1982	Washington	DS	I-414	Environmental Reform	Five cent refund on beverage containers.	Failed
1982	Washington	DS	I-435	Taxes	Sales, other business taxes replaced by franchise tax.	Failed
1983	Maine	IDS	1	Animal Rights	Repeal hunting season on moose.	Failed
1983	Ohio	DA	Issue No. 1	Alcohol Regulation	Minimum age, beer consumption: twenty-one.	Failed
1983	Ohio	DA	Issue No. 2	Taxes	3/5 majority of General Assembly to raise taxes.	Failed
1983	Ohio	DA	Issue No. 3	Taxes	Repeal all taxes passed since 1982.	Failed
1984	Alaska	IDS	N/A	Business Regulation	Regulate transportation.	Passed
1984	Arizona	DA	110	Health/Medical	Health care institutions, regulation	Failed
1984	Arizona	DS	200	Health/Medical	Regulate cost of health care.	Failed
1984	Arkansas	DA	64	Term Limits	Four year terms for state constitutional officers.	Passed
1984	Arkansas	DA	66	Gaming	Authorize gambling in Garland County.	Failed
1984	Arkansas	DA	67	Administration of Government	Sales/use tax for Fish and Game Commission.	Failed
1984	California	DS	24	Administration of Government	Legislature: rules, procedures, powers, funding.	Passed
1984	California	DA	36	Taxes	Forbids new property tax.	Failed
1984	California	DA	37	Gaming	Establishes state lottery.	Passed
1984	California	DS	38	Administration of Government	Voting materials. English only.	Passed
1984	California	DA	39	Apportionment/Redistricting	Revising apportionment of members of legislature.	Failed
1984	California	DS	40	Campaign Finance Reform	Campaign contribution limits.	Failed
1984	California	DS	41	Welfare	Public aid, medical assistance programs.	Failed
1984	Colorado	DA	3	Abortion	Ban the state funding of abortion.	Passed
1984	Colorado	DS	4	Election Reform	To provide for additional voter registration of qualified electors applying for a driver's license.	Passed
1984	Colorado	DA	5	Gaming	Establish casino gambling in Pueblo.	Failed
1984	Idaho	DS	1	Taxes	Sales tax exemption: food for consumption.	Failed
1984	Michigan	DA	N/A	Taxes	State/local tax rates set to those of 12/31/81.	Failed
1984	Missouri	DS	N/A	Utility Regulation	Electricity generation cost charges for consumers.	Passed
1984	Missouri	DA	N/A	Gaming	Establish Horse Racing Commission and regulate wagering.	Passed
1984	Montana	DS	I 96	Business Regulation	Milk price decontrol.	Failed
1984	Montana	DS	I 97	Business Regulation	Allowing practice of Denturitry.	Failed
1984	Nevada	DA	12	Taxes	Limit tax increases, all levels of government.	Failed
1984	North Dakota	DA	N/A	Gun Regulation	Right to bear arms as a state right.	Passed
1984	North Dakota	DS	N/A	Education	Three junior colleges to local school board control.	Failed
1984	Oklahoma	DA	563	Alcohol Regulation	Renaming Alcoholic Beverage Commission; taxation.	Passed
1984	Oregon	DA	2	Taxes	Property tax limit.	Failed
1984	Oregon	DS	3	Utility Regulation	Establish a citizens' utility board.	Passed
1984	Oregon	DA	4	Gaming	State lottery; profits for economic development.	Passed
1984	Oregon	DS	5	Gaming	Statutory provisions for State operated lottery.	Passed
1984	Oregon	DA	6	Death Penalty	Death penalty exempt: guarantees against cruelty.	Passed
1984	Oregon	DS	7	Legal	Death/mandatory imprisonment: aggravated murder.	Passed
1984	Oregon	DS	8	Legal	Criminal laws: police powers, evidence, sentences.	Failed
1984	Oregon	DS	9	Nuclear weapons/facilities/waste	Naturally occurring radioactive isotopes: disposal.	Passed
1984	South Dakota	IDS	1	Nuclear weapons/facilities/waste	Voter approval: nuclear waste disposal, compacts.	Passed
1984	South Dakota	IDS	2	Education	School begins day after Labor Day.	Passed
1984	South Dakota	M	3	Nuclear weapons/facilities/waste	SD mandates a verifiable nuclear freeze.	Failed
1984	Utah	DS	A	Legal	Cable television decency act.	Failed

Year	State	Type	Measure Number	Subject Matter	Description	Pass/Fail
1984	Washington	M	I-456	Business Regulation	Petition Congress to de-commercialize steelhead.	Passed
1984	Washington	DS	I-464	Taxes	Trade-in values; sales tax computation.	Passed
1984	Washington	DS	I-471	Abortion	No public funding of abortions.	Failed
1985	Maine	IDS	N/A	Nuclear weapons/facilities/waste	Would require a statewide referendum on any plan to dump low-level radioactive waste in the state.	Passed
1986	Alaska	IDS	1	Nuclear weapons/facilities/waste	Nuclear Weapons Freeze.	Passed
1986	Arizona	DA	103	Tort Reform	Personal injury damages, legislative limitations.	Failed
1986	Arizona	DS	200	Campaign Finance Reform	Limit campaign contributions.	Passed
1986	Arkansas	DA	65	Abortion	Limit public funding of abortion.	Failed
1986	Arkansas	DA	66	Administration of Government	Four year terms for elected County officials.	Failed
1986	Arkansas	DA	67	Taxes	Issuance of revenue bonds without election.	Passed
1986	California	DS	51	Tort Reform	Multiple defendants tort damage liability.	Passed
1986	California	DA	61	Administration of Government	Compensation of public employees, contractors.	Failed
1986	California	DS	62	Taxes	Taxation, local governments and districts.	Passed
1986	California	DA	63	Administration of Government	English as official state language.	Passed
1986	California	DS	64	Health/Medical	Acquired Immune Deficiency Syndrome (AIDS)	Failed
1986	California	DS	65	Environmental Reform	Toxic discharge into drinking water.	Passed
1986	Colorado	DA	4	Taxes	Voter approval for tax increases.	Failed
1986	Florida	DA	2	Gaming	Allow casino gambling.	Failed
1986	Florida	DA	5	Gaming	Establish a state operated lottery.	Passed
1986	Idaho	DS	1	Gaming	Establish state lottery and lottery commission.	Passed
1986	Maine	IDS	N/A	Utility Regulation	Ban mandatory local phone service; flat rates.	Passed
1986	Maine	IDS	N/A	Civil Rights	Obscenity law.	Failed
1986	Massachusetts	IDS	Question 3	Taxes	Limit state revenue tax increases: income surtax.	Passed
1986	Massachusetts	IDS	Question 4	Environmental Reform	DEQE to identify/clean hazardous waste sites.	Passed
1986	Massachusetts	IDS	Question 6	Election Reform	Mail-in voter registration.	Failed
1986	Montana	DA	CI 27	Taxes	Abolish property tax; popular vote for tax change.	Failed
1986	Montana	DA	CI 30	Legal	Concerning private liability.	Passed
1986	Montana	DS	I 104	Business Regulation	Decontrol of milk prices.	Failed
1986	Montana	DS	I 105	Taxes	Limit property taxes to 1986 levels.	Passed
1986	North Dakota	DS	N/A	Labor	Sunday grocery employees — from six to three.	Failed
1986	North Dakota	DS	N/A	Business Regulation	More businesses allowed open for retail on Sundays.	Failed
1986	North Dakota	DS	N/A	Gaming	Establish a state lottery.	Failed
1986	Oregon	DS	10	Legal	Criminal laws: victims, evidence, sentences, parole.	Passed
1986	Oregon	DS	11	Taxes	Property tax relief program; sales tax limitation.	Failed
1986	Oregon	DS	12	Taxes	State income tax changes, property tax relief.	Failed
1986	Oregon	DA	13	Election Reform	Twenty day pre-election voter registration cutoff.	Passed
1986	Oregon	DS	14	Nuclear weapons/facilities/waste	Nuclear Power: permanent waste site licensed.	Failed
1986	Oregon	DS	15	Nuclear weapons/facilities/waste	"Radioactive waste" defined; energy facility payments.	Failed
1986	Oregon	DS	16	Nuclear weapons/facilities/waste	Nuclear weapons funded by tax credits. Civil penalty.	Failed
1986	Oregon	DS	5	Drug Policy Reform	Legalize marijuana for personal use.	Failed
1986	Oregon	DA	6	Abortion	Prohibits state funding of abortions.	Failed
1986	Oregon	DA	7	Taxes	Sales tax. Funds schools, reduces property taxes.	Failed
1986	Oregon	DS	8	Utility Regulation	Mandatory local measured telephone service.	Passed
1986	Oregon	DA	9	Taxes	Limit property tax rate, assessed value increases.	Failed
1986	South Dakota	IDS	1	Administration of Government	Memorial Day observed last Monday in May.	Passed

Year	State	Type	Measure Number	Subject Matter	Description	Pass/Fail
1986	Washington	IDS	I-90	Taxes	Sales/use tax for conservation, recreation programs.	Failed
1987	Maine	IDS	N/A	Nuclear weapons/facilities/waste	No high-waste nuclear plants after July 4, 1988.	Passed
1987	Ohio	DA	Issue No. 3	Judicial Reform	Abolish election of Supreme, Appeals Court judges.	Failed
1987	Washington	IDS	I-92	Welfare	Charges to Medicare patients; reasonable charges.	Failed
1988	Alaska	IDS	2	Legal	Civil liability.	Passed
1988	Alaska	IDS	3	Education	Separate Community College from University.	Failed
1988	Arizona	DA	106	Administration of Government	English as official language.	Passed
1988	Arkansas	DS	1	Campaign Finance Reform	Conduct and disclosure act — lobbyist, state officials.	Passed
1988	Arkansas	DA	3	Abortion	Prevent abortion funding and restrict abortion.	Passed
1988	Arkansas	DA	4	Taxes	Repeal property tax on household goods.	Failed
1988	California	DS	100	Business Regulation	Reductions in auto insurance rates, regulation.	Failed
1988	California	DS	101	Business Regulation	Automobile accident claims, insurance rates.	Failed
1988	California	DS	102	Health/Medical	Reporting exposure to AIDS virus.	Failed
1988	California	DS	103	Business Regulation	Insurance rates, regulation, Commission.	Passed
1988	California	DS	104	Business Regulation	Automobile and other insurance.	Failed
1988	California	DS	105	Business Regulation	Disclosure to consumers, voters, investors.	Passed
1988	California	DS	106	Tort Reform	Attorney fee limit for tort claims.	Failed
1988	California	DS	68	Campaign Finance Reform	Legislative campaigns-spending and contribution limits.	Passed
1988	California	DS	69	Health/Medical	Acquired Immune Deficiency Syndrome (AIDS)	Failed
1988	California	DS	73	Campaign Finance Reform	Campaign bundling.	Passed
1988	California	DS	95	Welfare	Funding for hunger and homelessness programs.	Failed
1988	California	DS	96	Health/Medical	Communicable disease tests.	Passed
1988	California	DS	97	Health/Medical	State occupational safety and health plan.	Passed
1988	California	DA	98	Education	General fund financing — school funding.	Passed
1988	California	DA	99	Taxes	Cigarette and tobacco tax. Benefit fund.	Passed
1988	Colorado	DA	1	Administration of Government	English as official language.	Passed
1988	Colorado	DA	6	Taxes	Voter approval: increases in tax revenues.	Failed
1988	Colorado	DA	7	Abortion	Restore funding for abortions.	Failed
1988	Colorado	DA	8	Administration of Government	Referral of measures to committees.	Passed
1988	Florida	DA	10	Tort Reform	Limit damages in civil actions.	Failed
1988	Florida	DA	11	Administration of Government	English as official state language.	Passed
1988	Massachusetts	IDS	Question 2	Labor	Repeal prevailing wage law.	Failed
1988	Massachusetts	IDS	Question 3	Animal Rights	Regulate treatment of farm animals.	Failed
1988	Massachusetts	IDS	Question 4	Nuclear weapons/facilities/waste	Ban electric power plants that produce nuclear waste.	Failed
1988	Missouri	DA	N/A	Health/Medical	Trust fund for catastrophic, high-risk illness.	Failed
1988	Missouri	DA	N/A	Taxes	Extend use and sales taxes.	Passed
1988	Montana	DS	I 110	Health/Medical	Repeal the Montana Seatbelt Use Act.	Failed
1988	Montana	DS	I 113	Environmental Reform	Refundable deposits on beverage containers.	Failed
1988	Nebraska	DS	402	Environmental Reform	Central Interstate Radioactive Waste Compact.	Failed
1988	Nebraska	DA	403	Gun Regulation	Right to bear arms.	Passed
1988	Nevada	DA	9	Taxes	Prohibit a state personal income tax.	Passed
1988	North Dakota	DA	N/A	Gaming	Legislative assembly to establish state lottery.	Failed
1988	North Dakota	DS	N/A	Veteran Affairs	Restore Veterans' Postwar Trust Fund, 1987 balance.	Passed
1988	Oregon	DS	4	Legal	Full sentences, no parole; probation, repeat felonies.	Passed
1988	Oregon	DS	5	Taxes	Sin taxes to finance Intercollegiate Athletic Fund.	Failed
1988	Oregon	DS	6	Environmental Reform	Indoor Clean Air Law revisions — ban public smoking.	Failed

Year	State	Type	Measure Number	Subject Matter	Description	Pass/Fail
1988	Oregon	DS	7	Environmental Reform	Oregon Scenic Waterway System.	Passed
1988	Oregon	DS	8	Civil Rights	Revoke ban on sexual orientation discrimination.	Passed
1988	South Dakota	IDS	1	Taxes	Additional tax on surface mining.	Failed
1988	South Dakota	IDS	2	Environmental Reform	Surface mining reclamation.	Failed
1988	South Dakota	IDS	3	Animal Rights	Ban on corporate hog farms.	Passed
1988	South Dakota	DA	Constitutional Amendment B	Gaming	Permit gambling in city of Deadwood.	Passed
1988	South Dakota	DA	Constitutional Amendment C	Taxes	Add section limiting property taxes.	Failed
1988	Utah	DS	A	Taxes	Tax and spending limitations.	Failed
1988	Utah	DS	B	Taxes	Tax reductions.	Failed
1988	Utah	DS	C	Taxes	Income tax credit for private education.	Failed
1988	Washington	DS	I-518	Labor	Minimum wage increases: include agricultural sector.	Passed
1989	Maine	IDS	N/A	Campaign Finance Reform	Campaign finance — candidates for Governor.	Failed
1989	Maine	M	N/A	Nuclear weapons/facilities/waste	Stop cruise missile tests.	Passed
1989	Oklahoma	DA	620	Administration of Government	Legislative Session: dates and times.	Passed
1989	Washington	IDS	I-102	Taxes	$360K new taxes for family services, K–12 education.	Failed
1990	Alaska	IDS	N/A	Utility Regulation	Amendments to Alaska Railroad Act.	Failed
1990	Alaska	IDS	N/A	Drug Policy Reform	Penalties for marijuana sale/use.	Passed
1990	Alaska	IDS	N/A	Gaming	Regulate gambling.	Failed
1990	Arizona	DA	103	Education	Classroom Improvement program.	Failed
1990	Arizona	DA	104	Legal	Victims' bill of rights.	Passed
1990	Arizona	DA	105	Business Regulation	Vehicle accident compensation law.	Failed
1990	Arizona	DS	200	Environmental Reform	Arizona state Parks funded by lottery.	Passed
1990	Arizona	DS	201	Administration of Government	Establish Consumer Insurance Office.	Failed
1990	Arizona	DS	202	Environmental Reform	Hazardous waste disposal.	Failed
1990	Arizona	DS	203	Business Regulation	Motor vehicle insurance; rates and damages.	Failed
1990	Arkansas	DS	1	Campaign Finance Reform	Conduct and disclosure act — candidates and campaigns.	Passed
1990	California	DA	115	Legal	Changes criminal law, judicial procedures, expands capital offences.	Passed
1990	California	DS	116	Bonds	Authorizes bonds for passenger and commuter rail systems.	Passed
1990	California	DS	117	Animal Rights	Prohibit sport hunting of mountain lions and establishes fund for wildlife protection.	Passed
1990	California	DA	118	Apportionment/Redistricting	Changes procedures for redistricting.	Failed
1990	California	DA	119	Apportionment/Redistricting	Reapportionment by commission.	Failed
1990	California	DS	128	Health/Medical	Regulates chemicals in foods and pesticides.	Failed
1990	California	DA	129	Drug Policy Reform	Creates drug superfund and authorizes bonds for prison construction.	Failed
1990	California	DS	130	Environmental Reform	Authorizes bonds for forest acquisition and regulates timber harvesting.	Failed
1990	California	DA	131	Term Limits	Term limits for state officials, changes campaign finance laws, some public funding.	Failed
1990	California	DA	132	Environmental Reform	Establishes marine protection zone within three miles of coast.	Passed
1990	California	DS	133	Taxes	Increases sales tax to fund drug enforcement and prevention.	Failed
1990	California	DA	134	Alcohol Regulation	Alcohol surtax.	Failed
1990	California	DS	135	Environmental Reform	Pesticide regulation.	Failed

Year	State	Type	Measure Number	Subject Matter	Description	Pass/Fail
1990	California	DA	136	Taxes	State and local taxation.	Failed
1990	California	DA	137	Initiative and Referendum	Initiative and referendum process.	Failed
1990	California	DS	138	Environmental Reform	Forest acquisition. Timber harvesting. Bond act.	Failed
1990	California	DA	139	Labor	Prison inmate labor. Tax credit.	Passed
1990	California	DA	140	Term Limits	Term limits for state officials, limits on legislature's salary and operating costs. 6/8	Passed
1990	Colorado	DA	1	Taxes	To require voter approval for certain state and local government revenue increases.	Failed
1990	Colorado	DA	4	Gaming	Legalizing limited gaming.	Passed
1990	Colorado	DA	5	Term Limits	Term limits for elected officials. State legislature and Congress. 8/8	Passed
1990	Maine	IDS	N/A	Business Regulation	Stores open on Sundays/holidays; option to workers.	Passed
1990	Massachusetts	IDS	Question 2	Administration of Government	Limit state use of consultants	Failed
1990	Massachusetts	IDS	Question 3	Taxes	Change income tax law; regulate state agency fees.	Failed
1990	Massachusetts	IDS	Question 4	Election Reform	Establishment of political parties, nominations.	Passed
1990	Massachusetts	IDS	Question 5	Administration of Government	Regulate local aid fund.	Passed
1990	Missouri	DS	N/A	Environmental Reform	Regulation of streams.	Failed
1990	Montana	DA	CI 55	Taxes	Repeal existing taxes; charges on business exchange.	Failed
1990	Montana	DS	I 115	Taxes	Increase cigarette sales tax.	Failed
1990	Nebraska	DA	404	Gaming	Establish state lottery.	Failed
1990	Nebraska	DA	405	Administration of Government	Limits budget appropriations.	Failed
1990	Nevada	IDS	6	Taxes	Net profit tax, franchise fee for corporations.	Failed
1990	Nevada	DA	9	Taxes	1988 Measure 9 — prohibits a state personal income tax. 2nd vote as required by law.	Passed
1990	North Dakota	DS	N/A	Gaming	Regulates private games of chance: video gaming.	Failed
1990	North Dakota	DS	N/A	Business Regulation	Insurance agents can rebate their commission.	Failed
1990	North Dakota	DS	N/A	Taxes	Sales, use, motor vehicle taxes for education.	Failed
1990	North Dakota	DA	N/A	Gaming	Electronic video gaming, proceeds.	Failed
1990	North Dakota	DA	N/A	Gaming	Games of chance: proceeds, Roland Township.	Failed
1990	Ohio	DA	Issue No. 3	Gaming	Casino resort hotel in Lorain as pilot project.	Failed
1990	Oklahoma	DA	627	Administration of Government	Create five-member Ethics Commission.	Passed
1990	Oklahoma	DA	632	Term Limits	State legislative term limits. Twelve years limit.	Passed
1990	Oregon	DS	10	Abortion	Parental notice before minor's abortion.	Failed
1990	Oregon	DA	11	Education	Choice of public schools; tax credit, private schools.	Failed
1990	Oregon	DS	4	Nuclear weapons/facilities/waste	Prohibit Trojan operation until standards met.	Failed
1990	Oregon	DA	5	Taxes	Property tax limit; schools, government operations.	Passed
1990	Oregon	DS	6	Environmental Reform	Product packaging: recycling, hardship waivers.	Failed
1990	Oregon	DS	7	Welfare	Work in lieu of welfare benefits pilot program.	Passed
1990	Oregon	DA	8	Abortion	Prohibit abortion.	Failed
1990	Oregon	DS	9	Health/Medical	Requires use of safety belts.	Passed
1990	South Dakota	DS	1	Utility Regulation	Legislative approval: large scale waste facilities.	Passed
1990	South Dakota	DS	2	Environmental Reform	Permits for large scale gold/silver mining.	Failed
1990	Utah	DS	A	Taxes	Removal of state, local sales tax from food.	Failed
1990	Washington	DS	I-547	Environmental Reform	Growth and environmental protection goals, fees.	Failed
1991	Maine	IDS	N/A	Administration of Government	Reauthorize widening of the Maine Turnpike.	Passed
1991	Oklahoma	DS	639	Education	Repeal minimum standards for school accreditation.	Failed
1991	Washington	IDS	I-119	Physician assisted suicide	Allows a mentally competent adult who is suffering from a terminal illness to request and obtain medication from a physician to end that patient's own life in a humane and dignified manner.	Failed

Year	State	Type	Measure Number	Subject Matter	Description	Pass/Fail
1991	Washington	IDS	I-120	Abortion	Revise abortion laws — a woman's right to choose.	Passed
1991	Washington	DS	I-553	Term Limits	Term limits on state and federal officers. 6/12	Failed
1991	Washington	DS	I-559	Taxes	Adjust property value for tax purposes.	Failed
1992	Arizona	DA	107	Term Limits	Term limits. State legislature 8/8. Congress 6/12.	Passed
1992	Arizona	DA	108	Taxes	Public debt, revenue and taxation.	Passed
1992	Arizona	DA	110	Abortion	Pre-born child protection amendment; abortion.	Failed
1992	Arizona	DS	200	Animal Rights	Unlawful methods of capturing wildlife.	Failed
1992	Arkansas	DA	4	Term Limits	Term limits. State legislature 6/8. Congress 6/12.	Passed
1992	California	DS	161	Physician assisted suicide	Allows a mentally competent adult who is suffering from a terminal illness to request and obtain medication from a physician to end that patient's own life in a humane and dignified manner.	Failed
1992	California	DA	162	Administration of Government	Public employee retirement systems.	Passed
1992	California	DA	163	Taxes	End taxation of certain food products.	Passed
1992	California	DS	164	Term Limits	Term limits on Congress 6/12.	Passed
1992	California	DA	165	Administration of Government	Lets Governor reduce some expenditures to balance budget.	Failed
1992	California	DS	166	Health/Medical	Requires employers to provide basic health care coverage.	Failed
1992	California	DS	167	Taxes	Raises top income tax rates, repeals 1991 sales tax hike, renters' tax credits.	Failed
1992	Colorado	DA	1	Taxes	Voter approval of tax revenue increases.	Passed
1992	Colorado	DS	10	Animal Rights	Prohibit taking of black bears.	Passed
1992	Colorado	DA	2	Civil Rights	Repeal local laws passed to ban discrimination based on sexual orientation and prevent similar new laws.	Passed
1992	Colorado	DA	3	Gaming	Limited gaming; surtax.	Failed
1992	Colorado	DA	4	Gaming	Limited gaming.	Failed
1992	Colorado	DA	5	Gaming	Limited gaming.	Failed
1992	Colorado	DS	6	Education	Act for system of educational standards.	Failed
1992	Colorado	DA	7	Education	Vouchers for school funding.	Failed
1992	Colorado	DA	8	Environmental Reform	The Great Outdoors Colorado program.	Passed
1992	Colorado	DA	9	Gaming	Limited gaming.	Failed
1992	Florida	DA	10	Taxes	Limit homestead valuations.	Passed
1992	Florida	DA	9	Term Limits	Term Limits on state legislature 8/8.	Passed
1992	Idaho	DS	1	Taxes	Limit ad valorem property tax rates.	Failed
1992	Massachusetts	IDS	Question 1	Taxes	Tax on cigarettes and smokeless tobacco.	Passed
1992	Massachusetts	IDS	Question 2	Taxes	Public reporting of corporate tax information.	Passed
1992	Massachusetts	IDS	Question 3	Environmental Reform	All packaging to be recycled or recyclable.	Failed
1992	Massachusetts	IDS	Question 4	Taxes	Tax on oils, hazardous materials.	Failed
1992	Michigan	DA	B	Term Limits	Term limits on state legislature 6/8 and Congress 6/12.	Passed
1992	Michigan	IDS	N/A	Business Regulation	Amendment of auto insurance laws.	Failed
1992	Michigan	DA	N/A	Taxes	Exempt property tax from school funds; increases.	Failed
1992	Missouri	DA	12	Term Limits	Term limits on Congress 8/12.	Passed
1992	Missouri	DA	13	Term Limits	Term limits on state legislature 8/8.	Passed
1992	Montana	DA	CI 63	Taxes	Big Sky Dividend	Failed
1992	Montana	DA	CI 64	Term Limits	Term limits on state elected officials 8/8 and Congress 6/12.	Passed
1992	Nebraska	DA	407	Term Limits	Term limits on state elected officials 8 years. Congress 8/12	Passed

Year	State	Type	Measure Number	Subject Matter	Description	Pass/Fail
1992	North Dakota	DS	Measure 5	Term Limits	Term limits on Congress 12/12.	Passed
1992	North Dakota	DS	N/A	Taxes	Water development, sales and use tax.	Failed
1992	North Dakota	DS	N/A	Legal	Prohibit stopping/searching vehicles at random.	Failed
1992	North Dakota	DS	N/A	Environmental Reform	Environmental protection fund, fees on waste.	Failed
1992	Ohio	DA	Issue No. 2	Term Limits	Term limits on Congress 8/12.	Passed
1992	Ohio	DA	Issue No. 3	Term Limits	Term limits on Governor.	Passed
1992	Ohio	DA	Issue No. 4	Term Limits	Term limits on state legislature 8/8.	Passed
1992	Ohio	IDS	Issue No. 5	Business Regulation	Businesses to provide warnings for toxic substances.	Failed
1992	Oklahoma	DA	640	Taxes	Revenue bills approval by voters or 3/4 Legislature and Governor.	Passed
1992	Oregon	DA	3	Term Limits	Term limits on state legislature 6/8 and Congress 6/12.	Passed
1992	Oregon	DS	4	Business Regulation	Ban triple truck-trailers on Oregon highways.	Failed
1992	Oregon	DS	5	Nuclear weapons/facilities/waste	Close Trojan: waste, cost, and earthquake orders.	Failed
1992	Oregon	DS	6	Nuclear weapons/facilities/waste	Bans Trojan operation unless conditions met.	Failed
1992	Oregon	DA	7	Taxes	Raises limit on property tax; renters' tax relief.	Failed
1992	Oregon	DS	8	Animal Rights	Lower Columbia fish harvest.	Failed
1992	Oregon	DA	9	Civil Rights	Government to discourage homosexual "behaviors."	Failed
1992	South Dakota	DS	2	Environmental Reform	Regulation, reclamation: gold/silver mining.	Passed
1992	South Dakota	DS	3	Taxes	Various tax reductions, redistribution.	Failed
1992	South Dakota	DS	4	Gaming	Repeal the video lottery.	Failed
1992	South Dakota	DA	A	Term Limits	Term limits on state legislature 8/8 and on Congress 12/12.	Passed
1992	Utah	DS	A	Gaming	State-regulated horse races; pari-mutual wagering.	Failed
1992	Washington	IDS	I-134	Campaign Finance Reform	Limit campaign contributions, funding, campaigns.	Passed
1992	Washington	DS	I-573	Term Limits	Term limits on state legislature 6/8, Governor, and Congress 6/12.	Passed
1992	Wyoming	DS	1	Business Regulation	Ban triple trailers from State highways.	Passed
1992	Wyoming	DS	2	Term Limits	Term limits on state and federal officials.	Passed
1992	Wyoming	DS	3	Utility Regulation	Railroads: emergencies, toxins, hazardous materials.	Passed
1993	California	DA	174	Education	State education vouchers usable for public or private schools.	Failed
1993	Maine	IDS	1	Term Limits	Term limits for state legislators 8/8.	Passed
1993	Washington	DS	I-593	Legal	This measure imposes a "three strikes your out" rule for major criminal convictions.	Passed
1993	Washington	DS	I-601	Taxes	Limits state expenditures and provides for a popular vote on new taxes.	Passed
1993	Washington	DS	I-602	Taxes	This measure would limit state taxes and expenditures to a set formula, as well as repeal certain revenue measures.	Failed
1994	Alaska	IDS	4	Term Limits	Term limits on Congress 6/12.	Passed
1994	Alaska	IDS	N/A	Administration of Government	Relating to changing the capital to Wasilla.	Failed
1994	Alaska	IDS	N/A	Administration of Government	Relating to voters right to know the cost of moving the capital.	Passed
1994	Arizona	DA	103	Tort Reform	A Constitutional Amendment relating to the right to recover damages.	Failed
1994	Arizona	DS	200	Taxes	Proposing an act by Initiative Petition to increase state taxes on tobacco products.	Passed
1994	Arizona	DS	201	Animal Rights	Relating to the use of leg hold traps, poison and snares on public lands.	Passed

Year	State	Type	Measure Number	Subject Matter	Description	Pass/Fail
1994	California	DS	184	Legal	Convicted felons with 1 such prior conviction would receive twice the normal sentence for the new offense. Convicted felons with 2 or more such prior convictions would receive a life sentence. Three strikes your out.	Passed
1994	California	DS	185	Taxes	This measure imposes an additional 4% tax on retail sales of gasoline.	Failed
1994	California	DA	186	Health/Medical	Establishes health services system with defined medical, prescription drug, long-term, mental health, dental, emergency, other benefits.	Failed
1994	California	DS	187	Alien Rights	Makes illegal aliens ineligible for public social services, public health care services (unless emergency under federal law), and public school education at elementary, secondary, and post-secondary levels.	Passed
1994	California	DS	188	Health/Medical	Repeals and preempts local smoking and tobacco regulations. Repeals and replaces existing statewide smoking and tobacco regulations.	Failed
1994	Colorado	DA	1	Taxes	Would place an additional 50 cents per pack tax on the sale of cigarettes by wholesalers.	Failed
1994	Colorado	DA	11	Labor	Workers compensation benefits.	Failed
1994	Colorado	DA	12	Campaign Finance Reform	Placed limitations on elected officials compensation; enacted campaign contribution limitations.	Failed
1994	Colorado	DA	13	Gaming	To allow slot machines without a local vote in Manitou Springs.	Failed
1994	Colorado	DA	15	Campaign Finance Reform	Establish campaign contributions limits.	Failed
1994	Colorado	DA	16	Civil Rights	Would allow the control of the promotion of obscenity by the state and any city, town or County to the full extent permitted by the First Amendment to the United States Constitution.	Failed
1994	Colorado	DA	17	Term Limits	Term limits on Congress 6/12 and on all localities.	Passed
1994	Colorado	DA	18	Administration of Government	State medical assistance repayment.	Failed
1994	Florida	DA	3	Environmental Reform	Limit marine net fishing	Passed
1994	Florida	DA	4	Taxes	Governmental revenue limits.	Passed
1994	Florida	DA	8	Gaming	Legalize casinos in limited areas.	Failed
1994	Idaho	DS	1	Civil Rights	Act establishing state policies regarding homosexuality.	Failed
1994	Idaho	DS	2	Term Limits	Term limits on state legislature 8/8 and Congress 6/12.	Passed
1994	Maine	IDS	1	Term Limits	Term limits on Congress 6/12.	Passed
1994	Massachusetts	IDS	Question 1	Campaign Finance Reform	Regulating spending on ballot question campaigns.	Failed
1994	Massachusetts	IDS	Question 4	Term Limits	Term limits on state legislature 8/8 and on Congress 6/12.	Passed
1994	Massachusetts	IDS	Question 5	Business Regulation	Opening of retail stores on Sunday morning and certain holidays.	Passed
1994	Massachusetts	DA	Question 6	Taxes	Graduated income tax.	Failed
1994	Massachusetts	IDS	Question 7	Taxes	Personal income tax changes.	Failed
1994	Massachusetts	IDS	Question 8	Administration of Government	State highway fund changes.	Passed
1994	Massachusetts	DS	Question 9	Housing	Prohibiting rent control.	Passed
1994	Missouri	DA	N/A	Campaign Finance Reform	Establish campaign finance regulations.	Passed
1994	Missouri	DA	N/A	Environmental Reform	Property protection to require government reimbursement for lost revenue due to the acquisition on lands for park use.	Passed

Year	State	Type	Measure Number	Subject Matter	Description	Pass/Fail
1994	Missouri	DA	N/A	Taxes	Voter approval of tax increase.	Failed
1994	Missouri	DA	N/A	Gaming	Allow slot machine gambling on a riverboat.	Passed
1994	Montana	DA	CI 66	Taxes	Requires voter approval of all new or increased taxes.	Failed
1994	Montana	DA	CI 67	Taxes	Requires 2/3 vote of the legislature for any new or increased taxes.	Failed
1994	Montana	DS	I 118	Campaign Finance Reform	Lower the cap on campaign contributions and other revisions to campaign finance laws.	Passed
1994	Nebraska	DA	408	Term Limits	Term limits on state legislature 8 years and on Congress 6/12.	Passed
1994	Nevada	DA	10	Campaign Finance Reform	Defines and limits campaign contributions.	Passed
1994	Nevada	DA	11	Taxes	Require a 2/3 vote in the legislature and a majority vote by referendum for any tax increase.	Passed
1994	Nevada	DA	8	Term Limits	Term limits on judges and state legislature 12/12.	Passed
1994	Nevada	DA	9	Term Limits	Term limits on Congress 6/12.	Passed
1994	North Dakota	DS	N/A	Administration of Government	Provides that cities vote every four years whether to publish the minutes of their meetings.	Passed
1994	North Dakota	DS	N/A	Health/Medical	Provides for the repeal of North Dakota's mandatory seat belt law.	Failed
1994	Ohio	DA	Issue No. 4	Taxes	Prohibiting the current wholesale tax on soft drinks and other carbonated, non-alcoholic beverages.	Passed
1994	Oklahoma	DA	658	Gaming	Would create a state lottery	Failed
1994	Oklahoma	DA	662	Term Limits	Term limits on Congress 6/12.	Passed
1994	Oregon	DA	10	Initiative and Referendum	Legislature cannot reduce voter approved sentences without 2/3 vote	Passed
1994	Oregon	DS	11	Legal	Mandatory sentences for listed felonies; covers persons 15 and up	Passed
1994	Oregon	DS	12	Labor	Repeals prevailing rate wage requirement for workers on public works.	Failed
1994	Oregon	DA	13	Civil Rights	Governments cannot approve, create classifications based on homosexuality.	Failed
1994	Oregon	DA	14	Environmental Reform	Amends chemical process mining laws — adds requirements, prohibitions, standards, fees.	Failed
1994	Oregon	DA	15	Education	State must maintain funding for schools, community colleges.	Failed
1994	Oregon	DS	16	Physician assisted suicide	Allows a mentally competent adult who is suffering from a terminal illness to request and obtain medication from a physician to end that patient's own life in a humane and dignified manner.	Passed
1994	Oregon	DA	17	Legal	Requires state prison inmates to work fulltime.	Passed
1994	Oregon	DS	18	Animal Rights	Bans hunting bears with bait. Hunting bears, cougars with dogs.	Passed
1994	Oregon	DA	19	Civil Rights	No free speech protection for obscenity, child pornography.	Failed
1994	Oregon	DA	20	Taxes	"Equal Tax" on trade replaces current taxes.	Failed
1994	Oregon	DA	5	Taxes	Bars new or increased taxes without voter approval.	Failed
1994	Oregon	DA	6	Campaign Finance Reform	Candidates may use only contributions from district residents.	Passed
1994	Oregon	DA	7	Civil Rights	Guarantees Equal protection and lists prohibited grounds of discrimination.	Failed
1994	Oregon	DA	8	Labor	Public employees must pay part of salary for pension.	Passed
1994	Oregon	DS	9	Campaign Finance Reform	Sets contribution and spending limits and adopts other campaign finance law changes.	Passed
1994	South Dakota	DS	1	Taxes	Property tax reform.	Failed

Year	State	Type	Measure Number	Subject Matter	Description	Pass/Fail
1994	Utah	IDS	A	Term Limits	Term limits on state legislature 8 years and on Congress 8/12.	Failed
1994	Washington	DS	I-607	Business Regulation	Shall persons other than dentists be licensed to make and sell dentures to the public, as regulated by a new state board of denture technology?	Passed
1994	Wyoming	DS	2	Gaming	Local option gambling.	Failed
1994	Wyoming	DS	3	Administration of Government	Investment of state funds	Failed
1995	Maine	IDS	N/A	Civil Rights	Do you favor the changes in Maine law limiting protected classifications, in future state and local laws to race, color, sex, physical or mental disability, religion, age, national origin, familial status and marital status, and repealing existing laws?	Failed
1995	Mississippi	IDA	4	Term Limits	Term limits on all elected officials in the state.	Failed
1995	Washington	DS	I-640	Environmental Reform	Regulation of state fishing	Failed
1995	Washington	DS	I-651	Gaming	Should gambling be allowed on Native American lands?	Failed
1996	Alaska	IDS	3	Animal Rights	Bans same day airborne hunting of wolf, wolverine, fox or lynx.	Passed
1996	Alaska	IDS	4	Term Limits	Informed Voter Law.	Passed
1996	Arizona	DA	102	Legal	Requires juveniles ages 15 and older to be tried as an adult for murder, rape and armed robbery.	Passed
1996	Arizona	DS	200	Drug Policy Reform	Relating to laws on controlled substances and those convicted of personal use or possession of controlled substances.	Passed
1996	Arizona	DS	201	Gaming	Proposing an act concerning the use of uniform gaming compacts with Indian tribes.	Passed
1996	Arizona	DS	203	Health/Medical	Allocates lottery revenues for health programs.	Passed
1996	Arkansas	DS	1	Campaign Finance Reform	Establish campaign finance regulations.	Passed
1996	Arkansas	DA	4	Gaming	Would establish a state lottery; permit charitable bingo and raffles, provide for a local vote in Hot Springs concerning casino gambling.	Failed
1996	Arkansas	DA	9	Term Limits	Term limits on state legislature 6/8, Governor, and Congress 6/12.	Passed
1996	California	DS	198	Election Reform	Created open blanket primary voting.	Passed
1996	California	DS	199	Housing	Mobile home rent.	Failed
1996	California	DS	200	Business Regulation	No-fault motor insurance.	Failed
1996	California	DS	201	Tort Reform	Attorneys' fees in class action and shareholder suits.	Failed
1996	California	DS	202	Tort Reform	Limits on attorneys' contingency fees in tort cases.	Failed
1996	California	DS	207	Tort Reform	Attorneys fees. Right to negotiate. Frivolous lawsuits.	Failed
1996	California	DS	208	Campaign Finance Reform	Campaign contributions and spending limits. Restricts lobbyist.	Passed
1996	California	DA	209	Civil Rights	Ending racial preferences.	Passed
1996	California	DS	210	Labor	Minimum wage increase.	Passed
1996	California	DS	211	Tort Reform	Attorney — client fee arrangements, securities, fraud, lawsuits.	Failed
1996	California	DS	212	Campaign Finance Reform	Campaign contributions and spending limits. Repeals gift and honoraria limits. Restricts lobbyist.	Failed
1996	California	DS	213	Business Regulation	Limitation of recovery to felons. Uninsured motorists. Drunk drivers.	Passed
1996	California	DS	214	Health/Medical	Regulation of health care business.	Failed
1996	California	DS	215	Drug Policy Reform	Legalize marijuana for medicinal purposes.	Passed
1996	California	DS	216	Business Regulation	Consumer protection. Taxes on corporate restructuring.	Failed

Year	State	Type	Measure Number	Subject Matter	Description	Pass/Fail
1996	California	DS	217	Taxes	Reinstates expired higher tax rates on top incomes.	Failed
1996	California	DA	218	Taxes	Establish tax limits	Passed
1996	Colorado	DA	11	Taxes	Eliminates property tax exemptions of religious and nonprofit organizations.	Failed
1996	Colorado	DA	12	Term Limits	Term limits on Congress 6/12 and all localities.	Passed
1996	Colorado	DA	13	Initiative and Referendum	Expands initiative and referendum powers.	Failed
1996	Colorado	DA	14	Animal Rights	Concerns methods of taking wildlife; prohibits use of leg hold traps.	Passed
1996	Colorado	DS	15	Campaign Finance Reform	Limiting the amount of campaign contributions to candidate committees.	Passed
1996	Colorado	DA	16	Administration of Government	Concerns management of state's trust lands; expands membership of the State Land Board.	Passed
1996	Colorado	DA	17	Civil Rights	Grants constitutional status to parents' rights.	Failed
1996	Colorado	DA	18	Gaming	Allow limited gambling in the city of Trinidad.	Failed
1996	Florida	DA	1	Taxes	Requires a 2/3 vote for new constitutionally imposed state taxes or fees.	Passed
1996	Florida	DA	4	Taxes	Establishes a fee on Everglades sugar production.	Failed
1996	Florida	DA	5	Environmental Reform	Responsibility for paying costs of water pollution abatement in the Everglades.	Passed
1996	Florida	DA	6	Environmental Reform	Establishes and Everglade Trust Fund for conservation and protection of natural resources and abatement of water pollution.	Passed
1996	Idaho	DS	1	Taxes	Limit property taxes to one percent of value.	Failed
1996	Idaho	DS	2	Animal Rights	Prohibit the use of dogs or bait for hunting bear. Limit the bear hunting season.	Failed
1996	Idaho	DS	3	Nuclear weapons/facilities/waste	Require legislative and voter approval of agreements for the receipt of additional radioactive waste and nullifying a prior agreement.	Failed
1996	Idaho	DS	4	Term Limits	Informed Voter Law.	Passed
1996	Maine	IDS	1	Term Limits	Informed Voter Law.	Passed
1996	Maine	IDS	2A	Environmental Reform	Bans clear cutting.	Failed
1996	Maine	IDS	3	Campaign Finance Reform	Campaign finance reform; including voluntary spending limits and public funding.	Passed
1996	Massachusetts	IDS	Question 1	Animal Rights	Prohibits use of leg hold traps and snares. Prohibits use of dogs and bait in hunting bear and bobcats.	Passed
1996	Michigan	IDS	D	Animal Rights	Limits the bear hunting season and prohibits the use of bait and dogs to hunt bear.	Failed
1996	Michigan	IDS	E	Gaming	Permit casino gambling in Detroit.	Passed
1996	Missouri	DA	8	Taxes	Extends, for 10 years, a sales and use tax for soil and water conservation, state parks and historic sites and for payments in lieu of property taxes for park lands.	Passed
1996	Missouri	DA	9	Term Limits	Informed Voter Law.	Passed
1996	Missouri	DS	A	Labor	Increases the minimum wage, from $6.25, Jan. 1, 1997, to $6.75, Jan. 1, 1999 and an additional 15 cents per year thereafter.	Failed
1996	Montana	DS	I 121	Labor	Increases the minimum wage, from $4.25 to $6.25 by year 2000.	Failed
1996	Montana	DS	I 122	Environmental Reform	Increases requirements for treatment of water discharged from mines.	Failed
1996	Montana	DS	I 123	Legal	Allows lawsuits for civil damages for unlawful threats or intimidation. Prohibits filing of false liens against property.	Passed

Year	State	Type	Measure Number	Subject Matter	Description	Pass/Fail
1996	Montana	DS	I 125	Campaign Finance Reform	Prohibits contributions from corporations to ballot question committees.	Passed
1996	Montana	DS	I 132	Term Limits	Informed Voter Law.	Failed
1996	Nebraska	DA	409	Term Limits	Term limits on state legislature 8 years and on Congress 6/12.	Passed
1996	Nebraska	DA	410	Initiative and Referendum	Bases number of signatures required on citizen petitions on percentages of votes cast for governor rather than on percentages of the total number of registered voters.	Failed
1996	Nebraska	DA	411	Education	Makes "quality education" a fundamental constitutional right.	Failed
1996	Nebraska	DA	412	Taxes	Limits property taxes.	Failed
1996	Nevada	DA	10	Campaign Finance Reform	Campaign contributions limits. 2nd vote as required by law.	Passed
1996	Nevada	DA	11	Taxes	Amends constitution to require a 2/3 vote of the legislature to increase taxes. 2nd vote as required by law.	Passed
1996	Nevada	DA	17	Term Limits	Informed Voter Law.	Passed
1996	Nevada	DA	9A	Term Limits	Term limits on state legislature 12/12.	Passed
1996	Nevada	DA	9B	Term Limits	Term limits on judges. (Question 9 was split into two questions, by court order) 2nd vote as required by law.	Failed
1996	North Dakota	DA	Measure 4	Veteran Affairs	Makes the veteran's postwar trust fund a permanent fund.	Passed
1996	North Dakota	DA	Measure 5	Term Limits	Informed Voter Law and term limits on state legislature 8/8.	Failed
1996	North Dakota	DA	Measure 6	Term Limits	Direct application for constitutional convention to consider a term limits amendment.	Failed
1996	Ohio	DA	Issue No. 1	Gaming	Authorize moored river boat casino gambling.	Failed
1996	Oklahoma	DA	669	Taxes	Would limit property taxes.	Failed
1996	Oregon	DA	33	Initiative and Referendum	Prohibits the legislature from amending or repealing, for five years, statutes approved by the voters.	Failed
1996	Oregon	DS	34	Environmental Reform	Gives Fish & Wildlife Commission exclusive authority to manage wildlife; repeals 1994 initiative that prohibited the use of dogs or bait to hunt bear or cougar.	Failed
1996	Oregon	DS	35	Health/Medical	Restricts bases on which health care providers may receive payment.	Failed
1996	Oregon	DS	36	Labor	Increases minimum wage to $6.50 over three years.	Passed
1996	Oregon	DS	37	Environmental Reform	Broadens types of beverage containers that require deposits and refunds.	Failed
1996	Oregon	DS	38	Environmental Reform	Prohibits livestock in or near polluted waters or on adjacent lands.	Failed
1996	Oregon	DA	39	Health/Medical	Prohibits government and private entities from discriminating among health care provider categories.	Failed
1996	Oregon	DA	40	Legal	Victims' rights.	Passed
1996	Oregon	DA	41	Labor	Makes complete information regarding employer costs of public employees available to the public.	Failed
1996	Oregon	DA	42	Education	Requires annual testing of public school students, grades 4–12.	Failed
1996	Oregon	DS	43	Labor	Reinstates collective bargaining law for public safety employees.	Failed
1996	Oregon	DS	44	Taxes	Increases cigarette and tobacco product taxes; changes tax revenue distribution.	Passed

Year	State	Type	Measure Number	Subject Matter	Description	Pass/Fail
1996	Oregon	DA	45	Labor	Raises public employees' retirement age to qualify for benefits; reduces benefits.	Failed
1996	Oregon	DA	46	Taxes	Counts non-voters as "no" votes on tax measures.	Failed
1996	Oregon	DA	47	Taxes	Reduces and limits property taxes; limits revenue available for schools and other local services funded by property taxes; allows lost revenue to be replaced only with state income tax.	Passed
1996	Oregon	DA	48	Term Limits	Informed Voter Law.	Failed
1996	South Dakota	DS	1	Term Limits	Informed Voter Law.	Passed
1996	Washington	DS	I-173	Education	Scholarship vouchers.	Failed
1996	Washington	DS	I-177	Education	Provides for publicly-funded charter schools.	Failed
1996	Washington	DS	I-655	Animal Rights	Prohibits baiting of bear; prohibits hunting bear, cougar, bobcat or lynx with dogs.	Passed
1996	Washington	DS	I-670	Term Limits	Informed Voter Law.	Failed
1996	Washington	DS	I-671	Gaming	Allows limited electronic gaming on Indian lands.	Failed
1996	Wyoming	DS	1	Term Limits	Informed Voter Law.	Failed
1997	Colorado	DA	1	Taxes	Funding for transportation.	Failed
1997	Washington	DS	I-673	Health/Medical	Shall health insurance plans be regulated as to provision of services by designated health care providers, managed care provisions, and disclosure of certain plan information?	Failed
1997	Washington	DS	I-676	Gun Regulation	Shall the transfer of handguns without trigger-locking devices be prohibited and persons possessing or acquiring a handgun be required to obtain a handgun safety license?	Failed
1997	Washington	DS	I-677	Civil Rights	Shall discrimination based on sexual orientation be prohibited in employment, employment agency, and union membership practices, without requiring employee partner benefits or preferential treatment?	Failed
1997	Washington	DS	I-678	Business Regulation	Shall dental hygienist who obtain a special license endorsement be permitted to perform designated dental hygiene services without the supervision of a licensed dentist?	Failed
1997	Washington	DS	I-685	Drug Policy Reform	Shall penalties for drug possession and drug-related violent crime be revised, medical use of Schedule I controlled substances be permitted, and a dug prevention commission established?	Failed
1998	Alaska	IDS	5	Environmental Reform	Would prohibit billboards	Passed
1998	Alaska	IDS	6	Administration of Government	Would adopt English as official language.	Passed
1998	Alaska	IDS	7	Term Limits	Self Limit Law.	Passed
1998	Alaska	IDS	8	Drug Policy Reform	Would allow the medical use of marijuana	Passed
1998	Alaska	IDS	9	Animal Rights	Would prohibit trapping wolves with snares.	Failed
1998	Arizona	DA	105	Initiative and Referendum	Would prohibit the Governor's veto of initiative and referendum measures. Prohibits legislative repeal of I&R measures and requires 3/4 vote of legislature to amend I&R measures.	Passed
1998	Arizona	DS	200	Campaign Finance Reform	Would establish a five-member commission to administer alternative campaign financing system and provides for public funding and additional reporting for participating candidates and reduces current contribution limits by 20%.	Passed
1998	Arizona	DS	201	Animal Rights	Would outlaw cockfighting.	Passed
1998	Arizona	DS	202	Taxes	Would give Arizona candidates for federal office the option to pledge to support and vote for elimination of the federal income tax and IRS through the passage of a national consumption tax.	Failed

Year	State	Type	Measure Number	Subject Matter	Description	Pass/Fail
1998	California	DA	10	Health/Medical	Would create state commission to provide information and materials and to formulate guidelines for establishment of comprehensive early childhood development and smoking prevention programs.	Passed
1998	California	DA	223	Education	School districts to spend no more than 5 percent of all funds for administrative costs.	Failed
1998	California	DA	224	Administration of Government	Regulates state funded design and engineering contracts.	Failed
1998	California	DS	225	Term Limits	Informed Voter Law.	Passed
1998	California	DS	226	Campaign Finance Reform	Union member's permission required to use dues for political contributions.	Failed
1998	California	DS	227	Education	Ending bilingual education.	Passed
1998	California	DS	4	Animal Rights	Would prohibit trapping mammals classified as fur bearing or non-game with body-gripping traps for recreation or commerce in fur.	Passed
1998	California	DS	5	Gaming	Would specify terms and conditions of mandatory compact between state and Indian tribes for gambling on tribal land.	Passed
1998	California	DS	6	Animal Rights	Prohibiting any person from possessing transferring receiving or holding any horse or pony or burro or mule with intent to kill or have it killed.	Passed
1998	California	DS	7	Environmental Reform	Would authorize State Air Resources Board and delegated air pollution control districts to award $218 million in state tax credits annually until 2011 to encourage air-commissions reduction.	Failed
1998	California	DS	8	Education	Would create fund for reduction in class sizes. Requires teacher credentialing and testing.	Failed
1998	California	DS	9	Nuclear weapons/facilities/waste	Would prohibit assessment of utility tax bond payments or surcharges for payment of costs of nuclear power plants/related assets.	Failed
1998	Colorado	DS	11	Abortion	Would prohibit partial birth abortion	Failed
1998	Colorado	DS	12	Abortion	Would require parents be notified prior to a physician performed abortion.	Passed
1998	Colorado	DA	13	Animal Rights	Would establish uniform livestock regulations.	Failed
1998	Colorado	DS	14	Animal Rights	Establish regulations for commercial hog farms.	Passed
1998	Colorado	DS	15	Environmental Reform	Would regulate water flow meters.	Failed
1998	Colorado	DA	16	Education	Would require that payments by the Conservation District be made to the Public School Fund and School Districts.	Failed
1998	Colorado	DA	17	Education	Would establish Income Tax Credit for education expenses.	Failed
1998	Colorado	DA	18	Term Limits	Self Limit Law.	Passed
1998	Idaho	DS	1	Term Limits	Informed Voter Law.	Passed
1998	Massachusetts	IDS	Question 2	Campaign Finance Reform	Would establish public funding of campaigns.	Passed
1998	Massachusetts	IDS	Question 3	Taxes	Would cut state income taxes.	Passed
1998	Michigan	IDS	B	Physician assisted suicide	Allows a mentally competent adult who is suffering from a terminal illness to request and obtain medication from a physician to end that patient's own life in a humane and dignified manner.	Failed
1998	Missouri	DA	9	Gaming	Would overturn a Missouri Supreme Court ruling that games of chance including slot machines may legally be offered only on boats moored in the main channels of the Missouri.	Passed
1998	Missouri	DS	A	Animal Rights	Would make it a felony to bait or fight animals.	Passed

Year	State	Type	Measure Number	Subject Matter	Description	Pass/Fail
1998	Montana	DA	CI 75	Taxes	Would require voter approval of tax increases.	Passed
1998	Montana	DS	I 134	Taxes	Would repeal Montana Retail Motor Fuel Marketing Act.	Passed
1998	Montana	DS	I 136	Animal Rights	Would revise outfitter and hunter licensing.	Failed
1998	Montana	DS	I 137	Environmental Reform	Would prohibit cyanide process open pit mining.	Passed
1998	Nebraska	DA	413	Taxes	Would slow the growth of state and local government spending and cut taxes.	Failed
1998	Nebraska	DS	414	Utility Regulation	Would require long distance carriers to pass on for the benefit of long distance carriers mandatory reductions in access charges by local exchange carriers.	Failed
1998	Nevada	DA	17	Term Limits	Informed Voter Law.	Passed
1998	Nevada	DA	9	Drug Policy Reform	Would let adults on the advice of physicians use marijuana for curing or relieving pain in a number of illnesses such as cancer and AIDS.	Passed
1998	North Dakota	DA	Measure 2	Election Reform	Would set up a process for the election of Sheriffs	Passed
1998	Ohio	IDS	Issue No. 1	Animal Rights	Would ban the hunting of mourning doves.	Failed
1998	Oklahoma	DA	672	Gaming	To establish casino gambling.	Failed
1998	Oregon	DS	58	Administration of Government	Would require issuing copy of original birth certificates to adoptee.	Passed
1998	Oregon	DA	59	Campaign Finance Reform	Would prohibit using public resources to collect money for political purposes.	Failed
1998	Oregon	DS	60	Election Reform	Would require vote by mail in biennial primary and general elections.	Passed
1998	Oregon	DA	62	Campaign Finance Reform	Would require campaign finance disclosures and regulates signature gathering.	Passed
1998	Oregon	DA	63	Election Reform	Would establish super-majority voting requirements and require same super-majority for passage.	Passed
1998	Oregon	DS	64	Environmental Reform	Would prohibit many present timber harvest practices and imposes more restrictive regulations.	Failed
1998	Oregon	DA	65	Administration of Government	Would create process for requiring legislature to review administrative rules.	Failed
1998	Oregon	DA	66	Environmental Reform	Would dedicate some lottery funding to parks and beaches habitat and watershed protection.	Passed
1998	Oregon	DS	67	Drug Policy Reform	Would allow medical use of marijuana within limits and establishes permit system.	Passed
1998	South Dakota	DA	Constitutional Amendment A	Taxes	Would prohibit property taxes for school funding.	Failed
1998	South Dakota	DA	Constitutional Amendment E	Administration of Government	Would address issues relating to corporate farming.	Passed
1998	Washington	IDS	I-200	Civil Rights	Would prohibit state and local government't entities from discriminating against or granting preferential treatment to any individual or group based on race and sex and color and ethnicity or national origin.	Passed
1998	Washington	DS	I-688	Labor	Would increase the minimum wage for workers eighteen years and older.	Passed
1998	Washington	DS	I-692	Drug Policy Reform	Would permit the medical use of marijuana by patients with certain terminal or debilitating conditions.	Passed
1998	Washington	DS	I-694	Abortion	Would make it a felony to kill a fetus in the "process of birth" except when such procedure is the only way to prevent death of the mother.	Failed
1999	Maine	IDS	1	Abortion	Bans partial-birth abortions except when such an abortion is necessary to save the life of the mother.	Failed

Year	State	Type	Measure Number	Subject Matter	Description	Pass/Fail
1999	Maine	IDS	2	Drug Policy Reform	Authorizes an eligible patient diagnosed with one or more specified debilitating conditions, including cancer and acquired immune deficiency syndrome, to use marijuana for medical purposes	Passed
1999	Mississippi	IDA	9	Term Limits	Term limits on state legislature 8/8.	Failed
1999	Washington	DS	I-695	Taxes	This measure would establish license tab fees at $30 per year for motor vehicles. No new taxes without vote of people.	Passed
1999	Washington	DS	I-696	Environmental Reform	Prohibit certain commercial net, troll, and trawl fishing in fresh and marine waters, except tribal treaty fisheries.	Failed
2000	Alaska	IDS	4	Taxes	This bill sets the value of property at its assessment on January 1 of the first year the bill is in effect.	Failed
2000	Alaska	IDS	5	Drug Policy Reform	This bill would shield those 18 years or older from civil and criminal sanctions for the use of marijuana and other hemp products.	Failed
2000	Arizona	DA	106	Apportionment/Redistricting	Creates a new "citizens' independent redistricting commission" to draw new legislative and congressional district boundaries after each U.S. Census.	Passed
2000	Arizona	DA	108	Utility Regulation	End rate making by the Corporate Commission of local telephone rates where service is available from two or more competing providers.	Failed
2000	Arizona	DS	200	Health/Medical	Provide health insurance for uninsured working parents.	Passed
2000	Arizona	DS	202	Environmental Reform	This initiative would require cities and counties to adopt growth management plans to limit urban sprawl.	Failed
2000	Arizona	DS	203	Education	Requires that all public school instruction be conducted in English.	Passed
2000	Arizona	DS	204	Health/Medical	Funds the Healthy Arizona Initiative passed in 1996; increases eligibility of working poor at federal poverty level for health care coverage through AHCCCS.	Passed
2000	Arkansas	DS	1	Health/Medical	Will designate how the tobacco settlement proceeds are dedicated.	Passed
2000	Arkansas	DA	5	Gaming	An amendment to establish a state lottery; to permit charitable bingo games and raffles; to allow Arkansas Casino Corporation to own and operate six casino gambling establishments.	Failed
2000	California	DS	21	Death Penalty	Increases punishment for gang-related felonies; death penalty for gang-related murder; indeterminate life sentences for home-invasion robbery, carjacking, witness intimidation and drive-by shootings.	Passed
2000	California	DS	22	Civil Rights	Adds a provision to the Family Code providing that only marriage between a man and a woman is valid or recognized in California.	Passed
2000	California	DS	23	Election Reform	Provides that in general, special, primary and recall elections, voters may vote for "none of the above" rather than a named candidate.	Failed
2000	California	DS	25	Campaign Finance Reform	Expands campaign contribution disclosure requirements. Establishes contribution limits. Bans corporate contributions. Limits fundraising to period 12 months before primary election and ninety days after election.	Failed

Year	State	Type	Measure Number	Subject Matter	Description	Pass/Fail
2000	California	DA	26	Education	Authorizes school, community college districts, and County education offices that evaluate safety, class size, information technology needs to issue bonds if approved by majority of applicable district or County voters.	Failed
2000	California	DA	27	Term Limits	Self Limit Law	Failed
2000	California	DS	28	Taxes	Repeals additional $.50 per pack tax on cigarettes and equivalent increase in state tax on tobacco products previously enacted by Proposition 10 at November 3, 1998, election.	Failed
2000	California	DA	35	Administration of Government	Overrides constitutional restrictions to allow state, local contracting with private entities for engineering and architectural services in all phases of public works projects.	Passed
2000	California	DS	36	Drug Policy Reform	Requires drug treatment program and probation for certain non-violent drug possession offenses and similar parole violations not including sale, production or manufacture.	Passed
2000	California	DA	37	Taxes	Redefines as taxes any compulsory fees enacted by state or local government after July 1, 1999 to monitor, study or mitigate societal or economic effects of activity where such fees impose no regulatory obligation on the payer.	Failed
2000	California	DA	38	Education	Authorizes annual state payments of at least $4000 per pupil for qualifying private and religious schools as grants for new enrollees.	Failed
2000	California	DA	39	Education	Authorizes bonds for construction, reconstruction, rehabilitation or replacement of school facilities if approved by 55% vote.	Passed
2000	Colorado	DA	20	Drug Policy Reform	Legalizes marijuana for medical purposes.	Passed
2000	Colorado	DA	21	Taxes	Amends TABOR — creates tax cuts.	Failed
2000	Colorado	DS	22	Gun Regulation	An initiative amendment to require background checks for guns purchased at gun shows.	Passed
2000	Colorado	DA	23	Education	Providing Additional K–12 Funding	Passed
2000	Colorado	DA	24	Environmental Reform	Citizen Growth Initiative.	Failed
2000	Colorado	DS	25	Abortion	This measure insures the provision of complete and accurate information to allow a woman to make an informed choice as to whether to give birth or to have an abortion.	Failed
2000	Florida	DA	1	Environmental Reform	To reduce traffic and increase travel alternatives, this amendment provides for development of a high speed monorail, fixed guide way or magnetic levitation system linking Florida's five largest urban areas.	Passed
2000	Maine	IDS	1	Physician assisted suicide	Allows a mentally competent adult who is suffering from a terminal illness to request and obtain medication from a physician to end that patient's own life in a humane and dignified manner.	Failed
2000	Maine	IDS	2	Environmental Reform	Sets limits on timber harvesting on land subject to the Maine Tree Growth Tax Law and requires that a landowner obtain a permit from the Maine Forest Service prior to undertaking harvesting activities that will result in a clear-cut.	Failed
2000	Maine	IDS	3	Gaming	This initiated bill authorizes the operation of video lottery terminals at certain existing pari-mutuel facilities.	Failed

Year	State	Type	Measure Number	Subject Matter	Description	Pass/Fail
2000	Massachusetts	IDS	Question 3	Animal Rights	This proposed law would prohibit in Massachusetts any dog racing or racing meeting where any form of betting or wagering on the speed or ability of dogs occurs.	Failed
2000	Massachusetts	IDS	Question 4	Taxes	This proposed law would repeal the law setting the state personal income tax rate on Part B taxable income.	Passed
2000	Massachusetts	IDS	Question 5	Health/Medical	This proposed law would set up a state Health Care Council to review and recommend legislation for a health care system that ensures comprehensive, high quality health care.	Failed
2000	Massachusetts	IDS	Question 6	Taxes	This proposed law would allow a state personal income taxpayer a tax credit equal to the amount of tolls the taxpayer paid during the taxable year on all Massachusetts roads.	Failed
2000	Massachusetts	IDS	Question 7	Taxes	This proposed law would allow taxpayers who give to charity a state personal income tax deduction for those charitable contributions.	Passed
2000	Massachusetts	IDS	Question 8	Drug Policy Reform	This proposed law would create a state Drug Treatment Trust Fund, to be used, subject to appropriations by the state Legislature, solely for the treatment of drug-dependent persons. The Fund would include fines paid under the state's criminal drug laws; money and the proceeds from selling property forfeited because of its use in connection with drug crimes.	Failed
2000	Michigan	DA	1	Education	Create voucher system. Guarantee per-pupil funding in public schools; require testing of teachers in academic subjects.	Failed
2000	Michigan	DA	2	Administration of Government	Requires supermajority vote of legislature interfere in municipal affairs.	Failed
2000	Missouri	DS	A	Environmental Reform	Prohibits new billboards from being constructed and restricts existing outdoor advertising along all National Highway System highways in Missouri.	Failed
2000	Missouri	DS	B	Campaign Finance Reform	Allows candidates that abide by certain requirements (such as campaign spending limits) to receive taxpayer money for their campaigns.	Failed
2000	Montana	DS	I 143	Animal Rights	Prohibit all new alternative livestock ranches, also known as game farms. Existing game farms would be allowed to continue, but would be prohibited from transferring their license to anybody else.	Passed
2000	Nebraska	DA	415	Term Limits	Term limits on state legislature 8 years.	Passed
2000	Nebraska	DS	416	Civil Rights	Ban on Same Sex Marriage.	Passed
2000	Nevada	DA		Civil Rights	Ban of same sex marriage	Passed
2000	Nevada	DA	9	Drug Policy Reform	Would let adults on the advice of physicians use marijuana for curing or relieving pain in a number of illnesses such as cancer and AIDS. 2nd vote as required by law.	Passed
2000	Oregon	DA	1	Education	Accountability and equity in school funding.	Passed
2000	Oregon	DA	2	Administration of Government	Creates process for requiring legislature to review administrative rules	Failed
2000	Oregon	DA	3	Drug Policy Reform	Limits asset forfeitures and restricts use of proceeds.	Passed
2000	Oregon	DS	4	Health/Medical	An initiative statute to use tobacco settlement money for low-income health care.	Failed
2000	Oregon	DS	5	Gun Regulation	An initiative statute to require background checks at gun shows.	Passed

Year	State	Type	Measure Number	Subject Matter	Description	Pass/Fail
2000	Oregon	DS	6	Campaign Finance Reform	Provides public funding to candidates who limit spending.	Failed
2000	Oregon	DA	7	Environmental Reform	Requires payment to landowner if government regulation reduces property value.	Passed
2000	Oregon	DA	8	Administration of Government	Limits state appropriations to percentage of state's prior personal income.	Failed
2000	Oregon	DS	9	Civil Rights	Prohibits public school instruction encouraging, promoting, sanctioning homosexual and/or bisexual behaviors.	Failed
2000	Oregon	DA	91	Taxes	This measure makes all federal income tax paid by personal and corporate income taxpayers a deduction on the taxpayer's Oregon income tax returns.	Failed
2000	Oregon	DA	92	Campaign Finance Reform	Prohibits payroll deductions for political purposes without specific written authorization.	Failed
2000	Oregon	DA	93	Taxes	Requires Voter Approval Of Most New And Increased Taxes, Fees.	Failed
2000	Oregon	DS	94	Legal	Repeals Mandatory Minimum Sentences For Certain Felonies, Requires Re-sentencing	Failed
2000	Oregon	DA	95	Education	Job performance must determine public school teacher pay.	Failed
2000	Oregon	DA	96	Initiative and Referendum	Prohibits increasing expense, difficulty of initiative process except through initiative.	Failed
2000	Oregon	DS	97	Animal Rights	Restricts use of certain animal traps, poisons and commerce in fur.	Failed
2000	Oregon	DA	98	Campaign Finance Reform	Prohibits using public resources for political purposes. Limits payroll deductions.	Failed
2000	Oregon	DA	99	Health/Medical	Creates commission ensuring quality home care services for elderly and disabled.	Passed
2000	South Dakota	DS	1	Gaming	Initiated measure to change the maximum bet limit in Deadwood.	Passed
2000	South Dakota	DA	Constitutional Amendment C	Taxes	No tax may be levied on any inheritance, and the Legislature may not enact any law imposing such a tax.	Passed
2000	South Dakota	DA	Constitutional Amendment D	Gaming	Constitutional amendment prohibiting video lottery.	Failed
2000	Utah	DS	A	Administration of Government	Declaring English to be the official language for the conduct of government business.	Passed
2000	Utah	DS	B	Drug Policy Reform	Relating to forfeiture of assets and property; establishing uniform procedures for the forfeiture of property; forbidding forfeiture against innocent owners.	Passed
2000	Washington	DS	I-713	Animal Rights	This measure would make it a gross misdemeanor to capture an animal with a steel-jawed leg hold trap, neck snare, or other body-gripping trap.	Passed
2000	Washington	DS	I-722	Taxes	This measure would declare null and void tax and fee increases adopted without voter approval by state and local governments between July 2, 1999, and December 31, 1999.	Passed
2000	Washington	DS	I-728	Education	This measure would direct that certain existing state revenue, including all unobligated lottery revenue, be placed in a student achievement fund and in the education construction fund.	Passed
2000	Washington	DS	I-729	Education	This measure would authorize school districts and public universities to sponsor charter public schools.	Failed
2000	Washington	DS	I-732	Education	This measure would provide annual cost-of-living salary adjustments to school district employees.	Passed

Year	State	Type	Measure Number	Subject Matter	Description	Pass/Fail
2000	Washington	DS	I-745	Taxes	This measure would require that 90% of state and local transportation funds, including local transit taxes bus excluding ferry and transit fares, be spent on road construction, improvement, and maintenance. Road and lane construction and maintenance would be the top transportation priority.	Failed
2001	Colorado	DA	26	Administration of Government	Expends $50 million of 2001 tax refund revenues over a period of three years to fund a high-speed monorail.	Failed
2001	Washington	DS	I-747	Taxes	This measure would establish new "limit factors" for taxing districts in setting their property tax levies each year.	Passed
2001	Washington	DS	I-773	Taxes	This measure would impose an additional sales tax on cigarettes and a surtax on wholesaled tobacco products.	Passed
2001	Washington	DS	I-775	Health/Medical	Creates a "home care quality authority" to establish qualifications, standards, accountability, training, referral and employment relations for publicly funded individual providers of in-home care services.	Passed

Section F: Initiative & Referendum Institute's 2002
General Election Post Election Report[1]

So what did the voter's decide—were they cautious as we had predicted or did they disregard the concerns of war, terrorism and the economy and do as they pleased? In short, "cautious" was the word of the day. The voters once again defied party labeling and voted their conscience when it came to ballot measures. In a time of great uncertainty, voters picked through the list of statewide ballot measures and systematically made their feelings known while at the same time not revealing whether their underlying principles lean more liberal or conservative. The great race to categorize the voter's political beliefs will once again have to wait for another election day.

On Election Day 2002, voters cast their ballots on 202 statewide ballot measures in 40 states and approved approximately 60% of them. 53 were placed on the ballot by the people and 149 were placed on the ballot by the state legislatures.[2] Of the measures placed on the ballot by the people, 45% were approved. This number is a little higher than the 100-year average of 41%. In looking at the measures placed on the ballot by the state legislatures, the voters continued the trend of passing those at a higher percentage than citizen measures by adopting almost 66% of them. Arizona and New Mexico hold the top honor of having the most prolific ballot on Election Day—both with 14. The state that had the most issues from the people (commonly referred to as initiatives) was Oregon with 7—though a 60% decrease from 2000. Three of the top five most prolific ballots comprised of issues from lawmakers and not the people—New Mexico, Louisiana and Georgia. There was an average of 2.04 initiatives per state and an average of 2.94 legislative referendums per state on the ballot this election.[3]

This election was noticeable for many reasons but one that stands out is the fact that there were 30% fewer initiatives on the ballot than 2000 and the fewest number since 1986. The decrease in the number of initiatives making the ballot can be attributed to five distinct factors: 1) increased regulation of the initiative process has made it more difficult to use; 2) increased judicial action striking down initiatives on technical grounds has caused concern among potential users of the initiative process and has made them reluctant to use the process; 3) many potential users of the process were waiting to see what the new makeup of the state legislatures and Congress will be after redistricting and the mid-term elections. The new composition of these lawmaking bodies may be more receptive to their reforms and so therefore they would not have to turn to the initiative process; 4) some potential initiative supporters chose not to place initiatives on the ballot post 9/11 feeling that this was not the time to be challenging the government; and 5) due to the poor economy potential initiative proponents did not have the funds necessary to utilize the initiative process. However, even though the citizens placed fewer issues on the ballot, state legislators placed 10% more issues on the ballot than they did in 2000. The reason for this is hard to say, but it could be argued that the increase was due to a desire by state lawmakers to increase revenue for their states through new bonds or the expansion of lottery and gaming.

So how did the top initiatives do?

Drug Policy Reform—Coming into this election cycle, drug policy reformers had enjoyed a tremendous winning record but this year they suffered a clean sweep defeat on their statewide initiatives (they did win a local measure in Washington, DC and one in San Francisco). Ohio voters chose not to adopt Issue One that would allow for the treatment instead of incarceration for non-violent drug offenders while Nevadans chose to vote down Question 9 which would have legalized marijuana for recreational purposes. In one of the more surprising outcomes voters voted down Proposition 203 in Arizona that would have legalized medical marijuana.

Two other closely watched drug related initiatives in South Dakota, Amendment A which would allow a criminal defendant to argue the merits of the law and be found innocent because the jury found the law itself to be bad public policy and Measure 1 which would legalize industrial hemp (cannabis) were both defeated. Many have argued that the reason this election cycle has proven to be more difficult for the movement than previous elections is due to the extraordinary step by John Walter (Bush's Drug Policy Advisor) and Asa Hutchison (head of the DEA) in actively campaigning against

---

1. Special thanks must go to Shirley Starke for the preparation of this report. Shirley serves as the Institute's archivist and worked around the clock on election night collecting the information for this report.

2. This analysis was prepared by M. Dane Waters, President of the non-profit and non-partisan Initiative & Referendum Institute. Nothing in this analysis should be construed as an endorsement of any of the ballot measures mentioned and is being provided for educational purposes.

3. Only 24 states have the statewide initiative process and 50 states have the legislative referendum process.

these measures—a move that many believe will lead to litigation against the federal government's involvement in political campaigns.

According to Bill Zimmerman, Executive Director, Campaign for New Drug Policies, "of the four drug reform initiatives we were directly involved with in the last election, one won and three lost. While this represents a lower level of success than we realized in the three previous election cycles, we see it as a bump in the road, not a change of direction. Over the past six years, our initiatives have moved drug policy reform from the political netherworld to the political mainstream. Drug policy reforms are being debated by elected officials and legislatures across the country. We entered this cycle with a 17–2 record on drug policy reform initiatives. We come out of it with an 18–5 record." There is little doubt that the drug policy reform movement will continue to utilize the initiative process in its quest to raise awareness of the reforms they are seeking.

Animal Rights—Animal rights advocates fared well on Election Day. The animal protection movement emerged in the 1990s as a dominant issue at the ballot box. This election cycle was no exception. Voters in Oklahoma approved an initiative outlawing cockfighting while voters in Florida voted to ban the use of gestation crates for pregnant pigs. On the losing side was an Arkansas initiative that would have made cruelty to animals a class D felony instead of the current class A misdemeanor. The Florida win will help energize the movement to ban gestation crates across the country potentially leading to more ballot measures on this issue in the near future. "Voters again have demonstrated that they care about the protection of animals, whether the abuse involves intensive confinement on factory farms or staged animal fights," said Wayne Pacelle, senior vice president of the Humane Society of the United States.

Education—Another favorite at the ballot box has been education reform and this election cycle continued the trend. According to Kristina Wilfore of the progressive Ballot Initiative Strategy Center (BISC), "ballot measure results from this election clearly demonstrated voters' strong support for public education." Five initiatives are especially worth noting that prove this point. In California, Arnold Swartzenegger's Proposition 49 won handily. The initiative will "increase state grant funds available for before and after school programs." This impressive victory will no doubt give the "Terminator" the political prestige he wanted to launch his rumored gubernatorial campaign. In Colorado and Massachusetts voters decided on initiatives that would require children to be taught by using the English language in the classroom. These two initiatives follow wins on this issue in California and Arizona. The surprising thing about these two initiatives is where they won and lost. This issue, which is usually personified as a conservative issue, won handily in the liberal state of Massachusetts (Question 2) but lost in conservative Colorado (Amendment 31). This just goes to show that voters can't be expected to vote straight party ideology when voting on ballot measures. Floridians dealt with two high profile education initiatives. Measure 8, which will require that "every four-year-old child in Florida be offered a high quality prekindergarten learning opportunity" won by a narrow margin as did Measure 9. Measure 9, which will "provide funding for sufficient classrooms so that there be a maximum number of students in public school classes" had become a big issue in the Governor's race with McBride throwing his strong support behind it while Bush was caught in an unfortunate candid moment saying that he had already thought of several "devious ways" to keep the measure from going into affect. Now that it's the law all eyes will no doubt be watching for the "devious" Bush to appear.

Election Reform—One of the biggest losers on Election Day was election reform. In California and Colorado, voters said no to initiatives that would have put in place what is commonly referred to as "same-day voter registration." Three other Colorado initiatives are also worth noting. Amendment 29, which would change the way candidates are placed on the primary ballot by requiring nominating petitions instead of relying on nominating conventions, was defeated. Amendment 28, which would allow for mail ballot elections, was defeated as well. The third, Amendment 27, which would "reduce the amount of money that individuals and political committees can contribute", was victorious. According to Pete Maysmith, Executive Director of Colorado Common Cause, "voters in Colorado for the second time in six years overwhelmingly supported a strong, comprehensive campaign finance reform measure championed by the League of Women Voters and Colorado Common Cause. Although many politicians are reluctant to admit it, there can be no doubt—Coloradoans believe their campaign finance system is corrupted by big money and they want to see it fixed."

One of the more telling signs of the political feelings of the electorate was exemplified in Idaho with voters giving a controversial endorsement to a measure that would abolish term limits in Idaho. However, this victory for state lawmakers is being overshadowed by persistent stories of voter confusion over which way to vote on the ballot measure. According to Stacie Rumenap, Executive Director of U.S. Term Limits, "the narrow defeat in Idaho showed that the popularity of state legislative term limits is not always enough to sustain support for term limits on hundreds of state and local offices, from sheriff to school board members, as was the case in the Idaho term limits law. Additionally, there was a great deal of confusion over how to vote to keep term limits in place. However, it's clear that when voters are asked only about legislative limits, support remains strong. After being outspent by political elites 11 to 1 earlier this year, voters in California soundly defeated a measure intended to extend legislative limits. Across the county, the numbers are clear: the majority of voters continue to back legislative term limits every chance they get."

Gaming—Several ballot measures dealing with expanding gaming or creating a lottery were put before the voters, but as is usually the case didn't fare well. Those from the state legislatures will be discussed below but as far as initiatives were concerned, Arizona was the hotbed. In that state, three initiatives were voted on that dealt with gaming. Propositions 200 and 202 that dealt with expanding Indian gaming and dictating where and how the proceeds should be divided had mixed results. Proposition 200 was soundly defeated while Proposition 202 passed. The other initiative, Proposition 201 that would have allowed for "non-tribal gaming" in the state was defeated overwhelmingly. In Idaho, voters decided to allow video gaming on Indian land and voters in North Dakota decided to "direct the legislative assembly to authorize the state to join a multi-state lottery."

Taxes—Since 1978's Proposition 13 in California that cut property taxes, tax reformers have used the initiative process religiously. This election cycle was no different. However, it wasn't exactly a banner year for tax cut advocates at the statewide level. The voters of Massachusetts voted down Question 1 that would have abolished their state income tax—maybe in hopes of maintaining their title of "Taxachusetts"—while voters in Arkansas defeated an initiative that would have abolished certain taxes on their food and medicine. But tax cutters weren't without a few victories at the local level. According to John Berthoud, President of the National Taxpayers Union (NTU), "taxpayers were heartened by a number of strong victories at the local level in 2002. One of the most important was a resounding defeat of a proposed half-cent sales tax hike in Northern Virginia and Hampton Roads, Virginia for more transportation spending. Proponents of higher taxes pulled out all the stops. Developers poured in money and outspent taxpayer groups by at least ten to one. Politicians of both parties (well-funded by the same developers) lobbied hard for the measure. Still, taxpayers told them all that enough is enough."

Regardless of these outcomes at the statewide level, tax cutters will be back in future elections to carry on the legacy of Howard Jarvis and California's Proposition 13.

So how did the top legislative referendum do?

Revenue Enhancers—Over the last couple of election cycles, and especially since the fiscal impact of September 11th, state legislators have been looking at ways to increase the revenues in their state. At least forty states will have budget deficits this year and in this election cycle lawmakers were hoping that the voters would "ease their pain" and give them more money to spend. Well in short—the verdict is mixed. In Tennessee where lawmakers were hoping to establish a lottery (to escape having to implement an income tax), voters decided to help lawmakers by passing Amendment A-1. In Montana, South Carolina and Louisiana, where the voters were asked to give lawmakers greater latitude in investing in the stock market, the voters for the most part said no. With the exception of one measure in South Carolina, the voters told lawmakers that the stock market was too risky to be investing public funds. As to bonds, California voters adopted the largest bond measure in the state's history. Proposition 47 will raise $13 billion for an across the board overhaul of the state's public school facilities. Other bond measures across the country seamed to fare well also. According to the National Conference of State Legislatures (NCSL), 21 of the 24 statewide bond issues passed providing $22 billion dollars in funding for "everything from mortgage assistance for veterans, to transportation, education and environmental projects."

Initiative and Referendum Reform—As the Institute has highlighted over the last few years, state legislators have become more and more hostile to the initiative process. This election only emphasized the point with votes on amendments to make the process more difficult in Oklahoma and Montana. In Oklahoma, the voters defeated a measure placed on the ballot by lawmakers that would change the number of signatures needed to propose a constitutional initiative from 8% to 15% for initiatives pertaining to hunting, fishing or trapping. In Montana, voters decided two issues. They adopted one measure that would increase the distribution requirement for constitutional initiatives and another that would increase the distribution requirement for statutory initiatives.

A few honorable mentions.

Voters also showed their resolve to maintain the norm with the defeat of two high profile measures in Oregon—Measure 23 that would have called for universal health care and Measure 27 that would have called for the labeling of genetically modified foods. These defeats do not necessarily mean that voters don't support these reforms—it's just that given the uncertainty of the times these are items that they feel can be addressed in the future—but not now. Smoking was another area that voters spoke out on. In Florida the voters adopted Amendment 6 that would ban smoking in all public places. In Missouri, voters chose not to increase cigarette taxes while in Arizona the voters decided to make cigarettes $1.18 a pack—more than double the current rate. As to social policy, not much was on the ballot this election cycle with the exception of banning same sex marriage in Nevada. Nevadans voted once again (by law amendments must be voted on twice before becoming law) to adopt the ban.

So what does all of this mean?

Primarily, faced with uncertain economic times and the possibility of war, voters chose to be cautious and maintain the status quo—though with one obvious exception—education reform. The reason for this, many argue, is that during these tough fiscal times voters feel that big ticket road projects and other costly non-education related items can wait until economic times are better and they are more comfortable approving them. They also feel that items that would cause significant changes in their daily lives—like drug reform, labeling genetically modified food and establishing universal healthcare—can wait as well. However, they made it clear that what can't wait is the education of their kids.

Ignoring the hum drum factual analysis of Election Day 2002, what did we really learn about the voter—simply that the line between conservatives and liberals is blurring. You will always have your 10% hardcore conservatives and liberals at both ends of the political spectrum that not only vote the party line on candidates but also vote strict political conviction on ballot measures. But the other 80% is clearly thumbing their noses at those that want to label them. These voters may feel some loyalty to a specific party but when it comes to ballot measures they know that their vote will have an almost instantaneous impact on their daily lives and so are far less likely to vote strictly on party conviction. Though the repercussions of their vote for a specific candidate may be unknown for a long period of time, they can see clearly the impact of their vote on ballot measures almost immediately. Maybe this is the reason that voters love ballot measures so much—they know their vote will have an immediate impact—good or bad.

But what impact will these ballot measures have on government? Some, like those that gave governments more latitude in spending money, will help them deal with the tough fiscal crisis they are facing. Others that dedicated revenue for specific reforms—like education—will force governments to take a closer look at their budgets and make some tough choices in order to fund the citizens' mandate. However, there is no doubt that some governments will choose to ignore the people's mandates for various reasons—in most cases because they will argue that implementing the ballot measure will cause undue fiscal problems to the state. It will be interesting to see how the voters respond when this happens.

Overall, as with every election cycle in which ballot measures are voted on, the impact on the citizens and the government will be substantial and long lasting.

How the states rank

The following is how the states rank regarding number of statewide ballot measures voted on November 5, 2002.

The top five most prolific ballots this November by total number of *ballot measures*

State	Initiatives	Popular Referendum	Legislative Referendum	Total Number of Statewide Ballot Measures
Arizona	4	0	10	14
New Mexico	0	0	14	14
Louisiana	0	0	12	12
Oregon	7	0	5	12
Georgia	0	0	11	11

The rest of the country

State	Initiatives	Popular Referendum	Legislative Referendum	Total Number of Statewide Ballot Measures
Florida	5	0	5	10
Colorado	5	0	5	10
Nevada	2	0	7	9
Oklahoma	1	0	8	9
California	4	0	3	7
Montana	2	1	4	7
Utah	1	0	6	7

State	Initiatives	Popular Referendum	Legislative Referendum	Total Number of Statewide Ballot Measures
Alaska	2	0	4	6
Missouri	2	0	4	6
Rhode Island	0	0	5	5
Washington	2	1	2	5
Arkansas	2	0	2	4
Michigan	2	1	1	4
South Dakota	2	0	2	4
Virginia	0	0	4	4
Wyoming	0	0	4	4
Alabama	0	0	3	3
Hawaii	0	0	3	3
Maine	0	0	3	3
Maryland	0	0	3	3
Massachusetts	2	0	1	3
North Dakota	2	0	1	3
Idaho	1	1	0	2
Kentucky	0	0	2	2
Nebraska	0	0	2	2
New Hampshire	0	0	2	2
South Carolina	0	0	2	2
Tennessee	0	0	2	2
West Virginia	0	0	2	2
Mississippi	0	0	1	1
North Carolina	0	0	1	1
Ohio	1	0	0	1
Pennsylvania	0	0	1	1
Texas	0	0	1	1
Vermont	0	0	1	1
Connecticut	0	0	0	0
Delaware	0	0	0	0
Illinois	0	0	0	0
Indiana	0	0	0	0
Iowa	0	0	0	0
Kansas	0	0	s0	0
Minnesota	0	0	0	0
New Jersey	0	0	0	0
New York	0	0	0	0
Wisconsin	0	0	0	0

The top five most prolific ballots this November by total number of initiatives

State	Initiatives	Popular Referendum	Legislative Referendum	Total Number of Statewide Ballot Measures
Oregon	7	0	5	12
Colorado	5	0	5	10
Florida	5	0	6	11
Arizona	4	0	10	14
California	4	0	3	7

The top five most prolific ballots this November
by total number of legislative referendum

State	Initiatives	Popular Referendum	Legislative Referendum	Total Number of Statewide Ballot Measures
New Mexico	0	0	14	14
Louisiana	0	0	12	12
Georgia	0	0	11	11
Arizona	4	0	10	14
Oklahoma	1	0	8	9

State-by-state listing

ALABAMA— State does not have the initiative process. Total number of ballot measures currently certified for the November 2002 general election ballot: 3

State ID Number: Amendment Number 1
Type: Legislative Referendum
Summary: Proposing an amendment to the Constitution of Alabama of 1901, providing that any new proposed Constitution of Alabama adopted to replace the existing Constitution of Alabama of 1901, shall become effective only upon its ratification by a majority of the qualified voters voting on such ratification. Proposing an amendment to the Constitution of Alabama of 1901, providing that any new proposed Constitution of Alabama adopted to replace the existing Constitution of Alabama of 1901, shall become effective only upon its ratification by a majority of the qualified voters voting on such ratification.
Pass/Fail: P
Percent Yes: 81.03
Percent No: 18.97

State ID Number: Amendment Number 2
Type: Legislative Referendum
Summary: Proposing an amendment to the Constitution of Alabama of 1901, to establish the General Fund Rainy Day Account within the Alabama Trust Fund.
Pass/Fail: F
Percent Yes: 49.9
Percent No: 51.1

State ID Number: Amendment Number 3
Type: Legislative Referendum
Summary: Proposing an amendment to the Constitution of Alabama of 1901, to provide a means by which members of the sheep and goat industry may organize and by referendum levy upon themselves assessments for the purpose of financing promotional programs for the sheep and goat industry.
Pass/Fail: P
Percent Yes: 66.04
Percent No: 33.96

ALASKA— Total number of ballot measures currently certified for the November 2002 general election ballot: 6

State ID Number: Bonding Proposition A
Type: Legislative Referendum
Summary: State Guaranteed Veterans Residential Mortgage Bonds $500,000,000
Pass/Fail: P
Percent Yes: 70.03
Percent No: 29.97

State ID Number: Bonding Proposition B
Type: Legislative Referendum
Summary: State Guaranteed Transportation Revenue Anticipation Bonds and State General Obligation State Transportation Project Bonds—Total Bond Authorization $226,719,500
Pass/Fail: P
Percent Yes: 67.75
Percent No: 32.35

State ID Number: Bonding Proposition C
Type: Legislative Referendum
Summary: State General Obligation Educational and Museum Facility, Design, Construction, and Major Maintenance Bonds $236,805,441
Pass/Fail: P
Percent Yes: 59.60
Percent No: 40.40

State ID Number: Ballot Measure No.1
Type: Legislative Referendum
Summary: Shall there be a constitutional convention?
Pass/Fail: F
Percent Yes: 28.36
Percent No: 71.64

State ID Number: Ballot Measure No.2
Type: Initiative
Summary: Would move all sessions of the state legislature from Juneau to the Matanuska-Susitna Borough.
Pass/Fail: F
Percent Yes: 32.77
Percent No: 67.23

State ID Number: Ballot Measure No. 3
Type: Initiative
Summary: Would establish the Alaska Gas Development Authority to maximize revenues for Alaska and to promote jobs for Alaskans.
Pass/Fail: P
Percent Yes: 62.03
Percent No: 37.97

ARIZONA—Total number of ballot measures currently certified for the November 2002 general election ballot: 14

State ID Number: Proposition 100
Type: Legislative Referendum
Summary: A constitutional amendment relating to municipal debt limits. It would 1) remove the requirement for voting in political subdivision elections to approve indebtedness that the voters must be property taxpayers, but retain the requirement that they be qualified electors. This change would conform the Arizona Constitution to a United States Supreme Court decision; 2) specify that the last assessment for state and county purposes must be used in determining the value of taxable property in incorporated cities and towns, and; 3) allow incorporated cities and towns to include debt for the construction, reconstruction, improvement or acquisition of streets, highways or bridges and the acquisition of interests in land for rights-of-way for streets, highways or bridges in the twenty percent debt limit, with voter approval.
Pass/Fail: F
Percent Yes: 42
Percent No: 58

State ID Number: Proposition 101
Type: Legislative Referendum
Summary: A constitutional amendment relating to state lands.

Pass/Fail: F
Percent Yes: 48
Percent No: 52

State ID Number: Proposition 102
Type: Legislative Referendum
Summary: A constitutional amendment relating to residential property tax valuation.
Pass/Fail: P
Percent Yes: 80
Percent No: 20

State ID Number: Proposition 103
Type: Legislative Referendum
Summary: A constitutional amendment relating to bailable offenses.
Pass/Fail: P
Percent Yes: 80
Percent No: 20

State ID Number: Proposition 104
Type: Legislative Referendum
Summary: A constitutional amendment relating to school and community college district expenditure limitations.
Pass/Fail: P
Percent Yes: 70
Percent No: 30

State ID Number: Proposition 200
Type: Initiative
Summary: Would direct the Governor to enter into gaming compacts with Arizona Indian tribes asking for such compacts for the purpose of alleviating poverty on Arizona Indian Reservations and enhancing the self-sufficiency of Arizona Indian Tribes.
Pass/Fail: F
Percent Yes: 15
Percent No: 85

State ID Number: Proposition 201
Type: Initiative
Summary: Would permit Arizona non-tribal gaming operators a limited number of gaming devices.
Pass/Fail: F
Percent Yes: 20
Percent No: 80

State ID Number: Proposition 202
Type: Initiative
Summary: Would authorize agreements between Arizona tribes and the State to allow for the continuation of limited, regulated gaming on tribal lands.
Pass/Fail: P
Percent Yes: 52
Percent No: 48

State ID Number: Proposition 203
Type: Initiative
Summary: Would create a medical marijuana registry card system authorizing medical use of marijuana for people diagnosed with a debilitating medical condition; increase drug offender maximum sentences for violent crimes committed while on drugs by 50%; punish personal possession of marijuana with a civil fine; require a drug related conviction before forfeiture of property seized incident to possession or use of drugs; establish state administered system for distribution of marijuana to qualifying medical patients; require supervised release of non-violent offenders convicted of simple possession or use of controlled substances, unless such release poses a public danger.

Pass/Fail: F
Percent Yes: 42
Percent No: 58

State ID Number: Proposition 300
Type: Legislative Referendum
Summary: A measure relating to state school trust land revenues.
Pass/Fail: P
Percent Yes: 75
Percent No: 25

State ID Number: Proposition 301
Type: Legislative Referendum
Summary: A measure relating to the continuation of the state lottery commission. If adopted by the voters, the state lottery would extend the termination of lottery from 2003 to 2012.
Pass/Fail: P
Percent Yes: 72
Percent No: 28

State ID Number: Proposition 302
Type: Legislative Referendum
Summary: A measure relating to probation.
Pass/Fail: P
Percent Yes: 69
Percent No: 31

State ID Number: Proposition 303
Type: Legislative Referendum
Summary: A measure relating to the taxation of tobacco products.
Pass/Fail: P
Percent Yes: 66
Percent No: 34

State ID Number: Proposition 304
Type: Legislative Referendum
Summary: A measure increasing legislative salaries to $36,000.
Pass/Fail: F
Percent Yes: 33
Percent No: 67

ARKANSAS—Total number of ballot measures currently certified for the November 2002 general election ballot: 4

State ID Number: Proposed Constitutional Amendment 1
Type: Legislative Referendum
Summary: Would ensure the secrecy of individual votes cast in elections.
Pass/Fail: P
Percent Yes: 57
Percent No: 43

State ID Number: Proposed Constitutional Amendment 2
Type: Legislative Referendum
Summary: Revise certain constitutional articles pertaining to the executive branch.
Pass/Fail: F
Percent Yes: 45
Percent No: 55

State ID Number: Proposed Constitutional Amendment 3
Type: Initiative
Summary: Would eliminate taxes on food and medicine.
Pass/Fail: F
Percent Yes: 39
Percent No: 61

State ID Number: Proposed Initiated Act 1
Type: Initiative
Summary: Would amend Arkansas law concerning cruelty to animals to add a section establishing the offense of "aggravated cruelty to animals."
Pass/Fail: F
Percent Yes: 38
Percent No: 62

CALIFORNIA — Total number of ballot measures currently certified for the November 2002 general election ballot: 7

State ID Number: Proposition 46
Type: Legislative Referendum
Summary: Would establish the Housing and Emergency Shelter Trust Fund.
Pass/Fail: P
Percent Yes: 57.6
Percent No: 42.4

State ID Number: Proposition 47
Type: Legislative Referendum
Summary: Would authorize new bonds for educational purposes.
Pass/Fail: P
Percent Yes: 59.1
Percent No: 40.9

State ID Number: Proposition 48
Type: Legislative Referendum
Summary: Would set the guidelines for the consolidation of California courts.
Pass/Fail: P
Percent Yes: 72.9
Percent No: 27.1

State ID Number: Proposition 49
Type: Initiative
Summary: Increases state grant funds available for before and after school programs providing tutoring, homework assistance, and educational enrichment. Establishes priority for continued funding level for schools already receiving grants. Makes public elementary, middle and junior high schools, including charter schools, eligible for grants ranging from $50,000 to $75,000. Provides priority for additional funding for schools with predominantly low-income students. Declares that funding for before and after school programs shall be above Proposition 98 base funding, and at least $85 million for first year increasing to $550 million annually if state revenues grow. Summary of estimate by Legislative Analyst and Director of Finance of fiscal impact on state and local governments: This measure would have a major fiscal effect of additional annual state costs for before and after school programs that could exceed $400 million annually, beginning in 2004–2005.
Pass/Fail: P
Percent Yes: 56.7
Percent No: 43.3

State ID Number: Proposition 50
Type: Initiative
Summary: Authorizes $3,440,000,000 general obligation bonds, to be repaid from state's General Fund, to fund a variety of water projects including: specified CALFED Bay-Delta Program projects including urban and agricultural water use

efficiency projects; grants and loans to reduce Colorado River water use; purchasing, protecting and restoring coastal wetlands near urban areas; competitive grants for water management and water quality improvement projects; development of river parkways; improved security for state, local and regional water systems; and grants for desalination and drinking water disinfecting projects. Summary of estimate by Legislate Analyst and Director of Finance of fiscal impact on state and local governments: If passed, the measure would result in state costs to repay the bonds, which, if the bonds were issued with a maturity of 25 years, would equal approximately $5.7 billion to pay principal ($3.44 billion) and interest ($2.24 billion), with payments of approximately $227 million per year. The measure would also result in potential costs of an unknown amount to state and local governments to operate or maintain properties or projects acquired or developed with these bond funds.

Pass/Fail: P
Percent Yes: 55.4
Percent No: 44.6

State ID Number: Proposition 51
Type: Initiative
Summary: Reallocates 30% of certain state revenues collected on motor vehicle sales or leases from the General Fund to the Traffic congestion Relief and Safe School Bus Trust Fund. Allocates money for transportation programs including: highway expansion, specific freeway interchange improvements, mass transit improvements, purchasing buses, and expanding light and commuter rail. Provides funds for environmental enhancement, transportation impact mitigation programs, and transportation safety programs. Allocates money to 45 specific projects and for remainder specifies distribution percentages, restricts fund uses, and provides accountability measures. Summary of estimate by Legislative Analyst of fiscal impact on state and local governments: About $460 million in 2002–03 and $950 million in 2003–04, increasing annually thereafter, for state and local transportation-related purposes. Summary of estimate by Department of Finance of fiscal impact on state and local governments: Increases resources for state and local transportation-related purposes by about $460 million in 2002–03 and $950 million in 2003–04, increasing annually thereafter. Potentially increases resources for Proposition 98 purposes and reduces resources for other General Fund purposes by significant amounts that could exceed the amounts stated above.

Pass/Fail: F
Percent Yes: 41.4
Percent No: 58.6

State ID Number: Proposition 52
Type: Initiative
Summary: Allows persons who are legally eligible to vote and have valid identification to register to vote on Election Day at their polling place. Increases criminal penalty for voter and voter registration fraud. Makes conspiracy to commit voter fraud a crime. Requires trained staff at polling places to manage Election Day registration. Creates fund to implement measure, including training and providing personnel for Election Day registration. Allows a person to register or re-register during 28 days preceding Election Day at their local elections office. Provides more time to county election officials to prepare voter registration lists. Summary of estimate by Legislative Analyst and Direct of Finance of fiscal impact on state and local governments: This measure would result annually in about $6 million in state costs and no net costs to counties.

Pass/Fail: F
Percent Yes: 40.6
Percent No: 59.4

COLORADO — Total number of ballot measures currently certified for the November 2002 general election ballot: 10

State ID Number: Amendment 27
Type: Initiative
Summary: The proposed amendment reduces the amount of money that individuals and political committees can contribute; to candidates and various political organizations; limits the amount of money that political parties can contribute to candidates; creates small donor committees which may accept up to $50 per individual per year, and limits the amount of money they can contribute to candidates and political parties; sets voluntary spending limits for political races and establishes incentives for candidates to accept the spending limit; adjusts contribution and spending limits for inflation every four years; and requires reporting and disclosure of money spent for certain political advertisements.
Pass/Fail: P

Percent Yes: 66.51
Percent No: 33.49

State ID Number: Amendment 28
Type: Initiative
Summary: Would allow mail ballot elections.
Pass/Fail: F
Percent Yes: 42.41
Percent No: 57.59

State ID Number: Amendment 29
Type: Initiative
Summary: An amendment to the Colorado revised statutes concerning the use of petition to provide candidate access to the primary election ballot, and, in connection, therewith, requiring that all candidates for nomination at a primary election be placed on the primary election ballot by petition; eliminating the candidate designation and certification process from state, county, and district assemblies; specifying the signature requirements for nominating petitions for access to the primary election ballot; allowing a candidate to include a personal statement on his or her nominating petition; providing for examination of nominating petitions by the designated election official; and setting forth a procedure to protest the election official's decision regarding the sufficiency of nominating petitions.
Pass/Fail: F
Percent Yes: 39.84
Percent No: 60.16

State ID Number: Amendment 30
Type: Initiative
Summary: An amendment to the Colorado constitution concerning election day voter registration, and, in connection therewith, allowing an eligible citizen to register and vote on any day that a vote may be cast in any election beginning on January 1, 2004; specifying election day voter registration locations; specifying that an eligible citizen who registers to vote on election day shall register in person and present a current and valid Colorado driver's license or state identification card or other approved documentation; and directing the Colorado general assembly, in implementing election day voter registration, to adopt necessary protections against election fraud.
Pass/Fail: F
Percent Yes: 39.25
Percent No: 60.75

State ID Number: Amendment 31
Type: Initiative
Summary: An amendment to the Colorado constitution concerning English-language education in Colorado public schools, and, in connection therewith, requiring children to be taught by using the English language in their classrooms and requiring children who are learning English to be placed in an English immersion program that is intended to last one year or less, and, if successful, will result in placement of such children in ordinary classrooms; exempting from such requirements those children whose parents or legal guardians obtain annual waivers allowing the children to transfer to classes using bilingual education or other educational methodologies, but making such waivers very difficult to obtain because the school can grant them only in very restrictive circumstances and can deny them for any reason or no reason thereby reducing the likelihood that bilingual education will be used; requiring schools that grant any waivers to offer bilingual education or other educational methodologies when they have at least 20 students in the same grade who receive a waiver and in all other cases permitting students to transfer to a public school in which bilingual education or other methodologies are offered, with the cost of such transfer, excluding transportation, to be provided by the state; allowing a parent or legal guardian to sue public employees granting a waiver if the parent or guardian later concludes that the waiver was granted in error and injured the child's education; creating severe legal consequences identified in the amendment for such public employees who willfully and repeatedly refuse to implement the amendment; and requiring schools to test children learning English, enrolled in second grade or higher, to monitor their progress, using a standardized nationally-normed test of academic subject matter given in English.
Pass/Fail: F
Percent Yes: 43.78
Percent No: 56.22

State ID Number: Referendum A
Type: Legislative Referendum
Summary: Would exempt District Attorneys from the existing term limits law.
Pass/Fail: F
Percent Yes: 35.27
Percent No: 64.73

State ID Number: Referendum B
Type: Legislative Referendum
Summary: Would provide for the public ownership of health facilities.
Pass/Fail: F
Percent Yes: 40.76
Percent No: 59.24

State ID Number: Referendum C
Type: Legislative Referendum
Summary: Would set the qualifications for the Coroner.
Pass/Fail: P
Percent Yes: 70.92
Percent No: 29.08

State ID Number: Referendum D
Type: Legislative Referendum
Summary: Would repeal obsolete provisions from the state constitution.
Pass/Fail: P
Percent Yes: 71.89
Percent No: 28.11

State ID Number: Referendum E
Type: Legislative Referendum
Summary: Would establish the "Cesar Chavez Legal Holiday."
Pass/Fail: F
Percent Yes: 20.61
Percent No: 79.39

CONNECTICUT—State does not have the initiative process. Total number of ballot measures currently certified for the November 2002 general election ballot: None

DELAWARE—State does not have the initiative process. Total number of ballot measures currently certified for the November 2002 general election ballot: None

FLORIDA—Total number of ballot measures currently certified for the November 2002 general election ballot: 10

State ID Number: Constitutional Amendment No. 1
Type: Legislative Referendum
Summary: Would authorize the death penalty for capital crimes and authorize retroactive changes in the method of execution.
Pass/Fail: P
Percent Yes: 69.7
Percent No: 30.3

State ID Number: Constitutional Amendment No. 2
Type: Legislative Referendum
Summary: Would require an economic impact statement for initiatives before being voted on.
Pass/Fail: P
Percent Yes: 78.0
Percent No: 22.0

State ID Number: Constitutional Amendment No. 3
Type: Legislative Referendum
Summary: Would authorize amendments or revisions to the Miami-Dade home rule charter.
Pass/Fail: F
Percent Yes: 47.8
Percent No: 52.2

State ID Number: Constitutional Amendment No. 4
Type: Legislative Referendum
Summary: Would require that laws providing exemptions from public records or public meetings requirements must be passed by a two-thirds vote of each house of the legislature.
Pass/Fail: P
Percent Yes: 76.6
Percent No: 23.4

State ID Number: Constitutional Amendment No. 6
Type: Initiative
Summary: Would prohibit tobacco smoking in enclosed indoor workplaces.
Pass/Fail: P
Percent Yes: 71.0
Percent No: 29.0

State ID Number: Constitutional Amendment No. 7
Type: Legislative Referendum
Summary: Would allow counties to exempt from taxation an increase in the assessed value of homestead property resulting from constructing living quarters for parents or grandparents who is 62 years old or older.
Pass/Fail: P
Percent Yes: 67.3
Percent No: 32.7

State ID Number: Constitutional Amendment No. 8
Type: Initiative
Summary: Every four-year-old child in Florida shall be offered a high quality pre-kindergarten learning opportunity by the state no later than the 2005 school year. This voluntary early childhood development and education program shall be established according to high quality standards and shall be free for all Florida four-year-olds without taking away funds used for existing education, health and development programs.
Pass/Fail: P
Percent Yes: 59.2
Percent No: 40.8

State ID Number: Constitutional Amendment No. 9
Type: Initiative
Summary: Proposes an amendment to the State Constitution to require that the Legislature provide funding for sufficient classrooms so that there be a maximum number of students in public school classes for various grade levels; requires compliance by the beginning of the 2010 school year; requires the Legislature, and not local school districts, to pay for the costs associated with reduced class size; prescribes a schedule for phased-in funding to achieve the required maximum class size.
Pass/Fail: P
Percent Yes: 52.4
Percent No: 47.6

State ID Number: Constitutional Amendment No. 10
Type: Initiative
Summary: Inhumane treatment of animals is a concern of Florida citizens; to prevent cruelty to animals and as recommended by The Humane Society of the United States, no person shall confine a pig during pregnancy in a cage, crate or other enclosure, or tether a pregnant pig, on a farm so that the pig is prevented from turning around freely, except for veterinary purposes and during the pre-birthing period; provides definitions, penalties, and an effective date.

Pass/Fail: P
Percent Yes: 54.8
Percent No: 45.2

State ID Number: Constitutional Amendment No. 11
Type: Initiative
Summary: A local board of trustees shall administer each state university. Each board shall have thirteen members dedicated to excellence in teaching, research, and service to community. A statewide governing board of seventeen members shall be responsible for the coordinated and accountable operation of the whole university system. Wasteful duplication of facilities or programs is to be avoided. Provides procedures for selection and confirmation of board members, including one student and one faculty representative per board.
Pass/Fail: P
Percent Yes: 60.5
Percent No: 39.5

GEORGIA—State does not have the initiative process. Total number of ballot measures currently certified for the November 2002 general election ballot: 11

State ID Number: Constitutional Amendment 1
Type: Legislative Referendum
Summary: Would make someone who defaults on his or her taxes ineligible to hold public office.
Pass/Fail: P
Percent Yes: 78.7
Percent No: 21.3

State ID Number: Constitutional Amendment 2
Type: Legislative Referendum
Summary: Would allow separate valuations for qualified affordable residential developments.
Pass/Fail: F
Percent Yes: 46.1
Percent No: 53.9

State ID Number: Constitutional Amendment 3
Type: Legislative Referendum
Summary: Would allow tax incentives to encourage redevelopment of blighted property.
Pass/Fail: P
Percent Yes: 59.6
Percent No: 40.4

State ID Number: Constitutional Amendment 4
Type: Legislative Referendum
Summary: Would allow different tax rates for properties contaminated with hazardous waste to encourage their cleanup.
Pass/Fail: P
Percent Yes: 68.6
Percent No: 31.4

State ID Number: Constitutional Amendment 5
Type: Legislative Referendum
Summary: Would allow different tax rates for commercial dockside facilities used to land and process seafood.
Pass/Fail: F
Percent Yes: 43.3
Percent No: 56.7
State ID Number: Constitutional Amendment 6
Type: Legislative Referendum
Summary: Would establish a program of dog and cat sterilization funded by special licenses plates.
Pass/Fail: P

Percent Yes: 70.9
Percent No: 29.1

State ID Number: Statewide Referendum A
Type: Legislative Referendum
Summary: Would change the income limit for school tax homestead exemptions for those 62 and older.
Pass/Fail: P
Percent Yes: 79.6
Percent No: 20.4

State ID Number: Statewide Referendum B
Type: Legislative Referendum
Summary: Would extend the tax exemption for spouses of military personnel who die due to war.
Pass/Fail: P
Percent Yes: 83.0
Percent No: 17.0

State ID Number: Statewide Referendum C
Type: Legislative Referendum
Summary: Would exempt medical societies and museums in historic property of nonprofit corporations from property taxes.
Pass/Fail: F
Percent Yes: 44.8
Percent No: 55.2

State ID Number: Statewide Referendum D
Type: Legislative Referendum
Summary: Would exempt commercial fishing vessels from property taxes.
Pass/Fail: F
Percent Yes: 32.9
Percent No: 67.1

State ID Number: Statewide Referendum E
Type: Legislative Referendum
Summary: Would increase the tax exemption for tangible personal property from $500 to $7,500.
Pass/Fail: P
Percent Yes: 72.2
Percent No: 27.8

HAWAII — State does not have the initiative process. Total number of ballot measures currently certified for the November 2002 general election ballot: 3

State ID Number: Question 1
Type: Legislative Referendum
Summary: Would require candidate's seeking office in a senatorial or representative district to be required to become a qualified voter in that district prior to filing nomination papers.
Pass/Fail: P
Percent Yes: 83.9
Percent No: 9.1

State ID Number: Question 2
Type: Legislative Referendum
Summary: Would authorize the state to issue special purpose revenue bonds and use the proceeds for educational purposes.
Pass/Fail: P
Percent Yes: 59.7
Percent No: 33.0

State ID Number: Question 3
Type: Legislative Referendum
Summary: Would permit criminal charges for felonies to be initiated by a legal prosecuting officer and establishing the procedures for such act.
Pass/Fail: P
Percent Yes: 57.3
Percent No: 31.9

IDAHO—Total number of ballot measures currently certified for the November 2002 general election ballot: 2

State ID Number: Proposition 1
Type: Initiative
Summary: Would define tribal video gaming machines and provide for their use.
Pass/Fail: P
Percent Yes: 57.8
Percent No: 42.2

State ID Number: Proposition 2
Type: Popular Referendum
Summary: Would reinstate term limits for elected state, county, municipal and school district officials that were abolished by the state legislature.
Pass/Fail: F (listed as failed because it would leave the law challenged in place)
Percent Yes: 50.2
Percent No: 49.8

ILLINOIS—State has an unusable initiative process. Total number of ballot measures currently certified for the November 2002 general election ballot: None

INDIANA—State does not have the initiative process. Total number of ballot measures currently certified for the November 2002 general election ballot: None

IOWA—State does not have the initiative process. Total number of ballot measures currently certified for the November 2002 general election ballot: None

KANSAS—State does not have the initiative process. Total number of ballot measures certified for the November 2002 general election ballot: None

KENTUCKY—State does not have the initiative process. Total number of ballot measures currently certified for the November 2002 general election ballot: 2

State ID Number: Constitutional Amendment 1
Type: Legislative Referendum
Summary: Would allow the Supreme Court to designate one or more divisions of circuit court within a judicial circuit as a family court division.
Pass/Fail: P
Percent Yes: 75.5
Percent No: 24.5

State ID Number: Constitutional Amendment 2
Type: Legislative Referendum
Summary: Would allow the state legislature to provide by general law, the powers, rights, duties, and liabilities of corporations and the powers, rights, duties, and liabilities of their officers and stockholders or members.
Pass/Fail: P
Percent Yes: 60.7
Percent No: 39.3

LOUISIANA—State does not have the initiative process. Total number of ballot measures currently certified for the November 2002 general election ballot: 12

State ID Number: Number 1—Act 1231
Type: Legislative Referendum
Summary: Would propose to set general legislative sessions in even-numbered years and fiscal sessions in odd-numbered years. Would authorize each member of the legislature to introduce the following bills during what is currently a fiscal issue only session convening in an odd-numbered year: 1.) Up to 5 pre-filed bills on any subject; and 2.) An unlimited number of bills to enact a local or special law that is required to be and has been advertised in accordance with the present constitution and is not prohibited by the present constitution. Act requires this amendment to be first on the ballot.
Pass/Fail: P
Percent Yes: 55
Percent No: 45

State ID Number: Number 2—Act 88
Type: Legislative Referendum
Summary: Would change the individual and joint income tax schedule of rates and brackets, state sales and use tax reduction, and exemption on certain purchases.
Pass/Fail: P
Percent Yes: 51
Percent No: 49

State ID Number: Number 3—Act 1236
Type: Legislative Referendum
Summary: Would establish the procedure for the legislature to adjust appropriations to eliminate a projected deficit.
Pass/Fail: P
Percent Yes: 58
Percent No: 42

State ID Number: Number 4—Act 1231
Type: Legislative Referendum
Summary: Would allow for the removal of public employees from employment due to a felony conviction during employment.
Pass/Fail: P
Percent Yes: 70
Percent No: 30

State ID Number: Number 5—Act 89
Type: Legislative Referendum
Summary: Would authorize the State Board of Commerce and Industry, with the approval of the governor and the affected local governing authorities, to contract for ad valorem tax exemptions with developers of retirement communities.
Pass/Fail: F
Percent Yes: 39
Percent No: 61

State ID Number: Number 6—Act 1234
Type: Legislative Referendum
Summary: Would require the governor to submit a budget estimate to fully fund state salary supplements for full-time law enforcement and fire protection officers of the state.
Pass/Fail: P
Percent Yes: 63
Percent No: 37

State ID Number: Number 7—Act 87
Type: Legislative Referendum

Summary: Would delete requirement that persons qualifying for special homestead exemption assessment level must reapply annually.
Pass/Fail: P
Percent Yes: 68
Percent No: 32

State ID Number: Number 8—Act 1235
Type: Legislative Referendum
Summary: Would create an exception to permit institutions of higher education or their respective management boards to invest in stocks of up to 50%.
Pass/Fail: F
Percent Yes: 49
Percent No: 51

State ID Number: Number 9-1232
Type: Legislative Referendum
Summary: Would create an exception to permit investment in stocks of up to 35% of the Medicaid Trust Fund for the Elderly.
Pass/Fail: F
Percent Yes: 48
Percent No: 52

State ID Number: Number 10-1233
Type: Legislative Referendum
Summary: Would create programs to assist farmers for the development and enhancement of surface water resources, and create the Drought Protection Trust Fund.
Pass/Fail: F
Percent Yes: 46
Percent No: 54

State ID Number: Number 11—Act 86
Type: Legislative Referendum
Summary: Would create an exemption from ad valorem taxation on drilling rigs used in outer continental shelf waters.
Pass/Fail: F
Percent Yes: 48
Percent No: 52

State ID Number: Number 12-1230
Type: Legislative Referendum
Summary: Would establish qualifications for the office of coroner in Livingston Parish.
Pass/Fail: F
Percent Yes: 45
Percent No: 55

MAINE—Total number of ballot measures currently certified for the November 2002 general election ballot: 3

State ID Number: Question 1: Bond Issue
Type: Legislative Referendum
Summary: Would authorize general bonds to build a new correctional facility and provide maintenance to existing prison facilities.
Pass/Fail: F
Percent Yes: 37
Percent No: 63

State ID Number: Question 2: Bond issue
Type: Legislative Referendum

Summary: Would authorize general bonds for water pollution control and other assorted environmental issues.
Pass/Fail: P
Percent Yes: 57.2
Percent No: 42.8

State ID Number: Question 3: Constitutional Amendment
Type: Legislative Referendum
Summary: Would allow loans to be repaid with federal transportation dollars.
Pass/Fail: P
Percent Yes: 55.3
Percent No: 44.7

MARYLAND—State does not have the initiative process. Total number of ballot measures currently certified for the November 2002 general election ballot: 3

State ID Number: Question 1
Type: Legislative Referendum
Summary: Would expand the powers and duties of district court commissioners.
Pass/Fail: P
Percent Yes: 87.54
Percent No: 12.46

State ID Number: Question 2
Type: Legislative Referendum
Summary: Would authorize the state legislature to pass emergency laws creating or abolishing any office or changing the term of duties of any officer.
Pass/Fail: P
Percent Yes: 50.57
Percent No: 49.43

State ID Number: Question 3
Type: Legislative Referendum
Summary: Would authorize the Montgomery County Council to appoint a licensed and certified real estate appraiser to estimate the fair market value of property situated in the county that is subject to eminent domain.
Pass/Fail: P
Percent Yes: 59.34
Percent No: 40.66

MASSACHUSETTS—Total number of ballot measures currently certified for the November 2002 general election ballot: 3

State ID Number: Question 1
Type: Initiative
Summary: Would eliminate the state's income tax.
Pass/Fail: F
Percent Yes: 45
Percent No: 55

State ID Number: Question 2
Type: Initiative
Summary: Would promote choices in bilingual education for students and parents.
Pass/Fail: P
Percent Yes: 68
Percent No: 32

State ID Number: Question 3
Type: Legislative Referendum

Summary: Would ask voters if they want to retain the provisions of the state's clean elections law.
Pass/Fail: F
Percent Yes: 26
Percent No: 74

MICHIGAN—Total number of ballot measures currently certified for the November 2002 general election ballot: 4

State ID Number: Proposal 02-01
Type: Popular Referendum
Summary: Would reinstate straight party voting in the general election. The state legislature passed a law last year to stop letting voters choose all the candidates from one political party by checking one box, an option most often used by Democrats. This popular referendum will suspend the law until voters decide the issue in November.
Pass/Fail: P (listed as passed because it would overturn the law challenged)
Percent Yes: 40
Percent No: 60

State ID Number: Proposal 02-02
Type: Legislative Referendum
Summary: Would allow for the issuance of general obligation bonds to be used for great lake preservation.
Pass/Fail: P
Percent Yes: 60
Percent No: 40

State ID Number: Proposal 02-03
Type: Initiative
Summary: Would establish collective bargaining rights for state classified employees.
Pass/Fail: F
Percent Yes: 45
Percent No: 55

State ID Number: Proposal 02-04
Type: Initiative
Summary: Would reallocate tobacco settlement funds for health care programs.
Pass/Fail: F
Percent Yes: 34
Percent No: 66

MINNESOTA—State does not have the initiative process. Total number of ballot measures currently certified for the November 2002 general election ballot: None

MISSISSIPPI—Total number of ballot measures currently certified for the November 2002 general election ballot: 1

State ID Number: Amendment 1
Type: Legislative Referendum
Summary: Would increase the terms of circuit court judges and chancellors from four to six years.
Pass/Fail: F
Percent Yes: 38
Percent No: 62

MISSOURI—Total number of ballot measures currently certified for the November 2002 general election ballot: 6

State ID Number: Constitutional Amendment 1
Type: Legislative Referendum
Summary: Shall the Missouri Constitution be amended so that the citizens of the City of St. Louis may amend or revise their present charter to provide for and reorganize their county functions and offices, as provided in the constitution and laws of the state? The estimated fiscal impact of this proposed measure to state and local governments is $0.

Pass/Fail: P
Percent Yes: 69.4
Percent No: 30.6

State ID Number: Constitutional Amendment 2
Type: Initiative
Summary: Shall Article XIII of the Missouri Constitution be amended to permit specified firefighters and ambulance personnel, and dispatchers of fire departments, fire districts, ambulance districts and ambulance departments and fire and emergency medical services dispatchers of dispatch agencies, to organize and bargain collectively in good faith with their employers through representatives of their own choosing and to enter into enforceable collective bargaining contracts with their employers concerning wages, hours, binding arbitration and all other terms and conditions of employment, except that nothing in this amendment shall grant to the aforementioned employees the right to strike?
Pass/Fail: F
Percent Yes: 48.8
Percent No: 51.2

State ID Number: Constitutional Amendment 3
Type: Legislative Referendum
Summary: Shall Article III, Section 8 of the Missouri Constitution be amended to exclude, from the calculations of term limits for members of the General Assembly, service of less than one-half of a legislative term resulting from a special election held after December 5, 2002? The estimated fiscal impact of this proposed measure to state and local governments is $0.
Pass/Fail: P
Percent Yes: 54.3
Percent No: 45.7

State ID Number: Constitutional Amendment 4
Type: Legislative Referendum
Summary: Shall joint boards or commissions, established by contract between political subdivisions, be authorized to own joint projects, to issue bonds in compliance with then applicable requirements of law, the bonds not being indebtedness of the state or political subdivisions, and such activities not to be regulated by the Public Service Commission? This measure provides potential savings of state revenue and imposes no new costs.
Pass/Fail: P
Percent Yes: 57.8
Percent No: 42.2

State ID Number: Constitutional Convention Question
Type: Legislative Referendum
Summary: Shall there be a convention to revise and amend the constitution?
Pass/Fail: F
Percent Yes: 34.5
Percent No: 65.5

State ID Number: Proposition A
Type: Initiative
Summary: Shall Missouri law be amended to impose an additional tax of 2.75 cents per cigarette (fifty-five cents per pack) and 20 percent on other tobacco products, with the new revenues placed into a Healthy Families Trust Fund to be used for the following purposes: hospital trauma care and emergency preparedness; health care treatment and access, including prescription drug assistance for seniors and health care initiatives for low income citizens, women, minorities and children; life sciences research, including medical research and the proper administration of funds for such research; smoking prevention; and grants for early childhood care and education?
Pass/Fail: F
Percent Yes: 49.1
Percent No: 50.9

MONTANA—Total number of ballot measures currently certified for the November 2002 general election ballot: 7

State ID Number: C-36
Type: Legislative Referendum
Summary: Would authorize the investment of local government's insurance program assets.
Pass/Fail: F
Percent Yes: 39
Percent No: 61

State ID Number: C-37
Type: Legislative Referendum
Summary: Would amend signature-gathering requirements for initiatives. Would increase the distribution requirement for constitutional initiatives.
Pass/Fail: P
Percent Yes: 57
Percent No: 43

State ID Number: C-38
Type: Legislative Referendum
Summary: Would amend signature-gathering requirements for initiatives. Would increase the distribution requirement for statutory initiatives.
Pass/Fail: P
Percent Yes: 57
Percent No: 43

State ID Number: C-39
Type: Legislative Referendum
Summary: Would remove the restriction on investing public funds in private corporate capital stock.
Pass/Fail: F
Percent Yes: 35
Percent No: 65

State ID Number: IR-117
Type: Popular Referendum
Summary: Would repeal HB 474 relating to the electric industry.
Pass/Fail: P (listed as passed because it would overturn the law challenged)
Percent Yes: 40
Percent No: 60

State ID Number: I-145
Type: Initiative
Summary: Would acquire hydroelectric dams and operate them for the benefit of Montanans.
Pass/Fail: F
Percent Yes: 31
Percent No: 69

State ID Number: I-146
Type: Initiative
Summary: Would establish a statewide tobacco-use prevention program using tobacco settlement funds
Pass/Fail: P
Percent Yes: 65
Percent No: 35

NEBRASKA—Total number of ballot measures currently certified for the November 2002 general election ballot: 2

State ID Number: LR 4CA
Type: Legislative Referendum

Summary: Would authorize the use of revenue bonds to develop and lease property for use by non-profit enterprises as determined by law.
Pass/Fail: F
Percent Yes: 43
Percent No: 57

State ID Number: LR 1CA
Type: Legislative Referendum
Summary: Would clarify English language requirements in schools.
Pass/Fail: F
Percent Yes: 40
Percent No: 60

NEVADA—Total number of ballot measures currently certified for the November 2002 general election ballot: 9

State ID Number: Ballot Question 1
Type: Legislative Referendum
Summary: Shall the State of Nevada be authorized to issue general obligation bonds in an amount not to exceed $200 million in order to preserve water quality; protect open space, lakes, rivers, wetlands, and wildlife habitat; and restore and improve parks, recreational areas, and historic and cultural resources?
Pass/Fail: P
Percent Yes: 60.2
Percent No: 39.8

State ID Number: Ballot Question 2
Type: Initiative
Summary: Would provide that only a marriage between a male and a female person shall be recognized. This initiative was voted on in 2000 and passed but state law requires that it be voted on twice before becoming law.
Pass/Fail: P
Percent Yes: 66.3
Percent No: 33.6

State ID Number: Ballot Question 3
Type: Legislative Referendum
Summary: Shall the Sales and Use Tax Act of 1955 be amended to provide an exemption from the taxes imposed by that act on the gross receipts from the sale and the storage, use or other consumption of farm machinery and equipment employed for the agricultural use of real property?
Pass/Fail: F
Percent Yes: 38.8
Percent No: 60.9

State ID Number: Ballot Question 4
Type: Legislative Referendum
Summary: Shall the Sales and Use Tax Act of 1955 be amended to provide an exemption from the taxes imposed by that act on engines and chassis, including replacement parts and components for the engines and chassis, of professional racing vehicles and for certain motor vehicles used by professional racing teams or sanctioning bodies to transport certain items and facilities?
Pass/Fail: F
Percent Yes: 21.2
Percent No: 78.4

State ID Number: Ballot Question 5
Type: Legislative Referendum
Summary: Shall the Nevada Constitution be amended to repeal the constitutional rule against perpetuities?
Pass/Fail: F
Percent Yes: 40.4
Percent No: 58.8

State ID Number: Ballot Question 6
Type: Legislative Referendum
Summary: Shall the Constitution be amended to revise the term of office of a Supreme Court justice or district court judge who is appointed to fill a vacancy?
Pass/Fail: F
Percent Yes: 40.7
Percent No: 58.8

State ID Number: Ballot Question 7
Type: Legislative Referendum
Summary: Shall the Nevada Constitution be amended to allow an exemption from the state debt limit for state contracts necessary for the improvement, acquisition or construction of public elementary and secondary schools?
Pass/Fail: F
Percent Yes: 42.2
Percent No: 57.3

State ID Number: Ballot Question 8
Type: Legislative Referendum
Summary: Shall the Nevada Constitution be amended to authorize the Legislature to provide by law for a reduction in the property taxes on a single-family residence occupied by the owner to avoid a severe economic hardship to that owner?
Pass/Fail: P
Percent Yes: 57.7
Percent No: 42

State ID Number: Ballot Question 9
Type: Initiative
Summary: Would amend the constitution to provide that possession of three ounces or less of marijuana by a person who has attained the age of 21 years is not cause for arrest.
Pass/Fail: F
Percent Yes: 39
Percent No: 61

NEW HAMPSHIRE—State does not have the initiative process. Total number of ballot measures currently certified for the November 2002 general election ballot: 2

State ID Number: Question 1
Type: Legislative Referendum
Summary: Would provide that the Supreme Court may adopt rules that have the force and effect of law.
Pass/Fail: P
Percent Yes: 62
Percent No: 38

State ID Number: Question 2
Type: Legislative Referendum
Summary: Would ask the voters if a convention should be called to amend or revise the constitution.
Pass/Fail: F
Percent Yes: 49.9
Percent No: 50.1

NEW JERSEY—State does not have the initiative process. Total number of ballot measures currently certified for the November 2002 general election ballot: None
NEW MEXICO—State does not have the initiative process. Total number of ballot measures currently certified for the November 2002 general election ballot: 14

State ID Number: Constitutional Amendment 1
Type: Legislative Referendum

Summary: Would phase in additional exemptions from property taxation for honorably discharged veterans.
Pass/Fail: P
Percent Yes: 72
Percent No: 28

State ID Number: Constitutional Amendment 2
Type: Legislative Referendum
Summary: Would remove the prohibition against certain persons exercising the right to vote.
Pass/Fail: F
Percent Yes: 40
Percent No: 60

State ID Number: Constitutional Amendment 3
Type: Legislative Referendum
Summary: Would eliminate an outdated section in the constitution regarding the designation of judicial districts.
Pass/Fail: P
Percent Yes: 67
Percent No: 33

State ID Number: Constitutional Amendment 4
Type: Legislative Referendum
Summary: Would eliminate section of constitution that states that aliens cannot own land or any interest in land in the state unless otherwise approved by law.
Pass/Fail: F
Percent Yes: 43
Percent No: 57

State ID Number: Constitutional Amendment 5
Type: Legislative Referendum
Summary: Would exempt from property taxation the principal place of residence occupied by a veteran who has 100% permanent and total service-connected disability.
Pass/Fail: P
Percent Yes: 74
Percent No: 26

State ID Number: Constitutional Amendment 6
Type: Legislative Referendum
Summary: Would permit the state and local governments to provide land, buildings or infrastructure to create affordable housing.
Pass/Fail: P
Percent Yes: 57
Percent No: 43

State ID Number: Constitutional Amendment 7
Type: Legislative Referendum
Summary: Would designate the last Friday in March as a legal holiday honoring Cesar Chavez.
Pass/Fail: F
Percent Yes: 38
Percent No: 62

State ID Number: Constitutional Amendment 8
Type: Legislative Referendum
Summary: Would broaden eligibility for Vietnam veteran's scholarships.
Pass/Fail: P
Percent Yes: 70
Percent No: 30

State ID Number: Constitutional Amendment 9
Type: Legislative Referendum
Summary: Would change the name of the State Highway Commission to the State Transportation Commission.
Pass/Fail: P
Percent Yes: 51
Percent No: 49

State ID Number: General Obligation Bond A
Type: Legislative Referendum
Summary: Would authorize the issuance and sale of general bonds to make improvements to senior citizen facilities.
Pass/Fail: P
Percent Yes: 56
Percent No: 44

State ID Number: General Obligation Bond B
Type: Legislative Referendum
Summary: Would authorize the issuance and sale of state public educational capital improvements and acquisition bonds.
Pass/Fail: P
Percent Yes: 57
Percent No: 43

State ID Number: General Obligation Bond C
Type: Legislative Referendum
Summary: Would authorize the issuance and sale of public library acquisition bonds.
Pass/Fail: P
Percent Yes: 60
Percent No: 40

State ID Number: General Obligation Bond D
Type: Legislative Referendum
Summary: Would authorize the issuance and sale of state facilities improvement and equipment bonds.
Pass/Fail: F
Percent Yes: 39
Percent No: 61

State ID Number: General Obligation Bond E
Type: Legislative Referendum
Summary: Would authorize the issuance and sale of water project bonds.
Pass/Fail: P
Percent Yes: 55
Percent No: 45

NEW YORK—State does not have the initiative process. Total number of ballot measures certified for the November 2002 general election ballot: None

NORTH CAROLINA—State does not have the initiative process. Total number of ballot measures currently certified for the November 2002 general election ballot: 1

State ID Number: Constitutional Amendment 1
Type: Legislative Referendum
Summary: Would make a technical correction in the state's constitution to allow the dedication and acceptance of property into the State Nature and Historic Preserve by the General Assembly by enactment of a bill rather than by a joint resolution.
Pass/Fail: P
Percent Yes: 72
Percent No: 28

NORTH DAKOTA—Total number of ballot measures currently certified for the November 2002 general election ballot: 3

State ID Number: Constitutional Measure 1
Type: Legislative Referendum
Summary: Would change the taxable status of land held for conservation or wildlife purposes.
Pass/Fail: P
Percent Yes: 51.49
Percent No: 48.51

State ID Number: Initiated Constitutional Measure 2
Type: Initiative
Summary: Would direct the legislative assembly to authorize the state to join a multi-state lottery.
Pass/Fail: P
Percent Yes: 63.47
Percent No: 36.53

State ID Number: Initiated Statutory Measure 3
Type: Initiative
Summary: Would create a Bank of North Dakota administered program providing for partial reimbursement of student loan payments for employed North Dakota residents under thirty years of age who have graduated from accredited post secondary schools.
Pass/Fail: F
Percent Yes: 32.90
Percent No: 67.10

OHIO—Total number of ballot measures currently certified for the November 2002 general election ballot: 1

State ID Number: Issue One
Type: Initiative
Summary: Would establish new penalties for drug kingpins; require treatment instead of jail time for drug possession offenses.
Pass/Fail: F
Percent Yes: 33
Percent No: 67

OKLAHOMA—Total number of ballot measures currently certified for the November 2002 general election ballot: 9

State ID Number: State Question 687
Type: Initiative
Summary: Would ban cockfighting in the state.
Pass/Fail: P
Percent Yes: 56.19
Percent No: 43.81

State ID Number: State Question 693
Type: Legislative Referendum
Summary: Would allow local governments to issue bonds for economic development.
Pass/Fail: P
Percent Yes: 52.39
Percent No: 47.61

State ID Number: State Question 696
Type: Legislative Referendum
Summary: Would exempt storm shelters from ad valorem tax.
Pass/Fail: P

Percent Yes: 66.79
Percent No: 33.21

State ID Number: State Question 697
Type: Legislative Referendum
Summary: Would exempt county development from ad valorem tax.
Pass/Fail: P
Percent Yes: 55.41
Percent No: 44.59

State ID Number: State Question 698
Type: Legislative Referendum
Summary: Would change the number of signatures needed to propose a constitutional initiative from 8% to 15% for initiatives pertaining to hunting, fishing or trapping.
Pass/Fail: F
Percent Yes: 45.77
Percent No: 54.23

State ID Number: State Question 701
Type: Legislative Referendum
Summary: Would modify expenditures from the Tobacco Settlement Endowment Trust Fund.
Pass/Fail: F
Percent Yes: 46.06
Percent No: 53.94

State ID Number: State Question 702
Type: Legislative Referendum
Summary: Would authorize the legislature to enact laws providing for tax abatement under certain circumstances.
Pass/Fail: F
Percent Yes: 55.41
Percent No: 44.59

State ID Number: State Question 703
Type: Legislative Referendum
Summary: Would limit liability for information technology contracts.
Pass/Fail: F
Percent Yes: 45.19
Percent No: 54.81

State ID Number: State Question 704
Type: Legislative Referendum
Summary: Would allow for the use of building funds for inspection of property by the county assessor.
Pass/Fail: F
Percent Yes: 44.10
Percent No: 55.90

OREGON—Total number of ballot measures currently certified for the November 2002 general election ballot: 12

State ID Number: Measure 14
Type: Legislative Referendum
Summary: Would remove historical racial references in obsolete sections of the constitution.
Pass/Fail: P
Percent Yes: 71
Percent No: 29

State ID Number: Measure 15

Type: Legislative Referendum
Summary: Would authorize certain bonds for seismic rehabilitation of public education buildings.
Pass/Fail: P
Percent Yes: 55
Percent No: 45

State ID Number: Measure 16
Type: Legislative Referendum
Summary: Would authorize certain bonds for seismic rehabilitation of emergency services buildings.
Pass/Fail: P
Percent Yes: 55
Percent No: 45

State ID Number: Measure 17
Type: Legislative Referendum
Summary: Would make changes to requirements to run for office and reduce the age requirement to serve as state legislator from 21 to 18.
Pass/Fail: F
Percent Yes: 27
Percent No: 73

State ID Number: Measure 18
Type: Legislative Referendum
Summary: Would allow certain tax districts to establish permanent property tax rates and divide into tax zones.
Pass/Fail: F
Percent Yes: 39
Percent No: 61

State ID Number: Measure 21
Type: Initiative
Summary: Would revise the procedure for filing judicial vacancies and allows vote for "none of the above".
Pass/Fail: F
Percent Yes: 43
Percent No: 57

State ID Number: Measure 22
Type: Initiative
Summary: Would require Oregon Supreme Court judges and court of appeals judges to be elected by District.
Pass/Fail: F
Percent Yes: 49
Percent No: 51

State ID Number: Measure 23
Type: Initiative
Summary: Would create health care finance plan for medically necessary services.
Pass/Fail: F
Percent Yes: 21
Percent No: 79

State ID Number: Measure 24
Type: Initiative
Summary: Would allow licensed denturists to install partial dentures (replacement teeth); authorizes cooperative dentist-denturist business ventures.
Pass/Fail: P
Percent Yes: 75
Percent No: 25

State ID Number: Measure 25
Type: Initiative
Summary: Would increase Oregon minimum wage to $6.90 in 2003; adjusts for inflation in future years
Pass/Fail: P
Percent Yes: 52
Percent No: 48

State ID Number: Measure 26
Type: Initiative
Summary: Would prohibit payment or receipt of payment if based on number of initiative, referendum signatures obtained.
Pass/Fail: P
Percent Yes: 75
Percent No: 25

State ID Number: Measure 27
Type: Initiative
Summary: Would require labeling of genetically engineered foods (as defined) sold or distributed in or from Oregon.
Pass/Fail: F
Percent Yes: 30
Percent No: 70

PENNSYLVANIA — State does not have the initiative process. Total number of ballot measures currently certified for the November 2002 general election ballot: 1

State ID Number: Question 1
Type: Legislative Referendum
Summary: Approval of this question will authorize the state to incur an indebtedness of up to $100,000,000 for the purpose of establishing a program that utilizes capital and other related methods to enhance and improve the delivery of volunteer fire and volunteer emergency services.
Pass/Fail: P
Percent Yes: 73
Percent No: 27

RHODE ISLAND — State does not have the initiative process. Total number of ballot measures currently certified for the November 2002 general election ballot: 5

State ID Number: Question 1
Type: Legislative Referendum
Summary: Approval of this question will authorize the State of Rhode Island to issue general obligation bonds, refunding bonds, and temporary notes in an amount not to exceed $55,000,000 of which an amount not to exceed $56,400,000 will be for the State support of the construction of the new State Municipal Fire Academy and the remainder will be for the State support of the construction of the new State Police Headquarters facility.
Pass/Fail: P
Percent Yes: 59.78
Percent No: 40.22

State ID Number: Question 2
Type: Legislative Referendum
Summary: Approval of this question will authorize the State of Rhode Island to issue general obligation bonds, refunding bonds, and temporary notes in an amount not to exceed $14,000,000 for State support of recreational development, historical preservation and the Heritage Harbor museum.
Pass/Fail: P
Percent Yes: 53.64
Percent No: 46.36

State ID Number: Question 3

Type: Legislative Referendum
Summary: Approval of this question will authorize the State of Rhode Island to issue general obligation bonds, refunding bonds, and temporary notes in an amount not to exceed $563,500, 000 to match federal funds; provide direct funding for improvements to the State's highways, roads and bridges; replace and repair transportation maintenance facilities and purchase buses and/or rehabilitate existing buses for the Rhode Island Public Transportation Authority's bus fleet.
Pass/Fail: P
Percent Yes: 71.86
Percent No: 28.14

State ID Number: Question 4
Type: Legislative Referendum
Summary: Approval of this question will authorize the State of Rhode Island to issue general obligation bonds, refunding bonds, and temporary notes in an amount not to exceed $11,000,000 for road and utility infrastructure, building demolition, site preparation and pier rehabilitation at the Quonset Point/Davisville Industrial Park.
Pass/Fail: F
Percent Yes: 45.54
Percent No: 54.46

State ID Number: Question 5
Type: Legislative Referendum
Summary: Should the Rhode Island Constitution be changed to eliminate Article 6, Section 10, which preserves to the General Assembly today broad powers granted to it by King Charles II of England in 1663 and also be changed to expressly provide that the legislative, executive and judicial branches of Rohde Island government are to be separate and co-equal consistent with the American system of government?
Pass/Fail: P
Percent Yes: 75.77
Percent No: 24.23

SOUTH CAROLINA — **State does not have the initiative process. Total number of ballot measures currently certified for the November 2002 general election ballot: 2**

State ID Number: Amendment Question Number One
Type: Legislative Referendum
Summary: Must Section 16, Article X of the Constitution of this State relating to benefits and funding of public employee pension plans in this State and the equity securities investments allowed for funds of the various state-operated retirement systems be amended so as to delete the restrictions limiting investments in equity securities to those of American-based corporations registered on an American national exchange as provided in the Securities Exchange Act of 1934 or any successor act, or quoted through the National Association of Securities Dealers Automatic Quotations System or similar service?
Pass/Fail: F
Percent Yes: 45.28
Percent No: 54.72

State ID Number: Amendment Question Number Two
Type: Legislative Referendum
Summary: Must Section 11, Article X of the Constitution of this State relating to restrictions on pledging the credit of the State or its political subdivisions for a private purpose and the restrictions on the State or its political subdivisions from becoming a joint owner or stockholder of a business be amended so as to allow a municipality, county, special purpose district, or public service district of this State which provides firefighting service and which administers a separate pension plan for its employees performing this service to invest and reinvest the funds in this pension plan in equity securities traded on a national securities exchange as provided in the Securities Exchange Act of 1934 or a successor act or in equity securities quoted through the National Association of Securities Dealers Automatic Quotations System or similar service?
Pass/Fail: P
Percent Yes: 57.50
Percent No: 42.50

SOUTH DAKOTA — Total number of ballot measures currently certified for the November 2002 general election ballot: 4

State ID Number: Constitutional Amendment A
Type: Initiative
Summary: The Constitution currently guarantees certain rights to a person accused of a crime. Amendment A would amend the Constitution to state that a criminal defendant may argue the merits, validity, and applicability of the law, including sentencing laws.
Pass/Fail: F
Percent Yes: 21
Percent No: 79

State ID Number: Constitutional Amendment B
Type: Legislative Referendum
Summary: The Constitution requires the Legislature to establish legislative districts every ten years. Voters from each legislative district elect one state senator and one or two state representatives to the South Dakota Legislature. Amendment B would require the Legislature to adopt a new plan, in a regular or special legislative session, if a court invalidates the districts established by the Legislature.
Pass/Fail: F
Percent Yes: 39
Percent No: 61

State ID Number: Constitutional Amendment C
Type: Legislative Referendum
Summary: The Governor must veto legislation within five days of presentation while the Legislature is in session, and within fifteen days of presentation if presented within five days of adjournment or recess. Amendment C would alter these time periods by excluding weekends and holidays from the five-day presentation period, and would clarify when the fifteen-day time period is applicable.
Pass/Fail: P
Percent Yes: 54
Percent No: 46

State ID Number: Initiated Measure 1
Type: Initiative
Summary: Initiated Measure 1 proposes a law that would make it legal under state law, but not under federal law, for a person to plant, cultivate, harvest, possess, process, transport, sell or buy industrial hemp (cannabis) or any of its by-products with a tetrahydrocannabinol (THC) content of one percent or less.
Pass/Fail: F
Percent Yes: 38
Percent No: 62

TENNESSEE — State does not have the initiative process. Total number of ballot measures currently certified for the November 2002 general election ballot: 2

State ID Number: Constitutional Amendment 1
Type: Legislative Referendum
Summary: Would delete the current constitutional prohibition on lotteries.
Pass/Fail: P
Percent Yes: 58
Percent No: 42

State ID Number: Constitutional Amendment 2
Type: Legislative Referendum
Summary: Would allow the General Assembly to prescribe the maximum fine that, absent waiver, may be assessed without a jury.
Pass/Fail: P

Percent Yes: 53
Percent No: 47

TEXAS—State does not have the initiative process. Total number of ballot measures currently certified for the November 2002 general election ballot: 1

State ID Number: Constitutional Amendment—HJR 2
Type: Legislative Referendum
Summary: Would authorize the commissioners' court of a county to declare the office of constable in a precinct to be dormant if the office has not been filled by election or appointment for a lengthy period and providing a procedure for the reinstatement of the office.
Pass/Fail: P
Percent Yes: 80.2
Percent No: 19.2

UTAH—Total number of ballot measures currently certified for the November 2002 general election ballot: 7

State ID Number: Constitutional Amendment 1
Type: Legislative Referendum
Summary: Would make changes to the investment of state school funds.
Pass/Fail: P
Percent Yes: 62.62
Percent No: 37.38

State ID Number: Constitutional Amendment 2
Type: Legislative Referendum
Summary: Would change county boundaries.
Pass/Fail: P
Percent Yes: 72.75
Percent No: 27.25

State ID Number: Constitutional Amendment 3
Type: Legislative Referendum
Summary: Would amend the revenue and taxation provisions of the constitution.
Pass/Fail: P
Percent Yes: 70.0
Percent No: 30.0

State ID Number: Constitutional Amendment 4
Type: Legislative Referendum
Summary: Would require public notice prior to special sessions.
Pass/Fail: P
Percent Yes: 77.36
Percent No: 22.64

State ID Number: Constitutional Amendment 5
Type: Legislative Referendum
Summary: Would amend debt limits for political subdivisions.
Pass/Fail: P
Percent Yes: 66.15
Percent No: 33.85

State ID Number: Constitutional Amendment 6
Type: Legislative Referendum
Summary: Would expand the government property tax exemption.
Pass/Fail: F

Percent Yes: 42.41
Percent No: 57.59

State ID Number: Citizen's State Initiative Number 1
Type: Initiative
Summary: Would change Utah's regulatory and tax framework affecting the disposal and storage of radioactive waste. It provides stricter regulations, certain prohibitions, and new and increased fees and taxes.
Pass/Fail: F
Percent Yes: 31.93
Percent No: 68.07

VERMONT—State does not have the initiative process. Total number of ballot measures currently certified for the November 2002 general election ballot: 1

State ID Number: Question 1
Type: Legislative Referendum
Summary: Would set the retirement age of justices of the state Supreme Court.
Pass/Fail: P
Percent Yes: 65
Percent No: 35

VIRGINIA—State does not have the initiative process. Total number of ballot measures currently certified for the November 2002 general election ballot: 4

State ID Number: Proposed Amendment 1
Type: Legislative Referendum
Summary: Shall the Constitution of Virginia be amended to permit the Supreme Court to consider, as part of its original jurisdiction, claims of actual innocence presented by convicted felons in the cases and manner provided by the General Assembly?
Pass/Fail: P
Percent Yes: 72.68
Percent No: 27.32

State ID Number: Proposed Amendment 2
Type: Legislative Referendum
Summary: Shall the Constitution of Virginia be amended to allow localities by ordinance, rather than the General Assembly by law, to exempt property from taxation that is used for charitable and certain other purposes, subject to the restrictions and conditions provided by general law?
Pass/Fail: P
Percent Yes: 64.51
Percent No: 35.49

State ID Number: Proposed Bond Issue #1
Type: Legislative Referendum
Summary: Shall Chapters 827 and 859, Acts of the General Assembly of 2002, authorizing the issuance of general obligation bonds of the Commonwealth of Virginia in the maximum amount of $900,488,645 pursuant to Article X, Section 9(b) of the Constitution of Virginia for capital projects for educational facilities, take effect?
Pass/Fail: P
Percent Yes: 72.73
Percent No: 27.27

State ID Number: Proposed Bond Issue #2
Type: Legislative Referendum
Summary: Shall Chapters 854 and 884, Acts of the General Assembly of 2002, authorizing the issuance of general obligation bonds of the Commonwealth of Virginia in the maximum amount of $119,040,000 pursuant to Article X, Section 9(b) of the Constitution of Virginia for capital projects for parks and recreational facilities, take effect?

Pass/Fail: P
Percent Yes: 68.72
Percent No: 31.28

WASHINGTON—Total number of ballot measures currently certified for the November 2002 general election ballot: 5

State ID Number: Initiative 776
Type: Initiative
Summary: Would require license tab fees of $30 per year for cars, sport utility vehicles, motorcycles, motor homes, and light trucks.
Pass/Fail: P
Percent Yes: 51.47
Percent No: 48.53

State ID Number: Initiative 790
Type: Initiative
Summary: Would establish a new board of trustees to manage the law enforcement officers' and fire fighters' (LEOFF) pension system, plan 2.
Pass/Fail: P
Percent Yes: 53.02
Percent No: 46.98

State ID Number: Referendum Measure 53
Type: Popular Referendum
Summary: Would establish new rate classes and increase taxable wage bases for these classes; adopt tax array schedules for 2003 and 2004; adopt tax array schedules for 2005 and beyond; impose surcharge taxes if certain contingencies occur; require successor employers to use the previous owners' taxable wage base; require administrative expenses to be funded out of a separate account; and establish effective dates for various sections.
Pass/Fail: P (listed as passed because it would overturn the law challenged)
Percent Yes: 40.78
Percent No: 59.22

State ID Number: Referendum Bill 51
Type: Legislative Referendum
Summary: Would increase weight fees on trucks and large vehicles, fuel excise taxes, and sales taxes on vehicles to finance transportation improvements.
Pass/Fail: F
Percent Yes: 37.30
Percent No: 62.69

State ID Number: Constitutional Amendment HJR 4220
Type: Legislative Referendum
Summary: Would permit property tax levy propositions for fire protection districts to be submitted to voters for periods up to four years, or six years for fire facility construction, rather than annually.
Pass/Fail: P
Percent Yes: 68.14
Percent No: 31.86

WEST VIRGINIA—State does not have the initiative process. Total number of ballot measures currently certified for the November 2002 general election ballot: 2

State ID Number: Amendment 1
Type: Legislative Referendum
Summary: Would amend the State Constitution to permit the Legislature by general law to authorize county commissions and municipalities to use a new economic development tool to help create jobs.
Pass/Fail: P

Percent Yes: 56.8
Percent No: 43.2

State ID Number: Amendment 2
Type: Legislative Referendum
Summary: Would allow county and municipal governments to propose excess levies for the same time periods as boards of education, which is up to five years.
Pass/Fail: P
Percent Yes: 51.8
Percent No: 48.2

WISCONSIN—State does not have the initiative process. Total number of ballot measures certified for the November 2002 general election ballot: None

WYOMING—Total number of ballot measures currently certified for the November 2002 general election ballot: 4

State ID Number: Amendment A
Type: Legislative Referendum
Summary: Would allow a majority of the elected members of each house to convene a special legislative session.
Pass/Fail: P
Percent Yes: 66
Percent No: 34

State ID Number: Amendment B
Type: Legislative Referendum
Summary: Would allow legislative leaders of each house to call a special session to resolve a dispute or challenge to determine the presidential electors.
Pass/Fail: P
Percent Yes: 65
Percent No: 35

State ID Number: Amendment C
Type: Legislative Referendum
Summary: Would limit the governor's partial veto authority.
Pass/Fail: F
Percent Yes: 44
Percent No: 56

State ID Number: Amendment D
Type: Legislative Referendum
Summary: Would provide that amendments to the constitution proposed by the legislature be submitted to the voters without prior approval of the governor.
Pass/Fail: F[4]
Percent Yes: 53
Percent No: 47

---

4. In order to pass, a constitutional amendment must receive a majority of the total votes in the election. The unofficial total votes cast was 188,524; therefore, based on the unofficial number of total votes, cast, the majority needed is 94,263. The measure received 87,795 votes, and thus failed.

Overall State Rankings

State	Initiatives	Popular Referendum	Legislative Referendum	Total Number of Statewide Ballot Measures
Alabama	0	0	3	3
Alaska	2	0	4	6
Arizona	4	0	10	14
Arkansas	2	0	2	4
California	4	0	3	7
Colorado	5	0	5	10
Connecticut	0	0	0	0
Delaware	0	0	0	0
Florida	5	0	5	10
Georgia	0	0	11	11
Hawaii	0	0	3	3
Idaho	1	1	0	2
Illinois	0	0	0	0
Indiana	0	0	0	0
Iowa	0	0	0	0
Kansas	0	0	0	0
Kentucky	0	0	2	2
Louisiana	0	0	12	12
Maine	0	0	3	3
Maryland	0	0	3	3
Massachusetts	2	0	1	3
Michigan	2	1	1	4
Minnesota	0	0	0	0
Mississippi	0	0	1	1
Missouri	2	0	4	6
Montana	2	1	4	7
Nebraska	0	0	2	2
Nevada	2	0	7	9
New Hampshire	0	0	2	2
New Jersey	0	0	0	0
New Mexico	0	0	14	14
New York	0	0	0	0
North Carolina	0	0	1	1
North Dakota	2	0	1	3
Ohio	1	0	0	1
Oklahoma	1	0	8	9
Oregon	7	0	5	12
Pennsylvania	0	0	1	1
Rhode Island	0	0	5	5
South Carolina	0	0	2	2
South Dakota	2	0	2	4
Tennessee	0	0	2	2
Texas	0	0	1	1
Utah	1	0	6	7
Vermont	0	0	1	1
Virginia	0	0	4	4
Washington	2	1	2	5
West Virginia	0	0	2	2
Wisconsin	0	0	0	0
Wyoming	0	0	4	4
Total	**49**	**4**	**149**	**202**

Index